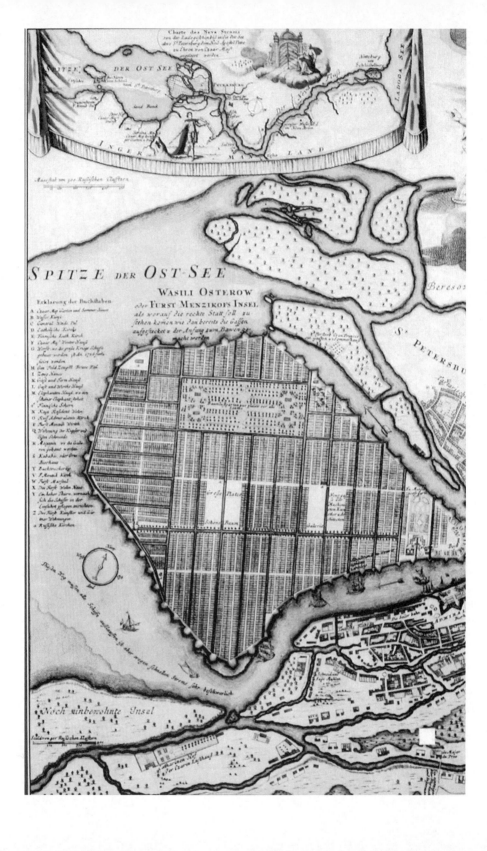

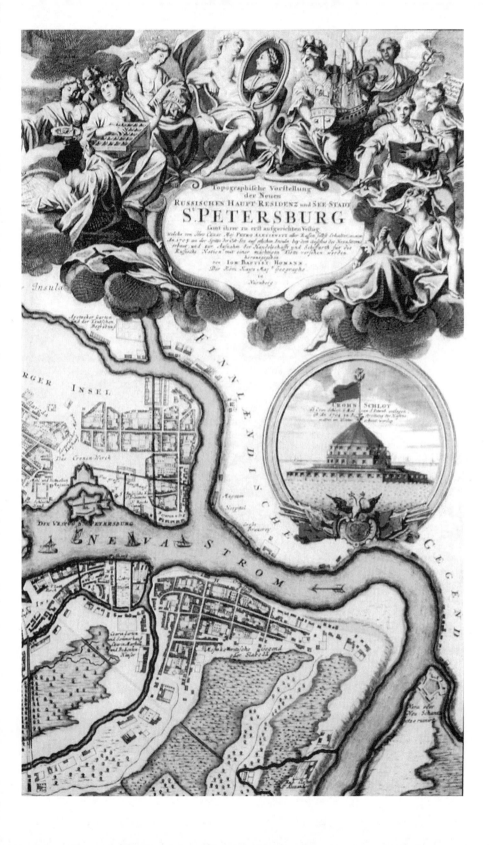

Topographische Vorstellung
der Neuen
RUSSISCHEN HAUPT RESIDENZ und SEE STADT
St. PETERSBURG

Samt ihrer zu erst aufgerichten Verlag
welche von Ihro Czaar: Maj: PETRO ALEXIEWIZ aller Reußen selbst Erhalter, anno
An 1703 an der Spitze der Ost-See auf etlichen Insuln bey dem Ausfluss des Neva-Strom
erbaut, und zur Aufnahm der Handelschafft und Schiffarth für die
Rußische Nation mit einer mächtigen Flotte versehen werden
herausgegeben
von JOH BAPTIST HOMANN
Ihr Röm Kays: Maj: Geographi
in
Nürnberg

St. Petersburg

St. Petersburg

Russia's Window to the Future
The First Three Centuries

ARTHUR L. GEORGE
WITH ELENA GEORGE

TAYLOR TRADE PUBLISHING
Lanham • New York • Oxford

Front endpapers: Plan of St. Petersburg, 1717–1721. Anonymous engraver, published by J. B. Homann. (Courtesy National Library of Russia, St. Petersburg)

Back endpapers: Center of St. Petersburg in 1913.

Photos #   1, 2, 5, 6, 8, 10, 11, 12, 14, 15, 17, 18, 20, 23, 24, 25, 26, 27, 29, 30, 31, 32,
          33, 39, 40, 41, 45, 46, 47, 52, 61, 62, 63, 68, 69, 71, 72, 73, 74, 75, 76, 77,
          78, 79, 81 Courtesy of National Library of Russia, St. Petersburg
   #   80 Courtesy of Gennady Golstein
   #   82 Courtesy of M. Milchik
   #   83 Courtesy of Vadim Shesterikov
   #   84 Courtesy of Irina Ganelina
   #   85,87 Courtesy of Valery Zarorotnyi
   #   86 Courtesy of Alexander Margolis
   #   88 Courtesy of Sergei Semenov
Unless otherwise noted, photos provided are from the private archives of the author, Lev Lourie, and Rimma Krupova.

First Taylor Trade Publishing edition 2003

This Taylor Trade Publishing hardcover editon of *St. Petersburg* is an original publication. It is printed by arrangement with the author.

Copyright © 2003 by Arthur L. George

Library of Congress Cataloging-in-Publication Data

George, Arthur L.
   St Petersburg : Russia's window to the future—the first three
centuries / Arthur L. George with Elena George.
        p. cm.
Includes bibliographical references and index.
   ISBN 1-58979-017-0 (cloth : alk. paper)
   1. Saint Petersburg (Russia)—History. I. George, Elena. II. Title.
   DK561 .G46 2003
   947'.21—dc21
                                                    2003001138

∞™ The paper used in this publication meets the minimum requirements of
American National Standard for Information Sciences—Permanence of
Paper for Printed Library Materials, ANSI/NISO Z39.48-1992.
Manufactured in the United States of America.

In Petersburg we'll meet again,
As if the sun we buried there. . . .

—OSIP MANDELSTAM

Petersburg is both the head and heart of Russia. . . . Even up to the present Petersburg is in dust and rubble; it is still being created, still becoming. Its future is still in an idea; but this idea belongs to Peter I; it is being embodied, growing and taking root with each day, not alone in the Petersburg swamp but in all Russia.

—FEDOR DOSTOEVSKY

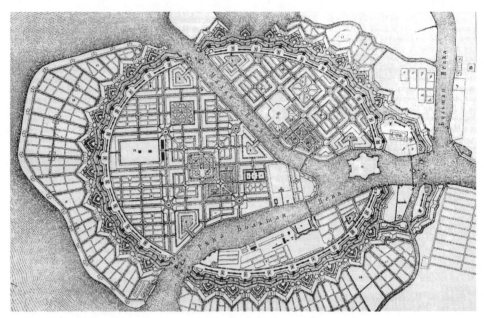

Jean Baptiste LeBlond. Plan of St. Petersburg, 1717

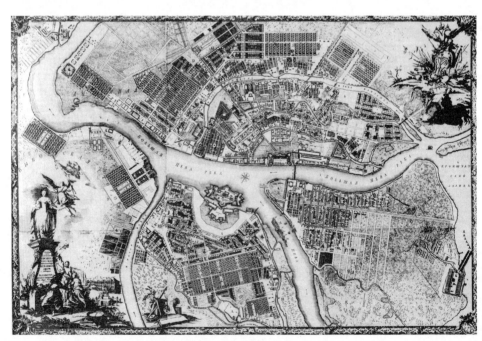

Map of St. Petersburg, 1753. Executed by I. F. Truscott, drawn by M. I. Makhaev

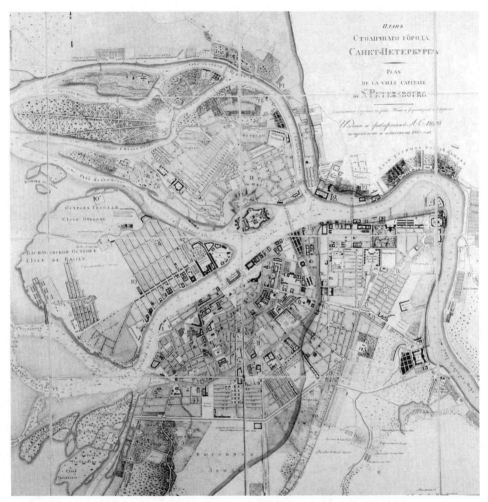

Map of St. Petersburg by A. Savinkov, published in 1825. It shows the flooded areas during the 1824 deluge.

Bird's-eye view of St. Petersburg, 1860s.

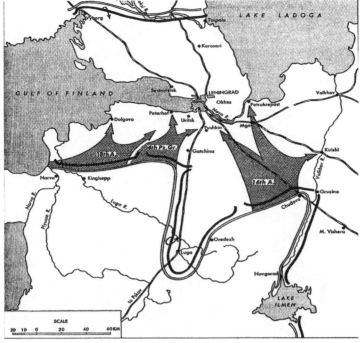

Situation on the Leningrad Front on August 21, 1941. (*Source*: Leon Gouré, "The Siege of Leningrad," RAND/R-0378, published by Stanford University Press, Stanford, CA, 1962. Copyright RAND, Santa Monica, CA, 1962. Reprinted by permission.)

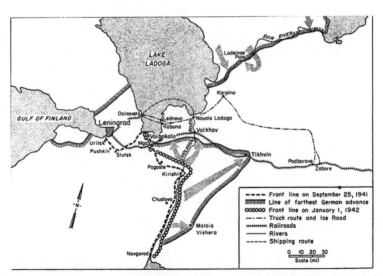

The German Advance to Tikhvin. (*Source*: Leon Gouré, "The Siege of Leningrad," RAND/R-0378, published by Stanford University Press, Stanford, CA, 1962. Copyright RAND, Santa Monica, CA, 1962. Reprinted by permission.)

Contents

PREFACE

I became enraptured with St. Petersburg (then called Leningrad) upon my first arrival there in 1979 as a student of history and Russian studying at its University. It was June and our plane had touched down at about 11:00 P.M. While our group waited outside Pulkovo air terminal for our bus, a lazy red sun still hung low over the runways, refusing to set, and as we drove into town the light held. After arriving at our dormitory near the Peter and Paul Fortress, I stashed my things in the room and immediately broke curfew to take a midnight stroll along the embankment of the silvery Neva and enjoy a few moments of solitude and reflection on that poetic White Night. I found no solitude, but there was much to reflect upon. On the embankment were scores of romantic couples, young and old, and other Leningraders strolling about in calm and contented silence, gazing and whispering in reverent, loving admiration of their surreal city. Upon seeing the 18th-century palaces lining the opposite shore (Palace Embankment), it seemed that had I been on this spot 200 years earlier, the scene and the feeling would have hardly differed. I recalled another midnight stroll through the bustling Latin Quarter of Paris upon my first visit to that city the year before. That too was a memorable experience, but it did not compare. It seemed to me that the wrong city is called the City of Light.

Soon afterwards I visited Moscow. I still remember how, as our bus lumbered into town from the airport, our local guide told us that we would enjoy Moscow more than Leningrad because it is a more "Russian" city. She espoused the view of many that Leningrad was somehow odd and foreign, not really Russia. Although I was already familiar with the differing histories and traditions of these cities, this was my first direct encounter with the clashing mind-sets that their pasts had imparted on their citizens. The topic of St. Petersburg's place in Russia fascinated me, and as I continued my studies I came to agree with those historians who found strong parallels between Russia's Muscovite past and the Soviet regime and explained much of the latter by the former. The pressing question was how to escape this wheel of history. It was therefore of interest that an escape had been tried before, in St. Petersburg.

During that first visit, the USSR was still ruled by Brezhnev. Years later, beginning in January 1989, I (together with my wife, who hails from St. Petersburg and with whom I was also stricken while a student there) lived nearly four years in

Moscow and then nearly five in St. Petersburg, where I opened and headed my firm's office. We lived through the era of Gorbachev's *perestroika* and *glasnost*, the loss of Soviet satellites in Eastern and Central Europe, the August 1991 coup with Yeltsin's speech from atop a tank outside the White House and the breakup of the USSR. We saw St. Petersburg reemerge as a leading progressive force with a new spirit of hope. Many sincere and enlightened Russians, particularly from St. Petersburg, strove mightily to turn Russia around, but they seemed outnumbered and crushed by the heavy weight of the past; many hopes were dashed. We saw the reemergence, in various forms, of the "Russian idea." We saw the brown-shirt nationalism of Pamyat and Vladimir Zhirinovsky, the continued appeal to the communist crusade, various other claims to Russia's special mission, suspicion of the West, continued corruption and cronyism in government, the struggle for the rule of law, and the emergence of the Mafia, the oligarchs, and others who considered themselves above society and restraint. Much of Russia still did not "get" what it took to be a modern, open society.

After moving to Chicago, I attended a luncheon with Sergei Kiriyenko shortly after Boris Yeltsin had replaced him as Prime Minister. Kiriyenko, an enlightened progressive who had found it difficult to implement reforms, told me that the most important factor holding Russia back is the mentality *(soznanie)* of most of its people, and that changing that mentality would be the key to progress and to Russia's joining the modern world and community of nations. Shortly thereafter I read a Russian newspaper article which quoted alienated St. Petersburg youth as holding that it is impossible to live in contemporary Russia and not be postmodern. Russia's fate was still in the balance. Peter the Great's vision was still a work in progress. Yet as I worked on this book, progress was being made in Russia, led by important reformers from St. Petersburg. The original vision was still there and beheld, increasingly within the nation's grasp.

During those historic years in the USSR and Russia, friends and colleagues often urged me to keep a diary and write an account of my experiences, particularly since my work as a lawyer put me at the cutting edge of developments and in regular contact with many leading figures of the day. Busy living history, I never seemed to find the time to write it. In truth, such a project did not inspire me. I did not want simply to compile a journalistic observation of famous events that I lived through and participated in. Instead, my interest kept returning to Russia's fundamental "accursed questions." Besides reading daily press accounts of revolutionary changes, I reread Gogol and remembered what had not changed. The age-old accursed questions were still playing themselves out before my eyes, and even made things difficult at my job. Historically, the drama of these questions had unfolded first and foremost in the city of St. Petersburg, and the ending was still to be written.

When the late Anatoly Sobchak was Mayor of St. Petersburg, he used to give a speech (which I heard several times) outlining his vision of how St. Petersburg would call upon its great past and potential and reemerge as Russia's locus of political and intellectual enlightenment and its center of trade, finance, shipping, and tourism, leading Russia into a prosperous, democratic, and enlightened future. Warming to the subject, he would add that this in turn would help ensure the stability of the central Asian subcontinent and lead to world peace in the 21st century. The first part of this was hardly original but rather was a St. Petersburg tradition—Peter the Great had instituted this same vision, and some of it came to pass. As to the second part, one can only hope so. Whatever the case, the challenges facing post-Soviet Russia had placed the city's original role and relevance to the new Russia front and center.

By the time I returned to America from St. Petersburg in late 1997, the city was already planning its tercentenary celebrations for 2003. This in itself, together with the fact that no English-language narrative history of the city yet existed, seemed to make publishing one timely. But ultimately it was my fascination with the city's role and meaning in Russia's tortuous history and my conviction that an understanding of this history can be instructive for the present that finally inspired me to write this book rather than another as the first literary fruit of my Russian studies and life there. In arriving at an organizing theme for this story, I was aided by the historian Aileen Kelly's observation that the city's tragic mythological aura that engulfs so many literary and prose writings about the city—however fascinating and which even as myth and literature forms an essential part of the city's history—is ultimately inadequate to explain Petersburg's overall historical significance or its potential role in the new Russia.[1] Rather, as I watched post-Soviet Russia struggle to modernize and move toward a civil society and new national life and as Petersburgers and their ideas assumed a leading role in this struggle, it seemed to me that the modernizing changes introduced beginning nearly three centuries earlier and of which Petersburg was to be the embodiment had acquired a new relevance, and that these changes and the values underlying them also stood apart from the values of what eventually became known as "Imperial St. Petersburg." In today's global information society, the idea that a single city as a geographical or economic unit can play the kind of unique vanguard role envisioned by Peter and dreamed of by Sobchak is a stretch. But Petersburg was nothing if not a city of ideas, and technology has shrunk Russia's geographical expanse that observers throughout history have believed necessitated despotism rather than government according to the liberal ideas that became associated with the city; perhaps the present heralds the first realistic opportunity for these ideas to be realized. It struck me that people would be helped by a better awareness of the instructive historical dramas played out in Petersburg's past, because some of them are being repeated. I became convinced that, in today's world of globalization, a book exploring the city's unique history from the perspectives of modernism, movement toward civil society, common human values and world culture would be interesting and timely. From this perspective, Petersburg is not just a Window to the West, but a Window to the Future, and not just Russia's.

Since Petersburg was founded in 1703 with a mission to change the national life, in order to understand Petersburg one must understand something of Russia before 1703. Thus, the book opens with a prologue recounting the formative themes of Russian history leading up to Peter the Great and the founding of St. Petersburg. Since through Nicholas I each sovereign in Petersburg left his or her unique imprint on the city and most progress (or regression) was driven by the imperial court, chapters 1–9 are organized around the reigns of Russia's rulers. Thereafter, the chapters are tied to major historical events and themes rather than to rulers. From the perspective of the city's social, intellectual, and political history, its story divides into four phases: the evolution of Peter the Great's vision and reforms until early in the reign of Catherine the Great; the emergence of a liberal opposition late in Catherine's reign culminating in the Decembrist uprising in 1825; the era of disparate searches for solutions, repression, radical opposition, and social and political unrest culminating in the establishment and consolidation of the Bolshevik regime; and the subsequent struggles of the city's people to escape from the Soviet regime and live in a modern, open society.

While political and intellectual history and the theme of modernism form much of this book's conceptual frame, the city's unique culture (and in particular themes of world culture) is also part of that frame and also provides much of the picture inside this frame. Indeed, most of the book is devoted to this fascinating picture, which does prominently include the story of the city's tragic mythological and mysterious aura, as well as what one can discern as its "soul." Peter the Great founded the city to be an ideal (utopia) of civilization and culture, a vanguard for Russia and even for Europe. While political and social reform ultimately lagged, in many respects Petersburg long ago achieved its purpose in the cultural sphere, synthesizing the best of Russia and Western Europe to create new art that stunned and conquered Europe. Petersburg developed its own special intellectual and artistic vigor, architecture, culture, beauty, mystery, spirit, and rhythm of life that form its soul, which is incomparable and stems from the city's unique place in geography and history, and from the daring, unbridled imagination and spirit of its people. It was embodied in such figures as Alexander Pushkin, Peter Tchaikovsky, Vladimir Nabokov, Kazmir Malevich, Alexander Benois, Pavel Filonov, Igor Stravinsky, Anna Akhmatova, Osip Mandelstam, Nikolai Gumilev, George Balanchine, Nikolai Antsiferov, Mikhail Baryshnikov, Joseph Brodsky, Dmitry Shostakovich, and Dmitry Likhachev. Alongside the political turmoil, this life has always gone on, and the city has stood patiently and beautifully on the banks of the Neva, hoping for the nation's political life to catch up and awaiting its chance again to play an important role in that process.

I wish to thank the many people who helped create this book. Among specialists who kindly offered their consultation, I wish to thank Lev Lourie, the prominent St. Petersburg historian; Blair Ruble, Director of the Kennan Institute for Advanced Russian Studies; Anatoly Belkin, noted St. Petersburg art historian;

Vladimir Sanzharov, Chairman of the St. Petersburg branch of the Union of Designers of Russia, a specialist on city planning and architecture; Andrei Burlaka, specialist on the history of Russian rock and roll; Gennady Golstein, famous jazz band leader and instructor at the Mussorgsky School of Music, for his consultation on the history of jazz in St. Petersburg; Richard Torrence, former advisor to Mayor Sobchak; the writer Valery Zavorotnyi for his assistance regarding the August 1991 coup; John Evans, former U.S. Consul-General in St. Petersburg and currently head of the Russia desk at the U.S. State Department; Evgeny Feodorov, Tatyana Pasynkova, Nina Tarasova, and Elena Korolkova from the Hermitage Museum; and Lydia Leontieva of the Astoria Hotel for information on the rich history of that hotel. I also wish to thank the following friends in St. Petersburg for their support, research assistance, and review of the manuscript: Boris Andreyev, Alexander Pozdnyakov, Vladimir Marinichev, and Lyubov Erigo. I thank Rimma Krupova and Yuri Ermolov for their assistance with the photographs and illustrations. Thanks also to the staffs of the Russian National Public Library in St. Petersburg (particularly Elena Nebogatikova and Natalya Rudakova), the Lake Forest Public Library, the Lake Forest College Library, the St. Petersburg office of my own firm, Baker & McKenzie, and to the firm as a whole for giving me the leeway to complete this project. Warm thanks also are due to my agent, Ed Knappman, and my editor at Taylor Trade Publishing, Michael Dorr, both of whom had the vision to see the book's potential and guided me through the minefields of the publication process. But most of all I thank my wife Elena, whose love and support got me through the project. Because of her love of and knowledge about her native city, she worked tirelessly in assisting with research, offered many stimulating ideas, and was my best critic and editor, all of which led to many late-night discussions and helped give the book the shape it has. Without her there would be no book.

Generally, the book gives dates from 1700 according to the calendar in use at the time. The Julian ("Old Style") calendar was used in Russia from 1700 until 1918, when the Gregorian ("New Style") calendar was adopted. To get New Style dates, one must add 11 days during the 18th century, 12 days during the 19th century, and 13 days during the early 20th.

In transliterating Russian words into English, I have generally followed a modified version of the Library of Congress system for general works described in J. Thomas Shaw, *The Transliteration of Modern Russian for English-Language Publications* (New York, 1967), without diacritical marks, while making some concessions to common usage to make the text more readable. Translations of quoted texts originally in Russian are my own unless otherwise indicated.

Lake Forest, Illinois
April, 2003

PROLOGUE

A Tale of Three Cities

There have been five periods in Russian history and each provides a different picture. They are: the Russia of Kiev; Russia in the days of the Tartar yoke; the Russia of Moscow; the Russia of Peter the Great; and Soviet Russia. The Moscow period was the worst in Russian history, the most stifling, of a particularly Asiatic and Tartar type, and those lovers of freedom, the Slavophils, have idealized it in terms of their own misunderstanding of it.

NIKOLAI BERDYAEV[1]

S t. Petersburg has often been considered a stranger in its own land, an unnatural aberration situated on the far edge of the nation—not really Russian. St. Petersburg is indeed unique, but Russia's three previous major cities—Novgorod, Kiev, and Moscow—also have lived separate and distinctive lives. In fact, St. Petersburg, Novgorod, and Kiev enjoy many similarities, while in important respects Muscovite civilization is the anomaly, particularly if viewed in terms of world history. Most major world cities, including capitals, lay either on the seacoast or not far up navigable rivers, because this facilitates trade, prosperity, and interaction with other nations, and stimulates culture. Novgorod, Kiev, and St. Petersburg followed this norm, while due to historical accident (the Mongols) Muscovy arose deep inland with no ready access to the sea. This had pernicious consequences that eventually had to be redressed.

Peter the Great's reforms and St. Petersburg itself should be understood not as unnatural aberrations but as logical and natural responses to the inevitable 17th-century crisis of Muscovite civilization. Later, in the 20th century, the rise and staying power of Soviet Communism can be understood as a reassertion and embracing of old Muscovite traditions and values and a rejection of those of St. Petersburg. The crisis of the Soviet system that led to its downfall has parallels to the crisis in 17th-century Muscovy. Many of the ideas and values required for Russia's post-Soviet revival and entry into the modern world of nations can be found in the history of St. Petersburg, beginning with its founder, Peter the Great. The city's history and meaning holds lessons for Russia's future and can help guide it.

It is thus important to begin the story of Petersburg by examining how Novgorod, Kiev, and Moscow each have bequeathed their unique traditions to Russia and St. Petersburg and enriched the city's life. Events and personalities from their histories appear in Petersburg's art, music, opera, ballet, literature, and poetry, as well as in political and intellectual controversies. Their histories help explain why Petersburg was founded and provide the context to give the city its meaning and interpret its development.

One can summarize the historical interplay among Novgorod, Kiev, and Moscow only by illustrating its complexity. There was no uniform historical line of succession or influence among them, and in many ways their civilizations were rival. Novgorod spawned Kiev, but Kiev grew close to Byzantium and adopted its religion, and then violently imposed it on Novgorod. Muscovy grew up largely outside the Kievan state but embraced and developed its religion. It matured under the Mongol yoke without meaningful contact with Constantinople or the West, becoming the dominant force in Russia in part because its princes represented the Khan in dealings with other Russian princes and nobles. Kiev fell to the Mongols in 1240, but when the Mongols were repelled, Kiev and what would become Ukraine were absorbed into the Polish-Lithuanian state. When Ukraine rejoined Russia four centuries later on the eve of the founding of St. Petersburg, the culture and learning that it had acquired while outside Muscovy's influence inspired fundamental departures from Muscovite culture and thinking, influenced Peter the Great's reforms, and contributed to the intellectual, religious, and political life of the new capital. For its part, Novgorod, previously part of the Kievan state, remained an absent, independent republic in the North with its own traditions. Muscovy not only drew little from it, but it became Muscovy's commercial and political rival, and Muscovy eventually decided to crush it.

NOVGOROD

Novgorod's initial contribution to Russian civilization was political and economic and came early. According to the *Primary Chronicle*, the tribes of the region constantly quarreled, and social and political disorder reigned in the land. Tradition held that the tribal leaders, unhappy with this state of affairs, invited a Viking prince, Rurik, who founded Novgorod ("New City") around 860 and ruled as its prince. His descendants and relatives, most notably Oleg, Sviatoslav, Vladimir, and Yaroslav the Wise, later ruled in Kiev and presided over its Golden Age. The Rurikid line of princes continued through most of the Muscovite period, until the death of Tsar Fedor (the son of Ivan the Terrible) in 1598.

In the same year that Kiev fell to the Mongols (1240), Prince Alexander led Novgorod to victory over the Swedes on the banks of the Neva near the future St. Petersburg, for which he acquired the sobriquet Nevsky. Two years later he de-

feated the Teutonic Knights on the ice of Lake Chud (now Peipus), thereby eliminating military threats from the north and west. Security thus assured, and essentially free of the Mongol yoke, Novgorod went on to prosper through trade and
contact with the West, particularly with the Hanseatic League, of which it became
a member. Novgorod was on the axis of the great north-south trade route between
the Vikings and the Greeks, and was also a center of trade with the East via the
Volga River. The northern section of the route ran from the mouth of the Neva
(where St. Petersburg was later founded), along the length of the Neva, through
Lake Ladoga, and down the navigable river Volkhov which connected Ladoga to
Novgorod and Lake Ilmen just south of Novgorod. So long as Novgorod controlled these territories, it grew and prospered, but when it lost them to Sweden
the city declined. To regain its position in international commerce, develop its national economy, and maintain effective contact with the West, Russia needed access to the Baltic, but this was not reestablished until the reign of Peter the Great.

As a cosmopolitan urban trading center not unlike Venice or other progressive
medieval Western European city-states, Novgorod developed an urban civilization
unique in Russia as well as democratic and tolerant political and cultural traditions.
It used a Germanic monetary system, a large community of foreigners lived unhindered in the city, its citizens traveled and established communities abroad, and
its princes and leading citizens often married foreigners. Women were generally
treated as the equals of men and participated in civic affairs. Wealth was sufficiently
high to maintain education and high literacy, and to support art and architecture. Unlike Muscovy, in Novgorod most wealth and power lay with a powerful merchant
class, which kept the ruling prince and the Church in check. Whereas Moscow's
Grand Princes gained power by "gathering" the Russian lands as their own and ad-
ministering them as their patrimony, in Novgorod property and sovereignty were
understood as separate, and institutions were created to curb and control the exercise of political power and protect property and citizens' rights in it. Novgorod's
prince was selected and hired by the people, and he functioned pursuant to a contract setting forth his powers and the restrictions on them; if the people grew dissatisfied, he could be replaced. All major decisions were made by democratic public assemblies called a *veche*, which assembled on both a city-wide and district level,
and at which each free householder had a vote. An advanced legal code was developed, criminal punishments were generally humane with an emphasis on fines, and
human life and the individual were held in high regard. Thus, a reciprocal relationship between the state and society was recognized, whereby the vital activity
within the state lay with its citizens, who created their government to protect their
rights and property, and provide security. This anticipated Western political thought
by centuries and was fundamentally different from the idea of a divinely ordained
monarch prevalent in Muscovy and the Old Regime in Western Europe.

Out of this economic, political, and cultural milieu grew a tradition of civic and individual independence (even irreverence), vigor, tolerance, and imagination. It stands

in stark contrast to the worldview of the rest of Russia during and after the Mongol period, until St. Petersburg. A poignant example was the fresco of the Savior in the main cupola of St. Sophia Cathedral in the city's kremlin: His hand was portrayed not, as usual in Moscow, partly open and relaxed as when crossing oneself, but as a fist symbolizing strength and independence, even defiance. Even the Orthodox monastery constructed on Perun hill outside town where pre-Christian pagan rites were held was named Our Lady of Perun, after the pagan god. This would have been unthinkable in Moscow. Before Moscow conquered Novgorod, the city's seal consisted of a flight of steps representing the *veche* tribune and a T-shaped pole representing the city's sovereignty and independence. Under Muscovite rule, the steps assumed the shape of the Tsarist throne, and the pole that of the Tsar's scepter.[2]

Feeling commercial competition, needing tax revenues, and demanding political subservience, Muscovy under Ivan III conquered Novgorod in 1471. He arrested thousands of Novgorodians, who were either killed or deported en masse, and confiscated their property. He eliminated the *veche*, and its famous bell was taken down and shipped to Moscow. In 1494 Moscow expelled the Hanse from the city, arresting its members and confiscating its property. When Novgorod recovered over the next century and once more was perceived as a threat to Moscow, it suffered utter devastation from Ivan the Terrible in 1570, when he (probably falsely) accused Novgorod of plotting with Poland to overthrow him. In an infamous incident, Ivan invited the town's leading citizens to dinner in the Faceted Chamber in Novgorod's kremlin, where his guards murdered them. About one-third of the city's population perished in a massacre that lasted weeks. Ivan then removed the city's main library, which contained many ancient and priceless manuscripts, and buried it in secret chambers under the Moscow Kremlin, where it remains lost to this day. Thus was smashed Russia's most important link to the West which had survived the Mongol invasion. Whereas Kiev had been lost to the Mongols, Novgorod was crushed by fellow Russians.

Peter the Great was impressed by Novgorod's history and traditions and held up many of them as models. After Petersburg was established, in 1724 Alexander Nevsky's remains were transferred to St. Petersburg's principal monastery, Alexander Nevsky Monastery, to symbolize Petersburg's links with Novgorod's history and traditions. St. Petersburg's main street, which connects the city's center to the Monastery, was eventually named after him (Nevsky Propsect). When legends about the founding of St. Petersburg first began to circulate, a popular one in the North was that St. Andrew the First-Called* had visited the future site of Novgorod

---

*The Apostle Andrew is the patron saint of Russia. According to the officially sponsored legend found in the chronicles, he visited the site of the future Kiev, introduced Christianity to Russia, and traveled to the area of the future Novgorod to preach. For Muscovy, this served to link Russian Orthodoxy directly to biblical times, thus avoiding links with Byzantium and the Viking princes of Novgorod and Kiev. While there is some evidence that Andrew traveled north into what is now Ukraine and Russia (and also Scotland), neither Kiev nor Novgorod existed at the time, nor did the Russian language or the Russians as a nationality.

as well as the mouth of the Neva, the site of the future "reigning city" *(tsarstvuyushchii grad)*.[3] This legend linked Novgorod and Petersburg as centers of Russian civilization. Later many Petersburg liberals, including Alexander Radishchev,[4] the Decembrists,[5] Alexander Herzen,[6] and playwrights,[7] identified with Novgorod's traditions when advocating their progressive agendas for Russia. Today, Novgorodians proudly assert that Peter the Great and St. Petersburg continued directly many of the essential traditions of Novgorod.

KIEV

The Kievan state was founded in 882 by Prince Oleg, one of a line of Viking princes related to Prince Rurik of Novgorod. Kievan civilization reached its zenith under Vladimir and his son Yaroslav the Wise from the late 10th to mid-11th centuries. Its failure to develop stable political structures and its economic dependence on trade with Byzantium ultimately led to its demise.

Whereas Novgorod's legacy is political and economic, Kiev's is largely cultural and religious. When the Kievan state was founded, Byzantium represented the height of civilization, and Christianity had not yet split into Orthodoxy and Catholicism. Thus, Kiev not only learned much from Byzantium, but it also developed political, cultural, and dynastic ties with the West. Kiev's prestige was so high at the time that many European monarchs sought alliances with Kiev through dynastic marriages. Vladimir's daughters Premislava and Dobronega-Maria married the kings of Hungary and Poland. Henry I of France, who was illiterate, married Yaroslav the Wise's daughter Anna, who was well educated and knew several languages. Yaroslav's two other daughters, Anastasia and Elizabeth, married the kings of Hungary and Norway. Vladimir Monomakh's daughter Praxedis married the Holy Roman Emperor, Henry IV. Indeed, Kiev's civilization in many respects was ahead of Western Europe. Its laws were humane, citizens enjoyed freedoms, public education was progressing, commerce was sophisticated, and women enjoyed high status. Had Kiev developed the political and military organization needed to withstand the Mongol hordes, Russian history would be very different.

The key civilizing and cultural development in Kiev was Prince Vladimir's adoption of Christianity from Byzantium in 988. One motivation for the conversion was Vladimir's immediate political goals. The conversion was facilitated by Vladimir's marriage to Princess Anna, the Byzantine Emperor's daughter, which cemented political ties between the two civilizations while preserving Kiev's political and cultural independence (by putting the Prince on par with the Emperor as his brother). More importantly, the conversion left permanent marks on Kievan and (later) Muscovite society, serving to unify the Russian nation culturally and politically.

The new religion had to be propagated through a language. Kievan Russia's alphabet, Cyrillic, received through Bulgaria, facilitated the development of the vernacular Slavonic into a written language, Church Slavonic, which remained the principal written language of Russia until the 17th century. Kiev's adoption of this vernacular for Church purposes rather than the Greek or Latin texts available in Byzantium meant that Greek was not well-known (and Latin virtually unknown) in Kievan and Muscovite Russia. Since these were the languages of classical and Western Christian philosophical, religious, and historical works as well as of Roman law, Muscovite Russia's access to and knowledge of much of classical and Western culture following the decline of Byzantium was severely limited. Kiev's own absorption into the Polish-Lithuanian state exacerbated this problem for Muscovite Russia, while Kiev itself would exploit this link to grow into a center of Greek and Western-inspired learning. As a result, classical thought had no meaningful influence in Russia until the St. Petersburg era, when Kievan scholars played an important role in introducing this learning into Russia.

Also significant was the manner in which Christianity was introduced and practiced. Since the society had no developed philosophical tradition or even literacy, Orthodox believers tended to adopt all aspects of doctrine and ritual uncritically, assuming that the religion's founders had worked out to perfection all essential and necessary truths and rituals. Further, since Orthodoxy was forced on the population from above, often violently, there was little scope for theoretical discussion and more attention to form, although some concessions were made to graft Orthodoxy onto pagan rituals and practices. Finally, the Greek and Slav churchmen dispatched to spread Christianity in this hinterland were by no means the best and most educated, and were often separated from their flock by language barriers. Consequently, they typically confined themselves simply to teaching the externals of ritual and collecting money for the Church.[8]

As a result, the mystical and ritualistic aspects of the new religion predominated. No sophisticated philosophical or theological tradition was transmitted from Byzantium or developed on its own. In a largely illiterate population in which pagan influences were still fresh and alive, the beliefs of Russian Orthodoxy came to be understood, conveyed, and appreciated not through theoretical or literary means but through its mystery and visual beauty, as represented by the service and by icons. (Indeed, it was the beauty of the religion's ritual which most impressed Vladimir's emissaries sent to Constantinople to evaluate its suitability for Kievan Russia.) Icons and the icon screens in Orthodox churches served as a constant reminder of God's power and constant involvement in human affairs, reinforced the social and political hierarchy in society, and, in the Muscovite period, supported the Tsar's place as the icon of God in the Orthodox empire, just as the Orthodox empire was the icon of the heavenly world.[9]

The focus on adherence to ritual and near absence of theology also meant that, unlike religion in Western Europe, deviations from the established beliefs and rituals were rare. When they did arise, they gained no large grassroots following and were short-lived, and while they did they were not tolerated. Due to this intolerance for change among both church leaders and believers, Russia's isolation from Byzantium and then Byzantium's decline, Russian Orthodox texts and rituals remained essentially unchanged until the mid-17th century.

When the Mongols eventually lost Kiev and the surrounding area, it went not to Moscow but to the emerging Lithuanian state (soon to be the Polish-Lithuanian state). Thus, although its later shedding of the Mongol yoke might have given Moscow the benefit of Kiev's civilizing and cultural influence, instead each developed along separate political and cultural lines for the next four centuries. Poland ceded Kiev to Moscow under the Treaty of Andrusovo in 1667, the same year that marked the end of the Great Schism. Thereafter, Kiev's learning helped Petrine Russia become a less religious and more secular, modern state.

Despite the future importance of these cultural and religious trends, they never dominated Kievan national life in the way they later did in Moscow. Kiev's culture remained cosmopolitan, and the focus of its life continued to be trade between the Normans and the Greeks. When trade dwindled as Byzantium declined and the Crusades opened the Mediterranean to trade from Western Europe, so did the Kievan state itself. The government was not organized well enough to govern such a large territory. The roles and responsibilities of the Prince relative to the *veche* (adopted from Novgorod) were ambiguous. The outlying towns and estates were not closely integrated into the state structure; the sole concern was whether they paid tribute to Kiev. Most importantly, no orderly scheme for princely succession was established, so that the land was constantly divided and ravaged by warring brothers and their supporters. This disorder made Kiev easy prey for the Mongols, who united under a strong leader. Moscow's princes took notice of Kiev's fate and were determined not to repeat the same mistakes. The result was an absolutism unparalleled in Europe.

MOSCOW

Historical sources first mention Moscow as a city in 1147, and Prince Yuri Dolgoruky is said to have laid the foundations of the town (i.e., the city wall) in 1156. At the time, the town was under the suzerainty of Suzdal, which lay outside the Kievan state. The Mongols invaded and destroyed it in 1237, just before Kiev met the same fate. Muscovy's inheritance from Kiev was limited and consisted mainly of the Orthodox faith and forms of land ownership; Kiev's political traditions and its civilized culture did not pass. Instead, the influences of the Mongols and Orthodoxy combined to foster at the top an arbitrary autocracy and at the bottom a conservative, passive, uncritical populace wedded to habit and tradition.

Moscow and the territory surrounding it were under Mongol control until the late 14th century; it was in these conditions that Muscovite civilization matured.

Mongol rule broke most contact with Western Europe and even with Kiev; it also eliminated the possibility of developing diplomatic and commercial contacts with Byzantium. The Mongol conquest and decline of Byzantium thus blocked what might otherwise have been a natural and continuous line of Russian political, economic, social, and cultural development more in line with that in the West. Instead, the new external elements introduced over the next two centuries were oriental traditions and oriental blood. No Moscow prince ever set foot in Constantinople, but they were regular visitors to their sovereigns in Sarai.

Mongol influences on Moscow included the Asiatic dress adopted by princes and nobles (known as boyars), a variety of Mongol words incorporated into the language (particularly those relating to state affairs), rampant corruption, and the low status and isolation of women. Another Mongol legacy was autocracy, obsequious loyalty to princes, and the rule that the people "pray only to one Tsar." Muscovite princes adopted from Sarai a model of governing that limited their role to tax collection, keeping public order, and administration of patrimonial domains. No further secular conception of responsibility for public well-being existed. When Mongol rule ended, the practice of collection of tribute did not end; it was continued by the Muscovite Prince, who kept it for himself. No notion existed of a society separate from the sovereign which had any rights or with which it had reciprocal relations.

Mongol influence over Moscow began to wane after the Muscovite victory over the Mongols at Kulikovo in 1380 and Tamerlane's campaigns ending in 1395. The yoke was formally broken in 1480, when Moscow refused to pay tribute. The Grand Prince designated himself autocrat (samoderzhets), meaning that he paid tribute to no one.

During the Mongol period, local "appanage" princes rose up who operated vast estates, maintained order, and governed their localities. In order to defend themselves against Mongols, Turks, Lithuanians, Poles, and other outsiders, it was necessary and inevitable for these princedoms to unite, with one of them emerging on top. Beginning in the 12th century and culminating in the late 15th century with Ivan III's subjugation of Tver and Novgorod, the inevitable shakeout occurred, and Moscow emerged as the victor.

Understanding this shakeout process and why Moscow emerged victorious is fundamental to understanding the nature of the Muscovite civilization which developed and which Peter the Great despised and sought to replace in St. Petersburg. The lands were owned and run by nobles under a hereditary system called votchina, which had originated in Kiev. Within his own lands, the owner was sovereign and law unto himself; he controlled not only property, but also the local economy, political power, and the administration of justice. In short, the land and its people were his patrimony. Yet the nobles owed little to the prince, who correspondingly had little formal control over or responsibilities to them, a fundamental weakness in the state. This situation differed from medieval Western Europe, where vassals bound themselves to lords by contract and an elaborate network of subinfeudation developed.

Moscow's Princes learned from Kiev's weakness. Their initial approach was not to change the *votchina* system, but to become the chief landowner, to gain control of the entire land and make the entire nation the Muscovite Prince's patrimony and the Prince its absolute sovereign. Over time they also succeeded in introducing primogeniture in order to avoid the breakup of holdings and to preserve princely power. Once such ownership and control was achieved, the Prince was able to reverse the process and grant landholdings, as typical in the West, on a nonhereditary basis in return for service. This system was called *pomestie*. Over time, the service nobility convinced the Prince (later Tsar) that they could best serve him if their peasants could not migrate. The rise in service obligations resulted in serfdom. V*otchina* declined, but the Prince's absolute authority was assured.

Since the entire nation (both land and populace) was essentially the Tsar's patrimony, the exercise of property rights and sovereignty (politics) were not separated. The distinction in Roman law between *dominium* and *imperium (*or *iurisdictio)* which had been preserved in the West and which led to private property and individual rights was unknown in Muscovy; political authority too was exercised as *dominium*. State finances, for example, were essentially those of the Prince himself; state administration was essentially that of the Prince's household *(dvor)* and properties. This process reached its apogee under Ivan III and remained fundamentally unchallenged and unchanged until the Petersburg era, when Peter sought to institute a new model based on Western conceptions of property, state, and society. Much of this Muscovite legacy, including the preference of many for state ownership of land, survived right through the Soviet regime.

Similarly, unlike the West, in Muscovy there was no developed concept of a society in which the ruler had a reciprocal relationship with his subjects, who had certain rights and to whom the ruler owed particular duties. Even the modern Russian word for society *(obshchestvo)* did not yet exist; there existed only the concept of *zemlya*, which today carries a narrow meaning of "land" but which at the time was understood as income-producing property and its people, the object of the Prince's exploitation.[10] The Russian word for state *(gosudarstvo)* comes from *gosudar*, which, prior to being used as the word for "sovereign" in reference to princes and Tsars, was the word for a slave owner and thus connoted authority in the private sphere *(dominium)*. In this climate, the nobility was never able to emerge as a separate estate or order with its own common interests (and eventually rights) which could eventually pave the way for a civil society. This would begin only after Peter the Great's reforms, in the reign of Catherine II.

The reasons why the prince of Moscow emerged as the leader have much to do with why it became the "soul of Russia," with which Peter the Great and St. Petersburg are contrasted. Although there is much to be said for the skill of Moscow's Princes, initially Moscow's most fundamental advantage was geographical: It was far enough into the interior so as to not be easily accessible from distant Sarai on the lower Volga, and it was located in dense forest at the junction of two rivers, conditions which rendered the Mongols' cavalry-based attack ineffective. These conditions forced the Mongols to rule with a lighter and more distant hand than in many other areas, which ultimately allowed Moscow's princes to gather strength. In particular, in gratitude for Moscow's assistance in crushing the 1327 revolt of Tver (Moscow's rival) against the Mongols, the Khan put Ivan I in charge of collecting their tribute from neighboring Russian princes. The Mongols bestowed on him the official title "Grand Prince," though he became known then and to posterity as Ivan Kalita ("moneybag"). His role as tribute collector gave Moscow authority over rival princes and isolated them from having direct relations with the Khan. Also, like any effective tax collector of the time, Kalita garnered more taxes than he remitted and enriched himself and Muscovy (which were hardly distinguishable). Once Mongol power began to decline and a challenge became possible, Moscow was well placed to "gather" Russia. By delegating their fiscal powers, the Mongols had created their own nemesis.

Another force which fueled Muscovy's rise to prominence, united its people, and determined the civilization's character was the Orthodox Church. Ivan Kalita added to his domain the town of Vladimir, which after Kiev's fall had become the seat of the Orthodox Metropolitan. After Metropolitan Peter died in 1326 and Moscow defeated Tver in 1327, Peter's successor aligned with Moscow and moved Orthodoxy's seat there. Thereafter, Moscow's princes and the Church worked hand in hand to increase each other's power and influence.

Understanding the religious character of Muscovite civilization is crucial to understanding Moscow as Russia's "soul" and how it differed from Peter the Great's ideas and the civilization of St. Petersburg. A first important feature was Orthodoxy's simple asceticism and the associated monastic movement, epitomized in the 1330s by St. Sergius of Radonezh, who eschewed rational theology and favored direct contact with God through achieving an appropriate mystical inner spiritual state.

Notwithstanding the mysticism and asceticism of the faithful, the Church hierarchy and the Grand Prince inaugurated a monastic crusade designed to consolidate Moscow's territorial gains with monastery-fortresses and spread a uniform Orthodox faith. In 1503 the abbot Joseph Sanin persuaded a Church council to allow monasteries to accept land grants (fully equipped with peasants) from the Grand Prince and nobles. These monastic landholdings were still under the protection and ultimate control of the Prince and remained his patrimony; in return, he expected and received ecclesiastical support. Sanin was also strict on matters of doctrine, sought to root out heresy, and resorted to torture and executions, which became accepted practice. Sanin's efforts were opposed by Nil Sorsky, whose adherents became known as the "nonpossessors" since they opposed gifts of land to monasteries. Sorsky sought to preserve a more pure and spiritual brand of Orthodoxy, uncorrupted by vast properties and involvement in temporal matters. He was thus tolerant in matters of belief and supported the church and state keeping to their separate realms.

But Sanin's approach, known as Josephism, was a winning proposition for the Prince and fused the alliance between Church and Tsar. Church holdings became immense and serfdom spread. Princes and nobles endowed the Church with their wealth to ease their consciences in the hope for salvation and also to avoid taxes. The Monastery of the Trinity founded by St. Sergius outside Moscow in 1335, for example, had at least 100,000 serfs cultivating its lands by 1600. Monasteries often focused more on their role as landowners than on religion. This process subjected the formerly loosely bound ascetic communities to the Moscow Metropolitan's power. With the victory of Josephism, Muscovy itself came to be conceived of as a national monastery under the direction of the Tsar, in whom "the opposition between Caesar and the will of God was overcome."[11] But in practice the Tsar dominated the Church. Josephism helped set the stage for Russian autocracy as it emerged under Ivan the Terrible.

Josephism also helped generate Orthodoxy's messianic ideology, which conceived of Russia as a divinely chosen, special and superior nation destined to lead the rest of the world to salvation. Once developed, it remained a fundamental part of the Russian mentality, including in 19th-century Slavophilism and indeed in Soviet communism. This vision coalesced in the mid to late 15th century. At the Council of Florence in 1437–39, Byzantium, hoping to attract Western help in its struggle against the Turks, agreed to compromises which it hoped would unify Catholicism and Orthodoxy. Moscow rejected the arrangement and arrested Isidore, the Greek Moscow Metropolitan who had attended the Council and agreed to it. Moscow believed that Byzantium had betrayed the faith, which Byzantium's fall shortly thereafter (1453) seemed to confirm. It was God's retribution against an unfaithful people, the result of a corruption of the Greek Orthodox faith and Greek society.

Moscow now viewed itself as Byzantium's successor, which Ivan III symbolized by marrying Sophia Paleologus, the niece of the last Byzantine emperor, in 1472, and by adopting the Byzantine double-headed eagle as the Imperial seal.* Ivan III took the title "Tsar" (meaning Caesar), symbolizing his claim to inherit all political and religious authority of the fallen Byzantium. Thus arose the theory and widespread belief that Muscovite Russia was the "Third Rome," a term first coined by Philoteus, a monk from Pskov, who called the Tsar "the only Tsar of Christians."[12] The first two (Rome and Constantinople) had fallen as a result of deviations from the faith and, because Moscow would last forever (or at least until the

---

*The double-headed eagle, with the two heads looking in opposite directions, symbolized Byzantium's position between East and West, with its eyes set in both directions. Muscovy, of course, was in a similar position.

Apocalypse), there could be no fourth. The Tsar's role was not merely that of autocrat but of the divinely ordained head of a religious civilization. Muscovite Russia thus represented the culminating stage of a preordained progression in sacred and world history, with the Tsar at its apex. Since Muscovy was God's and history's chosen repository of perfect and undivided Orthodoxy, there was no scope for further historical development, only the wait for the Second Coming and the end of earthly life, and there could be no dissent on the question. (Bolshevism held similar views.) Originally the doctrine of the Third Rome was principally a religious concept, deeming Russia the successor to the pure and right teaching,[13] charged with preparing humanity for the Second Coming and salvation. For the Tsar, however, it also implied the exercise of temporal authority. It was only a short step to make it an imperial doctrine as well. The Tsar must unite the Orthodox world and prepare it for the Second Coming. The doctrine justified extending Orthodoxy (and the Tsar's power) to new lands, and for rooting out opposition within his own. The Tsar's temporal pretensions and Orthodoxy's spiritual doctrines reinforced each other.

Thus arose Moscovy's conservatism, arrogance, and disinterest in and xenophobic suspicion of anything and anyone not Orthodox and not Russian. This attitude extended to intellectual activity in general and to science, as well as to innovations (seen as deviations) in elements of culture on which the Church touched, such as music and art, which were viewed as lower forms of activity, superfluous, and not to be tolerated. Muscovites fell into a Manichean worldview, under which anyone who was not a member of Orthodox faith was impure, an enemy and not to be trusted. This included, of course, all Westerners. It is this view which bred the arrogance and condescension shown toward foreigners at the Tsar's court and was remarked upon by so many foreign visitors and eventually led to the establishment of a separate quarter for foreigners outside Moscow. It also led to censorship to prevent wrong thinking, discouragement of free intellectual activity, and the banning of things foreign. These attitudes reemerged during the Soviet period.

A final aspect of Muscovite Orthodoxy was that its prophetic and apocalyptic quality, focusing on the messianic role of the Orthodox nation and cosmic redemption, downplayed the role and importance of the individual, even his own salvation. Individual souls needed only to purify themselves and prepare for the Second Coming of Christ, which was seen as a collective, national event. No well-developed notion of individual conduct, rights, and duties ever emerged. Morality was not paramount and no moral code developed. People were politically and economically passive, behaved slavishly and were prone to exploitation, and had little incentive to develop knowledge or their abilities. Correspondingly, Moscow's rulers treated people as masses and expendable fodder without legal rights.

Since the end of the Orthodox calendar, and therefore, according to many of the devout, the end of history, was to be in 1492, people began to expect and look for either good or bad signs, of the Second Coming or of the Antichrist.[14] As that date approached, various cranks and mystics prophesied the end of the world. Though

Muscovy survived 1492, this apocalyptic outlook persisted and rose to particular prominence during crises such as the Time of Troubles (1598–1613) and the Great Schism (1653–67). It also enabled Peter the Great's opponents to label him the Antichrist and Petersburg a cursed city.

Under Ivan IV, the Terrible, the Russian calendar was reconstituted and history proceeded anew. His reign (1533–84) began with certain steps toward a secular state, but ultimately it marked the apex of Muscovite autocracy operating in tandem with the Church. There being no ready models for law and governance (the Novgorodian model being considered unacceptable) or classical political knowledge, governmental (and Church) administration was indeed muddled, and legal codes and rational procedures were lacking. In order to decide how to remedy the problem, in 1550 Ivan convened the first *zemskii sobor*, a representative gathering of important personages of the realm to codify laws and carry out a number of reforms. The primary result was a new legal code, the *Sudebnik* of 1550. Ivan restored some ecclesiastical lands to his domain and curbed the Church's acquisition of new lands. He initiated military reforms and established detailed regulations for military service of the nobility, as a result of which the *votchina* system of landholding, already in decline, disappeared and it became impossible to be a landlord without owing service to the Tsar. In effect, nobles became glorified serfs with no contractual or legal rights to couterbalance the Tsar's power. Ivan purged the boyars and the Church, creating for seven years a virtual state within the state, the infamous *oprichnina*. He arrested and executed the Metropolitan of Moscow, subordinating the Church to princely power in fact if not in theory. His rule presaged the totalitarian state, complete with denunciations, interrogations, prisons, and terror.

It would be mistaken to view Ivan as simply another monarch creating a secular monarchist state at the expense of religion and the nobility on the Western European model. Rather, Ivan achieved his ends while embracing and even sincerely seeking to preserve Muscovite religious tradition. He never viewed himself merely as a political leader but, consistent with the old Muscovite ideology, as the anointed head of a monolithic religious civilization. He issued a 27,000-page church code and encyclopedia called the *Hundred Chapters* to codify prior Orthodox rules, traditions, and practices, and catalogue church history, readings, and the lives of saints, even while it formally purged material from Church tradition considered undesirable; it also tightened restrictions on secular art and music. Even a printing press set up in Moscow was declared an inappropriate method for reproducing copies of the Bible, and it was destroyed by a mob. Ivan also had his confessor, Sylvester, prepare a guidebook for private life called the *Domostroi* ("Household Manual"),[15] which prescribed forms and methods of dress, household economy, family relations, and overall behavior, even regulating how to beat one's wife (lovingly), preserve mushrooms, care for animals, spit, and blow one's nose. It promoted a near-monastic, passive religious life, and demoted women. The more enlightened customs of Novgorod and Kiev were disapproved, ignored, or simply lost.

During Ivan's reign, Muscovy was constantly at war with the increasingly large and sophisticated armies of Poland, Sweden, and Turkey. Ivan needed Western assistance in training and commanding his forces, as well as to help in developing industry and certain sciences such as medicine. This he sought mainly from England and Holland, Protestant countries to the west of his adversaries. In return, these countries received trade privileges which led to an increase in the number of foreigners in Russia. In 1558 Ivan started the Livonian* War against Protestant Sweden and Catholic Poland in an effort to gain access to the Baltic. After initial successes, this quarter-century effort ended in defeat and a net loss of territory, mainly due to the backwardness of Muscovy's army. Muscovy was now enmeshed in military, religious, and cultural conflict with the West, but its political, military, and economic institutions and its people were unprepared to cope with the challenge. In the short term, the struggle caused further antagonism to Latin civilization and the termination of meaningful civilizing contacts with the West until Peter the Great. When a century later Peter the Great waged another major war against Sweden for access to the Baltic, Russia won due to Peter's military and other reforms. In the victory parade held in Moscow, people carried portraits of both Ivan IV and Peter with the slogan "Ivan began, and Peter completed."

In light of Ivan's purposes, the irony of his reign is that he more than anyone else set in motion the processes which ultimately destroyed Muscovy as a monolithic and insular religious civilization. He drove Russia in incompatible directions. Although he escalated the Tsar's claims to authority over religion above any known in Byzantium, he eventually discredited his claim to leadership of a Christian civilization by murdering his son and heir and the Metropolitan of Moscow, and temporarily renouncing his divinity and his title in favor of a converted Tartar Khan. His reign indeed acquired many trappings of an Asiatic despotism. The moral, spiritual, and political ties between the Tsar and the Church began to fray. When Ivan drew Russia into irreversible military and ideological conflict with the West, he inadvertently put it on the path to European statehood and unavoidable contact with and influence from the West. Militarily, Russia was falling behind and lay dangerously exposed. Russia would have to face squarely the question of which direction its civilization must take. The answer became evident over the century between Ivan IV and Peter the Great.

Ivan the Terrible is said to have died while playing chess with Boris Godunov. History does not record who was winning, but it does record that it was Boris who moved the country the next square closer to the Russia of St. Petersburg. Brother-in-law to Ivan's weak son and successor Fedor, Boris ruled in fact from about 1588. When Fedor died without an heir in 1598, a specially convened *zemski sobor* elected Godunov as the new Tsar, and he proved to be a capable ruler. He initiated many

---

*Livonia was on the Baltic Sea roughly where present-day Latvia is located. Separate from Lithuania, since 1237 it had been run by the Livonian Branch of the Teutonic Order.

public works and was an enthusiastic Westernizer. He sent 30 promising Russians abroad to study, but all except two chose to remain there and never returned. He attempted to establish the first university in Moscow, but the proposal was defeated by the clergy. He tolerated other religions, expanded trade with the West by granting favorable trade conditions, and afforded protection to the foreign community in Moscow. He was the first to encourage the Western practice of shaving, later enforced (among the upper classes) by Peter the Great. But his initial popularity faded after famine struck Russia, the Church grew uneasy with his policies, and the nobles who originally had opposed him reorganized their resistance. Boris died suddenly in 1605 just as a serious challenge was being mounted; his relatives were quickly executed and his family's influence was eliminated. These events inaugurated what is known as the Time of Troubles.

In the vacuum of power, rival boyar clans contended for the throne, as did Poland, and eventually they resolved upon a Lithuanian claiming to be Ivan IV's son, Dmitry. Dmitry had died in 1591, and the pretender was really Grigory Otrepiev, a defrocked monk who had been in the service of the Romanov family. Despite the defects in "False Dmitry's" claim, his conversion to Catholicism, and his marriage to a Catholic Polish girl, his supporters were able to make him Tsar in June 1605. When Dmitry proved not to be the puppet of the boyars or anyone else, the boyars, led by Prince Vasily Shuisky and supported by the Church, sought to replace him with one of their own. They worked the populace into a frenzy and Dmitry was killed by the mob. His body was dragged through the streets, left exposed for days on Red Square and then burned, and his ashes were shot from a cannon in the direction of Poland.

Shuisky was then proclaimed Tsar in May 1606, but he failed to appease the populace and became unpopular. A breakdown in social and civil order ensued, which Poland and Sweden exploited. Rebellions and brigandage broke out, rival factions competed for power, crops were abandoned and went unharvested, and famine spread. Word spread once more about the end of the world and the coming of the Antichrist. When a second False Dmitry appeared and Poland supported him, Shuisky struck an alliance with Poland's enemy, Sweden. This gave Poland a pretext to invade Russia, take Moscow, and depose Shuisky in 1610. After that a seven-member boyar duma ruled while it looked for a Tsar, considering among others the Polish and Swedish Crown Princes.

A striking feature of this strife was the degree to which it unmasked the inability of the leading elements of Muscovite civilization—the Church and the boyar nobility—to exercise effective moral or political leadership or even influence. For a civilization said to be organic and unified under a religious mission, one would have expected more. Russia had been exposed as an oriental despotism that had failed to develop institutions that could provide unity, stability, and prosperity. The boyars, the Tsardom, and the Church were discredited as representatives of the true Orthodoxy—the Third Rome—in the eyes of much of the population. Thus were exposed the cracks in society which would erupt during the Great Schism later in the century.

In the wake of the failure of Muscovy's institutions, Russia's plight was miraculously saved by the uneducated, religious, and usually passive Russian masses. In one of Russia's greatest national moments, the common Russian people, tired of strife, united almost spontaneously under the leadership of a common butcher, Kosma Minin, and Prince Dmitry Pozharsky of Nizhny-Novgorod in a grassroots uprising to march on Moscow and drive out the Polish occupiers in 1612. Having saved the nation, the common people promptly ceded their position back to the boyars and went home. Notably, in the aftermath no serious thought or attention was given to reforming the country's political institutions or the Church. Instead, a *zemski sobor* was called to elect a new Tsar and return power to the boyars, or so they thought. It chose the 15-year-old boyar Michael Romanov, whose great aunt, Anastasia Romanova, had been Ivan IV's first wife. The boyars chose Michael principally because he was young and seemingly could be controlled by the boyars and service gentry in the absence of his powerful father, Metropolitan Philaret, who they thought had been killed by the Poles. In fact, Philaret was still alive but held captive in Poland. He returned in 1619, was made Patriarch and became the most powerful man in Russia. He put the boyars in their place and effectively ruled until his death in 1633. Thus was established rule by the Romanov family for the next three centuries.

Notwithstanding the deficiencies and divisions in Muscovy that were exposed during the Time of Troubles, no meaningful reforms ensued. To the contrary, thanks to Minin and Pozharsky catalyzing a nationalist uprising, the immediate legacy of the Time of Troubles was a national and religious revival and a renewed belief in the superiority of Muscovy's religious culture. Muscovy's xenophobia hardened, which cut its culture off from the West until late in the century. Russia's fear of the West and Catholicism was exacerbated by the fact that this was the time of the Counter-Reformation and religious wars throughout Europe. Behind the Polish army lay the support of the Vatican and the Jesuits, who hoped to expand Catholicism to Russia. In order to check Poland during the Time of Troubles and both Poland and Sweden thereafter, Russia increasingly had to turn for help to the Protestant countries of Northern Europe. From these nations the Tsar invited unprecedented numbers of foreigners to serve in the military and for construction, trade, and crafts. Before the Time of Troubles, beginning in the 1560s, in order to prevent contact with the local population, foreigners had been restricted to an enclave outside Moscow originally called the "lower city commune" but which later became known as the German Quarter.* During the

---

*This village was known as the German (or "foreign") quarter *(nemetskaya sloboda)* because foreigners were generally referred to as "Germans." The Russian word *nemets*, is derived from the word *nemoi* ("dumb"), and foreigners were regarded as such because generally they could not speak Russian. *Nemoi* is derived from the words *ne moi* ("not mine"), hence the alternative translation "foreign."

Time of Troubles, however, the settlement was destroyed. The new foreigners temporarily lived freely amongst the population in Moscow, where they were allowed to open their own businesses, taverns, and chapels. But Muscovites soon grew tired and suspicious of them and tensions mounted, eventually resulting in a rampage in which many foreigners were killed or driven from town. As a result, their businesses were closed, their chapels demolished, and the German Quarter was reestablished at its previous location in 1652. It was in that Quarter that Peter the Great became drawn to the West.

As the century wore on, Europe developed economically and grew more powerful and more secular. The technological, economic, and cultural gap between Russia and the West widened. Russia was finding it harder to keep up and increased its reliance on Western military assistance, technology, and goods. Increasing numbers among the elite felt that something was rotten, that Russian civilization was losing its bearings. The natural instinct of most Russians who considered what had gone wrong (but did not consider that Europe might be doing right) was to seek answers in the past, which meant some form of revitalization and renewal of Orthodoxy. As the Church sought to tighten its grip on the faith, two competing approaches emerged in the 1650s: one led by Patriarch Nikon and the other by Archpriest Avvakum, which led to the Great Schism.

Nikon's approach had two elements. The first was to increase the Church's authority in relation to the state and indeed assert its (i.e., his own) authority in temporal affairs, which went beyond Byzantine tradition. Nikon did succeed in dominating the Tsar for several years, until he foundered when implementing his reforms within the Church. The second element was principally religious. He endeavored to purify the faith by correcting, editing, and publishing religious texts and manuals, as well as to improve the discipline, education, and training of the clergy, all of which he sought to achieve by tightening central control over the ecclesiastical hierarchy and the monasteries. In order to implement his religious reforms, following the introduction of the printing press in Moscow Nikon decided to produce, print, and distribute Church books. Church ritual and texts contained many local variations, and translation and other errors had crept in over the centuries following the adoption of Orthodoxy from Byzantium. The production of a new set of books for nationwide distribution necessitated a uniform ritual and cleansing the texts of errors. Notably, Nikon did not attempt to change doctrine; he merely sought to replace one set of forms with another. Specifically, in 1653 Nikon proposed a variety of translation and editing changes to texts and in 1656 upped the stakes by demanding changes to ritual as well. This set off a firestorm of grassroots opposition led by Avvakum, who accused Nikon of heresy. Avvakum viewed Nikon as the Antichrist and saw the influence of foreigners behind the reforms and the end of the world as their result. Unfortunately for his own cause, Nikon had taken the scholarly but impolitic step of employing outsiders (Greek, Kievan, and Jewish scholars) in his research and seeking outside sanction from the patriarchs of Constantinople, Antioch, and Alexandria. Inevitably, imperfect research made it possible to expose some of his changes as incorrect.

Avvakum's supporters, who came to be called Old Believers, represented more than technical opposition to formal changes. First, since the reforms had the state's backing, opposition to them was tantamount to insurrection against the state, which the Tsar could not let pass. Further, the Old Believers adhered to the original model and value system of Muscovite Orthodox civilization for which Nil Sorsky had fought. They represented the common, suffering religious folk, the "Holy Rus" that had been left behind by Josephism, the imperial aspect of the Third Rome doctrine, and the Church's collaboration with the Tsar. They represented the disaffected who during the Time of Troubles had finally arisen to save Muscovy, an event which they now saw as pointing the proper direction for the nation. The essence of these folk and their faith must be preserved and permeate Russian civilization. Only by taking this step back could Russia regain her character and fulfill her prophetic and historical mission. The Old Believers thus embodied purist Russian Orthodoxy: its emphasis on the historical, its concern not with the words of scripture or even its message but with the form of worship and the ideal represented, its mysticism, its monastic tradition, its apocalyptic vision, and Russia's historical mission. In this context, not even the slightest changes to received texts and rituals could be tolerated, and they steadfastly opposed them.

A church council was convened in 1666–67 to resolve the crisis. On the important political question, it rejected Nikon's pretensions to authority and the establishment of a theocratic state and deposed him, but it approved the vast majority of his disputed reforms. Avvakum was likewise deposed. Both were exiled; Avvakum died a martyr's death at the stake in 1682, the year of Peter the Great's accession to the throne.

Nikon's persecution of Old Believers was seen by the latter as evidence of the coming end of the world, with Nikon as the Antichrist. The (Western) year 1666 was equated with the biblical year 666 marking the beginning of the end.[16] Thousands burned themselves to death in mass conflagrations. Because the Old Believers had lost the support and participation of the clergy, they soon found themselves without priests to conduct services, without a liturgy and sacraments, and even churches. Some decided that priests were unnecessary, and the Old Belief quickly divided into those who had priests (popovtsy) and those who did not (bespopovtsy), which in some ways resembled Protestantism. The Old Belief never entirely died out, and their communities of Old Believers survived through the October Revolution and constituted one body of opposition to Peter the Great and Petersburg culture.

The result of the Schism was the final subordination of the Church to the state and the predominance of secular power, thus presaging Peter the Great's reforms.

The religious parties had fought mainly against each other and destroyed one an-other, adopting in the fray methods and practices which themselves were inconsis-tent with Orthodox traditions. Nikon had his portrait painted; Avvakum wrote his autobiography. Both acts would have been unthinkable in the time of Ivan III. The pretense of Muscovy as an organic religious state was destroyed. This meant that the Tsar too was discredited as the representative of the Orthodox nation, the true creed and the path to salvation. Maybe God had forsaken the Tsardom, thought many. The Establishment was illegitimate and would produce the Antichrist. The true kingdom lay elsewhere, outside the Church and the state. Particularly among Old Believers, the legend of the invisible, ideal City of Kitëzh hidden at the bot-tom of a lake became popular and exemplified the people's vision of the true, lost Russia. Powerless anyway, many opted out of society and history, focusing on the true faith and their own salvation. In this twilight of Muscovite civilization, a breach had opened between the rulers and the ruled.[17] But in the popular mind the problem was linked to the influence of foreign ideas and learning. Many con-sidered that Peter the Great created a gulf between the elite and the ruled, but in fact a gulf already existed, and his enterprise was an effort to rectify the problem through a new model of civilization in which all Russian people would be en-franchised.

By the end of the Schism, the Muscovite state and civilization had reached a dead end. In the modern world, it could not maintain itself as a premodern civ-ilization essentially isolated and distinct from the rest of the world. Russia had to be put back together again, and fundamental change was inevitable. It needed a new paradigm, a clear break from the past. But too many vested interests were still tied up with the existing social and political structure, and few at the time were willing to admit openly that the Muscovite religious civilization was gone forever and had no future. Since no one of consequence dared advocate an al-ternative, the state muddled through, maintaining only cautious contacts with the West. (The Soviet leadership faced a similar dilemma and had adopted much the same policy by the 1970s.)

Thus, Tsar Alexis (ruled 1645–76) consolidated the autocracy and followed a cautious and sporadic policy of Westernization without tampering with the social and political structure. This was simply a somewhat enlightened continuation of the dual, contradictory policy of Ivan IV. An important event of Alexis's reign was the return of Kiev to Russia in 1667 following the defeat of Poland, which brought back to Russia Kiev's higher level of culture, scholarship, and enlighten-ment. Peter the Great would later draw on this resource, and many leading Kievans would later move to St. Petersburg. Fedor's reign (1676–82) followed the lines of Alexis and was notable mainly for the abolition of the family precedence system known as *mestnichestvo*, which later facilitated Peter the Great's creation of a class of service nobility.

It was Alexis's son, Peter the Great, who was both able to recognize the need for change and willing to exercise all means to effect it. He asked not simply what Russia was doing wrong, which produced answers in the past, but what the West might be doing right, opening a window to the future. He would not make piecemeal, convenient use of Western technology, personnel, and ideas, but would reject large parts of Muscovite civilization and replace them with Western models. St. Petersburg would be the icon of this new paradigm and the laboratory for the new Russia.

CHAPTER 1

A Giant's Vision:
A New National Life

Peter the Great . . . alone is universal history!

ALEXANDER PUSHKIN

I am a student and I seek teachers.

WRITTEN ON PETER THE GREAT'S PERSONAL SEAL

Suppose I have to harvest large shocks of grain, but I have no mill; and there is not enough water close by to build a water mill; but there is water enough at a distance. Only I shall have no time to make a canal, for the length of my life is uncertain. And therefore I am building the mill first and have only given orders for the canal to be begun, which will better force my successors to bring water to the completed mill.

PETER THE GREAT[1]

There is a legend that St. Petersburg—too miraculous to be the work of ordinary humans—was created by a Giant. Inspired by the sight of the setting sun over the silvery waters of the Neva as it flows into the Gulf of Finland, he decided to build there his paradise, the city of his dreams. There he built a house, but the Earth swallowed it. Undeterred, he built another house, but the Earth swallowed it too. The Giant furrowed his brow, realizing that the task would be harder than he thought, yet he refused to give up. Then, in a stroke of genius, he built the whole city on the palm of his hand and gently lowered it to the ground. This time the Earth sighed, but did not swallow the city. The Giant now had his paradise.

The Giant, of course, was Peter the Great. Indeed, at six feet seven inches tall, Peter towered over everyone else. Yet it was not simply his height that made him a giant. More important was his vision of a new Russia and what he did to bring it about. And central to it all was the creation of St. Petersburg, which Peter envisioned and created as the embodiment of all that he stood for, a laboratory and a model for the rest of Russia to follow, a catalyst for changing the national life. He called it his "paradise" and spared no effort or expense for it, personally supervising the details of its construction and laboring with his own hands to turn his dream into reality.

Peter the Great and St. Petersburg are inseparable.[2] To understand Peter takes one far in understanding his city in its proper context and full sense. The story of St. Petersburg thus begins with that of its founder: his upbringing, the influences upon him, his friends and helpers, his view of the world, his dreams and goals.

PETER'S CHILDHOOD AND YOUTH

Peter, the son of Tsar Alexis and his second wife, Natalya Naryhshkina, was born in the Terem Palace of the Moscow Kremlin on May 30 of the Russian year 7180,* the day of St. Isaac of Dalmatia. He was named after the Apostle Peter, and was christened four weeks later on June 29, the holy day of St. Peter, after whom he later named St. Petersburg.

Peter's father, Tsar Alexis, was the most educated, moderate, and well-traveled (within Russia) Tsar in recent memory. Intellectually curious, open-minded and interested in the arts, he borrowed tentatively and selectively from the West while hoping not to endanger Muscovite culture. According to his English physician, "had not he such a cloud of Sycophants and jealous Nobility about him, who blind his good intentions, no doubt he might be numbered amongst the wisest of Princes."[3]

Peter's mother, Natalya, was the daughter of a rural landowner, Kiril Naryshkin, who, in order to give his daughter a better life, had her brought up in Moscow in the home of his friend, Artamon Matveev. Matveev was not a boyar but a commoner who, thanks to his education and abilities, had risen to become Alexis's chief minister. Matveev loved intellectual discourse, socialized with foreigners regularly, and was married to Mary Hamilton, a Scot. Thus, Natalya grew up in a stimulating environment, and she in turn stimulated Alexis and Peter.

Peter's early childhood was not unusual for a potential heir to the throne. His education was less formal than usual for Tsarevichs—after all, he was third in succession behind his half-brothers Fedor and Ivan—but it was still better than that of the average nobleman. He was given a tutor, Nikita Zotov, who was not a scholar, professional tutor, or educator but a tax clerk incapable of giving Peter a formal classical education. But Zotov's knowledge of world and military history and foreign places piqued Peter's interest, and soon Zotov was regaling him with stories from Russian and foreign history, battles, and exotic places. Zotov became one of Peter's lifelong friends and servants, serving Peter in many capacities, ranging from Prince-Pope of Peter's All-Jesting Assembly to privy councillor and general-president of the Privy Chancellery.

When Alexis died in 1676, next in line for the throne was Peter's older half-brother Fedor, Alexis's son by his first wife, Maria Miloslavsky. Whereas after Alexis's

---

*June 9, 1672, under today's Gregorian calendar. Until Peter changed the Russian calendar at the turn of the 18th century, years were reckoned from the date of the creation.

marriage to Natalya the Naryshkins had enjoyed favor in court, once Fedor took power the tables were turned back in favor of the Miloslavsky clan. Matveev, as a Naryshkin supporter, was exiled to the far north of Russia. As Fedor's health was delicate, other members of the Miloslavsky family effectively ruled until his death in 1682.

Fedor died without a son or designating an heir, and a bloody struggle for power ensued between the Naryshkin and Miloslavsky clans. By law and tradition, Fedor's brother Ivan should have succeeded to the throne, but he was frail (lame, nearly blind, and with speech impediments) and incapable of ruling, and it seemed that his health would degenerate further. Moreover, the boyars were still upset at Fedor's (i.e., the Miloslavskys') abolition of *mestnichestvo*. In an irony of history, they looked to Peter as a guardian of the old ways. Since Peter was a minor, the boyars made Peter Tsar and Natalya Naryshkina his regent, in the hope that real power would be wielded by Matveev, who was recalled from exile.

The Miloslavskys reacted within a few weeks. The opportunity arose with the revolt of the *streltsy*, 22 elite regiments of 1,000 soldiers each who in peacetime served mainly as guards to the Tsar. They revolted initially against their commanders due to just grievances, but Miloslavsky supporters skillfully manipulated them against the Naryshkins. The *streltsy* went on a three-day rampage in which they stormed the Kremlin and hacked to pieces Matveev and many of Peter's relatives before his eyes; Peter was terrified and feared for his and his mother's life. Their Kremlin apartments were ransacked, and many of Peter's own possessions were destroyed or stolen. In the aftermath, Ivan was installed as Peter's co-Tsar, while Fedor's and Ivan's sister, Sophia, was appointed as their regent and assumed effective power.

The *streltsy* revolt brought the 10-year-old Peter's peaceful boyhood to a rude end and scarred him for life. Beginning with this incident he developed a growing hatred for the Kremlin and its court, Moscow, and the ways and trappings of Muscovite civilization. He longed to escape it, and eventually to destroy it. The ultimate realization of this desire would be the new world of St. Petersburg.

Sophia quickly obliged Peter's wish to escape. Following the Naryshkins' ouster from the Kremlin, Peter and Natalya were consigned to quasi-exile in the village of Preobrazhenskoe, a Romanov country estate just outside Moscow, near enough for them to be watched. This gave Peter free rein to pursue his own whims, ideas, and imagination without becoming heavily involved with or influenced by the rituals and obligations of the Kremlin court. His formal education was discontinued, however, from which he suffered later in life. Peter always lacked scholarly discipline and was never a theoretician, but he became a true visionary. Perhaps he would not have accomplished as much had his thinking been limited by a traditional Muscovite Kremlin education.

Peter's favorite pastime was war games. Initially these were mere child's play, but by using the resources of the state they became increasingly sophisticated and large, his "play soldiers" numbering over 1,000 by 1689. The games ultimately led to the formation of the famed Preobrazhensky and Semenovsky Regiments (after the nearby villages of Preobrazhenskoe and Semenovskoe which provided the initial recruits), which later served in St. Petersburg as the Emperor's personal regiments until the February Revolution. Through these games, in which he was often advised by his foreign friends, Peter learned a great deal about the art of war.

Peter's efforts to recruit knowledgeable commanders for his war games led to his first contacts with the German Quarter, located near Preobrazhenskoe. Over the years, Peter recruited there many foreign advisers who were to serve him loyally and well after he took power, including the Swiss Franz Lefort, the Scots Patrick Gordon and James Bruce, and the Dutchman Franz Timmerman.

Timmerman and another Dutchman, Karsten Brandt, awakened in Peter the desire to learn sailing and build ships and taught these skills to him. Whereas Russia had only primitive, flat-bottomed river sailboats, Peter and Timmerman built new vessels in the Dutch manner. In the summer of 1688 Peter went sailing almost every day in an "English" style boat that he and Timmerman found and Brandt restored. (Known as the "father of the Russian navy," this boat is now on display at the Naval Museum in St. Petersburg.) Thus was born Peter's love for sailing and, later, the sea.

Like Peter's war games, his shipbuilding and sailing enterprises became grand. Peter, now 16, spent most of the next summer (1689) sailing and shipbuilding at Lake Pleschev, some 80 miles from Moscow. Still more influential on him were the following two summers of sailing in Archangelsk on the White Sea, Russia's only northern port, where for the first time he saw the sea and oceangoing ships. From his Archangelsk experiences he acquired a love and awe of the sea and an even greater respect for Holland, whose ships dominated that port. The experience also heightened his appreciation for the West and his desire to see and learn from it, especially from Holland. Later, Peter liked to think of ships at sea as metaphors for his vision of Russia, with a ship under full sail, its synchronized crew functioning like clockwork representing his ideal of Russian society.[4] He saw his city of St. Petersburg as such a ship, and established as the city's official symbol the image of a caravel under full sail, which can still be seen atop the golden spire of the Admiralty.

Meanwhile, in August of 1689 a crisis arose. Peter's half-sister Sophia actually had governed well, but her favorite, Boris Golitsyn, had taken some Westernizing initiatives and invited numerous foreigners to Russia, which made him and Sophia unpopular with the conservative Patriarch Joachim as well as with much of Moscow's population. Golitsyn's loss to the Turkish-backed Crimean Tatars gave the Naryshkins and their supporters, who included Joachim, the opportunity to oust Sophia from power. The alarm sounded and a panic ensued when Sophia's departure from the Kremlin to Donskoi Monastery accompanied by a *streltsy* guard was mistakenly interpreted and immediately reported by Naryshkin supporters as a march on Preobrazhenskoe against Peter. Word of this reached Preobrazhenskoe in the middle of the night and Peter was hastily awakened. Dressed only in his bedclothes, Peter fled with his retinue to Troitsky Monastery outside Moscow. From there he skillfully issued orders and ultimatums and, over the course of a few days, gradually won over the soldiery and population and isolated Sophia. As a pilgrimage of officials, churchmen, and soldiers headed to Troitsky to join Peter's cause, Sophia's and Golitsyn's government crumbled. Natalya Naryshkina was once more installed as regent, and her relatives and supporters governed for the next five years.

While Peter, now 17, could have assumed power at this point, he had no desire to do so; indeed, his later ideas and reforms had not yet ripened in his mind. So Peter continued as before, sailing, playing war games, and visiting the German Quarter. Natalya was not pleased by Peter's lifestyle and, influenced by the conservative Patriarch Joachim, who in the wake of Golitsyn's downfall had convinced her to introduce discriminatory measures against foreigners and foster antiforeign sentiment, she limited Peter's visits to the German Quarter and convinced him to marry Eudoxia Lopuknina, from a conservative Muscovite family, in the hope that married life would both curb his excesses and produce an heir. Peter and Eudoxia were married in 1689 and soon had a son, Alexis, but Peter ignored his wife and son. When Joachim died in 1690, as if in belated protest against Joachim and to make up for lost time, Peter immersed himself in the life of the German Quarter.

In this microcosm of Europe, Peter personally began to bridge the wide cultural and psychological gap between Russia and the West. On the surface, the Quarter's attractions were the relief and enjoyment it provided through its gaiety, variety, companionship, drinking, and women. He soon took a mistress there, the German Anna Mons, and their relationship would last 12 years. For Peter, however, the deeper and more lasting attractions and influences of the Quarter were the stimulating conversations with foreigners about the world, foreign events and ideas, military escapades, and stories of the residents' experiences. There he also heard foreigners' views on Russia, what was wrong with it, and what should be done to improve it.

Peter quickly became the most popular and celebrated visitor to the Quarter, and his activities with his friends there soon became more elaborate and formalized. Most notable was the creation of the All-Jesting Assembly (*Vseshuteishnyi Sobor*), a private drinking and social society in which members were given formal ecclesiastical titles and responsibilities complete with elaborate entertainments, ceremonies, and rites. It continued to function actively on a larger scale in St. Petersburg right up to Peter's death. Organized nominally as a parody of the hierarchy of the Western Catholic Church, in fact it mocked the hierarchy of the Orthodox Church and gave vent to Peter's resentment against it. This was one means by which Peter sought to discredit Church institutions and officials and ridicule superstition.

It was in the German Quarter that Peter found his cast of foreign friends and advisors, chief among whom were Francis Lefort and Patrick Gordon. Lefort was a handsome and engaging Swiss adventurer and mercenary soldier from Geneva who had served in the Russian army since 1676. Fond of a good time, he quickly became Peter's guide and mentor in the Foreign Quarter and ultimately his closest and most trusted foreign friend. Lefort was given positions beyond his qualifications, serving as the first admiral of Russia's new fleet and as head of Peter's Grand Embassy. But in 1699 he died relatively young at 42, probably from excessive drinking. Gordon, a Scottish soldier, had begun serving in Russia's army even earlier, in 1661. He served as Peter's most reliable military lieutenant, a sage advisor, and a venerable drinking companion. Gordon first trained the young Tsar during his war games in Preobrazhenskoe, showed his loyalty to Peter and Natalya by leading the foreign officers to join Peter at Troitsky Monastery in the overthrow of Sophia and Golitsyn, served in the Azov campaigns, and quashed the *streltsy* revolt. But he too died in 1699, within weeks of Lefort. From then on, Peter would never again rely so closely on foreigners. While he was eager to learn from foreigners, throughout his reign Peter was careful never to put them in top positions. Whether in the military, the Colleges, or other posts, foreigners were generally in secondary or lower positions, available to render advice and expertise but never able to wield power.

Despite Peter's friendships with foreigners, most of his close companions were Russians, and this would continue throughout his life. It was during this period and the early years of his rule that he gathered his core group of Russian friends and supporters. For the most part, these were men chosen for their ability, with little regard for social class; many were of truly humble origins. From the upper classes Peter took Field Marshal Count Boris Sheremetev, Prince Jacob Dolgoruky, Fedor Apraxin, Gavriil Golovkin, Prince Mikhail Cherkassky, Prince Peter Prozorovsky, and Prince Fedor Romodanovsky. From more humble origins he took Alexander Menshikov (who reputedly had sold pies on the streets of Moscow), Peter Shafirov (a former store clerk), Pavel Yaguzhinsky (who had shepherded swine in Lithuania), and Alexei Kurbatov (an inventor).

By far the most important of Peter's Russian friends and servants was Menshikov. Probably descended from Lithuanian peasants, he is said to have attracted the attention of Francis Lefort while selling pies on the street, became a stable boy at Preobrazhenskoe, and enrolled as one of Peter's play soldiers. The able and dedicated youth attracted the Tsar's attention and became one of his personal orderlies. From that time until Peter's death he would be at the Tsar's side as his closest friend and most loyal and trusted servant, both on the battlefield and in government. Through his genuine ability, tact, charm, and acquired polish, he rose to become the most powerful man in Russia (besides Peter) and held numerous high military and governmental offices, including that of the first governor of St. Petersburg, and in many ways was a model of the new kind of man that Peter wanted to create. But Menshikov was far from perfect. While he became one of the wealthiest men in Russia, much of his wealth was ill-gotten. He was a master intriguer, often to his own ends rather than the state's. As his power grew, his conceit, pretense, self-indulgence, and rapaciousness became boundless, which after Peter's death became his undoing. But Peter could never stay angry with him for long. One day Peter became fed up with Menshikov's excesses and threatened to send him back to selling pies on Moscow's streets. That very evening, Menshikov appeared before Peter dressed in an apron with a tray full of pies hanging from his neck, crying out, "Hot pies! Hot pies! I sell hot, fresh-baked pies!"[5] Peter of course forgave him.

Such a medley of personalities from all levels of society would have been unimaginable in the days of *mestnichestvo*, where positions were dictated by strict family hierarchies. What mattered to Peter were personal qualities, qualifications and competence. Peter himself set the example, beginning his military career at the lowest military rank and advancing only gradually; he became a rear admiral in the navy and a senior lieutenant-general in the army only after his victory at Poltava in 1709. Peter once told a young naval trainee, "You see, lad, even though I am the Tsar I have callouses on my hands, all in order to show you an example so that I may see fitting helpers and servants of the fatherland, even if I have to wait until I am old."[6]

Peter's gay life ended in 1694 when Natalya died. At 22, Peter finally began to rule.

PETER'S INITIAL YEARS IN POWER

Peter's first venture was to wage war against Turkey, the protector of the Crimean Tatars who continuously raided Russian settlements in the South and blocked access to the Black Sea, rendering European Russia landlocked except for Archangelsk. Peter was also personally eager to lead a real military campaign instead of playing war games. But the first campaign, involving the siege of Azov on the Black Sea in 1695, failed because the city remained supplied by sea, which Russia could not cut off because it had no navy. Peter tried again in 1696, after he built Russia's first naval force and besieged the city from sea as well as land, and this time Azov fell.

But final victory against the Turks remained elusive. The need to secure Western allies against Turkey provided the pretext for Peter to embark, in 1697, upon the trip to the West for which he had long yearned. Called the Great Embassy due to its nominal diplomatic purpose, the expedition was organized and led by Lefort and consisted of some 250 people, including 20 noblemen and 35 commoners (among them Alexander Menshikov) who were to learn shipbuilding, military techniques, and the sciences. The trip lasted 18 months and included Poland, various German states, Holland, England, and Vienna. Peter traveled incognito as "Peter Mikhailov" to free himself from ceremonial functions and attention and to allow him to pursue his private interests, a ruse which succeeded only partially.

The trip made a tremendous impression on Peter and was one of the defining events of his life. He saw Europe at the height of the Age of Reason. It was the age of Descartes, Hobbes, Newton, Locke, Milton, and Leibniz. Discoverers were exploring the Americas, Africa, and the Far East, the arts and sciences were flourishing; the Church was in retreat. Peter spent much of his visit learning several crafts and trades, absorbing local techniques. Most famously, he spent several weeks working as a carpenter in the shipyards at Zaandam and Amsterdam, learning how to build ships. He also visited with many of the leading figures of the day, including key statesmen such as Frederick III and the English King, William of Orange, as well as with scientists (including Newton and Leibniz) and military men.

One of the lesser known aspects of Peter's Embassy is his contacts with Freemasons. At the time, Freemasonry was still an underground movement persecuted by the Church, and it would not go public until the establishment of the Grand Lodge of London in 1717. Many leading European statesmen, scientists, and thinkers of the time were Freemasons, including, in Britain, King William of Orange, Sir Isaac Newton, and Sir Christopher Wren, all of whom Peter met with privately and at length. Tradition holds that Wren, who was then Grand Master of London's secret lodge, initiated Peter into the Order.[7] Whatever the case, Peter was familiar with and influenced by Masonic precepts, and his civilizing work was certainly consistent with Masonic ideals, which included a moral life, good works, the search for truth, education, toleration, and in general the brotherhood and perfection of mankind. One result of the Grand Embassy was to give Peter and his key aides access to the network of Masons across Europe, a powerful asset for a Tsar seeking to bring Western civilization, or rather an improved version of it, to his country. Back in Russia, according to Russian Masonic tradition, many of Peter's helpers, including Menshikov, Lefort, Gordon, and James Bruce, were practicing Masons and together with Peter founded a lodge, the legacy of which was found in the "Song to Peter the Great" sung at Masonic lodges in the late 18th century to the words of the Petersburg poet Gavrila Derzhavin.[8] Among its many other attributes, St. Petersburg may have been established as a Masonic city devoted to realizing Freemasonry's universal ideals, with Freemasonry playing a role not unlike that in the subsequent foundation of America and the building of Washington, D.C. While Russians often considered that Peter was copying Europe, enlightened Europeans realized that Peter sought to avoid Europe's defects and create an ideal society that they considered impossible under existing European social and political conditions. For this reason they looked to St. Petersburg with great hope as a new beginning for civilized man, and only after the disappointments of Catherine II's reign did their hopes shift to America.

Peter returned from his trip convinced of the need to decisively overturn the societal model and practices of old Muscovy and transform Russia into a modern society and a great power. The need was urgent, as Russian's enemies threatened and at stake was the very survival of the Russian state, so he introduced a shock therapy of Western technology, methods, and ideas. While still abroad, Peter recruited over 750 foreigners, particularly from Holland, to return with him to serve in Russia, and he purchased boatloads of equipment, weapons, art, and other items. But he would reject many Western ideas and practices that he considered unsuitable for Russia. The excessive enthusiasm of his days in the Foreign Quarter had faded, and it was gone for good after the death of Lefort in 1699.[9]

Peter's determination to change Russia rose to outrage when his trip was cut short by reports that the *streltsy* had revolted against him. In addition to their rampage of 1682, still branded into Peter's memory, the *streltsy* had created trouble just before his trip and in fact had delayed it. This new revolt was the last straw. But it was also an opportunity to consolidate power and begin implementing the plans that he had formed over the course of his journey. As matters turned out, Patrick Gordon had put down the revolt before Peter's return (and indeed even before word of it reached Peter). When Peter arrived in Moscow, he did not waste time. He immediately required his courtiers to shave their beards and adopt Western dress. Peter regarded beards as unnecessary, unclean, and uncivilized, and Russian traditional dress, featuring long oriental robes with sleeves longer than one's arms, as cumbersome, impractical, and unbefitting for men of action. At a banquet attended by Moscow boyars in such dress, Peter took a pair of long cutting shears and cut off the long sleeves. "See," he admonished, "these things are in your way; you are safe nowhere with them; at one moment you upset a glass; then you forgetfully dip them in the sauce; get gaiters made of them."[10] Then he dispatched his wife Eudoxia, a tool of Peter's opponents, to a convent.

This done, Peter had the *streltsy* interrogated, tortured, and punished. The majority of the revolting *streltsy*, perhaps over one thousand, suffered agonizing public executions, others exile and confiscation of their property. Their mutilated bodies were publicly displayed to provide a graphic example of the price of opposing the new Tsar. Sophia, who had been instrumental in instigating the revolt, was forced into a nunnery. Thus was extinguished the last serious political threat to Peter's rule from the old Muscovite order. His power consolidated, Peter embarked on expanding Russia's borders to the Baltic Sea and introducing his reforms.

In order to protect Russia's southern flank and free his hand for this enterprise, Peter concluded a treaty with Turkey in July 1700 according Russia some territorial gains. He immediately declared war on Sweden, thus beginning Russia's long involvement in the Great Northern War lasting until 1721.* Peter's first battle with Charles XII of Sweden, at Narva in present-day Estonia, in November 1700, ended in disaster, as his yet-unreformed army panicked and was routed despite a numerical advantage. Fortunately, Charles did not take Russia seriously and failed to press his advantage. Many of his counselors advised him to march onward to Moscow, but Charles wavered and in 1701 decided to concentrate on Saxony and Poland, which he considered more formidable enemies.

Peter quickly and effectively exploited this reprieve. Over the next two years he reformed and rebuilt his forces from the bottom up using the advisors, tactics, and weapons he had acquired in the West. As a result of the military reforms, Russia's

---

*This war pitted Sweden against Denmark, Russia, Saxony, and Poland. Sweden, along with France, had been the chief victors in the Thirty Years' War of 1618–48, and its opponents again combined in an endeavor to curb Sweden and restore the balance of power in the region.

army under the command of Count Boris Sheremetev enjoyed its first victories against Sweden in a series of minor battles along the Baltic, which Charles had left weakly defended under less capable commanders. Peter would gain no outlet to the sea, however, until May 1703, when Russia captured the area around the mouth of the Neva River and Peter founded St. Petersburg. When Charles learned of the city's founding, he mocked: "Let [Peter] found new cities. Then there will be more of them for us to conquer."[11]

Among the acquisitions of this Baltic campaign was an attractive but illiterate 17-year-old Lithuanian peasant girl, Marfa Skavronskaya, who had been orphaned and brought up by a Lutheran pastor. She had married a Swedish soldier who was soon killed in the fighting, and she found herself among the prisoners taken by Russia's army. Noticed first by an officer by the name of Bauer, she soon entered the service of Sheremetev, and then of Alexander Menshikov. In 1703 she became the mistress of Peter himself and the love of his life. Peter married her privately in 1707 and publicly in 1712, and in 1724 she was crowned Empress. Upon Peter's death in 1725 she would rule Russia as Catherine I.

Following Poltava, the war shifted to land battles on historically Swedish territory and to naval warfare on the Baltic using Peter's new fleet. Peter was again victorious, most notably in a naval battle off Hangö (at the southern tip of present-day Finland) in 1714, with Peter in personal command of the Russian fleet. The Treaty of Nystadt finally brought victory and peace in 1721.

Once the war turned in Russia's favor, Peter could concentrate not only on building St. Petersburg, but also on introducing reforms, which were fundamental and wide in their scope. They touched virtually all aspects of Russian society and the life of each individual. This was best described by the 19th-century Russian historian, Mikhail Pogodin, in his essay, *Peter the Great*:

Yes, Peter the Great did much for Russia. One looks and one does not believe it, one keeps adding and one cannot reach the sum. We cannot open our eyes, cannot make a move, cannot turn in any direction without encountering him everywhere, at home, in the streets, in church, in school, in court, in the regiment, at a promenade—and it is always he, always he, every day, every minute, at every step.

We wake up. What day is it? January 1, 1841—Peter the Great ordered that the years be counted from the birth of Christ and the months from January. It's time to get dressed—our clothing is sewn in the fashion given by Peter the First, our uniform according to his model. The cloth is woven in a factory which he created; the wool is shorn from the sheep which he introduced into Russia. A book catches your eye—Peter the Great put the script into use and himself cut out the letters. Your start reading it—this is the language that under Peter was made into a bookish one, a literary one, at the time of Peter the First, superseding the earlier church language. Newspapers are brought in—Peter the Great introduced them. You need to purchase various things—all of them, from the silk neckerchief to the sole of the boot, will remind you of Peter the Great; some were ordered by him, others were brought into use or improved by him, carried on his ships, into his harbors, on his canals, on his roads. At dinner, all the courses, from the salted herring, through potatoes which he ordered to be grown, to wine made from grapes which he began to cultivate, will remind you of Peter the Great. After dinner you go out for a visit—this is an *assemblée* of Peter the Great. You meet ladies there—they were permitted into men's company by order of Peter the Great. Let us go to the university—the first secular school was founded by Peter the Great. You receive a rank—according to Peter the Great's Table of Ranks. The Rank gives me gentry status—Peter so arranged it. I must file a complaint— Peter the Great prescribed its form. It will be received—before Peter the Great's mirror of justice. It will be acted upon—on the basis of the General Regulation. You decide to travel abroad—following the example of Peter the Great; you will be received well—Peter the Great placed Russia among the European states and began to instill respect for her; and so on, and so on, and so on.[12]

One could see such changes first and foremost in St. Petersburg.

These visible changes were grounded on several fundamental reforms in the state and society, which were aimed at the heart of Muscovite civilization and designed to revolutionize it. In the context of St. Petersburg, other than the changes in daily life, the most important were Peter's reform of the state and its administration (and, correspondingly, his view of the individual and his role in society), his religious policy, and educational reforms.

A NEW KIND OF STATE

In Muscovy, the state and the governmental apparatus developed as a means to administer the Tsar's own patrimony and derive income from his lands. Thus, the executive organs of Muscovy, *prikazy*, were organized primarily along territorial lines or according to sources of revenue rather than according to governmental function. Officials in each *prikaz* were representatives of the Tsar's household *(dvor)* and exercised both private and public functions on his behalf, including the administration of justice. Nobles were viewed as the Tsar's personal servants *(kholopy)* and in theory were only well-off serfs. There was no national budget until Peter, little coordination of officials' duties, and their status and salary across *prikazy* varied. For services on lands outside the Tsar's personal domain, officials were paid wages in money or in kind by the population, a system known as *kormlenie* ("feeding"). This "system" inhibited rational centralized state administration as well as the development of local government, and fostered corruption and arbitrariness.[13] There was barely any conception of "government" as such. The ruler's purpose was religious and not oriented toward earthly progress, which required no effective government.

Peter replaced the old patrimonial model of the state and its administration with a new model drawn from Western experience and the philosophers of the Age of Reason, some of whom he knew personally. Chief among them were Leibniz, Hugo Grotius, and Samuel Pufendorf, whose treatise *On the Duties of Man and the Citizen According to Natural Law* Peter had translated and published in St. Petersburg. These thinkers developed what became known as "police science" (*la police* in France, *Polizeiwissenschaft* in the German states). This theory embraced the idea of human progress and held that the state is not of divine origin but is a human creation. Therefore, it may be constituted, reconstituted, and improved by humans applying their reason. Organizing the state in the most rational manner would strengthen the nation and maximize prosperity, happiness, and each individual's potential.

Peter viewed the ideal state as a well-oiled machine running according to rational laws. In reference to the collegial system of administration, Leibniz had written to Peter: "There cannot be good administration except with colleges: Their mechanism is like that of watches, whose wheels mutually keep each other in movement." The state should function on the basis of rational laws, administered and enforced by enlightened officials and judges and obeyed by citizens who understand them. Unlike Muscovy (or the Soviet Union) the state is not dedicated to any ultimate idea or goal to which it or its members must conform. Rather, the individual, possessed with reason and a will, is the real agent of human progress. Government's task is to organize and administer the state so as to maximize human potential. Once the monarch, much like the Deist God, sets the mechanism in motion, the government need not act in a repressive or intrusive manner; it need only modify laws to changing circumstances and educate the public, and people's talents and reason will take care of the rest.[14] Peter's theory of the state partly explains his adoption of the title of "Emperor," derived from Rome, the very embodiment of law and efficient state administration, and Petersburg's own imagery reflects this Roman theme. Both the city and its main cathedral were named after St. Peter, and the city's crest contains the crossed keys from the state flag of the Vatican.[15]

The state's subjects were not viewed as slaves but as more akin to citizens. While in Muscovy all Russians also owed service obligations, Peter revolutionized their basis. In Muscovy, service was a personal duty to the Tsar derived from his religious position, which in theory left little barrier between the rulers and the ruled but in reality made all Russians slaves and afforded no basis for reciprocal rights and obligations. Under Peter, each individual owed obligations of loyalty and service not so much to him as to the state (and ultimately society), so that its enlightened purpose could be realized. Both government and citizens held rights and owed obligations to each other as defined and guaranteed by law. The Tsar himself was viewed as the highest servant of the state and bore the most responsibilities. Peter set a personal example by taking only his military salary, regarding only this as his own money, and spending only this on his personal needs.[16] The crown (now better viewed as the state) retained vast property holdings, but the revenues went to the state budget (which Peter introduced) and were no longer regarded as personal to the Tsar. The nobles had the next highest duties and universally had to serve in military or civil capacities.

This theory implied that the state should be run by the most educated and qualified people, up to and including the Tsar. Thus, in February 1722, Peter decreed that each Tsar should choose his successor. Merit rather than divine right should determine the right to rule. To justify this, later that year Peter had Feofan Prokopovich write *The Justice of the Monarch's Will*, which outlined the theoretical basis for the Tsar's authority. Rather than simply ruling by divine right and demanding the loyalty of subjects to his person on religious grounds, his authority stemmed from a contract theory of law, under which in exchange for protection and wise rule, the people cede a part of their freedom and accord authority to their ruler.[17] This concept did not require that all sovereign power be exercised by the Tsar, but allowed it to be distributed across governmental institutions (which Peter did endeavor to accomplish). The full idea of the social contract was not far away, either conceptually or in time. Peter's theory did not explicitly recognize society as self-constituting or include notions of democracy, the right to political opposition, or broad individual freedoms as understood today, but it was pregnant with their seeds. It was an important conceptual step toward civil society (in which society forms its own government charged with protecting its and individuals' rights and well-being) because it embraced the idea of human progress, government was recognized as man-made and subject to change, individuals were viewed as creative driving forces in society, and education was considered paramount for the system to work. Peter did not see this as limiting his power, which he considered ceded to him permanently and totally; citizens' rights could be exercised against government bodies and officials, but the Tsar's authority was final. Peter was an early believer in and practitioner of the emerging idea of enlightened despotism, which was beginning to take hold elsewhere in Europe. But for Europe's 18th-century monarchs the contract theory was destructive, and soon they were waging a losing battle against peoples in Europe and America who considered it their right to replace monarchs who violated their rights and govern themselves according to a constitution. Russia took longer because it had to overcome its Muscovite inheritance.

With these principles in mind, Peter set about reforming the state and its government, principally through his General Regulation published in 1720. For the government apparatus, following largely the Swedish model, he introduced a collegial system of administration based on the current European theory of administration known as cameralism. Cameralism entailed organizing the organs of state administration according to function (subject matter) and collegiality (strict delineation of duties and responsibilities of staff, and uniformity of status and salary). Thus, he replaced the Muscovite *prikazy* with several colleges. Each was responsible for a particular field, including foreign affairs, war, the navy, justice, state income, state expenditures, financial inspection and control, commerce and manufacturing. In 1722 Peter created the famous Table of Ranks, according to which each civil servant and military officer was assigned one of 14 ranks, advancing upward through them in the course of his career based on merit, making it possible for commoners to advance to high positions and become nobles.

In 1711 Peter created the Senate, which was partly a cabinet to oversee financial, judicial, and administrative affairs, and also partly a legislature to enact the new laws.

Through the Senate, together with the reform of the law courts and the creation of the General Procurator's office, Peter separated the judicial from the executive (administrative) functions of government. This departed from the Muscovite model, where the Tsar and his personal agents dispensed justice. The actions of state organs and state officials were now subject to review by the bodies of justice. In practice this principle struggled to become a reality, but at least this separation of powers, and the dispersal of power across state institutions, had been recognized and established in principle.

Peter extended his administrative and judicial reforms to local administration, again along European lines. Russia was divided into administrative districts and subdistricts, each organized along the lines of and subject to the colleges. The status and salaries of officials were made uniform, and the system of *kormlenie* was formally abolished.

Peter's new ideas of government did not readily take hold (especially in local government) for several reasons. First, the major reforms came only shortly before Peter's death and he was not around to ensure that they were implemented. Second, the reforms depended on the availability of qualified human capital, which was scarce in Russia. Peter confronted, almost universally, a slavish, passive religious and peasant mentality, widespread prejudice and superstition, ignorance, sloth, an outright suspicion of learning, and no conception of or desire for earthly progress or the general welfare. Most state servants were unable or unwilling to take any initiative, and many were corrupt. Menshikov was one of the few people able to think independently and make decisions himself, thanks to which he rose to second position in Russia and was appointed Governor of St. Petersburg. It was for this reason that Peter made education and the furtherance of knowledge key aspects of his reforms, but their fruits would come too late to have much effect in his lifetime. Finally, when Russians were unable or unwilling to act as demanded by theory, Peter grew frustrated and resorted to the cudgel and overregulation, which created confusion and some paralysis. The very speed and scope of the reforms necessitated a strong hand and strict oversight, but Peter's personality made it excessive. When bureaucrats demanded instructions and decrees from their sovereign before acting, a frustrated Peter obliged them with, as Pushkin later phrased it, decrees "written as with the knout." While Peter demanded that people take initiative and responsibility, his own behavior inhibited it.

Peter's system of state service also tended to tie the nobility too closely to the monarchy. In the West, the nobility as well as the Third Estate emerged as independent forces in society which fought for their interests and rights, which ultimately led to the rule of law and the emergence of civil societies. But in Russia no noble, industrial, or merchant class having a meaningful degree of independence from the monarchy had ever existed. Muscovite culture, which called for the complete and organic unity of Orthodox civilization and made nobles slaves, was antithetical to any model which recognized competing interests in society. Although

Peter's model could accommodate separate estates with their own interests, in practice his reforms did little to overcome this heritage.

Peter also applied modern western ideas in commerce, although his understanding of economics was limited.[18] In foreign trade, he applied the prevailing European practice of mercantilism, which emphasized a favorable trade balance, protection of domestic industries (particularly a protectionist tariff law in 1724), and proactive government policies to develop them. During Peter's reign, Russian foreign trade increased fourfold, much of it running through the new port of St. Petersburg. Peter even purposely tolerated a level of smuggling and underground market activity in order not to snuff out the seeds of commerce. In one case, he refused to approve proposed harsh confiscations on smugglers in the port of St. Petersburg, reportedly remarking: "It is too early as of yet. Commerce is like a fickle girl, who must not be frightened or harshly treated, but requires, on the contrary, flattering caresses and enticement."[19] Although Peter's reign antedated Adam Smith, he sought to expand private property and private enterprise. In 1719 he abolished the state monopolies in all industries except potash and weedash, placing all other industries in private hands. In principle, anyone from any social class could engage in such industries, though in practice the major enterprises were in the hands of the favored.

While Peter understood the need for balanced economic development, he was hamstrung by the war economy—the military absorbed over 40 percent of state expenditures[20]—which lasted until four years before his death. The war also affected industry, where the main challenge was accessing a factory labor force. Since most potential workers were serfs working on rural estates, Peter faced a dilemma: If they were freed, the state would lose poll tax revenues, which constituted the primary source of state tax revenues and were essential given the financial straits of the state resulting from the war. Peter's answer was to allow serfs to be "temporarily" furloughed to industrial enterprises, including in St. Petersburg, but technically they remained serfs and retained their registration as such in their old localities so that the poll tax could still be collected. In other cases they were simply bought from their rural owners. Thus began the extension of serfdom to private enterprise and Russia's industrial revolution, and its consequent impediments to developing a Russian Third Estate. There were opportunities after Peter to reverse this trend, but under subsequent rulers it deepened.

A NEW MIND-SET: PETER'S RELIGIOUS BELIEFS AND POLICIES, AND EDUCATIONAL REFORMS

Peter's departure from the Muscovite past is perhaps most visible in the religious realm. Of all of Peter's achievements, his church reform constituted the most decisive break with the past.[21] The reform changed peoples' values and worldview, intellectual life, methods of education, publishing, and the arts. Through his initiatives in education, scholarship, science, social life, and culture, Peter secularized Russian civilization in all areas except religious worship and doctrine, in which he did not interfere. He aimed to cut deep and revolutionize the Russian mind-set inherited from Muscovy, but not to have his people simply copy European externals.

Peter's religious reforms derived from his own religious beliefs. Peter was a believer, though he was not a fervent worshipper or churchgoer; his faith was the product of the Age of Reason. "Reason," he said, "is above all the virtues, for without reason virtue is nothing."[22] He rejected Muscovite mysticism, empty ritual, passivity, and superstition. Reporting to the Synod, Peter explained:

> There is a straight path to salvation—through faith, hope and charity—but people know very little, or wrongly, about the first and the last, and haven't even heard of the middle one, since they place all their hope in singing in church, fasting and bowing and so forth, in the building of churches, candles and incense. They believe that the suffering of Christ was caused only by original sin; in fact, they will obtain salvation as a result of their own deeds.[23]

Thus, he was a believer in good works. "For just as words without deeds and deeds without faith are equally dead," he maintained, "so words without acts and improper and unnecessary labor are equally useless."[24] An important part of deeds was morality, to which the Orthodox Church had paid scant attention. Peter attached much importance to morals in setting his policies, although personally he did not always set a good example. He was also knowledgeable about both the Orthodox and foreign faiths, theology and religious controversies, and was able to hold his own in discussions with clerics anywhere.[25] Thomas Consett, the chaplain in an English factory in St. Petersburg during Peter's reign, observed:

> His natural great genius led him very early in his life to give himself satisfaction in the doctrines and discipline of the Greek church, and his travels afterwards gave him the opportunity of examining into the doctrines of foreign churches, and of comparing them with his own: By which enquiries he rubbed off the rust of that bigotry to his own religion, which his people seem generally to have contracted, and as was seen in all his conversation, he was both an impartial an excellent judge of any controverted points in religion.[26]

Peter was tolerant and open-minded in his religious views, demanded the same from others, and embodied these beliefs in his policies. He did not interfere in matters of doctrine, ritual, or even choice of faith, and he allowed the establishment of many non-Orthodox churches. Peter reportedly declared, "We shall exercise no compulsion over the consciences of men, and shall gladly allow every Christian to care for his own salvation at his own risk."[27] His tolerance derived from his exposure to various faiths in his youth in Moscow's Foreign Quarter and his trips to Europe, particularly his experiences in Holland. During a discourse on the example of Dutch religious toleration while visiting that country, he reportedly observed that religious observance is generally beneficial but of little consequence to the state: "This system of government is highly favorable to commerce; it contributes greatly to the influx of foreigners into Amsterdam, and consequently increases the public revenues. I cannot give sufficient praise to [such] conduct, which it is fully my intention to imitate in my city of Petersburg."[28] Peter's only firm policy in the realm of beliefs was to combat and eradicate common prejudices and superstition, which he considered necessary for society to be governed and function rationally. Thus, he discouraged excessive veneration of icons, worship of holy relics, and placed false relics on public display. He tried to stamp out belief in false visions and miracles, and required priests to report them and prosecuted offenders. He also outlawed physically harmful practices such as self-mutilation.

The political concern of Peter's religious policy was to accord the state free rein in secular matters and the ability to carry out the reforms without Church interference. Peter feared that the Church, as the torchbearer of Muscovite civilization, might become a leading force of opposition to his reforms and a convenient rallying point for his political opponents. Therefore, while on the one hand he initiated the separation of church and state in accordance with modern ideas, he also ensured control over Church administration. To a large degree this merely institutionalized the dominance of temporal power over the Church which had already existed in Muscovy.

Peter's key lieutenant and theoretician in his religious reforms was Feofan Prokopovich (1681–1733), whom the historian James Cracraft described as "the first authentic voice in Russia of the Early Enlightenment."[29] Born in Ukraine as the son of a tradesman, and soon orphaned, he graduated from the Kiev Academy. Since higher theological education was unavailable in Russia at the time, he had to study at Jesuit colleges in Poland, for which he had to take Uniate orders. He then studied for three years in Rome at the Greek college of St. Athanasius, where he converted to Roman Catholicism. In 1702 he returned to Kiev, converted back to Orthodoxy, and began teaching at the Academy, among other things mathematics, literary theory, and physics. He authored a dramatic play, *Vladimir*, which was first performed in 1705 by his students and attended by the future rebel Ivan Mazepa. Eventually Prokopovich became a professor of theology, rector at the Academy, and abbot of the Kiev Brotherhood Monastery. He knew Greek, Latin, and Polish, was well acquainted with the theories and writings of Western philosophers such as Spinoza, Descartes, Leibniz, Bacon, and Pufendorf, and accumulated a large library of religious and secular works. He was probably the most learned man in Russia at the time. Originally recommended to Peter by Menshikov in 1711 to serve in the Ukraine, in late 1715 Peter summoned Prokopovich to St. Petersburg. There he became the architect of Peter's religious reforms and more generally Peter's chief ideologist and propagandist. He gave speeches and lectures, composed odes, wrote commentaries, and authored *The Justice of the Monarch's Will* and the Ecclesiastical Regulation.

Peter's most systematic religious reforms came late in his reign, with the issuance of the Ecclesiastical Regulation in 1721. To govern the Church, the Ecclesiastical Regulation created the Holy Synod, consisting of several clerics and one lay official and headed by its President. Like secular state organs, the Synod operated according to collegial principles. It was to have equal standing with the Senate (rather than being equal to a mere college), with each operating in its own sphere, and each was overseen by a procurator general. Church officials and priests were considered and treated like any other state servants. The service obligations imposed on priests were manifold. Indeed, at ordination, priests had to take an oath of allegiance similar to that administered to civil servants. Their obligations included the dissemination of decrees, laws, and other public information, keeping registers of marriages, births, and deaths, monitoring tax collection and reporting on tax evaders (though not actually collecting taxes).

Peter sought to reduce the number of clergy in order to free individuals for more "useful" professions. Correspondingly, he limited the construction of new churches and parishes, which he allowed only by special permission, as the labor and materials were needed more urgently for the war effort and Peter's other enterprises, including the construction of St. Petersburg. He also reduced the number of religious holidays and fasts, as these made people idle and unproductive, and he even permitted some previously banned activities during fast periods (in St. Petersburg, even balls and assemblies). Peter also scaled back the vast network of landed, serf owning monasteries that had grown up since the time of Joseph Sanin. Peter valued good works, and in his opinion Russia's monks were spiritually underdeveloped, ignorant, well-fed parasites who contributed little either spiritually or materially to Russia, were far too numerous, and were a drag on the economy, the state, and society. He set up a state department which administered monastic lands, imposed new taxes on them to support the war effort, imposed discipline and rigor on monks and nuns, and administered almshouses and religious publishing. The Ecclesiastical Regulation imposed public service obligations on monasteries (monks and monastic serfs), including the establishment and administration of hospitals and orphanages and the quartering of retired soldiers. Peter also established age and educational requirements for entering monasteries and otherwise restricted recruitment to them, which improved the quality of monks but reduced their number. Between 1724 and 1738 the number of monks, nuns, and novices was reduced by almost half (from 25,207 to 14,282).[30]

Ultimately, Peter believed, the key to reforming the Church and eradicating superstition, ignorance, and sloth was education. This policy was stated directly in the Ecclesiastical Regulation: "When the light of learning is extinguished there cannot be good order in the Church; there cannot be but disorder and superstitions deserving of much ridicule, in addition to dissension and most senseless heresies. . . . Learning is beneficial and basic for every good, as of the fatherland, so also of the Church, just like the root and the seed and the foundation." Indeed, it was in the sphere of education that common Russians most directly felt Peter's ecclesiastical reforms. He imposed compulsory education and training of priests, and those who failed were drafted into the army. Once educated, priests were expected in turn to educate their congregations at new ecclesiastical schools, preach sermons at religious services (which was not done traditionally in Russia but which Peter had observed in the Protestant countries), and to encourage literate members of their congregations to read religious works on their own, in the Protestant manner. This required not only literacy but also something more to read, so Peter expanded the writing and publication of religious books and pamphlets, including Bibles.

Peter likewise turned his attention to secular education. Education was perhaps the most crucial element of Peter's program, without which it would ultimately fail. It was the key not only to acquiring the technical skills needed by the military, the economy, and government institutions, but also to general secular enlightenment, the advancement of science and technology, and the eradication of ignorance and superstition, in short, the reformation of Russian civilization. Yet it was in education and learning that Russia was perhaps furthest behind the West. In Muscovy, learning was largely a monopoly of the clergy, but even they were mostly poorly educated. Knowledge about events in other countries was largely the privilege of government officials (this would be repeated in the Soviet period), while ignorance of foreign science and religions was celebrated as piety and goodness. Peter, however, wanted knowledge to spread widely and deeply in order to create "new men" who could then remake Russia. The need was urgent, and he could not let national pride get in the way. Peter made himself the first and best example, putting on his personal seal the words, "I am a student and I seek teachers." To this end, he went to the extent of issuing a decree in 1714 forbidding noblemen to marry unless they had achieved at least a basic education. Educational opportunities opened for the common citizenry as well, particularly in technical disciplines such as engineering. In order to realize his educational goals, Peter took a threefold approach: founding educational institutions (mainly in St. Petersburg), sending Russians abroad for education and training, and bringing foreign scientists, craftsmen, and educators to Russia (again, mainly St. Petersburg). The latter included bringing foreign nannies and other upbringers of noble children, including for Peter's own daughters, Anna and Elizabeth. The children of the new generation grew up in a different world than their parents.

PETRINE (AND PETERSBURG) CONTROVERSIES

Peter's reforms were and remain controversial. Since many of the controversies extend to Petersburg itself, a history of the city that does not address them would be incomplete. One is whether Peter's new vision (or something similar) can be viewed as the next natural development in Russia's history, or whether it was so alien and incompatible as to be inappropriate for Russia. If the latter is true, then St. Petersburg too is a stranger in its own land and no model for the future. Notably, this question was originally debated not among historians but in circles of writers, churchmen, and social critics. That is, the question was posed as an ideological issue rather than as a matter of historical record. The notion that Peter's legacy was fundamentally at odds with Russia's civilization and its national consciousness, and therefore wrong, arose only in the first half the 19th century among romantically inclined intellectuals and Slavophiles.[31] It was not until the second half of the 19th century, when the issue became one not of politics and ideology but of serious historical scholarship, that the question was genuinely addressed. Beginning with Russia's greatest historian, Sergei Soloviev (1820–79), the fundamental links between Peter's efforts and the Russian past became established as undeniable,[32] as traced in the prologue.[33]

A related question is whether Peter became too enthralled by the West and copied it uncritically, needlessly introduced foreign elements into Russia, and unduly favored foreigners. If so, St. Petersburg too would be to that extent artificial. While there were certainly examples of excesses which needlessly aroused opposition, as a rule these excesses were in tangential, superficial matters. Further, many of the coveted "Russian" elements that Peter sought to remove were themselves imports. The traditional Muscovite robes of boyars were not really Russian but Asiatic and had their origin with the Mongols.[34]* The beards that he famously shaved from his courtiers also were not typical in Russia prior to the Mongol period.† In Peter's more substantive policies and legislation there was virtually no blind copying from the West, but rather a cool adaptation of Western principles to Russian circumstances and an outright rejection of certain Western practices which did not fit Russian reality. Peter wanted to tap the West for Russia's own purposes, and eventually exceed it, not to make Russia a copy of Europe. Europe too had problems, which Peter had witnessed and wished to avoid. Peter is famously quoted as having boasted: "We need Europe for a few decades, then we can turn our backs on her."[35] Like many quotes attributed to Peter, this one may be apocryphal, but there are abundant other statements to similar effect.[36] Ultimately, Peter's goal was

---

*The dispute over the Asiatic robes and sleeves, together with the shaving of beards, in fact have a long and involved history to which Peter's decision was merely the culmination. Boris Gudonov, an early Westernizer, had made many shave their beards, as a result of which the opposition took shape. Under Michael and Alexis, shaving became more common, but as a result of opposition Alexis eventually forbade shaving, as well as short hair by penalty of demotion. In 1681 Fedor decreed that all courtiers must wear short kaftans rather than the traditional long robes, at least when in the Kremlin. Historically speaking, this was the replacement of Asiatic dress with, not simply general European dress, but that of old Russia (Kiev, Novgorod). Soloviev, *Publichnie chtenia,* pp. 493–94.

†Early in the Muscovite period the beard came to be associated with the images on holy icons. By analogy, the beard was deemed to represent the image of God in men, and thus was itself holy. Cutting it off was considered by many as sacrilege, lowering a man's status to that of an animal.

not "Westernization" as such, but to base Russian society on universal laws and values of humanity, such as those espoused by Freemasons, which would be exemplified first and foremost in St. Petersburg. In this sense, no country in Europe was fully "Westernized" either, and in fact Peter meant to improve on Europe. Indeed, European intellectuals, recognizing that Peter was experimenting with the ideal, hoped that his new civilization would not repeat Western Europe's mistakes.

Another paradox is the contrast between Peter's modern theories and the manner in which he wielded autocratic power, regimenting the state and its citizens through coercion. Some have questioned whether Peter and his reforms really were modern and represented progress along Western lines, arguing that Peter aggravated and institutionalized Muscovy's coercive autocracy, which ultimately barred progress on crucial social, economic, and political issues, helped lead to revolution, and indeed that many characteristics of Peter's rule were prominent during the Soviet regime.[37] In this respect, Peter has been compared to the Bolsheviks and in particular to Stalin.[38] If this is correct, then the true St. Petersburg is that of Nicholas I, not that of modernism, enlightenment, and creativity.

This contention is only partly true. The problem was not in Peter's principles, his core values, his vision, or even the general structure of his reforms, the analogues of which did not lead to similar results in other countries. Unlike dictators such as Stalin, he wanted to disperse power across executive, legislative, and judicial government institutions, not aggregate it to himself (or to a party controlled by him that is not formally part of the government). But his personality did inhibit people from exercising the qualities of initiative, creativity, and responsibility that he wanted to develop. The problems specific to his personality did not outlive him. He faced a crude mentality, ignorance, and inertia, not to mention outright opposition, which could be overcome only with some degree of coercion and regimentation. Peter's natural impatience was made more acute by his realization that his own life was short, and that he had to achieve all he could while alive because he could not be confident that his successor (most of all his son Alexis) would complete the task. None of this makes him a precursor to Soviet rule. Had he lived longer or had Russia been in more capable hands after he died, the subsequent evolution of his system may have more closely resembled that in Western Europe.

A final question is whether Peter created a split between the top of society infused with ideas, dress, manners and exemplified by St. Petersburg and the great mass of the population, which further distanced the rulers and the elite from the ruled. At the time, such or similar divisions existed in most European countries by virtue of class, education, wealth, or other factors. In pre-Petrine Muscovy, the substantive gulf between the Kremlin elite and the population was already greater than in Western monarchies, as the Tsar and court were physically isolated from the people and society, emerging only for ceremonies, and the Tsar was not only the sovereign but also the proprietor of the realm. The reality of this gulf was not perceived or resented only because it was masked by a unified religious vision. In fact, it was the abandonment of the long-held myth of an organic, monolithic Russian society with its special religious purpose and quest, led by the Tsar, which Peter's critics lamented. During the Schism, this vision was exposed as irreparably hollow and Russia could not return to it. It was that event, not Peter's reign, which shattered the credibility and legitimacy of the old vision and made an alternative paradigm necessary and inevitable. Peter's model, both in theory and as implemented over time, was of a more open, less stratified society in which every citizen, regardless of social standing or wealth, could participate, rise in wealth and power based on merit, and also share in a common purpose of progress of the Russian state and people.

From Peter's perspective, his approach was more successful in realizing the greatness of the Russian people and the Russian state. Ironically, Peter did better than his Muscovite predecessors in realizing the imperial aspect of the Third Rome, though he never talked about it. But to his opponents Russia had lost its soul and ultimate religious purpose, rendering its many new achievements empty. The St. Petersburg period of Russian history would be a long and tortuous attempt to establish and maintain this modern paradigm in Russia. In the 20th century, Bolshevik ideology exploited old Muscovite values, especially the yearning for an organic Russian state without internal conflict, chosen in history and committed to a quasireligious messianic purpose. In its essence, the Soviet experiment was antimodern and equally a dead end. Post-Soviet Russia's most fundamental challenge is to extricate itself from this mind-set and embrace the universal, modern values pioneered in St. Petersburg.

CHAPTER 2

Building Peter's Paradise

There, by the billows desolate,
He stood, with mighty thoughts elate,
And gazed; but in the distance only
A sorry skiff on the broad spate
Of Neva drifted seaward, lonely.
The moss-grown miry banks with rare
Hovels were dotted here and there
Where wretched Finns for shelter crowded;
The murmuring woodlands had no share
Of sunshine, all in mist beshrouded.
And thus He mused: "From here, indeed
Shall we strike terror in the Swede;
And here a city by our labor
Founded, shall gall our haughty neighbor;
'Here cut'—so Nature gives command—
'Your window through on Europe; stand
Firm-footed by the sea, unchanging!'
Ay, ships of every flag shall come
By waters they had never swum,
And we shall revel, freely ranging."

PUSHKIN
The Bronze Horseman[1]

The delta of the Neva River lies in the Far North of Russia at nearly 60 degrees latitude, approximately that of southern Alaska and Oslo, Norway. Summer is short, but its days are long and its "nights" are only a brief twilight known as "White Nights." But winters are long and dark, and the snow and ice lasts long. Only in May does the ice break up in Lake Ladoga—Europe's largest lake and the source of the Neva—and for a few days ice floes parade down the river to the sea. Over its last few miles, the Neva forms a delta of several low, marshy islands. When strong westerly winds blow in from the Finnish Gulf, mostly in the autumn, a cap forms on the sea, rolls inland, and backs up the river's flow. The islands can be flooded for several hours, with some of them completely submerged. The area's early settlers took care not to build dwellings they could not afford to lose, and they were ready to retreat inland on a moment's notice. Much of St. Petersburg's history, mythology, and literature derives from its extreme climate and the Neva's infamous floods, beginning with the river's own name.

Many believe that the word "Neva" comes from an old Finnish word for "swamp" ("nevo"),[2] but that term appears to have been used first in reference to Lake Ladoga, originally called Nevo Lake,[3] rather than to the river.[4] According to Swedish sources, the word "Neva" derives from a combination of the ancient Swedish adjective "Nu" or "Ne" ("new"), and the Russian root "va" ("water"),[5] thus together meaning "new waters" or "new river";[5] corroboration comes from references to the river as "Nu" in 13th-century Novgorodian chronicles.[6] Geological history coincides with this interpretation, as the Neva indeed is very new—the newest river in Europe—formed just over 4,000 years ago after the area was already inhabited by man.[7] The eastern part of the Gulf of Finland, originally called Kotlin Lake,[8] earlier had a large bay extending almost up to Nevo Lake. Gradually the land rose and the bay receded, thus forming the "new" river which over the centuries increased in length and eventually became known as the Neva. The islands on which St. Petersburg is located rose from the water to form the Neva delta,[9] with new islands forming even during historical times.[10] Thus, the name "new waters" exactly describes the region's history, and it was only fitting that Peter's new city and Russia's new beginning be built on this new land along Europe's newest river.

Pushkin's poetic image of the Neva delta before Peter the Great is that of a desolate, uninhabited, mosquito-infested swamp, a blank slate on which Peter could build. Thus, the city, in legendary fashion, arose out of nothing through Peter's stroke of inspiration, making his achievement that much more dramatic. This and other legends have long been woven into the popular mind, but they are only half true: Much of the area was inhospitable swampland, but it had been inhabited for centuries because of its historically strategic location. The area's pre-Petrine history was long and eventful, and complements the city's heritage by illustrating the region's historical importance for Russia and by presaging certain themes in the city's history.

LIFE BEFORE PETER

The region of Russia around the Neva was originally known as Izhora, which derives from the name of the native population of the region which spoke a Finnish language.[11] The first recorded town in Izhora was Ladoga (later called Staraya Ladoga) in the 8th century. By one account, the legendary Rurik, Prince of Novgorod, had a base there, and it was from there that Prince Oleg set off to Kiev to establish the Kievan-Russian state in 882.[12] From the early 10th century the Izhorsky region was ruled by Novgorod.

Novgorod prospered because the Neva was located at the northern end of Kievan Russia's great trade route "from the Vikings to the Greeks" stretching from the Varangian ("Viking") Sea (now the Baltic Sea) to the Black Sea, and thus the mouth of the Neva held key economic and strategic importance.[13] Arab coins dating from the 9th and 10th centuries have been found on Vasilievsky Island.[14] Novgorod's possession of this section of the route was the main reason for the city's wealth and influence and led to its membership in the Hanseatic League. (In fact, the Vikings also called the Varangian Sea the Novgorod Sea.) Ships entered the Neva from the sea, sailed upriver to Lake Ladoga, along the south shore of the lake to the Volkhov River, and downriver to Novgorod. The Novgorodians built boats for trade and also served as local pilots to guide foreign vessels through the dangerous waters of the Volkhov River, Lake Ladoga, the Neva and the sea channels at its mouth.[15] To protect this route, in 1114 Novgorod fortified Ladoga, where the Volkhov River enters Lake Ladoga. On the island called Kotlin (now Kronshtadt), Novgorod established a maritime watchpost from which its escorts met foreign ships entering the area and guided them upriver.[16] In addition to the river route to Novgorod, there was also a land route, the "Great Novgorod Road," beginning along the present Ligovsky Prospect in St. Petersburg.[17]

From the 12th through 14th centuries, Sweden challenged Novgorod for control over the Neva lands and the trade route. By one count, between 1142 and 1446 Novgorod fought the Swedes 26 times.[18] But the Swedes were not the only enemy. Pope Innocent III had founded the Teutonic and Livonian Orders (which merged in 1237) to Catholicize and subjugate the Baltic lands. In 1237 the Pope issued a Bull calling for a crusade against the "pagan" Finns and Russians of the Baltic. Under this pretext, a Swedish expedition under the command of the Swedish general Jarl Berger was launched to conquer Novgorod and "Latinize" the population. But the Novgorodian Prince Alexander Yaroslavovich defeated them on the banks of the Neva in 1240 and thus became known to history as Alexander Nevsky. According to popular tradition, the battle took place on the site of the future Alexander Nevsky Monastery in St. Petersburg, though in fact it was fought somewhat upstream near the mouth of the Izhora River.[19] Seeking to reverse Sweden's defeat, the Teutons then marched toward Novgorod in 1242, but Nevsky defeated them in the famous "battle on the ice" on Lake Chud (now Peipus), later portrayed in the classic Eisenstein film with its score by Prokofiev.

According to Novgorodian chronicles, in 1300 a Swedish force under the command of the Swedish Field Marshal Torgel Knutsson, the founder of Vyborg, landed at the junction of the Okhta River and the Neva on the site of the future Nienshantz,[20] on the holy day of the Trinity,[21] which four centuries later would also be the date of the founding of St. Petersburg. Using Italian architects sent by the

Vatican (which still had designs on the region) to accompany the force, Knutsson established there a fortress which he named Landskrona ("Land of the Crown"), but Novgorodian forces under the command of Alexander Nevsky's son, Andrei, razed the fortress within a year. In 1323 Novgorod fortified Orekhov Island where the Neva flows from Lake Ladoga, naming the fortress Oreshek, around which a settlement of traders and craftsmen grew up, which became the center of the Izhorsky region.[22] In 1348 the Swedes launched a campaign against Oreshek, but they were repelled, after which the territory of the Neva remained solidly in Novgorodian hands for over two centuries. Oreshek grew into a flourishing town of craftsmen and traders, which by 1500 boasted 152 residences, 2 monasteries, and 4 churches.[23]

The Novgorodians held out against Sweden for a long time. Novgorod's subjugation, however, came at the hands of Muscovy, into which it was absorbed in 1471. Moscow treated the conquered region as a hinterland, and it lay exposed to attack. But the area continued to grow under the Russians and later the Swedes. According to Novgorodian records, in 1400 on the territory of the future St. Petersburg there were 419 settlements having 744 residences in which 1,191 males resided; by 1500 the figures had increased to 1,082 residences and 1,516 male residents.[24] The total population, counting women and children, was probably at least double this figure. What became the main settlement arose at the junction of the Okhta and Neva Rivers (well inside today's city limits) near the site of Knutsson's Landskrona, but the new town became known as the "Mouth of the Neva."[25] In 1500 it had only 15 dwellings, but since at the time the Okhta was navigable, the town grew quickly and soon became a lively trading post and port, which later continued under the Swedish occupation.

The Baltic area was again contested during the Livonian War, begun by Ivan the Terrible in 1558 to establish a Russian foothold on the Baltic and lasting through the Time of Troubles. Sweden occupied the Neva region in the first years of the 17th century, Muscovy eventually lost the war, and in 1617 the Stolbov Treaty ceded to Sweden all of the Baltic lands, including those around the Neva and Lake Ladoga. Izhora became known as Ingria (or Ingemarland), Oreshek was renamed Noteburg, and the main Russian town, Mouth of the Neva, was renamed Nien ("New," derived from the same root as "Neva"). Sweden's General Delagardi, who had held the town since well before the Treaty, proposed to Gustavus II Adolphus to fortify it so that, aided by tax privileges granted by the crown, the town could prosper and grow through trade. Its fortress was built by 1611, having a diameter of nearly a kilometer and a garrison of 500–600 soldiers,[26] and became known as Ny-skantze or Nienshantz ("New Fortress"). The fortress and town were replanned and expanded in the late 17th century, which demanded much labor. In a manner that anticipated Peter the Great's methods of raising labor to build St. Petersburg, in 1679 the Swedish King, Charles XI, decreed that every able-bodied peasant in Ingria and Karelia had to spend one month laboring on the fortress.[27]

The Swedish trade development effort succeeded, and by the 1630s Nien boasted nearly 400 buildings outside the fortress, including two Lutheran churches (one Finnish and one Swedish), located mainly across the Okhta River and connected by drawbridges.[28] Nien's port flourished, receiving at least 50 foreign ships per year[29] (according to one source, as many as 108 annual visits).[30] The town had a large trading fleet, which by one (probably exaggerated) account numbered in the hundreds.[31] In 1632 Sweden accorded Nien the status of a town with its own coat of arms, consisting of a lion straddling its two rivers, the Neva and the Okhta. Soon after the start of the Great Northern War, a major Swedish merchant in Nien, Fritsius, extended Charles XII a large loan to finance his war effort against Peter the Great's Russia.[32] Immediately before Peter's conquest of the town, the number of dwellings in Nien had risen to about 450[33] and its population had grown to approximately 4,000.[34]

Most of Nien's residents were Russians. In the 1630s an Orthodox parish was formed in town to serve them.[35] As tensions rose between Sweden and Russia, however, tax increases and other discriminatory measures were introduced against the Russian merchants, which lasted until Peter's arrival.

By 1700 numerous settlements besides Nien had arisen on the territory of present-day St. Petersburg, located on the highest, driest, and most desirable sites. Peter initially built on them, since they were the best natural locations and it was easier and more economical to begin with partially developed sites.[36] They included the spit (*strelka*) of Vasilievsky Island and the future sites of the Summer Garden, the Admiralty, the Smolny Convent, Alexander Nevsky Monastery, and Trinity Square.*

THE FOUNDING OF THE CITY

Following the Narva debacle of 1700, Peter quickly rebuilt his forces and recommenced his drive to the Baltic. By mid-1702 Peter was ready, and he chose to concentrate on the more weakly defended area around the Neva rather than the lands to the West. In August 1702 a Russian flotilla attacked a Swedish squadron on Lake

---

*Across the river from Nien, on the site of the future Smolny, was the village of Spassky, fortified with a *kronverk* (see p. 50 below), having its own Orthodox church, and to which a ferryboat ran from Nien. On the site of the present-day Admiralty was an unnamed settlement, and on the *strelka* of Vasilievsky Island was the estate of Delagardi. On the site of the future Alexander Nevsky Monastery lay the village of Vakhrovo-Fedorkovo. Near the mouth of what is now the Fontanka River (in Finnish called the Kemeyaki but called by the Russians the *Bezimenni Yerik* ["Unnamed Rivulet"], or simply *Yerik*) was the settlement of Kalinka, and at the upper end in what became the Summer Garden was the Swedish settlement of Konau (or Kandau). Nearby, at the present location of the Engineers' Castle, was a Swedish Major's estate, and part of the site of Peter's future Summer Garden was already occupied by a modest garden laid out in the Dutch manner. Across the Neva, where Trinity Square would soon appear, was the settlement of Birkenholm.

Ladoga and forced it to retreat down the Neva and along the gulf to Vyborg. This allowed Peter's forces, in October, to besiege, storm, and take Noteburg in a fierce battle, after which Peter gave it the Dutch name Schlüsselburg ("Key City"). He would indeed use this base as a key to open the last barrier to the Baltic, the fortress Nienshantz. It was already too late in the year for more campaigning, however, so Peter went south for the winter. During the winter, Peter's forces encamped on Lake Ladoga and built the boats that he would use in the spring campaign.

Peter returned to Schlüsselburg in March 1703. On April 23, after the ice had mostly cleared, a Russian force of at least 16,000 under the command of Boris Sheremetev headed down the Neva toward Nienshantz, where the Swedes were belatedly and hastily reinforcing the fortifications. Sheremetev arrived on the 26th and commenced siege operations. Later the same day Peter arrived with war vessels and a caravan of barges carrying artillery, bombs, and other materiel. On the 28th Peter sailed downriver for reconnaissance and got his first glimpse of the site of his future city. He left a detachment of three companies on Vitsasaari ("Vine") Island (now Gutuyevsky Island, where the city's port is now headquartered) and returned to Nienshantz on the 29th, by which time the siege works were completed and the artillery batteries were emplaced. On April 30 Sheremetev sent the Swedish commandant proposed terms of surrender, which were rejected. The Russian bombardment began that evening, with Peter participating in the battle as a lowly bombardier captain under the name Peter Mikhailov. The Swedes capitulated at dawn on May 1, and the terms of surrender were negotiated by midday. The Swedes surrendered their arms and departed for Vyborg. Peter's forces entered the town and fortress on May 2 and held a prayer service not only in thanks for the victory but also because "the desired outlet to the sea had been secured."[37]

Peter renamed the fortress Shlotburg (Dutch for "Lock City," to which Schlüsselburg had been the key), but the name would have no use since the fortress would soon be razed. By one account, Peter also immediately renamed the town outside the fortress Sankt Piter Burkh.[38] Even if so, however, this was also quickly forgotten, and the town, burnt to the ground and largely abandoned, eventually was absorbed into the greater city dedicated under the same name two weeks later.

On the evening of May 2 Peter received word from his detachment on Vitsasaari that a Swedish squadron of nine ships under the command of Admiral Nummers had appeared at the mouth of the Neva. On May 6 two of the Swedish warships, the *Astrel* and *Gedan*, sailed into the Neva, unaware that Nienshantz was in Russian hands. They signaled their approach with two cannon shots. The Russians responded with shots from the fortress as if the Swedes still held it. Thus assured, the Swedes dropped anchor downriver. But Peter had devised a daring plan to attack the ships using ordinary riverboats in the middle of the night. Under the cover of an unusually dark and rainy night, he positioned half of his 30 boats downriver to block escape while the other half attacked and boarded the enemy ships. So swift was the victory that only eight of Peter's ships managed to see action. Thus, in the early morning hours of May 7, 1703, was achieved Peter's—and Russia's—first "naval" victory. This was celebrated with honors, promotions, and the issuance of a medallion with the words, "The Unimaginable Happens."

With this battle Peter's dream of achieving a foothold on the sea was realized. But it was a tentative one that had to be secured quickly. The rest of Nummers's squadron remained anchored in the Gulf, and a Swedish detachment was encamped across the Sestera River to the north, ready to attack at any time. Peter sent Sheremetev's forces against nearby towns to the south, which were secured by the end of May. As for Schlotburg, Peter decided that its fortifications were too small, that the site was too exposed from the landward side, and that it was too far from the sea. The Swedes could bottle up the area by securing the mouth of the Neva. A new site had to be found downriver. Once such a fortress and settlement was established, Shlotburg was destroyed so that the Swedes could not threaten the new city by retaking it. Besides, Peter did not want to build the new on the foundations of the old; the razing of the fortress symbolized his destruction of the old in order to realize his new creation.[39] Its stones were brought downriver to be used in construction. Peter ordered four tall mast poles to be erected on the site to serve as a memory that a captured Swedish fortress had once stood there.[40]

Accordingly, Peter and his lieutenants set off in their boats and for a few days examined potential locations for a new and better fortress. With little difficulty Peter selected Hare *(Zayachy)* Island as the site. A settlement had existed there since the days of Ivan III. The island was originally known as Yannisaari* (Finnish for "Hare Island"), which the Russians later translated to yield the name Zayachy Island. By one account, during the Swedish occupation the Swedes began to call the island Liusteland ("Happy Island") because its Swedish resident had decided to turn it into a place for recreation and began building a garden there. After his efforts were destroyed by a flood, however, he called it Devil's Island.[41] After Peter built the Peter and Paul Fortress there, it was known as Fortress Island until the early 20th century, when the name of Hare Island was restored.

Strategically, Hare Island was ideal. It was near to the sea, and depth measurements confirmed that the Malaya Neva to the right and the Bolshaya Nevka behind it were not navigable by warships, making a location further upriver unnecessary. The navigable channel of the Neva ran close to Vasilievsky Island and then (moving upriver), after the tip (*strelka*, meaning "point" or "arrow") of Vasilievsky Island, veered toward the south bank of the river opposite Hare Island, well within the range of Peter's cannon but making the fortress unapproachable by large ships and a landing difficult. The back of the island was protected by swampland and a natural water channel that separated it from Fomin (now Petrograd) Island. Hare Island was also small enough that the fortifications could extend to the water's edge on all sides so that attackers could not stage a landing and establish a base.

---

*In Finnish, "saari" means "island."

Legends abound concerning the events of May 16 (27 New Style), 1703, the holy day of the Trinity, which is considered the date of the founding of the city. According to one account, it was on May 14 that Peter decided to locate the Fortress there when he spied an eagle—the imperial symbol—circling the island.[42] Peter is said to have grabbed the musket of one of his soldiers, and with its bayonet he carved out two strips of turf, which he laid in the form of a crucifix and on which he planted a wooden cross. He then announced, "Here shall be a city." He then crossed from Hare Island onto the southern tip of what is now Petrograd Island, where he cut down two willow bushes. On the site of one bush he would build Trinity Cathedral, and on the other—his own cabin.[43] The official founding of the city came two days later on May 16. Peter is said to have symbolically buried a golden box containing some gold coins and the relics of the Holy Apostle Andrew the First-Called, Russia's patron saint, who, according to legend, had visited the area.[44] The box was supposedly inscribed: "In the name of Jesus Christ on May 16, 1703, his Tsarist majesty and Grand Prince, Peter Alexeievich, autocrat of all the Russias, founded the Tsarist city St. Petersburg."[45] At this moment, the legend continues, the eagle again appeared overhead and dipped in flight, as was said to have occurred when Constantinople was founded by the first Christian Emperor, Constantine. It alighted on two birch trees that had been bent and tied together in the form of an arch, which supposedly became the location of the Peter's Gate to the Fortress.[46] This story is meant to place the event within Christian tradition by recalling the legends of the Emperor Constantine being led to Byzantium by an eagle and of the Apostle Andrew, traveling from Kiev to Novgorodian lands, planting his staff near the future St. Petersburg and blessing the region.[47] The elaborate tale also testifies to the immense importance that Peter's contemporaries placed on establishing this city on the Baltic.

Actually, no one knows what really happened on May 16th. There is a curious lack of reliable information concerning the foundation of the Fortress, ranging from Peter's whereabouts to the abnormal absence of a decree on the establishment of the Fortress. Some historians believe that Peter was not even present, having left earlier for Lake Ladoga to check on shipbuilding operations, and that the groundbreaking ceremony was performed by Menshikov.[48] Others believe, based on Peter's character, that he could not have stayed away from such an important event marking the realization of his lifelong dreams.[49] One possibility is that he was present on the 14th but not the 16th.

On June 29, 1703, on the holy day of St. Peter on which Peter the Great was baptized, inside the rising Fortress the foundation of the original small wooden Peter and Paul Cathedral (named after the two Apostles) was laid. On the same date, Peter gave the city the Dutch name of Sankt Piter Burkh.* By some accounts, both

---

*Peter in Dutch is "Piter." The fond nickname "Piter" for the city survives to this day.

the Fortress and the new settlement were first named "Petropolis" or "Petropol." While this name does appear in a few letters of the time and in one engraving, it seems that this was only an informal shorthand name used privately by some on occasion, but that the name was never official and in any event did not stick,[50] although the name later appeared in literature. The names Peter and Paul Fortress and Saint-Petersburg soon became universal.[51]

The city is named not after Peter the Great, but after St. Peter, who was the Tsar's patron saint after whom he was named. St. Peter is known as the keeper of the keys to Paradise. Peter the Great considered that if the holder of the keys to paradise was made the city's patron saint and protector, the city would be protected and remain Russia's key to the Baltic and to Europe.[52] Peter indeed thought of his new city as his paradise, writing in April 1706 to Menshikov: "I cannot help writing you from this paradise; truly we live here in heaven."[53]

Work on the Fortress proceeded at breakneck speed in order to make the area defensible against the Swedes. That summer approximately 20,000 men, mainly soldiers supplemented by local residents, were at work on the fortifications. The Fortress was built to a design by Joseph Gaspard Lambert, who had been in the service of Louis XIV.[54] The six bastions of earth and timber each were built under the personal supervision of Peter or one of his trusted commanders or friends (Golovkin, Menshikov, Prince Trubetskoi, Naryshkin, and Peter's former teacher, Zotov). When the bastions were later faced in stone, they were named after their builders, except that Peter's was named the Sovereign's Bastion.

As Hare Island was low and marshy, the ground had to be raised by driving thousands of piles and adding earth. Indeed, on August 19 a serious flood occurred in which the Neva rose two meters, setting back the work by weeks. Prince Repnin described it to Peter:

> Alas, my Sovereign, we have been hit by harsh weather from the sea, and it hits on our place where I stand with the regiments, with the water coming right up to my encampment. I'm spending the night with the Preobrazhensky Regiment and it is midnight, and amongst the cooks there are many sleepless people and their supplies are all waterlogged. And the local inhabitants tell us that at this time of year this place is always flooded.[55]

This was only the first of the many disastrous and legendary floods that plagued the life of the city, but which also helped give it its unique character and mythology.

The living and working conditions that summer were terrible. Workers were underfed, often slept on bare ground and worked in the water; disease was rampant. The later Hanoverian ambassador, Friedrich Weber (not an eyewitness), described the scene:

> There were neither sufficient provisions for subsisting such a number of men, nor care taken to furnish them with the necessary tools, as pick-axes, spades, shovels, wheelbarrows, planks, and the like, they even had not so much as houses or huts. . . . [T]he earth

which is very scarce thereabouts, was for the greater part carried by the laborers in the skirts of their clothes, and in bags made of rags and old mats, the use of wheelbarrows being then unknown to them.[56]

Despite the hardships, the Fortress was essentially completed by September 1703. It was officially dedicated, however, only in April 1704. A settlement quickly grew up around it. Whereas in 1703 only 15 major houses stood around the Fortress, in 1704 there were 150.[57]

Throughout the construction of the Fortress, the Swedes were never far away and constantly threatened. Fortunately, the main Swedish forces were occupied in action to the west and could not be spared for efforts to retake the area of the Neva. But the threat of a Swedish attack and the loss of the city loomed over St. Petersburg until 1710; until then, there was military action around the city on land and sea nearly every summer. The city's early development must be understood in light of the Swedish threat. It explains the early emphasis on military over civil construction, the location of the shipyard (Admiralty) in the very center of the city, the focus of the city's industry on military production, the city's modest growth during these years, and the initial slow development of the city as a commercial port.

Already in early July 1703 a Swedish force of 4,000 under General Kronjort approached from the Vyborg side and encamped on the north bank of the Neva, but on July 7 a Russian detachment of 7,000 infantry and dragoons under Peter's personal command repelled them, and the Swedes withdrew to Vyborg. They would return in 1704, 1705, and 1708, but with similar results.[58] At sea, meanwhile, throughout the summer of 1703 the Swedish Admiral Nummers kept his remaining ships anchored in the Finnish Gulf just outside the mouth of the Neva, blocking access by sea and threatening to proceed upriver at the first opportunity. All Peter could offer in response was to position cannon on the spit of Vasilievsky Island to bar passage upriver. In August, several Dutch trading ships appeared expecting to buy timber from the Swedes as in prior years, but their captains were surprised to learn that the Russians controlled the Neva. Although Menshikov managed to meet with them and agree to carry out the transaction, Nummers, fearing that the Russians would commandeer the ships, arm them and turn them against him, prevented the Dutch from entering the Neva, and they had to leave empty-handed. This was the last time the Swedes would block Russian access to the Neva.

Realizing the importance of defending the city by sea, immediately after defeating Kronjort, Peter traveled to the shipyards on Ladoga to supervise shipbuilding operations, where the keels of six frigates and many smaller ships were laid. He soon returned to St. Petersburg with one frigate and several smaller ships and dropped anchor in front of the Fortress. After the autumn weather forced Nummers to withdraw to Vyborg (still Swedish territory) in October, Peter ventured into the Finnish Gulf in his new ship, *The Standard*. The name was taken from that of the Tsarist flag, called the Standard. Until then the Standard had portrayed the double-headed eagle holding in its beak and claws the cards of the three seas belonging to Russia, but the new Standard flown on Peter's new ship and over the Fortress depicted a fourth as well: the Baltic. This was a historic step for Peter and for Russia: the first time a Russian Tsar sailed on a Russian ship in the Baltic. Still, flying the new Standard was somewhat premature and presumptuous, as the Baltic was still ruled by the Swedes.

Accordingly, though immensely gratified by this precedent, Peter wasted no time in locating a site in the Finnish Gulf to fortify and from which to guard the approach to the Neva. Kotlin Island (now called Kronstadt) was slightly too far from the navigable sea channel for cannon to defend it, so Peter chose a shallow spot south of Kotlin on which to create a small island and erect a small fort, which he named Kronshlot. Over the winter, Peter's forces brought containers of stones over the ice and constructed a mechanism which automatically lowered the stones as the ice melted.[59] When spring came, a round fortress with 14 cannon rose from the sea. It was finished and dedicated with Peter present on May 7, 1704, exactly one year after his first naval victory on the Neva. In both 1704 and 1705 Sweden sent fleets to attack Kronschlot and Kotlin, but they were successfully repelled by Peter's admiral Cornelius Kruys, a Dutchman of Norwegian origin, and his sailors, among whom were already hundreds of Dutch and other foreigners.

While the city was still being fortified, for safety Peter had his ships constructed in a makeshift shipyard upriver on Lake Ladoga. This proved ineffective, as the yards were far away and many ships foundered, ran aground and were damaged or lost in the shallow, stormy waters of the lake around Schlüsselburg or when sailing downriver, especially in the dangerous Ivanovskoe rapids. In October 1704, once St. Petersburg was more secure from the Swedes, Peter issued an order to relocate the main shipyard to St. Petersburg and to fortify it. Peter named it the Admiralty. "Admiral" was not a term previously used in Russia, but Peter understood that it was derived from the Arabic word "amiral" meaning "lord of the seas," which fit Peter's purpose of ruling the Baltic. Peter laid the foundations of the Admiralty in November 1704 on the Neva embankment across from the spit of Vasilievsky Island, on a rise of drier land where a small settlement had existed. Locating it on the south bank facilitated direct communication and transport to the Russian mainland. Although a location closer to the mouth of the river would have been better for shipbuilding, it was necessary to locate it somewhat upriver so that it could be protected by the Peter and Paul Fortress and by artillery emplacements on Vasilievsky Island, and also so that its own fortifications could be used to defend the southern approach to the city. For this purpose, Peter built ramparts guarded by cannon and surrounded them with a wet moat. These defenses were nearly as effective as those of the Fortress across the river. Since an open space had to be preserved on all sides of the fortifications so that attackers would have no place for cover, no housing or other buildings were permitted alongside the Admiralty. Initially, the nearest buildings were along the Moika River. These open spaces were the origins of the square to the south known as Admiralty Lug ("Field") (later the Alexander Garden) and what is now Senate Square to the west and Palace Square to the east. Both the ship-yard and the initial fortifications were completed by the autumn of 1705, as were over 100 nearby homes for naval officers. As it turned out, the Admiralty's artillery never saw military action. In these initial years, the two sides of the city (Gorod-skoi and Admiralty Islands) were effectively two separate settlements under two sep-arate administrations, because construction on Admiralty Island was almost entirely under the control of the Admiralty enterprise and the navy.[60]

Initially, the Admiralty was a crude three-sided wooden rectangle of about 250 by 130 meters with its fourth side on the Neva, inside which hulls were constructed and eased into wharves on the Neva for fitting out. Even at that time, the Admi-ralty featured a tall spire in the central section with a weather vane in the form of a caravel, attributes which it has retained throughout its history. The first ships from the Admiralty were launched in 1706, and it became known as the "cradle of the Russian navy." It produced the fleet that would defeat the Swedes and rule the Baltic.

In 1707–08, while the Peter and Paul Fortress was being reinforced with stone facing, the fortress of St. Alexander was built on Kotlin Island. This proved a wise step, as the Swedes launched a major sea and land offensive against the city in 1708 in which the fortress helped keep the Swedish navy at bay. The Swedish land cam-paign ended ignominiously, its force being driven to the sea, compelled to kill its approximately 5,000 horses so as not to leave them to the Russians, and rescued by the Swedish fleet waiting offshore in the Gulf. This proved to be the last serious Swedish threat to the city, as the next summer saw Russia's decisive victory over the Swedish army at Poltava in Ukraine. On the evening after that battle, Peter wrote to Admiral Apraxin, "Now, with God's help, the foundation stone of St. Petersburg has been laid." And to Romodanovsky he wrote, "Now, with the final defeat of the enemy, without doubt, your Excellency, your desire to have a residence in St. Pe-tersburg will be fulfilled."[61] The Swedish threat was finally removed in 1710 when the Russians captured Vyborg, Riga, and Reval (now Tallin). Control over the sea would come with the Russian naval victory off Hangö in southern Finland in 1714. Final peace came only in 1721 with the Peace of Nystadt.

But by 1705, with the construction of the Peter and Paul Fortress, Kronshlodt, and the Admiralty completed, the city already was defensible. Thus, although the Swedish threat remained, the city could now grow, and Peter threw what resources he could spare behind the effort.

BUILDING A NEW CITY

To build his dream, Peter needed labor. Some workers were permanently trans-ferred to the city with or without their families, while others, mainly unskilled, were conscripted temporarily, normally for part of the summer. It was already a practice in Russia to use temporary summer labor for urban and military construction, but in Petersburg the scale was larger.[62] For Petersburg, the annual edicts for temporary workers spread the burden over locales throughout Russia, calling for a specified number from each place. Accounts differ as to how many temporary workers (mainly serfs) came annually. Beginning with a decree of March 1, 1704, Peter demanded at least 40,000 workers per year, but in actuality he received nothing close to this, usually between 12,000 and 18,000.[63] When these numbers did not suffice, Peter resorted to using criminals; building St. Petersburg was their hard labor punishment.

Temporary workers served in shifts of several weeks each so as to lessen and spread the burden among communities and families. Initially there were three summer shifts of two months each beginning on the 25th day of March, May, and July, but in 1706 this was changed to two three-month shifts beginning April 1 and ending October 1.[64] Since the annual conscription was spread over these shifts, the total number of conscripts in the city at any one time actually was not as large as one might think. Because of the long summer days, the usual summer workday ran from "dawn" (by 5:00 A.M.) to 9:00 or 10:00 P.M., but with a three-hour break from 11:00 A.M. to 2:00 P.M. and a half-hour break at 7:00 P.M.; the winter workdays generally ran from 6:00 A.M. to 6:00 P.M. with a shorter break of one hour.[65]

Peter also retained permanent workers, consisting partly of skilled carpenters, masons, and stonecutters, but mainly of unskilled peasants. They were given food and an allowance by their owners for their travel to the city, and then paid wages once there. War finances meant that wages were not paid regularly, but the skilled workers enjoyed priority and so were paid first and lived better. While some were conscripts, Peter sought to entice others to come voluntarily. Peter decreed, for example, that carpenters (especially needed for shipbuilding) agreeing to move to Petersburg be given a free fenced *izba* (hut) with a land plot, in addition to their salary and a bread allowance. Similar incentives were accorded to other craftsmen. Over time, skilled workers were used more to staff the growing number of factories in the city rather than for city construction.[66]

Growing numbers of Swedish prisoners of war also were employed. Swedish prisoners were used in the construction of the Grand Perspective Road (later Nevsky Prospect), the *Gostiniy Dvor* and the Colleges on Trinity Square, the canals and docks on Kotlin Island, and several other buildings.[67] The more skilled Swedes who could perform important and sophisticated work were especially valued and enjoyed a special "parole" status. Such work included architectural and engineering drawings, construction of windmills, medical treatment of Swedish and Russian workers, and work on the Peter and Paul Cathedral and bell tower. When the war ended, Peter offered to have them stay under privileged conditions, and he directed Russia's ambassador to Stockholm to recruit skilled Swedes.

At least for the unskilled temporary workers at construction sites and in factories, the living and working conditions in the city's early years were harsh, and desertion was common. Workers were crowded into primitive huts without floors, and many died from disease. The mortality figures are hard to estimate. The popular myth is that Petersburg is a city "built on bones" (or, as Nikolai Karamzin put it, "on tears and corpses"), and some near-contemporary foreign estimates put the total death toll at 60,000 or even 100,000,[68] which was many times the city's population. Historians have long considered these figures greatly exaggerated, although until recently the estimates were still in the tens of thousands.[69] More recently one Russian historian, using the mortality figures from the annual lists of temporary workers from several sample regions who returned each year to work in the city, estimated only about 2,000 deaths of all temporary workers from across Russia between 1703 and 1715.[70] Even allowing for greater mortality in the first summer or two, the overall figure still would not be in the tens of thousands. In any event, by 1710 if not before, medical and other measures were taken to improve the situation,[71] and before long St. Petersburg would be one of the cleanest, best serviced cities in the world. The notion of a city built on the bones of its builders appears to be a myth generated, accepted, and promoted by Peter's and the city's opponents to bolster their positions and later continued by sensationalists. No myths of sensational mortality arose in the many other places in which the same methods were used.[72]

Vast quantities of building materials were needed for this enterprise. In 1714 Peter decreed that every carriage and vessel entering the city had to bring a quota of stones in addition to its normal load. Vehicles without such stones were not permitted to enter the city, and checkpoints to enforce the requirement and collect the stones were set up at all points of entry. Production of bricks and tiles was put under the control of the Chancellery of Urban Affairs, and several thousand workers were employed in this industry. Prodigious quantities were turned out (e.g., 11 million bricks in 1710), which far exceeded production in Moscow, but since quality was poor, the yield was significantly lower. Similar advances were made in the production of lumber, lime, glass, and cement. Still, production fell far short of the city's needs. Lumber, stone, and glass were brought from afar at great expense. As a result, only major government buildings and the private buildings of grandees could avail themselves of the new production or of "imported" materials. The vast majority of smaller buildings were wooden shacks with wooden shingles and windows covered with mica, animal bladders, or rags.

Until 1706, Peter's concern with planning his city did not extend much beyond the Peter and Paul Fortress and the Admiralty, but late that year he began to issue detailed instructions for the construction of buildings, wharves, and other structures. That year he also founded the Chancellery of Urban Affairs under the direction of Ulyan Akimovich Senyavin, conveniently located in Senyavin's own house. In 1723 it was renamed the Chancellery of Construction.

In order to design buildings and plan the city as he desired, Peter needed a qualified architect. He chose a Swiss-born architect of Italian descent, Domenico

Trezzini (1670–1734), who had recently worked for the Danish King Frederick IV on his palace in Copenhagen. Denmark and other Scandinavian countries at the time, and thus Trezzini himself, were well acquainted with and under the influence of Dutch architectural design, which met Peter's tastes exactly. Trezzini with his team of 10 engineers, master builders, and artisans arrived in Petersburg in October 1704. When the Chancellery of Urban Affairs was created in 1706, he was appointed Chief Architect, a somewhat misleading title since he was the *only* professional architect in the city until 1710.

Trezzini was the first in a long line of foreign architects to leave his mark on the city. His works include the Fortress and its Peter's Gate, the Peter and Paul Cathedral, the Summer Palace, Alexander Nevsky Monastery, the Narva Gates, the barracks at Schlüsselburg, the military hospital, and the Twelve Colleges on Vasilievsky Island. Peter's relationship with Trezzini was long and fruitful. Peter not only respected Trezzini as a professional but was personally close to him, was a frequent guest at his home, and even became the godfather of his son, who not surprisingly was named Peter. Trezzini adopted Russia as his second homeland and became known as "Andrei" Trezzini. He trained Russia's first architects, including Mikhail Zemtsov, who eventually produced such works as Mon Plasir and the cascades at Peterhof, the Anichkov Palace (in part), the Kunstkamera, the Observation Palace at the mouth of the Fontanka (in part), and (with LeBlond) the palace at Strelna on the Finnish Gulf.

Trezzini's Chancellery oversaw the city's planning and construction and brought about the Petrine revolution in Russian architecture. As the number of foreign and Russian architects in the city multiplied, Trezzini was able to limit (though not eliminate) the tendency toward a hodgepodge of styles and impose, at least in designed buildings, some uniformity in the city's architecture.[73] In addition to planning all significant projects and the city's development generally, the Chancellery handled the recruitment, training, and qualification of architects and other specialists, the conscription, deployment, and support of the thousands of laborers, the procurement of supplies and building materials, and the administration of funds for construction. The task was enormous; by 1721 approximately five percent of all Russian state revenue was being spent on St. Petersburg's construction.[74] Despite the formal structure, much still depended on Peter himself for direction. In fact, the Chancellery was his executive arm in the city, and he issued his instructions through it.

When Peter was absent, he put Menshikov in charge of the city, who in 1703 became the first Governor of St. Petersburg (and of the whole Izhorsky region). Menshikov's authority extended to construction matters, which led to legendary run-ins with the city architects. Consequently, many of Menshikov's decisions and actions rather than Peter's or the Chancellery's would shape the city's appearance and destiny. Except for Peter, he was First Citizen of the city.

Despite Trezzini's presence, early planning efforts, and exceptional projects such as Menshikov's palace, the early development of the city was generally haphazard and in many respects followed traditional Russian patterns. For years there was no master plan. The usual abode of workers was a square log cabin. These were prefabricated with notched logs so they could be assembled or disassembled in minutes, and they were sold as a commodity in street markets.[75]

Since most of the city consisted of simple wooden buildings close together, fires broke out constantly. Because the layout of streets was random, fires spread quickly, and sometimes entire sections of town were consumed. Peter instituted rules for housing construction designed to minimize the outbreak of fires. He regulated the construction of fireplaces and stoves, mandated chimney cleaning, and established the hours for lighting and dousing fires. He also set up a surveillance and alarm system under which each civil and military officer in town, including Peter himself, was given a firefighting assignment. It was not unusual to see the Tsar on rooftops amidst the flames wielding his hatchet and directing the firefighting effort. The Danish ambassador, Just Juel, described such scenes (and the character of Peter's subjects whom he was trying to reform) as follows:

> As his intelligence is extraordinarily quick, he sees at once what must be done to extinguish the fire; he goes up to the roof; he goes to all the worst danger points; he incites nobles as well as common people to help in the struggle and does not pause until the fire is put out. But when the sovereign is absent, things are very different. Then the people watch the fires with indifference and do nothing to help extinguish them. It is in vain to lecture them or even to offer them money; they merely wait for a chance to steal something.[76]

No formal fire brigade was established until 1722, by the Admiralty, which had its own firefighting equipment and a storehouse. The Chief of Police, the Portuguese Anton Devier, appealed to the Senate for resources to create other brigades in other parts of the city, but he was given little and the means for firefighting remained substandard.

Except for the frantic building of the Fortress, the city grew slowly in the early years. Although Peter wanted to build a carefully planned city with stone and masonry buildings according to European designs, it was premature to divert to building and populating the city much of the scarce money, materials, and manpower needed for the war effort until the city was secure from the Swedes.

This all changed after the victory of Poltava in 1709 and the conquest of Vyborg, Riga, and Reval in 1710. Petersburg was now safe. When Peter returned to the city and remained there for most of 1710, he immediately commenced serious efforts at city planning and development, and the pace of construction quickened. Prior to 1710, all major buildings other than the Admiralty were huddled around Trinity Square east of the Fortress, but that year construction began on the first notable buildings on Admiralty and Vasilievsky Islands, including the Summer Palace, Menshikov's and Golovkin's Palaces, Alexander Nevsky Monastery, and St. Isaac's Church. That year Peter also set up the Garden Bureau to manage the city's (meaning the Tsar's) gardens, also on the Admiralty side. The next year work on the Grand Perspective commenced, and in 1712 work on the stone Peter and Paul Cathedral began.

Nearly from the start Peter wanted St. Petersburg to be Russia's future capital city. While away in 1704, he wrote to Menshikov that he would soon arrive in "the capital, Petersburg." As early as 1708, Peter had begun moving members of his family, nobles, and government bodies to the city from Moscow. This process began in earnest after 1710, and the city effectively became the capital in 1712. Curiously, no official decree transferring the capital from Moscow to St. Petersburg was ever issued. Instead, that year Peter simply ordered the remaining government bodies, service nobility and courtiers to move to the new city, foreign ambassadors, and merchants began moving there as well. In 1714, Peter ordered 350 noblemen, each having over 100 peasants in his possession; 300 merchants from the upper and lower classes, and 300 craftsmen from all trades to move to the city, and also fancifully ordered the construction of 950 houses to be completed that summer to permit occupancy in the autumn.[77] The Senate was transferred to the city in 1713. The foreign diplomatic corps soon followed: England's resident Charles Whitworth in 1712, France's Lavi in 1715, Holland's in 1716, and Prussia's and Hanover's (Weber) in 1718. To make moving easier and more attractive, Peter offered the nobles free land plots, but they were still obligated to build their own homes, and according to prescribed designs. The city's population skyrocketed. From 8,000 in 1710, it had tripled by 1717, and in 1725 it was approximately 40,000,[78] which already constituted one-eighth of the country's urban population.[79]

Why did Peter make St. Petersburg Russia's capital rather than just a trading city and military outpost? Personally, Peter hated Moscow and loved the sea. But the more fundamental reason was that he needed a fresh start in a new capital to realize his vision of creating a new civilization and national life, a city whose design, appearance, culture, and life he could create and control as the embodiment of his ideal. St. Petersburg offered many advantages as the site of the new capital. Being on the Baltic made links to Europe and the absorption of Western knowledge easier, facilitated commerce with the West and would help turn Russia into a commercial power, and made it easier for Russia to exercise political influence in Europe. Moving the court and a significant proportion of the Moscow nobility there also would weaken the nobility in Moscow as a force of potential opposition to Peter's reforms. Peter's hold on power would be more secure there than amidst a unified group of conservative nobles in Moscow who had always plotted against him.

When construction accelerated after 1710, the city had all the earmarks of a boomtown. In the summer the workers' encampments on the outskirts were as large or larger than the main city. Weber's impression of the city upon first seeing it is typical: "When I arrived there, I was surprised to find instead of a regular city, as I expected, a heap of villages linked together, like some plantation in the West Indies."[80]

Peter was equally dissatisfied. He wanted to make his city regular, an ideal of the Age of Reason and a showpiece to Russia and Europe. A starting point was to regulate the design and construction of individual buildings, but for this to have any effect in the built-up areas (mainly Gorodskoi and Admiralty Island), most existing buildings would have to be torn down and replaced. This would have been expensive and impractical, and the homeowners would oppose it. To skirt this problem, he sought to start anew in what were still relatively undeveloped areas pursuant to comprehensive plans. From 1710 through 1716–17, Peter struggled for a solution and somewhat impulsively seized upon a number of successive comprehensive designs, none of which were fulfilled. Ultimately, after Peter the grand architecture of the city developed as individual ensembles, and most of the old construction was replaced only brick by brick. Peter preferred Dutch architecture and urban design, and initially he dreamed of creating an Amsterdam of the North. Interestingly, however, not a single Dutch architect worked in the city until the very end of his reign. Peter's tastes changed during his second trip to the West in 1716–17, which made a deep artistic impression on him and proved to be an architectural turning point for the city. Peter's tastes broadened to include Italian and French architecture, "regular" gardens, and architectural ensembles, all of which began to appear in and around the city and leave the original Dutch theme behind.

In planning his Amsterdam of the North, Peter had to begin with the reality that the region around the Fortress and Trinity Square was already built up and for this purpose spoiled; moreover, Vasilievsky Island had been gifted to Menshikov, was cut off from the mainland, and lay somewhat exposed to the sea and therefore to floods and the Swedish navy. So Peter focused on the Admiralty side, targeting the area along the Neva east of the Fontanka River in the region where Shpalnernaya, Zakharevskaya, Tchaikovsky, and Furshtatskaya Streets are now located, and began encouraging the upper classes to build there. Peter set an example by settling his sister Natalya and his son Alexis in that region, and by building his own Summer Palace by the Fontanka in the Summer Garden. Work began on a rectangular grid of streets and canals, along which a number of palaces, servants quarters, and other buildings were constructed.

For reasons that remain unclear, in 1712 Peter ventured upon moving the center of the city to Kotlin (Kronstadt), now that it appeared defensible against the Swedes. He issued several decrees calling for massive construction there as well as for the mandatory transfer of various nobles and other inhabitants. A city plan featuring a large network of canals surfaced, probably that of Trezzini. Peter's reasons for this foray were probably the fact that the city's harbor, still on the Neva, was unsuitable for large naval and merchant ships, Russia's naval base and a fortress were already on this island, and here his dream of Petersburg as a genuine maritime city might be best realized. But the Kotlin plan was economically and logistically unrealistic, and his nobles opposed it. Before long, Peter accepted the inevitable and refocused his attention on the original city, again focusing for a while on the Admiralty side.

Frustrated with progress and the irregular appearance of the city, Peter brought in more foreign architects. In 1713 Trezzini was replaced as Chief Architect by a German, Andreas Schlüter, who brought a team of his own architects, including J.F. Braunstein (who worked mainly at Peterhof), Georg Johann Mattarnovy (noted for the Kunstkamera), Johann Christian Forster, and Theodor Schwertfeger. In 1713 Gottfried Schädel also arrived and completed Menshikov's palaces in the city and at Oranienbaum.

After 1714, when the naval victory of Hangö gave Russia supremacy over the Baltic, the pace of construction accelerated further and Peter regulated it more closely. In April of that year, Peter forbade plain wooden construction in St. Petersburg; rather, buildings had to be constructed either in masonry or wattle and daub. In October he freed masons and construction stone for the capital by decreeing that, until further notice, no masonry buildings could be built anywhere else in Russia, even churches. Traditionally in Russia, the main dwelling was placed in the center of the lot and the auxiliary buildings such as kitchens, stables, and storage sheds were located by the street, which often made streets crooked and narrow, a product of individual owner's decisions, which often were to let the building encroach on the street.[81] Peter, however, now decreed that the main houses had to face the street, while stables and sheds must be located in the rear. He also established what became known as the "red line" along each street across which no building could protrude.[82] Houses had to be built according to specified plans approved by Trezzini, who designed model homes in a simple Dutch style, differing in size according to the size of the land plot. It is often stated that these designs were specified for various classes. Actually, they carried no class designation, although of course the larger designs were obviously too expensive for the lower classes.[83]

Also in 1714, Peter decided that Vasilievsky Island should be the center of the city, with its spit (strelka) which divides the Large and Small Neva as the city's architectural focus, and the governmental and commercial center behind it. He had originally given most of the island to Menshikov in 1710, which had effectively prevented development on the island by others. Peter revoked his gift in 1715 but let Menshikov keep his estate there. He feverishly began issuing decrees for impossible amounts of masonry construction there, and for the next year he granted free land plots only on that island.

Peter recognized that his Vasilievsky Island initiative would not succeed unless the island (and the rest of the city) was developed according to a comprehensive plan. The city's separate villages had to be integrated into an overall design, and the existing random and shoddy wooden construction would have to be replaced with buildings of stone. The plan should call for long, wide, straight streets with regular city blocks and, as in Amsterdam, many canals that would serve as the city's arteries for travel and commerce and to control flooding, except that here they would be long, straight canals intersecting at right angles. "If God will prolong my life and health," Peter mused, "Petersburg will be another Amsterdam."[84]

Therefore, in 1715 Peter ordered Trezzini to develop a comprehensive city plan having Vasilievsky Island as the center. Trezzini produced one, and Peter approved it on January 1, 1716, just before his departure on his second long European tour. It had few details other than for Vasilievsky Island, thus not requiring major reconstruction of Admiralty and Gorodskoi Islands. It featured seven north-south canals (one of which would cut Menshikov's estate from the east side so as to limit its growth) and one east-west canal along what is presently Bolshoi Prospect, so that the island would be divided into regular city blocks. The edge of the island was to be modestly fortified, with regular bastions. A large park was planned on the north side, while the eastern spit of the island facing the Fortress and Admiralty Island would feature a large square. Rather than having an open architectural ensemble that would be visible from the Fortress and Palace Embankment and be the focal point of the city, however, the square would have buildings on all sides and be closed on itself. Thus the Fortress, Trinity Square, and the Admiralty would retain their leading roles in the architectural scheme of the city.

Trezzini, however, had not been reappointed Chief Architect after the death of Schlüter in 1714; Peter was struggling with who might best occupy the position. A promising place to look for such an architect, as well as sculptors, painters, and garden designers, was France, where Louis XIV's death in 1715 had left many court artists in an unsure position. In Paris Peter's emmisaries learned of Jean Baptiste Alexandre LeBlond, a talented former pupil of André Le Nôtre. He had made a name for himself both as an author and a theoretician of architecture and garden design, and also as the designer and builder of several prominent works, including the Chateau Chatillon, the Hotel de Clermont, and the building for the Carthusian Order. Impressed, Zotov invited him to visit Peter, who was then taking a cure in Germany. After a two-week acquaintance and many long discussions, Peter retained LeBlond at five times Trezzini's salary and made him Chief Architect of St. Petersburg.

LeBlond's duties and powers were wide ranging. In LeBlond's letter of introduction to be given to Menshikov, Peter wrote:

> This master possesses extraordinary qualities and a great talent, as I could readily observe in a short time. . . . Therefore, all architects [in St. Petersburg] shall be informed that no future construction shall be commenced without his signature being affixed to the plans, including projects already started, provided that they can still be corrected.[85]

Above all, LeBlond wanted to build the city according to his own plan, which Peter invited him to prepare for consideration despite having already approved Trezzini's plan. Besides being charged with planning and construction, he was to organize the production of construction materials, and also train Russian craftsmen, builders, and architects, including through education abroad. LeBlond arrived in August 1716 with a large contingent of other artists and craftsmen and quickly set to work. Once he had a chance to observe the state of the city, he produced a memorandum to Peter entitled *Concerning the Poor Construction Practices Prevalent in the City of St. Petersburg*. He then developed an ambitious city plan rivaling those of Trezzini and others. LeBlond claimed to have prepared it in great haste (four days) so that it could be dispatched to Peter (still abroad) together with rival plans and be considered along with them. Under LeBlond's plan, the outline of the city would be dominated by an oval of fortifications encompassing most of Vasilievsky Island, Admiralty Island, and Gorodskoi Island, which also would serve as dams to control floods. To give some idea of the scale, these fortifications would be approximately the height of Kirov Stadium now located on Krestovsky Island.[86] Within the city walls would be a grid of canals wide enough so that two boats could pass, like in Amsterdam, and a rectangular grid of straight streets. The architectural focus of the city, in the middle of Vasilievsky Island, would be the Tsar's palace with a square formal garden with cathedrals at each corner.

LeBlond sent his plan to Peter in Paris in early 1717, confidently expecting it to be approved. Peter, however, formally deferred a decision on it until his return to Russia. In the end, Peter simply took no action on LeBlond's plan, meaning that technically Trezzini's plan remained in force. The LeBlond plan was too grand and expensive, and (unlike Trezzini's plan) it violated the initial premise that it would not be feasible to tear down most existing construction. Further, its military emphasis was extreme and unnecessary since final victory over Sweden seemed imminent. The fortifications would have corrupted Peter's vision of the city as a center of civilization, constrained its growth as a commercial center, and unduly cut the city off from the mainland.

For several years Peter continued to issue decrees in an attempt to make Vasilievsky Island the city's center, but these plans were realized only in small part, and not just because of insufficient resources. Because the land was low and swampy, residents preferred to build on the higher land of Admiralty Island, where many already had built expensive homes. Vasilievsky Island was also cut off from the mainland because there were no bridges. LeBlond's efforts also got caught up in jealousies and intrigues, most notably with Menshikov, who was both Governor of the city and still the major landowner on Vasilievsky Island despite having been deprived of most of it. Menshikov skillfully used his powers as Governor to sabotage the work,[87] which was made easier by Peter's long absences from the city. Menshikov saw to it that the canals were built too narrow and too shallow and that the houses were constructed right at their edge. In order to realize the original design, nothing could be done save to demolish the work and start again. Peter was enraged, but realized that he would have to abandon the plan. By Peter's death only about one-fourth of the planned buildings on Vasilievsky Island were constructed, most of them wooden, and the island was dotted with numerous unfinished buildings, most of which remained in that state for some time and made much of the island resemble a ghost town.

Although Peter did not adopt LeBlond's plan, some of LeBlond's and Trezzini's general ideas were implemented, and the appearance of Vasilievsky Island still bears their general imprint. And LeBlond's contributions were still tremendous, especially considering that he worked in the city for only 30 months before his untimely death in February 1719. He has to his credit Peterhof, the Summer Garden, the finishing of Nevsky Prospect, Apraxin's palace, and (in part) Strelna. LeBlond also implemented generally a number of important architectural concepts still visible in the city. These included the integrated system of canals and waterways used as the city's principal method of communication and transport, a focus on masonry structures facing the streets or embankments, and strict regulation of construction. LeBlond's other legacies include his vision (later implemented by others) of building long, straight boulevards, initially called Perspective Streets (from the Latin *pro-specto*, meaning to look into the distance) and later shortened to "prospect," and his concept of designing whole architectural ensembles. The first ensemble was the square on the *strelka* of Vasilievsky Island, later executed by Trezzini (see below). The notable streets were three prospects radiating from the Admiralty like spokes, from which one can see the Admiralty's spire miles away. This layout differed greatly from the traditional irregular "circular" pattern of Russian cities. Had LeBlond lived longer, the early architecture of the city would have been more French in style. LeBlond also is credited with initiating the formal education and training of architects in Russia. Finally, he improved construction techniques and the quality of building materials, improved city infrastructure, added finish and beauty to the city by installing street lighting, paving some streets, and organizing regular street cleaning, and implemented safety and police measures against fire, theft, and vagrancy.

Paving the city's central streets was essential, as the swampy land quickly turned into mire when it rained and during the spring thaw. The first streets were paved in 1710, on Gorodskoi Island, but progress was slow due to a shortage of stone and of qualified workers. Peter's 1714 decree on the mandatory bringing of stones to the city helped accelerate this work, and in 1715 the Grand Perspective Road was paved in stone. Still, more systematic street paving began only in 1717. Petersburgers were obligated to contribute to the paving effort in the areas in front of their homes. A decree of June 18, 1718, required "each resident to fill the streets and lanes in front of their homes with sand, and to pave them smoothly with stone according to directions issued by the master craftsmen."[88] They were also required to keep these areas clean or they would be fined. In those places where the paving was in wood, people were forbidden to wear nailed boots, since they tore up the wood. By the end of Peter's reign, much of the city center was already paved.

Street lighting began with four lamps in front of the Winter Palace, but it soon spread throughout the city. LeBlond developed a plan for street lighting that was approved in 1718, designs for the street lamps by Ivan Petling were approved in 1720, and they were manufactured in factories owned by Menshikov. By 1724, 595 street lamps had been installed, which were lit and maintained by 64 workers. Another innovation was outdoor street clocks placed in selected locations, some with chimes (but which had to be struck manually).

Originally, Petersburg by design had virtually no bridges. At least in respect of the Neva, this was due to natural conditions: the river's swift current of 1.2 meters per second,[89] the river's great depth, and the winter ice and ice floes in the spring, which would have made construction and maintenance difficult. Bridges (except for drawbridges) also would have impaired the growing traffic of boats on the waterways. Most important, however, were Peter's preferences, which initially led him actually to prohibit the construction of bridges. First, he wanted canals and the river rather than streets to be the city's primary transportation arteries, for which bridges were unnecessary and even a hindrance. Second was Peter's love of sailing and the sea. Peter wanted his subjects to learn seamanship by crossing the Neva by sail, and bridges would have eliminated this need. Thus, Peter had sailboats issued for free to the upper classes, of various sizes according to one's rank. For those without sailboats, 20 government ferries were constructed and plied the Neva. Operated by unskilled peasants, these vessels were a hazard to the population and there were many accidents, in which among others the Polish Minister de Koningsek, Major-General Kirchner, and Peter's own physician perished. Initially, even the use of oars was forbidden except to foreign diplomats, on pain of fines and corporeal punishment. Oars were permitted only after the accident involving Peter's doctor. In the wintertime, roads were cleared across the ice and were lined with evergreens, the seasonal opening of which was marked with a cannon shot. For transportation other than on the Neva and other natural waterways, Peter dredged numerous artificial canals. Initially they numbered over a hundred, but only a few remain today. Many of today's streets originally were either canals or *linyi* with canals between them.

Ultimately, Peter's preference for water transportation proved unworkable. When the weather was foul, or when the river was clogged with ice floes, communications within the city were cut off and the various islands were isolated from one another, often for days at a time. It was partially because of Peter's insistence on using boats for transport that construction of private residences began to shift to Admiralty Island on the mainland. His own transportation system helped frustrate his plan to make Vasilievsky Island the city's center. Eventually bridges had to be built.

Peter strove to make Petersburg safe, habitable, and pleasant. To this end he organized the police, establishing the General Policemeister's Chancellery in 1718. Peter's conception of the police was not simply that of crime prevention, law enforcement, or surveillance. In fact the city's police numbered no more than 100 persons.[90] Drawing on rationalist Western European concepts of the well-ordered police state, the police were given broad responsibilities designed to rationalize and civilize society.[91] The first General Policemeister was the Portuguese-born Anton Devier, a former ship's cabin boy whom Peter met while in Holland during a mock naval battle. Impressed by Devier's abilities, Peter invited him to Petersburg, initially as one of his orderlies. Devier served Peter loyally and zealously, and continued as

Policemeister after Peter's death. The German Bergholz observed of him: "Strict and quick in carrying out the Tsar's orders, he instills in the common folk in general and all the inhabitants of the town such fear that they tremble at the very mention of his name."[92] But Peter was also strict with him. One day Peter was riding in a carriage with Devier, and while crossing one of the city's few bridges noticed that some of its planks were missing or loose. Peter immediately ordered the carriage to a halt, and, while the coachman repaired the bridge on the spot, Peter caned Devier's backside in punishment for negligence in maintaining the bridge.

Peter issued Devier a detailed 13-part instruction outlining the Policemeister's obligations, which reflect police science's concept of the broad social role of the institution. Devier's duties included not only enforcement of criminal laws, but publication of all Peter's decrees, organizing refuse collection, setting up guards and patrols to keep vagrants and beggars off the streets (it was illegal to give alms to them; charitable donations were to be made to charitable organizations such as hospitals), suppressing street fighting, organizing firefighting measures, exercising quality control and imposing hygienic measures at markets, cleaning up the slaughterhouses, enforcing construction requirements, maintaining canals and docks, ensuring compliance by residents with their obligations to pave and maintain streets and sidewalks and strengthen embankments, enforcing rules on traders (including their dress), and combating desertion by workers, soldiers, and sailors. The General Policemeister's Chancellery effectively became the general administrative body of the city. The Governor's Office made larger decisions in the city and administered lesser details only outside the city proper.[93]

This vast effort was possible because the city's residents were drafted into supplementing Devier's small force to beautify and maintain the city, at their own expense. Citizens were subject to numerous burdensome requirements, and were fined or subject to corporeal punishment if they did not comply. They had to keep the streets and sidewalks in front of their homes clean. When trees were planted, they were responsible for supplying the trees, and when paving was being done they had to supply sand and other materials and prepare the area by their homes. Residents living on the river and canals had to reinforce the embankments, and were forbidden from polluting the waterways. A decree of September 3, 1718, required that "each resident shall, early each morning before people walk the streets, . . . sweep all dirt from bridges and streets in front of their homes so that there will be no refuse, and maintain the paving stones."[94] Special taxes and duties were imposed on city residents in order to fund municipal improvements, maintenance and repair, city lighting, sanitation, and other measures.

However burdensome, these efforts made Petersburg unique in Russia, and indeed in Europe. Its main streets were wide and straight, and many were paved and lit at night. It featured canals, parks, and gardens. And it was relatively safe, orderly, and clean. In these respects Petersburg was better than most Western European cities.

By Peter's death, many of the city's distinctive landmarks had been built, and each island had developed its own characteristics that survive until this day. Describing them up close as they appeared in Peter's time helps to gain a feeling for Peter's conception of his city, its geography, life there, and how it differed from the rest of Russia and compared to Europe. The description below moves through Gorodskoi, Vasilievsky, and Admiralty Islands, and finally to the outlying islands and the new palaces in the suburbs, as they existed during Peter's reign.

GORODSKOI ISLAND

The island behind the Peter and Paul Fortress, now called Petrograd* Island, was the first area of the city to be developed, and it remained the city's center into the 1730s. It featured the city's main square and served as the first port, the city's religious and social center, and the location of the government.

The first building in the city was Peter's log cabin on the riverbank about halfway between the Fortress and the Bolshaya Nevka. It was built quickly to Peter's simple tastes by three soldier-carpenters on May 24–26, 1703, and consisted of a study, dining room, and bedroom. It combined traditional Russian and Dutch features, including painting the outside walls like bricks to resemble buildings in Amsterdam. Over time, due to his travels and other residences in the city and elsewhere, Peter spent less and less time there, and once he married Catherine he never resided there again. Recognizing its significance, however, he had it preserved. Since 1724 it has been encased and protected by three successive pavilions and still stands there today.

The original heart of the city was Trinity Square adjacent to the east side of the Fortress, named after Trinity Cathedral built on it. The Square, as well as the bridge over the Neva leading to it, still bears this name today, after having been called Revolution Square during the Soviet period. According to tradition, the foundation of Trinity Cathedral was laid on the same day as the Fortress, May 16 (27 New Style), 1703, the holy day of the Trinity, hence the Cathedral's name. Though an Orthodox church, in a major break with Russian tradition it was built in the Dutch style and was the first building of many in the city to feature a tall, slender golden spire. The original wooden building lasted until 1750, when it burned, after which Empress Elizabeth ordered that a yet unconsecrated wooden church that had just been

---

*It was originally known as Tamminen ("Oak") Island, which the Novgorodians phonetically corrupted to Fomin Island; a new Finnish name also emerged, Koivusaari ("Birch Island"), but the name Fomin stuck and was reestablished by 1500. Once the city was established, the island's name changed from Fomin to Garrison Island, then to Gorodskoi (or Gorodovoi) ("City" or "Fortress," as the word for "city" still connoted a fortified settlement on an elevation; the Russian word for hill is *gora*) Island, Trinity Island, and finally in the 1730s to Petersburg Island. During World War I the name changed to Petrograd Island, which remains to this day.

built near her Summer Palace be transported to the site. It lasted until 1928, when it was destroyed by the Soviets.

Trinity Square was the site of holiday and victory celebrations, military parades, announcements of new laws and decrees, other public functions and outdoor social events, and public executions. One of the most notable executions was that of the noble Matvei Gagarin, who using pilfered state funds built himself a large stone mansion just east of Peter's log cabin. In February 1723 he was convicted of massive corruption and publicly beheaded in front of the College of Justice. His palace was confiscated and used for the Synod. Catherine's consort William Mons, the younger brother of Peter's former lover Anna Mons, and Mary Hamilton, one of Catherine's maids of honor, also were executed there in 1724, he for corruption and she for infanticide. But the Square was also the scene of happier events. Huge parades and masquerades, often lasting several days, were held there.*

On the river side of the Square was the city's first port. Opposite, at the back (north) of the square, approximately where the Mosque stands today, were trading stalls dating from 1705, which served both as an ordinary food market and as a place where merchants traded and were accommodated. In July 1710 the old market and trading stalls were consumed by a fire, and in its place grew up a secondhand market that became known as the "Tatar Camp" due to the area's ethnic makeup. In 1713 a large new two-story *gostiny dvor*† made of masonry replaced it, which also housed the city's first bookshop, opened in 1714. It was government owned and guarded by soldiers. In its courtyard the original exchange building still stood, which had been built in 1705 and survived the fire. This *gostiny dvor* lasted until 1737, by which time others had been built in other regions of the city.

On the east side of the Square, in 1714 construction began on the two-story building of the Colleges, built of wood faced with clay. It was designed in the Dutch style, based on the new concept of identical, repeating sections (symbolizing the equality of each College) which could be added to without destroying the architectural integrity of the building. (This pattern was later repeated in the Twelve Colleges on Vasilievsky Island.) Indeed, it was first built in four sections and later expanded to six. At the time, it was one of the largest governmental buildings in Europe. In 1718 the Senate, until then housed in the Fortress, also moved into the new building, but not for long. From 1723 it met in Peter's Winter Palace on the Admiralty Side, where it would remain until 1732, when it moved to Trezzini's Twelve Colleges building on Vasilievsky Island.[95]

---

*See chapter 3.

†The term *gostiny dvor*, still in use today, became popular to designate specially constructed trading stalls where finished goods, usually from elsewhere (called *gostintsy*, "souvenirs" because they were often presents or souvenirs), were traded, in order to distinguish them from an ordinary market (*rynok*) where food products were primarily sold.

On the west side of the Square was the Krasny Bridge, a drawbridge connecting the Square to the Fortress. Built in 1711, it was the first bridge in the city. Next to it on the Square stood two small buildings, the main printing shop, and the Austeria of the Four Frigates Tavern dating from 1705. Operated by a German,[96] the Four Frigates was owned, like other taverns, by the state.[97] There the townspeople and foreign merchants gathered to eat, drink, trade, and exchange news and stories. It was the city's most popular place for socializing. Peter was a frequent visitor, often turning up there after services at neighboring Trinity Cathedral to enjoy his favorite beverage of vodka and cayenne pepper.

Trezzini's first major project in the city was to improve the Fortress, on which work began in 1706 and at the time was the largest and most complex construction effort in Russian history. Over 40,000 piles were driven to support the new walls faced in stone and brick. The walls were heightened to 10–12 meters, and also thickened (to 20 meters) and redesigned to accommodate various offices, warehouses, and the Fortress's infamous prison cells. A canal was cut lengthwise through the middle, so that boats bearing materials could unload inside the walls. (It was filled in during the 19th century.) New buildings were added inside, including one initially housing the Senate. Trezzini also built the famous Peter Gate on the east side of the Fortress facing Trinity Square, which was designed after the triumphal gate in Narva and, through its depiction of the biblical subject of the Fall of Simon Magus, symbolizes Peter's victory over the Swedes. The project was completed only in 1740, six years after Trezzini's death. The present granite facing on the river side was added under Catherine II in the 1780s. By then the poor quality brick had begun to deteriorate, and in the 1760s Catherine had begun to uniformly decorate the Neva's embankments in granite. The river side of the Fortress had to match. After all this effort, it is notable that the Fortress never saw military action. It would, however, feature prominently in the later history of the city.

Under Peter began the city's tradition of daily cannon shots from the Sovereign's Bastion of the Fortress to mark the times of day. In Peter's time there were three shots daily year round: one at sunrise, another at 11:00 A.M. (when workers took their mid-day break), and another at sunset. The tradition is maintained to this day, but now there is only one shot, fired at noon.

In 1712, when St. Petersburg had become the capital of Russia, the question of having a suitable state cathedral in the city arose. Peter decided that this should be the Peter and Paul Cathedral, reconstructed in masonry. Trezzini designed it, and work began in June 1712. The first section to be built was the immense bell tower with its spire rising 122 meters into the sky. Peter wanted the spire to dominate the city's skyline. Because of the tower's great weight, it was built first so it could settle in the soft ground before the remainder of the Cathedral was built. The tower was finished only in August 1720, when Peter ascended it and for the first time surveyed his Petersburg from on high. The remainder of the Cathedral took over 10 years to complete. Like Trinity Cathedral, it deviated completely from the traditional onion-domed Muscovite churches, and rather resembled the Protestant churches of northern Europe.

Outside the Fortress to the north initially spread an empty field, kept clear so that no enemy could approach undetected or protected. But there was a weakness. Unlike the other sides of the Fortress, which were protected by expanses of water, on this landward side an enemy could place artillery close enough to bombard the Fortress and so had to be kept out of firing range. Thus, in December 1706 Peter ordered the construction of outer fortifications across the water channel on Gorodskoi Island to protect this side of the Fortress, and work began in 1707. These fortifications were named the Kronwerk (Swedish for "Crown Works") because of their crown pattern. They were completed within a year and featured 87 barracks and 78 cannon. The field to the north of the Kronwerk was extended to include the territory now occupied by the Alexander Park. The Kronwerk underwent capital reconstruction in 1752, and a new plan of 1757 called for the Kronwerk to be rebuilt, but the plan was only partially realized as the Kronwerk had already lost its military significance.

Beyond the Kronwerk, to the west, north, and east spread residential districts. St. Petersburg, in a manner traditional for Russian cities, initially developed into various quarters (sloboda), each populated by a group of people of a common vocation, ethnic background, or social class. The area immediately around Trinity Square was known as the Russian quarter. To the west of the Kronwerk was the Tatar quarter with its Tatar market, where Tatars and various other southern ethnic groups lived, which heritage is preserved today by the lane named Tatarsky Pereulok. Closer to the river to the west of the Fortress, where the Malaya Neva branches off, was the customs house. To the northwest of the Tatar quarter lay another Russian quarter where the temporary Russian workers for building the fortifications and other projects lived. The Preobrazhensky and Semenovsky regiments also were initially quartered to the northwest. To the northeast of the Kronwerk were several quarters populated by various kinds of tradesmen, and many streets of this district still reflect the trades carried out there, such as Ruzheinaya ("Gunsmith") Street and Monetnaya ("Mint") Street.

To the east of Trinity Square, on the embankments of the Neva and Bolshaya Nevka and along the present Kuibysheva and Michurina Streets (then called Big and Small Courtier Streets respectively) initially were the dwellings of most courtiers, including Peter's closest lieutenants such as Menshikov (before his Vasilievsky Island palace was ready), Golovkin, Bruce, Zotov, Buturlin, and Shafirov. Golovkin's was the first stone and masonry residence in the city, built in 1710 from stones taken from the ruined Nienshantz.

Medicinal herbs and medicines were needed in the new military and other hospitals and by the public, so Peter also established in St. Petersburg Russia's first publicly accessible pharmacy shops. The first pharmacy was established in the Peter and

Paul Fortress as early as 1704; the first public pharmacies were opened in 1722. Petersburg's climate was not ideal for growing medicinal herbs, but in 1714 Peter decided to establish a medicinal herb garden on what was then the edge of the city. The site chosen was across the Karpovka River, on what became known as Apothecary Island. The garden was established and operated by the Scottish doctor Robert Erskine, the scion of a noble family who had graduated from Oxford and established a successful and famous medical practice in England. Invited to Russia in 1704 by Menshikov, he also practiced medicine, serving first as Menshikov's and later (from 1713) Peter's personal physician. He ran Peter's Kunstkamera and headed the Pharmaceutical *Prikaz*, in which capacity he researched the medical properties of the plants and waters in the St. Petersburg area, including the famous Polustrovo mineral springs. He accumulated a large library, which Peter bought upon Erskine's death in 1718 and eventually donated to the new Academy of Sciences. In the mid-19th century, a botanical garden was established on the site, and it remains a botanical garden and park to this day. On the northeast part of Apothecary Island there was a Lutheran cemetery, as in the city's early days most Germans lived on adjacent Gorodskoi Island; they worshipped in the Lutheran Church of St. Anna not far from Trinity Square.[98]

Elsewhere on Apothecary and Gorodskoi Islands, it was still wild. Bears and wolves roamed there. In the winter large wolf packs roamed in search of food, attacking both animals and humans. Many homeowners erected fences around their properties for protection, and from the Kronwerk to the north toward Kamenny ("Stone") Island a fence was erected to keep the wolves out of that part of town,[99] but the incidents continued, in all parts of the city. In 1714 two soldiers were attacked and one of them killed as they stood guard in front of the central foundry, and the next year a woman was devoured by a wolf in broad daylight on Vasilievsky Island near Menshikov's palace.[100]

VASILIEVSKY ISLAND

The largest island in St. Petersburg was originally called Vasilievsky Island after Vasily Selezne, a well-known Novgorodian *posadnik* who was executed when Tsar Ivan III conquered Novgorod in 1471. Sometime after the 15th century, however, it became known (at least to the Finns and Swedes) as Hirvisaari ("Reindeer, or Elk, Island"). The name Vasilievsky reappeared after Peter's conquest of the city and has remained to this day.

The development of Vasilievsky Island was initially retarded by Menshikov. Peter granted him ownership of most of Vasilievsky Island in 1707, and thus construction there by others was largely precluded. For a while the island itself was known as Menshikov (or Prince's) Island. Peter retracted most of his gift in 1715 once he decided to make the island the city's center, after which it developed more rapidly though still not as desired.

Menshikov began the settlement of Vasilievsky Island in 1710 with the construction of his magnificent pink palace on the Neva embankment facing the Admiralty. Although it remains unclear who authored the building's plan, the work was begun by Giovanni Maria Fontan and completed by Gottfried Schädel. The palace was built largely according to contemporary European designs. It featured statues on the roof and in the interior, both firsts in Russia, although those on the roof did not last long because they were wooden. A canal was cut from the Neva into the courtyard with a boat landing by the palace entrance. To the east he built the Church of Resurrection of Christ, which stood until 1730. In the back were his "pleasure house" and a regular park stretching almost to the Malaya Neva, which rivaled the Summer Garden in its splendor.

For many years Menshikov's palace was the finest in the city. It, rather than Peter's palaces, was used for the city's main social and diplomatic events, and thus it became known as the Ambassadorial Palace. The first such event, held in 1710 before the palace was completed, was the wedding and reception of Peter's niece and future Empress, Anna Ioannovna, to the Duke of Courland, soon followed by a famous wedding of dwarfs.[101]

Beginning in 1716, Vasilievsky Island's development followed certain features of LeBlond's and Trezzini's plans. LeBlond worked actively there during his brief tenure in the city, and himself maintained a residence there from 1717. An entire French *sloboda* was built (by Trezzini, to his chagrin) behind Menshikov's palace along what became known as French Street, in which LeBlond's assistants, who knew no Russian, created their own community. Even today, the originally planned grid pattern remains. The main arteries of the island—Bolshoi, Sredny, and Maly Prospects—are as plotted by Trezzini. Running crosswise was the planned series of north–south parallel streets called "*linyi*" ("lines" or "rows"), which was also replicated in certain other parts of the city. The word "*linyi*" originally referred to the lines of houses, not the streets. Like in Amsterdam, across the street from the houses, and between each pair of streets, was supposed to be a navigable canal suitable for family and commercial traffic. Each house was to have a small dock on the canal, as in Amsterdam. The streets on either side would have a numbered name (3rd, 4th, 5th *Linya*, etc.). Due mainly to Menshikov's interference, the original design and purpose of the *linyi* were not fulfilled, and fewer were built than originally planned. When the too-narrow canals were later filled in to make a single, wider street, the designations as *linyi* survived, so that each side of the same street retained a different *linya* number, which still confuses visitors to the city.

Other prominent early buildings on the island included the palace of Fedor Soloviev constructed in 1713 just east of Menshikov's palace, which at the time was second only to Menshikov's in its splendor. In 1718, Georg Johann Mattarnovy began work on the palace of Praskovya Fedorovna, the widow of Peter's half-brother Ivan V and mother of the future Empress Anna Ioannovna, located on the *strelka* of the island. It was still unfinished at Peter's death in 1725, however, and two years later it was decided to house the Academy of Sciences there. The building lasted until the early 19th century, when it was demolished to build the Exchange Building. Around to the southeast and across from the Admiralty, in 1718 Mattarnovy began work on the Kunstkamera building. One of the first public buildings in Russia, it took the appearance of Western public buildings at the time, which featured a tower in the middle, but in this case the tower was used as an observatory. Mattarnovy died in 1719, and his various projects, including the Kunstkamera, were completed by Nicholas Friedrich Grebel. Construction proceeded slowly (Mattarnovy's central tower began to deteriorate in 1724 and had to be reconstructed). The building was opened officially in 1728, but work continued until 1732. Elsewhere near the *strelka* a vigorous trading area had developed, and there were even Dutch-style windmills, which were used to provide power for sawing wood.

The above buildings were not built as part of a planned ensemble on the *strelka*, but soon after Peter returned from Europe in late 1717, he demanded such a plan. He had been influenced by his long conversations with LeBlond and was impressed by Europe's architecture, particularly the squares, multi-building ensembles, and regular gardens in Paris. At the same time, his government had increased in size and was outgrowing its offices on Gorodskoi Island. Peter desired ensembles of magnificent public buildings in his capital, but saw that Trinity Square, itself rather haphazardly developed, would have to be reconstructed if it were to become a regular architectural ensemble. These factors, together with his earlier decision to make Vasilievsky Island the city center, led Peter in 1718 to decide to create a new main city square on the *strelka*. Since Peter had already decided not to adopt LeBlond's city plan, he ordered Trezzini to develop the plan for the *strelka*. This was the first time in Russia that part of a city was to be developed as a planned architectural ensemble.

When Trezzini developed his original city plan in 1715, he had taken pains to let the architectural focus of the city remain the Fortress and Trinity Square on the north shore, and the Palace Embankment and Admiralty on the south, and thus the *strelka* area was largely enclosed by buildings. Trezzini now needed to make it more open while also blending it with the Kunstkamera and Praskovya Fedorovna's palace. Trezzini presented his plan in 1722, and it was immediately accepted by Peter. The *strekla* would be dominated by a long, regular building back from the tip of the *strelka* perpendicular to the river and looking upstream, which would house the ten Colleges (later increased to twelve). In front of the Twelve Colleges would be a canal cutting the *strelka* off from the rest of the island, and in front of that a large square with a church dedicated to St. Andrew in the center and nearby Carlo Rastrelli's equestrian statue of Peter. To the north would be a new port and customs house.

In May 1723 Peter instructed Trezzini to begin work on the Colleges and some work was begun, but Peter then changed his mind and decided to hold an architectural competition (the first ever in Russia) for the design of the *strelka* ensemble. Trezzini's designs were used for the Colleges, the Customs House, and the *gostiny dvor*, but as none of the proposed designs for St. Andrew's church pleased Peter, this project was given to a Swedish architect. Due to Peter's death, ensuing political complications and a shortage of funds, the church was never built. The new port was constructed on the Malaya Neva around the north side of the *strelka* and began functioning in the 1730s. In 1730 the Senate ordered that the main customs be transferred there. The *gostiny dvor* also was completed, in 1736.

The concept for the Twelve Colleges was similar in concept to the Colleges on Gorodskoi Island. It featured 12 identical two-story sections on top of an arcaded basement, one for each College, with a hipped roof with an attic. The front was dominated by white pilasters. Work on the building proceeded unevenly, as each College had to pay for its section with its own funds, which were sometimes lacking; work was not completed until 1733. When Peter added a thirteenth College to his government, it was too late to accommodate this in the building's design. Instead, the new College was housed in a wing adjoining the west side of Menshikov's palace. It was painted not the pink color of Menshikov's palace, but a rusty red like the other Colleges, which can still be seen today. In 1730, as originally planned, a canal was cut in front of the Twelve Colleges running to the *gostiny dvor* to the north. A legend later arose that the Twelve Colleges were originally meant to face the Neva but that the jealous Menshikov changed the alignment to perpendicular—as he had foiled other plans for "his" island—because he did not want his own palace to be outshone, and that Peter was outraged when he learned about it. This is mere legend, but is still testimony to Menshikov's cunningness and history of intrigue. The Twelve Colleges building is now the main building of St. Petersburg State University.

The square itself, then called Senate Square, remained for a long time largely open, unpaved and swampy, which meant that Carlo Rastrelli's famous equestrian statue of Peter could not be placed on it as originally planned. The canal in front of the Twelve Colleges was filled in during the 1760s, but otherwise the general pattern of the Square remained unchanged until the early 1800s, when the Exchange Building was built and a garden with trees was laid in front of the Twelve Colleges building. On the very tip of the *strelka* was a platform on piles extending into the water called the Illumination Theater. From there fireworks were displayed and could be conveniently viewed from Gorodskoi Island, the Fortress, or from the Winter Palace on the Admiralty side.

ADMIRALTY ISLAND AND THE MAINLAND

The south shore of the Neva was known as the Ingemarland Side. The area between the Mya (now Moika) River* and the Neva became known as Admiralty Island. The city grew faster on Admiralty Island than elsewhere and became the city's center. Why? The city's largest enterprise, the Admiralty, was located there, meaning that its workers had to live on that side. This was also the mainland and thus was not cut off from the rest of Russia. The land was also higher and drier, and so better for building. Finally, beginning in 1710 until Peter turned his attention to Vasilievsky Island in 1714–15, Peter himself encouraged settlement of Admiralty Island. As a result, whereas in 1711 there were only 300 buildings on Admiralty Island, within 6–7 years the number of principal buildings exceeded 1,500.[102]

In the early years, the centerpiece of Admiralty Island was the Admiralty itself, the largest enterprise and employer in the city. Completed in 1705, its first ship, a small 18-cannon vessel designed for bombarding coastal defenses, was launched on April 29, 1706. Indeed, until the Poltava victory in 1709, only smaller naval vessels were built there. After that victory, Russia could turn its attention to the naval phase of the war and focus on controlling the Baltic. For this it needed a fleet of larger vessels suitable for the open sea. The Admiralty was re-equipped to produce them, but demand was so great that some vessels were built to the west of the Admiralty's walls where Decembrists Square is now located. The first such vessel was the 54-cannon *Poltava*, begun in 1709 and launched in June 1712. From 1712 the Admiralty focused exclusively on large vessels, so a new site for the construction of smaller vessels was chosen not far west of the Admiralty between the Moika and the Neva, where the famous New Holland complex was later built. Overall, from 1706 to 1725, St. Petersburg's shipyards are known to have built at least 59 large naval vessels (including 4 frigates) and 203 galleys and other smaller naval vessels.[103] At first shipbuilding at the Admiralty was exclusively under the direction of foreign masters from Holland, England, and Italy, but gradually they were replaced by Russians who learned there or who returned from training abroad. But all Admiralty workers wore the same foreign dress. Initially the Admiralty employed about 1,000 people, but this grew to 4,700 by 1711 and approximately 10,000 by 1715.[104] Affiliated with the Admiralty

---

*The name for the Moika River is popularly thought to originate from the root for the Russian verb *myt'* ("to wash") because of bathhouses located along its banks as well as the daily washing of laundry and other articles carried out there in early days. Documentary sources, however, show that long before Peter's time the river was already called "Mya" ("muddy"), and that the name "Moika" was thus suggested, if not derived from, the Izhorsk-Finnish words "Mya Ioki," meaning "muddy river (or stream)." Zavarikhin, *op cit.*, p. 11; Gorbachevich and Khablo, *op cit.*, p. 314; see also Stolpianskii, *op cit.*, p. 24. This is quite opposed to the notion of washing or bathing, but the similarity in the words made it easy for the Russians to associate the river with the washing and bathhouses and seize upon the name Moika. For convenience, the name "Moika" is used throughout this book, even though in Peter's time the name was "Mya."

were numerous other factories and workshops—both in and outside of town—which produced the materials used in shipbuilding, including lumber, bricks, rope, wax, tar, shingles, and gunpowder bags.

Generally, the construction of dwellings west (downriver) from the Admiralty was forbidden because Peter wanted to preserve the area for industry and warehousing to serve the Admiralty. He did issue decrees requiring construction of prominent residences right on the embankment to provide an impressive view for visitors arriving in the city, but as in many other places he encountered resistance and at least in Peter's time construction there was slow.

Further downriver to the west of the Admiralty ancillary industries and warehouses grew up, together with the new shipyard for smaller naval vessels. Originally it produced mainly small boats called *skampavi* and therefore was known as *Skampaveini* Wharf, but production soon shifted to galleys, formerly built at the Admiralty, and it became known as Galley Wharf (officially so in 1721).* Galley Street (still so named today) was created to connect it to the Admiralty. Beginning in 1717, a network of canals was dug in order to transport materials to the Admiralty from these storage areas. Connecting the Moika and the Neva† was the Kryukov Canal (so called to this day), named after Semyon Kryukov, the contractor for the canal's earth works. Further down, also connecting the Moika with the Neva, was the New Admiralty Canal. Parallel to Galley Street toward the Moika ran the Admiralty (later New Holland) Canal, which also connected the two shipyards, and parallel to it to the south ran another canal. Once shipbuilding ceased at the Admiralty and the Galley Wharf was moved to Vasilievsky Island, these two parallel canals were filled in and now form the two sides of Konnogvardeisky Boulevard separated by a park median. Under Catherine II, the New Holland complex was built on the site of Galley Wharf. The name "Holland" derives from a Dutch method of curing wood used in ships adopted by Peter. This was originally done on a plot just to the west of Admiralty, which people accordingly called "Holland." When Catherine II transferred this work to the island formed by the Admiralty and Kryukov canals, it became known as New Holland.

Because of the industry in the region to the west of the Admiralty, there were no important buildings there at the time; the notable buildings were far downriver. In 1711, as a gift to Catherine, Peter built a one-storied wooden palace near the mouth of the Fontanka at the site of his first naval victory over Sweden on May 6, 1703, in honor of that victory. He named it Ekaterinhof. Around the palace Peter laid out a park with a canal through it to the sea and a menagerie. This was the first

---

*In Russia at the time, "galley" meant any warship with oars. The harbor for the galleys was originally in the channel between the Fortress and Gorodskoi Island, but a new harbor on the west end of Vasilievsky Island was designed by Trezzini in 1720 and completed in 1724.

†The continuation of the Kryukov Canal connecting the Moika and Fontanka that one sees today was built only in 1782–87.

of many imperial summer palaces to be built on the outskirts of the city. Further downriver from Ekaterinhof Peter also built two one-story wooden palaces for his daughters Anna and Elizabeth. Finally, also near Ekaterinhof, on a small island at the very mouth of the Fontanka, in about 1720 Peter built the two-storied, towered masonry Observation *(Podzorny)* Palace. When he needed rest, Peter liked to spend time alone there observing ships entering his city.

Behind the Admiralty (to the south) stood the church of St. Isaac of Dalmatia, so named because Peter's birthday, May 30, was on that saint's day. The first such church was built of wood in 1710 on Admiralty Lug, approximately where the fountain in Alexander Park is now located. Peter's court attended services there, and in 1712 Peter and Catherine celebrated their public marriage there. It was torn down in 1717 and replaced by a stone church located approximately where Falconet's equestrian monument to Peter now stands on Decembrists Square, which at the time was nearer to the water's edge. It was designed by Mattarnovy, who used a Western design featuring a tall steeple and bell tower similar to that in the Fortress. Unfortunately, the ground was not reinforced sufficiently to support the stone structure, which soon began to subside. When it was struck by lightning in 1735, it fell into disuse, and it was demolished and eventually replaced by a new cathedral built under Catherine II further back from the river.[105]

South of St. Isaac's was the shipbuilders' quarter. This is still reflected in the names of the main streets in the area today, Malaya and Bolshaya Morskaya ("Small Maritime, or Navy" and "Big Maritime" Streets). Nearest to the Admiralty naval officers and master craftsmen received land plots and homes. Further away, and also to the east and west, lived the ordinary workers. Their quarters consisted of wooden shacks, which were a constant source of fires, which eventually facilitated their replacement by stone buildings beginning in 1738. Beyond the Moika, buildings extended up to the Krivushchi ("Curvy" or "Crooked") River (now named the Griboyedov Canal), consisting of several *sloboda*, including Pryadilnaya ("Spinners"), Kuznetskaya ("Blacksmiths"), Pushkarskaya ("Gunners"). On the northwest intersection of the Moika and the Grand Perspective Road, where the Barricade movie theater now stands, Mattornovy built a *gostiny dvor* in 1719, which lasted until 1736, when it was consumed by the great fire that ravaged that part of town. Across the Grand Perspective from the *gostiny dvor*, where the Literary Café now stands, was the home of the Dutch Admiral Cruys. Retained in 1698 as a result of Peter's visit to Holland, he was Peter's main naval commander and led Russia's navy to victory over the Swedes. Across the Moika from Cruys's house and slightly off the Grand Perspective was the Main Police Chancellery, which is why the nearby bridge over the Moika at this intersection eventually became known as Police Bridge. (Before that it was called Green Bridge.) Toward the Neva from Cruys's house, at the beginning of the Grand Perspective Road, was the Morskoi Market.

From the Morskoi Market along the Moika to the east, where the General Staff building now stands and across from Apraxin's palace, stood two series of row houses, one facing the Moika and the other facing the swampy field that would later become Palace Square, in which mainly foreign specialists lived. This area, and that to the east, became known as the German (or Foreign) Quarter. Petersburg's German Quarter contrasted sharply with that of Moscow in Peter's youth. Moscow's had been purposely located out of town, and foreigners were confined there so that their Western religious beliefs, political ideas, customs, and lifestyle would not corrupt Muscovites. In Petersburg, however, foreigners could live where they wanted, mingled freely within the city, attended the important social functions, and played important roles at all levels of society.

On the Neva embankment to the east of the Admiralty, the most prominent building was the thirty-room palace of Admiral Apraxin, which stood on the site of the present Winter Palace. Also in that area were the palaces of Alexander Kikin, head of the Admiralty, and Pavel Yaguzhinsky, another of Peter's "new men" who rose to become, among other things, Peter's eyes and ears in the Senate and a diplomat. In this area Admiral Cruys built a Lutheran church, where Dutch, Germans, Finns, and other northern nationalities worshipped. The first pastor was Wilhelm Tolly, who because of the various nationalities in his congregation conducted services in several foreign languages (he was said to speak 14). Located next to what is now called the Winter Canal, on the current site of the Hermitage theater, was Peter's Winter Palace, so named to distinguish it from his Summer Palace in the Summer Garden. The first Winter Palace was preceded by Peter's Winter House, built in 1708 by Trezzini, further back from the embankment and facing Middle Street. Peter located his home here in order to be close to the Admiralty. It was small (about 58 by 32 feet), wooden, built in a Dutch manner and was less ornate than the neighboring homes of his lieutenants. Still, it was too ornate for him and the rooms too high and spacious. Thus, to preserve decorum each story was as high as necessary for the facade to have the required proportions, but inside Peter installed false ceilings. In 1711 this wooden building was moved to Petrovsky Island, and what is often called the "first" Winter Palace was designed and built on the same site by Trezzini out of stone. It resembled one of Trezzini's model homes for the higher nobility. In 1716, a new Winter Palace designed by Mattarnovy was erected facing the river. In 1718 the Winter Palace Canal (later shortened to simply the Winter Canal) was cut alongside it, with a small boat landing. In front were installed four street lamps, the first in St. Petersburg.

In 1715 Peter issued a decree calling for the construction of a street along the Neva embankment between the Admiralty and Tsaritsyn Lug, now the Field of Mars. Prior to this, like Peter's Winter House, the row of palaces nearest to the Neva faced not the river but Middle Street, which ran between the embankment and the current Millionaya Street. Once the new street on the embankment was built, a new row of palaces appeared facing the Neva and presented an impressive view from the *strelka* of Vasilievsky Island or from the river. The embankment, at first unnamed and called informally the Upper Embankment, later was named the Palace Embankment, the name it bears today.

Behind this row of palaces toward the Moika was a second foreign quarter along what is now Millionaya Street. It was known as the Greek Quarter because of the many Ionian galley captains living there. The street thus became known as Greek Street, but also was called Nemetskaya ("German" or "Foreign") Street, Bolshaya ("Big") Nemetskaya or even simply Bolshaya. The facades of homes in this upscale neighborhood abutted the street as required, but many had their entrances from an interior courtyard accessed from the street through an archway, thus beginning a trend that spread throughout the city and is still seen today. This quarter also featured Catholic, Swedish, and Finnish churches. The quarter was destroyed by fires between 1735 and 1737, but the name Nemetskaya Street remained for some time.

At the river's edge on the east end of the Greek quarter, approximately where the Marble Palace now stands, stood the Post Office, with adjoining stables for postal horses. It was first built in wood in 1708, but was rebuilt in stone by Trezzini in 1716 after the wooden one burned down. After this too burned, the Post Office was moved to the west bank of the Winter Canal on Nemetskaya Street, which embankment was accordingly renamed Pochtovaya ("Post").

The city's postal service had a challenging task, as the city's streets had no official names until 1738. "If one asks for another's house," wrote Weber, "they give him direction by describing the place, or naming some person that lives thereabouts, till they hit upon one that he knows, and then he may go thither and inquire further."[106] Thus, letters came without a street address, and postmen had to roam around asking residents where the addressees lived. They had every incentive to succeed, however, because they earned no salary and were paid only by the addressees upon delivery. Mail was sent to the rest of Russia twice a week. In 1723 international service was initiated via Germany by two frigates coursing back and forth to Lubeck.

The Post Office served not only for mail delivery, but also was a hotel and a tavern frequented by Peter. It featured a ballroom in which Peter's "assemblies" and other social events were held. Following Dutch custom, a brass band often could be heard playing there at noon. Adjacent was a trading area featuring wines. In 1711, across Bolshaya Nemetskaya Street a menagerie grew up, complete with monkeys, bears, and big cats including lions, leopards, and a lynx that was caught right in the Summer Garden. In 1714, a small house was built there to house an elephant, complete with Persian attendants, that was presented to Peter by the Persian Shah. The elephant, however, did not survive long in the harsh climate, and after its death the famous Globe of Gottorp was initially housed in its building. In 1718 the menagerie was moved to the Summer Garden.

Just east of the Post Office was Bolshoi Lug ("Big Meadow"), soon renamed Tsaritsyn ("Tsarina's," meaning Catherine's) Lug* and today called the Field of Mars. The west side of Tsaritsyn Lug was initially bordered only by buildings, but in 1711 work began on the Krasny ("Beautiful") Canal cut along that border, to help drain the Lug. Contemporary accounts describe it as the widest canal in the city, hence its name, but this did not prevent it from being filled in during 1760. Between the canal and the Post Office, at the end of Bolshaya Nemetskaya Street, a basin and boat landing (principally for postal boats) were built, from which music was played on holidays. (This explains the fork and median at the east end of today's Millionaya Street.) Stone houses were built along the canal, around the basin and along Bolshaya Nemetskaya Street, which at the time were some of the most important in the city. These included the homes of the Duke of Holstein (the future husband of Peter's daughter Anna), Peter's daughter Elizabeth, Adam Veide, and Alexander Rumyantsev. By Empress Elizabeth's time, this had become the most aristocratic part of town, and the basin became known as the "Pas de Calais" (i.e., The Straits of Dover).[107] Eventually (in 1817–19) the famous Pavlovsky Regiment barracks would be built along on the western border of the former Krasny Canal, which building still stands there today.

Bolshoi Lug was bordered to the east by the Swan Canal (cut in 1711–16), thus separating it from the Summer Garden, and to the south by the Moika River, which in 1711 was dredged to make a clear, navigable connection through to the Fontanka. The Lug was used as a military parade ground once the canal system had sufficiently drained it.

Peter began work on what would become the Summer Garden as early as 1704, and it was improved and altered over decades and centuries by many designers. Initially, in 1703, Peter kept only a small cabin there and had no grand plans for the site. For him it was his personal hideaway in the city where he could relax, and his "gardening" activities there, though prodigious, were merely a private hobby.

The first plan of the Garden was developed by Peter's first Russian designer, Ivan Matveev, in 1707, but he died that same year. Trezzini took over, but did little because of his many other commitments and the fact that the Admiralty side of the city was not yet being developed. Once development of the Admiralty side accelerated after 1710, Peter appointed the Dutchman Yan Roozen to the project, who worked there from 1711 to 1716, and work went more quickly. Originally the Garden was wider, extending onto what is now the Field of Mars, but it extended southward only to about half of its present length. This was the "first" Summer Garden. The Swan *(Lebyazhi)* Canal was cut in 1711–16 to separate the Garden from Tsaritsyn Lug, while along the original south edge of the Garden a small canal

---

*It was also called Poteshnoe Pole ("Field of Entertainment") because fireworks, then called *poteshnie ogni* ("entertainment fires"), were often set off there to entertain revelers in the summer or at Catherine's Summer Palace.

was cut between the Swan Canal and the Fontanka. A new section of the Garden between this new canal and the Moika was added, which became known as the "second" Summer Garden or the "Red (or Beautiful) Garden," and which gave the Garden its present dimensions.

In 1710, to demonstrate his commitment to developing Admiralty Island, Peter began building his Summer Palace in the Summer Garden, which was completed in 1714. It was built where the Fontanka joins the Neva and originally featured a boat landing and water basin for small boats. This "Palace" was designed and built by Trezzini in the Dutch style and is one of his few remaining works in the city. It was small, simple, airy and full of light from its large latticed windows. Peter resided on the ground floor, which was simply decorated according to maritime themes; one room served both as his workshop and meteorological observation post. Catherine lived upstairs in more ornate and luxurious surroundings. From 1714 the Palace and an adjacent building also housed Peter's library and collection of curiosities, but the collection soon outgrew these premises and it was transferred to the Kikin Palace in 1718.

Peter was fanatically absorbed in the Garden's construction, issuing orders on minute details from afar even during the height of the war with Sweden. He ordered countless exotic trees, flowers, and other plants for it from faraway places, and sometimes brought them himself from his travels and campaigns. To the dismay of the workers, he often changed his mind and ordered redesigns and replantings.

Notwithstanding Peter's frenetic efforts, the Garden gained its full majesty only at the hands of LeBlond. By then, regular French gardens were the fashion in Europe, which Peter saw on his second European tour in 1716–17. This grand style differed from Peter's original concept of the Garden as his quiet refuge, and he initially rejected LeBlond's plan for a magnificent layout, which also incorporated Tsaritsyn Lug. But Peter had been impressed by the gardens in Versailles, Dresden, Greenwich, and elsewhere, and he wanted his Summer Garden (and the garden at Peterhof) to stand equal to the gardens of foreign monarchs. Thus, considerations of state, his desire to develop Admiralty Island and a certain amount of vanity convinced him to instruct LeBlond to lay out the garden in the formal French style, featuring carefully pruned trees and shrubs and intricate, curving lines. But the Garden would stay within its existing boundaries and be slightly less opulent than under LeBlond's proposal. Peter ordered seeds, bulbs, roots, bushes, and exotic trees brought in from all over Russia and abroad.

Exotic plants were not enough, however. LeBlond had written, "Fountains and water are the soul of a garden, and make the principal ornament of it; these animate and invigorate it, and if I may so say, give it new life and spirit." Thus, LeBlond built some 50 fountains in the Garden, many having sculptures of gods, mythical creatures, or animals. In order to supply the fountains with water, a canal was cut from the Liga River (and therefore called the Ligovsky Canal, which today is the route of Ligovsky Prospect) to a small man-made reservoir near today's Nekrasov Street. From this reservoir water was pumped through flues and pipes to the Bezimenni Yerik, which now became known as the Fontannaya ("Fountain") River (later shortened simply to Fontanka) and then across the river in pipes. Later an aqueduct was built to convey the water across the river. Originally, the water was fed by horse-powered pumps, but later it was fed from high water towers so that the fountains would function by force of gravity. They never worked very well, however, at least compared to those in Peterhof.

Another obligatory feature of European gardens at the time was a grotto, and so Peter had one built, begun by Schlüter and Mattarnovy but completed by LeBlond. It was said to be second to none in Europe, but it is no longer preserved and the Coffee House now stands in its place. Peter was also an admirer of Venetian sculptors, and so he lined the Garden's pathways with their works. The number of sculptures eventually reached about 250, but today only about 90 remain. The most notable was a nude statue of Venus by Bonazzi that had been unearthed in Rome in 1718 and secretly purchased for Peter in 1719 by Yuri Kologrivov, who had been sent there in charge of a group of young Russian painters. The governor of Rome forbade its export, so Kologrivov appealed to the Vatican and a deal was struck whereby the Pope donated the Venus to Peter in exchange for Peter's promise to obtain the holy relics of a 14th-century nun, St. Bridget, from Sweden. Venus made her way to St. Petersburg in a special coach ordered by Peter, but Peter never managed to obtain St. Bridget's relics. When the nude Venus was placed in the Summer Garden, many Russians, unaccustomed to nudity in art, were shocked and called her the "White Devil." Peter, fearing that the statue would be vandalized, had to post guards next to her. (She is now in the Hermitage.) Sixty of the other statues in the Garden, by Nicholas Pineau, depicted episodes form Aesop's fables, each having a plaque explaining the fable in question and its moral. (The same was done at Peterhof.) Each winter the statues were removed for safekeeping and brought back in the spring. This led to some amusing mistakes by the uneducated workmen, who did not always return the sculptures to their proper pedestals displaying the names of the works. The Italian visitor Francesco Algarotti noted seeing marble busts of "Ceres bearded and Domitian crowned," and Cassanova later reported seeing a statue of an elderly and bearded "Sappho." Many of these works can still be seen in the Garden today. A final detail was to move to the Garden the menagerie that had been located across from the Post Office. It was housed in eight buildings by the Oval Pond, and remained there until 1737, when it was moved to Mokhovaya Street. Artificial ponds at the southern end featured exotic fish, swans, other water birds, and a seal. Today only the swans remain as a reminder.

LeBlond nearly met his end due to the Summer Garden project.[108] The jealous Menshikov wrote Peter in 1717 that LeBlond was cutting down some of Peter's favorite trees in the Garden, when in fact LeBlond was only trimming their branches. When Peter returned, he confronted LeBlond before he had seen the Garden, went into a fit and struck LeBlond with his cane. LeBlond, upset as much by the affront as hurt by the blow, went into shock and a fever. When Peter learned the truth, he apologized, and when Peter next saw Menshikov he threw him against the wall, exclaiming, "You alone, you rascal, are the cause of his illness!"[109] LeBlond recovered, but he soon contracted smallpox and died in February 1719.

The Summer Garden became a social center of the city.[110] Peter held receptions and celebrations there,[111] as did the Empresses Elizabeth and Catherine the Great, during whose reign it became the fashionable place for the nobility to promenade; Catherine also enjoyed taking her morning walks there.

The land to the southwest of the Summer Garden and Bolshoi Lug, where Engineers Castle and the Mikhailovsky Garden are now located, and running nearly to the Grand Perspective, was given to Catherine. She had a "third" Summer Garden laid out here, which became known as Tsaritsyn ("the Tsarina's") Garden or the New Garden, and a bridge was built over the Moika to connect it to the second Summer Garden. In 1713 she had Zemtsov build her a wooden summer palace there facing the Moika and Bolshoi Lug where Rossi's pavilion now stands. Because of the new garden and palace, Bolshoi Lug soon became known as Tsaritsyn Lug. On account of the copious quantities of gold leaf used to decorate the palace, it became known as the "Golden Palace." It featured a large dancing hall, and social events were often held there.

Across the Fontanka from Catherine's garden was another garden, which became known as the Italian Garden. It got its name from a modest wooden palace that Peter had built there in 1712 for his daughter Anna, which was designed in the Italian style.[112] The wooden palace was replaced by a masonry palace of Niccolo Michetti built in 1721–23. The garden ran well south of the street which became known as Liteiny Prospect (see below). The section beyond Liteiny was actually the larger part, and boasted an orangerie and hothouses, and laurel, fig, and lime trees.[113] A Polish visitor described his visit there as follows:

> After lunch we set off to the Italian Garden, where we saw many adornments, fountains, and flowerbeds, between which stood large porcelain vessels. . . . Since this garden's establishment only 5 years have passed, but one must admit that such a garden as this is usually not seen after 20 years [of care] at a large noble's estate. In this garden were laid stone ponds, in which swim Indian geese, sea ducks and many other birds. . . . Thus we strolled in the garden until 11 o'clock in the evening until the fireworks began.[114]

To the east of the Fontanka beyond a small wharf was the Cannon Foundry, called the Arsenal after 1720, where cannon and eventually other metal articles, mainly military, were manufactured. The portion of the Novgorod Road between these Works and Grand Perspective Road became known as Liteinaya ("Foundry") Street (later Prospect), which it is still called today. The Foundry was established in 1711 and run by James Bruce. He was the son of a Scottish mercenary who had fled to Moscow during the English Civil War, and was born in Moscow in 1670.

He joined Peter's play soldiers at Preobrazhenskoe and rose in the military, distinguishing himself in fortress construction and in artillery, including at Poltava, for which he earned the order of St. Andrew. He was also something of a Renaissance man with a talent for math and science in the tradition of Benjamin Franklin and Isaac Newton, and, like them, was a Freemason. Accompanying Peter on the Grand Embassy, he remained behind to study astronomy in England before returning to Peter's service. He produced Russia's first almanac, ran a printing press, set up the Mathematical School and an observatory, and was a famed magician. He was the natural choice to head the Foundry, especially since it included many adjacent ancillary metallurgical and chemical laboratories, and even a pyrotechnics laboratory for producing the fireworks displays so frequently staged in the city.

To the east of the Foundry Peter created a specially designed region for the palaces of Peter's relatives and other nobility. Thus, in 1711, Peter laid down the Beregovaya ("Embankment") Linya several meters back from the Neva embankment, which today is the second street from the embankment, Shpalernaya Street (named after the factory near the street that produced tapestries, *shpaleri*).* Parallel to Beregovaya, Peter cut five other streets, now known as Zakharevskaya, Sergievskaya, Furshtadtskaya, Kirochnaya, and Pestel Streets. The first three were planned so that canals could be cut through their middle, which is why these streets are so wide today (some with medians). Perpendicular canals were to run along Voskresenskaya Street (now Chernyshevsky Prospect) and Tavricheskaya Street. The canals were never completed because Peter's focus soon shifted to Kotlin and then Vasilievsky Island. The main residences were located along the south side of Beregovaya Street and faced the Neva to the north. These included the palaces of Bruce, Praskovya Fedorovna, Tsarevich Alexis (completed in 1712), Peter's younger sister, Princess Natalya (completed in 1714), Marfa Matveevna (the widow of Tsar Fedor III and sister of Fedor Apraxin), and Gavril Golovkin. Two blocks south of her palace, Princess Natalya founded the city's first drama theater.

Further east and back from the embankment a palace was built in 1714 for Alexander Kikin, who in 1708 had become head of the Admiralty. His is the only one of the original palaces in this region preserved today. In 1718 he was executed for complicity in the affair of Tsarevich Alexis,† after which the building housed Peter's Kunstkamera and the state library. A mint was located in this region as well, until the country's main mint was moved from Moscow to the Peter and Paul Fortress in 1719. The quarters of the Preobrazhensky Regiment were also moved from Gorodskoi Island to the east of Liteinaya Street. Further east, on the site of the old Spassky settlement across from the former Nien, was the Smolny ("Tar") Works, so named because of the tar pits located there to produce tar for the Admiralty ships, and its corresponding *sloboda*. The name Smolny was retained for the

---

*Today's embankment extends further into the Neva and is called Robespierre Embankment.

†See chapter 4, pp. 89–90.

subsequent monastery, cathedral, and institute built on that site. Peter also built his own Smolny House by the Works, and after his death Catherine I turned it into a palace with a garden and ponds, which was later used by other royalty, including Peter's daughter Elizabeth. Factories and settlements of workers were located across the Neva by the Okhta River, as well as downriver from there.

Peter perceived that, in order for Petersburg to gain higher status in the minds of the people, it had to have a great monastery, and in 1710 he began building one. At first it was simple and wooden, but soon it was reconstructed in stone according to a 1715 plan of Trezzini with modifications by Theodor Schwertfeger. In 1720–32, its church was rebuilt as Trinity Cathedral. Peter named the monastery after Alexander Nevsky, who was the patron saint of the Izhora region. The Monastery was built near the site of Nevsky's legendary victory over the Swedes in 1240.* Thus, the establishment of the monastery on this land, only recently taken back from Sweden, symbolized Russia's ancient ties to this territory and its intent to remain there. After the Monastery's completion, in 1724 Peter had Nevsky's remains transferred with much pomp and ceremony to St. Petersburg from Vladimir, after which he was considered the city's patron saint. Henceforth, Nevsky was portrayed as a warrior rather than (as before) a monk, and his festival was set on August 30, the date of Peter's final victory over Sweden.[115]

Once work began on the Monastery, it had to be connected to the Novgorod Road and thence to city center. Also, now that the mainland was safe from Swedish attack and the pace of construction in the center could accelerate, traffic into the city would increase and the Admiralty and the rest of the city needed to be well connected with the Novgorod Road. Thus originated Nevsky Prospect. At Peter's order work began on an improved road from the Admiralty to the Novgorod Road, which was substantially completed in 1713. Most of the work was performed by Swedish war prisoners. Work on the shorter section from the Monastery side began in 1712, but due to difficult conditions and the scarcity of labor it took six years to complete. When the Monastery section was completed, it turned out that it did not meet the Novgorod Road in the same place as the Admiralty section, but intersected a short distance to the northeast. This did not please Peter, but he did nothing about it; eventually, in the 1760s an extension of the Admiralty section was built straight through until it met the Monastery section at what is now Suvorovsky Prospect, which explains its bend at this intersection. Both roads together were eventually named Nevsky Prospect. The "Admiralty" section initially was informally called the Grand Perspective, but in 1738 it was officially named Nevsky Perspective (later Nevsky Prospect, which remains today).

In 1721, the Grand Perspective was lined with two rows of birch trees on each side with side paths in between and ditches to provide drainage. It was 20 meters

---

*As explained earlier, the battlefield was actually somewhat further south near the mouth of the Izhora River, but Peter needed the monastery near the city.

wide, paved in stone, and (from 1723) was lit at night by gas street lamps. Foreigners marveled at the street's magnificence. The German general Bergholtz exuded that "it makes a more wonderful sight than any I have beheld anywhere,"[116] while the French visitor Aubry de LaMottraye remarked that it resembled the roads of ancient Rome. Indeed, there was nothing like it in the world.

Still, from the Novgorod Road to the Fontanka the Grand Perspective was bordered mainly by forest. Some nobles had begun erecting summer houses and small palaces on the southern bank of the river, which at the time was already the suburbs. The bridge across the Fontanka marked the southern border of the city. It was built in 1715 by soldiers of the Astrakhan infantry regiment commanded by Colonel Anichkov. Their adjacent settlement was known as the Anichkov *sloboda*, and so the bridge became known as the Anichkov Bridge. Since the bridge was the entrance to the city, at it stood a guardhouse and barrier, which was closed from 11:00 P.M. until sunrise. Visitors' documents were inspected here, and they had to pay a toll to enter.

Today, the next canal along Nevsky is the Griboyedova Canal, but in Peter's time it was a narrow, winding rivulet emerging from the swamp and did not connect to the Moika. Originally it was called the *Glukhaya Rechka* ("Out of the Way, or God-forsaken, River"), but once the area around it was built up and became less out of the way, it became known simply as the *Krivushaya Rechka* ("Curvy, or Crooked River"). Still, it was not made into a full canal until the reign of Catherine the Great, when it became the Catherine Canal.

THE OUTLYING ISLANDS AND SUBURBAN PALACES

Peter's paradise extended beyond the city limits, as he wanted to surround the city with beautiful suburban palaces, parks, and gardens. He began by giving plots of land as well as entire islands to relatives and wealthy favorites who had the means to develop them. His gifts of Vasilievsky Island to Menshikov and of plots of land on the south bank of the Fontanka were part of this scheme. Also important were Peter's gifts of the city's other three major islands, now called Krestovsky, Elagin, and Kamenny, whose eventful histories began at that time.

The largest of these islands, Krestovsky ("Cross") Island, was given to Peter's younger sister, Natalya, and for a time was known as Saint Natalya's Island, but the name Krestovsky arose early and remains to this day; no one knows exactly why.*

---

*One theory is that one of the ponds near the center of the island was roughly in the shape of a cross. Another points to the first stone building on the island being built in the shape of a St. Andrew's cross. A third notes that the main paths, later roads, on the island from an early time were laid out at right angles to each other in the form of a cross. Other versions speculate on man's past on the island, one holding that a large cross of unknown origin was found on the island, another that a small 17th-century chapel with a cross existed there.

Natalya built a two-story summer home on the eastern shore of the island across from Apothecary Island. After her death in 1716 the property remained in the royal family, until Anna Ioannovna gave it to Field Marshal Münnich in the 1730s. Following Münnich's downfall and Elizabeth's accession, Elizabeth gave it to her favorite, Razumovsky, who held it until his death, after which it passed to his brother Kyrill, who was the first to devote substantial efforts to developing the island and began holding entertainments there which Empress Catherine II attended.

Elagin Island was first known as Mishin ("Bear") Island. According to legend, Russian soldiers on reconnaissance there in 1703 spied movement in the bushes. At first they thought Swedish soldiers were hiding there, but instead a large gray bear emerged. It seems that this name was much older, however, as the island was inhabited by Finnish fishermen who called it Mistulasaari ("Bear Island"). Under Peter the island was first given to Peter Shafirov, then to Pavel Yaguzhinsky. The next owner was Senator Alexei Melgunov, who received it through the influence of his friend Ivan Shuvalov, another of Elizabeth's favorites, after which the island was known as Melgunov Island. It then passed to Catherine the Great's lover and statesman, Grigory Potemkin, and then to her courtier Ivan Elagin, after whom the island is still named.

Kamenny ("Stone") Island has always been so named, but no one is certain why. According to one version, a large underwater stone outcropping was visible in the Malaya Nevka near the island. The other version simply holds that an abnormally large number of rocks deposited by the retreating glaciers were visible on the island. In support of this version, some historians note that the whole region of the Bolshaya Nevka was sometimes called Kamenka. Peter gave the island to Gavril Golovkin in 1703 or 1704, who built a summer house there across from Apothecary Island. Golovkin was careful with his money and thus initially did little to develop the island. He was, however, careful to cut a road from his palace across the island to eastern Krestovsky Island so that Natalya and Peter could visit him if they ever desired. Peter's journal records that he did visit the estate in 1715 to attend a masquerade there.[117] While visiting on another occasion, Peter presented Golovkin with a young oak tree, which Peter planted there with his own hands. The tree is now dead, but its stump is still preserved as a monument in the middle of one of the island's streets. Eventually Golovkin replaced the small home with a larger, two-story estate that resembled one of LeBlond's model homes for nobles, and laid out several pathways which evolved into today's streets. In 1734 Golovkin's eldest son Alexander received the island under his father's will. He laid out a formal plan for the eastern tip of the island and built the first true estate there. He also constructed stables, fishing huts, pavilions, and other structures and laid out a formal garden. Golovkin kept the island until 1746, when he sold it to Alexei Bestuzhev-Rumin.

Further afield on the mainland, after Poltava, Peter also began giving plots of land to his favorites along the south shore of the Finnish Gulf between the mouth of the Neva and Kronstadt, on which they built palaces, agricultural estates, and country houses. A few hundred meters from the sea, a long ridge about 60 or 70 feet high runs for many miles, atop which numerous palaces were built which afforded a spectacular view of the Gulf; from the water the view of the many palaces was also beautiful.

As one would expect, the first of the major suburban palaces to be built was Menshikov's, which he named Oranienbaum ("Orange Tree"). It was designed and constructed by the German Gottfried Schädel (who also worked on Menshikov's palace in the city), beginning in 1713. It was grand in style and, with the possible exception of his own home in the city, it was the first building in or around St. Petersburg that was a genuine palace by European standards. It still stands today, though it is only partially restored.

Next in line was Peterhof, yet another contribution of LeBlond. The site had its origin as an embarkation point with a wharf and small cottage for Peter when visiting Kotlin during its construction when the sea was too rough to sail there from the Neva. Once Menshikov constructed the immense Oranienbaum, however, Peter decided he needed a country palace there befitting a Tsar, and so he assigned LeBlond the task of building what became a Russian version of Versailles, complete with French gardens. It took nearly 10 years to build and was opened as a residence only in August 1723. As in the case of the Summer Garden, LeBlond focused on the use of water as the ensemble's essential characteristic. He constructed dozens of imaginative fountains and waterfalls, which were fed through wooden pipes from miles away and functioned through force of gravity. Chief among these fountains is the immense central cascade dominated at the bottom by a fountain with a golden statue depicting Samson opening the jaws of a lion, from which a jet of water spurts over 50 feet into the air. The approach from the sea was awe inspiring.

In contrast with all this grandeur, which made Peter uncomfortable, was Monplaisir. This small summer house still stands to the front and side of the main Peterhof palace, right on the sea embankment. Like his Summer Palace in town, Peter decorated it in a simple Dutch fashion on maritime themes. It featured many windows and French doors to let in light, and a terrace right at the water's edge. When at Peterhof, Peter spent most of his time there.

Slightly nearer to the city, in 1708 Peter had built (partly with his own hands) a wooden house for himself in the settlement of Strelna Myza, by the Strelna rivulet, which flowed into the Gulf. Next to it was a large lime tree, in which Peter built an arbor reached by a ladder, where he would relax with a smoke and a drink and gaze at the Gulf. Charmed by the place, he ordered the large Strelna palace to be built, which would have overshadowed Peterhof (in its original design) had the project been realized as intended. Originally, it was to contain immense gardens to rival Versailles, and so LeBlond was engaged there and developed his own design. For a time up to 10,000 laborers were said to work intensely on the project.[118] However, when it was determined that the elevations at the spot would not support the magnificent fountains that Peter wished to construct there, completing Peterhof took precedence. A more modest palace was built with a lower garden and canals featuring thousands of lime trees. Instead of fountains, a grotto was built under a large terrace in front of the palace facing the sea, in which a large wine cellar was constructed for the court's Hungarian wines. In fact, after all the effort, the palace was not inhabited until 1803–04, when Grand Duke Constantine Pavlovich (son of Paul I) acquired it; its only use until then was as a wine cellar. In 2000, after decades of neglect, President Putin ordered that it be renovated to serve as a presidential palace.[119]

Further inland, south of the city, were the beginnings of another famous palace. About 10 miles from town was a modest Swedish homestead known (in Swedish) as Saarskaya Myza ("Sarah's Homestead").* When Russia captured the area, Peter gave it to Catherine and for several years it was largely forgotten. Then, while Peter was on one of his military campaigns, Catherine secretly had the house reconstructed. When he returned, Catherine told him that she had seen a wonderful spot on which to build a country house and wanted to show it to him. If it pleased him, she said, they would then build there. Peter agreed, and one day a party set out for a picnic on the site. When they arrived, however, Peter was presented with this fait accompli and was delighted, remarking, "I see that you wish to show me that there are beautiful places around Petersburg even though they are not on the water."[120] After showing Peter the house, Catherine raised a toast, and when the glass touched her lips 11 cannon saluted the event. Empress Elizabeth later renamed the estate Tsarskoe Selo ("Tsar's Village"), as a play on the original Swedish name.

---

*By another account, the original name was "Saari Mojs," Finnish for "high island (or place)," which indeed it was compared to the flat land around it. A. Kennett, *The Palaces of Leningrad* (New York, 1973), p. 120; S. Massie, *Pavlovsk: The Life of a Russian Palace* (Boston, 1990), p. 14 (hereinafter cited as *Pavlovsk*).

CHAPTER 3

Life in Peter's Paradise

. . . this great window recently opened in the north through which Russia looks upon Europe.

FRANCESCO ALGAROTTI[1]

Russia entered Europe like a newly launched ship, to the blows of axes and the thunder of cannon. . . . and European enlightenment became moored to the banks of the conquered Neva.

PUSHKIN[2]

I n its early years, St. Petersburg was populated mainly by soldiers, sailors, craftsman, workers, and prisoners living in barracks and huts. Life was spartan, crude, and often short. People's main concern was their own and the city's survival. This environment was not conducive to commerce, higher culture, sophisticated social life, or fine manners. Early social life was limited to holiday celebrations, churchgoing, drinking and card games in taverns, raucous music and singing, and all-night drunken parties.[3] Peter joined in all of them.

For most of his reign, Peter had to focus on the military, industrial, and financial measures needed to win the war and make Russia a European power. But Peter was not just a technocrat; he wanted to build a new culture and world outlook in Russia.[4] He recognized that behind the useful things that he took from the West stood a civilization, mentality, and way of life that was responsible for generating them. Russia's task in the long run was not to collect Western gadgets and ape its habits, but to develop its own civilization with a way of life that would yield its own fruits. This civilization could not be a mere copy of anything in the West. Petersburg was intended to and did become a unique synthesis of Russian and foreign elements that would stand on its own.[5] The change had to cut deeply, to the essence of the society and into people's mentality, spirit, and philosophy, in order to create a new breed of Russian.[6] To achieve this, Peter had to establish an environment of intellectual freedom, tolerance, creativity, and innovation. Given that Peter needed to initiate and shepherd this change from above, it was a delicate task not to crush the flower he was trying to nurture, and he did not always get it right.

70

St. Petersburg was the laboratory for this grand enterprise, and the icon of the renewal of Russia.[7] It was a city of ideas,[8] a center of a new culture through which Russia would be transformed and brought into the modern world.[9] In founding his capital, Peter intended to establish and spread from there enlightenment across the entire Russian empire.[10] "My desire is to implant in this capital crafts, sciences and art in general,"[11] Peter said. To attempt this in Moscow would have been futile.[12] In Petersburg, however, he created a blank slate where his vision could blossom relatively free from Muscovite influence and tradition.[13] The Petersburg idea was the antithesis of the "Russian idea." It stood for a secular over a theocratic and mystical society, but was not atheistic. It meant cosmopolitanism over isolationism, but without rejecting all that is Russian. It stood for modernism, innovation and creativity, humanism and individuality, education, tolerance, intellectual freedom, scholarship and scientific progress, and support of the arts and culture. Petersburg was a gateway through which Western ideas, people, and goods flowed in and Russian travelers, students, and traders ventured out. Petersburg's civilization was not meant as a copy of Europe but as a model of the universal ideals and values of mankind. The idea took hold, and the unimaginable happened. Scarcely a century after the city was founded, Russia's army entered Paris as the preeminent power in Europe, and a century later Petersburg's culture conquered Paris. Petersburg had not only transformed Muscovite Russia, but made Russia a leader in Europe.

ECONOMIC LIFE AND COMMERCE

In order for St. Petersburg to succeed in its mission, it had to prosper economically and become a thriving commercial port. Peter realized this from the start and immediately set about realizing this goal. Thus, already in May 1703, immediately after taking Nienshantz, Peter announced rewards for the first, second, and third foreign ships to call on St. Petersburg—500 golden ducats to the first, 300 to the second, and 100 to the third. In November 1703, a Dutch ship under the command of the skipper Vibes appeared, carrying salt and wine sent by Peter's old friend Cornelius Calf of Zaandam. When Peter learned of the ship's approach and who owned its cargo, he was ecstatic. He rushed to meet the ship and piloted it upstream himself. In addition to providing the previously announced reward of 500 golden ducats, he exempted the ship—which was renamed *The St. Petersburg*—from all Russian port fees and customs duties forever.

Before 1710, however, foreign trade with St. Petersburg grew slowly and erratically because the Baltic was a war zone and Sweden controlled it. Ships trading with Russia could be turned back, boarded, seized, or lost, and their cargoes confiscated. Foreign merchants trading with Russia, mainly English and Dutch, preferred to send their ships north around Scandinavia to Archangelsk. That port was closed due to ice in the long winter and the trip was long, but at least the route was peaceful.

Russia's merchants also preferred Archangelsk, as the interior routes to that port were well developed and far from Sweden's armies and navy, and Russia's merchants had already invested their capital and developed business networks there.

From the beginning, however, Peter did what he could to encourage trade with and a shift of trade patterns to his new city. He reduced port fees to less than half of those which the Swedes charged elsewhere in the Baltic. In 1714 Peter staffed the St. Petersburg customs office with experienced merchants in order to increase efficiency. Russia's ambassadors abroad sought to negotiate commitments to trade through St. Petersburg instead of Archangelsk. But due to the dangerous shipping conditions on the Baltic, Russia's entreaties met with no interest and considerable resistance.

Peter was careful not to mandate shifting trade from Archangelsk to St. Petersburg so long as the war raged and trade in the Baltic remained dangerous. But after the victories on land in 1700–10, at least land trade with the city became safe and he could not wait any longer. Thus, in anticipation of Baltic shipping soon becoming safe and in order to expand the city's trade with Russia's interior, in 1710 Peter ordered the transfer of members of many prominent Moscow merchant families to St. Petersburg, including Ivan Filatev, Semyon Pankratev, and Ilya Isaev.[14] In November 1713, Peter issued a series of decrees which called for transferring most port activity and trade from Archangelsk to St. Petersburg. In 1714 came Peter's naval victory of Hangö, which gave Russia effective control over the Baltic. In 1716 Peter ordered that at least one-sixth of all of Russian exports had to go through St. Petersburg. In 1718, he decreed that at least two-thirds of all goods exported from the two ports be exported through St. Petersburg and only one-third from Archangelsk.

Peter's efforts succeeded in stimulating Russia's foreign trade generally, but the pattern of trade shifted from Archangelsk to Petersburg only reluctantly and gradually. In fact, Archangelsk's volume of trade doubled between 1710 and 1718.[15] Even in 1717–19, an average of between 130–140 ships per year called at Archangelsk but only 52 annually in St. Petersburg. By the end of the war, however, Peter's policies had the desired effect, and the trading pattern reversed markedly in favor of the new capital.* In 1722, Peter forbade the import of all but a few goods through Archangelsk. While foreign governments were concerned by Russia's emergence as a power on the Baltic, their merchants quickly shifted their business to the nearer and more advantageous port. As a result, Russia's merchants too had no choice but to move to St. Petersburg, and they soon prospered there.

---

*In 1720, just before the Treaty of Nystadt, only 75 foreign ships called at St. Petersburg, but by 1722 the number had risen to 119 and in 1724 the number had more than doubled to 240 while only 50 called at Archangelsk. *PPV*, p. 81. By 1726, exports from St. Petersburg had risen to 2,403,423 rubles and imports to 1,549,697, while Archangelsk's had declined to only 285,387 and 35,846 respectively. *Ibid.*, p. 80.

Petersburg's main exports were hemp, lard, certain leathers (but so far not furs), iron, linens, and sailcloth.[16] The city's main imports were various fabrics (silk, wool, linens), dyes, coffee, sugar, and wines.[17]

International shipping, however, was still largely in the hands of foreigners. In Peter's time the foreign trade experience of most of Russia's merchants stopped at the water's edge. With considerable difficulty they gradually accumulated capital to purchase oceangoing ships, made other investments and gained in experience, grew in number, and within a few decades they took their place amongst the foreigners.[18] In 1716 Peter established the Commerce College, which was operational by 1718. Though dedicated to commerce and economic development in Russia at large, part of its function was to manage commerce within St. Petersburg and expand and administer its foreign trade.

A commodity exchange *(birzha)* was established from the very foundation of the city in 1703, initially located on Trinity Square. This was one of the world's first such exchanges, and in Europe was predated only by those in London, Holland, and certain French cities (Lyon, Toulouse); the famous exchanges in Paris, Vienna, and Berlin were established later.[19]

Peter also needed to link Petersburg with the interior of Russia. Thus, in 1703 he began construction of the Upper Volga Canal, completed in 1709, which connected the city to the Volga River. But this still required crossing turbulent and stormy Lake Ladoga, where each year many ships and lives were lost. In 1718, when nearly 1,000 small vessels were lost,[20] Peter decided that a canal along the lake's shore was indispensable and began its construction. According to Weber, up to 12,000 men annually worked on this project under the direction of the German engineer Burkhard Christopher Münnich. It was completed in 1732. On land, Peter built a new road from St. Petersburg to Narva and onward to Riga. He also improved the road between St. Petersburg and Moscow, shortening it by 200 versts.[21]

CULTURAL LIFE, SCIENCE, AND EDUCATION

Peter was a practical man who most liked useful things, and he drew a close connection between art and science.[22] Thus, Peter's personal interests lay mainly in architecture, science, exploration, publications, museums, and education. Theater, literature, painting, and classical music were less interesting to him, but he still recognized their value and importance to his quest and sought to advance them too.

It all began, however, with the Russian language that would have to carry the new civilization, and the challenge extended well beyond Peter's famous reform of the alphabet and the calendar. In Peter's time, the Russian language lacked the vocabulary needed to express Western culture and ideas. The word *nauka*, for example, now translated as "science," at that time referred simply to skilled technique rather than theoretical knowledge or scientific method.[23] The closest Russian word for "architecture," *zodchestvo*, referred merely to the activity of building, and a *zodchii* was simply a builder. The notions of architecture as design, a profession and a form of art, and of an architect as an artist and a professional, emerged in Russia only in Peter's time.[24] By the end of Peter's reign, these native terms had become nearly synonymous with the Western terms, which also entered the Russian language as *architektura* and *arkhitektor*. This evolution of Russian words combined with the adoption of many foreign words allowed Russia to transform its culture. Peter's reform of the alphabet freed the Russian language from the yoke of Church Slavonic and allowed a living literary language to develop.

Peter introduced new Western scientific discoveries, ideas, and learning to his people and established new academic and scientific institutions in St. Petersburg. He purchased several scientific collections and many books from the West during his travels and sent emissaries, most importantly his librarian Johann Schumacher, to do the same. His most important acquisitions were the collection of animals, insects, reptiles, and birds purchased from the Dutch apothecary Albert Seabee for 30,000 guilders, and the scientific collection of the Dutch anatomist Ruysch, whom Peter had met while in Holland. These and other acquisitions eventually became the basis of the Museum of the Academy of Sciences. For this museum and library, in 1718 he commissioned the construction of the Kunstkamera on Vasilievsky Island. The choice of that site was inspired by two pine trees that had miraculously grown up one inside the other at that location, a curiosity in itself which was later exhibited in the museum.[25] In the meantime, from 1719 until 1727, the Kunstkamera collection and the state public library were housed in the former Kikin Palace on First Embankment (now Shpalernaya Street). Peter loved to spend his early morning time in this temporary Kunstkamera studying his prizes, in which he was loath to let other affairs interfere. Once he scheduled an early morning audience with an Austrian ambassador from the Court of Vienna at the museum. When the ambassador's chancellor objected to the site and proposed the Summer Palace instead, Peter replied that the ambassador "is sent on an embassy to me, and not to one of my palaces, and can tell me whatever he has to say in any place." The ambassador was duly received at 5:00 A.M. on the appointed day.[26]

The Kunstkamera was the world's first museum open to the general public.[27] It was free of charge, and guides were provided. When Yaguzhinsky suggested charging admission, Peter objected. He decided that the museum should not only be free, but that visitors should be lured there by free refreshments (vodka and snacks), for which Peter paid personally about 400 rubles per year.[28] The museum's foreign collections were complemented by antiques and articles from Russia, including fossils, pagan idols, and finds from ancient ruins. Whenever and wherever Peter traveled, a train of books, curiosities, specimens, and artwork would follow him back to Petersburg. He expected his subjects to show the same enthusiasm. In February 1718, he issued a decree stating:

If anyone shall find in the earth, or in the water, any ancient objects, such as unusual stones, or the bones of man or beast, or of fishes or of birds, unlike those which are with us now, or such as are larger or smaller than usual, or any old inscriptions on stones, iron or copper, or any ancient weapons not now in use, or any vessel or such like thing that is very ancient or unusual, let him bring all such things to us, and ample reward shall be given to him.

Another important acquisition was the Great Globe of Gottorp. Made in 1664 for the Duke of Holstein, it was a hollow mechanical globe with the Earth's map on the outside and a map of the heavens inside, representing the Copernican system. It was nearly 12 feet in diameter so that people could climb inside, whereupon it would revolve around them. To Peter's delight, Duke Charles Frederick presented it to him as a gift. Once the new Kunstkamera was built, the Globe was placed there in a room in the tower specially designed for it, where it remains to this day.

Peter's lifelong appetite for collecting books was insatiable. He acquired them individually and in whole collections. The books covered every imaginable subject, including military studies, science and medicine, state administration and finance, history, philosophy and religion, and law. Initially the collection was kept in the Summer Palace, but when it grew too large it too was moved to the former Kikin Palace with his collection of curiosities, and it became Russia's first public library. Founded in 1719 with approximately 2,500 volumes on the basis of Peter's personal collection, it expanded to over 12,000 volumes by 1725. Unfortunately, the library was underused, with only five readers borrowing books in 1724.[29] In 1722, Peter decreed that the country (meaning mainly monasteries) be combed for old books, chronicles, and other writings and historical documents. These together with Peter's original collection became the nucleus of the library of the Academy of Sciences following his death. Many nobles followed his example and also amassed collections. Some, like Bruce, had serious intellectual interests, but for others, like the half-literate Menshikov, the volumes remained largely unread and served only as symbols of their modernity. The most impressive collection was that of the polyglot Feofan Prokopovich, who in addition to his religious offices was a true scholar, educator, and part-time dramatist. Amazingly, less than one-third of the churchman's over 3,000 titles were theological works, and only 44 were in Church Slavonic.[30]

After 1710, Peter focused on creating the educational and academic institutions needed to develop and support his new society. Prior to then, Peter had focused on sending Russians (200 of them between 1697 and 1714) abroad for training, mainly in Holland and England, and had set up the Mathematics and Navigation School in Moscow in 1701. Peter established the first Petersburg school in 1709, and by 1711 four others were operating in the city, including the first private schools. These were complemented by an artillery school in 1712, an arithmetic school and naval school in 1714, a language school for children of workers at the Admiralty in 1715, the Naval Academy also in 1715, the school under the Commerce

College for merchants by 1716, a medical-surgical school and military hospital in 1716, the architectural school also in 1716, and a higher engineering school in 1719 (transferred from Moscow). In 1720 chemical and pharmaceutical laboratories were established as departments of the Liteiny Works under James Bruce. In 1721, the Karpov School was established near the Apothecary Garden by Feofan Prokopovich using his personal funds. Although his students were largely poor children or orphans, it was perhaps the best school of its time and produced prominent academicians. The curriculum included Russian and foreign languages and grammar, arithmetic, geometry, geography, history, rhetoric, logic, drawing, and music. Also established in 1721 at the Alexander Nevsky Monastery was the Philology School for the children of servants, readers and scribes of the Monastery. At first it taught mainly language, religion, and arithmetic, but soon the curriculum broadened and the institution became the Slavo-Greek-Latin Seminary.

Peter's crowning educational and academic institution, however, was the Academy of Sciences. Peter had been impressed by the Paris Academy (to which he was elected in 1717), and Leibniz, who had founded the Prussian Academy of Science in Berlin in 1700, had long urged Peter to found such an institution in Russia. Peter had first raised the idea of a Russian Academy in 1698 to Patriarch Hadrian who responded coolly, and with the war and other exigencies demanding higher priority the idea lay dormant for many years. Finally, in 1721 with the war over, Peter decided to realize his dream and sent his librarian Johann Schumacher to Europe to recruit foreign staff for an Academy. Schumacher and Lavrenty Blumentrost, a medical scholar and son of the doctor of Peter's father Alexis, developed a program for the Academy, which Peter accepted with minor changes. The Academy was to lead secular enlightenment, working in tandem with Peter's scheme for religious education set up by the Ecclesiastical Regulation. Peter sought a marriage of religion and science but without confusing them. This would facilitate change within a stable order, as envisioned by the so-called Leibniz-Wolff cosmology, under which the revelations of knowledge were held to glorify God.[31]

Peter issued the decree establishing the Academy in January 1724, and it opened in December 1725. Its first President was Blumentrost. The Academy performed research (mostly scientific) and educated future scholars and scientists. Under Blumentrost's scheme, the Academy would consist of a research department, a "university" for higher education, and a gymnasium to prepare students for education at the university.* Unlike foreign academies, Peter's was founded and funded by the government. The research section, though underfunded, was functional and was responsible for virtually all of Russia's 18th-century scientific achievements. Originally the Academy hosted 17 academicians from France, Germany, and Switzerland. The first full Russian member, Mikhail Lomonosov, was admitted only in 1741.

---

*Although the Academy was effectively Russia's first university, the first institution to be formally organized and named as such was the University of Moscow founded in 1755. See chapter 5, p. 152.

The university section was not as successful. Since no Russians were qualified for university-level instruction and since the lectures were read in Latin, which required translators (also in short supply), the students were also imported. In order that audiences for lectures could meet the quorum required by the Academy's charter, the academics often had to attend each other's lectures. The gymnasium, initially not part of Peter's concept, was quickly established once the lack of even a few Russian students qualified to enter the university became obvious. Its initial class had 120 students, but the number steadily declined after that and many students never graduated.[32] After Peter, the problem of finding qualified and interested Russian students to attend the university was never satisfactorily resolved, as the nobility preferred that their children be educated at institutions specially created for them. Even under Catherine II, only 56 of 500 students and only 20 of 72 instructors at the Academy were Russian.[33] Vasily Tatishchev had criticized the Academy for this very reason, remarking to Peter, "You are trying to construct a powerful Archimedean machine, but you have nowhere on which to rest it." Peter responded with a metaphor:

> Suppose I have to harvest large shocks of grain, but I have no mill; and there is not enough water close by to build a water mill; but there is water enough at a distance. Only I shall have no time to make a canal, for the length of my life is uncertain. And therefore I am building the mill first and have only given orders for the canal to be begun, which will better force my successors to bring water to the completed mill.[34]

Peter's program of enlightenment also included the writing, translation, and printing of books and other printed materials. The first printing shop in Russia was established in Petersburg in 1711 in the home of its head, Mikhail Petrovich Avramov, and in 1713 was moved near the Peter and Paul Fortress next to the Austeria Four Frigates Tavern. Its first publication was the newspaper *Vedomesti* in May 1711, and it printed its first books in 1713. The first bookshop opened in 1714 in the Gostiny Dvor by Trinity Square, as a branch of the main printshop. The secular books, journals, and newspapers utilized Peter's reformed alphabet.* Since the printshops were government-owned, profit was not a principal motivation and books were affordable. Peter said that the printing shops were founded "not for any profit, not only for state and utilitarian matters but also for people's education."[35] Book publishing in the Petrine era was wholly devoted to reforming the country.[36]

As literacy rose, so did the number and circulation of publications. During Peter's reign, approximately 600 books were published in Russia. In the last 25 years of Peter's reign, 100 times more books, pamphlets, prints, maps, plans, and drawings

---

*Established in 1708 by eliminating duplicative letters (reducing their number from 42 to 32) and simplifying the characters. Religious works, the printing of which was left in Moscow, still used the old Church Slavonic alphabet.

were produced than in the entire prior century.[37] Eighty-six percent of the books published were secular. By comparison, from the installation of printing presses in the 1560s until Peter's reign, only three books not specifically religious in character had been published.[38] Most books and pamphlets were translations of secular works in foreign languages. Qualified translators were scarce, so even scholars from the Synod were called upon to translate Western secular works.

Most publications were technical in nature, but many served broader educational and cultural purposes, including *The Honorable Mirror of Youth, or Guide for Worldly Living, Collected from Various Authors* (1717), *The First Study for Young Boys* (by Feofan Prokopovich, 1722), *The Bequest of Father to Son* (1719), *The Dialogue of Two Friends about the Usefulness of the Sciences and Educational Institutions* (1730), and *The Complete Letter Writer*, a guide to the etiquette of writing letters, congratulations, marriage proposals, and similar social writings. *The Honorable Mirror of Youth* was especially important and makes a stark comparison with the Muscovite *Domostroi*. It was a guidebook, translated from German, on social manners and conduct in public as well as at home. It covered personal cleanliness, eating, the use of eating utensils and handkerchiefs, how to converse, how to blow one's nose, and similar topics. It became a popular and de rigueur manual for Petersburg's upper classes and went through many printings right through Anna Ioannovna's reign.

Religious life in St. Petersburg reflected Peter's overall religious policy. Peter did not discourage religion but kept it out of secular affairs. He also campaigned against, and condemned in the Ecclesiastical Regulation, what he considered superstitious excesses, such as the inordinate number of religious holidays and fasts, excessive devotion to alleged magical qualities of holy relics and icons, and false miracles. In one famous incident in Petersburg, an icon of the Virgin was said to be weeping tears and pleading that a church be dedicated to her in the city. (Most churches in Petersburg were dedicated to military victories or royal anniversaries.) Peter's opponents interpreted this as the Virgin's opposition to Peter's reforms and Petersburg itself. Peter visited the church and inspected the icon, only to find that his opponents had "planted" the tears using a receptacle in the back of the icon. He had it removed immediately to the Kunstkamera, where it joined a growing number of other exhibits of superstition such as fake saintly relics. Peter also reduced the number of fasts, and even during the remaining fasts assemblies and balls were still held.

Peter encouraged religious toleration and diversity in his city, where, in contrast to Moscow, Russians and foreigners of different faiths lived together, worked side by side and socialized freely. St. Petersburg featured churches of many religions and foreign congregations. The church buildings themselves had Western architectural styles. Alexander Herzen, the 19th-century thinker, would later remark that one could live for a couple of years in the city and still not know what was the religion of the people.[39]

Peter's favorite art form was architecture. It was functional, beautiful and public, and could trumpet the new culture for all to see. He wanted the capital to reflect the rationalistic principles of his age, and he brought in architects who could express this vision. Peter was open to all kinds of classical and modern styles, including Russian influences, and in Petersburg he gave no overriding preference to any one style, even the Dutch. In fact, only one Dutch architect, Steven van Zwiedten, is known to have worked in the city under Peter, and then only late in his reign.[40] Although Peter utilized foreign architects initially, he favored Russians once they were trained and up to the task. Their training in the new architecture occurred both at home and abroad, and they would not build according to Muscovite tradition.

Painting and other secular fine arts were not yet well developed, as demand for them was private (there were no art museums). Two notable Russian engravers, the brothers Ivan and Alexei Zubov, originally from Moscow, moved to Petersburg to improve and practice their art and produce many vistas of the city, most notably Alexei's 1716 panorama of the city presented to Peter upon his return from Europe in 1717. Peter gave importance to this form of pictorial art because it was inexpensive, and because the works, reproduced in copies of convenient size that could be distributed widely within Russia and abroad, had propagandistic value.

The first painter of any note in the city was Gottfried Dannhauer, a German who had studied in Venice and Holland. He was appointed court painter in 1710 and produced portraits and a depiction of the battle of Poltava, but his talent was deemed wanting and Peter soon was looking for a replacement. Peter offered the position to several painters who refused, but Louis Caravaque from Marseilles accepted in 1715 for a three-year stint. The principal Russian painter in town under Peter was Ivan Nikitin, considered the father of Russian portraiture. His early training in Russia is obscure, but eventually he studied in Venice and Florence, returning in 1720 to become master portraitist of the court, painting several portraits of the Tsar, his daughters, his sister Natalya and other court personages. Peter had sent another talented Russian, Andrei Matveev, to Holland for training. Peter died before he returned in 1727, but would have been proud of the direction in which Matveev took Russian painting, as his *Allegory of Painting* (1725) is considered the first Russian allegorical painting and is one of the first Russian paintings of a nude.

Russian secular sculpture also had its origins in St. Petersburg, although the output during Peter's time was tiny and most sculptures were wooden. The only notable sculptor of stone in the city was Carlo Bartholomeo Rastrelli, the father of the famous architect. His main works are a bust of Peter in armor and an equestrian statue of Peter that now stands in front of the Mikhailovsky Castle. The training of Russian sculptors drew less attention than that of architects or even painters, but finally in 1724 Peter sent four young sculptors to Italy for training. In the meantime, most stone sculptures in the city were imports, mainly from Italy, as in the Summer Garden.

Peter had hoped to create an academy of arts in order to train Russian artists, but this did not come to fruition in his lifetime and the project would have a long and tortuous history before being realized in 1758. Various attempts to create such an institution during and after Peter's lifetime failed, until the Academy of Sciences' charter was modified in 1747 to turn it into the Academy of Sciences and Arts, which had an art faculty for painting, engraving, and architecture. The Academy of Fine Arts became separate in 1758.

The performing arts also entered the city's life. The city's first drama theater was founded by Peter's younger sister Natalya by 1714 and was open to the public without charge. This was a makeshift affair in a large converted house near Natalya's home at what is now the corner of Tchaikovsky Street and Chernyshevsky Prospect. She, together with the actor Semen Semenov, also wrote many of the original plays performed, with titles such as *The Comedy of St. Catherine* and *The Comedy of the Prophet Daniel*. Peter included plays which ridiculed the faults of the clergy or the greed and bribe taking of government clerks, while another was a moralistic tale directed against rebellion (hinting at an insurrection that had erupted in 1707). Given the meager resources and poor training of the actors and musicians, the quality of the productions, in the opinion of Westerners who attended, left much to be desired. Weber described a performance of a *Compound of Sacred and Profane History* as follows:

> The actors and actresses were . . . all native Russians who had never been abroad, so that it is easy to judge of their ability. The tragedy itself, as well as the farce, were in Russian, and of the Princess' own composition, being a compound of sacred and profane history. I was told that the subject related to one of the late rebellions in Russia, represented under disguised names. The piece was interspersed with the drolleries of a Harlequin, who was an officer in the army, and ended with an epilogue, setting forth the contents of the tragedy, and concluding with a moral reflecting on the horrors of rebellion, and the unhappy events it commonly issues in. The orchestra was composed of sixteen musicians, all Russians, whose performance was suitable to that of the rest. They are taught music, as well as other sciences, by the help of the *batogs*,* without which discipline nothing goes down with them, as I have been told by diverse officers, and is confirmed by daily experience. If a General pitches upon some spare fellow in a regiment, whom he will have to learn music, notwithstanding he has not the least notion of it, nor any talent that way, he is put out to a master, who give him a certain time for learning his task. . . . If [he] has not learnt his lesson during the term prefixed, the *batogs* are applied, and repeated till such time as he is master of the tune.[41]

Shortly after Natalya died in 1716, her theater closed, although the building remained and a visiting German troupe would perform there in 1719. In 1723 Peter ordered a theater and opera house built on the Moika near Green Bridge. The theater operated sporadically for several years, performing largely translations or imi-

---

*A *batog* is a small rod or stick about the thickness of a man's finger often used to punish minor crimes. The offender would lie shirtless on the floor with his legs and arms spread. Two men would stand in front and back and beat him rhythmically in turn. Such punishment could cause serious injury or even death, though this was rare.

tations of foreign plays. To remedy the situation, Peter invited professionals from Prague to become the theater's permanent troupe, but the plan fell through when they demanded too much money. Shortly after that the theater failed. For the time being, the city had to make do with visiting foreign troupes, mainly from Germany, France, and Italy, and amateur performances, mainly by students.

Secular music also appeared. In Muscovy, the public performance of secular music was illegal, but in the new capital Peter could enjoy a German ensemble playing at his favorite tavern. Most of the new music was not high art, but, to Peter's liking, consisted of either popular songs for drinking and celebrating or military tunes. Beginning in 1711, each military unit had its own brass and wind orchestra, and those of Guards regiments regularly performed during lunchtime at the Admiralty. More refined secular music also entered Russian culture, however. One could enjoy it at the new assemblies, and Peter maintained a group of Italian singers who performed at court. The first orchestral concert, that of a chamber orchestra from Holstein, was heard in 1721. That group became very popular during its stay and could be heard performing somewhere in town nearly every evening. Permanent Russian orchestras, however, were established only in the 1750s.

No Russian secular literature had developed by Peter's death, but his reforms had sown its seeds in Petersburg. The Academy of Sciences was crucial to the birth of Russian secular literature, as its press provided the leading outlet for literary works, and many budding literary figures worked and taught there. Many of the Russian literary figures and intellectuals who would later rise to prominence were products of Peter's reign.[42]

SOCIAL LIFE

St. Petersburg's social life was also novel and driven by Peter, but at the time there was no royal court on the European model around which high social life could focus. Peter shunned such pretense; he did not even have a throne room in his palaces. Instead, social life revolved around particular occasions, and was secular in character. Initially, his purpose was simply to provide welcome diversions to lessen the hardships and discontents of living in the new capital, especially in the winter. In time, however, he structured such events so as to elevate the knowledge, manners, and morals of his people. He used social life to instill the new culture among the new service nobility. The new manners left not only a new outward appearance, but also hopefully would affect people's psychology. At the same time, Peter's taste for grand spectacles and simple, rollicking fun ensured ample social opportunities for all citizens.

Inspired by the salons he had seen in Paris on his second European voyage, in 1718 Peter instituted a new type of social gathering called the assembly. These were held during the winter, two or three times a week, usually at nobles' households.

Because the institution was unfamiliar and people would not know how to behave, Peter, in typical fashion, issued a decree on assemblies governing their conduct, and he usually attended them in order to ensure that they went right. Since the decree is both short and descriptive, it is worth quoting in full:

Assembly is a French word which cannot be rendered in a single Russian word. To state it in more detail: it is a voluntary gathering or meeting in someone's home; it is held not merely for amusement but also for affairs, and there people may see one another and discuss whatever is necessary, hear about what is going on, and also amuse themselves. And the manner in which we will conduct these assemblies, until it becomes a habit, is explained in the paragraphs below:

The person in whose home the assembly will be held shall in writing or by other means announce to people, of both sexes, where to go.

The assembly shall not begin earlier than four or five o'clock in the afternoon, and it shall not continue after ten in the evening.

The host is not obligated to greet, accompany or feed guests, and is not only not obligated as to the above but is also not obligated to provide anything except for all necessary tables, candles, drinks requested by the thirsty, and the usual table games and what is needed therefor.

There is no fixed time at which one must be there. One may be present when one desires, so long as it is not earlier or later than the fixed time. One may stay as long as one desires and leave when one desires.

While one is at the assembly, one may freely sit, walk around, and play. No one shall hinder or take exception to what another does, on pain of standing up and being penalized.* And one must bow when others enter and leave.

Only persons of certain ranks shall be entitled to attend assemblies, namely: from the highest ranks down to superior officers and nobles, also notable merchants and headmasters and notable Chancery officials, together, of course, with regard to the female sex, their wives and daughters.

Lackeys or servants shall not enter the premises but shall remain in the sleds or in such other place as the host shall designate.

Churchmen and foreigners also were often invited, in order to elevate the cultural level of clerics and encourage Russians to interact with foreigners. Peter also wanted to break down the conceit of the old Moscow boyars, so at assemblies distinctions of rank and status had to be left at the door. Anyone could invite anyone else to dance (though traditionalists considered dancing immoral), and one might see a noble drinking with a doctor, a general playing board games with a merchant, or a naval officer conversing with an untitled academic.

The beginning of an assembly was announced by a drum roll on the city's streets and squares. The guests then filtered into several rooms of the host's residence. Some danced, others conversed, and others snacked or played games (but usually

---

*The penalty consisted of having to drink wine or brandy from a large eagle-shaped goblet.

not card games, which were supposed to be forbidden at assemblies). Though not mandated by Peter's decree, in practice food was usually served at least by wealthier hosts, usually toward the end. Unlike most other social affairs, drinking was light by Russian standards, and drunkenness was frowned upon. As the evening wore on, the dancing tended to take center stage. The dances were normally either "Ceremonial" (minuet or Polish dance) or "English" (anglaise, allemande, contradance). Peter and Catherine (and their daughters Anna and Elizabeth) were adept dancers and would often take the lead. At first, the music was provided by wind and brass instruments and kettle drums. Later, stringed instruments made their appearance.

Both sexes dressed to the extent possible in the Western style. At first, such clothes had to be imported and were expensive. Men wore stockings and embroidered coats, while women wore fashionable dresses and rouge. The women in particular quickly rivaled foreign ladies in their dress, manners, makeup, and hairstyles, and the French language soon became popular among them. The historian Milukov observed that in order to meet a notable woman without a hairdo, one had to go to Moscow, and that in Petersburg a Russian costume was worn only at a masquerade.[43]

Assemblies quickly caught on and became especially popular amongst women. Indeed, a major purpose of assemblies was to bring the two sexes together in a refined setting for genteel social intercourse. This was a far cry from the Muscovite seclusion of noble women in the *terem*. Peter wanted to elevate the status of women, and St. Petersburg ladies eagerly exploited their new freedom. Relations between the sexes at assemblies were initially awkward. Men were not used to women being present at social affairs and did not know how to behave. At first, the sexes would come together for dances but then the men would retreat to one side of the room, leaving the women to socialize by themselves. If dinner was served, however, the ladies and gentlemen were seated alternately to foster social interaction.

The holding of assemblies also transformed the homes and households of nobles. In order to hold these gatherings, the size of homes and the amount of space in them designed for social functions increased. Art was also needed to adorn these rooms, which stimulated the demand for paintings, engravings, and tapestries, even though most homeowners were only beginning to understand and appreciate these new arts. New types of furniture were also needed, and at first most of it had to be imported.

In addition to assemblies, a focus of higher culture and a precursor to the famous St. Petersburg literary, intellectual, and artistic salons of later years existed in the social gatherings that Feofan Prokopovich held at his large and fashionable home near his school. Here a circle of intellectually oriented clerical and secular Russians, which Prokopovich dubbed his "Learned Guard," would gather with foreigners to discuss scientific, political, literary, and other ideas and topics in a social atmosphere.[44]

An old Russian tradition remained, however, in the popularity of Russian baths. The Russian custom was to bathe once weekly, which actually kept Russians cleaner than most Europeans at the time.[45] Bathhouses were operated by the government and generated a handsome revenue. Weber described the typical scene:

> Behind the Finnish *sloboda* in the forest along a little river are built upwards of thirty *banyas*, one half for men, and the other half for women; on the tops of the houses are placed children who cry that their *banyas* are thoroughly heated. Those who have a mind to bathe, undress under the open sky, and run into the *banya*. After having sufficiently sweated and got cold water poured upon them, they go to bask and air themselves, and run up and down through the bushes sporting with one another. It is astonishing to see not only the men, but also the women unmarried as well as married . . . running about, to the number of forty or fifty, and more together, stark naked without any sort of shame or decency, so far from shunning the strangers who are walking thereabouts, that they even laugh at them.[46]

Peter himself participated. Even in the winter, when the river froze, the Tsar and his retinue could be seen frolicking naked in the snow.[47]

In the summer, most social life was outdoors. For the lower classes, besides drinking at taverns, fights were popular, particularly on Sundays and holidays. These were not just boxing but mass affairs where inebriated men and boys divided into teams. Weber said they fought "in the most barbarous manner, the ground lies full of blood and hair, and many of them are carried off lame. When they fall on [each other], they make such a dreadful and wild noise, that they may be heard a mile off."[48] But for Peter and the nobility, the main social events outside holiday celebrations were parties in the Summer Garden, weddings, yachting parties, and launchings of new ships, each of which was often accompanied by fireworks.

The Summer Garden parties were often held around events dear to Peter, such as his name day or the anniversary of Poltava. The guests would gather at about 5:00 P.M. and the affair would begin slowly, with people strolling along the many alleys, among the many statues, through the aviary and menagerie, and gathering at their favorite fountains or corners of the Garden to catch up on the latest news. One fountain was known as the Women's, where Catherine would usually sit with her court ladies, while the adjacent one was for Peter. Along one alley was a small pond surrounded by miniature houses for geese and ducks and with a pavilion in the center, to which Peter would row his companions to drink Hungarian wine. It even had a miniature boat for court dwarfs. After the guests had relaxed for a while, there would be music, dancing, and often fireworks. Toward the end, dinner would be served. Since Petersburg's summer "White Nights" were short and never quite dark it was always light during such parties.

Trinity Square, however, remained the most popular outdoor location for large-scale events, especially public celebrations, and it served as the center of public life in the young city. The affairs on this Square were not just for nobles but involved the soldiery and populace at large. The most famous was a combination of the celebration of victory in the Great Northern War and the wedding of Peter Ivanovich Buturlin to the widow of his predecessor as Prince-Pope of the All-Jesting Assembly, held in October 1721 and which lasted over a week.[49] It began with prayer services in Trinity Cathedral. When Peter emerged from the Cathedral, a drum signaled to the crowd on the Square, and everyone took off their long coats to reveal their masquerade costumes: Roman soldiers, abbots, monks, nuns, Turks, Chinese, harlequins, nymphs, boyars, shepherds, shipwrights, miners, Neptune, giants dressed as babies, and Bacchus in a tiger skin draped with vine leaves. Peter was dressed as a ship's drummer, as was Menshikov, while Catherine was dressed as a Friesian peasant. There followed a masquerade procession across Trinity Square in carts drawn by bears, dogs and pigs, naval parades on the Neva, military parades, and cannon salutes. Finally, there was a fireworks display, which a contemporary described as follows:

[O]n Petersburg Island across from the Senate a Janus temple was made as a large theater ringed with torches of many colors, and behind it was a figure of the ancient, all-powerful Janus with a fuse on it. Opposite it were [the figures of] two important personages, the first bearing the seal of Peter the Great and the other the seal of the Swedish king, also fused, and beside them were pyramids, pinwheels and other various ground fireworks leading all the way to the Senate gallery, atop which was fastened an eagle. All of this was prepared by the Tsar himself. . . . At midnight the Tsar lit the eagle, which flew straight into the Janus temple and lit up the structure and the statues, and they burnt such that the personages moved forth with extended arms and shut the gates of the temple, from which suddenly flew out over a thousand skyrockets. And then from the city and from galleys anchored along the Neva came cannon fire which seemed like thunder and lightning, which continued for an hour. And then two more rigs were lit, one on a ship heading toward the harbor bearing the slogan: "The End of the Affair is Crowned," and on another the Russian and Swedish crowns united on a pillar, with the inscription "The Unity of Friendship." And as their flames died out, the fun began of lighting the line of pyramids and other ground fireworks, and on the top of one pyramid was the Russian crown, and atop another the Swedish crown, and the fun continued for four more hours.[50]

It is difficult nowadays to appreciate the significance and role that fireworks played in Peter's time. In that age, before Man's conquest of the skies, and when most of the population was illiterate, fireworks substituted for written propaganda. Hugely impressive, and frightening to the uninitiated, they were used not merely to demonstrate the glory and power of the state but also to convey messages and stories of events. If a crowd of thousands saw a rocket launch from a soaring eagle and land on a lion and blow it to bits, even the simplest among them would understand that the eagle was Russia and the lion was the Swedish crown, and that Russia had foiled Sweden's plans to subjugate Russia. So spectacularly enacted, the event would remain long in people's memories. And so Peter did not hesitate to spend lavishly on such events.[51]

Another favorite social event was weddings. With the royal family and a growing court and nobility, large wedding celebrations were common. Most were serious, but many were held for jest and entertainment, such as weddings of jesters, dwarfs, or the wedding of the 84-year-old Nikita Zotov, Peter's former tutor and Mock-Pope, to a widow of 34.

Prior to Peter's own public wedding to Catherine, the most notable wedding in the city was that of his niece, the future Empress Anna Ioannovna, to Frederick Wilhelm, Duke of Courland, both 17 years old. The marriage was celebrated on October 31, 1710, in a specially built "chapel" in Menshikov's still incomplete palace, with Peter as Grand Marshal. The ceremony was followed by a banquet, also in the palace, with 17 toasts accompanied by 13 cannon shots. The banquet was followed by an elaborate fireworks display designed by Peter himself, which he accompanied with a narrative explanation for the audience. Staged on rafts anchored in the Neva, the display featured two columns crowned by wreaths, under one of which appeared the letter "F" and under the other the letter "A," and in between them the letter "P." Then emerged two palm trees topped with crowns, above which blazed the words "Love Unites." Then a cupid appeared by a forge on which lay two hearts. Cupid fused the two hearts with a smith's hammer, and above the forge appeared the words "From two I make one whole." This was followed by a finale of rockets. After the display was over, a lavish ball was held until midnight.[52]

The couple's wedding was followed two days later by an elaborate wedding, also planned personally by Peter, of his favorite dwarf, Euphemius Volkov, and one of Praskovya Fedorovna's. For this event Peter needed more dwarfs than were available in the city, and so he ordered others to be brought from Moscow and around the country. Over 70 dwarfs attended the wedding, which was held in the Peter and Paul Cathedral, with Peter himself holding the wedding crown over the bride's head. The subsequent banquet was held in Menshikov's palace and was much like Anna's, except for the miniature tables at which all the dwarfs sat in the middle of the hall, all served by dwarf waiters. As in Anna's wedding banquet, there were cannon salvos to accompany the toasts and fireworks.

Peter's public marriage to Catherine on February 19, 1712, was notable not merely for the festivities but for its contrast with his first marriage to Eudoxia in 1689.[53] This time he was married in a private ceremony in the Church of St. Isaac of Dalmatia, wearing a naval uniform (that of a rear admiral) rather than the traditional coronation robes. The couple's daughters Anna and Elizabeth were bridesmaids. After the ceremony, the royal couple visited Menshikov's palace and then returned to the Winter Palace in sledges accompanied by drummers and trumpeters. When their sledge drew up to the Palace, Peter hopped out and rushed inside to hang over the head table his wedding gift to Catherine, a candelabrum made of ivory and ebony which he himself had made. A banquet attended by hundreds of guests and spread over several Palace rooms was then held. Most men were in naval dress, while the ladies were in wigs and décolleté dresses. The feast with toasts and dancing lasted from six until eleven. According to one guest, the English Ambassador Charles Whitworth, that evening "the company was very splendid, the dinner magnificent, the wine good, from Hungary, and what was the greatest pleasure, not forced on the guests in too large quantities."[54] The feast was followed by fireworks, which featured a tableau spelling "Vivat," two entwined columns with the couple's monograms, a representation of Peter as Hymen, the god of marriage, with a torch and eagle at his feet, and one of Catherine carrying a burning heart and kissing doves, above which was a crown with the words "United in your love."[55]

With his love for the sea and desire to have his people master seamanship, Peter especially liked yachting parties. He distributed to virtually everyone in the upper classes sailboats of various types and sizes according to one's rank, and in 1718 imposed rules for their operation and upkeep as well as for attendance at mandatory sailing lessons, and for the conduct of yachting parties. These outings were announced by hanging special flags at street intersections, which signaled all boat owners to assemble on the river by the Fortress on the appointed morning. A flotilla of up to 60 or so yachts with Peter's in the lead would set off downstream and venture into the Finnish Gulf. The party usually stopped for a picnic before returning, often near Catherine's country palace Ekaterinhof, where benches were set up in the garden for this purpose. Sometimes the weather turned foul, and some outings nearly ended in disaster.

Peter also loved to celebrate the launching of new ships from the Admiralty, which provided an occasion to honor shipbuilders and seamen. These were all-day parties for the citizenry with food, drink, and fireworks, and were attended by as many as 20,000 people. Peter used these occasions to speak and remind his citizens of their common enterprise. One of these speeches, given at the launching of the ship *Ilya Prorok*, has a Gettysburg-like brevity and grace, and elegantly sums up what Peter and his city were all about:

> Who among you, my brothers, would have dreamed 30 years ago that we would be here together, on the Baltic Sea, practicing carpentry in the dress of foreigners, in a land won from them by our labors and courage, erecting this city in which we live; that we would live to see such brave and victorious soldiers and sailors of Russian blood, and such sons who have visited foreign countries and returned home so bright; that we would see right here so many foreign artists and craftsmen, or that we would live to see the day when you and I are respected by foreign rulers? Historians believe that the cradle of all knowledge was Greece, from which (with the vicissitudes of time) it spread to Italy and then to all European lands, but this did not go beyond Poland and our ancestors were left in ignorance. The Poles like the Germans had wallowed the same impenetrable and dark ignorance that we remained in until later. And only by the extraordinary efforts of their leaders did they open their eyes and assimilate the

earlier Greek art, science and way of life. Now it is our turn, if only you will support me in my important enterprises, if you will obey me without any reservations, and if you can get accustomed to easily discerning and learning good from evil. I liken this transmigration of learning to the flow of blood in the body of mankind, and it seems to me that over time it will leave its current location in England, France, and Germany, stay a few centuries with us and then return again to its true homeland, in Greece. Meanwhile, I recommend that you remember the Latin saying *ora et labora* (pray and toil) and earnestly hope that perhaps even in our own century you will put other educated countries to shame and raise to a new height the glory of the Russian name.[56]

History records that the sailors listening to this quickly nodded in assent, saying "'tis very true," and then quickly forgot it and returned their attention to the brandy bowl.[57] In many ways this was the pattern in Russia generally after Peter's death. Nevertheless, by the end of Peter's reign there had arisen among leading St. Petersburgers great satisfaction and pride about their own and their country's progress and achievements, their place in the world, and their city.[58] The future did hold promise. But the path would not be straight or easy.

CHAPTER 4

Decline and Rebirth

Petersburg will stand empty!

PETER THE GREAT'S ESTRANGED FIRST WIFE,
EUDOXIA, LAYING A CURSE ON THE CITY

Petersburg is like a part of one's body that has been seized with gangrene and which must be amputated so that the rest of the body does not become infected by it.

PRINCE GOLITSYN OF MOSCOW[1]

One can find no other city besides Petersburg where so many people speak in so many different languages, and so poorly. One constantly hears even servants speak first in Russian, then in German, then in Finnish. . . . A German speaking in Russian and a Russian speaking in German commit so many mistakes that their speech could be taken by strict critics as a new foreign language. The young Petersburg, in this regard, can be compared to ancient Babylon.

PEDER VON HAVEN[2]

PETERSBURG'S OPPONENTS

The city, its way of life, Peter's reforms, and their acceptance by the Russian people were fragile, like new shoots of grass in the spring. Peter would soon be gone, but his foes would remain.

Peter's opponents were many, and to find them he did not have to look beyond his own family. Peter's son Alexis, born of Peter's unfortunate union with Eudoxia, grew up under the influence of Peter's adversaries in Moscow. Because he hated Eudoxia, Peter ignored Alexis when he was young, which certainly helped turn Alexis against him. But once Alexis was older, Peter did try to educate him under foreign tutors and personally teach him his beliefs. Peter took him along on several of his trips around Russia, including to the battle of Narva when Alexis was 13. On the eve of that battle, Peter, already aware of his son's leanings, wrote him a prophetic letter:

> I may die tomorrow, but be sure that you will have little pleasure if you fail to follow my example. You must love everything which contributes to the glory and honor of the fatherland; you must love loyal advisers and servants, whether foreigners or our own people, and spare no effort to serve the common good. If my advice is lost in the wind and you do not do as I wish, I do not recognize you as my son.[3]

But Alexis was one of those sons who always managed to disappoint. He was not a natural leader but was passive and weak-willed, and he ignored his German wife, preferring to spend his time with his mistress Afrosina, an illiterate Finnish peasant. In a letter to Peter in 1716, he offered to refuse the throne, confessing that he was "unqualified and unfit for the task." But Peter insisted that Alexis accept the succession, otherwise he would be sent to a monastery. Peter's opponents rallied around Alexis, who reluctantly was drawn into a vague plot led by the conservatives Alexander Kikin and Nikifor Viazemsky, the priest Yakov Ignatiev (Alexis's confessor), and his uncle Avraam Lopukhin. While traveling abroad later in 1716, Alexis received from Peter a letter of ultimatum demanding that he choose either the throne or a monastery. Alexis panicked and fled to Vienna to seek refuge at King Charles VI's court, which was an act of defection and treason. The plotters in Russia, who actually had not yet made concrete plans for Peter's overthrow, were gratified, but Charles VI declined to get involved. This made it possible to dispatch Peter's able diplomat Peter Tolstoy to Vienna to lure Alexis back to Russia on promises of a pardon and a comfortable married life with Afrosina. When Alexis returned, Peter deprived him of the succession, and he was told that his pardon depended upon his revealing the names of his accomplices. He was interrogated, imprisoned, and tortured in the Peter and Paul Fortress, the main charge being the treasonous act of seeking Austrian help to overthrow and assassinate Peter. The other plotters were also identified and interrogated. Afrosina betrayed Alexis, reporting that, among his other vows, he had stated, "I shall bring back the old people and choose myself new ones according to my will; when I become sovereign I shall live in Moscow, and leave St. Petersburg simply as any other town; I won't launch any ships."[4] Peter remained aloof from the tortures and trial, which was held openly as an example and involved as many officials and churchmen as possible in deliberating and consenting to the verdict. On June 24, 1718, the Senate found Alexis guilty and sentenced him to death. But he died the next day before the sentence could be carried out or commuted. The official cause of death was a seizure, but ultimately it was from the weakening effects of torture. The ordeal was painful for Peter too. Peter met with Alexis earlier on the day of his death, forgave and blessed him, and upon hearing of Alexis's death he wept openly. He had sacrificed his own son for the sake of his principles, his city, and Russia's future.

In a country still beset with superstition and mysticism, it did not help Peter's cause that Petersburg was uniquely menaced by nature: the disastrous floods that ravaged the city. In Peter's reign, the city suffered major floods in 1706, 1713 (two), 1715, 1720, 1721, and 1725.[5] In some cases the entire city would be under several feet of water, and whole islands would disappear for hours. Since the floods were caused by strong winds from the gulf blowing water into the city and backing up the Neva, they were usually accompanied by raging winds and waves. Vessels would be ripped off their moorings and float around the city like ghost ships, settling in strange places when the waters receded. People's furniture and personal belongings, goods from stores and markets, animals, bridges, and even newly buried coffins with cadavers could be seen floating about the city. No land would be visible, only the city's buildings protruding from the tops of the waves, with the city's residents huddled in the upper floors and attics or perched on roofs or in trees. In the flood of 1706, Peter himself was briefly in danger, and afterwards wrote Menshikov:

Three days ago the southwest wind drove in such water as is beyond description. In my home the water was 21 inches above the floor, and around town and on the other side [of the Neva] people freely traveled in boats. And it was fascinating to see people, not only men but also women, sitting on roofs and perched in trees as if it were the [biblical] deluge.[6]

Russians had never seen anything like this, and to them the floods indeed assumed biblical proportions. To Peter's opponents, it was easy to connect the floods with their vision of Peter as the Antichrist, as God's punishment for the Tsar's sins, and as a harbinger of the end of the world. Prophecies spread that the city would be destroyed and disappear into the sea. Many such prophesiers were punished and tortured by Peter's Secret Chancellery before and after his death for spreading such stories, but such talk persisted. Rumors spread of the kikimora, a mythical creature which supposedly lived in the bell tower of Trinity Cathedral and foretold the end of the city.[7] Peter's first wife, Eudoxia, was said to have laid a curse on the city: "Petersburg will stand empty!"

In one case, a story arose that, in 1701, before the city was founded, on Christmas Day many burning candles had suddenly appeared in a large tree standing at what would soon be the edge of Trinity Square. Upon seeing it, the native Chukhni residents immediately tried to cut the tree down to get the candles, but after a few blows of the axe the candles went out and disappeared; all that remained was a scar on the tree trunk. But in 1720 an elderly prophet appeared on Trinity Square and predicted that on September 23 of that year a large wave would rise from the sea and flood the city to the top of the tree's branches, destroying the city in punishment for abandoning Orthodoxy in favor of Peter's godless way. Word of the prophecy spread and many city residents believed it; some began evacuating the city. When Peter learned of this, he ordered that the tree be publicly cut down by Preobrazhensky Guards in his presence, after which the false prophet was publicly flogged beside its stump. Peter then lectured the onlookers about the harm that comes from believing superstitious fables. The prophesied day of the flood came and went without incident, although a "normal" flood did occur later that year.[8] It was in such an atmosphere that the city struggled to survive after Peter was gone.

PETER'S DEATH AND REACTION

By 1724, Peter began to slow down, and he grew moody and irritable. Since so much had depended on his personal example and energy, Petersburg and the Russian state lost momentum too. Gradually, it became clear that the problem was his health. Beyond the mileage that his ceaseless toils, torment, and revelry had put on him, his lifelong nervous disorder still bothered him, and he had an affliction in his left arm from medical malpractice which left it either painful or, at other times, without feeling and half-paralyzed. He also suffered from an infection in his urinary tract which often rendered him unable to pass urine. In mid-1724 the infection worsened, and Peter often lay immobilized and in great pain.

By autumn, however, he felt better and, against his doctors' advice, set off on an inspection tour of the region ending on the Finnish Gulf. One day during this last excursion he spied a boat carrying about 20 soldiers lose control and run aground on a shoal in high winds and large waves. After sailors sent from his own ship were unable to assist, in typical fashion Peter took matters into his own hands. He set off toward the imperiled boat in his own skiff and, as he approached, he jumped into the icy waist-deep water to direct the rescue. The soldiers' lives and the boat were saved. After these heroics, Peter's ship anchored at Lakhta and he retired, but during the night he developed chills and a fever. This, in turn, caused his infection to reappear, and this time it never left. Although he had a remission around Christmas, his condition worsened by mid-January. From January 16 he was bedridden in the Winter Palace and realized that he was probably dying. He finally succumbed between 4:00 and 6:00 A.M. on January 27, 1725.

A commission headed by James Bruce was appointed to organize a funeral in the European style, borrowing mainly from funeral ceremonies in the German states. Peter had ordered that he be entombed in Peter and Paul Cathedral rather than the Uspensky Cathedral in Moscow where his predecessors lay. Like many of Peter's undertakings, the Cathedral lay unfinished, and Trezzini had to hastily build a temporary wooden chapel inside the Cathedral walls for the ceremony. While preparations were made for the funeral, Peter's body lay in state (not a Moscow tradition) on a bier in the Winter Palace. Set up by Bruce, who was a Freemason, the room was filled with imagery from Masonic funerals. Peter was dressed in breeches, a shirt of silver brocade, lace cuffs and a cravat, boots with spurs, his sword, and the Order of St. Andrew. The room itself was in black, with black and white flowers, and lit by candles. Peter was surrounded by nine tables containing Peter's orders and regalia, four statues depicting Russia weeping, Europe mourning, Mars grieving, and Hercules in contemplation holding a club, four pyramids of white marble, at the bottom of which were marble figures of genies and children representing Faith, Death, Time, and Glory and bearing legends in tribute to Peter's many accomplishments. Next to the pyramids stood statues of the seven virtues (Wisdom, Bravery, Piety, Mercy, Peace, Love of the Fatherland, and Justice).[9] Beside Peter stood two men holding halberds, dressed in hooded black capes, and bearing unsheathed swords. Overhead hung a great chandelier with many candles, but only one was lit.

For over a month people filed by to pay their last respects. Peter's coffin was so large and the space in the Winter Palace so modest that it could not be taken downstairs, so on the date of the funeral it was passed outside through the second story balcony and down a temporary outdoor staircase. The funeral was held on March 10. For the procession a wooden road (more like a bridge) was built across the Neva ice. The ceremony began at 8:00 A.M. in the twilight of an early morning snowstorm. On either side of the river stood two rows of musketeers (1,250 in all) holding burning torches. It began with a procession of over 10,000 soldiers across the ice, followed by Catherine and her ladies, government officials, members of the court, military officers, and foreign envoys. The cortege was so long that it took two hours to cross the Neva, all members bareheaded in the snowstorm. Feofan Prokopovich gave a stirring eulogy, reminding Russians, "O Russia, seeing what a great man has left you, see also how great he has left you."[10] Peter's coffin lay in the chapel for six years, and it was interred only on May 29, 1731.

Those who were personally or politically close to Peter felt a great loss, and feared for their careers and well-being. Peter's opponents, of course, rejoiced and looked forward to abandoning St. Petersburg and returning to the old ways. The bulk of the population, both in Petersburg and in Russia as a whole, simply felt relief. Peter had for so long demanded so much and imposed such financial, military, service, and personal burdens on his people that, despite Russia's victories and great accomplishments, they needed a rest.[11] The general reaction was later wittily portrayed in the popular engraving entitled "How the Mice Were Burying the Cat," which parodied both Peter's reign and his own parodies of religious ritual. The drawing portrayed a cortege of mice (Peter's subjects) in a funeral procession for a large cat (Peter). The procession features shaving, smoking, new ways of drinking, music, and a cabriolet—all things introduced by Peter. But some cannot participate in the festivities because they are cripples, victims of the cat's reign, of which it is said that "he used to swallow an entire little mouse in one gulp."

PETERSBURG UNDER CATHERINE I

Peter never formally chose his successor, though many consider this implied by his coronation of Catherine as Empress in 1724. While Peter still lay alive, the group of key men who had risen under Peter reached a consensus in favor of Catherine as the safe choice for his successor. They included Menshikov, Apraxin, Tolstoy, Yaguzhinsky, Prokopovich, and General Buturlin. Catherine herself had courted their support, as well as that of the Guards regiments, in particular by paying all of their back wages in her own name. She realized that whoever enjoyed the backing of the Guards would carry the day.

The only other serious candidate for the throne was nine-year-old Grand Duke Peter Alexeevich, the son of Peter's disgraced son Alexis. He was supported by many of the old Moscow nobility, who sought to reestablish their prominence and reverse much of Peter's program. They included the Princes Golitsyn, Dolgoruky, and Repnin. The debate and confrontation came into the open at the Winter Palace on the night of January 27, only hours before Peter's death. In preparation, Catherine and her supporters had the Preobrazhensky and Semenovsky Guards ready and assembled outside the Palace. Seeing that Grand Duke Peter's supporters did not have the backing to assert his claim directly, Golitsyn proposed a compromise under which Catherine would simply serve as regent. Tolstoy, knowing that he had the support to reject this, countered that at this crucial time Russia needed

> a sovereign who is courageous, firm in the affairs of state, who would be able to defend that importance and glory won through the long labors of our Emperor, and who, at the same time, would be distinguished by a concern for making our people happy and loyal to the government. All these necessary qualifications are united in the Empress: She has learned the art of governing from her husband, who confided to her the most important secrets. . . . Moreover, her right to rule is confirmed by her coronation.[12]

By this point, several of the Guards had slipped into the room and cheered Tolstoy. Prince Repnin, the commander of the St. Petersburg garrison, angrily demanded why the soldiers were there without his knowledge or orders. "Am I not the Field-marshal?" he asked. But at this moment drums sounded outside the Palace, reminding all inside that the regiments backed Catherine. "I commanded them to come by the will of the Empress, whom any subject must obey, including yourself," answered Buturlin, commander of the Guards. The discussions continued for a while longer, but the conclusion was foregone. Apraxin, the senior Senator, proposed that Catherine be made Empress without restrictions on her power, like Peter. An act to this effect was drawn up and signed by all Senators.

Once on the throne, Catherine declared her intention to rule in the spirit and according to the policies of her late husband. She meant this and tried to do so, not intending to be a mere figurehead. But she was not up to the job and could not control her ambitious ministers. Worse, her health began to deteriorate within the first year of her reign. Finally, her close association with the hated Menshikov roused the ire of the nobility and generated intrigue. In an attempt to gain more authority, in February 1726 she replaced the Senate with the

Supreme Privy Council, to which she appointed a narrower group (six) of her more trusted advisors who had worked for Peter: Menshikov, Tolstoy, Golitsyn, Apraxin, Golovkin, and the German Baron Andrei Ostermann. All except Golitsyn were exponents of Peter's views and opponents of the old Muscovite aristocracy. Despite this relative unity of ideology, Menshikov's unabated rapaciousness and desire for the Empress's attentions and favor soured relations with Council Members and other nobles and paralyzed the Council's work. One day in March 1725, Menshikov got into an argument with Yaguzhinsky, then General Procurator of the Senate, and threatened to arrest him and make him surrender his sword. Distraught, that evening Yaguzhinsky had too much to drink and ended up at the Peter and Paul Cathedral, where Peter the Great's coffin still lay exposed, and he spent the entire night commiserating with the deceased Emperor about Menshikov's behavior.

Catherine's renewed relationship with Menshikov and its character were not entirely his initiative. Catherine's own personal life was falling apart. Not only had Peter died, but so had her youngest daughter, Natalya, in March 1725. Her friend, confidant, and lover, William Mons, had been beheaded by Peter in November 1724. She was not succeeding in her rule, took to alcohol, and her health began to fail. In these circumstances, she looked increasingly to Menshikov for support and comfort. And since Menshikov's own position depended increasingly on her, he obliged.

Menshikov had risen by virtue of his many talents and loyalty to Peter. But he was also a selfish upstart, often corrupt, and eventually managed to offend virtually everyone else around Peter. Thus he was overly dependent on Peter's protection, and when Peter died he sought patronage in Catherine. But in Catherine's case he dominated the ruler, thus increasing the ire of his enemies.

Catherine's contributions to the city were modest. In reality, her feelings about the city were ambivalent, and she spent much of her time in Moscow.[13] She followed through with the establishment of the Academy of Sciences, which opened in December 1725, and continued existing construction in the city, but she began no major new projects except for the third Winter Palace, constructed 1726–1728 by Trezzini.[14] Generally, Catherine sought to reduce the burdens on the population and improve the state's finances by reducing expenditures. This was a popular policy, but it limited the possibilities for new projects in the city.

Catherine's death, like Peter's, was brought about by the elements. In November 1726, she made an escape from her palace during a flood, wading through the cold, knee-deep waters. Shortly thereafter, in January 1727, she attended the Blessing of the Waters celebration on the icy Neva and remained outside and exposed for hours as she reviewed the troops. She came down with a severe fever and was bedridden for two months. As her health was already wracked by venereal disease, fatigue, and excessive drinking, she never fully recovered. She died on May 6, 1727, only two years and three months after her husband.

THE CAPITAL WITHOUT A TSAR

Before her death, Catherine had named Grand Duke Peter Alexeevich (the son of Alexis) as her successor. Since Peter was only 11 years old at the time, she also appointed the Supreme Privy Council as his regent. Peter represented the hopes of the old Moscow aristocracy and thus was not favored by Peter the Great's new men. It was difficult to make a persuasive case for an alternative candidate, however. Peter's two remaining daughters, Elizabeth and Anna, were tainted by illegitimacy, having been born long before Peter's public marriage to Catherine. Moreover, Anna had married the Duke of Holstein-Gottorp in 1725, and many feared that, if Anna were chosen, the Duke would gain too much power and even might make a grab for the throne. Similarly, it was feared that Elizabeth might marry a foreign prince. Thus, after complex negotiations and intrigues, Peter II was made Tsar on May 7, the day after Catherine's death. As Catherine had decreed, the Supreme Privy Council, which Menshikov still controlled, was appointed Peter's regent.

In the first months after his accession, Peter was firmly under Menshikov's thumb and the Moscow princes were unable to exercise their hoped-for influence. Menshikov moved Peter into his own palace so he could watch over him, had him engaged to his daughter Maria, and even had Trezzini begin building a new palace for Peter on Menshikov's palace grounds. Menshikov behaved imperiously, making state decisions in Peter's name without consulting him. But Peter had a mind of his own, quickly came to resent Menshikov, and sought to avoid his impending marriage to Maria. One day Menshikov intercepted gifts meant for Peter. When Peter learned of this, he warned, "We shall see who is Emperor, you or I."[15]

Peter and his Moscow allies got their chance in July 1727, when Menshikov suddenly fell ill. Peter moved to Peterhof with Elizabeth, where he began exercising his powers without Menshikov. Menshikov recovered, but by then the situation had changed. When he visited Peter at Peterhof after his condition had briefly improved, the Emperor remarked to his astonished courtiers in Menshikov's presence, "You see, I am at last learning how to keep him in order." Then, on July 17, urged on by Elizabeth, Peter refused to attend a celebration in honor of his own birthday at Menshikov's summer palace, Oranienbaum. Instead, he went hunting that day with Elizabeth and then moved from Menshikov's palace to the Summer Palace in apartments next to Elizabeth's. Peter also disclaimed his intentions of marrying Maria. Menshikov's illness worsened in late August, so he was unable to save himself. On September 8 Peter issued decrees stripping Menshikov of his titles and placing him under house arrest at Oranienbaum. He was soon exiled to Ukraine with his family under comfortable conditions. In April 1728, however, when the Moscow aristocracy was firmly in charge, Menshikov was charged with treason (alleged contacts with Sweden), all of his property was confiscated, and he was exiled permanently to the village of Berezov in Siberia, where he died in November 1729.

After Menshikov's fall, Peter moved to Moscow, where he was coronated in January 1728, and he never again saw St. Petersburg. Still young and not well educated, he spent most of his time hunting outside Moscow. Power and day-to-day government devolved to the Supreme Privy Council, now dominated by the Dolgorukys. Peter was particularly close with the young Prince Ivan Dolgoruky, which Ivan's family exploited to the full, quickly arranging Peter's marriage to Princess Dolgorukaya. But on the very day of the wedding in early 1730, Peter died of smallpox without having designated a successor.

Peter never formally moved the capital back to Moscow, although there was much talk that he would do so. (But then, it had never been formally transferred to St. Petersburg.) The effect was nearly the same, however, because the entire court joined Peter in Moscow, and in mid-1729 he began to transfer various government agencies there. Peter had no love for his grandfather's city. "What am I to do," he asked, "in a place where there is nothing but salt water?"[16] "I do not intend to sail the seas like my grandfather."[17] The city would be without a Tsar for four years, until Anna Ioannovna's return in 1732.

St. Petersburg suffered greatly between Peter the Great's death and Anna's return. Catherine did not abandon it, but was unwilling to devote state funds (i.e., impose tax burdens) to fund construction, and so the pace slackened. With Peter I's strong hand gone, officials ceased to enforce measures designed to maintain the city. Even the previously fastidious Devier was unwilling to test public opinion by enforcing the requirements for mandatory building of homes. Several incidents of arson occurred, and security had to be tightened.[18] In the spring after Peter I's death, a mass exodus began, led by many nobles who had been brought there unwillingly. With the tempo of construction decreasing, many workers also left.

The situation deteriorated further when Peter II removed the court and government to Moscow. Local industries and trade lost state support, and many factories closed. The Academy of Sciences barely functioned due to lack of funds, students, and foreign academics. The number of students at the Naval Academy fell to 150 in 1731 from its high of about 350 in Peter I's reign.[19] Construction in the city essentially stopped, even on such fundamental projects as the Kunstkamera. Many homes and palaces stood half built, with weeds growing in them. Grass grew on many streets, and some sections of the city, particularly Vasilievsky Island, resembled a ghost town. A contemporary account of the wife of the British resident, Thomas Ward, from 1729 described the scene:

[On Vasilievsky Island] the merchants were designed to live; but though the houses and streets are very handsome, they are uninhabited. . . . A mile from the town is the monastery of St. Alexander Nevsky . . . and [it] will be very fine if ever it is finished. . . . There are many fine houses in the town belonging to the nobility, but now, in the absence of the court, quite empty.[20]

Soon the city's population was only half of what it had been at Peter the Great's death.[21] After Catherine's death, in the summer of 1727 the students that Peter the Great had sent to study abroad were recalled. Russia's window to the West was closing.

When Peter II moved to Moscow, he made a German, Burkhard Christopher Münnich, Governor of the city. Münnich was a native of Oldenburg from a gentry family with a long engineering tradition. He began as a professional soldier and fought in the Austrian army in the War of the Spanish Succession and was captured by the French, after which he fell under the spell of French culture, language, and manners, which he awkwardly affected for the rest of his life. Upon returning to Germany, he became an engineer like his ancestors, and was soon constructing canals. In 1720 he presented a proposal to Peter the Great for an ambitious system of fortifications in the newly acquired Baltic provinces. Peter rejected that proposal but offered him a lieutenant–generalship in the Engineers. Münnich accepted and moved to Petersburg in 1721. He was soon put in charge of constructing the Ladoga Canal, work on which had begun in 1718 but had proceeded slowly. Münnich would labor on this thankless task through the reigns of Catherine and Peter II and complete it only in 1732 shortly after Empress Anna Ioannovna's return to St. Petersburg, when he finally received due recognition for his efforts and favor at Anna's court. This 65-mile artery linked St. Petersburg with the vast interior of Russia and protected ships from Ladoga's stormy waters. The easier transport of supplies to the city lowered the price of goods and, beginning with Anna's reign, made life there less costly and less of a hardship.

In the absence of the court, St. Petersburg functioned principally as a port city dominated by merchants and the military. During Peter II's rule, Münnich did what he could to improve and enliven the city. He tirelessly hosted dinners, balls and celebrations of holidays, and launchings of new ships (now much fewer in number), and arranged inspections of troops. In addition to his work on the Ladoga Canal, he completed the stone bastions of the Peter and Paul Fortress, and continued work on the Twelve Colleges. He also initiated a better system of communications between the city and Europe by establishing a regular schedule of postal and passenger ships commuting between Kronstadt and Danzig and Lubek. But he could not stem the city's decline.

By mid-1729, even Peter II, no friend of the city, realized that the situation had deteriorated too far. Accordingly, on July 15, 1729, he issued a decree calling for the mandatory return of merchants, craftsmen, coachmen, and others, together with their children, who had deserted the city, and also forbade those who had remained from leaving. The penalty for noncompliance was confiscation of property and exile to hard labor. The reaction was an epidemic of incendiarism.[22] Despite Peter's efforts, the city continued to stagnate until Empress Anna returned there in January 1732.

ANNA IOANNOVNA'S ACCESSION

Anna Ioannovna, born in 1693, was the second daughter of Ivan V, Peter the Great's older half-brother, and his wife Praskovya Fedorovna. Anna grew up in her mother's palace at Izmailovo on the outskirts of Moscow. She saw Petersburg for the first time in the spring of 1708, when Peter invited the dowager Empress and her family there to see where they would soon live. Peter personally guided them around town and presented the palace that was being constructed for them. They moved to Petersburg in the autumn of that year.

The family's arrival in the city was eventful. It began with a cannon salute followed by a reception in the old Governor's palace in which they were to be guests until their own palace was ready for them. One night after everyone had gone to bed, however, the Governor's palace caught fire and burned to the ground. With nowhere else to go, the family moved into their own damp and airy unfinished home. Soon thereafter, in 1710, the palace next door was burnt down by arsonists, who were caught and hung on the gallows built on the site, where they could be seen outside Praskovya's windows.

Life brightened for Anna later in 1710 when she married Frederick William, the Duke of Courland. Courland was a small Baltic state in present-day Lithuania which had long been a pawn between the neighboring states of Prussia, Poland, Sweden, and Russia. With Russia's ascendancy in the region following Poltava, the Duke sought to ally himself with Russia for protection against Prussia, and Peter also wanted to consolidate control over the duchy. Normally, the Duke would have married Praskovya's older daughter, Catherine. But she was Praskovya's favorite, and Praskovya could not bring herself to part with her. Instead, she persuaded Peter to offer Anna. Anna had always been and would remain Praskovya's bête noire,[23] and each was pleased to be rid of the other.

After their lavish wedding, the happy couple departed for Courland. Unfortunately, Frederick died on the journey only about 30 miles from St. Petersburg, a victim of the excesses of the celebrations. Seventeen and unattractive, Anna would spend 19 lonely years living in near poverty in her late husband's Teutonic castle in Mitau, fighting off foreign pretenders to the duchy, creditors, and boredom. She had few contacts with her relatives from St. Petersburg; her correspondence with them was mostly one-way, with Anna's entreaties for money usually going unanswered.

When Peter II died in 1730, Anna was an aging widow. As the daughter of Ivan V, Peter's older brother, she had a strong claim to succeed Peter, but there were other candidates, all women: Peter the Great's first wife Eudoxia; Princess Dolgorukaya (whom Peter II was to marry); Anna's sisters Catherine and Praskovya; and Peter the Great's daughter Elizabeth. It was Peter II's regent, the Supreme Privy Council, now dominated by the Dolgorukys and Golitsyns, which met to decide the matter, still hoping to control Russia under whichever new Empress it would appoint. Anna had the right credentials, and it appeared from her record of behavior in Mitau that she would be docile, easily influenced, and eager to escape from there under almost any conditions, and thus be easily controlled by the Council. And since she was single and childless, she was not associated with any Russian or foreign families, which could have provoked jealousy and intrigues. She was a neutral choice on whom a consensus could be reached.

The Council decided to offer her the position only if she would accept a number of "Conditions." The Conditions required that she undertake certain actions only with the Council's prior consent, including declaring war or making peace, marrying, appointing her heir, levying new taxes, promoting men to civil and military ranks above colonel, depriving nobles of their titles, lives, or estates, granting estates, or spending state revenues. The capital, of course, would be Moscow. In their form, the Conditions represented an effort toward constitutionalism, but in the short run would have turned Russia into an oligarchy of Muscovites whose goal was to turn back the clock on Peter's reforms.

With little alternative, Anna signed the Conditions without argument and prepared to go to Moscow for her coronation. But the Council had acted in the narrow interests of its members and to the exclusion of other interests in society such as the military, the Church, and, in particular, the lesser nobles and gentry. The Conditions were not public, but they soon became known to these groups. Since the lesser nobles and gentry depended directly on the Tsar for their positions and privileges, they felt safer with an autocracy than under a clique of dominant, rival noble families. Word of their opposition to the Conditions reached Anna by secret messenger before she came to Moscow in February 1730. Thus, when she arrived, she began acting without regard to the Council and secretly plotted with its opponents to eliminate the Conditions. When the plotters were ready, they, with the support of the Guards, "demanded" an audience with Anna in the Council's chamber, in which they presented a petition signed by a large number of nobles asking her to restore the autocracy and destroy the Conditions. Anna, feigning surprise, asked, "Do you mean that the conditions that were brought to me in Mitau did not reflect the desires of all my subjects?" When she was told that they did not, she turned to Prince Vasily Dolgoruky and said, "Then that means that you, Vasily Lukich, have deceived me."[24] She granted the petition and had the members of the Council publicly consent to it. She then had an aide retrieve the Conditions, and she tore them to pieces in front of everyone.

Within a few days Anna was Empress. The coronation was held on April 28, at a ceremony the lavishness of which exceeded those of all her predecessors. On the same day, Münnich held celebrations in St. Petersburg. He began with a celebratory dinner at his residence, which was followed by a fireworks display on a scale never before seen in Russia.[25]

Anna quickly moved to consolidate her power. On March 4, 1730, only days after becoming Empress, she eliminated the Supreme Privy Council. She also reinstated the government bodies established by Peter the Great: the Senate, with Yaguzhinsky at its head, the Colleges, and the Synod. Anna also created her own loyal regiment, the Izmailovsky, named after the village of her family's palace in Moscow. Its officers were drawn from loyal and reliable Baltic nobility. Peter the Great's security police, which had been abolished by Peter II, was revived as the Privy Chancery. With these supports in place, Anna's power was secure.

Although traditional government institutions during Anna's reign were in Russian hands, she installed many German favorites to high positions at court. Her Cabinet of Ministers consisted of three foreigners: Biron, Münnich, and Ostermann. Chief among them was her lover and favorite, Count Biron. Born Ernst Johann Bühren in 1690, he became an ardent Francophile and changed his name to Biron (stress on final syllable) and, according to some, took the coat of arms of an extinct French noble family of the same name in order to conceal his low ancestry. An adventurer, he surfaced in St. Petersburg in 1714 seeking a position at the Court of Charlotte of Wolfenbüttel, but his arrogant manner was offensive and he was refused. Since his ancestors had been grooms in the service of the Dukes of Courland, he migrated to Mitau, obtained a position in Anna's court and soon gained her favor and affections. Russians almost universally disliked him. According to one contemporary, "[h]is character was full of faults: he was haughty and ambitious beyond all bounds; abrupt, and even brutal; avaricious; an implacable enemy, and cruel in his revenge."[26] Count Ernst Münnich, the son of Gerhard, recalled that "there was not a single language which he could speak properly."[27] Biron rarely attended social functions; his only passions were power and horses. The Austrian Ambassador, Count Ostein, reportedly observed that "when the Count Biron talks of horses, or to horses, he speaks like a man, but when he speaks of men, or to men, he speaks as a horse might do."[28] When Anna traveled to Moscow to be crowned, she was forbidden to bring him along. Once she gained autocratic power, however, he joined her and would never leave her side. Biron's influence over Anna was so great that he dominated the rule of Russia until the end of her reign. In 1737, Anna arranged Biron's election as Duke of Courland. Anna's reign dominated by foreigners is known among Russians as the *Bironovshchina* ("the rule of Bironism").

Anna began her reign by committing to follow the policies of Peter the Great. But Anna's government often did poorly in this regard and the *Bironovshchina* is viewed as a dark period in Russia's history. In her eight short years in St. Petersburg, however, she saved the city and set it permanently on the path to greatness. It was Anna who established Russia's first royal court. She would repair the city's decaying buildings and infrastructure, replan and rebuild it following several disastrous fires, complete Peter the Great's unfinished projects, and add new architectural monuments of her own. And it was Anna who would initiate the city's long heritage as a center of opera, music, theater, and ballet, expanding from Peter I's preponderantly utilitarian outlook. Her reign was indeed a frustrating juxtaposition of repression and vulgarity on the one hand and efforts to achieve a higher level of culture and increase Russia's glory on the other. Insofar as her lasting impact on the city of St. Petersburg is concerned, it is these positive contributions which prevailed and are described below.

ANNA IOANNOVNA'S PETERSBURG

Anna, the court, and the government initially remained in Moscow following her coronation, and at first it was not certain whether she would return to St. Petersburg. According to one account, Anna was inspired to return to St. Petersburg after her carriage hit a large hole on a road outside Moscow and overturned; she miraculously escaped serious injury or death, and she took the episode as an omen. In reality, she probably never intended that the capital be anywhere but in Petersburg. She remained in Moscow long enough to allow the political turmoil surrounding her accession to dissipate, for her enemies to be punished, and to give by her presence in Moscow some attention to the Moscow nobility who longed for the capital to be returned there.[29] She needed St. Petersburg for many of the same reasons that Peter did. In Moscow, she could not escape the local nobility and would risk being swallowed by them. She had to get away from her enemies and gather in Petersburg her own loyal following. But in Anna's case, in light of recent experience, she felt that she could not trust Russians and therefore surrounded herself with foreigners whose positions were wholly dependent upon her.

Thus, already in the spring of 1731, Anna summoned Governor Münnich to Moscow and instructed him to prepare Petersburg and its palaces for the return of the court nearly a year later.[30] That autumn the Guards were moved to Petersburg. They were followed by Anna's sister Catherine, Duchess of Mecklenburg, and shortly after that by Tsarevna Elizabeth. Finally, in January 1732, Anna herself was ready.

Münnich had made grand preparations for this special event marking the restoration of Petersburg's position. On January 15 the Empress and her retinue were met two miles outside town by the members of the courts of justice, the land and sea officers, the foreign merchants, members of the Academy, and the foreign ministers. A long and grand procession was formed, which made its way down the Novgorod Road and onto the Grand Perspective. On this route stood five triumphal arches through which the procession passed, and along the Grand Perspective lines of foot soldiers stood at attention in the cold. The procession passed through the last of the triumphal arches by the Admiralty and stopped in front of St. Isaac's Church. All church bells in the city rang, and cannon saluted from the Fortress. Anna entered the Church and spent a long time there in prayer while the procession waited patiently outside. When she exited, she and the procession proceeded to her palace, which was the former Apraxin palace between Peter's Winter Palace and the Admiralty. There she was again welcomed by a salute of artillery and muskets. Welcoming and congratulatory speeches were followed by a dinner for 80 guests, consisting of court ministers of the first rank and foreign diplomats and their wives. The tables were spread over several rooms because the palace was not large enough to accommodate everyone in one room, a situation which Anna would soon remedy. Dinner was followed by a ball and fireworks.

Three days later a larger court ball was held, and beginning from January 23 balls were held in the palace every Sunday that winter. To entertain the court on this first occasion, Münnich had also staged a mock seizure of a snow fortress built on the frozen Neva in front of the palace. At the end of the attack, the soldiers conducted elegant maneuvers which ended by their forming a large letter "A."

The city which Anna had inherited was largely wooden, muddy, and run down, and many buildings stood unfinished. Such an appearance would not do for the imperial city, and immediately she set to work restoring, improving, planning, and expanding it. In the old sections of town, Anna concentrated on replacing wooden buildings with stone ones, on repairing, widening and paving the streets, building bridges, installing other infrastructure, and improving markets and other public places. The wider, smoother, and straighter streets led to reckless high-speed sleigh riding in the wintertime, but regulations were passed to control it. She issued several decrees calling for the cleanup of the Moika and Fontanka and forbidding the discharge of waste into them and for reinforcing their embankments, which like under Peter was made the responsibility of the inhabitants. She also took measures against street vagrants and beggars, and to care for them she set up almshouses.

Rather than undertake massive new construction projects, Anna focused on completing those of Peter the Great, namely the Peter and Paul Cathedral, the stone facing of the Fortress, the Kunstkamera, the Twelve Colleges, and the Ladoga Canal. Since the city was expanding, however, Anna did undertake new construction at the city's limits, which were then extended. On the Admiralty side, by the end of Anna's reign, Bolshaya Zagorodnaya ("Beyond the City") Street had become the city's boundary.

For the court's own needs, at Biron's recommendation Anna appointed Bartolomeo Rastrelli as Court Architect, one of the wisest decisions of her reign which had profound importance for the city. His first project in St. Petersburg, completed in time for Anna's return to the city, was a new Summer Palace for her in the Summer Garden by the Neva embankment. Rastrelli's talent was also recognized by Münnich, who in 1731 had retained him to construct a theater, which was completed in only two months. Rastrelli also built for Biron the Manezh, a large riding school located at the edge of what is now Palace Square near the Grand Perspective which could accommodate up to 75 horses and riders. It became a fashionable, almost obligatory social gathering place for the elite. Biron's love of horses brought to the city many good breeds and made Russia's royal stables first class.

Rastrelli's major project in the city during Anna's reign was the reconstruction and expansion of the Winter Palace, which he undertook once he completed the

Manezh. Peter's Winter Palace, even as expanded by Catherine, was modest and far inadequate for Anna's designs. Mrs. Rondeau, the wife of the British Ambassador, had described it in 1729 as "small, . . . far from handsome, [with] a great number of little rooms ill-contrived, and nothing remarkable either in architecture, painting or furniture."[31] For such reasons, upon her arrival Anna chose to reside in the former Apraxin palace, which Apraxin, who had died childless in 1728, had willed to Peter II. While today it may seem natural that the principal royal residence must be on the site of the present Winter Palace, it is unclear whether, without such bequest, the residence would have remained there. Part of the credit goes to Rastrelli, who proposed to Anna that the Winter Palace be reconstructed. In 1732 he presented a plan, which Anna approved. The project was completed in 1736, but modifications continued well into Elizabeth's reign. Rather than demolish the old buildings and start anew or simply modify the existing Winter Palace, Rastrelli redesigned and combined into one larger structure the existing Winter Palace, the Apraxin palace, the old Kikin palace, and several minor buildings. The result was an unbalanced and complex composition which did not disguise the separate origins of its parts. Algarotti, a follower of Palladio who disliked the baroque, viewed the building in 1739 and characterized it as "half Italian and half French, or rather it is in the modern, foolish Italian taste, like most of the buildings of Petersburg."[32]

Rastrelli was better able to apply his talent in the interior of the palace, which he decorated exquisitely. The colonnaded grand hall was 180 feet long and featured a beautiful ceiling painting by Louis Caravaque. Mrs. Rondeau left a description of Anna's birthday ball:

> Though it was very cold, the stoves kept it warm enough, and it was decorated with orange-trees and myrtles, in full bloom; these were ranged in rows that formed a walk on each side of the hall and only left room for the dancers in the middle. The walks on each side gave the company opportunity to sit down sometimes, as they were hid from the presence of the sovereign. The beauty, fragrance, and warmth of this new-formed grove, when you saw nothing but ice and snow through the windows, looked like enchantment. . . . The walks and trees filled with beaux and belles, in all their birthday finery, instead of the shepherds and nymphs of Arcadia, made me fancy myself in a Fairyland, and Shakespeare's Midsummer Night's Dream was in my head all evening.[33]

Anna also redesigned the region surrounding the palace. She razed many of the wooden buildings behind the palace to enlarge that part of Admiralty Lug (today's Palace Square).[34] She had intended to enclose the new area with a colonnade and to erect in its center a large bronze statue of herself, of which a wax model was produced by Rastrelli's father, the sculptor Bartolomeo Carlo Rastrelli, but this project never came to fruition.[35] (A smaller bronze version completed in 1741 after Anna's death now stands in the Russian Museum.) The neighboring Admiralty, originally constructed of wood and mud, had deteriorated, and the view from Anna's windows was unsightly. She had it rebuilt in masonry between 1732 and

1738. The Russian Ivan Korobov reconstructed the central block and placed a new tower with a golden spire and a caravel weather vane at its top. On the upriver embankment east of the Palace (now named Palace Embankment but then called simply the "Upper Embankment"), Anna decreed that only stone buildings could be constructed. Several other decrees calling for stone construction in other regions of town also were issued, but usually with results not much better than under Peter I.[36] She was reluctant to enforce the decrees over clear opposition, but did so as occasion permitted.

One place where Anna's decrees did work was the embankment of the Neva below the Admiralty, then known simply as the Lower Embankment. Peter the Great had also wanted to develop that embankment as a showpiece for visitors arriving up the Neva, so in 1714 he issued a decree granting free plots of land to select nobles and ordered them to build houses there, which were mostly wooden. He also required them to reinforce the embankment in front of their homes by driving evenly spaced wooden piles, placing sturdy boards in between them, backfilling the wall with earth, and painting the face of the boards with black and white stripes. Later, in 1718, the owners were ordered to pave the portion of the embankment in front of their homes.

Under Catherine I and Peter II, the area became run down, but in June 1732 Anna issued a decree requiring nobles, on pain of punishment for noncompliance, to rebuild the embankment with stone houses and reinforce the embankment in front of them. Free plots of land were also granted for new construction. A 1738 decree required the destruction of all wooden buildings on that embankment. The nobles reluctantly complied, but since most were already comfortably housed elsewhere in the city and did not want to move, they leased the new homes out to wealthy foreign merchants. (At the time, foreigners were not allowed to purchase houses.) The favored tenants were English, because in 1735 Anna had issued a decree designed to foster better trade relations with England, which exempted English merchants from the quartering of troops (to which both Russians and foreigners were generally subject) in their homes. By leasing to the English, the owners could avoid having troops live in and perhaps spoil their new mansions. As a result, over time a thriving English settlement developed in this area complete with shops, taverns, the English Embassy, the famous English Club, and an Anglican Church designed by Giacomo Quarenghi. It was in this English community that the city's first Masonic lodge (foreigners only), with the Scottish General James Keith as Grand Master, was established in 1739 or 1740.[37] As a result, the area became known as the English Embankment. (Known in Soviet times as Red Fleet Embankment, the original name was restored in 1994 on the occasion of Queen Elizabeth's visit to the city.) By the 19th century it was perhaps the most fashionable and elite area of town, surpassing even Nevsky Prospect, and was the center of grand entertainments both on land and water. In Anna's time, nobles such as Ostermann, Trubetskoi, Naryshkin, Golitsyn, Dolgoruki, and the architect Eropkin owned houses there.

The Lower Embankment was also the site of the first bridge over the Neva, St. Isaac's Bridge, erected in 1727 on pontoons while Menshikov still held effective power. Not so coincidentally, it connected Menshikov's palace (directly across the river) with many of his profitable shops near the current site of the Senate and Synod building. The bridge was lost to the river's current within a year, and a new one built by Anna in 1732 suffered the same fate. A replacement was erected by the naval engineer Solovev in 1733, and this one would last for nearly a century. All three bridges were made of pontoons linked together with rope, on which a wooden decking was placed. The bridge had to be disassembled before each winter in order to avoid destruction by the ice—a bridge was unnecessary in the winter anyway—and was reassembled each spring.

Anna's selection of the Admiralty side for her palace made it inevitable that her development of the city would focus on that side. The initial impetus came when Anna's court, growing in size, could not feasibly be housed within the royal palace but had to be located in the region immediately to the south, which had to be redeveloped. But this region was the site of a number of *sloboda* of tradesmen, including the Morskaya, Greek, Novaya, and Perevedenskaya. They lived in closely packed wooden homes located on crooked, muddy streets. The area was an eyesore, not befitting what should be a splendorous center of the city surrounding the royal residence. But among these groups was a high level of discontent, and Anna was afraid to precipitate unrest.

Anna's dilemma was resolved fortuitously in 1736 and 1737 when several disastrous fires swept through the Admiralty side of the city. The stone or brick buildings were concentrated along the Neva embankment above the Winter Palace and below the Admiralty, on Nemetskaya Street (now Millionaya) running parallel one block to the south from the Winter Palace to the Summer Garden, and on Lugovaya Street bordering Admiralty Lug. The rest of the Admiralty side was built in wood. Firefighting measures, though formally in place, were not as rigorously organized as they had been under Peter the Great.[38] The first of the two major conflagrations, in August 1736, reportedly was started through the negligence of servants at the residence of the Persian ambassador. According to one version, the servants were smoking a pipe in the courtyard when a spark fell on some straw which caught fire,[39] while a contemporary source believes that they may have been conducting an ancient (i.e., pre-Islamic) Persian fire worship ritual around a large fire.[40] In any event, the blaze erupted at around noon and raged through the night. It destroyed about 1,000 houses and many of the best shops in the city, in an area stretching roughly from Green Bridge to behind the Admiralty down to the Kryukov canal. Two other major fires broke out in June 1737 in an area upriver from the Admiralty in the Greek *sloboda* and along Nemetskaya Street and over to the Moika up to Tsaritsyn Lug. Among the destroyed or damaged homes were those of many notables, including Tsarevna Elizabeth, Prince Kantemir, Field Marshal Trubetskoi, Count Apraxin, General Ushakov, Prince Cherkassky, and several foreign ambassadors. The British Ambassador, whose home barely escaped ruin, wrote:

> My house, which is in the finest street in the town, was in such great danger that I was obliged to move all my furniture, which has suffered very much by being carried away in such great haste. Nobody can imagine the continual frights we are in for fear of being burnt, and the great misery vast numbers of people are reduced to by the late fire. Though several persons have been taken on suspicion of being incendiaries, as yet none have been convicted of it.[41]

Indeed, many considered the latter fires suspicious and suspected arson,[42] but their cause was never determined and no one was ever arrested or punished.

The fires were a blessing in disguise because they afforded an opportunity to re-design and rebuild the city's center in stone, which in turn provided an opportunity to reorganize the city's governance and administration. In order to organize the re-building of the city and carry out other government functions, the Commission on the Construction of St. Petersburg was created, with the Russian architect Peter Eropkin as its chief. Eropkin had been sent to Italy for training by Peter the Great, where he had remained for nearly 10 years and thoroughly learned his art. When he returned in 1725, he was put in charge of the construction of several buildings and worked on canal construction and water drainage. Well read, he had a vast library, translated Palladio's works into Russian, edited Russian architectural treatises, and taught architecture. As head of the Commission, he oversaw the preparation and drawing of the general plans for the incinerated and new regions of town, including streets, squares, and public and private buildings. The remaining members of the Commission were also all Russians, including Zemtsov and Korobov. In fact, al-though Rastrelli as court architect held many important commissions, under Anna the city's development, construction, and architecture was under the control of Rus-sians, which had been made possible by Peter's efforts to train them.

The replanning work continued through Anna's reign, and it would be left mainly to Elizabeth to implement the plans. According to the Soviet architectural historian Bronstein, this effort had no equal in the worldwide history of city plan-ning up to that time.[43] Among the Commission's other achievements, it conferred the first official names upon the city's streets, in 1738. The Commission also di-vided the city into several administrative regions run by regional offices of the po-lice, each of which was responsible for keeping public order, firefighting, and pro-viding amenities in its region. The *slobodi* were legally terminated. Eropkin also used the Commission as a basis for establishing formalized institutional architectural training within Russia, and himself taught students.

Under the Commission's direction, the tradesmen were moved out of the Ad-miralty region to outlying areas. Similarly, in light of Anna's concern for conserva-tion of nature and trees, she ordered that no further factories be built in town, and many existing ones were closed and relocated. Henceforth, the city center was developed first and foremost as Russia's capital in a planned manner, in stone, and became the residence of the court, aristocracy, and prominent merchants. The Commission's principal design concept for the central region was the radial (or "spoke") design of three long prospects running from the Admiralty away from the Neva.[44] This pattern had emerged under Peter I, beginning with the Grand Perspective. Under Anna, however, in 1738 it became a formal centerpiece of the city plan. Complementing the Grand Perspective were Middle Perspective and the Voznesensky Perspective. These three prospects made the Admiralty, and in particular its tall golden spire, the focal point of the city's design and skyline. From anywhere along them, no matter how far away, the Admiralty's spire could be seen.

Under Anna's scheme, the existing portion of Middle Perspective was to be straightened, and a new portion extended across the Moika and Fontanka to connect with Zagorodnaya Street at the city limits. At its terminus the Semenovsky Regiment would be quartered. The name of the Middle Perspective eventually changed to Admiralty Prospect, and in the late 18th century it became known as Gorokhovaya Street ("street of peas"), which name survives today. (Under the Soviets it was named after Felix Dzerzhinsky, the head of the infamous *Cheka*.) The name Gorokhovaya came from the name of a merchant (some say Count[45]) Harrach (which resembled the Russian word *gorokh,* "pea"), who in 1756 built on that street a stone building containing a well-known shop.[46] The street previously known informally as the Third Perspective was also straightened and lengthened, and at its end was housed the Izmailovsky Regiment. In 1738, this street was officially renamed Voznesensky Perspective because on it was located the Church of the Ascension (*Voznesenie*) of our Lord. In time, the segment of the street near the Regiment became known as Izmailovsky Prospect.[47] The deployment of the regiments along these prospects was strategic, as the monarchy depended upon their support on a moment's notice; hence the well-constructed bridges across the canals along these streets. Anna, and later Elizabeth, made sure the Guards were well taken care of. They were housed in regular homes together with their families, which resulted in whole regions laid out in a rigid grid pattern still visible today.

It was the Grand Perspective, in 1738 renamed Nevsky Perspective, which received the most attention. Before Anna, it was out of the way and undeveloped, so plots along it were available for construction. The city's need for foreign and Russian churches provided one opportunity. In 1727, permission had been granted to construct an Evangelical Church and school, and under Anna permissions were granted to construct French, Swedish, Dutch, and Catholic churches. The Dutch church stood on the corner of Nevsky and the Moika by Green Bridge (now Nevsky No. 20), and since then the site has always been under the control of or associated with the Dutch. Since these churches were for foreign denominations, the Russian treasury could not finance their construction, so their pastors took an inventive approach. Once the sites were allocated, they obtained permission to construct temporary wooden buildings (an exception, since wooden construction was generally prohibited), where the pastors both lived and held services, taking up collections from their congregations. Once the churches collected enough money to construct a stone church, the wooden churches were razed and the permanent churches were erected.[48] A large number of foreign churches is a rarity for the main street of any city, but Nevsky was exceptional. When Alexandre Dumas visited St. Petersburg in the 1860s, he called Nevsky Prospect the "street of religious toleration."[49]

As for a Russian church on Nevsky, Anna decreed that the famous icon of the Blessed Mother of Kazan, which had been brought to Petersburg in 1710 and kept in Trinity Cathedral on the Petersburg side, be moved to the Grand Perspective into a newly built church consecrated in 1737. The church was named the Church of the Holy Virgin of Kazan, and lasted until Kazan Cathedral was built on the site under Alexander I. This gesture symbolized Anna's intention to develop the Admiralty side and make Nevsky Prospect more than just the road out of town.

Another opportunity for developing Nevsky was markets. The earlier Gostiny Dvor built by Mattarnovy in 1719 by Green Bridge over the Moika had become too small, and in any event was consumed by the great fire in 1736. The Commission decided to build a new one by the northeast corner of Anichkov Bridge, which later became impossible because Empress Elizabeth built her labyrinth there. Meanwhile, a temporary Gostiny Dvor was built in 1737 at the intersection of Nevsky and what is now called Sadovaya ("Garden") Street (then called the New Perspective). It was wooden, but the traders were soon obligated to construct new trading stalls in masonry according to an approved plan.

Sennaya ("Haymarket") Square, made famous by Dostoevsky, has its origins in Anna's reign. This outdoor market was established in haste in 1736 after the Morskoi Market near Admiralty Lug was consumed in the great fire and was relocated to behind the new wooden Gostiny Dvor. Here traders sold not only food products but also firewood and hay, which presented a danger of fire. The worried traders in Gostiny Dvor complained, and Sennaya Square was relocated, initially near the current Yusupov Garden and in the 1740s to its present location.[50]

On Vasilievsky Island, Anna did follow through on Peter I's plan to locate various government and other official buildings there. The Twelve Colleges and Kunstkamera were completed, as was Trezzini's Gostiny Dvor, after which the city's original Gostiny Dvor on Trinity Square was razed. The Customs House was also transferred to Vasilievsky Island, temporarily (in 1730) to the former Naryshkin home on the Malaya Neva and in 1733 to a building of its own. On the *strelka* of the island the large "Illumination Theater" was reconstructed, on which illuminations were displayed and fireworks were set off during celebrations for spectators at the Winter Palace. Menshikov's Palace had been confiscated by the state, and was now used to house the new Corps of Cadets. Like Peter, however, Anna was less successful in settling the island, despite decrees forbidding landowners from disposing of their homes there and calling for the construction of new houses.

Thanks to Anna's return to the city and her efforts to develop it, its population grew rapidly. Whereas the population had stood at approximately 40,000 by Peter I's death prior to its downturn under Peter II, by 1737 it had grown to approximately 70,000,[51] and the figure was of course higher by Anna's death in 1741.

THE COURT AND SOCIAL LIFE

In Anna's Petersburg, as in Peter the Great's time, the city's main social life and culture revolved around the imperial household. But it was Anna who created Russia's first true imperial court on the European model. A chamberlain's office was created under Biron, and a complicated hierarchy of court officials and attendants, right down to large numbers of pages, heyducks, and footmen was organized. Soon the court was many times larger than Peter's. The court's style was defined by the personalities of Biron and Anna. Biron loved luxury and pretense and urged Anna to acquire it, to which Anna was receptive. Before becoming Empress she had lived a sad life and always lacked money, so it was not surprising that she sought refuge from her past through extravagance and diversions. She strove to make her court the most brilliant in Europe, and in some respects she succeeded.

First came lavish dress. Anna ordered that the court dress only in happy, bright colors such as light blue, pink, pale green, and yellow, and no one was allowed to appear at court twice in the same outfit. This required importing huge quantities of silks, brocades, gold embroidery, and other fine cloth, and with them tailors and seamstresses. The British Ambassador Rondeau observed, "I cannot well describe how magnificent this court is in clothes. I never saw such heaps of gold and silver lace laid upon cloth. . . . I cannot imagine that this magnificence will last many years, for if it should, it must ruin most part of the Russian nobility, for several families are obliged to sell their estates to buy fine clothes."[52] Algarotti noted that "special care is taken at Lyons to put gold and silver by the whole ounces into the tissues intended for Russia."[53] As a result, Rondeau reported, "Your Excellency cannot imagine how magnificent this Court is since the present reign, although there is not a shilling in the Treasury and nobody is paid."[54] Foreign diplomats complained that their allowances did not permit them to maintain themselves as required, and their correspondence was filled with pleas for more funds. The men were nearly as affected as the women. Uniforms were required of schoolboys, the Corps of Cadets, and even of foreign diplomats for their work. It was forbidden to appear at court in uniform; separate court dress was required. Anyone appearing at Biron's riding school on Mondays, Thursdays, and Saturdays, when the Empress also was present, had to wear a uniform of yellow buffalo skin embroidered with silver galloon, with a blue vest and all the trimmings.[55] The palace servants likewise were richly attired, initially in green laced with gold and later in yellow and black velvet laced with silver.[56]

To accompany the new dress one needed new hairstyles. Many Parisian modistes and coiffeurs were imported, but there were not enough of them. They were in such demand that before balls many women had no choice but to have their dresses sewn on and hair done up as many as three days in advance and then sleep upright in chairs to avoid ruining their hairdos. Of course, expensive jewelry also was needed, so finished jewels, precious stones, and jewelers were also imported.

Despite these efforts, the overall result was uneven in a country where taste was undeveloped and access to all the finishing necessities was difficult. The sights were often comic. As Christoph von Manstein observed:

> The richest coat would sometimes be worn together with the vilest dressed wig; or you might see a beautiful piece of stuff spoiled by some clumsy tailor; or if there was nothing amiss in the dress, the equipage would be a failure. A man splendidly dressed would appear in a miserable coach, drawn by the wretchedest hacks. The same want of taste reigned in the furniture and neatness of their houses. On one side, you might see gold and silver plate in heaps, on the other a shocking dirtiness. The dress of the ladies was on par with that of the men; for one well-dressed woman, you might see ten frightfully disfigured.[57]

There were also new styles in furniture and interior decoration, particularly since homes were becoming larger and intended as sites of social gatherings. Fancy English and French mahogany and walnut furniture now replaced the primitive oak furniture typical under Peter. The walls were adorned with wallpaper, mirrors, paintings, and linen or damask hangings. Tapestries again became popular, especially since they could be produced locally and relatively cheaply.

Anna held court twice a week, on Thursdays and Sundays, at which she received officials, guests, and foreign ambassadors. Her remaining time was spent in her chambers either alone with Biron or at court entertainments (which Biron rarely attended). Other than holidays or special celebrations, the highlight of social life was the royal balls, which in the cold months were held twice a week in the Winter Palace. After some brief socializing, dancing would begin. The dances were not only Western; Russian folk dances were on the program too, much to the delight of the foreign guests. After the dancing, all would dine, which was followed by more dancing. Anna rarely danced herself, but instead liked to observe and talk with the guests. One remarkable colloquy occurred with visiting Chinese envoys. When they entered the room, observed Mrs. Rondeau, they "seemed to observe everything with an air of curious rather than ignorant people."[58] After greeting them, Anna asked the first who he thought was the prettiest woman there. "It would be difficult in a starlight night to say which star was the brightest," but observing that Anna expected a straight answer, he bowed to Anna's rival, Tsarevna Elizabeth, and said that "among such a number of fine women, he thought her the handsomest, and if she had not quite so large eyes, nobody could see her and live." Maintaining her composure with difficulty, Anna then asked what, among the things they saw in Russia that differed from their own customs, appeared the most extraordinary. "Seeing a woman on the throne," he answered. Anna finally inquired whether the masquerade did not appear odd to them. "No," they answered, "for all was masquerade to them."[59]

The balls and celebrations frequently included illuminations and fireworks displays, often accompanied by cannon fire from the Fortress and naval flotillas. Such shows were staged on the Empress's birthday, name day, coronation, New Year's Day, and on special occasions such as to celebrate the capture of Azov from the Turks in 1739. The festivities often went on for several nights. For the larger celebrations the illuminations were not restricted to the Illumination Theater on the *strelka* of Vasilievsky Island but also were laid out on the walls of the Fortress across the river from the palace, as well as on the adjacent Admiralty. On their walls were depicted allegorical symbols or written the names of the honored, all ultimately in praise of the Empress. Often all Petersburgers joined in by lighting candles or lamps in their windows, so that the whole city would be lit. Accidents sometimes occurred. Once fireballs from a rocket crashed through the window of the Winter Palace where Elizabeth was watching the display, and the shattered glass cut her on the forehead by her right eye. Fortunately, the resulting scars were hardly noticeable.

In the winter of 1736 Anna introduced a new pastime to the court: tobogganing. Wooden chutes were constructed either from the tops of houses or from specially built towers on the Neva anywhere from 30 to 50 feet in height, onto which was poured water, which froze into a layer of ice. The members of the court had to mount flat sleds and hurtle down the chute. If the occupant was unbalanced or if the sled hit a slight bump, he or she would be thrown off head over heels, which of course was the highlight of the fun. The Russians loved it, but the more sensitive foreign ladies were horrified. "I was terrified out of my wits," wrote Mrs. Rondeau, "for fear of being obliged to go down this shocking place, for I had not only the dread of breaking my neck, but of being exposed to indecency too frightful to think of without horror."[60] Fortunately for her, she was granted a reprieve on account of being pregnant.

As under Peter I and in other European courts, Anna's court had its share of dwarfs, hunchbacks, cripples, buffoons, and other humans deemed curious or entertaining. Her court was more notable, however, for the debasement of several members of ancient Moscow boyar families against whom she continued to wreak revenge, including the Apraxins, Volkonskys, and Golitsyns. The duties of these unfortunates included looking after Anna's pet white rabbit, lining up in rows and kicking each other, pulling each other's hair, taking part in fistfights, going on all fours and braying like donkeys, mounting one another and engaging in bloody jousting matches, and squatting in rows and cackling like hens.

The unluckiest of these victims was Prince Mikhail Golitsyn, whose family had been most associated with the Conditions. This Prince, Anna learned, had married a Roman Catholic while in Italy. This offense provided the excuse for

Anna to force him to join the court in the mock role of official cupbearer of the Empress for *kvass*, after which he became known as Prince Kvassnik. He was later demoted to the rank of page and given the task of sitting like a hen on eggs for hours at a time in a specially made basket and cackling like a hen. When Golitsyn's wife died, Anna did not relent but used this as an excuse to force him to marry again in what would be her coup de grâce. "This time," Anna said, "I will choose you a bride myself. And what is more you shall have a wedding the like of which has never been seen, and I shall pay for it out of my own purse."[61] Anna's choice was an elderly Kalmuk serving woman, as ugly as could be found, known as Anna Buzheninova (after her favorite food, *buzhenina*, a peasant pork recipe).

The marriage was celebrated in January as the main social event and entertainment of the winter of 1739–40, for which no effort or expense was spared. Since the marriage was held just after Anna's celebration of her victory over the Turks, the event was arranged with a political purpose to impress foreign dignitaries with the wide range and variety of the Empress's dominions. Much in the tradition of Noah's Ark, she ordered her regional governors to dispatch couples representing the various native peoples from Russia's provinces, including Finns, Lapps, Tartars, Cossacks, Samoyeds, Bashkirs, and Kalmucks. The ceremonies began with a long procession to the church. At its head rode the bride and groom in a cage strapped to the back of an elephant. They were followed by a parade of the representative couples from Russia's native peoples, riding in carts and sleighs drawn by a bizzare assortment of reindeer, dogs, wolves, bears, goats, pigs, and oxen. After the marriage ceremony a large banquet was held at Biron's riding school where everyone's national dish and beverage was served, which was followed by dancing where everyone's national dance was performed to native music. Finally, late at night, the bridal couple, once again in their cage on top of the elephant, were escorted to their specially built wedding abode.

This structure was one of the shortest lived architectural marvels in history. It was an ice palace constructed on the frozen Neva in front of the Winter Palace measuring 80 feet long, 23 feet wide, and 33 feet high. The ice was carefully selected for transparency and the blocks were cut precisely to fit together seamlessly, joined by instantly freezing water so that the house appeared to be made from a single block of ice. The door and window frames were colored to resemble bluish-green marble, as was a row of pillars along the roof. The palace's historian, George William Kraft of the Academy of Sciences, wrote that "it was infinitely more beautiful than if it had been constructed of the finest marble. . . . The transparency and bluish tone of the ice gave it the look of some precious stone, rarer than any marble."[62] The window panes were made of the thinnest possible ice and were essentially transparent. Outside, the palace was surrounded by a balustrade of ice columns topped with balls of ice. In front of the balustrade stood ice cannons and mortars mounted on ice carriages. These were guarded by two ice dolphins, an ice elephant ridden by an ice

Persian, and two ice Persian sentries. Next to them on pedestals stood two hollow transparent ice pyramids lit from the inside by paper lanterns on which were depicted odd figures which may have been obscene. Behind the balustrade, in ice pots, stood ice trees, in the branches of which roosted ice birds, all of which were painted in their natural colors. Behind them was an ice stairway flanked by ice dolphins leading to the entrance, over which was a frontispiece decorated by four ice putti. At night the palace was illuminated by ground fireworks and torches.

The entrance led into a foyer which divided the building into two halves. On one side was a drawing room, in which were arranged a sofa, statues, and a card table with cards, all made of ice, on which stood a working ice clock, the mechanism of which could be seen through the ice "cabinet," and a dining room complete with ice dishes and an ice tea service. On the other side was a bedroom with an ice-curtained four-poster ice bed, on which were an ice mattress, ice pillows and carved ice bedclothes and nightcaps; on the floor were placed ice bed slippers. The windows had ice curtains, and in the corner was an ice fireplace with ice logs, which for short periods actually "burned" using a petroleum mixture poured over them. Adjacent were a dressing room and a lavatory complete with ice toilet utensils.

As the procession approached with the court and public watching, the ice cannons fired wooden cannon balls and the ice dolphins breathed fire. The ice elephant turned out to be a fountain (utilizing a plumbing system laid from the nearby Admiralty), a jet of water streaming from its trunk high into the air while a man hidden inside the beast blew a trumpet to imitate the sound of an elephant trumpeting. At night, a petroleum mixture was used so that the jet was flaming. The pair was escorted to the bedroom, stripped naked and placed on the ice bed to survive the night. Guards were placed at the entrance to prevent escape.

Afterwards the palace was opened to the public and proved so popular that it had to be ringed by a fence to prevent overcrowding. Adjacent was a bathhouse made from ice logs, also open to the public, which could be heated and on occasion was used. The structure remained intact until March before beginning to melt, but even into the summer some of its walls could still be seen submerged in the Neva.

While there is much to criticize about Anna's court, she set a better example in her private life, which in fact could be favorably compared with her popular successor, Elizabeth. While Anna spent much time at frivolous activities such as cards, she was relatively free from vices and drank little; thus, drinking was moderate at her court entertainments. Anna rose early in the day and was ready for business by nine. She would dine privately with Biron (and his wife) around noon, and on days when she did not hunt or there were no court entertainments she would spend the afternoons and evenings with Biron or her maids. Much of the official entertainment was left to her ministers. To cheer her up, she often had her girls sing to her for hours, usually simple peasant songs.

Anna's personal passion was animals and hunting. A crack shot since her youth, she hunted whenever she could. And for those days when she could not, she kept loaded guns at her windows both in the city and in the country in order to take aim at passing birds. At Peterhof, she had a special pavilion erected, called the "Temple," from which she shot game driven past her. (Such methods were repeated in Soviet times for Brezhnev.) She also built a large aviary in which birds were let loose for her to shoot. To prevent depletion of herds, Anna introduced many conservation measures, prohibited private hunting within 20 miles of the capital, and imported animals from elsewhere in Russia. Her collection of hunting dogs came to rival Biron's collection of horses.

Anna also put a large variety of birds and beasts on exhibit for the court and the public. Her foremost passion was birds. In and around her palaces she had vast collections of domestic and exotic birds, including peacocks, parrots, canaries, finches, nightingales, even ostriches. Smaller birds flew freely about indoors. Pagoda-shaped aviaries were maintained in the Summer Garden for the exhibit of exotic birds. Anna also loved to keep other animals at home, including dogs, monkeys, and rabbits. In the city, a zoo was built in 1736 on the Fontanka near where the circus is now located. It was called the *Slonovy Dvor* ("Elephant's Home") because it featured a gift of the Persian Shah: an elephant together with its attendants. According to the records, the elephant consumed not only grain, hay, and sugar, but 340 buckets of wine and 60 buckets of vodka per year,[63] but history does not record how much of this was consumed by the attendants rather than the beast. The elephant was taken for walks nearby, usually along Nevsky, and attracted large crowds of onlookers. Learning of the beast's popularity, the Shah sent 14 more elephants in 1741 with his embassy to St. Petersburg,[64] for which the zoo had to be expanded, and the Anichkov and other nearby bridges had to be reinforced or rebuilt in order to withstand their weight. Once one elephant escaped and roamed all the way to Vasilievsky Island, where it wreaked havoc in a neighborhood before being caught.[65] When Empress Elizabeth had Rastrelli build her wooden Summer Palace on the current site of the Mikhailovsky Castle, she also built her famous labyrinth behind it, and therefore in 1744 the *Slonovy Dvor* was relocated further south along Nevsky by the present Suvorov Prospect. That *Dvor* lasted until 1778, but its memory remained for over a century, as the street on which it was located continued to be named Elephant Street; only at the end of the 19th century was it renamed Suvorov Prospect, after the famous generalissimo. Nearby Caravannaya Street derives its name from the arrival of the Shah's caravan, and the attendants named their residence Caravan-Sarai.[66]

EDUCATION, LEARNING, AND CULTURE

Anna was not well educated, but she was keen to be viewed as following in Peter's footsteps and needed educated Russians in government service, so she made education, at least for the nobility, a priority. Noble families were clamoring for new institutions to educate their children in the new Western culture and manner, and thus demanded curricula that transcended the technical disciplines. Anna responded in 1732 by founding the Corps of Cadets to educate the young nobility. It had both military and civil faculties, but in both cases offered a broad education in subjects such as languages, music, mathematics, history, geography, military science, riding, fencing, drawing, and dancing. The Italian composer Francesco Araja directed the music curriculum, while the French dance master Jean Baptiste Landé taught the dancing (the most popular class except for German language), and his dancers performed in the royal theater beside the more experienced Italians and would replace the foreigners as they left. The number of students in 1733 was already nearly 250.

Even before returning to St. Petersburg, Anna increased funding for the Academy of Sciences, over the opposition of many who failed to see its value. The increase, however, was not enough to upgrade the Academy's facilities and laboratories to Western standards. In contrast to the disinterest at home, scholars and scientists abroad took great interest in the St. Petersburg Academy's work. One Swiss member of the Academy, upon returning home, observed: "I have not words enough to describe how eagerly people everywhere inquire about the St. Petersburg transactions," and Condorcet described Leonard Euler's *Mechanica*, published by the Academy in 1736, as "the first Great work in which analysis has been applied to the science of motion."[67] The Academy also performed useful practical work. It published helpful historical information about China in advance of a visit of a Chinese delegation, assisted in the allegorical composition of fireworks displays, and prepared an itinerary and maps for Bering's second Kamchatka expedition which began in 1734 and was responsible for the discovery of Alaska. The Academy also began to publish its proceedings, called the *Komentarii*, and took over publication of the St. Petersburg *Vedomosti* ("Gazette"), a newspaper published in Russian and German that carried items of general interest and official court and government announcements. The Academy also published the *Primechania* ("Notes"), a monthly journal intended mainly for members of the court, government servants, and students which contained light articles on science, etiquette, music, the arts, recreation, and biographies.[68]

In 1735, the Academy sponsored the Russian Council to stimulate the development of Russian literature. Its initiator and secretary was the Russian poet Vasily Trediakovsky (1703–69), who had traveled in Holland and Germany and studied three years at the Sorbonne during 1726–30, after which he returned to St. Petersburg, made a name for himself by translating a famous French novel, and became Anna's court poet. In 1735 Trediakovsky presented to the Academy a treatise proposing a new system of versification of Russian poetry, and also made proposals to incorporate ordinary Russian speech into literature and produced philological works. Many of his ideas were later developed by Mikhail Lomonosov, considered the founder of modern Russian language.

Lomonosov (1711–65), a giant in Russian literature, academics, science, and the arts and the leading figure in the Russian Enlightenment, got his start under Anna. Born a peasant in the Far North, he learned to read and made his way to study at the Slavonic-Latin Academy in Moscow. In 1735 the St. Petersburg Academy decided to transfer a select group of top students to its Gymnasium for scientific training, and Lomonosov was one of the chosen. He arrived in St. Petersburg on New Year's Day 1736, but later that year he was already on his way to Germany for education in mining engineering. While there, however, he soon mastered other disciplines of the sciences, was heavily influenced by the rationalist Christian Wolf, and became interested in language, poetry, and literature as well. Lomonosov took with him to Germany Trediakovsky's treatise on Russian versification, and in 1739 he produced his own *Epistle on the Rules of Russian Versification*, which in eight short pages (accompanied by a sample ode) elaborated the system of Russian syllabotonic versification as it has been practiced ever since.

Another key figure was the historian and satirist Vasily Tatishchev (1686–1750), who had worked under Peter the Great, and as a Guards officer helped bring Anna Ioannovna to the throne. A model of Peter's new man, Tatishchev was one of Prokopovich's "Learned Guard" who promoted secular culture and thought.[69] His *Conversation on the Usefulness of Science and Educational Institutions*, based on the arguments and ideas of Grotius, Pufendorf, and other European thinkers, is considered the Russian first systematic defense of the secular way of life.[70]

But perhaps the most interesting literary figure and man of letters during Anna's reign was Tatishchev's friend Antiokh Kantemir (1708–44), also a member of the Learned Guard. He actually spent most of his time during Anna's reign abroad, but from there he worked extensively with the Academy, and the city featured prominently in his famous satires. He was the son of the erudite hospodar (viceroy) of Moldavia who fled to Russia in 1711 after Peter the Great's Pruth campaign collapsed. He was well educated and familiar with the classics, and is said to have known six or seven foreign languages, including Latin and Greek. A translation of a French work on the Copernican system and his first satires attracted the attention and acquaintance of Feofan Prokopovich and other supporters of Petrine policies in the capital. Anna appointed him as ambassador to England (1732–38) and then France (1738–44), where he mingled with leading French writers and intellectuals such as Montesquieu. Unfortunately he died in France in 1744. His nine annotated satires styled after those of Horace were biting caricatures of universal stereotypes and traditional Muscovite Russian traits and prejudices which impeded reform and progress, as well as of the hardships of a Petersburg courtier. While these works were known to and circulated freely among the upper crust, they were considered too critical for general publication in Russia during his lifetime. He also wrote fables, epigrams, erotic verse, odes, and poetry, including an unfinished epic poem about Peter the Great, called the *Petride*. While his writings did support Westernization in Russia, their aim was more generally to promote toleration, reason, classical learning, education, and the importance of good works as the measure of a person's worth.

Other Petersburg culture in Anna's reign—music, theater, opera, and ballet—either served as or was built around court entertainment. Peter I had brought drama theater to his city, but it did not survive. Anna had to start anew, and it was under her auspices that the permanent roots of St. Petersburg's traditions in the performing arts were established, and in the case of ballet it was to her reign that the origins of Russia's school of ballet can be traced. At the time, such arts were viewed more as court spectacles and entertainments than as high culture. Anna herself was not well read or highly cultured, but she wanted to bring to Russia the best entertainments that Europe could offer and to match or outdo rival courts in the West. Doing so demanded a high level of talent and training, and consequently the institutions to develop it, all of which Russia lacked. Anna began this process, and with it a more discriminating taste and appreciation of high art emerged.

Anna had been exposed to theater and court music in her youth thanks to Peter, and she was well aware of their popularity in the West. Thus, it took her little over a month after her coronation (while she was still in Moscow) to decide to establish a court theater. The easiest way was to import an entire troupe, and so she appealed to Frederick Augustus II, Elector of Saxony and King of Poland, who maintained at his lavish court a famously large number of actors, dancers, singers, and musicians consisting of several troupes in various locations, some of which had earlier performed for Anna in Mitau. Augustus agreed to lend Anna a group of 36 players, mostly Italian, from his Warsaw troupe. Their first performance, in Moscow on March 9, 1731, consisted of a comedy together with musical and comic interludes *(intermezzi)* and was deemed a success. When asked what she thought, Anna remarked that she was extremely pleased and that, since she does not understand Italian, she hoped to have the plays translated into Russian so that she could "better understand the subject of the pieces and the gestures that accompany them." That summer the troupe staged numerous performances, and its musicians provided the music at the almost daily court social events. Anna found such players indispensable, and by 1735 she had formed in St. Petersburg a resident troupe, again mostly Italians. Theater, mainly comedic, became a regular entertainment for the court.[71] The performers would remain Italian for some time, as Italian comedy was the most popular theater in Europe at the time. A Russian national theater would be founded only under Elizabeth.

For the performance of drama, opera, and ballet, Anna needed theaters. Early in Anna's reign, the theater built in 1723 by Peter the Great near Green Bridge collapsed from erosion of its foundations, somewhat prophetically, immediately after a performance of the ballet *The Destruction of Babylon*. Performances were temporarily moved to a reconstructed riding school further up Nevsky near to where Kazan

Cathedral now stands. By 1736, however, two new theaters had been built, one in the Summer Garden for summertime performances outdoors, and the other in the Winter Palace, which became known as the House of Comedy.[72] The Winter Palace theater was large—Algarotti estimated it as twice the size of the Paris Opera—and accommodated an audience of a thousand, and it was heated in the winter by eight large stoves. Although it was richly decorated, the guests sat on hard wooden benches. The acoustics were said to be excellent, as were the performances. At this time, the court's entertainments were the only expressions of drama and music in Russia other than in church and in folk songs. Performances were rarely open to the public, but the court, the nobility, and well-dressed foreigners attended for free as invited guests. Anna and her entourage attended religiously; only hunting took priority and could keep her away.

The Winter Palace theater was inaugurated in January 1736 by the performance of an opera, the first ever performed in Russia. Entitled *La Forza dell' Amore e dell' Odio*, it was composed by the Italian Francesco Araja to a libretto by Bonacci. It was actually composed in Italy a couple years before his arrival, but it was premiered in Russia and Araja let the Russians assume it was created there. The first opera actually composed in Russia was Araja's *Semiramide* of 1737. Araja, born in Naples in 1700, was a successful composer of operas in his homeland, and notable performances of his work were staged in Naples, Florence, Rome, and Venice. In Rome he attracted the attention of the Russian ambassador, who in 1735 offered him the position of director of the new St. Petersburg opera company that Anna was forming. In St. Petersburg, his company, about 70 in number, consisted not only of Italians but also of many Russians, including many young noblemen, mainly Cadets who were his students. He and other star performers, especially the castrati and female singers, were highly paid. His first Russian effort, the above-mentioned *La Forza dell' Amore e dell' Odio*, was a lavish production but was received coolly by the audience and was staged only twice. Its distinguishing feature was ballets rather than *intermezzi* between the acts. Araja remained the leading light of Russian opera through most of Elizabeth's reign. Under Anna, opera was chiefly a foreign import to be appreciated by Russians but not performed by them.

Not so with ballet. Opera, so far sung in foreign languages, often left audiences cold, but ballet had a universal appeal. It required no translation, had more action and lively music, and could be combined with Russian folk traditions. It could appeal even to the relatively illiterate, of which there were still many, including at court. It quickly became the most popular of the performing arts.

The origin of ballet in St. Petersburg goes back to slightly before Anna, in 1727, when performances were held in the theater by the Green Bridge.[73] At that point all dancers were Russian under the tutelage of Otto Fürst. Anna sought to upgrade dancing and ballet in the capital by inviting notable foreigners to teach. In quick succession, Philippe Martin Bazancourt, Johann Jacob Schmidt, and Konrad Menk were put in charge of teaching this art, but with unsatisfactory results. Then a

Frenchman, Jean Baptiste Landé, was invited to St. Petersburg in 1734 on a three-year contract, and this time it worked. One of his functions was to teach ballroom dancing and ensure the smooth running of dances at court functions. He reportedly once said that nowhere else in Europe had he seen the minuet danced with such grace. His pupils included Princess Elizabeth, other members of the court, lesser nobility, and, during Elizabeth's reign, the future Catherine the Great. He also trained other pupils specifically for the ballet, both as soloists and for the corps. At the core of this group of dancers were a dozen talented amateur dancers from the Corps de Cadets, where he taught. He also choreographed ballets performed for the court to great approbation.

Landé's success enabled him to propose to Anna founding a separate ballet school under his direction. Landé's proposal was calculated to be modest. He requested only to be allowed to train 12 young Russians, 6 of each sex, in order to create "a ballet for theatrical dances." As a nod to the court preferences, he stressed that he would train the Russian students to act in comedies to be performed in Russian and to combine their dancing skills with those of comic acting. After just one year, he claimed, the students would dance as well as the Cadets; after three years, they would achieve perfection. Anna approved the proposal, and the question of who would be selected as pupils then arose. Landé suggested that "the long and strenuous training would be burdensome for the children of the nobility," an opinion that Biron shared. Therefore, Anna chose the 6 boys and 6 girls, all under 12 years old, from amongst the children of court servants. Both teacher and students were housed in Peter's old Winter Palace, together with the artists of the Italian companies. The school, founded in 1738, flourished until Landé's death in 1747.[74] Thus was planted the seed of Russia's hegemony in world ballet.

Music was not confined to a supporting role for stage performances and court entertainments, however. Music was the one art of which Anna had some understanding, she promoted it as an art form in itself, and beginning in 1733 she held concerts at court twice a week.[75] At first, she had no experienced Russian classical musicians, so she had to import them. She created the first regular classical orchestra in Russia,[76] which she began organizing in Moscow prior to her return to Petersburg. She dispatched her musical director, the Viennese-trained Prussian conductor Johaan Hübner, to Germany to recruit top musicians. When to Biron's distress the Germans' music proved less popular than the more lively Italian tunes, Anna sent Hübner to Italy in 1732 to recruit Italians, who were both talented and popular. Among them was Pietro Mira, who soon doubled as a court jester under the name Pedrillo. He quickly gained Anna's trust and was sent to recruit more Italian musicians in 1734. Anna also established Russia's first secular school of music, also under Hübner's direction, whose best students went on to play in the court orchestra.[77] Anna's support of music attracted the interest of leading nobles, who began to learn to play instruments or have their serfs instructed and form small orchestras. Music lovers began to gather in nobles' homes to socialize and play music.[78]

The final cultural highlight of Anna's reign was the visit of the popular German troupe of the actress Caroline Neuber. They arrived in April 1740 on the occasion of the anniversary of Anna's coronation, when Anna was already ailing. The visit was arranged by Biron, who was by now plotting to preserve his power after Anna's death. The play appears to have been Joseph Addison's *Cato*,[79] a tragedy about treachery and conspiracy in high places, featuring such lines as:

> *Know, villains, when such paltry slaves presume*
> *To mix in treason, if the plot succeeds,*
> *They are thrown neglected by: but if it fails,*
> *They're sure to die like dogs, as you shall do . . . .*[80]

For the anxious courtiers in the audience already scheming to contend for power, it must have been a long evening.

Anna rescued St. Petersburg from the tumult of 1725–30 and potentially from oblivion. She made valuable contributions in city planning and construction on which her successors would build, created the first royal court resembling those in the West, and introduced to the city and Russia many Western art forms. But ultimately she failed to give the city a more genuine European look or feel. Outside the performing arts, the foreign elements that she introduced were too artificial and associated with hated Germans to be popular and take hold, and the style of her reign was ultimately crude and unenlightened. It would be up to her successor Elizabeth to make the city at once both more European and more Russian.

CHAPTER 5

Looking Like Europe: Elizabeth's Petersburg

You're the spark of Peter the Great.

BISHOP LOPATINSKY, recognizing Elizabeth
upon returning from imprisonment
under the *Bironovshchina*[1]

Russia regained her consciousness.

HISTORIAN SERGEI SOLOVIEV,
summarizing Elizabeth's reign[2]

WAITING FOR THE THRONE

In 1740 Anna was dying, and those around her were scheming to take power. For years Anna and her circle had sought to neutralize Peter the Great's daughter Elizabeth, either by sending her to a nunnery or marrying her off to a foreign prince, but these plans had been foiled only by luck. Elizabeth had every reason to claim the throne upon Anna's death and enjoyed wide support in the city and among the Guards. But she displayed no inclination to do so, perhaps because Anna had legally designated her successor. In 1731 Anna had decreed that the first-born child of her yet unmarried thirteen-year-old niece, Catherine Elizabeth Christina of Mecklenburg, would be her own successor. For this purpose Anna arranged Catherine's conversion to Orthodoxy under the name of Anna Leopoldovna and moved her to St. Petersburg. In 1739 Anna Leopoldovna married Prince Anton Ulrich, Duke of Brunswick-Wolfenbüttel, and in August 1740, she gave birth to a son, Ivan. In early October 1740, just six days before her death, the Empress named Ivan as her successor and Anna Leopoldovna as regent and ordered the Guards regiments to swear allegiance.

When it became clear after a second stroke that the Empress would soon die, Biron remained constantly at her bedside. Realizing his unpopularity, Biron shuddered at what would happen to him should his enemies gain control, so he decided upon a high-stakes gambit. He presented Anna with his own version of her last will and testament, which among other things replaced Anna Leopoldovna with Biron as regent. He persuaded the weakening Empress to grant his last wish, and she signed it, upon which she reputedly told him, "My heart is sad for thee, for thou encompasseth thine own ruin."[3] Upon Anna's death on October 26, Biron assumed effective control of Russia.

Like Menshikov after the death of Catherine I, Biron was widely hated. He made matters worse by bullying Anna Leopoldovna and her family, assigning his spies to watch her and the court, and arresting and torturing those suspected of opposition. His enemies were quick to act. Chief among them was Münnich, who had always taken care to appear as Biron's supporter but in fact coveted Biron's role as the power behind the Empress. Seeing no future with Anna Leopoldovna, Münnich had eluctantly supported Biron in his bid for the regency, hoping to be rewarded. Once in power, however, Biron was afraid to raise him to a powerful position and granted him nothing. Disappointed, Münnich deftly changed sides.

In the time available, the plotters' only option was to restore Anna Leopoldovna's rights as regent. The 21-year-old Anna, frustrated and confused, was prepared to leave the country with Ivan rather than continue enduring Biron's torments.[4] Münnich, however, persuaded Anna to reassert her claim to the regency with his support, hoping to become the power behind her. Anna left the plot's execution in Münnich's capable hands.[5]

Münnich struck quickly on November 9, just two weeks after Anna Ioannovna's death and even before her funeral. In a remarkable feat of daring and hypocrisy, that evening Münnich had dinner with Biron and his family at Biron's home. Over dinner Biron asked Münnich whether in his life's adventures he had "ever undertaken any affair of consequence during the night." Münnich recoiled, fearing that Biron had learned of the plot, but he recovered his composure and replied that he did not recall having done so, but that his "maxim was to seize all times that appeared favorable."[6] After bidding Biron a good night at around 11:00 P.M., he strode over to the nearby Winter Palace with his aide-de-camp, Colonel Christof von Manstein, and several officers to visit Anna. Münnich announced that they would act that evening, obtained Anna's assent, and then had his officers swear allegiance to her. They then returned to Biron's mansion with about 80 soldiers and announced their intentions to Biron's guards. Conveniently, the guards were from Münnich's own Preobrazhensky Regiment, so it was not difficult to convince them to join in. Manstein, with about 20 men, slipped into Biron's bedchamber, threw aside the bed curtains, woke Biron and his wife, and announced his arrest. Biron resisted but was subdued by the butts of a few muskets and led out in his bedclothes to confront Anna at the Winter Palace. Münnich then had Russia's senior officials wakened and summoned to the Winter Palace, where Anna presented herself to them as regent and they swore allegiance to her. Biron and his family were imprisoned in the fortress of Schlüsselburg, where they remained for six months awaiting Biron's conviction and sentence. The sentence was death by quartering, but Anna commuted this to exile in Pelim, Siberia, in a house that had been designed by Münnich himself.

The nation was relieved to be finally rid of Biron, but the young Anna Leopoldovna proved unfit to rule. Manstein, though he helped bring her to power, characterized her as "naturally prone to indolence and self-indulgence, [having] too much dislike of business, and too much love of pleasure, to undertake willingly the least affair requiring any effort of mind."[7] Power devolved to a group of minor, impoverished German princelings who exploited Russia for their own gain. Meanwhile, Anna concentrated on her liaison with her lady-in-waiting, Julie Mengden. When this passion cooled, she turned to Count Maurice Lynar, ambassador of Saxony, after which to preserve appearances she sought to marry Lynar to Mengden. Anna's welcome soon wore thin, and in about a year she would be out of power. During her brief rule, she did nothing for the city. It was time for the daughter of Peter the Great to claim her father's throne.

Elizabeth was born in Kolomenskoe, then a suburb of Moscow, on December 18, 1709. She and her older sister Anna were brought up largely by Russian and Karelian peasant nannies and wet nurses and thus learned much about the common people and were comfortable among them. Because of Peter's and Catherine's travels, the Tsarevnas were often left at Ismailovo, just outside Moscow, under the care of the Dowager Empress Praskovya, a traditional, conservative Muscovite, and they lived in St. Petersburg for only part of the year. Elizabeth's childhood experience of Moscow was much better than her father's, and she always retained a fondness for it. She held a balanced and politic view of the traditions of the old and new capitals and appreciated the best of each. As Tsarevna and during her reign, she would spend much of the year in Moscow or in the surrounding countryside. In this way she came to understand and gain the love of her subjects to a degree not seen since her grandfather, Tsar Alexis.

For the first time in Russian history, the education of a Tsar's children was placed in the hands of foreigners, to prepare them for good marriages to foreign princes.[8] Beginning in 1716, the Tsarevnas were given foreign governesses, were taught by foreign teachers and dance instructors, and learned foreign languages and court etiquette. Elizabeth spoke French and German fluently, and also had an understanding of Italian, Swedish, and Finnish. When Empress, she would address many foreign ambassadors in their own languages. She had a quick mind, learned fast, and could read and write at an early age, but she lacked her father's intellectual curiosity. In fact, her formal education was still subpar by European standards and she was not an avid reader, but she had a genuine interest in and knowledge of the fine and performing arts. Elizabeth was deeply religious, and throughout her life her many pleasures were punctuated by long, pious retreats to monasteries and convents. Her piety came from the peasants who cared for her in her youth, and during the difficult years between her mother's death and her seizure of the throne she regularly sought solace by attending long Orthodox services. Perhaps taking such religiosity as a cue, Anna Ioannovna had favored making Elizabeth a nun in order to get her out of the way, a fate from which she was saved only by Biron's intercession. Anna

Leopoldovna threatened to do the same if Elizabeth would not marry Prince Lewis of Brunswick, whom Anna had brought to St. Petersburg to be made the new Duke of Courland.

As Britain's ambassador Edward Finch observed, however, Elizabeth had "not one bit of nun's flesh about her."[9] In a similar vein, the Duke de Liria commented that "she shamelessly does things that would make even the most uninhibited individual blush."[10] From her childhood Elizabeth was always fun loving and gay, and her great beauty and grace was apparent from an early age. The Saxon resident remarked that she was "always with one foot in the air."[11] The French portraitist Louis Caravaque painted an extraordinary nude portrait of the seven-year-old Elizabeth as Venus, which still hangs at Tsarskoe Selo outside St. Petersburg. When Elizabeth came of age, she found herself the center of attention at social gatherings and the object of male admiration, and she reveled in it. Mrs. Rondeau described Elizabeth as

> very handsome. She is very fair, with light brown hair, large sprightly blue eyes, fine teeth, and a pretty mouth. She is inclinable to be fat, but is very genteel, and dances better than any one I ever saw. She speaks German, French and Italian, is extremely gay, and talks to every body, in a very proper manner, . . . but hates the ceremony of a court. . . . I have a veneration for her, and fondness in my heart, that make the visit to her a thing of pleasure, not of ceremony. She has the affability and sweetness of behaviour that insensibly inspires love and respect.[12]

Contrary to popular legend, Elizabeth was not promiscuous (her known lovers were only seven in number),[13] but she did enjoy male company, ardently valued and sought romantic love, and enjoyed a number of romantic liaisons. Beginning with her father's failed plans to marry her to Louis XV, various efforts were made to marry her to a foreigner, but due to her illegitimacy, the deaths of some candidates, her own rejection of others, and other quirks of fate, this was never to be.

Although Elizabeth failed in marriage, she was successful in romance. Her first lover was Peter Buturlin, a young officer in Peter II's suite, but Peter, who himself adored her, soon became jealous of Buturlin and sent him off to the Ukraine to fight the Crimean Tatars. She then fell for a young sergeant, Alexei Shubin, but when Anna Ioannovna learned about it she was enraged, so when Shubin apparently made some critical remarks about Anna she used this as a pretext to arrest, torture, and banish him to Kamchatka. Elizabeth's next lover, Alexei Razumovsky, would remain her companion for life. He was born Alexei Razum (which means "reason") into a rural Cossack family in the Ukraine the same year as Elizabeth (1709). He became the village shepherd, but was attracted to books and secretly was taught to read and write by a priest in a neighboring village. His father, a drunkard, opposed erudition. Upon returning home drunk one day, he discovered Alexei reading, beat him and chased him out of the house with an axe. Alexei was lucky to escape, and he ran away from home to live with his teacher. The priest put him in the church choir and discovered Alexei's real gift: his wonderful singing voice. Soon a Russian military officer visited the priest while returning from Hungary to St. Petersburg with a shipment of Tokay wines for Anna Ioannovna, and upon hearing Alexei sing he was so impressed that he brought him to St. Petersburg, where he received proper voice training and became a chorister in the Imperial Chapel. This was in 1731, and Elizabeth was 22. When she heard this handsome man sing, her heart melted, and she persuaded Anna to attach him to her (Elizabeth's) household. He became her lover soon after Shubin was exiled. Razumovsky, as he was now called, was a warm and honest man without worldly ambitions, and their relationship was entirely personal; he never interfered in Elizabeth's imperial duties or in government. Once Empress, she bestowed great gifts on him, and he soon owned several estates. According to some accounts, Elizabeth secretly married Razumovsky outside Moscow in the autumn of 1742 at the instigation of her confessor, Feodor Dubyansky. They may have had a child before Elizabeth became Empress, but even if so there is no credible evidence that the child survived long. Alexei's younger brother Kyrill, however, became an important figure. He was sent to Europe for two years of education in Köningsburg, Berlin, and Paris and returned in 1745, worldly and refined, to become a favorite of the court. He later served as president of the Academy of Sciences, was made a Count and Grand Hetman of the Cossacks, and played a crucial role in bringing Catherine II to power.

Elizabeth's romantic nature was complemented by her ability, both instinctive and learned, to keep her thoughts and intentions to herself, dissemble, be diplomatic and not commit, through which she appeared unthreatening and could survive. Mrs. Rondeau discerned this quality, writing in 1735:

> In public she has an unaffected gaiety, and a certain air of giddiness that seem entirely to possess her whole mind; but in private, I have heard her talk in such a strain of good sense and steady reasoning, that I am persuaded the other behavior is a feint; but she seems easy; I say *seems*, for who knows the heart? In short, she is an amiable creature, and though I think the throne very worthily filled [by Anna Ioannovna], yet I cannot help wishing she were to be the successor, at least.[14]

Elizabeth's history is replete with instances in which people misjudged and underestimated her, and historians too have had trouble determining her intentions and beliefs. She is often depicted as lazy, neglectful, and indecisive, letting official papers awaiting her signature lie for long periods even though she found the time to attend court entertainments, but in significant part this was simple cautiousness, care and a desire to consult all involved.[15]

While Elizabeth had all the guile, sophistication, and refinements needed for the court, politics, and high society, she also had a kind heart, an easygoing manner, and the ability to relate to and communicate with the common people and soldiery, who lovingly called her their *Matyushka* ("Little Mother"). Elizabeth was Russian to the core, even in her personal habits and in romance; all her lovers were Russian. Although she had a liking for things French, she never preferred foreigners in anything. In Petersburg, she could often be seen walking about the streets and fraternizing with the Guards officers and soldiery. She cultivated their friendship, received Guards officers into her home, and even stood as godmother to the children of some of them. In the wintertime the soldiers would often jump onto the runners of her sleigh to ride as unofficial escorts. Elizabeth was also widely popular among the city's people, and after Anna Ioannovna died, city residents often called to her on the street urging her to assume the throne.

As Anna Leopoldovna's regency grew more troubled and unpopular, many looked to Elizabeth as their rightful ruler. The initial impetus for her bid, however, came not from Russians but from France. At the time, Russia was allied with Britain and Austria against France, so France sought a less threatening, weaker Russia that would not and could not intervene in Europe against French interests. France believed that these goals would be best served if the seemingly pro-French, religious Elizabeth were on the throne. Instructions were sent to the new French ambassador in St. Petersburg, Marquis Jacques Joachim Trotti de la Chétardie, who had arrived in 1739, to identify Elizabeth's supporters in Russia and encourage if not organize a coup. Since being seen meeting with Elizabeth would arouse suspicion, Chétardie established a contact with her through her French doctor, Armand Lestocq. Chétardie had been given funds for his efforts, and some of these certainly went to pay Lestocq, but there is no evidence that any French money went to Elizabeth or any of her Russian supporters. Through Lestocq, Chétardie and Elizabeth conducted a clandestine correspondence in code language. Eventually, in April they agreed to meet at night in Elizabeth's boat on the Neva, but when her boat passed his villa by the river he missed her signal to join her. Beginning in June, however, Lestocq was able to arrange a series of private meetings, to which Chétardie came in disguise. Chétardie sought an ally in Sweden and hatched a plot with Sweden's ambassador, Baron Nolken. Sweden hoped to regain some of the territories surrendered to Peter I, including St. Petersburg, so Chétardie convinced Sweden to attack Russia and help place Elizabeth on the throne. Sweden declared war in July 1741.

Elizabeth was well aware of the plot and neither discouraged nor became actively involved in it. She cagily refused to give concrete promises of territorial concessions or to sign any documents supporting the plot or even expressing good feelings toward Sweden, and she never communicated directly with the Swedes. In the end, she tricked both them and Chétardie, who had been afraid to tell his King that Elizabeth had made no written commitments. Sweden would lose the war and receive nothing for its efforts, as neither the Swedes nor Chétardie played a direct role in the actual coup. Except for Lestocq in his personal role, the coup turned out to be a wholly Russian affair.

Even before the Swedes declared war, in June 1741 a group of Preobrazhensky Guards officers had met with Elizabeth in the Summer Garden to declare their support for her and urge her to strike. "Little Mother, we are all ready and are only awaiting your orders," they told her. She replied, "Disperse now and conduct yourselves peaceably; the time is not yet ripe for action. I will let you know beforehand."[16] By early autumn, however, rumors of a coup as well as some fairly accurate suspicions and information about the actual plot had begun to circulate. The British Ambassador, Edward Finch, sought to counter the French and Swedes by confiding this information to Count Ostermann, who conveyed it to Anna Leopoldovna. Lestocq's behavior did not help. According to Manstein, he was "the most giddy man alive and the least capable of keeping a secret, [and] had often said in a coffee-house, before a number of people, that there would soon be seen great changes in St. Petersburg. The minister [Ostermann] did not fail to give notice of all this to [Anna]."[17] At first Anna dismissed such reports, but as their number increased and began coming even from abroad, she could no longer ignore the danger. On November 20, Anna confronted Elizabeth with the allegations. Since Anna's information contained much that was untrue, Elizabeth was able to convincingly deny the charges. She shed sufficient tears during this encounter to convince Anna that she had been wrongfully accused, but Anna nevertheless declared her intention to arrest Lestocq the following day (but which was not carried out).

Upon arriving home at the Summer Palace, Elizabeth related the whole encounter to Lestocq, who urged her to act immediately. Since the soldiers had been dispersed to their quarters, however, nothing could be done that evening. Elizabeth realized that she would have to act and set the Twelfth Day (January 6) for her coup, as on that day the soldiers supporting her would all be gathered on the Neva ice for the Blessing of the Waters ceremony. She would arrive there at the head of the Preobrazhensky Guards Regiment, whose leaders would be part of the plot, harangue the soldiers, and have the whole Regiment declare for her, hopefully to be followed by the other regiments.

But events moved more swiftly. Elizabeth soon learned that Anna had decided to declare herself Empress. Then the regiments upon which Elizabeth was depending were ordered to activate and proceed without delay to Vyborg to fight the Swedes. Without them, there could be no coup. There was now no choice but to act.

On the morning of November 24, the day before the regiments were to depart, Lestocq entered Elizabeth's chambers and presented her with a card. On one side, drawn in pencil, Elizabeth appeared with a crown on her head; on the other she appeared in a nun's veil and was surrounded by gibbets and racks. He then told her: "Your highness must now absolutely choose one of these two things, to be Empress, or to be put into a convent, and to see your faithful servants perish under tortures." Just after this several Guards burst into her room to report that their regiment had been ordered to depart for Vyborg the following day. There was no choice. Elizabeth decided to act at midnight.

There were no preestablished arrangements in place, nor was there even a large number of conspirators. Only about 30 Guards figured among Elizabeth's active supporters, and she had to depend on them and herself to win over the rest. Other than Lestocq, no French, Swedes, or other foreigners were involved. Hasty arrangements were made to meet at an appointed time, arrest Anna's chief supporters, and converge on the Winter Palace. At about midnight, Elizabeth knelt in her chambers before a holy icon, asked for divine guidance, and is said to have vowed to abolish capital punishment in Russia if she assumed power. She donned a Guardsman's cuirass, grabbed a silver cross, and left to meet her destiny.

She was met in her outer rooms by Razumovsky and her main supporters: the three Shuvalov brothers, Mikhail Vorontsov, Lestocq, and Vasily Saltykov. As the city slept, they boarded sleighs and set off through the snow for the nearby Preobrashensky Guards barracks. Their sudden arrival at the barracks sent the place into confusion. One guard started beating his drum to summon the soldiers. Lestocq, realizing that this could alert the city that something was amiss, leapt from his sleigh and slashed the drum. The 30 or so grenadiers who were already in the plot rushed to Elizabeth as she rose and stepped down from her sleigh. "Lads!" she said. "You know whose daughter I am! They want to force me into marriage or put me into a nunnery! Will you follow me so that doesn't happen?" The Guards shouted back: "We're ready, Little Mother! We'll kill them all!" "If you are planning to kill people," Elizabeth replied, "then I won't go with you. I don't want anyone's death." Raising her silver cross, she declared: "I shall swear to die for you and you shall vow to give your lives for me. But let no blood be shed unjustly." "We swear!" they shouted back, and prostrated themselves before her to kiss her cross.[18]

These Guards quickly rounded up over 300 men to join them, took an oath of loyalty to Elizabeth, and set off in their sleighs and on foot along Nevsky Prospect toward the Winter Palace. As they made their way down the wide, desolate, lamplit street bordered by rows of snow-laden trees, groups of 25 or so each slipped off to arrest Anna's chief advisers—Münnich, Ostermann, Karl Gustavus Löwenwolde, and Mikhail Golovkin—at their residences. Small guards were also stationed at the homes of Elizabeth's other opponents. As the main group crossed the Moika and neared the Winter Palace, all dismounted from their horses and sleighs, left them behind, and continued silently by foot so that the sound of horses would not alert guards at the Palace. But the snow was deep and the already stout Elizabeth found the going slow. Finally the soldiers lifted her onto their shoulders and carried her the rest of the way. On reaching the Palace, Elizabeth led her men into the guard rooms, approached the guards and commanded them to lay down their arms and follow her. They offered no resistance and replied that she could do as she wished. Elizabeth proceeded directly to the chambers of Anna and her family. She and seven men entered, went over to Anna's bed and awakened the sleeping woman. "Little sister, it is time to rise," she whispered. Anna offered no resistance. She and her husband dressed and were led downstairs to a sleigh, Anna's infant daughter and Ivan were placed in another sleigh together with their nurses, and they followed Elizabeth back to the Summer Palace.

Upon returning to the Summer Palace, Elizabeth drafted a manifesto to deliver to the people. Only when this was finished were the prisoners summoned and told that they were charged with depriving her of her hereditary rights. Dawn was already coming. At eight o'clock Elizabeth read her manifesto to the members of the Senate, other high officials and the military assembled in front of the Palace, and they took an oath of loyalty to her. Elizabeth then returned inside to pack her things, and by mid-afternoon she was installed in the Winter Palace. Chétardie, whom Elizabeth had kept informed of progress by dispatches during the night, came to pay his respects that evening, bringing with him a song of praise for the Empress newly composed by his secretary, Valdancourt.

Elizabeth then distributed the spoils. The grenadier company of the Preobrazhensky Regiment that brought her to the throne that night was renamed "Her Majesty's Own Company" *(Leibkompaniya)* with the Empress as its captain. Its members were promoted, ennobled, and given money and estates. Lestocq was made a Privy Councillor, Physician in Chief to the Empress, and President of the Imperial College of Physicians, but in 1747 he would be exiled to Siberia for disloyalty (being in the pay of Prussia). Chétardie was awarded the Order of St. Andrew, but in 1744 he would be expelled from Russia for his involvement in a plot to undermine Russia's foreign alliances. Never again would a foreigner have a prominent role in Russia's governmental and military affairs.

More important was Elizabeth's new group of Russians. Mikhail Vorontsov was made a count and was appointed to the College of Foreign Affairs; he would later become Grand Chancellor. The brothers Peter and Alexander Shuvalov, both longtime friends, supporters, and former members of Elizabeth's household at Izmailovo, were given high positions. Alexander headed the Secret Chancery located in the Peter and Paul Fortress, which functioned as the secret service. Peter was made a Senator and played a key role in state finances and administration, legal reform, and the development of Russian industry and the economy, particularly by abolishing internal tolls in Russia and improving the roads. He also brought the army back to the high standards and size it had seen under Peter I and invented a new type of howitzer which Russia used effectively in the Seven Years' War. Peter and Alexander Shuvalov brought their cousin Ivan to St. Petersburg from Moscow. He began as a page to Grand Duchess Catherine (the future Catherine II), and through their shared interest in books they became friends.[19] Ivan then charmed Elizabeth herself, and beginning in about 1751 they would carry on a long-standing liaison. Next to Mikhail Lomonosov, Ivan Shuvalov was perhaps the best educated man in Russia, and more charming. Ivan became President of the Academy of Fine Arts founded in 1758, cofounded (with Lomonosov) Moscow University in 1755, and played a leading role in developing Russian culture. A Francophile, he corresponded with, among others, Voltaire, Diderot, and Helvétius, and stimulated the use of the French language at the court. Count Alexei Bestuzhev-Rumin, an old protégé of Elizabeth's father, was made Vice-Chancellor and later Chancellor, from which positions he ably conducted Russia's anti-French foreign and military policy. Alexei Razumovsky was made a count and appointed as Court Chamberlain and Master of the Hunt, but he did not desire any position of power. When Elizabeth offered to make him a field marshal, he declined, explaining, "Your Majesty may create me a field marshal if you so desire, but I defy you or anybody else to make even a tolerable captain out of me."[20]

The coup had been bloodless, and so would be its aftermath. Anna Leopoldovna's ministers were tried and sentenced to death in the usual Russian fashion: Ostermann to be broken on the wheel, Münnich by quartering, and the others by decapitation. But just before the executions were to be carried out, Elizabeth made good on her oath on the evening of the coup to eliminate capital punishment and commuted the sentences to exile in Siberia. Anna and Ivan were initially freed and sent off to Germany, but they made it only as far as Riga, where they were stopped. There they lived under guard until January 1744, when they were exiled to the north of Russia, first in Oranienburg and then in Kolmogori. Anna died in childbirth in 1746 and was buried at Alexander Nevsky Monastery. The unfortunate Ivan remained in exile until he was transferred to Schlüsselburg in 1756, when Grand Duke Peter's bizarre behavior and unpopularity made Elizabeth grow nervous about potential coup attempts in Ivan's favor. Ivan remained in Schlüsselburg for the remainder of Elizabeth's reign, but was killed there in 1764 pursuant to long-standing orders (which Catherine II had reconfirmed) when his guards saw that a rescue attempt and coup were under way.

The city was overjoyed to be rid of Anna's German clique, and nationalistic feelings ran high. Elizabeth played on this in a second manifesto to the nation three days after the coup, in which she promised to deliver Russia from the control of foreigners. Unfortunately matters got out of hand. Many foreigners were molested on the streets, and Elizabeth had to restore order and arrest the offenders. Politics dictated that she expel some token foreigners from Russia, although this was never her desire. In fact, for all of the Western appearance of Elizabethan Russia, relatively few foreigners of importance came there during her reign. Lestocq was the only foreigner to achieve any position of significance in her court and government. The others were from the arts, or served at the court as cooks, tailors, hairdressers, and the like.

Elizabeth's being was strongly rooted in Russia and its people. Russians did not doubt her patriotic credentials and knew that she had Russia's interests foremost in mind. Having this trust gave her greater scope for action, which was fortunate in light of her plans. As Peter the Great's daughter, she was the first ruler of Russia since Peter to understand and believe in his vision, and she came to power committed to restoring it. But whereas conservatives, particularly in Moscow, had viewed Peter as the Antichrist and plotted against him, they largely let Elizabeth proceed to restore and solidify his creations. Elizabeth's main accomplishment in domestic affairs was to achieve in politics, society, and culture a sophisticated and comfortable synthesis of the Petrine vision and Russia's heritage, first and foremost in St. Petersburg. In the words of the historian Sergei Soloviev, under the daughter of Peter the Great "Russia regained her consciousness."[21] It was under Elizabeth that the St. Petersburg of which Peter had dreamed became reality and the foundations of Catherine the Great's age were laid. And she fostered the legend by commissioning Voltaire to write his history of Peter the Great's reign.

URBAN DEVELOPMENT UNDER ELIZABETH

Anna Ioannovna had already prepared and begun to implement sophisticated and well-planned urban development schemes, and for Elizabeth it remained only to complete the work. She left Anna's Commission on the Construction of St. Petersburg intact and let it continue its work of paving, straightening, and lengthening streets, draining swamps, strengthening embankments, and rebuilding the burnt-out districts. With this process already in hand, and since Russia lived in relative peace and prosperity, Elizabeth and prominent St. Petersburg families had the opportunity and resources to devote to building architectural marvels. The city's popularity rose with that of the new sovereign. No longer was Petersburg regarded as the outpost of the Antichrist or gangs of usurping foreigners. The city was now well supplied, the expense of living there was less out of proportion to the rest of the country than previously, and it was now a more attractive place to live. Prior to Elizabeth, most nobles built homes in St. Petersburg only because the sovereign commanded it, and they built them slowly and spent as little as possible on them. As late as June 1741, just prior to Elizabeth's accession, Britain's ambassador wrote of the city's Moscow nobles, "there is not one of them who would not wish St. Petersburg at the bottom of the sea . . . so they could but remove to Moscow."[22] Under Elizabeth, however, nobles grew eager to build lavish palaces in Petersburg and competed for prestigious architectural talent to design them. The city's population grew quickly from about 75,000 at the beginning of Elizabeth's reign[23] to 95,000 in 1750,[24] and rose steadily thereafter.

The result was a building boom. While Algarotti, writing in 1739, could truthfully speak of "bastard architecture" and coin the witticism that "elsewhere ruins make themselves, while in St. Petersburg they are built,"[25] this would not be true of Elizabeth's new buildings. "Though so lately a morass," wrote a British merchant around 1745, St. Petersburg was "now an elegant and superb city, very beautiful, and abounding in all the necessities, and many of the pleasures, of life."[26] As the city expanded and new construction replaced the old, forests were felled and many features of the older city, such as its wooden buildings and the *sloboda*, disappeared. The names of many streets, which originally described local residents or landmarks, were already anachronistic. A popular rhyme from the 1740s went:

All along Garden Street I searched
But I found not a single birch.
On Pea Street I looked all around
But there was not a pea to be found.
I wanted the sea as my view
So over to Sea Street I flew.
But no matter where I would stop
Of sea water there was not a drop.[27]

On Nevsky Prospect, not only was it now forbidden to construct in wood, but owners had to raze or reconstruct older buildings that did not conform to strict requirements, and to plant and maintain trees and greenery in front of their buildings so that the street would be enveloped in green in the summer. The ground along Nevsky was further drained in order to pave it properly and to facilitate stone and masonry construction along it. The draining of the area where the Krivushchya ("Crooked") Rivulet crosses Nevsky (by Kazan Cathedral) gave the rivulet defined embankments, which was the genesis of what is now the Griboyedov Canal. Upstream, where the rivulet divided in two and blended into a marsh, it was decided to make a cut through to the Moika River just south of the royal stables, which were called the *Konyushni*, and so the canal was initially called the Konyushenni Canal.

Construction of the large Gostiny Dvor that still stands on Nevsky began under Elizabeth. In 1748 it was decided to replace the wooden Gostiny Dvor with a large, one-story masonry structure on the same site. But the project dragged and in 1752 Bartolomeo Rastrelli was commissioned to redesign it as a two-story building. But a design was approved only in 1757 and work began again in 1759. With Elizabeth's passing and Rastrelli's fall from favor in 1761, the project was reexamined again. It was decided to keep Rastrelli's basic plan but to have the French architect Vallin de la Mothe reconfigure the façade along more classical lines. Construction moved slowly, and the building was finished only in 1784–85. Today it is the city's largest department store.

On May 26, 1761, at about 11:00 A.M., a fire erupted on the Meshchanskie Streets south of the Blue Bridge over the Moika and burned until dusk, ruining several city blocks. Elizabeth herself rushed to the scene and personally directed the firefighting efforts, much like her father used to do. After this, she took extraordinary measures to rebuild the stricken area and improve systems for firefighting. All public construction except for the Winter Palace was suspended, and the materials were used instead to rebuild the burnt zone. Favorable construction loans were dispensed to the owners by the recently established commercial bank. Elizabeth ordered all merchants at their expense to post fire watchers and to have firefighting equipment and a sufficient quantity of water on hand. It was forbidden to go into or near trading places with anything lit.

Elizabeth also imposed public order measures. It was forbidden to travel at a trot or at high speeds along city streets, and harnessing horses to carriages in tandem or greater numbers was forbidden except for foreign ambassadors entering and leaving the city. Strict tariffs for cabmen were established to prevent price gouging, and in order to better identify them they had to purchase for two rubles leather patches showing their registration number and their region of the city. Hotels and taverns were classified into five grades according to the quality of their offerings and they paid an annual tax accordingly. While private residents and businesses had long been required to clean and repair the sidewalks, streets, and embankments in front of their buildings, government bodies had not. As a result, the condition of streets in front of government buildings was noticeably dirtier and often dangerous. Elizabeth extended the requirements to government departments, to be funded by their own budgets. Another eyesore was the variety of unsightly signs hanging on peoples' homes; this was now forbidden on the city's main streets. When the growing numbers of residents along Nevsky Prospect began hanging their laundry to dry on the trees lining the street, Elizabeth issued a decree forbidding it.

Fighting crime in the city also became a priority under both Anna and Elizabeth. Robberies, burglaries, and grave robbing were a constant problem. People traveling on the edge of town were particularly vulnerable, as brigands hiding in the woods could descend upon them in surprise. Gangs of thieves were encamped in the forests just beyond the city limits, which at the time was still not far from the center; many of them lived in the woods just beyond the Fontanka. To protect homeowners, pedestrians, and travelers, Elizabeth ordered that the areas surrounding the homes on the Fontanka be cleared of trees. The same was done on the sides of roads leading in and out of town. One Cossack neighborhood on the Vyborg side known to be a haunt of criminals was simply moved. Soldiers were posted as guards along Nevsky. Punishments became more severe and included disfigurement, exile, and (under Anna) execution. To set an example, two incendiaries were burnt alive where they had started a fire in the Morskaya region.

Elizabeth, influenced by clerics, also considered the regulation of public morals in the city within her purview. Many of her decrees in this sphere appear to be the result of pressure from her confessor, Feodor Dubyansky. In one instance, in June 1750, he brought to her attention the existence of a house of ill repute operating in the city, and she ordered the proprietress, a Ms. Felker (known as the "Dresden-sha"), and her girls all be jailed, and the police arrested over 50 "procuresses and loose women."[28] Later that year a general order was issued to round up all women and girls of ill repute in the city. Dubyansky convinced Elizabeth to set up a special commission to take charge not only of that effort, but also to investigate instances of rape, pandering, and adultery, and in 1750–51 alone over 200 such investigations were conducted.[29] Elizabeth also forbade a number of other disreputable activities in public, including the staging of fistfights, raising tame bears, riding fast on horses, collecting alms, cursing in public, and spreading the streets with juniper during funeral processions. Taverns were no longer allowed on major streets.

CITY ARCHITECTURE: THE AGE OF RASTRELLI

The Elizabethan age marked the culmination of the career of the Russian architect Mikhail Zemtsov, as well as the rise of new Russian stars such as Savva Chevakinsky and Andrei Kvassov. A Briton who visited the city in this period, however, observed that "the taste of Italy is adopted in almost all their houses," thanks to the efforts of "an Italian architect some years since established in Russia."[30] This architect indeed needed no introduction. Above all others it was Bartolomeo Rastrelli who defined the appearance of Elizabethan St. Petersburg. During her reign, she employed him on every major building project in St. Petersburg and its suburbs. Rastrelli was Elizabeth's one great exception to favoring Russians for high positions, yet he had lived in Russia practically since his birth and Russians considered him almost one of their own; moreover, he trained many gifted Russians who would later rise to prominence. But after Elizabeth's premature death in 1761 his style fell out of favor, to be replaced by classicism. He left Russia in 1764 to work in Mitau (on the palace of Biron, whom Catherine II recalled from exile) and then in Italy, but he would return to St. Petersburg as an old man and die there in relative obscurity in 1771. Instead of resting in a place of honor, he lies in an unmarked grave somewhere in the city that he did so much to define. Had Elizabeth lived longer, Rastrelli's Baroque style would be still more pronounced in St. Petersburg today, at the expense of classicism. His creations embody the spirit of the city at the time, and most of them are still standing today, which merits treating them in some detail.

Rastrelli's first project after Anna Ioannovna, the new Summer Palace, was begun by order of Anna Leopoldovna, for which after Biron's arrest Rastrelli was recalled to St. Petersburg from Mitau, where he had been working on Biron's palace.[31] Now that a Western-style court had developed, the lack of a proper Summer Palace in the city had become a source of complaint and embarrassment. The site was just across the Moika from the Summer Garden where it intersected the Fontanka, and Anna Leopoldovna chose it because her lover, Count Maurice Lynar, lived nearby. Moreover, here Catherine I had built her small wooden "Golden" Palace, which subsequently had been enlarged, so it was natural to build upon this tradition. Thus, when Elizabeth became Empress, a larger wooden palace, known as the Third Summer Palace, was rising on the site. Elizabeth instructed Rastrelli to revise the design and complete the project, which he did in 1744. It stood until 1797, when it was razed in order to build Paul's ill-fated Mikhailovsky Castle. Fortunately, its image is preserved in several fine engravings from the period. Its style was the Russian Baroque* for which Rastrelli became famous. Though built mainly of wood, which was still common in the city due to the shortage of stone, its scale was grand. Its great ballroom is said to have been longer (though narrower) than that in Versailles and could hold more people. Great attention was also paid to its grounds. Behind the palace, a formal, regular garden in the French style featuring carefully shaped trees and bushes, ponds, fountains, and pathways stretched nearly to Nevsky. At its back an enormous, complicated labyrinth was laid out, which can be seen depicted on city maps of the period. Accommodations for the many servants were constructed across the Fontanka, over which a decorated aqueduct was constructed to supply the Summer Garden, the palace, and their fountains with water.

With the construction of the Summer Palace and its gardens, the entire central section of St. Petersburg from the Neva nearly to Nevsky was now owned and developed by the crown. This included Tsaritsyn Lug (now the Field of Mars), the Summer Garden, the Summer Palace and Gardens, other gardens later occupied by the Mikhailovsky Palace (now the Russian Museum), and the royal carriage house and stables just to the east of the Winter Palace.

The Winter Palace was also not up to European standards of the time. Rastrelli had patched it together for Anna Ioannovna from several buildings, and its main façade faced the Admiralty, which was no longer important and which left little space in the front. In June 1754 Elizabeth gave up on the building and ordered Rastrelli to raze it and design a new one on the site. He was thus afforded the rare opportunity for an architect to redo his own work. Construction began in 1754, and though work progressed at an amazing pace given the scale of the project, the new Palace was completed only in 1762, shortly after Elizabeth's death. She toured it in the autumn of 1761 when it was essentially ready, but never got to live in it. It is this palace which stands in St. Petersburg today.

While the project was proceeding—indeed for the rest of her reign—Elizabeth needed a temporary wooden Winter Palace. Rastrelli built it on the northwest corner of Nevsky Prospect and the Moika where the Barricade Theater now stands; conveniently, this nearby site was available because the wooden Gostiny Dvor that had stood there had perished in the great fire of 1736.[32] Work on the temporary palace was begun in February 1755 and was completed quickly: Elizabeth moved in on November 5 of that year.[33] It was large enough to contain the usual royal

---

*Rastrelli's style was very late baroque and is sometimes called rococo because of the emphasis on elaborate decoration. E.g., G. Hamilton, *The Art and Architecture of Russia* (Frome, United Kingdom, 1983), p. 276. Since Rastrelli synthesized late Western Baroque and the new rococo styles with traditional Russian motifs, in Russia specialists usually reserve the term "Russian Baroque" for the most developed of the baroque styles in Russia that was carried to its highest level by Rastrelli, and it is in this sense that the term baroque rather than rococo is used in this book. See Cracraft, *Petrine Revolution*, pp. 170–71, also pp. 79–110.

trappings, including a ballroom, throne room, grand staircase, chapel, and, as a stone addition, a royal theater. At the time Admiralty Lug stretched south from the Admiralty's moat all the way to the northern façade of the new palace, so that the Admiralty was visible through a row of large windows. The temporary Winter Palace was dismantled in stages by Catherine II beginning in 1765, and in its place was built the elegant home of the Elisyeev brothers which survives today.

The new Winter Palace was in the very center of the city, bounded by the river on one side, the Admiralty on another, and mansions on a third. It was not possible to surround the structure with a large park or garden as with the palaces in the suburbs or even like the Vasilievsky Island palaces envisioned in LeBlond's and Trezzini's city plans. Instead, Rastrelli settled upon a closed structure with court-yard gardens. To create openness, he gave the palace two main facades, one facing the Neva and the other facing Admiralty Lug to the south. The Palace was meant to be viewed from any side, but already in 1764–67 Catherine II had Veldten erect the adjoining Small Hermitage that permanently eliminated the view from the East. Rastrelli planned a circular colonnade to enclose most of Admiralty Lug and to place his father's statue of Peter I in the center, but this plan was never effected following Elizabeth's premature death and Rastrelli's ensuing departure.[34] The finished palace was huge: It had 1,054 rooms with over 2,000 windows and covered over 400,000 square feet of ground. On the Neva side, in order to support the Palace's great weight, the embankment was enlarged and faced with the city's first granite quay.

Work proceeded on a hectic pace and monumental scale that recalled the founding of the city itself. As under Peter the Great, skilled workmen were brought in from around the country, and soldiers served as laborers. The center of the city—all of Admiralty Lug from Millionaya to St. Isaac's Church—was turned into a work camp for the workers and storage site for materials. At any one time about 4,000 workers could be found toiling on the edifice.[35] Many of them lived in tents and shacks on or near the site, and some died from disease. Others toiled outside the city cutting trees and transporting them and other materials, for which the entire fleet of barges on the Neva and Lake Ladoga was placed at Rastrelli's disposal. Huge sums were appropriated for the project, about 120,000 rubles per year, but less (70,000 rubles or less) was actually dispensed. While Rastrelli raced against ambitious deadlines, he had to fight tooth and nail and appeal personally to the Senate for the money, labor, and materials needed to meet them. He was under great stress and his health suffered.

Cleanup at the end of the project took only a matter of hours, when at Policemeister Nicholas Korf's suggestion Peter III invited the city's residents to the site to carry off and keep whatever items they wanted. As Peter watched in amazement from his palace window, great throngs converged on Admiralty Lug, arriving on foot, in carriages, and by boat. People swarmed over the site like ants, carrying off bricks, lumber, logs, metal, and whatever else they could dislodge, and then returned for more. By the end of the day hardly a scrap could be found. The cleanup had cost the state treasury nothing.[36]

The building's design was essentially as is preserved today, except that the ground level around it has risen over time, thus covering much of the structure below the base of the lower rank of columns and destroying much of the architectural effect of the palace resting above street level. In order to break up the potential monotony of the Palace's great length—a problem made worse by the flat square on one side and the horizontal of the embankment on the other—the façades are dominated by numerous bays and projections and hundreds of superimposed Ionic and Doric columns in two ranges divided by a string course, which emphasized the building's considerable height. (At that time the building towered over all others.) The sensation of height is enhanced by a balustrade along the roof dotted with hundreds of larger-than-life-size bronze statutes in various poses gazing over the city. These figures have indeed witnessed great events, and on summer White Nights they are a dominating and haunting presence. In between the columns are rows of windows, the designs of which vary by façade and by floor. The Palace's color was originally yellow and white. This color scheme remained for about a century and then changed to green and white, then to brick red all over early in the twentieth century, and finally to today's pale sea green and white.

The prominence of color typical of St. Petersburg architecture, particularly in this period, had its reasons. It was not feasible to bring to St. Petersburg in large quantities the colorful marble, granite, and other stone used in Western Europe. The shortage of all kinds of stone meant that many prominent buildings and palaces, even Imperial ones, had to be built of wood or of brick coated with plaster, both of which had to be painted. Moreover, pure stone construction would have accentuated rather than provided relief from the city's gray, bleak climate, winter snows, and the silvery or frozen waters of the Neva. Thus, in St. Petersburg buildings were painted in bright, even pastel colors such as turquoise, pink, orange, the ubiquitous yellow, or shades of green (sea, emerald, or pistachio), all of which were typically combined with white to produce an overall polychromatic effect that is particularly striking in the snow. Only over time did the colors of some buildings become darker and more subdued.

Another work of Rastrelli, the Anichkov Palace, is directly associated with Elizabeth's coming to power and her lifelong favorite, Alexei Razumovsky. For the site of the palace, in 1741 Elizabeth purchased from the merchant Lukyanov the headquarters of the Preobrazhensky Regiment, on the northwest corner of Nevsky and the Fontanka. The palace took its name from the Anichkov Bridge, which crosses the Fontanka at that point. Work began in 1742 or 1743 under Zemtsov according to a design of his student and assistant, Grigory Dmitriev. After Zemtsov died in 1743, the project was temporarily in the hands of Dmitriev and then Guiseppe Trezzini (the nephew of Domenico), but in 1744 Elizabeth appointed Rastrelli to complete the palace according to his own revised design. It was ready for occupation by 1746, but it was formally completed and presented to Razumovsky only in 1750, when its chapel was consecrated. By the time Rastrelli took over construction, the walls of the second floor had already been erected, so he was constrained by the original design and had to focus his originality on the interior and the roof. To outfit and furnish the palace, Elizabeth ordered that the decorations from Biron's palace in Mitau be brought in. Outside, the original design had called for a central and two lateral projected facades which looked virtually identical, resulting in an uninteresting appearance. Since Rastrelli could do nothing to increase the size of the center section, all he could do to differentiate side from center was to top the two wings with cupola-like crowns and then add statues, crowns, and trophies to the central portion. Despite its defects, the palace was popular, as its height made it visible from all over town, much like the Admiralty and Peter and Paul Cathedral.

On the Fontanka side of the palace stood a colonnade with a small canal cut through it leading to the entrance of the palace so that one could row to the palace steps. In back of the palace was a large garden extending all the way to Sadovaya ("Garden") Street and westward to Chernyshev Bridge, which encompassed the area of the current Pushkin Theater, Ostrovsky Square, and the Public Library. Where the Pushkin Theater now stands, Razumovsky had a large pavilion with a gallery of paintings in one room. The pavilion's other room was a large hall in which concerts, masquerades, balls, and other affairs were held. On the corner where the Public Library now stands was Razumovsky's orangerie and nursery.

The palace has been reconstructed several times, first by Ivan Starov in 1778, who altered the wings and their roofs, and most recently under Alexander II in 1866. Its original appearance has been lost and the canal has been filled in. The colonnade was rebuilt into a grating said to have been designed by Frederick William III of Prussia, and later another colonnade was erected by Quarenghi which obscures the view of the palace from the Fontanka. The gardens grew smaller as other buildings were erected on the grounds.

Rastrelli's success with the Summer Palace and the popularity of the Anichkov Palace made him all the rage. The city's elite clamored to have him design and build their mansions, even if only in general sketch or if his supervision was from afar. Only the most influential were able to gain his personal attention and get him or his main assistants to build palaces for them. Among them were Sergei Stroganov, Mikhail Bestuzhev, Mikhail Vorontsov, and to a lesser extent Boris Sheremetev and Ivan Shuvalov. The most famous and enduring of these buildings is the Stroganov Palace.

Baron Sergei Stroganov was from a rich and respected family of Ural industrialists and Siberian pioneers dating from the 15th century. He was close to Elizabeth but did not covet high office or a place at court. Highly cultivated, his inclinations were more intellectual and cultural, so he served as president of the Academy of Sciences and amassed one of the best art collections in Russia, which needed to be housed in a new palace. He commissioned Rastrelli to build it on the southwest corner of Nevsky Prospect and the Moika, just across the Moika from Elizabeth's temporary wooden Winter Palace. It was begun in 1752, but Sergei died in 1756 only two years after its completion. The *Academic Gazette* honored him with the epitaph: "He was an eye to the blind, a leg to the lame, and a friend to everyone." His son Alexander, who would serve four sovereigns with distinction, moved into the palace, and under him it became a beacon of the Russian Enlightenment. The building is unique among nobles' palaces in the city in that it abuts the sidewalks of Nevsky and the Moika embankment and has no grounds or park other than a modest interior courtyard. In this courtyard Alexander served free dinner daily to any cleanly dressed member of the public, and himself dined with the many anonymous guests. Unfortunately, like the Winter Palace, its appearance has suffered due to the rise in the elevation of the street over time, which has cut off much of the lower row of windows. Originally the palace was painted in bright orange and white, not the pea green and white seen today. Rastrelli's interior, which featured one of the country's best libraries, was mostly lost in a fire.

Grand Chancellor Mikhail Vorontsov's palace was built in 1749–57 on Sadovaya Street (now No. 26) on the northwest edge of the Anichkov Palace's gardens. It is considered one of the purest expressions of Rastrelli's taste in architecture. (Rastrelli showed his own taste and restraint in not burdening private palaces with the ornate and often excessive decoration demanded of him for royal palaces.) A Francophile, Vorontsov furnished his palace lavishly with French furniture, including that of Madame Pompadour, and decorated it with French art. During Paul's reign the building would become the headquarters of the Knights of Malta and from 1810 served as the college of the Imperial Corps of Pages. In 1798–1800 Giacomo Quarenghi built as an addition a Catholic Maltese chapel, which still stands today and is considered one of his best works.

In the spring of 1746 Alexei Bestuzhev-Rumin purchased Kammeny ("Stone") Island from Alexander Golovkin. Bestuzhev spent vast sums of money beautifying and developing the island and hired the best park designers and architects to do so. On the tip of the island facing up the Malaya Neva he had Rastrelli build a splendid summer palace with surrounding gardens and pavilions, which began the tradition of nobles building palaces on the city's outlying islands. Bestuzhev's palace, completed in 1750, combined the style of a suburban villa with the features of Rastrelli's more grandiose works. It consisted of two separate two-storied wings joined by an elaborate colonnade, which stands unique among Rastrelli's creations. It became the city's showcase suburban residence for Baroque design. In 1765, Catherine II bought the island back from Bestuzhev and gave it to her son, Grand Duke Paul. The Imperial family gradually had the palace rebuilt into a larger structure that became known as the Stone Island Palace and it lost its Baroque features, but its original appearance is preserved in a set of engravings by Makhaev.

The Sheremetev palace on the Fontanka, often called the Fountain House, had its origins in July 1712, when Peter gave the site to Fieldmarshal Boris Sheremetev with instructions to build a mansion on it. But Sheremetev built only a modest wooden home together with some stone structures before his death in 1719. His son Peter replaced it with a one-story palace. Once Elizabeth built her Summer Palace across the Fontanka, Peter felt a need to expand his own, and his marriage in 1743 into the Cherkassky family provided him with the means to do it. He reconstructed it into a two-story structure in the Baroque style, which was completed in 1750. The building is well set back from the Fontanka, and behind it a large garden stretched to the current Liteiny Prospect and beyond, in which the Russian architect and painter Ivan Argunov (born as Sheremetev's serf) built a grotto, a Hermitage, and a Chinese pavilion. The authorship of this palace is not certain. While some credit it entirely to the Russian Savva Chevakinsky and Argunov, the similarities of its features to the Strogonov, Anichkov, and Vorontsov palaces lead others to detect Rastrelli's hand, although Rastrelli himself did not list it among his works.[37] The palace still stands today with at least its outward form intact, and it houses, among other things, the Anna Akhmatova Museum in her former apartment in one of its wings.

Rastrelli also turned his attention to religious buildings. His most famous such work in St. Petersburg is the Smolny Cathedral and convent. His initial design was approved in 1746 and he soon began site work, but in 1749 Elizabeth ordered a redesign along more traditional Russian lines, including an enormous (140 meter high) bell tower similar to the Ivan the Great bell tower in the Moscow Kremlin. The Russianness of the design was dear to Elizabeth, because throughout her life she would often retreat to convents, and she had ordered Smolny built thinking that she might retire there in her old age. The modified design with the bell tower is preserved in a wooden model that survives today and can be viewed in the Cathedral. The ambitious project had to be scaled back due to a shortage of funds, however. The bell tower was never built, and the elaborate interior of the Cathedral that Rastrelli planned was never realized; an extremely simple interior decoration was later furnished by the Russian architect Vasily Stasov, which itself suffered during the Soviet period. Still, the outside of the Cathedral and the monastery complex were completed marvelously in 1764 and, at 85 meters in height on the bank of the Neva, it provides one of the city's most stunning sights. It is said that when passing the Cathedral in his carriage, Giacomo Quarenghi, the classical architect who later built the adjoining Smolny Institute and disliked the Baroque, would nevertheless doff his hat in homage and exclaim, "Now *there's* a cathedral!"

The Nikolsky Cathedral of the Sea is normally attributed to Rastrelli's most talented pupil, Savva Chevakinsky, but it is built squarely in the Rastrelli Baroque style and recalls Rastrelli's own church near Strelna. It was built on the embankment of the Kryukov Canal for the Admiralty workers, who lived in that region of town. A series of smaller churches had occupied the site since Peter I's reign, also named after St. Nicholas, the patron saint of sailors. The design for the new cathedral was approved in 1752, and work was completed in 1762. It is surrounded by a park and outbuildings, including a bell tower, that occupy a large city block. The complex has survived in preserved condition to this day. It is still a functioning cathedral and was one of the few in which services were held during the Soviet period.

Under Elizabeth, defining work was also done on the city's suburban palaces. In 1728, shortly after Catherine I's death, Elizabeth had been given the small palace that Catherine had constructed for Peter at Saarskaya Myza, but for lack of resources she had never been able to do anything with it. Shortly after her accession, Elizabeth renamed the site Tsarskoe Selo ("Tsar's Village"), signifying her intent to make it the chief suburban summer residence of the imperial family. She assigned Zemtsov to redesign and enlarge Peter and Catherine's original palace, but he died in 1743 and the work was reassigned to Chevakinsky and Andrei Kvasov. The project was nearly complete when in 1751 Elizabeth announced that she was dissatisfied with the results and reassigned the project to Rastrelli with instructions to redesign it himself. He completed it in 1756. Elizabeth then named it the Catherine palace after her mother, placing Catherine's monogram in the pediment in "eternal and happy memory."

Rastrelli retained the original structure for the central portion of the palace, but greatly extended it on each side to a total length of over 900 feet, breaking up the long façade by dividing it into sections and placing the chapel on the north end of the main axis. He gave the building an entirely new Baroque façade, covering the original front of the center section with a portico and the remainder with prominent columns and pilasters. The main section was three stories high, with a vast courtyard on the west side enveloped by curved one-story wings (for servants' quarters) leading to an iron grating and a large central gate. He painted the building pale blue (which remains today), with white columns and gilded details and roof sculptures. The large, gilded windows reflected the sun in such a way that they looked like fire, and the Empress's fire brigade sometimes rushed to the palace mistakenly thinking it was aflame.

Inside, the great hall alone was over 150 feet long, with rows of alternating windows and gilded mirrors imported from France. At night the effect was spectacular as the light from over a thousand candles was reflected throughout the room. The most famous of the smaller rooms was the Amber Room. It had its origin in 1715 when Peter I was visiting Frederick I at Monbijou and admired a room paneled in amber carved in 1707 by the Dresden craftsman Forfrin Tusso to the designs of Andreas Schlüter. Peter asked to have the amber panels, and his gracious host agreed, in return for 55 selected grenadiers of exceptional height. Peter indeed trained, inspected, and sent the grenadiers to Frederick, but he never got around to installing the amber panels and for a while they were forgotten after his death. Elizabeth located the panels and Rastrelli designed a room around them. He interspersed the panels with mirrors and other decoration in order to highlight the panels as ornament, with results that stunned visitors. During WWII, the original amber panels were removed by the Nazis and are probably lost forever, but the room has now been restored with new panels based on drawings and photographs.

The grounds of the palace were equally splendid, consisting of formal French gardens directly in front of the palace while to the south grew up an irregular network of ponds and rivulets, numerous sculptures, a grotto, and various other pavilions, some of which Rastrelli designed and others which were added over time. The masterpiece of the grounds was the Hermitage located in the formal garden, which was used mainly for royal entertainments and dinners. It was two stories high in Rastrelli's Russian Baroque style with statues and a gilded cupola on top, painted in green and white, and surrounded by a wet moat. The interior featured ceiling paintings by Giuseppe Valeriani, Antonio Battista Peresinotti, and Gradizzi. The dining room and anterooms had five tables seating up to 35 people, the central sections and placings of which could be lowered downstairs using an elevator mechanism so that an entire dinner could be served and enjoyed in the absence of bothersome and eavesdropping servants. Downstairs, servants would clean the setting, load the next course, and return it upstairs to the delighted guests. Guests with requests could note them on a slate and pull a string to have their wishes fulfilled. After dinner the entire tables could be lowered and parquet placed on top so that the entire hall could be used for dancing. This innovation was repeated at Peterhof and copied by many Western courts.

The palace grounds were also distinguished by the famous sliding hill (Katalnaya Gorka). Tobogganing had been a favorite winter pastime of Elizabeth since her youth, and in fact was a traditional Russian activity during Butter Week that had been introduced to the St. Petersburg court by Anna Ioannovna. Rastrelli designed an elaborate pavilion with a permanent brick and stone slide nearly 90 feet high and 900 feet long running off one side, on which in the summertime wheeled cars would roll down. It lasted until 1792.

The story at Peterhof on the Finnish Gulf was similar. Its original design had been defined by Peter the Great's modest tastes, and many now considered it dull and unbecoming for the proper European court that the imperial household had become, nor did it suit Elizabeth. Renovations began shortly after her accession and were based on the existing layout, but in 1746 Elizabeth grew dissatisfied and here too turned matters over to Rastrelli and instructed him to fundamentally redesign and enlarge the palace. The new plan was ready the next year and he proceeded with work, which would take nearly 10 years to complete. Unlike at Tsarskoe Selo, he did not redesign the façade but retained much of the character of LeBlond's design. Onto LeBlond's original central section Rastrelli grafted a third story, altered somewhat the roof and window design, and lengthened the wings. To the extended wings he added galleries leading to side pavilions with cupolas. One was a church, and the other was known as the "Coat of Arms" wing with its cupola gilded with

600 pounds of gold. Rastrelli painted the palace pink and white. He substantially modified the interior of the palace, which Elizabeth demanded be lavish. He accommodated her wishes with elaborate gilded décor, carved woodwork, mirrors, chandeliers, statues, and other artwork that was overdone to such an extent that some suggest that he did it mockingly.[38] Rastrelli also added new buildings, fountains, and other structures in the upper and lower parks.

At Oranienbaum, no major reconstruction or redesign was undertaken, but considerable repairs were necessary because it had deteriorated following Menshikov's downfall.[39] Elizabeth gave it to her nephew, Grand Duke Peter (the future Peter III) and his wife Catherine (the future Catherine the Great) as their summer residence.

SOCIAL LIFE AND THE COURT

Under Elizabeth, Petersburg's social life continued to be driven by the royal court, but she changed the court dramatically, and with it social life. Both became more civil, sophisticated, tasteful, and cultured. Gone were the dwarfs and buffoons and in came the poets. Elizabeth eliminated the uncouth behavior and most of the gauche excesses of Anna's court, even setting limits on the amount of gold and decoration on the clothing of courtiers. But it was lavish nevertheless and was recognized as one of the most splendid in Europe.[40] Throughout her reign, it would strain the state's finances.

Elizabeth left most day-to-day governance in the hands of her capable ministers, which gave her more time for traveling through her realm, religious worship, and cultural and social events. When in town, she held court twice a week, on Thursdays and Sundays, and some form of entertainment was held almost nightly. Concerts were held twice a week, theater (usually a French comedy) once a week (twice a week in the winter), and court balls twice a week.[41] Many balls were hosted not by Elizabeth but by various nobles in their mansions. If the host's home was not large enough, one of the royal palaces might be used instead, especially if the ball was in the Empress's honor.[42] Balls were the highlight of court and city social life, although many found them tiresome and boring,[43] and for everyone they were expensive.

Masquerades had been popular in Russia since Peter the Great's time, but in 1744 Elizabeth had the idea of having the male guests dress as women and the women as men, and without masks. Holding such balls unmasked altered the meaning of the masquerade as it had been practiced throughout Europe until then, as guests were no longer coming as someone they were not, but rather as different versions (or aspects) of themselves. These affairs, called "metamorphoses," were held regularly. Elizabeth was enthusiastic about them as she had "well turned" legs and was seemingly the only woman (other than Grand Duchess Catherine) who looked becoming in male attire, which helped maintain her superiority over the other ladies and reinforced female dominance over the court. Catherine the Great later observed:

The only woman who looked really well and completely a man was the Empress herself. As she was tall and powerful, male attire suited her. She had the handsomest leg I have ever seen on any man and her feet were admirably proportioned. She dressed to perfection and everything she did had the same special grace whether she dressed as a man or a woman. One felt inclined to look at her and turn away with regret because nothing could replace her.[44]

Elizabeth's favorite costume was that of a Dutch sailor, in which character she called herself Mikhailovna, which signified that she was the daughter of Mikhailov, the name her father Peter had adopted for his military roles and during his Great Embassy to the West. But most of the men and many of the women disliked these events. "As a rule," Catherine wrote, "the men were in a churlish humor at these masquerades, and the women were in constant danger of being knocked over by some frightful Colossus, for the men moved about most clumsily in their gigantic hoop-skirts."[45]

One individual who probably attended these affairs, however, would have been right at home with this role reversal. He was a Frenchman, the Chevalier d'Eon de Beaumont, who had assumed the role of a woman for much of his life, in part to work as a spy. Following England's alliance with Prussia, France dispatched him to Petersburg in June 1756 to serve as secretary to the new French chargé d'affaires, Alexander Douglas. According to d'Eon's own account, he disguised himself as a woman (Lia de Beaumont, indeed reportedly seen in Douglas's company) in order to infiltrate the court, become a French tutor and confidante of Elizabeth, and promote a Russian alliance with France. If this is true, he would have appeared at metamorphoses as the man he really was. Whether he really assumed a female identity in Russia or simply made this up in his memoirs is still a matter of debate.[46] Whatever his choice of dress, he served his country well and became a trusted private messenger between the Empress and Louis XV, the man Peter I had hoped Elizabeth would marry. D'Eon played a key role in the reestablishment of diplomatic relations between Russia and France and in reaching a treaty in 1758.

Even more than when a Princess, the lively Elizabeth as Empress was the life of the balls, and not merely because of her position. Her dancing remained the envy of all despite her increasing weight. Catherine wrote in her memoirs:

At one of those balls, I watched her dance a minuet; after it was over she came up to me. I took the liberty of telling her that it was lucky for all women that she was not a man, for even a mere portrait made of her in that attire could turn the head of any woman. This compliment was expressed in full sincerity and she accepted it with grace, replying in the same tone and in the sweetest manner, that had she been a man, it would have been to me that she would have given the apple.[47]

Dancing was not limited to European minuets and quadrilles, however. Elizabeth took pains to include native Russian folk dances, and late in her reign English folk dances.[48]

In the summer the court would retreat to one of the city's suburban palaces for rest, relaxation, and a more subdued social life. Elizabeth's favorite retreat was Tsarskoe Selo, at which she emulated the idyllic lifestyle of the French nobility portrayed in the paintings of Watteau and Fragonard and to which Russia's aristocrats now aspired. One description from Catherine the Great's memoirs, complete with swing, captures this mood:

> At Tsarskoe Selo we tried as well as possible to amuse ourselves; during the day we promenaded or went hunting. The swing played an important role; while swinging, Mademoiselle Balk, a lady-in-waiting of the Empress, aroused the interest of Monsieur Sergei Saltikov, Chamberlain of the Grand Duke. He made her a proposal of marriage the next day, which she accepted, and they were married soon afterwards.[49]

Not all social life was empty entertainment, however. Through the almost daily social events Elizabeth sought to create a more cultivated, intelligent, and European society. A sign of some success was that a core group of intellectuals and literati had coalesced in the city and began to gather socially amongst themselves for enlightened conversation. The great minds in the city were no longer foreigners but rather Russians who had seen Europe, been educated abroad or at the Academy, and were already making original contributions in their fields. The center of their gatherings was the mansion of Ivan Shuvalov, who was the first to hold the salons for which Petersburg would become so well-known. The home itself, just off Nevsky and designed by the Russian architect Alexander Kokorinov, reflected the neoclassicism already prevalent in France.* His housewarming masquerade was held on October 25, 1755, for which Lomonosov composed and recited an ode. A Francophile, and known to his contemporaries as the "Russian Maecenas," Shuvalov outfitted his home in French décor and in it amassed a huge library and collection of paintings. In this setting gathered such literati as Alexander Sumarokov, Mikhail Lomonosov, Vasily Trediakovsky, the poet Emile Kostrov, and the author and translator of Homer, Hippolyte Bogdanovich. As happens among intellectuals, they often disagreed with one another and hot disputes would erupt. The loud arguments between the rivals Lomonosov and Sumarokov, from which guests derived a certain pleasure and came to expect, became legendary, and Shuvalov would have to try and make peace. Still, these gatherings were recognized at the time as embodying the height of social manners and good taste. They also marked the beginnings of a vital social and intellectual life in the city separate from the court.

Shuvalov was the vanguard of French culture in St. Petersburg society, beginning a fascination and style in the capital that would last from the Diplomatic Revolution of 1756, which aligned Russia with the ancien régime of France,

---

*This mansion should not be confused with another one of his built by Chevakinsky described earlier in this chapter. See A. Platunov, *Tak stroilsia Peterburg* (St. Petersburg, 2000), p. 136.

through most of Catherine II's reign until she became disillusioned and alarmed by the French Revolution. In this period French replaced German as the preferred foreign language of the court and aristocracy, the court adopted Versailles modes of behavior, and men and women alike wore the latest French fashions. The French influence brought Russia's elite into the mainstream of European culture, and soon Russians were also reading French literature, watching French plays, and absorbing French philosophical ideas. To be sure, much of this Francophilia was superficial and as time went on served as fruitful material for satire, a genre that was itself adopted from France. The prevalence and influence of French language and culture at court was not as great or deep as is sometimes stated. Catherine II, for example, typically used French in the presence of foreigners and when speaking or corresponding with them, but she spoke and corresponded with her officials in Russian.

The most brilliant social event in Elizabeth's St. Petersburg was the marriage of Grand Duke Peter to Catherine in August 1745. Elizabeth was determined to make it the most splendid wedding in Europe and spared no expense. It was modeled on the recent wedding of the French Dauphin at Versailles, but she intended to surpass it in both richness and solemnity through the ritual of the Orthodox Church. Indeed, the French resident in St. Petersburg observed that "[o]ne could scarcely behold anything more splendid and more stately."[50] Elizabeth directed top nobles and officials to employ extra heyducks and footmen, prescribed elegant dress, and advanced the salaries of officials so they could afford it. She ordered shiploads of elegant carriages, costumes, and textiles from abroad. She personally supervised Catherine's dress, hair, and jewelry (which Elizabeth gave her). The wedding day began at Admiralty Lug by the Winter Palace, from which, with a drumroll and fanfare, at about 10:00 A.M. the long wedding procession set off along Nevsky toward the Church of Our Lady of Kazan (now the site of Kazan Cathedral), where the wedding ceremony would be performed. Rows of finely dressed hussars, dragoons, cuirassiers, and horse-guards guarded the route, restraining the large, cheering crowds. The procession featured 120 elegant carriages, each surrounded by many retainers, and it took three hours for all of them to cover the short route. The elegant and solemn Orthodox marriage ceremony was equally as long. Alexei Razumovsky held the wedding crown over Catherine; he would later carry her crown at her coronation.[51] The procession then returned to the Winter Palace. Outside on Admiralty Lug, temporary fountains flowed with wine, and masses of Petersburgers dined at rows of tables on food cooked at hearths set up in the square. Inside the palace, a banquet and ball was held which lasted past midnight. Elizabeth, eager for an heir to the throne, urged the pair to retire to the bedroom somewhat early. Catherine did so, but Peter remained behind to dine. When he finally joined his bride in bed, he promptly fell asleep. Of this Catherine would write: "In this state matters remained . . . without the least alteration."[52]

THE PERFORMING ARTS AND LITERATURE

Elizabeth brought the level of the performing arts in Petersburg to a new height. Her love of dancing and music and her reputation for good taste attracted foreign artists to St. Petersburg in great numbers and led to the national development of the performing arts. She invested large sums to attract foreign performers and to develop Russia's own. Whereas Elizabeth's father had to send agents to the West to entice artists into his backwater, now Europe was beginning to beat a path to St. Petersburg.

In the case of theater, royal theaters were attached to each of Elizabeth's palaces in town, and regular performances were held in them. Elizabeth also encouraged nobles to include music and theater performances at the parties held in their homes, which eventually led to the tradition of home theaters. French comedies remained popular, and a well-paid permanent French troupe performed once or twice a week and attracted much interest and discussion, as much for their behavior offstage as for their performances on it. Soon all of Petersburg was familiar with the works of Voltaire, Jean-Baptiste Molière, Jean Racine, and Thomas Corneille. Italian and German performers also appeared, among them the famous Giovanni Antonio Sacco in 1742. The city's large German community was able to support a German theater on Bolshaya Morskaya Street.

More significant, however, was the people's growing desire for native Russian theater. Elizabeth commissioned Vasily Trediakovsky to write, among other things, tragedies for her theater, and his neoclassicist tragedy (Russia's first), *Khorev*, was premiered by the Cadets in 1749. Lomonosov also tried his hand at plays. But it was Russia's first literary critic, Alexander Sumarokov, who really fathered Russian drama by authoring 26 major plays and establishing Russia's national theater. Sumarokov's tragedies and comedies closely followed French and German models and only one was performed into the 19th century, but they provided performers at the time with a suitable initial repertoire. The key and timely impetus to the establishment of a Russian national theater came from Feodor Volkov. A native of Yaraoslovl, he visited St. Petersburg when he was young and attended the theater, where he saw the Cadets perform Sumarokov's *Sinave et Trouvore*. Inspired, upon his return home he immersed himself in drama and music and in 1750 set up a local theater and began giving performances. News of this reached Elizabeth within a year, and she invited him and his troupe to perform in Petersburg, which they did in February 1752 at the German theater. The debut of the provincials from Yaroslavl did not exactly enthrall audiences brought up on the more sophisticated foreign fare and better actors. The lack of a national theater, however, had been for Elizabeth a point of embarrassment that hurt Russia's prestige and which Alexander Shuvalov had been urging her to remedy. Indeed, she had commissioned Trediakovsky's and Sumarokov's plays in anticipation of having one. Since Volkov's troupe showed promise, she assigned them to be trained at the Corps of Cadets under Sumarokov in the hope of developing them into Russia's national theater.[53] When they were deemed ready, in August 1756 Elizabeth issued a decree establishing Russia's national theater, with Volkov's group as the nucleus and Sumarokov as the theater's director. Their first performance was given in January 1757 in their own theater, in the former Golovkin mansion on Vasilievsky Island where the Academy of Fine Arts now stands. By 1760, their repertoire included more than 60 plays. When Sumarokov fell out of favor after Elizabeth's death, Volkov himself became director, and when he died in 1763 the theater continued under the direction of one of his chief actors. Although the theater would suffer from lack of funds for many years, it was this institution which eventually grew to occupy the Alexandrinsky Theater (now the Pushkin Theater) on Nevsky Prospect.[54] Elizabeth also took an interest in Russian amateur performances. Prince Yusupov drew her interest to the plays staged by the young actors at the Corps of Pages which he directed.[55] Meanwhile, the performances of the Cadets in the royal palace continued, with Elizabeth taking a personal interest in the young actors, helping them at her own expense, even lending them her jewelry for their costumes.[56]

Russian opera also broke new ground and gained in popularity under the continued direction of Francesco Araja, who under Elizabeth retained his post as director of music until 1759, when he returned to Italy with a considerable fortune.[57] Many new operas were staged, but typically they were Russian translations from the original libretti. The signature event for Russian opera was the production and performance in 1751 of the first opera composed in Russia to an original Russian text, *The Clemency of Titus*.[58] Composed by Araja, its libretto was written by Fedor Volkov. And in 1755 Araja's *Cephalus and Procris* was performed using entirely Russian actors, with Sumarokov as the librettist. In 1757 the Italian Giovanni Battista Locatelli brought an opéra bouffe and ballet company to the city, which was so popular that it leased out the wooden opera house by the Summer Palace and charged nobles a high annual rent for boxes; the lower classes paid handsomely by performance. Elizabeth often attended incognito, and was so pleased that she granted Locatelli an annual stipend of 5,000 rubles. Regular theatergoers became fans of particular performers and displayed their admiration by wearing small cards inscribed with their favorites' names.[59]

The ballet remained popular, and it was not limited to Locatelli's troupe. When the Italian *maître de ballet* Antonio Rinaldo Fuzano learned of Elizabeth's accession and the demise of the pro-German faction that had driven him from Russia,* he returned to St. Petersburg in 1742. He was confident of being retained since in Elizabeth's youth he had been one of her dancing instructors, and he was not disappointed. He was appointed second court *maître de ballet* in charge of comic

---

*Fuzano had come to Petersburg in 1736 with his troupe and initially enjoyed success, but Biron and his clique forced his resignation and departure in 1738.

ballets; Landé, whom Elizabeth admired, retained first position in charge of dramatic ballets. The French dancer Thomas Lebrun remained popular and himself produced allegorical ballets. Of the female dancers, Fuzano's wife Julia, already known throughout Europe, was a star, as was the Russian talent Aksina Sergeyeva. After Locatelli's company declined and Russia became allied with Austria, the Viennese court sent the Austrian *maître de ballet* Hilferding to St. Petersburg in 1759. His ballets were popular and his company succeeded Locatelli's as the leading foreign ballet troupe in the city. He worked with Russian dancers as well and provided them with valuable training. The ballets performed by students at Landé's ballet school also remained popular well beyond his death in 1746.

Music as a separate art form grew in stature, but it was not yet Russian. An orchestra was now a fixture at most court and other high society entertainments. The Italian violinist Domenico Dalloglio conducted the Italian court orchestra. A native of Padua, he had lived in Russia since 1735, apparently having arrived with Araja, and departed in 1764 not long after Elizabeth's death. During his stay he composed many symphonies, concertos, and solo works. Elizabeth invited famous French and Italian singers to perform. Elizabeth also sought to train Russian singers, but none of importance had yet emerged. The Russian choir in the Imperial Chapel performed at a high level, however.

The state of Russian poetry under Elizabeth was somewhat complex. On the one hand, it enjoyed unprecedented popularity and was composed on a wide scale. Seemingly everyone, including Elizabeth herself, tried their hands at it. At both court and private entertainments, recitations of verse specially composed for the event became ubiquitous and nearly obligatory. Trediakovsky, who had pioneered Russian versification and become professor of eloquence at the Academy, once complained that poets' work was regarded "like the fruits and the sweets which appeared on the tables of the rich."[60] As a result, the art form was cheapened and little of artistic merit was produced by these so-called "pocket poets." On the other hand, this phase in Russian poetry's development broadened people's familiarity, knowledge, and liking of this art form and gave it a wider base on which it would later flourish. For Petersburg the one important work was Trediakovsky's ode, *Praise to the Izhorsk Land and the Imperial City of St. Petersburg* (1752), which inaugurated the long tradition of poetry and literature devoted to the city.

THE FINE ARTS

In Elizabeth's time Russian painting had not yet developed to a high level, and a group of foreign artists dominated painting in the city. These included the French portraitist Louis Caravaque, from whom Elizabeth commissioned many portraits of herself, including a dozen upon her accession to send to Russia's embassies abroad. Others included the German brothers Georg and Johann Grooth, the Italian Count

Pietro Rotari, the Frenchman François Tocqué, and the Italian decorative painter Giuseppe Valeriani. There were also some promising Russians in Ivan Vishniakov, Alexei Antropov, and Ivan Argunov, the former serf, but they did not reach the level of the best foreigners. But Russia still lacked a higher school for training painters.

To this end, Peter I had planned to establish a national academy of the arts but had managed to establish only a drawing school as part of the printing office. Little was done until Elizabeth, who in 1747 added to the Academy of Sciences a faculty devoted to the arts, and so the institution was briefly known as the Academy of Sciences and Arts.[61] Ultimately, however, with Ivan Shuvalov's advice and assistance, Elizabeth decided to found a stand-alone national Academy of Fine Arts. It was founded early in 1758 and housed temporarily in quarters on Vasilievsky Island, with Shuvalov as its first president, and by that summer it had 38 students. Its faculty and student body grew rapidly, and under Catherine II it acquired magnificent new quarters on the Neva embankment, where it remains today.

In Elizabeth's time, of greater influence than Russian painting was the vast quantity of Western paintings purchased and brought to Russia and the number of commissioned paintings executed in St. Petersburg by foreign artists. These were ubiquitous, and their subjects included portraits, landscapes, classical mythology and other classical scenes, and depictions of great historical events.[62] This was an extreme departure from the Russia of only a half century earlier, when virtually all culture was dominated by Orthodoxy and painting was limited largely to icons. Petersburg had opened Russia to a new world of art. It would take more time to develop top-flight native painters, but meanwhile the growing general abundance and popularity of paintings on secular themes was an important aspect of stimulating and opening people's minds and changing their tastes and psychology. The portrayal of classical subjects and increased knowledge of classics during Elizabeth's reign eventually resulted in classicism's replacement of the Russian Baroque under Catherine II, which would change the face of the city.

EDUCATION AND INTELLECTUAL LIFE

Elizabeth strove to improve the level of education, professional qualifications, and culture of her people. Unlike her father, she invited few foreigners to Russia, but like him she sent many Russians abroad for training. So many were sent to Paris that the Russian Embassy in Paris had an Orthodox church built there to service them.[63] Elizabeth also created new educational institutions at home. She created the Corps of Pages in 1759 to train youths to serve at court and in the government, for which a special building was built near Nevsky. The Academy of Sciences continued to instruct students but struggled as many nobles now preferred to send their children to the Corps of Cadets. But this made it easier for commoners to attend the Academy and its Gymnasium. In 1750, the ethnographer and botanist Stepan

Krasheninikov took over the Gymnasium. He was able to increase attendance by obtaining more funding for stipends, and replaced foreign teachers with Russians. In 1754 Ivan Shuvalov and Lomonosov convinced Elizabeth to establish as a branch of the Academy a university in Moscow. The Senate quickly approved the project, and it was founded in 1755 with Shuvalov as its curator. It had faculties of law, medicine, and philosophy, but no theological faculty, making it the only European university at the time without one. The university was open to students of all social classes (except serfs), religions, and nationalities. In St. Petersburg, with students and teachers spread across many operating educational institutions and its highest one operating (as Peter had intended) as an Academy rather than a true university, no proper university would be established in Petersburg for some time.

In light of St. Petersburg's vanguard role in enlightenment, the choice of Moscow for the nations's first true university may seem odd, but it made a certain sense. Lomonosov and Shuvalov wanted a degree of independence and freedom in realizing their plans, and this was best achieved far away from the scrutiny and politics of the St. Petersburg court. This distance would also allow intellectual life to grow and flourish in a quieter environment. Indeed, one purpose in founding St. Petersburg was to facilitate the spread of enlightenment throughout Russia, and the prime target was Moscow. This policy succeeded all too well among Moscow's intellectual circles, which over the next century would become hotbeds of progressive thought and dissent.

The Corps of Cadets, though military in name, in fact was designed mainly to prepare youths for life in high society and provided only superficial military education. In order to improve military education, in 1752 Peter I's Naval Academy was transformed into the Naval Corps of Cadets, which 360 students attended in Münnich's former palace on Vasilievsky Island.[64] Later the artillery and engineering schools were merged into the Artillery and Engineering Corps of Cadets. A medical school was established as part of the city's main hospital, which served mainly the army and navy. Elizabeth sought to upgrade education for the broader population as well, by improving religious texts and religious schools, by founding a school for the sons of soldiers, and by requiring some factories to establish schools for the children of their workers.

Elizabeth succeeded in creating a stimulating climate for the mind. It was in her reign that an intellectual and cultural life of the type of which her father had dreamed of began to emerge in the city, with Ivan Shuvalov and Lomonosov at its head. Lomonosov had returned from abroad by 1741, was elected to the Academy in 1744, established his laboratory for chemistry and physics experiments in 1748, and did his best work as a philologist and grammarian during this time. In 1745 the Academy published the first atlas of Russia. Shuvalov worked tirelessly at establishing and improving educational institutions and in sponsoring promising intellectuals, founded the Academy of Fine Arts, and, as in his own salons, brought an intellectual and artistic element to social and court life in the capital. It was in this period that private journalism began, with the appearance of the *Monthly Contributions* and *The Busy Bee*, which Sumarokov edited. In addition to news of events in Russia and abroad, these journals published literary pieces, including poetry, light scholarly articles on science, history, and geography, and some social commentary and criticism. They expanded readers' minds and helped break down old prejudices. More confident about Russia and themselves, people grew more relaxed and less suspicious of foreigners and their practices and ideas, facilitating a more honest fusion of Russian and Western culture and ideas in place of the initial superficial overlay. For Elizabeth, the sign that Russia had become part of Europe came in 1746, when Voltaire asked to be elected as a corresponding member of the Academy of Sciences. She regarded this as only natural and fitting, and Voltaire was elected without fanfare.

It was in Elizabeth's St. Petersburg that Russians and the world could first see Peter the Great's vision pay dividends. In virtually every sphere—military, politics, the court, intellectual life, architecture, and culture—the willingness to open up to and draw on the offerings of the West was elevating Russia to a new level which in some respects was beginning to rival the West. Catherine the Great's achievements would be based more than she would ever admit on foundations laid by Elizabeth. Elizabeth's reign marked the beginning of the golden age of the Russian aristocracy, running approximately to 1855. At the same time, in the background lay inheritances from the past which Elizabeth was not capable of confronting, most notably the growing problem of serfdom and the political relationship of the autocracy with the other elements in Russia's society, and which would plague her successors, the city, and Russia as a whole. The intellectual achievements under Elizabeth were as yet apolitical, but Peter the Great had introduced in St. Petersburg new and provocative political and social ideas with implications that could and eventually would rock society and the autocracy itself. The reign of Catherine II marked a turning point in which these themes came to the fore.

CHAPTER 6

Thinking Like Europe:
The Petersburg of Catherine II

If Peter had opened a window to Europe and Elizabeth had decorated it with Rococo frills, Catherine threw open the doors and began to rebuild the house itself.

JAMES BILLINGTON[1]

[Catherine] has compiled for herself a code of political convictions, quite elevated ones, but which are not applicable to actual affairs. The implementation into practice of such an administration would be the more difficult and even dangerous, inasmuch as one would have to deal with a coarse people which, instead of ideas, possesses only superstitious traditions, and instead of manners—slavish fear and stupid submission. These forces are quite alive, and it would be irrational to endeavor to replace them with others.

JEAN LOUIS FAVIER, French agent
in St. Petersburg, writing in early 1762[2]

A large empire presupposes a despotic authority in the one who governs.

MONTESQUIEU[3]

PETER III AND CATHERINE'S COUP

Elizabeth died on December 25, 1761, of natural causes, and power transferred smoothly to her 33-year-old nephew Peter, whom she had named as her successor. Peter Karl Ulrich was born in Kiel on February 10, 1728, the son of Peter the Great's daughter Anna and Karl Friedrich, the Duke of Holstein-Gottorp. Anna died only 10 days after Peter's birth, his father in 1739. Peter's childhood was unhappy and unstimulating. His father ignored him, and the boy grew up among Holstein guards officers. Even though he was the potential heir to both the Russian and Swedish thrones, no serious effort was made to educate him. Instead, he grew up on the parade ground and became enamored of military drill.

When Elizabeth became Empress, an urgent concern was to designate Peter as her successor in order to eliminate any claim of Ivan VI, who was still a prisoner in Schlüsselburg. She virtually abducted Peter from Holstein and had him travel incognito to St. Petersburg, where he arrived in January 1742. When Elizabeth met Peter, she was shocked at his ignorance and boorish manners; moreover, he spoke no Russian and knew virtually nothing about Russia or the Orthodox faith, nor did he seem to care. She immediately put him in the care of tutors to provide remedial education and teach him the art of governing, but by then his character had been formed, his attention span was short, and his interests were limited to Holstein, military drills, Prussia and its ruler Frederick II, and the violin (since Frederick played one). He learned passable Russian thanks to his good memory, but little else. Although he converted to Orthodoxy in November 1742, he continued to consider himself a Lutheran. Elizabeth had him renounce the Swedish throne and then declared him her heir.

Elizabeth's next task was to find Peter a wife who could produce a successor to Peter. After considering various candidates, Elizabeth settled upon a German, Sophia Augusta Fredrike, princess of Anhalt-Zerbst, who had also been recommended by Frederick of Prussia. Born on April 21, 1729, Sophia was the daughter of Christian August, Prince of Anhalt-Zerbst, and Johanna Elizabeth of Holstein-Gottorp, whose brother Karl Augustus had been engaged to Elizabeth but had died from smallpox in Petersburg in 1727. Johanna was also a first cousin of Peter's father Karl, so Peter and Sophia were also cousins. Elizabeth invited Sophia and Johanna to Russia, where they arrived in February 1744 and quickly assumed their roles at court. Sophia pleased Elizabeth and the court, and devoted herself to learning Russian and learning about her new country. In June 1744 she converted to Orthodoxy, taking the name Catherine Alexeevna, in a ceremony which was a personal triumph marked by her perfect performance of the Orthodox ritual and nearly perfect Russian. The royal couple was betrothed the next day, and they were married in St. Petersburg on August 21, 1745, in the Church of Our Lady of Kazan on Nevsky Prospect.[4]

Although, according to Catherine, the marriage was never consummated, relations between Catherine and Peter initially were cordial. But Catherine proved far more intelligent and the more dominant personality, and their interests differed; inevitably they drifted apart. Peter was the first to take other consorts, although at first he was probably unable to be physically intimate with them.* When the royal couple produced no heir after several years, Elizabeth essentially ordered that one be produced.[5] If the marriage produced no heir, Elizabeth was prepared to disinherit Peter, and both his and Catherine's positions would be lost. The eventual result, to Peter's astonishment, was the birth of Grand Duke Paul on September 20, 1754, who, according to Catherine, was fathered by her first lover, the chamberlain Sergei Saltykov.

---

*After the court belatedly realized that the lack of an heir was Peter's fault, an operation was performed on Peter's foreskin, which was thought to be overly constrictive and perhaps the source of the problem.

With the burden of the succession behind the couple, the pressure on them eased, and they settled into a leisurely life, each spouse turning to his and her interests. Peter's passion was military games at Oranienbaum, which he turned into a military encampment with its own mini-fortress, where he drilled a favored Holstein unit, much to the displeasure of Petersburg's Guards. He took on more consorts, finally settling upon the unattractive and foolish Elizabeth Vorontsova, the niece of Elizabeth's Grand Chancellor Mikhail Vorontsov. Peter's public behavior grew more offensive, and it became evident to all that he was mentally unbalanced. Peter's open adulation of Frederick II of Prussia, with which Russia had been at war since 1756, was offensive to Russians, many of whom had lost their sons to Prussian bullets. But Peter called Frederick "my master," secretly passed Frederick Russian military secrets, and once told a Prussian prisoner in St. Petersburg that "if I were sovereign you would not be a prisoner of war."[6] Russia's statesmen abhorred the prospect of a sovereign who would reverse the policies and accomplishments of the past several years.[7]

When Elizabeth died, Peter was overjoyed and did not hide it. He ordered that bright clothing be worn at the oath of allegiance ceremony only hours after the Empress's death, after which he held a large banquet. When he called the Guards regiments to the Winter Palace to administer the oath of allegiance, he turned it into a military review. Peter was delighted and thought he had discerned enthusiasm and devotion in his subjects' faces. "I did not think they had so much love for me," he declared upon returning to the Palace.[8] But the young Princess Dashkova thought they looked "gloomy and dejected," and thought that "the confused, stifled murmur which arose from the ranks sounded so menacing and alarming, so desperate even, that I could not help wishing myself a hundred miles away."[9] Peter rarely visited Elizabeth lying in state, and when he attended memorial masses for her, Catherine wrote, he "made faces, acted the buffoon, and imitated poor old ladies whom he had curtsy in the French style instead of inclining their heads as is the Russian custom. These poor old ladies were hard put not to stumble when they had to bend at the knee."[10] Even at the funeral he smiled, joked, and played crude pranks. Foreign ambassadors observed that the new sovereign "seemed to make it his aim to be criticized and perhaps finally to be despised."[11]

Some of Catherine's supporters and Peter's opponents were resolved to strike upon Elizabeth's death to deny Peter the throne and make Catherine either Empress or Paul's regent. Prince Mikhail Dashkov, a young captain in the Preobrazhensky Guards, wrote Catherine: "Give the order, and we will place you on the throne!"[12] Catherine had long before (as early as 1756) decided to usurp Peter or perish,[13] but she saw that the time was not ripe: Peter's rule would inevitably deteriorate. Moreover, unknown to most, she was six months pregnant with her lover Grigory Orlov's child and in no condition for such an undertaking. So she replied to Dashkov, "For God's sake, do nothing foolish. All will happen as providence wills. But your undertaking is premature and untimely."[14] Instead, she donned a commodious black mourning dress to conceal her condition and bided her time. Only after the child was born in April did she begin actively plotting Peter's overthrow.

In fact, Peter took a number of measures to modernize Russia in the best St. Petersburg tradition, including freeing nobles from mandatory service obligations except during wartime, giving them full liberty to travel abroad, and encouraging them to engage in commerce and industry.[15] In St. Petersburg itself, his reign was too brief to have any significant effect. He initiated no new building projects except at Oranienbaum, but he did remove the chief naval yards from the city to Kronstadt and improved street lighting.[16] He also introduced a number of police measures which brought greater order in the streets, lowered crime, and improved sanitation.[17] Of course, soldiers were ubiquitous. As the young Russian officer Andrei Bolotov observed, "What with the marching and exercising of troops, and the rolling of carriages, and the traffic and concourse, St. Petersburg seems to have undergone a complete change, and all its circumstances are so altered that we seem to be breathing quite a different atmosphere."[18]

Peter's more enlightened policies were undermined by his unwise and offensive behavior. He immediately ended the war against Prussia, thereby rendering futile the efforts, successes, and sacrifices of the past several years. When peace came, Peter held lavish celebrations marking the friendship of the two nations and their sovereigns.[19] He began dressing and reorganizing the whole army on the Prussian model.[20] The Saxon minister in St. Petersburg observed: "Here at St. Petersburg the King of Prussia *is* Emperor."[21] Peter disbanded Her Majesty's Own Company, formed by Elizabeth from select Preobrazhensky Guards after her coup in 1741, and replaced them with his favored Holstein Cuirassier Regiment.[22] The Guards feared that they too would be disbanded, which indeed Peter apparently was contemplating.[23] Then Peter declared war on Denmark in order to secure for Holstein the territory of Schleswig, in which Russia had no interest. Used to safety and comfort in the capital, soldiers looked for a means of averting a journey to Denmark to risk death fighting for Peter's dear duchy.

Peter next offended the Church and the religious sensibilities of the nation by shaving the beards and changing the dress of churchmen, removing icons from churches, imposing new burdens on the Church and secularizing its lands, and generally appearing to be trying to change Russia's religion and impose Lutheranism. Then he deprived the Senate and other government bodies and their officials of their now traditional powers, concentrating power in a coterie of favorite Russian generals, civil officials (Dmitri Volkov, Nikita Trubetskoi, and Mikhail Vorontsov) and three Germans (including the octogenarian Burkhard Münnich, whom Peter had brought back from exile, and two Holsteiners).[24] He replaced many freed service nobility with pen-pushing commoner bureaucrats.[25] This concentration of power among "accidental people" brought back memories of Menshikov's Supreme Privy Council of 1725–27 and the *Bironovshchina* under Anna Ioannovna. Also unsettling was Peter's failure to mention Paul (or Catherine) in the loyalty oath upon assuming power[26] and his March 1762 visit to the imprisoned Ivan VI in Schlüsselburg,[27] all of which set off speculation that Peter would deprive Paul of the succession. No one, even within Peter's select group, could be assured of his position and future.[28] The revolt against Peter was one in favor of the routinization and stabilization of power within regular institutions.[29]

By June 1762 Peter not only had not created his own power base, but had managed to alienate all principal constituencies. Catherine had courted all these interests, and they began to look to her as the solution, either as regent for Paul or as Empress outright.

The plot began in the Guards units and was led by Grigory Orlov, a dashing young officer in the Izmailovsky Guards who had become Catherine's lover sometime in 1761. He was a military hero, was a natural leader and organizer, enjoyed the unquestioning loyalty of his men, and had four brothers in other Guards units to assist. From the government Catherine recruited the cosmopolitan and experienced diplomat Nikita Panin. In 1759 he had returned from a 12-year stint as ambassador to Sweden to become Grand Duke Paul's tutor, but had been personally insulted by Peter and dismayed by his rule. He would secure the support of disaffected Senators and other civil officials. From the new nobility came Kyrill Razumovsky, brother of Elizabeth's favorite, Alexei. He was one of the unfortunate civilian nobles to be given a military command (in the Izmailovsky Regiment) and forced to drill with the rest, and as such became the butt of the Emperor's crude military humor,[30] which drove him to defect. From the more established nobility came the 19-year-old Princess Catherine Dashkova, the niece of Grand Chancellor Mikhail Vorontsov and sister of Peter's lover Elizabeth Vorontsov. She therefore served as a useful spy and source of connections. Catherine had met the young (fourteen years her junior) and intelligent Dashkova in 1759, they had quickly become close friends due to their shared intellectual interests, and she became Catherine's confidante. At some point, the Archbishop of Novgorod (whose jurisdiction included Petersburg) was made aware of the plot and promised to lend his and the Church's support insofar as his office permitted.[31] He had been offended when Peter told him that he planned to set up a Lutheran chapel at court for the use of his Lutheran domestics; when the Archbishop objected, Peter had heaped abuse on him, calling him a fool and claiming that a religion good enough for Prussia was good enough for Russia too.[32] Catherine and Orlov worked with these supporters directly and kept them apart until the actual execution of the plot.

Initially, the plotters had no date in mind, but in late May and early June matters became more urgent in light of Peter's measures against the Senate, the Prussian peace, and the preparations for war with Denmark. Also, Peter's high-handed treatment of Catherine in public gave support to rumors that he would divorce her or send her to a nunnery and marry Vorontsova. A turning point came in early June, when at a banquet in celebration of the peace with Prussia Peter raised a toast "to the Imperial Family." Catherine did not rise, as the toast was in part to her and her son. Peter objected, however, on the ground that the Imperial Family included his relatives in Holstein, and called her a "fool" (*dura*) loudly enough for most to hear. Following this incident, the conspirators decided to strike as soon as Peter departed for Denmark.

But events soon compelled them to act sooner. On the evening of June 28, one of the conspirators, Captain Peter Passek, was arrested for suspected complicity in the plot. Word of the arrest reached Grigory Orlov during the night, who consulted Panin, who urged Orlov to act immediately before Peter could learn of the plot and react. Alexei Orlov was dispatched in a carriage to fetch Catherine, who was then staying at Mon Plaisir at Peterhof. (Peter was at Oranienbaum.) Meanwhile, Panin and Grigory Orlov readied the city for what they hoped would be Catherine's triumphal entrance and proclamation.

Alexei Orlov arrived at Mon Plaisir by 6:00 A.M. and woke Catherine. "The time has come, all is ready for your proclamation," he announced. "What do you mean?" asked Catherine, sitting up in bed. "Passek is arrested," he replied. She needed to hear no more and did not hesitate. She quickly donned her black dress one last time, exited through the back door and hurried through the gardens to Orlov's carriage, and they set off for the city at breakneck speed. She arrived at the Izmailovsky Guards Regiment, of which Peter had unwittingly made the coconspirator Kyrill Razumovsky its colonel. It was still before 9:00 A.M. and only a few soldiers were up and about when Catherine arrived, but soon the soldiers were streaming out to kneel before their new Empress and kiss her hands, dress, and feet. The regimental chaplain Father Alexei joined them and administered the oath of allegiance; then Razumovsky arrived and swore his allegiance.

Catherine and the Izmailovsky soldiers formed a column led by Father Alexei and set off for the nearby Semenovsky Regiment barracks. Word of Catherine's arrival in the city now preceded her procession, and large crowds were waiting at the barracks to receive and proclaim her. The growing throng made it impossible for Catherine to continue on to the barracks of other regiments, so her procession set off along Nevsky Prospect toward the Church of Our Lady of Kazan, where Catherine and Peter had been married 17 years earlier. As they neared the Church the soldiers of the Preobrazhensky Regiment joined Catherine.

At Kazan the Archbishop of Novgorod was pleased formally to proclaim Catherine Empress and Grand Duke Paul her successor. A short prayer was said, and amid hurrahs and the pealing of church bells the multitude continued down Nevsky to the Winter Palace. By now word of the coup had spread through the city and crowds were thronging into the square by the Palace, Admiralty Lug. When Catherine arrived, the soldiers were set on guard outside, while inside she greeted the Senate and Synod, which Panin had assembled and which swore allegiance to her. She then proceeded upstairs to the balcony overlooking the square to present herself and Paul to the thousands of soldiers and citizens. She held up Paul and read to the people a manifesto justifying her actions. It was aimed at the very groups that Peter had offended and who had turned to Catherine: she explained that Orthodoxy had been endangered, Russia's military glory had been sullied by the peace with Prussia, and the government's institutions had been undermined.

Around the city things were remarkably calm; the only sign of anything unusual was the extra pickets and patrols on the streets. The only serious looting was of Prince Georg of Holstein's home. He was later compensated and simply sent back to Holstein with a number of his compatriots. The foreigners in town feared an anti-foreign backlash as had occurred after Elizabeth's coup, and so they were quick to voice their support of Catherine. Some foreigners brought free liquor to drinking establishments to placate the Russian crowd, which was hardly necessary as the tavern keepers were already serving free vodka and beer. This was apparently done with Catherine's knowledge and approval, and they were later reimbursed.

In the afternoon Catherine reviewed her troops on Admiralty Lug. To her surprise and the delight of all, they had already discarded their Prussian uniforms and were wearing their Russian uniforms from the time of Elizabeth. Catherine and her suite then moved to the wooden Winter Palace on Nevsky that Rastrelli had built for Elizabeth, where they could work more effectively. They sent Admiral Ivan Tazylin to Kronstadt with plenipotentiary powers to take charge of the naval base, which was dangerously near Oranienbaum and could be accessed by Peter to mount a resistance. Others were sent to navy and army units (even those in Prussia) to take command, secure their loyalty, and block any escape by Peter.

That morning Peter had risen late at Oranienbaum, with a hangover. It was his name day and he looked forward to the afternoon's celebrations at Peterhof. After drilling his troops, and still in his Prussian uniform, he and his retinue left for Peterhof at about one o'clock. But when he arrived at Monplaisir he could not find his wife, and a frantic search of the building and grounds yielded only her abandoned gala dress to have been worn at the day's festivities. "I told you she was capable of anything!" he shouted. Then a boat arrived from the city with supplies for the celebration, which brought the news that Catherine had entered town and been proclaimed Empress with the support of the Guards. Perhaps sensing a chance to escape, three of Peter's top officers, Grand Chancellor Vorontsov, Nikita Trubetskoi, and Alexander Shuvalov, volunteered to go to Petersburg and dissuade Catherine from her folly. But when they met Catherine, they made only half-hearted protests. Catherine led Vorontsov to the window, showed him the crowd outside the Palace, and suggested that he try delivering his message to them.[33] Realizing the situation, they swore allegiance to their new Empress.

Meanwhile, Peter and his suite lounged impatiently in Peterhof's lower gardens, waiting for news. But none of his couriers returned; all had been intercepted by Catherine's troops, and Peter was cut off. He began to drink. The numbers of his demoralized suite began to diminish. Sensing the worst, he resolved to move to Kronstadt in the hope of mounting resistance from there, and sent for his Preobrazhensky Guards uniform. At about 11:00 P.M., Peter, now in his unfamiliar Russian uniform, and about 50 of his remaining entourage clambered aboard a galley and a yacht and embarked for Kronstadt. Approaching the harbor of Kronstadt's fortress after midnight (just after sunset and still light), Peter found it closed to larger vessels by a boom. Peter, Münnich, and two or three others climbed into a rowboat and approached the fortress walls. The guard on duty, midshipman Mikhail Kozhukov, ordered the boat to retreat or he would fire. Peter then stood up, threw open his cloak to reveal the blue ribbon of his Order of St. Andrew and shouted: "I am your Emperor!" "We have no emperor!" replied Kozhukov. "Long live Catherine!" Catherine's men had gotten there first. He ordered Peter not to come closer or he would fire, and then sounded the alarm in the fortress. Peter panicked and retreated to his galley, where he fainted. Since the navy had blocked escape by sea, Peter set off for Oranienbaum.

Back in town, Catherine and her advisors resolved to go to Peterhof or Oranienbaum to capture and arrest Peter, leaving the city and Paul in the capable hands of Panin and the Senate. An advance guard of cavalry and hussars headed by Alexei Orlov departed early in the evening to secure Peterhof and Oranienbaum, while Catherine personally commanded the rear guard. For the occasion Catherine chose masculine garb: the uniform of a colonel in the Preobrazhensky Guards (Peter the Great's rank). Mounting astride her white-grey stallion Brilliant, she set off with Princess Dashkova, Razumovsky, and the recently converted Shuvalov and Trubetskoi at her side. As everyone was tired, they stopped at the Krasny Kabachok tavern about six miles from Petersburg for a few hours' rest. They set off again at about 5:00 A.M., and along the route they met deserters from Peter's camp. Before long Prince Golitsyn galloped up to them bearing a letter from Peter apologizing for his conduct and offering to share his throne with her. Catherine only smiled and did not deign to reply, at which point Golitsyn submitted and swore allegiance to Catherine. She then learned that Alexei Orlov's advance guard had secured and sealed both Peterhof and Oranienbaum without bloodshed. At around 10:00 A.M. Catherine and her suite galloped triumphantly into the grounds of Peterhof to the sound of loud hurrahs and cannon salutes. Soon Peter's adjutant, General Ivan Izmailov, arrived with a second letter from Peter, this time renouncing the throne and requesting permission to return to Holstein with Vorontsova. Catherine had a formal abdication drafted on the spot, which Izmailov and Grigory Orlov delivered to Peter, had Peter copy it in his own hand and sign. Peter was then taken to Peterhof, where he surrendered his sword, orders, and uniform. He was then transferred to his nearby estate at Ropsha under the guard of Alexei Orlov until permanent accommodations could be readied at Schlüsselburg.

The next morning Catherine entered Petersburg on horseback in grand fashion at the head of her suite and soldiers. The whole city turned out for her ceremonial entry. The clergy blessed her, bands played, and cheering crowds lined the streets and rooftops. She arrived at the Summer Palace at noon and, conscious of the religious sensibilities of the nation, immediately retired to the court chapel for prayers. Meanwhile, the city celebrated into the night.

Catherine's coup had been bloodless, without the mass arrests, punishments, and confiscations characteristic of earlier coups. But on July 6 Catherine received word that Peter had died. The official cause was an attack of hemorrhoidal colic, while an apologetic letter from Alexei to Catherine claimed that it was the result of a simple brawl. No one claimed that Catherine had ordered Peter's death or even knew of any plan to kill him, but most people in Russia and abroad believed that he had been strangled by Orlov's men acting in what they considered her best interests. In reaction, European wits of the day characterized the government of 18th-century Russia as a "despotism tempered by assassination."

It was the day after Peter's death that, in the taint of this crime, Catherine had the unenviable task of presenting to Russia her second, detailed manifesto elucidating the principles of her reign in which she would strive to bring greater civilization and enlightenment to her adopted country.

ST. PETERSBURG AND THE ENLIGHTENMENT

Catherine was a child of the Enlightenment. Her governess, Elisabeth Cardel, from a French Huguenot family, immersed her in French culture. She taught Sophia French and then had her read and memorize Racine, Molière, and Corneille. At the tender age of eight, Sophia had met the supreme "enlightened despot," Frederick the Great, and had impressed him with her intelligence, curiosity, and memory. From then on she frequented his court. Shortly before her summons to Russia, she met the Countess Charlotta Bentinck from Oldenburg, who had befriended Voltaire during his stay in Prussia and later corresponded with him. Bentinck was not an intellectual, but she was quick-witted, a free bohemian spirit who spurned all conventions. The Countess's nature rubbed off on Sophia. "She stimulated my natural vivacity which was already sufficiently developed and needed to be restrained," Catherine later recounted.[34]

As Grand Duchess, Catherine was well educated, curious, and had a philosophic bent of mind. The Swedish ambassador, Count Adolf Gyllenborg, called her his "fifteen year old philosopher." She took to reading, beginning with simple French romances and then the letters of Madame Sévigné. "After I had devoured them," Catherine wrote, "I read the works of Voltaire and never again got loose from them."[35] She would later write to Baron Grimm that Voltaire "is my teacher, or, better said, his works have formed my mind and spirit."[36] Upon finishing Voltaire, she remarked, "I looked for something similar, but since I could find nothing like it, I read in the meantime whatever fell into my hands."[37] She also formed a stimulating friendship with the Francophile Ivan Shuvalov, who, Catherine remarked, always seemed to have a book in his hand.[38] After giving birth to Paul in 1754,

Catherine was left more to herself and her reading intensified, at which point she read, besides more Voltaire, the *Annals* of Tacitus and Montesquieu's *Spirit of the Laws*,[39] which she later termed "the prayer book of monarchs with common sense."[40] The *Encyclopédie* was her constant companion.[41] The Chevalier d'Eon called her "a natural blue stocking" and remarked that "it is enough for a book to be condemned in France for her to give it her full approbation."[42]

When Catherine ascended the throne, therefore, she was already seeped in Enlightenment thought. Enlightenment thinkers applied reason and scientific method to law, government, economics, society, and individual human beings in order to achieve progress and, ideally according to Condorcet, the perfection of man and society. In the long run, these ideas would challenge the entire European order: its Christian civilization, monarchical government, aristocracy, and other hierarchical divisions, privileges, and inequalities of Old Regime society. Eventually, Enlightenment thinkers sought to replace the Old Regime and even so-called "enlightened despots" with a civil society, meaning one which is self-generated "from below" by equal citizens who create their government, which in turn is charged with protecting citizens' rights. No longer should society need a monarch at its apex to impose rational organization on "subjects" from above.

Even in the West, however, the full implications of these ideas were not foreseen until the eve of the French Revolution. In the meantime, enlightened rule meant the application of police science by an enlightened monarch to achieve the rational organization of government and society according to law. So far, the only social contract was that the nobility would serve the state, and in return the sovereign as "chief servant" of the state would enact rational laws and protect the rights and privileges of those who serve.[43] But even this theory tended to undermine divine right, as it implied duties and limitations on the monarch, and that subjects had the right to expect certain things from their government. Peter the Great had set Russia on this course, and it was still work in progress when Catherine assumed the throne.

Catherine was eager to apply early to mid-Enlightenment ideas to reform Russia's institutions and civilize its people. Sometimes she is portrayed as dilettantish and an intellectual coquette.[44] While this description might apply to her literary efforts, she had a solid understanding of Enlightenment ideas and writings, and her intentions were serious. She would spend thousands of hours over many years personally drafting the law codes through which she hoped to realize her ideas. At least until the French Revolution, her principal hesitations were limited to the questions of autocracy and serfdom, and it is well-known that she would have abolished serfdom had she considered it practical.

Catherine also recognized the propaganda value of being seen as a paragon of enlightenment in Russia and abroad. Also, the figure of Peter the Great loomed over her, and she wanted to outdo him. And she had to repair the tarnish that Peter III's murder (and, later, Ivan VI's murder) had put on her image. She was also vain. She was determined to stun Europe and remake her own and Russia's image. Within days after her accession she launched a massive and systematic public relations campaign.* The campaign would soon come to include massive investments in St. Petersburg designed to turn it into a showcase of enlightened Russian civilization.

Catherine began by entering into correspondences with notable philosophes such as Voltaire, Denis Diderot, Jean D'Alembert, and Baron Frederick Melchior Grimm, and invited them to Russia. (She also corresponded with a young Corsican named Napoleon Bonaparte, who for a time considered joining Catherine's service.[45]) D'Alembert, invited to be Grand Duke Paul's tutor, politely declined. Referring to the official cause of Peter III's death, he explained to Voltaire, "I am also prone to hemorrhoids; they take too serious a form in that country and I want to have a painful bottom in safety."[46] Voltaire also would never go, pleading old age. But others, most notably Grimm and Diderot, made the journey, and while there they were both elected to the Academy of Sciences. Catherine bought Diderot's library in order to relieve his financial difficulties but let him keep it for life, and even paid him a pension for maintaining it. Diderot thanked her profusely: "Oh Catherine! Remain sure that you rule as powerfully in Paris as you do in St. Petersburg."[47] The library finally arrived in St. Petersburg in 1785. When Voltaire died, she bought his library too, which arrived in the capital in 1779 and now resides in the Public Library. She published works of the philosophes that were banned in France, including the *Encyclopédie,* which she hoped to use as a tool for widespread public enlightenment. "What astonishing times we live in!" Voltaire wrote to Diderot. "France persecutes philosophy and the Scythians offer it their protection."[48] When a smallpox epidemic hit Russia in 1768, Catherine resolved that Russia would be the first to utilize a newly discovered vaccination that was untried even in the West. For the event Catherine invited from London the famous Dr. Thomas Dimsdale, and at great risk to herself she set the example by being the first to be inoculated, after which her court and others were obliged to follow. The tide of acclaim abroad was just as hoped. Voltaire exclaimed: "Ah! Madame, what a lesson Your Imperial Majesty has given to our fops, to our learned Professors of the Sorbonne, to the Asclepiuses of our medical schools! You had yourself inoculated with less ceremony than a nun taking an enema."[49] But the inoculation was not mere show: Some two million of her subjects eventually underwent the procedure, and Dimsdale was later brought back in 1781 to inoculate Grand Dukes Alexander and Constantine.[50]

---

*The public relations campaign was not just Catherine's. The philosophes, who were persecuted, saw their works banned in France, and whose ideas were getting nowhere with their king or government, wanted to put France and its monarch to shame by publicizing how even a "backward" country like Russia compared more favorably. They were not Catherine's servile publicity agents, but rather were holding up her example to press their own agenda both at home and in Russia. They regarded Russia as a tabula rasa on which their ideas could and should be tried out. The philosophes understood that in building Petersburg Peter I had not set out to copy Europe but to realize the ideals of a common humanity, and they were committed to the same.

Diderot accepted Catherine's invitation and visited St. Petersburg for five months in 1773 when he was already 60 years old, after a long and hard journey during which he fell ill from colic. He arrived on the eve of Grand Duke Paul's wedding, but since his luggage had not, he could only attend one of the post-wedding masquerades, where he was introduced to Catherine. Diderot wore his black philosopher's suit as usual, which provoked some sniggers among the guests. But Catherine soon met him at length, and they hit it off. She so enjoyed their conversations that she would receive him at least three times a week in her Hermitage between three and six o'clock.

Since Catherine's Legislative Commission (see below) had recently been disbanded, Diderot sought to refocus the Empress on the need to complete the task of enacting an enlightened code of laws. He decided to approach the task by showing her how to arrive at practical proposals from first principles. For each meeting, he would compose a short paper called a "memoir" on the day's topic, which he would read to her and they would then discuss. The topics included the morality of princes, despotism, serfdom, creating a Third Estate, building streets, and how to write. Diderot often became overly animated and enthusiastic, walking all over the room, throwing off his wig, and grabbing Catherine's knees and slapping her thighs. "Your Diderot is a most extraordinary man," Catherine wrote to the patroness of the philosophes, Mme. Geoffrin. "I emerge from my conversations with him with my thighs bruised and quite black and blue. I have had to put a table between him and me to keep myself and my limbs out of the range of his gesticulation."[51] Ultimately, the old philosopher's ideas proved too theoretical and impractical for the sovereign; they disagreed on many things though they continued to be on the best of personal terms. It did not help Diderot's cause that the Pugachev rebellion* erupted in the middle of his visit. Catherine would later famously describe these meetings to a later French ambassador, Count Ségur:

> I frequently had long conversations with him, but with more curiosity than profit. Had I placed faith in him, every institution in my empire would have been overturned; legislation, administration, politics and finance all would have been changed for the purpose of substituting some impracticable theories. . . . Then, speaking to him freely, I said: "Monsier Diderot, I have listened with the greatest pleasure to all that your brilliant genius has inspired you with; but all your high principles, which I understand very well, though they will make fine books, would make sad work in actual practice. You forget, in all your plans for reformation, the difference between our positions: You work only upon paper, which submits to everything; . . . but I, a poor Empress, work on human nature, which is, on the contrary, irritable and easily offended."[52]

---

*Emelian Pugachev, a Don Cossack, exploited the local grievances of Ural Cossacks to assume the mantle of Peter III and lead a revolt beginning in the autumn of 1773. The insurrection spread through much of the country and included most disaffected elements of the population. The rebellion was finally quashed in late 1774, with Pugachev being taken prisoner, tried and executed.

Despite their differences, upon his return to France Diderot, still on Catherine's payroll, renewed his praises of the Empress.

Grimm also visited St. Petersburg in 1773 for Grand Duke Paul's marriage and to some extent competed with Diderot for the Empress's attentions; he visited again in 1776 for almost a whole year. Catherine courted his favor because his journal, *Correspondance littéraire,* was widely read throughout Europe, and she subscribed to it. Catherine found Grimm more practical, worldly and closer to her heart than Diderot, and she met with him, usually in the evening, even more often than with Diderot. They would remain friends and maintain an active correspondence for life. He returned from his first visit waxing enthusiastic about Catherine, whom he called "the nourishment of my soul, the consolation of my heart, the pride of my mind, the joy of Russia, and the hope of Europe."[53]

Catherine had to give substance to her image, and soon she was at work putting her ideas into practice, first and foremost in the role of lawgiver. Catherine sought to rationalize Russian government and society through a new code of laws. A foundation of both police science and Enlightenment political theory was the belief in law as the means to rationalize government and society.[54] In Russia, the last comprehensive revision of the legal code, Tsar Alexis's *Ulozhenie* of 1649, had long been rendered obsolete by Peter the Great's reforms.[55] Russia's laws were in a state of confusion, which confounded efforts toward rational state administration and the rule of law. One Russian wit of the time observed that the government of Russia must be directed "by God himself—otherwise it is impossible to explain how it is even able to exist."[56] So Catherine spent nearly two years holed up with her books (up to three hours a day, she would claim[57]), in particular with Montesquieu's *Spirit of the Laws* and Cesare Beccaria's *Essay on Crimes and Punishments,*[58] in order to compose for Russia's lawmakers a broad outline of the principles that should underlie Russia's laws. The result was the *Nakaz* ("Instruction"),[59] a grand instrument penned by Catherine herself consisting of (including two supplements) 655 articles.

Montesquieu had considered Russia an Asian country and, due to its expanse and climatic conditions, consigned it to the category of necessary despotisms.[60] This found expression in Article 9 of the *Nakaz,* which stated: "The Sovereign is absolute; for there is no other Authority but that which centers on his single Person, that can act with Vigor proportionate to the Extent of such a vast Dominion." Indeed, in Catherine's reign Russia's domains would extend from Poland to the Canadian Yukon and northern California. But Catherine was at pains to deem Russia European. Thus the *Nakaz* began by proclaiming that "Russia is a European state." This meant that Russia need not be and was not a despotism, but rather a monarchy on the European model with some limitations on royal authority, a rational and enlightened system of government and, presumably, a European culture. Indeed, like Peter I she based imperial authority on utilitarian philosophic principles rather than hereditary right or divine sanction.[61] Thus, the *Nakaz* contained a tension between absolutism and the legal (ultimately constitutional) limits on sovereign power that would come to underlie civil society.

Catherine's conception of the rational state was the European system of a "society of orders," in which each segment of society—the nobility, the clergy, and the merchants and others in the Third Estate—were accorded their specific places and roles. This is reflected in the *Nakaz* itself, as well as in Catherine's later legal codes dealing with various elements of society, including the Provincial Statute (1775), the Charter of the Towns (1785), the Charter of the Nobility (1785), the Police Code (1782), and the drafted but unenacted Charter on the State Peasantry. She especially sought to develop a Third Estate, hoping to create a dynamic social and economic force that would stimulate the national economy and provide qualified servitors and governing bodies in the towns and provinces to carry out imperial policies; certainly it was not her plan to create a class that would undermine monarchy itself. But the merchants and other commoners did not aspire to a political role. Much as in France, the initial challenges to Russia's monarchy would come from the aristocracy. Since nobles were no longer bound to serve the state, many began devoting their lives to helping the Russian people instead and became Russia's first intelligentsia.[62] The nobility did not, as Catherine hoped, take to commerce.

Thus, Catherine's *Nakaz* on its surface as well as subsequent legislation sought to formalize in Russia an ancien régime structure of society that was already becoming outdated in the West and being undermined by the very Enlightenment principles that Catherine was advocating. Nevertheless, it called for many reforms in the areas of the judiciary, crimes and punishment, the treatment of serfs, the subjection of all persons to the rule of law, and radically progressive government institutions. The *Nakaz* sought to place Russia on par with the most progressive of European regimes, and exceed them. When she submitted early drafts to her advisors, they were shocked at its liberalism. Nikita Panin warned her: "These are axioms that will break down walls!"[63] In fact, it was so liberal that it was banned and confiscated in France.[64] Catherine realized the propaganda value of her creation and so had it translated into several foreign languages and bound in luxury leather editions for consumption in the West.[65] This had the desired effect. Giving Catherine the title of "Semiramis of the North" and St. Petersburg that of the "Northern Palmyra," Voltaire called the *Nakaz* the "finest monument of the age" and ridiculed the French government for banning it (thus ensuring its popularity there), and went on to observe that "we have never heard of any Female being a Lawgiver. This Glory was reserved for the Empress of Russia."[66]

In 1767, Catherine convoked the Legislative Commission to begin the work of lawmaking based on the *Nakaz*. Before it convened, however, she toured Russia's provinces in order to learn more about her adopted country. She entered a different world from that of St. Petersburg and was dismayed by what she saw: backward economic development, poor local governance, illiteracy, religious persecution and, especially, vast ethnic diversity and differences in customs and beliefs. She began to doubt the practicality of her lawmaking endeavor before it even began. On May 29 she confided to Voltaire:

> These laws about which so much as been said are in the first analysis not yet enacted. Well, who can answer for their usefulness? It is posterity, not we, who in truth will have to decide that question. Consider, if you will, that they must be applied in Asia as well as Europe, and what difference of climate, peoples, customs, and even ideas! Here I am in Asia: I wanted to see it with my own eyes. In this city there are twenty diverse peoples, which in no way resemble one another. We have nevertheless to design a garment to fit them all. . . . I have come to realize that we have to create a world, unify and conserve it. I shall not finish and here there are too many of all the patterns.[67]

And again a few days later: "This is an Empire to itself and only here can one see what an immense enterprise it is as concerns our laws, and how little these conform at present to the situation of the Empire in general."[68]

Catherine convened the Legislative Commission in Moscow not only because it was a central location, but also in order to better mobilize public opinion (so that it would not be seen as a St. Petersburg or "Petrine" enterprise) and to challenge Muscovite backwardness and lethargy in its own backyard. The Commission was unique first because it consisted of *elected* delegates from throughout the empire. It was also reasonably representative of the nation, with only the nobles' serfs unrepresented (on the theory that their masters represented them; state peasants were represented). In many ways it resembled the French Estates General of 1789. Indeed, in preparation for the event, delegates were tasked with canvassing their constituents and drawing up their own subsidiary *nakazi* ("instructions") outlining their positions and complaints, much like the *cahiers* in France in 1789. The substantive debates broke down along class lines. Thus, the merchants opposed the nobility's participation in trade and manufacturing and even the nobility's use of serfs as commercial agents. The nobles demanded exclusivity over agriculture and ownership of serfs, claiming that merchants should hire free labor, and supported autocracy as their protector. Thus, the delegates were (to Catherine) surprisingly conservative. They favored stable and hereditary divisions between the orders rather than social mobility. Their worldview still reflected the medieval Muscovite notion of an organic, harmonious, and static Russian society without conflict, not Catherine's of altering the social structure into a more dynamic one, admitting the potential for diverse interests and conflict, aimed at progress and development of the country's potential.[69]

The Commission divided into various subcommittees responsible for particular areas of legislation, but the delegates were unprepared and unqualified for the task and they became bogged down in debate. Catherine recessed the Commission briefly and, believing that the atmosphere in Moscow was partly to blame, moved it to St. Petersburg in the hope of better results. But fewer delegates made the trip to the capital, and the plenary sessions there were suspended indefinitely in 1768 when the First Turkish War began and many delegates had to leave to serve in the military. While the Commission was disappointing in terms of its grand design, its work proved useful for drafting Catherine's later legislation, especially during her second period of "legislomania" in the early 1780s. By then she had also become enamored with William Blackstone and Jeremy Bentham, leaving behind French natural rights theories (already becoming dangerous) in favor of more utilitarian principles.[70] More broadly, the Commission had a lasting effect on the country's educated elite, and it stimulated and defined much of the social and political debate for decades to come.[71] Many participants in the Commission's work, such as Nikolai Novikov, would later emerge as leading thinkers and social reformers who drew on the *Nakaz*'s principles.

It was under Catherine that Peter the Great's conception of applying the modernization achieved in St. Petersburg as a springboard to modernize the rest of Russia became a reality and was systematically and fairly successfully carried out.[72] Catherine saw the development of towns and cities as the key to creating the numbers and classes of citizenry who would modernize her agrarian country, which led to the Provincial Statute of 1775 (to strengthen local government following the Pugachev rebellion) and the Charter of the Towns of 1785 (dealing mainly with local economics).

Moscow is perhaps the most poignant example of Catherine's effort to expand modernization beyond Petersburg and remake other cities in its image. From her first experiences in Moscow she had quickly come to detest its backwardness, superstition and fanaticism, shabby construction, and dirt, a city in which "sloth and indolence are the chief employments."[73] She liked to call it Ispahan, in reference to the city from which the Persian voyagers in Montesquieu's *Persian Letters* traveled to France in search of enlightenment.* She wrote that "it often happened that I saw from the windows of the Summer Palace two, three, four, sometimes five fires at the same time in different parts of Moscow."[74] During her trip there in 1753, the palace in which she stayed was "filled with every kind of insect"[75] and burned to the ground. As she fled, she observed that "a prodigious number of rats and mice were filing down the stairs, not even hurrying much."[76] She realized that she had "spent a month in circumstances like those that Peter the Great lived under for thirty years"[77] and understood how he must have felt. When she returned to the capital in January 1768, she was thrilled to be home and told Panin, "Petersburg seems paradise in comparison to Ispahan, and especially the palace."[78] Later, in 1771 when a plague broke out in Moscow that ultimately killed 100,000 people, a fanatical mob murdered the city's Archbishop and trampled many people to death when he tried to stop charlatans from bilking donations from a crowd that they had raised to a

---

*Ispahan, now normally spelled Isfahan or Esfanan, is located just over 200 miles south of Tehran. Alas, Montesquieu's travelers were confused and disappointed by what they found in France, as the author used their trip as a device to criticize what he considered wrong in France.

fever pitch. Catherine wrote Voltaire: "Moscow is a world of its own, not just a city. . . . The famous Eighteenth Century really has something to boast of here! See how far we have progressed!"[79] In 1772 she wrote a comic play, *Oh, Our Times!*, satirizing the conservative nobility of the city. At around this time, Catherine also penned her *Reflections upon Petersburg and Moscow* setting forth her more considered thoughts on the subject:

> I do not like Moscow at all, but I have no prejudice against Petersburg; [in appraising both] I shall take as my guide the good of the Empire. . . . Moscow is the seat of sloth. . . . The nobility who have made the place their home love it: that is no surprise; but from their most tender youth they assume the tone and allurements of laziness and luxury; they become effeminate, always driving around with a coach and six horses, and they see only sorry sights capable of enfeebling the most remarkable genius. Furthermore, never has a people held before its eyes more objects of fanaticism, such as miraculous icons at every step, churches, priests, convents, pilgrims, beggars, thieves, useless servants in the houses—what houses, what disorder there is in the houses, where the lots are immense and the courtyards are filthy swamps. . . . There you have that rabble of a motley crowd, always ready to oppose good order, which from time immemorial has rioted at the least pretext and which cherished stories of these uprisings, nourishing its spirit thereby. . . . By contrast Petersburg, one must admit, cost many men and much money; it is expensive to live there, but in forty [years] Petersburg has given more circulation to money and industry in the empire than Moscow has in the 500 years since it was built; a great many people are employed in construction there, in exchanging foodstuffs and merchandise, and they spread a great deal of money to the provinces; the people there are more docile, more polite, less superstitious, more accustomed to foreigners, from whom they continually acquire one fashion or another, and so on.[80]

Catherine was determined to improve construction in Moscow and elsewhere and, with it, raise the level of civilization. Thus, in 1762 she created the Commission on Masonry Construction of St. Petersburg *and* Moscow. After a fire leveled Tver in 1763, the Commission's jurisdiction was expanded to cities in all of Russia and was placed under the control of the Senate. In 1764 a decree required the preparation of urban plans for all towns, and by the end of Catherine's reign the Commission had developed and approved comprehensive plans for over 300 Russian towns and cities.[81] Among other things, manufacturing was to be moved out of Petersburg and Moscow into provincial towns, and in the centers of cities would be ensembles of governmental buildings. In addition to replanning existing cities, Catherine founded scores of new towns and cities, including Sevastopol, and populated them with soldiers, citizens, and foreigners (especially Germans). By 1781 Catherine counted 29 provinces (*gubernii*) reorganized according to her reform and 144 new towns.[82] Russia's urban population doubled in only 13 years between 1769 and 1782.[83] These efforts succeeded in enabling Westernization and European culture to penetrate Russia to an unprecedented degree, not only in the towns and cities but also into the countryside.

These policies were also applied in St. Petersburg. In accordance with the Provincial Statute, the government of St. Petersburg was reorganized on the basis of home rule. With new local self-government featuring an *elected* City Duma and City Chief, the direct role of the Emperor or Empress and the Senate in the city's affairs was significantly diminished, and many rights and functions previously carried out by them were transferred to the municipality. The city now had the right to own land on its territory that was not privately owned, to found schools, establish mills, restaurants, taverns, markets and regulate local trade. For the first time in history the city had its own budget. In 1780 the city's official coat of arms was approved.[84] Used unofficially since 1722 and still in use today, it consists of a scepter with the royal double-eagle emblem topped by the royal crown, with crossed sea and river anchors behind it on a red background symbolizing the city's role as a sea and river port.

The city's new government exercised its powers to improve life in Petersburg. The paving of city streets became more systematic and was carried out by approved contractors, although building owners still had to pay for paving to the middle of the street in front of their buildings. By the end of Catherine's reign, virtually all streets on the Admiralty side between the Neva and the Fontanka were paved, while in other regions only the principal streets were paved. The number of street lamps was increased from 1,257 in 1770 to over 3,400 by 1794, and a special team of lamplighters was created to light and maintain them. The street addresses of buildings were also renumbered, and street names were engraved in marble tablets. The number of bridges was greatly increased, many of which were now built in stone. Regular street patrols were organized to maintain safety and order. In 1763 the city's first fire department with municipal firefighting equipment was founded, though it consisted mainly of managers; troops and residents were still called upon for the actual firefighting. Fires thus became less of a threat to the city; the only major fire in Catherine's reign was in 1774, which consumed about 150 buildings between the Admiralty and the Moika. Beginning in 1784, the city also founded public hospitals and other medical facilities; previously they had been founded by individual organizations, especially the military, principally to serve their members.[85]

Notwithstanding self-rule, Catherine personally played a crucial role in the architectural plan of the city during her reign. Her ultimate goal for St. Petersburg was to make it a glorious showcase of her reign for both Russia and Europe to behold, in its architectural appearance, prosperity, and vibrant cultural and social life.

BRINGING CLASSICAL ARCHITECTURE
TO ST. PETERSBURG

Prior to Catherine's reign, the only sophisticated urban planning had been on the Admiralty side following the fires of 1736–37; other efforts, like the *strelka* of Vasilievsky Island near the end of Peter's reign, were only on the ensemble scale.

Moreover, except for the grand palaces constructed mainly under Elizabeth, most construction was still shoddy. Visiting in 1764, Giacomo Casanova observed that the city was still in its "infancy" and that "everything seemed to me ruins built on purpose."[86] No comprehensive plan had yet been implemented to unite all three parts of the city—Vasilievsky Island, the Petersburg side, and the Admiralty side—and the Neva itself into a cohesive and grand appearance. Catherine needed to address these challenges in order to realize her vision of a grand capital, and she was impatient to begin.

Thus, even before the formation of the Commission on Masonry Construction of St. Petersburg and Moscow in December 1762, a new plan for St. Petersburg was hastily drawn up and approved by her government.[87] But once the Commission was formed it was decided to take a more deliberate approach. In November 1763 Catherine announced an open international competition for the planning of the city. Each participant had to submit two designs. The first could not alter the existing conditions in the city, leaving all major streets and buildings largely untouched except where absolutely necessary, the goal being mainly to bring the existing elements of the city into greater harmony. In the second design, participants were given full rein to propose whatever scheme they thought best regardless of existing conditions. The proposals received were put on public exhibition for 15 days, after which the entries were to be judged by the Commission. The surviving records of the competition do not reveal the results, but the Commission's later planning of the city owed much to the ideas of the competitors.[88]

From this effort emerged a plan by Alexei Kvasov, then Chief Architect of the Commission. It focused on developing five central squares on the Admiralty side of the city as unified architectural ensembles, including what are now Palace Square on the south side of the Winter Palace, Decembrists Square to the west of the Admiralty, and St. Isaac's Square to the south of St. Isaac's Cathedral. Fundamentally this plan was realized,[89] but it took nearly a century. Separate plans were approved in 1766 and 1768 for other districts of the Admiralty side. For the Petersburg side, an idea arose to lay three radials spreading outward from the spire of the Peter and Paul Cathedral, just as the radials on the Admiralty side spread out from the spire of the Admiralty,[90] but this would have entailed destroying too much existing construction and expensive rebuilding. More fundamentally, a unified solution to the overall design and appearance of the city could not be achieved through isolated schemes and ensembles within various islands without reference to the Neva. Rather, a unified design had to exploit the Neva itself, focusing on the visual interrelationships of the islands, each as seen from across or on the river, which was the city's main transportation artery from which residents and visitors regularly viewed the city. This approach would require integrating into a unified whole the *strelka* of Vasilievsky Island, the Fortress, the twin spires of the Admiralty and Peter and Paul Cathedral, the river embankments, and the façades and skylines of the buildings built upon them.

The project began with facing the central embankments of the city in pink Finnish granite, the design and construction of which was carried out by the German architect Georg Veldten from 1764 to 1788. The project required great artistry to prevent the embankments from appearing cold and faceless. This was avoided partly through the bright color of the granite, which provided a welcome contrast to the gray river and the silver sky, and partly by exploiting the fact that the Neva was still the main transportation artery of the city with no permanent bridges across it, constructing numerous boat landings along the embankments, most of which were of a uniform, graceful design and accessed by granite staircases. He also designed in 1763–69 picturesque arched bridges over the Winter Canal (Hermitage Bridge), Swan Canal (Upper Swan Bridge), and the Fontanka (Prachechny Bridge). In 1779–87 Veldten complimented the new embankment by facing the Fortress with the same granite.

While the new embankments provided a stunning frame, the picture had to be provided: an architectural focus for the riverscape and the city. The Fortress offered no such potential, and the *strelka* of Vasilievsky Island was too small. The obvious choice was Palace Embankment running between the Admiralty and the Summer Garden, which extends for nearly a mile and already boasted the Winter Palace and other palaces of the court and aristocracy. In 1765 the Commission presented a report to Catherine outlining the Palace Embankment project. There would be an unbroken line of palaces along the embankment, as well as a new face to the Summer Garden. The height of all buildings needed to be relatively uniform, which meant that many existing buildings had to be heightened and their cornices redesigned, and their facades should not clash.

This last requirement meant that Catherine had to select an overall architectural style through which to make her mark on the city and give it a uniform character. While Grand Duchess, she had come to regard Elizabeth's Russian Baroque style as overdone and in bad taste. As Empress, she wanted to distance herself from her predecessor. She took as her point of departure the new paradigm in thought and civilization that she sought to bring to Russia. In the West, especially in Italy and France, the Enlightenment's interest in the classical world, coupled with the discoveries of Herculaneum and Pompeii, had led to a revival of classicism and Palladio in architecture that would reach its height under Napoleon. This purer, simpler yet stately style suited Catherine. An early Petersburg example was a small palace designed and built in 1753–54 for Ivan Shuvalov by the Russian Alexander Kokorinov (1726–72), which in important ways departed from traditional Baroque elements in favor of classical themes.[91] The turning point, however, was the building for Shuvalov's brainchild, the Academy of Fine Arts on the Vasilievsky Island embankment (1764–88), designed by the Frenchman Jean-Baptiste-Michel Vallin de la Mothe (1729–1800), whom Shuvalov had invited to Russia in 1759, and Kokorinov, who in 1761 had become the Academy's director. This edifice featured two full stories atop a rusticated basement, straight, clean lines broken only by a low dome in the center, and large porticoes with Tuscan columns. It served as an example of classical design for the Academy's students. Another point of departure was the early work of the Italian Antonio Rinaldi (1709–94), who had become architect to the court of Grand Duke Peter and Grand Duchess Catherine in 1756. Peter, who opposed Elizabeth in everything, gave Rinaldi full reign to design and build outside the Baroque style. He put Rinaldi to work on a small palace and other buildings at Oranienbaum, including the Chinese Palace for Catherine. His *Katalnaya Gorka* ("Sliding Hill") at Oranienbaum was a key early expression of neoclassicism. It retained Baroque elements but is marked by a reserved elegance that makes an interesting comparison to Rastrelli's Hermitage at Tsarskoe Selo. Rinaldi's early work at Oranienbaum endeared him to Catherine, influenced her architectural tastes, and gained him commissions after Elizabeth's death.

Thus, from the start Catherine worked with a group of prominent architects, mostly foreign, who leaned toward classical design. At first the key figures were Veldten (1730–1801), Vallin de la Mothe, Rinaldi, and the Russian Vasily Bazhenov (1738–99), whose emergence is a testament to the training of young Russian architects initiated by Peter the Great and continued under Elizabeth. Late in Catherine's reign, as classicism grew more pure and became linked to a Palladian revival, Catherine's key architects were the Italian Giacomo Quarenghi (1744–1817), the Scot Charles Cameron (1740–1812), and the Russian Ivan Starov (1743–1808).

Many of the architectural masterpieces seen along Palace Embankment today are the result of Catherine's plan to make it the architectural focus of the city. She began by adding a complex of buildings to the east of the Winter Palace which now is part of the Hermitage Museum. The first was the long and narrow Small Hermitage adjacent to the east end of the Winter Palace and running along its side perpendicular to the Neva. It was built in 1764–67 by Vallin de la Mothe as a private retreat to which Catherine could withdraw for peace and quiet. Atop the first story in the interior was a hanging garden, still preserved today, along which galleries were soon added to house artwork. But its main façade (really its end) facing the Neva is monumental in the style of the architect's Academy of Fine Arts, with a tall first story and a grand portico spanning the second and third stories. These proportions repeated those of the adjacent Winter Palace so that its more classical style would not noticeably clash with its neighbor. Next upriver, Veldten was commissioned to design a "building in line with the Hermitage" to house most of Catherine's growing art collections, which came to be known as the Old Hermitage. It too is long and narrow but, unlike the Small Hermitage, runs along the Embankment, up to the Winter Canal. Its proportions, height, and cornice match those of the Small Hermitage, but it is more reserved in style and lacks columns or pilasters. Finally, across the Winter Canal, on the site of Perter I's Winter Palace, Quarenghi built the Hermitage Theater in 1783–87. It is connected to the Old Hermitage by an arched bridge on the second story matching the arch of the Hermitage Bridge just below, and the curved bulge on the Winter Canal side trumpets the building's function. Harmony with its neighbors to the west is retained in the height and proportions of its stories: Its height, like that of the Small Hermitage, is emphasized by large engaged columns, while prominent string courses and its cornice complement the horizontal of Veldten's Embankment and the adjacent buildings. With its statues and busts in niches and corniced windows, it is the most classical building of the ensemble.

Catherine also decided finally to regularize the square behind the Winter Palace and surround it with a regular architectural ensemble. Rastrelli had designed a kind of park with a large circular colonnade with two rows of columns of white marble on the still unpaved square, with his father's equestrian statue of Peter the Great in its center. He had planned to start on it immediately after finishing the Winter Palace, but his patron Elizabeth died before then and Catherine did not employ him. In 1779 Catherine held a competition of architectural designs, and Veldten's won. His buildings formed an arc encircling the opposite side of the square. It was these buildings which Carlo Rossi later reconstructed into his General Staff Headquarters with the grand arches between them still seen today.

While the profile of Palace Embankment was well framed by the Winter Palace ensemble on the west, it needed a magnificent structure on the east by Tsaritsyn Lug. For this Catherine turned to Rinaldi, and the result was the Marble Palace built between 1768 and 1785. She gave it to Grigory Orlov in 1772, long after he had ceased to be her lover, in gratitude for his many services to the state. The palace was unusual in utilizing only pure stone for its exterior rather than masonry coated with painted plaster. The lower portion was built in pinkish-red granite to match Veldten's embankment, while the upper stories were clad with rare marble from Siberia in various colors, mainly bluish gray and pink. Still more types and colors of marble were used in the spectacular interior, which is largely preserved today. The roof was made of sheet copper which reflected the sun's rays and gave the appearance of gold. (The Soviets sequestered the copper in the 1930s for state needs.) The palace actually faced Tsaritsyn Lug (now the Field of Mars), but its Neva façade with its giant pilasters and roof decoration is monumental and makes a breathtaking sight from the river or its opposite bank.

The scheme for the embankment continued upriver from the Marble Palace. Just to the east Quarenghi built the palace of the merchant Groten in 1784–88, which now houses the Institute of Culture, and Veldten built the palace of Ivan Betskoi, who headed both the Academy of Fine Arts and the Commission on Masonry Construction. Catherine also wanted the Summer Garden to present a grand visage to the Neva. For this she commissioned Veldten to build a grand iron grille, which was framed by his new arched bridges across Swan Canal and the Fontanka. Until then the Garden itself extended to the water's edge, but now a street was laid down between Veldten's new granite embankment and his grille. The grille is constructed in sections between granite columns. The ironwork is stately and beautiful in its simplicity; the bronze rosettes and other detailing add lightness and avoid monotony. According to legend, an eccentric Englishman traveled to St. Petersburg by ship just to see the beauty of Veldten's grille. When he arrived he immediately sailed upriver and dropped anchor to admire it. Satisfied, he returned to his homeland, never having set foot in the city.

In the Summer Garden itself, however, little new work was done. This is because the English-style garden, in which the man-made elements of a park blended into the natural surroundings, had become more popular than the earlier French style in which the Summer Garden was originally laid out. New gardens at Tsarskoe Selo and Peterhof, and later Pavlovsk and Gatchina, gave more scope for designing in the English manner. These suburban palaces were also the preferred residences of royalty in the summer months, and their gardens were now the site of outdoor summer entertainments. Thus, the Summer Garden, originally the preserve of royalty and their guests, lost much of its original function, and it became more like a public park. Beginning in 1755, Elizabeth opened it to the public twice a week and on holidays, and public access increased over time. Boatloads of well-dressed aristocratic girls from the Smolny Institute would dock in front of the Garden and stroll in it, a sight which inspired a series of portraits of the girls by Dmitry Levitsky now hanging in the Russian Museum. Catherine often went there for her morning walks. In 1777, one of the city's worst floods destroyed the Garden's fountains, many works of art, as well as exotic shrubs and trees. The French style having passed, Catherine decided not to rebuild the fountains, but retained the existing layout and the surviving artworks. She replanted trees but eliminated the more exotic types; contrary to popular tradition, she did not let the trees grow naturally (like today) but kept them trimmed.[92]

Catherine also developed the Neva embankment downriver from the Winter Palace, which Veldten also encased in granite as far as New Holland. Not much could be done to beautify the river side of the Admiralty. Having a naval shipyard in the very center of a capital city and adjacent to its royal palace was an anachronism and an eyesore, and it contradicted her cameralist principle of locating industry outside city centers. After a fire there in 1783, Catherine ordered that the Admiralty be moved to Kronstadt. The Admiralty staff, which coveted their place in the city, opposed this move but did not dare openly oppose the Empress. Instead, they prepared a study showing that the cost of moving the Admiralty to Kronstadt would be exorbitant. Impressed, and with her treasury strained, Catherine relented and let the Admiralty remain, but in consequence the Admiralty was not rebuilt until the next century.[93]

Just downriver from the Admiralty was one of the open areas that Kvasov had proposed making into one of the city's main squares. On the west side of the Square, in 1763 the palace of Bestuzhev-Rumin was passed to the state, and after renovations the Senate moved into it from Vasilievsky Island. On the Square itself stood Mattarnovy's St. Isaac's Church. But it fell into disrepair, was torn down in 1763, and a new one was begun by Rinaldi in 1768 just to the south, where the current St. Isaac's Cathedral now stands. The new church was never finished by Rinaldi or even fully according to his design, and was completed by Brenna in 1801. But the Square was now open to the Neva and its center was bare. It needed a monument.

For years there had been discussion of building a grand monument to the city's founder. Peter and his contributions had been so manifold, complex, and controversial that prior to Catherine no one could agree on how to represent him. But Catherine, eager to be seen as Peter's heir, was determined to erect it. Lomonosov, Diderot, and others had proposed not a mere sculpture but a grand panorama replete with allegorical figures representing both Peter's many virtues as well as the barbarism and many enemies that he overcame. But Catherine, never enamored with allegory, wanted a more timeless, pristine, and personal representation in line with her classical tastes. Fortunately, Russia's highly cultured ambassador in Paris, Prince Dmitri Golitsyn, knew just the man to create it.

Etienne-Maurice Falconet, born in 1716 of a Parisian craftsman, studied sculpture from 1734 and was elected to the French Academy. Like Catherine he had a philosophic bent of mind and thus frequented the circles of Diderot and other philosophes, and had even contributed an article on sculpture to the *Encyclopédie*. So when Diderot learned that Catherine needed an artist for what would likely be her grandest commission for a monument, it was easy for him to recommend Falconet to his friend Golitsyn. Falconet, by then 50 years old, arrived in St. Petersburg in mid-1766 with his 17-year-old student assistant, Marie-Anne Callot, for what all thought would be an eight-year project. But the job was larger than anyone had imagined. He would not return to Paris until he was 62, and he never saw the unveiling of his masterpiece.

Falconet began designing the statue before leaving Paris and conceived it relatively quickly. He shared Catherine's aversion to an allegorical panorama and wanted to represent only Peter himself. Taking inspiration from the equestrian statues of Marcus Aurelius in Rome and Frederick II in Berlin, Falconet placed Peter on a horse which had just galloped up onto a wavelike cliff, rearing. To Diderot he explained:

> The monument will be simple. . . . Peter the Great is both the subject and the attribute: One need only show him. I therefore stand for a statue of this hero whom I envision not as a great general or warrior, although he was one. It is necessary to show mankind a more splendid sight, that of a creator, lawgiver, and benefactor of his country. . . . My Tsar does not hold a baton in his hand: He extends his beneficent hand over the country over which he soars, and climbs onto the cliff which serves as his support—an emblem of the difficulties that he overcame.[94]

Great thought and care went into the details. Peter's mount, representing the wild Russia over which he ruled, was unruly, rearing and barely in his control, seeming ready to plunge into the void and challenge fate. Peter's garb was neither Russian, nor European nor Roman, but rather (in line with Peter's ideas) universal with hints of each. Peter's dress had to be "that of all nations, of every man in any time," Falconet wrote. "In a word, it is [to] be purely heroic."[95] Thus, Peter's loose robes and laurel crown only evoked Rome, while his boots vaguely suggested an old Russian style that Alexander Nevsky himself might have worn. The sculptor did allow himself one allegorical figure, which doubled as a third point of support for the statue: a large snake—the allegory of evil and envy—writhing around the horse's hooves, which Peter in his greatness had trampled. But not completely or for all time, as history would prove. As the 20th-century poet Innokenty Annensky would write in his *Petersburg*:

> The tsar did not manage to kill the snake,
> And it survived to be our idol.

Falconet's greatest challenge was Peter's head. He produced three versions, all of which Catherine rejected. Finally, he turned to Callot, who utilized Carlo Rastrelli's famous plaster mask of the Tsar to design the final version. It expressed a delicate and critical tension between the calm and confident demeanor of the supreme ruler and his inner fire. His eyes, as Pushkin would later observe, seemed transfixed on the Emperor's vision in the distance yet glared down at the viewer.

The project was the subject of continual attention, debate, and speculation. People flocked to Falconet's studio, especially for the presentation of the model in 1770. Most observed in silence and departed without comment, which confused Falconet until he came to understand the restrained character of the city's residents: "all buttons buttoned," unsentimental and tending toward irony and sarcasm, traits which one still finds today.[96] On the other hand, this reaction may have simply evidenced a still undeveloped level of sculptural criticism in Russia.[97] When Diderot saw the model in 1773, it pleased him greatly. He perceptively observed in a letter to Falconet: "The Hero and the Horse make together a beautiful Centaur, the human and thinking part of which contrasts marvelously, in its tranquility, with the fiery and animal part."[98]

More challenging was Falconet's relationship with his conservative and unimaginative overseer, Ivan Betskoi, head of the Academy of Fine Arts and a fine bureaucrat but no artist. Fortunately, over Betskoi stood Catherine, who approved all main features of the design. She was quick and decisive in approving the overall design and in understanding what was needed for Peter's head, but was stymied by whether to approve the inclusion of the snake. At first she waffled, saying that it "neither pleases nor displeases me," but after more argumentation and flattery from Falconet she finally agreed: "There is an ancient song which says: if it is necessary, then it is necessary, and that is my answer regarding the snake."[99] For the dedication on the pedestal, which was in Russian on one side and in Latin on the other, Catherine the propagandist wanted to give herself nearly equal prominence and clearly align herself with Peter's legacy. Whereas Falconet had proposed "To Peter the First erected by Catherine the Second," she changed it to "To Peter the First from Catherine the Second," thus stressing their first-second continuity and her place as his heir.[100]

For the cliff-pedestal, Falconet chose a giant hunk of granite that had been discovered by a peasant eight miles up the Gulf of Finland and five miles inland near the village of Lakhta. According to legend, it was so prominent that lightning had hit it during a thunderstorm, leaving a prominent and auspicious gash on it, and thus it became known locally as the "thunder-stone" (*grom-kamen*). It is also said that Peter had once climbed atop it during his many travels in the area, thus presaging his own monument. Even after preliminary hewing on the site, the thunder-stone still measured 30 feet in height and weighed 1,500 tons. In a miracle of engineering, it was detached and dragged on bronze rollers by hundreds of laborers over the rugged land during the cold season when the earth was firm. It took six months to cover the five miles to the sea, whereupon it was placed on a barge suspended between two large ships. On September 26, 1770, the thunder-stone was ceremoniously rolled onto land before cheering crowds. Falconet then did the final carving, reducing the stone's mass nearly by half, and partially buried it on the site.

The finished monument, which became known as the Bronze Horseman, was unveiled on August 7, 1782, the 100th anniversary of Peter's accession to the throne. But Falconet was gone. Tired of red tape and arguing with Betskoi, he had departed an angry man in 1780 and would never see his finished creation in its place. Legend has it that he took with him pieces of his thunder-stone, which he distributed to friends back in France. Once the monument became famous, jewelry inset with small pieces of it became fashionable among the Parisian ladies.

The day of the unveiling dawned rainy and windy, but as the hour of the ceremony approached the rain stopped and the sun came out. The guards, dignitaries, foreign ambassadors, and the common people filed into the square. Large sheets of cloth fastened onto tall wooden frames concealed the monument. At about 5:00 P.M. Catherine arrived by water on the imperial yacht. Other city residents watched the ceremony from the Neva on their yachts. When Catherine strode onto the Senate balcony, she waved her hand, a rocket was launched, and as it exploded the panels fell away to reveal the Bronze Horseman.

Catherine proclaimed the day a holiday, declared an amnesty for jailed debtors and criminals, and held a special service in the Peter and Paul Cathedral over Peter's tomb. Metropolitan Platon struck the sarcophagus with his staff and called to Peter: "Arise now, great monarch, and behold your favorite invention: it has not withered with time, nor has its glory dimmed."[101] According to legend, an impressionable Grand Duke Paul apparently took Platon's solemn words at face value and feared that "grandpa will arise from his coffin."[102*] More believable is the story that

---

*This legend assumes that Paul was young, but in fact Paul was already 28 at the time, so the story is far-fetched.

Kyrill Razumovsky joked to those next to him, "Why is he calling him? Once he gets up, he'll get us all!"[103]

Since that day the Bronze Horseman has been the best-known image and symbol of the city, and of its and Russia's fate. It has been interpreted variously and portrayed endlessly in verse, prose, paintings, and song. In his *Bronze Horseman,* for example, Pushkin would ask:

> *Proud charger, whither are thou ridden,*
> *Where leapest thou? And where, and on whom,*
> *Wilt thy plant thy hoof?*

In modern times it is an obligatory stop for newlyweds immediately after weddings for photographs, smiles, and good wishes.

Catherine's last project along the Neva embankment was New Holland. The Galley Wharf had been moved to Vasilievsky Island, and the remaining wooden warehouses, which had stored wood for ships and other materials, were in disrepair. Catherine decided to reconstruct the complex in stone and make it a showpiece. Cheviakinsky redesigned the interior, while Vallin de la Mothe designed the famous façade with its famous archway spanning a canal into the interior of the complex. Construction began in 1765, but work dragged on into the 19th century due to lack of funds and it was never completed as designed. In 1828–29, a military prison was built inside its walls, which became known as "the bottle" due to its shape. In post-Soviet times, the city has sought to develop this popular landmark into a commercial complex, but as of this writing no investors had taken on the project.

New buildings, especially churches, also rose along Nevsky Prospect. Work on the Gostiny Dvor, which Elizabeth had begun to reconstruct according to Rastrelli's Baroque design, was halted when Catherine took the throne. She had Vallin de la Mothe redesign it in a more stark, classical style. Work was recommenced in 1765, and it would take until 1785 to complete. It is essentially this design which survives today, though a restoration in the 19th century shortened the columns. St. Petersburg continued to be a city of few churches, but some notable ones were built along Nevsky, including Veldten's Armenian Church (1771–80), conceived at the initiative and expense of the Armenian Ovanes Lazarian, a wealthy merchant and fighter for Armenian independence from the Turks. Further down Nevsky toward the Center was built the (Polish) Roman Catholic Church of St. Catherine, which was consecrated in 1783. Originally designed by Pietro Trezzini as a Dominican monastery with an ensemble of three-story residential side buildings, it too was set back from the street. The residential buildings were built according to Trezzini's design, but Catherine had Vallin de la Mothe redesign the church, which was completed by Rinaldi as de la Mothe left Russia in 1775. It has had a long and tortuous history of varying uses. The Soviets made it into a recreation hall complete with a swimming pool, but it is now restored as a functioning church. At the far end of Nevsky, in Alexander Nevsky Monastery, Domenico Trezzini's Trinity Cathedral had fallen into disrepair and was near collapse, and Catherine decided to rebuild it. After rejecting several designs of others, she turned to Ivan Starov, who in 1778–90 built a larger cathedral in a noble classical style which remains today.

The purest expression of classicism within the city was the Horse Guards Palace built by Starov in 1783–89. Catherine built it for Potemkin, who had become known as the Prince of Tauris (Crimea), in honor of his victories in the South in the Second Turkish War. She named it the Tauride Palace after his death, purchased it, used it as her own autumn residence, and completed the palace's interior in 1795. Its site was chosen well east of the city center near Smolny in order to accommodate its large size and expansive gardens. At the time, the palace was set back from but faced the Neva and was connected to it by a canal, while its front gardens dominated that part of the embankment. The palace has a simple elegance, clear lines and a graceful dome, and is marked by rows of mostly Tuscan columns inside and out. Its central rotunda was inspired by the Pantheon in Rome, in the back was an expansive winter garden with a large skylight, and in between them was the columned Catherine Hall, a ballroom that could accommodate 5,000 persons. This was indeed needed when Potemkin returned in triumph from the Crimea in 1791. On April 28 he staged perhaps the grandest ball of Catherine's reign at a reported cost of 150,000 rubles. It included a comedy performance with ballet (with the musicians hidden in giant chandeliers), a masquerade ball, dinner and dancing, and a concert by 300 musicians which included a victory hymn composed for Catherine. Potemkin was striking in his scarlet kaftan and cape of black lace, but his hat was so laden with diamonds that he could not keep it on his head, and he had a servant carry it behind him. Around the palace spread a large garden designed by the Englishman William Gould, much of which remains in altered form as a city park today.

It was also under Catherine that the great work was done on St. Petersburg's main canals and rivers on the Admiralty side that made them into the beautiful and romantic waterways that one sees today. From 1764 to 1790, the Catherine Canal (now the Griboyedov Canal) was created out of the Crooked Rivulet, and its embankments were faced in granite. It was built by the military engineer Golenishchev-Kutuzov, an ancestor of the Field Marshal who would defeat Napoleon. Connecting the Moika with the Fontanka, it winds its way through the central and picturesque parts of the city and is the most romantic and mystical of St. Petersburg's waterways. Between 1780 and 1790, the Moika and Fontanka embankments also were faced in granite. Along the edge of each river and canal embankment was erected a wrought iron grille and railing, each having its own unique design which remains today. Each waterway was given new granite bridges, with the Fontanka having seven new identical three-span bridges. Like the Neva embankments, the lesser rivers and canals also had boat landings, which are still used today by water taxis.

In order to complete the grand plan of making the Neva's riverbanks the architectural focus of the city, a complementary redesign of the *strelka* of Vasilievsky Island was a key. This demanded that the ensemble look outward to the opposite shores.[104] A fire that destroyed much of the Kunstkamera in the 1770s provided the opportunity to replan the area. Several plans were considered, but in 1782 Catherine put the design into Giacomo Quarenghi's hands. He designed a new Exchange Building as the *strelka's* centerpiece, and since the Palace Embankment was now the city's architectural focus, he aligned the Exchange not along the axis of Vasilievsky Island but toward the Summer Garden. Work began in 1782, but funds dried up and work slowed; the exposed elements of the structure began to deteriorate. When Catherine died, Paul was glad to stop work altogether. A final architectural solution for the *strelka* would not come until the early 19th century.

Some of the best architecture of Catherine's reign, and the purest expression of classicism, was to be found in the royal palaces in the suburbs, particularly in the works of Charles Cameron. Born in Scotland in 1740, he spent much of his youth and training in Rome, among other things excavating the Imperial Thermae at the behest of Pope Clement XIII. He returned to London to enjoy much success, became a Freemason, invented a noble ancestry, and wrote a book in which he proposed to improve upon Palladio. He soon attracted Catherine's attention, came to Russia in 1779, and became her favorite architect. His first project was to reconstruct Catherine's apartments in the Catherine Palace at Tsarskoe Selo in classical motifs, highlighted by the Green Dining Room. This interior work was followed by the famous two-storied Cameron Gallery with its line of Ionic columns and row of busts of famous personages running perpendicular to the end of the Palace, the Agate Pavilion, and other pavilions and bridges in a largely English-style park to the south of the original regular French park. Through these structures and decor Catherine and Cameron sought to create an idealized, elevated, and stimulating world where one could stroll, sit, and read in peace and contemplation. In fact, adjacent to the royal complex Catherine created in 1780 the model village of Sophia (Catherine's name by birth), as an example of Enlightenment life as it should be for ordinary citizens, complete with model factories, craftsmen's shops, and trading places. Unfortunately, it had disappeared by 1808. Cameron was not the only active architect in Tsarskoe Selo. In 1792–96 Quarenghi built the magnificent Alexander Palace for Catherine's favorite grandson, Alexander.

ECONOMIC AND BUSINESS LIFE

St. Petersburg grew quickly under Catherine. From 95,000 residents in 1750, the city's population had more than doubled to 192,000 by 1784, and in 1800 it stood at 220,000.[105] Nearly half of the population (41 percent) lived on the Admiralty side between the Neva and the Fontanka.[106] Men outnumbered women by approximately two to one, mainly because of the many soldiers and invited workers in the city.[107] As of 1789, approximately 32,000 of the city's residents were foreigners, over half of them Germans.[108] The military with their families made up over one-fourth of the population,[109] which attracted nobility from all over the country.[110] The number of merchants in the city had grown rapidly from slow and difficult beginnings under Peter the Great to about 3,000 (including family members) by the 1750s, and by 1790 had risen as high as perhaps 7,000.[111] There were relatively few clerics, much lower in proportion to the population than in Moscow or elsewhere in Russia.[112] The remainder of the population consisted mainly of craftsmen, construction and factory workers, traders, and government employees.

In her effort to modernize Russia's economy, Catherine also drew upon Enlightenment economic thinking, including the theories of Adam Smith and the Physiocrats. She sent many students to study economics and finance abroad, including with Adam Smith. In order to provide a forum to discuss and implement reforms, in December 1763 Catherine created the Commission on Commerce, which in the economic sphere served a function analogous to the later Legislative Commission in law, but unlike the latter would last for her entire reign. She reduced state regulation of the economy by abolishing most state monopolies, eliminated the need for state permission to establish enterprises and factories, and sought to promote the use of free labor rather than serfs at urban and rural manufactories. This policy paid off. During her reign the number of production enterprises in Russia rose from 600–700 to over 2,000. In and around St. Petersburg the growth of free labor at its enterprises was by far faster than elsewhere in Russia.[113] In October 1762, in accordance with cameralist theories Catherine forbade the construction of new manufactories in the city, instead providing them land in nearby towns such as Schlüsselburg, Krasnoe Selo, and Slavyanka.[114]

Since Russia was a rural and agricultural society, the theories of the French Physiocrats Dr. Francois Quesnay and Le Mercier de la Riviere were of special interest to Catherine. It was Diderot who referred Catherine to their writings and arranged for de la Riviere to visit St. Petersburg to advise Catherine. The visit turned out badly as Catherine found him impossibly arrogant, but she nevertheless sought to apply Physiocratic principles to Russia. Physiocracy, which meant "The Rule of Nature," held that land was the greatest source of national wealth, which meant not only that agriculture must be made efficient by leaving it free of regulation and restrictions, but also implied the elimination of internal customs and other internal barriers to trade, eliminating excise taxes, and abandoning export restrictions and tariffs. This stood to benefit St. Petersburg as Russia's primary port.

In order to stimulate ideas and discussion of how best to bring these ideas to life in Russia, in 1765 Catherine founded the Free Economic Society, located on Nevsky Prospect near the Winter Palace. Through the Society, she sponsored an international essay competition with a prize of 1,000 gold pieces for the best set of proposals on how to organize Russia's agricultural system for the common good.

There were 164 entries, with the largest number and the winning essay coming from France.

In the end there was no wholesale reorganization of agriculture, not to mention any serious talk of abandoning serfdom, but Catherine took many other steps recommended by Physiocrats such as minimizing internal barriers, authorizing the export of grain, and greatly reducing export duties. She also modified the customs tariff in 1766 to reduce or eliminate tariffs on raw materials or components that could be processed into finished goods in Russia, while maintaining reduced, targeted protective tariffs on goods which were actually produced or whose equivalents were produced in Russia. These policies stimulated foreign trade. In Catherine's reign, the number of Russian-registered merchant ships rose from 20 to 400, and total foreign trade turnover during Catherine's reign rose from 20 million to over 100 million rubles.[115] Most of these benefits accrued to St. Petersburg, where both the foreign and Russian merchant communities thrived. Imports and exports in St. Petersburg's port rose from about 13 million rubles in 1768 to over 51 million in 1797 and came to account for over half of Russia's imports and exports.[116] The number of ships calling in St. Petersburg rose from 338 in 1760 to 1,267 in 1797, over half of them English.[117] In order to handle this volume, the main port was moved to Kronstadt; smaller vessels ferried cargoes between Kronstadt and the city. While St. Petersburg's merchants now owned ships, they still had insufficient capital to acquire the largest, long-distance vessels, and they manned their ships mainly with foreign sailors. Long distance shipping remained principally in the hands of the foreign merchants. The city's exports were mainly iron, leather goods, linen and flax, canvas, rope, hemp, and lard.[118] Imports were mainly for merchant trade and consumption by the court and nobility, and consisted principally of raw sugar, silks, woolens and other fabrics, alcoholic drinks, tobacco, coffee, and fruits.[119]

St. Petersburg and its suburbs also grew as an industrial center. Between 1761 and 1780, nearly 100 new manufactories were established, mainly in light industry in the city's environs.[120] The large military enterprises remained in state hands, while light industry was almost entirely private and used mainly hired rather than serf labor.

THE ARTS, CULTURAL AND SOCIAL LIFE

Like Peter I, Catherine considered it her ultimate goal to civilize Russia, and Petersburg would be the showcase of the nation's new civilization. As Catherine was the chief sponsor of the fine and performing arts and other areas of culture, cultural life in St. Petersburg continued to revolve around the court.[121]

The area of culture in which Catherine was determined to make her biggest and most lasting mark was in the fine arts. She sent large numbers of Russians abroad to study painting, sculpture, and architecture, and at home supported the Academy of Fine Arts, inviting prominent foreigners such as Vallin de la Mothe to teach there. This effort, actually commenced under Elizabeth, began to pay dividends. The best Russian painter of the time was Dmitry Levitsky, who eventually became professor of portraiture at the Academy. His portraits of the architect Alexander Kokorinov, Diderot, Smolny Institute girls, and Catherine herself brought him both local and international renown. The best sculptor to emerge from this system was Mikhail Kozlovsky, who created many works on idealized classical themes such as his caryatids in the throne room at Pavlovsk.

Under Catherine, an appreciation for painting and sculpture spread widely among the nobility. Grand Duke Paul began collecting in the 1760s and added considerably to his collections during his European trip in 1781–82. Prince Alexander Bezborodko, Prince Nikolai Yusupov, and Count Peter Sukhtelen began their large collections in the 1780s. The Stroganovs, Vorontsovs, and Shuvalovs had already begun their immense collections under Elizabeth. Many of these collections are now in the Hermitage.

Most spectacular, however, was Catherine's own compulsive collecting of Western art. She sought to acquire the best collection in the world and make her court a monument of world art. She did this not simply from her knowledge and appreciation of art, which was in fact limited, but also to bring glory to Russia abroad and favorably impact diplomatic relations. For this she spared no expense. Nowhere else was so much money lavished on the fine arts, and no one else in Europe could compete with her. She had her agents, chief among them Diderot and Grimm, scour Europe for opportunities to buy whole collections.

Catherine began collecting in 1764 with the purchase of 225 Old Masters paintings, including works of Rembrandt, Hals, and Steen, from a dealer in Berlin who had originally collected them for Frederick the Great, who could no longer afford them after the crippling Seven Years' War. In Paris, ambassador Dmitry Golitsyn bought a variety of contemporary works including those of Greuze and Chardin, and Rembrandt's *Return of the Prodigal Son*. When Golitsyn was transferred to the Hague, he began acquiring Dutch works. Unfortunately, one of his shipments of treasures, including works of Rembrandt, Steen, and Esaias van de Velde, sank to the bottom of the Baltic. Through Diderot, in 1768 Catherine acquired for 500,000 francs the famous collection of Pierre Crozat, which boasted about 1,000 works, including by Raphael (*Holy Family*), Rembrandt, Van Dyck (including his *Self Portrait*), Giorgione (*Judith*), Veronese, Rubens, and Poussin. This was followed by some 500 paintings from the Duc de Choiseul, and in 1769 by the collection of Count Heinrich von Bruhl, former chancellor of Augustus III of Saxony, which included five paintings by Rubens and Watteau's *Embarrassing Proposal*. Her last great acquisition was the massive collection of Sir Robert Walpole in 1779 which included works of Rubens, Titian, Van Dyck, Velasquez, Hals, Raphael, Poussin, and Veronese. She also did not neglect sculpture, though these works were generally acquired one by one. Her acquisitions included Michelangelo's *Crouching Boy* and Jean-Antoine Houdon's seated Voltaire. She filled out her collection with engraved gems, cameos, Scythian gold, coins and medals, books, prints, bronzes, silver, porcelains, tapestries, and furniture. Many such objets d'art were commissioned by her and crafted by shops and artists in Russia, such as her own Imperial Porcelain Factory, or abroad, including porcelain by Wedgwood and Sèvres, tapestries from the Gobelins factory, furniture from David Roentgen in Germany, and silver from Roettiers in Paris.[122] All in all, by around 1790, she had collected 4,000 Old Masters, 38,000 books, 10,000 engraved gems, 10,000 drawings, and 16,000 coins and medals.[123]

Catherine originally intended to house all this in the Small Hermitage, but she quickly ran out of space. She first added galleries along its hanging gardens but even by their completion she realized that a new building was needed, which led to building Veldten's Old Hermitage.

The Small Hermitage was also the setting for Catherine's private social events for selected guests. Some were small dinners among a dozen or so people followed by private theater, others were soirees for 60 to 80 guests which she called *Petits Hermitages,* while less often she held *Grandes Hermitages* for up to 200 people. These affairs were meant to be purely relaxing and pleasurable in order to encourage lively and enlightened conversation. Taking a page from Peter the Great, she drafted rules for such affairs resembling those for Peter's assemblies: "All ranks shall be left behind at the doors," as well as all "parochialism and ambitions." "One shall speak with moderation and quietly so that others do not get a headache."[124]

The grandest social life in the city naturally still focused on the court, but other high social life expanded beyond it. Royal balls continued to be held regularly and on a massive scale much in the tradition of Elizabeth—only without the cross-dressing—and Catherine was hard put to better them. There were now bigger and better palaces in which to hold them, such as the new Winter Palace and Potemkin's Tauride Palace. Petersburgers' taste in dress and manners was more refined, the quality of the entertainments was better, and the influence of French language and culture was more pronounced. Catherine tried to introduce French Enlightenment ideas in part through the city's social life, but the results were inevitably superficial.

In addition to social events at nobles' homes, a variety of social clubs sprung up at which various classes of Russians as well as foreigners could gather to socialize. The most famous was the English Club, founded in 1770 by the merchant Francis Gardner. It met first in the home of one of its German members, Conrad Kuzel, on New Isaac Street near the Moika and St. Isaac's Square, and it moved to other locations as its membership grew. It began with 50 founding members and grew to over 300 by 1780. Its membership included all nationalities and the British were never in the majority; in fact, the Club's minutes were kept in German. At first no one *above* the fifth position on the Table of Ranks could be admitted, but this was eventually relaxed to include higher ranks, and soon the Club was meeting at

Count Buturlin's house. The Club was open daily and members could dine there on designated days of the week.

The English Club inspired the formation of many other private clubs. The Bourgeois Club opened in 1772 on Admiralteisky Prospect, and the Commercial Club opened in 1785 on the English Embankment. The Musical Club formed in 1772 on Nevsky Prospect, and soon after that the Dance Club. An American Club opened in 1783 on Bolshaya Morskaya. A Nobles Club opened in 1789—just as the nobility was being eradicated in France—having various branch locations in the city. The Masonic lodges also served as social clubs for their members. Their meetings were held at nobles' mansions such as Elagin's and Stroganov's.

The other major foci of high social life in the capital were the many cultural events, including theater, opera, ballet, and concerts. Music and opera were popular at court, but music as art was still not developed among Russians. No notable Russian composers, or compositions, or musical school had yet emerged, but well-known foreign composers such as Cimarosa, Paisiello, Galuppi, and Sarti worked in Russia for long periods. (A planned visit by Mozart was prevented only by his premature death.) Most opera music was that of these foreign composers, but native Russian or Ukrainian composers such as Pashkevich and Sokolovsky also wrote operatic scores. Catherine herself wrote librettos for many operas. In 1763 the Royal Choral Cappella was opened just across the Moika River from the Winter Palace (where it remains today), beginning a long and glorious tradition of Russian choral music which combined Russian church and folk music with foreign influences. Ballets continued to be popular and were performed not only in theaters, where they were often fit into operas and plays, but also at grand balls such as Potemkin's at his Tauride Palace in 1791 and at educational institutions by their students. The St. Petersburg *Vedomosti* described part of a 1775 performance by the young ladies of the Smolny Institute:

> When the guests arrived they saw the Temple of Benevolence, its entrance hidden by a mountain; and shepherdesses went down the mountain to present gifts to the Rosiere. They expressed their joy by pastoral dances. When Benevolence crowned the shepherds with flowers to the sounds of music, the mountain opened and revealed the inside of the temple, where stood an alter on which a sacred flame was burning. It was surrounded by an amphitheater with seventy Vestals in it who attended to the fire. Forty shepherdesses and forty peasant girls, who were seen on the lowest steps, danced. Three Graces and the Vestals joined them. These concluded the play with a dance in which they held garlands of flowers above their heads and moved them so that they resembled a living garden.[125]

Foreign directors and dancers such as Pierre Grandjé, Charles Le Picq, and Joseph Canziani composed ballets and held prominent positions, but Russian dancers such as Ivan Valberg were also accomplished and among the stars. It was also under Catherine that the painting of theatrical scenery became the high art for which St. Petersburg's theaters and stage artists would later become so famous.

Under Catherine, drama theater and opera (the line between which was often blurred) assumed an unprecedented and important role in society. The playhouse became the principal arena of ideology and social criticism under Catherine,[126] and there was an explosive number of new Russian plays and operas. Foreign troupes continued to perform, but increasingly the plays and actors were Russian. Court performances were held at the royal theater in the Winter Palace (located in the palace itself until Quarenghi's Hermitage Theater was completed), at the Small (Wooden) Theater on Tsaritsyn Lug and (in the summer) in Tsarskoe Selo. Plays, as well as operas and ballets, were also performed at the Academy of Fine Arts, the Theater on New Isaac Street, at the Corps of Cadets on Vasilievsky Island, and at a People's Theater for the general public, built in 1765 on a vacant lot on Bolshaya Morskaya Street. In 1775–83 the Bolshoi Stone Theater was built on what is now Theater Square. In 1771–72 an English Theater organized by the city's British community and built next to the Wooden Theater on Tsaritsyn Lug staged many popular plays by an English troupe. From 1766, the Imperial Theaters were directed by Catherine's councilor and secretary Ivan Elagin, who replaced the quarrelsome Sumarokov. It was Elagin who confronted the challenge of borrowing from foreign plays with his theory of "adaptation to our customs," in which the main lines of the plot were kept intact but Russian names and characters, customs, and situations were added.

Early in Catherine's reign, the spectacles consisted mainly of foreign productions, Sumarokov's dramas, and light satirical comedies and comic operas, many authored by Catherine herself. Gallomania, the thoughtless aping of European manners, and the shallow understanding of Western ideas at court were popular targets, particularly from the pens of Moscow writers (although the form and characters of these plays were themselves those of French classical comedy). In the first comedy of the young Moscow noble playwright Denis Fonvizin (1744–92), *The Brigadier* (1769), a character asks: "I was never there, but still I already have a very good idea of what France is like. Isn't it true that mostly Frenchmen live in France?" Fonvizin, who by his own admission could read the play masterfully, himself read this play in aristocratic homes and salons throughout St. Petersburg and finally to Grand Duke Paul and the Empress herself. Fonvizin's most popular and longest lasting play, and probably the best Russian dramatic work of the 18th century, was his satirical masterpiece *The Minor* (1782), which portrayed the boorishness of Russia's provincial gentry. Like *The Brigadier,* it contended that bad people are such due to lack of education, hence the importance of true enlightenment. But it went further to argue that the social environment is also important, and that backwardness and lack of culture in Russia could not be overcome (or even reach the level of those satired in *The Brigadier*) by those involved in the system of serfdom. Thus, social reform, not just efforts to improve individuals, is needed to perfect man.[127] Another important comedy was *The Arcades of St. Petersburg* (1792) by Mikhail Matinsky, who had been born a serf but had studied in Italy and rose to teach at the Smolny Institute. The play traced the escapades and intrigues of dishonest merchants and corrupt civil servants, and is notable for its originality (no foreign model), dramatic scenes, and fine music and choruses.

As Enlightenment ideals penetrated amongst the educated in the face of Russian social conditions, however, satirical comedies (especially Catherine's own increasingly frivolous and tiresome efforts) were not enough to satisfy playwrights and increasingly sophisticated audiences. Plays became more sophisticated, serious, and critical. Naturally, tragedies assumed a more prominent role, and they served as an early sign of the alienation of Russia's aristocratic intellectuals. Sumarokov had originated Russian tragedy during Elizabeth's reign. While staying faithful to the classical forms of Greece, Rome, and France, he stressed as his themes secular enlightenment, moral principles, and spiritual edification. Taking inspiration from Marcus Aurelius and other Stoics, he held that the purpose of tragedy is "to lead men to good deeds," "cleanse passion through reason," and achieve "true wisdom."[128] True wisdom looked beyond mere cultivation of taste and manners and Voltairean skepticism to higher principles which might put one at odds with one's monarch. Sumarokov was soon joined by other Russian tragic playwrights, including Vasily Maikov (1728–78), Alexei Rzhevsky (1737–1804), Mikhail Kheraskov (1733–1807), Yakov Knyazhnin (1742–91), and Nikolai Nikolev (1758–1815), the adopted son of Princess Dashkova. Their works dealt with a wide variety of moral, social, and political themes. Maikov's *Agriope* (1769) built a tragedy of national oppression and betrayal around a Byzantine princess's imprisonment in a Turkish seraglio. Rzheveky's *The False Smerdius* (1769) was a variation on the False Dmitry theme. Kheraskov's *The Nun of Venice* (1758) denounced religious intolerance. Nikolev's *Sorena and Zamir* (1784) criticized the messianic conversion to Christianity of native peoples, pleading for religious tolerance and denouncing tyranny, observing that "we do not always find a father in our monarch." The commander of the Moscow garrison found this line offensive and initially forbade the play's performance, but Catherine overruled him, commenting, "I am astounded, dear Count. . . . The meaning of the verses you indicated has no relation to your sovereign. The author protests against the abuses of tyrants, and you yourself have called Catherine mother."[129]

Catherine's reign, like Elizabeth's, still featured so-called "pocket poets" at court, but it also saw more original, sophisticated, and beautiful poetry emerge from more talented and independent poets. Poetry was encouraged by the emergence of artistic and literary salons in the capital, which were based on the earlier pioneering examples of Feofan Prokopovich and Ivan Shuvalov, as well as those in Paris. Chief among them in Catherine's time was the salon of Nikolai Lvov (1751–1803), himself a poet, beginning in the 1770s. The gatherings of Lvov's circle were held not only at his home but also at those of its other members, including Gavrila Derzhavin (on Italyanskaya Street), the painter Dmitry Levitsky (on Vasilievsky Island), and the poet Mikhail Muravev (on the Fontanka Embankment). The circle also included Ivan Khemnitser (1743–1784) and Vassily Kapnist (1758–1823). Another literary circle was formed at the Corps of Cadets.

Kapnist was from the Ukrainian gentry but moved to St. Petersburg to enter the Preobrazhensky Guards and joined the Lvov circle, where his thought and poetry matured. His poems ranged from classical comedy to bitter social commentary before becoming sentimental in his later years. His *First and Last Satire* (1780), in which he attacked highly placed "thieves," was considered overreaching and too personally directed at members of the court, and for it he was told to return to his estate in the Ukraine. But his political verses continued in his *Ode to Slavery* written in 1783 upon the extension of serfdom to the Ukraine, which contained the following portrayal of the new serfs:

> *In chains of slavery they sadden,*
> *Nor dare to overturn the yoke.*

Kapnist would eventually return to St. Petersburg to become director of imperial theaters and continue writing poetry until his death in 1823.

Ivan Khemnitser, an admirer of Diderot, was an original ironic and satiric poet in the best St. Petersburg tradition. Born of a Saxon army officer in Astrakhan, he enlisted underage and had a brief military career before moving to St. Petersburg in 1769 to become a translator. In 1776–77 he toured Western Europe with Nikolai Lvov and absorbed its art, literature, and theater. After penning some early ponderous odes, he found his talent for witty satire, fables, and anecdotes in the late 1770s and achieved popularity in 1779 with his two Horatian satires, *On Bad Judges* and *On the Bad Conditions of the Civil Service and how Even Appointments to Government Posts Are at the Pleasure of Corruption*. His fables portrayed the virtues of independence, intelligence, and not acquiescing to evil, and ridiculed stupidity, greed, and vice. In *A Trap and a Bird*, a caged and a free bird sing differently, in *Freedom and Unfreedom* a wolf prefers freedom to the price of a dog's life, and in *The Parrot* the exotic bird nearly perishes when it falls into the hands of superstitious peasants. In *The Metaphysical Student*, he ridicules the uselessness of abstract school learning. A student who falls in a ditch is thrown a rope, but instead of using it to climb out, ponders: "What is the nature of a rope?"

Ippolit Bogdanovich (1743–1803) was famous essentially for a single inspired work, *Dushenka, an Ancient Tale in Free Verse* (1783), which illustrates the revival of classical themes in the city under Catherine and the high level to which the art of versification had now risen. Originally from the Ukraine, he first gained recognition as a translator of Voltaire. He soon settled in St. Petersburg, where he joined the circle of Nikita Panin, and then served in the Russian legation in Dresden in 1766–69 before returning to the capital to hold other government positions and write poetry. *Dushenka* was styled on the classical legend of Psyche and Cupid, and most directly on La Fontaine's treatment of the legend in *Les Amours de Psyche at de Cupidon* (1669). The poem does not strike social themes and is notable mainly for its beautiful versification and elegant combination of classical legend with native Russian elements.

St. Petersburg's greatest poet laureate of the time, however, was Gavrila Derzhavin (1743–1816). He was able to stand strongly for truth, justice, and independence and satirize Catherine and her court while also staying in their good graces through his laudatory odes. Born in Kazan, he moved to St. Petersburg and entered the Preobrazhensky Guards (serving in the campaign against Pugachev), became the poet of the regiment, and joined Lvov's circle. He held several civil posts both in and outside of the capital, with uneven results because his high liberal principles and uncompromising style often brought him into conflict with his superiors. But in 1791 he was made a Senator and in 1801 became Minister of Justice. In 1783 he first attracted Catherine's attention in his satirical *Ode to the Wise Princess Felitsa*, in which he praised her (Felitsa)* but satirized her courtiers. This inaugurated a whole Felitsa cycle of poems. His most famous ode was *The Waterfall,* written ostensibly to commemorate the death of Potemkin in 1791. In it he portrays both the human condition and nature through the metaphor of a Karelian waterfall, at whose beauty and wonder he marvels like a Deist at any of God's creations. He upholds the Enlightenment ideals of the dignity of man and the human spirit, as depicted in Potemkin's heroic exploits, while at the same time lamenting our mortality and the transience of temporal glory. The waterfall attracts the forest animals whom it nourishes with its waters and beauty, but these beings are mortal. Only the truth is eternal, greater than man who can only partake of it, and will remain after we perish just as the waterfall will continue to flow. In *The Monument* (1795), based on Horace's *Exegi monumentum,* Derzhavin described his own odes in lines which are understood as his declaration of the poet's stand for truth, independent from any earthly ruler:

> *I was the first who dared in Russian style diverting*
> *The virtues to proclaim that our Felitsa has,*
> *To chat of God as with a friend in heartfelt candor,*
> *And tell the truth with smile when speaking up to kings.*[130]

EDUCATION, INTELLECTUAL LIFE, FREEMASONRY, AND THE RISE OF SOCIAL ACTIVISM

Under Catherine, education, intellectual life, and scholarship in St. Petersburg blossomed, and Russian journalism and social and literary criticism were born.

---

*He wrote this while temporarily out of favor at court. The name Felitsa for Catherine was taken from her own story, *The Tale of Prince Khlor,* written for her grandson Alexander, in which Catherine portrayed herself as the Khan's daughter, who sends Reason to accompany the hero in his search for the rose without thorns, or virtue.

While Catherine sought to spread enlightenment through society from atop her throne and in a controlled manner, she ran into a contradiction: Enlightenment philosophy presupposed the equality of all people and thus expected private initiative and creativity to spring from society itself and ultimately to become its driving force. Almost by definition, being an enlightened autocrat should be a short-term profession, and indeed this dynamic arose in her reign. For the most part, at first she let this process take its course, but she often found herself in a quandary whether to place some activities, such as education, under the wing and control of the government, a debate which continues in free societies today. In the end, Catherine pursued whatever ideas she thought useful and important without waiting for others to show the initiative, while in other instances she found herself trying to recover the initiative from others. Inevitably, not all freethinking people lined up behind the autocrat, and many expressed a variety of critical views which Catherine could not control. Indeed, for the first time Russia's leading writers and thinkers functioned outside the court and government. The spread of critical views was accelerated and brought to a head by the advent of the French Revolution, against which Catherine recoiled.

The ennobling and liberating power of education was a central tenet of Enlightenment thought, and Catherine's educational initiatives stand as one of the more successful legacies of her reign. Since Peter, the educational curriculum in most institutions had broadened to include what today are called liberal arts, as well as music, dancing, and other subjects as in the case of the Cadet Corps, but no systematic educational program for broad-based nationwide schooling had emerged. Catherine adopted a systematic and nationwide program for primary and secondary schools, first as part of the 1775 Provincial Statute, then through the activity of the new Commission on National Education beginning in 1782, and finally through the Statute of National Schools in 1786. Special schools to train teachers were established, textbooks were written and published on a large scale, and private schools were made to conform to state guidelines of quality and curriculum, which included the prohibition of corporeal punishment. From virtually nothing when Catherine started, by the end of the century Russia had approximately 315 primary and secondary public schools with approximately 20,000 students, one-tenth of which were girls.

The goal of education and the curriculum also changed under Catherine. These were reflected early in a 1764 work authored by her minister in charge of education, Ivan Betskoi, in which the Empress herself closely collaborated, entitled the *General Plan for the Education of Young People of Both Sexes.* In addition to the existing goal of preparing qualified persons for civil or military service, education now also aimed at broadening the Third Estate by educating more doctors, lawyers, merchants, architects, apothecaries, engineers, and teachers and so on. Further, education now contained a socializing and moral element. The curriculum was designed to develop good moral character, a curious and reasoning mind, and general knowledge that every citizen of a civilized country should possess. In other words, education was now geared toward forming the total human being—mind, body, and soul—in order to create the new kind of citizen and nation that Peter the Great had envisioned. In order to best achieve this end, where feasible students were to be boarded in order to control their environment. This was not possible in the common public schools and in the provinces, but it was practiced widely in St. Petersburg, including in a number of new foundling homes.

The technical and military schools that Peter had established in St. Petersburg continued to function, but their curricula broadened into the liberal arts. The Cadet Corps was given a new charter in 1766 that reflected Catherine's new approach to education. Now the goal was "to make a person healthy, to beautify his heart and reason, [and] create distinguished citizens . . . just as a field becomes beautified with flowers."[131] On this basis the Corps continued to flourish: by 1793 its number of teachers rose to 73 and its student body rose to 680.[132] The Gymnasium of the Academy of Sciences also continued to function, but as before with a small number of students. Its University was closed in 1767, however. (Even the University of Moscow had difficulty filling its halls with students. The nobles preferred the institutions designed for them, while it was difficult to interest many commoners in a general university education.)

New educational institutions also appeared in the city. The most prominent was the establishment in 1764 of the Imperial Society for Daughters of the Nobility, known as the Smolny Institute, designed to elevate the education and status of women in Russian high society. Approximately 200 girls from 6 to 18 years old were boarded and schooled at the Smolny Convent (though the Institute was secular). Later, in 1806–08, Quarenghi would construct his famous Classical building immediately to the south to house the Institute, where it remained until 1917. The curriculum was wide ranging and included not only traditional subjects but manners, music, art and architecture, and home economics. The early example of Smolny led to the establishment of other schools for noble girls in the city, as well as some for bourgeois children. A school attached to the Academy of Fine Arts was also established for non-noble children, as the Academy drew most of its students from non-nobles. Taking matters further to the primary education of commoners of both sexes, in 1777 Nikolai Novikov founded in St. Petersburg the Catherine School and later the Alexander School. Originally intended to subsist on revenues from his journal *Morning Light,* they ultimately were funded by charitable contributions, mainly from Freemasons. These private efforts spurred the Empress to open public primary schools, which she considered a government task. By 1781, on the eve of the establishment of the Commission on National Education, seven new primary schools were functioning in various regions of the city teaching 485 students; by 1792 the numbers had risen to 13 public schools in which 3,198 boys and 535 girls studied.[133] Even with such improvements, this still meant that the vast majority of commoners in the city remained illiterate. In 1784 the city's private schools, which then totaled 18 Russian and 28 foreign, were placed under government regulation, and eventually the Russian private schools were closed and their students were transferred to public schools.[134]

The Academy of Sciences languished early in Catherine's reign under Grigory Orlov and then Sergei Domashnev, whose inefficient administration, financial dishonesty, and limited intellectual abilities did not bring the institution honor. This changed in 1782 when Catherine replaced Domashnev with the startling choice of her friend, Princess Dashkova. At first Dashkova resisted the appointment on the ground that her gender rendered her unfit for the position. "Put me at the head of your washerwomen," she told Catherine, "and you will see with what zeal I shall serve you."[135] But the educated and enterprising Princess eventually accepted and brought to the Academy a new vigor. She was able to exploit her many acquaintances with leading intellectuals in Europe for its benefit. She improved its finances, erected new buildings, instituted a new series of lectures, attracted additional academics from abroad, expanded the Academy's literary and scientific output (including several scientific expeditions), and gradually increased the number and proportion of Russian students and academics.

Dashkova served so well in this position that Catherine also made her Director of the Academy of Language when that institution was established the next year (1783). Its scholars built upon the contributions that Sumarokov and Lomonosov had made to the Russian language under Elizabeth. One of Catherine's keen interests was languages and linguistics, and she had taken up a patriotic interest in her adopted country's language. In 1771 the Free Russian Society had been established at Moscow University for the purpose of enriching the Russian language, but in order to give linguistic studies separate high status, she decided to establish the Academy, in St. Petersburg. Its principal initial task was to produce the first comprehensive dictionary of the Russian language, but it also carried out other scholarly projects and instruction and published periodicals containing articles on a variety of subjects, not merely linguistics.

Catherine promoted literature, poetry, and criticism as a means of spreading the intellectual currents of the time. Periodicals were ideally suited for this task, as had been shown in England by the satirical weeklies *The Spectator*, *The Rambler*, and *The Tatler*. Catherine began by founding her own journal, *Odds and Ends*, in 1769, to which she contributed anonymous articles. The journal satired Russians, especially courtiers, who aped European manners but took no serious interest in Enlightenment thought. Catherine encouraged other writers to follow suit, and 15 new journals appeared between 1769 and 1773, mostly in St. Petersburg. Chief among them was *The Drone* (taken from the name of a character in a popular play), founded in 1769 by Nikolai Novikov with encouragement from Catherine. But to Catherine's displeasure these other journals quickly went beyond her own tame satire to criticize corruption at court, social injustices, the ineffectiveness of Russian courts, the failings of the bureaucracy, and other ills. By late 1770, all of the initial weeklies, including Catherine's own, had failed and shut down. While it is tempting to see only the Empress's hand in their closure, there is no evidence of imperial interference in their operations; rather, it seems that the journals were not financially viable, as they competed with each other for a small readership.[136]*

New periodicals emerged in subsequent years in the capital and in Moscow, and again Novikov, one of the most fascinating figures of Catherine's reign, was at the forefront. He was born in 1744 to impoverished provincial gentry and attended a secondary school attached to Moscow University but did not complete his studies; he never mastered foreign languages. Nevertheless, he had a brilliant mind and was an able networker, and he secured a job as a secretary at Catherine's Legislative Commission, where he developed a thorough understanding of Catherine's reform efforts, the opposition to them, and Russia's many social ills. It was after this formative experience that he threw himself into publishing satirical journals and writing essays for them, which coincided with Catherine's own efforts to promote the ideals behind the Commission in print. But Novikov quickly went beyond the tame satire and criticism that the Empress had in mind. Catherine had written and had performed in St. Petersburg in 1772 her satirical comedy, *Oh, Our Times!*, in which she ridiculed conservative Moscow opponents of her reforms. By flattering Catherine for this effort and ingratiating himself with her, Novikov obtained permission to open a new St. Petersburg journal, *The Artist,* in which he published a key satirical piece, *Fragment of a Journey to . . . ,* which anticipated Alexander Radishchev's *Journey from St. Petersburg to Moscow* in its portrayal and criticism of Russian life and social conditions, including serfdom. This story also outlined Novikov's own view of a Russian utopia. Unlike Radishchev, who would recognize competing interests in society and advocate the rule of law as the road to a better government and a more just society, Novikov's utopia was an idealized portrait of pre-Petrine Muscovy, in which a patriarchial monarchy united the entire people in harmonious activity behind a common national cause.[137] Because of this and his dislike of France, of the merchant class, and of industrial capital, he shared little with the proponents of the Enlightenment. But thanks to his overt nationalism, the increasingly patriotic Empress tolerated him and supported his establishment of the *Ancient Russian Library,* which published pieces on Russian history. In 1774 he was

---

*In fact, there was no general censorship in Russia until the very end of Catherine's reign; individual printing presses exercised their own judgment over what to print, without governmental oversight. There were a few isolated instances of central control over publications, such as when the Senate forbade Rousseau's *Émile* and an account of the death of Peter III in 1763 when Catherine was not yet secure on the throne. Initially, there were no private printing presses not because they were forbidden but because no one had even thought of establishing them; but in 1783 a law was passed specifically authorizing and encouraging private presses, requiring only that publications printed on them be submitted to the police to check for anything likely to offend the person of the sovereign, the Orthodox faith, and public decency. While these criteria were vague and capable of abuse, in practice they were interpreted narrowly, and many publications critical of absolutism and Russian conditions rolled off the private presses. See Madariaga, *Catherine,* pp. 94, 97–98; Madariaga, *Russia in the Age of Catherine,* pp. 332–35.

also allowed to open a new journal, *Koshelek ("Bag-wig")*, named after the bag in which fashionable men carried their French-style wigs. Its purpose was expressed succinctly in one of his satires published there, in which he mused that "if only some human force could give back to the Russians their former morals that have been destroyed by the introduction of bag-wigs; then they would become a model for mankind."[138] It was in this year, in the aftermath of the Pugachev rebellion, that Novikov underwent a spiritual crisis and decided that this human force was Freemasonry. He became a Freemason in 1775, and in 1779 would move to Moscow to join forces with like-minded thinkers. In the meantime, in 1777, he opened a new journal in St. Petersburg, *Morning Light,* where he published his famous essay *On the Dignity of Man in his Relationship to God and the World,* a humanist work in which he affirmed the Masonic ideals of the dignity, perfectibility, and essential equality of each individual, and argued that as such an individual is not just an end, but also a means who should work for the common good.[139] In fact, "every thing in the world is both an end for all others and a means to all others."[140] Anyone focusing on self-perfection only as an end (not to mention anyone not even seeking self-perfection) is a parasite—a "drone," as expressed in the title of his first journal.

During this period, most prominent Russian thinkers and writers, as well as some members of the royal family and of the government, were either Freemasons or were influenced by its precepts. Freemasonry helps explain how social and political thought in St. Petersburg developed from the mid-1770s and eventually translated into social and political activism. The differing strains of Freemasonry which developed in St. Petersburg and Moscow also explain how the latter formed the basis for Slavophilism (based mainly in Moscow), against which St. Petersburg intellectuals would do battle in the next century. The activities of Freemasons also help explain Catherine's often inconsistent and virulent reactions to the publications and activities of some of her most enlightened subjects, as well as to the French Revolution.

Freemasonry's origins are still not entirely proven, but the first official and open lodge, the Grand Lodge, was opened in London in 1717. Many leading lights of Western Europe and America of the time were Freemasons, including Sir Isaac Newton, Sir Christopher Wren, Francis Bacon, Goethe, Voltaire, Byron, Mozart, Benjamin Franklin, George Washington, and Thomas Jefferson. In an Enlightened Europe in which traditional religion had been discredited but where reason provided scant refuge for the soul, Freemasonry offered thinking people a new concept of the spiritual, a set of moral principles, and a sense of higher calling through its commitment to philanthropic and educational work geared toward realizing the Enlightenment's ideal of the perfection of man. A Freemason was obligated, first,[141] to dedicate himself to study, living a clean, moral and high-minded life, and maintaining his relationship with God, all aimed at perfecting his soul; second, to take some responsibility for helping and bettering, and hopefully perfecting, one's fellow man and society through education, and charitable and other good works. This aspect attracted people thirsty for social reform and could easily be transformed into a political program.

Freemasonry varied according to location and nationality. In England and America, Freemasonry was relatively free from mysticism and elaborate ritual, but as one moved east members felt a greater need for their own distinctive aims and ritual, so new degrees of membership were added to the original three and the ritual became more extravagant. It attracted mystics and occultists such as Henri de Saint-Martin, the leading "anti-Voltaire" of French thought. He inspired what became known as "higher-order" Masonry, characterized by ever higher orders of membership and esoteric secrets, extravagant ceremony, mysticism, and occultism. It reached its height in the less-developed German states, where it became entwined with the pre-romantic, nationalistic Germanic reaction against France and its Enlightenment, which in literature was reflected in sentimentalism and the *Sturm und Drang* movement. Especially prominent in Prussia were the mystical Rosicrucian ("Rosy Cross") Order and the *Illuminati*.

The influence of Freemasonry on thoughtful Russians seeking a more meaningful life and a better world is perhaps best known in the West through Pierre Bezukhov's soul searchings in *War and Peace,* but lodges in which Russians participated as members were operating in St. Petersburg by mid-century, the principal one being founded in 1756 with the Anglophile Count Roman Vorontsov as Grand Master. Its membersip list reads like an honor roll of the future intellectual and political leaders and prominent nobles of Catherine's reign, including Roman Ilarionovich Vorontsov (Grand Master), Prince Mikhailo Dashkov, the brothers Zakhar and Ivan Chernyshev, Prince Mikhail Shcherbatov, the Panin brothers, and Alexander Sumarokov.

It was in Catherine's reign, however, that Freemasony truly flowered, particularly in the mid to late 1770s as social consciences were raised by the Pugachev rebellion. In St. Petersburg, the lodges flourished under the wealthy and influential courtier of Catherine, Ivan Elagin, Grand Master of the Russian Empire. By 1774, his 14 lodges boasted about 200 Russian and foreign aristocrats, almost all of them leaders in the civil and military service. The number of Masons in Russia soon rose to approximately 2,500, nearly all of them in the military or civil services (meaning mostly in St. Petersburg). Since the number of such officials ranged from 6,000 in 1777 to 12,000 in 1787, Masons accounted for one-sixth to one-third of government servants, mainly at the upper levels.[142] Prominent Russian Freemasons in Catherine's reign included Sumarokov, Alexander Radishchev, Nikolai Karamzin, the playwright Mikhail Kheraskov, Prince Mikhail Shcherbatov, Ivan Lopukhin, Alexander Suvorov, Mikhail Kutuzov (the future conqueror of Napoleon), Prince Alexander Kurakin, and several Stroganovs.

Freemasonry became the largest and most influential organization in Russia independent of the government. In time, it also became the primary inspiration and organizing point of aristocratic opposition to Russia's autocratic form of government and the country's growing social ills, the first ideological class movement of the Russian aristocracy.[143] Many Decembrists had Masonic backgrounds. And in its educating and civilizing mission, it became Russia's first and most successful nongovernmental organization to spread Western ideas widely in all classes of society,[144] in line with St. Petersburg's mission.

Why was Freemasonry so popular? To begin with, it had come from the West and thus held the usual attraction of new Western ideas and movements. Amongst the nobility, who, unlike their Western counterparts, had no chivalric tradition, the brotherhood and ceremonies of Freemasonry provided a structured setting in which to gather and develop a class consciousness and aristocratic code of behavior.[145] Since the nobility was no longer obligated to serve the state, and since the government was increasingly run by the bureaucracy, the focus of many educated nobles shifted from loyalty and service to the sovereign to a commitment to serving and bettering the life of the Russian people. Freemasonry's commitment to improving the life of one's fellow man and perfecting society found a responsive chord among Russians eager for social and political reform and feeling social guilt. Most fundamentally, however, Freemasonry held a great spiritual attraction. In an age when Orthodoxy was discredited and in retreat while cold Enlightenment ideals seemed to do little for one's soul, Freemasonry redefined what it meant to be a good Christian. Following the Pugachev rebellion, many began to question the personal or social efficacy of liberal ideals alone, and sought to complement them. "Finding myself at the crossroads between Voltairianism and religion," Novikov wrote of his decision to join, "I had no basis on which to work, no cornerstone on which to build spiritual tranquility, and therefore I unexpectedly fell into the society."[146]

Freemasony in St. Petersburg was relatively free of higher-order mysticism. Elagin's own definition of a good Mason was "a free man able to master his inclinations . . . to subordinate his will to the laws of reason."[147] As such, Freemasonry was a vehicle for infusing society with the ideals of the Enlightenment and for performing charitable work. Still, Elagin did establish elaborate initiation rituals, which, he explained, helped substitute for the solemnity of Church rites. These ceremonies were often held at his palace on Elagin Island on the outskirts of town.* In 1779 Elagin was favored with a visit by the notorious Count Cagliostro, widely viewed as a charlatan who promoted his "Egyptian Order" of Freemasonry as its highest and most ancient order. He, often with a female medium, performed before large gatherings of Masons, including on the grounds of Elagin's estate. But he was received cooly by the worldly and skeptical Petersburgers, and St. Petersburg stands as the only major European city that he visited in which he failed to establish a branch of his Egyptian Order.[148] According to tradition, he had to flee the

---

*Recently an archeological dig unearthed evidence of these ceremonies. "Na strelke u masonov," *Nedvizhimost i stroitelstvo Peterburga*, July 22, 2002.

city after he offered to cure the dying baby of a Russian noblewoman for 5,000 louis on the condition that he take it into his exclusive care, substituted another baby when the sick one died, and was exposed when the "cured" baby was recognized as different. When asked for the dead child, Cagliostro could not produce it, claiming to have burned it "to test the theory of reincarnation."[149] He is said to have paid back the 5,000 louis with bills of exchange of a Prussian banker which were subsequently dishonored. Soon after Cagliostro's flight, Catherine wrote two plays performed in 1786, *Obmanshchik* ("The Deceiver") and *Obolshchennii* ("The Deceived"), lampooning these escapades. Notably, Catherine tolerated and took no measures against Petersburg's Freemasons.

But higher-order Freemasonry found a welcome home in Moscow.[150] The mystical and ceremonial side of Freemasonry appealed to Muscovites still attached to Orthodox ritual and mysticism. The city was also Russia's center of Francophobia, opposition to Enlightenment ideals, and of nationalist glorification of the Muscovite past.[151] The writings of Saint-Martin and Jakob Boheme, who opposed rationalist French Enlightenment ideals and claimed that the real world was that of spirit, were translated and widely read. In 1776, a 25-year-old German-educated Transylvanian occultist and higher-order Mason, Johann Georg Schwartz, was given a teaching position at Moscow University. He lectured, among other things, on mystical philosophy and the philosophy of history, and soon attracted a large following which included Novikov. Schwartz later established in Moscow a Russian branch of the Rosicrucian Order, with which he had become associated while in Prussia in 1781. Novikov and Schwartz published two journals, *Moscow Press* and *Twilight Glow,* in whose opening issue Novikov wrote that "comparing our present position with that of our forefather before the fall who glistened in the noon-day light of wisdom, the light of our reason can hardly be compared even to the twilight glow."[152] The light of Adam is still within us, and we can reveal it through self-purification and the study of the "hieroglyphics of nature" and of older history, in particular pre-Petrine Russia, which still contained reflections of this lost light.

Twilight Glow became Schwartz's mouthpiece for popularizing his teachings. Like Novikov, Schwartz sought to gain mystical insight into the secrets of nature. The elevated and the select brotherhood of Rosicrucians, he held, could be a vanguard to lead man to this knowledge and rebirth.[153] To this end, Schwartz and Novikov published mystical books in order to acquaint minds corrupted by Voltairianism with the road to truth.

Such Germanic doctrines were seductive to Muscovites who already were beginning to hold idealized notions of the Orthodox religious civilization of pre-Petrine Muscovy and seemed to validate traditional Muscovite notions that many held dear: the thirst for absolutes, mystical contemplation, union with the forces of nature, the organic unity of the entire nation set on a common religious messianic destiny, the Third Rome, and the union of the "true" monarch with the nation. But this was what Petersburg had been created to oppose and overcome.

The 19th-century struggle between Westerners and Slavophiles was prefigured in the differences between higher and lower order Freemasonry as practiced in Russia,[154] and the vanguard role in a messianic national quest to which the Rosicrucians aspired was later taken up by the Bolsheviks.

By the mid-1780s Catherine had seen enough and launched a public relations campaign against all Freemasonry and conducted investigations of it, although she did not persecute it. In 1785–86 she wrote two comedies ridiculing the movement, *The Deluded* and *The Siberian Shaman,* and published anonymously a critical brochure entitled the *Secrets of a Preposterous Society.*

Why did Freemasonry strike such a raw nerve with Catherine? Peter III's being a Freemason certainly got things off on the wrong foot. More fundamentally, she opposed any obscure, mystical, and secretive doctrines, and she conveniently lumped all Freemasons into the higher-order category. Catherine was also uncomfortable with any large, independent organization engaging in a broad social program, which she regarded as the sphere of government and desired to control. The mere fact that such efforts were being undertaken drew attention to society's ills and was an implied criticism of her. Indeed, as time went on, the criticisms of many Freemasons became explicit, and she began to fear the movement as a source of political opposition. In this regard, it worried Catherine that Freemasonry was an international movement linking prominent and wealthy individuals and members of royal families throughout Europe. She began to see signs of a possible international conspiracy to replace her with her son Paul, and there was at least some basis for this fear.[155]

In addition to its important role in intellectual life and social activism, Freemasonry also influenced the architectural appearance of St. Petersburg and its fine arts. Many of the city's leading architects of the time were Freemasons, including Quarenghi, Cameron, Bazhenov, and Voronikhin. One aspect was in park design, as the English style of park was conceived in England by Freemasons, and such parks in and around the city were built largely by Freemasons. The style was designed to blend nature with the beautiful, graceful, and restrained art and architecture of man in order to encourage peaceful contemplation and higher thoughts. Another aspect was Egyptian themes, partly because some believed that Freemasonry's origins could be traced to Egypt and partly because the construction of temples—the mason's craft—originated in Egypt. This could be seen in the many obelisks (not a traditional Russian artistic or architectural form) erected in the city, sphinxes, the importation and placement of ancient Egyptian artifacts in the city, and hieroglyphs and other Egyptian designs in exterior and interior decoration, such as the Egyptian Gates at Tsarskoe Selo. Finally, purely Masonic symbols appeared on the exterior and interior of many buildings, including Kazan Cathedral. In the fine arts, Freemasonry stimulated the art of portraiture, which was facilitated by the fact that the longtime head of the Academy of Fine Arts, A. Labzin, as well as the leading painters Dmitry Levitsky, Fedor Rokotov, and Vladimir

Borovikovsky, were Freemasons. It was the practice of Freemasons to give their portraits to one another as symbols of brotherhood, which greatly stimulated the demand for "intimate" portraiture portraying the "hieroglyphics" of the subject's nature and not simply base appearance. This helps explain the multiple portraits of the same individuals, as a result of which portraits of virtually all leading Freemasons of the time survive today.

ST. PETERSBURG AND THE FRENCH REVOLUTION

Catherine's latter years were marked by a series of crises which left their mark on the city. The first was the two-year Swedish war. Soon after the onset of the Second Turkish War (1787–92), Turkey persuaded the King of Sweden, Gustavus III—Catherine's "cousin Gu"—to open a second front in the Baltic in order to detain Russia's navy in the north so it could not threaten Turkey. The Sultan's promises of payments to finance the war (never received) and the fanciful hope of reclaiming the territories lost to Peter the Great—first and foremost St. Petersburg itself—convinced the simpleminded Gustavus to commence hostilities in June 1788. He sent Catherine an ultimatum in which he demanded all territories lost to Russia since Peter the Great and that Russia accept Swedish "mediation" in the Turkish conflict and restore to Turkey lands taken in the First Turkish War. Catherine could only laugh and call him "Don Quixote the Knight Errant." When leaving Sweden for the front, Gustavus boasted to the ladies of Stockholm that he would soon invite them to a ball at Peterhof.[156] From Peterhof he would then go to Petersburg itself and overturn all monuments to "Russian insolence" except for the Bronze Horseman, "in order to engrave upon the pedestal, and immortalize, the name of Gustavus."[157] When Catherine heard of this she remarked that her foe was indeed "Sir John Falstaff."[158]

Catherine's own boasts were soon forgotten once the Swedish navy approached and threatened the city. Catherine immediately took emergency measures. Emergency provisioning of the city was organized, and Swedish trading vessels were seized and sequestered. She also commandeered the horses of local peasants and even those from the royal stables. Citizen militias were formed from local tradesmen, churchmen, state peasants, palace servants, and lamplighters. They could be seen drilling and marching at all hours and standing guard over the city. Catherine even pardoned and released 153 court-marshalled Russian sailors in order to strengthen the defenses of Kronstadt. She wrote to Potemkin: "Petersburg has at this moment the look of an armed camp, and I myself am like the quartermaster-general; [on] the day of the naval battle of 6 July the smell of gunpowder was scented in town; and so, my friend, I too have smelled gunpowder."[159] The more important battle was on July 9 off the more distant island of Hogland, which went to Russia and for a while gave the city a reprieve.

The war then drifted on for over a year due mainly to the timidity of the Russian naval and army commanders, with victories and losses on both sides. These desultory naval battles gave Grand Duke Paul his only military experience. He was generally kept at a safe distance from the main action, but some musket balls did whistle past his ears and thus he could claim his baptism of fire. When the Swedes heard about this, they apologized for firing at him.[160]

To invigorate the naval effort, Catherine summoned to St. Petersburg none other than John Paul Jones, the naval hero of the American Revolution. He had already been serving under Potemkin's command in the Turkish war with notable success, but the headstrong admiral inevitably fell out with Potemkin, and it was decided that his talents could be put to better use against the Swedes. Had he seen action, perhaps the war would have been shorter. As matters went, however, he arrived in the city only in December 1788, and before the next year's campaign season began he was accused of raping a young girl. Circumstances suggested that he was framed by the British, and he was never tried. But since his reputation was ruined, including with the Empress, and Russian naval officers resented him, he was simply asked to leave Russia. He went to revolutionary Paris for more adventure, where he died three years later.

The year 1790 began more brightly with the performance in the Hermitage Theater of a comic opera written by Catherine, *The Errant Knight*, with foreign ambassadors in the audience. It was a burlesque of Gustavus, who was portrayed as a blustering dwarfish captain in an oversize uniform who was misguided by the advice of a mischievous fairy into attacking a three-man garrison and was put to flight by the commandant with no weapon other than his crutch.[161] When the ice broke, Russia was ready for the final campaigns of the war. The hostilities culminated in naval battles just outside St. Petersburg beginning in late May. Ensconced in Tsarskoe Selo on May 23, Catherine and her suite listened all day to what she termed a "terrific cannonade" as couriers came and went with dispatches. The fighting continued for several days. Finally, on the morning of May 28, Catherine went to Peterhof and thence at great risk to herself to Kronstadt, where she surveyed the battles all day long through a telescope. That same day, inside the city a large accidental explosion in an artillery laboratory panicked the city's residents, who thought the battle had reached the city's streets. Hundreds of windowpanes were shattered, including in Potemkin's Tauride Palace. To prevent further unrest, a prohibition was issued against the shooting of any cannon, fireworks, rockets and the like (which were a popular pastime in the dachas surrounding the city). The Swedes were put on the defensive, but unfavorable winds prevented a decisive victory until late June. Despite a subsequent Swedish victory on June 28 (the anniversary of Catherine's coup), a peace was signed on August 3 which confirmed the prewar status quo. Catherine's and cousin Gu's enmity did not last long. Within a year, they would unite as allies against revolutionary France.

Indeed, while Catherine fumed at her generals' inability to close either the Swedish or Turkish wars, she and all of St. Petersburg had watched closely and nervously as the revolutionary events in France unfolded. Initially Catherine had been sanguine about the prospects for a peaceful resolution of the demands of the National Assembly, but as events spun out of control she and her statesmen were horrified at the atrocities and anarchy, and she feared the spread of the Jacobin cancer to Russia.

Catherine had reason to be concerned. Most of Petersburg's noble youth had been educated by the French and were seeped in French Enlightenment thought, which was still in vogue. Many Russians were studying in France at that very time. The French Ambassador in Petersburg, Count de Ségur, was a popular figure, and was liked by the Empress and often in her company,[162] but he had come out in support of the revolution and could gain a local following.

The account of the storming of the Bastille was published in the St. Petersburg Gazette on August 17. The ensuing events, including the nobility's voluntary abandonment of feudal privileges, were reported in detail. The Declaration of the Rights of Man, Article III of which proclaimed that "[s]upreme power derives from the people," was printed in full in Russian translation. French publications describing the events in Paris as well as revolutionary pamphlets were also available, widely read, and even on open display in the library of the Corps de Cadets. These events riveted Petersburg's citizens. The French Ambassador de Ségur reported:

> The news spread with rapidity, and was listened to with very different feelings, according to the condition and opinions of the persons to whom it was communicated. At court, the agitation was violent and the discontent general; in the town, the impression was altogether the reverse; and, although the Bastille, could not, assuredly endanger the safety of the inhabitants of Petersburg, I cannot describe the enthusiasm which was excited among the merchants, the tradesmen, the citizens, and some young men of a more elevated rank, by the destruction of that state-prison, and the first triumph of a stormy liberty.
>
> Frenchmen, Russians, Danes, Germans, Englishmen, Dutchmen, all congratulated and embraced one another in the streets, as if they had been relieved from the weight of heavy chains.[163]

Among many the revolution became fashionable. Revolutionary clothing was in vogue, and revolutionary jargon was on people's tongues. Society ladies were spied at the English Club wearing red Jacobin hats. An Italian artist in town was said to be organizing a Jacobin club (and therefore was placed under surveillance). French revolutionary songs such as "Ca ira" were sung in the royal palace in Catherine's presence.[164] Open debates were heard on how best to draft the French constitution.[165]

As France degenerated into anarchy and terror, Catherine could not let this trend continue, especially after a report in 1791 of a French plot to assassinate her. Russia joined the international coalition (including Prussia, Austria, Britain, The Netherlands, and Spain) that was waging war with revolutionary France. The importation, sale, and distribution of French publications, including even the Encyclopédie and works of

Voltaire, were banned,[166] though no general censorship was yet established. Catherine forbade the sale and wearing of French revolutionary clothing. In 1790–91 she recalled all Russian students and other citizens from Paris and Strasbourg after learning that Paul Stroganov, living in Paris and already a Freemason and member of the Club of Friends of the Law, in August 1790 had attended Jacobin meetings and perhaps joined the organization. In the same period, her correspondents in Germany fed her information that Freemasonry lay at the root of the French Revolution.[167]

In 1791 de Ségur quit St. Petersburg, and Catherine bade him the following farewell:

> I regret much your departure; you would do better to remain with me, and to keep away from those storms of which you do not, perhaps, foresee the full extent. Your predilection for the new philosophy, and for liberty, will probably incline you to support the cause of the people; I regret it; for aristocracy is my profession, and I must adhere to it.[168]

He was replaced by his secretary of legation, Edmond Genet, later infamous in the United States as "Citizen Genet." The French legation in Petersburg was virtually under house arrest. Genet was generally despised, treated as a pariah, forbidden to appear at court, and his house was often surrounded by unruly crowds bearing, he said, "daggers, pistolets and poisons." There was some reason for this treatment, as the Russians, who had broken the French cypher, saw his inflammatory dispatches claiming that Russian society at every level was rife with revolutionary ferment.[169] Catherine and her ministers had to wonder if he was right. But they made sure Genet would play no part in it by expelling him in July 1792. "They say he left Petersburg cramming a red wool cap down over his head," Catherine wrote Grimm.[170]

The situation worsened after Sweden's Gustavus III was assassinated at a masked ball in 1792 and Louis XVI was guillotined in January 1793. In February 1793, Catherine broke all relations with France. Among other measures, she abrogated a 1787 trade treaty, banned the importation of French goods, and ordered all French citizens who would not take an oath forswearing revolution to leave Russia (but of the 1,500 or so French in Russia, only 42 refused).[171] The citizenry of St. Petersburg also eventually turned against France, and something of a witch-hunt for French ensued.[172] French were detained and interrogated. Marriages to French were disapproved. In July 1794, barrels of French vodka were dumped into the Neva in St. Petersburg's equivalent of the Boston Tea Party, and French wares were burned.[173] Catherine had already (in 1789) smashed her bust of Voltaire in the Cameron Gallery at Tsarskoe Selo; now she consigned Houdon's Voltaire in the Hermitage to the attic.

St. Petersburg became a haven for fleeing French nobles, who unlike ordinary French in the city were honored as victims and welcomed with open arms. A veritable parade of titled names such as Esterhazy, Richelieu, de Villeneuve, Saint-

Priest, Choiseul-Gouffier, and Sénac de Mailhans flowed into town. The most notable among them was Louis XVI's brother, the Comte de Artois, who would later occupy the French throne as Charles X. He arrived in early March 1793 while the Russian court was still in mourning attire in memory of Louis XVI and was treated as royalty. Petersburg also became a refuge for French clerics such as the Abbé Lharidon de Penguilly, whom Grand Duke Paul had met on his European tour, as well as noble Poles fleeing from the revolutionary unrest there. Many of these French entered the Russian service. A later arrival, in mid-1795, was the famous French court portraitist Louise-Elisabeth Vigée-Lebrun. "Altogether, St. Petersburg took me back to the times of Agamemnon, partly through the grandeur of the buildings and partly through the popular garb, which reminded me of the dress of antiquity," she wrote of her first impressions of the city in her memoirs.[174] She would remain there until the spring of 1801 and leave behind many portraits of the Imperial family and nobility which now grace the walls of the Hermitage.

The French émigrés changed the complexion of life in the city. "One might have believed oneself at Paris, so many French were there at the fashionable gatherings," wrote Vigée-Lebrun.[175] The Comte de Puibusque remarked that on Nevsky Prospect

> I would have thought myself in Paris, on the Terrasse de Feuillans or the Boulevard de Goblentz. I heard French spoken everywhere. The attire of the lords and ladies . . . is precisely the same as in Paris. The civility and brilliance of their conversations, this agreeable chatter of a joyous and contented crowd, made me forget the distance which separates us.[176]

Catherine realized that the greater threat to Russia was not from France directly but from neighboring Poland, which she saw as an Eastern European manifestation of the French contagion that had to be snuffed out in its incipience. On May 3, 1791, reformers in Poland had succeeded in enacting a new constitution which, though it preserved a hereditary monarchy, made it a constitutional one including a full legislature. Its opponents from the old order invited Russia to intervene, which resulted in the second partition of Poland in January 1793. This led to an uprising in March 1794 led by Tadeusz Kosciuszko (who had served in the American Revolution), in which the Russian garrison in Warsaw and over 3,000 Russians in that city were killed or captured. Catherine was denounced as a tyrant and her portrait was trampled on the streets. They proclaimed the equality of all men and called for freeing the serfs (and mobilizing them). Catherine was convinced that the "hydra of Jacobins" had infected Poland, and that the French were behind it and other planned revolts throughout Europe. This fear was confirmed when news of an abortive Jacobin coup in Naples and rumors of another in Genoa reached Petersburg. She was determined to crush the hydra. She sent in Generalissimo Suvorov to do the job, which resulted in the third partition that eliminated Poland from the map of Europe until the 20th century.

It was in this inauspicious atmosphere of near hysteria and a fortress mentality, with the Empress now over 60 and losing her grip, that some Russian intellectuals, many of whom subscribed to Enlightenment thought and Catherine's own earlier ideals, decided to take their stand against the continuing injustices in Russia. It was very bad timing.

A rather mild example was the publication in 1793 of a 1789 play by Yakov Knyazhnin, *Vadim of Novgorod,* which recalled the old values of Novgorod and whose hero proclaimed the virtues of republicans and denounced autocracy:

> *Autocracy is everywhere the cause of evil,*
> *As it corrupts even the purest virtue,*
> *And as it gives free rein to human passion,*
> *Gives license to a king to be a tyrant.*[177]

Since the French Revolution broke out just as Knyazhnin finished the play, he tactfully withdrew it from presentation. In 1793, however, Knyazhnin's widow begged Princess Dashkova, still head of both the Academies of Sciences and Language, to publish the play so that the proceeds could benefit her children. It was cleared internally by those responsible for self-censorship at the Academy of Sciences and published on its press. Had the play been published years earlier, no one would have noticed, but in the current atmosphere, which included Dashkova's brother's patronage of the now-exiled Alexander Radishchev (see below), Catherine took it as an attack on her monarchy. She gave Dashkova a severe dressing down and ordered all copies destroyed.[178]

In April 1792, Novikov was detained on suspicion that he had secretly published a book about the Old Believers containing lies about the Orthodox Church. But other banned literature was found in his apartment, links with Grand Duke Paul were discovered, as well as evidence that the Moscow Rosicrucians with whom he was connected were being directed from Prussia by Johann Christoff von Wöllner, a minister of King Frederick Wilhelm. In Catherine's mind, this was evidence of the long-suspected international Masonic conspiracy to place Paul on the throne, and Novikov and some of his associates were arrested.[179] Novikov was sentenced without trial to 15 years imprisonment in Schlüsselburg, but he was released four years later during Paul's reign. After his release he seemed a broken man and retreated into religious mysticism and theosophical, magical, and cabalistic writings.[180]

The most important case, however, was that of Alexander Radishchev, who was a pure product of Catherine's own Russian Enlightenment and of St. Petersburg. From a noble family, he had grown up in the provinces and studied in Moscow before being chosen after Catherine's coronation in 1762 as one of 40 to study in St. Petersburg at the Corps of Pages. As a page at court, he could observe firsthand court manners, intrigues, and corruption. In 1767 he was sent by Catherine as one of 12 to be trained as an elite group of jurists at the University of Leipzig. There he thoroughly studied the works of the Enlightenment, particularly Helvétius and Raynal. By the time he returned to Russia in 1771, he regarded autocracy as simple despotism that violated natural law and the social contract. In St. Petersburg he served in the department of the Senate dealing with appeals and revisions to sentences, and then in the legal staff of the Department of War. In 1777 he joined the College of Commerce and rose to become the director of St. Petersburg Customs.

During this period he published several works, including a translation of Mably's *Reflections on Greek History*, his *Ode to Freedom* in praise of the American Revolution, and a number of essays. In these he openly condemned absolutism (in the abstract), but in the liberal atmosphere of the time they caused no stir. In 1773 he became a Freemason, of the original St. Petersburg variety. He regarded the higher-order Freemasons in Moscow as nothing more than the latest manifestation of Muscovite religious mumbo jumbo. "If you open the latest mystical writings," he observed, "you imagine yourself to be back in the age of scholasticism and theological disputation, when the human mind busied itself with preachifying, without stopping to reflect on whether there was any sense in what was preached."[181] Instead, he focused on helping his fellow men.

In 1790, he self-published anonymously his novel, *Journey from St. Petersburg to Moscow*,[182] which used the device of a travelogue to criticize a wide variety of social ills and government abuses and to advocate change. The book began: "I looked around me—and my soul was troubled by sufferings of humanity. . . . I felt that it was possible for anyone to strive for the well-being of his fellows."[183] With these words, proclaimed Nikolai Berdyaev, "the Russian intelligentsia was born."[184] From then on, Russian thought would be focused on the transformation of the actual state of affairs, and on the well-being of the people rather than merely of the state. For the first time, the principles of the Enlightenment which Catherine had espoused and which had matured in St. Petersburg were turned against Russia and its ruler in an open challenge. Radishchev took these principles to their logical end to demand equality of all citizens before the law, the end of absolutism, and the freeing of the serfs:

> Every man is born into the world equal to all others. . . . But when he puts limits to his own freedom of action, he agrees not to follow only his own will in everything, he subjects himself to the commands of his equals; in a word, he becomes a citizen. . . . If the law is unable or unwilling to protect him, or if its power cannot furnish him immediate aid in the face of clear and present danger, then the citizen has recourse to the natural law of self-defense, self-preservation and well-being. . . . If the law, or the Sovereign, or any power on earth should tempt you to falsehood or to depart from virtue, remain immovably true to it. Fear not ridicule, nor torture, not sickness, or exile, nor even death itself.[185]

But Radishchev was not merely talking in the abstract. Through his graphic depiction of conditions in Russia, like Hans Christian Andersen's little boy he told Catherine the truth that no one else dared: her subjects were suffering and unhappy, and she and her regime had many failings. And this gauntlet from a noble whom she had groomed to be a loyal state servitor! Catherine fumed: "He's a Martinist! He's worse than Pugachev! He extols [Benjamin] Franklin!" "The questions brought up here," she wrote in her own notes on the book, "are the ones over which France is now being ruined."[186] In earlier years Radishchev might not have suffered, but in the atmosphere of 1790 he was tracked down and arrested, held in the Peter and Paul Fortress, interrogated (by the interrogator of Pugachev), tried, and sentenced to death—the first such sentence imposed on a nobleman since Catherine's Charter of the Nobility in 1785 (under which any corporal punishment of a noble was illegal). As usual since the time of Elizabeth, however, the death sentence was commuted to exile. By the time the episode was over, Catherine seems to have realized that she had overreacted, but she was not about to reverse any decisions. Radishchev was allowed to remain in Petersburg and then Moscow for some months before departing to Siberia, and once outside Petersburg his fetters were removed by imperial order. His patron, Alexander Vorontsov, then President of his employer (the College of Commerce) and brother of Princess Dashkova, was allowed to aid him and make his life in Siberia comfortable. Radishchev returned from Siberia in 1797, and in 1801 Alexander I appointed him to his Commission on Laws charged with redrafting Russia's laws—what some hoped would be the basis for a Russian constitution—but the Commission generally consisted of conservative nonentities and Radishchev's proposals were rejected as too radical. According to Pushkin, its head, Count Peter Zavadovsky, was astonished "at the youthfullness of his grey hairs" and admonished him: "Eh, Alexander Nikoliavich, so you really want to talk the same old nonsense? Didn't you have enough of Siberia?"[187] In September 1802 Radishchev concluded that the Commission was going nowhere, that his efforts were in vain, and possibly that he could be sent back into exile. He committed suicide by poison, an end which Pushkin observed "could be foreseen long ahead of time and which he himself had prophesied."[188] Indeed, in light of Radishchev's own writings in which he had discussed suicide and a note found in his documents following his death stating that "posterity will avenge me," his act seems to have been not the result of simple depression but a considered act of political defiance.[189]

Radishchev marked the logical culmination in 18th-century Russia of the principles which Peter the Great had introduced and on which St. Petersburg was founded and modeled. The blueprint for a civil society in Russia was now ready and apparent for all to see. But as of yet there was no developed Third Estate or social institutions upon which to create it, much less the political will to do so. The lines of political and social debate in Russia from then up to the present time can be seen as stemming from the challenge thrown down by Radishchev: a tortuous series of efforts to build a civil society in the face of oppression and in competition with alternative visions mainly derived from old Muscovite values.

Despite Catherine's usurpation of the throne, her reign had held great promise. She began her reign believing in the urgent need to move Russia along the Petrine path, calculating that prudently progressive policies would reinforce her hold on the throne.[190] By the time her power was secure in the late 1770s, she could have pressed a more progressive agenda if she truly wanted to make it hers. Peter the Great had not shrunk from controversy. But Catherine decided to avoid confrontation and any attendant risks to her throne, and as a result the state began to drift and her reign degenerated to some extent into maintenance of the status quo, tolerance of corruption, and court favoritism and intrigue. Perhaps Catherine rationalized that the ideas and legislation that she introduced would naturally result in evolutionary social and political change—after her.

Although Catherine proved a disappointment, she had planted important ideas and seeds of progress in St. Petersburg. The mere fact that she had promoted Enlightenment ideals, classical architecture, education, and literature was enough to stimulate thinking people and move the city and its people to the next stage along the path implied by Peter the Great's founding principles and strengthened the city's role as a vanguard of change within Russia. Even had she proved more progressive, Catherine could not have conferred enlightenment, culture, or freedom of mind by decree. But she could and did reveal it for members of society to see and take up. And thus it was in Catherine's reign that many of Peter the Great's initiatives in education, the arts, and culture came to fruition, and that a large segment of the St. Petersburg aristocracy was soon far more modern and progressive than the Empress. Thus, St. Petersburg did become the grand showcase of modern Russian civilization that Catherine envisioned; for the rest of the country it stood as a model to which one might aspire (or reject). And in the social and political spheres for the first time Russian citizens began to feel enfranchised, realize that Russia's future was in their hands, and that Russia was already great and could be made greater. In 1696, a century before Catherine's death, the young Peter the Great was only dreaming of visiting Europe. Now Russia was a major European power with a large empire, had absorbed much of Western thought and culture, and Europeans were coming to marvel at and work in its capital. Like Western Europeans, Russians now had the intellectual ammunition needed to advocate and pursue the social and political changes needed to overcome the past, and soon they—with or without the support of their sovereign—would seek to do so. As Sumarokov wrote, "Peter gave us existence, Catherine—our soul."[191]

CHAPTER 7

Petersburg under the Errant Knight

There is but one important person in Russia. That is the person whom I happen to address, and this importance lasts only while I am addressing him.

EMPEROR PAUL I

This beautiful capital, in which people used to move about as free as air, which had neither gates nor guards nor customs officers, is transformed into a vast prison.

COUNT GOLOVKIN

When Catherine died of a stroke on November 6, 1796, the full implications of the modernization for which St. Petersburg stood were apparent to all. A more liberal Russia free of serfdom was the dream of many, but it was a threat to many more. Paul ascended the throne as the first Emperor to face such a stark ideological and political choice. The country held its breath, awaiting Paul's direction. It did not take long to find out. Paul's views on what was wrong with Russia had long been formed. He knew what he wanted to do, and he was eager to begin. Paul threw himself headlong into furious activity to realize his vision, which was unique and came from a special personal background.

PAUL'S UPBRINGING

Paul, born on September 20, 1754, was probably the son of Catherine's first lover, Sergei Saltykov. Paul almost certainly realized that he was not Peter III's son, but he put this out of his mind and always regarded Peter as his father. In fact, he idolized him, even though Peter had failed to designate Paul as his heir, in which case Catherine at most would have been Paul's regent for a few years.

Paul was short (not over 5'3") and not particularly attractive, but neither was he ugly or deformed. He had a small pug nose, receding hair, and gained weight as he aged. As a child he was frail and often ill. When he matured he maintained an iron discipline, was free from vices, rarely drank, and was not corrupt. But he was one of those children who grew up with a chip on his shoulder, was sensitive to

210

any slight, and was quick to take offense and revenge. He was headstrong and seemingly certain in his opinions, but in fact he was easily influenced by others and thus often changed his mind. He held his more fundamental values and beliefs strongly, however, and whatever he did, outrageous as it seemed to others, he did because he thought it was right, without ulterior motives. He was capable of great feeling and human warmth, though he rarely showed it. Countess Golovina wrote about him:

> [A]mid this chaos of punctiliousness, pettiness, and unreasonable demands, the Emperor had great and chivalrous ideas. There were in him two beings quite different. His mind was a labyrinth in which reason went astray. His natural disposition was noble and virtuous, and when it was in ascendancy, his actions evoked respect and admiration.[1]

Paul grew up in the shadow of Catherine's coup. Catherine had no claim to the throne, and many believed that in 1762 Paul should have been proclaimed Emperor with Catherine only his regent. Paul held this grudge against Catherine from the start, and it only festered as he came to detest his mother's corrupt and immoral court. He also disagreed with most of her policies, and grew frustrated with his lack of state responsibilities and political isolation. Thus, Paul's desire to undo Catherine's work became the salient feature of his program and reign. This desire was personal as much as ideological, as shown by his immediately freeing Novikov, Radishchev, Kosciuszko, and others whom Catherine had exiled or imprisoned, although he violently disagreed with their views.

Catherine had taken care to provide Paul with the best possible education in the liberal ideas of the Enlightenment. In 1759, when Paul was five, she appointed Nikolai Panin as his Governor, who both elaborated a detailed educational program and ran Paul's household. Panin was chosen at the recommendation of Chancellor Mikhail Vorontsov because both were champions of aristocratic constitutionalism and wanted to influence Paul in that direction.[2] Panin's progressive program indeed reached a new height in Russian educational thinking. It included technical subjects such as mathematics, science, history, languages (French and German), and literature, but also included sports and entertainment such as fencing, horseback riding, attendance at the theater, and moral and religious instruction.

Panin got along well with Paul, but he was never able to bring his charge over to his liberal political views. One reason was that, by the time Paul was of age to understand political theory and receive practical instruction in governing, it was not provided because Catherine and Potemkin opposed it. Potemkin coveted the military and governmental positions that Paul otherwise might hold, and obtained them. Catherine did not want to think about death, of which preparing Paul to rule would remind her. Moreover, as Paul was the hope of Catherine's opponents she did not want to encourage them by making Paul ready to govern just yet, nor did the liberal Panin want to appear to be aligning with them.[3] Thus, Catherine removed Panin as Paul's tutor and occupied Paul with a wife.

In October 1773 Paul married a German princess who took the Russian name Natalya Alexeevna. She turned out to be headstrong, spoiled, spendthrift, immoderate, and carried on a liaison with Paul's close friend Andrei Razumovsky, which was a blow to his self-esteem and sense of personal security, after which he no longer trusted anyone. Natalya died in childbirth in 1776, and within months Paul had married another German princess, who took the name Maria Fedorovna. Their marriage was long and fruitful and produced Grand Dukes Alexander, Constantine, Nicholas, and Mikhail.

In late 1776 Paul visited Berlin and met Frederick the Great. This was Paul's first trip abroad, and he was impressed by how Frederick's court, the military, and Prussian society differed from Russia's. Frederick kept strict order, the military was kept in top form, the population was disciplined and hard working and the country prospered. Paul concluded that "Prussia has two more centuries of civilization than we do."[4] In 1781–82 Paul toured Austria, Italy, France, and the Low Countries. He returned from the trip impressed with Europe's Old Regime and determined to remold Russia's aristocracy on that model: to create and preserve a static society of orders with a paternalistic reforming autocrat on top.

Paul was tolerant in religious matters, but he was an uncompromising moralist. He regarded Catherine's court as licenscious, immoral and corrupt, overrun with sycophants and favorites, wasteful and disorderly. But the rural gentry were little better. He saw them as lazy, corrupt, profligate in living beyond their means and in contracting unpayable debts, and as a burden on the nation. The military too was soft, disorderly and corrupt, especially the Guards.

Paul also had a mystical and romantic streak, a trait shared with his friend Crown Prince Frederick Wilhelm of Prussia. While Paul was initially attracted to higher-order Freemasonry, he later lost interest in it and renewed Catherine's prohibitions on the movement as it was too independent of imperial authority and too associated with liberal social reform. He preferred instead the chivalry and pomp of the Knights of Malta, a true anachronism.

Paul was a convinced autocrat and considered monarchy the natural form of government. He believed in a natural, organic, orderly, and static type of society in which each element had its place and in which the autocrat stood at its apex. To prosper, society needed discipline, strict morals, and strict acceptance of authority. He accepted the authority of his superiors, and he expected the same from others when he would be Tsar. Paul believed in the rule of law as a means to establishing his ideal society, but his conception of the term differed fundamentally from the Enlightenment liberal-constitutional understanding advocated by Panin and other liberals. For Paul, the rule of law simply meant order imposed by the autocrat. When he struck his chest and declared "Here is the law!" he literally meant it. In France, order had broken down because the monarch was weak, the aristocracy had grown profligate and failed in its duties, and morality had been subverted by destructive Enlightenment ideas. He saw Russia as destined for the same fate unless this trend was arrested. Russia had to put its house in order to prevent an uncontrollable revolution in which countless Pugachevs would arise, influenced by subversive ideas from the West. Further, Russia should serve as a bastion of opposition to revolution in Europe. But Russia should concentrate on rebuilding itself and refrain from foreign military adventures. Though a militarist, initially Paul was not bent on achieving military glory.

In overturning Catherine's model, Paul could not turn back to Muscovite Russia. Nearly a century after Peter the Great, this would no longer be credible. Instead, he created a hybrid. He drew on some of Muscovy's fundamental values such as the idea of an ordered, organic, and static society rooted in religion and headed by an autocrat, and overlaid them with European Old Regime forms. Though he introduced modern features such as a modern military and Western models of state administration, he did so in the service of a conservative cause.

Paul had to wait a long time to put his ideas into practice as Tsar, but before then he was able to do so in miniature at his estate at Gatchina. Gatchina was a village about 28 miles southwest of St. Petersburg originally owned by Peter the Great's sister Natalya, but by Catherine's reign it was held by Prince Boris Kurakin. When Kurakin died in 1765, Catherine bought it as a gift for her favorite Grigory Orlov, who commissioned Antonio Rinaldi to build a palace there to serve as his wilderness hideaway for hunting with close friends. It was begun in May 1766 and finished in 1781. The main palace was unique as it had the outlines of a castle complete with twin towers and was faced with local limestone rather than the usual stucco and paint. Rinaldi gave the castle a classical flavor by including Doric and Ionic pilasters on the exterior. The interior was tastefully decorated in classical style with elaborate inlaid wooden floors, intricate moldings, and painted ceilings. It also had a large garden reminiscent of castles in England. After Orlov died in 1783, Catherine purchased the estate from his family, and she presented it to Paul on the occasion of the birth of his first daughter, Alexandra. Paul was delighted. He lavished his attention on the estate for the 13 more years that he would wait to become Tsar, much as his wife Maria made Pavlovsk her project. Paul made many changes to Gatchina's castle and grounds, which were carried out by Vincenzo Brenna (1747–1819), Charles Cameron's former assistant. Paul decorated his castle with busts and statues of classical heroes, especially Roman emperors and generals, while portraits of his heroes (including Peter the Great, Frederick the Great, Sully, and Henry IV) hung on the walls. He also imposed a more geometrical and orderly form on the gardens and created there the first arboretum in Russia.

At Gatchina Paul created his own utopia which he ruled like a medieval prince, and a new phase in his life began. What gave Gatchina its essential character was Paul's private army. At first it was only a battalion extracted from Catherine to defend the village against local brigands, but eventually it numbered about 2,000 enlisted men and about 130 officers. He hoped to create what could become the nucleus of a properly disciplined and trained army once he became Tsar. They were primarily poor nobles from the regular army for whom a career in the Guards was not possible, or men with flawed character who were unable to advance in the army. Paul gave them a chance for advancement and glory. Among the notables who got their start at Gatchina were the later Counts Alexei Arakcheev, Fedor Rostopchin, and Ivan Kutaisov. Paul lavished love and attention on them, and they grew loyal to him as a father figure despite his strictness and frequent outbursts. Under the influence of the Prussian commander Baron Stienwehr, Paul dressed them in old Prussian-style uniforms from the time of Frederick the Great and imposed a strict Prussian military regime and drill. At both Gatchina and Pavlovsk he would set up a telescope in the palace from which he would survey the grounds and call attention to any defects in the gait of soldiers, the buttons on their uniforms, or the length of the strap on their muskets. He imposed a strict dress code, which forbade "immoral" styles (including round hats), and any dress inappropriate for the wearer's class. He invited his sons Alexander and Constantine to participate in maneuvers, and to Catherine's chagrin they much enjoyed it. His wife Maria also took part. Replicating medieval chivalry, Paul placed her in a tower to play the damsel in distress and his battalion would proceed to save her. Alexander Herzen later called Paul "Don Quixote with a crown."

Paul's world at Gatchina was well-known at court and became an object of ridicule. "The officers of the Grand Duke's entourage are like figures cut out of an old scrapbook," remarked the Duchess of Saxe-Coburg of his anachronistic soldiers.[5] Catherine forbade the Gatchina uniforms at court. But Gatchina proved to be a blessing for her, as it completely occupied Paul and kept him out of her court's and government's affairs.

On November 5, 1796, Paul related to his friends over dinner a recurring dream he had the night before in which he had been lifted up out of his bed by some unknown force. His wife Maria was excited because she had the same dream. On the way back from dinner, a hussar rode up and excitedly told Paul that Count Nikolai Zubov had arrived and wanted to see him urgently. Since Zubov was the brother of Catherine's reigning favorite at court and therefore his rival, Paul suspected the worst and thought he was being removed from the succession and that Zubov had come with troops to arrest him. "We are lost!" he exclaimed, grasping Maria's hand. But he was relieved to hear that Zubov was alone. When Paul presented himself to his visitor, Zubov immediately kneeled before him and reported that Catherine had suffered a stroke, was near death, and that Paul was urgently needed at the Winter Palace. The moment that Paul had awaited for 42 years had finally arrived.

Paul and Maria jumped into their carriage and headed toward the city. Messengers from the Winter Palace came regularly with news. Importantly, no one was rallying around Alexander as Catherine's successor. Rostopchin rode out from town to join Paul in his carriage. "Monsignor, what a moment for you!" he exclaimed. Paul pressed his hand and thanked God: "Perhaps he will give me the strength to support the state to which he destines me." Paul arrived in the Winter Palace at about 8:30 P.M., where he was received as Emperor. He first kneeled beside his dying mother, who was spread out on the floor. According to some, Paul was truly moved, wept openly and repeatedly kissed his mother's hand. But then Paul set himself up in a makeshift office in an adjacent apartment and began conducting business and giving orders, one of which was for new army uniforms in the Gatchina-Prussian style. Those who filed in and out would pass through Catherine's chamber as she lay dying on the floor, which to Catherine's suite seemed rather profane. Paul had ordered a number of his *Gatchiniki* to follow him to the Winter Palace, and they soon began arriving. Countess Golovina commented:

> The Empress' apartments filled up at once with servants devoted to the Grand Duke Paul. For the most part persons of obscure origin, to whom neither their talents nor their birth gave any right to aspire to the places and favors that in imagination they already saw being showered upon them. The crowd in the ante-rooms grew from moment to moment. The *Gatichinese* (as the persons I have just alluded to were called) ran about and knocked up against the courtiers, who asked each other in amazement who these Ostrogoths could be.[6]

After Catherine expired at about 9:45 P.M. the next evening, Paul became Emperor.

Paul's first actions were to begin reversing his mother's legacy and to revive his father's memory. Within days after Catherine's death, he had Peter III's remains unearthed from the cemetery at Alexander Nevsky Monastery (he had not been interred at the Peter and Paul Cathedral like other sovereigns beginning with Peter I) and transferred to the Church of Kazan. For the event Paul orchestrated a solemn procession of about 30 black carriages drawn by horses in black shrouds down Nevsky Prospect, which was lined on both sides by soldiers from the Guards regiments with black veils on their bayonets. Paul made Prince Fedor Baryatinsky (a conspirator who had figured in Peter's death at Ropsha), the famous Peter Passek, and other of Catherine's conspirators from 1762 draw Peter's coffin. Paul also designated the now elderly and infirm Alexei Orlov (responsible for Peter's death) to carry Peter's crown. At first, Orlov could not bear to do it and retreated to a dark corner of the church, where he wept, but he was brought out and was soon seen walking bareheaded behind the coffin bearing Peter's crown on a gilt cushion. As the procession moved along Nevsky, church bells rang solemnly throughout the city, and three artillery salutes rang out from the Fortress. Later, Peter's remains were put on display in the Winter Palace next to Catherine, with an honor guard of Peter's surviving officers guarding the coffin. Soon Peter and Catherine were interred side by side in Peter and Paul Cathedral. Paul explained, "My mother, having been called to the throne by the voice of the people, was too busy to arrange for my father's last rights. I am remedying that oversight."[7]

Paul did not follow up with a wholesale purge and arrest of Catherine's favorites and officials, but Catherine's conspirators of 1762 felt his wrath. Baryatinsky and Passek, whose arrest had prompted the coup, were removed from their offices and eventually exiled. Princess Dashkova had to leave her Moscow estates (to which she had moved following the *Vladimir of Novgorod* scandal) and live in semi-exile in Novgorod to "ponder on the events of the year 1762."[8] On the other hand, many of those whom Catherine had exiled or imprisoned, including Radishchev, Novikov, and 12,000 Polish prisoners, including Kosciuszko (who left for America), were freed. Paul brought from Moscow the only surviving supporter of Peter III, Peter Izmailov, a former Preobrazhensky officer who had sided with Peter against Catherine, and made him general aide-de-camp.

Paul then distributed appointments to his loyalists, including Alexander Kurakin, Count Bezborodko, Arakcheev (who became city commandant for St. Petersburg), and Rostopchin, and embarked upon a period of intense lawmaking designed to sweep away the rot of Catherine's regime and restore order. Over 48,000 orders, laws, and regulations were issued in Paul's first year, the most intense phase being the first five months before his coronation.[9]

PETERSBURG LIFE UNDER PAUL

Life in St. Petersburg, which Paul meant to turn into a model for his new regime, literally changed overnight. Paul disapproved of virtually the whole lifestyle of the capital under Catherine, and within a week after his accession his new order was already in place. The poet Derzhavin compared the scene to a conquest of the city by Paul's Gatchina battalions. The capital was sealed, with barriers and new guards placed at the entrances to town. Guards were also placed on major streets and at the entrances to public buildings. The uniforms were now the tight-fitting Prussian uniforms of a bygone age. To gain support, Paul called upon Suvorov to introduce them. Suvorov did so, but under protest, noting that curls are not cannon and queues are not bayonets. The British Ambassador, Charles Whitworth, observed that "the Court and the town is [*sic*] entirely military, and we can scarcely persuade ourselves that instead of Petersburg we are not in Potsdam."[10]

Paul also quickly changed the ordinary life of the city's residents. "Never before have all the decorations been changed so quickly at the sound of a whistle as happened when Paul ascended the throne," observed Prince Adam Czartoryski. "Everything was changed in a day—costumes, hairdos, looks, manners and occupations."[11] Paul issued detailed regulations prescribing how people were to dress, imposing the regime which had been in force at Gatchina for years. He favored the Old Regime style of breeches and stockings, buckled shoes, tricorn hats, and powdered hair; straight trousers, top boots, laced shoes, and round hats were prohibited.[12] The police and 200 dragoons sent into the streets of the city were instructed to confiscate nonconforming garb. Paul regulated the height of collars, styles in other neckwear; hair had to be combed back from the forehead. The dress of servants was prescribed. Foreigners were technically exempt from the new dress codes, but who was a foreigner was not immediately obvious to the police so there was little choice but to comply. Paul closed private printing presses, imposed censorship, banned the import of French books and even musical scores, and forbade the use of certain words such as *citizen*, *club*, and *society*. He proscribed the waltz, regarding it as immodest. Couples dancing at court balls twisted themselves into contortions to avoid turning their backs to him. Paul disliked male ballet dancers, so females had to dance the male roles. Russians could no longer travel abroad. Street traffic had to move slowly and decorously, carriages could be drawn only by a single horse, and only German harnesses were allowed. Officers had to ride on horseback or in open carriages, not in enclosed carriages. Whenever the Emperor's subjects met him in the streets, whether in a carriage, on horseback or on foot, they had to remove their hat, descend to the ground and kneel before him, otherwise they would be arrested. (This was a revival of a Muscovite custom.) When Paul encountered the 18-month-old Alexander Pushkin (the future poet) in a bonnet being pushed in his baby carriage, he scolded his nurse for not removing the bonnet. Lunchtime for city residents was prescribed for 1:00 P.M. Paul also imposed a curfew under which lights were to be extinguished and people were to be in bed by 10:00 P.M., but Petersburgers continued to make merry behind tightly curtained and blinded windows.

The regulations were numerous and unrelenting, often were not published, and enforcement was arbitrary. People did not know what was expected of them. No full version of the dress codes was published until 1798. The city became a social minefield as people were afraid to set foot in public lest they violate some new and unknown rule.[13] Countess Golovina observed:

> [T]he just liberty of the individual was fettered by a sort of terrorism, and the multiplicity of the rules of etiquette and the empty marks of respect to be observed no longer permitted one to breathe freely. . . . In a word, everything, down to our hats, bore the hall-mark of restraint.[14]

Indeed, many contemporaries traced Paul's downfall to such petty tyranny. "A sovereign can do many wrongs without exposing himself to death," explained Czartoryski, "[b]ut when the sovereign authority weights at every moment on each individual . . . and continually disturbs the peace of families, passions are excited which are more formidable. . . . This was the real motive of Paul's assassination."[15]

For his more substantive reforms, Paul began with reforming the military on the Prussian model, and he indeed made it more efficient. Paul spent 2–3 hours daily, usually on Tsaritsyn Lug (soon renamed the Field of Mars), drilling his troops. Paul imposed extraordinary strictness and arbitrary punishments. Officers and ordinary soldiers could be demoted or exiled for slight imperfections in dress or drill. Before military reviews, officers got into the habit of saying good-bye to their wives and families and bringing with them extra money for a long journey. When the performance of one unit displeased him, Paul ordered the entire unit to begin marching at once, in full uniform and in formation, to Siberia, which it obediently did for several days until Paul was persuaded to recall it. Officers began resigning en masse. By late in Paul's reign, over half of the Guards officers had resigned. The tough new regime was felt most by the educated, influential, and affluent, the very types who would later launch the conspiracy against Paul. "Our way of life, the officer's way of life, has changed utterly," lamented one Izmailovsky Guards officer. "Under the empress we thought only about going to the theater and to parties and walked around in coats and tails; now we have to sit from morning to evening in the regimental yard and be instructed in everything, like recruits."[16] Paul's favored *Gatchiniki* effectively became the new Guards. Paul planned to integrate the original four Guards units into the regular army.[17] Over two-thirds of the conspirators against Paul would come from Guards units.[18]

In the civil sphere, Paul eliminated Catherine's system of decentralized local government and brought it under direct supervision from the center. He formed a state council to centralize decision making and reformed the Senate to make it more efficient. In 1797 he formed in St. Petersburg an institute for training future government servants which would later evolve into the Imperial School of Law. He sought to reform landowners' treatment of serfs, limiting work for the landlord to three days per week. This displeased the gentry, who feared that Paul was on the path to abolishing serfdom, while giving rise to false hopes among the serfs, which led to the most significant peasant unrest since the Pugachev rebellion. Although he did not formally repeal the Charter of the Nobility, in practice Paul ignored most of it, again forcing nobles into state service and subjecting them to corporeal punishment. In order to bring the nobility into financial order, he created the Land Bank of the Nobility. It was ostensibly designed to consolidate and refinance the mounting (largely bad) debt of the gentry to give them a fresh start while paying off their creditors. But the scheme imposed such unrealistic repayment terms in light of nobles' meager incomes that foreclosure was a certainty in most cases, and the scheme was exposed mainly as a social policy designed to impose discipline on the nobility. The Bank became a scandal in which Paul was seen as lacking judgment or any understanding of economics.

In foreign policy, Paul initially joined Austria and other European powers in opposing the French contagion, but as he grew frustrated with his allies' caution and saw Bonaparte as a conservative force that could restore order and thwart revolution, in 1800 he switched sides and allied with him. He lifted the ban on trade with France, dismissed the Austrian and British ambassadors from St. Petersburg, and imposed a trade embargo against England, which deprived the English and much of the Russian merchant community in St. Petersburg of its livelihood and denied the landed gentry grain exports. He then launched a bizarre and unpopular military campaign against India, Britain's colony. Finally, Paul publicly proposed to resolve the issues of war and peace in Europe by challenging several European sovereigns to a series of duels.[19] This may have been done in jest, but in St. Petersburg it was taken seriously. Such actions confounded Russia's experienced statesmen who understood them as harmful to Russia's commercial and diplomatic interests. Fonvizin would later note that the plot against Paul was a "truly patriotic affair."[20] The recalled English ambassador, Charles Whitworth, commented to his government that "the Emperor is literally not in his senses. . . . [His] actions are guided by no fixed rules or principles, consequently nothing is, or can be, stable."[21]

Indeed, as time went on Paul's actions became more bizarre and capricious. Within the first few months of his reign, he had set in place virtually all that he had intended to do.[22] Beyond imposing order, he had little idea of what to do with Russia and was not committed to real progress. This was eventually betrayed by increasingly erratic decisions which had little to do with Russia's state interests. A cartoon circulated underground at the time depicted Paul holding a document in each hand. On one was written "Order," on the other was written "Counter-order," and on Paul's forehead was written "Disorder."[23] Grand Duke Alexander confided to his tutor LaHarpe in a letter in September 1797:

> When my father ascended the throne, he wanted to reform everything. It is true that he began quite brilliantly, but his later actions have not corresponded to the first. Everything has been turned upside down all at once, and that has only increased the confusion of affairs, which was already too great. The military waste almost all their time on parades. In other areas, there is no coherent plan. An order given today will be countermanded a month hence. . . . There is only one absolute power, which does everything without rhyme or reason. . . . My poor country is in an indescribable state: the farmer harassed, commerce obstructed, liberty and personal welfare reduced to nothing. That is the picture of Russia. Imagine what I suffer in my heart.[24]

At bottom, the problem was that, for all his commitment to order, the idea of the sanctity of and respect for law was alien to him and he recognized no one's rights.

A prime example of bizarre behavior at odds with Russia's interests is Paul's involvement with the Knights of Malta, which provides insight into Paul's vision for Russia and what he wanted St. Petersburg to become.[25] Paul had been fascinated with this chivalric order as a child, when he had read its histories. In Catherine's reign, Malta had been used as a training base for Russian naval officers, and a prominent Maltese naval officer, Count Giulio Litta, served Catherine with distinction in the war with Sweden (1788–90), for which he was decorated twice. Litta returned to St. Petersburg in 1796 to negotiate the status of the Knights' lands in Russian-held Poland following the third partition, but Catherine soon died. Paul received him enthusiastically, and on January 4, 1797, a convention with the Knights was inked recognizing the Order's claims over the Polish lands and obligating Russia to pay all back dues owed by the Polish priory. The Polish priory was moved to St. Petersburg and renamed the Grand Priory of Russia, and the Knights sent a special delegation to St. Petersburg to thank Paul, recognize his contributions to the Order, and to get the Russian priory running.

Paul gave great importance to the event and made elaborate preparations, involving the court, military and civil officials, and the Russian nobility in the pomp and ceremony. The delegation made its ceremonial entrance into the capital on November 29th in 36 ordinary and four royal carriages, some of which carried Russian nobles. A gala was held that evening in the Winter Palace with Paul dressed in the costume of the Order. After Litta gave a stirring speech, Paul was given the honorary office of Protector of the Order, a title shared only with the Holy Roman Emperor and the King of the Two Sicilies. He was also presented with an ancient and valuable Maltese cross that had belonged to one of the Order's legendary Grand Masters, la Valetta, and a coat of arms. Paul knighted his sons Alexander and Constantine. Maria Fedorovna received the grand cross of the Order. Since the Order had strict qualifications for membership (like being a Catholic) that Paul could not meet, he could not be a member of the Order or hold office in the Russian priory, so Prince de Condé, who headed the French emigré army in Russia, was named its Grand Prior. Litta remained in St. Petersburg as Paul's advisor on Maltese affairs. Paul soon gave the priory premises at the former Vorontsov mansion on Sadovoya Street and commissioned a Maltese chapel, which Quaranghi designed and built in 1798–1800 on the mansion's grounds and which still stands.

Seven months later Malta fell to Bonaparte with hardly a shot being fired, for which the Grand Master Ferdinand Hompesch came under criticism. The harshest criticism came from the Russian priory, which was essentially the mouthpiece of Litta. The priory issued a declaration withdrawing its recognition of Hompesch as Grand Master and threw itself "into the arms of our August and Sovereign Protector Paul I." Litta also wanted the Order's international headquarters to be St. Petersburg and for Paul to be Grand Master. This would require papal sanction, and for this purpose Litta took advantage of the visit of the papal nuncio to St. Petersburg, whose mission was to arrange diplomatic relations with the new Tsar. The nuncio was Litta's brother Lorenzo, and he quickly saw Paul's interest in the Knights as his means to achieve his own mission. Thus, the brothers gave Paul the impression that the Pope would approve their plans, and on October 27, 1798, the Russian priory, in the name of the entire Order, formally proclaimed Paul Grand Master, while in return Paul offered St. Petersburg as the Order's capital. Paul formally accepted the post on November 13 in a grand ceremony in the Great Throne Room at the Winter Palace, where in his full imperial dress Paul received the Maltese Crown and Staff, the Seal of the Order, and the Knightly Sword. Paul then drew the sword, traced the figure of a cross over himself, and took the Knightly oath.

When Pope Pius VI received the documentation for his approval, he agreed to suspend Hompesch pending an investigation and accepted Paul's offer to make St. Petersburg the Order's capital, but he withheld sanctioning Paul's appointment, maintaining that only the Order as a whole, with the participation of priories in other countries, could depose or elect a Grand Master. The embarrassed Litta did not report this to Paul, but the Tsar soon found out through an unciphered papal letter that was probably meant to be intercepted. Paul reacted by withdrawing the concessions to the Vatican then under discussion and expelling Lorenzo Litta from Russia. He sought and obtained the support of most foreign priories,[26] while he maintained cordial relationships with the Pope and actively pursued diplomatic efforts to obtain papal sanction for his Grand Mastership. These efforts were cut short by Paul's death.

Paul not only never renounced the office, but upon his acceptance he immediately created a second, Orthodox priory in Russia that was open to Russian nobles of all religious faiths. He then appointed officials for the priory and his own sacred council. The new priory had 98 commanderies compared to the Catholic priory's ten, and so would overwhelm the latter. The members of the new priory were subjected to the discipline of an order "whose laws and statutes . . . inspire love of virtue, contribute to strong morals, strengthen the bonds of subordination, and offer a powerful remedy against thoughtless love of novelty and unbridled license in thinking."[27] Paul also added the Maltese cross and crown to the coat of arms of the Russian empire, and he regularly wore the cross.

These actions reveal why it was important to Paul that he be Grand Master rather than merely the ceremonial protector of the Order. Without that office he would not be empowered to mold the Russian priory according to his vision. The Knights stood for the kind of old world order in which Paul believed, and by controlling the order in Russia he could bring Russia closer to that ideal. Within Russia, Paul wanted to make the Knights an organizational center for enlisting the Russian nobility into his worldview and version of absolutism, with St. Petersburg as its hub and symbol. The order would be one means of restoring discipline, morality, and honor to Russia's depraved nobles. On the international stage, Paul wanted to exploit the Knights to establish Russia as Europe's leading bulwark against revolution and modernity abroad. Instead of being a symbol of modernism and liberal, enlightened values, St. Petersburg would be the capital of international reaction.

As matters turned out, however, the nobility took no interest in the Knights, the Order never served as an instrument of policy, and Paul's fascination with the Order proved unpopular. He continued extravagances in their name and seemingly adopted the Maltese cross as his unique symbol. Rumors spread that Paul would convert to Catholicism and seek to unify the two branches of Christianity. Countess Golovina commented:

> The nation was displeased to see the Emperor prouder of being Grand Master of the Order of Malta than of being ruler of Russia, and when he added this cross to the arms of the Empire, the fact was made a subject of general jest, as likewise the almost theatrical scenes that the ceremonies of the Order occasioned. Moral disorder had taken the place at Court of the austerity that the Emperor had appeared up to that time to insist upon, he himself setting the example of laxity and encouraging his sons in the same evil courses.[28]

CITY BUILDING AND ARCHITECTURE

In his brief reign, Paul did not have time to build much or change the appearance of the city. In fact, Catherine's stately classical style suited him well, though he did try to disassociate himself from her favorite architects and use those of his own choice. He and his wife Maria Fedorovna had already left their architectural mark on the city's suburbs at Gatchina (discussed above) and Pavlovsk, only three miles from Tsarskoe Selo.

Pavlovsk got its start in 1777 when Catherine gave the tract of land to Paul and Maria in celebration of the birth of their first child, Alexander. The couple began modestly by building two simple wooden dachas there and then began developing gardens. Maria had acquired a passion for garden design at a young age as it had been a family tradition. She learned the art from her father at the family's summer estate, and by the time she moved to Russia she had the competence of a professional. In 1780 Catherine loaned the services of Cameron, her architect at Tsarskoe Selo, to Paul and Maria to help design and build the garden and its pavillions. Over the ensuing years Cameron would style a large and beautiful English garden over Pavlovsk's gently rolling terrain and waterways, complete with numerous statues and pavilions (15 by Cameron alone) placed strategically and designed in pure classical style, most notably his Temple of Friendship, the first Doric building in Russia. Today the park is largely intact and is popular with Petersburgers and tourists.

Since the gardens soon outstripped the couple's modest dachas, in 1781 they instructed Cameron to design and build a palace. In contrast to the opulence of Tsarskoe Selo, Cameron designed a smaller and more subdued building that had the more intimate flavor of a country estate, which seems to have been inspired by Palladio's unfinished Villa Tressino at Meledo in Italy.[29] No sooner had the couple approved the design when they embarked on a 14-month European tour. While on the trip, they acquired other artistic ideas for Pavlovsk, long distance communication with Cameron was difficult and led to misunderstandings, and relations with the architect deteriorated. While in Italy, Paul and Maria had met the architect Vincenzo Brenna, were impressed with him, and invited him to Russia in 1783. Paul favored Brenna and his Roman and Italian Renaissance leanings over the pure classical Greek style of Cameron; moreover, Brenna was Paul's own man rather than Catherine's. When Catherine summoned Cameron to the Crimea in 1786, Brenna finished the palace, and although Cameron would return, from then on Brenna dominated construction at Pavlovsk. He altered some of Cameron's designs, especially in the interior, resulting in a mixture of styles that made the palace heavier and more martial, and less in harmony with the park than under Cameron's design. But it is still a remarkable building, consisting of a central three-story block with a low dome supported by slender columns, flanked by curved galleries running to pavilions on either side.

In St. Petersburg itself, the principal new public building downtown was the Public Library on the corner of Nevsky and Sadovaya Street, classically designed and built in 1795–1801 by the Russian architect Yegor Sokolov. Paul also had Brenna build the Mikhailovsky Manezh and Stables in 1798–1800 on what later became known as Manezh Square near where the Catherine Canal joined the Moika. The most notable new private home in Paul's reign was Arakcheev's mansion completed in 1800 by the Russian architect Fedor Demertsov on the intersection of the Moika and the Winter Canal. Plans were also being drawn up for Andrei Voronikhin's Kazan Cathedral, which would take until 1811 to complete but reflected Paul's tastes though he did not live to approve the final plans.

The military focus of Paul's reign also was felt in the city's appearance. Paul made Tsaritsyn Lug into a military parade ground, for which it would soon be called the Field of Mars after the Roman god of war. On it Paul erected in 1799 Brenna's Rumiantsev Obelisk dedicated to Count Peter Rumyantsev's victories against the Turks, which today can be seen on Shevchenko Square on the University Embankment of Vasilievsky Island. In 1799 Paul commissioned the Russian sculptor Mikhail Kozlovsky to design a bronze monument to Generalissimo Alexander Suvorov. Suvorov died in 1800, and the sculpture was unveiled on May 5, 1801, the first anniversary of Suvorov's death. It portrays him in the aspect and garb of the Roman god, with sword and shield in hand. Originally it stood on the Field of Mars near the Moika, but in 1818 the architect Karl Rossi moved it to its present location just north of the Field of Mars toward the Neva. Paul also built a number of barracks in town for his soldiers.

Apart from new construction, Paul put some old buildings to different uses. Thus, he took revenge on Potemkin's memory by giving the Tauride Palace to the Horse Guards, who used it partly as a stable, the damage from which the palace never fully recovered. The favored imperial suburban residences also changed. Since Catherine had preferred Tsarskoe Selo, Paul virtually abandoned it and moved many of its beautiful effects to his favored Pavlovsk and Gatchina. Virtually deserted, the palace deteriorated rapidly, its magnificent grounds became overgrown with weeds, and its ponds began to look like marshes. In Pavlovsk, new buildings, mainly of wood, were hastily erected to accommodate the court. Thus, whereas at Tsarskoe Selo Catherine had built the magnificent Alexander Palace for the Grand Duke, in Pavlovsk Alexander and his wife had only a small wooden house.

The project dearest to Paul's heart, however, was his Mikhailovsky Castle, a fortress-like affair built as Paul's palace because he associated the Winter Palace with his hated mother. It was built on the site of Elizabeth's wooden Summer Palace where Paul had been born, at the intersection of the Moika and Fontanka by the Summer Garden. According to legend, on the first day of Paul's reign a sentinel at the Summer Palace had a vision of the Archangel Michael (the protector of the Romanovs), and for this reason the palace/castle which Paul wanted to embody his reign was built on that site. (For the same reason, he vowed to name his next son Mikhail, who was born in January 1798.) Paul commented, "On that spot I was born and there I wish to die."[30] He would get his wish. As Karamzin later remarked, "He wanted to build himself an inaccessible palace—and built himself a tomb instead!"[31]

Paul burned the Summer Palace down in 1797 to make way for the castle. Paul commissioned the project to his favorite architect, Brenna, who used in part some earlier designs of Bazhenov. The castle was painted in Paul's favorite shade of dark rusty red. According to legend, at a ball his favorite, Anna Lopukhina, dropped her glove, which was of that color. Paul gallantly picked it up for her, but as he was about to give it back he noted the color, admired it, and instead gave the glove to the nearby Brenna as a sample of the color that the Castle should be painted.[32] Since Paul was paranoid about potential attempts on his life, and also because he was a romantic, he called his palace a castle and gave it medieval features such as deep water moats, four drawbridges, and secret passages. When he moved in, he instituted a strict security regime to protect himself, pursuant to which the drawbridges were lowered only once a day at noon. It did him no good however. Just over a month after he had moved in, he was assassinated in his bedroom. The project, unlike any other in the city, was viewed at court and by city residents as another of the Emperor's crazy schemes and drew much ridicule.

Paul spent lavishly to rush the castle to completion, and he moved in on February 1, 1801. Much of the plaster was still moist and green, the walls sweated, and the moisture fogged up the rooms and windows. As a housewarming celebration, Paul held a large masked ball. Hundreds of candles lit the rooms, but the fog was so thick that one could barely make out their flickering flames. The dancers moved like ghostly shadows through the glow of semidarkness, their numbers multiplied by the many mirrors in the hall. The guests, many of whom were already plotting against the Tsar, had a terrible sense of foreboding.

PAUL'S END

Late one spring night Paul, while still Grand Duke, was walking through the city with Prince Alexander Kurakin when he felt a chill on his left side and saw there a dark figure walking between himself and a wall. He pointed it out to Kurakin, who said he saw nothing. Paul looked harder, but he could not make the figure out as he was in a large cloak and had pulled his hat down to shadow his face. The stranger identified himself to "Poor Paul" only as "someone who is interested in you," and then warned him "not to become too attached to this world, for you will not remain here long." He advised Paul to "live justly if you wish to die in peace." He then opened his cloak to reveal himself as none other than the ghost of Peter the Great. According to Paul, Peter then disappeared just opposite the site soon to be occupied by the Bronze Horseman.[33] This was one of the early premonitions leading Paul to believe that he would die prematurely, which is why he built the Mikhailovsky Castle and rushed it to completion. Another legend holds that a year before Catherine's death a Solovetsky Monastery monk named Avel had prophesied her imminent death to her, for which she imprisoned him in the Peter and Paul Fortress. After her death, Paul freed Avel and ordered that he be brought before him. Not having learned his lesson, Avel then prophesied Paul's early death, for which Paul immediately returned him to the Fortress.[34]

By late 1799, Paul's rule indeed was deteriorating. The number of arrested and exiled officers and officials was now enormous, while others were self-exiled out of fear. The city seemed deserted to many contemporaries.[35] The ranks of Paul's supporters were growing thin, and even they wondered whether they would be the next victims. Paul's behavior was increasingly capricious, irritable, and erratic, and so were the resulting policies. Rumors spread that he was going mad. The consensus of historians and psychologists is that Paul was not clinically insane,[36] but he was clearly unbalanced, paranoid, and a microphiliac. Finally, the principles of morality and good order for which Paul stood were being undermined by his scandalous liaison with Anna Lopukhina, highlighted by the apartment he kept for her in the Mikhalovsky Castle with a secret passage to his own chambers.

Some kind of plot against Paul was inevitable. One contemporary, Count Dietrichstein, wrote that speculation on who might lead a plot against Paul and when "forms a primary topic of conversation in every society from the first to the last."[37] The plot was conceived by the nephew of Paul's former governor, Count Nikita Panin, a diplomat who unsuccessfully attempted to prevent Paul from turning against Austria and England. Bitter over Paul's decision to ally with Bonaparte, he returned to St. Petersburg and began talking of Paul's overthrow with the British Ambassador Whitworth and the Neapolitan Admiral and adventurer Joseph Ribas. Yet success depended on the defection of Paul's closest advisor and Governor of St. Petersburg, Count Peter von der Pahlen,[38] a Baltic German who became the chief organizer of the plot. Years earlier Paul had dismissed and exiled him from his post as Governor-General of Riga, and with Paul's increasingly erratic behavior in which increasing numbers were being arrested, Pahlen did not feel secure. Better to place Alexander on the throne, who would be indebted to him.

It was Panin who first informed Alexander of the conspiracy and sought his support of it, but Paul soon exiled him in November 1800 for continuing to oppose his foreign policies. Whitworth had now been recalled to England, and Ribas suddenly died on November 16. Suddenly Pahlen was left alone to mastermind the conspiracy. Fortunately, earlier that month, the numbers of the disaffected in St. Petersburg swelled when Pahlen convinced Paul to amnesty a number of exiles, including the Zubovs, and most were unable to find work upon returning to the capital. With grievances against Paul and no livelihoods, they eagerly joined the plot. This help was critical because Pahlen, an outsider from the Baltics, lacked strong ties amongst the Petersburg nobility, and depended heavily upon the Zubovs to recruit key supporters.[39] Pahlen also lobbied Alexander to support the plot. He obtained the Grand Duke's support only after convincing him that his and Constantine's own lives were now in danger, explaining that the goal was only to force Paul's abdication, and promising that Paul would not be harmed. From the beginning, however, Pahlen was prepared to kill Paul if necessary. Asked about this promise later, he replied laconically that one cannot make an omelet without first breaking some eggs.[40]

There were at least 68 known members of the conspiracy, but undoubtedly there were many more.[41] They were representative of Russia's upper nobility and included such distinguished names as Dolgoruky, Golitsyn, Tolstoi, Kutuzov, Khitrovo, and Muraviev. Most were Guards officers, but there were also many civil officials, including six Senators. Two, including Nikita Muraviev, were future Decembrists, while two others later served under Mikhail Speransky. Many had personal grievances against Paul, but the general reasons behind the coup were Paul's petty tyranny under which no one felt secure, dissatisfaction among the Guards and military in general, opposition to Paul's foreign policy, the threat to the familiar way of life and interests of the nobility, and a feeling that Paul's mind was literally becoming unhinged. The conspirators had no ideology or platform,[42] and they demanded nothing from Alexander as their price for placing him on the throne. They were aware of Alexander's liberal background and leanings and were confident that things would be better under his rule, from which they expected a return to the more enlightened Catherinian policies.

It is a mark of the near universal opposition to Paul that so many were involved in the plot yet it was not betrayed. Thus, with a flair for history, Pahlen chose the Ides of March (March 15th), when Brutus killed Caesar, as the date of the coup. About a week before then Paul became suspicious that something was afoot so the date was moved up to the 11th, when the Semenovsky Guards loyal to Alexander (their commander) would be on guard at the Castle. Indeed, Paul, already suspecting Alexander, is said to have discovered on his son's reading table a copy of Voltaire's *Brutus*, opened to the last page where it proclaims: "Rome is free: it is enough . . . let us thank the gods." Upon seeing this, Paul had his aide Kutaisov give Alexander a copy of a history of Peter the Great, marked at the section describing the treason, punishment, and death of Peter's son Alexis.[43] On March 11th, Paul summoned Alexander and Constantine and had them renew their oaths of loyalty.

Paul also had a famous confrontation with Pahlen (who was responsible for Paul's security) on the eve of the coup, which has many versions. In one, Paul claimed to know of a plot, to which Pahlen responded that he knew about it and the people involved, that in fact he was a member of it, but that it was not a serious threat. He assured Paul that he enjoyed wide support, and that he would take action if and when necessary. In another version, Pahlen reveals the names of all involved, including Alexander and Constantine, and arrest warrants are issued on the spot, including for the Grand Dukes, which Pahlen then showed Alexander to obtain his final assent to the coup.[44]

On the evening of the 11th, most of the conspirators dined together at Colonel Talyzin's apartments at the Winter Palace. They fortified themselves with drink and raised many toasts to their success and the reign of Alexander. There was even some talk of constitutions. They had Paul's abdication statement already drafted for him to sign, and a carriage stood outside Mikhailovsky Castle to take Paul to his place of detention. Neither would be needed. Pahlen arrived at the dinner about 11:30 P.M., raised a toast and reviewed last minute details.

The plotters broke into two groups. One, headed by Platon Zubov and Leo Bennigsen, a Hanoverian officer in Russia's service, was to enter the castle through the rear gate while another, headed by Pahlen, would secure the other drawbridges. In the event, Pahlen's group arrived 15 minutes late, after Paul was already dead, probably so that Pahlen could "rescue" Paul if Zubov's group ran into trouble. Zubov's group arrived at about midnight, gave the password to cross the draw-bridge, entered the castle, and headed toward Paul's bedchamber. Pahlen had taken care to see that security was light that evening, but a servant in the antechamber to Paul's room shouted a warning to Paul. When Bennigsen and Zubov entered the room, Paul was nowhere to be seen. "The bird has flown," remarked Zubov. But Bennigsen, feeling the warm sheets, replied, "The nest is still warm, the bird can-not be far." Holding their lamps higher, they looked around the large room. At that moment the moon emerged from behind a cloud, its light streamed through the room's window, and Paul's feet could be seen protruding below a Spanish screen behind which he was hiding. They went behind the screen and pronounced him under arrest on Alexander's orders. The Tsar, in his white shirt and cotton night-cap, protested and demanded explanations. By this time, other officers had entered the room and gave Paul their explanation: "You have tortured us for four years!" Zubov suddenly left the room, probably to get Alexander. A brief standoff was bro-ken when several others burst into the room, turned over the screen, knocked over the lamp, and threw themselves upon Paul in the dark, perhaps thinking that he had been resisting. Bennigsen rushed out for another lamp, warning Paul not to resist. But the conspirators beat Paul up, smashed his head on his marble work table, and strangled him with one of their scarves. One of them seized the dead emperor's head by the hair and banged it on the floor, exclaiming, "There is the tyrant!" Then they began to desecrate the corpse, but Zubov arrived and stopped them.

Pahlen found Alexander in his apartment with his wife Elizabeth, awake and still dressed. Upon learning of his father's death, Alexander burst into sobs of guilt and remorse. Pahlen admonished him in French: "Enough of playing the child. Go reign. Come show yourself to the Guards! The well being of millions of people de-pends upon your firmness." Reluctantly, he got up and presented himself to the Guards assembled in the courtyard. Once the Guards were convinced that Paul was dead, they swore loyalty to Alexander to the sound of loud hurrahs. Alexander then left for the Winter Palace at about 2:00 A.M. The next day he read a brief mani-festo promising to govern "according to the laws and spirit of Catherine II." The official cause of death was given as apoplexy, but the plotters barely concealed what happened and the fact that Paul was assassinated became widely known.

The next morning in the city, public notices were posted announcing Paul's death, and word of it spread like wildfire. So did the rejoicing. It was like a holi-day. Indeed, storekeepers congratulated their customers on Paul's passing much like they did on public holidays. Residents filed out of their homes onto the streets, taverns, and clubs, and began to celebrate. A weight had been lifted from their shoulders. Residents began to openly flout Paul's regulations. Horses and carriages raced through the streets at high speed, with their once-forbidden bells ringing loudly. A Hussar on his horse was seen galloping on a sidewalk shouting, "Now we can do what we like!"[45] In the evening, people spontaneously lit their windows late into the night in belated protest over Paul's curfews. Even the following day, when the French painter Vigée Lebrun returned to the city from Moscow, she wrote that "I found that city in a delirium of joy; people were singing and dancing and kissing one another in the streets; acquaintances of mine ran up to my carriage and squeezed my hands, exclaiming 'What a blessing!'" Soon Russians who had been living abroad began to return, bringing with them the latest Western ideas and fashions. A wave of adoration and high expectations surrounded the young Emperor Alexander.

Paul considered Peter the Great one of his heroes, but he never really understood him. Peter recognized Russia's society as backward and not viable, so he embarked upon modernization. He built St. Petersburg and wielded his autocratic powers to realize change. For Peter and Catherine, the past, whether Russia's or Europe's, was to be overcome, not emulated. Paul, however, saw no need for change and even tried to turn the clock back. He used the powers of autocracy to this end. His "reforms" were designed to make the old order workable, institutionalize it and ultimately to perfect it, not to work fundamental change.[46]

Paul's reign is significant because it was his vision of preserving order and a static society at the expense of real development and modernization, and not the vision of Peter and Catherine, which would come to dominate Russia under Nicholas I until 1855, and which the Crimean War would prove bankrupt and incapable of keeping Russia viable.[47] Paul's approach was antithetical to the St. Petersburg idea, yet it was this vision which came to be associated with the capital under Nicholas I. In this aspect, the city would become known as "Imperial St. Petersburg" and serve as an inviting target for the satirical literature of Gogol and others, and later for political radicals as well. The city's image would become more confused and complex. The fact that Alexander would spend his reign wavering between these two competing visions was one of the causes.

CHAPTER 8

Crossroads: Alexander I
and the Decembrist Rebellion

The apparition of such a man on the throne is one of the phenomena which will distinguish the present epoch so remarkable in the history of man. But he must have a herculean task to devise and establish the means of securing freedom and happiness to those who are not capable of taking care of themselves. . . . Alexander will doubtless begin at the right end, by taking means for diffusing instruction and a sense of their natural rights through the mass of his people.

THOMAS JEFFERSON[1]

The Russians, too, want to participate in the destinies of enlightened Europe; they want to know not only of its prosperity and miseries, but also of their causes. In this respect the last war had a decisive impact on Russia. Peter the Great forced us to march together with Europe. We have followed the direction [he gave us]; we have marched along an open path, but we did not know where to and we had no goal. The events of 1812, 1814, 1815 have brought us closer to Europe. We—at least many of us—have seen the aims of national life, the purpose of the states' existence; and no human force can make us turn back.

NIKOLAI TURGENEV, Decembrist[2]

DASHED HOPES

Few monarchs upon their accession have been greeted with such love, acclaim, and high expectations as Alexander I. The cream of St. Petersburg looked forward to his reign as a watershed in creating the modern society that Peter the Great visualized. But his reign turned into an excruciating drama for which St. Petersburg was center stage.

Alexander had promising beginnings. Tall, blond, and strikingly handsome, he was a dashing figure on both the parade ground and in the ballroom. He was well educated, sophisticated, charming, and spoke French better than Russian. He seemed the ideal monarch to advance Russia into the modern world, liberalize the government, and eliminate serfdom. "Now, thank heaven, Russia is going to be like the rest of Europe," wrote his wife Elizabeth to her mother.[3]

When Alexander was born on December 12, 1777, Catherine II believed he was destined for greatness and took personal charge of his upbringing. She named him after Alexander Nevsky (some say also Alexander the Great). At the time Catherine was still an enthusiast of the Enlightenment, and she wanted him to continue her civilizing work after she was gone. Catherine herself read to Alexander the first French constitution and had him learn it by heart (but told him not to tell anyone).[4]

Catherine asked Grimm to locate a European intellectual to take charge of Alexander's education, and he recommended Frédéric César de LaHarpe, a well-known Swiss republican, who served as Alexander's tutor from 1784 until 1795. La-Harpe worked hard to school Alexander in the works and ideas of the Enlightenment, of which his pupil did develop a good understanding. Alexander was a reasonably good student, though he lacked Catherine's passion for learning and would not pursue questions to their end. On the other hand, LaHarpe instilled in Alexander a sensitivity, moral principles and a conscience that his grandmother lacked. LaHarpe made Alexander into a man first and a sovereign second. Contemporary critics complained that he was trying to make Alexander into a Marcus Aurelius when what Russia really needed was a Tiberius or even a Ghengis Khan. As Alexander grew into adolescence, he noted the contradiction between the high-minded principles that Catherine espoused and the deteriorating atmosphere at her court with its lax morals, waste and population of sycophants and favorites. In this Alexander agreed with his father. Alexander became attracted to Paul's love of good order and military drill, and he began spending some time nearly each week at Gatchina drilling troops and learning the military craft. His friend Adam Czartoryski would later comment: "The trivia of [this sort of] military service, and the practice of attaching extreme importance to them, perverted the mind of the Grand Duke Alexander. He developed a liking for them from which he never recovered."[5]

Alexander thus matured in two antithetical worlds—the relatively enlightened but dissolute court of Catherine in Petersburg and the more principled but militaristic and Prussianized world of Gatchina—and he had to stand on good terms with each. He learned to listen patiently, dissemble, and to say what people wanted to hear. To Catherine's amazement, he once convincingly performed three separate roles in a play called *The Liar*. He would remain an actor throughout his life and it became difficult to discern his true thoughts, for which Napoleon would call him the "Sphinx of the North." One can quote him in support of virtually any political view current at the time.

Alexander's education ended at the age of 15 when in September 1793 he married a beautiful princess from Baden who took the name Elizabeth Alexeevna. When Paul became Emperor, he made Alexander, among other things, Military Governor of St. Petersburg, a Senator, President of the War College, and honorary colonel of the Semenovsky Regiment. Suddenly, at 19, he was thrust unwillingly into an adult's world and had to assume an adult's responsibilities.

What he saw in Russia and at court dismayed him. His reclusive and moralistic side asserted itself, and he was not sure he would be up to the job of ruling. In 1795, not long before Catherine died, he wrote to his good friend Victor Kochubei:

> Our affairs are in unbelievable disarray, and we are being plundered from all sides. It is an absolute impossibility even for a genius, let alone an ordinary person like me, to deal with these problems, and I have always held to the principle that it is better not to take on a task than to do it badly. Thus my plan is that, having at some point renounced this scabrous place, I shall set myself up with my wife on the banks of the Rhine, where I shall live a life of peace and simplicity, devoted to the company of my friends and to the study of nature.[6]

Dismayed by how Paul's rule was turning out, he agreed to the plot against Paul. But after the assassination his conscience was heavy and initially he was inconsolable. As the weeks passed, however, he drowned himself in work, hoping that his devotion to the well-being of his people would rehabilitate him in his own and the nation's eyes. What did he believe in and want to do?

One must begin with LaHarpe, an impassioned republican who nevertheless concluded that monarchy was still best for Russia. But he believed that monarchical government must be based on fundamental laws to which even the sovereign must be subject. He taught Alexander that when thrones have been based on fundamental laws faithfully observed, they had been stable. When not, they have resulted in unstable despotisms, against which the people have the right to revolt.[7] Remembering Paul, Alexander declared to LaHarpe, "I shall do much more to work at making my country free and by this to prevent her in the future from serving as the plaything of madmen."[8] But he had to decide how and under what kind of government. Initially he theorized that enlightenment would lead to a liberal constitution in the Western sense, government by national representation and eventually to his abdication:[9]

> [T]his would be the best kind of revolution, being brought about by a legal power which would cease to be such as soon as the constitution was finished and the nation had representatives. . . . Once my turn comes, we shall have to work, gradually of course, to assemble representatives of the nation who, with guidance, will draw up a free constitution, after which my power will cease absolutely. . . . This is my idea. I have communicated it to some enlightened persons who, for their part, had been thinking of the same thing for a long time.[10]

Who were these enlightened confidantes? There were four, and they exemplified the kinds of men that the Petersburg era had produced. The first was the Polish Prince Adam Czartoryski (1770–1861), a tall, handsome and cultured young man who had traveled widely and was educated in Western Europe. A

Polish patriot and liberal who had fought in the failed Polish revolt of 1792, he then came to Petersburg to avoid confiscation of his family's estate; instead, Catherine gave him a court appointment to ensure his family's loyalty. There he befriended Alexander, who absorbed his friend's liberal views. Alexander told Czartoryski that he hated despotism, that all men had a right to liberty, and that the French Revolution, despite its excesses, had some beneficial effects.[11] He even instructed Czartoryski to prepare a draft proclamation for his accession embodying his liberal ideals.[12]

The youngest of Alexander's confidantes was the flamboyant Paul Stroganov (1774–1817), born in Paris and raised mostly abroad. He barely spoke Russian. His father Alexander was a prominent St. Petersburg Freemason, one of the most cultured men in Russia, and probably the richest. He entrusted Paul's education to the Frenchman Gilbert Romme, who took him to Switzerland in 1787, and in 1789 to revolutionary Paris. The two quickly became wrapped up in the wave of revolution. Paul visited the Jacobin Club and worked in its library, purported to give up his noble title, founded with Romme the Friends of Law, sported a Phyrgian hat, and became the lover of the infamous Théroigne de Méricourt. When Catherine learned of these escapades, she ordered all Russian students in France to return to Russia. Paul's father dispatched the older and more sober Nikolai Novosiltsev to Paris to bring him back. Reflecting on Paris, Paul wrote:

> I have seen a whole people raise the banner of liberty and shake off the yoke; no, I shall never forget that moment. I cannot shut my eyes to the fact that despotism exists in my country, and I look upon its hideous specter with horror. . . . My blood and my fortune belong to my fellow citizens.[13]

Back in St. Petersburg, he married Princess Golitsyna and some of his revolutionary ardor cooled, but he continued active discussion of political ideas with Alexander and other friends.

Nikolai Novosiltsev (1768–1838), the oldest of the four, was Stroganov's older cousin, which is why Paul's father entrusted him with recovering his son from Paris. Novosiltsev grew up in St. Petersburg and was educated at the Corps of Pages before serving in the Swedish and Polish wars. He spent most of Paul's reign safely in England, where he attended university classes and absorbed the latest thinking of that country. Novosiltsev was the most educated, disciplined, and systematic thinker of Alexander's circle. When Alexander became Tsar, Stroganov wrote him: "Alexander I reigns. Come, my friend, we are going to have a constitution. . . . The nation will have representatives."[14]

The last was Victor Kochubei (1768–1834), who grew up in the home of Bezborodko in St. Petersburg and completed his education abroad in Geneva. After briefly serving in the Preobrazhensky Guards, he embarked on a diplomatic career. By the time of Alexander's accession he had already served in Sweden, London, and Constantinople, from which posts he had corresponded with Alexander.

But Kochubei was one of the unfortunates dismissed from service by Paul, and Alexander's accession found him in voluntary exile in Dresden, whence Alexander summoned him to St. Petersburg.

Alexander quickly reversed Paul's repressive measures and unpopular schemes. On the first day of his reign, he freed some 12,000 people who had been imprisoned or exiled under Paul. Many others who had fled on their own accord also returned. The repressive regulations on life in the capital also were eliminated. The city, seemingly empty in the last months of Paul's reign, was full again, and life returned to normal. Alexander also abolished Paul's secret police, reaffirmed the Charter of the Nobility, recalled the troops marching to India, reopened the private printing presses, allowed Russians to travel abroad once more, allowed the importation of foreign books and musical scores, and rescinded the bans on export of many products. He reversed the Prussianization of the military and brought back the former styles and traditions. Even the Maltese decoration was removed from Paul's garments as he lay in state. The Michailovsky Castle was abandoned and no one from the imperial family ever set foot in it again. In 1823 it became the Engineering Institute, whose most famous graduate was Fedor Dostoevsky.

But Alexander never punished those close to Paul, nor did he lavish rewards on the plotters or his other supporters. Unlike Paul, he did not grant serfs or estates to nobles. "The vast majority of our peasants in Russia are slaves," he said, and "I have vowed not to increase their numbers."[15] The plotters were given no major positions, and over the ensuing months many were simply eased out of the capital. Alexander set a more relaxed and subdued tone in the capital, with fewer pompous displays and lavish social events. Alexander often walked or rode around town alone, especially early in the morning, and would engage passers-by in conversation. The city's residents began calling him "our little father" and "our beautiful sun."

The harder task was to continue with reforms from where Catherine had left off. For ideas and advice he called upon Czartoryski, Novosiltsev, Kochubei, and Stroganov. Initially they were not given official governmental positions and met in secret, fearing that the reforms would be harder to implement if word about them leaked out in advance. The group became known as the *Neglasni Komitet*, usually translated as the "Unofficial Committee" but also having the connotation of "secret." Suspicious and resentful conservatives called it a "Jacobin gang," while Alexander jokingly referred to it as the "Committee of Public Safety."*

Alexander also set up the Permanent Council to advise and coordinate government policy and commissioned a Charter of the Russian People to be proclaimed at his coronation that September. It would set forth the fundamental "rights of citizens" modeled on the French Declaration of the Rights of Man and the Citizen of 1789, which while a pupil of LaHarpe he had defended against conservative French émigrés.[16] He asked the Senate to prepare its own proposals to reform that

---

*Robespierre's 12-man committee that ran revolutionary France during the Terror.

institution, which implied an expansion of its legislative and judicial powers at the expense of the Emperor's. And in June he established a Commission on Laws charged with a comprehensive recodification of Russia's laws, for whose work Radishchev was invited back to St. Petersburg.

A renewed spirit of reform spread amongst Petersburg's expectant aristocracy and became the talk in the city's salons, clubs, and private homes. The latest Western political ideas were on everyone's tongue, especially since so many had just returned from abroad. This was no longer the superficial and stylish social chatter of Catherine's St. Petersburg. This time it was serious and in earnest. A new publication, *The St. Petersburg Journal*, was soon (1802) established by the new Ministry of the Interior headed by Kochubei, which published proposed new laws and critiques of them. Since French Enlightenment ideas had lost their sheen in the aftermath of the French Revolution, Russians looked increasingly to England, where the ideas of Jeremy Bentham and Adam Smith reigned, parliament and courts were developing, and nobles' rights were protected. Soon prominent former officials from Catherine's time as well as new faces were making their own proposals for how to reform Russian government and society.

One of them, Count Bezborodko, even before Alexander's accession had proposed that the Emperor retain autocratic powers but establish the rule of law by which the autocrat would voluntarily limit these powers,[17] establish the equality of all citizens before the law and the security of each subject's person and property, accord rights and protections to serfs (envisaging serfdom's gradual elimination), and expand the legislative role of the Senate.[18]

The Senators indeed proposed according the Senate a limited right of legislative initiative as well as a right of remonstrance (limited judicial review) against the Emperor's violations of fundamental laws. Meanwhile, Alexander's Charter of the Russian People was prepared. It focused on civil rights rather than the operation of government. The initial draft was prepared by Radishchev, but it was considered too radical and had to be toned down; the final edit was in the hand of a talented newcomer, Mikhail Speransky. Modeled on the rights accorded to English gentlemen at the time, it proclaimed the legal protection of person and property, the freedom to travel and reside where one desired, unhindered freedom of thought, religion, and speech, and equality before the law. It embraced basic judicial protections such as the right to counsel, the right to release on bail, recusal of judges, and the presumption of innocence until proven guilty. It also prohibited double jeopardy or detention for more than three days without being charged.[19]

The approach to reform followed by the Senators and in the Charter was essentially that followed in the West, particularly England (with which many Senators had close connections), in which rights were accorded to a powerful class at the expense of the monarch and the state apparatus in order to protect its rights and property and prevent abuses of power, which in turn would lay the groundwork for extending rights to the rest of the nation.[20]

With these proposals either in hand or under way, in late June the Unofficial Committee eagerly set to work. In the beginning, with Alexander's coronation not far off, they convened a few times a week. They gathered in the Winter Palace late in the day after others had left, in Alexander's private quarters. They began with thoughts of at least partially representative government (for nobles), legal reform, local government reform, a constitution in the liberal Western sense, and the abolition of serfdom. But as their deliberations progressed they began to confront unpleasant Russian realities which they, having lived abroad so long, had not well understood. There were extremely few educated, qualified Russians to serve in reformed national or local government institutions or in any representative capacities. The nobility in general did not aspire to a political role but preferred to rely on the autocrat to protect its interests, and, as Catherine had found out, except for the progressive upper nobility in the capital it was vehemently opposed to ending serfdom. The serfdom question foundered on the issue of who would own the land on which the peasants worked. It seemed unfair to deprive the landowners of their property, and compensation would be too expensive, but freeing peasants without land could deprive them of their livelihood and perhaps worsen their material condition. The Emperor was not only naturally reluctant to give up his powers, but he saw in the Senate's proposal political opposition and a power bid to elevate an aristocracy of which he was suspicious. The traditional model of an enlightened autocracy began to sound more appealing after all. That way, the Emperor reasoned, he would retain the power to impose the desired reforms, and they would be designed and implemented objectively in the best interests of the nation rather than in response to narrow interests. The Committee also found attractive the idea, increasingly popular among conservatives wanting to pay lip service to reform, of the need to reform gradually in accordance with the "national spirit" and traditions of Russia, which if taken to its logical extreme would mean no proactive reform effort.[21]

Thus, in the vocabulary of the Unofficial Committee, as elaborated in Stroganov's "Principles of Government Reform,"[22] the term "constitution" came to mean not a representative government with full separation of powers and checks and balances in the liberal Western sense, but rather an enlightened and well administered rule of law with the framework of a monarchical and nearly autocratic system. Even so, fully implementing this approach would gradually lead to the accumulation of more rights by citizens and more limitations on government, and eventually to a constitution tending toward the Western model.[23]

The reform effort ended with a whimper, and only some disappointing half measures were enacted. The Charter was never proclaimed. The Senate's proposals were mostly set aside and that body never gained the right of legislative initiative. Instead came merely administrative reforms such as the gradual replacement of Colleges with Ministries whose ministers were responsible directly to the Emperor. No central policymaking body was ever established. The only action on serfdom was the Free Agriculturalists Law of 1803, which permitted serfs to buy their freedom by agreement with their masters, but the price was so high that only a fraction of one percent of all male serfs (37,000 out of some 10 million) were able to utilize it by the end of Alexander's reign.[24] The recodification of laws stagnated. Unlike Catherine with her Commission, Alexander provided no leadership or guidance to his Commission on Laws. Headed by the old and unimaginative Count Zavadovsky and composed largely of nonentities, the Commission lacked direction, its work was uninspired and nothing was accomplished. This drove Radishchev to suicide in 1802. The Unofficial Committee was disbanded in 1803, and most of its members moved on to other callings. The one bright spot was Alexander's educational reforms, including the eventual establishment of St. Petersburg University in 1819, initiated in an attempt to remedy the paucity of qualified state servants.

Alexander realized that he had failed and disappointed his people. It was not for lack of political convictions; he continued to place constitutional reform on the agenda from time to time nearly until the end of his reign, and he in fact granted constitutions to subject peoples in the Ionian Islands (1803), Finland (1809), and Poland (drawn up by Czartoryski and proclaimed in 1815). But he lacked backbone and was never willing to risk controversy and major confrontations, however sincerely he held his beliefs in private. Thus, his reign became an exercise in muddling through.

Unable to reform Russia, Alexander then tried to save Europe from Napoleon's France. During 1804–07, he spent most of his time out of the capital in Europe. But Alexander did not fare any better there. He and his allies lost the key battles, and instead he returned to the capital after the ignominious meeting at Tilsit (1807), where he had allied with his new friend Napoleon, offered his sister Anna's hand to him in marriage, and (like Paul) obligated Russia not to trade with France's enemy, England. The country's landowners and Petersburg's merchants, who depended on trade with England, were incensed (though the lack of competition from English finished goods helped Russian manufacturers). Used to victory under Catherine, Russians could not understand or tolerate military defeat. Much less could they understand why their Emperor was making common cause with the progeny of the French Revolution. To make matters worse, wartime finances and the printing of money had led to high inflation. Alexander's popularity had plummeted, and he felt insecure on the throne. He had to redeem himself.

Thus, Alexander reassumed the mantle of reformer and in 1808 made another run at constitutional and legal reform. This time he placed his faith in Mikhail Speransky (1772–1839), a talented and progressive official who had rocketed through the ranks of the bureaucracy. The son of a village priest in the province of Vladimir, Speransky had entered the seminary at Vladimir and quickly distinguished himself. In 1790, a central theological seminary for advanced training was set up at Alexander Nevsky Monastery in St. Petersburg, and Speransky found himself in its first class. Here too he rose to the top, and soon he was delivering his own lectures, which went beyond religion to include mathematics, physics, and philosophy. Though religious, the institution was saturated in 18th-century European thought, and Speransky became well versed in the theories of Locke, Descartes, Leibniz, Kant, and Condillac, as well as with Western literature and the classics. He developed a talent for clear, concise, and logical oral and written exposition of complex subjects, which endeared him to his superiors and eventually to the Emperor. Soon he was noticed by Prince Alexei Kurakin, who took him from the seminary to be his private secretary. When Catherine died, Kurakin became Procurator General of the Senate, and he took Speransky with him. Speransky advanced quickly and within months he achieved noble rank. At the Senate he learned much about government, and even hastily prepared a draft commercial code for Paul (which was shelved when Paul quickly lost interest). When Alexander became Emperor, Speransky contributed to the ill-fated first round of reforms, in particular the Charter of the Russian People. He became acquainted and worked with Radishchev, valued his ideas, and recommended that he be appointed to write a history of Russian law. When the Ministry of the Interior was established in 1802 with Kochubei as Minister, Kochubei took Speransky with him. At the Ministry Speransky helped establish the *St. Petersburg Journal* and drafted some of Alexander's most important legislation, including the Free Agriculturalists Law. He attracted Alexander's personal attention when Kochubei fell ill in 1807 and delegated Speransky to present to Alexander the weekly oral report on the affairs of the Ministry. He impressed Alexander with his clarity, intelligence, efficiency, and polite and pleasant manner. When Alexander went to Erfurt to meet Napoleon in 1808, he took Speransky with him, which opened Speransky to the possibilities that Napoleon's legal reforms held for Russia. When Alexander asked him what he thought of France, Speransky supposedly replied, "Their institutions are better, but we have the better people."[25] Soon he became Alexander's right-hand man in domestic affairs.

In most respects Speransky was the epitome of the educated, cultured, and refined St. Petersburg man and a product of the Petrine system. Though of modest origins, he had become refined and could hold his own in the highest society. But he lived modestly in a small apartment and spent wisely. His friends were mainly from the clerical, merchant, and intellectual community rather than from high noble society, which he failed to cultivate. High society felt snubbed and resented him, for which he would eventually pay dearly. In 1798 he married an Englishwoman, Elizabeth Stephens. They led a quiet and happy life and within a year had a daughter, also named Elizabeth. But his wife, a frail woman who suffered from tuberculosis, never recovered from the strain of childbirth and died a few months later. His wife's death nearly broke him. He vanished from home for days, appearing only briefly each day to visit the funeral bed. Friends reported seeing him wandering about outlying sections of town, disheveled and dirty, and they feared for his sanity and his life. Recognizing his responsibilities to his daughter, however, he returned and soon lost himself in his work. He steadfastly refused to remarry, and lived a secluded bachelor's life with few friends. His polite, aloof yet ingratiating manner was often interpreted as insincere, many incorrectly believed he was a slippery manipulator, and his opponents took every opportunity to portray him as such. It is this vivid image of him that has come down to us in Tolstoy's *War and Peace*. In fact, he was sincere and straightforward. He had become a Freemason in 1810 at the Fessler Lodge, known for its idealistic Christianity. He remained loyal to his religious and moral principles throughout his life, and they guided his ideas and work.

One of Speransky's notable accomplishments was the establishment in 1811 of the Lyceum, designed to educate "young men destined for high office in the state, chosen from among the best which the foremost families had to offer."[26] Housed in a wing of the Catherine Palace at Tsarskoe Selo and having a curriculum designed by Speransky, the Tsar's personal library donated to it, professors of impeccable repute and free tuition, it was an ideal environment to train the country's elite. Many graduates did enter state service or the military, but its most famous graduate was Alexander Pushkin, and other graduates included future Decembrists such as Ivan Puschin and later Nikolai Gumilev.

But Alexander looked to Speransky mainly for legal reform and ideas for restructuring the government. Though politically constrained by the legacy of the Unofficial Committee, Speransky believed strongly in the separation of executive, legislative, and judicial powers. He argued that "it is impossible to base a government on law if one sovereign power both composes and executes the law," and claimed that his proposals consisted "not in hiding autocracy in external forms only, but in limiting it by the internal and substantial force of institutions."[27] Thus, Speransky envisioned a Council of State to coordinate government and with at least some ability to initiate legislation, a hierarchy of national, regional, and local Dumas made up of representatives elected on the basis of property qualifications to act as consultative bodies, and the Senate as the supreme judicial body with various levels of courts below it. The powers of each in relation to the Emperor's were modest, but it was clear that their future evolution would be along Western constitutional lines, which made the proposal radical. This was all done in secrecy, the proposal was submitted to Alexander alone, and few knew about it. This provoked resentment amongst powerful figures who were excluded from the process.[28]

Meanwhile, Speransky also was assigned to give new life to the recodification effort of the Commission on Laws. The atmosphere at the Commission changed nearly overnight. Previously, the Commission had proceeded by assembling and synthesizing centuries of Muscovite and Imperial laws, without questioning them and analyzing what needed to be changed. Speransky turned the focus around and asked what first legal principles *(principia juris)* modern Russia's laws should be based on and proceeded to redraft the laws accordingly. For the most part, modern and enlightened principles were not to be found in Russia, however, so he looked to the West for inspiration and found not only recent codifications in Prussia and Austria but also the new Code Napoleon, which represented the state of the art. Speransky took the outline of the Code Napoleon as a framework for his own new code, which he hoped to populate to the extent possible with suitable parallel provisions taken from existing Russian laws, but these were not always available. Work proceeded quickly and efficiently, and in 1812 the new draft Civil Code was submitted to the new Council of State for review. Unfortunately, its hasty preparation exposed it to easy criticism, and its French inspiration was soon apparent to all. Karamzin and Speransky's other enemies had a field day, claiming that he had merely translated the Code Napoleon and had imposed upon autocratic and Orthodox Russia a set of foreign laws developed under fundamentally different social, economic, and political conditions.[29] Worse, the model was that of Russia's enemy, revolutionary and atheistic France. There was some truth to this charge, but the exaggerations that Speransky was essentially a French agent stuck and helped lead to his downfall.

The campaign against Speransky began in Moscow, to whose nobility Speransky represented an alien force that epitomized what they feared most about St. Petersburg and its culture, as brilliantly portrayed in *War and Peace*.[30] If Speransky got his way, they believed, Russia would take another fundamental step away from national traditions of autocracy, orthodoxy, and national identity. The nobility's prerogatives and way of life would be threatened, and so eventually might be the institution of serfdom. This opposition found intellectual expression in Karamzin's famous *Memoir on Ancient and Modern Russia*, commissioned by Alexander's own sister Catherine, a court intriguer who had few beliefs but resented Speransky's favor with her brother and wanted to oust him. The *Memoir* accused Speransky, and by association Alexander, of disregarding Russia's past, repudiating its spiritual tradition, and threatening the ruin of its landed nobility. He argued for preserving autocracy unlimited by any laws, restoring the nobility to its traditional role of the Tsar's personal servants, and reducing the bureaucracy that had displaced much of that nobility. The *Memoir* was at bottom a threat, and it did have some influence on Alexander. This "Moscow Fronde,"[31] as it became known, in turn inspired other attacks on Speransky. One quarter of opposition was the bureaucracy, which resented Speransky's imposition of civil service exams. They circulated a libelous pamphlet about Speransky signed "Rostopchin and Muscovites."[32] (Rostopchin was by then Governor of Moscow.) Court intriguers longed to unseat him, as did many diplomats and other foreigners who suspected that he was a Francophile. This suspicion was fueled by the fact that Foreign Minister Nesslerode's diplomatic correspondence from Paris was sent to St. Petersburg through Speransky. Not only was Speransky not supposed to see it, but once he carelessly left some of it in plain view on his desk at home, which was noticed by his houseguest, Mikhail Magnitsky. Rumors soon spread that Speransky was spying for France.[33] Nor did the more progressive St. Petersburg high society, among whom Speransky had no friends, come to his aid. In the end, most of the country was arrayed against him, and now he could look only to Alexander for support. This was in 1812, when war with France appeared inevitable. Alexander needed to restore confidence in the government and unite the country, and the Speransky controversy was dividing it. To Alexander there was only one solution.

On March 17, Speransky was summoned to the Winter Palace early in the evening. Several men were waiting for an audience in the anteroom of the Emperor's study when Speransky arrived, and he was immediately whisked past them to Alexander. He and Alexander remained in the study for two long hours while the others waited outside. When Speransky emerged, his face was full of tears. Saying nothing, he turned his back to the others to hide his face as he stuffed his papers into his briefcase. As he was about to leave, Alexander burst out of his study, his face also in tears. He rushed over to Speransky and embraced him. "Once more, Mikhail Mikhailovich, Good Bye!" "When I left him," Speransky later remarked, "my cheeks were still wet with his tears."[34] Alexander knew that his dear friend and trusted advisor did not deserve dismissal and exile, but he had no choice. The next morning Prince Alexander Golitsyn found Alexander in a mood of deep depression and inquired why. "Would it not hurt you if someone cut off your right hand?" he asked his visitor. "Last night they made me part with Speransky and he was my right hand."[35]

Speransky spent the next four years in Siberia.

ST. PETERSBURG DURING NAPOLEON'S INVASION

One morning in mid-March 1812, at about the time Alexander was dismissing Speransky, the American ambassador in St. Petersburg was out for his morning walk along the Neva Embankment. He was John Quincy Adams, the future President. He came upon the Emperor, who also liked to take morning walks or rides alone in the city. The two often encountered one another this way early in the morning, and they usually made small talk, in French. But on this morning military matters were on Alexander's mind, and he mused: "That war is coming which I have done so much to avoid—everything. I have done everything to prevent this struggle, but thus it ends." "But are all hopes vanished of still preserving the peace?" asked Adams. "At all events we shall not begin the war," Alexander replied. "My will is yet to prevent it; but we expect to be attacked." Indeed, Adams had observed that seven or eight regiments had already left St. Petersburg in the past three weeks for the frontiers, and that others were following twice or three times each week.[36]

A French invasion seemed unavoidable. Frictions between Russia and France had arisen all over Europe. Napoleon had deposed the Duke of Oldenberg (Alexander's relative) and annexed the duchy. His annexation of West Galicia threatened Russia's position in Poland as established by the third partition. Napoleon had married Marie Louise of Austria, not, as Alexander had proposed, his sister Anna. Napoleon had not supported Russia's policies in the Balkans, the Near East, the Danubian principalities, the Straits, and the eastern Mediterranean. Most fundamentally, however, France and Russia stood as the two great powers on each end of the continent. It was inevitable that the Titans would clash.

Napoleon thought he knew Alexander, remarking in March 1812 in reference to Tilsit, "I once had influence over him, and it will come back."[37] Alexander had perceived Napoleon's attitude at that time, writing to his sister Catherine, "Napoleon pretends that I am nothing but a fool," but "he who laughs last laughs best!"[38] Napoleon hoped not to have to march far into Russia, but instead gain a decisive victory early in the campaign and secure an advantageous treaty, perhaps wintering in Smolensk if necessary. But if there was no early victory, he was prepared to proceed to Moscow. But why focus on Moscow and not St. Petersburg, which, after all, was the capital? Napoleon at least understood the meaning that Moscow held in the hearts of most Russians. "Moscow is not a military position; it is a political position,"[39] he remarked. "A single blow delivered at the heart of the Russian Empire, at Moscow the Great, at Moscow the Holy, will instantly put this whole blind, apathetic mass at my mercy."[40] Napoleon had his spies of both sexes in each city, and they had heard, especially in Moscow, grumblings against the St. Petersburg court and government. If the Emperor would not negotiate, then Napoleon would negotiate instead with the Moscow "boyars," playing them off against Alexander in an attempt to unseat him. "Moscow hates St. Petersburg," he claimed. "I shall take advantage of this rivalry. The consequences of such competition are incalculable."[41]

But Napoleon misjudged both Alexander and the mood of the Russian nation. Alexander was unpopular and another Tilsit would not be forgiven. In St. Petersburg the salons bristled with talk that the Emperor would be incapable of coping with the coming storm, and some ventured that perhaps he should be replaced.[42] Alexander knew that this time he must emerge from the conflict with his own and the nation's honor intact, which may mean a fight to the end. The alternative was to lose his throne, and Russian history had shown that Tsars who lose their thrones do not live long. Signing another treaty with Napoleon other than with Russia as victor was unthinkable. "I shall not lay down my arms so long as a single enemy soldier remains in my domains,"[43] he announced in a declaration published in the *St. Petersburg Gazette* after the invasion had commenced. Alexander had told as much beforehand to the French ambassador in St. Petersburg, General de Caulaincourt, but the message went unheeded.[44] As Clausewitz observed, of all of Napoleon's mistakes, the largest was in thinking that if he occupied Moscow, Russia's leadership would fall apart and that Alexander would be compelled to sue for peace.[45] Napoleon misjudged the patriotism, unity, and staying power of all Russians with a foreign force on their soil; Napoleon's plan of dividing the nation between the two capitals never materialized.

Napoleon crossed the Niemen on June 24th with over half a million men. At first the Russians were far outnumbered, so with a vast territory to fall back on and the Russian winter in reserve, they followed a strategy of measured retreat and attrition. Count Rostopchin, the Governor of Moscow, wrote Alexander, "Your

Empire has two powerful defenders in its vast space and its climate. The Emperor of Russia will be formidable at Moscow, terrible at Kazan, and invincible at Tobolsk."[46] And St. Petersburg? Less known to history is that a corps of 30,000 under Marshal Macdonald also crossed the Niemen at Tilsit, 80 miles to the northwest of Napoleon, and headed toward St. Petersburg. Another force of 28,000 under Marshal Oudinot was to unite with Macdonald and proceed through Riga and on to the capital. Guarding the road to St. Petersburg was a force of only 25,000 under General Wittgenstein.

When the residents of St. Petersburg first learned of the invasion, the rapid retreat of the Russian armies, and Macdonald's march toward Riga, their worst fears about Alexander's leadership seemed confirmed. Napoleon seemed invincible, and panic spread through the city. As the daily news flowed in they counted the distance to Moscow. When Napoleon took Moscow and it began to burn, the capital's residents thought Napoleon would now veer north and march on St. Petersburg. Many in the court and aristocracy packed and fled the capital right away, while others simply prepared and waited, as Joseph de Maistre reported, "with one foot in the carriage."[47] Everyone, from the Dowager Empress to the girls at the Smolny Institute and the young men at the newly opened Lyceum, packed their clothes and household belongings and arranged boats, horses, and carriages in which to flee the city at a moment's notice. Arrangements were made for the Imperial family and court to be transferred to Kazan, together with Falconet's Bronze Horseman. No paintings in the Hermitage remained in their place; its treasures as well as most major libraries were packed and shipped into the interior. The banks closed. Foreign diplomats burned their secret papers, and most left Russia. The Sardinian envoy, Joseph de Maistre, wrote to his government:

> Here we continue to be on the go. Everything of any value is packed; all the stables are full of horses; my small packets have already been done up and their destination settled. It is now that one can repent at leisure over having wasted or lost money. In the past twenty years I have witnessed the obsequies of several dominions, but nothing has struck me so forcibly as what I see at this moment, because I have never seen anything so large trembling. . . . This past month in St. Petersburg more paper has been burnt than would be required to roast all the cattle of the Ukraine. I have burnt all I could on my own account. . . . On all sides I can see boats and wagons loaded. I hear the voice of fear, resentment, and sometimes malice. I see more than one terrible sign. In truth, Sire, all this is not rosy.[48]

He secured his own place on a large barge that was already laden with bronzes, silver, paintings, and other artworks which would be sent into the Russian interior at a moment's notice.[49]

While the city waited, it was gripped by a patriotic fervor. Collections of money, precious metals, and anything else that could be of help to the army were taken up. So many silver dinner services were received from private donors that the mint could not keep up in turning them into currency.[50] Countess Nesslerode wrote of a religious service at Kazan Cathedral:

> A *Te Deum* was sung and prayers were offered for the success of our arms. Next the clergy read a moving address aimed at persuading the nobles to make sacrifices. You should also see the manifesto written for the occasion. Our clergy are setting a very fine example. Out of the money they have put by, they have offered a million and a half. The Metropolitan of the town is having all his silver melted down, and that is valued at fifty thousand roubles. . . . [A]ll the silver in the convents and religious houses which is not in use—in other words, everything held to be the treasure of these institutions—will be given up for the good of the state. The Russian and foreign merchants have already offered two millions.[51]

The popular Mikhail Kutuzov was elected commander of the city's militia, and a collection was also taken up for them.[52] Men volunteered for home guard brigades. Levies of additional troops to send to the front also were imposed, which John Quincy Adams witnessed:

> They are organizing the new armament for the defence of the country, and the nobility of the governments of St. Petersburg and Moscow have given one man in ten of their peasants for the army. I saw many of them this morning, just in from the country, with the one-horse wagons, and the families of the recruits taking leave of them. The number of volunteers is very great; and if they find it as easy to organize and discipline them as they find it to raise the men, there is little danger for the country to apprehend from the invasion under which it now suffers.[53]

Naturally, anti-French feelings ran high. "Everything French, even the language, has become an object of their abhorrence," wrote Adams in his diary.[54] When a performance of Racine's *Phedre* by a French drama troupe premiered, there was so much noise and abuse from the audience that the play had to be stopped. "What barbarians, not to want to see Racine's *Phedre!*" exclaimed the exiled Madame de Staël, then resident in the city. But there would be no more performances of French works that summer; now the troupe had to perform Russian patriotic works translated into French. When captured French standards were placed on display in the new Kazan Cathedral, an unruly crowd was let in to see them and soon it was noticed that the captured baton of the French Marshal Davout was missing. A rumor soon arose that it had been found with one of the French actors. Eventually the French troupe had to leave the city for Sweden under the government's protection.[55]

So far Alexander had been out of town at the front, but in late July he went to Moscow to rally the nation and finally returned to the capital at the beginning of August. With his army still in retreat, Alexander was not only dour but very unpopular. So were his generals. The city clamored for Mikhail Kutuzov, the popular commander of St. Petersburg's militia, to be appointed Commander-in-Chief. Finally, on August 17 Alexander yielded, explaining, "The public wanted him to be appointed, so I have appointed him. As for myself, I wash my hands."[56] Soon Kutuzov reported the battle of Borodino as a victory, and the city was awash with pride. A *Te Deum* was sung in Kazan Cathedral with a hopeful Alexander present, followed by cannon salutes and fireworks. But then came the news of Kutuzov's withdrawal from Borodino and the mass casualties, Napoleon's entry into Moscow and the burning of the city. The mood in Petersburg changed to one of gloom and distrust of the Emperor. Only a few days later came the anniversary of Alexander's coronation. At the *Te Deum* at Kazan Cathedral to mark that event, the Emperor feared bodily harm and so arrived in a closed carriage under the gaze of a silent and hostile crowd. "We could hear our footsteps as we went up the steps of the cathedral," wrote one of his suite.[57] At the service too the crowd maintained a hostile silence. "One could have heard a pin drop," wrote Empress Elizabeth, "and I am sure that a single spark would have put this crowd aflame."[58] Shaken, Alexander withdrew from the Winter Palace to his summer villa on Kamenny Ostrov. He would remain there fretting over his uselessness until after the threat had passed. He had learned better than to try and command himself. After the humiliating defeat at Austerlitz in 1805, Czartoryski had told Alexander bluntly that his presence on the battlefield had been worse than useless. Now, even his sister Catherine wrote him: "For God's sake, do not try to command yourself. We need to have a leader in whom the troops have confidence immediately, and you inspire none at all!"[59] With nothing else to do and spiritually shaken, he began fervently reading the Bible.

Fortunately, the war turned in Russia's favor. Stuck in Moscow and with Alexander refusing to negotiate, Napoleon resolved to join with Macdonald's forces and march on the capital. "Only the occupation of St. Petersburg will open the Emperor's eyes," he claimed.[60] But this would have meant a winter campaign by an overextended force with Kutuzov threatening his rear. Napoleon's marshals vetoed the idea, and he did not insist. This left Macdonald's force near Riga as the remaining threat to Petersburg. In order to advance, Macdonald had to unite with Oudinot. But Wittgenstein had intercepted and defeated Oudinot's force near Jacobuvo on July 30, and Oudinot had to withdraw south to Polotsk to await reinforcements. Wittgenstein attacked him again at Polotsk in mid-August and the armies fought to a standoff. This was enough to keep Macdonald immobilized between Riga and Dünaburg for the rest of the campaign. In mid-October, just as Napoleon was abandoning Moscow, Wittgenstein took Polotsk. As Napoleon had abandoned Moscow, Macdonald too fell back to unite with him. His forces fell apart in the Lithuanian forests, and only a few stragglers made it back across the Niemen.

St. Petersburg was overjoyed. The news that Napoleon had abandoned Moscow was announced to the accompaniment of cannon from the Fortress, and the capital was illuminated for two nights. But the city would not see the return of its heroes for over two years. Seeing the opportunity to become Europe's liberator, Alexander now vowed to pursue Napoleon to the end. On March 31, 1814, scarcely a century after Peter the Great had founded St. Petersburg and set his reforms in motion, Alexander marched down the Champs-Elysées on his white horse at the head of the Russian Army. Marching alongside him as officers were the sons of St. Petersburg's aristocracy. A century before, unreformed Russia could not even gain the Baltic and scarcely knew Europe. Now it was Europe's savior and most powerful member. Such an achievement would have been impossible without the century-long drive to modernization under new ideas begun by Peter the Great and symbolized by St. Petersburg. Peter and his city seemed vindicated. Russia's success disguised its many unremedied ills and seduced many into the complacent belief that Russia's system was fundamentally sound, but soon the system would again be under attack.

BUILDING AN IMPERIAL CITY

Alexander inherited Catherine's fascination with architecture as well as her good taste. During his stays in Europe he saw its great buildings, studied the current styles, and met leading architects. Like Catherine, he loved St. Petersburg and was determined to make it more beautiful and grander than any other European capital. Even during his military campaigns the building of the city was always on his mind. Messengers constantly traveled between him and the capital bearing progress reports to Alexander and his instructions to architects, and work was barely affected by his absence. Also like Catherine, Alexander relied primarily on one set of architects early in his reign (Andrei Voronikhin, Thomas de Thomon, and Adrian Zakharov), and another group late in his reign (Vasily Stasov, Carlo Rossi, and Auguste Montferrand), due mainly to the deaths of the former group in 1811 through 1814. Thus, architecturally Alexander's reign consisted of two phases divided roughly by the Napoleonic war. The latter group of architects, which also worked under Nicholas I, perfected the style known as Alexandrian Empire, named after the Empire style in France that reached its height under Napoleon.

Alexander's first phase was one of transition from the pure and refined classicism of Catherine, was inspired more by Greece than Rome, and reflected the influence of Cameron. The first transitional project, Kazan Cathedral on Nevsky Prospect, built in 1801–11 to replace the Church of Our Lady of Kazan, was commissioned by Paul I shortly before his assassination and reflects his rather than Alexander's tastes. For this project Paul chose Andrei Voronikhin (1760–1814), who was originally a serf of Alexander Stroganov and probably his son. When Voronikhin showed an early talent for drawing, his master sent him to Moscow to study painting, but when his interest in and talent for architecture became paramount he was enrolled in the Academy of Fine Arts in St. Petersburg. Soon, in 1784, he found himself studying in Europe, accompanied by Stroganov's son Paul, and in 1790 returned with him to St. Petersburg from revolutionary Paris. Kazan Cathedral evidences the influence of

Catholicism and the Knights of Malta and Paul's personal desire to unite Catholicism and Orthodoxy. As such, it is designed on a Latin cross plan parallel to Nevsky and combines the influences of ancient Rome and Renaissance Italy. Its large bronze doors at the main (north) entrance are exact replicas of Lorenzo Ghiberti's Gates of Paradise at the baptistry of Florence Cathedral. But its most striking exterior feature is its vast semicircular colonnade of 144 Corinthian columns in four rows facing Nevsky with an obelisk (now gone) in front, inspired by Bernini's piazza at St. Peter's in Rome. At the back of the colonnade stand in niches four large statues of St. John the Baptist, St. Andrew, and Saints Vladimir and Alexander Nevsky. According to the original design, there were to be two similar colonnades on other sides, but they were never built. The interior of the cathedral is equally stately. It features 56 granite columns with bronze Corinthian capitals, an iconostasis bearing two tons of silver, and overlooking it all a long frieze depicting Christ bearing his cross to Golgotha. Also figuring in the design were many symbols of Freemasonry, such as the triangle with rays on the frieze facing Nevsky. During the war with Napoleon it became a pantheon in tribute to Russia's war heroes and the repository of a display of captured French war banners, batons, keys to captured cities and fortresses, and other trophies, which can still be seen there today. The Cathedral also serves as the tomb of Marshal Kutuzov, who was laid to rest there in 1813 on the very spot where he had knelt to pray before departing to do battle with Napoleon. In 1837 Boris Orlovsky's statues of Kutuzov and Barclay de Tolly were unveiled in front of the Cathedral. On the whole, the Cathedral is a curious mix of Orthodox and Catholic imagery and architectural styles from various places and eras, designed as much to glorify the temporal, Romantic glory of the nation as that of God. Somehow it is not surprising that in Soviet times it was chosen to house the Museum of Religion and Atheism.

Voronikhin's chief work for Alexander, the Mining Institute built in 1806–11 on Vasilievsky Island, reflects classical Greek style. It was inspired by the Temple of Poseidon at Pasteum and has a similar simple and clean elegance, featuring a portico with twelve Doric columns and a pediment decorated with only the royal double-eagle, all framed by a flat wall. Voronikhin's other contributions were mainly interior work and small buildings at Pavlovsk, Peterhof, and the outlying islands.

It was Alexander who finally resolved the question of what to build on the tip (strelka) of Vasilievsky Island. For this he chose the Frenchman Thomas de Thomon (1754–1813), who had trained in France and Italy and worked for the Comte d'Artois and in Vienna for Prince Esterhazy. An ardent royalist, de Thomon had moved to St. Petersburg in 1790 following the French Revolution. His first commission from Alexander was to reconstruct the Bolshoi ("Great") Theater on Theater Square (1802–05) where the Conservatory is now located. Rinaldi had completed the Theater for Catherine in 1783 as the first large building in Russia built solely as a theater, and as such was a model for Europe. But by Alexander's time the Theater was already too small, and he commissioned Thomon to enlarge and reconstruct it. Thomon's design, inspired by the Odéon in Paris, featured a portico of eight Ionic columns and two stories of Palladian windows. Unfortunately, his work burned down in January 1813 and we know it only from drawings. When investigating the causes of the fire the following day, he fell from high up and was paralyzed, after which he was frequently ill, and he died in August of that year. The Theater was reconstructed in 1818, and again in the 1830s by Albert Kavos, who also designed the Bolshoi Theater in Moscow.

The *strelka* had stood since Catherine's time as the unfinished element of the city's central panorama linking Palace Embankment with the Fortress and the Petersburg side. When Alexander assumed the throne, Quarenghi's Exchange building lay unfinished and was deteriorating, and he soon gave Thomon a free hand to redesign the whole *strelka* as an ensemble. Thomon responded by reshaping the whole tip of the island to form the semicircular Exchange Square bounded by a granite embankment with arcing stone ramps leading to boat landings on the water. In the center he replaced Quarenghi's Exchange with his own in 1804–10. Like Voronikhin's Mining Institute, it was inspired by the temple of Poseidon at Pasteum, and it is dominated by rows of large unfluted Doric columns on all sides standing on a high base, topped on the front (east) side by a large statue of Neptune in a chariot drawn by sea horses, and on the west side by a statute of Mercury, the god of trade. Thomon framed the Exchange with two large rostral columns, from which projected bows of ships to commemorate the city's role in Russian sea power, and at the foot of which sat four statues representing Russia's four great rivers, the Volga, Dneiper, Volkhov, and Neva. The *strelka* became a monumental setting for outdoor ceremonies and festivities and presented an impressive vista to ships arriving in the city. On holidays the rostral columns were lit and spouted fire high into the air, illuminating the Exchange and the Neva and providing a vista unequalled in Europe. Today the Exchange Building serves as the Naval Museum, which contains Peter the Great's first boat on which he sailed with Franz Timmerman in 1688.

Alexander's last great project before the French invasion was to reconstruct the Admiralty. No work had been done since Korobov's reconstruction in 1732–38, and the building was dilapidated, still surrounded by fortifications and a moat that served no purpose. The Admiralty's centennial in 1805 seemed like a logical time to reconstruct the building, and the transformation of the Admiralty into the Ministry of the Navy provided the need for suitable offices for the new institution. For this project Alexander commissioned Adrian Zakharov (1761–1811). Zakharov had entered the Academy of Fine Arts at the unusually young age of six, graduated in 1782 and went to Paris to study for four more years and then traveled to Italy. After returning to St. Petersburg in 1787, he taught architecture at the Academy until his death.

Formally, Zakharov's commission was termed only a replacement of the façades, and he had to preserve the spirit of Peter the Great's creation and its unity with the spire of the Fortress across the river. Zakharov thus retained much of Korobov's structure, including his spire, but gave the intermediate detail leading up to the spire sharper, cleaner lines. He also enlarged the tower's base, which now projected from the rest of the building, and added to it a high cornice and large central arch. These changes gave the tower greater mass and sharper outlines for viewers from Admiralty Island's three radial prospects and made it the architectural center of the city. Zakharov left the façade otherwise uncluttered except for twin porticoes near each end. On and in front of the tower Zakharov added relief and statues depicting Russia's naval successes and, on each side of the archway, Feodosy Shchedrin's triads of nymphs gracefully bearing the weight of heavenly and earthly spheres on their shoulders. Since the Admiralty was still building ships and no embankment could run along the Admiralty by the river, the English and Palace Embankments each terminated respectively at Senate and Razvodnaya Squares by the sides of the Admiralty. Thus, for the terminal architectural foci of the two Embankments, Zakharov built columned and arched pavilions at each end of the Admiralty by the Neva. Originally the pavilions were to be closer to the Neva, but they were relocated 18 meters further back from the river when Alexander realized that they would block the view from the Winter Palace downriver to the English Embankment. This was fortunate since it allowed room for a street on Admiralty Embankment once shipbuilding ceased. Another proposal for the Neva side was to hide the work area behind a façade having several large arches through which ships could be launched. This would have presented a beautiful façade to the river, but the plan was never implemented.

On the south side of the Admiralty the earth fortifications were removed,* thus creating an open square where the Alexander Garden (created in 1872–74) now lies. Thus was formed an L-shaped continuum of squares nearly a mile long from Palace Square by the Winter Palace and then along the Admiralty to Senate Square where Falconet's Bronze Horseman stands, which covered about 100 acres, the largest such area in Europe. This presented the challenge of integrating the complex of squares into an architectural whole, which brought Alexander to his second phase of architecture, Alexandrian Empire.

This challenge coincided with Alexander's triumph over France. After so long being looked upon as inferior to the nations of Western Europe, Russians now felt better about themselves and an air of national self-satisfaction and pride filled the capital. National dances and dress were now popular at high society balls, and national themes would soon dominate literature, historical writing, and music. Alexander wanted a new architectural style built upon classicism but also monumental and heroic to symbolize and reinforce Russia's newfound power and status, and as usual

---

*The moat was not filled until 1840, but as it was narrow and below street level it did not detract from the architectural unity of the area or from the functionality of Admiralty Boulevard as a parade ground.

he wanted to outdo Europe. A lover of military parades since his days at Gatchina, Alexander now had many festive occasions to hold them, and the Field of Mars was neither large enough or close enough to the city center for this purpose. Also, the many new ministries that Alexander had created needed large and prestigious office quarters. For these reasons, Alexander decided to turn the large central area into parade squares bounded by a unified architectural ensemble in which would be housed the General Staff Headquarters, the Senate, the Synod, and various ministries.

Since by 1814 Voronikhin, Thomon, and Zakharov had all died, Alexander needed a new architect to conceive and build a unified scheme, and he found him in Carlo Rossi (1775–1849). Rossi was born the son of an Italian ballerina popular in St. Petersburg during Catherine's reign, so popular that it is not clear who his father was. (The candidates include Paul I.) As a child he grew up in the household of Paul's favorite architect, Vincenzo Brenna, was trained by him and worked as his assistant at Pavlovsk, Gatchina, and on the Mikhailovsky Castle, thus bypassing the Academy. After Paul's death, Brenna retired from Russia and in 1802 he and Rossi went to Italy, where Rossi studied for two years. Upon his return, he worked in Moscow until he was summoned to St. Petersburg in 1816. More than any other architect, including Rastrelli, it is Rossi who has left the largest mark on the historical center of today's St. Petersburg, and therefore his work deserves discussion in detail. There are two main reasons for his influence besides his sheer talent and the monumental size of his works. First, whereas most large projects under Elizabeth and even Catherine were private or royal palaces, Alexander focused on government or other public buildings such as theaters, the Exchange, St. Isaac's Cathedral, and churches, and he made them architectural focal points of the city. Second, Alexander gave unprecedented attention to creating linked ensembles of buildings, streets, and parks, and at this Rossi was a master. In order to coordinate the new projects in the city's center, in 1816 Alexander formed the Committee of Construction and Hydraulic Works with General Augustine Béthencourt as its chairman and Rossi as its chief architect, and separate subcommissions were established for specific ensembles such as Palace Square (1819) and St. Isaac's Square (1818).

By then Palace Square already had a long and unresolved history. Under Catherine, Veldten's design of 1779 had established the graceful arc at the back of the Square, but many of the buildings were out of scale with the Winter Palace and the new Admiralty, they varied in height and architectural style, and the entry of Bolshaya Morskaya (then Malaya Millionaya) Street into the square was unsatisfactory. Rossi demolished its buildings and erected his monumental four-story General Staff Building (1819–28), which runs the entire length of the square along Veldten's original arc. Like the palaces on Palace Embankment built in Catherine's time, it was designed to match the height and overall scheme of the facade of the Winter Palace. In the center and directly opposite from the main entrance of the Winter Palace Rossi built a huge archway flanked by columns leading to Bolshaya Morskaya Street, behind which he placed a second archway where the street bends toward Nevsky Prospect. The archway was so large and massive that some believed it could not support itself, but when it was completed Rossi himself confidently stood on top of it as the supports were removed. Atop the arch stands a massive bronze sculpture of Victory in a chariot drawn by six horses. Though monumental in size, except for the arch the building does not draw attention to its details, letting the Winter Palace and the vast space of the Square itself take center stage.

But this stage was incomplete without a monument in its center to provide a focal point when looking from Admiralty Boulevard. Thus, from the outset in 1819 it was decided to erect in the center of the square a column dedicated to the war of 1812, usually called simply the Alexander Column. Designed by the Frenchman Auguste Montferrand in 1829, it was unveiled in 1834. It is made of a single piece of granite from quarries near Lake Ladoga, and like the Bronze Horseman's Thunder Stone in Catherine's time, its quarrying, transportation, and erection stand as one of the engineering marvels of the time. Designed to surpass both Trajan's column and that on the Place Vendôme in Paris, at over 150 feet in height and weighing 600 tons, it is the largest in the world. Atop it stands a solemn angel with bowed head supporting a large cross, hand pointing to heaven. The face of the angel is popularly thought to resemble Alexander's. Though one can fault the column's intrinsic artistic merit, its overall design beautifully complements the rest of the square. Its vertical orientation provides a welcome contrast to the horizontal scheme of the rest of the square's ensemble, the simplicity of its design does not divert attention from the Winter Palace, and its narrow profile does not obstruct views across the square or interfere with parades. The redesign of Palace Square was finally completed in 1840 with the construction of Alexander Briullov's Staff Building of the Royal Guards Regiments on the eastern side.

Rossi's other early masterpiece was actually his first major commission from Alexander, the Mikhailovsky Palace for Grand Duke Mikhail built in 1819–23 and which now houses the Russian Museum. It stands in what until then was known as the Third Summer Garden across the Moika from the Field of Mars, which one of the Palace's façades faces. Rossi redesigned the garden and designed for it a charming pavilion by the Moika which still stands today. The main (south) façade faces a new square created by Rossi soon called Mikhailovskaya Square, which Rossi connected to Nevsky Prospect by a new street soon called Mikhailovskaya Street, on which the Philharmonic and Grand Hotel Europe stand today. Around the square Rossi placed many prominent buildings designed by Rossi and other architects, including the Mikhailovsky Theater (now the Mussorgsky Theater) and the Society of the Nobility (which now houses the Philharmonic). Because the square is surrounded by a theater, concert hall, and museums, in 1940 it was renamed the Square of the Arts. Appropriately, in 1957 a statue of Pushkin was erected in the center of the square.

This grand architecture heralded the dawn of a grand aristocratic age. Russia and St. Petersburg stood proud at the apex of Europe, and its society was grand. Theatergoing had never been so popular, and people went there to be seen as much as to watch. But the glitter obscured deep questions and problems which had begun to fester in aristocratic society. Some were continuations of the issues debated during Catherine's reign, while others were brought on by Alexander's increasingly reactionary policies. The trauma of invasion and ultimate victory over Napoleonic France had produced two nearly irreconcilable reactions, a conservative mystical and religious nationalism supported by the government and the Church, and a Europe-inspired drive by the city's enlightened aristocrats for reforms. Over the next decade and through Alexander's death these two visions of the old and new Russia would vie over Russia's form of government and for the hearts and minds of the Russian people. The battle not only raged mainly on the stage of St. Petersburg, but it was about the city's meaning.

IMPERIAL REACTION

In the dark days of 1812, while isolated at his Kamenny Ostrov palace, scorned by his subjects and feeling useless, Alexander underwent a spiritual crisis. The toll from his father's assassination, his failures at home and abroad, and the invasion culminating in the burning of holy Moscow had been high. But one day his friend Prince Alexander Golitsyn came to him with a Bible in his hand and recommended that he read it. Golitsyn, formerly an ardent Francophile and devotee of the Encyclopaedists, had been appointed Procurator of the Holy Synod, and therefore decided he had better read the New Testament for the first time. Unexpectedly, in its pages he found inspiration and revelation, and he underwent a spiritual transformation. He came to believe that the Protestant Pietists and other sectarians were practicing a better kind of Christianity than Orthodox believers. He therefore resigned his position at the Synod shortly before the war and took a position as supervisor of foreign confessions in Russia. He founded his own interconfessional chapel and began propagating his version of Christianity. The Emperor was Golitsyn's greatest convert. As the war dragged on through the summer of 1812, Alexander read scripture with increasing ardor and found revelation: "I simply devoured the Bible, finding that its words poured an unknown peace into my heart and quenched the thirst of my soul."[61] And when the French began their retreat, he wrote his sister Catherine that "God has done everything. It is He who has turned things in our favor so suddenly."[62] He and Golitsyn came to believe in the establishment of a universal, pure Christian faith, and they set their minds to bringing this about. Together they founded the Russian Bible Society in St. Petersburg, with the express goal of promoting a single Christian faith uniting all denominations.

The new religious outlook was not limited to the two friends or even to Russia. It originated in Western Europe in reaction to the French Revolution and Napoleon, which were held to be the result of the harmful rationalist, skeptical, and atheistic doctrines of the French Enlightenment. In the West, this belief united Catholics, higher-order Masons, mystics, and Protestant Pietists, all of which had an impact in Russia as well. The Catholic influence was led by Joseph de Maistre, a Savoyard noble and Mason who had fled the French Revolution in 1797 to St. Petersburg during Paul's reign, where he was partly responsible for Paul's interest in the Catholic faith. He remained in Petersburg for 15 years as ambassador of Sardinia, and thus was well-known to and met with Alexander. He set forth his beliefs in a famous dialogue, *Evenings of St. Petersburg.* He believed that the universe is not ordered and that man is inherently flawed and corrupt, meaning that optimistic doctrines based on reason and liberty rather than faith and fear of God are harmful and had led to the upheavals in France. In *Evenings*, he painted a picture of the flames reaching to St. Petersburg, of the sun rolling "like a flaming chariot over the somber forests which crown the horizon, and its rays reflected by the windows of the palaces give the spectator the impression of an immense conflagration."[63] A royalist, he argued that authority and tradition are not stultifying but rather prevent extremism and ensure the stability and prosperity in which creativity can thrive.

More influential in Russia were Europe's Protestant Pietists and related mystics and higher-order Freemasons, whose adherents in Russia took up where Schwarz and Novikov had left off in their attacks on "the pale light of reason." The most popular of these was Karl Eckartshausen, whose *Cloud over the Sanctuary* (1802) preached a mystical primal religion anterior to all others and therefore higher and universal. Another of Alexander's close friends, Rodion Koshelev, a mystic and occultist who had been an enthusiast of higher-order Freemasonry while living in Western Europe, in the aftermath of 1812 gave up his imperial posts in order to devote himself to the study of arcane doctrines. It was he who presented Alexander with *Cloud over the Sanctuary*, which the Emperor avidly read as he was conceiving the Holy Alliance. Alexander thanked Koshelev by letter in December 1815: "You have powerfully contributed to make me adopt the course I am now following by conviction and which alone has brought me success in the most difficult task the Very High One has assigned me."[64] Mystics and Pietists whom Alexander met while in Western Europe also captured his imagination. He visited the Moravian Brethren in Livonia and Quakers in London. Most influential on Alexander was the exotic Livonian Baroness Juliana von Krüdener, the widow of a Baltic diplomat in the Russian service who wandered through Europe as a prophetess establishing her own salon wherever she stopped. A strong personality attuned to human nature and practiced in the art of persuasion, she claimed to be in direct communication with God and brought Alexander over to her cause at a three-hour midnight meeting with him at Hieilbronn. She told Alexander that he was God's chosen agent to lead Russia and Europe through these troubled times.

Another important influence was the Bavarian mystic Franz von Baader, who among other things argued that all education and political rule should be suffused with religion and that the true religion should be an assimilation of the vital elements of all religions and mythologies.

The religious and spiritual revival and spread of varied forms of mysticism became a national phenomenon that also swept St. Petersburg by storm. The French Embassy reported from the capital:

> A number of society women—most of them reformed from a wanton past—are now seeking the excitement of mysticism. They write to the Emperor, they gather to read *Le Pur Amour*, Madame Guyon's *Théologie astrale*, Fénélon's *Maximes des Saints*, the works of the Bavarian illuminist Jung-Stilling, and those of the famous Saint-Martin. The court bookseller, Saint-Florent, told me that he could not keep up with the demand for these works.[65]

One of these women, Catherine Tatarinova, who often met with the Emperor, soon founded her own group that met in her drawing room in the Mikhailovsky Castle and practiced rites resembling those of the whirling dervishes in which she recited her prophesies in a trancelike state.[66] The Old Belief also enjoyed a revival, at first tolerated by the Emperor, while some of the more extreme cults from Muscovite Russia made their reappearance, such as the *skoptsy* ("the castrated") headed in St. Petersburg by the eunuch Kondraty Selivanov (who was sponsored by Golitsyn), the *Molokane* ("Milk Drinkers"), and *Dukhobory* ("Spirit Wrestlers"), who recognized no church institutions or even that of marriage.[67] Alexander Labzin, who had worked with Novikov in Moscow at *Twilight Glow*, now in St. Petersburg repopularized the mystical and occult doctrines of Jacob Boheme in his journal *Herald of Zion*, to which Alexander subscribed. Other spiritual journals such as *Christian Reading* and *Friend of Youth* were soon published in the city.

The trauma of the war had shaken the fragile new foundations of civilization that Peter the Great and Catherine II had laid in St. Petersburg, which began to unravel among some segments of society who retreated into cults of unreason. But neither was the movement a true return to Orthodox spirituality. Russian Orthodoxy too had long lost its hold on most of the educated public, and, as with the rise of Masonry under Catherine, the people's yearnings for alternatives evidenced Orthodox civilization's decay.

For Alexander it was not at first clear what his and his country's new destiny meant in practice or how to translate his new beliefs into state policies. At first, he simply took a page from Muscovite ideology: "It is to the cause of hastening the true reign of Jesus Christ that I devote all my earthly glory."[68] But policy quickly settled around his belief that godless revolutionary extremists holding rationalist, liberal ideals were responsible for the French Revolution, Napoleon, and all that Russia and Europe had suffered. A universal Christianity could be advanced by

Europe's monarchs working together, and realizing this Christian civilization would ensure lasting peace and prosperity. Thus, Europe's monarchs must join in stamping out conspiracy and rebellion wherever it may arise.

This doctrine found expression in Alexander's brainchild, the Holy Alliance, signed in September 1815 and announced in Russia on Christmas Day as "the Christian answer to the French Revolution." It proclaimed that the policies of the great powers should be based in morals and the Christian religion, which would lead to a unified and peaceful pan-European community of nations. But in practice the Alliance only served as one basis for the allies to subdue the national and political aspirations of the peoples who had been conquered by Napoleon and the Ottoman Turks. Alexander's Holy Allies were only interested in the political agenda and gave only lip service to the Christian one. Other allies refused to have anything to do with it. Thus, while Russia, Austria, and Prussia signed the document, the British foreign minister, Viscount Castlereagh, labeled it "a piece of sublime mysticism and nonsense."[69] The Pope also declined to sign it, explaining that no new lay interpretations of Christian doctrine were needed. Alexander soon fell under the sway of Austria's foreign minister, Prince Metternich, Europe's leading exponent of preserving the status quo and suppressing revolution, and was soon drawn from the religious to the political agenda of suppressing a wave of nationalist uprisings throughout Europe. "The present evil is still more dangerous than the devastating despotism of Napoleon because the present doctrines are more seductive for the masses than the military yoke under which Napoleon held them," Alexander wrote to Golitsyn. "Only now do I understand why the Lord God has kept me here until this moment!"[70] But when the Greeks revolted in 1821 for independence against the Ottoman Turks, Russia's longtime enemy, Alexander was caught in a dilemma between his commitment to oppose revolution and his religious duty to support his Orthodox brethren. Russian public opinion was squarely behind Greece. The country's young, romantic progressives were inspired by Lord Byron's joining the cause to command Greek soldiers and his death while in service of the cause at Missolonghi in 1824. He was immediately immortalized by the Decembrist poet Kondraty Ryleev in On the Death of Byron (1824). But Alexander, under Metternich's influence, to his nation's dismay declined to support Greece for years and resolved to fight the Turks only in the last months of his reign.

In Russia too Alexander adopted a conservative political stance in line with the Memoir of Karamzin. His regime became one of repression, managed by the Emperor's loyal factotum, Alexei Arakcheev. According to one contemporary, Arakcheev was "of average height, stooped, with thick hair cut short and bushy; small, cloudy, cold eyes beneath a low, furrowed brow; a large, boot-shaped nose; thin, tight lips over which it seemed no smile had ever played."[71] Of lowly origin, he was one of Paul's original "Gatchina men" and as fastidious as Paul; he was said to have ripped off the mustaches and bitten the noses of soldiers at Gatchina reviews and bitten his servant on the ear. He became a specialist in artillery whose guns were a key to defeating the French. Alexander had come to know Arakcheev and see his talents, and when he veered toward reaction he tapped Arakcheev as his new right-hand man. Tireless and loyal to the Emperor, colleagues said he was as "industrious as an ant, and venomous as a trantula." Arakcheev brought back Paul's militaristic mentality, operated a revived secret police and spy network under which thousands were imprisoned or exiled, and conceived and established the unpopular military colonies. As such, he became the archenemy of the country's liberals and intellectuals. Pushkin soon flayed him in his epigram, *To Arakcheev*:

> *To all Russia an oppressor,*
> *To the Governors a tormentor,*
> *To the Council a master,*
> *But to the Tsar—a friend and brother.*
> *Full of malice, full of revenge,*
> *Without wit, feeling or honor,*
> *Who is this whom they call "faithful but not a flatterer"?*
> *At best, a common foot soldier.*

The capital seethed with stories of rebellion and mistreatment of colonists, which helped turn military officers in the capital into Decembrists. Similarly, in 1820 officers and soldiers in the Semenovsky Guards Regiment in St. Petersburg revolted unsuccessfully against the harsh treatment of their commander, Colonel Schwartz, and the famous unit was disbanded.

Constitutional reform was now largely off the agenda, at least at home. Russians saw constitutional monarchies established in France, several German states, and in Poland, often with Alexander's support, but looked in vain for the same in Russia. When Alexander appeared before the Polish Diet in 1818, he gave hope to Russians by hinting that a constitution finally might be in store for them too. He told the Poles:

> The customs already existing in your country have made it possible for me to introduce this constitution. . . . Thus you have furnished me with the means of giving to my own country that which I have long been preparing for it, and which it will possess as soon as the time is ripe for this matter of capital importance.[72]

Though liberals knew better than to trust Alexander by now, many wanted to hold him to his promise. Besides, to many the speech seemed condescending to Russians, implying that they were not yet up to the level of civilization of the subject Poles, who had fought on Napoleon's side in the war. Nevertheless, wrote Karamzin, "the Warsaw speeches have deeply stirred the hearts of the young. They see the constitution in their dreams, they debate, they fancy themselves competent judges on every question. . . . It is at once sad and ridiculous."[73] The gradualist Speransky also thought the enthusiasm excessive: "The danger is that the great, obscure mass of the people have now become convinced not only that freedom has been promised to them, but that it is already theirs, and only the landowners are preventing it from being openly proclaimed. . . . It is terrifying and all too easy to imagine what the result of this could be."[74] But the only attempt at constitutional reform at home was Novosiltsev's proposed constitutional charter drafted in 1818–20. Even this focused on administrative reorganization and was not a progressive document, claiming that "the sovereign power is indivisible [and] is concentrated in the person of the Monarch" and that "the Sovereign is the sole source of all authority in the Empire: civil, political, legislative, and military."[75] This was a far cry from the liberal regime in Poland. But even this mild document, like its predecessors, was shelved.

But perhaps most destructive to the St. Petersburg idea was when the new religious impulse and resurgent nationalism were co-opted by Orthodoxy and combined with Arakcheev's political reactionism to impose new educational policies and censorship. At first, Alexander had made serious efforts to transform Russian religion and society in accordance with his original principles of the Holy Alliance. For this purpose he appointed Golitsyn to a newly created position of Minister of Education and Spiritual Affairs, who organized an effort aimed ultimately at a religious reeducation of the population.[76] Religious-philanthropic societies such as the Lovers of Humanity founded by Alexander spread spiritual instruction. Alexander supported a revival of higher-order Masonry, the lodges of which Alexander visited in both Prussia and Russia and which again thrived. Golitsyn and the Emperor maintained contact with such Western mystics as Baader, who was asked to write a manual of instruction for the Russian clergy. Seeing Alexander's policies and sensing opportunity, other foreign mystical leaders came to Petersburg on their own accord. These included Ignatius Lindl, the leader of the Bible Society in Bavaria who arrived in 1819, and Johann Gosner, another Bavarian mystic, who moved to St. Petersburg in 1820 and launched a preaching career and published a manual for the new faith, *The Spirit of the Life and Teaching of Christ*. Ignatius Fesler returned to Petersburg from the south to publish a new liturgy and other works.

The Orthodox hierarchy watched this extremism and panoply of doctrines with horror. To Orthodox clerics, the new movement threatened the established church order and was un-Russian. Though the phenomenon derived from traditional Muscovite religious impulses, it entailed a heretical change in doctrine. Thus, clerics soon invoked the newfound Russian nationalism resulting from the war and implored the government to reestablish traditional Orthodoxy. Their arguments eventually had their effect on the Emperor. Alexander saw that his initiative, begun with conservative intentions, had led to extreme and scattered beliefs, and it was becoming clear that his dream of a universal church in Russia was unrealistic and un-Russian and threatened to divide the country. Some of his advisors suspected that a plot lay behind the heretical sects. Alexander decided to back a retrenchment.

Alexander now linked the extreme sects with the ideas that had caused Europe's political unrest and revolutions. One of his advisors, Alexander Sturdza, had written a study arguing that such mystical doctrines were the cause of political disorder in the Germanic states and that such disorder had begun in the universities.[77] Another, Mikhail Magnitsky, a former colleague of Speransky who was exiled along with him in 1812 (but in his case to Vologda), like Speransky became a local civil servant and rose to become governor of Simbirsk on the Volga. He became a conservative and in his government capacity soon began investigating Masonic lodges and the University of Kazan, where the ideas of Lopukhin were popular. In his report, which made its way to Alexander, he portrayed the University as a hotbed of dangerous Germanic philosophy. He proposed closing it. "The human word, that is what transmits this diabolical force; the printing press is its arm. Godless university professors are distilling the atrocious poison of disbelief and of hate towards legitimate power for unhappy youth," he fumed. Russia should "separate herself from Europe so that not even a rumor about the horrible events taking place there could reach her."[78] He wanted to turn from Europe not only toward Orthodoxy but also toward Indian and other Eastern religious teachings, which he proposed to be taught at a new school set up in place of the University of Kazan. He even took issue with Karamzin for writing that the Mongol period was one of decline for Russia.

Alexander did not approve Magnitsky's extreme proposals, but he did appoint him head of Kazan University, from which position he launched a purge that spread throughout the educational system of Russia. One after another the country's universities were "purified" by firing professors, removing banned titles from libraries, and revising the curricula to remove dangerous political and philosophical content and substitute religious teachings. The curator at the University in St. Petersburg, D. Runich, soon fell into line and became known as "Magnitsky's echo."[79] In 1822 he dismissed three outstanding professors on grounds such as atheism, pro-constitutional inclinations, explaining philosophical systems while failing to refute them, and for having stated that lands tilled by free peasants have higher yields than others. Under Magnitsky's enthusiasm for the East, a chair of Arabic was established there. At the Lyceum at Tsarskoe Selo Pushkin's favorite professor, Alexander Kunitzyn, Professor of Moral Philosophy who had only recently presented Alexander with his book, *Natural Law*, and to whom Alexander had awarded the St. Vladimir Cross, was dismissed for teaching Rousseau. Such measures caused deep indignation among students with liberal ideas, many of whom would become Decembrists. But no student unrest was tolerated. At the least sign of trouble, students were threatened with exile, imprisonment, or conscription into the army, which some in Petersburg suffered. Soon only about 40 students remained at the University of St. Petersburg.

Censorship technically had been in force since 1804 but was not oppressive in practice until the war of 1812, and it only worsened afterwards. Journalists were ordered to write in accordance with government policies and not to publish material about government activities without prior authorization. Some journals in Petersburg were closed down, as in the case of the *Dukh Zhurnalov* ("The Spirit of Journals") which had published articles on the United States Constitution and representative government. Many philosophical and literary works were banned as immoral or subversive. These included Aristotle's *Politics*, Lamartine's *Méditations Poétiques*, Goethe's *Egmont*, Schiller's *Jeanne d'Arc*, and Griboyedov's play *Woe from Wit*, which was banned on stage and became known through circulation of unauthorized handwritten copies. The antigovernment poems of Alexander Pushkin and Kondraty Ryleev also circulated only in underground copies. Newly hired, uncultured, and nervous censors often banned harmless works such as a treatise on mushrooms (on the ground that mushrooms were a favorite item on Lenten menus).

Eventually the campaign came under the control of zealous Orthodox churchmen, whose leader was the archimandrite Photius. He was of little learning, but through his fanaticism and imperial support he quickly rose to act as a kind of Russian Torquemada to combat the enemies of a true, militant Orthodoxy. Pushkin portrayed him in verse:

> *Part fanatic, part pickpocket,*
> *The only spiritual weapons he waves*
> *Are opprobrium and cross, sword and knout.*

The campaign began with obvious and easy targets. Tatarinova was evicted from Mikhailovsky Castle. The eunuch Selivanov was banished to a monastery in Suzdal. Alexander refused to see Baroness Krüdener when she visited St. Petersburg. When Baader tried to visit his disciples in St. Petersburg, he was turned back at Riga. But soon government officials became targets, and the biggest target was Golitsyn, whose dismissal was secured in 1824 under circumstances resembling the dismissal of Speransky 12 years before. The coup de grace came when Photius secured Magnitsky's own downfall by accusing him of Illuminism, exposing faults in his administration at the University of Kazan, and revealing that he had employed a Jew as supervisor of studies.

It was against this background of obscuritanism, reaction, backwardness, and dashed hopes that St. Petersburg's enlightened nobility returned from Western Europe beginning in 1814–15. This was not what they had fought for, and they soon sought to do something about it.

THE CHILDREN OF 1812

The flower of St. Petersburg's youth had joined Alexander on his glorious campaign in Europe, simply as military officers on a military mission. "In 1812 I had no formed thoughts other than a flaming love for the Fatherland," wrote the Decembrist Nikita Muraviev.[80] But they returned charged with liberal political ideas.

What had happened? One of them, Mikhail Lunin, later testified merely that "A liberal cast of thought took shape in me from the moment I began to think; natural reason strengthened it."[81] Most, however, pointed to their experience in Europe as a turning point.[82] "We were the children of 1812," remarked the Decembrist Matvei Muraviev-Apostol.[83] Another Decembrist, Mikhail Fonvizin, explained:

> During the campaigns though Germany and France our young men became acquainted with European civilizations, which produced upon them the strongest impression. They were able to compare all that they had seen abroad with what confronted them at every step at home: slavery of the majority of Russians, cruel treatment of subordinates by superiors, all sorts of government abuses and general tyranny. All this stirred intelligent Russians and provoked patriotic sentiment.[84]

This generation of young men was already well educated in European history, thought, and languages, and had absorbed a Western mentality from a young age. For them classical models of Greece and Rome were not limited to the arts and topics for superficial social chatter, but were sources of inspiration to be applied in human affairs. This laid the basis for absorbing what they saw in the West. There they had a chance to meet their fellow officers from other allied countries. They became acquainted with the latest Western political debates, theories, writings, and political parties, and witnessed the formation of constitutional monarchies. They saw the dignified and independent bearing of Westerners, even among those of low social rank, and the relative economic prosperity in Europe even as it recovered from war. They explained this by the rule of law which had taken hold there, which was the result of a high degree of general enlightenment.[85] At the same time, they had fought alongside Russia's peasant soldiers in the campaign and came to respect them, and believed they had understood and formed a bond with them. The victory was a national one, shared by all classes. Many officers now believed that the peasantry deserved the rights of citizens.

These youths compared Europe to the Russia to which they now returned. Except for war damage, conditions in Russia were not worse than before the war, but they returned to their homeland with opened eyes and awakened minds and were sickened by what they saw. The Decembrist Ivan Yakushkin provided a graphic example of his return to St. Petersburg:

> From France we returned to Russia by sea. The First Division of the Guard landed at Oranienbaum and listened to the *Te Deum* performed by the Archpriest Derzhavin. During the prayer the police were mercilessly beating the people who attempted to draw nearer to the lined-up troops. This made upon us the first unfavorable impression when we returned to our homeland. . . . Finally the Emperor appeared, accompanied by the Guard, on a fine sorrel horse, with an unsheathed sword, which he was ready to lower before the Empress. We looked with delight at him. But at that very moment, almost under his horse, a peasant crossed the street. The Emperor spurred his horse and rushed with

the unsheathed sword toward the running peasant. The police attacked him with their clubs. We did not believe our own eyes, and turned away, ashamed for our beloved Tsar. That was my first disappointment in him; involuntarily I recalled a cat transformed into a Beauty, who, however, was unable to see a mouse without leaping upon it.[86]

Though the officers were home again, much was now alien to them. The capital, now dominated by Arakcheev's lackeys and religious fanatics, seemed grand and gay on the surface but to thoughtful people was oppressive. The poet Vasily Zhukhovsky complained that the city's residents "were mummies, surrounded by majestic pyramids, whose grandeur exists not for them."[87] Yakushkin continued:

> In 1814 life for youth in Petersburg was tiresome. During the two years events had passed before our eyes which had determined the fate of nations and to some degree we had been participants in them. Now it was unbearable to look at the empty life in Petersburg and listen to the babbling of the old men who praised the past and reproached every progressive move. We were away from them a hundred years.[88]

These years marked the beginning of the image of "Imperial St. Petersburg" as the cold and inhuman seat of a repressive regime. But this period also saw the city emerge as the country's leading hotbed of liberal thinkers opposed to the regime, as well as of cutting edge writers and artists standing for originality, individuality, and creativity, a city tradition that would hold through the Soviet regime.

The formerly frivolous young officers had been transformed into serious, thinking citizens. As Yakushkin explained, "In 1811, when I joined the Semenovsky Regiment, the officers, when they gathered amongst themselves, either played cards, cheating each other without a twinge of conscience, or drank and caroused recklessly." Before the war, they frequented the city's salons, but now, back from the war, "after dinner some would play chess while others read aloud from Western newspapers and followed events in Europe. Such a way of spending our time was a real innovation."[89]

Soon they needed more structured ways to spend their time. Sharing common values, experiences, and dissatisfaction with the regime, they needed outlets through which to discuss their concerns and what might be done. They began to gather regularly in social circles at their homes, often in the company of like-minded intellectuals and writers, and naturally politics was at the forefront of conversation. Eventually their views crystallized. They formed secret societies, the purpose of which was explained by Nikolai Turgenev, an economist, high official in the Ministry of Finance, and future theoretician of the Decembrists, in his essay *Ideas on the Organization of a Society:*

> Where can a Russian obtain the necessary general rules of civil society? . . . Previously (namely, in the period of Catherine II) we looked for nourishment in Freemasonry, mysticism, alchemy. Now, when as a result of big events, the mind of the nations has given up the barren field of gloomy *reverie* and has turned toward earnest reality, now when the spirit of the times has flown over several centuries in a few years, the moral

requirements of our compatriots have acquired another character. . . . [O]ne cannot but agree that the joining together of several Russians who love their fatherland, its glory and happiness, and who are true to their obligations and to the laws of honor, may be of some use to Russia, provided their active, selfless striving toward a noble goal is crowned with some success.[90]

Usually the societies were formed on Masonic models and incorporated Masonic terminology, ceremonies, and principles of organization; many fathers of Decembrists had been prominent Freemasons.[91] They were also inspired by similar secret patriotic and political societies in the West, especially the short-lived German *Tugendbund* ("Society for Virtue") formed under Napoleonic rule, which had been dedicated to the moral regeneration of society in preparation for political liberalization, which itself had been inspired by Benjamin Franklin's proposed Junto society in Philadelphia.[92] By breaking ranks with the rest of the nobility, such officers (and noble writers like Pushkin) were heeding Radishchev's call to serve the nation rather than the regime, taking the first steps toward an intelligentsia in opposition.

One early society established in 1814 involved 15 or 20 officers of the Semenovsky Regiment, including the future Decembrist Ivan Yakushkin. Another, called the "Sacred Artel," was founded by Alexander Muraviev, an officer at military headquarters and included many officers from there as well as Alexander Pushkin's fellow student at the Lyceum, Ivan Pushchin, who attended their meetings in his school uniform. The meetings were held in a republican atmosphere harking back to democratic Novgorod, and the room featured a *veche* bell which any member could ring to have his proposal considered. A third was the Order of Russian Knights, cofounded in 1814 by General Mikhail Orlov and Matvei Dmitriev-Mamonov, with the goal of achieving a limited aristocratic monarchy. But the Order never got off the ground as Dmitriev-Mamonov went insane.

One evening shortly after the Order of Russian Knights failed, a number of officers were gathered at the home of Sergei Muraviev-Apostol. One of the guests, Nikita Muraviev, suggested forming a single secret society devoted to a political program. Six of them—Alexander Muraviev, Nikita Muraviev, Prince Sergei Trubetskoi, Ivan Yakushkin, and Matvei and Sergei Muraviev-Apostol—agreed to found it and to draw up its constitution. It was established in February 1816 as the Union of Salvation, and its numbers soon included the future Decembrists Pavel Pestel and Mikhail Fonvizin.

The original stated aims of the Union are not clear since its constitution is not preserved, but in any event its agenda soon became dominated by a debate engendered by the fiery Pavel Pestel (1793–1826). Born the son of a corrupt governor-general in Siberia, Pestel was first educated in Germany and returned four years later to attend the St. Petersburg Military Academy, where he graduated with special honors. In the war of 1812 he participated in the battle of Borodino, where he was seriously wounded. After the war, he served as aide-de-camp to General Wittgenstein and in 1821 became Colonel of the Viatsky regiment in the South. He was intelligent, strong-willed, and highly opinionated, which made him persuasive to others and a natural leader, to the point where he became something of a dictator and in St. Petersburg became known as the "Southern Napoleon." Yakushkin wrote that "Pestel always talked wisely and stubbornly defended his opinion, in the truth of which he always believed as is usually believed of a mathematical truth."[93] He was also practical, a superb organizer, and an adept conspirator with no patience for long-winded discussions having no useful outcome. He was a fierce republican inspired by the Jacobins, whose political organization he sought to replicate, and he was ready to resort to the most radical means, including regicide, to achieve his political ends. As such, he differed from his fellow Decembrists and rather was the grandfather of the long line of iron-willed radical Russian revolutionaries who would emerge over the next century, culminating with Lenin.[94]

When the members of the Union met, they agreed on the moral and educational aims of the society but quickly split into two camps over its political program. Most members preferred a liberal but moderate program aimed at achieving in due course limited constitutional monarchy by legal rather than revolutionary methods. To this Pestel sardonically remarked that Russia seems to need an *Encyclopédie* before it can think of revolution, but to many in the St. Petersburg group this was exactly the point. Pestel's faction favored a revolutionary action, including regicide if necessary, in order to found a republic. On this question the Union broke within a year, but this issue remained the central point of difference amongst Decembrists and eventually led to a formal split between the North and the South.

But the members would not give up, as repression in Russia seemed to dictate haste while Alexander's speech in Poland raised hopes. Thus, the officers redoubled their efforts, deciding to reorganize the society under a new constitution. They obtained a copy of the *Tugendbund's* constitution from Germany and within four months had drafted their own, which became known as the Green Book from the color of its binder, chosen because green is the color of hope and regeneration. The new society, established in 1818, was called the Union of Welfare, and eventually it included over 200 members.[95]

Since Pestel was not made a member of the committee which prepared the Green Book and some radicals withdrew rather than submit to a moderate program, the constitution reflected the moderate views of the majority of St. Petersburg officers and the moral and educational program of the *Tugendbund*. The Green Book called upon members to act in four fields—philanthropy, education, justice, and the national economy. It evidenced the influence of Freemasonry, as many Decembrists, including Alexander Muraviev, Ryleev, Pestel, and Wilhelm Küchelbecker were Freemasons and held to its tenets of philanthropy and education though they recoiled from higher-order mysticism. They also hoped either to recruit members from the Masonic lodges or turn the lodges themselves into centers of political activism, but the Masons as a whole preferred gradual reform to immediate revolution, and in any event Alexander banned the lodges (and all secret societies) in 1822.[96]

To fulfill these goals, the Union of Welfare either sponsored or cooperated with several other societies active in particular fields, especially in letters and literature from which they took inspiration. One was the Free Society of Amateurs of Russian Letters, formed in 1816 by the poet and Decembrist Fedor Glinka (cousin of the composer Mikhail). It included the future Decembrists Kondraty Ryleev, Wilhelm Küchelbecker, and Alexander Bestuzhev and published the journal *The Champion of Enlightenment and Philanthropy*. Another group was Arzamas, formed in 1815 among a group of progressive linguists and poets, including Vasily Zhukovsky, Prince Peter Vyazemsky, Alexander Turgenev, Baron Anton von Delvig, and the young Alexander Pushkin. It was originally founded as a riotous circle to parody Admiral Alexander Shiskov's "Conversation of Lovers of the Russian Word," a literary circle of conservative rivals opposed to linguistic innovations, and thus to promote their own new language and literature. But by 1818 Arzamas had wearied of its own joke and the original target and raison d'etre of the club, Shishkov's Conversation, had become defunct. Under the influence of the new members and future Decembrists, General Orlov and Nikolai Turgenev, the group agreed that their aims should become more civic. Thus, most of them formed a new society in 1818, known as the Green Lamp since it gathered every fortnight at the home of the millionaire Nikita Vsevoloshsky in a room lit by a green lamp. Members each wore a special ring with the lamp engraved on the stone. The society's statutes invited members to discuss all political, social, literary, and other questions of the day in complete freedom under a guarantee of complete secrecy. The group consisted mainly of young officers such as Prince Trubetskoi, and due to the need for secrecy could admit only a few select poets such as Delvig and Pushkin, who were excluded from the more sensitive political discussions. Both the genuine poets and dilettante officers read their verses, some lectured on Russian history, others reviewed plays and discussed the possibility of staging some. Many such works criticized and parodied Alexander's government. Of these meetings the young Alexander Pushkin wrote in his *Epigram to Engelhardt* (1819):

> There we spoke with open hearts
> Of the fool, the wicked dignitary
> Of the inveterate kowtower
> Of the king in the heavens
> And sometimes, too, of the earthly one.

After the meetings, the friends would dine, drink, and sing together and have a riotous time. Pushkin later wrote fondly of the bonds thus formed:

> It was there, in that hospitable retreat
> That retreat of love and free muses,
> Where with a mutual oath
> We bonded in eternal union,

> *Where we knew friendship and bliss,*
> *Where in red bonnets at a round table*
> *We sat in sweet equality.*

Out of that group sprang revolutionary poetry that became a rallying cry for the Decembrists. Some of it was officially published, but much circulated underground in handwritten form and was committed to memory. Chief among these poets was the brash Alexander Pushkin (1799–1837), from an old, noble, but nearly impoverished family. Born in Moscow, he was fortunate to have a well-educated father with a large library, and the young Alexander took to reading and learned French almost as a second native language. He soon displayed a unique talent for poetry, which he began writing by age eight. But his father treated him harshly and his mother did not pay him much attention, favoring her other children. This, combined with his mixed feelings about his maternal African ancestry, his short, somewhat pudgy stature and generally unattractive appearance made him somewhat a loner with an "otherness" about him. As he matured he became better looking, charming and witty, but instead of using his assets to fit into Petersburg's high society, he developed a love-hate relationship with it, desperately wanting to be adored but at the same time being the aloof artist and savage critic who recognized no rules and would challenge anyone and everything. His short life would be a continuous firework.

In 1811, when he was 12, he had the good fortune to be accepted in the entering class of Alexander's new Lyceum at Tsarskoe Selo, where he studied for six years while the war raged and graduated in June 1817. In most subjects he was a slightly better than average student, but he excelled at literature and fencing. His poetry was soon recognized as exceptional and attracted the attention of the city's literati, which led them to invite him into Arzamas and the Green Lamp. By the time he graduated, he was already writing some of his more mature work such as *Ruslan and Lyudmila*. He took an undemanding job at the Foreign Ministry, which he largely ignored, and divided his time between writing poetry and living the dissipated life of a dandy. He became not only famous for his poems but infamous for his behavior, which included drunkenness, carousing with friends and getting into fights, dueling, charming respectable ladies, and visiting brothels. "More or less I have been in love with all the pretty women I have ever known," he confessed.[97] But his status as Petersburg's enfant terrible only put him in greater demand among the high society in which he could barely afford to circulate. He was regularly a guest at balls, literary salons, and private homes. To the dismay of many, he also frequented the theater, where out of disdain for the quality of the spectacles and the low cultural tastes of the audience, which usually included young officers who attended only to attract the attentions of ballerinas, he would circulate through the crowd in the theater during the performance, acting bored, yawning, commenting on the performance, and joking with people. Once, when his head was still shaved after an illness, he appeared in a wig but during the performance took it off and ostentatiously fanned himself with it. But inside that shaved head and behind all the shenanigans lay an immense talent and serious ideals.

Pushkin's first famous political poem, *Ode to Liberty* (1817), took its title from Radishchev's ode *Freedom* that had been partially included in his *Journey*. The poem made him an instant hero and celebrity, and the Decembrists knew it by heart. It ended:

> And now know this, O Tsars:
> Neither punishments nor rewards
> Nor prison bars nor altars
> Will protect you any more.
> Be the first to bow your heads
> To the trustworthy force of the Law,
> And then the eternal defender of your throne
> Will be the peace and liberty of the people.

This was followed by *Fairy Tales* (subtitled *Noël* as it was written for Christmas in 1818), in which Pushkin openly mocked Alexander's recent Warsaw speech hinting at a constitution for Russia, likening the Tsar's promises to a fairy tale being told to the Christ child. Returning from abroad, the Tsar first proclaims that he has brought with him new Prussian and Austrian uniforms, and assures his listener that he is well fed, overweight, and not overly pressed with affairs. But as an "afterthought" the Tsar promises to retire the chief of police Lavrov, grant human liberties to the nation, and erect the Law on Golgotha:

> At these words, the baby wriggles
> Vigorously in his cradle:
> "Is it really true?
> Is it not a joke?"
> And his mother says: "Bye-bye! Close your eyes
> It is time to finally sleep,
> Now that you have heard how our Tsar-father
> Tells fairy tales."

Finally, in *The Village* (1819), Pushkin spoke out against serfdom and the cruelty of landowners. The poem ended with a dream:

> Do I see—Oh friends!—the people freed,
> And slavery abolished by the hand of the Tsar,
> And will a brilliant dawn of enlightened freedom
> At last burst forth over the fatherland?

Such poems, complemented by his barbed epigrams targeted at figures such as Arakcheev, Golitsyn, and Photius, made Pushkin a popular hero. Not only were his poems sacred hymns to the revolutionaries, but they were known to all of St. Petersburg society right down to actors, painters, intellectual serfs, and coachmen. "There was not at the time a literate ensign in the army who did not know them by heart," wrote the Decembrist Ivan Yakushkin.[98] Soon other revolutionary poems in circulation were wrongly attributed to him.

Pushkin's poems also became known to Alexander, Arakcheev, and the police, and by 1820 Pushkin was considered politically dangerous. A police agent tried to bribe Pushkin's valet into turning over the poet's papers, but he refused and instead warned Pushkin, who quickly burned them. The next morning he was summoned to appear before Count Mikhail Miloradovich, the Governor of St. Petersburg. On his way there Pushkin bumped into his friend Fedor Glinka, just outside Glinka's home on Theater Square. Glinka, who worked in Miloradovich's office, told Pushkin that Miloradovich is "no poet" but at heart is a chivalrous romantic. He advised Pushkin that if he would be open and fearless and play to Miloradovich's noble heart, the Governor would not betray him. It worked. Miloradovich had been ordered simply to arrest Pushkin and seize his papers, but thought it would be "more elegant" to invite Pushkin in person and ask him to hand over his manuscripts. But when Pushkin arrived, he told the Governor: "Count, my poems have all been burned!—so nothing will be found in my home. But if you like, I have them *here* (pointing to his head). Send for some paper, and I will write down everything that has ever been written *by me* (other than what has been published, of course), and I will point out what is mine and what has been circulated *under my name*." The paper was brought, and Pushkin wrote and wrote, until he had filled a notebook. He had omitted only his epigram to Arakcheev. Miloradovich could not arrest him. "You know," he told Glinka right after the meeting, "Pushkin utterly charmed me by his nobility of speech and demeanor."[99] But Miloradovich would have to deliver Pushkin's notebook to the Tsar, who would finally decide Pushkin's fate, and the Tsar's advisors were not so favorably disposed or so easily swayed. Pushkin's friends and all of liberal St. Petersburg trembled, fearing that the poet would be imprisoned or exiled. Some influential friends, including his Lyceum schoolmaster Yegor Engelhardt, and Capo d'Istria, his superior at the Foreign Ministry, lobbied Alexander to be lenient. Even Karamzin interceded on his behalf after extracting a promise from the poet not to write antigovernment poems for two years. "Having long since tried every means I know of to subdue this daredevil, I had already abandoned the wretch to his fate and to Nemesis," Karamzin wrote in April 1820. "Out of compassion for his talent, however, I agreed to intercede personally on his behalf."[100] Pushkin's friends argued that exile would have a counterproductive effect on the poet's impassioned nature, whereas magnanimity would help reform it and allow him to bring glory to Russian literature. The Tsar liked to imagine himself as a ruler of enlightened generosity and found the arguments compelling. He ordered Pushkin "transferred" (rather than formally exiled) from St. Petersburg to Yekaterinoslav in the South. Pushkin would remain outside the capital in various provinces until 1826. Because Pushkin left town so long before the Decembrist uprising of 1825, he was not directly implicated in the conspiracy and was spared.

Another inspiring and more revolutionary poet was Kondraty Ryleev (1795–1826), who mostly wrote romantic historical narrative poems. The son of an impoverished landlord near Kiev, he attended the Corps of Cadets and then traversed Europe as an army officer, but at heart he was a poet, not a soldier. So in 1818 he resigned from the army on principle and moved back to St. Petersburg. There he eked out a living as an assessor in the Criminal Court and then as a manager at the Russian-American Company, and served as editor of the Union of Welfare's journal, *The Polar Star*. "I saw Russia enslaved," he wrote. "With her head bowed, her chains rattling, she prayed for her Tsar."[101] In 1820 he became an active Freemason and, seeing Pushkin's example, became politically active and decided to put his talent at the service of the revolutionary cause. "I am not a poet, but a citizen," he now declared. His revolutionary poems were not even submitted to the censor but circulated widely. The memorized verses were put to music and sung at meetings of the secret societies; others were initially composed as songs. His principled example eventually inspired his comrades to make him the leader of the Decembrists, and he would become a revolutionary martyr.

To posterity, however, the most famous literary product of the Green Lamp group is not a poem but a short story by the musician and future Decembrist Alexander Ulybyshev called *The Dream*, in which he portrayed St. Petersburg as a utopia some three centuries hence. "It seemed to me that I was in the streets of St. Petersburg," he wrote, "but everything had been changed so much that I had difficulty in recognizing them." On the façade of the Mikhailovsky Castle he saw in large golden letters "Palace of the State Assembly." Public schools, academies, and libraries had taken the place of the innumerable military barracks. Along Nevsky Prospect the Anichkov Palace was turned into a kind of Russian Pantheon with statues and busts of people who had distinguished themselves by their talents and services to their country. And at the end of Nevsky, instead of the Alexander Nevsky Monastery, he saw "a triumphal arch which seemed to have been erected on the ruins of fanaticism." Behind it rose a temple "but I could not guess of what religion." Except for a few elderly worshippers, all traces of Russian Orthodoxy had disappeared: no priests or monks, no vestments, no icons, and no elaborate ritual. Instead, he heard only Haydn's Hymn to Creation being sung by female voices,* as music was the only art admitted in the temple. The religion featured only pure worship and direct communication with God the creator, removed of all barriers and superstition. Instead of priests, high government officials worked in shifts there as part of their official duties. "After leaving the temple I shall be busy with judicial matters," one remarked.

---

*Russian Orthodoxy prohibited women from singing in church choirs.

"Is not the guardian of order on this earth the most deserving representative of God, source of order in the Universe?" And finally, atop the Winter Palace, he saw a new national emblem in place of the double-eagle. There, a phoenix soared against the sky, holding in its beak a wreath of olive branches and immortelles. "As you see," said the storyteller's companion, "the two heads of the eagle denoting despotism and superstition have been cut off and from their blood rose the phoenix of freedom and true faith."[102] A true national literature, dress and other culture had developed which reflected neither Muscovite extremes nor blind copying of Europe.

The more radical members of the Union of Welfare indeed viewed the majority as dreamers. Seeing no concrete political program or ultimate goal, they would still ask, "But where is stated the aim of the Society?"[103] Indeed, the program's authors believed that preparing Russia for political change would require nearly a generation and that the revolution would occur only around 1840.[104] The radicals, mostly in Ukraine and led by Pestel, whose regiment was stationed there, grew impatient. Pestel visited St. Petersburg in 1820 and met with the Union's local leaders, but was unable to persuade them into a more radical program and political action. Another attempt at reconciliation at a conference in Moscow the next year also failed, at which point the Union was officially dissolved.

Pestel resolved to continue the organization in the South under his own agenda. Eventually his group became known as the Southern Society. He drafted a proposed constitution for Russia entitled *Russian Justice*.[105] It called for a republican form of government open to most citizens and the abolition of serfdom with land, but also featured retention of government supervision over economic life and forced Russification of nationalities. Establishing this republic would require assassinating the royal family, after which a dictatorial provisional government headed by Pestel would rule for eight or more years before the republic could be formed. Although Pestel always insisted that he would never become a despot, his behavior did not dispel such fears.

But Pestel knew that any successful revolution had to occur in the capital and be led by the St. Petersburg group. It was led mainly by high aristocrats who held responsible government or military offices and did not want the revolution to threaten their standing, whereas the Southern Society had more lower, impoverished army officers and nobility or members of no rank, as well as many disaffected officers from the disbanded Semenovsky Regiment, who had greater grudges against the existing system, held their republican and democratic ideas due to their economic status, and had little to lose. Both societies, however, being familiar with the excesses of both the French Revolution and of past peasant revolts in Russia, and fearing retribution against landowners, were opposed to a mass rebellion involving the whole population and therefore both favored a "surgical" revolution involving only the conspirators and the military.

In 1822 the St. Petersburg leaders of the disbanded Union of Welfare established what was known as the Northern Society headed by Nikita Muraviev, this time with overt political goals. From a leading noble family, Muraviev had joined the army at 17 in 1813, fought in Europe, and followed Alexander into Paris. Back in St. Petersburg he joined Arzamas and later the secret societies. A republican, he was more radical in his thinking than most of his St. Petersburg comrades, but unlike Pestel he was not doctrinaire and would work for compromise, which is why he was chosen the Society's leader. He authored a proposed constitution for Russia which was finalized through debate within the Society. It is based squarely on Enlightenment principles and constitutional precedent, most clearly the Constitution of the United States. It began by proclaiming that the source of sovereign power lies in the people, that all citizens are equal before the law (with no distinctions between commoners and nobility), and that serfdom and slavery are abolished. Citizens' civil rights included the right to engage in any trade, protection of property, the right to free speech, and various judicial protections. The government was to have three branches, including an elected bicameral legislature (the People's *Veche*) invested with all legislative power. The Emperor would be the chief executive, whose powers would be similar to those of the U.S. President, including conducting foreign relations, acting as commander-in-chief, appointing ambassadors, judges, and the heads of all executive bodies, and securing enforcement of the laws. He could veto legislation passed by the *Veche*, but the veto could be overcome by a two-thirds vote of each chamber. Russia would be a federal state divided into 13 states and two regions, each also having the three branches of government. In order to bring the new constitutional regime into being, the Emperor would need to accede to it, and a provisional government headed by a Directory appointed by the Senate would rule until elections could be held, which was thought to be a matter of months rather than several years as under Pestel's proposal. What to do if the Emperor refused was never satisfactorily agreed upon? Some favored arrest and exile to the West, while others were willing to resort to regicide. As a partial escape from such a hard choice, there was vague agreement that the death of Alexander would be the time to present the ultimatum. But they thought this was far off.

When Muraviev became temporarily unable to function because of family matters, the poet Kondraty Ryleev became leader of the Society and revitalized it. Ryleev was a visionary republican patriot passionately committed to the Society's cause. His political views were never clearly worked out even in his own mind, nor was he well suited to organize the logistics of revolution. But he emerged as a true leader through his tireless efforts at propaganda, recruitment of new members, and his inspiring example. If Muraviev was the Society's brains, Ryleev was its heart and soul.[106] Inspired by Byron's martyrdom in Greece, he was a romantic figure of fearless destiny, foretold in his poem *Nalivaiko*:

> *My coming doom I feel and know*
> *And bless the stroke which lays me low,*

And, father, now with joy I meet
My death; to me such end is sweet.[107]

It was through Ryleev's efforts that the four Bestuzhev brothers, the poet Prince Alexander Odoevsky, the writer and lecturer Wilhelm Küchelbecker, the economist Baron Stiengel, all from the lower nobility, joined the cause. The class makeup of the Society broadened, which helped move it toward revolutionary action. In early November 1825 Prince Sergei Trubetskoi arrived from the South reporting that the Southern Society was organized and ready to rise, and the North agreed to rise together with the South sometime in mid-1826.

But events soon overtook both Societies. On November 19, 1825, Alexander suddenly died while in the South at Taganrog, news of which reached St. Petersburg on November 27. His death precipitated a succession crisis because he had no sons and his oldest brother, Constantine, to whom the succession would normally go, in 1822 had secretly renounced the throne in favor of his younger brother Nicholas due to his morganatic marriage to the Polish Countess Ioanna Gruzdinskaya. Nicholas, known as a martinet in the tradition of Paul and Colonel Schwartz, had questionable support among the Guards. Thus, he was cautious and refused to claim the throne and take oaths of loyalty until Constantine renounced it publicly. This interregnum, which lasted over two weeks, gave the Decembrists their chance to act.

Alexander's death took the Society by surprise. Planning to revolt at the earliest in mid-1826, they were completely unprepared for action and their numbers were still small. But they realized that if they let this opportunity escape, there would not be another for a long time. Inaction probably would have meant the end of the Society and potential arrest under Nicholas's regime. Thus, led by Ryleev and the Bestuzhev brothers, they decided upon rebellion. They exploited Constantine's (largely undeserved) appeal to recruit new members. Since they had attracted only small numbers of troops to their cause and the key conspirators were mainly lower officers unable to commit or influence large units, they embarked upon a grassroots campaign among the soldiers, visiting them by night to rally support. Ryleev and the Bestuzhevs spent two sleepless nights on "promenades" through military barracks. They told the soldiers that Nicholas was usurping the throne to defeat Constantine, who they said favored a constitution, would free the peasants and institute shorter terms of military services which Alexander had promised but denied. They coined for the soldiers the popular slogan "Constantine and Constitution." The soldiers were sympathetic, but since the Society had still not decided on how to revolt, Ryleev could not explain to the soldiers what was expected of them and the rebels lost this opportunity. They suspended their propaganda for the moment and began meeting daily in more or less continuous sessions in Ryleev's or Obolensky's apartments to make concrete plans for the revolt. Since Ryleev was not a practical or military man, they appointed Prince Trubetskoi as "dictator" to execute whatever plan was adopted. Besides, Ryleev had caught a severe cold from his nighttime visits to the soldiers, which had developed into angina and he could barely speak.

The Society's frantic efforts to recruit support were difficult to conceal, and by December 12 Nicholas learned of the plot. But paradoxically he saw this as further proof of his low standing among the troops, and it convinced him in the correctness of his policy of refraining from any provocative actions in the capital* until Constantine publicly renounced the throne. When the plotters learned that Nicholas knew of the conspiracy, they realized that the moment of truth had come: either abandon the plan, dissolve and perhaps flee, or press on gallantly to an uncertain end. Realizing that they were already compromised, they decided that it was "better to be seized on the street than in bed."[108] Once Nicholas learned of the plot, his accession was hastily announced for December 14, by which time Constantine would have returned from Warsaw and Nicholas could take the oaths of allegiance on Senate Square by Falconet's Bronze Horseman. Nicholas could have arrested the rebel leaders beforehand, but he shrank from this. "I do not wish the oath [to me] to be preceded by arrests," he told his War Minister. "Think of what an ugly impression that would make on everyone."[109] In retrospect, his lenience was a mistake and an uglier impression was in store.

Their plot revealed, the Society had to make its final decision. They met for the last time on the night of the 13th–14th in Ryleev's apartment in an atmosphere of romantic delirium. Ryleev, still barely able to talk, rose and began to speak quietly but movingly of the justice of their cause, of their service to the fatherland, and of their patriotic duties. "How beautiful Ryleev was that evening!" Mikhail Bestuzhev later wrote in his memoirs:

> When he came to his favorite theme—love for the fatherland—his physiognomy came to life, his coal-black eyes shone with a heavenly glow, and the words flowed freely like a flood, and at that moment one could not but love him. And so on that fatal evening which decided the hazy question, 'To be or not to be,' his visage was like a pale moon bathed in a supernatural light, appearing and then disappearing in the stormy waves of this sea, boiling with manifold passions and urges.[110]

While admitting the group's unreadiness and the high risk of failure, Ryleev explained that they had gone too far to turn back and that now they must either succeed or die. After Ryleev finished, Prince Odoevsky exclaimed, "We shall die, oh, how gloriously we shall die!"[111]

The plan was to assemble troops on Senate Square early enough to prevent the administration of the loyalty oaths to Nicholas, rally bystanders to their cause, and send a delegation (Ryleev and Ivan Pushchin) to the Senate to present their demands.

---

*In the South, Pestel was arrested on December 13. The Southern Society revolted in the Ukraine two weeks after the revolt in the North and was easily put down.

For this purpose, Trubetskoi had prepared a short manifesto summarizing their de-mands based on Muraviev's constitution.[112] They also made plans for soldiers of the Izmailovsky Regiment and sailors under Yakubovich to seize the Winter Palace and the royal family pending resolution of the new form of government.[113] They de-cided also to send a detachment to seize the Fortress under the leadership of Colonel Bulatov, Ryleev's former schoolmate at the Corps of Cadets.[114]

But among some of them the romantic fervor either never took hold or soon wore off when the prospects for success dimmed. By December 12th it had be-come apparent that the number of military units committed to revolt was much smaller than hoped. While many officers supported the cause, they could not promise to deliver their units. They could only pledge to bring as many men as possible; many lost heart and would never appear. On the eve of the revolt, the commanders of the newly re-formed Semenovsky Regiment and the Finlandsky Regiment pulled out on the ground that the revolt was certain to fail. In the mid-dle of the night, Mikhail and Alexander Bestuzhev made one last desperate visit to the Moskovsky Regiment soldiers in order to shore up support. "I spoke heat-edly and they listened to me with passion," Alexander Bestuzhev later recalled.[115] At least one of its battalions promised to refuse to take the loyalty oath to Nicholas and to come to Senate Square. In the end, the rebels could count only on the Grenadiers, the Marine Guards, and parts of the Moskovsky Regiment. In a moment of desperation, Ryleev asked one colleague, Peter Kakhovsky, to pen-etrate the Winter Palace in a borrowed uniform and assassinate Nicholas. Kakhovsky at first agreed, but just as quickly thought better of it. Just after Kakhovsky refused, Yakubovich appeared before Ryleev and refused to seize the Winter Palace on the ground that the sailors would likely kill Nicholas, for which he did not want to be responsible.[116]

That night Nicholas was holding an emergency meeting of the State Council in the Winter Palace. He had waited for Constantine's arrival into the evening of the 13th but finally, after midnight, began the meeting without him. Nicholas ex-plained the situation and the plot, and arranged for the commanders of the Impe-rial Guards to swear allegiance to him in the Palace at 5:00 A.M., which they did. Nicholas then told them, "You shall answer to me with your heads for the tran-quility of the capital. As far as I am concerned, even if I shall be Emperor for only one hour, I shall show myself worthy of the honor."[117] He then had the Senate and Synod pledge allegiance on Senate Square around 7:00 A.M., before the rebels could assemble there. Constantine finally arrived late in the morning.

Early that morning Trubetskoi and Pushchin met with Ryleev at his home. They had just learned that Nicholas had administered the loyalty oaths early in order to avoid a confrontation. The conspirators were thus too late to execute a key part of their plan. Moreover, the hoped-for support from the soldiers had not materialized. The takeovers of the Winter Palace and the Fortress were called off. They made last minute plans, pinning their hopes on Trubetskoi inspiring a popular insurrection on Senate Square. Trubetskoi then left, promising to join Ryleev and Pushchin on the square.

But Trubetskoi had learned that no high government officials would join in support of the revolt. After leaving Ryleev's home, the demons of fear and doubt overcame the "dictator" who had been entrusted to lead the revolt. He lost his nerve and abandoned the cause and his comrades. He never appeared on the Square as promised, and instead went to his General Staff office to see how he could still take a loyalty oath to Nicholas, and then wandered aimlessly about the city. In the evening he was found seeking refuge in the Austrian Embassy, where his brother-in-law was Ambassador. It would be up to the inexperienced Ryleev to improvise the rebellion.

As he was preparing to depart for the square from his home, Ryleev, ever the romantic, was thinking of appearing on the square in a peasant's costume and knapsack with a rifle in his hand, to symbolize the union between peasant and soldier "in the first act of their mutual liberty." But Nikolai Bestuzhev arrived and dissuaded him: "The Russian soldier will not understand these delicacies of patriotism, and you'll probably hit yourself with the rifle butt."[118] Ryleev dressed in normal clothes, and as they headed for the door Ryleev's wife burst into the room with their six-year-old daughter, Nastenka. Grabbing Bestuzhev by the arm, she shouted to him, "Leave my husband with me, don't take him! I know he's going to his death." As Ryleev tried to calm her, she turned to their daughter and cried, "Nastenka, beg your father for yourself and my own sake." The sobbing girl embraced her father's knees, begging him not to go; her mother collapsed into Bestuzhev's arms. Ryleev picked up his daughter, sat her on the divan, hugged them both, and ran out with Bestuzhev toward the square.[119]

On December 14 dawn came late (after nine), it was cold (eight degrees below freezing), and an icy wind blew over the city. Senate Square was already empty following the taking of the loyalty oaths a couple hours before. At around 9:00 A.M. the first units of the Moskovsky Regiment began to dribble into the Square and gather around the Bronze Horseman. They were joined by some Grenadiers and Marine Guards, but that was all. By noon only about 3,000 rebels had assembled. Some rebel leaders such as Bulatov, seeing the disappointing turnout, immediately fled to take the loyalty oath to Nicholas. The others looked in vain for Trubetskoi. Realizing that he was probably not coming, the rebels debated who should take command but no one volunteered; only late in the afternoon did Prince Evgeny Obolensky take charge. By then the rebels were surrounded by three times as many government troops, with cannon and cavalry. At that point Yakubovich left the rebels, claiming that he had a headache. "Apparently the atmosphere of the new Sovereign has hurt his sensitive nerves," Alexander Bestuzhev commented to his brother, gesturing to Nicholas's ranks.[120]

As word of the revolt spread throughout the city, Petersburgers converged on the square and drew as close as they could. As one witness recalled, "All of Petersburg flowed toward the Square, and all of the first Admiralty Region, consisting of up to 150,000 people, acquaintances and strangers, friends and enemies, forgot their personal affairs and gathered in groups, discussing the matter at stake with grave looks."[121] The rest of the city had a ghostlike emptiness about it, said eyewitnesses. Many if not most bystanders were sympathetic to the rebels, but most were separated from them by government troops; only those few who had gathered early in the morning stood beside the rebels.

Without sufficient forces to carry the day themselves, the rebels pinned their hopes on winning government troops and the civilians over to their side and staging a mass demonstration. In this they saw that time was on their side and hoped for defections. If they could hold out until dark (around 4:00 P.M.), overnight they might convert more to their side and the next day they would be stronger. But the rebels, without leadership, failed to seize the moment and accord the crowd a role in the uprising.

The government troops also were indecisive. For a couple of hours there was a standoff known to posterity as the "standing revolution." Government representatives, backed by troops on the Admiralty side of the Square, first tried to negotiate. The Governor of St. Petersburg, the same Mikhail Miloradovich who had helped Pushkin, approached the rebels to persuade them to leave. Obolensky, who had finally taken charge of the rebels, told him to leave or his life would be in danger, and as Miloradovich turned away, the hothead Peter Kakhovsky shot and killed him. Metropolitan Serafim and Kiev's Metropolitan Evgeny next approached the rebels in their diamond-studded green and crimson church robes, which stood out against the white snow. The rebels told Serafim not to meddle in political affairs and instead asked him to pray for their souls. "What kind of Metropolitan are you when you swear loyalty to two Emperors within two weeks? You're a traitor, a deserter, Nicholas's stooge," they replied. Shaken, the churchmen beat a hasty retreat through an opening into the construction site of the new St. Isaac's Cathedral at the back of the Square and took a carriage back to the Winter Palace. Entreaties by Grand Duke Mikhail Pavlovich were equally unavailing, and he might have been shot had the poet Küchelbecher's pistol not misfired as he tried to "graze" him with a bullet.

At first Nicholas was not on the Square with his troops and learned of Miloradovich's death only as he was leaving Palace Square with the Preobrazhensky Guards. At that moment a group of rebel Grenadier Life Guards rode past, intent on seizing the Imperial Family, only to see that the Palace was already heavily guarded.* As they were riding out of Palace Square past Nicholas's column, Nicholas ordered them to halt. "We are for Constantine!" they cried. "Very well," Nicholas reportedly replied, gesturing toward Senate Square, "your place is over there!" Fortunately for Nicholas, the Grenadiers did not recognize him or they might have taken him prisoner then and there.[122]

---

*The troops guarding the palace had barely arrived. If the rebels had come only shortly before, the royal family would have been in their hands.

When Nicholas arrived on Senate Square, he surveyed the situation and ordered the cavalry to charge and disperse the rebels. They charged three times, but the attacks turned into a comedy because of the confined area, because the horses were not properly shorn for the icy surface, and because the soldiers were bearing unsharpened parade sabers. As the horses and riders slipped and fell, bystanders pelted them with rocks and firewood, and the cavalry retreated to the laughter of the rebels and the crowd. Nicholas then sent General Sukhozanet to parlay with the rebels, who told them to lay down their arms or else they would be fired upon, but the rebels asked him whether he had brought a constitution.

The day was growing long. Onlookers, including some government troops, were voicing sympathy for the rebels and urged them to hold on until dark, after which, they said, all would go well for them. Some government soldiers began to defect. Nicholas heard that other units were on their way to the Square to join the rebels. Nicholas saw the danger, and he had 36 artillery pieces at his disposal. Finally General Toll approached him. "Your Majesty," he pleaded, "either let us clear the Square with gunfire or abdicate."[123] Nicholas's aide-de-camp Prince Ilarion Vasilchikov agreed: "Sir, there is not a moment to lose. You must give the order to fire!" "Do you wish me to shed the blood of my subjects on the first day of my reign?" Nicholas asked. "To save the Empire," was the reply.[124] Nicholas gave the order to ready the cannon to fire canister shot. "That's a happy beginning to my reign," he muttered in French.[125]

When the rebels saw this, some suggested storming the guns before they could fire, but most were either indecisive or did not believe that their brethren would fire upon them, so they stayed put. After a final warning, Nicholas gave the order to fire. The cannoneer lit the fuse, but he could not bear to insert it into the cannon. As his superior officer approached, he turned and handed the burning fuse to him, saying quietly, "It's yours, your honor." The officer inserted the fuse. The first shot was aimed over the heads of the rebels as a warning and merely pelted the Senate's roof and broke windows, but the rebels stood firm. The second volley burst into the heart of the rebel ranks. They quickly broke ranks under the hail of canister shot, which also hit civilian bystanders. Between rounds and amid the cries, blood could be heard oozing onto the white snow and melting it, red on white. Rebels and civilians alike fled along narrow Galernaya Street (which became a deadly shooting gallery as the government artillery trained its fire along the length of the street), along the English Embankment and across the Neva ice toward Vasilievsky Island. Many were simply trampled to death in the melee. Those fleeing on land tried to hide in private homes, but most owners denied them entry, fearing arrest for harboring traitors. Out on the river ice Mikhail Bestuzhev tried to assemble his troops for an attack on the Fortress, from which they might mount an effective defense, but cannon placed on the bridge across the Neva fired at them. When the cannonballs hit, the ice broke and many of his soldiers fell through and drowned. He led his remaining troops into the Academy of Fine Arts building where they hastily began setting up defenses. But when they saw the vastly superior government forces bearing down upon them, they saw that they were lost and Bestuzhev gave the order, "Every man for himself!" Most rebels who managed to escape were soon apprehended. No one will ever know exactly how many died that day, but the report compiled by the Ministry of Justice showed a death toll of 1,271 soldiers and civilians.[126]

Some of the leaders made their way back to Ryleev's home, where they met one last time in despair. Thinking that they would either succeed or die, they had given no thought to how to conduct themselves if they failed. They quickly discussed this and dispersed, but they had no chance to flee the city, nor did they attempt to do so. Meanwhile, back at Senate Square, the government attempted to erase all evidence of the revolt by daybreak. Fires burned on the square throughout the night as troops and police removed the dead from the square and tried to scrub away or cover up the bloodstains. In his haste, the chief of police, Alexander Shulgin, ordered many of the dead thrown into the Neva through the ice; some suffering this fate were only wounded. Their corpses would reappear on the riverbank in the spring.

The rebel leaders were rounded up in the course of the evening and brought straight to the Winter Palace, where Nicholas himself skillfully conducted the initial interrogations through the night. Others were arrested over the ensuing days and weeks, and almost all of them were presented to the Emperor. Nicholas performed as a royal chameleon, treating each prisoner differently and exploiting their individual personalities and vulnerabilities (he knew many of them personally). Based on their answers to his questions and degree of guilt, Nicholas penned instructions (some 150 of them) regarding the conditions of their detention in the cells of the Fortress. Some were not manacled, were held in better cells and could communicate with the outside world; others suffered in solitary confinement with little food in inhuman winter conditions. No one was tortured, but those who failed to cooperate suffered harsher conditions of confinement. Eventually, the Decembrists were given a series of written questions to which they replied in writing, including such broad inquiries as "When and where did you acquire liberal ideas?" Their answers, which are largely preserved, form a remarkable record of the Decembrists beliefs, the influences on their thought, their grievances and their proposals for reforming Russia. In fact, Nicholas's government quickly recognized the value of this record and had the Investigating Commission compile from the testimony a frank and honest report,[127] in response to which some reforms were later made.

The Decembrists conducted themselves variously. Some such as Yakushkin and Pestel bravely stood fast and would not betray their comrades. Others like Trubetskoi broke down—some immediately and others only after repeated interrogation. They confessed to errors and delusions, pleaded for mercy, and named their co-conspirators and even some innocents. Sometimes the prisoners were simply acting to save themselves, but in many cases they were truly repentant and ashamed for what they had done, concluding that they had followed the wrong approach to realizing their goals by revolting instead of remaining loyal to the state and the Emperor and working within the system.[128] Ryleev seems to have been in this category. In light of the 30 years of Nicholas's repression in reaction to the revolt, their conclusion may have been right.

Russia then held its first political trial, but it was not really a trial. (When the convicted Decembrists were later assembled inside the Fortress to hear their sentences read to them, they did not know they had been tried in absentia.) In early June 1826 a special Supreme Court was convened from members of the State Council, the Senate, the Ministry of Justice, and the Synod to consider the evidence and issue sentences. Its membership included Mikhail Speransky, whose name had been associated with the rebels (many of whom were his friends) and whose loyalty his enemies and Nicholas himself wanted to test. The court met for only a week to consider the guilt of 579 defendants and issued its sentences based solely on the written record. Of them, 290 were acquitted. Of the remaining 289, a majority were found guilty of minor offenses, but 121 were deemed the most responsible conspirators and received severe sentences. The Court's sentences included 31 death sentences by decapitation, with the remainder to be exiled to Siberia, but Nicholas reduced many of the sentences. Given that the rebels' acts were treasonous, the overall harshness of punishments was not extreme. Only five—Pestel, Ryleev, Kakhovsky, Mikhail Bestuzhev-Rumin, and Sergei Muraviev-Apostol— would suffer death, by hanging. (But for military men, death by hanging rather than by firing squad was an undignified insult.) Of the others, 31 were sent to hard labor in Siberia, and the remainder simply exiled for various terms, most of whom in Russian tradition were accompanied by their wives and families.

The executions were not publicly announced and were administered in the early morning hours of July 13 in order to avoid a spectacle. No prisoner had been put to death in Russia since Pugachev. Russia did not even have an experienced hangman to build gallows and carry out the sentences, so one had to be imported from Sweden. Most people, including the prisoners, believed that Nicholas, following tradition, would commute the sentences to exile at the last minute, but this would not come to pass. On the eve of the executions, gallows were constructed in the light of bonfires at the Kronverk just across the water channel from the Peter and Paul Fortress. At 3:00 A.M. the morning dawn was already breaking through a drizzle and light fog. The condemned were led out from the fortress to the gallows in front of some assembled soldiers, while relatives and a few civilians looked on from a distance. The prisoners were stripped of their insignias, their uniforms were removed and thrown into a bonfire, and they were given loose robes instead. One by one, their swords were then broken over their heads and also thrown into the bonfire. The five then mounted the scaffold, stepped onto the stools, and the nooses were slipped over their heads. The executioner kicked away the stools. Pestel and Bestuzhev-Riumin died, their necks broken, but Ryleev, Kakhovsky, and Muraviev-Apostol each slipped through their nooses and fell to the scaffold floor. The rain during the night had swollen the rope, and the executioner had not tightened the wet nooses enough. The fall broke Muraviev-Apostol's leg. "Poor Russia!" he cried in pain. "She cannot even hang a man decently!"[129] But new ropes were brought, the condemned were lifted back onto their stools, and the sentence was completed. The five bodies were taken away and buried in a secret location which remains unknown to this day. The verdict called for their graves to be marked not with crosses but with scaffolds declaring the eternal disgrace of their names, but instead on the site of the execution now stands a memorial in tribute to the martyrs and their cause.

The failure of the Decembrists in 1825 represented the defeat of liberalism in the political sphere; it was the religious, educational, and cultural purge culminating in 1824 which set the tone for the state's ideology for the rest of the 19th century. Though Nicholas's reign is famous as the beginning of a period of repression and turning inward, this was not simply the product of Nicholas's personality or of simple political fear in response to the Decembrist revolt; it had its clear origins as a national movement in the postwar reign of Alexander and even Paul I. The patriotism evoked by the French invasion and eventual reassertion of Orthodoxy evolved into a militant Russian nationalism led by a newly revitalized autocracy triumphant over the Decembrists and their ideals. From there it was only a short step to both the "Official Nationality" of Nicholas I and the doctrines of the Slavophiles. Like the old Muscovite ideology, both held that Russia was a special, even superior, civilization with a special destiny largely exempt from European principles of social and political organization.

The events of 1824–25 did not merely set the stage for Nicholas's reign but dealt a severe blow to the St. Petersburg idea from which it is still recovering. The clear line of development toward civil society for over a century beginning with Peter the Great and leading through Elizabeth, Catherine, and the young Alexander to the Decembrists was cut off, after which only occasional flickers would erupt until the post-Soviet era. Though the 19th century in Russia was one of intense intellectual and revolutionary ferment, it is characterized by the complete absence of liberal political and other intellectual thought inspired by the Western ideas that had matured in St. Petersburg from 1703 through 1825 and on which the world's modern, civil societies built themselves in the 19th and 20th centuries. Even the revolutionary political thought in the century between the Decembrists and the Russian Revolution, though it drew on then-fashionable Western (or at least German) thought and considered itself modern, was underpinned by traditional Muscovite notions of Russia's special nature and destiny, extreme mystical-religious devotion to a cause, and a messianism under which Russia would save the world.

But there is more to modernism than politics. In fact, the virtual shutdown of political possibilities caused many of Petersburg's best minds to seek alternative outlets in literature, literary criticism, scholarship, and culture. Though Nicholas sought to close Russia's window to the West, this would prove futile. From 1825 until the Russian Revolution, among the city's fertile minds and talented artists and writers, the latest trends in European culture and thought continued to mix with native ideas and traditions to produce original and modern creations. The traditions of the city's first century would pay handsome dividends in an unprecedented flowering of creativity that produced world-class literature, music, painting, and dance. St. Petersburg therefore shifts from being the vanguard of liberal political ideas to being the crucible of new and stunning Russian cultural achievements leading to the Silver Age at the beginning of the 20th century in which the city truly did equal or better Western Europe.

CHAPTER 9

Pushkin's St. Petersburg, Imperial St. Petersburg

A century—and that city young,
Gem of the Northern world, amazing,
From gloomy wood and swamp upsprung,
Had risen, in pride and splendour blazing . . .
To that young capital is drooping
The crest of Moscow on the ground,
A dowager in purple, stooping
Before an empress newly crowned.
I love thee, city of Peter's making.

PUSHKIN, *The Bronze Horseman*[1]

He is the soul of our people.

ALEXANDER TVARDOVSKY, at the 125th anniversary
of Pushkin's death

Two men above all others defined St. Petersburg in the second quarter of the 19th century: Alexander Pushkin and Nicholas I, the Poet and the Tsar. Their fates were intertwined, and each left his mark on the city. Some call the age Pushkin's Petersburg, but it also marked the height of Imperial St. Petersburg. This era began symbolically when the two first met right after Nicholas's coronation, which had taken place on August 22, 1826, in Moscow. During the post-coronation celebrations, Nicholas sent for Pushkin, who was still living in exile at his Michailovskoe estate for writing antigovernment poems. Pushkin was lucky to be around to be invited, because only his superstitions had saved him from the fate of his Decembrist friends.

Pushkin liked to tell the story of how he almost ended up on Senate Square on the day of the uprising. When he learned of Alexander I's death, he decided to visit his friends in Petersburg. Although he was still barred from the capital, he hoped that in the commotion surrounding Alexander's death and funeral nobody would notice him. He planned to take precautions by traveling at night and not staying in hotels, and once in Petersburg he would go directly to the apartment of his poet friend, Kondraty Ryleev, who lived quietly and outside of high society, and stay there. Only his closest friends would know he was in town. After instructing his servant to prepare for departure, Pushkin took a carriage to his neighbors to bid farewell, but on the way a hare dashed across the road in front of his coach—a bad omen. On the way back home another hare crossed the road, but Pushkin kept his resolve to go to Petersburg. When he returned home, however, he learned that the servant who was supposed to go with him had suddenly been stricken with white fever. Desperate, Pushkin ordered another servant to accompany him. Finally he set off, but just then he saw a priest coming to see him, yet another bad omen. This was the last straw, so he turned back and stayed at Michailovskoe. Had he continued to Petersburg, he would have arrived at Ryleev's apartment late on December 13, the eve of the Decembrist uprising, when the conspirators held their famous meeting at Ryleev's apartment. In that case, Pushkin certainly would have joined them on Senate Square. Thus, two hares, a servant, and a priest had saved Pushkin from Siberia.

When news of the uprising reached Pushkin, he knew he was in trouble and expected to be summoned to Petersburg for interrogation. But nothing happened. In May, once the investigation was over, Pushkin wrote to Nicholas asking forgiveness for his youthful indiscretions and to end his exile. Pushkin promised never to join a secret society or express antigovernment opinions.[2] But by July Pushkin still had no response, and confided his fears in a letter to his friend, Prince Peter Viazemsky: "I don't have high hopes. It is true that I never liked uprisings and revolutions, but I was in contact with almost everybody and corresponded with many of the conspirators. . . . If I were called to stand before the Commission, I would have cleared my name, but I was left alone, and I do not think that this is a good sign."[3] The silence continued through August, but early in September a messenger from Nicholas arrived with orders to bring Pushkin to Moscow. At that moment Pushkin was sitting by the fireplace, and when he was told that the messenger had arrived from Moscow he thought he was being arrested. He grabbed his papers and threw them into the fire, burning his notes and many poems. The messenger informed Pushkin that they must depart for Moscow immediately. There was no time to pack any bags. Pushkin grabbed some money, put on his coat, and off they went.

THE TSAR

Nicholas Romanov, the third son of Paul I and Maria Fedorovna, was born in June 1796. Even as a baby he had an exceptional physique. This pleased his grandmother, Catherine the Great, who said that "in all my life I have never seen such a knight."[4] To Baron Grimm she wrote: "I have become the grandmother of a third grandson who is also, I think, destined, thanks to his unusual strength, to reign, even though he does have two older brothers."[5] Indeed, although Nicholas was

Alexander's brother, he was 19 years younger and practically from a different generation. Both Catherine and Paul died too soon after his birth to have any influence on him. Empress Maria Fedorovna, in whose care Nicholas grew up, was no intellectual match for Catherine the Great, and Nicholas's early teachers were Baltic German women from military families. From 1800 his governor was Count M. I. Lansdorf, a military man from Courland of little learning but who had gained Paul's favor. Slated for an army career, Nicholas grew up in a military atmosphere, and like Paul and Alexander he became enamored of military drill, parades, and other military trivia. Maria Fedorovna tried to combat this fascination and insisted that he and his younger brother Michael wear civilian clothes and study the sciences at the university level. Nicholas also liked to draw and had a talent for it. He even taught himself how to engrave his drawings, which can still be seen at the Russian National Library, and his paintings could pass for the work of a professional artist. He knew four languages, liked to read, and played the flute well. But his first love remained the military.

To complete his education, Nicholas traveled all over Russia and Europe, as was the custom at the time. In England, ostensibly on a mission from Alexander, he was supposed to observe the English constitutional system in action. Although Nicholas enjoyed England's aristocratic countryside estates, he was nonplussed by its political institutions and spent most of his time in the company of British army officers. In Prussia, however, he was impressed by the country's order and militarism, which he would later emulate in Russia.

In Berlin Nicholas met Princess Charlotte, the daughter of the Prussian King Frederic-Wilhelm III. They fell in love and in 1817, she converted to Orthodoxy under the name Alexandra Fedorovna, and they were married in St. Petersburg on Charlotte's 19th birthday in the chapel of the Winter Palace. Nicholas worshiped his wife, they had seven children whom he adored, and for many years he rigorously set aside about two hours a day for his family. Not long before her death, remembering her wedding day, Alexandra wrote: "I felt very, very happy when our hands were finally joined; I gave my life with complete trust into the hands of my Nicholas, and he never betrayed that trust."[6] Indeed, Nicholas had a strong moral fiber and work ethic, and was deeply religious. He had simple tastes, worked in modest surroundings, and regarded the ostentation of court life as a duty rather than a pleasure. In his study he kept only a desk, sofa, simple chairs and tables, a cot with a straw-filled leather pallet on which he always slept, and a few personal mementos.

If within his family Nicholas was kind and loving, in public he bore a different countenance, revealingly described by a contemporary:

Nature has endowed him with one of the best gifts she is able to give those whom destiny has endowed with a high place: he has a most noble appearance. His usual expression reflects something stern and even forbidding. His smile is the smile of condescension rather than the result of a cheerful disposition or of fondness. His habit of dominating these feelings has become so much a part of his being that you will not notice in him any sense of constraint, nothing out of place, nothing overly studied, although his every word, like his every movement is measured, as if he were reading from a musical score. There is something unusual about [him]: he speaks with animation, simplicity and to the point; everything he says is intelligent; there is not a single vulgar joke, never a single funny or inappropriate word. Neither in the tone of his voice nor in the structure of his speech is there anything that would reflect pride or secretiveness. Yet you sense that his heart is closed, that the barrier is insurmountable, and that it would be foolish to try to penetrate to the depth of his thinking or to expect his complete trust.[7]

The Marquis de Custine perceived much the same, remarking that Nicholas "cannot smile at the same time with the eyes and mouth, a want of harmony which denotes perpetual constraint. . . . Nicholas . . . desires to be obeyed, where others desire to be loved."[8]

Suspicious of, but otherwise disinterested in the West, Nicholas loved his homeland and his subjects dearly and was committed to serving them as best he knew how, but only according to his own beliefs. What were they? Whereas Catherine and Alexander had struggled to justify autocratic rule using Western political theory, Nicholas had no doubts or qualms: He had received his power to govern directly from God and was accountable only to Him for his actions, just as his subjects had to submit without question to their Emperor and serfs had to bow to their masters. Nicholas also regarded Orthodox Russia not as part of Europe but as fundamentally different and superior. To him, Russia was naturally the supreme power among nations, as well as the repository of the most perfect morality and justice. Therefore, it was only proper that Russia stand as the arbiter of Europe, and he supported Alexander's Holy Alliance. Affairs at home and abroad must be kept in good order through the military and a large state bureaucracy, which also should be run in a military fashion. Nicholas had stated his views early on in a famous letter to his betrothed Charlotte:

Here [in the army] there is order. . . . All things flow logically one from the other. No one here commands without first learning to obey. No one rises above anyone else except through a clearly-defined system. Everything is subordinated to a single, defined goal, and everything has its precise designations. That is why I shall always hold the title of soldier in high esteem. I regard all human life as being nothing more than service because everyone must serve.[9]

THE POET

Alexander Pushkin was born on May 26, 1799, only three years after Nicholas. On his father's side he belonged to one of Russia's oldest noble families. Five of his ancestors signed the name of Pushkin on a document in 1613 electing the first Romanov Tsar, Michael. On his mother's side he traced his lineage to Abram Hannibal, an African boy of a princely descent, who in his eighth year was abducted to

Constantinople, where the Russian Ambassador rescued him and sent him to Peter the Great, who immediately took a liking to the boy. When Hannibal grew up, he studied in France and became the best military engineer in Russia. He also had a talent for writing, which Pushkin inherited from him together with his passionate nature. Pushkin was never close to his parents, but he adored his nanny, Arina, who loved him like a son and told him many stories and fairy tales which captivated Pushkin's imagination, even as an adult when he stayed at Mikhailovskoe. Pushkin's connection with rural Russia shone in his works, helped him advance the Russian language, and endeared him to aristocrat and commoner alike.

In 1811 Pushkin was enrolled in the new Lyceum founded by Alexander I at Tsarskoe Selo. The Emperor wanted his younger brothers, Grand Dukes Nicholas and Mikhail, to attend the Lyceum, but Maria Fedorovna categorically rejected the idea. Had Alexander gotten his way, Pushkin and Nicholas would have been schoolmates. Instead, Pushkin's most memorable schoolmates and friends were several future Decembrists. He held these friendships dear to his heart until the day he died, but now, in 1826, he had to explain this to Nicholas, and his loyalty to his friends would be tested.

Fortunately, while still at the Lyceum Pushkin also became friends with Vasily Zhukovsky, then Russia's leading poet, who became like a father and mentor to him. Zhukovsky quickly recognized Pushkin's genius, writing to Prince Peter Viazemsky that Pushkin "is the hope of our literature. . . . We should all unite in order to help grow this future giant, who will outgrow us all."[10] Nicholas liked and trusted Zhukovsky, and hired him as tutor to his son, the future Alexander II. Zhukovsky was thus in a position to protect Pushkin and intervene on his behalf with the Tsar.

Pushkin was about five feet, six inches tall, with dark curly hair and blue eyes. He was not classically handsome. Early in his life he reportedly looked in the mirror and exclaimed: "What a monkey!" Indeed, the censor Alexander Nikitenko* noted that "at first glance nothing about him stands out. . . . and you will search in vain for evidence of a poet's gift, until you see his eyes. But his eyes instantly arrest you: In them you see the rays of that fire which burns in his poems—wonderful, like a bouquet of fresh spring roses, resonant, full of strength and feeling."[11] Indeed, when he was in a good mood, his eyes sparkled and his face became beautiful, and he shone as a witty conversationalist. Add to this his poetry and he was irresistible to women, who loved him passionately. Pushkin loved them too, seemingly was al-

---

*Nikitenko, born in 1804 as a serf of Count Sheremetev, was determined to gain his freedom and become well educated. He was freed in 1824 with the help of Ryleev and other future Decembrists so that he could enter St. Petersburg University (forbidden to serfs). He eventually became a professor at the University and also a censor for Nicholas. Throughout his life he kept a diary, a compelling account of his life and the times. He lived to see the abolition of serfdom in 1861. His youth is described in A. Nikitenko, *Up from Serfdom: My Childhood and Youth in Russia 1804–1824* (New Haven, 2001).

ways in love, and kept a list of the women he loved (known as his *Don Juan* list), which was long. His amorous nature inspired him to write some of the best love poems ever written. He was also very perceptive and understood the depths of human nature. A free and colorful spirit, he dreamed of traveling to far away places, but never was allowed to do so. He loved to gamble, carouse, and fight duels, which only enhanced his reputation and fame. He became a celebrity sought by all, comparable to today's movie stars, and he died the most famous man in Russia.

As a boy, Pushkin, together with a friend, visited a famous fortune-teller, who predicted that he would be very famous, get money unexpectedly, receive an unusual proposition, be exiled, and die at the hands of a blond-haired man. When Pushkin and his friend left the fortune-teller, they joked about it, but within only a few days two of the predictions came true, and then he became famous. Now he was in exile. As his carriage hurtled toward Moscow and his reckoning with the Tsar, he wondered whether Nicholas, who had blond hair, would bring him death.

THE FIRST MEETING

When Pushkin arrived in Moscow on September 8, he was immediately escorted, dirty, in his traveling clothes, and unshaven, into the Chudov Palace at the Kremlin, where Nicholas was staying with his family. In his pocket Pushkin carried a copy of his unfinished subversive poem *The Prophet*, which as then drafted ended with God speaking to the prophet and alluding to the hanged Decembrists:

> *Arise, Prophet of Russia*
> *Don your shroud of shame,*
> *Go, the noose around your neck,*
> *To face the execrable assassin.*

If Nicholas decided to send him to Siberia, he would give the copy to the Emperor and go out in a blaze of glory.

But Nicholas thought of himself as noble and gracious, and wanted to repair his damaged reputation with Russia's educated elite in the wake of his punishing the Decembrists only two months before. Nicholas knew that Pushkin had not been involved in the conspiracy and had not known about it, but from the testimony and papers of the Decembrists Nicholas also knew that Pushkin's powerful poetry had helped inspire the Decembrists to action. Perhaps Nicholas wanted to understand what made Pushkin tick, but most of all he realized that Pushkin could still be a dangerous man. Both Zhukovsky and Karamzin had already appealed to Nicholas's noble side, arguing that pardoning Pushkin would be an ornament to his new reign, while punishing him would alienate educated society. Thus, Nicholas was in a mood to be gracious, if only Pushkin would meet him halfway. But Pushkin had resolved on the bold, honest, and noble approach that had worked so well years before with Governor Miloradovich.

Pushkin was escorted into the Emperor's office, where they met alone for over two hours. Unfortunately, neither left his own account of the meeting. What we have was written by Pushkin's friends and their accounts differ somewhat, but it went something like this: The Emperor greeted him: "Hello, Pushkin, are you pleased to be home?" Pushkin answered politely. Nicholas then asked what he was writing. "Hardly anything, Your Majesty. The censor is very strict." Not wishing to founder on such questions, Nicholas quickly moved to the main point: "You were friendly with a number of the men I sent to Siberia, were you not?" "Yes, Your Majesty, I esteemed many of them and my feelings toward them have not changed." "Would you have taken part in the rebellion of December 14 if you had been in Petersburg?" Nicholas asked. "I certainly would have, Your Majesty. All my friends were in on the conspiracy and I could not have stayed out of it. It was my absence alone that saved me, for which I thank God," Pushkin replied. "You have been foolish long enough," Nicholas remarked. "I hope you will be more sensible after this, and there will be no more quarrels between us. You will send everything you write to me. From now on, I shall be your censor." We do not know what else they talked about at that long meeting, but almost certainly about Russia, its fate, and its future. Reportedly Nicholas sought to impress the young poet by seeking his opinion about his planned reforms, perhaps hoping that Pushkin would see him as a reformer like Peter the Great. The Tsar and the Poet, of course, were very different, as was their purpose in life. But they both valued in people, above all else, goodness, directness, and honesty, qualities extremely rare in those days, but which each of them possessed. And that would lie at the heart of their unusual relationship.

When they were finished, Nicholas proudly escorted Pushkin into the adjoining room and declared to the assembled guests: "Gentlemen, here is the new Pushkin for you. Let us forget about the old." That evening, he would proudly tell guests at a ball, "Today I had a long conversation with the most intelligent man in Russia: Pushkin."

For his part, the disheveled Pushkin was also touched and rushed out of the Tsar's offices with tears in his eyes. "How I would like to hate him! But what can I do? For what can I hate him?" he thought. Pausing to catch his breath on the staircase, he thrust his hand into his pocket. *The Prophet* was gone! Had he left it in Nicholas's study? But then he looked down on the staircase and saw that it had fallen out only a moment earlier. A few days later he penned a lighter ending to the poem:

> *Arise, prophet, listen and behold!*
> *Fill yourself with my will*
> *And travel, over land and sea*
> *To burn my will into people's hearts.*

Pushkin stayed in Moscow for two months and became the talk of the town. Everybody who was anybody knew him, everyone was interested in him, and wherever he went he was the center of attention. When he came to the theater, the audience watched him and not the performance on stage. Pushkin's years in exile were finally over, and he soon returned to St. Petersburg to create his masterpieces. The city would become his world, the stage that he would fill with unforgettable, fantastic characters, blending reality with fiction.

IMPERIAL ST. PETERSBURG

Nicholas inherited Russia from Alexander I in the midst of turmoil, and the scope of the problems he faced shocked him. He was unprepared and at first unwilling to rule, but after surviving the uprising he concluded that this was God's will. His dreams of a quiet happy family life and military career over, Nicholas resolved to do his best, and, equipped with his motto "Firmness and Hope," he set to work. He began his day early. In the winter, people walking past the Winter Palace around 7:00 A.M. could see the Emperor working at his desk by candlelight, reading and signing mounds of papers. At 9:00 A.M. ministers came with their reports. In the afternoon, he inspected educational institutions, workshops, barracks, and other establishments.

Nicholas, like Alexander, at the outset of his reign formed an informal committee of close associates outside of the formal state apparatus, known as the Committee of December 6 (St. Nicholas's Day, when it was formed), to study the state of affairs and set his policy agenda. Nicholas kept in his study his bound volume of testimony from the Decembrists, in which they had frankly spoken out on what was wrong in Russia, and he consulted it often. He also traveled the country widely early in his reign in order to survey its condition. It was not good. Russia's social and economic system was backward and falling behind the rapidly industrializing West, the aristocracy was on its way to economic ruin, and state administration was in disarray and rife with corruption and arbitrariness. Russia's prominence in Europe was due only to its armies.

Unfortunately, Nicholas was incapable of understanding either the problem or what needed to be done and never developed solutions. His beliefs did not allow him to question the fundamental soundness of Russia's social and political order. In 1833 his principles were officially crystallized into the doctrine of Official Nationality, consisting of the trinity of Orthodoxy, Autocracy, and Nationality. Other than to try and find ways to free the serfs, Nicholas dealt only with details of administration and never contemplated fundamental reforms. Even his greatest accomplishment, Speransky's law code of 1833, was essentially a compilation and reorganization of prior laws, not a legal reform. He developed a proclivity for the minutiae of military and bureaucratic procedures to create at least the semblance of order. Eventually, Nicholas became the prisoner of his own bureaucratic machine and was misled as to the true condition of the nation. He never addressed the key question of avoiding arbitrariness in government, as was done in the West, by providing citizens with individual rights and political guarantees. Rather, he was convinced that Russia would resolve its challenges and prosper if Official Nationality was followed strictly, and believed that the main threat lay in subversive foreign ideas.

To combat subversion, in 1826 Nicholas formed the infamous Third Section of His Majesty's Own Chancery to serve as the ideological and political guardian of the nation. He gave it wide and vague powers, characterized by the probably apocryphal story that he once presented the Section's Chief, General Benckendorff, with a clean white handkerchief and announced, "Here are your orders. Take this and wipe away the tears of my people." Driven by bureaucratic careerism and the self-fulfilling notion that subversion must exist if the Emperor had formed the Section to root it out, the Section's zealous minions became ubiquitous. Mail was opened, spies were everywhere, and books were censored. Nicholas, as God's anointed representative, thought himself an expert on everything from the army to art, and considered it his government's right to interfere in anything. This view rubbed off on the Third Section's overzealous agents who often got out of hand and began to open the mail even of members of the Imperial family. Yet there was never an atmosphere of terror. Nicholas's reign is much maligned for repression, but in fact there were relatively few arrests, very few were imprisoned or exiled in comparison to some reigns of the 18th century, and executions were virtually unheard of. Rather, everyone simply knew the rules and usually abided by them.

Nicholas's fear of sedition and foreign ideas also affected higher education. Philosophy and other liberal arts faculties were cut back. The curriculum now focused on technical subjects (as a result of which there were notable scientific achievements) and on training government bureaucrats, for which there was such a need that the number of university students quickly multiplied. But higher education was to be only for the few that the government needed. In 1826 Nicholas proposed a law preventing peasant children from attaining higher education, which might enable them "to rise above their station,"[12] but the more enlightened Victor Kochubei, Alexander I's former confidante, convinced him to control university admissions instead. Observing that young aristocrats studying in Europe "return from there with a spirit of criticism," Nicholas also limited study abroad.[13] He decreed that students sent abroad must be of "pure Russian background" and that students between the ages of 10 and 18 must study within Russia.[14] Nicholas had no interest in St. Petersburg being Russia's window to the West, and the window did close somewhat. But the ever increasing contact between Petersburgers and Europeans, whether through travel, education, commerce, or in the arts and literature, was a tide that could not be stopped. In the end, Nicholas only alienated educated society and denied Russia the benefits of government collaboration with it.

Russia under Nicholas became a complex bureaucracy. The government was small through the late 18th century, but the military bureaucracy expanded greatly during the war against Napoleon, the civil bureaucracy began growing quickly late in Alexander's reign, and the trend only accelerated under Nicholas. Between 1800 and 1850 the size of the state bureaucracy increased fivefold,[15] and at the heads of most civil ministries Nicholas appointed trusted military men. By 1855, the number of officials in the Table of Ranks had risen to over 82,000,[16] most of whom lived in and around the capital. To this must be added a large number of petty clerks and copyists who labored at the most menial tasks. The avalanche of paperwork became numbing. In the Ministry of the Interior alone, in a single year (1849) over 31 million official papers were produced,[17] and each one had to be signed, sealed, copied by hand, delivered, and registered according to procedures prescribed in volumes of regulations. By the early 1840s, the backlog of unresolved decrees and matters not acted upon in the state apparatus exceeded 3.3 million.[18]

At the center of this vast machinery stood Imperial St. Petersburg, which was dominated by the military and a parallel army of bureaucrats. The city's new public buildings—however magnificent on the outside—inside were dark, cavernous warrens piled with mountains of files overseen by petty bureaucrats overseeing armies of copyists and clerks. Messengers hurriedly delivered documents along long corridors, to government offices across town, or out to the provinces. The Marquis de Custine described the city's morning street scenes:

> The movements of the men whom I met appeared stiff and constrained; every gesture expressed a will which was not their own. The morning is the time for commissions and errands, and not one individual appeared to be walking on his own account. . . . Now appears a cavalry officer passing at full gallop to *bear an order* to some commanding officer; then a chasseur carrying *an order* to some provincial governor, perhaps at the other extremity of the empire. . . . Next are seen foot soldiers returning from exercise to their quarters, in order to *receive orders* from their captain. This automaton population resembles one side of a chessboard, where a single individual causes the movements of all the pieces, but where the adversary is invisible. One neither moves nor respires here except by an imperial order; consequently everything is dull, formal, and spiritless.[19]

More than ever, Petersburg itself became a mecca for provincials who left family and friends to seek fame and fortune, or just to bask vicariously in this picturesque center of imperial glory, mystery, and intrigue. The novelist Mikhail Saltykov-Shchedrin captured this attraction in his *Diary of a Provincial in St. Petersburg:* "We provincials somehow turn our steps towards Petersburg instinctively. . . . It is as if Petersburg all by itself, with its name, its streets, its fog, rain, and snow, could resolve something or shed light on something." Legions of lowly clerks eked out a lonely and wretched subsistence, living in crowded flats on meager salaries that were a small fraction of what their superiors earned. "I still do not understand why I came to St. Petersburg," confided one provincial to his diary. "Among the city's half million inhabitants, I had not a single friend or acquaintance."[20]

With this influx of bureaucrats, the city's population exploded, and in fact surpassed that of Moscow a few years before the French invasion. From 220,000 residents in 1800, the figure rose to about 300,000 in 1811 (compared to 275,000 in Moscow), and about 524,000 by 1853, all the while maintaining about a two-to-one ratio of men to women.[21] As a result of Nicholas's xenophobic policies, the number of foreigners in the city, which had stood at 35,000 in 1818 (about 10% of the population), scarcely rose during Nicholas's reign; only the numbers of Germans increased while the presence of most other nationalities declined.[22]

The armies of officials revered their Emperor and believed that their machine was working toward some great purpose that they could not hope to comprehend. They labored with the utmost seriousness and air of urgency, each hoping to be noticed by his superior and get ahead. But movement often was mistaken for progress. The burden of bureaucratic minutiae became so overwhelming that officials could not focus on their main tasks and deal with the real challenges. Even Nicholas might wait months for action in response to his requests, and he soon began operating through committees of trusted aides functioning outside the formal bureaucracy.

CITY ARCHITECTURE UNDER NICHOLAS I

Nicholas's reign saw the last of Petersburg's great civic architecture sponsored by the crown. Alexander's style never quite suited him, as it was derived from classical antiquity and the West rather than Russia. He finished Alexander's projects and then, consistent with Official Nationality, looked back to Muscovy to promote a revival of old Russian styles. Fortunately this style never took hold in Petersburg, and the examples of it there are few.

Carlo Rossi spent his last active years working for Nicholas. His main project for the new Emperor was Senate Square, which had to be redesigned since it was conspicuously at odds with Zakharov's new Admiralty bordering the Square and did not measure up to the Empire style and the government's needs. But nothing was done on Senate Square until Rossi's General Staff Building on Palace Square was a confirmed success. In 1827 Nicholas ordered a competition for a redesign of Senate Square based on that model. Not surprisingly, Rossi's design won, and the project was built in 1829–34. Like his General Staff Building, the design called for two buildings linked by a central arch (this time spanning Galernaya Street) and extending along the entire west side of the square. The Senate would occupy the building nearest to the Neva, and the Synod would take the other. Rossi designed the front corner of the Senate building by the river to be curved and faced it with prominent white columns because it extended closer to the river than the Admiralty's wings and thus functioned to close the perspective from the corner of the Winter Palace and the Palace Embankment.

Rossi's greatest masterpiece was the ensemble on Alexandrinskaya Square on the southwest side of Nevsky Prospect between the Public Library and the Anichkov Palace. At its center stands the Alexandrinsky Theater (now the Pushkin Theater). In 1811 Alexander decided to build a theater on the site and a competition was announced, but the war interfered. By 1816 Rossi was working on his plan which encompassed not merely a theater but a redevelopment of the whole area from Nevsky to the Fontanka. The plan went through many variations, and Nicholas approved the final design only in 1828. Rossi had difficulty getting approval for his novel use of iron rafters in the theater, but convinced the skeptical bureaucrats after volunteering to be hanged from them in case of an accident.[23] The theater building was finished in 1832. Its dramatic front façade features six unfluted Corinthian columns with statues of muses in niches on either side, all crowned by a chariot of Apollo; similarly dramatic porticos grace either side of the building.

On the north side of Alexandrinskaya Square in front of the theater Rossi built an extension of the Public Library with a long row of Ionic columns, between which stand statues of ancient poets and philosophers, conforming the façade to that of the original library building on the corner of Nevsky. On the south side of the Square he built two small garden pavilions, one of them right on Nevsky Prospect. Eventually, in 1873, a memorial statue to Catherine the Great was erected in the center of the Square, and in 1923 the Square was renamed Ostrovsky Square in honor of the great Russian dramatist. Behind the theater leading to what Rossi designed as Chernishev (now Lomonosov) Square on the Fontanka, Rossi built Theater Street (in 1923 renamed Rossi Street) with two long columned government buildings along either side. In 1836 the Imperial School of Ballet moved into one of them, where it has remained ever since, producing such legends as Anna Pavlova, Rudolf Nureyev, and Mikhail Baryshnikov. Rossi Street is unique in its proportions, as its width (22 meters) equals the height of the buildings on either side, and the street's length of 220 meters is exactly 10 times that.

The edifice which completed the west end of the city's central squares, St. Isaac's Cathedral, was the work of Auguste Montferrand, and it was being constructed throughout Nicholas's reign. In 1815 Alexander I decided to replace Rinaldi's old and deteriorating St. Isaac's Cathedral with a massive landmark boasting a large dome that would dominate the city's skyline like St. Paul's in London or St. Peter's in Rome. In 1817 a competition was held and a design of Montferrand was selected. Montferrand, formerly in Napoleon's Imperial Guard, had arrived in St. Petersburg in 1816 with little or no architectural or building experience. But he was an excellent draftsman who could produce beautiful and appealing drawings of projects. For the competition Montferrand submitted a beautiful album with attractive drawings depicting the cathedral according to various classical and national styles, including those of China and India. Through the help of his patron and countryman at Alexander's court, Augustine Béthencourt, Montferrand's designs got Alexander's attention and he was hastily appointed as architect of the project.

This choice bewildered the city's community of seasoned architects, who could not understand how an unknown neophyte could receive the most important commission in town. When Montferrand made his drawings public in 1820, his critics had a field day and quickly identified serious defects in the designs. In 1824 a committee was formed to investigate and actually held a new competition for designs, but Montferrand outflanked his enemies and saved his appointment by correcting the problems while preserving the basic design that Alexander had so liked; his critics were relegated to making minor improvements. Because of the difficulties in design, a succession of changes by Nicholas I, and the cathedral's vast size, work dragged on for over 30 more years and was completed only on May 30, 1858, just a month before the architect's death. The aged and ill architect was unable to attend the ceremony, but at least the cathedral's dome could be seen from his window. Montferrand's last wish was to be entombed in his cathedral, which in Western Europe was something of a tradition amongst architects of churches and cathedrals. But Alexander II would not permit this, considering it too high an honor for a mere architect. Instead, at his funeral, attended by his colleagues and ordinary laborers on the cathedral, its doors were opened and the strains of choral music filled the square outside. Then his body was carried once around the cathedral and then to rest in St. Catherine's (Catholic) Church on Nevsky Prospect; his body was taken to Paris, where he was buried at a location now unknown.[24] But on the west portico the presence of Montferrand lives on in the form of a sculpture of him presenting a model of the cathedral to St. Isaac, in which he is the only figure present not bowing his head to the saint.

The cathedral is indeed massive (the heaviest building in the city) and its grand gold dome does dominate the city's skyline. Its design attacked the difficult problem of building an Orthodox Church in classical style. It also stands, together with the Marble Palace and Kazan Cathedral, as one of the few architectural monuments of St. Petersburg built in natural stone rather than brick and painted plaster. Its footprint is slightly rectangular, while each of its walls has a large central portico modeled on the Pantheon in Rome featuring massive granite columns 54 feet high and seven feet thick and large bronze doors. The cathedral's interior plan is that of a Greek cross with a large central dome and four subsidiary domes in a square around it, which was traditional in Orthodox churches. Its stately interior is mainly marble and features a guilded iconostasis over 200 feet long.

As St. Isaac's Cathedral rose, St. Isaac's Square to the south had to be redesigned, as it had a triangular shape and narrowed to nothing where Voznesensky Prospect crosses the Moika. Rossi originally thought he would be building a palace for Grand Duke Mikhail just at that point across the Moika, but nothing was done until Nicholas retained the Russian Andrei Shtakenschneider to build on the same site the Mariinsky Palace for his eldest daughter Maria in 1839–44. The Square was then opened up and two ministry buildings were also built on the east and west sides. The Blue Bridge over the Moika (named after the color of the original wooden drawbridge on the site) was widened to make it part of the square in front of the palace, which at 100 meters wide became the widest bridge in the city.

Once the square was opened up, it needed a monument in its center, and after the death of Nicholas I a bronze equestrian statue of him by the sculptor Peter Klodt was erected in 1859. It depicts Nicholas I on his mount, mildly rearing, so that the statue has only two points of support. It stands atop a high base that frames bronze reliefs depicting Nicholas's glories, around which sit four allegorical female bronze statues of Wisdom, Strength, Justice, and Faith, whose faces are those of his wife and three daughters. A controversy arose over which direction the statue should face. The Synod objected to the horse's and Nicholas's backsides facing the cathedral, while Maria had the same objection as to herself and her palace. The Synod won out, Maria was insulted, and thereafter she refused to live in the palace. The statue also naturally invited comparison with the Bronze Horseman of Peter the Great "ahead" of Nicholas on the other side of St. Isaac's. According to legend, on the morning after the unveiling, a wooden sign was placed on the statue with the words, "You'll never catch him."

The last architect to embody Alexander's Empire style and Nicholas's militarism was Vasily Stasov (1769–1848). Alexander sent him to study in England, France, and Italy for six years, and he arrived in St. Petersburg in 1808. He first worked on renovations and small buildings at Oranienbaum, Peterhof, and Tsarskoe Selo, and eventually received his largest commission, the Pavlovsky Barracks on the west side of the Field of Mars in 1816–19. Under Nicholas, he also built the Trinity Cathedral for the Izmailovsky Regiment on Izmailovsky Prospect (1827–35), the Church of the Transfiguration for the Preobrazhensky Regiment near the Tauride Palace (1827–29), the Narva Gate on the road to Peterhof commemorating the victory of 1812 (dedicated in 1834), and on Tsarskoe Selo Road (now Moscow Prospect) the cast iron Moscow Triumphal Gate (1834–38) commemorating Nicholas's victory over the Turks in 1828.

While Nicholas's Slavic revival style flourished in Moscow, in Petersburg it had little appeal. Except for a few churches, most examples lie outside of town at the imperial estates, such as the Nicholas Cottage at Peterhof (1834). By that time most important architectural commissions were for either the homes and palaces of wealthy nobles and merchants or commercial buildings constructed with private capital, whose owners had their own tastes. The crown could not impose uniform designs on private citizens, and in the 1840s Nicholas repealed all such requirements. From then on, builders in the city only had to comply with building codes and zoning ordinances. As a result, the variety of styles proliferated. Some private buildings, such as Shtakenschneider's Beloselsky-Belozersky Palace on the corner of Nevsky and the Fontanka, were magnificent and still grace the city, but most were unremarkable. Also, a revolution in building materials had begun; buildings and other structures with iron and steel frames, often exposed as in the case of factories, railway stations, and bridges, made their appearance. Fortunately, the city's historical center was already essentially complete and the new styles did not significantly alter its appearance.

One of these modern iron structures was the first permanent bridge across the Neva, built in 1842–50 by Stanislav Kerbedz to connect the English Embankment with Vasilievsky Island just below the Academy of Fine Arts. It features a cast iron grille below the railing, which began the tradition of such grilles on the bridges over the Neva. Originally called Annunciation Bridge and after Nicholas's death Nicholas Bridge, in 1918 it was renamed Lieutenant Schmidt Bridge.

Under Nicholas the city and Russia saw its first railroad. Since Nicholas did not encourage rapid industrialization, he did not appreciate the value of a railway network, even for military use, so at first he rejected proposals to build one as too costly. His Finance Minister even considered railroads a danger to public morals because they would encourage "frequent purposeless travel, thus fostering the restless spirit of our age."[25] But finally Nicholas agreed to build Russia's first railway, a short line linking St. Petersburg with Tsarskoe Selo with a spur to Pavlovsk, which opened in 1837. This hardly served the nation's economy, and critics remarked that the line's only function was to "connect the capital with the cabaret." Indeed, the station complex at Tsarskoe Selo, designed by an English architect, featured a concert hall and expansive pleasure gardens named after those at Vauxhall in London. (Thus the word *vokzal* became the Russian word for railroad station.) Finally, in 1842, Nicholas approved a rail line between St. Petersburg and Moscow. It took nearly a decade to build, and service began in 1851. In Petersburg the line terminated at the south end of the main section of Nevsky Prospect, where the architect Constantine Ton built the Nikolaevsky Railway Station in 1844–51. The building remains today as Moscow Railway Station.

On December 17, 1837, Petersburg nearly lost its architectural centerpiece when the Winter Palace was consumed by a terrible fire. Nicholas was attending a French ballet at the Bolshoi Theater that evening when he learned that his palace was in flames. He quickly took Alexandra back to the Anichkov Palace in their carriage, then he mounted his horse and galloped down Nevsky to the burning Winter Palace, which by then was illuminating snowy Palace Square in an orange hue. He rushed into the flaming building to direct his Imperial Guards' efforts to save the palace's furnishings and other contents, which they piled up by the Alexander Column. When asked what papers he most wanted from his study, he said only the love letters from Alexandra that she had written to him as his fiancée. Once he saw that it was too dangerous to continue the rescue efforts, he ordered everyone to abandon the building. When the Guards continued to struggle amidst the flames to save a large mirror, Nicholas threw a pair of binoculars at it, shattering the glass. "See, lads," he cried, "your lives are worth more to me than a mirror, so I ask you to get out!"[26] The fire soon threatened the adjoining Hermitage and its art collections, which were saved only by destroying the two connecting passages to the Winter

Palace, by building a temporary wall between the buildings, and continuously dousing it with water from the frozen Neva and Moika Rivers. The paintings in the 1812 Gallery were safely removed, although the room was destroyed. In the end, virtually everything of value in the palace was saved, although the building burned on for three days and was nearly ruined. Nicholas vowed that the palace, which had taken Rastrelli eight years to build, would be rebuilt in little over a year—by Easter of 1839. He made good on the promise, but only at the cost of the lives of many workmen who toiled to exhaustion and in merciless heat generated to dry the new mortar and plaster more quickly. The project was headed by Vasily Stasov, who preserved most of the original plan and interior designs. With Petersburg's central shrine rebuilt as good as new, city life returned to normal.

LIFE IN THE IMPERIAL CITY

At least for the well-to-do in the capital, the reign of Nicholas I was a time of peace, stability, and prosperity. The memories of 1812 and the Decembrists soon faded in the minds of most, and there were no more wars or insurrections until the Crimean War of 1854–55. It was a gilded age in which Russia basked in the achievements and glories of the past before its underlying weaknesses were exposed. With the peasants still tied to the land in the provinces and Nicholas not promoting industrialization, the city was not yet marred by the industrial squalor and teeming masses of the proletariat associated with Dostoevsky's age onward. Even the city's floods were not serious. Fires still broke out, but none on the scale of the prior century.

The only citywide calamities during Nicholas's reign were two epidemics of cholera in 1831 and 1848. The first epidemic, which at its height claimed 600 lives per day and even by conservative official statistics ultimately claimed over 10,000 lives, reached St. Petersburg on June 14, 1831. "The city is in anguish," wrote the censor Alexander Nikitenko in his diary a few days later. "Almost all activity is disrupted. People emerge from their homes only in emergencies or when their duties require it."[27] Top government officials and the nobility withdrew to their residences in the outlying islands or more distant suburbs. The inner city was left to commoners and to police and soldiers charged with maintaining order. There were not nearly enough doctors or hospital beds, and corpses littered the streets and were collected each night. Wild rumors spread that there was no cholera, but only a plot by evil people or even the government, and that the doctors were poisoning patients.[28] On June 22 a riot erupted on Haymarket Square. To restore order, Nicholas himself sped to the city from Peterhof on his yacht and drove to the square, where, standing in his carriage, he bravely addressed the unruly mob. Unable to promise a solution, he adopted a stern tone, chastising the people for believing false stories, turning away from the religion of their forefathers and creating disorder, and telling them that they should be ashamed of themselves. The tactic worked and the crowd dispersed. The 1848 epidemic was even worse, infecting over 22,000 Petersburgers, of whom over 12,000 (one in 36) died.[29]

Despite the epidemics, the city's population grew rapidly, and with it the demand for goods and services. All basic goods and produce were inexpensive and abundant. The city's economy thrived as merchants traded their goods from Russia and abroad. Open markets teemed with peasants hawking their wares and produce, and large arcades of new shops opened. The most famous was the Passage department store on Nevsky Prospect, which opened in 1848, with two stories of fashionable stores and cafés under a glass-roofed arcade. Stylish customers came to buy stylish goods and socialize in the cafés to the strains of a small orchestra that played there daily. Scores of factories opened on the outskirts of town to produce goods for the city's new residents, which demanded still more workers from the provinces. But in Nicholas's time, the city was dominated by government servants and the military. When strangers met and asked about each other's professions, the question was not, as in Moscow, "What do you do?" but "Where do you serve?"[30] Even the city's famous writers and artists such as Pushkin, Gogol, Dostoevsky, and Glinka at one time or another held government jobs, and for some, like Alexander Griboyedov, government service remained their main profession.

When the weather was fair, the city's main streets—Nevsky, Admiralty Boulevard, and the English Embankment—turned into veritable stages where officers, aristocrats, and rich merchants promenaded and socialized in the afternoons and early evenings. Men dressed in top hats and tails and sported canes; officers and soldiers were in uniform and wore their swords. The ladies wore long dresses in the latest European fashion and carried parasols. Each year on the first of May, the arrival of the warm weather was celebrated by a mass public promenade attended by the Emperor at Ekaterinhof, which Governor Miloradovich had restored into a beautiful park. A traffic jam of carriages crowded the road there and back and in the "procession" through the park, where there was a restaurant, street food, music on bandstands, and fireworks. Commoners attended the festivities too, but off to the side from the main attractions, where they conducted themselves, in the words of a contemporary feuilletonist, "quietly and decorously."[31] During the rest of May until residents left for their summer residences, the Summer Garden, which now boasted Rossi's Coffee House, was the favorite place of the elite for a quiet stroll within the city. It was now a public park, but dress codes kept out the riffraff.

By June people of means who were not required to work in the summer moved out of the city to summer homes, usually taking with them large quantities of furniture and other household effects, as few families had enough to outfit two residences. The inner city during the summer was one of commoners, civil servants, and soldiers. Landowners went off to their estates in the provinces, while other aristocrats owned palaces or large country houses (*dachas*) on the "islands" or outside

Petersburg. The road to Peterhof was now studded with miles of estates perched along the ridge overlooking the Finnish Gulf. Closer in were the many palaces and *dachas* on Apothecary, Krestovsky, Elagin, and Kamenny Islands, which were close enough that one could still commute to work in the city center. The most prestigious island was Kamenny, where Nicholas maintained the royal summer palace. Each summer a community would come alive on that island. The pastime of promenading moved to Kamenny's embankments, performances were held in a new wooden theater built in 1827, and parties at the island's private residences complete with music, dancing, and fireworks became daily events.

The main social pastime in the cold months was balls and masquerades. Alexander had not been fond of them and held them only occasionally, but Nicholas revived them. He held royal balls on major Russian and family holidays such as Christmas and the anniversary of his accession, as well as on special occasions such as visits of foreign dignitaries. On New Year's Nicholas even opened the Winter Palace to a fête for some 30,000 ordinary residents of the city, where for several hours the Emperor and court mingled with craftsmen, shopkeepers, coachmen, and servants.

But Petersburg's balls were no longer focused or dependent on the court. Some were not even by invitation but were organized as charitable or commercial events for any member of the public who could afford a ticket. Beginning in 1830 such public balls were held at Vasily Engelhardt's large home on Nevsky Prospect to benefit the Philharmonic Society, but soon the Theater Directorate saw profit in such events, and after 1835 they were held in the Bolshoi Theater, where up to 12,000 revelers paying ten rubles a head could be accommodated on the stage, parterre (stripped of seats), and in the foyer.[32] Another favorite venue was Demidov Sad, an open-air garden with dancing and theater halls on what is now Decembrists Street. On Wednesdays and Sundays any member of the public could for one ruble attend a masquerade and dance; on some evenings one could also see acrobats, strongmen, or plays on such subjects as Captain Cook and "New Year's in India" performed by itinerant troupes of actors.

More impressive, however, were the many private balls and masquerades in the mansions of the rich, sometimes several in one evening. "Every day there are balls," wrote one party goer in February 1834. "Today at the Shuvalovs, tomorrow at the Lazarevs, and the French artists are giving a masquerade for some widow at which many also will gather; Wednesday at the Austrian ambassador's, on Friday at Prince Volkonsky's, on Saturday a children's masquerade at the Palace, and on Sunday they are preparing for a small ball in the Anichkov Palace as Prince Kochubei is no longer healthy and may not be able to give his usual day of dance that day."[33] Such balls were magnificent affairs, with both men and women dressed to impress, adorned with jewels, colorful hairdos with feathers, and satin dresses embellished with crepe and flowers. Guests danced, flirted, joked, gossiped, plotted, and watched each other attentively, because more than anything else, a ball was a performance in which all participants played their parts. Well-understood rules governed what was acceptable and what was not, the conversation had to be witty rather than profound, smiles and poses were rehearsed, and each movement of a lady's fan had a particular meaning. It was a sophisticated, often cruel game in which high society participated with abandon. Hosts also competed to outdo each other and spent lavishly, conspicuously, and carelessly. Pushkin noted in December 1833, when there was hunger in the countryside: "Kochubei and Nesselrode received [from the government] 200,000 rubles each to feed their hungry peasants, but this 400,000 remains in their pockets. . . . Society grumbles, but at Nesselrode's and Kochubei's there will be balls."[34]

The fall and winter seasons were also the height of smaller private evenings and entertainments, highlighted by the many salons and "literary evenings" held in the homes of notable socialites, literati, and intelligentsia. Social life in the city was dominated by circles of friends and acquaintances having common occupations or common interests. Thus, the playwright and director of the Russian troupe Alexander Shakhovsky would host the city's actors, playwrights, and theater enthusiasts at his penthouse apartment near the Bolshoi Theater. After the historian Karamzin died in 1826, his widow Catherine began hosting what became the leading salon in the city, frequented by the cream of the city's aristocrats and Russian and foreign literati from about 10:00 P.M. until 1:00 or 2:00 A.M. There she continued the family tradition of hospitality, good manners, polite and elevated conversation, and light entertainment while the guests sipped tea. "These evenings were the only ones in Petersburg where people spoke Russian and did not play cards," remarked one contemporary. "At Karamzin's the topics of conversation were not philosophical, but neither were they empty Petersburg gossip or tales. . . . These evenings freshened and fed our minds and spirits, which in the stifling Petersburg atmosphere of the time was especially useful."[35] The salons were not the place for shop talk or serious debate, but rather witty banter and flirting, as portrayed eloquently by Pushkin in *Eugene Onegin*:

> *The conversation sparkled bright;*
> *The hostess kept the banter light*
> *and quite devoid of affectations;*
> *Good reasoned talk was also heard,*
> *But not a trite or vulgar word,*
> *no lasting truths or dissertations—*
> *And no one's ears were shocked a bit*
> *By all the flow of lively wit.*[36]

Still more interesting and important were the less formal literary "evenings" at the apartments of the city's most gifted writers and critics, including Vasily Zhukovsky, Anton Delvig, Peter Pletnev, and Vladimir Odoevsky. They rarely began before 11:00 P.M., and the conversation was more open and freewheeling. Zhukovsky's Saturday evenings at his home on Millionaya Street were the earliest, dating from 1818, and proved helpful to the careers of Gogol and the composer Mikhail Glinka. But the evenings hosted by Delvig, Pushkin's best friend from their Lyceum days, became the most important, held on Wednesdays and Sundays at his home on Zagorodny Prospect. Delvig always graced them by telling a story of his own, usually based on some scene or incident he had experienced in the city. Sometimes musicians, including Glinka, attended and performed before the intimate audience. But most importantly, the poets and writers read their latest poems, stories, plays or, as in the case of Ivan Krylov, fables. These gatherings provided the main opportunity for the city's literary elite to keep abreast of artistic and intellectual trends and happenings, exchange ideas to develop their art, and commiserate about the hand of the censor. Once at Zhukovsky's, the censor Alexander Nikitenko saw Nicholas's own mark-up of Pushkin's *Boris Godunov* with its many redactions. "That is what made many critics call the published play a collection of excerpts," he remarked.[37]

In the wintertime, sleigh races were held on the Neva on a course set up just above the *strelka* of Vasilievsky Island in front of the Winter Palace. Also popular, especially during Shrovetide, were the many tobogganing hills erected around the city on Admiralty Boulevard, the Field of Mars, on the Neva ice, and even on the outlying islands. Tobogganing was no longer the pastime of the court and nobility that had so terrified Mrs. Rondeau in Anna Ioannovna's time; now the aristocrats usually preferred to spectate while they took their daily walks. Shrovetide through Easter was also a popular time for street carnivals featuring skits, puppet shows, dancing bears, and other trained animals brought in from the provinces. Sometimes entire zoological exhibits came to town. In the 1830s a small permanent zoo was established featuring an African lion, a Bengal tiger, jaguars, zebras, gnus, hyenas, and a trained elephant. In 1827 a circus was established on the Fontanka Embankment at Simeonovsky (now Belinsky) Bridge on the site of Elizabeth's old labyrinth, where it remains to this day.

LITERARY ST. PETERSBURG:
THE WORLD OF PUSHKIN

On May 23, 1827, just three days before his 28th birthday, Pushkin returned to Petersburg to create his major works and become a legend. Until his marriage in 1831, he lived at the Demuth Hotel on the Moika, the most popular and famous hotel of its kind in St. Petersburg; Pushkin's friends Peter Chaadaev and Alexander Griboyedov also stayed there. When Pushkin returned to Petersburg, his friends embraced him warmly and he was welcomed everywhere, yet he felt deep sadness and emptiness because so many of his old friends were gone. Still, Pushkin had more friends than anybody else. They included actors, students, scholars, officers, and, of course, writers and poets. He went to the theater, drank and caroused with officers, played cards and dined at the English Club, and frequented salons and literary evenings at his friends' homes.

One such place was the home of the widow of his old friend Karamzin, the linguist, writer, and historian who had interceded on his behalf with Alexander in 1820 and again with Nicholas in 1826. But Karamzin had died on May 22, 1826, before Pushkin's famous meeting with Nicholas. Karamzin held a special place in Pushkin's heart, and he dedicated his historical tragedy *Boris Godunov* to him. Earlier in the century, Karamzin, a linguist on par with Lomonosov, together with poets such as Zhukovsky, had reformed the Russian language into a form suitable for modern literature. But conservatives thought that Russian had already been contaminated with too many innovations and foreign words, and wanted to remove them from the language and return to something akin to Church Slavonic. One of them, Admiral Shishkov, in 1811 had founded in St. Petersburg a society that he called the "Conversation of Lovers of the Russian Word," which held pompous and solemn gatherings in his home on the Fontanka. After one member wrote a comedy, *The Waters of Lipetsk*, parodying Zhukovsky, one of Zhukovsky's friends retorted with a pamphlet called *The Vision in the Cabaret at Arzamas*, named after a small town near Karamzin's estate. In 1815 Karamzin's modernists founded their own society, Arzamas, which Pushkin joined. Meeting at Karamzin's, the Arzamas writers and poets read and discussed their works and practiced their principle that patriotism and Orthodoxy should not dictate linguistic usage. The young modernists proved unstoppable and, building on the century of progress since Peter the Great, they ushered in the Golden Age of Russian poetry.

The Golden Age began with Zhukovsky himself, the illegitimate son of a rural landowner and a beautiful captured Turkish slave girl. He was the first of Russia's modern poets and the father of Russian Romanticism, but his reputation was built equally on his talents as a translator of classical and Western literature, through which Russians became familiar with Western Romantic works such as Byron's *Prisoner of Chillon*. Beyond his work, Zhukovsky was a noble and kind man, a gracious host, and always ready to help those in need. He unselfishly encouraged young talent, and spent many evenings patiently listening to the immature works of aspiring writers.

Pushkin also often met and was friends with two other notable writers of the time: the critic, playwright, and fabulist Ivan Krylov (1768–1844) and the playwright Alexander Griboyedov (1795–1829). Krylov was born in Moscow but moved to St. Petersburg in 1782, where he discovered his literary interests and talents. He began with satirical plays in the 1790s in the classical manner, including *The Fortune Teller from Coffee Grounds*, *The Mischief Makers*, *Dido*, and *Trumf*, and in the same period he founded and ran his own literary journals, including the *Mail of Spirits* (1789), *The Viewer* (1792), and *The St. Petersburg Mercury*. In 1806 he published his first volume of fables, and from that point concentrated on that genre.

Krylov had a unique talent for fables, which were reminiscent of Russian folk stories, and it is for these that he became so famous. By the time Krylov died, he was
so well loved that charitable donations poured in to erect a statue to him. Sculpted
by Peter Klodt in 1854, it depicts Krylov surrounded by animal characters from his
fables. It still stands in the Summer Garden.

   Griboyedov was born and educated in law in Moscow, served in the cavalry during the war with France, and then moved to St. Petersburg to join the foreign service in 1817. Griboyedov was an able diplomat with a successful career, and was
more a government official with an interest and talent for writing than a writer
who held a government job to make ends meet. Griboyedov's single famous work
before his untimely death was his play, *Gore ot Uma* (1824), usually translated either
as *Woe from Wit* or *The Misfortune of Being Clever*, although the Russian *um* connotes
not merely cleverness and wit but also a deeper intelligence and presence of mind.
It is a comedy in the classical style of the prior century, in rhymed verse, and is
more notable for its character portraits, social commentary, and witty aphorisms
(many of which remain on people's tongues today) than for its overall literary merit.
The title arises directly from the plot, in which the protagonist, the intelligent and
witty Alexander Chatsky, returns to Moscow after three years in Europe like a Petersburg idealist, only to confront the primitive and banal mind-set of its backward
people. Sophia, to whom he returned in fond hopes of marriage, he now sees as a
simpleton who is satisfied with the attentions of his father's lowly servant. After a
few days of wasting his arguments and witty barbs jousting with conservatism, petty
intrigue, hypocrisy, and gossip, he flees the city:

> *Away from Moscow! I won't come again.*
> *I'll run, I won't look back, I'll search until I've found*
> *A place to hide my outraged feelings from all men!*
> *Boy, bring my carriage round!*

In the aftermath of the Decembrist rebellion, the play was kept from publication
but circulated widely in manuscript copies. The play was too controversial to be
staged during Griboyedov's lifetime, but it was finally staged in St. Petersburg in
1831, published with cuts in 1833, and the full text was published only in 1860.

   In 1828 Griboyedov left Petersburg for Persia to become Russia's ambassador to
the Shah. Pushkin recalled that when they parted, Griboyedov "was sad and had
strange premonitions."[38] On January 30, 1829, an angry mob in Tehran stormed
the Embassy and massacred Griboyedov and his staff. In June of that year, when
Pushkin was traveling in the Caucasus, he met the wagon carrying Griboyedov's
body back from Persia. In 1923, the Catherine Canal was renamed after Griboyedov because he once lived on its embankment.

   Nicholaevan Petersburg saw the first important poetry and literature about St. Petersburg as a city—its natural surroundings and climate, its White Nights, the floods,

its dark and snowy winters, its waterways and islands, its architecture, its unique society and culture, and the St. Petersburg idea—which became a genre in itself. No one did this better than Alexander Pushkin. Like a magician who could see through time and space and knew both the future and the past, he created masterpieces behind whose seeming simplicity lurked such depths of meaning that readers continue to unravel them today. His unforgettable words have etched themselves in the minds of generations of Russians.

The most famous and important of his works dedicated to the city is *The Bronze Horseman* (1833), subtitled *A Petersburg Tale*, centered on a flood (inspired by the flood of 1824) and Falconet's statue of Peter the Great. In 1827, Pushkin and the Polish poet Adam Mickiewicz had stood before the monument under a single cape debating the merits of the Tsar-Reformer, and Mickiewicz had gone on to author his poem *To the Monument of Peter the Great*, while Pushkin worked for years on a history of Peter, which he never completed. Instead, Pushkin's thoughts about Peter were bestowed to posterity mainly in his poem named after the monument. It was inspired by a legend recounted to him by Count Mikhail Vielgorsky. According to the story, in 1812, when Napoleon was thinking of marching on Petersburg, Alexander I wanted to move the statue out of the city. But a certain Major Baturin had a dream that recurred for several nights in a row, in which the statue of Peter the Great came alive and rode through the city. It came to Alexander I and warned him, "While I am in my place, nothing will happen to the city!" When Baturin told Alexander about this dream, he changed his mind and left the statue in the city. When Pushkin heard this legend, he grew excited and kept exclaiming, "What poetry! What poetry!"[39]

Pushkin's poem begins with a prologue in tribute to Peter and his city, but which ends by foretelling, "Sad will be my tale." The poem proper begins with the "cold autumn breath of November," which turns into a gale and a flood. Eugene, a lowly clerk, lies awake in his bed thinking of his betrothed Parasha, who lives in a hut on the other side of the Neva. When he gets up the next morning, the city is underwater and he sees boats, houses, and coffins drifting through the streets. When the water subsides, Eugene has a boatman ferry him to Parasha's island, but both Parasha and her hut have been swept away and are no more. As Eugene staggers through the fog, he starts laughing and goes mad. For days he wanders aimlessly through the city until one evening he finds himself on Senate Square facing the Bronze Horseman. Eugene blames Peter for his misfortune and raises his fist at him in rebellion. "Very well, builder and miracle worker," he whispers. "Just you wait!" But then Eugene, in his delirium, sees the statue come alive. Terrified, he flees, but the statue pursues him through the city's moonlit streets:

> *Illumined by the pale moonlight,*
> *With arm outflung, behind him riding*
> *See, the bronze horseman comes, bestriding*

The charger, clanging in his flight.
All night the madman flees; no matter
Where he may wander at his will,
Hard on his track with heavy clatter
There the bronze horseman gallops still.[40]

Hounded by the statue, Evgeny cannot escape, and his body is eventually found on an offshore island.

The Bronze Horseman has provoked more commentary and interpretation than any other Russian poem, beginning with Pushkin's censor, Nicholas himself. The Tsar, suspecting that Pushkin's references to Peter were aimed at him, demanded changes and omissions. Like Evgeny, Pushkin too must bow to the monarch. But he would not accept the edits and so only the prologue was published in his lifetime. A toned-down version of the full poem appeared in 1837 after the poet's death, but it became possible to publish a full, uncensored version only in 1917 once the monarchy had fallen. The poem introduces an ambiguous and tense dual vision of the city that is a natural response to the rise of the autocratic state, symbolized by Imperial St. Petersburg, which had affected Pushkin so personally. While in the prologue Pushkin expresses admiration for Peter and love for his city, in the eyes of Evgeny the two symbolize the oppressive state that Russia had become and which so easily squashed individuals. Pushkin, who always remained a monarchist though he opposed tyranny, does not clearly take Evgeny's side, and the degree to which the poem distinguishes Peter from Nicholas is naturally left unclear.

In Pushkin's other Petersburg stories, *Eugene Onegin* and *The Queen of Spades*, he depicts typical Petersburg figures: young officers gambling and chasing attractive, superfluous young women, a spoiled dandy, the court, old officers and bureaucrats, and their trophy wives. The importance of *Eugene Onegin* is hard to overestimate. This "novel in verse," as Pushkin called it, is the forerunner of the great Russian novel, just as Onegin is the first of Russia's literary heroes. Behind the easily flowing, playful, and slightly ironic verses lies a deep psychological portrait of the Petersburg society that Pushkin knew so well, and the city is brought alive. The first chapter is a day in the life of Onegin, but it is also a day in the life of the city. Together with Onegin, we see Petersburg wake up early in the morning, drive through the city's streets and squares, and follow the hero to the theater and a ball.

Onegin, a Byronic hero, is a sophisticated but aimless and cynical dandy. He visits a provincial estate, where the young and naive Tatyana falls head over heels in love with him. She declares her pure, passionate love to him in a letter, but he rejects her and in the meantime kills in a duel his best friend, the poet Lensky, who was about to marry Tatyana's sister. Years later, back in Petersburg, now aging and lonely, Onegin sees Tatyana at a ball, but now she is the beautiful, charming, and sophisticated wife of an old general with whom she shares respect but not love. Onegin now declares his love and pursues her. She still loves him, but resolves to remain faithful to her marital vows and in a painful ending rejects him. Most of Pushkin's readers were disappointed: They would have preferred a happy ending. But in 1837, when Pushkin was killed at a duel, people found so many similarities between Pushkin's duel and the one he imagined in *Eugene Onegin* that many identified Lensky with Pushkin, and over 40,000 copies of the work were sold in Petersburg alone following the poet's death.

The subject which frames Pushkin's major prose work on the Petersburg theme, *Queen of Spades* (1833), is cards, a major Petersburg pastime. Pushkin was a passionate card player and gambler, but usually he lost. He was fascinated by how, in the game of cards, Fate played with human lives. In a sense, gambling was akin to a duel, because not only money, villages, and palaces could be lost in a blink of an eye, but also lives: For a loser who could not pay his debt, the only honorable way out was a bullet in his head. Gambling was like a disease, and in desperation a loser was ready to sell his soul to the Devil. In 1802, Petersburg society was shocked when Prince Alexander Golitsyn lost his beautiful wife to Count Lev Razumovsky at cards. When Pushkin proposed to his future wife, Natalya Goncharova, her mother opposed the marriage because Pushkin was a gambler.

In the *Queen of Spades*, a Russian officer of German origin, Hermann, is poor and needs money to live respectably in the splendid city and win the heart of his secret love, Liza, who lives with her rich relative, an old Countess. Hermann learns that when the Countess was young, she was a beauty and lived in Paris. She was a passionate gambler, and one night lost a vast sum of money. When her husband refused to give her more money, she visited the famous and mysterious St. Germain, who told her the secret of three cards. Knowing these three cards, the Countess played again and won her money back. One night Hermann makes his way to the Countess's bedroom, points his gun at her and demands that she name the three cards, but she dies in shock without revealing the secret. Later her ghost visits Hermann and tells him the three cards: Three, Seven, and Ace. He wins with the first two cards, but then instead of an Ace, he gets the Queen of Spades. He stares at the Queen, stunned, and it seems to him that she resembles the Countess and is grinning at him. He realizes that he is lost. The Countess has reached from beyond the grave to destroy him. Delirious, Hermann walks the streets of the mysterious, threatening, and cold city, indifferent to his fate, and he goes mad. The story was an immediate hit. "My *Queen of Spades*," Pushkin wrote in his diary, "is in big vogue. Gamblers bet on the Three, Seven and Ace. At the court, everybody found similarities between the old Countess and Princess Natalya Petrovna Golitsyna, and don't seem to mind." Later, Tchaikovsky made *Queen of Spades* into an opera.

Pushkin was working on his history of Peter the Great, Hannibal's biography, and several other projects when in January 1837 his life was cut short by a man with blond hair, just as the fortune-teller had predicted in his youth. The underlying cause of the tragedy was that he stood in opposition to, offended, and threatened high society in the capital. He was forever linked to the disgraced Decembrists, had turned his back on the noble's way of life by writing for a living, and his poetry was suspect and feared. He was always an outsider.

Pushkin's beautiful wife Natalya, whom he loved dearly, became the tool in the intrigue. The inevitable fate of having a beautiful wife in St. Petersburg's high society was to see swarms of men, from young officers to the Emperor himself, fawn over and pursue her. Though Natalya, like any other society woman at the time, enjoyed the attentions of men, she remained faithful to Pushkin. A young French exile, the dashing but arrogant George-Charles d'Anthes, was especially obsessed with her (or pretended to be) and relentless in his pursuit. In fact, he was bisexual and also the lover of the Dutch Ambassador, Baron Louis van Heeckeren, who became his adoptive father. Heeckeren conspired with d'Anthes in his pursuit of Natalya, and even threatened her in an attempt to make her give in to him. In November 1836 d'Anthes tricked Natalya into a private meeting where he brandished a pistol and threatened to blow his brains out if she would not have him. Terrified, she ran away and told Pushkin about it. Pushkin realized that his wife was being used to hurt him, and that d'Anthes and Heeckeren were not alone but were supported by Pushkin's powerful enemies in high society. A few days later Pushkin and several of his friends received an anonymous letter in French announcing that he had been elected to The Most Serene Order of Cuckolds. Pushkin held d'Anthes and his protector Heeckeren responsible and immediately challenged d'Anthes to a duel. There followed two months of letters, scandal, and intrigue which fixated all of Petersburg high society up to and including Nicholas. Friends, relatives, and even the Emperor interceded and prevented the duel. Meanwhile, d'Anthes unexpectedly proposed marriage to Natalya's older sister Catherine, claiming that all the time she and not Natalya was his love interest. Nobody believed him and few believed the marriage would take place, but Catherine was an old maid, poor, and in love with d'Anthes, so she accepted. The marriage became the talk of the town, and it seemed that all of high society, except Pushkin, came to the wedding just to be there. Because the circumstances of the marriage were so strange, false rumors arose that Catherine was pregnant. For his part, d'Anthes renewed his open pursuit of Natalya. By late January Pushkin had had enough and wrote another letter of challenge to Heeckeren, which d'Anthes accepted.

The duel, which Pushkin kept secret, was held at about 5:00 P.M. on January 27, 1837, at in isolated spot near the Black River on the Petersburg side, then on the edge of town. At the Wolff and Berange Café on Nevsky Prospect (in honor of Pushkin now called the Literary Café) Pushkin waited for his second, Constantine Danzas, a schoolmate from his Lyceum days. When Danzas arrived, the two set off and on the Palace Embankment passed Natalya's carriage coming the other way, but she failed to notice them. Once at the site, the seconds cleared away the knee-deep snow, Danzas dropped his hat to start the duel and the brothers-in-law advanced toward each other brandishing their pistols. D'Anthes, a crack shot, realized that he would be ruined if he killed the famous poet, so he only intended to wound him in the leg. But Pushkin was intent on killing d'Anthes and rushed toward the barrier to shoot from close range. With Pushkin taking aim so quickly, in order to avoid his own death d'Anthes had to fire before he was ready. His aim was thus faulty, and the bullet struck Pushkin in the abdomen. Pushkin dropped to the ground and the seconds rushed to him, but he motioned them away as d'Anthes started to leave his spot. "Wait!" Pushkin gasped. "I have enough strength to take my shot." D'Anthes stayed in his place, protecting his heart with his arm as allowed by the rules. Pushkin took careful aim and fired, saw d'Anthes drop to the snow and, believing he had killed him, threw his gun in the air and shouted "Bravo!" But the bullet, after going through d'Anthes arm, was deflected by a button and only managed to break two of his ribs. It was Pushkin who was mortally wounded, though at first he did not realize it.

A sleigh brought Pushkin to his home on the Moika, where the doctors, including Nicholas's own Dr. Arendt, pronounced the situation beyond hope. Resting in his study, Pushkin was asked whether he wanted to say farewell to his friends. He looked around him and said farewell to his books. He saw Natalya and assured her that he did not hold her guilty in the matter and that it was his own responsibility. Natalya was delirious from grief and fell ill. News of the duel spread through town like wildfire and Pushkin's friends rushed to his apartment and stayed with him until the end. Outside on the street the growing crowd began a night vigil. The police had to be dispatched there to maintain order.

Through Dr. Arendt Pushkin asked Nicholas to forgive him for breaking his promise not to fight a duel. Nicholas replied in a note, in which he wrote: "My Dear Friend Alexander Sergeevich: If it is God's will that we not see one another again in this world, please accept my last advice: Try to die as a Christian. As for your wife and children, do not worry, I will take care of them."[41] Through Arendt, Nicholas inquired about Pushkin's debts, which were many, and which Nicholas paid after Pushkin's death. Pushkin lingered in great pain for another day, then said good-bye to Natalya, his four children, relatives, and friends. He told Natalya to go to the country for two years and then marry a good man. He died at 2:45 P.M. on January 29.

For the Russian people Pushkin's death was a national tragedy, and their grief was inconsolable. Thousands filled the streets by Pushkin's house, which was opened to the public, while others paid their respects as he lay in state at the nearby Konnyushennaya Church on the Moika. The authorities did not expect such a demonstration of love and grief for a poet, and they feared disorders. Thus, though a memorial service had been planned, the gendarmes now considered this too dangerous. Instead, Pushkin's body was secretly spirited out of town at night, accompanied by his friend and relative, Alexander Turgenev, to Mikhailovskoe, where the poet was buried in accordance with his wishes.

Two months after Pushkin's death, a 16-year-old Fedor Dostoevsky moved to Petersburg, and right away visited the site of Pushkin's duel and his apartment at

Moika No. 12 in order to see where he had died. But the apartment was already rented to someone else and everything inside had changed. Later, however, Pushkin's apartment was turned into a Pushkin museum and opened to the public. Today "Moika 12" is the most famous address in Russia.

Among the crowd gathered outside Pushkin's house as he lay dying stood a 23-year-old military officer and poet, Mikhail Lermontov. Five years earlier Lermontov had transferred from Moscow University to join the St. Petersburg School of Cavalry Cadets, and after graduation had lived a dissolute life while the censor was rejecting his work. He was ill on the day Pushkin was shot, but when he learned what had happened he put on his fur coat and rushed to Pushkin's house. It is not clear whether the two poets ever met, but Lermontov felt a personal loss when Pushkin died, and he blamed his death on what he saw as a corrupt Petersburg high society. He put his pain and anger into a poem, which he entitled *Death of a Poet*.

> Yet—are you blameless, you who banned
> His free, brave talent out of spite,
> And smoldering flames to white heat fanned
> That should have been extinguished quite?
> Come, be content, then—such a refinement
> Of pain was more than he could bear.
> The lamp of genius is no longer shining,
> The laurel wreath is fading now and sear.[42]

Lermontov's poem was so brilliant and powerful that he was immediately hailed as Pushkin's heir. Everybody wanted a copy, including Pushkin's wife. People made handwritten copies of the poem and circulated them throughout the city and to friends and relatives all over Russia. Somehow this new talent helped to fill the emptiness left by the loss of Pushkin.

But the targets of the poem were not pleased to see another troublesome poet arise so quickly to attack them, and they fought back. Before circulating the poem, Lermontov had his friend Svyatoslav Raevsky show it to Benckendorff, who had no objection. Once it was circulated, court intriguers passed a copy anonymously to Nicholas, but he too saw nothing wrong with it. Soon afterwards, at a social gathering at which Benckendorff was a guest, he was asked, "Count, have you read the new poem aimed at all of us, *la crème de la noblesse*?" But Benckendorff quickly changed the subject. Not giving up, the intriguers penned on the top of another copy the words "A Call to Revolution" as if it were Lermontov's subtitle and sent that copy anonymously to Nicholas, which had the desired effect. Before Nicholas realized that the affair was a court intrigue, Lermontov had been arrested, court-martialed, and exiled to the Caucasus, but Nicholas had him pardoned and within a year Lermontov returned to Petersburg in triumph.[43]

Lermontov's other works about St. Petersburg portrayed the city in a similar vein. His society novel set in St. Petersburg, *Princess Ligovskaya*, was never finished though its fragments contain rich descriptions of the city. His best work about Petersburg and its society was his play *The Masquerade* (1835), set at the famous masquerades in Engelhardt's house on Nevsky, which portrayed the city's high society as empty and depraved. It is a melodrama of jealousy, betrayal, and intrigue in which a husband ends up poisoning his wife for an adultery that she did not commit. For years it was rejected by the censor and finally published posthumously in 1842, and it was staged only in 1862. The play's most famous staging was that by Vsevolod Meyerhold during the tumult of the February Revolution in 1917, when it literally brought the curtain down on Imperial St. Petersburg. Lermontov, who painted for a hobby and liked to portray Petersburg engulfed in a raging tide, would have thought this appropriate.

The more Romantic works for which Lermontov is more famous are set in the Caucasus, but they were mainly composed in St. Petersburg, and reflect the alienation that Lermontov saw in Nicholaevan Russia, including his own. This is best expressed in *A Hero of Our Time*, whose jaded hero, Pechorin, has experienced all that life has had to offer and has no higher purpose. Bored, disillusioned, and cynical, he wastes his time on trifles and on toying with and ruining others, although the more authentic life in the Caucasus does make an impression on him. As Lermontov explained, Pechorin "was a portrait compounded of the vices of our whole generation in their full development."[44] In 1840 Lermontov dueled in Petersburg with the son of the French Ambassador, for which he was sent back to the Caucasus, where he died in another duel in 1841. He was only 27 years old. Having lived, written, and died as a true romantic, he became a cult figure second only to Pushkin.

Another writer and friend of Pushkin filled the streets of Petersburg with characters even more fantastic that Pushkin's. His name was Nikolai Gogol, and since his school days he had dreamed of meeting his idol Pushkin. When the 19-year-old Gogol moved from his native Ukraine to Petersburg in 1828 to seek his fortune, he immediately went to see Pushkin at home. But the closer he got, the more nervous he became, and before getting there he suddenly turned around, ran to a nearby coffeehouse, and ordered a stiff drink. His courage thus fortified, he was soon at Pushkin's threshold. A servant opened the door and told Gogol that Pushkin was asleep, though it was already late in the day. "He must have worked all night," Gogol surmised. "Yeah, he worked," grinned the servant. "At playing cards!"

But they met soon enough and became friends. Pushkin recognized Gogol's great talent and imagination and took him under his wing to develop his talent, even suggesting subjects for some of Gogol's works (including *The Government Inspector* and *Dead Souls*). For Gogol, Pushkin's death was a severe blow. "All the joy of my life, all my highest joy is gone with him," wrote Gogol after Pushkin's death. "I never did anything without seeking his advice. I never wrote a line without imagining him in front of me."[45]

When Gogol arrived in Petersburg, few could make a living at writing, and he still was not sure what he wanted to be. It could be something else—a prominent statesman, painter, or actor—so long as he could achieve distinction. But he had come with no friends or connections, could not circulate in aristocratic society, and succeeded at none of these vocations though he tried them all. Instead, like so many others he languished as a minor government clerk, though he did manage to teach medieval history briefly at the University. The cold, heartless, and hostile city would not accept him, he concluded, and in turn he came to hate it. At one point he re-solved to abandon Petersburg and seek his fortune instead in America, but once on the road he turned back. He settled into another undemanding government post, in the evenings began writing in his spare time, and found his real talent. He soon enjoyed success, recognition, and a means of living with his Ukrainian stories, *Evenings on a Farm near the Dikanka River* (1831–32), but the setting and subject of his writing soon became St. Petersburg itself. In 1835 he published his short stories *Nevsky Prospect* and *Diary of a Madman*, followed in 1836 by *The Nose* and in 1842 by *The Overcoat*.

These works present for the first time in prose an alternative, negative image of the city which from then on would compete with the Petrine or "Palmyra of the North" vision. Drawn from Gogol's own experience, these stories portray the cap-ital as dominated by smug, callous careerists while the pure of heart are crushed by the unbearable chasm between their dreams and revolting reality.[46] In his pages the city assumes a grotesque, perverse, irrational, demonic, and mystical character. Its regular streets, magnificent buildings, and elegant high society mask a corrupt and seamy underbelly and turbulent disorder. "The idea of the city," he once wrote, "is emptiness taken to the highest degree."[47]

Thus, in *Nevsky Prospect*, named after Petersburg's main and most elegant street, Gogol colorfully describes its many splendors, but concludes:

> Oh, do not trust this Nevsky Prospect! . . . It's all deceit, all dreams, it's not what it seems! . . . It deceives at all hours, this Nevsky Prospect, but most of all when night falls in masses of shadow on it, throwing into relief the white and pale walls of the houses, when all the town is transformed into noise and brilliance, when myriads of carriages roll off the bridges, postilions shout and jump up on their horses, and when the devil himself lights the street lamps to show everything in false colors.

In the story, the young artist Piskarev becomes enraptured with an elegantly dressed, fresh looking girl walking along Nevsky and follows her to her house, only to be deflated when it turns out to be a brothel and she—one of its prostitutes. But he is captivated by her beauty and convinced in her underlying goodness, so he pursues her and proposes marriage. She is unable to understand him, however, and after she rejects him the artist falls into delirium and commits suicide. Meanwhile the story's other protagonist, the smug rake Pirogov, chases after a German tin-smith's wife, and though he is eventually thrashed by her husband and his friends, he quickly resumes his ways as if nothing had happened. Thus, the city crushes the sensitive and honest while sinners can thrive unscathed.[48]

The Nose was published in Pushkin's journal *Sovremennik* ("The Contemporary"), where the poet was chief editor, and it appeared under a note by Pushkin: "N.V. Gogol would not agree for a long time to the publication of this joke; but we found so much that was surprising, fantastic, hilarious and original in it that we persuaded him to permit us to share with the public the pleasure which his manuscript gave us."[49] In it a middle-level bureaucrat awakes one morning to notice that his nose has disappeared, but soon he observes it going about the city in a carriage, dressed in the uniform of a civil councilor (a higher rank), and attending services at Kazan Cathedral, while wild rumors of the nose's more extravagant escapades spread through the city. These escapades serve as a device for satirizing the lives of bureaucrats, the omnipresent city police, and the city's press. This tale became so popular that an outdoor sculpture of the nose now lives on in the city.

In *The Overcoat*, Akaky Akakievich, a low-level copyist in his fifties, finally saves up enough money for a fine overcoat but enjoys less than a day of pride and happiness with it, as thieves mug him and steal it on a snowy city square on the first evening he wears it. Deprived of his metaphor of protection, he is left lying to face the cold and hostile city, whose white snow falling on him is identified with the shower of papers in which bureaucrats are immersed. When he asks a high ranking superior in his ministry to intercede with the police to give their investigation of the theft due attention, Akaky is rebuked for bothering him about it and soon dies from anguish. At first the city does not notice his absence (a new face readily appears on his seat at the office), but Akaky's ghost is said to haunt the city, though in fact it is the man who stole his overcoat. At one level, this story of the underdog gives Gogol a device to portray the lonely and meaningless lives of the city's vast army of petty servants and the foibles of its inhabitants.

But it would be wrong to read *The Overcoat* and Gogol's other Petersburg tales simply as venom directed against the city that he disliked. The important themes in these stories are universal to mankind, and his handling of them advanced Russian literature to a new level. The stories are existential, focusing on how imperfect individuals deal with the inevitable flaws and elements of absurdity in the world and life itself. The city and its individual souls are thus inextricably linked, but not as opposites. Both have imperfections, an ultimate irrationality, and a deep mystery underneath a mask (or overcoat) of seemingly contented rationality and order. Gogol's protagonists are driven by their realization of their imperfect and seemingly futile existence to the brink of lunacy to seize upon some idea, object, or person that hopefully will make life better, but never does. Complementing this angst is the image of Petersburg as a surreal, haunting, and absurd city, one in which the wind, "in accordance with St. Petersburg custom, blew at him from all four quarters" (impossible), where a door to a home might open and a pig will emerge, and where a uniformed nose having eyebrows rides in a carriage to church. In *Nevsky Prospect*, when Piskarev followed the object of his affection, "the sidewalk seemed to be moving under his feet, carriages drawn by trotting horses seemed to stand still, the bridge stretched out and seemed broken in the center, the houses were upside down, a sentry box seemed to be toppling toward him, and the sentry's halberd, and the gilt letter of the signboard and the scissors painted on it, all seemed to be flashing across his very eyelash." Gogol's magnificent interplay between our inner state of existence and the city's surreal surroundings was a truly novel and modern art form not only in Russia but for world literature, and paved the way for Dostoevsky's deep psychological stories and novels set in the city. Dostoyevsky supposedly once said that "we have all emerged from under Gogol's overcoat."[50] Petersburg, after all, was the perfect city for Gogol and his art.

Gogol complemented his Petersburg tales with his *Petersburg Notes of 1836* (1837), in which he compared St. Petersburg and Moscow, and his satirical dramatic masterpiece, *The Government Inspector* (1836), of which, he once explained, "I decided to gather into one heap everything bad in Russia . . . and laugh at it all at one stroke."[51] Read by Gogol himself to friends at Zhukovsky's literary evenings before being staged in 1836, it premièred in Rossi's Alexandrinsky Theater in the presence of Nicholas, who interpreted it as parodying government officials who failed to measure up to his standards and even demonstrating the need for his secret police. This was actually not far from Gogol's own view. He was a monarchist, convinced that imperial authority was needed, among other reasons, to control the worst in people. It was when *The Government Inspector* began to be interpreted among intellectuals as a radical satire of Romanov rule that he fled to Italy, to escape both their misdirected adulation and the risk that the Third Section might also adopt that interpretation. He lived mainly in Italy, where he wrote *Dead Souls*, conceived as the *Inferno* of a Russian *Divine Comedy* that he never finished. The work's purpose was to portray the ideal holy Russia to which the nation should aspire, but in the end he realized that "this is all a dream which vanishes once one shifts to what things are really like in Russia,"[52] a realization which drove him insane.

After Gogol, it became common and even fashionable for poets and writers to bash the city. Apollon Grigoriev, a Moscow Freemason and Slavophile critic and poet who moved to St. Petersburg, portrayed the city as a den of bad taste and philistinism. In his poem *The City* (1845), even the city's quiet White Nights are painted as a deceptive mask of evil:

> *And in those hours when night descends on*
> *My city without darkness or shadow,*
> *When everything is transparent, then a swarm of revolting visions*
> *Flickers before me. . . .*
> *Let the night be as clear as day, let everything be still,*
> *Let everything be transparent and calm—*
> *In that calm an evil illness lurks—*
> *The transparency of a suppurating ulcer.*[53]

After Pushkin's *Bronze Horseman*, Falconet's statue was fair game. In one poem, Nikolai Scherbin, a government official, portrayed Peter as having trampled not the snake but Russia's common people. Another poet, Mikhail Dmitriev, wrote a poem, *The Underwater City* (1847), in which he relished in describing the flooding of Petersburg and gleefully foretold that the deluges would never end. A flood also featured in Vladimir Odoevsky's *A Joker from the Dead* (1844), in which a Princess abandons her young lover for a secure life with an older state official. But a flood delivers her dead lover's coffin into the middle of a ball. She faints, the ballroom collapses, and the city is swept into the sea. Alarmed at this negativism, Nicholas's government could fight back only with the publication of engravings with beautiful panoramas of the city, portraying it as orderly and clean in accordance with the Emperor's ideal and without any of the ugliness that writers had started to reveal.[54]

The city of St. Petersburg as a literary subject, whether positive or negative, was growing into a genre of its own. Soon there was a need for criticism too. Gogol had published his *Petersburg Notes of 1836*, while Herzen penned his essay *Moscow and Petersburg* in 1842. In 1845, the young poet Nikolai Nekrasov wrote *Petersburg's Corners*, which he included in a two-volume anthology about the city that he edited, entitled *The Physiology of Petersburg*, which also contained an introduction by the leading literary critic, Vissarion Belinsky. Featuring literature, criticism, and essays on the city and its customs and society, including Belinsky's own essay *St. Petersburg and Moscow*, *Physiology* was so successful that the next year another volume appeared as the *Petersburg Anthology*. The year 1845 also saw E. Kovalevsky's *Petersburg by Day and Night*, V. Krestovsky's *Petersburg Slums*, and Yakov Butkov's *Petersburg Summits*. The young Fedor Dostoevsky added his own four-part feuilleton, *Petersburg Chronicle*, which was published in the *St. Petersburg Gazette* in 1847.

THE ARTS

Nicholas was divided about art. He recognized that art, like Pushkin's poetry, could wield great power over people. Thus, on the one hand he exploited the arts to glorify Russia and promote Official Nationality, turning the New Hermitage into Europe's first art museum. On the other hand, he prevented overly critical artistic expression and reduced most theater to diversion. Thus, while he purported to encourage the arts, his fears and his conservative, simple tastes straightjacketed them. Petersburg's artists struggled in the stifling atmosphere, but true genius still shone through.

Theatergoing had become a passion in Alexander's time, especially after 1812, and continued through Nicholas's reign. Theater was supported by the state and managed by the Theater Directorate, which built and operated the theaters, hired the Russian and foreign performers, provided for their accommodation and even their transport to and from the theaters, in special green theater carriages. The city now boasted permanent Russian, French, and German drama troupes.

Under Alexander the repertoire consisted of translated French works, especially Racine and Voltaire, Russian historical dramas, comedies and tragedies, and Shakespeare. Under Nicholas, the repertoire changed, and even the atmosphere at performances grew stiff and vacuous. Foreign and Russian tragedies and other thought-provoking dramas were de-emphasized, replaced by original Russian melodramas and vaudevilles, which Nicholas personally liked but critics like Gogol cautiously bemoaned.[55] Plays of true artistic merit such as Griboyedov's *Woe from Wit* and Gogol's *Government Inspector* were rare, but when they appeared, they became immediate hits. After *The Government Inspector* opened in 1836, it was performed 272 times that year.

March marked a change of seasons in city life when the theaters were closed during the six weeks of Lent, but the city was opened to musical concerts. In Nicholas's reign, due to the Church's influence, formal public concerts were generally banned; they were permitted only as an alternative to theater during Lent,[56] although late in his reign this rule was relaxed. The Lenten season became a veritable "festival of musicians," with world-famous artists streaming in from all over Europe.[57]

Unlike other art forms, music was not supported by the state, and there would be no conservatory in the city until 1862. Music was thought of as entertainment rather than high art, as an ornament of the court and aristocratic salons, much as poetry had once been treated. As a result, ever since music had become a part of St. Petersburg culture under Anna Ioannovna and Elizabeth, it had been dominated by foreigners, especially the Italians. But late in the first half of the 19th century Russian music came into its own.

It emerged in the homes of Petersburg aristocrats, intelligentsia, and musicians, where hosts arranged private concerts and informal musical entertainment, which were not forbidden. Songs, especially romances, developed as a native art form and soon became a permanent fixture at salons and literary evenings. Romances developed as a fusion of Russian folk and gypsy songs with the Italian music that had long dominated Petersburg. A pure creation of Petersburg culture, romances became the pop music of the time. The city's most famous musical salon was at the home of Counts Mikhail and Matvei Vielgorsky, where 300 or more guests could be accommodated to hear even symphonic concerts. Beethoven's Ninth Symphony had its Russian première there, and Lizst, Robert Schumann, Berlioz, and Wagner all dazzled its audiences. Nicholas himself often attended. Petersburg's other famous musical salon was at the home of General Alexei Lvov, who was head of the Capella, composer of Russia's anthem "God Save the Tsar," and founder of the Concert Society. The popularity of playing music in private homes put music teachers in high demand, and the growing numbers of musicians stimulated demand for instruments and musical scores. Soon numerous music shops had opened in the city. Since scores were expensive, most shops also maintained musical libraries where scores could be rented out. It was only a matter of time before an extraordinary talent would emerge.

Orchestral music also began to flourish outside the court and private settings. In 1802 the Petersburg Philharmonic Society was founded by musicians in order to introduce and popularize classical music and raise money for the widows and orphans of deceased musicians. Beginning in 1830 its concerts were held in the spacious home of Vasily Engelhardt, Pushkin's enlightened friend from the Green Lamp society. He had married into money, acquired a large home on the corner of Nevsky Prospect and the Catherine Canal, and renovated it into a shrine of culture and entertainment which became the center for concerts in the city. Eventually the concert season came to include not only Lent but the entire autumn and early winter. When the building opened, the *Northern Bee* boasted that "now we can decisively say that no other capital in the world, including Paris and London, has such a wonderful public cultural establishment."[58] At that time, however, the repertoire was limited to the works of foreign composers such as Handel, Haydn, Mozart, Beethoven, and Rossini. There was a crying need for native Russian classical music, and Russia's first great composer was about to emerge.

Russian music as high art finally arrived with Mikhail Glinka (1804–57), the cousin of Pushkin's and Ryleev's friend Fedor. He was the son of a wealthy landowner near Smolensk, but moved to St. Petersburg to study music while working as a civil servant. In 1828 he left for five years of travel and musical study in Italy, Vienna, and Berlin, and returned to St. Petersburg determined to give the Russian stage a monumental national work of art. In nationalistic Nicholaevan Russia, a popular figure of legend was that of Ivan Susanin, a peasant martyr who during the Time of Troubles had led a unit of Polish soldiers astray into the forests to protect Michael Romanov, and was killed by them when they discovered his trickery. Ryleev had written poems about Susanin, and when Glinka returned to the city in search of a subject for his opera, his friend Zhukovsky suggested Susanin. Glinka, who reputedly once said that "nations create music, composers only arrange it,"[59] threw himself with abandon into arranging his opera. It was not the first Russian opera, but it was Russia's first "national" opera, complete with a Russian subject, about peasants and using Russian folk melodies. Nicholas was delighted to learn of it, as it seemed to support Official Nationality and his ideal union of Tsar and People. But he had Glinka change the name from *A Death for the Tsar* to the more upbeat *A Life for the Tsar*. It premièred in St. Petersburg's newly reconstructed Bolshoi Theater in November 1836 with a proud Nicholas in attendance. It was an astonishing success in Russia and abroad and showed that Russian music could stand with the best in Europe. "A new period is beginning in the history of art," crowed one St. Petersburg critic. "It is now the era of *Russian* music."[60]

Glinka went on to compose a variety of symphonic works, piano compositions, works for other instruments, and songs, many of which he loved to perform himself, especially at the evening gatherings of his poet and writer friend Nestor Kukolnik and later at gatherings of the Petrashevtsy circle (see below). But none of his work would ever rise in the public's eye to the level of *A Life for the Tsar*, and he began to tire of the city. In 1840, when he thought of escaping to Paris, he wrote a cycle of 12 songs entitled *Farewell to St. Petersburg* with lyrics by Kukolnik, but after they were completed he decided to stay in town. The cycle was an immediate success. The songs are a musical depiction of colorful Petersburg scenes of love, sprees among friends, and even a ride on the new railroad to Tsarskoe Selo, and reflect the city's cosmopolitanism by utilizing a variety of Italian, Spanish, Jewish, and folk melodies. His next great work, the opera *Ruslan and Lyudmilla* (1842), based on Pushkin's poem, was musically more sophisticated than his first opera, but it was too advanced for both Nicholas and the public, who did not understand it. Nicholas left the première before it ended, thus giving it the kiss of death. The applause was so subdued that Glinka did not know whether to take his bows, but his companion in the director's box persuaded him, saying, "Go on, Christ suffered more than you."[61] Glinka turned against the "vile" city, complaining that "the local climate is definitely harmful to me, or perhaps, my health is even more affected by the local gossips, each of whom has at least one drop of poison on the tip of his tongue."[62] Seeing where he was more appreciated, in 1844 Glinka left for Europe, where he spent most of the rest of his life but did little composing. When he left Petersburg for the last time in 1856, as he crossed the city's boundary, he stopped the carriage, stepped out and spat on the ground that, in his opinion, had never given him his due. He returned only in a coffin, and only about 30 people attended his burial.

As the number of aristocrats who appreciated painting grew and needed more paintings for their homes, the ranks of artists in the city multiplied as well. Artistic training still centered on the now-conservative Academy of Fine Arts, although by now drawing and painting was also taught elsewhere, such as at the School of Engineers and Corps of Cadets. In 1821 the Society for the Encouragement of Artists was formed by several rich aristocrats to sponsor the development of promising young artists and (from 1826) to hold exhibitions of new works. Famous artists who received pensions from the Society included Karl and Alexander Briullov, Alexander Ivanov, and the sculptor Peter Klodt. The Society's exhibitions provided important exposure, because the Academy exhibited the works of its graduates and teachers only once every three years, in September. Each year the six top graduates of the Academy were sent abroad for training to perfect their talents. Study abroad was crucial because under Nicholas the Academy barely strayed from the classicism of Catherine's time except to encourage national themes, and the horizons of the young artists needed to be widened. As Gogol observed in his story *Nevsky Prospect*, Petersburg artists "often nourish a genuine talent, and if only the fresh air of Italy were to blow on them, it would probably develop as freely, broadly, and brilliantly as a plant which is finally brought out of a room into the fresh air."

Such was the good fortune of the painter Karl Briullov (1799–1852), who, like Glinka in the case of music, raised Russian painting to European standards. He was born and raised in St. Petersburg to French emigré parents, who enrolled him (and his four brothers) in the Academy of Fine Arts. Karl excelled and in 1823 graduated with the gold medal that entitled him to study abroad. He studied in Rome for seven years, during which a visit to the ruins of Pompeii, Giovanni Pacini's 1825 opera about its destruction, and Pliny the Younger's description of it inspired him to paint *The Last Day of Pompeii* (1833), a huge canvas (now in Petersburg's Russian Museum) portraying the dramatic destruction of the ancient city in a hail of fire and ash. Utilizing both color and light to brilliant effect and melodramatic images, it was the first Russian painting to have as its subject a group of anonymous figures and no single protagonist. First praised highly in Italy, in Paris the painting won the French Academy's gold medal for 1834. Sir Walter Scott is said to have sat in front of it for an hour, pronouncing it not a painting but an epic. Following its triumphs in Europe, it was then taken to St. Petersburg on the ship *Tsar Peter* and exhibited at the Academy of Fine Arts, also to rave reviews. Petersburgers from all walks of life flocked to see it, the artist became known as "Divine Karl," and Nicholas awarded him the Order of St. Anna. Gogol devoted an article to it, calling Briullov "one of the brilliant phenomena of the 19th century" and his canvas a "brilliant resurrection of painting, which for some time had remained in some half-lethargic state."[63] Pushkin began (but did not finish) a poem dedicated to the painting. But many Russians, especially those who disliked the capital plagued with its own natural disasters, saw it as allegorical of St. Petersburg and its ultimate fate. Alexander Herzen, in his essay *Moscow and Petersburg*, commented that Briullov, "who developed in St. Petersburg, selected for his brush the terrible image of a wild, irrational force, destroying the people in Pompeii—that is the moving spirit of St. Petersburg!"[64]

The ambitious Briullov then tried to surpass *Last Day* with his even grander *The Siege of Pskov by Stefan Batory in 1581*, but he could never regain his earlier form and the work was never finished. Meanwhile, he painted many notable portraits of leading figures in Petersburg, including the poet Zhukovsky, his mutual friend with Glinka Nestor Kukolnik, the fabulist Ivan Krylov, and Prince Alexander Golitsyn. But he never again enjoyed his former fame. After painting his self-portrait in 1848 in which his dissatisfaction, disdain, and torment are apparent, he left Russia to live on the island of Madeira and finally in his beloved Rome.

Petersburg's other leading painter of the period was Alexander Ivanov (1806–58), the son of Briullov's teacher at the Academy of Fine Arts and a close friend of Gogol. Ivanov studied at the Academy for 10 years but like Briullov tired of its conservative traditions and of his father, who also was his teacher. He left for Rome in 1830 in order to experiment, remarking, "A Russian cannot remain in a city like Petersburg which has no character. The Academy of Fine Arts is a survival of a past century."[65] In St. Peter's city, he became increasingly religious and in the 1830s switched from classical to religious themes. His masterpiece was *The Appearance of Christ to the People*, on which he worked for 20 years (1837–57), during which Nicholas visited him at his studio during his own trip to Italy in 1845. *The Appearance* is a realistic group portrait of Christ appearing before a mixed crowd, who suddenly confront the decision whether to accept or reject the new faith. After it was finished, Ivanov returned to St. Petersburg in 1858 in order to exhibit it. He died there only a few days after its first showing.

Closer to Petersburg life were the paintings of Pavel Fedotov (1815–52). Born in Moscow, he moved to Petersburg at 18 to join the military, but soon took up drawing and painting, for which he had a natural talent. His formal training was thin, but he easily developed a popular realistic style that for the first time made Russian secular painting accessible to a broader audience. He produced numerous small paintings depicting typical, often comical, scenes from daily life set in Petersburg's homes, military barracks, eateries, and shops. Fedotov incisively portrayed human foibles, vulgarities, and tragedies as well as broader social problems, and thus became to St. Petersburg painting what Gogol was to its literature. Thus, *The Major's Courtship* (1848) depicts an embarrassed impoverished aristocrat asking for the hand of a merchant's daughter in order to stay financially afloat. *A Poor Aristocrat's Breakfast* (1849) shows another poor aristocrat sharing quarters with his trimmed poodle, eating bread like a commoner while looking at advertisements for expensive oysters. *The Newly Decorated Civil Servant* (1846) portrays a proud bureaucrat standing before his wife in their shabby flat the morning after his promotion, proudly wrapping himself like a Roman senator in his worn bathrobe "toga" on which he has pinned his new medal. And *The Fastidious Bride* (1847) recreates Krylov's fable of a middle-aged bride who in her youth had proudly rejected all suitors, but now humbly accepts the proposal of a hunchback. In his later years, following Nicholas's repressions of 1848 and censorship of his own work, Fedotov grew despondent, and his last works such as *The Young Widow* (1851–52) and *The Gamblers* (1852) reflect his final depression and pessimism. He eventually went mad and entered a psychiatric clinic, where he died in 1852 at the age of 37.

Portraying the city itself also became something of a genre. Portraits of the city in oil, watercolor, lithographs, or simply drawings by such artists as Fyodor Alexeyev, Andrei Martynov, Stephan Galaktionov, and the former serf Vasily Sadovnikov became immensely popular and were encouraged by the government. Most famous is Sadovnikov's series of detailed colored lithographs published in 1830–35 providing an unbroken panorama along both sides of Nevsky Prospect, which depicted every building and shop right down to the signs.[66] The drawings were joined into two continuous scrolls 47 feet long and mounted on reels so that viewers could look through an eyepiece and "roll" along the street. At about the same time, the popular monthly journal *The Magic Lantern* first appeared, which featured colorful lithographs of the city and street life accompanied by detailed captions and even dialogues.[67]

The number and size of the city's art collections continued to grow, but the largest continued to be those at the Academy, the Strogonov Palace, and the Hermitage. All could be seen by invited guests. The general public could attend temporary exhibitions, but the only permanent exhibition other than at the New Hermitage was the so-called "Russian Museum" founded in 1819 by the writer and publicist Pavel Svinin in order to popularize native Russian art. It was housed in

Svinin's own apartment on Mikhailovskaya Square and contained contemporary paintings as well as older works dating back to Elizabeth's time. The Hermitage, in contrast, exhibited only foreign paintings until the 1830s. By then its collection had grown to 222 French, 302 Flemish, 472 Italian, and 482 Dutch paintings; its Russian paintings numbered only 23.[68] Unfortunately, Nicholas, considering himself an expert in art as in all things, applied his own tastes to redefine the collection and sold off 1,220 paintings, including some of major importance, and even had some others destroyed. He also melted down some of Catherine's gold and silver dinner services to make others in a style that he preferred. Among the works to be disposed of was Houdon's seated statue of Voltaire, regarding which Nicholas ordered: "Destroy this old monkey!" Fortunately the staff disobeyed him by "hiding" it in the library, where they knew Nicholas would never venture.[69]

In 1826 the Winter Palace itself also gained a permanent hall of art in its Gallery of 1812. Designed by Rossi at Alexander I's behest, the Gallery was a pantheon containing life-size or larger portraits of 332 heroes from the Patriotic War of 1812. Ironically, the paintings were executed by an English artist in the service of the Duke of Kent, George Dawe, because Alexander had met him in Europe and was impressed by the speed at which he could produce quality portraits in the dashing, romantic style that he wanted. Dawe was paid handsomely (one-fourth the cost of constructing Kazan Cathedral) in order to complete the job quickly and left Russia in 1829 to retire a rich man.

INTELLECTUAL FERMENT, THE REVOLUTIONS OF 1848, AND THE PETRASHEVTSY AFFAIR

It took a while for Petersburg intellectual life to recover from 1825 and develop in spite of Nicholas's system. For over a decade, intellectual life in Moscow, where the Decembrists had never struck a chord, overshadowed Petersburg's, but by the late 1830s the center began shifting back to the capital. After 1825, most thinkers stopped focusing on politics and constitutions. Western political ideas had not made headway in Russia, and people began to wonder whether they were naturally unsuitable for Russia. Also, since 1812 there had been a resurgence of national pride and interest in Russia's past. When searching for solutions to Russia's problems, many thinkers began to reexamine Russia as a nation and ask not whether the problem, but rather the way forward may lay in the deepest reaches of Russia's nationhood. Peter the Great had his own answers to these questions, which led him to create St. Petersburg. Until the failure of the Decembrists, most thinkers agreed that Russia's future lay in completing Peter the Great's work, in realizing the St. Petersburg idea. But now that vision was questioned. The result was one of the most intense and fruitful periods of thought in Russian history, described by Herzen as an "extraordinary age of external constraint and inner liberation."[70]

That age began with a great friend of Pushkin, Peter Chaadaev (1794–1856), who wrote eight *Philosophical Letters* which were largely completed by 1831. But the first was published only in 1836, and then only anonymously and thanks to a censor's oversight. Herzen called that *Letter* "a shot that rang out in the dark night . . . one had to wake up."[71] Chaadaev wrote:

> Historical experience does not exist for us. To behold us it would seem that the general law of mankind had been revoked in our case. Isolated in the world, we have given nothing to the world, we have taken nothing from the world, we have not added a single idea to the mass of human ideas; we have contributed nothing to the progress of the human spirit. And we have disfigured everything we touched of that progress. . . . [F]rom the inventions of others we borrowed only the deceptive appearances and the useless luxuries.[72]

Chaadaev blamed this on Russia's turning to Byzantium for its religion and culture.[73] While the West over centuries had developed universal ideas and turned to Antiquity for its forms of beauty, "we locked ourselves up in our religious separatism."[74] The solution for Russia, Chaadaev concluded, was "contact with other nations,"[75] which would enable Russia "somehow to repeat the whole education of mankind."[76] Chaadaev meant turning not to the ideas of the Enlightenment but to the precepts of Christ as developed by Western Christianity, especially Catholicism. If Russia could eschew the West's atheism and materialism that had developed since the Enlightenment and recapture the true and universal Christian faith, Russia's destiny could even be to save Europe.

Chaadaev's pronouncements were an affront to all of Muscovite history, the Orthodox Church, Official Nationality, and Nicholas. Chaadaev was not only arrested, but officially declared insane. Later, aptly, he wrote *Apology of a Madman* (1845), which was less an apology or recantation than an explanation and updating of his views in the hope of making them more palatable. He abandoned the Catholic model as politically and historically impossible. Rather, now somewhat influenced by Hegel, he acknowledged that Russia's past had some positive elements (or at worst that Russia was a "blank sheet of paper") and hoped that Petrine ideas would catalyze the nation and eventually yield a unique national culture.[77] He pointed to certain achievements of the Petersburg period such as Lomonosov and Pushkin as hopeful signs.

There were two principal responses to Chaadaev, which reflected the intellectual gap between the two capitals.[78] The first, confined largely to circles in Moscow, was to assert that Chaadaev was wrong and identify historical traditions that held a future for Russia, and map out a future based on them. These Slavophiles, as they were called, insisted that a worthy national identity existed in Orthodoxy and in the common people in whom it authentically inhered. It was reflected, they claimed, in the peasant commune *(mir)*, which embodied a communal spirit *(sobornost)* in which the individual identified himself both with his community and with God. Thus, Russia had been on the true path until the Petersburg period; Western

Europe suffered from the same disease and should not be Russia's model. Rather, by returning to this past and practicing *sobornost*, Russia could not only renew itself but fulfill its destiny as Europe's savior. The Slavophiles propagandized the virtues of the past, searched for historical relics, and even wore traditional Russian peasant costumes.

The other response to Chaadaev's challenge, more typical in Petersburg, was to continue synthesizing useful foreign ideas in an effort to forge for the first time a worthy and unique national political, religious, social, and cultural life—in short, the original Petersburg idea. Chaadaev himself wrote in his *Apology* that "our fanatical Slavists . . . now and then exhume curios of our museums and libraries, but it is doubtful that they will ever draw from the entrails of our historic soil the wherewithal to fill up the void in our souls, to condense the fog in our minds."[79] This group became known as the Westernizers, due more to their common opposition to Slavophilism than because they agreed among themselves.

Russia's leading Westernizers at the time were Vissarion Belinsky and Alexander Herzen. Herzen left for Europe in 1847, but his writings were widely read in Petersburg and his spirit was always present. His main work about Petersburg was his essay *Moscow and Petersburg* (1842), which circulated widely in manuscript form and was read in meetings of the Petrashevtsy circle. But it was not a deep analysis, and Herzen diplomatically avoided giving preference to either city. Instead, he peppered his essay with witty aphorisms such as, "In Moscow people take every foreigner for a great man, whereas in Petersburg people take every great man for a foreigner."[80] The serious Belinsky expected more, and in 1845 responded with his own essay, *Petersburg and Moscow*.

Belinsky's importance in Petersburg's intellectual life at the time is hard to overestimate. He was born the son of a poor doctor in Finland in 1811 and grew up in the provinces before entering Moscow University in 1829. He was thin, frail, stooped and eventually developed consumption, which would strike him down in 1848. Deadly serious, he rarely smiled, and impressed his teachers with his single-minded and unprejudiced devotion to literature, its role in society, and the search for truth. He was a truly independent mind, not a joiner (or founder) of movements. His pursuit of truth at times led him to change his mind, of which he commented that "if a man does not alter his views about life and art, it is because he is devoted to his own vanity rather than the truth."[81] His consistency was moral above all else.[82]

Belinsky originally fell under the spell of Moscow's romantics and idealists, but in 1840 he moved to St. Petersburg, where Herzen paid him a visit in order to wake him from this slumber. He hardly had to try. "I am so stupid I should not have known how to begin" our conversation, he told Herzen. "You've won. Three or four months in Petersburg have done more to convince me than all the arguments. Let us forget this nonsense."[83] Petersburg had stimulated him not because its atmosphere was so enlightened, but because there he came face to face with the deadening realities of the Nicholas system, which convinced him of the futility, even immorality of the passive and impractical speculations of Moscow's romantic circles. As Herzen commented in connection with Belinsky's epiphany, "Petersburg, like all mature people, does not listen to babblers, but demands action."[84] Belinsky would later say the same, explaining that it seemed to be Petersburg's destiny to work and do, and Moscow's to prepare the doers.[85] From this moment Belinsky never looked back and embarked on an illustrious though tragically short career as Russia's leading literary critic and Westernizer.

Because overt political activity and commentary was impossible, Belinsky became a literary critic writing for *Annals of the Homeland* and *The Contemporary*, veiling his commentary in literary articles that could get past the censor. More importantly, he regarded political activity as fruitless in contemporary conditions. "To give Russia in her present state a constitution is to ruin her. . . . To our people liberty . . . simply means license. The liberated Russian nation would not go to a parliament, but run to the taverns to drink, break glass, and hang the gentry because they shave their beards and wear European clothes . . .—education, that is the road to happiness."[86] Writers and artists had a social and moral duty to educate and build the moral conscience of society, and thus better it and ready it for political reforms. Their work must be judged in part by such standards, yet he did not favor producing art crudely as a social weapon. "Do not worry about the incarnation of ideas," he warned. "If you are a poet, your works will contain them without your knowledge."[87] He mercilessly skewered hacks while hailing new talents such as Turgenev and Dostoevsky. With his wit, intense and penetrating analysis, and moral stands he soon attracted a large and loyal following. Petersburg's readers eagerly awaited his next articles and could be seen devouring their pages in the city's cafés. Personally, Belinsky was clumsy and uncomfortable in society and shunned the limelight, but he regularly attended literary evenings in his friends' homes, where he would usually sit quietly until someone said something with which he disagreed, at which point he would pounce on his opponent and begin an impassioned argument. As his fame grew, he became the star of the literary evenings at his friends Ivan and Avdotia Panaev.

Belinsky best expressed his mature views in a famous 1847 letter to Gogol in response to Gogol's *Selected Passages from Correspondence with Friends*, in which Gogol had espoused conservative religious and monarchist views in common with the Slavophiles, disappointing many who had idolized him. Having grown up in the provinces amidst poverty, illiteracy, and serfdom, one of Belinsky's peeves was the Slavophiles' glorification of Orthodoxy, the peasants, and nonexistent traditions. To Gogol he explained:

Russia sees her salvation not in mysticism or asceticism or pietism, but in the successes of civilization, enlightenment, and humanity. What she needs is not sermons (she has heard enough of them!) or prayers (she has repeated them too often!), but the awakening in the people of a sense of their human dignity lost for so many centuries amid dirt and refuse; she needs rights and laws conforming not to the preaching of the church but to common sense and justice, and their strictest possible observance.[88]

He leveled his harshest criticism against Russian Orthodoxy, which had "always served as the prop of the knout and the servant of despotism."[89] Christ had taught freedom, equality, and brotherhood, but the church was "the champion of inequality, a flatterer of authority, and the enemy and prosecutor of brotherhood among men."[90]

In his essay *Petersburg and Moscow*, Belinsky portrayed Petersburg and its tradition as the moral antidote to Russia's past. He loved Moscow, but thought it could not tame new ideas and went to extremes. The carrier of new ideas, he realized, must be Petersburg because it can handle them to good purpose, "and in this lay its great significance for Russia":

> Petersburg is not carried away by ideas; it is a practical and sober man. It will never mistake its flannel frock-coat for a Roman toga; it would rather play at cards than busy itself with the impossible; you will not stun it with theories or speculations, and it cannot tolerate dreams; it does not like to stand in its swamp, but this is still better than to hang in the air without support. . . . In a word, Petersburg doesn't believe, it demands action. In it each person strives toward his goal and, no matter what it may be, achieves it.[91]

Belinsky's hope and approach was exemplified by St. Petersburg's main group of intellectuals and social critics during Nicholas's reign, the Petrashevtsy, who were active from 1845 to 1849. The group's most famous alumnus was Fedor Dostoevsky, but it was named after its founder, Mikhail Butashevich-Petrashevsky (1821–66). The son of a prominent army physician, Petrashevsky, like Pushkin, attended the Lyceum (graduating in 1839) and took a minor position at the Ministry of Foreign Affairs. In his spare time he attended lectures at the University, where he met the immensely popular young professor of political economy, Victor Poroshin, to whose lectures the youth of Petersburg flocked. Poroshin was well acquainted with the latest European thinking and propounded the theories of the French utopian socialist, Charles Fourier. Soon Petrashevsky too was preaching the ideas of Fourier and other French socialists to all who would listen. By 1845 he and like-minded friends began gathering on Friday evenings at his wooden home on Pokrovskaya Square just off Sadovaya Street. At first the gatherings were informal and mainly social, often with large numbers of invitees, not the narrow "circles" of a few intense intellectuals characteristic in Moscow. One participant described them as follows:

> We did not have any sort of organized society or general plan of activity, but once each week at Petrashevsky's there was a gathering . . . and it was always possible to meet new people there. . . . The city's news was brought there and everyone spoke loudly about everything, without any reservations whatsoever. . . . At these gatherings, no

specific projects or proposals were worked out, but judgments about the existing order were expressed, jokes were often told, and complaints about our present condition were voiced. . . . Our small circle, centered around Petrashevsky at the end of the 1840s, carried within it the seeds of all the reforms of the 1860s.[92]

Another member, the satirical writer Mikhail Saltykov-Shchedrin, recalled the "long winter evenings and our friendly modest conversation, lasting long after midnight. How easy it was to live in that time, what a deep faith in the future, what various hopes and ideas inspired us . . . a new life blew over our souls."[93]

The core Petrashevtsy had serious intentions of somehow bringing about change, and they went to Petrashevsky's to debate it. They amassed a large multilingual library of books on philosophy, economics, and social and political thought. This was not hard, as the city's bookstores, especially the secondhand booksellers, either secretly carried or could obtain forbidden publications. People from all walks of life became associated with the group, including rich landowners, students and recent Lyceum graduates, civil servants, Imperial Guards officers, merchants, economists, as well as literary figures such as the literary critic Valerian Maikov and his poet brother Apollon, and the young writers Dostoevsky and Saltykov-Shchedrin. Some members were the sons of Decembrists. The Petrashevtsy estimated their members and known sympathizers at between 500 and 800,[94] which made their influence wide.[95] Individual members published in the city's many journals, while as a cooperative effort they published the popular *Pocket Dictionary of Foreign Terms* in two installments in 1845 and 1846, the entries in which were used as vehicles to expound on their ideas. Dedicated to Grand Duke Michael in order to gain favor, after publication the book was deemed subversive and an order was issued to confiscate copies from the bookstores, but this was never carried out.[96] They planned eventually to have their own printing press.

The Petrashevtsy held widely differing views. According to Dostoevsky, nobody at Petrashevsky's ever agreed with anyone else about anything.[97] But they shared the Enlightenment belief that man's nature is good, as well as Fourier's that man had been corrupted by social and political systems, which Fourier thought could be put right by life in socialist communities known as phalansteries. (Petrashevsky, a landowner, in 1847 tried to transform one of his villages into a phalanstery, but the suspicious peasants burnt it down.) The Petrashevtsy were cosmopolitans rather than nationalists and held universal values, to whom the dignity and freedom of each individual (rather than *sobornost*) was paramount; religion was unimportant. Like the Freemasons, they advocated and practiced education of the people, were the first to conceive of "going to the people" to realize social change, and proposed reforms of serfdom and the judiciary.[98] Only a few extremists like Nikolai Speshnev preached armed revolt. Like the Decembrists, they valued Novgorodian rather than Muscovite traditions; in 1847, they even installed a *veche* bell with a figure of Liberty on it to convene their meetings. Their opinion about St. Petersburg was

ambivalent. Because Fourier, following Rousseau, had taught that large cities corrupt the human spirit and should be destroyed, the Petrashevtsy were bound to dislike Petersburg, even as they upheld its Westernism. Moreover, Imperial St. Petersburg represented despotism.

Their downfall began in February 1848, when Petrashevsky distributed to the
nobles in Petersburg's Duma copies of his pamphlet proposing reforms of serfdom.
His proposals were modest, but they struck at the privileges of the landed nobility.
This attracted Nicholas's and the police's attention, after which the Petrashevtsy
were closely watched. Nor was the general environment conducive to toleration.
In mid-summer a cholera epidemic hit, and a drought had led to a harvest failure,
famine, suspicious fires, and peasant unrest. But most of all, just when Petrashevsky
was distributing his brochure on serfdom, word reached Petersburg of the socialist
revolution in Paris, followed by the news two days later of Louis Philippe's abdication and the declaration of a republic. Saltykov-Shchedrin recalled the moment:

> I was at a matinee at the Italian opera when suddenly, like an electric spark, the news
> penetrated the whole audience . . . the old men waved their spectacles, twisted and
> twirled their mustaches, threatening to take up arms, the young could scarcely restrain
> their ecstasy. . . . France seemed the land of miracles.[99]

Revolutions soon erupted in Italy and the Hapsburg domains and seemed to be
heading toward Russia.

The exciting events in Europe riveted the city's attention and became the talk of
the educated public. The atmosphere in Petersburg resembled that under Catherine in 1789. The city's educated youth almost universally supported the revolutions.
They put aside their "thick journals" and read whatever newspapers they could get
their hands on. Demand for newspapers, especially foreign ones, far exceeded supply, and their price tags became exorbitant. The city's cafés and confectioneries—
the new Passage, the Wolff and Berange, Izler's, Dominique—became meccas for
those who could read foreign languages because the proprietors provided foreign
newspapers to customers, who passed the precious copies amongst themselves and
guardedly shared impressions while agents from the Third Section listened for un-
restrained talk. The more daring climbed onto tables to read aloud the news and
the speeches of French radicals such as Louis Blanc. Shopkeepers were soon selling
portraits of Europe's revolutionaries, which were hung in the homes of many Petrashevtsy. People also flocked to Petrashevsky's home, not merely to learn the news
but to discuss and plan how to respond.

Nicholas was naturally displeased. Revolution in Europe not only threatened to
inspire unrest in Russia but also implicated his foreign policy of standing as the gen-
darme of legitimacy in Europe. Thus, when Nicholas received the news of the new
republic at a court ball, according to legend he told the officers in attendance,

"Gentlemen saddle your horses. A republic has been declared in France!"[100] As the revolutions spread into central Europe, Nicholas feared that he would have to resort to military action. (Eventually, in June 1849, he did dispatch troops to Hungary, Gallacia, and Transylvania to quell unrest there.) In Petersburg, he notified all French citizens that they were free either to stay or to leave, but if they stayed they must promise not to foment revolution in Russia. Rumors spread that the University would be closed.[101] At first Nicholas also tried to eliminate the many foreign newspapers and periodicals from the city and restrict domestic reporting on the revolutions, but he soon gave up. Nicholas reasoned that he could deal with educated Petersburg society, while the illiterate could not read the publications anyway. Instead, Nicholas drew the line at discussing the revolutions in a way that might provoke general unrest. In March he warned the city's nobles to be careful about what they said and where, explaining, "These conversations, harmless among educated people, often inspire in your servants thoughts that would never have occurred to them on their own. This is very dangerous."[102]

Much like the Decembrists when confronted with Alexander I's sudden death, the Petrashevtsy were now put on the spot. Should they seize the opportunity to foment revolution like their European brethren or continue along gradualist lines? Naturally, opinions differed. A few radicals like Speshnev advocated armed rebellion and an immediate campaign of propaganda to agitate the people. They argued that gradual reform was hopeless given Nicholas's reactionary response to the revolutions in Europe, and they also claimed to have detected in that summer's peasant unrest a revolutionary spirit. Meetings now grew more organized and were dedicated to deciding upon concrete actions, but the number of Petrashevtsy began to dwindle as the less committed began to fear the Third Section. This fear was justified, as one of the Section's spies, Peter Antonelli, infiltrated the group in March 1849. The debates over what to do became fierce and reached their climax in mid-April 1849, at which point the Petrashevtsy split into factions, and the extremists led by Speshnev began conspiring for armed revolt (though the government did not learn the extent of this). Dostoevsky was one of his followers. Speshnev exploited talented writers for propaganda purposes, and even bound them closer to him by giving them loans, which Dostoevsky too accepted. "I am with him and his," Dostoevsky admitted. "From now on I have my own Mephistopheles."[103] Dostoevsky later used Speshnev as the prototype for Stavrogin in *The Possessed*.

When Antonelli reported on what he had seen and heard, the authorities decided that matters had gone far enough. On the night of April 23, 1849, Petrashevsky and several others were arrested as they emerged from his home. More arrests followed, and eventually the authorities questioned no fewer than 252 individuals. Lacking any evidence of concrete plans to overthrow the state, the authorities instead charged the Petrashevtsy with a "conspiracy of ideas." Among the accused was Dostoevsky, whose main offense had been to read a copy of Belinsky's letter to Gogol at the climactic April 15 meeting. Dostoevsky's cell in the Peter and Paul Fortress has become a city landmark. He and 20 others were sentenced to death by firing squad, while 51 more were to be exiled. Nicholas turned the execution into a cruel charade in which the condemned were subjected to the psychological torment of impending death. At dawn on December 22, 1849, the prisoners were led out of the Fortress to Semenovskaya Square, where the sentences were read, a priest called on the condemned to repent, and they were dressed in white hooded cloaks. The first three were led and tied to their posts, their heads were covered, the drumroll began, and the firing squad began taking aim. But at that very moment a messenger arrived bearing a last-minute reprieve from Nicholas. The sentences had been commuted to exile and hard labor in Siberia. The prisoners were immediately shackled and put in the covered carriage that took them to Siberia.

In light of what the moderate majority of Petrashevtsy might have achieved and the later over-radicalization of Russian social and political thought and activism, the breakup of the Petrashevtsy circle stands along with that of the Decembrists as one of the great tragedies and turning points of Russian 19th-century intellectual, social, and political history. Still, their influence was sizable, and they are recognized as the forerunners of the populists of the 1860s and 1870s, many of whom (such as Chernyshevsky) were originally associated with the Petrashevtsy.

Nicholas's reign thus ended as it had begun, with the forcible suppression of Petersburg's most enlightened and reform-minded citizens. In the interim, instead of modernizing the country, Nicholas had tried to create a future based in the past, and failed. The proof came in the debacle of the Crimean War (1854–55), when Russia's army proved no match for the technologically advanced armies of the West's rapidly industrializing powers. Peter the Great never would have let Russia fall behind, and so Russia's defeat once again put the Petersburg idea front and center on the country's agenda.

In his waning years, Nicholas came to realize that he had failed, though he could never quite understand why. The ray of hope that had opened when he first met with Pushkin was extinguished when he sent Dostoevsky to Siberia. Nicholas's censor Nikitenko perhaps summarized it best when he confided to his diary that "the main shortcoming of the reign of Nicholas Pavlovich lay in the fact that it was all a mistake."[104] As Nicholas lay dying of pneumonia, he admitted his failure to his son, the future Alexander II. "I wanted to take everything difficult, everything serious, upon my shoulders and to leave to you a peaceful, well-ordered, and happy realm. Providence decreed otherwise."[105] Some even suggest that Nicholas's death was a suicide, but this would be inconsistent with Nicholas's beliefs and character. But even to suggest this illustrates how his death symbolized to many that his system and set of beliefs had reached a dead end. In truth, as Nikitenko observed, Nicholas, devastated by his army's defeat in the Crimea, really "died from shame and despair."[106]

History has not been kind to Nicholas, but Pushkin's importance and fame have only grown over time. And it has been Pushkin's Petersburg that has been so fondly remembered and brought to life in so many later books and works of art. Be that as it may, the complex ties between the Poet and the Tsar did not stop growing with their deaths. In 1891, Nicholas's grandson, Grand Duke Mikhail, married Pushkin's granddaughter, Sophia Merenberg, and in 1895 Pushkin's grandson, Georgi Merenberg, married Nicholas's granddaughter (Alexander II's daughter), Princess Olga Yurievskaya.

CHAPTER 10

Dostoevsky's St. Petersburg

This is a city of half-crazy people. If we were a scientific people, doctors, lawyers and philosophers could make the most valuable investigations in Petersburg, each in his own field. There are few places where you'll find so many gloomy, harsh and strange influences on the soul of a man as in Petersburg.

SVIDRIGAILOV IN DOSTOEVSKY'S
Crime and Punishment

Petersburg is the touchstone of a man: whoever, living in it, has not been carried away by the whirlpool of phantom life, has managed to keep both heart and soul but not at the expense of common sense, to preserve his human dignity without falling into quixoticism—to him you can boldly extend your hand as to a man.

VISSARION BELINSKY[1]

When Dostoevsky returned to Petersburg from exile in 1859, he was a changed man. But by then the city too had changed, and there was a new Emperor, Alexander II. When Dostoevsky was exiled in 1849, the capital still had the aristocratic and orderly imperial sheen of Pushkin's Petersburg. In 1848 Dostoevsky had written *White Nights*, a lovely romance set in a Petersburg of classical beauty, in which the city's night sky was "so bright and starry that when you looked at it the first question that came into your mind was whether it was really possible that all sorts of bad-tempered and unstable people could live under such a glorious sky." But within two decades the city was beset with the blights of the early industrial revolution already familiar in the West, only made worse by Russian conditions and Petersburg's location and climate. Growing numbers of the proletariat labored in the city's belching factories, lived in crowded tenements and cellars, and were ravaged by disease; the city's high life went on, but it was becoming dominated by rich industrialists and merchants rather than aristocrats. Young radicals like those in *The Possessed* clamored for revolution. This welter of rapid and confusing change, human suffering, contradictions, and extremes inspired much of the city's great art, music, and literature of the time, none greater than the works of Dostoevsky. Beginning with *Poor Folk,* Dostoevsky's Petersburg was one of dreamlike gloom and mystery, commotion, squalor, and lost souls, including the radical groups of misdirected youth.

Petersburg was fortunate that Dostoevsky was not only a novelist but also a journalist writing for local newspapers and journals, including two which he founded and ran himself or with his brother, Mikhail: *Vremya* ("Time") in 1861–63, and *Epokha* in 1864–65. The city was his "beat," and he knew all the key goings on. He was fascinated by cities, how they affect people, and how society develops in them. While a follower of Fourier, he had come to regard large cities as unnatural creations which corrupt man's essentially good nature. For a talented writer interested in art more than social issues, this was an opportunity to create great literature. Dostoevsky loved to watch life in whatever city he visited and walked their streets endlessly, looking for ideas. His daughter later wrote that Dostoevsky "would roam down the darkest and most remote streets of Petersburg. In the course of his walking he would converse with himself and gesticulate, so that passers-by would turn around to watch. Friends who ran into him considered him a madman. He would stop, suddenly struck by the smile of a stranger that had imprinted itself on his brain," and likewise with the striking outlines of the city's landscape, the form of an expressive building or a bend in a canal.[2] He knew intimately the city's neighborhoods, especially the lower-class districts along Voznesensky Prospect and around Haymarket Square with their narrow streets and alleys, noisy street trade, lodging houses and brothels.

While traveling abroad he did the same thing. When in the summer of 1862 he spent a week in Florence with his friend Nikolai Strakhov, they visited the Uffizi, but Dostoevsky quickly grew impatient, and over Strakhov's protests they abandoned the museum to walk the streets, which is how they spent the rest of their stay. Beautiful as they were, Florence's landmarks interested him only as a backdrop to the human drama being played out on the city stage. He liked most of all the most crowded and bustling parts of town where he could study the faces and what they told about people's inner conflicts. It was likewise in London. There he was fascinated by the city's Haymarket, where among other things he observed mothers bringing their young daughters to the street to be sold to men. (He later portrayed this image in his Petersburg story *The Dream of a Ridiculous Man*.) He also visited the World Exposition at the Crystal Palace, that icon of capitalist industrialization, which both awed and horrified him by its soulless materialism and affected his opinion of the West and of where Russia might end up if it followed that example. He was convinced that the West's bourgeois order was doomed to come crashing down, like Babylon, feelings expressed in his essay *Winter Notes on Summer Impressions* (1863):

> You look at these hundreds of thousands, these millions of people humbly streaming here from all over the face of the earth—people who come with a single thought, peacefully, persistently and silently crowding into this colossal palace—and you feel that here

something final has been accomplished, accomplished and brought to an end. It is a kind of biblical scene, something about Babylon, a kind of prophecy from the Apocalypse fulfilled before your very eyes. You feel that it would require a great deal of eternal spiritual resistance and denial not to succumb, not to surrender to the impression, not to bow to fact, and not to idolize Baal, that is not to accept what is as your ideal.[3]

Since his Petrashevtsy days, Dostoevsky had viewed cities as concentrations of man-made miseries and corruption of the human spirit. His art was dedicated to exploring the many faces and deepest reaches of this spirit and the means for its renewal. Russia's social critics of the time were arguing that political and constitutional reform was useless without social and economic reform. Dostoevsky went further, holding that true social reform could not occur, and that attempts at it would be useless, without the spiritual regeneration of individuals and the Russian people as a whole. Thus, his fiction acknowledges but does not dwell on the characteristics of Petersburg itself or its social problems in the manner of Western realists such as Dickens, and generally his characters are not social. Rather, the city's role is as a backdrop whose beauty, dreamy moods, weather, bustling crowds, and the harsh conditions of industrialism are important only insofar as they influence the spirit, psyche, and actions of the characters. Dostoevsky once said, "They say I am a psychologist. Not true. I am a realist in a higher sense, that is, I depict the depths of the human soul."[4] To Dostoevsky, Petersburg was "the most abstract and premeditated city in the whole world,"[5] and as such it was the most perfect city for his art. Over it reigned the new Tsar, Alexander II.

THE TSAR LIBERATOR

Alexander II (1818–81) was not brought up to be a reformer or liberator, but unlike his father at least he was brought up to rule. Alexander was originally slated for a military career, but when Nicholas became Emperor, suddenly Alexander was heir to the throne, and his education had to be broadened to prepare him to rule. In 1826 Nicholas selected Pushkin's mentor, the poet Vasily Zhukovsky (who had freed his serfs), to supervise his son's education, and he drew up a detailed plan under which Alexander received the most comprehensive education of any Romanov ruler to date. Unfortunately, Alexander was an inattentive and mediocre student, like his ancestors preferring the parade ground.

When Alexander's education was declared complete in 1837, he toured Russia, and then Europe, where he visited every major country except France, Spain, and Portugal. He was especially impressed with Germany, and, while in Darmstadt he fell in love with Princess Marie of Hesse, known to be the offspring of one of her mother's lovers of low origin. Nicholas and Alexandra were aghast and opposed the marriage. As Emperor, Alexander was too often weak and backed down in the face of opposition, but not so in love. He would not give up and eventually overcame his parents' objections. In 1841 Marie, now Maria Alexandrovna, and Alexander were wed in the Winter Palace.

Alexander was appointed to several civilian and military positions to give him experience, and from 1842 he essentially served as Nicholas's deputy and as his regent during his absences from the capital. As a result, Alexander became something of a creature of the Nicholas system and a believer in it. Like Nicholas, he firmly believed in autocracy, revered military principles, and held to Orthodoxy and considered himself God's anointed representative. Alexander's beliefs were well-known, and Russian progressives held little hope that his regime would differ in substance from his father's, though it might have softer edges.

But when Alexander assumed power in February 1855, Russia's defeat in the Crimean War was only months away. The Nicholas system had failed, and it was clear that Alexander would preside over its dismantling. Russia was rapidly falling behind the West and needed to modernize. Much as Peter the Great had realized that the viability of the Russian state was in jeopardy around 1700, Alexander now understood the same, and like Peter he responded with reforms. Unlike Peter, however, he reformed reluctantly rather than enthusiastically, and when faced with opposition, like Catherine II and Alexander I he usually backed down.

Alexander's reign began with a symbolic victory for St. Petersburg's progressives when the new Emperor amnestied the Petrashevtsy, including Dostoevsky, as well as the surviving Decembrists. But the most pressing need was to reform Russia's semi-feudal economic and social system, which was holding back industrialization, economic growth, and prosperity. To the moral arguments against serfdom were now added the economic, and these were enough to overcome the opposition of the landowners. But the opposition was still intense, intrigue was rife, the terms and implementation of the emancipation were extremely complicated, and so it took several years to finalize the program. The effort initially proceeded in a secret committee, but in December 1857 Alexander publicly announced his intentions to a group of St. Petersburg nobles and the debate became public. The city's intellectuals hailed the announcement, with Nikolai Chernyshevsky comparing Alexander to Peter the Great and Herzen chiming in with praise from abroad. The young future revolutionary, Peter Kropotkin, then a Cadet, later wrote that "the whole disposition of St. Petersburg, whether in the drawing rooms or the streets, was such that it was impossible to go back."[6]

Finally on February 19, 1861, Alexander signed the statutes of emancipation, which were announced on March 5, a Sunday. The manifesto proclaiming the emancipation was posted all around town and read in city squares and from the pulpit in the city's churches, in one location by Alexander himself. Kropotkin, not a churchgoer, learned about it when his servant burst into his bedroom and woke him, shouting: "Prince, Freedom! The manifesto is posted on the Gostiny Dvor. . . . People stand around; one reads, the others listen. It *is* freedom."[7] It was also an emotional day for the censor Nikitenko, a former serf himself. After reading the act aloud to his family at home, he felt compelled to go out to the streets:

> I could not remain at home. I had the urge to go out and stroll in the streets and, so to say, merge with the renewed people. At intersections the announcement from the Governor-General was posted, and around it people crowded, and while one read the others listened. . . . To my ears continuously came the words "declaration of liberty" and "freedom." . . . From among my acquaintances I met Galakhov. "Christ has risen!" I said to him. "Christ has risen!" he replied and we exchanged our joy. Then I called on Rebinder. He ordered champagne and we raised our glasses in honor of Alexander II.[8]

As the excitement spread, many Petersburgers feared unrest and stayed indoors. But the city was well patrolled and there were no incidents, only joy and celebration. Nikitenko saw everywhere only "joyous but quiet faces."[9] That evening in the theaters the performances were accompanied by repeated renditions of the national anthem, "God Save the Tsar," sung by the audiences so loudly that they drowned out the musicians, while outside crowds still lined the lamplit streets. A few days later a ceremony was held on Palace Square in which a deputation of peasants formally thanked the Tsar for granting them freedom. Alexander then addressed the crowd: "The work was already begun in my father's day, but he was unable to accomplish it in his lifetime. With God's help, it fell to my lot to complete the task for your good. Now, my children, go and thank God; pray for the eternal repose of my father; prove yourselves useful to the fatherland."[10] This was followed by a parade, after which Alexander, still on horseback, called out, "The officers to me!" As they gathered around him, he reminded them of the need for the nobility to make sacrifices to remedy centuries of injustice and for the good of the country.[11]

The emancipation was followed by other reforms. In 1864 Alexander created local elective bodies (*zemstvos*) responsible for local administration of police functions, social services, and public health. Also in 1864 Alexander reformed the court system, introducing trial by jury to replace the former secret proceedings, and making judges independent by giving them permanent tenure and setting standards for competence and honesty. In 1874 he introduced universal compulsory military service, which ended the forced recruitment of peasants for what was essentially lifelong military service. Higher education in the city had stagnated under Nicholas, especially after 1848, but Alexander liberalized university education to accord new rights to both professors and students.

The reforms bred expectations that were impossible to satisfy, and soon Alexander recoiled from further reform efforts in an attempt to keep matters from spinning out of control. In the provinces, many *zemstvo* leaders sought to build on electoral local government to push for constitutional government at the national level. But as before, the effort foundered on autocracy, with Alexander opposing their efforts toward a civil society. He denied local leaders the right to make representations to central authorities, which stifled efforts to modernize rural life. In Petersburg, enlightened officials, merchants, professional associations, and intellectuals also agitated for constitutional reform, also were rebuffed, and were unable to organize. Eventually, the disappointment bred an extremism that would result in Alexander's assassination and eventually the monarchy's downfall.

MODERNIZATION IN ST. PETERSBURG

Unlike his father, Alexander saw rapid industrialization and development of the country's infrastructure as the key to regaining Russia's greatness and making it competitive with the West. His reforms paved the way. State enterprises largely yielded to private companies, and the advent of joint-stock companies meant that many enterprises were formed not by a single owner but with capital raised from investors. The main drivers of industry were Russia's expanding network of railroads and the military, as Russia's army and navy were being modernized. Demand for iron, steel, armaments, machinery, and rolling stock skyrocketed. St. Petersburg became a center for heavy industry (whereas light industry and trading prevailed in Moscow), focusing on metallurgy, machinery, and shipbuilding, traits which the city retains today. But lighter industry also grew, especially textiles, tanning, tallow and soap, chemicals, food and tobacco products, and (for the bureaucracy and publications) paper and printing.[12] Since the late 18th century, industry had been kept largely out of Petersburg's center, a process that was completed by the closures of the Admiralty shipyard in 1844 and of the Foundry on Liteiny Prospect. By mid-century the city was surrounded by a ring of factories centered on the mouth of the Fontanka and Neva, the northern Vyborg, Petersburg, and Vasilievsky (Island) regions, along the Obvodny Canal, and along the Neva on the road to Schlüsselburg.[13] To support industrial development, several technical institutes, such as the Technological Institute and Institute for Transportation Engineers, were established in which scholars, inventors, and scientists such as Dmitry Mendeleev (who developed the periodic table) worked and students studied, beginning a city tradition of high-level technological research, scholarship, and education which remains to this day.

The city's heritage as a haven of foreign ideas and innovations, capitalistic reforms of Alexander's Minister of Finance, Count Mikhail Reutern, that made investment in Russia attractive and more reliable, a wide range of investment opportunities, the prospect of high returns, and economic stagnation abroad attracted a growing flow of foreign investment to Petersburg, and much of the city's new industry came to be owned by foreigners and funded with foreign capital. After the Admiralty ceased its shipbuilding activity, the new ironclad steamships were built by new enterprises such as the Baltic Shipbuilding and Mechanical Factory, established by the foreigners Carr and McPherson on Vasilievsky Island in 1856. In 1883 the German Heinrich Kamp formed the St. Petersburg Iron and Wire

Works.[14] In 1862 Ludwig Nobel founded the Phoenix metallurgy plant and steel mill on the Vyborg Embankment. The Russian-American Triangle Rubber Manufactory, founded in 1860 on the Obvodny Canal, employed over 11,000 workers and held a monopoly on rubber production in Russia. Other American companies such as International Harvester and the Singer Sewing Machine Company established operations in the city. Even Heinrich Schliemann, the discoverer of Troy, was based in Petersburg in 1846–69, beginning as the agent of a Dutch trading firm and then becoming a successful independent merchant trading mainly in indigo.[15] Foreign investment increased tenfold from 9.7 million to 97 million rubles from 1860 to 1870, more than doubled to 214.7 million by 1890, and then exploded to 280.1 million in 1895 and 911 million in 1900.[16]

But most new industry was Russian owned, and the city came to have its share of rich native industrialist families such as the Semyanikovs, Poletikas, Obukhovs, Kudriavtsevs, and Putilovs. Chief among them was Nikolai Putilov, originally an engineer at the Admiralty who made a name for himself during the Crimean War as the designer of steam-powered gunboats. After the war, the government sold him a foundry in the hope that he could harness modern technology to support the railroad and armaments booms. He succeeded beyond expectations, and his family became one of the wealthiest in St. Petersburg, living like aristocracy in palatial homes staffed with servants, furnished lavishly, and stocked with fine food and wines.

Together with industry grew commerce and banking, which continued to employ more people than industry until late in the century.[17] Traffic at the city's port grew rapidly, its value doubling between 1850 and 1870. In 1872–83 a new port was built in its present location, to which a sea channel was dredged from Kronshtadt and railroad tracks were laid from land. While St. Petersburg's port remained the largest in Russia, it lost ground to those in Riga, Reval, and Odessa, and sea transport as a whole was partially supplanted by the new international network of railroads which could operate year round and likewise connected Russia with Europe. Thus, the Petersburg port's traditional dominance over Russia's foreign trade faded, falling from one-third of Russia's foreign trade in the 1860s to one-fifth in the 1880s. Railroads also dislocated much of the city's river traffic, which had traditionally hauled grain, firewood, hay, construction materials, and lumber into the city.

To support commerce, a sophisticated financial infrastructure grew up which included dozens of joint-stock commercial banks, brokers and agents, credit and insurance companies, and, of course, the Exchange on Vasilievsky Island. By late century, there were 28 banks on Nevsky Prospect alone.[18] Many were affiliates of major Western banks such as Credit Lyonnais. The city became one of Europe's largest banking centers, behind only London, Paris, and Berlin.

The city now bristled with technological innovations. In 1855 the first telegraph station went into service on Admiralty Embankment; by 1858, Alexander had installed telegraph connections between the Winter Palace and all other imperial res-

1. Peter the Great. Engraving by J. Hubraken (1724) after the original by Karl Moor, 1717.

2. Feofan Prokopovich was the most educated man in Russia at the time and a firm supporter of Peter's reforms. He understood Peter's genius and significance better than anyone else. Engraving by Loira.

3. Catherine I entered Russian history as a prisoner of war, became Peter's mistress, then wife and, finally, the Empress of Russia. Portrait by J. M. Nattier, 1717.

4. Alexander Menshikov made a dizzying career from a pie seller to the Governor of Petersburg and second in Russia only to Peter I himself, but he ended his life in exile and poverty.

5. *Ships on the Neva with the Peter and Paul Fortress in the background. The maritime theme figures prominently in the art of Peter I's time. Engraving by Alexei Zubov, 1717.*

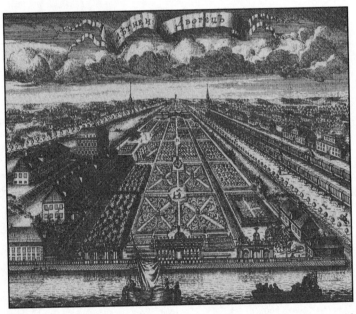

6. *The Summer Garden during Peter's time. Like many panoramas and maps of the city in its first century, the image is idealized. Engraving by Alexei Zubov, 1717.*

7. Peter II by unknown artist after a painting by I.P. Ludden, 1725.

8. Burkhard Christopher Münnich, Governor of St. Petersburg under Peter II and Anna Ioannovna, later exiled and then brought back as advisor to Peter III. Engraving by M. Bernigeroth, 1740.

9. Empress Anna Ioannovna. Engraving by J. Mentzel after an original by M. Bernigeroth, 1733.

10. Ernst Biron, Anna Ioannovna's lover and virtually a co-ruler. Engraving by Ivan Sokolov, 1740.

11. The Winter Palace as reconstructed by Rastrelli for Anna Ioannovna, by Mikhail Makhaev, mid 18th century.

12. The Twelve Colleges. Construction began under Peter I and was completed by Anna Ioannovna. Engraving by E. Vnukov after a drawing by Mikhail Makhaev, 1753.

13. *Empress Elizabeth. Engraving by Evgraf Chemesov after an original by Louis Tocque, 1761.*

14. *Bartolomeo Rastrelli by Pietro Rotari, late 1750s.*

15. *Mikhail Lomonosov by unknown artist, mid 18th century.*

16. *Peter III, an engraving after a painting by F. Rokotov, 1758.*

17. Elizabeth's wooden Summer Palace constructed by Rastrelli at the junction of the Moika and Fontanka, where the Mikhailovsky Castle now stands. To the left in the distance is the Anichkov Palace. Engraving by A. Grekov after a drawing by Mikhail Makhaev, 1753.

18. Anichkov Palace, with a view down tree-lined Nevsky Prospect toward the Admiralty. Engraving by Yakov Vasiliev after a drawing by Mikhail Makhaev, 1753.

19. *Catherine II by F. Rokotov, 1780s.*

20. *Gavrila Derzhavin, engraving by I. Pozhalostin after a painting by V. Borovikovsky, 1811.*

21. *Emperor Paul I as Grand Master of the Maltese Order by S.Tonchi, 1801.*

22. *Alexander I. Portrait by unknown artist, early 19th century.*

23. Rastrelli's Winter Palace from the Neva. It was built for Elizabeth, but she died before the palace was completed, and Catherine II was the first ruler to occupy it. Painting by I. Charlemagne.

24. The unveiling of the Monument to Peter the Great (the Bronze Horseman) on Senate Square in 1782. Engraving by A. Mylnikov (mid-19th century) after a drawing by A. Davidov, 1782.

25. *Mikhail Speransky, engraving by Thomas Wright.*

26. *Carlo Rossi. Portrait by B. Mitoire, 1820s.*

27. *The Palace Square. The blessing of the Alexander Column on August 30, 1834. Painting by V.E. Raev, 1834.*

28. *Kazan Cathedral in winter. The street is Nevsky Prospect, and the Catherine (now Griboyedov) Canal flows under Kazan Bridge. Lithograph by L.J. Arnout, 1840s.*

29. *The Triumphal Arch of the General Staff Building from Palace Square. Lithograph by Karl Beggrow, 1822, done before the Arch was completed and therefore depicts atop it Rossi's original conception of two female figures supporting Russia's coat of arms. Nicholas I changed this to the sculpture of Victory in a chariot.*

30. Gostiny Dvor at the intersection of Nevsky Prospect (right) and Sadovaya Street. To the right is the tower of the City Duma building. By Benjamin Paterssen, 1802.

31. The strelka *of Vasilievsky Island during Pushkin's time, with Thomon's new Exchange building and the rostral columns. Engraving by an unknown artist published in 1827.*

32. Zakharov's reconstructed Admiralty building during Alexander I's reign. The corner of the Winter Palace (right) appears nearer than in reality. Engraving by unknown artist published in 1827.

33. Police Bridge on Nevsky Prospect across the Moika during Alexander I's reign. To the left across Nevsky is the Stroganov Palace. Engraving after a drawing by M.F. Damame-Demartrais, 1812.

34. *The great flood of 1824, which inspired Pushkin's* Bronze Horseman. *To the left is the Bolshoi Theater and in the background is Nikolsky Morskoi Cathedral. Painting by Alexander Alexeyev (1826-1835).*

35. *The Decembrist rebellion on Senate Square. To the left are construction works for St. Isaac's Cathedral. Copy of a watercolor by Karl Kollmann, 1825.*

36. *Nicholas I by Franz Kruger.*

37. *Alexander Pushkin by unknown artist after an original by Orest Kiprensky, 1827.*

38. *Natalya Pushkina. Watercolor by Vladimir Gau, 1842-43.*

39. *The composer Mikhail Glinka. Lithograph by R. Berendgoth after a drawing by N. Breze, 1857.*

40. Anichkov Bridge on Nevsky Prospect across the Fontanka late in Nicholas I's reign, with Shtakenshneider's Beloselsky-Belozersky Palace in the background. By L.J. Jakottet and G.L. Regamey, from a drawing by Joseph Charlemagne, 1850s.

41. The Dutch Church on Nevsky Prospect. By an unknown artist, mid-19th century.

43. Alexander III. Photo by Levitsky, 1883.

42. Alexander II by I. Tyurin, 1874.

44. Feodor Dostoevsky. Etching by V. Bobrov, 1883.

45. Peter Tchaikovsky. Photo by A. Fedecki, 1898.

46. Haymarket Square. Lithograph from an original by F. Perrot, 1840s.

47. The assassination of Alexander II on March 1, 1881, on the embankment of the Catherine Canal. Lithograph by D. Rudnev, 1881.

48. Interior of the Eliseev grocery store on Nevsky Prospect in 1901.

49. St. Isaac's Square and Cathedral at the beginning of the 20th century.

50. *Alexander Benois by Léon Bakst, 1898.*

51. *Sergei Diaghilev by Léon Bakst, 1906.*

52. *Cover of an issue of* Mir Iskusstva, *1899.*

53. *Tamara Karsavina in 1916.*

54. Alexander Blok by Léon Bakst, 1907.

55. Andrei Bely in 1905.

56. Nikolai Gumilev (in center) shortly before his murder in 1921, together with members of his poetic circle,"The Resonant Shell." Photo by M. Nappelbaum, July 1921.

57. Osip Mandelstam in 1914.

58. *Dmitry Merezhkovsky in 1913.*

59. *Zinaida Gippius by Léon Bakst, 1906.*

60. *Anna Akhmatova by Nathan Altman, 1914.*

62. Sergei Prokofiev in 1926.

61. Igor Stravinsky around 1904.

63. Bloody Sunday (1905) on Palace Square.

64. Nicholas II.

65. Empress Alexandra Feodorovna.

66. Grigory Rasputin (center) with Prince Poutiatin and Colonel Loman, two of the many court officials with whom Rasputin established close relations.

67. Maxim Gorky in 1914.

68. Rebel soldiers during the February Revolution 1917.

69. The July Days (1917) at the corner of Nevsky Prospect and Sadovaya Street, with the Public Library in the background.

71. Lenin speaking on Palace Square July 19, 1920. He came to Petrograd for the opening of the 2nd Congress of the Komintern.

72. Sergei Kirov

73. Dmitry Shostakovich

74. During the blockade, many famous landmarks became military emplacements. St. Isaac's Cathedral is in the background.

75. Citizens supplemented the army in defending the city.

76. Home destroyed.

77. The Road of Life.

78. Cleaning up the city in the spring of 1942.

79. Peterhof destroyed.

80. Famous jam session between members of Benny Goodman's band and Russian jazz artists in 1962. In the center are Phil Woods (piano) and Zoot Sims (saxophone). Local musician Gennady Golstein in photo with saxophone near Sims.

81. Military parade on Palace Square on November 7, 1969.

82. Joseph Brodsky on the balcony of the Muruzi house in 1966. Photo by A.I. Brodsky.

83. Boris Grebenshikov. Photo by Vadim Shesterikov, 1986.

84. Dmitry Likhachev.

85. Demonstrator by Mariinsky Palace taking up a collection to support the defenders of Mariinsky Palace.

86. Mayor Anatoly Sobchak addressing citizens on Palace Square during the coup, August 20, 1991.

87. Rally on Palace Square protesting coup attempt by GKChP, August 20, 1991.

88. President Vladimir Putin.

idences in and around the capital. By the 1860s gas street lamps had replaced the smouldering oil lamps. In 1879 the first electric street lamps were installed, on Palace Bridge, and by the 1880s they were installed on Nevsky Prospect. The first water tower and waterworks were built in 1862 by the Neva in front of the Tauride Palace, from which the city's new water supply system extended. The first horse-drawn trams went into service in 1860, and served the city for the rest of the century. The world's first electric tramway was invented and demonstrated in St. Petersburg in 1880, but they could not be installed on the city's streets for many years because the company which operated the horse-drawn trams had a long-term contract which it refused to give up. But no one had ever thought of extending that contract to the Neva, so eventually in the winter of 1894–95 an enterprising company built electric trams on the Neva ice. They ran successfully for several winters, and finally in 1907 the first electric trams began running on the city's streets.

The rapid growth of industry and commerce in Petersburg led to a population explosion. The city's population doubled from nearly half a million in 1850 to about 1 million in 1890, and it doubled again to about 2 million by 1914.[19] Since the city's death rate approximated its birthrate due to poor health conditions, this growth came almost entirely from immigration.[20] By 1900, two-thirds of the city's residents had been born elsewhere.[21] The proportion of factory workers grew. By 1867 the number had grown to about 35,000 in the city limits alone (with more in the suburbs), about 74,000 in 1890, and by 1914 there were about 200,000 factory workers, which was about one-tenth of the city's population.[22] Since the influx initially was mainly peasants on leave from their communes, the vast majority were males, and so for a while the overall proportion of men to women in the city remained at least two to one.[23] Once female labor became widespread, it became more common for whole families to move to the city. The proportion of women then grew, and by 1890 they accounted for about 45 percent of the city's population.

The overall architectural face of the city's center did not change under Alexander II and Alexander III, but styles proliferated as designs were increasingly driven by technology rather than academic schools. To some extent, as in Louis Sullivan's designs in America, form began to follow function. In the city center many facades were redesigned to prevailing tastes, while new buildings in many styles were built in the outer regions as the city expanded outward, especially on the Petersburg Side. "You really don't know how to define our current architecture," complained Dostoevsky in 1873. "It's a sort of disorderly mess, entirely, by the way, appropriate to the disorder of the present moment."[24] After shipbuilding at the Admiralty ceased, the shipyard was filled in, buildings sprung up in its place, and Admiralty Embankment was created. On the south side of the Admiralty, the canal was filled in and the Alexander Garden was created, which like the Summer Garden was populated with busts, especially of famous Petersburgers such as Zhukovsky, Lermontov, and Glinka. The Foundry was torn down, allowing Liteiny Bridge to be built across the Neva. A number of canals were filled in, including Ligovsky, which was replaced by the long boulevard now known as Ligovsky Prospect. New public statues were erected such as Opekushin's of Pushkin on the new Pushkin Street (1884), the Monument to Glory in front of Ismailovsky Cathedral, its column formed from captured Turkish cannon (taken down in 1930), and, on Vasilievsky Island the statue of Admiral Kruzenshtern (1873), the first Russian to sail around the world, and who in the process made many scientific discoveries. But the most prominent statue was Mikhail Mikeshin's statue of Catherine the Great on Alexandrinskaya Square (1873), the pedestal of which depicts bronze figures of her many friends, statesmen, and lovers, including Dashkova, Orlov, Suvorov, Potemkin, and Derzhavin.

The most ambitious project of the age was Alexander II's plan, approved in principle 1869, to fill in the Catherine Canal and create Alexander II Boulevard between the Moika and Nevsky Prospect and Emperor's Boulevard to the west of Nevsky. The boulevard was to be divided by an alley featuring large bronze busts of Russian rulers from Rurik through Alexander II himself. At the Moika terminus of the boulevard there was to be a grand monument portraying the apotheosis of Russia, with two women on either side with a cross and anchor symbolizing faith and hope. But the project was too expensive and was shelved.[25] Had it gone forward, today there would be no Griboyedov Canal.

POOR FOLK

Industrialization and the influx of factory workers and others from the countryside resulted in classic Dickensian urban blight and hardship which at first was beyond the ability of city authorities to control. The aristocratic and imperial city became more than ever one of contrasts. Side by side with imperial magnificence stood pollution, labor abuses, atrocious living conditions, vice, and disease. Haymarket Square, the inner city's pit of squalor and vice made so famous by Dostoevsky, lay right in the center of town by the Catherine Canal and Sadovaya Street at the beginning of the road to Tsarskoe Selo (now Moscow Prospect). The square was a teeming market with hundreds of street merchants and peasants hawking their wares, produce, and baked goods, street performers, streetwalkers, drunks, and pickpockets. "In that neighborhood," wrote Dostoevsky in *Crime and Punishment*, "nothing could surprise anybody. Close to the Haymarket, thick with whorehouses, it swarmed with a population of tradesmen and jacks-of-all-trades who combined to make those central streets of Petersburg flash with a panorama in which almost nothing or nobody could cause any surprise." The German traveler J. G. Kohl described an "unwashed throng, by which it is filled to such a degree that the police have some trouble to keep a passage clear in the centre for the equipages constantly coming and going."[26]

But much of the worst was out of sight at the edge of town where many of the city's factories and communities of factory workers were concentrated, living in crowded wooden tenements. One would see this only when entering or leaving the city. One mid-century English travel guide warned that "for some time after entering the suburbs the tourist will pass through dirty and wretched streets, until a sudden turn brings him in view of the massive walls and batteries of the citadel."[27] When it rained, these streets turned into a mire in which carriages and wagons sank up to their axles.

Economics and the rapid influx of workers meant that most buildings both in the center and in the outlying regions were wooden, mostly one story affairs without plumbing. People drank from the polluted river and canals. Because of the housing shortage and high rents, workers crowded into flats in large numbers. In the poorer districts, around mid-century on average between 15 and 20 people lived in one apartment, but the figure could go higher;[28] the average was still around 16 per room around 1900.[29] Around the Haymarket in 1869 on average 247 people lived in each house.[30] Such numbers were achieved by stuffing tenants into attics, closets, below staircases, and in cellars. As the shortage worsened, slumlords built or converted whole buildings into large dormitories consisting only of rows of bunks reminiscent of a prison camp. Even these spaces were leased out in shifts during the day and night so that the same bunk would be occupied by two or three people in the course of 24 hours. But even such an abode was preferable to the cellar apartment, which prior to the industrial boom had been considered unfit for human habitation. Now they were quickly converted into apartments, and by 1871 over 30,000 people lived in the city's cellars,[31] which number doubled by the end of the century.[32] These dungeons were dark, rat infested, lacked light and ventilation, and, worst of all, were often flooded with water tainted with excrement. But many people were simply homeless, and so doss-houses became common. By World War I the city had 34 doss-houses providing a roof for over 8,000 people, which fell far short of the need for such shelters.[33]

Another blight was pollution. Discharges from factories and human wastes poured into the Neva and the canals, which were still the source of most residents' drinking water and which one foreign visitor termed "perfectly pestiferous."[34] Public notices warned residents not to drink unboiled water. Only in 1914 did the city council approve a project to pipe in water from Lake Ladoga and build a new drainage system.[35] Excrement and garbage piled up in the city's courtyards and alleys and was only irregularly removed, while waste from outhouses and latrines penetrated water supplies and houses.[36] Meanwhile, hundreds of smokestacks spewed smoke and ash into the air which settled on the surrounding territory. When the wind was still, a yellowish-gray pall hung over the city.

The combination of climate, poor housing conditions, bad diet, and pollution soon gave St. Petersburg the unenviable distinction of being the unhealthiest large city in Europe, with the highest death rate.[37] Diseases such as cholera, typhoid fever, diptheria, smallpox, measles, tuberculosis, typhus, syphilis, and alcoholism were rampant and by the late 1860s accounted for one-half of all deaths in the city.[38] Typhus was especially deadly, killing 20,000 per year in the 1890s, a rate that was at least eight times that of Moscow's.[39] But syphilis infected 30,000 per year;[40] in one factory three workers in ten were found to be infected with the disease.[41] People's health was worsened by a shortage of medical care, the cost of which was out of reach for most residents and usually was not provided by employers. In fact, employer-enforced working conditions were responsible for much of the problem. Sick employees were usually not let off, and scenes of women giving birth on the factory floor were not uncommon.[42] Thousands suffered and died from treatable diseases.

In this atmosphere, crime and vice reached crisis proportions and public morals deteriorated. By 1866, the number of crimes resulting in arrest and confinement had reached 130,000 per year, nearly one person in four.[43] Drunkenness became a bane of the city, whose per capita consumption of vodka was the highest anywhere in Russia.[44] Especially on payday, workers congregated in the city's now prodigious number of taverns (1,840 by 1865) and drank until dawn, often ending up in brawls.[45] The result was a high number of arrests for drunkenness, which reached nearly 35,000 in 1869, nearly five percent of the city's population.[46] Prostitution was legal and flowered. The number of registered prostitutes first exceeded 2,000 in 1868 but by the end of 1870 already exceeded 4,400; the real figure including unregistered prostitutes was far higher.[47] By the end of the 1860s, one-fourth of the births in the city were illegitimate.[48] As a result, the number of foundlings also sky-rocketed, reaching 7,600 by 1872.[49] The city's suicide rate rose too, from an average of 61 per year from 1858–69 to 167 in 1872.[50]

The response of the city's authorities to these conditions was slow and ineffective. The challenge was enormous even for the most well-intentioned city government, but the city's Duma was populated by many of the employers and landlords who were profiting from the status quo.[51] Finally, a cholera epidemic in 1866 spurred officials into action, but they found that they could do little because the bureaucratic Ministry of the Interior still held too much power over local affairs. In 1870, reforms were approved that opened the electorate to anyone over 25 who owned real estate or engaged in commerce or a trade. They elected a Duma, which chose an executive committee and the City Chief, the first of whom was the merchant Pogrebov.[52] The new local government, first elected in 1873, received new powers from the federal government and from that point began addressing the city's many challenges.

Gradually the new city government attacked the worst problems in housing, water supply, pollution, and public health. The biggest success was in public education. Dozens of new elementary and secondary schools were opened[53] and literacy in the city rose to nearly 80 percent by 1910.[54] This rise of literacy was reflected in a vast increase in the number and variety of newspapers, journals, and magazines published and sold in the city, which by the end of the century numbered in the thousands. The proportion of society engaged in the debate of social and economic questions increased likewise, and citizens began taking responsibilty for their lives and community, even as the autocrat kept a lid on political reforms. The years following the accession of the reactionary Alexander III became known as the era of "small deeds." Professions such as law and medicine matured, and their practitioners formed associations in Petersburg which studied and took positions on public issues, proposed reforms, served as vehicles for expressing public discontent, and were consulted by the government.[55] Side by side with the more famous radical movements, in the capital a dynamic between society and its elected government (paralleled in the provinces by the *zemstvo* movement) was developing almost unnoticed that could have formed the basis for a civil society in Russia.[56] But education and civic-mindedness proved to be a double-edged sword and led to greater demands for reform from which the Emperor recoiled. The hope of such peaceful evolution to a better world would founder on the Scylla of autocracy and Charybdis of radicalisim.

THE POSSESSED

By the accession of Alexander II intellectual life in the capital was in turmoil. The arrest and exile of the Petrashevtsy, Russia's defeat in the Crimean War, the unresolved question of serfdom, general backwardness, and the increasing number of social ills provoked disappointment and anger against the regime. Beyond the age-old "accursed questions" of Russia's essence and place in the world, which had generated speculation rather than action, Russia faced burning social and economic problems in need of immediate concrete solutions, and thinkers became more practical. In Europe, the revolts of 1848 had been a disappointment, and in the aftermath the abuses of early industrialization continued unabated. The fact that many of these countries now had constitutional government did not seem to help address the social abuses. Legal reform, democracy, and political rights seemed irrelevant even abroad and provided no model for Russia. In 1848 Proudhon had opposed a proposed constitution in France "not because it is bad, but because it is a constitution."[57] Suddenly the model of the West since the Age of Reason with which enlightened Petersburg had always been associated seemed discredited. Russia's Westernizers, most of whom lived in the capital, had to rethink their beliefs, because the West itself was split. The capital soon found itself populated with everyday characters straight out of Dostoevsky's novels, revolutionaries like those portrayed in *The Possessed*, and individuals who considered themselves and their deeds beyond good and evil, like Raskolnikov in *Crime and Punishment*.

Even in the West, leading thinkers had begun searching for more fundamental social and economic forces that were responsible for society's injustices. At the time it was easy to blame capitalism itself, and socialism in various forms came to dominate Europe's intellectual climate, especially in France and Germany. The French utopian socialist Fourier, harking back to Rousseau, held that human nature is good but had been corrupted by society. Theorists such as August Comte sought to apply scientific methods to develop a science of society (sociology). This implied that social injustices and the corruption of the human spirit could be eliminated by reforming the social and economic system. Only after such reform could just laws be passed, true democracy exist, and political rights be meaningfully exercised.

In Russia, Petersburg's Petrashevtsy were the first group of thinkers to follow this line of thought. By Alexander II's reign, industrialization had begun to take hold but the overwhelming social and economic problem was the plight of the peasantry. The emancipation did not remedy the misery of most peasants and came to be regarded as a half-measure. Following Europe's lead, most of Russia's intelligentsia focused on social and economic rather than mere political change. To speak of constitutionalism and political rights to illiterate and starving peasants seemed to mock their despair. Thus, leading intellectuals departed from the liberal line of progressive thought that Petersburg had represented from its beginning through the Decembrists.

In such a climate, Russia's social thinkers reached a broad consensus on the solution, at least in regard to the peasantry, for which they became known to history as the populists. They saw in the peasant commune a ready-made embryonic start for applying socialism and creating a just social, economic, and political order. Turning their backs on the aristocracy and capitalists, they embraced "the people." This approach appealed to Slavophiles because it seemed to uphold and even return to Russian tradition and peasant values, while Westernizers liked it because it applied modern European socialist thought. And since many of Alexander II's reforms already had been built around the commune, to moderates cooperation with the government was not excluded and reform might be achieved by evolutionary means. Since Russia was the only major European state in which such communes existed, it also seemed that Russia was uniquely positioned to apply the new socialist doctrines and could lead Europe into a new era. Some even argued that Russia could overleap the capitalist stage of economic development. In the minds of some this revived the mystical Muscovite notion of Russia's special nature, destiny, and mission, but most populists were not concerned with this and did not believe in a unique character of the Russian people.[58] Orthodoxy was entirely missing from the populists' equation.

But who would lead change and how? Traditionally, the autocrat had played this role because only he or she could rise above narrow class interests and providentially impose difficult and just reforms. But at least since the Decembrists, most progressives had lost faith in this notion, a feeling confirmed when Alexander recoiled from his initial reforms. For its part, the intelligentsia had grown in numbers and become more practical. The Romantic, higher Masonic and German idealist notions that an intelligence rules the universe and is the moving force of history still held wide sway. This was an appealing concept to the intelligentsia, who believed that they best understood and embodied intelligence and intellect and could harness it, enabling them to serve as the vanguard of change.[59] One branch of populism was conceived as orchestrating the flow of intelligence to the people,[60] laying the basis for reforming the social and economic order. Equally, however, repentant gentry emphasized that the flow could work in reverse. Society and liberal education had corrupted urbanites, whereas the peasantry was the last repository of uncorrupted spirit and goodness. Thus, the intelligentsia should flow out among the people not so much to teach and propagandize socialism, but to learn and redeem themselves.[61] (Which of these tendencies dominated varied from individual to individual.) Moreover, because the intelligentsia were not out to enrich themselves, hold political office, and were not beholden to any class interest, they were the ideal dedicated servants of humanity to replace the autocrat as the benevolent agent of historical change. No longer would they be "superfluous men" as in the 1830s and 1840s (and many would be women). Most populists believed that, by taking such steps, change would come naturally and spontaneously, through revolutionary uprisings if necessary, after which a just order would arise naturally from a regenerated human nature.[62] Initially they did not face the dilemma of to what extremes they should go to achieve their ends if the people did not understand or embrace their teachings. Since their socialism was "subjective" (i.e., moral) rather than objective and deterministic (as in Marxism-Leninism) and they upheld the primacy of human rights, at the outset virtually none would have been willing to trample over an unwilling people in their name.

The populist movement was centered in St. Petersburg, and its leading apostle, whose commitment, spirit, and ideas dominated it from the beginning and even during his imprisonment and exile, was Nikolai Chernyshevsky (1828–89). He had been born in Saratov to a priest and had studied at a seminary, but his formidable linguistic abilities enabled him to move to St. Petersburg to attend the University (1846–50), where he became acquainted with the Petrashevtsy and absorbed many of their ideas. He found his calling in journalism, in 1853 joined the realist writer Nikolai Nekrasov at the *Contemporary*, and became coeditor with him in 1859. From this pulpit throughout the 1850s and into 1861 following the emancipation he expounded on his ideas and inspired followers, grew in popularity and stature, and became the heir to the great Belinsky, despite his lack of natural literary flair and methodical empirical approach that often made his writings tedious.

The year 1861 was a turning point, beginning with the emancipation itself. Chernyshevsky was distressed by its terms, especially by what he considered a woefully insufficient land grant, and led a campaign of protest. One of the fruitful recruiting grounds for protest movements is universities, which in Russia at that time was facilitated by recent liberal reforms which increased the number of students (many coming from the provinces). The student body at St. Petersburg University tripled between 1855 and 1861, and women were now admitted. Students were accorded rights against the administration, and the curriculum was liberalized. By the late 1850s, Petersburg's students had assembled libraries of forbidden books, were steeped in populist ideas, often lived together in student communes, and were able (from 1857) to form student organizations and hold student meetings. Student uniforms were abolished, and many of them now dressed in peasant costumes to show their solidarity with the people. But in the climate of tumult and discontent following the emancipation, in May 1861 the government imposed new restrictions on student assemblies and libraries and limited the number of students granted free tuition. The indulgent and popular Prince Gregory Shcherbatov was replaced as the university's Curator by a retired general. In September 1861 students forced their way into a lecture hall and held a meeting to plan the first ever student demonstration at the University to protest the new measures. When the police closed the campus the next day, the demonstration was held instead on the city's streets. According to one of the participants,

> A sight like it had never been seen. It was a wonderful September day. . . . In the streets the girls who were just beginning to go to university joined in together with a number of young men of differing origins and professions who knew us or merely agreed with us. . . . When we appeared on the Nevsky Prospect, the French barbers came out of their shops and their faces lit up and they waved their arms cheerfully, shouting, "Revolution! Revolution!"[63]

The University's Curator then met them on the street and agreed to negotiate with a delegation of the students back at the University. The procession returned to campus and some concessions were preliminarily worked out, but that evening several students were arrested, including some who were in the delegation and had been promised immunity. The authorities' uncoordinated, incompetent, and harsh actions gained sympathy and support for the students from the public and the intelligentsia, most importantly from Chernyshevsky. Students began picketing key locations around town, demanding the release of their comrades being held in the fortress, but the arrests only continued. The administration attempted to reopen the University in October by issuing special entry tickets to the students. Some students refused to accept them, and some professors refused to distribute them, but when the University reopened even the students with tickets tried to stop the lectures and flung down their tickets at the University gates. The students were now arrested en masse (some 130 in total), many of them shouting at the police to carry them off to prison. But the punishments were mild. Five students were exiled, 32 were barred from the University but were able to take their exams as external students, and the rest were merely reprimanded.[64] The University was soon closed, and most faculties did not reopen until August 1863. The intoxicating experience of brief imprisonment and mild martyrdom only served to solidify the students' ranks and bound them more closely. With the University closed, they continued to gather secretly, and soon Petersburg was covered with a network of their secret meeting places in homes and private clubs. They organized a free university which several prominent professors agreed to join and to which Chernyshevsky was invited to lecture, but the authorities kept him and many other potential troublemakers away. The free university lasted only a month, folding when the students boycotted lectures following the arrest of one of its professors who had supported them.[65]

The authorities now sought an excuse to arrest Chernyshevsky. His *Letters without an Address* (i.e., addressed to the Emperor) from January 1862, in which he predicted widespread peasant revolt, attacked the bureaucracy, and advocated political freedoms, provided the pretext. The censors did not clear it. In April the *Contemporary* was shut down, and Chernyshevsky was arrested and eventually imprisoned in the Peter and Paul Fortress, where he remained until May 1864, when he, like Dostoevsky, underwent a mock execution and was exiled to Siberia. But he was allowed to write while in the Fortress, and it was there that he penned his novel *What Is to Be Done?* It was published only by fluke, because the censors at the Fortress and the now-reopened *Contemporary* each passed it thinking that the other would suppress it. (Even after it was passed, the manuscript was given to Nekrasov, who lost it in a cab and was able to recover it only by placing an ad in the official gazette of the St. Petersburg police.) The novel ostensibly traced the emancipation and intellectual coming of age of a young Petersburg woman, Vera Pavlovna, but in the course of the novel Chernyshevsky managed to expound on a wide range of ideas and answer the question in the novel's title. A key part of his answer lay in establishing student communes and production cooperatives through which the intelligentsia could reach out to the people, which later helped inspire the populist "movement to the people." Despite its (partly intentional) lack of literary merit, the novel was not merely popular but became the Bible of the populist and radical movements and the most influential novel in 19th-century Russia, bettering in this respect Gogol, Dostoevsky, Turgenev, and Tolstoy.[66]

The events of 1861–63 and Alexander's eventual refusal to continue peasant reforms provoked radical action. Even Alexander's truly progressive judicial and local government reforms frightened radicals precisely because the liberal constitutional order that they implied would result in victory of the bourgeois capitalists as in the West.[67] Better to strike now before such reforms succeeded. In this world turned upside down, Russia's radicals even took inspiration from the 1865 assassination of another liberator of the enslaved, Abraham Lincoln.[68] Throughout Russia, radicals began to form secret circles dedicated to violent revolution, and many came to St. Petersburg to strike their blows. One of them was Dmitry Karakozov, an unstable personality who had been expelled from Kazan and Moscow Universities, served as master at a free school in Moscow organized by the radical Nikolai Ishutin, and was active in Ishutin's radical group called "The Organization," in which a plot was hatched by a subgroup called "Hell" to assassinate the Emperor. Early in 1866

Karakozov traveled to St. Petersburg with a pistol but without a passport (and so lived in the city as a transient), began associating with local radicals who gave him money to buy gunpowder and bullets, and wrote his manifesto while he awaited his opportunity to strike down Alexander. It came on April 4 when the Emperor was ending an afternoon stroll in the Summer Garden. When Alexander emerged through Veldten's gate onto the Neva embankment to get into his carriage, Karakozov stepped to the front of the crowd and shot at the Emperor but missed. According to the newspaper reports the next day, a peasant named Osip Komissarov standing next to Karakozov had jostled him and spoiled his aim. The would-be assassin was immediately seized, and he and his coconspirators were arrested and tried in the fortress. On October 3, Karakozov was hanged before thousands of spectators.

A spate of patriotic fervor followed Karakozov's attack. The peasant Komissarov became the latest of many peasant folk heroes credited with saving the sovereign. Glinka's *Life for the Tsar*, in which a peasant saved Tsar Michael Romanov from the Poles, enjoyed an enthusiastic revival in the city's theaters. Russia also saw the rise of militant nationalism and pan-Slavism, mainly in Moscow as a prophetic alternative to St. Petersburg's populism.[69] For its part, the government exploited the radicals as a smokescreen for reaction and repression which halted movement toward civil society.[70] In response, again mainly in Moscow, radicals inaugurated the tradition of revolutionary Jacobinism based on the theories of Sergei Nechaev, the ringleader of his own radical group.[71] It was Nechaev's circle on which Dostoevsky modeled the band of revolutionaries in *The Possessed*. But Petersburg was barely affected by Nechaev's group, and it was with the capital's populists that the peaceful movement "to go to the people" originated.[72]

The leading circle propounding this idea was established by a medical student at Petersburg's School of Medicine, Mark Natanson. The group first surveyed the peasantry to determine their readiness for revolution as Bakunin and Nechaev had claimed, but the negative results convinced them to adopt the more gradual approach of propaganda and infiltration; Natanson actually weaned away several of Nechaev's radicals. But in 1871 he was arrested and exiled to Archangelsk, and was succeeded by the more famous Nikolai Chaikovsky, who recruited more members, including several women. Principal among the women was Sofia Perovskaya, daughter of the Governor of St. Petersburg at the time of Karakozov's assassination attempt (as a result of which he was dismissed), and who seemed to epitomize the heroine in *What Is to Be Done?* Soon the core group in Petersburg numbered around 30, while affiliated circles sprung up in other cities. Chaikovsky preached the moral message of a "religion of humanity" and urged the educated to go among the people where they could become godlike.[73] The Chaikovtsy first agitated among the peasant workers in St. Petersburg, hoping that as new urbanites they would be especially capable of mental and moral development and carry the message back to their villages. But when the workers did not respond, in early 1874 they called upon fellow populists, known in Russian as *narodniki*, to go directly among the peasantry in the countryside.

The response was so spontaneous and overwhelming that the Chaikovtsy could not centrally control it and instead were drawn along by the tide. That summer students left in droves for the countryside, often dressed in peasant costumes, ready to renounce their careers and privileges to pay their debt to the people. They served as teachers, doctors, veterinarians, nurses, scribes, field laborers, foresters, even storekeepers, and spoke of social change. The Chaikovtsy tried to organize propaganda with a directed message, but to no avail because that was not the real nature of the movement. As the historian Franco Venturi described it:

> Nothing like it had ever been seen before or after. It was a revelation rather than propaganda. . . . It was a powerful cry that arose no one knows whence and that called living souls to the great work of redeeming the Fatherland and the human race. And the living souls, when they heard this cry, arose overflowing with grief and indignation for their past. And they gave up their homes, their riches, honors and families. They threw themselves into the movement with a joy, an enthusiasm, a faith which one can feel only once in one's life and which, once lost, can never be found again. . . . It was not yet a political movement. Rather it was alike a religious movement, with all the infectious nature of such movements. Men were trying not just to reach a certain practical end, but also to satisfy a deeply felt duty, an aspiration for moral perfection.[74]

But the peasants did not see it this way. Most of the young idealists had only read about the peasants that they idolized and knew little about them. The oddly dressed youths cut comic, out-of-place figures. Neither side understood the other at any level; most peasants were interested in getting rich, not in philosophy or revolution, and no uprisings were forthcoming. The peasants viewed the *narodniki* with suspicion and often turned them in to the police. Indeed, the suddenness and size of the movement threw the government into a panic. Soon the *narodniki* were being arrested en masse and the movement was quickly crushed. Approximately 2,500 *narodniki* had gone to the people, but some 4,000 individuals were interrogated or harassed by the police. Of these, 770 (612 men and 158 women) were handed over to justice, 53 managed to escape, 452 were given provisional liberty, and 265 were imprisoned.[75]

Many populists drew lessons from the failure of the movement to the people and the arrests of the *narodniki* that drove them to extremes. Many decided that mere propaganda is ineffective, and that only well-organized, centrally directed conspiratorial tactics would work. The failure of the peasants to understand what was for their own good made the radicals more willing to act on their own in the people's name, without the people's involvement and even over their opposition. Finally, many concluded that the government could be defeated and change would come only by violent means. Thus, while most populists remained moderate, a number of extremists split and formed a small group dedicated to waging a campaign of terror against the Russian state. Over the next few years, Petersburg was the bloody battleground in this struggle to the death. Not only did the terrorists kill, but they publicized their plans and targets ahead of time, took credit for the acts and publicly defended and rationalized them afterwords. For a while they were able to create the illusion that they constituted a large and formidable movement, when in fact at any one time the St. Petersburg group never numbered more than 30 and had almost no money, weapons, or expertise in their calling.

They first struck against local Petersburg officials. In January 1878 Vera Zasulich shot and seriously wounded the Petersburg City Chief, Fedor Trepov. Then they targeted the police chief, Mezentsov, and the city prefect, Zurov. It was only a matter of time before the terrorists tired, as Vera Figner put it, of "beating the servants for doing the bidding of the master" and targeted the man ultimately responsible for the corrupt system, the Emperor himself. If he were shown to be vulnerable and eliminated, perhaps the people would rise up, topple the whole state edifice and replace it with a just system. So in 1879 they vowed to "substitute the will of the people for the will of one individual" and formed a group called the People's Will, headed by Andrei Zhelyabov, with the sole purpose of assassinating Alexander II.

The group pursued Alexander all over Russia. First they shot at him on Palace Square and missed. Then they tried to dynamite his train, but the explosives did not go off. They tried it again but blew up the wrong train. Then they decided to blow him up right in the Winter Palace to demonstrate that the Emperor was not safe even in his own home, the very symbol of imperial power. One of their members, Stepan Khalturin, was able to get a job as a workman in the Palace, which he proceeded to case while he collected dynamite, at first in his apartment where he kept it among other places in his mattress under his pillow(!), then gradually smuggled it into the Palace. When by January 1880 the conspirators thought he had enough explosives, he set up a charge two floors below Alexander's dining room, lit the fuse as dinner was being served, and calmly walked out through the workers' entrance. But Alexander had been detained and was not in the dining room during the explosion (although 11 other people died and 56 were injured). For this feat, the Soviets would rename adjacent Millionaya Street after Khalturin in 1918. But in 1880 the city was thrown into panic. Alexander could not understand why he was hunted like a wild animal. But Dostoevsky at least understood the real Possessed: "We say outright: these are madmen, yet these madmen have their own logic, their teaching, their code, their God even, and it's as deep set as it could be."[76]

Following this incident the People's Will decided to hunt Alexander down on the streets of the city. For months they studied his comings and goings and the routes that he took. A favorite route was along Malaya Sadovaya Street from the Field of Mars where Alexander often reviewed his troops on Sundays. They decided to plant a charge of dynamite under that street and blow up his carriage or sleigh. Two of the terrorists, posing as man and wife (the "Kobozevs"), leased space at 56 Malaya Sadovaya and opened a cheese shop as a front, while from the basement at night they and their comrades proceeded to dig a tunnel under the street in which to plant the explosives. But soon neighbors noticed that the Kobozevs knew little about cheese, sold it too cheaply to make a profit, and that strange people came and went at night. The police soon paid a visit posing as sanitary workers to inspect, but they failed to notice the dirt stored in the basement barrels. One of the terrorists, Nikolai Kibalchich, had invented the world's first fuseless hand grenade. Zhelyabov recruited four volunteers to throw grenades at Alexander in case the underground explosives failed, and if the bombs failed, Zhelyabov himself would intervene with a dagger and a pistol. They also arranged for one of their members, none other than Sofia Perovskaya, who by then was Zhelyabov's lover, to direct the throwers to nearby streets by hand signals in case the Emperor changed his route. When Zhelyabov was arrested in late February, they feared capture and accelerated the assassination date to March 1.

That morning Alexander was in good spirits. Not only was Zhelyabov behind bars, but the finishing touches had just been put on a series of reforms developed by his chief minister, Count Mikhail Loris-Melikov, under which elected representatives from around Russia would participate in the deliberations of central government bodies. Alexander himself understood that this was the first step toward national representative government (already in existence on the local level). He signed the document, noting: "I have given my approval, but I do not hide from myself the fact that it is the first step toward a constitution."[77] But the reform had been kept secret and the People's Will did not know about it, nor would they have cared.

Before Alexander set off to review his troops, his wife, fearing for her husband's safety, made him promise to change his route and return to Nevsky along the Catherine Canal rather than Malaya Sadovaya. This he did, frustrating the cheese shop plan. But since he stopped at the Mikhailovsky Palace for a social visit on the way, Perovskaya had time to redeploy the bomb throwers along the Catherine Canal. When shortly before 3:00 P.M. Alexander emerged onto the Canal embankment in his special bombproof carriage (a gift from Napoleon III), the bombers were ready. The first, Nikolai Rysakov, threw his bomb under the carriage. It exploded and injured several bystanders, but Alexander was unhurt. As Rysakov was being seized by the police, Alexander stopped the carriage to step out and confront him and check on the wounded. One officer, failing to recognize the Tsar, asked him whether he was hurt. "No, thank God," he replied, motioning to a wounded man on the ground. "It's too soon to thank God," retorted Rysakov, whereupon the second bomber, the Pole Ignacy Hyrniewicki, who had been standing by the Canal railing, approached to within a couple steps of Alexander and threw the bomb at his feet. The explosion destroyed Alexander's legs and mortally wounded Hyrniewicki. Alexander was placed on a sleigh and taken to the Winter Palace, where he died less than an hour later.

Most of the conspirators were caught, tried, and hanged about a month later, though some like Vera Figner remained at large for some time. Those still at large issued a famous letter to Alexander III demanding the convocation of a national assembly, a constitution, and various freedoms. But neither he nor the nation had any sympathy for the rebels' cause. Instead of catalyzing either reform or revolution, the terrorists' extreme acts had set back the cause of both. The city and the nation were left horrified, and the dead Emperor's son Alexander assumed the throne as Alexander III.

ALEXANDER III'S PETERSBURG

Alexander III (1845–94), like Nicholas I, was not born to be Emperor, but he became heir to the throne in 1865 when his elder brother, Grand Duke Nikolai, died of tuberculosis. Nikolai's death was a tragedy for Russia, as he was considerably brighter and more liberal than Alexander. Alexander, in Nice with the Imperial family when Alexander II died, was proclaimed Emperor within hours. He also soon married Nikolai's fiancée, Princess Dagmar of Denmark, and their marriage was happy; Alexander III was the only Romanov Emperor to date not to have a mistress. Alexander was a tall, burly, and strong man, known for his feats of strength such as bending horseshoes with his bare hands and holding up the falling ceiling of the imperial train carriage after a crash so that his wife and children could escape. But Alexander was a conservative reactionary, a devotee of his grandfather's Official Nationality, and a Russian chauvinist; his father's assassination only made him more so. An iron-fisted ruler, in his 13-year reign he undermined his father's reforms and instituted a police state that both squashed radical opposition and halted moderate political reform toward a civil society. One of his first acts was to revoke the Loris-Melikov reform that Alexander II had signed on the morning of his murder. Throughout the multinational Russian Empire he followed a policy of Russification and even pogroms against Jews and other minorities.

For the city of Petersburg, however, his reign was somewhat brighter. The city grew in conditions of peace and prosperity. Seeking to promote Russian national culture, Alexander patronized the arts and regularly attended the opera, ballet, concerts, and theater when he was in town. He conceived and initiated what a year after his death would become the Russian Museum. His most famous legacies in the city, however, are the Church of the Resurrection built in honor of his father and Paolo Trubetskoi's equestrian monument to him.

Out of shock and sympathy for the dead Alexander II, on the day after his death the city Duma petitioned Alexander III for permission to erect a chapel or monument in honor of the fallen Emperor on the spot of the murder. Alexander replied that this was not enough: a church should be built. While that idea was still being worked out, however, by April the city's wealthy merchants had funded and built a temporary wooden chapel there. But a competition was soon held for the design of a large church on the site, and Alexander demanded that the design be in the pure Russian (Muscovite) style of the 17th century, which would make the church an anomaly in the new Westernized capital. The winning design was the joint submission of the Archimandrite Ignaty Malyshev, who was not an architect but (like Montferrand) had an attractive vision of how the church should appear, and Alfred Parland, an experienced architect who brought Malyshev's ideas to architectural life. The church is formally named the Church of the Resurrection of Christ, but because of its association with Alexander's murder Petersburgers usually call it the Savior's Church on the Spilled Blood. Reminiscent of St. Basil's on Moscow's Red Square, it features traditional onion domes and tent roofs complemented by vivid colors and lavish details using colored brick, tiles, and mosaics. Inside, the appearance is stately and showy rather than intimate and spiritual, highlighted by the use of mosaics and over 20 types of colorful semiprecious minerals from Russia and abroad, including jasper, rhondonite, porphyry, and Italian marble. A side chapel honors the spot where Alexander II was murdered, which necessitated a prominence of the embankment. The Church was closed for much of the Soviet period, but it was reopened to the public in 1997 after over 20 years of renovations.

Alexander III's image was preserved in the equestrian statue to him unveiled on Znamenskaya (now Uprising) Square on Nevsky Prospect in front of the Nikolaevsky (now Moscow) Train Station in 1909. It was the work of an Italian sculptor of noble Russian ancestry, Prince Paolo Trubetskoi, who moved to St. Petersburg in 1897. He depicted Alexander as a lethargic, unthinking hulk in a heavy coat and hat atop an equally burly workhorse with its four hooves firmly planted on the ground and its head bowed. Trubetskoi's design was controversial and barely won the competition, and when the work was unveiled it caused a citywide scandal. Conservative royalists vilified it as an insult to imperial dignity, while progressives admired its honesty. As for Trubetskoi, he simply remarked: "I do not deal in politics. I just portrayed one animal on top of another."[78] Finally the City Duma had to decide upon the right of the statue to remain. The monument soon provoked a popular poem called *The Scarecrow:*

> On the square is a commode,
> On the commode is a hippopotamus,
> On the hippopotamus is a brute.

In 1937 the Soviets redesigned the Square, cut up the monument's large pedestal (the commode) to make statues of Lenin, and consigned the statue to obscurity, in a corner of an inner courtyard at the Russian Museum where it could be viewed only by visitors who knew enough to part and peer through stairway window curtains. Finally, in 1994 it was moved to the pedestal in front of the Marble Palace (by then part of the Russian Museum which Alexander was responsible for creating) to replace the armored car on which Lenin had stood when he arrived at the Finland Station.

A REVOLUTION IN ART

Populism cast a long shadow over literature, painting, music, and the performing arts for the remainder of the century. The populist aesthetic was conceived by Chernyshevsky in his 1855 doctoral thesis at St. Petersburg University, "The Aesthetic Relationship of Art to Reality," in which he affirmed that "beauty is life," that "reality is not only more animated, but also more perfect than imagination," and also claimed that art can have as a purpose to "explain life" and to "pronounce judgment on the phenomena of life."[79] He called upon artists to abandon tired classical and biblical themes and portray the real Russia with all its flaws, thus bringing art and artists closer to the people. Artists have a social mission to change the world. The notion of pure art must yield to life, and artists should not aspire to creating beauty apart from life. Some, like Dostoevsky, disagreed, but at the time the populist aesthetic framed the debate.

But even within this aesthetic lay a classic artistic tension between truth (current Russian reality) and beauty (in this case the future that art should help create). Even the best realist art might seem impotent before real human suffering, doing nothing to relieve it, but the populist drive for social change asked artists to look to the future and imagine things as they should be. For their part, painters, like the formerly "superfluous" intelligentsia, wanted to be relevant. So they went beyond objective realism to what became known as "critical realism," painting canvases pregnant with other meanings, with calls for hope, or even prophecy. This fruitful combination of objective reality and subjective messages (not yet, as in Soviet times, in the service of any ideology) produced the most original and meaningful paintings that Russia had yet seen. But for some art would never be enough. The dilemma was illustrated in a short story of Vsevolod Garshin, *The Artists* (1879), which contrasts an ordinary landscape painter with a realist artist who portrays the sufferings of workmen, but who in the end abandons painting in order to genuinely help the people by becoming a village schoolmaster. But the best art transcends the moment, and the best artists did not limit themselves to populist themes. Amongst the cascade of paintings about peasants and villages one could also find innovative landscapes, riveting portraits, deeply psychological biblical scenes, and portrayals of defining moments in Russia's history, including Peter the Great.

This atmosphere provided fertile ideas for painters and an opportunity finally to break with the classicist aesthetic tradition of the Academy of Fine Arts. By the reign of Nicholas I, the Academy's adherence to classicism was not merely aesthetic but political: Realizing the power of art, the authorities did not want Russia's artists criticizing the regime or inspiring unrest, and classical art was safer. But in the meantime realist art had arisen in industrial Europe, and in Russia provided artists with its own examples of human suffering and injustice to portray. Russian artists outside the Academy began responding to Belinsky's and Chernyshevsky's call to portray life as it is, with all its flaws.

The painter who most inspired this revolution in Russian art, Vasily Perov (1834–82), originally was from Moscow, where the art school was freer and less bureaucratic. But after graduating he came to Petersburg for a year's work at the Academy, where in 1861 he painted *A Village Sermon* and *The Easter Procession*. The first painting was rather tame and inoffensive, and despite its departure from classicism won the Academy's Gold Medal. But Perov was committed to struggling against the decay in Russian life, and his *Easter Procession* proved a bombshell. In it he portrayed Russia's priests as corrupt, immoral, ill-mannered, and illiterate, much as Belinsky had done in his letter to Gogol. Perov's canvas depicted a group of priests exiting a dirty village tavern in various stages of inebriation. Yet he pays no homage to the peasants. The central figure, a young peasant woman, is equally inebriated and holds an icon mindlessly, while another man holds his upside down. Yet off to the side in the shadow is a mentally alert young man standing upright and reading, the hope for the future. When the painting was exhibited in St. Petersburg the next year (1862), it caused a sensation among artists and a storm of protest amongst the authorities and the Church, and it was quickly removed. Many believed Perov would be arrested and exiled, which would have been a first for a painter, but this did not transpire. Perov became a hero, and from then on Russian painting would play a new role in Russian society.

This style of painting as a movement began in that already turbulent year of 1863, when the Academy of Fine Arts was preparing for its Gold Medal painting competition. Because of the recent scandal involving Perov, the Academy decided not, as was traditional, to allow the students to choose their own subjects for their entries. Instead, the Academy chose for the competition a safe subject from Scandinavian mythology, The Banquet of the Gods at Valhalla. The students, inspired by Perov's example, motivated by events in the real world, and chafing under the Academy's aesthetics, protested. A group of them led by Ivan Kramskoi applied for permission to choose their own individual subjects instead. This was not a nihilistic rejection, but a protest against the inferior societal role that the Academy had assigned to art and an assertion of artistic freedom. But the examiners refused, and in what became known as the "Rebellion of the Fourteen," Kramskoi, 12 other painters and one sculptor collectively resigned from the Academy, forfeiting their diplomas, studios, and potential commissions, and struck out on their own. The resulting scandal and embarrassment were so great, and the fear that the event and the rebel artists might provoke social unrest was so high, that the authorities prohibited mentioning their departure in the press, and the artists were put under covert police surveillance.

Undeterred, Kramskoi's group of rebels, following the example of Chernyshevsky's heroes in *What Is to Be Done?*, formed in St. Petersburg an artists commune called the St. Petersburg Artel ("Cooperative") of Artists. They rented a large house on Vasilievsky Island, where they lived together and shared the expenses. For several years they fulfilled commissions together, exhibited their works, read about and discussed new artistic ideas, the new literature, and social issues. Inspired by the aesthetic ideas of Chernyshevsky, they staged a creative revolution in Russian art by realistically and meaningfully portraying the life of Russia's common people. As an enterprise, the Artel was a huge success. The demand for such works in Petersburg among people who could afford them was great, and the Artel painters became the dominant force in Petersburg art. They also held evening gatherings in the home reminiscent of the literary evenings of Pushkin's time and the early meetings of the Petrashevtsy, only the main subject was art. Articles about art were read aloud and discussed, music was played, dinner was served, and sometimes the guests danced.

The group continued as the Artel for several years, but eventually its purpose had been served. By then other artists with similar ideas had graduated from the Academy or soon would, such as Ilya Repin and Arkhip Kuindji; another, Nikolai Ge, had graduated in 1857 before the Revolution of the Fourteen. Moreover, the populist goal was to bring art "to the people," which was hardly achieved by selling their works to Petersburg's wealthy merchants and aristocrats. Thus, having conquered Petersburg, in 1870 the Artel was closed, and Kramskoi, together with Perov, Ge, and Grigory Miasoyedov established the Society of Wandering Art Exhibitions, through which they would exhibit their art each year not only in Petersburg and Moscow but also in the provinces. Their first exhibition, held in Petersburg in 1871, was a tremendous success. From then through 1923 the Wanderers, as they were called, put together 48 nearly annual traveling exhibitions which circulated throughout the Empire, including to such cities as Kiev, Odessa, Kursk, Saratov, and Kharkov.

The soul of the Wanderers and their best painter was Ilya Repin (1844–1930). Originally from Chuguyev in Kharkov province, he attended the Academy in St. Petersburg from 1864 to 1871, where he won the Academy's Gold Medal for his *Resurrection of Jairus' Daughter*. The influential critic Vladimir Stasov, who, as the times dictated, by now was mocking Karl Bruillov's *Last Day of Pompeii* as "superficial" and "Italian fake declamation instead of honest feeling,"[80] hailed Repin as the artist of Russia's future, declaring that he was "totally absorbed in the very depths of the lives, interests, and crushing burdens of the masses"[81] and thus promised to create a Russian national school of painting. In 1873–76 Repin studied briefly in Vienna before settling in Paris during the height of Impressionism. While he found the Impressionists' technique pleasing, as a populist he considered their works ultimately shallow and meaningless[82] and their influence on him was not great, his only nod in their direction being *On the Turf Bench* (1876). Rather, upon his return to Russia he urged Russian artists to go to the peasants: "You will see for yourself . . . how our Russian reality . . . will begin to glitter right before your very eyes [and] how its poetic truth will draw you in to the very core of your being."[83] In a fashion that would have made Chaadaev proud, Repin had drawn from the West without being overtaken by it, to help create a truly Russian national art. Thus was born the third crucial element of populist art in addition to populism and realism, that of national consciousness. This was seen most fully in his historical paintings, especially *Tsarevna Sophia* (1879), *Ivan the Terrible and His Son Ivan* (1885), and *Zaporozh Cossacks Writing a Reply to the Turkish Sultan* (1891). His portrait of Ivan the Terrible shows the Tsar in that horrible moment when he realizes he has killed his own son in a fit of madness and ended his family's royal dynasty. It was first exhibited in Petersburg's Yusupov Palace at the 1885 Wanderer's exhibition, and was so impressive, wrote one observer, that women fainted when they saw it and high-strung observers lost their appetites.[84]

The icon of populist painting was Repin's *Bargehaulers on the Volga* (1871–73), a version of which hung at the Wanderers' first Petersburg exhibition in 1871. It was inspired in 1868 when he was walking on the banks of the Neva in Petersburg with his student friend and future Wanderer Konstantin Savitsky and they noticed a gang of boat haulers trudging past a group of young picnickers. *Bargehaulers* portrays the suffering and hopelessness of peasants of various ages, backgrounds, and nationalities—a cross section of the Russian Empire. Most are miserable, exhausted, and beaten men. Even Dostoevsky, who considered most populist art a crude appeal to emotion and propaganda rather than true art, was impressed by the painting's restraint. "I was ready to meet [the haulers] all in uniforms with well-known labels on their foreheads," he told the readers of *The Citizen*, but instead he found art that "will recur in one's dreams; it will be recalled some fifteen years hence!"[85] But Repin also held out hope. One hauler in the center of the canvas is a younger lad standing up straight and proud, one hand grabbing his harness as if ready to throw it off, with his eyes and attention focused on a point outside the picture as if gazing into the future. Populists understood him as the hero heeding the populist call to action.

Repin did not stop with portraying peasants, but went on to paint truly revolutionary art after his move back to Petersburg in 1882. *The Propagandist's Arrest* (1880–92) depicts the arrest of a populist agitator, *Spurning Confession* (1879–85) portrays the moral triumph of a tortured populist facing execution in refusing to confess to a priest, while *They Did Not Expect Him* (1884–88) shows the unexpected return of an exiled populist to his family's rural estate following Alexander III's amnesty of the exiles upon his coronation. Perhaps surprisingly, Repin remained unmolested and would live in and around Petersburg, Petrograd, and Leningrad until his death in 1930. His suburban dacha-studio on the Gulf of Finland in the village of Repino (named after him) where he spent the last years of his life is now a museum in his honor. The Academy, where he taught from 1894 to 1907, in 1944 was officially renamed the Repin Institute of Painting, Sculpture, and Architecture.

The other principal Petersburg Wanderers were Nikolai Ge (1831–94) and Arkhip Kuindzhi (1842–1910), neither of whom concentrated on the populist peasant themes. Ge focused at first on novel depictions of traditional biblical themes, such as in his *Last Supper* showing the scene *after* Judas's betrayal as he is about to leave, portraits of prominent Russian cultural figures such as Herzen and Saltykov-Shchedrin, and Russian historical paintings, the most famous of which is his *Peter the Great Interrogating Tsarevich Alexis at Peterhof* (1871). In his later years, rather than let his talents decline he produced radically new, emotional depictions of biblical themes that adumbrated Europe's turn-of-century Expressionism. Kuindzhi, on the other hand, made new strides in landscape painting through his novel perspectives, arrangements of subject, and use of light. His paintings became popular amongst Petersburg's elite and drew high prices. One day when he had just completed one landscape, a young naval officer peered into his Vasilievsky Island studio and asked to buy it. "It is beyond your means," Kuindzhi replied with some irritation. But the officer persisted and asked Kuindzhi to name his price. "Nothing less than five thousand," he responded, naming an exorbitant sum just to get rid of his visitor. "Fine, I'll take it," the officer said without question. He was Grand Duke Constantine.[86]

Art and its appreciation in the capital did not stop with the Wanderers, but grew more general and public. In 1863 the St. Petersburg Society of Artists was established to support artists regardless of their school, followed by the St. Petersburg Society of Architects in 1870. In 1882 a women's artists' circle was founded and began holding annual exhibitions, and in 1887 even a society of watercolor painters was set up.

The Hermitage too recovered from years of neglect and decline under Nicholas I. Alexander II turned it over to the Ministry of the Court, and in 1866 it became a public museum and its doors were finally opened to all. Alexander II renewed acquisitions, although the budget was modest and paled in comparison to Catherine's and Alexander I's spending. His most famous acquisition was not of paintings, however. Rome's Giampetro Campana had amassed the century's largest collection of classical antiquities and art, buying them from Italian tomb robbers mainly with funds embezzled from the Monde de Pieta Bank, of which he was director. When the Pope arrested him in 1857, his collection was sold off. Stepan Gedyonov, then in Rome to supervise Russian art students, negotiated the purchase of many of its choice works, for which he was rewarded with the Directorship of the Hermitage in 1863.[87]

Acquisitions accelerated under Alexander III. He began collecting on a large scale, often out of his personal fortune since the state allowance for acquisitions at the Hermitage was paltry. His most famous purchase was the collection of medieval and Renaissance art of Alexander Basilewski, a wealthy Russian then living in Paris. Alexander was outbid by an American collector, but patriotism carried the day and Basilewski sold to the Tsar.[88] But Alexander, a Russian nationalist, was especially interested in Russian paintings, and soon the collection was sizable. The Russian collection never became part of the Hermitage collection because Alexander dreamed of creating a separate museum to showcase Russian art. Thus, instead he housed the Russian works in the Mikhailovsky Palace. In 1895 Nicholas II turned the collection into the Alexander III Museum in honor of the Tsar who dreamed of creating it, and since 1917 it has been known as the Russian Museum.

LITERARY PETERSBURG: DOSTOEVSKY'S CITY

With Chernyshevsky's social novel enjoying the greatest vogue in the late 19th century and nihilist and populist aesthetics dominating the intellectual climate, true literature in Petersburg went into a recession. Poetry all but disappeared, few writers were producing literature of merit, and there was little reason anymore to hold literary salons. Count Leo Tolstoy came to the city to study in 1849 at the time of the Petrashevtsy affair, living at the Napoleon Hotel on Malaya Morskaya. At first he reveled in its order and gay life and loved making the rounds in the salons of high society, but eventually he got into debt, tired of Petersburg and left, after which he visited the city only occasionally. Ivan Turgenev lived in Petersburg when he wrote his *Notes of a Hunter* (1852), a popular condemnation of serfdom that served as Russia's *Uncle Tom's Cabin* (which had appeared only four months earlier), but Nicholas I sent him away to his estate and eventually he left for France, where he spent most of the rest of his life.

In order to write great literature in the Petersburg of the 1860s and 1870s, one had to courageously rebel against the modish utilitarian aesthetic of the populists and to some extent also their social and political ideas. Only Dostoevsky, Petersburg's greatest writer of the time, and the greatest writer ever about the city, did so. That literary age belonged to him, and his unforgettable images of the city still haunt readers over a century later.

Dostoevsky was born in Moscow in 1821, and grew up there and on his father's small estate in Tula province. His father wanted him to be an engineer, so in 1837 at 16 Dostoevsky moved to Petersburg and enrolled at the new Engineering School at the Mikhailovsky Castle. But his real love was poetry and literature, and he spent most of this time reading, writing, and dreaming. More than anything he dreamed of becoming a famous writer, as soon as he could give up his army engineering career, which he did in 1844. Meanwhile, he read the classics of Antiquity and Western Europe, including Homer, Shakespeare, the French dramatists and Enlightenment writers, the Germans Goethe and (especially) Schiller, and later the new realists Dickens and Balzac. Among Russians he loved Karamzin, Pushkin, Lermontov, and especially Gogol, from whose oeuvre Dostoevsky's early works were a transition. When he was not reading and writing, like Pushkin, he liked to gamble. In his youth Dostoevsky was an atheist and one of the more radical Petrashevtsy, but in exile he abandoned such views and adopted a personal version of Christianity. Having grown up on a rural estate, spent a decade in Siberia, and seen his father murdered by his peasants, unlike the populists he held no romantic illusions about peasants and did not see in them the solution to Russia's problems.

As an active journalist, Dostoevsky knew Petersburg intimately and wrote articles about goings on for the local newspapers and journals. He witnessed the rise of the feuilleton as a journalistic genre in Europe, and was stimulated by Eugene Sue's 1842 feuilleton *Les Mysteres de Paris* in *Journal des Débats*. Belinsky and Gogol had just written their own essays about Petersburg, other writers penned feuilletons describing the "physiology" of the city, and Dostoevsky was not about to be left out. In 1847 he wrote his own feuilleton, *Petersburg Chronicle*, published in four installments in the *Petersburg Gazette*. This was Dostoevsky's principal prose work characterizing and portraying the city. Realizing that he had much to observe and learn about his city both in order to write the piece and portray the city in his fiction, he hit the streets for weeks in search of material. The result was an entertaining variety of not altogether consistent impressions and ideas, some of which he later abandoned and others which would figure in his later works. In one passage, he suggested that Gogol's dualist vision of the city must yield to the Northern Palmyra idea of Peter I and Catherine II:

> It may be that in some respects everything here is chaos, . . . but on the other hand, everything is life and movement. Petersburg is both the head and heart of Russia. . . . Even up to the present Petersburg is in dust and rubble; it is still being created, still becoming. Its future is still in an idea; but this idea belongs to Peter I; it is being embodied, growing and taking root with each day, not alone in the Petersburg swamp but in all Russia.[89]

But later he disowned Petersburg as a Window to the West because he grew critical of the West itself.

The remainder of his feuilleton touches on classic Dostoevskian themes. Of Petersburg's climate, he said that the capital is a city "in which nature forgot to arrange itself for the best."[90] Walking through the Haymarket one raw misty morning, he wrote, melancholy gnawed at him, and the city assumed the personality of an irritable living being. "Petersburg had gotten up ill-tempered and angry, like an irritated society maid turned yellow from spite at last night's ball," and at 1:00 P.M. there was still such a dismal twilight over the city that "the city's chimes themselves could not understand by what right they were compelled to strike such an hour in such a darkness."[91] Petersburg is portrayed as an abode of reclusive dreamers with miserable daily lives, but who, stimulated by the fantastic city, in private give full rein to their pent-up idealism and imaginations. Such dreams he calls a "Petersburg nightmare" because in the end one must come back to reality, which only causes the dreamer to crave more dreams. Like a narcotic, dreaming becomes an addiction: "Sometimes whole nights pass unnoticeably in indescribable delights; often within a few hours one lives through a paradise of love or a whole enormous life, gigantic, unheard-of, marvelous as a dream, grandly beautiful. . . . But the moments of sobering up are terrible; the unfortunate cannot bear them, and immediately takes his poison in new, larger doses."[92] Most of all, the city is one of mystery and the fantastic. For the dreamer (and also for Dostoevsky as an artist), "even the most ordinary everyday trifle, the most empty routine matter, immediately assumes for him a fantastic coloring. His glance is already attuned to see the fantastic in everything."[93] He later called Petersburg "the most fantastic city, with the most fantastic history of all the cities on the face of the earth."[94]

In his only other feuilleton, *Petersburg Dream-Visions in Verse and Prose* (1861), Dostoevsky recounted how he had discovered this "fantastic city." It happened in a creative epiphany while walking home along the Neva early one winter evening, just as the sunset was dying and night was descending over the city:

> It seemed, finally, that this whole world with all its inhabitants, strong and weak, with all their domiciles, the shelters of the poor or gilded mansions, at this twilight hour resembled a fantastic, magic vision, a dream which in its turn would vanish immediately and rise up as steam toward the dark-blue sky. Some strange thought suddenly stirred in me. I shuddered, and my heart was as if flooded at that moment with a hot rush of blood that boiled up suddenly from the surge of a powerful but hitherto unknown sensation. I seemed to have understood something in that minute which had till then only been stirring in me, but was still not grasped; it was as if my eyes had been opened to something new, to a completely new world, unfamiliar to me and known only through certain murky rumors, by certain mysterious signs. I suppose that my existence began from just that minute. . . . There have been no minutes in my life more full, more sacred, and more pure.[95]

The first of Dostoevsky's Petersburg works, the novella *Poor Folk* (1845), was highly praised by the leading critics Nekrasov and Belinsky, who hailed him as the successor to Gogol. Indeed, with a lowly government clerk, Devushkin, as its hero and its portrayal of the city, *Poor Folk* builds on *The Overcoat* and even includes Gogol's story in the plot. The familiar theme of the little man versus the city is quickly struck when Devushkin muses: "Hurrying to work early in the morning, I sometimes take a look at the city, to see how it wakes, gets up, starts to smoke, to fill with life and noise—and sometimes you feel so small before such a spectacle that it's as though somebody had given you a flip on your inquisitive nose, and you plod quieter than water, humbler than grass, and shrug!" But the descriptions are from the hero's immediate perspective and the novella is not simply social commentary. Dostoeveky's focus is psychological, and the hero's poverty is treated more as a spiritual than material state. Thus from his first work Dostoevsky develops further the human existential themes that Gogol had opened and departs from the classic realism of the West.

White Nights (1848), Dostoevsky's most charming work, deals with the theme of the dreamer, again evoked by the city's beauty:

> There is something indescribably moving in the way nature in Petersburg, suddenly with the coming of spring, reveals herself in all her might and glory, in all the splendor with which heaven has endowed her, in the way she blossoms out, dresses up, decks herself out with flowers. . . . She reminds me somehow rather forcibly of that girl, ailing and faded, upon whom you sometimes look with pity or with that certain compassionate affection, or whom you simply do not notice at all, but who in the twinkling of an eye and only for one fleeting moment becomes by some magic freak of chance indescribably fair and beautiful. . . . But the brief moment passes, . . . And you feel sorry that the beauty, so momentarily evoked, should have faded so quickly

and so irrevocably, that she should have burst upon your sight so deceptively and to so little purpose that she should not have given you time even to fall in love with her.

Naturally, over the space of four White Nights, the story's young dreamer falls in love with a charming and sincere but fickle young girl, Nastenka, whom he discovers crying on the railing of a canal. He deludes himself that her love is constant, only to see her vanish in the arms of her former flame who reappears from Moscow. The dreamer will return to his room with his memory of a few days of bliss to fantasize anew. But which is really the dream, that or his "real" experience in the city?

After his exile, a changed Dostoevsky returned to the theme of the Petersburg dreamer in *Notes from Underground* (1864). By now the city had no dualism, no redeeming traits. The protagonist, a clerk, stays in his pitiful flat and out of society, his condition and spirit so debased that he consciously acts against his rational self-interest simply to assert his individuality and free will. (This was, among other things, a swipe at Chernyshevsky and Nekrasov, who sought to apply scientific principles of rational self-interest and determinism to resolve the social and ethical problems of the day.) Only outside the real world of Petersburg, in his dreams, does the protagonist experience the sublime, the beautiful, and love. "Though it was a fantastic love, though it was never in fact applied to anything human, there was so much of it, of this love, that afterward one did not even feel the need to apply it in practice: that would have been a superfluous luxury." Here Dostoevsky was caricaturing and ridiculing such dreamers as a Petersburg phenomenon. As the story's protagonist tells the reader at the end of the story, "we have all lost touch with life, we are all cripples, every one of us, more or less. . . . I have, after all, only carried to an extreme in my life what you have not dared to carry even halfway, and what's more, you have taken your cowardice for prudence, and found comfort in that self-deception." The phenomenon of the story's antihero, on the one hand, arises from the complex irrationality of human nature that Russia's social activists refused to acknowledge, but on the other is a product of unnatural societal conditions that drive people into such a state, of which the epitome is Petersburg. Thus, the analogue of the story's antihero is the contrived city built in service of an idea and in violation of the natural laws of human life. As Dostoevsky explains in his introductory note to the story, "such persons as the author of these notes not only may, but must exist in our society, when you consider the circumstances under which our society was in general formed."

The city provokes a seemingly opposite but ultimately similarly self-destructive reaction in the dreamer-hero of *Crime and Punishment* (1866), the first of Dostoevsky's four great novels and the ultimate and most famous embodiment of Dostoevsky's portrayal of St. Petersburg. The novel's plot is barely fictional; it was inspired by an actual murder of two old women with an ax, which was the subject of a famous trial in the spring of 1865 followed by St. Petersburg's newspapers and public. The novel opens with the hero being oppressed by the city:

Outside, the heat had grown ferocious. Closeness, crowds, scaffolding, with lime and brick and dust everywhere, and that special summer stench familiar to every Petersburger who cannot afford a summer cottage; it all jarred instantly and unpleasantly on the young man's nerves, which were tense enough already. The intolerable stench of the saloons, especially numerous in that part of town, and the drunks he came upon continually in spite of the fact that it was a working day, contributed to the melancholy and repulsive tone of what confronted him. An expression of the deepest loathing flashed for a moment across his sensitive face.

Like the antihero in *Notes from Underground*, the protagonist's individuality and ego rebel against Petersburg's realities. A gifted student, he thinks he is separate from and superior to all this, that he is not responsible for it. Yet he is poor, and so is his mother and his sister, who is about to marry a despicable businessman to escape from poverty. He reasons himself into ax-murdering an evil elderly pawnbroker woman to steal her ill-gotten money, but in the event he surprises her innocent sister who is unexpectedly in the apartment and must kill her too. This leads to an ascent, through a variety of characters including the noble prostitute Sonya and a police investigator who understands the criminal mind, into the instinctively decent, compassionate and humane, and ultimately dominant, side of the hero's character. His name, Raskolnikov, comes from *raskol* ("schism"), thus signifying his divided character. Ultimately the only alternative to confession (in every sense) is suicide (or spiritual death), exemplified by the suicide of another murderer, Svidrigailov. Raskolnikov chooses life, repentance, and the resurrection of his spirit. As the novel ends, he decides to turn himself in, and on the way to the police he stops in the middle of Haymarket Square, kneels down "to all the suffering in the world" and "kisses that filthy earth with joy and rapture." A nearby drunken artisan of the type he had previously scorned remarks, "He's bowing down to all the world and kissing the great capital of St. Petersburg and the ground it is built on." Like Dostoevsky in his own life, Raskolnikov eventually finds in a Siberian prison camp the reconciliation and peace that he could not find as a young man in Petersburg.

MUSICAL LIFE

Russian national music was inaugurated by Glinka, but without a state-sponsored national school no one else had emerged. Even Glinka had been trained largely abroad, and his operas were mainly a product of his Italian schooling with just enough Russian flavor added in. When Alexander II assumed the throne, Russia was nearly bereft of competent musical teachers or books on musical theory, had only a handful of largely self-taught amateur musicians, and the repertoire was almost entirely Western.

A talented young piano prodigy named Anton Rubenstein (1830–94), who as a boy had performed in the Winter Palace for Nicholas, changed this. With several years of training in Berlin and Vienna and many foreign tours, his spirit and compositions were steeped in the Western academic tradition, especially that of Mendelssohn, Schumann, and Chopin. His *Ocean Symphony* was one of the most popular orchestral works in Europe in the last half of the 19th century, and it bore no trace of Russian nationalism.

Rubenstein realized that in order for music to advance in Russia, it needed a national school, which would require state support. He found his imperial ally in Grand Duchess Elena Pavlovna, the wife of Nicholas's younger brother Mikhail. Originally a German princess, she had been raised on Western music and in Petersburg had become the royal family's main patroness of the arts, especially of music, and so became known as the "muse Euterpe." Rubenstein often played at her popular salon, and the two became friends. During their long evening conversations on Kammeny Island, where Rubenstein lived and Elena had a palace, they conceived of founding a conservatory in Petersburg, but under Nicholas nothing came of it. On the contrary, when Rubenstein arrived in Petersburg in 1849 from revolutionary Berlin, his compositions were confiscated at customs on suspicion that they contained something seditious, the city's governor threatened to send him to Siberia, and by order of the chief of police Rubenstein, already a European star, had to vindicate himself by playing a piece to prove that he was really a musician.[96] While waiting for his chance to found a school, Rubenstein wrote several popular piano works capturing the city's beauty and the spirit of its aristocratic social life, including *Kammeny Island* (1853–54), *The Ball* (1854), and *Soirées a St. Petersburg* (1860).

In 1859, Rubenstein founded the Russian Musical Society with the help of Elena Pavlovna, who became its chairwoman. That same year the old prohibition on concerts except during Lent was lifted so that the Society could hold regular symphonic and chamber concerts, which Rubenstein conducted. The Society also began to hold musical classes, and in 1862 it was converted into the St. Petersburg Conservatory, the first in Russia, located on Theater Square. (In 1866 Rubenstein's brother Nikolai founded another in Moscow.) Its inaugural class included Peter Tchaikovsky. Now supported by the state, Rubenstein was able to staff the Conservatory with foreign teachers, who taught a rigorous curriculum based on those in the West. A true cosmopolitan, Rubenstein believed that passions and creativity are not national, and he sought to ensure that Russian music maintain strong ties with Europe. He had good reason to fear that it might not, because a group of amateur nationalist Russian musicians led by Mily Balakirev had just emerged to whom Rubenstein's views were anathema.

Balakirev (1837–1910) grew up in Nizhny-Novgorod and Moscow, discovered his natural talent for music, but received no formal training. Inspired by Glinka's operas, he decided to devote himself to music and moved to St. Petersburg, where he was fortunate to befriend the great Glinka and became active as a pianist and composer. When Glinka died in 1857, the mantle of leader of Russian music passed to him (Rubenstein was again living abroad in 1854–58). A nationalist and romantic, he wanted to create truly national Russian music, which, he believed would spring more from native inspiration and natural talent than mastery of musical theory derived from the West, which in fact might prove a hindrance. Strong in his opinions and dictatorial by nature, he was able to gather around him four like-thinking and similarly untrained but talented amateur musicians, who by profession were a doctor and chemist (Alexander Borodin), a fortifications engineer (César Cui), a Preobrazhensky Guard (Modest Mussorgsky), and a naval officer (Nikolai Rimsky-Korsakov). Together they flowered into the most creative composers of the time, who thanks to the group's ideologue and publicist, Vladimir Stasov, became known as the "Mighty Handful" (in English usually called the "Mighty Five"). In the same year that Rubenstein founded the Conservatory, Balakirev and his friend Gavriil Lomakin founded the competing Free Music School on Nevsky Prospect, which was open at no cost to anyone with an interest in composing and sponsored concerts which introduced new works, eventually including some by Tchaikovsky.

In a manner not unlike painters of the Artel, the Five became a close-knit group of friends (Mussorgsky and Rimsky-Korsakov roomed together for a while), who taught and helped each other, shared ideas, and even completed each others' works. Borodin once wrote: "In the relations within our circle, there is not a shadow of envy, conceit or selfishness. Each is made sincerely happy by the smallest success of another."[97] They would meet at least once a week at one of their homes or those of friends such as the wealthy connoisseur Nikolai Purgold, who had two musically talented daughters, the singer Alexandra and the pianist Nadezhda. It was in their home that much of the Five's music was first performed. Romance sprung up between Nadezhda and Rimsky-Korsakov, and they were married in 1873.

The Five emerged out of musical evenings in the home of their older friend, Alexander Dargomyzhsky (1813–69). From an older generation, he was more Petersburgian than his young nationalist friends, having composed a number of songs in the city's aristocratic cultural tradition, and had gathered a following among the capital's dilettantes. One popular series of choral songs, entitled St. Petersburg Serenades, was set to the verse of such poets as Delvig, Pushkin, and Lermontov. Another set of songs, composed to the translated verse of the French poet Pierre-Jean Béranger, included such titles as The Old Corporal and The Worm, attacking Nicholas's army and bureaucracy. The Titular Councillor, about a miserable and timid clerk, recalled Gogol's humble characters. These works made him the darling of Petersburg's intelligentsia. Dargomyzhsky was at his most inventive in opera, where he sought to reform and modernize the genre. As his target he chose nothing less than Mozart and his Don Giovanni, and as his vehicle Pushkin's The Stone Guest. In his view, music should only frame the changing moods in such a work of art and remain subordinate to the human word, which should be spoken naturally more than sung in order to be truer to human experience. This implied a music stripped of ornamentation. "I do not intend to debase music to the level of mere amusement . . . I want the notes to express exactly what the words express. I want truth."[98] Here one detects the populist aesthetic. Thus, The Stone Guest was largely recitative and closely followed Pushkin's original text. He performed portions of it at home to the delight of his young friends, himself singing the part of Don Juan and Mussorgsky that of Leporello. Stasov later recalled, "It was delight, awe, it was an almost prayerful bowing before a mighty creative force, which had transformed that weak, bilious, sometimes petty and envious man into a powerful giant of will, energy and inspiration." But in 1869 the composer died in bed with the unfinished opera open on his lap. Cui finished the final scene and Rimsky-Korskov scored it. Dargomyzhsky's novel ideas influenced Mussorgsky and represented the beginning of Petersburg's long avant-garde musical tradition.

Since Dargomyzhsky was frail of health and lacked Balakirev's leadership abilities, Balakirev became the group's leader and steered it in a nationalist direction. As a composer, he completed two symphonies, several overtures, and symphonic poems such as *Tamara*, a number of piano works including the brilliant *Islamey*, and many songs. As his friends matured, they needed him less and began to think and act independently, which distressed him and led him to be more demanding and offensive to his friends. "I don't understand why Balakirev turns away so stubbornly," complained Borodin in 1871. "It doesn't seem possible for him to acknowledge freedom and equality. He wants to impose his yoke on everyone and everything. . . . And yet he is quite aware that we all have already grown up." Eventually, the Five broke up. Balakirev never understood why, but to Borodin "this is nothing but a natural situation. As long as we were in the position of eggs under a sitting hen (thinking of Balakirev as the latter), we were all more or less alike. As soon as the fledglings broke out of their shells, they grew feathers. Each of them had to grow different feathers; and when their wings grew, each flew to wherever his nature drew him." In 1872 Balakirev abandoned music for a while to become a railroad clerk and religious fanatic, but he eventually returned to the fold to finish several uncompleted works, compose new ones, and resume his position at the Free School.

César Cui (1835–1918), an army officer and fortifications engineer who had graduated from the same institute as Dostoevsky in the Mikhailovsky Castle, likewise became more famous for his art and became the first of Balakirev's disciples, in 1856. He was the least talented but most prolific of the Five, composing no less than 10 operas, 30 choruses, 200 songs, and a number of minor works. But they were consistently mediocre, and except for some salon pieces never made it into the repertoire. Eventually, he became more notable and influential as a music critic for one of the city's prominent newspapers, and his articles often appeared abroad. In this role he was able to direct the Five's efforts toward opera as the finest expression of Russian national music, believing that the symphonic form had already been perfected in the West.

Modest Mussorgsky (1839–81) was a well-bred, dashing Preobrazhensky Guards officer with a promising military career and a talent for the piano, with which he charmed guests at social gatherings. Soon Balakirev noticed Mussorgsky and convinced him to resign his commission in 1857 to devote himself to music. The most original of the Five, Mussorgsky had well-formed musical as well as political ideas, and sought to create a higher form of music that embraced Russian nationality and religion, art, philosophy and politics, yet he was free from populist dogma and his art was never ideological. Influenced by the works of Gogol, Dostoevsky, and Chernyshevsky (he once formed and lived in a student commune like that described in *What Is to Be Done?*) he believed that great music must emerge straight out of life and be the equivalent of written prose or human speech in its pure state, without the glamour of poetry or classical ornamentation. Indeed, his music is vivid, feverish, and shrouded with mystery, just like Dostoevsky's prose, and his characters, like Dostoevsky's, are frenzied and haunting. This quest also made Mussorgsky the most modern and futuristic of the Five, anticipating the literary ideas of the Silver Age and Petersburg's musical avant-garde. As he explained in the dedication of his opera *Boris Godunov*, "The artist believes in the future because he lives in the future."[99]

Opera was the perfect medium for expressing Mussorgsky's vision. He was able to combine his musical ideas with themes derived from Russia's folklore and mythology, folk music, religion, and national heritage, in which he had been steeped while being raised on his family's country estate by a peasant nanny. The result was the national operas *Boris Godunov* and *Khovanshchina* (completed by Rimsky-Korsakov), symphonic works such as *Night on Bald Mountain*, and song cycles such as *The Nursery* and *Songs and Dances of Death*.

Some of his works evoked life in Petersburg. Two unfinished operas, *The Marriage* and *Sorochinsk Fair*, depicted Gogol's stories of the same name, the former being set to Gogol's original prose. His song *Forgotten* was based on a famous painting of the same name by the antiwar painter Vasily Vereshchagin, a favorite of Petersburg intellectuals, most of whom denounced war. The painting, which portrayed a dead Russian soldier with vultures hovering over him, was included in a dramatic 1874 exhibit of Vereshchagin's works in Petersburg, which unfortunately coincided with the hysteria surrounding the arrests of the populists. The painting was cheered by Petersburg's intellegentsia (including Mussorgsky) but denounced by the military establishment, and the artist consigned the canvas to the flames. But Mussorgsky resurrected it in music, in a somber song of only 27 measures. The initial fate of the song was not unlike that of the painting, however, as it was immediately banned by the Petersburg censors, which in the composer's mind only confirmed his belief in the broad mission of his art. Mussorgsky's most Petersburgian work, however, was his autobiographical song cycle *Sunless*, composed in 1874 to the poetry of his friend Prince Arseny Golenishchev-Kutuzov. The ghosts of Gogol and Dostoevsky are felt in these songs about loneliness and alienation in the large city. One song in the cycle, *An End to the Futile, Hectic Day*, begins:

> *An end to the futile, hectic day;*
> *And human life, now silent, slumbers.*
> *All is quiet. The May night's shadow*
> *Shrouds the sleeping city.*

Another, *In the Crowd*, about a woman spied in a fleeting moment on the street, recalls Gogol's *Nevsky Prospect*, while *Within Four Walls* portrays the hovels inhabited by Dostoevsky's characters:

> My little room is tiny, peaceful, welcoming,
> The shadows are impenetrable and unanswering,
> My thoughts are deep and my song is melancholy,
> Yet in my beating heart hope lies hidden.

Mussorgsky himself was something of a Dostoevskian character. Always fond of drink, he deteriorated into an alcoholic, portrayed as such in a famous portrait by Repin painted only days before the composer's death.

The music of Alexander Borodin (1833–87), the illegitimate son of a Caucasian prince, was more upbeat and is known for its pleasing and memorable melodies. But he was committed to his career as one of Europe's most prominent chemists, and to the dismay of his colleagues scarcely had time to give range to his considerable musical talents. He called himself a "Sunday composer" for whom "science is my work and music is my fun," and once claimed that he could write music "only when I am too unwell to give my lectures" at Petersburg's Medical-Surgical Academy where he was a professor and head of the chemistry department.[100] Rimsky-Korsakov later recalled trying to discuss music with him in his apartment "in the midst of which he used to jump up, run back to the laboratory to see whether something had not burned out or boiled over; meanwhile he filled the corridor with incredible sequences from successions of ninths or sevenths. Then he would come back, and we proceeded with the music."[101] Borodin returned from his chemical studies in Europe in 1862, promptly married a young Russian pianist whom he had met in Italy, and joined Balakirev's circle. His musical output was not large, consisting mainly of his nationalistic opera *Prince Igor* (completed by Rimsky-Korsakov and Alexander Glazunov), two symphonies, two string quartets, and the symphonic poem *In Central Asia*, all of which remain in today's repertoire in Russia. His *Polovtsian Dances* from *Prince Igor* and the Nocturne from his Second String Quartet remain popular in the West. In 1887 Borodin's life was cut short at 54 when he dropped dead of a heart attack while joking with friends at a Petersburg benefit ball, dressed in Russian national costume.

Nikolai Rimsky-Korsakov (1844–1908) ultimately emerged as the brains and strongest musician of the Five, composing what still stands as perhaps the finest collection of Russian national classical music of any single composer, including operas such as *The Snow Maiden, The Maid of Pskov, The Tsar's Bride, Sadko, The Legend of the Invisible City of Kitezh*, and *The Golden Cockerel*, and orchestral works such as the *Russian Easter Festival Overture* and *Scheherazade*. A unifier, he was the only member of the Five to cross over and make peace with Rubenstein, who in 1871 appointed him to teach composition at the Conservatory. Rimsky-Korsakov, having only a scant knowledge of musical theory, was petrified by the appointment and spent sleepless nights in fear of embarrassment. "I was a dilettante and knew nothing," he later recalled. "At the time I could not decently harmonize a chorale; not only had I not written a single counterpoint in my life, but I had hardly any notion of the structure of a fugue; nay, did not even know the names of augmented and diminished intervals, of chords (except the fundamental triad), of the dominant and chord of the diminished seventh."[102] But he could hardly refuse the honor, which Rubenstein seems to have made easier by making his title that of Professor of *Practical* Composition and Instumentation. Teaching in his naval uniform, he applied himself and managed to stay one step ahead of his students. Eventually he became one of Russia's greatest masters of orchestration, wrote a book on the subject, and influenced such foreign masters as Ravel, Debussy, and Holst, not to mention Russians. He also used these talents to complete unfinished works of his friends Mussorgsky, Borodin, Dargomyzhsky, and Cui.

But it was left to Peter Tchaikovsky (1840–93) to synthesize the best traditions of the Conservatory and the Five and become the century's greatest Russian and, despite long stays in Moscow and abroad, most Petersburgian composer.[103] Born in the Ural mining town of Votkinsk into lower gentry, his family moved permanently to St. Petersburg in 1850, when he was impressed by *A Life for the Tsar* and *Giselle*. In 1852 he entered the School of Jurisprudence (on the Fontanka across from the Summer Garden) and graduated in 1859. He began work at the Ministry of Justice, where he showed talent, was promoted and had a promising career ahead of him. But from an early age he had displayed a love and sensitivity for music, and now this interest and talent came to the fore. In 1861, after a trip abroad, he began his first formal musical training at Rubenstein's new Russian Musical Society under Nikolai Zaremba, a musician of the German school, showed promise and attracted Rubenstein's attention. When the Conservatory opened in 1862, Tchaikovsky found himself in its first class. He distinguished himself, decided upon a musical career, and resigned from the Ministry in 1863. Upon graduating in 1866, he got a job teaching harmony at Nikolai Rubenstein's new Moscow Conservatory, and lived with him there for six years while he absorbed the Russianness of the old capital. Having obtained a thorough European-style musical education, he dismissed the Mighty Five and their methods, preferring rigorous musical method and discipline. "One must always *work* rather than wait for inspiration," he claimed. "That is why, in spite of their great gifts, they produce so little and in such a desultory way."[104] But like the Five, Tchaikovsky was a fountain of inspiration, had a talent for melody, and admitted to struggling with form.[105] When he visited Petersburg in 1868, he met with Dargomyzhsky and the Five and was received surprisingly well.

Tchaikovsky loved Petersburg and its ethos. He felt at home in its society, looked upon its aristocratic heritage with nostalgia, and saw that it held great material for his art. "I admit I have a great weakness for the Russian capital. What can I do? I've become too much a part of it. Everything that is dear to my heart is in Petersburg, and life without it is positively impossible for me."[106] Thus it is not surprising that he chose Pushkin's quintessential Petersburg tales, the still popular *Eugene Onegin* and *Queen of Spades*, as the subjects for his two major operas. Even as penned by Pushkin, the stories portrayed an aristocracy (and hence Petersburg as an aristocratic city) already in decline. In Tchaikovsky's versions half a century later this theme naturally resonated more loudly, even as Tchaikovsky in Dostoevskian fashion focused the stories on the psychological torments and personal fates of key characters. When Tatyana sends Onegin quietly away and the curtain falls, or when in Tchaikovsky's new ending to *Queen of Spades* Herman and Liza take their own lives,* the audience is also bidding farewell to the city's bygone age. Tchaikovsky's *Onegin* has been termed the *Cherry Orchard* of Russian opera.[107] And like Dostoevsky, he could be more critical than Pushkin, who did not know that he would die at the hands of that society. Tchaikovsky did not express such feelings except through his works, but they were summed up well by his biographer Boris Asafyev:

> The poison of Petersburg nights, the sweet mirage of its ghostly images, the fogs of autumn and the bleak joys of summer, the coziness and acute contradictions of Petersburg life, the meaningless waste of Petersburg sprees and the amorous longing of Petersburg's romantic rendezvous, delicious meetings and secret promises, cold disdain and indifference of a man of society for superstition and ritual right up to blasphemous laughter about the other-worldly and at the same time the mystical fear of the unknown—all these moods and sensations poisoned Tchaikovsky's soul. He carried that poison with him always, and his music is imbued with it.[108]

But to some like the aspiring artist and writer Alexander Benois, Tchaikovsky's glimpse into the past provided an uplifting revelation of the city's unique poetics:

> Now the city's past suddenly opened itself before me. Until being enraptured by *Queen of Spades*, I somehow did not fully realize my soul's connection with my native city. . . . I had instinctively adored Petersburg's charms, but other things about it offended my tastes with their severity and "officiousness." Now through my delight with *Queen of Spades* I saw the light. . . . Now I found all around me that captivating poetry whose presence before I had only guessed at.[109]

Similar moods haunt Tchaikovsky's Piano Trio in A Minor (1882), dedicated to Nikolai Rubenstein "in memory to a great artist" after his death, and his last three symphonies, of which the Fifth (1890) and Sixth (1893) premiered in St. Petersburg. Each symphony deals with man's confrontation with Fate (ultimately death), and each was written at a time of personal crisis.† But above the introspection and doom is a

---

*In Pushkin's ending, Hermann (spelled differently) simply goes mad and is last seen living at a mental hospital, while Liza marries well and presumably lives a happy life.

†The Fourth was written as he was extricating himself from his disastrous marriage, the Fifth as he witnessed the deathbed struggle of his friend Nikolai Kondratiev, and the Sixth while being abandoned by his longtime patron Nadezhda von Meck.

portrait of the capital: imperial majesty and triumph, the gaiety of high society, and Russian melodies. The Fifth Symphony was greeted enthusiastically by the city's audiences, though not by critics. His Sixth, the *Pathétique*, was so innovative that audiences did not know what to make of it. When at the premiere its final mournful bars died out into a somber silence and Tchaikovsky lowered the baton in the Hall of the Nobility, the stunned listeners just sat silent to the sound of sobbing. Only nine days later the composer was dead, the victim of cholera contracted from drinking unboiled the city's contaminated water. Some writers have completed the story melodramatically by making Tchaikovsky's death a suicide, but there is no evidence for this.[110]

The opera that had so impressed Benois at the Mariinsky was the result of state support of that theater, which revived its Imperial Ballet. After ballet's strong start under Russia's 18th-century Empresses, at the turn of the 19th century Russia found its own talent in the ballet composers Alexei Titov and Stepan Davydov and the Russian dancer and ballet master Ivan Valberg (Leisogorov), who, particularly after the Patriotic War of 1812, was the first to synthesize Russian folk dance and national culture with European technique. The Emperor convinced the internationally renowned French dancer and ballet master Charles-Louis Didelot (1767–1837) to work in Petersburg, where he worked from 1801 to 1811 and again from 1816 to 1829. Working with his talented Russian students, he revolutionized ballet instruction, costume, dance technique, choreography, story development, and ballet staging and special effects, and broadened the themes of ballets to include both classical and Russian myths and fairy tales, the poetry of Pushkin, and historical subjects. He pushed his dancers to their technical limits, having both the male and female dancers pioneer solo flights as well as group flights. By the time he left, the training and virtuosity of Russia's dancers surpassed those in all of Europe.

Didelot's heritage set the stage for French-born Marius Petipa (1818–1910), whose almost 50 productions at the Imperial Theater dominated Russian ballet in the latter third of the 19th century and into the 20th. Handsome, romantic by nature, always immaculately groomed and a naturally talented dancer, he was a naturally expressive showman who joined the troupe in 1847, rose to be lead dancer in the 1860s, and was appointed Ballet Master in Chief to the Tsar in 1869. In that position he created classical ballet as it is known today, choreographing many of the great ballets still in the repertoire such as *Don Quixote*, *Giselle*, and Tchaikovsky's *Sleeping Beauty*, *The Nutcracker*, and *Swan Lake*. Drawing on Russian folk dance, Romantic story lines, and native Russian expressiveness, he transformed the rigid virtuoso Italian style brought to its height by Didelot into a more deeply expressive, flowing style emphasizing plasticity of the arms (known as the "dance of the arms"), seamless integration of movement between the soloists and the corps, exploitation of music to enhance mood and expression, and light, gossamer costumes that evoked lightness, dreams, and the unreal. This style was best suited to Romantic themes, which tended to be either interplays between dreams and reality as in Tchaikovsky's ballets, or stories of adventurers, pirates, or outcasts as in *Don Quixote* or *Le Corsaire*. *Sleeping Beauty* premiered at the Mariinsky Theater in 1890 and disconcerted balletomanes accustomed to the old style of dancing to simpler, rhythmical music that served principally as background; to them Tchaikovsky's music was too complex to be *dansant*, as well as boring. But the new style won the hearts of audiences, and soon *The Nutcracker* (1892) and the reworked *Swan Lake* (1895) also came to the Petersburg stage.

DOSTOEVSKY'S FINAL YEARS

In 1881 both Dostoevsky and Mussorgsky died, Alexander II was assassinated, and the dark reign of Alexander III began. Once the weight of that reign was lifted, what would lie in the future, and what road should Russia take? In *Crime and Punishment*, Dostoevsky had attacked nihilism but had not elaborated an alternative, positive vision; his readers were left hanging. In Dostoevsky's last two novels, one, *The Possessed* (1872) portrayed the road that Russia eventually took, while in the other, *The Brothers Karamazov* (1880), Dostoevsky began to reveal his own vision.

The main setting of *The Possessed* is a provincial town rather than Petersburg. It was inspired by the rise of radicalism in the capital and the trial of Nechaev's terrorist group, and its main protagonist was modeled on none other than Nikolai Speshnev, the Petrashevtsy radical that Dostoevsky had followed into Siberia. Like *Notes from Underground* and *Crime and Punishment*, it depicts people's reactions to an unnatural society with many social ills, but it does so at the group level and focuses on the devastating consequences of trying to remedy social problems through utopian, radical social and political movements. A revealing portrayal of the psychology of a revolutionary, the novel is seen by many as prophesizing how Petersburg became the cradle of the Russian Revolution.

In *The Brothers Karamazov*, intended as the first part of a larger work, the mature Dostoevsky began to sketch his final vision of the reconciled and ideal human being that the repentant Raskolnikov had set off to become. At the end of the novel, one of the Karamazov brothers, Dmitry, stands between the traditionally religious Alyosha and the rationalistic Ivan. Influenced by Schiller* and his *Ode to Joy*, Dmitry had developed a keen aesthetic sense and a delight in play that enables him to experience the wonder of children, with whom he plays. Through Dmitry, Dostoevsky holds that one must not love or founder on the "meaning of life," but simply love life itself, rejoice in spontaneity, and enjoy "the game for the sake of the

---

*Friedrich Schiller, in his *Letters on the Aesthetic Education of Mankind* of 1794–95, argued that a balanced combination of the rational and sensual faculties is necessary to form the complete human being, and that such balance is achieved by an aesthetic education focusing on the instinct for play and spontaneity, the ultimate fruit of which is love. Disharmony and worse results when this side of man's self (in today's vernacular, the left brain) is repressed. Schiller was a major influence in Dostoevsky's youth, and Dostoevsky later said that Schiller had inspired his finest dreams.

game" and all creation. Such people are not the reclusive dreamers portrayed in Dostoevsky's early works, but live and flourish in society and thereby reach their full potential. Indeed, they feel responsible for the whole world (exemplified by Ivan accepting his conviction and suffering for a murder that he did not commit), and only with enough such people in society will genuine social change and a just, civil society be possible. Here Dostoevsky had come full circle back to his *Petersburg Chronicle* of 33 years earlier, in which he said that

> life as a whole is art, that to live means to make of oneself a work of art, that only in the presence of generalized interests, in sympathy for the mass of society and for its direct, immediate demands, and not in somnolence, not in indifference, from which the mass is falling apart, not in isolation, can his hidden treasure, his capital and his kind heart be polished into a precious, genuine, gleaming diamond.[111]

This is what Dostoevsky meant when he said that beauty will save the world. Peter the Great, who lived such a life, would have been proud to see such ideas take hold in his city. Dostoevsky's most final vision is neither an idealization of the Muscovite and Orthodox past,[112] nor a rejection of Peter the Great's vision, which he had embraced in his *Petersburg Chronicle*. Originally formed in the Age of Reason, the Petersburg idea rather needed to be updated and complemented by the left brain. Indeed, it would be exactly this kind of delight in beauty, art, and life itself which would underlie Petersburg's next generation of artists, musicians, writers, and poets, exemplified by the World of Art movement, in which Petersburg culture flowered to stun Europe.

CHAPTER 11

From World of Art to Apocalypse

St. Petersburg, where they guess things that are not guessed even in Paris!

NIETZSCHE

We are a generation thirsting for beauty.

SERGEI DIAGHILEV

We feel the apocalyptic rhythm of the times. We strive toward the Beginning through the End.

ANDREI BELY[1]

FIN DE SIÈCLE ST. PETERSBURG

Like many European cities, turn-of-century St. Petersburg was a city of contrasts and contradictions. But in Russia everything is Big, often a matter of life and death. A new struggle was brewing for the soul of Petersburg and Russia. While lifestyles of the newly rich industrialists and merchants reached new levels of extravagance and the economy boomed, the misery of a growing, restless urban proletariat deepened. Creative geniuses like Diaghilev, Chaliapin, Bakst, Fokine, Pavlova, Stravinsky, Nijinsky, and Benois produced innovative art, music, opera, and ballet that stunned Russia and Europe alike, thus realizing in culture the Petersburg idea of synthesizing East and West into something new and original which surpasses both. But political life was paralyzed, as the heirs of Radishchev and the Decembrists fought for liberal constitutional reform against an entrenched but disintegrating and disreputable autocracy on the one hand and radicals on the other. Professors and scientists at the city's university and institutes made new discoveries—Ivan Pavlov even won a Nobel Prize—but their students were rebelling on the streets. While the radicals agitated on the streets and in factories for revolution, the city's highbrow intelligentsia literally sat in its own tower, isolated from the people. And the people? The formerly aristocratic city was now overwhelmingly one of masses of peasant-workers from the countryside. The Petersburg of Gogol and Dostoevsky was still alive, but now was more complex and impatient. It was a fast-paced and exciting age of grand ideas, the bizarre, and tumult in every sphere that made one's head spin. Pushkin and Lermontov had deserving heirs in poets like Blok, Gippius, Akhmatova, Mandelstam, and Gumilev, whose thoughtful and often prophetic poems devoted to the city and its fate carried on the Petersburg myth. As the city entered the new century, burning political and social issues, as well as deep questions of civilization and culture, had to be resolved, which in turn could determine whether St. Petersburg's distinctive culture and idea would triumph (or at least survive), or whether, in Akhmatova's words, the city would be "transformed into the opposite of itself."[2]

THE ST. PETERSBURG OF NICHOLAS II

Nicholas II, born on May 6, 1868, was ill suited to bring Russia into the new century. As a boy of 13, he saw the shattered body of his grandfather, Alexander II, brought into the Winter Palace and watched him breathe his last breath. He was educated under the supervision of Alexander III's conservative minister Constantine Pobedonostev, admired his father and was determined to carry on his policies and defend autocracy, which he saw as divinely ordained. But unlike his father, who was a giant of a man with an iron will, Nicholas was short, slight of build, never confident in his opinions, and could not command loyalty or respect. Nicholas never understood and was not comfortable with Petersburg, preferred Moscow, and was fascinated with the Muscovite period. He preferred the title "Tsar" to that of "Emperor," named his son after Tsar Alexis, the last Tsar of Muscovy, and when he appeared at balls, he liked to wear 17th-century Muscovite costumes. He admired the military but was otherwise uninterested in state affairs, preferring safer and more private pursuits like chopping wood, skating, sailing, theater, opera, and ballet.

Nicholas especially liked ballet, the art form most capable of creating an enchanted dream world. He was particularly taken by *Sleeping Beauty*, which he saw three times in the month after its première, and he often attended Mariinsky rehearsals; chatting with the dancers. One of the great events of Petersburg's ballet world was the graduation performances of the students at the Imperial School of Ballet, which the imperial family attended. The School's star was Matilda Kshesinskaya (1872–1971), a tiny, vivacious sprite with lovely dark eyes and a coquettish smile that men and audiences found irresistible and naturally made her the center of attention. After the graduation performances in 1890, the royal family greeted the students in the rehearsal room. Alexander III singled her out, holding out his hand to her and saying, "Be the glory and adornment of our ballet."[3] That evening, the royals hosted a dinner for the dancers, at which Kshesinskaya sat between the Emperor and 21-year-old Grand Duke Nicholas, whom she captivated. The feeling was mutual. "It was like a dream," she later wrote. "I fell in love with the Tsarevich on the spot! . . . I did not sleep a wink the whole night."[4] The affair moved slowly as Matilda's parents sent her to Europe and Nicholas departed on a nine-month world tour, but eventually she became his mistress. There could be no question of marriage, however, as Nicholas had to marry into a European royal house. After Nicholas's engagement to Princess Alix of Hesse-Darmstadt in 1894, he had to break off the liaison with Kshesinskaya but wrote to her, "Whatever happens to my life, my days spent with you will ever remain the happiest memories of my youth."[5] She went on to become the shining star of the Mariinsky and the consort of Grand Duke Sergei Mikhailovich and later the mistress of Grand Duke Andrei Vladimirovich, whom she married in Paris after the Russian Revolution. Royal patronage ensured her fame and fortune, and she lived lavishly, first in a house at 18 English Prospect that Nicholas secured for her, and later in a *style moderne* mansion on Trinity Square (which still stands today). At the Mariinsky, she shone in the title roles to the raves of audiences and critics alike, and all of Petersburg high society came to her performances. When Tchaikovsky saw her dance the role of Aurora in his *Sleeping Beauty*, he rushed backstage to congratulate her and promised to write a ballet for her. She had a flair for stardom, dressing in alluring costumes that breathed sensuality. Publicly known as the demimonde of two Grand Dukes, on stage she seemed to be inviting audiences into her world, which for the fleeting moment seemed almost accessible. Naturally, she was as famous off the stage as on it, controversial for her lifestyle as well as her performances, both of which some considered vulgar. But nobody could deny her talent and continuing dedication to her art.

As Nicholas ended his affair with Kshesinskaya, he was already preparing to marry Princess Alix, four years his junior and his distant cousin whose grandmother was Queen Victoria of England. Alix was smart and well educated, but following the traumatic loss of her mother became serious, aloof, introverted, and prone to the influence of mystics and quacks. The French Ambassador in Petersburg, Maurice Paléologue, saw her as follows: "Moral disquiet, constant sadness, vague longing, alternation between excitement and exhaustion, constant thought given to the invisible and supernatural, credulousness, superstition."[6] They were betrothed in April 1894, and looked forward to a happy and carefree life together while the iron-fisted Alexander III held Russia together and led it into the next century.

It was not to be. When Alix arrived in Russia in early October 1894, Alexander suddenly fell ill and on October 20 died from nephritis. "Sandro, what will I do!" Nicholas confided to his cousin, Grand Duke Alexander Mikhailovich. "What will happen to Russia now? I am not yet ready to be Tsar! I do not know how to run the empire. I don't even know how to talk to the ministers."[7] Indeed, Nicholas's first act was to mismanage his father's funeral, while Alix's first public appearance was in the funeral cortege, in a carriage behind the hearse. A peasant woman observing on the sidewalk was heard to utter, "She has entered our land behind a coffin. She brings misfortune with her."[8] Indeed, tragedy struck at Nicholas's coronation celebrations in Moscow, when thousands were trampled in a deadly stampede at Khodynka Field; Nicholas then alienated others by continuing the festivi-ties as if nothing had happened. As time went on, the royal couple isolated them-selves from the people, rarely appearing in public or holding balls, and living most of the time not in the Winter Palace in Petersburg but in the Alexander Palace at Tsarskoe Selo, even in the winter. With Nicholas detached physically from the cap-ital and neglecting affairs of state and the urgent need for reform, Russia was rud-derless. Russia had a Tsar but no ruler.

Yet upon taking power Nicholas had reason to be optimistic. Russia had been at peace for years and no conflicts loomed. The revolutionary movement that had taken his grandfather's life had been crushed. Thanks to the policies of Alexander III's finance minister Sergei Witte, who later served Nicholas, the pace of industri-alization in Russia was exploding. The growth rate of Russia's industry during 1890–1899, at over eight percent, was probably the highest in the world.[9] The trans-Siberian railroad was being built, and overall railroad expansion outpaced even that in the United States. Russia's production of coal, oil, and steel was rising faster than in either Europe or the United States.[10] Foreign capital invested in Rus-sia was surging, rising from 280.1 million rubles in 1895 to 911 million in 1900.[11] And while agriculture lagged, Russia had recovered from a recent famine and no major crises or peasant unrest seemed likely.

With the economy booming, turn-of-century St. Petersburg was rich and gay. Its life not only mirrored that of Europe, but in some respects surpassed it. Trains and steamships now made visits to the West easy and inexpensive, and by then tra-ditional travel restrictions were largely abolished. Businessmen, intellectuals, artists, writers, and government officials frequented Europe, experienced firsthand its lifestyles, art, ideas, and growing material riches, and they brought these influences back to Petersburg. The court, aristocrats, and the nouveaux riches industrialists and merchants demanded striking buildings, beautiful art, and fine things. Aesthetic tastes shifted from realism to a desire for the beautiful that celebrated life. Peters-burg was entering a new age of art and beauty.

Eclectic new styles of architecture and interior design—neo-Renaissance, neo-Greek, Russian Revival, Louis XVI, Moorish, Scandinavian *moderne*, but most of all variations on *style moderne* (as Art Nouveau was called in Russia)—now adorned the façades and interiors of homes, shops, and public buildings, enriching the city's ap-pearance and adding to its enchantment. This was made possible by the now prodi-gious numbers of professional architects who were trained in the city's institutions and joined the Petersburg Society of Architects, which published the country's lead-ing architectural journal, *Zodchii* ("The Architect"), and its weekly supplement, *Nedelia stroitelia* ("Builder's Weekly"). Architectural criticism also appeared in the Pe-tersburg art journals, *Mir iskusstva* and *Apollon*. Thanks to professionalization and the influence of the Petersburg art world, the initial disorganized, dilettantish eclecticism of architecture in Dostoevsky's time evolved into a sophisticated modernism, marked by Vladimir Apyshkov's book *The Rational in the Latest Architecture* (1905), in which he synthesized the various styles into a coherent aesthetic movement. While recognizing that the needs of commerce and economics had to influence modern architecture, he maintained that "the task of a true artist is . . . not to struggle with the practical and expedient but rather to transform them into the aesthetic."[12] Thanks to Apyshkov and creative colleagues like Fedor Lidval, Pavel Siuzor, Ippolit Pretro, Nikolai Vasiliev, Leonti Benois, and Nikolai Dmitriev, some of the city's finest buildings went up. Nevsky Prospect now boasted the magnificent Eliseev Building hosting the city's finest grocery store, the Singer Building (now the House of Books), and a remodeled Hotel Europe. The Mertens Building, innovative apartment buildings, and a mosque now graced Petersburg and Vasilievsky Islands, and the rich Vollenweider, Gausvald, Belzen, Meltser, and Schöne families resided in modernistic dachas on Kamenny Island.

On the city streets, imported delicacies stocked the shelves of grocers like Eliseev's, while the well-off dined in fine restaurants like Donon's, Palkin, Barel, The Bear, and Vienna. The city's nightlife rivaled Paris, offering on any given night a wide choice of plays, operas, concerts, and cabarets. The traditional Petersburg balls and masquerades were still popular, though they were now almost entirely private functions rather than affairs of the court. European fashions were broadly available in off-the-rack clothing. Even beautiful jewelry was now made and sold on a mass scale, thanks to newly discovered deposits of gold and gems and improved technology for jewelry making, and numerous Russian and foreign jewelers set up shop in the city. "In those days there were no crude or awkward corners in St. Petersburg," reminisced one Englishman in the city at the time. "Everything went with a swing, all things flowed, as it were, one into the other, to make of the whole city's life one unending sweep of dignity and poise. And if you wished to see this state of affairs at the very pinnacle, you went to Fabergé's at 24 Morskaya."[13]

Peter Karl Fabergé (1846–1920) epitomized the Russian artist who learned his craft in Europe and absorbed its influences, only to return and create truly original and genuinely Russian art and then export it to the world. From a French Huguenot family that found comfort in St. Petersburg, he was born to Gustav Fabergé, a goldsmith who ran a basement jewelry shop on Bolshaya Morskaya. After the family moved to Germany in 1860, Karl perfected his art in Dresden and Frankfurt before moving back to Petersburg in 1870 to take over his father's shop. Eventually he became Russia's leading goldsmith and jeweler, his enterprise boasting some 700 craftsmen and located in an elegant building opened in 1900 at 24 Bolshaya Morskaya which still stands today. Fabergé's workshop produced magnificent original works for Russian and foreign royalty, aristocracy, and other wealthy clients. Fabergé's works stood out from the fine work of other Russian and foreign jewelers and goldsmiths by their uncompromising fine workmanship, opulence, color and originality of their designs, and their identity with Russia. His creations included such diverse items as jewelry, snuff and cigarette boxes, binoculars, serving dishes, parasol handles, fans, vases, clocks, frames, match holders, furniture, goblets, baskets, crosses, wedding crowns, triptychs, figures of plants, animals, people, and gods, and miniature sedan chairs. Most famous was his series of Easter eggs designed as the Tsar's gift to the Empress every year beginning in 1884, each intended to surpass its predecessors in beauty and extravagance. Other masterpieces included a crystal vase with forget-me-nots made of golden stems, nephrite leaves, and flowers in turquoise and diamonds, a jadeite Buddha studded with rubies and rose diamonds, figures of dancing peasants with sapphire eyes, and gypsies, chimpanzees, and even anteaters with diamond eyes. Through such creations Fabergé and other artisans helped deepen people's appreciation for beauty and the arts and popularize Russian semiprecious stones.

But Fabegé's creations were only the tip of the iceberg. The two decades in St. Petersburg's life known as the Silver Age produced a remarkable revival in poetry and literature, architecture, music, ballet, theater, and intellectual life. Many brought their groundbreaking creations not only to St. Petersburg but also to the West, thus realizing at least in the realm of culture St. Petersburg's original purpose. The age seemed to herald a Russian renaissance, a cause which in Petersburg was championed by Dmitry Merezhkovsky, the poet and theoretician of Russian Symbolism, and his wife, the poet Zinaida Gippius.

THE DIONYSIANS: SYMBOLISM IN PETERSBURG

By the end of the 19th century, the left intelligentsia's realist aesthetics derived from Chernyshevsky and Nekrasov vied with Dostoevsky's religious and spiritual notions of beauty, but for true creative artists only the latter view held promise. In Petersburg in the early 1890s, Merezhkovsky and Gippius led the break from realism into the new century.

They were a unique pair of opposites. Before they met, she had read his poetry and hated it; he had seen her portrait and exclaimed, "What a mug!" Their first meeting, while each was on vacation at Borzhom, a spa in the Caucasus, turned into an argument, and so did their almost daily meetings during the rest of their stay. But something was special, and while on one walk in the park, she recollected, "We—and it is important that it was both of us—suddenly began to speak as if it had been decided long ago that we would marry and that it would be good if we did." The marriage too happened "by itself," in Tiflis in January 1889. After the ceremony, Merezhkovsky retired to his hotel, she to her own bed in the cottage where she was staying with her mother. When Dmitry called on Zinaida the next morning, her mother awakened her: "You're still sleeping and your husband is already here. Get up!" "My husband?" she said to herself, "How astonishing!"[14] But the two would spend an extraordinary 53 years together, and never again were they apart for a single night.

Creatively they formed a complementary pair. She was the inspiration and source of ideas, the more artistically creative and better poet of the two, while he was the better scholar, theoretician, and critic. While Dmitry was slight, bookish, and shy, Zinaida was anything but. She was a tall, beautiful, self-assured, and flamboyant dark blonde who often colored her hair flaming red. She radiated sensuality despite her masculine manner and way of thinking and writing (she wrote in the masculine gender), usually dressing either in male attire or in revealing feminine, skin-tight clothes. She confessed that "spiritually, I am more a man, but physically, I am more a woman,"[15] and much of her poetry concerned uniting the male and female in order to transcend traditional sexuality. Notoriously haughty, mean, and quick to pronounce judgment, she was variously called the Decadent Madonna, the Petersburg Hedda Gabler, the Russian Messalina, a witch (by Trotsky), and a white she-devil (by churchmen). But this behavior, dress, and manners masked a vulnerable and serious woman. "It is no joy to peer into the murk of my own difficult, dark soul," ran one of her poems. Taking inspiration from her favorite writer, Dostoevsky, and Lermontov (especially his *Demon*, with which she identified), her quest was to overcome the Devil and achieve union with God, spiritual regeneration, and cosmic love. For her, art was real when it guided one toward the spiritual, and poetry was a form of prayer and personal confession:

> *I'm close to God, and yet I cannot pray,*
> *And I want love, but cannot love a soul.*

Much of her poetry is pessimistic, and she conceived of the coming regeneration of Russia, like her own, not as linear progress or a renaissance, but as "a new death, and a new resurrection."[16]

The Merezhkovskys and Moscow's Symbolists initially took their inspiration from the West: Charles Baudelaire, the French Symbolist poets Paul Verlaine, Arthur Rimbaud, and Stéphane Mallarmé, and the "decadent" paintings of the Englishman Aubrey Beardsley. In Russia, French Symbolist thought and aesthetics merged with the influential philosophy and aesthetics of Vladimir Soloviev to create a uniquely Russian form of symbolism which dominated fin de siècle poetry and literature in the capital.

Symbolists viewed the visible world in Neoplatonic terms, as consisting of mere manifestations of a deeper underlying reality and truth which is inherently inexpressible. Symbolist poets expressed the eternal in the temporal and the underlying mystery of existence through images and metaphors which, though imprecise, reflected the artist's personal link with the ultimate. Thus, in authentic art, form and content are inseparable. Beauty resides in the symbol itself, which should not be broken down into emotions or discursive ideas.

Soloviev, a Muscovite who lectured at St. Petersburg University before traveling abroad in the mid-1870s, was a Christian who was also influenced by the German mystics Jacob Boehme and Franz Baader (who had influenced Moscow's higher-order Freemasons a century before). Like these mystics, he believed in a deeper reality underlying the visible world, and thus presaged Symbolism in some of his own poems:

> *Everything visible to us*
> *Is only a flash, only a shadow*
> *From what cannot be seen by the eye.*

Soloviev believed that man, transfused by the divine spirit, is the link between God and the material world. Ideal humanity embodying divine wisdom takes real, earthly form in Sophia, who Soloviev identified with the eternal feminine. (Soloviev claimed to have actually seen her three times in his life: once in childhood, once at the British Museum, and again in the deserts of Egypt.) Humanity must align itself with Sophia and thereby attain world spiritual unity. Since the divine is the ultimate expression of beauty, artists, poets, and writers play a crucial role in Man's quest for perfection. Creating a work of art is to commune with a higher world. Art aimed at expressing such communion can help individuals achieve their own. Thus, art becomes a theurgic force capable of transforming the world to align it with the divine, literallly spiritualizing matter to create beauty on earth. Thus, man too can become godlike. Russians now recognized the crucial importance of perceptive and gifted individuals who, fully aware of their powers, could achieve the highest form of communion and lead mankind to higher levels.

Not surprisingly, therefore, the ideas of Nietzsche (despite his atheism) also took Petersburg by storm,[17] Berdyaev called him "the strongest Western influence on the Russian Renaissance."[18] Nietzsche's principal influence in Russia was not his theory of the superman but his theories about ancient Greek art, culture, and theater as explained in his *Birth of Tragedy*. Nietzsche contrasted the musical intoxication of the Dionysian festival, through which individuals (or the group) could lose their ego and unite with the divine without the mediation of the artist, with the dreamlike Apollinian impulse toward classical perfection: beauty, harmony, and measure. It was by uniting in a work of art these ultimately irreconcilable poles that the highest achievement of Greek culture—classical tragedy—was achieved. Petersburg's literati were schooled in Nietzsche's theories and viewed their own ideas and work through this paradigm. One outgrowth of these trends was Prometheanism, based on the legend of Prometheus who brought fire and the arts to humanity and was seen as a model for artists and art. Merezhkovsky translated Aeschylus's *Prometheus Bound*, the Petersburg Symbolist Vyacheslav Ivanov wrote a play called *Prometheus*, and the legend inspired several other artistic works of the time.[19] In short, artists could not only express ultimate reality but use their insight, wisdom, and will to transform the visible world. Symbolists believed that the new art would give rise to a new renaissance in Russia and perhaps for all of mankind. "We saw the glow of a new dawn," recalled Nikolai Berdyaev, "and the end of an old age seemed to coincide with a new era which would bring about a complete

transfiguration of life."²⁰ Their outlook was at odds with the established left intelligentsia who saw Symbolism (and later the World of Art movement) as a reactionary betrayal of the social struggle in the name of the people. The two sides
waged a war on all fronts, with the now ancient Stasov still the spokesman of the
realists. But in the heady years of the fin de siècle, in Berdyaev's estimate "Soloviev
conquered Chernyshevsky."²¹

From this point of departure Russian artists, poets, writers, and musicians could
go in various directions, including extremes. The moderate ("Apollinian") approach which came to dominate in St. Petersburg, typified by the World of Art
movement and Acmeist poetry, was to use the arts to create beauty, enrich and celebrate life, and draw humanity together, which in turn would contribute to bettering social, political, and economic life. The more extreme ("Dionysian") tendency
of Symbolism, more pervasive in Moscow, was metaphysical, mystical, grandiose,
and in many cases Slavophile and nationalistic. Soloviev's ideas appealed to
Slavophiles who believed in Russia's spiritual superiority over the West and special
relationship to the divine. For them, Soloviev had only confirmed their long-held
messianic belief that Russia was destined by history to unify and save mankind. This
theme was explored in a novel by the Moscow Symbolist Andrei Bely, who was fascinated by Petersburg, visited it often, and was destined to become a fixture in the
city's heritage. Entitled *The Silver Dove* (1909), the novel was conceived as the first
part of a trilogy entitled *East or West?*, the second part of which was *Petersburg*; the
third, *Invisible City*, was never written. In *The Silver Dove*, a Russian symbolist poet
rejects the West to go live and seek the truth in the "East" of Russia amongst peasants (as Bely did when writing the novel), and falls in love with Matryona, a pock-
marked, breasty, and lustful peasant woman representing Mother Earth and who is
destined to be the progenitor of a pastoral apocalypse that will unite East and West
by producing a savior, the "dove" who can rise to heaven. But when the poet fails
to impregnate Matryona, a local religious sect kills him, and Russia's proper direction (East or West) is left ambiguous. Back in Moscow, Bely and his friend Sergei
Soloviev founded a literary circle called The Argonauts to popularize their beliefs.
Perhaps the most grandiose example of this messianic direction was the Muscovite
composer Alexander Scriabin (1872–1915), who began as the composer of imaginative, modern piano pieces and ended his days as a mystic hoping to unify all the
arts and religions and become the savior of the world. He once wrote that his Third
Symphony (1902–04), a choral work entitled *The Divine Poem*, expressed "the evolution of the human spirit which, torn from an entire past of beliefs and mysteries
which it surmounts and overcomes, passes through pantheism and attains to a joyous and intoxicated affirmation of its liberty and its unity with the universe." He
sought to surpass this vision in his *Poem of Ecstasy* (1907) and *Prometheus: The Poem
of Fire* (1910–11). In his uncompleted final work, *Mysterium*, a massive score and
synthesis of the arts, two thousand musicians, singers and dancers were to perform
without an audience in a semicircular temple on the shore of a lake in India, with

the lake itself completing the circle. Through this intoxicating Dionysian festival of music, dance, light, color, architecture, and smell in which the ego would dissolve, he literally hoped to bring about the culmination of human history, the end of the material world and the triumph of spirit, raising man to the level of the gods.[22] By his sudden death in 1915, he was divorced from humanity, living in the realm of abstraction. By contrast, also in Moscow, Valery Briusov, the initiator of Symbolism in that city, was nearly alone in viewing Symbolism as a literary rather than mystical philosophical movement, but, lacking philosophical, religious, or social ideas, his formalistic poetry ultimately grew stale and empty, and eventually he gave it up. It was Petersburg's Symbolist and other poets—Gippius, Blok, Akhmatova, Mandelstam, and Gumilev—who eventually married original and inspired content with form, and synthesized the Dionysian with the Apollinian, to create the greatest poetry of the early 20th century.

Merezhkovsky authored the earliest Symbolist manifesto, *On the Reasons for the Decline and New Trends in Contemporary Russian Literature* (1893), in which he gave poetry primacy as an elemental force and "gift of God" and attacked the populist-realist view of art as a means for conveying a moral: "The highest *moral* significance of art does not lie in affecting moral tendencies but in the selfless, incorruptible veracity of the artist, in his fearless sincerity. The beauty of an image cannot be untrue and therefore cannot be immoral; only deformity, only vulgarity in art can be immoral."[23] Rather than look to Russia's past for inspiration, he found it in the beauties of classical antiquity and the rites of paganism. He traveled to Greece, and on his first visit to the Acropolis experienced a communion with the divine and a peace he had not before found in the modern world. New gods had to be created that combined paganism (really Hellenism and Nietzsche) with Christianity, which he explored in his novel trilogy *Christ and Antichrist* (1896–1905), which among other things pitted Peter the Great against his son Alexis to show that Christ and Antichrist had been at war in modern Russia and that this conflict could be resolved only by an apocalypse raising man to a higher level. As Berdyaev summarized it, "The Renaissance upheld the banner not only of the Spirit but also of Dionysis, and in it a Christian renaissance was mingled with a pagan renaissance."[24] An important part of this new spiritual union was to restore sex to its natural role, which Merezhkovsky claimed Christianity had suppressed, turning that religion into one of death. As the natural combination of divine creation and nature, sex is a natural bridge between the human and the divine.

In order to achieve their desired union of Christianity and paganism—what they called the Third Kingdom of God—in 1901 the Merezhkovskys founded in St. Petersburg the Religious-Philosophical Society, where clerics in cassocks and monks in cloaks mingled with the city's literati, philosophers like Berdyaev, and chic socialites. Since the Merezhkovskys dominated the meetings, Berdyaev recalled, "the subject of sex predominated."[25] Indeed, at its first meeting, held in the hall of the Geographical Society on the Fontanka, Gippius appeared in what seemed at first glance to be a modest black dress, but it had pleats that opened up at the slightest movement to reveal a pale pink lining that made it appear that she was naked underneath. The churchmen were not amused. Soon the large statue of Buddha overlooking the hall was covered up in order "to avoid temptation."[26] Needless to say, no union was ever achieved, although the discussions were serious and enlightening.

But most famous and influential was the Merezhkovskys' salon at their elegant second-floor apartment in the building on the corner of Liteiny Prospect and Panteleimonovsky (now Pestel) Street, called the Dom Muruzi ("Home of Muruza," after its owner, Prince Alexander Muruza, who built it in 1874[27]). The salon became the first circle of Russian Symbolists and lasted until the Merezhkovskys fled Russia after the October Revolution. The city's leading writers, artists, and critics gathered there each Sunday after midnight. Gippius reigned over the soirées like a lioness. Dressed provocatively and sporting French perfume, her blond mane flowing like a Rusalka's, smoking scented cigarettes through a long, slender holder, and glancing coldly through her lorgnette with her green mermaid eyes, she circulated langourously among her guests or lay on her chaise longue, pronouncing often deadly aphoristic judgments on artists and their works. She became a feared arbiter of taste in the city's modernist circles, and for most new, aspiring artists a pilgrimage was mandatory. (Akhmatova was a notable exception, declining to come when Gippius invited her.) Merezhkovsky was more gracious and deferential than his wife and paid less attention to ceremony and dress. He was so preoccupied with his work that he often retreated to his study to read or write, emerging only when he had something important to say. Those who gathered there were out to change the world, sure of their importance, serious and egocentric; the atmosphere was heady. As Berdyaev recalled, "The Merezhkovskys' drawing-room was not a place where you would meet a real person."[28]

The Merezhkovskys also initially allied themselves with the World of Art movement and worked on their journal *Mir iskusstva*, but grew dissatisfied both with the group's focus on the plastic arts and aesthetics and scant attention to poetry, literature, and philosophy. Thus, in 1903 the Merezhkovskys established their own literary journal, *Novyi Put* ("The New Path"), and then the more philosophical *Voprosy Zhizni* ("Questions of Life") (1904), edited by Nikolai Berdyaev, for which purpose he moved to St. Petersburg.

Complementing the Merezhkovskys was Petersburg's other main theoretician of Symbolism, Vyacheslav Ivanov. An erudite scholar, classical philologist, and translator, he studied history in Germany under Mommsen, once wrote a thesis on the Roman fiscal system, and became influenced by Nietzsche and Prometheanism; his doctoral dissertation was "Dionysis and Pre-Dionysianism." For him, Symbolism was not merely a literary school as in France, but a way of understanding the world by stripping away the symbols contained in visible reality. Like Merezhkovsky and Gippius, he sought to unite Christianity with elements of pre-Christian paganism. While Merezhkovsky and Gippius lived for several years in Paris following the 1905 revolution, Ivanov established his own literary and intellectual salon at his large apartment at 35 Tavricheskaya Street. He assumed leadership of Petersburg Symbolism, and his salon became an intellectual center in the city. It became known as "The Tower" because it was on the seventh floor and at its corner had a rounded tower with a view over the adjacent Tauride Palace gardens. The salon was held on Wednesdays from midnight to dawn, beginning with a presentation on a philosophical or artistic theme followed by discussion. When the formal part of the night was over, usually about 2:00 A.M., dinner was served and alcohol flowed to intelligent conversation and readings of poetry and criticism of it. The handsome Ivanov was an attentive, charming, and gracious though manipulative host, circulating gracefully among his guests in his pince-nez and black gloves (to cover his chronic eczema). The poet Sergei Gorodetsky described one of these evenings, at which the young poet Alexander Blok, at the time (1907) under the influence of Ivanov, read poems from *The Snow Mask:*

> A large garret with a narrow window straight to the stars. Candles in candelabra. L.D. Zinovieva-Annibal* in a tunic. . . . We assembled late. After twelve, Vyacheslav and Anichkov or someone else gave reports on the themes of mystical anarchism, collective individualism, the suffering god of Hellenic religion, the collective theater, Christ and Antichrist, etc. We argued violently and at length. Toward morning, after the debate, the reading of poems began. . . . In his long frock coat, with the soft necktie tied with elegant casualness, in a nimbus of ashen-gold hair, Blok was at that time romantically handsome. . . . He would go slowly to the table with the candles, look around at everyone with his stony eyes and would himself turn to stone until the silence became complete. And he began to speak, holding the verse steady agonizingly well and slowing the tempo slightly on the rhymes. . . . Everyone was in love with him.[29]

On another night, recalled Chukovsky, the company of writers and artists proceeded outside onto the roof of the Tower as a White Night was brightening into dawn to hear Blok recite his *Unknown Woman*:

> Intoxicated by poetry and wine—and in those days poetry was as intoxicating as wine—we emerged under the white sky, and Blok, slowly, with outward calm, and young and tanned (he was always tanned by early spring), climbed onto the large iron frame used for telephone lines, and as if leading us in prayer recited three or four times his immortal ballad in his restrained, muffled, monotone, resigned, tragic voice. And we, having drunk of those sound-songs of genius, were already suffering as they ended as we wanted them to continue for hours, but suddenly, just as he uttered the last word, from the Tauride Garden just below a waft of air carried up to us the song of nightingales.[30]

Blok, the son of a gentry jurist and law professor, studied law at St. Petersburg University, but fell in love with the theater (playing Hamlet, Romeo, and Chatsky

---

*Ivanov's wife, a descendant of Pushkin.

from *Woe from Wit*) and then poetry. After discovering the poetry and philosophy of Vladimir Soloviev, he transferred to the historical-philological faculty in 1901. "I did not know a single line of modern poetry until my entry into university," he wrote, but "Soloviev's poetry filled my being, closely responding to my feelings of mysticism and romanticism."[31]

A family friend of the Bloks was the great St. Petersburg chemist Dmitry Mendeleev, creator of the periodic table, who had a country estate, Boblovo, on a hill near Blok's estate, Shakhmatovo. Alexander first met Mendeleev's daughter Lyubov* at age five, but for many years they did not meet again. One summer day in 1898 when Alexander, now a handsome, blond-haired, and grave-faced aesthete, was riding his white horse through the pastures, dressed in a white tunic and sporting a riding crop, he came upon Lyuba in a birch grove. Now Blok saw a tall, beautiful golden-haired goddess, who reminded him of Soloviev's lines:

> *Know that here, descended to earth,*
> *Is the Eternal Feminine in flesh incorruptible.*

Immediately visualizing her as Soloviev's Sophia, he began to idealize and worship her. She became his Muse, his Beatrice, and his first poems were dedicated to her, which culminated in his first collection of poems, *Verses about a Beautiful Lady* (1904). Lyuba shared his love for the theater and began acting in plays, and likewise she studied in the philology faculty at the university. But she was aloof, and for a long time rejected his advances. Blok pursued her on the streets of Petersburg like Dostoevsky's dreamer in *White Nights*; eventually she relented, and they got married in 1903. Also in 1903 his poems were first published, in the Merezhkovskys' journal, *The New Path*, and in Moscow in Bryusov's review, *Northern Flowers*.

Blok's fame also grew in Moscow, especially among its Symbolists, just as the works and ideas of Moscow's Symbolists interested Blok. Blok and Bely each decided to become acquainted with the other, and they first wrote each other on the same day; their letters crossed in the mail. They corresponded regularly and became close, but they met only in January 1904, when Alexander and Lyuba traveled to Moscow. Their first meeting was awkward, as neither was what the other expected; they seemed like opposites. Blok, handsome and immaculately dressed, was somber, pensive, and talked little. But when he spoke, it was slowly and gravely, and his words were of consequence. Bely, in contrast, was a chatterbox, was always moving about in a dance-like way, and had a decadent air and forced eccentricity highlighted by his pince-nez. The Petersburg couple was welcomed by Bryusov, Balmont, Bely, and the Argonauts, who like Blok quickly began to worship a some-

---

*Her name means "love" in Russian, and in common speech is usually shortened to Lyuba.

what embarrassed Lyuba as the Universal Soul.* The group held merry dinners, read their poems, talked about a great future, plied Lyuba with flowers, swapped shirts according to Russian custom, and visited Vladimir Soloviev's grave at Novodevichi Convent. But most evenings were spent at serious meetings devoted to the Symbolists' mystical quest, one of which Bely described colorfully:

> At the meeting at Sokolov's M. Ertel was present—historian appointed to the university upon graduation, occultist, Sanskritologist; the theosophists later considered him a "secret teacher"; he combined deep erudition and charlatanism. At some point, approaching a state of ecstasy, Ertel began to yell that all Moscow is enveloped in theurgy. Some theosophist proclaimed that the Initiated are already marching, and a mystically disposed barrister whispered: "Gentlemen, the table is shaking."[32]

"Blok turned gray from suffering," Bely noted. After another meeting of a university circle, Blok mused, "No, that's not the thing: there's something painful among all these people."[33] He longed for Petersburg: "I want the holy, the quiet, and the white," he wrote to his mother. "I want *books*; I don't expect anything from the people in Petersburg but 'literary conversations' in the best case, and banal mockery or 'winking at something else' in the worst."[34]

The experience of Moscow had been memorable, but Blok's creativity did not stand still. His early mysticism had played itself out Moscow, and his art and vision of Lyuba had to change. Then came the revolution of 1905, which opened his eyes to real life. Walking the streets of Petersburg, he observed, "Dostoevsky comes back to life in every corner of the town."[35] Blok became a man of 20th-century Russia, with a conscience and suffering personal anguish. Yet he admitted to his father: "I will never become a revolutionary or a 'builder of life,' not because I see no sense in one or the other, but simply due to the nature and quality of the emotional experiences in my soul."[36]

Blok buried his mystical past and the Beautiful Lady in his 1906 tragic play *Balaganchik* (translated variously as "The Puppet Show," the "Fair Show Booth," or simply "The Showbooth," a ubiquitous feature at Petersburg's carnivals) about Pierrot's ill-fated love. The opening parodies a rite of mystics who await the coming of a beautiful maiden from a distant land. That maiden is Death. But when she appears, Pierrot thinks they are mistaken about her and claims her as his bride Columbine. She follows him, but Harlequin appears and steals her away. While the rivals contend for her, they realize that she is only a cardboard doll. Everything turns out to be a lie, and all characters face disaster, especially Pierrot, whose dreams and life fall to pieces. When Blok read it to his friends, they recognized it as a

---

*Bely soon fell in love with Lyuba. At first the Bloks were merely amused, but Bely continued to pursue her and at one stage she almost left Blok for him. Even though she resolved to stay with Blok, Bely would not give up. This drama left deep scars and tormented them for the rest of their lives.

masterpiece, but Bely saw more: In the broken-hearted Pierrot Blok had portrayed himself, Columbine was Lyuba, and Bely—Harlequin. What Blok had once held holy was shattered. But not for the last time. It would happen again with the October Revolution, and then it would kill him.

Blok was not alone in challenging Symbolist conceptions of beauty and the role of art (for which Symbolists cared little outside poetry and literature). As Symbolism rose and realist art declined in the 1890s, a new group of Petersburg artists emerged and gained a following. It was led initially by Alexander Benois, who explained the new movement to Merezhkovsky:

> Whatever you say, for you the history of the world is coming to an end, is almost finished. . . . But our attitude is quite different. For us the world—despite triumphant Americanism, railroads, telegraphs, telephones, all this modern brutality and vulgarity, all this despicable transformation of the earth—still contains great charm and, most important, is full of promise.[37]

THE APPOLINIANS:
THE WORLD OF ART MOVEMENT

Benois's roots were European and cosmopolitan: French and German on his father's side, Venetian on his mother's. His family had moved from Venice to St. Petersburg late in the 18th century and quickly established its artistic and intellectual pedigree. His great grandfather was "director of music" in St. Petersburg for Nicholas I. His grandfather, an architect, had built the Bolshoi and Mariinsky Theaters in St. Petersburg, and his father was also a notable, wealthy architect who among other things had designed the Imperial Stables at Peterhof. Alexander grew up among books and the arts. Raised as a Lutheran, he was an erudite cosmopolitan, spoke foreign languages, and was a consummate aesthete. He especially loved St. Petersburg: its history, architecture, and culture, and particularly Pushkin and Tchaikovsky. He saw Petipa's groundbreaking *Sleeping Beauty* countless times (once four times in one week), and as seen earlier *Queen of Spades* was a defining moment in his life. He attended the gymnasium of Karl May, which taught music and painting in addition to the usual subjects, and became a notable if not top-rate painter. There he became friends with other aesthetically minded students, including the future critic Dmitry Filosofov, the future music critic Walter Nouvel, and the painters Konstantin Somov and Nikolai Roerich.

After graduating in 1889, the friends, still in their late teens, began meeting a few times a week at the Benois home on the corner of Nikolskaya Street and Ekaterinhofsky Prospect. Soon they were joined by others, including the artist Lev Rozenberg (soon to become famous as Léon Bakst, after his grandfather), Benois's nephew (nearly his age) Eugene Lancéray, the half-English future writer and art critic Alfred Nourok, and Filosofov's cousin Sergei Diaghilev, a recent arrival from the provinces. Calling itself the Society for Self-Education (and later jokingly the Nevsky Pickwickians), the group held formal meetings on art, literature, music, and philosophy. Nouvel was its "president," but Bakst usually moderated the discussions, while its acknowledged pedagogue was Benois, whom one of the group once called "a one-man artistic university."[38] In the tradition of Novgorod, Pushkin's literary societies and the Petrashevtsy, Benois installed a bronze bell in the room to bring the meetings to order. At their meetings, one of them would make a presentation which the group would then discuss and debate. Since the Benois household proliferated with European art and literary journals, the friends read them avidly, and their articles often formed the topics of discussion. The friends rightly considered themselves Petersburg's (and Russia's) leading group of artistic cosmopolites. Out of these countless discussions emerged a discernible aesthetic orientation mostly reflecting Benois's own tastes, as well as concrete ideas on how to move Petersburg's art world in that direction. But Benois and most of his friends were artists, writers, and scholars rather than practical organizers. "Nothing would have come of it further, except a muddle, were everything confined to friendly chats," recalled Benois. "Our personal qualities and temperaments were largely responsible. [We] were spoiled, fastidious 'lordlings' or extremely impractical dreamers."[39] It fell to the ambitious, practical, and imaginative Diaghilev to realize the friends' ideas.

Diaghilev was born into a musical family of gentry and spent his early childhood in St. Petersburg, where he met Mussorgsky and Tchaikovsky, but when he was 10 his family moved to Perm, where his father was to command the garrison. After graduating from the gymnasium there, he returned to St. Petersburg in 1890 to study law at the university and lived with his cousin, Dmitry Filosofov, who introduced him to Benois's circle. At first Sergei cut an odd figure amongst the sophisticated Petersburgers. He was intellectually behind them and knew virtually nothing about art and literature, though he did have some background in music (and eventually studied composition at the St. Petersburg Conservatory). Benois later admitted that the group might not have taken him in but for the fact that he was Filosofov's cousin.[40] But Diaghilev was determined, brimmed with self-confidence, and had great willpower. He polished his manners, improved his wardrobe, and with Benois as his tutor he passionately plunged into study in order to make up the intellectual gap. Within a few years he could hold his own with the others in the group, except in one respect: he was neither an artist, musician nor writer, and therefore amongst his friends felt somewhat profane and a dilettante.[41] But he found his talent soon enough. As he himself put it in a letter to his stepmother, "I have no real gifts. All the same, I think I have found my true vocation—being a Maecenas."[42] He would be the leader and organizer who would bring the group's ideas (which now included Diaghilev's own) to Petersburg, Russia, and the world. Their movement was called *Mir iskusstva* ("The World of Art"), and its members the *miriskusniki*. What was their message?

Benois and his friends each had different artistic talents, beliefs, and interests, but they all joined the Symbolists in opposing the realists. "It's time for these anti-artistic canvases to stop appearing—with their militia-men, police officers, students in red shirts and girls with cropped hair," complained Diaghilev in 1897.[43] "Russian art of the 1860s is simply one big slap in the face of Apollo."[44] In response to Chernyshevsky, they adopted the motto: "Art is free; life is paralyzed."[45] To them, socialism was a leveler and enemy of art. They shared the Symbolists' conviction that art and beauty should be integral elements in human life and could change the world, but they were more restrained and dispensed with Symbolists' metaphysics, religion, and the theurgical nature of art. For them the hoped-for renaissance did not entail an apocalypse but meant making art and a developed aesthetic sense integral to life. "Beauty and art shall merge with life," they proclaimed.[46] Art is a unifying force for Man, but this is because human nature gives us the capacity to see and be moved by beauty, not because art connects man with some mysterious ultimate reality. Rather than seek the absolute, *Mir iskusstva* had the more immediate goal of making life richer, happier, and more beautiful, which in turn could play an important role in improving social, political, and economic life. The *miriskusniki* were not indifferent to social questions, but they believed that they could make a better contribution to society by remaining true to art and creating beauty than by putting art at the service of political and social movements (like the realists) or by making it a religion (like some Symbolists). Thus, their purpose was to spread knowledge of and an appreciation for art among the people and, as Benois put it, "to teach the public to respond artistically to works of art."[47] They also sought to help develop a national school of true art, in part by reforming the Academy (for which Benois made several unsuccessful proposals). As it turned out, however, the new and original Russian art of the early 20th century developed spontaneously from individual creativity stimulated by a new awareness of contemporary European art trends and pre-realist art. Indeed, the *miriskusniki* considered an individual's own personality and experience (not ultimate reality) the ultimate source and inspiration of art, of which one's nationality is only one element. Thus, *Mir iskusstva*'s aesthetics were by nature cosmopolitan, and there need be no fundamental gap or rift between Western and Russian art. Thus, the *miriskusniki* sought to build bridges between East and West through exchange and collaboration in order to stimulate creativity and new art forms. This meant not just receiving Western and classical influences into Russia as in the past, but also bringing Russian art and culture to the West.

To achieve their aims, in 1898 the *miriskusniki* decided to publish a journal of the arts called *Mir iskusstva* ("The World of Art"), hold art exhibitions through an art exhibition society of the same name, and form a concert society called the Evenings of Contemporary Music. The focus of most *miriskusniki* was the new journal, which Diaghilev proclaimed "must create a revolution in our artistic life and must do the same, more or less, amongst the general public."[48] Like Petersburg itself, their journal would be a "window on Europe." Benois had first broached the idea of a journal in 1895 to Princess Maria Tenisheva, a rich patroness of the arts. He secured financial backing from Tenisheva and the wealthy Moscow merchant and art patron Savva Mamontov, and the financial contract was celebrated at a formal banquet at Tenisheva's house in March 1898.

Because of their credo, the *miriskusniki* gave careful thought to the title, considering such titles as *Beauty, Pure Art, Forward, Radiance,* and *New Art,* all of which signaled a break from the realists. Benois favored *Renaissance* both to suggest their purpose of reviving true art as well as to help shed the label of "decadents" with which they were saddled. Finally they settled on *Mir iskusstva,* which suggests that art is a self-sufficient and important sphere of human activity and also signals its universal meaning and capacity to unite human beings: Europe and Russia formed (or should be) one continuous World of Art. Bakst designed their emblem, a lonely eagle perched on a snowy peak, on a triangular black field. Describing it in a letter to Benois, he said that "The 'World of Art' is above all earthly things, in the realm of the stars; there it reigns, proud, secret, and lonely like an eagle on a snowy peak."[49] The first issue was published in November 1898.

The *miriskusniki* were not ideological and did not represent a school. They had eclectic tastes, and they were careful to embrace all styles in the journal. They also wanted to promote crossover and fusion between the various forms of art, and looked forward to the creation of the "total work of art" *(Gesamtkunstwerk).* Thus, the journal was to have sections devoted to literature (initially to be headed by Merezhkovsky and Gippius), art and art history, architecture, and music. Consistent with their holistic aesthetics, they wanted the journal itself to be a work of art, which distinguished it from most other literary and art journals of the day. One of them, *Rodina* ("Homeland"), had such a low level of typography and illustrative design that it became known instead as *Urodina* ("Monster"). The *miriskusniki* devoted extraordinary time and care to their journal's design, and invested in high quality paper and printing and reproduction equipment. Foreigners put it on par with famous English and German journals, such as *The Savoy, Studio, Yellow Book, Pan,* and *Die Insel.* The project attracted the interest of the influential art critic Igor Grabar, who joined the group after being impressed with the first issue. He served as an important spokesmen and theoretician of the group, regularly contributed "letters" to the journal, and attracted others, including the painter Mstislav Dobuzhinsky.

Initially the journal was run out of Princess Tenisheva's "Hermitage" or "conspiratorial apartment," a flat adjoining her main house on Galernaya Street where she could indulge in her artistic activities out of her husband's sight (he was not allowed inside). She was a gracious hostess, and after work the *miriskusniki* liked to remain there, often joined by other guests from the art world or high society. There they relaxed to music or a game of cards, enjoyed snacks, tea and drinks, or perhaps had dinner, often departing only after midnight. But eventually Tenisheva's support for the project waned because she disliked her cosponsor Mamontov, Diaghilev began taking her for granted and behaved boorishly toward her, and the local press wrote unfavorably about her association with such "decadents," once caricaturing her as a cow being milked by Diaghilev. Her patronage ended in 1900, and after her withdrawal Diaghilev's own flat on the corner of Liteiny Prospect and Semenovskaya Street (and beginning in 1901 on Fontanka Embankment No. 11) became the unofficial office of the journal. The friends gathered amidst the clutter of newly acquired paintings, drawings, and souvenirs from Diaghilev's travels for "editorial Tuesdays" and "Sunday teas" to plan the upcoming issues. "The mere fact that they took place during tea-time, to the accompaniment of the hissing samovar, gave them a very homely, unofficial character," Benois recalled.[50] The informal atmosphere typified their combination of high ideals and professionalism mixed with a dash of dilettantism.

The first issue in November 1898 was a sensation. The journal was unreservedly and unrelievedly polemical, and from the beginning contained articles by *miriskusniki* such as Diaghilev's "Complex Questions" which were really manifestos declaring the movement's artistic platform. They conducted a constant debate with *Art and Art Industry*, a journal published by the aging realist critic Stasov between 1898 and 1902, and jousted as well with Repin. Each issue usually featured a particular artist, containing many high quality reproductions of his or her works. A favorite theme was St. Petersburg itself, and several issues included articles and artwork devoted to the city. Several of the artists loved to paint historical works depicting the city and the Imperial court, such as Benois's *Peter the Great Walking in the Summer Gardens* (1910), Lancéray's *Empress Elizabeth Petrovna in Tsarskoe Selo* (1905) showing the aging Empress exiting the Catherine Palace into the gardens, Serov's *Peter II and Princess Elizabeth Riding to Hounds* (1900), and his famous *Peter the Great* (1907) depicting the Tsar striding along the Neva shore with bowing servants in his train. Anna Ostroumova-Lebedeva, who in 1898–99 worked under James Whistler in Paris, was famous for her many romantic, moody watercolors, drawings, and woodcuts of St. Petersburg landscapes, such as *The Admiralty under Snow* (1901). Mstislav Dobuzhinsky, on the other hand, was known for his modernistic urban paintings portraying the onset of impersonal industrialism and the threat it posed to beauty and personality, as in *The City* (1904), *A Cottage in St. Petersburg* (1905), *City Types (City Grimaces)* (1908), and *The Kiss* (1916). He was influenced by Dostoevsky, made the classic set of illustrations to Dostoevsky's *White Nights*, and many of his portraits of the city evoked Dostoevsky's moods. A 1904 issue of the journal published Benois's illustrations to Pushkin's *Bronze Horseman*, which are still the classic illustrations of the poem.

Despite its artistic success, the journal struggled financially because it was expensive to produce and pricey. Its circulation rarely exceeded 1,000. Mamontov's support ceased at the end of 1899 due to his financial collapse, and Tenisheva withdrew in 1900. It was saved only when Nicholas II himself was persuaded to give the journal an annual subsidy beginning in 1900. This occurred because Serov had the good fortune at the time to be painting Nicholas's portrait (later displayed at the 1901 *Mir iskusstva* Exhibition) and had earned the Emperor's sympathy and interest for the movement. Diaghilev suggested that Serov ask Nicholas to subsidize the journal, which he did at 10,000 rubles a year.[51] But after the subsidy was terminated in 1904 because of the Russo-Japanese War, the journal folded. But for the *miriskusniki* the journal's closure was no tragedy. It had already served their main purpose, and its members were already actively pursuing their own artistic interests and careers.

The journal was gone, but the other prongs of *Mir iskusstva*, the staging of annual art exhibitions and the Evenings of Contemporary Music, continued. The *miriskusniki* considered turn-of-century Russian music overly academic, imitative, and stale, especially compared with the "new music" in the West. In order to stimulate musical creativity, in 1898 the more musically oriented *miriskusniki*, Nouvel, Nourok, and Vyacheslav Karatygin, founded the Evenings of Contemporary Music, dedicated to the performance of innovative, modern music of composers such as Debussy, Richard Strauss, Gabriel Fauré, Paul Dukas, Maxmilian Reger, and, later, Schönberg, as well as avant-garde Russian works such as Nikolai Makovsky's pieces set to poems by Gippius. Their ideological opponents were the musicians of the Belyaev circle, which had succeeded the Mighty Five as the dominant force in St. Petersburg's musical world.

That circle got its name from Mitrofan Belyaev (1834–1903), a Petersburg timber millionaire and amateur violist who, along with Mamontov in Moscow, was Russia's leading patron of music and composers. He first attracted Anatoly Liadov, who had been associated with the Five, then Alexander Glazunov, and gradually took a large number of lesser composers and musicians under his patronage. Since most of them had studied at the Conservatory under Rimsky-Korsakov, he too became associated with the circle and inevitably stood as its elder statesman. Belyaev set up both a music publishing house, founded an organization named Russian Symphonic Concerts to organize concerts of his musicians in Russia and abroad, established the Glinka Prize, and beginning in 1898 chaired the Petersburg Society of Chamber Music. He also continued Petersburg's tradition of private musical evenings, which he organized on Fridays at his home on Nikolayevskaya Street (now 50 Marat Street). The usual musical fare was string quartets, with Belyaev himself on viola. After the performances, the guests would retire to the dining room for a lavish dinner. Musically, however, the circle was overly influenced by Belyaev's conservative tastes and made no significant innovations. Rimsky-Korsakov diplomatically compared the circle with the Five by explaining that "Balakirev's circle was revolutionary, Belyaev's, on the other hand, was progressive,"[52] but in fact it was reactionary. It was academic and focused on technical perfection and opposed innovations. Inevitably, a major young talent would stand up in opposition. He was Sergei Prokofiev.

Prokofiev (1891–1953) was born in Ukraine but was such a musical prodigy that he was sent to study at the St. Petersburg Conservatory in 1904 at the age of 13, by which time he had already composed four "child's operas," a symphony, two sonatas, and numerous other piano works. He was tired of Romantic music in the Lizst-Chopin tradition in which Scriabin had been trained, and set off to pioneer new forms of composition and a new style of playing. He was under intense pressure to conform and compromise and was constantly criticized by conservatives such as Liadov, but fortunately he was headstrong, stubborn, and supremely confident in his abilities and tastes. He composed works with rapid, assertive rhythms and sharp dissonances which presaged works such as Stravinsky's *Rite of Spring*, while developing a crisp, percussive style of playing the piano, which ran alien to all of musical St. Petersburg except the avant-garde Evenings of Contemporary Music. He joined the Evenings in 1908, and at one of them gave his first public concert. His compositions (one aptly named *Diabolical Suggestions*) and style stunned listeners and set off a musical firestorm in the capital. While the Belyaev circle and Conservatory were appalled, Karatygin hailed him as "the antithesis to Scriabin— and thank God that the antithesis has appeared."[53] Prokofiev went on to compose his first sonata in 1910 and his Piano Concerto No. 1 in 1911, which he played to win the Rubenstein Prize for piano playing in 1914. At this point he attracted the interest of Diaghilev, who following the *Rite of Spring* commissioned him to write a ballet on the theme of Scythian myths for the *Ballets Russes*. But when Diaghilev heard it, he rejected it on the ground that it was too similar to the *Rite*. Prokofiev reworked the piece into his *Scythian Suite*, but he later composed two ballets for Diaghilev in the 1920s. Little of his work is on Petersburg themes, but he did compose the lyrical *Five Poems by Anna Akhmatova* (1916).

In attendance at Prokofiev's debut at the Evenings of Contemporary Music was another promising musician, Igor Stravinsky, already 26 and still trying to make his mark. But soon he would be adopted by Diaghilev and become the first Russian to be the world's leading force in modern music. Like the Five, he developed as a musician largely outside the music establishment and for years was little known, though he too became associated with the Evenings and some of his compositions were performed there. His musical pedigree was impeccable. Born at Oranienbaum in 1882, his father was a leading bass singer at the Imperial Opera, where among other roles he sang the part of Boris Godunov. Though Igor showed an interest in music, he did not seem to be a prodigy so his father sent him to study law at the University of St. Petersburg. But he had no interest in law and soon began taking lessons in composition. Fortunately, Rimsky-Korsakov had also sent his son Andrei to law school, where he and Igor became friends. Andrei introduced Igor to his father in 1902, who encouraged him to pursue his musical studies. Soon Rimsky-Korsakov, perhaps remembering his own past, agreed to instruct Igor himself, which he did until his death in 1908. But Stravinsky never obtained a formal musical education. While Rimsky-Korsakov was the prime early influence on Stravinsky, he was increasingly attracted to the modern French composers popular at the Evenings of Contemporary Music, especially Franck, Faura, Dukas, Chabrier, and Debussy.

Stravinsky did not fully develop his talent until he began composing for the theater. He began in 1908 with *Le Rossignol*, based on the Andersen story of the Chinese emperor, which he eventually completed in 1914 when Diaghilev made it into a ballet. But his big break came when Diaghilev was planning to stage a ballet for the 1910 season of his *Ballets Russes* based on the Russian legend of the firebird, so called because of its wings of golden flame. Diaghilev initially commissioned Liadov for the score, but after several weeks Liadov had not even begun. Diaghilev, who had heard a 1908 work of Stravinsky called *Fireworks* and had an eye for new talent, offered the commission to Stravinsky, who completed it quickly and went to Paris for the rehearsals. His novel score made the ballet a smashing success and catapulted Stravinsky to international fame. Much to his dismay, the suite derived from the ballet became the most popular work he ever composed, and it remains in the repertoire today. Stravinsky followed *Firebird* with the entirely original *Petrushka* (1911) and *The Rite of Spring* (1913). In *Petrushka* he explored polytonality, polyrhythms, and polyharmony, all stated with unprecedented boldness and clarity. The *Rite* went further to turn Russian folk melodies into strident, wild, and unsentimental musical statements full of dissonance, percussion, and driving rhythms. Ultimately, his most fundamentally national ballet was *A Peasant Wedding* (1923), which was based on painstaking ethnographic and musical research and faithfully re-created time-honored peasant traditions. Composers and critics who understood his music hailed him as the new apostle of modernism, and he accepted his fame and status gracefully. But some resented the unschooled newcomer's success. Debussy, whose music in fact most heavily influenced the *Rite*, snickered that Stravinsky is "a spoiled child who sometimes cocks a snook at music. He is also a young barbarian who wears flashy ties and treads on women's toes as he kisses their hands. When he is old he will be unbearable."[54] Closer to home, the Russian critic Boris Asafyev recognized that Stravinsky's music (to date) was purely Russian and was "only an ultrarefined synthesis of previous achievements," and looked rather to Prokofiev as the composer of the future. Prokofiev did better exemplify *Mir iskusstva's* emphasis on pure, modernist, cosmopolitan innovation, but Stravinsky better understood their concept of the total work of art, and he worked with Diaghilev to create it.

The final prong of *Mir iskusstva* was art exhibitions. Diaghilev had organized his first art exhibit, of German and British watercolors, in 1897 at the new Stieglitz Museum, but the first official *Mir iskusstva* exhibition, also at the Stieglitz, was the Exhibition of Russian and Finnish Artists in January–February 1898. The exhibitions included not only Russian artists of various styles, but initially also leading foreign artists. Their January 1899 International Exhibition included paintings by the American Whistler and the Frenchmen Degas, Monet, Renoir, and Moreau, and glasswork by Tiffany. Not only was the art novel, but the shows made groundbreaking improvements in exhibition technique and management. Previously, exhibitions were laid out haphazardly and with little consideration for the surroundings. But just as the group's holistic aesthetics led them to turn their journal into a work of art, they wanted their exhibitions to be a total aesthetic experience, so great care went into planning the color schemes, plants and other décor, and the layout and sequence of paintings. *Mir iskusstva's* exhibitions were always popular and artistic successes, and were visited by the Tsar.

Diaghilev's grandest and most successful exhibit was the Exhibition of Historical Russian Portraits in the Tauride Palace in 1905, which traced through approximately 3,000 portraits the histories of the Romanovs and other prominent Russian families. This massive undertaking required him to collect portraits from museums and private owners throughout Russia and abroad. Diaghilev researched public records and libraries, advertised for information about portraits, and wrote hundreds of letters to the heads of noble families. He traveled throughout Russia, rooting through the homes and attics of minor nobles in remote villages to look for treasures that their owners may have forgotten. Fortunately, Grand Duke Nikolai Mikhailovich was president of the exhibition committee, so wheels turned and the magnificent Tauride Palace was secured as the site, which the exhibition completely filled. But the preparations were not without incident. Grand Duke Nikolai accidentally put his foot through a portrait standing on the floor, and as he walked away simply ordered, "To be restored."[55] Another time, a workman fell from a ladder onto the large portrait of Alexander I that he was about to hang, ripping the canvas across Alexander's stomach. When Diaghilev rushed to the scene, his first concern was for the worker: "Did this unfortunate break his neck?" Fortunately the worker was not injured and was given a tip for his trouble, and the painting was perfectly restored.[56] Diaghilev published a lavish and scholarly eight-volume catalogue of the exhibition. Great care was taken in the design of the exhibition, especially the section dedicated to the Romanovs. Each ruler had a full-length portrait under a canopy, which was surrounded by portraits of his or her ministers and court. The setting for Paul I's portrait, depicting him as Grand Master of the Maltese Order and wearing his crown crooked, was done sinisterly in black.

The Exhibition was a sensational success, was praised by critics, and did great service to the Russian art world and Russian history. Visitors returned repeatedly to marvel at the many paintings, which could not possibly be viewed in a single visit. But in that time of strikes, the 1905 revolution, and Russia's defeat in the Russo-Japanese war, many visitors sensed that the spectacle was a monument to a bygone age and the beginning of the last act in the tragedy of the Romanov dynasty. Diaghilev said so in a speech at an exhibition banquet given in his honor:

There is no doubt that every tribute is a summing-up, and every summing-up is an ending. . . . Don't you feel that this long gallery of portraits of big and small people that I brought to life in the beautiful halls of the Tauride Palace is only a grandiose summing-up of a brilliant, but, alas, dead period of our history? . . . [W]e are witnesses to the greatest moment of summing-up of history, in the name of a new and unknown culture, which will be created by us, but which will also sweep us away. That is why, without fear or misgiving, I raise my glass to the ruined walls of the beautiful palaces, as well as to the new commandments of a new aesthetic. The only wish that I, an incorrigible sensualist, can express, is that the forthcoming struggle should not damage the amenities of life, and that the death should be as beautiful and as illuminating as the resurrection![57]

Indeed, the transition to the new age occurred at the site of the exhibition itself. Within a few months after its opening the exhibition was prematurely closed so that the Tauride Palace could house the new Russian Duma, which for the first time limited imperial power under a constitution. Political change came about not through art but through the combined efforts of workers and other reform-minded citizens who marched and died on the city's streets.

REVOLUTION ON THE STREETS

While Petersburg basked in its cultural renaissance, the rumblings of economic, social, and political discontent grew louder. Just as in 1861, the trouble started with the city's students. Already in 1897, the student Maria Vetrova had burned herself to death in the Peter and Paul Fortress, and had become a martyr in the minds of her successors and inspired future revolutionaries like Trotsky. Another ugly portent of things to come occurred on March 4, 1901, when students, joined by a number of socially conscious public figures, including the dramatist Vsevolod Meyerhold and Prince Leonid Vyazemsky, demonstrated in front of Kazan Cathedral to protest so-called "Temporary Rules" denying military deferments to students guilty of political misconduct. Police and Cossacks on horseback descended on the unarmed crowd, beating them with their sheathed swords, and some 1,500 were arrested and carted off to jail for about three weeks. The excesses created a scandal in the capital, inspired Gorky to write his *Song of the Stormy Petrel*, and convinced Nikolai Burenin, from the family of one of Petersburg's largest magnates, to embark on a revolutionary career. From then on the city's activist students were dead set against the Tsarist "system" and became a key bastion of revolutionary agitation.[58] The liberal Pavel Milyukov warned in 1904 that "the revolution is, as it were, insistent within the walls of our universities and academies."[59] The authorities struck back. In the spring of 1901 alone following the Kazan disturbance, some 16,000 were exiled from the city, and for the two years of Dmitry Sipyagin's tenure at the Ministry of the Interior, Milyukov estimated the total at 60,000.[60] For these efforts, Sipyagin was assassinated by a radical student in April 1902, and from that time forward the Ministry led a policy of unflinching confrontation with "society" on behalf of the autocracy, creating an atmosphere of a police state and tolerating pogroms against Jews.[61]

Petersburg's factory workers also asserted themselves. In fact, the formerly refined and aristocratic capital had become a city of peasants and workers. With rapid industrialization, hundreds of thousands of emancipated peasants had poured into the city to take factory and other menial jobs. By 1914 nearly 75 percent of Petersburg's 2.2 million inhabitants were peasants, compared to half a century before when they constituted less than one-third of the populace.[62] The number of factory workers had risen to nearly 74,000 in 1890,[63] and by 1914 they would number around 200,000,[64] a dangerous force to be reckoned with. When the war came, another 200,000 peasant-workers streamed in from the countryside together with 160,000 recruits and reservists for St. Petersburg's garrison, mainly of the same origin.[65] Barely able to eke out a living, their concerns were economic and immediate, and there was little room for enlightenment, culture, or Western democratic ideals. The intelligentsia began to take notice, and grew worried about the city's and culture's fate. "Who are they, these strange people, unknown to us, who have unexpectedly revealed themselves?" asked the literary critic Chukovsky. "No, they're not even savages. . . . Savages are visionaries, dreamers, they have shamans, fetishes, and curses, while this is just some black hole of nonexistence. . . . I'm even afraid to sit among these people. What if they suddenly neigh or I see that they have hooves instead of hands?"[66] Merezhkovsky dubbed them "The Coming Boor." But others like Blok looked to them with hope as an elemental force that would bring about an upheaval that would regenerate Russia. A battle for the city's soul—between high and low civilization, East and West, the traditions of Muscovy and those of Petersburg—was underway.

In 1905, the city's workers had much to complain about, as living conditions for many were worse than in Dostoevsky's time. Factory workdays were long, but even through such toil men were usually not able to feed and clothe their families because the cost of living and housing was high and many wages were lost through fines imposed by employers. Female and child labor thus became a necessity, with its attendant abuses. Factories were unsafe and unsanitary. So was worker housing, where plumbing was often lacking and people often slept in shifts and shared beds. As the new century neared, the city's workers began organizing into unions, which at the time was illegal. Beginning with the strike of textile workers in 1896–97, union-sponsored strikes became more common. Whereas in the year Nicholas became Tsar there were only 66 strikes in Russia, by 1903 their number had reached 550.[67]

At first the workers' demands were not political, and had they been addressed probably would not have become so. Following the suggestion of Sergei Zubatov, head of Moscow's political police, the Ministry of the Interior recognized that by meeting workers' economic demands and improving their lot, radical revolutionaries might not gain influence over them. The Ministry sponsored the formation of workers' unions (which became known as "Zubatov" or "police" unions) in the hope of both improving working conditions and controlling the workers' movement. In Petersburg, the head of the Zubatov union, formed in early 1904 and called the Assembly of Russian Factory and Plant Workers, was a charismatic and popular priest, Father Georgi Gapon, who genuinely took up the workers' cause and distanced himself from the police and government. He set up union halls around the city, where he not only held union meetings but organized dances and other social activities, readings of newspapers for the illiterate, and even set up lending libraries. From monthly union dues he began establishing insurance and vacation plans and other benefits. He truly became a father figure to whom his loyal workers were devoted, and when the time came for political action they were ready to follow him through fire and brimstone. While radical socialists sat on the sidelines and bickered among themselves, within the course of a year Gapon had become the most outstanding labor leader in Russia.[68]

Potentially most fruitful in the area of political reforms was the movement of constitutional liberals in the tradition of Radishchev and the Decembrists. By the turn of the century, Russian liberalism had two principal centers. One was in St. Petersburg among various associations of lawyers, doctors, engineers, and other professionals, who conducted political activity under the guise of professional associations because it was otherwise forbidden. Their leader was Peter Struve (1870–1944), from Petersburg. Formerly a radical student at St. Petersburg University who had suffered arrest, he began as a Marxist. But while in the West he noted that worker movements were in fact wresting concessions from capitalists and governments and increasing their share of output by bargaining rather than by revolution, which refuted Marx's labor theory of value and doctrine of increasing misery, and therefore he came to favor evolutionary political and economic reform.[69] If change is achieved by a brutalized proletariat, he argued, workers would not live in Marx's utopia but fall victim to a political dictatorship.[70] History would prove him right. Through his journal *Liberation* published abroad and smuggled into Russia, he gained a constituency among the professionals for democratic political reforms of the type they saw in the West. In 1903 the groupings of professionals had formed in Petersburg the underground Union of Liberation to press their demands. After Bloody Sunday, Struve returned to Petersburg, where he became a professor at the Polytechnical Institute and edited *Russian Thought*. In August 1905 the Union became the Constitutional Democratic Party (Cadets, or CDs), and Struve served as a Cadet deputy in the Second Duma.

The other branch of liberalism arose from the *zemstvos* (and therefore the gentry), called itself the Group of Zemstvo Constitutionalists, and had its power base in provincial centers and Moscow. Unlike the Union, that grouping included a wing of Slavophiles, which resulted in internal differences and a more conservative and ambiguous position on a constituent assembly and a constitution than the Union ("popular representation in an organic unity of the monarch with the people").[71] Also an unofficial organization, it held various private meetings and congresses, leading up to a national Zemstvo Congress in St. Petersburg in November 1904. Since the Congress was not governmentally sanctioned, the deputies met in private residences, including that of Vladimir Nabokov (the writer's father) on Bolshaya Morskaya, and was watched by the police. They called for freedom of the press, speech, and assembly, and rule of law, though they proved unable to agree on resolutions dealing with the Tsar's role under a constitution, a constituent assembly, and the nature of suffrage. In the following weeks, these issues were carried to Russian society by the Union of Liberation through a series of 46 banquets of professionals, intelligentsia, and businessmen (called the "banquet campaign"), at which proponents of the reform spoke, resolutions were adopted, and petitions were signed. The first and most important banquet was held on November 20, 1904, in St. Petersburg, which attracted 676 guests, who signed a petition calling for a constitution and constituent assembly. The proposals, more liberal than the Zemstvo Congress resolutions, made their way to Nicholas, but he wavered and in the "reform" legislation enacted in December he struck out the provisions providing for representative government. Nicholas's government was discredited in the minds of liberals, but this paled in comparison to the disrepute suffered in the minds of the populace a week later when Port Arthur surrendered to the Japanese.

Russia's provoking war with Japan is often explained by Interior Minister Plehve's famous quote that, "In order to hold back revolution, we need a small victorious war."[72] The deeper reasons lay in Russia's imperialism leading to the laying of a railroad across Chinese Manchuria and annexation of that territory in February 1903, which threatened Japan's sphere of influence. When negotiations with Japan failed, on February 8, 1904, the Japanese attacked the Russian fleet moored at Port Arthur, sinking several ships, and laid siege to the port. In response, a wave of patriotism swept Russia which indeed silenced all strikes and criticism of the regime. Four days after the attack, even the students of St. Petersburg University paraded across the Neva to the Winter Palace carrying flags and banners and singing Russia's national anthem, "God Save the Tsar," and other hymns, and raising cheers in support of the army, the fleet, the Tsar, and the motherland. Nicholas and his family stepped onto the palace balcony overlooking Palace Square to receive the crowd's salute, and he sent the palace commandant to personally thank the students. The crowd then turned up Nevsky Prospect to the Anichkov Palace, growing in numbers. They stopped at Anichkov Bridge and, overseen by Klodt's famous statues of horses, again broke into cheers and songs. "Generals and tramps marched side-by-side, students with banners, and ladies, their arms filled with shopping," wrote one enthusiastic participant. "Everyone was united in one general feeling. Everyone sang."[73] Nobles and merchants made monetary and in-kind contributions to the Red Cross and other charitable defense funds, the city's merchants alone donating half a million rubles.[74] The rooms of the Winter Palace were transformed into workrooms where people came to sew and knit clothes for the Russian soldiers. Empress Alexandra often joined the women in their work. The New Hermitage became a depot for medical and other supplies to be sent to Russia's sick and wounded soldiers.

But all of this was to no avail. Russia's army and navy were not as modern and well trained as Japan's. They were undersupplied, outgeneraled, and Japan's intelligence was superior. Defeat followed defeat. On December 20, 1904, the besieged Port Arthur fell and on March 10, 1905, Russia lost the greatest land battle of the war, at Mukden, where some 89,000 Russian soldiers were lost (compared to 71,000 Japanese). But the worst was yet to come. Nicholas had dispatched the Baltic Fleet to the war, but on May 14, 1905, it was surprised by Admiral Togo in the Strait of Tsushima and nearly annihilated in a short battle. But by then both sides were exhausted, and peace came with the Treaty of Portsmouth in August.

The shock of the surrender of Port Arthur put the Tsar and his regime in disrepute and encouraged liberals and workers to cooperate in pressing their demands. Impressed by the Zemstvo Congress and banquet campaigns, Gapon saw democratic political reform as being in the workers' interests and in November 1904 established contact with the Union of Liberation, whose members began advising him.[75] He began distributing the resolutions of the Congress to members of his Assembly. The opportunity for action came in mid–December when four Assembly workers at the Putilov Plant were fired and Gapon took up their cause, arguing that they were wrongly dismissed because of their membership in the Assembly (which was officially sanctioned and legal). When the Plant gave no satisfaction, on January 3, 1905, some 12,500 Putilov workers walked out on strike. Word spread like wildfire, and workers at other plants, usually led by Assembly members, walked off in solidarity, at the same time demanding an eight-hour day, increased workers' rights, and better pay. By January 7, 382 factories had closed and at least 120,000 of Petersburg's workers stood idle.[76] The city came to a standstill. There was no electricity, and all public establishments were closed. Since the newspapers too had shut down, there were no sources of information and rumors ran rife.

Gapon seized the moment and called for mass action to achieve broad demands. He met continuously with Assembly workers in their union halls throughout town, racing from one to the other to debate demands and tactics. They decided to march. Gapon prepared a petition of worker grievances and political demands based on the Zemstvo Congress resolution, sent it to the authorities, and announced that on the morning of January 9 the workers would form a peaceful procession to the Winter Palace to present it to the father-Tsar, to whom they looked for their salvation:

> We, workers and residents of the city of St. Petersburg, of various ranks and stations, our wives, children and helpless old parents, have come to Thee, Sire, to seek justice and protection. We have become beggars; we are oppressed and burdened by labor beyond our strength; we are humiliated; we are regarded, not as human beings, but as slaves who must endure their bitter fate in silence. . . . Is it better to die—for all of us, the toiling people of all Russia, to die, allowing the capitalists (the exploiters of the working class) and the bureaucrats (who rob the government and plunder the Russian people) to live and enjoy themselves? This is the choice we face, Sire, and this is why we have come to the walls of Thy palace. Order these measures and take Thine oath to carry them out. . . . And if Thou does not so order and dost not respond to our pleas we will die here on this square before Thy palace. We have nowhere else to go and no purpose in going.

At the Assembly meetings, Gapon and the workers had considered the eventuality that Nicholas might not receive them or deny their demands. In that case, they decided, "then we have no Tsar."[77] Indeed, on January 9 there was no Tsar. Nicholas knew about the procession and petition, yet on January 8 he went to Tsarskoe Selo, considering the matter inconsequential and leaving it in the hands of the police and soldiers. The city's intellectuals and liberals were more alarmed, fearing an uncontrolled, destructive upheaval. They hurriedly formed a delegation of writers (among them Gorky), historians, lawyers, and publicists—some of them veterans of the banquet campaign. They met with government officials, including Witte, as well as Gapon's representatives in an attempt to reach a compromise and stave off disaster, but positions had hardened, and on the 9th they could only stand by helplessly while the tragic events unfolded.

Although Gapon's union was officially sanctioned and had declared its peaceful intentions, the authorities distrusted Gapon and ordered his arrest, but he managed to hide in a worker's apartment. On the morning of the 9th, the workers were to gather at six assembly points around the city and proceed in separate columns to Palace Square. Petersburg's Governor, General Fullon, with some 12,000 troops and thousands more police at his disposal, gave orders to block each column at key intersections and bar access to Palace Square, and to shoot if necessary to hold the lines.

Despite the tension in the air, the streets of St. Petersburg on the night of the 8th–9th were somehow serene. "On this night," wrote one observer, "Petersburg was the very heart of Russia."[78] The sky was clear, and a large, blood-red moon rose over the horizon. The wind was still, the temperature crisp at five degrees below zero. Bivouacs of troops formed on the streets and squares; pots of soup boiled in mess kitchens. Detachments of troops stood around campfires, sipping vodka, swapping stories, dancing, and singing camp songs; soon they received extra vodka and live ammunition. Ambulances arrived to take away the wounded. Gapon spent the night at the apartment of a Putilov worker surrounded by guards. Andrei Bely was on the night train from Moscow, never suspecting what he would face the next day. Workers consoled their families; some wrote farewell letters. "If I am killed, then do not weep," wrote Ivan Vasiliev to his wife. "Raise Vaniura, and tell him that I died a martyr for the freedom and happiness of the people."[79] He never returned.

January 9 dawned a Sunday, "Bloody Sunday." The day was clear and beautiful, and as the church bells tolled, cupolas and frosted roofs shone in the morning sun. Workers from outlying regions had been gathering since before dawn and proceeded toward the assembly points. Some made speeches. One with a sense of Russian history shouted, "You remember Minin who turned to the people in order to save Russia?* . . . Now we must save Russia from the bureaucrats under

---

*See prologue, p.xxxviii.

whose weight we suffer."[80] They were confident that they would not be fired upon, but to help prevent this and proclaim their peaceful intentions they placed women and children in the front ranks. They came dressed in their Sunday best. Red banners and other revolutionary symbols were banned, as were any kinds of arms, even penknives. Gapon's column, estimated at anywhere from three to fifty thousand and including the Putilov workers, assembled in the southwest part of town, and at about 11:00 A.M. began marching down Peterhof Prospect toward the Narva Gate. At the front marched Gapon in his long white cassock, carrying a crucifix. Beside him workers carried crosses, icons, and portraits of Tsar Nicholas and the royal family. A white banner beseeched: "Soldiers! Do not fire upon the people." As the procession marched they sang hymns, and police were seen to doff their caps and stand at attention as they passed. But when they reached the bridge over the Tarakanovka River in front of the Narva Gate, where the troops were ordered to stop them, cavalry from the Horse Grenadier Guards charged. But at each pass the crowd parted and again drew together and the sides were not engaged. Finally a bugle signaled the infantry to fire. At first they did not heed the command, then they fired twice into the air, but the column kept advancing. Finally they fired into the procession at close range. Gapon, protected in front by bodyguards, was knocked down by someone hit by a bullet and was still on the ground when the shooting stopped. Shocked and dazed, he managed to get up and, standing amidst his fallen comrades, cried, "There is no God any longer! There is no Tsar!"[81] Then he fled to the nearest courtyard.

The scenes were similar in other parts of the city. Another column, which included Maxim Gorky and Lenin's sister, approached from the St. Petersburg side along Kamenoostrovsky Prospect, intending to cross Troitsky Bridge. As Witte watched from his balcony, the soldiers confronted the marchers in Trinity Square by the fortress. When the marchers refused to disperse, the infantry fired volleys, the cavalry charged with open sabres, and nearly 50 men, women, and children were killed and over 100 wounded. On Vasilievsky Island, the procession of some 6,000 approached the Nikolaevsky Bridge by the Academy of Fine Arts, where the *miriskussnik* painter Serov watched from his window. (He later portrayed the day in his paintings.) When the marchers sent deputies waving white handkerchiefs to parlay with the Finnish Life Guard Regiment, the cavalry charged, the infantry opened fire, and the crowd scattered. But this was the student region, and before long the students were rallying the workers with fiery speeches, breaking into shops to seize weapons, and erecting barricades. The soldiers too regrouped and got orders to clear the barricades. After minor shooting, resistance crumbled into occasional revolver shots and bricks thrown from rooftops. The column from the central region, some 5,000 strong, marched down Nevsky Prospect, mingling with the usual Sunday morning crowds. When the procession reached Bolshaya Morskaya Street, some marchers turned right toward the arch of the General Staff Building while others continued toward the end of Nevsky by the Alexander

Garden, where citizens were taking advantage of the fine weather to take a stroll or go skating. Before long the crowd of demonstrators and onlookers around Palace Square swelled to some 60,000 as survivors from the other columns arrived with their horror stories, which only seemed to strengthen their resolve. Some 2,300 cavalry and infantry blocked the way into Palace Square, while cannon surrounded the Palace, which was flying the imperial standard indicating (wrongly) to the crowd that the Tsar was in the city. "Disperse or we'll shoot," the commanding officer shouted to no avail. "Shoot! We've come in search of the truth," someone retorted.[82] As the appointed hour when Gapon was supposed to arrive and present the petition approached, two sides faced one another in an eerie hush, waiting. Two o'clock struck and Gapon did not appear. After a few more minutes, the Preobrashensky Guards and cavalry tried to clear the crowd with whips and the flats of their sabres. When this failed the Preobrazhensky infantry moved into position, kneeled and took aim at the demonstrators by Alexander Garden. Some workers in the front, seeing the rifles pointed at them, fell to their knees and crossed themselves. A bugle sounded and the soldiers fired. The bodies of men, women, and children, many of them onlookers perched on fences, statues, and in trees, fell to the ground, their blood oozing over the snow and ice. The soldiers continued firing, now at other demonstrators by the Admiralty, Palace Bridge, and the General Staff arch.

The crowd by the Square scattered, but not merely in terror. Witnesses saw how panic quickly turned into resolve and rage.[83] Their faith in the Tsar shattered, groups rampaged through on the streets, and for a few hours the center of the city was in open rebellion. The crowds broke windows, looted stores and homes, and destroyed property. They attacked officials in uniform and hurled abuse at the Cossacks who patrolled the streets with their drawn swords. Revolutionaries spoke to the applause and cheers of now-receptive crowds, and red flags unfurled. Barricades started going up, one of them across Nevsky right in front of Kazan Cathedral, made from park benches. But darkness came (some said rather suddenly after the shooting on Palace Square) and it began to snow. The city streetlights did not come on, and darkness enveloped the capital. The crowds, leaderless and exhausted, went home, and by midnight the streets were again quiet.

Rumors flew that Gapon was dead. In fact, he had fled with Peter Rutenburg, an engineer and Socialist Revolutionary agent, and other workers. After ducking into a corner, Rutenberg hurriedly cut Gapon's beard and hair with a knife and small pair of scissors, dressed him in a worker's coat and cap, and took him from one hiding place to another, eventually ending up at Gorky's apartment. "Give me something to drink. Wine. Everyone's dead," Gorky recalled Gapon gasping as he entered.[84] Gorky summoned Asif Tikhomirov, director of the Art Theater, who shaved off Gapon's beard, trimmed his hair, put on makeup, and gave him a disguise. Gorky recalled that Tikhomirov did not quite understand the tragedy of the moment and made Gapon look like "a hairdresser or a salesman in a fashionable shop."[85] In order to disprove rumors of his death, Gapon decided to appear, so disguised, at that evening's meeting of the Free Economic Society, where St. Petersburg's intelligentsia would be gathered.

During the day the city's intelligentsia had congregated at the Merezhkovskys' apartment, where visitors shuffled in and out, bringing with them the latest news or rumors. Gippius lay on her divan in a black satin dress, surveying the comings and goings through her lorgnette. When Bely arrived from Moscow, she turned to him and remarked languidly, "Well, you sure picked the day!"[86] That evening Bely and the Merezhkovskys went to the meeting of the Free Economic Society, where they hoped to gain some understanding of the day's events. The disguised Gapon was there, together with Gorky perched on a balcony, and he began to speak. "Peaceful means have failed," he shouted to the assembled crowd. "Now we must go over to other means."[87] Some in the crowd recognized him. "It's Gapon himself," they whispered.[88] He called for money to help the workers in their struggle, and then invited all "honest chemists" to join him presently (presumably to make bombs). Bely glanced at Gippius: "I'm also a chemist. Should I go?" Bely "understood nothing," Gippius later recalled. "Moscow and Petersburg are different countries."[89] Later that night Gapon escaped to Finland and then abroad.*

At dawn the following morning the American dance innovator Isadora Duncan arrived at the Nikolaevsky Train Station from Berlin, on the first of her visits that would help inspire another Petersburg revolution—Diaghilev's in ballet. As her cab made its way along Nevsky Prospect to the Hotel Europe, she later recalled, "I beheld a sight equal in ghastliness to any in the imagination of Edgar Allan Poe." A long procession of men, women, and children, dressed in black, were bearing the coffins of the victims from Palace Square. The driver stopped and crossed himself while they watched. "The tears ran down my face and were frozen on my cheeks," she recalled. "How useless even my Art, unless it could help this."[90] Such feelings later led her to welcome the Bolsheviks, move to Petrograd, and put her art at their service.

The public and the press also were outraged by the carnage, which probably totaled about 200 dead and 800 to 1,000 wounded.[91] The Tsar's image was irreparably damaged. Workers staged the largest strikes in Russia's history. Students too walked out, and all universities in Russia were closed. After Bloody Sunday and the defeats in the Far East, all hopes of staving off political reforms were dashed. The liberals, still seething after their defeat in December, had not given up on constitutional reform, and they and the workers continued to press their demands. Reeling from the unrest, the government decided to appoint a com-

---

*He fled to Geneva, where he met Lenin, then wrote his "autobiography" with the help of a hack ghostwriter, and then returned to Russia after the amnesty granted following the October Manifesto. He was soon assassinated (by hanging) at the hands of Rutenberg (who had stood by his side at the Narva Gate), on orders of the head of the Socialist Revolutionary terrorist arm, which considered him a rival.

mission including representatives of workers to investigate the causes of the tragedy, for which some 145,000 St. Petersburg workers cast ballots. Though the commission accomplished nothing, its very creation legitimized the workers movement and their right to representation, which paved the way for convening the St. Petersburg Soviet of Workers' Deputies later that year.[92] Late in February Nicholas invited his subjects to submit to him what were in effect *cahiers* containing suggestions for the nation's well-being, and also announced that he intended to "involve the nation's worthiest men, endowed with the nation's confidence and elected by the people," in passing the nation's laws.[93] This meant a real legislature, soon called the Duma. In response, the liberals resumed the banquet campaign and the *zemstvos* held a second congress (this time in Moscow) to debate proposals. In May, the St. Petersburg City Duma passed its own electoral reforms. But just as in December 1904, Nicholas backed away from a full constitutional monarchy, and in August passed a law calling for a Duma to be elected by extremely limited suffrage and with only a consultative role and no real powers. It was too little too late. In response, students and workers went on strike nationwide, and Russia ground to a halt. In the capital, thousands of workers gathered each night at St. Petersburg University where they were harangued by the students, their numbers growing each day. The stock exchange and most businesses were closed. There were no newspapers, no streetlights, no trams, and no electricity. Nevsky Prospect was illuminated by a single searchlight installed on the Admiralty's spire, which was powered by naval turbines. Other public services ceased, except for the supply of running water, which was preserved only by locking the workers inside the waterworks.

On October 13 the city's workers formed a coordinating council *(Soviet)*, which held its first session at the Technological Institute. Although the Soviet was a creature of the moderate Union of Unions, the more radical Trotsky quickly emerged as its dominant figure. The Soviet gathered strength daily, started acting as a rival government rather than as a strike committee, and launched its own underground newspaper, *Izvestia*. On October 9 the alarmed Witte met with Nicholas and advised him either to appoint a military dictator under whom the army could crush the rebellion or to make concessions and establish constitutional government. Witte favored the latter option, if only because at the moment there were only about 2,000 troops in the capital to defend the government. Supposedly, Nicholas responded by saying, "I have nothing against a constitution so long as I can preserve the autocracy."[94] Initially Nicholas favored dictatorship and offered the position to his uncle, Grand Duke Nikolai Nikolaiovich. But the Grand Duke refused, brandishing his pistol and swearing to shoot himself on the spot if the Tsar would not change his mind. The Tsar backed down, and on October 17 he issued what became known as the October Manifesto, which established a constitutional monarchy. It guaranteed inviolability of the person and freedoms of press, conscience, speech, assembly, and association. It created the State Duma to be elected by universal suffrage and stated that no measure may become law without its authorization. The radicals, including Trotsky, wanting nothing short of the Tsar's abdication, objected and agitated further, but the government put a stop to it, disbanding the city Soviet and arresting and exiling its leaders, including Trotsky. For the time being, at least, it seemed that the liberals had won, that the dreams of Radishchev and the Decembrists had been realized.

After the October Manifesto, on the surface city life returned to normal. The general strike was called off, the economy recovered and local prosperity resumed, the theaters reopened, and the scene on Nevsky Prospect seemed like old times. Famous foreign writers, artists, and performers beat a path to the city, among them Gustav Mahler, Sarah Bernhardt, Pablo Casals, Jerome K. Jerome, Anatole France, Johann Strauss, and the American cinema actor Max Linder. The tango became the dance of choice. The American-style roller skating rink was a craze. During Easter Week 1910 the first airplanes flew at the city's Kolomyashsky hippodrome, and aviation became the danger sport of the daring few and a spectacle for the public. The poet Nikolai Gumilev never missed an air show while in town, and the flights inspired Blok's poem *The Pilot*. For the well-to-do, the years before World War I were a time of carefree gaiety. They dined at fine restaurants, sported European fashions, traveled abroad in the summer, and spent winters at an endless succession of balls and dinners.

Mass culture also sprung up, thanks to a literacy rate that approached 80 percent by World War I. The number of newspapers, magazines, and journals in the city exploded, reaching 555 in 1913, as did the newsstands and bookstores. One tabloid daily, called the *Gazeta-Kopeika* ("Kopeck Gazette"), really did cost only a kopeck and enjoyed a circulation of 250,000 by 1910. Popular illustrated periodicals such as *Niva* ("Cornfield") and *Ogonek* ("Little Flame") reached circulations of 275,000 and 700,000 respectively. Special-interest periodicals, including *The Stock Exchange News*, *Theater Review*, *Family Health*, *Accessible Fashions*, and *Knowledge and Art* now also thrived. A city directory called *All Petersburg* came out annually.

With the lifting of censorship, society's appetite for sensation and eroticism erupted into the open. It was quickly satisfied as Russian authors began generating pulp novels charged with crime and sex. Soon thousands of books on not only simple erotic themes but also homosexual and lesbian love, pederasty, bestiality, and masochism were available in the stores (a phenomenon that would be repeated in the 1990s). The role of sex was also a theme among serious intellectuals and writers, most of whom opposed the crude sensualism of mass culture. In his hugely successful novel, *The Petty Demon* (1907), the Petersburg schoolteacher and Symbolist writer Fedor Sologub caricatured the new mass sensualism as mere corruption, perversion, and common vulgarity, portraying it as merely a heightened expression of the general condition of man. Mikhail Artsybashev had a similar goal in his racy *Sanin* (1907), which featured an amoral, lecherous, and cynical antihero who caroused, drank, fought, deceived, and loved women. At least in part, Artsybashev intended the work as a statement about the condition of man in the tradition of Lermontov's Pechorin or Dostoevsky's protaganist in *Notes from Underground*, but neither the authorities nor the public understood it as such. Artsybashev was arrested on charges of pornography and blasphemy, which only turned the book's author and protagonist into heroes and inspired the formation of Sanin clubs throughout the city.

Soon one did not even have to be literate to enjoy the new mass culture. The first public demonstration in Russia of the Lumières Cinématographe took place at Petersburg's Aquarium theater in 1896. Russia's first feature film (at only 10 minutes) was made in Petersburg in 1908, about the rebel Stepan Razin, and by the end of 1916 some 500 films had been produced in the city's studios. By 1914 Petersburg boasted well over 100 movie theaters (23 on Nevsky Prospect alone) with seating for up to 800 and having names like Paradise, Piccadilly, and Lightning.[95] Unlike the other performing arts, movies were viewed by people from all classes. Adaptations of the classic works of the city's writers—Pushkin, Lermontov, Gogol, Dostoevsky, and others—began appearing on the silver screen. Soon avant-garde artists were tapping this form of artistic expression. As in America, critics lamented the era of the silver screen as marking an inevitable decline of reading and cultural standards. In fact, it marked the beginning of the glorious history of the city's film studios. But as people flocked to the theaters, a greater drama was unfolding in real life: the disintegration of Tsarism, and with it, Imperial St. Petersburg.

THE DECLINE OF IMPERIAL ST. PETERSBURG

All of Petersburg was shocked when the members of Russia's first legislature, the Duma, arrived in the city in April 1906. Nearly one-half of the deputies were rural peasants, many holding radical ideas. They differed markedly from the idealized peasant of the populists, Wanderers, and left intelligentsia. One reform-minded official, Sergei Kryshanovsky, described the horror felt by many as the deputies descended upon the capital:

> It was enough to take a look at the motley mob of "deputies" . . . to experience horror at the sight of Russia's first representative body. It was a gathering of savages. It seemed as if the Russian land had sent to St. Petersburg everything that was barbarian in it, everything filled with envy and malice. . . . [I]n this mass any consciousness of statehood, let alone of shared statehood, was totally submerged in social hostility and class envy.[96]

He went on to describe how deputies placed constituent-petitioners in deputies' seats, sold tickets to the proceedings, spread radical propaganda in factories and organized street demonstrations, got drunk in taverns and engaged in brawls, sometimes appearing at the Duma the next day in bandages. To avoid arrest, they invoked their immunity as deputies, which mattered little to one tavern owner who thrashed one deputy, telling him, "For me, you are quite violable, you SOB."[97] Upon investigation, about 40 (or 8 percent) of the deputies were disqualified from running for election because earlier they had been convicted of pecuniary crimes.[98]

With such human material, one could not expect the Duma to carry on productive work, but neither the more sophisticated deputies nor the Tsar made the task easier. Nicholas never believed that he had agreed to constitutional government. In order to hamstring the First Duma, just days before it convened Nicholas enacted the Fundamental Laws, a kind of constitution designed to preserve royal prerogatives. He even retained the title of "Autocrat." The Laws created an upper house (never mentioned in the October Manifesto) called the State Council, a conservative institution of nobles meant to serve as a brake on the Duma, which thus became known as "the graveyard of Duma hopes."[99] Both the Council and the Tsar had to approve any legislation passed by the Duma before it could become law. Ministers would not be a parliamentary cabinet but be appointed solely by the Tsar. The Tsar could dissolve the Duma, and, under Article 87 of the Laws, if the Duma was not in session he could enact emergency legislation himself, which he did on occasion.* Nicholas evidenced his disdain for the Duma at its opening ceremony by holding it in the Winter rather than the Tauride Palace, where the Coronation Hall was decked in royal and Church regalia, and a choir sang "God Save the Tsar" again and again. When the royal procession arrived, the members of the court and government cheered, while the Duma deputies, many dressed in national or folk costumes, maintained a frosty silence. Never deigning to glance at the parliamentary side of the hall, Nicholas gave a short speech promising to uphold the principles of autocracy, and promptly left. The next decade of Russian political life was an unresolved battle between the parliamentarians and the monarchy.

From the start, the Duma was a revolutionary body devoted to weakening or abolishing the monarchy. Even the Cadets,† who might have worked within the existing order for gradual change, shifted to the left. They were incensed by the Fundamental

---

*In 1906, Nicholas invoked Article 87 to enact landmark agrarian reform legislation authored by Peter Stolypin, which eliminated the last vestiges of serfdom.

†Most of the deputies were members of one of several parties or factions. The Socialist Revolutionaries (SRs for short) came from the tradition of populism and the Peoples Will, and had a terrorist arm. It claimed to represent the peasantry. The Social Democrats (SDs) were Marxian socialists focused on the urban proletariat. They were divided into Mensheviks, who believed in a more evolutionary transition to socialism through a bourgeois revolution and liberal democracy. The Bolsheviks had a narrower ideology devoted to an imminent revolution led by themselves, a tightly organized vanguard of professional revolutionaries. The largest party in the First Duma was the Constitutional Democrats (Cadets) led by Pavel Milyukov, who stood for true liberal constitutional democracy and therefore to the left of the October Manifesto. To their left was the loosely organized Trudovik ("Labor") Party, of which most of peasant deputies were members, which advocated a radical solution to the land question: expropriation of the landlords' properties and distribution to the peasants. Those Cadets who were willing to work within the framework of the October Manifesto and Fundamental Laws split off and so became known as Octobrists.

Laws, which they regarded as an "unconstitutional" violation of the October Manifesto, and sought to reverse them. Simple politics also drove them to the left. Since the radical socialists had boycotted the elections, the Cadets sought to gain much of their constituency and neutralize the Trudoviks. Finally, they played on the regime's fear of revolution to advocate a compromise solution under which the monarchy would cede more power to the Duma. Flush with their electoral victory and believing, or at least arguing, that they spoke for "the people," the Cadets waged an aggressive and unremitting campaign against Nicholas and his government, and demanded a constituent assembly to draft a proper constitution. After 72 days and 40 sessions of deadlock, Nicholas dissolved the Duma and called new elections. In response, some 200 deputies, mostly Cadets, adjourned to Vyborg, Finland, just beyond the jurisdiction of Russia's police, to issue a manifesto denouncing the dissolution as illegitimate and calling on all Russian citizens to stop paying taxes and providing recruits. The country ignored them, and the signatories only succeeded in spending three months in jail and disqualifying themselves from election to the Second Duma, thus depriving it of needed talent and leadership.

The Second Duma, which convened in March 1907, was even more radical and intransigent than the first since the socialists participated in the elections and many moderates had been disqualified. The socialists arrived with the intention not of pursuing legislative work but of utilizing the Duma as a platform for fomenting revolution among the masses under the protection of parliamentary immunity.[100] The Duma was incapable of working internally or with the government, and in June Nicholas dissolved it. Before convening the Third Duma, he changed (unconstitutionally) the electoral laws to ensure a more pro-government parliament with less representation of national minorities. It served its entire five-year term, and the Fourth Duma nearly did as well, cut short only by the February Revolution. The Cadets, who had been the hope of liberal democrats and enlightened Petersburg, returned to their roots as the party of business, but by then they had squandered the opportunity to steer Russia and its people on a moderate course and given liberalism a bad name. Democracy in Russia would not recover from the blow for over 80 years.

For their part, Nicholas and Alexandra did nothing to repair their reputation after 1905. Everything they did seemed to bring the monarchy into further disrepute and closer to destruction. Disliking Petersburg and its society, they rarely lived in the Winter Palace, staying most of the time at Tsarskoe Selo, where Nicholas had built a model medieval Muscovite village. Preferring to spend time with his family and dominated by the possessive Empress, Nicholas left government to his ministers, leaving unresolved the country's many problems and giving the impression that he did not care.

In February 1913 Nicholas and Alexandra had a chance to repair their image at the celebrations of the 300th anniversary of Romanov rule. Under Nicholas, royal fêtes were rare, so Petersburgers looked forward to the event with great anticipation. The city was decked out in royal colors of red, white, and blue, portraits of the royal family and the first Tsar, Michael, were seen everywhere, and garlands adorned statues. Strings of lights hung from buildings and across city streets, some of them spelling out slogans like "God Save the Tsar" or forming royal symbols. The façade of the Admiralty facing the Winter Palace was draped in imperial purple with the imperial coat of arms topped by a crown. Thousands of dignitaries of all nationalities and regions of the Tsar's vast empire made the pilgrimage to the capital to pay their respects, and dressed in their local national and folk costumes. The hotels and restaurants were jammed, the traffic was the worst ever seen, and hordes of provincials walked the city's sidewalks gaping at the splendors of the capital. The city's elite and invited dignitaries celebrated with royal receptions at the Winter Palace and balls at the Assembly of the Nobility and at private mansions. The Mariinsky staged *A Life for the Tsar*, for which Nicholas's former mistress Kshesinskaya made a special appearance to dance the mazurkas in the second act. On the anniversary day itself, factories closed and people were given the day off to enjoy free meals and fairs and concerts in the parks. As evening fell, masses crowded the city center. Searchlights illuminated key landmarks like the Admiralty spire and large portraits of the royal family on the Winter Palace. Then there was a fireworks display.

But even on such an occasion the monarchs did not take advantage of the opportunity to foster reconciliation with the people. The Tsar granted no amnesties or similar concessions as other Tsars had customarily done on great occasions; women waited in vain outside the city's jails hoping their husbands would be released. The elite were disappointed when the royals made the distinctly un-Petersburgian decision to hold no imperial balls. The royal couple did attend the ball at the Assembly of the Nobility, but the Empress did not dance; she worked herself into an emotional frenzy and asked to leave early. As the door closed behind them, she fainted into Nicholas's arms. The couple's only step toward communing with the people was to ride on the street in an open carriage—the first time since 1905—from the Winter Palace to the service at Kazan Cathedral which began the celebrations. But here as everywhere the royals were stiff, grave, expressed no joy, and did not bond with the crowd. The daughter of the British Ambassador, Meriel Buchanan, described Nicholas at Kazan as having an "almost stern gravity [that] gave to the celebration no sense of national rejoicing," while at the Mariinsky that evening Alexandra was "expressionless, almost austere. . . . Not once did a smile break the immobile sombreness of her expression when, the Anthem over, she bent her head in acknowledgment of the cheers that greeted its conclusion."[101] Then she withdrew to the back of the royal box to be seen no more that evening. And at the Kazan Cathedral service, Nicholas played political games, relegating Duma deputies to seats at the back, far behind those of his government. When the Duma's President, Mikhail Rodzyanko, protested, noting that it was a people's assembly that had elected Michael Romanov in 1613, the Duma's seats were moved forward. But when

Rodzyanko went to take his newly assigned seat, he found it already occupied by a dark-haired, bearded man in peasant dress. His name was Grigory Rasputin.

The royal family's scandalous and secretive relationship with Rasputin was the dominant story in Petersburg in the few years before his death in December 1916. Today it is difficult to appreciate the degree of hatred and revulsion occasioned by the spectacle of a dirty, ignorant, and drunken peasant penetrating the sacrosanct corridors of the highest royalty and gaining their loyalty at the expense of Petersburg's usual ruling circles. Yet many from these circles ended up competing for Rasputin's patronage and favors. The story fixated the public, high society, the clergy, the military, and the government alike. Petersburgers watched every move, scrambled and competed for information, and the rumors flew. Rasputin stories sold newspapers, which printed rumor and fact alike, Rasputin cartoons, and "interviews" that he never gave.

The relationship arose due to Alix's mysticism and propensity to rely on charlatans, together with the discovery that the Tsarevich Alexis had hemophilia. At the same time, she had a type of populist faith in the mythical common folk of Russia who were the repository of a hidden truth and were dedicated to their sovereign, but who were artificially separated from each other by the corrupt bureaucracy and court. (In fact, Nicholas held similar beliefs.) Thus, before discovering Rasputin, Alix had made failed attempts to "connect" with the common people, first through one Khlopov who promised to reveal corruption of provincial officials but could not, through "Blessed Mitya," a simple Man of God whose prayers failed to help Alix give birth to a boy, and "Matryona the Barefoot," who supposedly had a miracle-working icon that would achieve the same.[102] Alix then turned to a French charlatan known as Monsieur Philippe, who at one point claimed Alix was pregnant with a boy, only to discover in the ninth month that she was not. After that scandalous episode Philippe fled to France and soon died, but predicted he would return in another's body. But in the meantime Alexis was born in July 1904, a hemophiliac. Because his illness jeopardized the succession, it was made a state secret, and the need to maintain secrecy (which was successful) became another reason for the couple's isolation at Tsarskoe Selo. Feeling guilt and desperate for treatment and possibly a cure for the heir's ailment, Alix looked for Philippe's reincarnation.

Rasputin was born on January 10, 1869, in Pokrovskoe, a village about 200 miles east of the Urals. Like many peasant teenagers, he began a dissolute life of drinking with male friends, frequent fistfights (including with his father), petty theft, and fornication. He eventually married and had three sons and two daughters, but at 28 he was inspired by a seminary student that he met by chance on the road to Tyumen. He took up a religious life, gave up drinking, and for a few years spent most of his time wandering through villages and monasteries like a typical Russian holy fool. For a time he fell in with the sect of *Khlysti* ("Flagellants"), who generally were ascetics but practiced group whirling and dancing and a rite euphemistically called *radenie* ("rejoicing"), which consisted of promiscuous sex among sect members for the purpose of experiencing repentance after sin; without the sin, there could be no repentance. (Later in Petersburg, this became his pick-up strategy with women.) Rasputin gained a local reputation and following because he actually had a healing effect on people, hypnotic powers, magnetic piercing eyes, and a calm but commanding demeanor that riveted one's attention.

Rasputin was introduced to Alix and Nicholas through mutual friends and clerics on November 1, 1905, just as the turmoil from the October Manifesto was settling, and made a favorable impression. Before long he was successfully relieving the Tsarevich's sufferings and had made himself indispensable. Gradually, Alix and then Nicholas turned to him for advice on other matters—personal, spiritual, and state. Meanwhile, he attracted his own circle of followers in Petersburg, mainly divorced or lonely society women, with whom he held court almost daily in his apartment on English Prospect. As his influence and notoriety grew, petitioners and others asking for royal favors or action came to him, and began paying him to place the request before the Tsar or Empress. He was seen going to bathhouses with women, soliciting prostitutes, and taking women into his apartment, all of which reached the press. To Alix, such behavior and the "cross" of public ridicule that he had to bear only evidenced of Rasputin's image as a "holy fool," placing him beyond reproach. The court and wider circles, not knowing about the Tsarevich's affliction, could not understand the presence of this scandalous figure in the royal couple's midst. His enemies in the government and the Orthodox Church, one after one, tried to scandalize and oust him, but each time Alix dug in, and it was Rasputin's enemies who were dismissed. Rasputin now had the opportunity and the need to replace these officials and clerics with those friendly to him, and to oust other enemies. Rasputin was able to control the appointment and dismissal of key ministers and clerics, most of them obsequious nonentities. To complain to Nicholas or Alix about their "Friend" only ensured one's downfall. In this situation, the only solution was to eliminate him, and Rasputin's days were numbered.

WARTIME: PETERSBURG BECOMES PETROGRAD

The final downward spiral which ended Petersburg as it had been known for over two centuries began with World War I, which Russia entered on July 20, 1914, on the side of France and Great Britain against Germany and Austria-Hungary, and eventually its old enemy Turkey. In the capital, anti-German and patriotic sentiments ran high, and people expected a quick victory that would have Russia's army in Berlin by winter. Nicholas went to the Winter Palace to announce Russia's declaration of war. For the occasion the icon of the Virgin of Kazan was brought from Kazan Cathedral for a special mass in St. George's gallery before a crowd of 5,000. Nicholas recited the oath made famous by Alexander I in 1812: "I solemnly swear that I will never make peace so long as one of the enemy is on the soil of the fatherland."[103] He then stepped onto the balcony overlooking Palace Square, where an immense throng of some 250,000 had gathered to cheer the war, bearing icons, flags, and portraits of Nicholas and Alexandra. When the royal couple appeared on the balcony, the crowd sank to its knees as one, and sang "God Save the Tsar," Russia's national anthem. At least at that time and place, Russia felt united in a moment of *sobornost*. "You see," Nicholas remarked shortly afterwards, "there will now be a national movement in Russia like that which took place in the great war of 1812."[104]

Indeed, all strikes ceased and the workers began working overtime to support the war effort. The local press fanned patriotic fires. Even some of the intelligentsia were inspired, seeing it as the conflagration that would bring about Russia's spiritual renewal. Gumilev, seeking adventure and danger, volunteered immediately, soon saw battle and was decorated with the Cross of St. George; Mayakovsky tried to join, but was turned down and had to settle for writing inflammatory articles against the Germans. Gippius dissented: "Everyone has gone out of their minds," she lamented. "Why is it that, in general war is evil yet this war alone is somehow good?"[105] For his part, Blok saw the war as the fulfillment of his apocalyptic premonitions, as the beginning of what he called "incinerating years" in which Russia would see "Unprecedented changes/Unparalleled revolts." "In hearts once rapturous," he wrote, "there is a fateful void."[106] In May 1916 he was called into military service, and served in a construction division overseeing laborers building fortifications in East Prussia.

Naturally, the patriotic fervor turned into anti-German frenzy. Within a few days, people began vandalizing and looting German shops and offices. On July 22, the German Embassy on St. Isaac's Square, completed only two years earlier, was stormed by an angry crowd as Petersburg's governor and police stood only a few feet away and let it happen. Inside the mob destroyed furniture, paintings, and anything made of glass, and hurled the ambassador's collection of Renaissance bronzes out through the now broken windows. They continued onto the roof, where they pried away the bronze statues of horses and giants perched on the building's cornice and pushed them onto the square. People with German-sounding names began changing them to Slavicized versions. On August 19, the city itself suffered the same fate when at Nicholas's initiative its name was changed to the Slavicized "Petrograd" without any serious debate or opposition. The change was mistaken, first in that the original name "Sankt Piterburkh" was a Dutch rather than German name, and second in that the city was originally named after St. Peter, not Peter the Great, but it became so when "St." was dropped. This was ironic since Nicholas never cared much for the city's founder, once remarking that Peter "is the ancestor I like least of all for his enthusiasm for Western culture and violation of all purely Russian customs."[107] Indeed, Peter the Great had never intended his paradise to be a Slavicized city.

Russia's army stood at 5 million men and its navy had been rebuilt after Tsushima, but the lessons of Japan were never learned and neither force was modernized. Moreover, supplies of weapons, munitions, food, horses, and just about everything else were short and exacerbated by poor transport to the front. From the start the Prussian campaign went badly. Already in August Russia lost the major battle of Tannenberg, and in the first 10 months of the war even official counts put Russia's losses at a mind-boggling 3,880,000.[108] The initial wartime exuberance dissipated into despair, finger pointing, and the humiliation and exposure of Nicholas and his hollow and corrupt regime. Waves of wounded soldiers and deserters flowed into the capital, telling their horror stories of incompetence, waste, and carnage from the front. Prices escalated, and when the cost of living rose workers began to strike. The first food shortages arose while war profiteers and speculators reaped millions.

THE TRAGEDIANS

The debacles of the Russo-Japanese War and the 1905 Revolution shook Petersburg's artistic and cultural life. Before those events, both the Symbolists and the aesthetes seemed aloof from social and political concerns. But just as the events of 1905 drew Blok away from Symbolism, they forced some *miriskusniki* to reconsider their stance of aesthetic purity, challenging them to be more relevant to real life without abandoning true art. But the *miriskusniki* changed their position only slightly in a 1905 manifesto entitled *The Voice of Artists*, authored by Dobuzhinsky and co-signed by Benois, Lancéray, and Somov, who feared that

> beauty will be abolished and forgotten in the mighty wave of urgent, practical needs.
> . . . In constructing the new life, artists must contribute to the common cause, but not only as citizens. . . . Artists are confronted with the task: to decorate this new, unknown life. . . . Our appeal must be not for artists to revert to the simple life, but for the masses to be educated in the spirit of beauty.[109]

Some *miriskusniki* became involved with the revolutionary and satirical journals of 1905–07 such as *Zhupel* ("Bugbear") and *Adskaya pochta* ("Mail from Hell"), and began to give some of their works (some of which were simple cartoons) social and political content, such as Dobuzhinsky's *October Idyll* (1905), showing a blood spattered wall, a dropped girl's doll and lost shoe (manufactured by the Red Triangle factory and presumably lost by one of its workers) on the corner of Nevsky Prospect, Serov's *Soldiers, Heroes Everyone, Where Is All Your Glory* (1905), showing hesitant soldiers about to attack a huddled dark mass of demonstrating citizens, and his *After the Suppression* (1905), showing Nicholas II, his tennis racket under one arm, awarding medals to soldiers while corpses from Bloody Sunday lie next to them. Meanwhile, in Moscow Bryusov and Bely spoke (not necessarily negatively) of a new Mongol horde from the East leading to a final cataclysm (and rebirth).

During 1905, many writers and artists, seeing either danger, hopelessness, or opportunity, left for long stays in Europe. Benois left with his family to visit France even before the portrait exhibition had closed, and Merezhkovsky and Gippius also went to Paris for five years. But Diaghilev was always one to focus on opportunities, and he used this one to begin exhibiting Russian art abroad and put together with other *miriskusniki* his greatest creation, the *Ballets Russes*, which one specialist has called "basically *Mir iskusstva* transplanted from Petersburg to Paris."[110]

Indeed, it was through ballet above all other art forms that the *miriskusniki* summed up their work and most closely approached their ideal of a *Gesamtkunstwerk* and the kind of revolution in culture of which Diaghilev spoke in his dinner speech of 1905. Diaghilev had the best possible base to draw on, for ballet in Petersburg had already developed into the world's best, thanks to lavish funding from the imperial treasury which had attracted the best Russian and foreign talent to train dancers and choreograph the ballets, especially Marius Petipa. Petipa's art was made possible by the scores of talented and well-trained dancers emerging from the Imperial Ballet School on Theater Street behind Rossi's Alexandrinsky Theater, where master instructors such as Lev Ivanov, the Italian Enrico Cecchetti, Ekaterina Vazem, and the Swede Christian Johannson produced such stars as Tamara Karsavina, Anna Pavlova, Vatslav Nijinsky, Mikhail Fokin (soon Frenchified to Michel Fokine) and, of course, Kshesinskaya.

Diaghilev's leadership, organizational abilities, and contacts at *Mir iskusstva* led Prince Volkonsky, head of Imperial Theaters, in 1899 to employ him at the Mariinsky. Diaghilev in turn invited Bakst, Benois, and other *miriskusniki* to create scenery and costumes for its ballet and opera productions. He turned the previously dull *Theaters Annual* into a stunning publication with artwork by Bakst, Serov, Somov, and even Repin, and articles by Benois. Kshesinskaya, the same age as Diaghilev, became a great friend, and their fortunes were to be linked for over a decade. "I liked him from the first, both for his intelligence and culture," she later declared. "Diaghilev had a rich head of hair with a greying lock in front, which earned him the name 'Chinchilla.' . . . Diaghilev nearly always accompanied me home after the performance."[111]

While at the Mariinsky, Diaghilev also met the great bass, Fedor Chaliapin, who first performed there on December 20, 1899, and thereafter always performed to a full house. With his stunning voice, the skills of a tragic actor, and directorial talents, one contemporary called him "a performer of genius, an artist of unsurpassed talent on the operatic stage! In all his roles he was inimitable, original and grandiose!"[112] Together with Diaghilev and the *miriskusniki*, he revived opera in Petersburg, which in recent decades had been outshone by the ballet. In 1901 he became the first Russian singer to tour abroad and rocketed to international fame. When as an international unknown he was to debut at La Scala in Milan (in Arrigo

Boito's *Mephistopheles*), the local press so attacked the theater's management for inviting a presumably untalented and untrained Russian to perform at that acme of European opera that the director stayed away on opening night. But when Chaliapin began singing the prologue, the audience was transported into such ecstasy that they made him repeat it, the audience applauding throughout, before the opera could continue.[113] Beginning in 1909, Chaliapin would team up with Diaghilev in the *Saisons Russes* to showcase Russian opera to the world.

In 1901 Benois had Diaghilev convince Volkonsky to stage a production of Léo Deslibes's *Sylvia* as a vehicle to showcase the talents of the *miriskusniki*. Volkonsky initially agreed to let Diaghilev direct the production, but he quickly retracted and assumed the nominal direction himself. Though Diaghilev had Kshesinskaya and Grand Duke Sergei Mikhailovich lobby with Nicholas to overturn the decision, he was soon shocked to learn from the newspaper of his dismissal from the Theater on grounds that suggested improper conduct. Ultimately, the incident proved a godsend to both Diaghilev and world culture. His stint at the Mariinsky proved to be only Act One in the creation of the *Ballets Russes*. There he learned how to stage ballets and collaborated with the *miriskusniki* on the productions. He also became acquainted with the Mariinsky dancers Pavlova, Karsavina, Nijinsky, and Fokine, the key soloists who would later leave the Mariinsky to join him in Paris.

Following his triumphal exhibition of portraits in 1905, in 1906 Diaghilev, uninspired by recent exhibitions in Paris, introduced Russian paintings to the West in a large exhibition at the Salon d'Automne in Paris, which was followed in 1907 with a series of five "historical concerts" at the Opéra. In 1908, he brought Russian opera to Paris with the Western première of *Boris Godunov* in Rimsky-Korsakov's orchestration, which also launched the international career of Chaliapin. Finally, for the 1909 season, Diaghilev was ready to launch the *Ballets Russes*.*

By the time Diaghilev joined the Imperial Theaters in 1899, Petipa's career was declining and the Mariinsky's ballet productions were growing stale. Convinced that he had a natural vocation for the theater, Diaghilev aspired to reinvigorate Russian opera and ballet with a new creativity, which is why he had fought so hard for *Sylvia* and his directorship of the production. Such creative possibilities of dance were impressed upon the *miriskusniki* when the King of Siam's dancers performed in St. Petersburg in 1904. Bakst drew inspiration from their designs and costumes and painted pictures of scenes from the performances, while Fokine found ideas for choreography. Fokine also took inspiration from the visit to Petersburg of the American dance innovator Isadora Duncan, the self-proclaimed enemy of classical ballet. Indeed, Fokine had already been experimenting with new forms in his *Chopiniana* (1907), inspired by Duncan's 1906 composition *The Flight of the*

---

*The broader term *Saisons Russes* is technically more correct as it encompasses the company's operatic productions as well, but *Ballets Russes* is adopted here (except when referring to opera) as it has entered general use and the company's principal artistic contributions were in ballet rather than opera.

Butterflies, which she performed in Petersburg to the music of Chopin; he later turned *Chopiniana* into the plotless *Les Sylphides*. Fokine did not abandon classical forms, but he rebelled against fixed poses in favor of movements that better expressed emotion, expanded the types of dance music, and introduced new costumes, and bare legs and feet (forbidden at the Mariinsky). The *miriskusniki* finally got their chance to stage a ballet together at the Mariinsky when Benois's ballet *Le Pavillon d'Armide* (1907) was premiered to the music of his friend Nikolai Tcherepnine, Fokine's choreography, and Benois's sets. After seeing it, Dhagiliev shoved his way through the excited crowd, hugged Benois and exclaimed: "This is what must be shown in Europe, this is what we will take to Paris!"[114] When in 1909 Diaghilev was ready to launch the *Ballets Russes*, it was not hard to attract the Mariinsky dancers, who were restless under the Mariinsky administration, inspired by the *miriskusnikis*'s innovations, and longed for international travel and fame. As Karsavina recalled, "I went to all the exhibitions of the *Mir iskusstva*, and a wonderful revelation they gave me. I did so long to penetrate into that holy of holies, where now they all worked together."[115]

The *Saisons* were launched in May 1909 at the Théâtre du Châtelet in Paris. They were held every year, even in wartime, until 1929. Some performances were also staged in other European cities, including London and Vienna, and some seasons included operas featuring Chaliapin. The company drew on most of the *Mir iskusstva* artists, especially Bakst, Benois, Roerich, Dobuzhinsky, and Korovin, and the former Mariinsky dancers, Fokine, Karsavina, Pavlova, Nijinsky, and the newcomer Ida Rubenstein. Fokine was chief choreographer in the initial years, retaining Petipa's approach of emphasizing the artistic interpretation of music over simple technical virtuosity but applying it to modern music, new choreography, and new subjects. (Eventually Petipa himself choreographed some productions.) But Diaghilev and Fokine broke with Petipa's style by conceiving short ballets to artistic sets, which facilitated a closer and more concentrated link between all artistic elements of the production.

The highlights of the inaugural season, besides Benois's *Pavillon d'Armide*, were the *Polovtsian Dances* from Borodin's *Prince Igor*, to Fokine's choreography with sets and costumes by Roerich, and *Les Sylphides*, to Chopin's music and Fokine's choreography, sets and costumes by Benois, and danced by Pavlova, Karsavina, and Nijinsky. In 1910 the most important productions were in *Schererazade*, set to Rimsky-Korsakov's music and based on a tale from *The Thousand and One Nights*, and Stravinsky's *Firebird*. Stravinsky followed this with *Petrushka* in 1911, derived from the pre-Lenten "Butter Week" carnivals in St. Petersburg during the age of Nicholas I, during which magicians, performing animals, and puppet shows entertained the public in the city's squares. Through the device of a puppet which comes to life and battles a Moor for the love of a ballerina, the Western public saw a slice of Petersburg life combined with a touching love story. The puppets, as products and symbols of man's creative imagination, reflect *Mir iskusstva*'s belief in the superiority of imagination over reality, shown in Petrushka's final grimace at the magician. *The Rite of Spring* (1913) brought to life the wild, primal, though mythologized, traditions of Russian paganism. Despite the *Rite*'s setting off the greatest uproar in the history of music, the stunning artistry and success of Diaghliev's productions made Diaghilev and his dancers stars and household names and injected new life into Western ballet. But the ultimate compliment came when the West's leading composers and artists joined in the phenomenon. Soon the productions included original musical compositions by Debussy, Falla, Satie, and Ravel, librettos by Jean Cocteau, and sets and costumes by such artists as Picasso, Derain, and Matisse (whose conception of the dance was close to Fokine's). Diaghilev's productions were influenced by Western art, the *Rite of Spring*, for example, being inspired in part by the paintings of Gauguin. In Paris, *Mir iskusstva*'s dreams of a union of East and West into one World of Art, of combining elemental Dionysian Russia and Apollinian Western art forms, and of the fusion of all art forms into a *Gesamtkunstwerk* had come to fruition. In the *Ballets Russes*, the opening of Russia's window to the West had come full circle. Petersburg had drawn from Europe an art form, transformed it into a more beautiful, powerful, and modern means of expression, and returned it to the West and all the world.

Back in Petersburg, Diaghilev's shoes as the Maecenas of Petersburg culture were mostly filled by the influential critic and aesthete Sergei Makovsky, who in 1908 began organizing modern art exhibitions, beginning with a salon at the Menshikov Palace in 1909, moving on in 1910 to exhibitions of Russian art in Brussels and Paris, and returning to Petersburg in 1912 with an exhibition of French paintings. In 1909 Makovsky and the young poet Nikolai Gumilev, with the help of former *miriskusniki*, also founded a new artistic and literary journal, appropriately named *Apollo*, still hoping that the new Russian art would bring about an aesthetic renaissance. As a quality journal publishing articles by leading artists and critics and leading edge prose and poetry, *Apollo* became the focus of Petersburg's artistic and literary life, around which former *miriskusniki* founded a new exhibition society in 1910 retaining the name *Mir iskusstva*. The re-formed *miriskusniki* also formed the Antique Theater (1907–12), to which the usual cast of Benois, Dobuzhinsky, Roerich, Lancéray et al., contributed their designs. That theater revived the classic forms of Western European theater going back to the Middle Ages—the miracle play, the morality play, and the pastorale—preserving the historical and ethnographical authenticity of the productions through careful scholarship and tasteful restraint.

The Symbolist movement, on the other hand, continued, mainly in Moscow under Bely and Briusov. They founded the journal *Scales* under Bryusov's editorship, and in the Argonaut tradition in 1906 also established *The Golden Fleece*. In Petersburg, the movement was dying a slow death, and only Ivanov managed to continue his peculiar version of the faith. Former Symbolists such as Mikhail Kuzmin started defecting or trying to redefine the movement, Kuzmin contributing to *Apollo* his manifesto "On Beautiful Clarity," in which he called upon Symbolists to descend from the clouds to earth, to abandon foggy mysticism for the sake of beautiful clarity. In 1909, Innokenty Annensky, a classical literary scholar, translator of Euripidies and French Symbolists, poet, and tragic playwright, had contributed to *Apollo*'s initial issues "On Contemporary Lyricism," an influential survey of the Symbolist legacy in which he advocated a return to the original French Symbolism that drew inspiration from the inner workings of the human mind. The end of Russian Symbolism as a viable force (formally it lasted until the Russian Revolution) was marked by the defection in 1910 of its own founder, Bryusov. Older than the other Symbolists and always more in the 19th-century tradition, he had always remained in the French Symbolist tradition and now declared that he was "with all my heart with the clarists"[116] and that art must be autonomous, without any message—mystical, political, or otherwise.[117]

With Annensky's untimely death in 1909, leadership of clarists fell to his former student at the Lyceum, Nikolai Gumilev (1886–1921), a natural leader and organizer. He published his first verse, the romantic *Path of the Conquistadors*, in 1905. He then studied at the Sorbonne in Paris in 1907–08 where he started a journal, from which he returned to cofound *Apollo* and enter Petersburg's literary world. At heart Gumilev was a restless romantic adventurer in the tradition of Hemingway, always in need of excitement for his soul and manhood and of stimulation for his artistic mind, which eventually led him to Egypt and the inner reaches of Africa, as well as a lifetime of love affairs. Not a handsome Apollo, he was insecure about his physical appearance and tried to make up for it through his immaculate dress and pretentious manners. By nature he was combative, arrogant, and, inspired by Nietzsche, out to change the world. Not long after his return from Paris, he fought a duel with another Petersburg poet which has become part of St. Petersburg lore.

The scandal began when Makovsky received at *Apollo* a set of poems purportedly authored by an aristocratic lady named Cherubina de Gabriac. A telephone liaison began and Makovsky became infatuated with the mysterious lady. "Her" poems were published in *Apollo*, they created a stir in the city, and were praised by Ivanov. But the affair turned out to be a hoax perpetrated by a minor poet, Maxmilian Voloshin and his lover Elizabeth Dmitrieva in order to embarrass the Symbolists. When Dmitrieva visited Makovsky to apologize, she turned out to be ugly, lame, and overweight, deflating Makovsky's dreams. But there was another twist. Earlier in the year she had had an affair with Gumilev and left him for Voloshin, thus inciting Gumilev's wrath. In November a number of poets, including Ivanov, Gumilev, Voloshin, Blok, and Annensky, were gathered in the studio of the painter Alexander Golovin in the upper floors of the Mariinsky Theater to have their group portrait painted. Chaliapin was rehearsing below, and as he finished an aria from *Faust* Voloshin stepped up to Gumilev and slapped his face. Gumilev, an aficionado of duels, immediately challenged him, already visualizing it as a reenactment of Pushkin's duel. He ordered pistols from Pushkin's time, and of course the duel was held on the same site. Fortunately, the duelers were better poets than marksmen: Gumilev missed, and Voloshin misfired. The confrontation became the talk of the town, and local press mocked it: "The Duel? Absolutely fabulous. Especially in winter," commented the popular newspaper *Speech*. "How can there be a duel in winter without cognac and champagne? And certainly the very best. Duels support the wine industry. . . . [T]here were seven seconds. And not a hint of danger."[118]

Gumilev had frequented Ivanov's Tower since 1908, but one evening in early 1910 he came prepared to declare war on Symbolism. Attired impeccably in his dress coat and top hat, which rested on his knees as he spoke in his lisping voice, he announced in measured, consequential tones that Symbolism was dead, and that a new literary movement was about to replace it. The offended Ivanov derisively suggested calling Gumilev's movement "Adamism" to suggest its Edenic innocence, or perhaps "Acmeism," taken from the Greek "acme," meaning "summit." After that the two were sworn enemies, and when Gumilev's new movement needed a name he "favored" Ivanov by calling it Acmeism. Later that year in *Apollo* he elaborated on his ideas in his "Letter on Russian Poetry," in 1911 he established the Poets Guild in opposition to Ivanov's Academy of Verse, and soon he had gathered a following of poets, including Anna Akhmatova, Osip Mandelstam, and Sergei Gorodetsky. In the March 1913 issue of *Apollo* the group inaugurated the new movement by publishing their works. The Acmeists stood for refined taste, talent, and poetic craft, all aimed at the precise embodiment of emotional experience and a harmonic balance between image and form. As Gorodetsky expressed it, "For the Acmeist, the rose has once more become beautiful in and of itself. Its petals are beautiful, its fragrance and color, and not the thoughts, correspondences, mystical love and other things of that sort which are evoked by it."[119] While Akhmatova and Mandelstam were nominally Acmeists and Blok never fully abandoned his Dionysian-Symbolist past, each transcended labels and represented a rich union of the Apollinian and Dionysian. If one focuses on the Acmeists' poems rather than their theories, one discovers an incomparable lyricism based on deep human feelings and a fine sense of taste.* Mandelstam always maintained that it was the tastes and not the theories of the Acmeists that killed Symbolism.[120] All were ultimately romantic tragedians in their art, and all met tragedy in their personal lives.

Akhmatova (1889–1966), born Anna Gorenko, believed that she was descended from Khan Akhmat, the last Tatar to whom Muscovite princes paid tribute, and so adopted the pseudonym Akhmatova. She grew up in Tsarskoe Selo but attended the Bestuzhev courses in St. Petersburg. Gumilev, who attended the Lyceum, in

---

*While the Acmeists were often accused of elevating craft over content, it was actually a group founded in 1914 by the poet Victor Shklovsky, the *Opyaz*, which had this honor. To them, like the Futurists, the "art" lay not in the content but in the devices and processes used around it and into which the content should dissolve. It was this group which the Soviets eventually condemned most of all for "formalism," in which the content of Communist ideology had no place.

1903 became her childhood friend, and through him she came to know the Lyceum's Director, the poet Annensky, and like Gumilev grew up under his influence. She sensed that she was destined for greatness, once declaring as a child that a plaque would be placed on the modest house where she was born (which came true). She also sensed that she was fated to marry Gumilev. He loved her desperately even as a teenager, proposed several times and nearly committed suicide in consequence of her rejections, but she finally relented and they were married in April 1910 and spent their honeymoon in Paris. But within a year he was back on safari in Africa, while she was in Paris, in the arms and on the canvases of the then unknown Modigliani. Though not classically beautiful, she was tall, svelte, and elegant, and no matter what she wore a quiet sensuality and inner beauty shone through. With her long tight dark dresses, shoulders draped in a shawl, dark bangs over her forehead and trademark bump on her nose, she cut a famous and unmistakable profile. "She was more than beautiful, something better," wrote Georgi Adamovich, a friend from the Poets' Guild. "Never did I see a woman whose face and entire appearance so stood apart from any of the beauties in her expressiveness and authentic spirituality, which somehow immediately captured one's attention."[121]

She soon gained prominence in Petersburg's literary world, though she entered it only as Gumilev's wife. Her debut was at Ivanov's Tower in June 1910. Ivanov had read her poetry, told her he liked it, and encouraged her to read. When she did, he turned on her and critiqued it mercilessly. But he recognized her talent and viewed her as the heir to Annensky who would realize the potential embodied in his ideas and poems. Her first collection of poems, published in 1911 as *Evening*, concerned the many aspects of love and immediately made her famous. Her trademark style, derived ultimately from Russian psychological prose literature, was to express inner feelings using poignant images from the outside world. In the words of one contemporary, Akhmatova, "without writing a single abstractly generalized line, gives our descendants the most profound picture of our age—by describing a feather in a hat."[122] She also developed a flair for the tragic, both in expressing her personal traumas and in sensing the artificial calm before Russia's impending storm. Many poems were devoted to her turbulent relationship with Gumilev, which had developed into a struggle between two strong and independent personalities with their own artistic tastes, but who realized (he from the very beginning and she later in life, years after his death) that they were somehow fated for each other, bound together for eternity by invisible threads. One verse went:

> *Because I shared with you*
> *The primal darkness . . .*
> *No matter whose wife you became*
> *Our criminal marriage*
> *(I'll hide it no longer) endured.*[123]

Together with Pushkin, Akhmatova stands as the quintessential poet of Petersburg who drew inspiration from it.

> My blissful cradle was
> A dark city on a menacing river
> And the triumphal marriage bed,
> Over which young seraphim
> Held bridal wreaths—
> Was a city loved with bitter love.
>
> Solium of my prayers
> You were, misty, calm, severe.
> There my betrothed first appeared to me,
> Pointing out my shining path,
> And my melancholy Muse
> Led me as one leads the blind.

Unlike many before her and her contemporaries Bryusov and Blok, who in their respective cycles *Urbi et Orbi* (1903) and *Gorod* (1904–08) portrayed St. Petersburg (and all cities) as a source of alienation and a cause of spiritual chaos, she loved her "cradle." To her Petersburg was man's and nature's transcendent work of art, a deserving source of artistic and spiritual inspiration, and often of optimism, love, and even salvation. To capture its mystique, she utilized the city's concrete details and images: clouds, light, White Nights, mist, the Neva, enchained embankments, empty balconies, monuments in shadows, palaces, flowers. For someone who so deeply and perceptively felt the city's rhythms and integrated them into her own life, the images came naturally and she knew, like Pushkin, which word or expression to call up. In her poems the seemingly cold face of the city lit up and smiled. When war and revolution threatened, she never saw Petersburg as accursed or as Peter's misguided venture. Instead, she portrayed pain intimately and vividly in the lives of its citizens. As the Petersburg scholar Nikolai Antsiferov put it, "In the quiet before the storm, there appeared a poet who looked affectionately into the face of the city fated for ruin and described it with tenderness, as a participant in its life."[124]

The poet with whom Akhmatova was closest, and who was perhaps her dearest lifelong male friend, was Osip Mandelstam, whom she first met at Ivanov's Tower in 1911. Born in Warsaw, he was raised in Petersburg and went to the Tenishev Commercial School, where he was inspired by its director, Vladimir Gippius, a critic, poet, and future member of Gumilev's Poets' Guild. After graduating, he studied in Paris and then in Germany, returning to Petersburg in 1910 in the midst of the Symbolist-Acmeist debates in which he participated and sided with the clarists. He was the epitome of the young, sensitive, romantic poet. Short and thin, he had wispy red hair, sparkling eyes, dressed well and in good taste, and was wholly without pretense. His manner was polite and endearing, and he had a flair for conversation. "He listened to his interlocutor with his lowered long lashes, as if he were listening not to words but what was hidden behind the words," remarked the art critic Nikolai Punin, Akhmatova's future consort. "A conversation between him and other people very often turned into a poetic improvisation in, if one can use the term, a special spiritual space. . . . I was often present at conversations between Akhmatova and Mandelstam. It was a brilliant dialogue which made me both excited and envious—they would speak together for hours, perhaps without saying anything remarkable, but it was a genuine poetic game so intense that it was totally inaccessible to me."[125] Yet his politeness never kept him from challenging his peers on matters of artistic belief, and he became a standout at Ivanov's. His poetry, first published in 1913 in *Apollo* and in the collection *Stone*, was immediately recognized as brilliant. Combining his original perceptions with technical elegance and vivid details and images, he focused his early poems on human situations and culture and its creations: chance human encounters, the human body, cathedrals, a tennis match, music, Akhmatova reading her poems. He was equally talented at reading poetry, which Akhmatova considered the highlight at meetings of the Poets' Guild. After sitting sometimes for hours listening to mediocre poems, she recalled, "suddenly your attention would be distracted . . . as if some swan flew in above you . . . Osip reads."[126]

Both among critics and the public, "decadence" was "in," and the bohemian poets became like latter-day movie stars and were the subject of society and gossip columns. Every word of their poetry was scrutinized for hints of their personal lives and affairs. None more than Blok. Readers sensed his talent instantly, and the handsome Apollo soon became the darling of the public. "Blok's poetry affected us the way the moon affects lunatics," wrote the critic Kornei Chukovsky.[127] (Gippius called him her "lunar friend.") Crowds flocked to his readings, his picture appeared on postcards, his lines graced the pages of popular magazines, and Blok clubs were formed where youngsters imitated his reading style. "In those days, there wasn't a single 'thinking' woman in Russia who wasn't in love with Blok," wrote one female contemporary.[128] The poets' portraits were painted and became well-known from exhibitions and reproductions in magazines. Somov famously painted Blok (1907), but the sitter most sought was Akhmatova. To meet the demand many portraits and engravings of her were turned out in various styles, but none was better executed or more famous than that of Nathan Altman (1915), which was exhibited by the revived *Mir iskusstva* to wide acclaim.

Altman, however, was aligned not with *Mir iskusstva* or Acmeism, but with Petersburg's modernist, avant-garde circle, which had a fundamentally different aesthetic. Just as *Mir iskusstva* had its benefactor in Princess Tenisheva and Petersburg musicians had their Belyaev, the modernists had theirs in Levky Zheverzheev. He came from a rich family that manufactured lamé fabric and owned a store which sold church vestments, but his passion was the arts. An amateur artist himself, on the one hand he looked to the past, collecting antique books and old souvenirs from theater productions, but on the other had a passion for starting something new. So he began inviting to his home on Fridays young, cutting edge artists absorbed in the latest trends in Russia and abroad, each of whom wanted to make a name for himself, start a movement, and outdo Europe. One of them, the painter Pavel Filonov, proclaimed that Picasso "had come to a dead end."[129] In 1910 Zheverzheev formed the group into an artists' society called the Union of Youth. They took inspiration not only from Europe but also from Moscow's version of Futurism, led by the poet Vladimir Mayakovsky, who strove to shock and overturn all conventions. According to their aesthetic, daily life can be so banal and routine that it stultifies one's being and life passes by unnoticed, typical of the bourgeoisie and general public. To regain a sense of life people should be stimulated, even shocked, by seeing familiar images out of context, words used in incongruous ways or neologisms. From this perspective, the process of perceiving the new can be more important than the object that is experienced or the content of art, which itself might have no inherent meaning or be utter nonsense.[130] Their 1912 manifesto, *A Slap in the Face of Public Taste*, declared: "Throw Pushkin . . . Tolstoy and all others overboard from the ship of modernity." Like the Symbolists, they were prophets out to change the world and looked forward to a new dawn when man would be reawakened. To achieve this, they wrote shocking poetry and paraded around Moscow with painted faces, dressed in futurist yellow and other outrageous outfits, and descended on society banquets and meetings simply to disrupt and shock them. One critic called them "hooligans with a vengeance," whereas Petersburg's Acmeists were merely "dandies with a certain defiance."[131]

In Petersburg, the Union of Youth, like *Mir iskusstva*, staged art exhibitions, published a magazine and books, and held debates. Their growing reputation attracted the attention of Moscow's then-Futurists, Mayakovsky, the artists Kasmir Malevich and Vladimir Tatlin, and the poet Alexei Kruchenykh, who during 1912–13 joined the Union and moved to the capital. Soon they, together with the Petersburg artist Pavel Filonov and art critic Nikolai Punin, were regulars at Zheverzheev's "Fridays." Their collaboration produced in Petersburg some of the most remarkable art of prerevolutionary Russia, including the emergence of Suprematism.

In 1913, the poets Velemir Khlebnikov and Alexei Kruchenykh and the musician and painter Mikhail Matyushin developed a new vocabulary and transrational language called *zaum* (from *za-um*, "beyond the mind," or roughly "non-sense") composed neologisms from Slavic roots and simple sounds, all designed to overcome convention and reason and communicate directly without reference to objects in the real world. But mere words were not enough to convey their message. Inevitably, the circle's talents combined in what became the circle's forté, the performing arts, where words, artistic decoration, and music could be merged into the total artistic experience (as with *Mir iskusstva*). For this purpose, in 1912 Zheverzheev founded the Troitsky Theater of Miniatures, managed by Alexander Fokine, the flamboyant brother of Diaghilev's choreographer and former race car champion.

In Petersburg theater at the time the shadow of the innovative dramatist Vsevolod Meyerhold (1874–1940) loomed large. A former actor in Stanislavsky's Art Theater in Moscow, Meyerhold departed in 1902 to exercise greater artistic freedom. After several years of touring the provinces, he established himself in the capital under the auspices of the wealthy actress Vera Komissarshevskaya, where he produced Blok's *Balaganchik* with himself playing Pierrot. Initially, he wanted to realize Symbolism on stage, but soon developed a style wholly his own. He thought of theater as total art, and thus at the expense of traditional dialogue brought to the fore innovative lighting and stage decor, avant-garde music, and a dancelike movement of the actors bordering on pantomime. When Komissarshevskaya could not tolerate his modernistic experiments, she abandoned him. Within a year, however, he became head of the imperial opera and drama theaters in Petersburg, where he staged the traditional repertoire. But he also led a separate life as Russia's most innovative dramatic director under the pseudonym "Doctor Dapertutto,"* which included running the short-lived Strand (1909), the House of Interludes (1910–11), heading a troupe in nearby Terioki Finland, an abortive stint at the new Stray Dog cabaret, and then his own studio theater after the war began. Blok's wife Lyuba followed him everywhere and was a regular in his productions. Though inspired by Meyerhold, the Union of Youth artists wanted to stage productions themselves (a mistake), relegating Meyerhold to the audience. Except for Meyerhold and some interesting satirical productions at Nikolai Evreinov's Crooked Mirror cabaret,[132†] Petersburg dramatic theater indeed needed stimulation by a new aesthetic.

Matyushin, already in his 50s but "futuristically trying to look young,"[133] was the elder statesman of the Union. He had a dacha in Russian Finland, to which he invited Union members. While there in summer of 1913, he, Malevich, and Kruchenykh proclaimed that their meeting was really the First All-Russian Congress of Futurists and decided to write an opera called *Victory over the Sun*, and, of course, issued a manifesto which quickly made its way into the Petersburg press. It proclaimed that their goal was to "swoop down on the bastion of artistic sickliness—the Russian theater— and to transform it decisively."[134] At the same time, Mayakovsky was writing a play, *Vladimir Mayakovsky, a Tragedy*.‡ Both works were staged by the Union in December

---

*From a character in E. T. A. Hoffman's *Adventure on New Year's Eve*.

†The name conveys "that grotesque mirror of parody and satire which, by reflecting distorted images, makes fresh vision possible." Segal, *op cit*., p. 280. Generally, theater in Moscow was still hewed to the realism of the late 19th century, while Petersburg theater had evolved to a more parodic-satirical orientation. *Ibid.*, p. 281.

‡Originally, Mayakovsky intended the title to be *The Rebellion of Objects* or *The Railroad*, but in haste he sent it in to the censors with only a descriptive cover page stating, "Vladimir Mayakovsky. A Tragedy." The censors took that as the title and, once they had approved the play, the title could not be changed.

at a packed Luna-Park Theater. "All Petersburg" and some of Moscow was in attendance, including Meyerhold, Blok, and the young Boris Pasternak.

Mayakovsky's play was a two-act drama in verse depicting himself as a poet joined by alternative versions of himself—"the man without an eye and a leg," "the man without an ear," "the man without a head," and "the man with black dry cats (several thousand years old)." Appearing before backdrops by Pavel Filonov and Ilya Shkolnik depicting St. Petersburg, Myakovsky, in his trademark yellow shirt, played himself as a literally mutilated poet, suffering like Christ for the poor, enslaved citizens of the large city, gathering up their tears into a large suitcase. Already at 20 an accomplished actor, Mayakovsky performed brilliantly, but the production otherwise left the audience cold because it was ineptly staged and the other actors, all volunteers, had not rehearsed it well. But critics looked beyond the staging to the play's brilliant content and Filonov's innovative scenery. One critic called the sets "the truest depiction of a city I had ever seen. . . . I felt a movement inside myself, I felt the movement of the city in eternity, its full horror as part of chaos."[135] As in the case of Bely and his *Petersburg*, a Muscovite had come to Petersburg and made himself a part of its myth.

Victory over the Sun was more daring and ambitious, and sought to realize more fully the Union's aesthetic vision, but like Mayakovsky's play it was marred by a poor supporting cast and insufficient rehearsal. (The piano was also out of tune and the chorus sang off key, but the artists claimed that this was intentional.) The opera is set in the 35th century, when mankind is waging a battle against the sun, the traditional symbol of Apollinian beauty but in Matyushkin's conception also representing all convention and "cheap appearances."[136] Two futurist heroes manage to stab and capture the sun, after which mankind lives in a lighter condition. Malevich made the scenery and costumes, which he lit innovatively with colored stage lights. Striving for abstractness, he dressed the actors in geometrical, brightly colored cardboard costumes. One of the backdrops included early versions of his famous *Black Square* and *White Square*. The actors performed to Kruchenykh's *zaum* libretto and Matyushin's sometimes atonal, sometimes quarter-tone music. Malevich claimed that Matyushin's score "smashed to pieces the crust of the old music . . . while the words and word-letters of Alexei Kruchenykh turned the stock word to dust. The façade was shattered and in the same moment the wail of the consciousness of the old brain was shattered as well."[137] The audience indeed felt shattered. Some applauded, but most hissed and booed, and the local critics had nothing good to say about it. But the style was not forgotten and would be revived by Leningrad's *Oberiuty* in the late 1920s.

With the "futurist festival" of *Mayakovsky* and *Victory*, the alliance between the Union of Youth and the Muscovites reached its pinnacle, the artists went their separate ways, and the Union itself dissolved in 1914. For Malevich, it was an important stepping stone for his career and his artistic development. He remained in Petersburg, and it was here that he transitioned from Cubo-Futurism to Suprematism. When the war broke out in 1914, many Russian avant-garde artists who had been living and working abroad had to return home, including Altman, Ivan Puni, and Zhana Boguslavskaya, all from Paris to Petersburg. Under their influence avant-garde art took off in Petersburg. In March 1915, the artist Ivan Puni organized the *First Futurist Exhibition of Pictures: Tramway V,* at which both he and his Constructivist Moscow rival, Vladimir Tatlin, exhibited. Then in December Puni organized at the Artistic Bureau of Russia's first art dealer, Nadezhda Dobychina, the famous *Last Futurist Exhibition of Paintings: 0–10 (Zero-Ten),* so called since the Futurists seemingly could go no further with their experiments. Indeed, it seemed that Malevich's Suprematism, unveiled at this exhibition, represented the ultimate in abstract art, the reduction of painting to pure color and shapes. High in the corner of the room containing some 40 of his paintings, where in Russia icons are usually placed, was his *Black Square,* which indeed became an icon for Russia's avant-garde set. In another room were Tatlin's new counter-reliefs. Because Malevich had abandoned Cubo-Futurism just before the show and had urged his artist friends to do the same, the remaining artists exhibited as part of either the Malevich Suprematist faction or the Tatlin Constructivist faction. Malevich and Tatlin became famous rivals both in their aesthetics and personally and competed for favor in Puni's and other Petersburg salons of culture, once reportedly coming to fisticuffs. Malevich in particular loved to expound on his philosophy to whomever would listen, insistently pressing his points like a Belinsky. Malevich strove for a pure art of color and form which abandoned the visual phenomena of the everyday world in order to stimulate in viewers pure feeling and elevate them into a kind of spiritual space.[138] He spoke of it in mystical terms, once remarking that his art enabled viewers to "cut loose from the terrestrial globe. . . . My new art does not belong to the world exclusively, Earth has been rejected as a home." "I can't wait to hear that breaking off," he wrote Matyushin. "When will we take off?"[139] His abandonment of the object in painting paralleled the abandonment of content in Russian Futurism's theater and poetry. Tatlin, on the other hand, was so down to earth that he eventually eschewed color and even painting as such. He insisted upon the right of natural materials to be objects of art, molding, bending, cutting, and stretching them into shapes of refined beauty.

Malevich and Tatlin eventually returned to Moscow, but another alumnus of the Union of Youth, Pavel Filonov (1883–1941), grew up in Petersburg and was one of those artists like Vrubel whose creative originality truly defied categorization and did not start or join movements. An orphan, he was raised by his older sister, took classes at the Society for the Encouragement of the Arts and later studied at the Academy, from which he was expelled in 1910 essentially for his nonconformism. Having grown up in tumultuous turn-of-century Petersburg, he viewed the world as basically chaotic. Therefore, it had to be understood intuitively and holistically, not merely according to form or color, on which Constructivists, Futurists, and Suprematists were focused to different degrees. Rather, the artist must paint based on an inner conviction derived from a plethora of visible and invisible phenomena, which in turn must be meticulously reflected on canvas with an emphasis on line like a modernist Dürer, a concept he called "madeness." It was this sensitive and all-encompassing vision which inspired his backdrops of Petersburg for *Vladimir Mayakovsky*, reflecting the psychology of the suffering city. (Ironically, they were destroyed in the city's peculiar form of chaos, a flood, in 1924.) Though distinctly modern in style, Filonov's works shunned abstraction in order to focus on portraying the predicament of bewildered, suffering people in a chaotic time and place. He was Petersburg painting's modern counterpart to Dostoevsky. Whereas Dobuzhinsky, also influenced by Dostoevsky, had focused on the city itself, Filonov concentrated on more modernist psychological portraits of the city's affected people. He also evoked classic Petersburg themes in other paintings like *East and West* (1912–13), *West and East* (1912–13), and *The Rebirth of the Intelligentsia* (1913), depicting its transformation from the dandies of Pushkin's time into the "superfluous people" and finally the leftist advocates of the urban proletariat. Moving to revolutionary times, in *Victor of the City* (1914–15), he pictures the face of a proletarian standing out from a chaotic human mass, fixedly staring into the future/eternity, thus prophesying that the city's fate and future lies in such hands.

As the war continued, poets and artists lost faith and hope. Literary life became less elevated and intellectual, more decadent and bohemian. The poets began to write of the ominous and decadent times. Poets and artists now gravitated not to pretentious literary evenings and formal meetings, but to the cafés and cabarets as in prewar Paris. Their favorite haunt moved from the Tower to the cellar, a cabaret named the Stray Dog. Created from an abandoned wine cellar in the former Dashkov mansion on the corner of Mikhailovskaya Square and Italyanskaya Street, it was so named because the "stray dogs" of Petersburg's art world who lived unorthodox lives could gather and be welcomed there. As one habitué, Benedikt Livshits, wrote, it was "the only islet in nocturnal Petersburg where the literary and artistic youth, without a cent to their name as a rule, felt at home."[140] Akhmatova wrote of it in a poem that she read there on New Year's Eve, 1913:

> *We are all carousers here, debauchees,*
> *How joyless for us together!*
> *Flowers and birds on the walls*
> *Long for the clouds.*

As the Dog's fame grew, it also attracted famous foreign artists and musicians visiting Petersburg, including Arnold Schoenberg, Richard Strauss, and the founder of Italian futurism, Filippo Marinetti. Seemingly only Blok shunned it, though his wife Lyuba frequented it with Meyerhold's troupe and read her husband's poems there.

The Stray Dog was opened on New Year's Eve, December 31, 1911, by Boris Pronin, a former associate of Meyerhold, and soon it became a mecca. The cabaret had two long, narrow rooms, their walls and the vaulted ceiling brightly painted with flowers and birds by the artist Sergei Sudeikin, a small stage, a piano, small tables, a buffet on the side, and no waiters. During wartime prohibition, only coffee and pineapple juice were served. After it opened at midnight, arriving guests signed their names in a thick pigskin book, which the poets often inscribed with their latest poems. The crowd was divided into two unequal groups: the artists, who came for free and provided the entertainment, and people from all other walks of life, known as the "pharmacists," who paid often exorbitant prices for the privilege. The pharmacists were typically wealthy businessmen (who soon included war profiteers) and professionals joined by their wives or girlfriends, most of whom had little idea of culture but who relished the opportunity to rub shoulders with famous names in an intimate, bohemian setting.

As an actor and former colleague of Meyerhold, Pronin was a master at organizing plays,* music, dancing, poetry readings, and lectures nearly every evening. He devoted evenings or whole weeks of entertainment around specific themes: Musical Mondays, Marinetti Week (on the occasion of his visit to the city), Oriental music, Caucasus Week, "Extraordinary" Wednesdays and Saturdays, or Karsavina coming to dance in the off-season of the *Ballets Russes*. When Karsavina appeared, some 50 balletomanes consented to be relegated to the status of pharmacists for 50 rubles each and watch her. Dancing to the music of Couperin in the middle of the hall, she was encircled by garlands of fresh flowers and wooden 18th-century cupids, and at the end she let a live child-amour out of a cage made of real roses. "The poets have written their madrigals to me, and some fresh ones were made and recited at supper," she recalled.[141]

The formal program was one thing, but most often the highlight of the evenings was the spontaneous performances of the local musicians, poets, and other artists seated in the crowd. These improvisations were dominated by Petersburg's Acmeist poets and their friends, who the ballet critic Andrei Levinson described thus: "On a precarious stage in the midst of tobacco smoke loomed then-new figures, the supple apparition of a Tatar princess—Akhmatova—the shaggy poet Mandelstam with the rhythmic howl of bronze verses, the unsociable Gumilev with the sharp skull of a Pericles of the decadent period."[142]

Akhmatova's best friend at the time, Olga Glebova-Sudeikina, the wife of the artist Sergei Sudeikin, was the belle of the cabaret. Beautiful, elegant, and charming, with braided golden hair and sparkling gray-green eyes, usually dressed in décolleté, and famous in her own right as a dancer, actress, and singer, she was described by Chukovsky as "the living embodiment of her desperate and piquant epoch."[143] Like the other artists both a guest and a performer, she sang, danced, and recited French and Russian poetry to throngs of admirers.

---

*The Stray Dog was originally conceived by Meyerhold and Pronin as the latest vehicle for staging Meyerhold's avant-garde plays, but the space proved too cramped, and Pronin drove the establishment more in a commercial and literary direction.

If Sudeikina was the Stray Dog's belle, Akhmatova was its muse, whose every movement and glance was watched, each of her poetic syllables relished. The poet Benedict Livshits once described an "entrance" by Akhmatova and her womanizing Gumilev:

> In a tight-fitting black silk dress, with a large oval cameo on her waist, in floated Akhmatova, pausing at the entrance to write her latest poem in the "pigskin" book handed her by the insistent Pronin, while the unsophisticated "pharmacists," their curiosity piqued, wildly guessed who's who in the poem. . . . Attired in a long frock coat and black boater's cap, not leaving a single beautiful woman without his attention, Gumilev retreated, moving backward among the tables, either to observe court etiquette or to avoid "dagger looks" at his back.[144]

Strangers in the cabaret often came up to Akhmatova just to touch her hand; men declared their love for her. Her poetry reading, itself poetry, entranced audiences. After hearing her read at the Stray Dog, Mandelstam penned his poem *Akhmatova* (1914):

> *Half-turned, oh grief,*
> *She gazed at those indifferent.*
> *Falling off a shoulder,*
> *The neo-classical shawl turned to stone.*
>
> *Ominous voice—bitter intoxication—*
> *The soul unfetters its entrials*
> *Thus—Rachel once stood—*
> *As indignant Phaedra.*[145]

Avant-garde music, often improvised, was another important attraction, and the cabaret was the inspiration of interesting if not always enjoyable creations designed to break free from both classical conventions and Scriabin's grandiosity. The city's music critics attended and critiqued the compositions and performances in the city's newspapers and reviews. Ilya Sats, a professional composer for Stanislavsky's Art Theater who wrote music that some considered only dissonance, tampered with the piano to create new sounds, often inserting metal sheets and other objects between the strings, composed and performed parody operas, and most notably a small ballet, *The Goat-legged*, in which Sudeikina starred. Arthur Lourié, who soon would have an affair with Akhmatova, considered his compositions musical Futurism and lectured at the Stray Dog on "the art of noise," proclaiming that all sounds in the outside world should be viewed as art, and he experimented with twelve-tone music, as well as quarter and eighth tones, in an effort to recreate natural sounds and synthesize music with life. Mikhail Kuzmin, famous as a poet, also composed music and sang his songs at the Stray Dog, accompanying himself on the piano. The music of the new foreign composers popular at the Evenings of Contemporary Music also spilled over into the Stray Dog; one journalist reported hearing ragtime there.[146]

The Stray Dog was also a haven for Mayakovsky and other Moscow Futurists. Mayakovsky migrated to Petersburg in the autumn of 1912 and began spending his evenings at the Dog, attired in Futurist yellow or other outrageous clothes. Typically he would survey the scene from a corner, reclining in the position of a wounded gladiator against a Turkish drum which he banged every time a stray Futurist entered the cabaret. He too recited his poems, which the Acmeists detested. On one occasion as he started to read in his flamboyant and pretentious style, Mandelstam walked up to him and demanded that he stop, telling him: "You're not a Rumanian orchestra!"[147] On another occasion in February 1915, by which time the war was going badly and Mayakovsky had come to oppose it, he whirled around in fury at the pharmacists and angrily declaimed *Vam!* ("To You!"), which ended with these lines:

> *To you, living through orgy after orgy*
> *Who have bathtubs and warm toilets!*
> *Aren't you ashamed to read in newspaper columns*
> *About the presentation of St. George crosses? . . .*
>
> *To please you, loving vulgar women and good food,*
> *Would I give my life?*
> *I would rather serve pineapple water*
> *To the whores at the bar!*

This was an attack not only on the war profiteers and other bourgeois pharmacists in the audience, but also on allegiance to the Tsar and the patriotism that he asked of the nation. A scandal ensued, and many pharmacists informed Pronin that they would never return. A month later, in March 1915, wartime censorship was imposed, and the police closed the Stray Dog down. Its place was taken in October of that year by the Comedian's Halt, a cellar cabaret off the Field of Mars, but the cast had changed and the Dog's special creative atmosphere never returned.

While the best artists and poets clung to their art, culture and civilization in the capital generally degenerated as people lost their sense of restraint and began living only for the moment, called in Russian *ogarochny*—roughly meaning burning the candle at both ends. The rich spent lavishly and recklessly at fancy restaurants and held expensive parties, not knowing what tomorrow would bring. A group of modernist artists, formerly optimistic, now gathered nightly at the Vienna Café to drink themselves senseless. One night, according to the press, they stole a friend's cat, tortured it "to extract a confession," tried and convicted it, and hung it from a gallows. After that, regulars at the Vienna were called "cat fanciers."[148] New salons emerged which were no more than dens of debauchery, bribery, drug dealing, gambling, profiteering, and spying, frequented by corrupt officials, double agents, criminals, influence peddlers, speculators, and Rasputin. The most popular were those of Baroness Y.M. Rosen and Boris Stürmer, soon to be appointed Premier thanks to Rasputin. Rasputin's own favorite haunt was a gypsy restaurant, the Villa Rode.

Although poets were well-known and even cult heroes, their artistic life existed as if in a vacuum and the true culture never reached the people. Neither *Mir iskusstva* nor Futurism stimulated a mass aesthetic movement, and the more introverted Symbolists barely tried. Since 1905, increasing numbers of intellectuals, artists, and literati had lost faith in the Russian renaissance. They did not understand and even feared the unruly masses, who were perceived as an unpredictable and dangerous primal force arising from deep within Russia's soul. Blok grasped this sooner and more deeply than anyone else. He now believed that his art, which by now he simply termed romanticism, "is nothing but a means of arranging or organizing man, the bearer of culture, in a new connection with the elemental force. . . . Romanticism is culture which is in ceaseless struggle with the elemental force."[149] In a famous 1908 lecture at the Merezhkovskys' Religious-Philosophical Society entitled "The People and the Intelligentsia," he pointed to an insurmountable barrier between the intelligentsia and the people, who constitute "not only two different concepts but truly two realities: the people and the intelligentsia; one hundred fifty million on one side and several hundred thousand on the other, people who do not understand one another at the most fundamental level."[150] Referring to Gogol's famous troika passage,* he asked: "What if this troika . . . is flying straight at us? What if in rushing to the people we are rushing straight under the hooves of that mad troika to our certain death?"[151] In his opinion, the intelligentsia held a "will to death."[152] The audience, most of whom still believed in the "Apollinian dream" of Culture, was thunderstruck. A commotion erupted and the police prohibited discussion, which was put off until the next meeting, which was animated, nearly violent. Blok was already prepared with his rebuttal, entitled "Elemental Force and Culture." In typical fashion, he did not confront his opponents point by point logically, but argued the only way he knew how, symbolically and musically:

> The vengeance of Culture was ignited. . . . This is only a sign that another vengeance was also ignited—an elemental and earthly vengeance. We live between the two bonfires of ignited vengeance, between the two camps. . . . We are living through a terrible crisis. We still don't know exactly what events to expect, *but in our hearts the needle of the seismograph has already been deflected.* We already see ourselves as if on the background of the glow, on a light, circling airplane high above the ground. And under us is a rumbling and fire-spitting mountain along whose slopes, behind clouds of ash, crawl unleashed streams of red-hot lava.[153]

Indeed, another Petersburg writer, Alexander Grin, wrote a story in 1914, *Land and Water*, portraying the city being destroyed by an earthquake during which one heard "the screams of dying Petersburg."

---

*From the end of part 1 of *Dead Souls*, where Gogol likened Russia to a wild, speeding *troika* whose direction is unclear.

But the supreme artistic statement of the imminent doom of the city came, quite naturally, from a Muscovite, Andrei Bely, in his novel entitled (at Ivanov's suggestion) *Petersburg*, published in serial form in 1913 in the journal *Sirena* ("The Siren") and in book form in 1916. Following Gogol's and Dostoevsky's depictions of Petersburg as an unreal city, Bely added Symbolist visions and technique to create a whirlwind of ghostly, haunting impressions of the city at the time of the 1905 revolution. The plot itself is unremarkable: Radicals give a confused student a bomb to blow up his father, an ossified and conservative Senator representing Imperial Petersburg. But Bely flexes his poetic talents to create a masterful linguistic kaleidoscope of images and sounds, to the extent that the work is virtually untranslatable. Bely's Petersburg is a phantom city, its famous elements dissolving into the mist before the reader's eyes in the face of primal forces, marked by the haunting "oo-oo-oo" sound of the wind and the hoofbeats of Mongol hordes nearing the city gates. The book opens with the contention that "if Petersburg is not the capital, then there is no Petersburg. It only seems to exist." It is defended by the Bronze Horseman, here a figure of the Apocalypse. As the bomb ticks, the assassination plot dissipates into farce and scandal, which embarrasses the father and forces his retirement, while the bomb explodes harmlessly. "Petersburg" can now be exorcised from the souls of the estranged family of characters, their authentic humanity comes forth and they are reunited, albeit imperfectly. The same can happen for Russia once it sheds Petersburg. In the meantime, for Petersburg itself the bomb was still figuratively ticking, and the city was kept from disintegrating only by the iron will of the Bronze Horseman.

But Nicholas was not a Peter the Great.

CHAPTER 12

Cradle of Revolution and Despair

What happened to our capital,
Who lowered the sun to earth?

ANNA AKHMATOVA

In the West, there are many books; in Russia there are many unspoken words. There is that in Russia which destroys books and smashes buildings and puts life itself to the fire; and on that day when the West comes to Russia it will be totally consumed by fire; all will burn that can be burned because only from the ashes of death does the Zhar–Ptitsa, the Firebird, fly to heaven.

ANDREI BELY, *The Silver Dove*

THE LAST GASPS OF IMPERIAL ST. PETERSBURG

By 1916, Nicholas and Alexandra had alienated most friends and supporters and seemed resigned to fate. The war effort was failing, the army under Nicholas's command was in disarray, and deserters flocked into the capital. Shortages of food, fuel, and goods appeared and prices skyrocketed. Duma members made speeches predicting ruin. "The dynasty is risking its very existence . . . by means of terrible destructive work from within," warned the Cadet Duma Deputy Vasily Maklakov in 1916.[1] Rasputin's opponents in the highest aristocracy and the Romanov family felt that he was dragging Tsarism to destruction, and they saw that they had the most to lose should that transpire. Many wished Rasputin dead.

The first assassination attempt on Rasputin came in July 1914 while he was staying in Pokrovskoe, when a peasant woman stabbed him with a knife. He nearly died, but slowly recovered and returned to the capital. The traumatic experience drove him to drink, he became less stable, and his behavior grew ever more scandalous as he became convinced that his days were numbered. Now he held wild, night-long parties in expensive restaurants, spent lavishly and ostentatiously, and bragged about his sexual conquests and influence at court. Once Nicholas assumed command of the army, he was rarely home, and Alix and

431

Rasputin assumed effective control of affairs in Petersburg. Everyone knew that Rasputin wanted Russia to withdraw from the war and many feared that now he was in a position to achieve this. Late in 1916, Rasputin's enemies hatched another plot.

The plot seems to have originated with Grand Duke Dmitry Pavlovich, the Tsar's cousin, and Felix Yusupov, who had married the Tsar's beautiful niece, Irina. Felix was a colorful epicurean who had been educated at Oxford, was bisexual and enjoyed dressing in women's clothing, in which he sometimes appeared in restaurants, nightclubs, and the opera. The ballerina Anna Pavlova once told him that "you carry God in one eye and the Devil in the other."[2] But he still had a sense of duty to his family and country, and did not hesitate to act to protect them. In November 1916, the Duma deputy Vladimir Purishkevich, an ardent patriot and monarchist, warned Nicholas of the dangers that Rasputin posed for the monarchy and Russia, and on November 19 he went public with the same message in a sensational and popular speech in the Duma. This attracted Felix's attention. He met Purishkevich two days later and recruited him into the plot.

Felix had met Rasputin years before and had found him revolting, but now he feigned a friendship with him, even allowing him to treat his ailments. Using his wife as bait to lure Rasputin to the Yusupov Palace where he could be killed, Felix told Rasputin that she also needed treatment. Perhaps Rasputin had lost his edge and was overly trusting of his newfound friend, perhaps the idea of intimacy with a member of the royal family clouded his judgment, or perhaps he sensed the danger but abandoned himself to fate, but whatever the reason, the temptation was too great and the trick worked. They agreed that Felix would come to Rasputin's apartment after midnight, when the guards had left, and Felix would escort him to the Yusupov palace for the rendezvous. (In fact, Irina, in the Crimea when the plot was hatched, backed out at the last minute and never came to Petersburg.)

Since Yusupov's palace on the Moika was across from a police station, the plotters decided against shooting Rasputin. Instead they would use poison (potassium cyanide), and with that in mind they recruited into the plot Dr. Lazavert, a physician trusted by Purishkevich. Once Rasputin was killed, they would tie weights to him and throw him into a branch of the Neva through a hole in the ice, so that the episode would look like a disappearance rather than a murder. For the event Yusupov specially renovated and decorated a basement room reached by a narrow, curving staircase. When Rasputin came, they would tell him that Irina was upstairs, occupied by unexpected guests, and invite him down to this room to wait. Felix took great care to outfit the room with a fireplace, elegant antique furniture, an Italian rock crystal crucifix from the 16th century, Persian carpets and, in front of the fireplace, a polar bear rug. In the center was a table at which Rasputin was to eat poisoned sweet cakes and drink poisoned wine.

After midnight on December 17, Felix went to Rasputin's and escorted him to the Palace. Because Irina was not there, the plotters played "Yankee Doodle" repeatedly on a phonograph from upstairs to make it appear as if there were a gathering. Alone in the basement with Rasputin, Felix offered him the cakes and wine. At least initially, Rasputin declined the cakes and had some wine, but it only made him sleepy and thirsty.* A panicked Felix excused himself and went upstairs twice to confer with Dmitry and Purishkevich, and after the second time he returned with Dmitry's pistol and shot Rasputin in the side.† Leaving him for dead, the plotters began to celebrate, but when Dmitry checked the basement, Rasputin revived, stood up, and climbed up the stairs and through a side door while the stunned Felix watched. "He's getting away!" Felix shouted to the others. Indeed, Rasputin was already outside, staggering across a small courtyard toward a gate by the street on the Moika embankment. According to the accounts of Purishkevich and Yusupov, Purishkevich stepped into the courtyard and began firing at Rasputin with his revolver, missing twice, then hitting him in the back and finally in the head. Rasputin collapsed and they brought him into the house, where he was tied and bundled up to be thrown into the Neva, but not before Felix at one point lost control and began beating Rasputin savagely with a dumbbell handle. Finally, Rasputin was put in Yusupov's car, taken to a bridge across the Malaya Nevka, and thrown through a hole in the ice. But the murderers forgot to weigh him down and left one of Rasputin's boots on the bridge, which enabled the police to discover and identify the body two days later. When his frozen corpse was taken from the water, it turned out that his hands had broken free and that he had struggled under the ice. He was still alive when he was thrown into the river.

News of Rasputin's disappearance spread through town like wildfire, and attention soon focused on the murderers, who had not been careful about concealing the plot and left clues all along the way. An investigation was instituted, but the Tsar, realizing that a trial would turn the murderers into heroes, stopped it and meted out punishments himself. Dmitry was exiled to military duty in Persia. Yusupov was sent into internal exile and later escaped to Paris. Because Purishkevich became a popular hero and was a Duma member enjoying immunity, Nicholas dared not punish him. Rasputin was buried secretly at Tsarskoe Selo on December 21, but after the February Revolution the corpse was discovered and exhumed, and eventually taken outside of Petersburg to be reburied in a secret location somewhere along the

---

*The legend that Rasputin survived doses of poison that would kill an ox is surely not true. While Rasputin may have had small amounts of wine mixed with other liquids, he did not like sweets and probably never ate any of the cakes. But Yusupov, the only witness, built this into his account to make the deed seem more sensational. Radzinsky, *op cit.*, pp. 477–78. Alternatively, Lazavert may have lost heart and never poisoned the cakes or the wine.

†More recent evidence from testimony in the file of the Provisional Government's Extraordinary Commission that investigated the murder suggests that Grand Duke Dmitry fired the latter two shots, but that Yusupov and Purishkevich agreed to take responsibility for the actual killing upon themselves in order to protect the royal family from the taint of murder. Radzinsky, *op cit.*, pp. 474–89.

Vyborg highway. But on the way the truck broke down. It was decided to burn the corpse, and Rasputin's ashes were scattered in the wind.

Rasputin was gone, but not Russia's troubles. The episode showed the depths to which the monarchy and Russia had fallen. And so with the city, which legend said would remain so long as the Bronze Horseman stood. But in 1916, Blok and Lyuba walked past the Bronze Horseman and beheld a scene: "On Falconet's statue is a horde of boys, hooligans, holding onto the tail, sitting on the serpent, smoking under the horse's belly. Total decay. Petersburg is *finis*."[3]

They were right. Revolution was now inevitable, predicted Maklakov. "It will not be a political revolution, which might follow a predictable course, but a revolution of rage and revenge of the ignorant lower classes, a revolution that cannot be anything but elemental, convulsive and chaotic."[4] But the Duma was internally paralyzed and powerless to act. A feeling of decline and resignation to fate had set in amongst the city's intelligentsia and high society. Most ominously, unrest and criticism of the Government was spreading amongst the common people, and strikes were breaking out. Not long before Rasputin's murder, the Tsar's own Security Police, the Okhrana, had warned him that Russia stood before an abyss, in danger not from organized revolutionaries but from the "broad dark body" of the common people. "The alarming mood grows stronger each day," reported the Okhrana. "It penetrates all the principal levels of the population. Never has there been such dissatisfaction." Should bread not appear in the stores, "this will touch off in the capital . . . the strongest kind of disorders with pogroms and endless street riots," which would have the support of "two-thirds of the former and present soldiers."[5] And thus it happened. And like the French Revolution it was sparked by a parade of women.

THE FEBRUARY REVOLUTION

The winter of 1917 in Petrograd was especially harsh, with unusually cold temperatures, heavy snowfalls, and blizzards. The failing railroad system which had plagued the war effort now threatened the cities as well. In such cold, locomotives had difficulty building up steam, railroad tracks lay covered in snowdrifts, and rail cars laden with supplies stood immobile. Supplies of flour, food, firewood, and fuel to Petrograd dwindled. By early February the city was receiving only one-twelfth the usual supply of flour and the bakeries only about one-third their usual supply.[6] The prices of essentials—potatoes, butter, sugar, meat, candles, firewood, kerosene, boots—rose well beyond the means of the average worker. By January, reported the Okhrana, the mood in the city had taken on an "exceptionally threatening character."[7] Strikes broke out. Bakeries, which lacked fuel for their ovens, could not work full time, and in any event their supplies of flour fell far short of the city's needs. Wives and grandmothers formed bread queues at night despite the bitter cold, often only to be told in the morning that there would be none for the day. "At a bakery on the Liteiny this morning I was struck by the sinister expression on the faces of the poor folk who were lined up in a queue, most of whom had spent the whole night there," wrote the French Ambassador Paléologue in his diary.[8]

When in mid-February the city authorities announced that rationing would begin on March 1, panic buying emptied the shelves of bakeries and food stores. Speculation and a black market appeared, and rumors flew that the shortage was artificial, engineered by the government (to justify peace with Germany) or by speculators. The police feared bread riots. Meanwhile, lacking fuel, many factories had to close or slow down; the all-important Putilov Works (where there was already a labor dispute) shut its doors on February 21. Tens of thousands of idled, hungry, and unhappy workers now milled about the streets daily.

When February 23 dawned unusually warm and sunny, Petrograders took advantage of the thaw to stroll on the streets and go shopping. It was also International Women's Day, a socialist holiday, and several groups of women—workers, society ladies, female students, peasants—had organized processions to celebrate the holiday and demand equal rights. They marched peacefully and in good spirits, but as they approached the center others joined and began clamoring for bread. The atmosphere grew uglier in the afternoon when the women were joined by groups of workers. About 100,000 demonstrated, leaderless and without specific demands other than for bread. Cossacks on horseback and police dispersed some crowds, but there was no shooting and only a few injuries. "It seems as if this is an ordinary hunger riot," wrote Gippius in her diary that evening, but "as when in water, especially turbid waters, we look and cannot see how far away we are from *the collapse*."[9]

Remembering 1905, the city's military commander, General Sergei Khabalov, and its governor, Alexander Balk, sought to contain the demonstrations without resorting to force and politicizing what so far were simple bread riots. But the perceived lack of resolution emboldened the workers, and on the 24th, incited by their leaders overnight, they turned out in greater numbers (about 200,000) and ready to cause trouble, and they did smash some windows and loot shops. Now they demanded not only bread, but chants of "Down with the War!" and "Down with the autocracy!" were heard. A large, festive rally was held on Znamenskaya Square in front of the Nikolaevsky Train Station, where Trubetskoy's famous equestrian statue of Alexander III stood. (For Petersburgers, this had become a symbolic and favorite spot for protests because Alexander III represented the epitome of autocracy and repression.) As the crowd mounted the statue and fiery orators spoke, the people's actions bespoke of revolution, and they began to sense their power. By the time they left that day, they had painted "Hippopotamus" (the locals' name for the statue) on the statute's plinth. Cossacks were seen fraternizing with the crowd.

By the 25th, the capital was in the grip of virtually a general strike. As in 1905, nearly all factories were closed, newspapers failed to appear, city transport was interrupted, many shops and restaurants had closed their doors. Again, Nevsky was lit at night by a searchlight from the Admiralty spire. The crowds on the streets neared 300,000 and now included people from all walks of life. Though they were still leaderless and not organized, their demands had become political and more radical. "Bread was unnoticeably being forgotten," observed Gippius that day, "it was forgotten, as a happenstance."[10] Red flags and banners began appearing. In front of Kazan Cathedral students led renditions of "La Marseillaise." Both the demonstrators and the authorities grew more aggressive and in spots violence erupted. Three civilians were killed at Gostiny Dvor, some grenades went off, and police chief Shalfeev was pulled off his horse and killed near Liteiny Bridge while Cossacks passively looked on. At the demonstration that day in front of Kazan Cathedral, a young girl had stepped forward from the crowd of demonstrators to present a bouquet of red roses to the Cossack officer in charge. He smiled at her and leaned down from his horse to accept it. The relieved crowd shouted "Hurrah!"[11] But the most telling breakdown in authority occurred on Znamenskaya Square, when revolutionary demonstrators at a mass meeting defied the demands of mounted police to tear down their red banner and disperse. As the police prepared to charge and their commander, Lieutenant Krylov, drew his pistol and took aim at the orator, the Cossacks charged the police, killing Krylov. The crowd cheered and the Cossacks waved their caps.[12] The demonstrators began avoiding confrontations with the "comrade Cossacks" and other soldiers and turned their wrath on the police, whom they called "pharaohs." The soldiers, on the other hand, were called *nashi* ("ours"), a term of endearment which conveys a sense of patriotism and unity. These were not army regulars, most of whom were off fighting the war, but mostly young reservists recently called up and who had little training. Most were peasants or workers, many of them from within St. Petersburg who had friends and relatives among the crowds. Some had been impressed into service as punishment for striking or creating disorders. "The Petersburg soldier of those days," observed Victor Shklovsky, "was either a dissatisfied peasant or a dissatisfied city-dweller. These men were not even dressed in their new gray overcoats, but just hastily wrapped in them, then lumped into crowds, bands and gangs and called reserve battalions."[13] When soldiers showed sympathy for the crowd, Khabalov failed to discipline or remove them from town; they began losing their fear of authority.[14] The psychology on the streets turned in favor of the crowd.

For their part the intelligentsia were, as Gippius phrased it, "off board."[15] In the absence of newspapers, they congregated at their apartments to share the latest information and impressions. For the leftist intellectuals, Gorky's apartment on Kronverksy Prospect became a meeting center, his telephone ringing off the hook as acquaintances called in with reports. For the artists, the Merezhkovskys' was still the place, as in 1905. As in 1905, Bely had the fortune or misfortune to be in town and staying with them. Having now written his novel about the disintegration of Petersburg at the hands of dark masses, he could now see it come true.

Akhmatova was also downtown on the morning of the 25th at the dressmakers; that evening she was going to Meyerhold's première of Lermontov's *Masquerade*. She tried to take a cab home to the Vyborg side, but the driver refused. "Lady, I'm not going over there. They're shooting and I have a family."[16] So for hours she wandered aimlessly and fearlessly amongst the troops, orators, and fires on the streets, gathering impressions that would later shine in her poems. But in the evening she, Kshesinskaya, and all of Petersburg's wealth and nobility turned up at the Alexandrinsky Theater, as if for one last fling. The streets outside were nearly empty; cries and shots were heard in the distance. The trams were not running, and most theatergoers walked to the performance in an eerie desolation. But at the theater entrance were lights and a line of black cars, and the theater was packed with enthusiasts who had paid top prices for tickets. While a dead student lay in the theater lobby, on stage the audience witnessed the spectacle of a bygone age of Petersburg's splendor: a palace hall ready for a masquerade, complete with huge mirrors and gilded doors. One Meyerhold scholar described the moment:

> Autocratic Russia was collapsing before everyone's eyes. Its imperial grandeur became a phantom and everything smelled of decay. . . . The entire solemn ritual of the Court, the magnificent uniforms, the bewitching power of rank, the strict etiquette, the indestructible preeminence of tradition, the arrogance of the nobility, heraldry, orders, epaulettes, review parades—it was as if they had been licked off by a cow's tongue. . . . Everything that had been indubitable, substantial, and weighty reality became mystically ephemeral, dubious: everything was in question. It was all drowning in the Rasputin business, reverses on the front, in corruption, bribery, espionage mania, in the loud spasmodic patriotism of the newspapers, in drunkenness. . . . Meyerhold and Golovin showed worn-out, perishing Imperial Petrograd a splendid and fearful vision, at once opulent and tragic. . . . The spectacle prophesied disaster and the end of the world. It was called the "sunset of the Empire," "the last spectacle of Tsarist Russia."[17]

Akhmatova had trouble getting home that evening. "There were shots on Nevsky Prospect and horsemen with bared swords attacked passersby," she recalled. "Machine guns were set up on roof tops and in attics."[18]

That evening the authorities lost control of the workers' districts, where rioters burned police stations; the government now held only the city center. Nicholas telegraphed Khabalov: "I order you to bring all of these disorders in the capital to a halt as of tomorrow." Khabalov was horrified. To do so was impossible, at least without major bloodshed. At that evening's meeting with his subordinates, Khabalov ordered that "if the crowd is in any way threatening, and if it carries banners, then you are to act according to regulations. You are to give three warnings and then—open fire."[19] In a show of force, he turned the city's center into an armed camp, posting emplacements of soldiers at major intersections and in front of the Winter Palace, some with machine guns. Ambulances were brought in. He raised the bridges, declared a total curfew, and plastered the city with posters warning, "All meetings or gatherings are forbidden. . . . I have given the troops fresh authority to use their arms and stop at nothing to maintain order."[20] The 26th was a Sunday and the city rose late. At around noon, the emboldened crowds, ignoring the warnings, marched on the city center. The police and soldiers initially followed orders and fired on the crowds. All along Nevsky Prospect—at Kazan Cathedral, Gostiny Dvor, the intersection with Vladimirsky Prospect, and, again at Znamenskaya Square—people fell to bullets. A student buying a ticket to *Masquerade* from a scalper on Nevsky was struck by a stray bullet.[21] The bloodiest scene was at Znamenskaya, where 40 or 50 were killed and as many wounded by a training detachment of the Volynsky Regiment. (For this in 1918 the square was renamed Uprising Square.) A group of citizens broke into the barracks of the Pavlovsky Regiment, whose soldiers were responsible for the killings at Kazan Cathedral, crying that their trainees on the street had been firing on the people and asking it to be stopped. About 100 soldiers responded, broke into the arsenal at the barracks to seize guns and ammunition, and set off toward Nevsky along the Catherine Canal. Not far from where Alexander II was killed, they encountered a police patrol and fired at them until they ran out of ammunition. When they returned to the barracks for more, Khabalov's loyalists were waiting, arrested them and sent them to the dungeon of the Peter and Paul Fortress, by then known as the Russian Bastille. But by the end of the day, the show of force seemed to have had the desired effect, and calm set in over the city.

That evening, Paléologue went to a fancy dinner, and while returning home along the Fontanka he saw a line of parked cars and carriages, including that of Grand Duke Boris, outside Princess Radziwill's home. Lights were ablaze within; her party was in full swing. "There was plenty of gaiety in Paris on the night of the 5th October, 1789!"[22]* he recalled. The next morning he awoke to a din outside his window by the Alexander (now Liteiny) Bridge over the Neva.

> [A] disorderly mob carrying red flags appeared at the end [of the bridge] which is on the right bank of the Neva, and a regiment came towards it from the opposite side. It looked as if there would be violent collision, but on the contrary the two bodies coalesced. The army was fraternizing with revolt.[23]

The revolution had begun. What had happened during the night?

Had the soldiers remained loyal, the disorders might have died out after the prior day's show of force. But that evening the soldiers of the Volynsky Regiment who had killed so many on Znamenskaya Square had returned to their barracks full of remorse. They also learned of the Pavlovsky Regiment mutiny earlier that day. One sergeant, a peasant named Kirpichnikov, spoke up. "Our fathers, mothers, sisters,

---

*The date of the march of women from Paris to Versailles. It was shortly before then when, upon hearing at a banquet that the people had no bread, Marie Antoinette supposedly said "Let them eat cake."

brothers, and brides are begging for bread. Are we going to kill them? Did you see blood on the streets today?" he asked. "I say we shouldn't take up our positions tomorrow. I myself refuse to go." And the others cried out, "We shall stay with you!"[24] On the next morning when their Commander, Lashkevich, ordered them out, they resisted. Lashkevich panicked, started fleeing across the barracks yard and was shot in the back. Suddenly the soldiers were mutineers, and there was no turning back. They quickly sent word to the Preobrazhensky and Lithuanian Guards, who joined them. The soldiers took to the streets, broke into the Arsenal on Liteiny Prospect and helped themselves to some 40,000 rifles and 30,000 revolvers, and also broke into the major weapons factories where they took thousands more. By March 1 virtually the entire Petrograd garrison of 160,000 had rebelled.

The soldiers and people were one, and the streets erupted in scenes of celebration. Soldiers wore red cockades in their hats, red ribbons, on their shoulders, and red stripes on their sleeves, and to the icons on their regimental standards were added red flags.[25] People wore red armbands, ribbons, or anything else red they could get their hands on to show solidarity. Even the Mariinsky dancers started calling one another "Comrade"; Karsavina was elected president of their worker's council.[26] Cafés and restaurants opened their doors to soldiers and demonstrators and fed them for free. A sign on one read: "FELLOW CITIZENS! In honor of the great days of freedom, I bid you all welcome. Come inside, and eat and drink to your hearts' content."[27] Shopkeepers offered their shops as bases and refuges for soldiers. Cabdrivers said they would transport only "leaders of the revolution."[28] Most cars and trucks in the city were commandeered. They cruised the city with soldiers perched on their hoods and fenders and banners waving. But the peasant soldiers not only did not know how to drive but were often drunk. Gorky called the vehicles "huge hedgehogs running amok."[29] "The city resounded with crashes" in what the writer Shklovsky called the "slaughter of the innocent cars."[30]

While many celebrated, on the 27th the battle with the police turned ugly, and street fighting with them continued for another couple of days. Hundreds of police snipers took up positions in windows, on roofs, and even in church belfries, and they had to be hunted down one by one. Other police were tracked down like animals, beaten and killed. Police stations and the Palace of Justice went up in flames.* The soldiers took over the telephone and telegraph exchange and most railroad stations. The prisoners were released from the Peter and Paul Fortress (the Pavlovsky mutineers turned out to be the only prisoners) and Kresty prison (mostly common criminals, but also several imprisoned revolutionary leaders). With the prisons emptied of criminals and authority collapsing, on the 27th a wave of looting and vandalism hit the city. Stores were emptied of goods. Imperial double-eagles and symbols of

---

*Among the buildings burned was the courthouse and prison on Liteiny Prospect. In the 1930s the NKVD (later KGB) building was erected on the site, which became another local symbol of oppression.

imperial power were attacked and destroyed. Kshesinskaya's mansion on Trinity Square, which had become a hated symbol of the imperial order, royal favoritism, and waste, was sacked. Having been warned of the danger, Kshesinskaya slipped out of the house in the plainest coat she could find with only a suitcase and her purse containing a few jewels and other valuables, and her fox terrier, Dzhibi.[31] (The Bolsheviks soon made the mansion their headquarters.) Government officials and loyalist forces bunkered down in pockets of resistance throughout the city, including the Winter Palace, the General Staff Building, the Admiralty, and the Astoria Hotel. In the Astoria were huddled loyalist officers and their families, protected by snipers on the roof. When the unruly crowd gathered outside, the snipers opened fire, and revolutionary soldiers responded by firing machine guns mounted on armored cars. The crowd stormed the building and shot and bayoneted several officers, wrecking and looting the fine interior in the process.[32]

So far the revolution had been little more than a large *bunt*, a spontaneous rebellion of the masses without leaders or clear goals. As the soldiers began restoring order on the streets, they and the people, who sensed that the monarchy was now doomed, looked for political leadership. Most initially looked to the Duma, which during the crisis had stood by helplessly, caught between the crowds and a Tsar who would not listen. Gippius likened its challenge to that of "taking control of a tramway car when it is already standing crosswise on the rails."[33] Moreover, Nicholas had prorogued the Duma on April 26, so officially it could not act and faced the question whether to act illegally or declare a provisional government. Although its leaders for years had been making speeches against the autocracy, now they were reluctant to seize power or even meet officially. But during the afternoon of the 27th thousands of expectant soldiers and citizens flowed toward the Palace and into its courtyard; a few got inside. They milled about impatiently, waiting for leadership. So pressured, the Duma leaders decided to hold a "private" meeting and formed a Provisional Committee, nominally for the purpose of restoring order in the capital. They also telegraphed the Tsar and gave him the misimpression that they were restoring order. In fact, they controlled nothing.

Also that afternoon, several workers' delegates and radical socialist leaders (though not yet any Bolsheviks), some just out of prison, made their way into the Tauride Palace. They decided to form a Petrograd Soviet as in 1905. For this purpose they appointed a Provisional Executive Committee of the Soviet, which convened the Soviet's first session for 7:00 that evening in the palace, called upon workers to elect deputies, published and distributed on the streets a makeshift issue of *Izvestia* to carry the announcement, and took the first steps to create a military organization to protect the revolution. That evening, the Soviet met in the Catherine Hall where the Duma normally sat, an ominous sign. About 250 people were present but only 40 or 50 were properly delegated and authorized to vote. It was disorganized, with many impromptu speeches and much cheering. But they managed to choose a permanent Executive Committee (none of whom were factory delegates), impound state funds under the Soviet's control, and add soldiers to the body to constitute it as the Petrograd Soviet of Workers' and Soldiers' Deputies.[34] The eventual election of some 3,000 members produced a Soviet overwhelmingly made up of moderate socialists and soldiers, with soldiers having two-thirds of the representation.[35] Their sheer numbers and inexperience made effective action impossible; the body resembled an unruly peasant village assembly. All meaningful work and effective power devolved to the Executive Committee, which eventually included about 40 members, who were never properly elected by the workers and soldiers of the Soviet. Rather, they were appointed from the various socialist parties, and could be withdrawn and replaced by them at any time. The Soviet never voiced concerns about it. Like Minin and Pozharsky centuries before, the "saviors of the people" ceded their power to a narrow clique, this time to a coordinating committee of radical intellectuals from socialist parties which had barely participated in the revolution but now purported to speak in the people's and Soviet's names.[36] Thus was set in motion the party-dominated pattern of politics that would prevail in the Soviet Union for some 70 years.

As the Soviet debated through the night of the 28th–29th, the Duma members a few rooms away wrung their hands, unsure whether to take power. The Provisional Committee feared that if the Duma did not seize power, the Soviet would, but the Committee decided to do so only when the Preobrazhensky Regiment placed itself at the Duma's disposal.[37] But the rebel soldiers on the streets feared counterrevolution from the Duma, turned to the Soviet for protection and made a deal with it. This resulted in the Soviet's famous Order Number One, which granted soldiers rights against and better treatment by officers, called for the organization of Soviet-type committees in each military unit, and subordinated the military to the Petrograd Soviet, specifically allowing it to countermand decisions of the Duma's Military Commission. Thus, the Petrograd Soviet held effective power in Russia. But still it did not seize formal power. The socialists were not prepared to take full responsibility for events before the unpredictable crowds, a power grab might provoke counterrevolution from the Tsar's army, and according to socialist doctrine it was still too soon for the socialist revolution. Therefore, they allowed a "bourgeois" Provisional Government to be formed by the Duma. The arrangements were agreed to in an eight-point document negotiated on the night of March 1–2, which among other things called for the prompt convocation of an elected Constituent Assembly to determine the form of government and constitution of Russia, and in the meantime the abolition of all police organs (to be replaced by the militia) and organs of self-government. The soldiers who had participated in the revolution were allowed to keep their weapons and were exempted from serving at the front. The Provisional Government was headed by Prince Georgi Lvov, with the socialist Kerensky as Minister of Justice.

The Tsar was a bystander to the events in Petrograd. When he learned that the disturbances in the capital were getting out of hand, on the 27th he dispatched his trusted General Ivanov to secure Tsarskoe Selo and then lead a force of eight regiments into the capital. But then he heard that the situation could be settled and his throne preserved through negotiations with the Duma, so he called Ivanov's operation off; soldiers at Tsarskoe Selo began defecting to the rebels. By March 1, it was clear that no accommodation was possible, that regaining control of the city would be impossible without a major military offensive and much bloodshed, and that to attempt to do so would risk full revolution in the army and threaten the war effort. Nicholas agreed to step down and issued his abdication manifesto on March 2nd. He abdicated on behalf of himself and his son Alexis in favor of his brother, Grand Duke Mikhail Alexandrovich. In Petersburg, the mob at the Tauride Palace protested that they wanted "no more Romanovs," and on March 3rd Provisional Government leaders convinced Mikhail to abdicate as well. Within the space of two weeks, the Romanov dynasty and an entire way of life were gone. Imperial St. Petersburg was no more.

The closing act of the February Revolution was the mass burial of the Revolution's victims at the Field of Mars on March 12, the second Sunday after the Revolution. All in all, some 1,400 to 1,500 had been killed, and another 6,000 wounded.[38] About 180 of these martyrs were buried in a ceremony that in this heady atmosphere of purification and spiritual renewal witnesses said resembled an Easter holiday. Some people even gave each other the Easter greeting, "Christ is risen!" or adapted it to "Russia is risen!"[39] They would soon change their minds. Indeed, Gippius realized at the time that the path to resurrection would be fraught with obstacles and temptations. "Russia is free—but not yet purified," she wrote. "The first cry of a baby is *always* a joy, even one realizes that both mother and child still might die."[40]

THE ROAD TO RED OCTOBER

The dyarchy of the Petrograd Soviet and the Provisional Government was unworkable. The two bodies had different goals, the Government wanting to contain the revolution and the Soviet seeking to deepen it. The Government had responsibility without power, the Soviet power without responsibility. Time was thus on the Soviet's side, and it was in no hurry to convene the Constituent Assembly, which would presumably deprive it and its leaders of power. Except for the Bolsheviks, the socialists in the Provisional Government and Soviet sought to unite. And unlike the Bolsheviks, they had to focus on the real issues of running the country. The Bolsheviks, essentially out of power, could blame Russia's problems on their opponents. They embarked on a strategy of infiltrating soviets and military units throughout Russia and recruiting workers and soldiers to their cause, tapping the age-old Russian craving for truth and social justice. Not willing to share power and unsure whether the Bolsheviks could gain control peacefully, Lenin shunned the political process and eventually imposed a strategy of taking power through an armed coup.

Lenin's start was not auspicious. Living far away in Zurich, he had not been following the press accounts of events in Russia and was not even aware of the February Revolution until an acquaintance informed him about it on March 2, and at first he was convinced that it was the result of an Anglo-French conspiracy.[41] Soon Bolshevik prisoners, including Stalin and Lev Kamenev, were freed, and arrived in Petrograd in mid-March. (Trotsky was in New York and arrived only in May.) They joined the Bolshevik Central Committee and began planning strategy and operations, largely ignoring Lenin, who they correctly viewed as out of touch. Lenin realized that he must return to Petrograd quickly or lose his leadership of the movement. Germany, whose foreign policy encouraged revolutionary activity in Russia, arranged his transit to Sweden. From Stockholm he traveled through Finland and then to Petrograd, where his train, draped in red, arrived at the Finland Station just after 11:00 P.M. on April 3.

A hastily assembled crowd of Bolsheviks, sailors, and other supporters waving red banners greeted him at the station. A woman gave him a bouquet of red roses, and the crowd asked him to speak. He made brief, sharp remarks outlining his position. The members of the Provisional Government, he cried, "are deceiving you, just as they deceive the whole Russian people. . . . The people need peace. The people need bread and the people need land. . . . Sailors, comrades, you must fight for the revolution, fight to the end, for full victory of the proletariat. All hail the world Socialist Revolution!"[42] In front of the Station, Lenin mounted a captured armored car and rode it to the Kshesinskaya mansion, now the Bolshevik headquarters. The route was lit by searchlights from the fortress, crowds surrounded the procession, and he stopped to speak a few more times en route. When he arrived at the mansion, orators were haranguing the crowd from the balcony overlooking Trinity Square, and before long Lenin was doing the same. Once, back inside, for nearly two hours he detailed his program to the Bolshevik leadership, which was reflected in his famous "April Theses" issued the next day: transition to the "second" phase of the revolution; refusal to support the Provisional Government; all power to the Soviets, including over production and distribution of goods; peace with Germany; abolish the army in favor of a people's militia; seize the landlords' property and nationalize all land; combine all banks into one National Bank under Soviet control; adopt the name "Communists"; create a new Socialist International and work toward world revolution.[43] When he finished, he called upon everyone to sing the "Internationale," but no one knew it.[44] Most of the faithful were skeptical, but only some voiced even mild criticism that night. In the succeeding weeks, after endless disputes and many stormy meetings Lenin was able to impose unity under the essential points of his program, though only in October was he able to convince the Central Committee to stage an armed coup.

The Bolsheviks feared a spontaneous, uncontrolled uprising, which they would not control and could spoil their plans. They needed to postpone the revolution until they knew they could manage it and gain sole power. In the meantime, they walked a fine political line, fomenting eventual revolution while discouraging a premature one. At times they canceled demonstrations, which confused and discouraged workers. But anarchists ensconced at the Durnovo mansion on the Polyustrovskaya (now Sverdlovskaya) Embankment were eager to whip up fervor. On June 5 some 70 of them armed with machine guns and grenades seized the printing plant of a right-wing newspaper. When government troops responded by laying siege to the Durnovo mansion, the anarchists called upon Petrograd's soldiers, sailors, and workers to go on strike and revolt. They began doing so, looking to the Bolsheviks to join in and lead them. But the Bolsheviks, caught by surprise, considered the uprising premature and backed down, calling off a demonstration. The crisis subsided, the Bolsheviks lost face, and Lenin retired to Finland for a rest.

No sooner had Lenin settled down in Finland when he learned, on July 4, that army units in Petrograd had mutinied because the Provisional Government had decided to send some units to the front in violation of Order Number One. The mutineers rallied other troops, sailors, and workers, who called for a seizure of power. Lenin slipped back into Petrograd and again confronted the dilemma of whether to attempt his coup. He paid lip service to the rebels but was able to avoid committing to full-scale revolt, which was fortunate because the Soviet failed to back the rebels and frontline troops arrived to quell the revolt. Since the Government had issued a warrant for the arrest of key Bolsheviks on July 1, Lenin went into hiding outside Petrograd and then once more in Finland, and would return only in early October. Trotsky was imprisoned on July 22.

But the paralyzed and powerless Government was never able to catch up with events, and there were several reshuffles. The July revolt led to the resignation of Prince Lvov, and on July 11 the ambitious socialist Alexander Kerensky became Premier. He took on a retinue of aides, moved into the Winter Palace, lived in the Tsar's suite, and slept in his bed. He secretly moved the real Tsar and his family to Tobolsk in Siberia, without informing the Government. Previously as War Minister, he had courted the army and visited the front to rally the troops. In July he began an offensive against Austria which at first was a success, gaining him wide support and dampening the revolutionary mood. His Government scheduled the long-awaited Constituent Assembly for November, but Kerensky seems to have been setting himself up to become dictator of Russia before then.[45]

Others had similar aspirations. One was the army's Commander-in-Chief, General Lavr Kornilov, a flamboyant Cossack with conservative views who wanted to restore law and order and eliminate the soviets. In August, Kerensky ordered Kornilov and his forces to Petrograd to restore order in the capital, hoping to use them to take power. But Kornilov had the same idea for himself. Kerensky realized Kornilov's ambitions only as his troops were advancing on the city. Kerensky immediately dismissed

Kornilov, who refused to step down. Kerensky then made himself Commander-in-Chief and appealed to the people and loyal soldiers to "save the revolution." The city rallied its defenses under the leadership of the Soviet, which after the July Days had moved to the Smolny (as had the Bolsheviks). The Soviet and the Government under Kerensky needed maximum support, including that of the Bolsheviks, who took full advantage of the opportunity to extract concessions. The Soviet formed a Committee for the People's Struggle Against Counter-Revolution, in which the Bolsheviks became the driving force. The Bolsheviks assumed the leading role in rallying the workers, and persuaded the Soviet to allow arming the workers with between 20,000 and 40,000 rifles. As a result, the Bolsheviks expanded their Red Guards to about 25,000. They also secured the release of all Bolsheviks still in prison, including Trotsky on September 3, whereupon he became chairman of the Soviet. Kerensky also asked the Bolsheviks to use their influence with the soldiers, both to defuse the mutiny of Kornilov's army and secure the loyalty of Government troops. As a result, Bolshevik orators were allowed to harangue the troops and present their message. The soldiers were receptive because the Bolsheviks were the only party that unambiguously opposed the war and promised to bring the troops home. This message resonated with the soldiers, who in September elections to the Moscow City Duma voted 90 percent in favor of Bolshevik candidates, though most of them probably had little idea what Bolshevism meant. As a result of Bolshevik propaganda and Kerensky's high-handed treatment of the army command, his own standing with the military plummeted, and in the October crisis they would not stand by him. Meanwhile, Kornilov's march on the city dissolved in the southern suburbs, partly on its own accord when soldiers defected and partly due to a railroad strike which prevented mass transport of the soldiers.

Lenin, in Finland, was inspired by these events, as well as by gains in the August 20 elections to the Petrograd City Duma, in which Bolshevik representation jumped from one-fifth to one-third. Lenin now was convinced that the moment for the Bolshevik coup had come, and decided to turn the fight against Kornilov into a revolutionary one. "The development of this war alone can lead *us* to power," he wrote his comrades at the end of August, "but we must speak of this as little as possible."[46] The perceptive Gippius realized that the die was now cast, observing in her diary on September 1 that "Kerensky is now entirely in the hands of the maximalists and Bolsheviks. The ball is over. They have not yet 'raised their heads,' they sit. Tomorrow, of course, they will get on their feet—to their full height."[47]

Lenin now called upon the Bolshevik Central Committee to launch an armed coup and take power. Most other Bolshevik leaders opposed him, because the All-Russian Congress of Soviets had been scheduled for October 20 (later postponed to October 25) at Smolny, for which the Bolsheviks were engineering a large majority, which would make the Bolsheviks the dominant political force in Russia and allow them to force through their program. But Lenin did not want to share power

with others and subject the Bolsheviks' fate to the political process; he was not confident of gaining a majority in the Constituent Assembly in November. He wanted
first to seize power, present the "stacked" Congress of Soviets with a fait accompli,
and render the Constituent Assembly irrelevant. Only in early October, after he had
secretly slipped back into Petrograd, did he convince the Central Committee to
stage the coup, but then they closed ranks and organized it within a couple of
weeks. The Soviet, now controlled by Trotsky, formed a Military Revolutionary
Committee which functioned as a legitimate cover for the Bolsheviks as they armed
their supporters and planned coup operations. Meanwhile, Trotsky led a propaganda campaign to solidify support of soldiers, sailors, workers, and common citizens, appearing at outdoor rallies and in packed indoor auditoriums, including at
the cavernous Cirque Moderne on the Petrograd side. With Lenin in hiding, it was
Trotsky who "made" the revolution. The Bolsheviks tried not to speak openly of
the upcoming coup, but it became common knowledge in the city by late September. Gippius observed in her diary, "Exactly when will come the slaughter, the
cannonade, the uprising, and pogrom in Petersburg—is still not clear. But it will
come."[48]

The mood in the city was ripe for change, even if only to end the months of
tiresome strife, endless debates, broken promises, and government reshuffles. The
overwhelming sentiment was one of weariness, fears arising from an uncertain future, and a sense of hopelessness and powerlessness. The July offensive against Austria had collapsed and thousands of deserters wandered the streets. Shortages worsened, lines grew, and prices soared, but the cold months had not yet made this
unbearable. Most Petrograders had no choice but to go about their daily business
and seek distraction in the city's new movie theaters; the rich still dined in restaurants and held dinner parties. The opera, ballet, and drama theaters still functioned.
A week before the coup, the Bolsheviks discovered to their dismay the workers
were hardly in a revolutionary mood. In the event, the coup was carried out almost
entirely by soldiers.

Finally, on the night of October 24–25, Bolshevik units began occupying the
weakly guarded strategic points in the city: bridges, train stations, the post office,
power stations, the telephone exchange. Lenin, disguised in a wig and worker's cap
and with a bandage over his face, came out of hiding and slipped into Smolny, now
heavily defended and ablaze with lights. By the morning of the 25th all of Petersburg was in the Bolsheviks' control except for the Winter Palace and the area immediately around it. The takeover had been accomplished with virtually no force,
not a shot was fired, and no one had been killed. Kerensky's troops, not functional
as a military force, were unwilling to defend him and his Government. The city's
defense had collapsed like a house of cards at the lightest touch. In its essence, the
coup was as much the implosion of the Government and its forces as a takeover by
Bolshevik soldiers. The Bolsheviks' victory was assured when the Fortress garrison
of 8,000 came over to their side and the city's famous Guards regiments declared

neutrality. Some other units opposed the Bolsheviks, but to do so would be to defend Kerensky. So they stayed in their barracks. As Gippius watched the Revolution unfold, she observed, "It is so boring and disgusting that there is not even any fear. And there is no element of struggle—anywhere."[49] Indeed, Lenin later remarked that carrying out the Revolution was as easy as "picking up a feather."[50]

When a gray dawn came on the 25th, one could hardly notice that a coup had occurred. Life went on as normal, with no unusual numbers of troops on the streets. The trams were running, and the stores were open and crowded with shoppers. Akhmatova remembered being on Liteiny Bridge that day when it was suddenly raised in broad daylight. "It was the first time in my life I had seen the bridge separated during the day. Trucks, trams, people—everything hanging over the suddenly gaping bridge. I looked. Under the bridge were torpedo boats. People in the crowd said, 'The Baltic Fleet is going to help the Bolsheviks.'"[51] The Merezhkovskys too went out for a walk and saw posters containing Lenin's announcement:

> The Provisional Government has been overthrown. State Power has been taken into the hands of the organ of the Petrograd Soviet of workers and soldier deputies—the Military Revolutionary Committee, standing at the head of the Petrograd proletariat and Garrison.
> Hail the Revolution of workers, soldiers and peasants!

But unlike in February, few people cared what was going on.

What was left of the Government was holed up in the Winter Palace, weakly defended by a motley assembly of teenage cadets, Junkers, Cossacks, and the Women's Battalion. Kerensky himself awoke in the Tsar's bedroom that morning, looked out the window and saw Palace Bridge guarded by Bolshevik sailors. His telephone was cut off. Abandoned, he decided to flee Petrograd, hopefully to rally troops at the front and return with them to retake the capital. Desperate for transportation, he commandeered a Pierce-Arrow belonging to the American Embassy and sped out of the city at around 9:00 A.M., without telling the rest of his Government. According to their plans, the Bolsheviks were supposed to have taken the Palace by then. Lenin was beside himself with rage, issuing demands to storm the Palace. The Congress of Soviets, at which he wanted to announce the Revolution would be meeting later that day, and the coup, had already been announced on the streets.

But the Bolsheviks had few troops and Red Guards by Palace Square, and it took until late evening to ready an attack. But by then no storm was necessary. Over the course of the day and evening, most Palace defenders slipped out through its many entrances, leaving only a token force to guard the remaining Government officials. An ultimatum demanding surrender was sent to the Government inside, but it went unanswered. Only a few Bolsheviks stood around Palace Square as another quiet evening descended on the city. So far hardly a shot had been fired. Chaliapin sang that evening at the Narodny Dom, while Karsavina danced at the Mariinsky.

Finally, by 11:00 P.M., the cruiser *Aurora*, manned by Kronstadt sailors and moored downriver by the Nikolaevsky Bridge, did signal an assault by firing a blank round (due to an oversight, it had only blanks). Cannon from the Fortress, cleaned and made operable only hours before, fired some three dozen shells at the Palace, hitting it only twice. Soldiers and Red Guards were to storm the Palace from Palace Square, but the legendary storming of the Palace in fact never occurred. Rather, earlier in the evening the Bolsheviks were able to slip in through side entrances and unlocked windows, mainly on the undefended Hermitage side of the Palace, many in search of loot. Thus, the Palace was already largely occupied by Bolsheviks when the stragglers wandered through the main entrance from the Square. Only minor struggles erupted inside, though on the Square machine guns strafed the Palace walls from time to time. By then Karsavina was already having dinner at the home of her friend, Edward Cunard, on Millionaya Street just off Palace Square. "Machine guns rattled with renewed zest," she recalled. "I had an uncomfortable feeling that I might get hit on the shinbone."[52] Thus, the Palace was secure by around 2:30 A.M., after which the victors looted some of its contents.

Meanwhile, at Smolny the Congress of Soviets had begun its session. Lenin waited eagerly for news from the Winter Palace, letting others speak until he knew that the Palace and power was theirs. The Congress was in an uproar not only due to the coup but over underrepresentation of the moderate socialist parties. In protest, the Menshiviks, most SRs, and the other left factions walked out, leaving only the Bolsheviks and Left SRs. The news that the Palace had been taken arrived only at about 3:00 A.M., after which Anatoly Lunacharsky read a proclamation of Lenin announcing Soviet power, peace, land for the peasants, and worker control of production. The session ended only shortly before 6:00 A.M. and reconvened late in the evening of the 26th. With only his allies now in the audience, Lenin was greeted with tumultuous applause and announced a new all-Bolshevik Provisional Government called the Soviet of People's Commissars, which was to rule until the Constituent Assembly convened.* He also presented his famous decrees on peace and on land, which were passed by acclamation. The Revolution was over. "Petersburgers," wrote Gippius that evening, "are in the hands and under the control of the 200 thousand [man] band of the garrison, headed by a group of swindlers."[53]

RED PETROGRAD DURING THE CIVIL WAR

The Revolution plunged Russia into a bloody Civil War from which it would emerge only in 1921. With the Bolsheviks in firm control of Petrograd, fortunately the war was waged entirely outside the city. The closest threat came in the autumn

---

*The Assembly was convened in Petrograd on January 18, 1918, with the Bolsheviks a distinct minority, so Bolshevik troops dispersed it the next day.

of 1919 when General Nikolai Yudenich led a small army of Tsarist soldiers, Estoni-ans, and British advisers to Pulkovo Heights just south of the city. Stalin had been charged with the defense of the city, and Lenin regarded Yudenich's appearance so close to town as a failure of Stalin. He sent Trotsky, now Commissar of War, to take Stalin's place, and he quickly gathered forces and drove Yudenich away within four days. The only war action that the city itself saw came from the Germans. By late February 1918 the Germans had advanced close to the city and it seemed that they might try to take it. On March 2, 1918, they dropped bombs on the city from air-planes. This was hardly necessary; the city was already being decimated both phys-ically and by hunger and disease, and on March 3 peace was signed. About a week later, Lenin announced that Russia's capital would be moved to Moscow, remark-ing that "worker-peasant power should be completely consolidated here."[54] Soon the Bolsheviks were calling Petrograd merely the Petrograd Labor Commune.

Ostensibly, the capital was moved to Moscow as a temporary expedient because the Germans threatened Petrograd, but in reality it marked Russia's turn against the West and Petersburg's traditions. Lenin detested Petersburg. To him it symbolized the Tsarist regime, cosmopolitanism, and an independent intelligentsia. In a rever-sal of Peter the Great's reasoning for establishing St. Petersburg, Lenin realized that he needed a fresh start far away from the Imperial capital and its independent-minded citizens—in Moscow, whose ancient traditions, it turned out, were more akin to the policies of the Bolshevik regime. Soon after the move to Moscow, Lenin expressed his feelings about Petersburg in a letter to his friend Gorky, in which he urged the writer to abandon the city. The former capital, Lenin told him, was in-fested by "an embittered bourgeois intelligentsia, understanding nothing, forgetting nothing, and learning nothing, and *in the best case*—and the best case is a rarity—is perplexed, desperate, groaning, repeating old prejudices, fearful and frightened of itself. . . . Here, as an artist, you cannot observe or learn anything."[55] The former capital's intellectuals think they are the mind of the nation, Lenin wrote, but in fact, they are "the droppings."[56]

When Bely wrote, "If Petersburg is not the capital, then there is no Petersburg," he probably did not expect this literally to come true. It now seemed that it would. With the capital in Moscow, the city and Russia turned inward, away from the West, in many ways taking Russia back to the Muscovite past, "undoing" Peters-burg. It began the day after the coup.

The new regime's first actions in the capital the morning after the coup set the tone. Copies of non-Bolshevik newspapers in the city were confiscated and burned in the streets, and their offices were closed. But authority on the streets soon broke down, far more so than after the February Revolution. Crowds of soldiers, sailors, and workers went on an orgy of looting, pillaging, and destruction. At one point robberies reached 800 per day.[57] Shops were emptied and burned, palaces and man-sions were defaced and stripped of their valuables, and the wine cellars and liquor stores and warehouses were emptied. The Winter Palace had thousands of barrels and tens of thousands of bottles, as did the residences of rich merchants and nobles and the city's restaurants. The soldiers and workers went on drinking binges. The Bolsheviks, convinced that their enemies were encouraging this to besot the Bolshevik soldiers and undermine the Revolution, sent more soldiers to guard the others, but they too succumbed to temptation. Then firemen were sent to flood some cellars, but they got drunk instead.

Nor was life sacred. The rioters were ready to kill on the least pretext: for food, clothing, small amounts of money, and before long, firewood. One street vendor was shot by soldiers who did not want to pay the price of apples.[58] Even the Bolsheviks' new chief of security police in Petrograd, Moisei Uritsky, fell victim one night when crowds pulled him out of his sleigh, stripped off his clothes, and left him naked on the street.[59] The Bolsheviks eventually imposed order by force. In order to fight "sabotage" and political opposition, at the end of 1917 they created the notorious Cheka, based at No. 3 Gorokhovaya Street and headed by the prison-hardened and iron-willed Felix Dzerzhinsky. From modest beginnings, he built it into the mammoth machine of repression that made the Soviet reign of terror possible. In his honor, in 1927 Gorokhovaya Street was renamed Dzerzhinsky Street, which it remained until 1991 when the original name was restored.

The pillaging threatened the city's many art treasures, first and foremost in the Winter Palace and Hermitage. Fortunately, after the Germans occupied Riga in September 1917, it was decided to remove the art treasures of the Hermitage to Moscow as a precaution. Two trainloads made it out, the second only days before the October Revolution, while the third was delayed and the plan was overcome by events.[60] While the Hermitage and its treasures escaped largely unscathed, many rooms in the Winter Palace itself were damaged, and much of its artwork and valuables were defaced or stolen by the Bolshevik occupiers. In the estimate of Benois, not an admirer of imperial artistic taste, the loss was not significant.[61] He did, however, help secure the protection of the city's real treasures, which in the wake of the February Revolution were threatened by the revolutionary tumult. In March 1917, he, Gorky, Chaliapin, and leading artists formed a Commission of Beaux Arts. They proposed a Ministry of Arts with Diaghilev as Minister, and worked out a plan to preserve the city's art and historical monuments. They presented the plan to Prince Lvov, who approved it and even gave them the right to form a special militia to protect art and museums, which was never done. But they did form the Council for Protection of Cultural Treasures of the Provisional Government, headed not by Diaghilev (busy in Paris) but of Fedor Golovin. When the Bolsheviks took power, it became the Collegium for the Preservation of Monuments and Museum affairs.[62] Over the years the body's name changed, but it survives today to guard the city's art and architectural treasures.

But most people were concerned with survival, not art. The Revolution and Civil War disrupted transportation, supplies of food, fuel and other necessities, and public services. The country's rail and transport network was in worse condition than in February 1917, and the Petrograd winter got off to a frosty start with four blizzards in December. The food and fuel crisis grew far worse than that of 1917. Real famine set in. The city's animal population—horses, dogs, cats, birds, and the animals in the zoos—disappeared. Horse meat was called "civil war sausage." The Acmeist poet Nikolai Otsup remembered that "it was no longer necessary to remove carrion from the streets—dogs grew thin tearing it apart, and people growing thinner would pull it apart."[63] Lacking fuel, many factories shut down or worked short shifts. The supply of electricity was erratic, usually available to citizens for only a few hours each evening. To keep from freezing, people tore down wooden fences and houses for precious firewood, and felled trees in the city's parks and outskirts. Some 3,000 wooden houses in Petrograd disappeared in 1919–20.[64] As the city's water supply, plumbing, and sanitation systems deteriorated and people's constitutions weakened, epidemics of diseases like typhus, cholera, dysentery, and influenza spread and killed thousands. "Petrograd is dying as a city," Gorky lamented in 1918. "Almost daily they pick up people who have dropped from exhaustion right in the streets. . . . Dead horses lie in the streets. The dogs eat them. The city is unbelievably dirty. The Moika and Fontanka are full of rubbish. This is the death of Russia."[65] In 1919, Petrograd's death rate was 80 per thousand.[66]

In addition to suffering from hunger and cold, the former aristocrats, Tsarist officials and soldiers, and priests were singled out for psychological punishment. Nobles who still had provincial estates fled the city and some escaped abroad, but many remained. They lost their homes, money, possessions, and inches off their waistlines. Those who were able to retain valuable antiques and works of art were soon peddling them at fire-sale prices, in depreciated currency or for barter, in order to acquire simple necessities. Some ended up selling their last possessions on the streets. The Bolsheviks purposely set these "former people," as they were known, to street cleaning and other menial labor before the public eye, in order to wreak revenge, humiliate and degrade them, and demonstrate the reversal of fortunes to the people.

In these conditions, inflation spun into hyperinflation and the economy disintegrated. By 1920 the city's industrial production stood at only one-eighth of that eight years earlier.[67] The port, already immobilized during the war, remained dormant. The average Petrograd worker's real wage in 1918, already only one-fourth what it had been in 1913, by the end of 1919 was only ten percent of that in 1913 and in some cases was as low as two percent.[68] Peasants were unwilling to sell their produce for paper money. People survived through the black market and barter, with flour emerging as the currency of choice. Unable to make ends meet through their regular jobs, workers spent much of their "workdays" moonlighting, dealing in the black market or fabricating simple articles for barter to peasants in the provinces, while their factory supervisors either turned a blind eye or joined in. Absenteeism at factories in Petrograd rose to an average of 30 percent.[69] To obtain food, residents packed up goods and scrambled onto crowded trains to trade with peasants in the countryside, a practice known as "bagging." Sometimes factories sent whole brigades of workers to barter with the peasants.[70] Many of the city's women, including from respectable families, were reduced to prostitution, their number reaching 30,000 in 1918. Nevsky Prospect was lined with teenage girls selling themselves for a loaf of bread, a piece of soap or chocolate; many were sent there by their own parents or husbands. For the privileged Bolshevik elite, conditions were ideal for corruption. Most of the new officials, flush with power, could not resist temptation and began operating more like mafia than government servants. In 1919 Lenin was shocked to learn that officials in the department responsible for provisioning the city had diverted supplies of foodstuffs to the city and were selling them by the truckload to black marketeers out of the back of Smolny.[71]

For most Petrograders life became unbearable, and they fled in droves to the countryside, by foot, in carriages, on horseback, or train. Between 1918 and 1920, the city's population plummeted from 2.3 million to 720,000.[72] Most who left were peasants or laid-off worker-peasants who had arrived in recent years and still had ties with their native villages, the very people in whose name the Revolution was staged. Indeed, to the new government's dismay, many of the refugees were Bolsheviks. In the six months after the Revolution the number of Bolsheviks in the city dropped from 50,000 to a mere 13,000.[73] While people clamored to leave, the railway system was in a state of collapse and few trains were running. When trains left for the countryside, crowds descended upon the stations and fought for spots on the trains. Overcrowded trains departed with passengers perched on car roofs, hanging out of windows, wedged between train cars, or clinging to the undercarriages. In one case, an overcrowded, unbalanced train toppled off a bridge into the Neva, drowning hundreds of passengers.[74] Abandoned by so many, and with its factories and trams not running, few cars, and little electricity, the city became like a ghost town. Its skies, in the past clouded by smoke from factory chimneys, became brilliantly clear by day, but at night the city was plunged into darkness and residents huddled around wood stoves for warmth and candles for light. In the warm months, grass grew on the city's streets. The poet Vladislav Khodasevich remembered that "pavements caved in, plaster peeled off, walls wobbled, hands broke off statues."[75] The émigré anarchist Emma Goldman, whom America deported back to Russia in 1919, described Petersburg in 1920 in her autobiographical *My Disillusionment in Russia*:

> It was almost in ruins, as if a hurricane had swept over it. The houses looked like broken old tombs upon neglected and forgotten cemeteries. The streets were dirty and deserted; all life had gone from them. . . . The people walked about like living corpses; the shortage of food and fuel was slowly sapping the city; grim death was clutching at its heart. Emaciated and frost-bitten men, women, and children were being whipped by the common lash, the search for a piece of bread or a stick of wood. It was a heartrending sight by day an oppressive weight by night. The utter stillness of the large city

was paralysing. It fairly haunted me, this awful oppressive silence broken only by occasional shots.[76]

Akhmatova painted a similar portrait:

> The old Petersburg signboards were still in place, but behind them there was nothing but dust, darkness, and yawning emptiness. Typhus, hunger, execution by firing squad, dark apartments, damp wood, and people swollen beyond recognition. You could pick a large bouquet of wildflowers in Gostinny Dvor. The famous Petersburg wooden pavement was rotting. The smell of chocolate still wafted from the basement windows of Kraft. All the cemeteries had been pillaged. The city had not just changed, it had turned into its exact opposite.[77]

Some found a perverse beauty in such scenes. "It had a new tragic beauty of desolation," wrote Karsavina, "its long vistas forsaken, its arches like mausoleums."[78] Similarly, Khodasevich believed that "Petersburg became more uncommonly splendid than it had ever been and might ever be again. . . . There are people who look better in their coffin: so it was, it seems, with Pushkin. Doubtlessly, so it was with Petersburg."[79] The thought was echoed by Otsup: "For us the dying Petersburg was sad and beautiful, like the face of a loved one on his deathbed."[80]

Such conditions could not continue for long without a popular rebellion. It happened right after the Civil War had ended (except in Poland), four years to the month after the February Revolution. Although the country was now supposedly a worker's regime, the scenario was almost identical to February 1917. The winter was harsh and the snows heavy, Russia's transport system failed, and Petrograd was hardest hit by fuel and food shortages; many factories closed. On January 22 the bread ration was cut by one-third, while Communist Party members enjoyed privileged rations. Strikes broke out, and rallies were held at the major factories, docks, and shipyards. Workers clashed with Bolshevik troops on Nevsky Prospect and Vasilievsky Island. Thousands of soldiers joined the strikers. Even the crew of the *Aurora*, moored in the city for winter repairs, joined the demonstrators. The analogy with the February Revolution was not lost on the Bolsheviks, so unlike their Tsarist predecessors they acted resolutely and ruthlessly. On February 24 power was placed in a three-man Committee of Defense headed by the local Party chief, Gregory Zinoviev. On February 25, the city was placed under martial law, which imposed a curfew and forbade gatherings at any time. The Cheka arrested hundreds of strikers, as well as all leading Menshiviks and SRs in the city. The workers responded by demanding the overthrow of the Bolshevik regime. On February 27, the fourth anniversary of the overthrow of Tsarism, they posted the following proclamation on the city's streets:

> A fundamental change is necessary in the policies of the government. First of all, the workers and peasants need freedom. They do not want to live by the decrees of the

Bolsheviks. They want to control their own destinies. Comrades, support the revolutionary order. In an organized and a determined manner demand:

Liberation of all arrested socialists and nonparty workingmen; abolition of martial law; freedom of speech, press, and assembly for all who labor; free elections of factory committees, trade unions, and soviets.

Call meetings, pass resolutions, send delegates to the authorities, bring about the realization of your demands.[81]

News of the revolt in the city spread to the 10,000 sailors of Kronstadt, whom Trotsky had once called "the pride and flower of the Revolution." Most of them were veterans of the October Revolution,[82] but now they were disillusioned with the regime that they had brought into power. Half of Kronstadt's Bolsheviks had torn up their Party cards in 1920, and in January 1921 some 500 of them deserted the naval base. When news of the uprisings in Petrograd reached them, the sailors sent a delegation to town to investigate and report back. When they returned, a meeting was held aboard the battleship *Petropavlovsk*, and the sailors issued a resolution siding with the rebels. Declaring that the soviets "do not express the will of the workers and peasants," the sailors demanded, in addition to the usual civic freedoms, new elections by secret ballot and the right to campaign freely in advance of the vote, a *nonparty* conference of the workers, soldiers, and sailors in Petrograd by March 10, abolition of all political departments "because no party should be given special privileges in the propagation of its ideas," abolition of the Communist fighting detachments in all branches of the army and the Communist guards kept on duty in factories and mills, and full freedom of the peasants in regard to the land.[83]

On March 2 the sailors rose in full mutiny. They knew that they stood no chance as an isolated force, but they had felt the pulse of the people in the city, in whom they placed their hopes. They called upon all Russians to rise up and overthrow the Bolshevik regime. On the island, they formed the Kronstadt Revolutionary Committee, dismantled the Communist apparatus, called for new elections, and published their own version of *Izvestia*, which printed a manifesto entitled "What We Are Fighting For," which proclaimed:

In carrying out the October Revolution the working class hoped to achieve its liberation. The outcome has been even greater enslavement of human beings. . . . The glorious emblem of the toilers' state—the hammer and sickle—Communist authority has in truth replaced with the bayonet and [the barred window], created to protect the tranquil and carefree life of the new bureaucracy, the Communist commissars and functionaries. But basest and most criminal of all is the moral slavery introduced by the Communists: they have also laid their hands on the inner world of the working people, compelling them to think only as they do. By means of state-run trade unions, the workers have been chained to their machines, so that labor is not a source of joy but a new serfdom. To the protests of peasants, expressed in spontaneous uprisings, and those of the workers, whom the very conditions of life compel to strike, they have responded with mass executions and an appetite for blood that by far exceeds that of tsarist generals. Toiling Russia, the first to raise the red banner of liberation of labor, is thoroughly drenched with the blood of the victims of Communist rule.[84]

The Bolsheviks realized that their regime was at stake, and there was no room for compromise. After ultimatums failed, on March 7 the Red forces, led by Trotsky, opened an artillery barrage on Kronstadt from the shore near Oranienbaum and dropped bombs from airplanes, while in the city the sailors' families were taken hostage. The bombardment could be heard in downtown Petrograd. The sympathetic but demoralized Petrograd workers, who were already being subdued by the authorities and placated by promises that free trade would be restored, could only watch helplessly as the drama unfolded. Emma Goldman, then in the city, watched groups of workers walk past her hotel window. "Their step had lost its spring, their hands hung at their sides, and their heads were bowed in grief."[85] The Soviet press had boasted that the sailors' resistance "will go down at the first shot,"[86] but they were mistaken about the will of the sailors, who held on against overwhelming odds. The Bolsheviks were running out of time, as the ice on the Finnish Gulf would soon melt, making the island nearly impregnable and allowing it to be re-supplied by sea. The Bolsheviks launched assault after assault over the ice, its soldiers dressed in white camouflage and with machine gunners placed at their rear to shoot them should they retreat. The rebel sailors pummeled them with artillery, which broke the ice, drowning many. The final assault came on the night of March 16–17, when some 50,000 Bolshevik troops advanced across the ice. The battle raged for 18 hours, but by midnight on the 17th Kronstadt's guns fell silent. Over 10,000 of the Bolshevik attackers were killed. The next day, rebels were paraded through Petrograd and 500 of them were shot without trial. Eventually, another 2,000 would be executed, mostly without trial. Others were sent to the Solovki concentration camp on an isolated island in the White Sea.

Thus was crushed the city's last resistance to the Communist regime. It remained to see whether the Bolsheviks could capture the city's best minds.

SPIRITS IN THE MATERIAL WORLD (PART I)

The elemental upheaval that Blok and Bely had foreseen and awaited had come. But was it the new dawn that the city's artists and writers should embrace, or false like the cardboard doll in *Balaganchik*? Most *miriskusniki* and Acmeists opposed the Bolshevik regime. They saw no beauty in the Bolsheviks' idealized lowbrow culture and only ugliness in their methods. To them, true human progress must begin within individual human souls, not in collectivist ideology and economics. But the Futurists and other avant-gardists figured large among the new regime's supporters, just as many Futurists in Italy later supported Fascism there. Though they hated the banality of mass culture under the Tsars, they joined the socialists in blaming this on capitalism and in wanting to change the world, and they shared a passion for large spectacles. Whereas the Bolsheviks were the vanguard of the people in the political realm, avant-garde artists considered themselves the same in culture. They looked to partner with the Bolsheviks to create the new society, a dizzying opportunity in itself and especially welcome when the artists were starving. And what about the Symbolists? Some, like Merezhkovsky and Gippius, immediately repudiated the new regime and left Russia. Ivanov remained, waging a losing battle to channel the new culture toward a Nietzschean epiphany. Bely and Blok, having awaited and written of the coming apocalypse for so long, could not but be enthusiastic at first and they gave Bolshevism a chance. But soon they recognized it as both the cardboard doll of hope and the real Maiden of Death.

The Revolution and Civil War thinned the ranks of the city's art community and intelligentsia. The cream of the ballet remained abroad with Diaghilev. Stravinsky was in Switzerland and never returned. Merezhkovsky and Gippius, implacable foes of Bolshevism, in 1920 made a daring escape to Paris through Poland; Filosofov, who went with them, remained behind in Poland to join anti-Bolshevik forces in the Civil War. After Lenin moved the capital to Moscow, many writers and artists, including Mayakovsky, Meyerhold, Malevich, Tatlin, Altman, Alexei Tolstoi, and Alexander Rodchenko, believed the Bolsheviks would make it the center of their new culture and moved there to seek greater, government-sponsored opportunities, only occasionally returning to the former capital. But many of the literati who loved the city and were its creatures—Akhmatova, Blok, Gumilev, Mandelstam— would not even think of leaving. Akhmatova expressed their feelings in a poem:

> But not for anything would we exchange our splendid
> Granite city of glory and misfortune,
> The glistening ice of broad rivers,
> The sunless, gloomy gardens
> And the barely audible voice of the Muse.

Also remaining in Petrograd were a number of Bolsheviks and sympathizers who espoused their own vision of what culture under the Bolsheviks should be. They operated through several organizations, including the army and navy, the semi-autonomous Proletcult, and the Commissariat of Enlightenment (Narkompros). Narkompros was headed by the truly cultivated, tolerant, and humane Anatoly Lunacharsky (1875–1933). A literary critic and playwright, he became a revolutionary in 1892, eventually joined the Bolsheviks, and was briefly imprisoned in the Peter and Paul Fortress with Trotsky after the July Days. Even before the October coup, when a Bolshevik victory seemed probable, he had met with about 40 of the city's leading actors at the apartment of Yuri Yuriev, the Alexandrinsky Theater's leading actor, to assure them that a Bolshevik victory would leave the city's theaters and theater life untouched. After the Revolution, he toiled valiantly to protect the city's buildings (even churches) from the ravages of the Civil War, preserve its culture, and feed its cultural figures. By exploiting their influence with Lenin and other Bolsheviks in Moscow, Lunacharsky and Gorky were able to keep Petrograd's artistic and literary life relatively free from bureaucratic and ideological interference during the Civil War. Petrograd intellectual and cultural life in the early Bolshevik years was able to develop away from the shadow of the central government and more independently from it. These writers and artists were determined to preserve the city's rich cultural heritage, and its culture did remain vibrant.

But life was still hard. In 1920 the local writer Evgeny Zamyatin published a short story called *The Cave*, set "where St. Petersburg had stood ages ago" and where "tomorrow" is a "word unknown." The story's characters had been reduced to caveman status, hunger reigned, and families huddled for warmth around their "greedy cave god: the cast iron stove." In Alexander Grin's story *The Ratcatcher*, an allegory of the city fighting for survival, the hero does battle with evil and powerful rats who are trying to take over dying Petrograd. Such was the grim life of the city's artists, intellectuals, writers, and musicians. Most were impractical, vulnerable people with few employable skills. Fortunately, Gorky rescued many. He was one of the few intelligentsia with a practical mind, common sense, and political acumen, and he was a personal friend of Lenin. His relationship with the Bolsheviks was ambivalent. While having strong revolutionary credentials dating from 1905, he spoke his mind, championed artistic freedom, and tried to do what he considered right and humane even if it was unpopular. Initially he opposed the October Revolution. He had a regular column in the Menshevik newspaper *Novaya zhizn* ("New Life"), in which on the morning after the coup he warned in his headline "CULTURE IS IN DANGER!" On November 7 he wrote that "Lenin, Trotsky and their companions have already become poisoned with the filthy venom of power, and this is evidenced by their shameful attitude toward freedom of speech, the individual and the sum total of those rights for the triumph of which democracy struggled. . . . Lenin and his associates consider it possible to commit all kinds of crimes . . . and senseless arrests—all the abominations which Phleve and Stolypin once perpetrated."[87] As a result of such articles, the journal was closed down in July 1918. In September 1918, after an assassination attempt on Lenin, Gorky reconciled with him. Again enjoying Lenin's support, Gorky undertook to save the city's culture. (But when in 1921 the Bolsheviks no longer allowed him to work and write as he wished, he left for the West.)

Gorky worked tirelessly to save culture and intellectual life in the city, as well as the very lives of the artists and scholars. To this end he lobbied with the Bolsheviks, even Lenin personally, to obtain food rations, accommodations, and other necessities for the starving artists. Many of Petersburg's greatest talents, including Gumilev, Khodasevich, Mandelstam, Chukovsky, Blok, Piast, and Zamyatin, owed their well-being if not their survival during these years to him. Gorky began by taking as many people as he could into his large apartment on Kronverksky Prospect. In September 1918, under the loose auspices of Narkompros he transformed and combined his existing publishing house, The Sail, and the recently closed journal *Novaya zhizn* into a larger publishing organization, World Literature, which published affordable editions of classics for the broad public. There, hundreds of the city's writers, literary scholars, and translators found employment to earn money and feed their families. In December 1918, the city's writers and journalists (largely independently of Gorky and Narkompros) organized the Writers' House, which had about 600 members by early 1922. It had a dining room where 500 persons a day dined at reduced prices, warm work and reading rooms where writers could work, a library of 70,000 volumes, and a bookstore; its members began collecting materials for a literary museum. Separately, in December 1919 Gorky established for writers, artists, and musicians the House of Arts at the former Eliseev mansion on the corner of the Moika and Nevsky. When lit at night, it had the appearance of the prow of a ship and thus became known as the "Crazy Ship." Akhmatova wrote in this vein of the city and its remaining writers and artists:

> *And in truth you are the capital*
> *For us mad and radiant ones.*

The House might indeed seem like a ship of fools to an outsider dropping in on Friday evenings, when its members could be seen gathered around the piano listening to Strauss waltzes played by Albert Benois (Alexander's brother), dancing in intoxicated rapture, for a few happy moments oblivious to the hard times, their ragged clothes and heavy boots clomping on the floor.

Since Gorky viewed the Writers' House as a refuge of old generation writers who longed for the old order, it did not satisfy his artistic goals. Thus, his House of Arts was a more selective organization composed of the city's best talents and promising young writers. Gorky hoped it would be a hotbed for creativity, and it was. The House held meetings, discussions, lectures, readings, concerts, debates, and courses. New trends did emerge from the House when in February 1921 several of its young writers who stood for experimentation, free creativity and fantasy, humaneness, and brotherhood formed a loose group (not a "school") called the Serapion Brothers (taken from the name of a hermit in E.T.A. Hoffmann's tales) and began writing experimental novels and stories. Many of the House's members, including Mandelstam, Gumilev, Shklovsky, Khodasevich, Alexander Grin, and Zoshchenko, lived at the House and received rations secured through Gorky's other project, the Scholars' House. Located in the palace of former Grand Duke Vladimir on Palace Embankment, it was created in January 1920 to provide impoverished scholars with food rations, clothing, firewood, medical care, and other necessities. But like the Writers' House it had a dual purpose. It fostered scientific work and spread knowledge, and sponsored meetings, discussions, and lectures.[88]

The Revolution had provided fertile subjects for art, and the artists needed to decide what to say. So did the Bolsheviks. Only days after the Revolution, Lunacharsky invited the city's writers and artists to a meeting at Smolny to discuss ideas for a new culture. He expected an enthusiastic response, but most voted against the Revolution with their feet—only five or six came to Smolny, mainly the usual suspects from the avant-garde—Mayakovsky, Altman, Meyerhold—but also Blok. Why Blok?

Shortly before the Revolution, during the hot, dry summer of 1917, peat fires burned outside Petrograd and the smoke wafted through the city. In Blok the fires inspired a prophetic dream in which the fire of "Russian Bolshevism is stalking, but there is no rain, and God does not send it."[89] He saw the fire as purifying, and now understood his duty to Russia as an artist. "Here is *the task of Russian culture*," he wrote in his diary on August 7—"to direct this fire toward what must be burnt down; to transform the violence of Stenka [Razin] and Emelka [Pugachev] into a spontaneous musical wave; . . . to organize this violent pressure in which the possibility of violence lurks and direct it into the Rasputin corners of the soul and there to fan it into a sky-high bonfire, so that cunning, lazy, servile carnality is consumed."[90] To Blok the Revolution was not about Bolshevism, Marx, or Lenin, and it had only begun. The fire might sweep away the Bolsheviks too before it was over. Blok thought of the Revolution as an elemental, triumphal cleansing of biblical proportions of the type that the Symbolists had prophesied, essential for Russia's rebirth. And so, despite the violence and suffering, the Revolution gave reason for hope. And so Blok came to Smolny.

Soon the snows came and the city was shrouded in white. Blok once told a friend that he loved to walk through Petersburg at night during blizzards, when whirlwinds of snow enveloped the city and made it nearly disappear.[91] The sound of the Petersburg wind had been a haunting presence in Bely's *Petersburg*, promising to usher in the Apocalypse. At night the city was dark from lack of electricity and kerosene, cars and trams were few, and the city resounded with footsteps, and shots—those of Red Guard patrols on the streets. Like others, Blok was starving, unable to feed his family, and his apartment was cold. But the less fortunate roamed the streets, begging. Surely the holy Revolution must mean more than this, he thought, so Russia must have hope and press on.

Such were the thoughts and images in Blok's mind as he sat down at his desk in January 1918 to compose his epiphany of the Revolution, *The Twelve*, which began:

> *Black night.*
> *White snow.*
> *Wind, wind!*
> *A man can't stand.*
> *Wind, wind—*
> *All over God's world.*

Twelve Red Guards appear from this cold black-and-white night and a drama unfolds to a cacophony of sharp sounds in changing rhythms: cries, shots, shouts, songs, the wind. The Twelve pass by fires, then a beggar. A soldier sleeps with a prostitute, an argument erupts, and she is shot in the fray. They march on, past a downtrodden bourgeoisie and a hungry dog, finally receding back into the black and white from which they came. Only then does one learn that at their head, unseen in the blizzard, impervious to bullets, bearing the bloodied red flag of revolution, and wearing the white rose crown of the Apocalypse, walks Jesus Christ; the Twelve are disciples. And throughout the poem Blok exhorts, *"Forward, Forward/Working people."*

The Twelve was published on March 3, the day when peace was signed with Germany, but it was Blok's poem that stuck in people's minds. The Bolsheviks did not know what to make of it. But it resonated deeply with people as Russians, so the Bolsheviks made it their poem, too. Blok encored with *The Scythians*, defiantly addressed to Europe, the "slanderer" of the Revolution and Russia and with whom Russia was still at war when the poem was completed on January 30. He first proclaims Russia's essence as still Asian and violent, and then turns to the theme of East or West:

> For you—ages, for us—a single hour.
> We, like obedient slaves,
> Held a shield between two hostile races
> The Mongols and Europe.
>
> . . . .
>
> Russia—is a Sphinx. Rejoicing and grieving,
> And steeped in blood
> She looks, looks, and looks at you
> With both hatred and love.

He then calls upon Europe to come from the war with sheathed sword and embrace Russia before its is too late so they can "become brothers." The poem is overshadowed as much by the war as by the Revolution, but clearly Blok is suggesting that the Revolution may represent a turning back to Russia's Eastern heritage and the undoing of Petersburg.

While Blok was finishing *The Twelve*, Gippius and Akhmatova met each other for the first time, at a Red Cross fund-raising event; hardship and charity had achieved what the city's fractured highbrow intellectual life had not. The event occurred shortly after the Bolsheviks' dissolution of the Constituent Assembly, which had been convened in the city, and so what was ostensibly a charitable function became something of a protest against the Assembly's dissolution. There Akhmatova read one of her few overtly political poems:

> Your spirit is clouded by arrogance,
> And that's why you can't see the light.

You say that our faith is—a dream,
And this capital—a mirage.

You say that my country is sinful,
And I say your country is godless.

She had penned these verses in 1916, aimed at Rasputin. But now she saw (like Blok soon would) the Bolsheviks as the new Rasputin devil that had to be driven out. Akhmatova became Petersburg's Cassandra, a role that Mandelstam had assigned to her in a December 1917 poem.[92] She foresaw that hard times and suffering would befall the city and threaten its ruin, but also that its spirit, like her own, would remain strong. She proudly refused to work for the Bolsheviks, generously shared her meager fare with others, and grew still thinner. Chulkov observed in a letter to his wife that Akhmatova had "turned into a horrible skeleton dressed in rags,"[93] but hardship did not silence her pen. Both she and Mandelstam dedicated poems to the city and its sufferings. Mandelstam, who liked to call the city Petropolis, wrote:

On a terrible height a wandering fire,
But is that really how a star glimmers?
Transparent star, wandering fire,
Your brother, Petropolis, is dying.

Gumilev was in Paris serving as the Provisional Government's military attaché when the October Revolution erupted, but he could not stay away from his native city and returned in April 1918. When asked why, he replied, "I fought the Germans for three years and I hunted lions in Africa. But I've never seen a Bolshevik. Why shouldn't I go to Petrograd? I doubt it's more dangerous than the jungles."[94] More seriously, Vyacheslav Ivanov explained Gumilev's return by noting that "a great poet always shares the fate of his nation."[95] When Gumilev arrived, Akhmatova asked him for a divorce. It hurt his pride, but he did not fight it. He then dove headlong into many projects, as always. He worked at World Literature, started a new journal, *New Hyperborea*, and formed a literary circle called the Resonant Shell. He took Blok's place as head of the Petrograd branch of the All-Russian Union of Poets, and later joined the House of Arts. He gave lectures and readings of his poems (even to sailors and workers), taught the art of translation, as well as poetry. He did not expect his students to become great poets, but considered it important to enrich their lives. Sometimes his work fell under the auspices of Bolshevik organizations, but he acted as if the Bolsheviks did not exist and seemed to dare them to touch him. He openly declaimed his monarchist poems, ostentatiously crossed himself when passing a church, and maintained his aristocratic manner and, to the extent possible, his exquisite dress. He once remarked, "The Bolsheviks despise conformists. I prefer to be respected."[96] Khodasevich left an apt description of Gumilev's entrance at one function:

> With befitting lateness, Gumilev appeared with a lady on his arm, who was shivering from the cold in a black dress with a deep slit. He walked, tall and arrogant in his frock coat, passing through the hall. He was trembling from the cold, but he bowed grandly and politely to the right and left and conversed with acquaintances in a worldly tone. . . . His entire appearance said: "Nothing's happened. The Revolution? I haven't heard anything about it."[97]

His poetry grew richer and more profound in these years, his great talent reaching its full power. Now his verses were not only beautiful and well crafted, but were fuller in meaning and drew on his greater human experience. Sometimes he also touched on politics, as in *The Wayward Tramway*, in which contemporary Russia, turned upside down under the Bolsheviks, was likened to a tramway hurtling out of control, not unlike Gogol's famous troika.

In the aftermath of the Kronstadt revolt, deviations from the Bolshevik line were dangerous, and the Cheka was eager to make an example of at least one artist. They found him in Gumilev, an easy target after having penned *The Wayward Tramway*. To the end Gumilev spoke his mind, visualizing himself as a 20th-century equivalent of Pushkin honestly and courageously confronting Nicholas I. But the Bolsheviks were qualitatively different and would never tolerate the equilibrium reached in Imperial Petersburg between the rulers and the city's cultural elite. They demanded complete submission. Apparently Gumilev was asked by anti-Bolshevik plotters to help organize officers and the intelligentsia against the Bolsheviks in case of a popular uprising, but the apolitical poet declined the invitation. When the Cheka learned of this, they arrested Gumilev on August 3, 1921, simply for having failed to report it to the authorities. In fact, there was no organized plot, but the Cheka invented one, claiming a vast conspiracy led by the "Petrograd Military Organization." Gumilev's friends and colleagues, not knowing the reason for his arrest, did not consider the situation urgent or dangerous, but out of principle lobbied hard for his release through the House of Arts, the Poets' Union, the Union of Writers, and Proletcult. Gorky unfortunately was in Moscow and could intervene with Lenin only at the last minute, too late to have any effect. On August 25 Gumilev and some 60 others were put up against the wall and shot without trial. His friend Adamovich observed that "no one imagined that the end would be so sudden and fatal. We petitioned for him never thinking that there would be an execution—there was absolutely no reason for it. Even by the Cheka yardstick."[98] But as one Chekist later explained, "In 1921 seventy percent of the Petrograd intelligentsia had one foot in the enemy camp. We had to burn that foot!"[99]

But the Bolsheviks did not need to resort to arrest and execution to kill off independent artists. The increasingly stifling atmosphere itself became enough. *The Scythians* was Blok's last poem; his pen was now silent. He found work at the Bolsheviks' new cultural institutions and Gorky's World Literature, partly to bring his ideal of culture to the people, partly to earn a wage. Meanwhile, Lyuba recited *The Twelve* to audiences for bread money. While Blok was glad to be able to work with his enlightened acquaintances, within months he was disillusioned with the new regime. It held Russia in a grip of terror, and its leaders had no conception of or interest in culture as he understood it. "What one cannot deny the Bolsheviks is their unique ability to exterminate life and destroy individuals," he wrote in his diary in 1919.[100] For Blok the music of the revolution had stopped. "The old music has gone but the new music has not yet come,"[101] he told a group of the city's actors in February 1921. When he realized that the new music would not come, it broke his spirit. He grew weaker and his heart ailment worsened. "I'm suffocating!" he told Annenkov. "The world revolution is turning into world angina pectoris."[102] "The louse has taken over the world; this is already a done deed," he wrote in his diary. "And now life is going to change, but not in the way we had hoped, not in the way we would like and for which we have lived— in another way entirely."[103] Blok sat in stunned depression and hunger in his cold apartment, each day carrying firewood up several flights of stairs like a packhorse. He needed treatment in the West for his heart, but Lenin delayed issuing his passport, fearing that he would speak out against the Bolsheviks in the West. Lunacharsky and Gorky intervened on his behalf, but too late. He died in Petersburg on August 7, 1921, four days after Gumilev's arrest. His passport came that evening. The clinical cause of death was endocarditis, but this was treatable and in truth he died from depression, nervous exhaustion, and malnutrition. The music gone, he had no reason to live. His death was as spiritual as his life.

Like Pushkin, Blok was driven to destruction by a society in which he could not live and breathe, and when citizens learned that Blok had died, the outpouring of grief in the city resembled that after Pushkin's death. But unlike in Pushkin's case, Blok's funeral was held in the city, and he was buried at Smolensky cemetery. Men of letters carried his coffin, among them Bely and Pyast, followed by a cortege of some 200 friends and thousands of admirers. Akhmatova was there too, in a simple gray dress, large hat with a veil, her tears flowing without restraint; it was at this funeral that she learned of Gumilev's arrest. Annenkov recalled her standing out from "among thousands in the crowd, though we had never met, and she left a wonderful impression of herself! . . . I thought for the first time in my life I had seen real beauty—and that such beauty really 'could save the world.'"[104] There were no speeches at Blok's grave; the greatest voices of Russia were at a loss for words, considering them worthless to express their feelings. But the crowd sang quietly to the strains of Tchaikovsky, perhaps trying to find the right music. After Pushkin's death, Lermontov had captured people's feelings in verse. Now, Akhmatova wrote:

We have brought to the Holy Mother of God,
In our hands in a silver coffin
Our sun, extinguished in torment—
Alexander, pure swan.

"We felt it was the end of a life, the end of a city, the end of a world," wrote one participant, Blok's friend Nina Berberova.[105]

Indeed, the deaths of Blok and Gumilev marked a crossroads in the relations between the city's intelligentsia and the Bolsheviks. Culture was on the edge of the abyss. From then on, the Bolsheviks insisted, artists must do their bidding or perish. To an intelligentsia that had built up a tradition of independence since the 18th century, this was a declaration of war. The regime could not be overcome, but neither could the intelligentsia's spirit. The city might no longer be the capital, but the few proud artists who remained, especially Akhmatova and Mandelstam, would preserve the city's traditions. The city itself became a martyr, and they along with it.

But others simply left in anger or disillusionment: Chaliapin, Balanchine, the pianist Vladimir Horowitz, the violinist Nathan Milstein, Dobuzhinsky, Glazunov, Alissa Rosenbaum (Ayn Rand), and, in 1926, even Benois. Dobuzhinsky paid his farewell tribute to the city in his remarkable series of lithographs entitled *Petersburg in 1921*. Describing them in his memoirs, he explained, "The city was dying before my eyes a death of incredible beauty, and I tried to the best of my powers to capture its terrible, deserted and wounded look. This was the epilogue of its entire life. It was turning into another city—Leningrad, already with completely different people and an entirely different life."[106]

CHAPTER 13

Becoming Leningrad: The Revenge of Muscovy

Russia, an autocracy with a great deal of slavery . . . contains the main element of socialistic and communistic theories. . . . Attempts to realize such dreams threaten society with destruction, its reversion to savagery, and eventually a one-man dictatorship. . . . As the saying goes, "extremes meet."

DECEMBRIST MIKHAIL FONVIZIN
writing from exile in 1849[1]

With Stalin in the Kremlin, Moscow at last wreaked its revenge on St. Petersburg, seeking to wipe out the restless reformism and critical cosmopolitanism which this "window to the West" had always symbolized.

JAMES BILLINGTON[2]

> *That was when the ones who smiled*
> *Were the dead, glad to be at rest.*
> *And like a useless appendage, Leningrad*
> *Swung from its prisons.*
> *And when, senseless from torment,*
> *Regiments of convicts marched,*
> *And the short songs of farewell*
> *Were sung by locomotive whistles.*
> *The stars of death stood above us*
> *And innocent Rus writhed*
> *Under bloody boots*
> *And the wheels of the Black Marias.*

ANNA AKHMATOVA, *Requiem*

THE ROARING TWENTIES ON THE NEVA

After years of war, revolution, civil war, and the harsh policies of War Communism, Russia was exhausted. The unrest in Petrograd and Kronstadt in February–March 1921 had shown Lenin that people's suffering, patience, and appetite for Great Causes had reached its limit. He admitted to his comrades at the Tenth Party Congress in March 1921: "We have failed to convince the broad masses."[3] In order to allow the country to recover and regain the people's support, that month Lenin introduced as a temporary expedient his New Economic Policy (NEP). In the countryside, peasants were again allowed to keep and sell their produce (after paying a new tax), which allowed the consolidation and increased efficiency of agriculture under the kulaks (begun under Stolypin) to resume. The state retained ownership of medium and large manufacturing enterprises but allowed small plants and retail outlets to be privately owned, and about 75 percent of retail trade ended up in private hands. A new currency, the *chervonets*, was introduced, which by 1924 was used for 90 percent of all accounts,[4] and inflation was brought under control. New laws were enacted to stabilize business. NEP was an economic success and lasted until the first Five-Year Plan was implemented beginning in 1928 and forced collectivization of agriculture in 1929.

Petrograd and its economy also revived. The city's infrastructure was repaired, the streets were cleaned and paved, the buildings painted. New trees were planted and colorful storefront signs replaced those which had become firewood. Fuel deliveries resumed, and beginning with the 1922 harvest food again became plentiful. During NEP some 8,000 privately owned small workshops were established, though heavy industry lagged due to lack of capital, loss or obsolescence of equipment, and the reluctance of foreign investors to reenter Russia. Thousands of new retail shops, supermarkets, and restaurants opened their doors. The city's population recovered from its low of 720,000 in 1920 to 1,775,000 in 1929.[5]

With their material needs met, the city's residents could enjoy life again and the city returned to its former bustle. Akhmatova observed that "everything started to look as before—restaurants, smart cabmen, beautiful young women in furs and diamonds."[6] And these women were usually escorted by the classic figures of the age, the newly rich, mostly small-time businessmen called "NEPmen," who in Russian conditions, whether by necessity or choice, operated partially on the far side of the law. Not knowing what would come tomorrow, they spent their newfound riches lavishly and conspicuously on luxuries, fine restaurants, cabarets and other night-clubs, casinos, and women, provoking the ire of the rest of society. (This would happen again in the 1990s.) They also became the target of scorn and satire by the city's artist community. Nevsky Prospect at that time was popularly called "NEP-sky," and the theater designer Boris Erbstein once walked down that street on all fours on a dare just to shock the "NEPman shits."[7] Indeed, Akhmatova perceived that the city's new life "was all pretend—it was only pretending to be like it had been before. It was all spurious. The past had disappeared irrevocably. Its spirit, its people—the new was only an imitation of the old."[8]

Be that as it may, city life teemed with excitement and new things, aided by a new generation that had only been in its teens during the period of war and revolution and passionately wanted to be modern and start or be part of something new. For this they turned to the West, especially America, and emulated the Roaring Twenties. They took their cue from the many American movies playing in the city's theaters. In 1922 the city received 300 titles from the West, mainly American, and hundreds more poured in over the rest of the decade and became the main fare on the city's silver screens.[9] Charlie Chaplin and Buster Keaton became household names, and Petrograders became more familiar with the faces of Hollywood stars than those of Russian culture or politics. Their favorites were the swashbuckling hero Douglas Fairbanks (called "Mr. Electricity"), who starred in adventure films like *Robin Hood* and *The Thief of Baghdad*, and his actress wife Mary Pickford.[10]

In 1924 American jazz became the rage after Meyerhold used a jazz band to titillate the audience in his production of an otherwise anticapitalist play, *The Trust D.E.*, at Petrograd's Conservatory. American jazz singers, musicians, and dancers visited the city, and jazz fashions caught on and were sold in the city's haberdasheries. Soon the city had its own Concert Jazz Band, which played on American instruments brought by its founder, Leopold Teplitsky, from his tour in New York and Philadelphia.[11] American dances like the fox-trot (which many Communists considered decadent, even pornographic), the shimmy, and the Charleston entered the city's nightclubs. The cabaret too developed floor shows to new levels, with an erotic flavor to satisfy the tastes of the NEPmen (also replicated in the 1990s) being performed regularly at the Hotel Europe, Comedy Theater, and at the Gambling House. Western influence was felt here too, but dance was an art in which Russia had always excelled. The young and entrepreneurial George Balanchine choreographed some cabaret floor shows while still in ballet school, once shocking the audience with the then-racy move of the male lead lifting his partner in an arabesque and carrying her offstage.[12]

City readers were also addicted to contemporary Western literature. The adventure stories of Jack London were by far the most popular, with Conan Doyle detective stories and pulp adventure novels not far behind. But the Soviets were quick to match them with their own Communist adventures and pulp stories, which became known as "Red Pinkertons." The most popular of these was *Mess-Mend, or A Yankee in Petrograd* (1924), by the Petrograd writer Maria Shaginyan under the pseudonym Jim Dollar, set in the city. In it a group of American factory workers save Petrograd (now bearing the utopian name Radio City) by thwarting a conspiracy of capitalist millionaires who are plotting the destruction of socialism, a conspiracy which goes awry when some of them visit Radio City and are captivated by that socialist utopia. Indeed, after the October Revolution a new movement of revolutionary culture had emerged devoted to building the new utopia through the arts.

SPIRITS IN THE MATERIAL WORLD (PART II)

Chekhov once said that if a Russian does not believe in God, it is only because he believes in something else. In this case, many of the city's writers and artists, especially the Futurists and other avant-gardists, were intoxicated by the Revolution. And because there was no other ready revolutionary aesthetic, they initially dominated revolutionary culture by default. They saw the overthrow of Imperial and bourgeois culture as the new dawn of which so many of them had spoken, and they seized the opportunity to realize their ideas for Russia's new culture. The avant-garde composer Arthur Lourie, who became Commissar of Music, expressed this enthusiasm:

> I heard the music of the revolution. Like my friends, the avant-garde youth—artists and poets—I believed in the October Revolution and immediately joined it. At first the young fanatics said they could now realize our dreams, and that in pure art neither politics nor any kind of force would intervene. We were given full freedom to pursue whatever we wanted in our sphere; nothing like this had ever happened before . . . anywhere in the world. . . . It was a fantastic and improbable time.[13]

Initially, no one imposed conformity, and no one had any inkling of the horrors to come. In fact, the heady artists visualized themselves as a cultural revolutionary vanguard analogous to the Party in the political and economic sphere, but which would work independently in parallel with the Party. The Bolsheviks' theme of proletarian culture seemed to mean raising the cultural level of ordinary Russians, not the leveling of art under political direction.

The artists got their first chance in the May Day celebrations in 1918 when Nathan Altman and other avant-gardists literally painted the town red with banners and posters, with novel Cubo-Futurist images of workers, soldiers, and peasants, and again in the first anniversary of the October Revolution when the Winter Palace (now renamed Palace of the Arts since it had been made part of the Hermitage) and Palace Square were draped with their designs.[14] Describing the decorations, one observer remarked that "legs walked by themselves, the head remained behind, while the arms, also separate from the torso, waved overhead. . . . Especially memorable for me was the enormous red cap worn by the tower of the City Duma. Exactly like a clown in the circus."[15]

But as before the Revolution, the avant-garde believed that theater was the best vehicle for expressing their vision. In their view, revolutionary content demanded revolutionary forms as well, for which theater provided the most scope. The theater combined various forms of art, was a mass spectacle that could be used for education and breaking down class divisions, and performances could be staged almost anywhere, by anyone and with little investment of money or technology. Moreover, unlike Russia's stars of music and ballet, theater producers and actors were not in a position to emigrate and practice their art abroad, so the talent had remained at home. The municipal theaters were put in the capable hands of Gorky's common-law wife, Maria Andreeva, which helped ensure state support and subsidization. This financing allowed Petrograders to attend performances for free or nearly free, and the city's theaters were packed every night. Many new theaters were opened; their number reached 45 offering a total of over 40 productions each evening.[16] These included the famous Bolshoi Drama Theater established in 1919 on the Fontanka, though in civil war conditions most were makeshift affairs reminiscent of the city's first theater established by Peter the Great's sister, Natalya.

With the theaters freed from commercial concerns, artists focused on producing what they wanted. The first and natural reaction of the intelligentsia in control of theater—Gorky, Lunacharsky, Blok, and Andreeva—was to stage the classics: Shakespeare, Sophocles, Aeschylus, Aristophanes, Hugo, Schiller, as well as Russian classics such as Gogol's *Inspector General*. One reason for this was that at first no works from the post-Revolutionary era yet existed. Russia's first revolutionary play was Mayakovsky's *Mystery-Bouffe*, staged by Meyerhold in Petrograd's Communal Theater of Musical Drama on the first anniversary of the Bolshevik Revolution, with sets by Malevich. The plot, based loosely on the theme of Noah's Ark weathering the Flood, portrayed a group of proletarians and capitalists who had survived the Revolution; the workers begin to rid society of parasites and to build their paradise, the vision of the new socialist city of which the audience was given a glimpse. Though the play's creators eschewed *zaum* language, the spectacle was sufficiently opaque to expose them to the charge that their work was unintelligible to workers. A backlash ensued which kept the avant-gardists out of the May Day celebrations of 1919, but they were back in force in 1920, when they staged five mass spectacles, this time making sure that the entertainment could be understood by all. In these spectacles, the producers built on the city's tradition of carnival as well as the Greek Dionysian festivals in order to break down the barriers between the performers and audience and create a feeling of *sobornost*, subordinating the individual to the common good and portraying Petrograd itself as a happy commune.[17] But in practice it more resembled the circus theater of the Roman Coliseum.

The first such mass spectacle was *The Mystery of Liberated Labor*, performed on May Day on the steps of Thomon's Stock Exchange on the *strelka* of Vasilievsky Island, which traced through world history the various rebellions against exploiters, beginning with the Spartacus revolt and culminating with the October Revolution. For the third anniversary of the Revolution in November 1920, Nikolai Evreinov staged *The Storming of the Winter Palace*, reinterpreting the non-event which had become legend. For the spectacle Nathan Altman draped Palace Square (now called Uritsky Square in honor of a fallen Bolshevik) with Futurist canvas panels of workers and peasants which were illuminated by giant arc lights, and surrounded the Alexander Column with a bright orange and red rostrum that made it appear that the Column, representing the old order, was going up in flames. The sets were designed by Tatlin, Meyerhold, and Yuri Annenkov. The square was thus transformed into an open-air auditorium in which thousands of performers representing workers (blacksmiths brandishing hammers), capitalists (in tall hats and carrying money bags), 25 identical Kerensky puppets, and the Red and White armies reenacted the Red victory before an audience of 100,000. The *Aurora* reprised its famous shot, soldiers (many more than took part in the actual "storming") fired machine guns and overcame the Whites. After the Bolsheviks entered the Palace, 50 of the upper story windows were illuminated so that the audience could watch a shadow play of the struggle inside accompanied by the crackle of gunfire. Then a rocket signaled victory, Kerensky fled in women's clothes, and in the finale everyone on the square sang the "Internationale."

The city authorities played up the international socialist theme in those early years. Since the city had lost its capital status, the ambitious Petrograd Party chief Zinoviev wanted the city, the cradle of the Revolution, also to become the center of the international socialist movement and eventual capital of a commonwealth of socialist states, a role for which the city's cosmopolitan traditions suited it. And for messianic Russians, it was not hard to transform the Muscovite Third Rome into the Communist Third International, which likewise was to be dominated by Russia.[18] Petrograd would be not a window to Europe, but the *center* of the new Europe in which the old Muscovite messianic national idea would be realized, and Zinoviev would be its Bronze Horseman. This utopian vision reached its peak with Tatlin's proposed Monument to the Third International, the model for which was exhibited in Petrograd during the third anniversary festivities in November 1920. Meant to surpass the Eiffel Tower, it was to be an open, conical, spiral-shaped structure reminiscent of the Tower of Babel but aligned off-vertical, 400 meters tall and spanning the Neva. Inside, high off the ground and stacked on top of each other would be three glass chambers—a cube, a pyramid, and a cylinder—which would revolve at speeds of once per year, once per month, and once per day respectively. The cube would house the legislative meetings and large conferences of the International, the pyramid was for its executive and administrative offices, and the cylinder on top would contain a visitor and press center, publishing offices, a radio station and movie hall. But the project remained a utopian dream due to lack of resources and engineering questions about its design. The image of Petrograd as the utopian Radio City in Shaginyan's *Mess-Mend* was borrowed from Tatlin, also taking on a three-tiered tower design with a radio antenna on the top to broadcast its vision to the world. In Radio City, man had conquered nature: its residents grew their own food, manufactured their own products, disease and death were unknown, and even the Petersburg swamps had been drained. But the rest of the world has not caught up, and thus the city is a revolutionary vanguard that must defend socialism at home and carry the revolution abroad. Such a utopian achievement was for the moment out of reach, but Petrograd's artists still visualized the city as the leader of world socialism as well as of the international avant-garde movement in the arts. One of Petrograd's mass spectacles in 1920 was *For a World Commune*, staged in July for the delegates of the Meeting of the Third International.

But the common people and many Bolshevk loyalists never warmed up to the highbrow "revolutionary" art of the avant-gardists, whom they regarded as show-off bohemian intellectuals with bourgeois origins who were out of touch with the worker. Some ideologists believed that the worker's state required a more down-to-earth proletarian culture divorced from Russia's past culture and aligned with the programs of the Party. The dominant early force in this movement was the Petrograd organization Proletkult ("Proletarian Culture"), a semi-autonomous organization under Narkompros. It was founded by Lunacharsky's brother-in-law, the Petrograd writer and thinker Alexander Malinovsky, who had taken the surname Bogdanov ("God-gifted") and wrote two socialist utopian novels, *Red Star* (1918) and *Engineer Menni* (1919). Bogdanov instituted cultural programs in factories, the army and the navy, organized lectures and worker-oriented plays and art exhibits. He recruited into the effort many of the initially enthusiastic poets, including Bryusov, Blok, Bely, and Khodasevich. Courses were set up to train actors, directors, and instructors on a mass scale. A movement called "people's theater" invited mass participation in plays, including street theater. A proletarian-oriented though modernist People's Comedy Theater was also established in 1920 by Sergei Radlov. Within a short time Proletcult had branches throughout Russia and had some 80,000 activists at work.

The Bolsheviks also sought to transform the plastic arts. In April 1918, in order to break down traditionalist imperial art, they abolished the Academy of Fine Arts, creating in its place the Free Art Studios. The Studios were open to all rather than to a privileged group. Art now spread to elements of everyday life, a realm in which the ideas of the avant garde and proletarian artists were closer. Constructivists in particular advocated immersing the people in an environment saturated with the new art and culture to create a new consciousness, so their designs appeared in industrial art, furniture, china, packaging, and couture, including idealized (often unisex) worker's clothing designed by artists like Rodchenko, Tatlin, and Varvara Stepanova. The city's old Imperial Porcelain Factory, by then renamed the Lomonosov Porcelain Factory, geared up to produce dinnerware and commemorative plates with avant-garde designs, slogans, and symbols of the Revolution, and portraits of its leaders, known as "propaganda procelain."

Bogdanov and his follower Alexei Gastev were also proponents of the super-science of "tectology," which he had championed in his multivolume treatise, *The Universal Organizational Science (Tectology)* (1913–22). He advocated, through the application of scientific studies, transforming man's work routine, personal life, and even speech into an idealized symphony of efficient, beautiful, and perfect movements, both as an individual and in the work collective. Gastev proposed that everyone sleep and rise in unison and mechanize their speech to use shorter expressions and acronyms (which in fact became a mainstay of Soviet culture). He founded an organization called the Time League whose members carried time cards to record the day's activities down to the minute in order to achieve greater efficiency. His ultimate vision, set forth in 1919 in the journal *Proletarian Culture*, was indeed a scary inversion of the Communist theme of capitalist dehumanization of the worker:

> The psychology of the proletariat is strikingly standardized by the mechanization not only of motions, but also of everyday thinking. . . . This quality lends the proletarian psychology its striking anonymity, which makes it possible to designate the separate proletarian entity as A, B, C, or as 325, 075, and 0, etc. . . . This signifies that in the proletarian psychology, from the one end of the world to the other, there flow powerful psychological currents, for which, as it were, there exist no longer a million heads but a single global head. In the future this tendency will, imperceptibly, render impossible individual thinking.[19]

By late 1920 many had had enough of proletarian culture, which had produced no real art and soon degenerated into a kind of political correctness. That year the Petersburg writer Evgeny Zamyatin completed his dystopian novel *We*, parodying visions such as Gastev's through its hero, named D-503, who forms an "irrational" attachment to a woman, I-303. Many yearned for a more substantial new culture that could compete with Europe and America. But to many the avant-garde did not fill the bill. Another direction was needed.

It was at this point when Lenin, now free from the distractions of the Civil War, took stock of Bolshevik culture and was distraught, declaring that "the Communist kernel lacks culture."[20] Lenin had traditionally conservative artistic tastes and was offended by much avant-garde art. But if the avant-garde was bad art, proletarian art to him was non-art, a banality that was the antithesis of revolution. In an October 2, 1920, speech to the Communist Union of Youth, Lenin dismissed Proletkult's theories as "utter nonsense" and argued that "proletarian culture must be the logical development of those resources of knowledge that mankind has produced under the yoke of capitalist society. . . . One can become a Communist only when one has enriched one's memory with the knowledge of all the riches that mankind has produced."[21] Lenin called for greater cultural differentiation, autonomy in art, and more recognition of the role of the individual.[22] Trotsky too, in *Literature and Revolution* (1923), popularized the notion of the old intellectual elite as sympathetic but apolitical "fellow travelers" *(poputchiki)* of the Revolution, who would have to be the mainstay of culture until the classless society was achieved. Petrograd's cultural establishment complained about state interference in art. "D'Anthes bullet didn't kill Pushkin at all. The absence of air killed him," argued Blok in 1921. "*Peace* and *freedom*. They are indispensable to the poet for the liberation of harmony. . . . Let those officials who intend to direct poetry along some channel of their own, encroaching on its secret freedom and hindering it from fulfilling its mysterious purpose, beware of worse nicknames [than the 'mob']."[23]

Proletkult was closed; Bogdanov went into medicine, dying in 1928 from an experiment that he performed on himself.[24] Mass spectacles were scaled down, cultural programs in the armed forces were curtailed as the soldiers and sailors were decommissioned, as were cultural programs in factories. A Union of Writers was formed, dominated by the old literary establishment. Narkompros's budget was cut, and the Party and the Young Communists' League (Komsomol) assumed a greater funding role. Not all Communist artists agreed with Lenin's new pluralism, and a group of them, mainly from Moscow and led by Mayakovsky, formed the Left Front of the Arts (LEF) to promote utilitarian art and literature that served the Soviet state. But for the time being Lenin's views became the policy.

Lenin's decision also marked a turning point for Petrograd. On the one hand, the greater role of the Party and Komsomol meant greater cultural funding for Moscow at Petrograd's expense, and over the next two decades Moscow replaced Petrograd as the center of most state-sponsored, mainstream Soviet Party culture and academics. Students at Moscow's State Institute for Cinematography, for example, received stipends, while those in Petrograd's Institute for Screen Art did not; the Soviet film industry gravitated toward Moscow.[25] Other institutions like the Academy of Sciences (headquarters) were moved to Moscow. On the other hand, Lenin's decision helped the city's culture maintain its distinctiveness. In Petrograd, artists and writers, whether the traditionalists of Old Petersburg on the right or the experimental, avant-garde artists of the left, were out of the limelight, preserved more independence and pursued, for a time at least, their bliss. Over the succeeding years and until the fall of the USSR, the city became home of the country's more independent, out-of-favor, Western-oriented cultural trends, whether of the right or the left.

THE REVIVAL OF OLD PETERSBURG

The traditional cultural elite who loved Petersburg moved quickly after the Revolution to preserve the city and its heritage. In 1918 Narkompros created its Department for Museums and the Preservation of the Historical Heritage, focused largely on Petrograd and headed by Alexander Benois. In 1921, the Society for Old Petersburg was reestablished by, among others, Benois and Count Valentin Zubov, and in 1923 also became affiliated with Narkompros. The Society worked to preserve the city's architecture, organized lectures and excursions around the city, and fostered Petersburg-oriented literature through its Circle of the Bronze Horseman.[26] The old role of the Merezhkovskys' Religious-Philosophical Society was to some extent taken up by another society, Petrograd's Resurrection, which published a journal called *Free Voices* and boasted at its peak some 200 members. Dominated by the historian and religious thinker Georgy Fedotov, it sought to fuse religion and communism in the Christian Socialist tradition of Hugues Lamennais.

The ballet circle of Vladimir Dmitriev and the young George Balanchine revived classical ballet traditions and the phantasmagorical "Petersburg Hoffmanniade," while Dmitriev and Mikhail Bakhtin through their literary meetings and books revived interest in Gogol and Dostoevsky.[27] Publications about Petersburg flooded the shelves. A new edition of Bely's *Petersburg* came out in 1922, and in 1923 an unexpurgated edition of the *Bronze Horseman* was published with illustrations by Benois. Chief among the new books was *The Soul of Petersburg* (1922) by the Petersburg scholar Nikolai Antsiferov, who became known as the bard of Petersburg. Written to heighten awareness of the city's rich culture, traditions, and meaning, the book traces the evolution of the city's mythos over time as expressed in the words of its poets and writers.

Part of the revival was aimed at preserving the city's art and architectural treasures, first and foremost those of the Hermitage. From the start Lunacharsky took the Hermitage and the Winter Palace under his protection and looked after them personally. After the October coup a quick inventory of the Palace was taken, and about half of the items looted from the Palace were recovered from markets in the city and the baggage of people fleeing the country.[28] In 1918 the Palace became part of the Hermitage, whose collections were soon nationalized. In 1918 Nikolai Punin was appointed Commissar of the Hermitage and Benois curator of its picture gallery. Meanwhile, the Bolshevik government wanted many of the Hermitage paintings to grace their new capital, Moscow, which lacked a state art museum. After difficult negotiations, an exchange was agreed under which some 400 Hermitage paintings were given to Moscow to found the new Pushkin Museum while the Hermitage received a lesser number of modern paintings from private collections in Moscow, which is how the Hermitage acquired its impressive collection of Impressionist and early 20th-century works. Other Hermitage works were sent to Ukraine and other Soviet republics. On the other hand, the Hermitage reaped a windfall from the confiscated collections of the Romanov family and Petrograd's nobility and merchants, including those of the Yusupovs, Stroganovs, and Vorontsovs. A much sadder fate befell the Museum's objets d'art. Thousands of silver and gold crosses, icon covers and other church art, jewelry, book bindings, and even the original iconostasis of Kazan Cathedral, were melted down and sold by weight to finance the new Soviet government. Even Alexander Nevsky's silver sarcophagus was barely saved, when curators convinced the authorities that it had propaganda value and offered other silver to melt down in its place.[29]

Later on, in the 1920s and early 1930s, thousands of paintings, Fabergé creations, and other artworks were sold to collectors in the West, including Marjorie Merriweather Post, Andrew Mellon, Armand Hammer, and Calouste Gulbenkian. The sales began in the early 1920s and reached their height when massive infusions of foreign currency were needed to finance Stalin's first Five-Year Plan. But in conditions of worldwide depression the masterpieces fetched only a pittance. Rembrandt's *Christ and the Samaritan at the Well*, for example, brought less than $50,000 when auctioned in 1931. Fortunately, however, many of the paintings ended up in Western museums.

THE BRONZE AGE

After the Civil War, a new generation of modernist Petrograd poets, writers, dramatists, painters, and composers brought fresh ideas to the city's culture, inaugurating what some have termed the Bronze Age. Most of their works were non-Marxist and traditionally Petersburgian, but the artists generally worked through officially sanctioned institutions. Chief among them was the State Institute for the History of the Arts, which had been founded in 1912 by Count Zubov as an aristocratic institution. But in 1920 it was accredited by Lunacharsky, and Zubov let the organization have his mansion on St. Isaac's Square, after which he became known as the "red Count" and the Institute the "Zubov House." It was divided into Departments of Fine Arts (dominated by retrospectivists), Verbal Arts (a bastion of the Formalists), the History and Theory of the Theater, and the History and Theory of Music under the famous critic Boris Asafyev. The Academy of Fine Arts was also restored in 1921; many traditionalists returned while many avant-gardists exited. The Petrograd branch of the new Union of Writers was dominated by non-proletarian writers from the old literary establishment.[30]

Literature again became the queen of the arts, supplanting the theater. Prose rather than poetry now predominated, much of it about the old and new city; even poets like Mandelstam became noted for their prose. One group that was infatuated with pagan, Dionysian Russia, calling themselves the Scythians, saw the Revolution as an expression of Russia's Eastern, Asian heritage, a revolt against the repressed, structured civilization of Europe.[31] The most creative and dominant movements of the period, however, emerged among former Acmeists and their younger followers at the House of Arts. The Opayaz movement led by Victor Shklovsky, a resident at the House, matured into Formalism, which focused on literature, especially poetry, as a linguistic craft with less attention to the content and the author's inspiration. They conducted valuable studies in versification and thus made good teachers and mentors for the younger generation, epitomized by the Western-oriented Serapion Brothers, the age's purest example of artists in the Petersburg tradition.

This group of talented writers and poets, whose mentor was Zamyatin and members included Vsevolod Ivanov, Lev Lunts, and Mikhail Zoshchenko, originally wanted to call themselves Nevsky Prospect, but decided that the term "Serapion Brothers" better described their outlook on art and life. The name was taken from E.T.A. Hoffmann's *Die Serapionsbrüder*, in which a group tells exotic tales while gathered around the hermit Serapion. Though the Serapions discussed each of their works and published as a group, they had no group ideology, were apolitical, stood for absolute artistic independence and freedom, and chafed at the Communist expectation that literature serve the regime's cause. In his 1922 polemical essay *Why We Are the Serapion Brothers*, Lunts declared:

> We came together in days of revolutionary and powerful political tension. "Who is not with us is against us!" they told us from the right and the left. "With whom are you, Serapion Brothers? With the Communists or against the Communists? For the Revolution or against the Revolution?" With whom then are we, Serapion brothers? We are with the hermit Serapion. That means—with no one? That means—a quagmire? That means—intellectual esthetes? Without ideology, without conviction, in an ivory tower? No. Each of us has his own ideology, his own political convictions; each one paints his home his own color. So it is in life. And so it is in stories, novellas, dramas. But together we, the brotherhood, demand one thing: that the voice not ring false. That we believe in the reality of a work of literature whatever its color may be.[32]

They wrote experimental, exotic, and fast-paced stories, novels, and poems of excellent craftsmanship in the Western manner with names like *Hollow Arabia*, *Envy Bay*, *The Purple Palimpsest*, and *The Emery Machine*, as well as critical essays such as Lunts's *Go West!* They satirized the philistinism of the NEP age as well as the proletarian orientation of the authorities, utilizing a technique called *skaz*, which parodied Soviet newspeak and the crude speech of the contemporary uneducated philistine or proletarian. Zamyatin wrote numerous stories, novellas, and novels highlighted by *We*, which went unpublished in Russia but circulated underground. Not surprisingly, the Serapions had continuous battles with the censors.

The Serapions' most well-known writer, whose popularity in Russia was second only to Gorky, was Mikhail Zoshchenko (1895–1958). The son of a Ukrainian gentry painter, he moved to St. Petersburg in 1904, studied law at St. Petersburg University, and briefly served as commandant of Petrograd's Post Office. He volunteered for the Red Army in the Civil War "to fight against the nobility and landlords, a milieu I know quite well enough," but he was deemed physically unfit. Instead, he joined the House of Arts, where he became a Serapion, developed his writing talents and emerged as the master of ironc *skaz* and the contemporary heir to Gogol, with whom he was often compared. Petrograders began copying his vignettes and style in their own speech. His method was so ambivalent and tongue-in-cheek that he could pass off with the censors as proletarian literature what was really satire of Bolshevik philistine culture.

When state subsidies for theaters ended after the Civil War, many of Petersburg's theaters could not make ends meet and closed down. Radlov's People's Theater was one of the casualties. Balanchine recalled that in one of its last productions, it had to stage the *Polovtsian Dances* with only two dancers from the troupe, who invited Balanchine and his friend from the audience to join in.[33] But Petersburg's theater culture survived and even flourished, in both its traditional and avant-garde varieties. The most innovative theaters were the Factory of the Eccentric Actors (FEKS), founded in 1922, and the Theater of Worker Youth (TRAM), also founded in 1922 and headed by Mikhail Sokolovsky. FEKS was the most traditionally Petersburgian of the two with its Western orientation and style of performance. It also drew on the style of Radlov's short-lived People's Comedy Theater, from which it hired its now-unemployed circus acrobat Serzh. FEKS was thoroughly modern and avant-garde but not of the left; rather, it was down-to-earth, topical but only mildly political, and generally evocative of the fast-paced life of NEP Petrograd. Its productions celebrated boulevard culture, American dance, jazz and film, the circus, Pinkertons, and the new technology of everyday life. When FEKS staged Russian works, they were turned inside out. The first major production of FEKS was its 1922 adaptation of Gogol's play *The Wedding*, but the public barely recognized it among the barrage of blinding lights, shouts, sounds, action that included pantomime and acrobatics, and a backdrop which at one point turned into a screen showing a clip of Charlie Chaplin fleeing from the cops.[34]

TRAM, on the other hand, became the haven of the theater world's radical utopian left once the mass spectacle had run its course and strictly proletarian, people's theater had fizzled. Sokolovsky preferred to work with new talent from the working class rather than "spoiled" professional actors. Capitalizing on the theater's name and its personnel as impeccable proletarian credentials, Sokolovsky in fact proceeded to stage unorthodox, experimental, and improvisational works, usually short pieces utilizing music, songs, and novel lighting and including audience participation. For several years its musical director was a talented, promising young composer named Dmitri Shostakovich, a true child of the theater.

Born in 1906, Shostakovich was also Russia's first musical child of the Revolution. A prodigy, he grew up in confusing and difficult times, and as an adult was the 20th century's most tormented composer. When in 1919 he entered the children's classes at Petrograd Conservatory, Rimsky-Korsakov was gone and Glazunov was in charge, then the leading influence on Petrograd music. Thus, whereas Stravinsky and Prokofiev had studied there under the influence of Rimsky-Korsakov at the expense of Tchaikovsky, Shostakovich drew heavily from Tchaikovsky (also Mussorgsky) even as the Communists sought to marginalize him as a Tsarist relic. Glazunov's Conservatory was still conservative and academic in the tradition of the Belyaev Circle, but Asafyev's Music Department at the Zubov House had entered the 20th century never looking back. With the Institute's literature section dominated by the Opoyaz and its theater section by the school of Meyerhold, its musicians, influenced by these trends, were equally modern, devoting their studies to the works of Europe's leading contemporary composers—Schoenberg and the Second Vienna School, Paul Hindemith, Eric Satie, Darius Milhaud, and Stravinsky. The atmosphere was heady as the Petrograd music world collaborated through intense discussions, lectures, and concerts to create its own brand of modernism.

Shostakovich knew them all and attended the discussions and concerts. In the early 1920s, many of Europe's leading composers, including Béla Bartók, Alban Berg, Hindemith, Milhaud, and Alfredo Casella visited the city.[35] Shostakovich absorbed it all and by age 19, still a student, he was ready with his First Symphony.

It premiered at the Leningrad Philharmonic on May 12, 1926, in the former Assembly of the Nobility, under the baton of Rimsky-Korsakov's former student, Nikolai Malko. Shostakovich's mentor Glazunov was in attendance, about to lose his place as the city's leading composer. The symphony was composed on a grand scale, joyous, youthful, and melodic, showing traces of Tchaikovsky and Russia's more recent masters, Rimsky-Korsakov, Stravinsky, and Prokofiev, as well as Richard Strauss and Mahler, yet the composer had fused them into a style uniquely his own. The symphony's success with the Leningrad audience and critics was spectacular, and soon it was being conducted by Bruno Walter in Berlin and Leopold Stokowski in Philadelphia. The city and the world had a new musical hero.

The city's ballet tradition suffered a worse fate. Because of the Revolution the Mariinsky had lost its patron, the Tsar, as well as its main audience—the court, aristocracy, and bourgeoisie. Its star dancers had fled abroad, and the Communists at first gave preference to other art forms more attuned to the worker's state. Isadora Duncan, now in her early 40s and a supporter of the Revolution, at Lunacharsky's invitation moved to Petrograd amidst the hardships of the Civil War to start her own dance school and help transform Russian culture. In the absence of electricity, sometimes she danced only to the light of torches brought onstage before a shivering audience wrapped in overcoats. She often performed to the "Internationale" and other revolutionary songs, now clothed in a red rather than white tunic and waving a red banner, and converting Tchaikovsky's *Slavonic March* into one of the proletarians. But her flame blew out when she died in an auto accident in 1927. Petersburg's real hope lay with a young dancer who once said that Duncan danced "like a pig."[36] He was Georgi Balanchivadze, a promising student at the Mariinsky school, who later changed his name to George Balanchine. About a year after graduation, he and several other young dancers, mainly from the Mariinsky, emerged from the artistic circle of Vladimir Dmitriev to form Evenings of the Young Ballet, dedicated to reinvigorating ballet in the city. Their first production at the aptly named Experimental Theater in the old City Duma building on Nevsky, in which they performed in novel costumes to Balanchine's modern choreography, was a sensation. He attracted a large following, and soon he and a group of his dancers were invited on a foreign tour in 1924. By then having made enemies at the Mariinsky and seeing greater artistic opportunities abroad, Balanchine defected to the West during the tour to work with Diaghilev and embark on his long and amazing career there. Like Diaghilev, Stravinsky, and Vladimir Nabokov, he became an ambassador of Petersburg and acquainted the world with its culture.

Petersburg's school of painting also lagged under the Communists and produced no new major talents. As the members of the left avant-garde fell out of favor and left the city for Moscow or abroad, Pavel Filonov stood out as the city's remaining independent genius. He initially welcomed the Revolution, considered himself its "soldier," and offered his Analytical Art in its service, but at heart he was an independent. He organized exhibitions of modern artists, taught his methods at the restored Academy of Fine Arts, in 1925 opened the Collective Masters of Analytical Art (known as the Filonov School), and also did sets for theater productions, including Igor Terentyev's famous adaptation of Gogol's *Inspector General*. But over the years he grew disillusioned, which yielded his largely abstract yet emotionally poignant watercolor, *Formula of the Revolution*.

LENINGRAD AND STALIN

The year 1924 was a year of transition for the city in more ways than one. The winds of change began blowing in from abroad in October–November 1923 with the failure of the German revolutionary uprising, which dashed hopes of an international socialist revolution any time in the near future and, consequently, Petrograd's presumed role in leading it. Thus, after Lenin died on January 21, 1924, it was somewhat in desperation that Zinoviev, with Stalin's agreement, pushed a resolution through the Petrograd Soviet calling for the city to be renamed Leningrad ("City of Lenin") in honor of the Revolution's leader. By linking the city with Lenin and reminding of its status as the cradle of the Revolution, he hoped to elevate the city's status and preserve its new revolutionary mythos as the torchbearer of Communism. (The city authorities periodically lobbied for returning the capital to the city using this argument.) The name change was made official two days later at the Second All-Union Congress of Soviets, which claimed to be "fulfilling the unanimous request of the workers of Petrograd." But the Congress also voted to entomb Lenin on Red Square, showing that Stalin and the Party really intended to make Moscow the new shrine of Communism. Soon Stalin proclaimed his inward-looking policy of Socialism in One Country. The window to the West was closing.

Another blow came in September 1924 when the city suffered a horrendous flood accompanied by high winds. As floors of buildings disappeared below the rising waters, the electricity went out, and human activity came to a silent standstill, the city was transformed into a scene of primal chaos where the only sounds were those of crashing waves and the haunting "oo-oo-oo" of the wind like that in Bely's *Petersburg*. The flood came almost exactly 100 years after the November 7, 1824, flood made famous by Pushkin's *Bronze Horseman*. The point was not lost on the city's residents and press, who made all sorts of comparisons, even noting that the flood level of 13 feet fell just seven inches short of that in 1824. Some considered the flood punishment for the name change, some as reflecting the chaos into which the Revolution had thrown the country, while others conjured up the usual visions of a doomed city. In the *Bronze Horseman* Pushkin had been ambivalent over the tension between the individual and the monolith of the state. As the Soviets tightened their grip, the city now feared that the monolith would dominate as never before. Stalin proved them right.

After Lenin died, Stalin became Chairman of the Central Committee of the Communist Party, and within a few years he had eliminated his principal rivals. Like Lenin, Stalin hated the city that now bore Lenin's name, considering it a den of independent intellectuals with Western, oppositionist views. But unlike Lenin, Stalin had a primitive, provincial mind, did not understand the West, and was extremely xenophobic, dogmatic, and would not tolerate opposition. To him the city's cosmopolitanism was anathema. He would not even visit the city, and instead installed a new lieutenant there to do his bidding.

Stalin found him in Sergei Kirov. Born in 1886 in the small town of Uzhum in Vyatka Province, Kirov studied engineering at the University of Kazan, became a Bolshevik in 1905, and spent time in Tsarist prisons. Kirov was an avid reader (at his death he left a library of 20,000 volumes) and loved to write, so when he was freed he went into journalism in the town of Vladikavkaz in the Northern Caucasus, where he rose to become senior editor of a newspaper. He remained there during the Revolution, but rejoined the Bolsheviks during the Civil War. Charismatic, persuasive, and perhaps the Bolsheviks' best orator, Kirov was already heading the Party in Azerbaijan when Stalin decided that Zinoviev must be removed.

Stalin dispatched Kirov to Leningrad in early January 1926, charging him with bringing the city's Party members over to Stalin's side. Living initially in the Hotel Europe just off Nevsky, Kirov spent all his waking hours canvassing the factories and Party offices campaigning against the Zinovievites and for Stalin. Waging the struggle at the grassroots Party level, Kirov, assisted by members of the Central Committee visiting from Moscow, had the Zinovievites voted out of the Party organizations one-by-one until on February 13, 1926, Kirov was elected as the new secretary of the Leningrad Party Committee and the Northwest Regional Party Bureau. Although in their hearts most Leningrad Communists sympathized with Zinoviev, they submitted to the will of the Kremlin. In October 1927 Stalin had Zinoviev (and Trotsky) expelled from the Politburo and dismissed as president of Comintern. At the Fifteenth All-Union Congress of the Communist Party in December 1927, Stalin finally consolidated his power. Now he could implement whatever policies he desired. One of them was announced at that same Congress, the First Five-Year Plan.

While NEP had allowed the country to recover, it had left large industry untouched, and without central direction the nationalized factories had not grown. Massive investments were needed to industrialize the country, but the capitalist route of development was precluded. Centrally planned investment offered a method of building socialism quickly in one country, without waiting for the world revolution. Declaring that the Soviet Union was 50 to 100 years behind the advanced countries, Stalin called upon the nation to close the gap in only a decade.

To achieve this, Stalin drew up the first of several Five-Year Plans, which lasted from October 1, 1928 to December 31, 1932. Achieving rapid industrialization in the absence of the profit motive of capitalism necessitated turning the effort into a national crusade and creating the requisite combination of enthusiasm and coercion for it. Thus, Stalin turned the effort into a mystical poetic with its own socialist aesthetic (myth) which portrayed the crusade in terms of Russian proletarian messianism.[37] This also entailed regimentation of public and private life, orthodoxy of thought, intolerance and repression, and bringing the people to a condition of state serfdom.

Nevertheless, Leningrad, as the city's historical center of heavy industry and associated technical institutes, played a key part in the Plan. The region had gotten somewhat of a head start in December 1926 with the opening of the Volkhovstroy hydroelectric plant on the Volkhov River, which helped realize Lenin's dream of electrifying the country and provided the city the electricity needed for new industry. In 1927 numerous conferences were held in the city when developing the Plan in order to decide how to implement industrialization. After the Plan was announced, the city's Gipromez Institute designed four out of five of the Plan's largest projects. But domestic resources proved inadequate, and Stalin resorted to foreign specialists and technology, which he funded in part by selling art treasures from the Hermitage. In the conditions of the Great Depression in the West, foreign companies and specialists were happy to receive such commissions. In the end, most major projects of the Plan were designed by or in association with foreign experts and utilized foreign equipment (although the generators for which the city later became famous were used in some power stations). Even Gipromez was packed with visiting foreign specialists.

The result was an explosion of industry. The city's overall industrial production, which stood at only 1.4 times the 1913 level in 1928, increased to 4.3 times by 1932, 9 times by 1937, and 12.3 times by 1940.[38] In some sectors the city dominated the rest of the country. By the early 1930s, Leningrad production accounted for 80 percent of the country's telephones and 90 percent of its hydrogenerators, while the "Red Putilov" and "October" plants produced tens of thousands of new tractors for Stalin's new collective and state farms.[39]

The intense industrialization program brought great changes to the city. The effort required hundreds of thousands of new workers, who flocked into the city from the countryside. By 1932 the number of workers was eight times that of a decade earlier. The city's population skyrocketed from 1,775,000 in 1929 to 3,119,000 in 1939,[40] mostly in the newer industrial regions in Malaya Okhta east of the Neva and the southern regions of Avtovo, Shchemilovka, and International Prospect. City authorities raced to build new housing, schools, and transport to keep up with the influx.

Just as in former times when the city's Emperors and Empresses undertook major urban development programs, the question of overall architectural planning of the city arose. In Moscow, Stalin was replacing the original socialist Constructivism with a combination of Neoclassical, Gothic, and Russian national styles which eventually culminated in the monumental "seven sisters" buildings and eventually much of Moscow's architecture and street layout was destroyed as the Communists converted the city into their showpiece. (The Kremlin remained as their headquarters only because the immense Palace of Soviets could not be built and the site was eventually turned into a swimming pool.) Fortunately, mainly for economic reasons, the historical center of Leningrad was left largely untouched by Communist designs and today retains most of its prerevolutionary appearance. Demolishing and replacing the old buildings would have cost scarce resources and would be more expensive than building anew. While Communist ideologists considered the city's center a tainted reminder of Tsarism, most recognized its historical and architectural value, and there was little sense in fighting over it. Thus, it was decided that the center would be an inappropriate setting for building an ideal proletarian community and the new seat of local Communist power.

Instead, in 1936 a plan was approved to develop a new region of town according to socialist ideals, along what had originally been the old Tsarskoe Selo Road but by the 1930s was called International Prospect (now Moscow Prospect, leading to Pulkovo Airport). This area was largely undeveloped, but was an emerging workers region conveniently near to the many factories along that Prospect and also reachable from nearby suburbs. Designed as a complex of government buildings, parks, residences, stores, medical facilities, and entertainment spots covering 99 acres, it was to become nothing less than the city's new architectural and administrative center. Its dominating edifice would be the House of Soviets, which would house the city government. Budgetary limitations and the war intervened, and eventually the project was scaled down to 28 acres and the old historical center was never abandoned. The House of Soviets was eventually completed in 1941 but it would never house the main city government. The adjacent Victory Park, completed after the war, is also a legacy of the project.

But the city's historical center did see some changes. After the Revolution, most of its residential buildings formerly inhabited by the aristocracy and bourgeoisie, including such landmarks as the Stroganov Palace and Fountain House, were converted into communal apartments and resettled with working families from outlying regions.[41] Many churches and monasteries were torn down or blown up, though generally those having the most historical and architectural value remained. Thus the city lost Znamenskaya Church on Nevsky Prospect, the Church of the Savior on the Water on Red Fleet (formerly English) Embankment, and Nicholo-Mirlikiiskaya Church, while the Reform Church on the Moika was redesigned into a cultural palace. (Stalin had also marked the Church on the Spilled Blood for destruction but the war intervened before the order could be carried out.) Churches left standing became warehouses and fell into disrepair. The Mosque was closed, as was the Buddhist temple which had been built in 1913; its Lamas were arrested.

Kazan Cathedral was closed as an operating cathedral in 1929, and in 1932 it became the Museum of Religion and Atheism. Monuments from Tsarist times were also demolished or moved, and in many cases monuments to the heroes of socialism were erected in their place.

After the October Revolution, the names of most major streets, squares, and parks were also changed to honor Communist heroes or great events. Thus, Nevsky Prospect became October 25th Prospect, Palace Embankment became January 9th (1905) Embankment, Millionaya Street became Khalturin Street (after the terrorist who nearly blew up Alexander II in the Winter Palace), and Gorokhovaya Street became Dzerzhinsky Street (after the founder of the Cheka). One could chart 20th-century history in the city's new street names.

The 1930s also saw the construction of the NKVD* headquarters on Liteiny Prospect. In Tsarist times on the site had stood the hated Regional Court and detention prison, but it was burned in the February Revolution and the lot had stood undeveloped through the 1920s. The cold and faceless late-Constructivist NKVD headquarters became the local symbol of the Terror, which made the hardships suffered in its Tsarist predecessor seem like child's play. To city residents it became known as the *Bolshoi Dom* ("Big House"), and residents joked that it was the highest building in the city because from it one could see all the way to Siberia.

Stalin also turned his attention to building a pure "socialist" culture, known as the Cultural Revolution. It had been awhile in coming. Ever since the October Revolution Communist purists had fumed while avant-gardists and others experimented with non-proletarian culture. Beginning in 1922, mostly in Moscow, cultural organizations such as the All-Russian Association of Proletarian Writers (VAPP) and LEF sprung up devoted to eliminating "non-Soviet" modernists, and they waged militant campaigns against them.[42] They joined forces with the Komsomol, which was composed of young careerists eager to show their ideological purity and make their mark. In Petrograd, the main targets were the Serapions, the Zubov House, and NEP phenomena like Red Pinkerton literature and FEKS. Proletarian cultural journals like *Worker and the Theater* arose to compete with the city's leading cultural journal, *Life of Art*.

Gradually the purist Soviet groups had their revenge. World Literature was closed in 1924, the Institute for Artistic Culture, a bastion of the avant-garde, was closed in 1926, and in the same year several of the city's arts and humanities institutes were brought under the control of a Moscow umbrella organization, the

---

*The acronym for the political police, the People's Commissariat of Internal Affairs, into which the former OGPU (United State Political Administration) had been reorganized only a month before Kirov's murder in preparation for the purges. The OGPU had replaced the GPU, which had succeeded the Cheka. The organization became the NKGB in 1943, the MGB in 1946, and the KGB in 1953. Today its successor is the FSB ("Federal Security Service").

Russian Association of Research Institutes in the Social Sciences.[43] The fall of Zinoviev and his dismissal from Comintern marked an anti-Western turn, and the installation of Kirov and purge of Zinovievites signaled that Leningrad would become Russia's first Stalinist city, a point brought home by Eisenstein's 1927 film *October*, which opens with the dismantaling of a statue of Alexander III and goes on to dramatize the storming of the Winter Palace, figuratively demolishing it and the Old Petersburg mythos.[44] Another film directed by Vsevolod Pudovkin, called *The End of St. Petersburg*, made the message even more explicit. Meanwhile, writers and artists from elsewhere were producing art that anticipated Socialist Realism, including the 1925 novel of Fedor Gladkov, *Cement*, about a Civil War soldier who returns to revitalize a cement factory, Eisenstein's film *The Battleship Potemkin* (1925) about the 1905 mutiny in the Black Sea fleet, Dmitri Furmanov's *Chapaev* (1923) about an actual peasant soldier-hero-martyr from the Civil War (made into a film in 1934), and paintings by the David of the Russian Revolution, Isaac Brodsky.

The year 1929, when the Plan and forced collectivization were under way, was a turning point. *Life of Art* was absorbed into the upstart *Worker and the Theater*. This marked a reemergence of theater and mass spectacles with a quasi-religious content (replacing Orthodox holidays) at the expense of literature. TRAM, now under the control of the Komsomol, was deemed by Moscow a model of proletarian theater, so it set up branches throughout Russia and, late in 1929, was convinced to form an alliance with Moscow theater organizations to eliminate all vestiges of traditional theater in favor of proletarian, agitational theater. The First Musical Conference was held in Leningrad in 1929, designed to promote the creation of music for the masses. For a while, cultural and professional norms were turned upside down. Intellectuals, scientists, engineers, and other specialists were demoted while ordinary workers rose to prominent positions. Hundreds of workers were assigned to the boards of Leningrad institutes and cultural bodies. But no sooner had the Party succeeded in establishing its policy of "leveling" when it realized that intellectuals and other specialists were essential after all. It turned out, for example, that the many workers assigned to institutes and cultural organizations needed remedial courses in basic culture in order to be able to function in their new positions.[45] But the basic Party line remained. The year 1929 culminated with the arrest of most members of Petrograd's Resurrection, who disappeared in prison camps, and the ouster of the more tolerant Lunacharsky. Long before Churchill or even Stalin's Terror, the city's religious philosopher Vasily Rosanov spoke of an "iron curtain" descending, but over Russia itself.[46]

The reaction of Leningrad's cultural establishment to the events of 1924–29 was varied. A few towed the Party line. Many emigrated or defected. Those leaving the city included: Balanchine in 1924; Annenkov, who had staged *The Storming of the Winter Palace*, in 1924; Evreinov, also of *Winter Palace* fame, who defected in 1925 while his troupe was on a European tour; the philosopher Georgy Fedotov in 1925; Benois in 1926; Glazunov in 1928; Zamyatin in 1931; and, in 1926, Alisa Rosenbaum, later known as Ayn Rand, who in the West waged an unremitting war against collectivism, which among other writings featured her novel of the Russian Revolution, *We the Living*. Some like the poet Sergei Esenin committed suicide, in Room 5 of the Angleterre Hotel in 1925. But many others remained to carry on their art, and Leningrad became the country's center of resistance to the Sovietization of culture.[47]

Some of the city's intelligentsia like Mikhail Bakhtin and his circle, which was apolitical and merely discussed Dostoevsky, Freud, Kant, Bergson, and Eastern philosophy,[48] went into a persecuted underground. An underground network of intelligentsia arose, which lasted until the final days of the Soviet regime. But others, including several former Acmeists, preferred to make their stand in the open. They were epitomized by the members of the Association for Real Art *(Oberiu)*, formed in 1927 just prior to the announcement of the First Five-Year Plan and led by the Leningrad poet and writer Daniel Kharms,* then only 22, and included Nikolai Zabolotsky, Constantine Vaginov, and Nikolai Oleinikov. In the tradition of making one's life a work of art, Kharms was the classic Petersburg eccentric poet whose appearance stood out: English-style gray jacket, starched white collar, vest with a large pocket watch on a chain, cavalier's hat, a chain of amulets around his neck, walking stick and crooked pipe, and at one time sporting long hair. He was also superstitious and believed that he was a wizard.

In the best Petersburg artistic tradition, the *oberiuty* held private literary evenings in which they formulated their creed, and in 1928 published their Manifesto in *Posters of the House of Poets*.[49] They were apolitical though they considered their art in harmony with the original aims of the Revolution, while they opposed mundane proletarian art and insisted on artistic autonomy, variety, and experimentation. Against the "literariness" of Formalism they advocated restoring content from the real world to the literary arts, at the same time freeing it from conventional associations between objects and words as a means to creativity and new meanings—to make the ordinary extraordinary. But rather than use *zaum*, which by definition was "beyond" actuality, they paralleled the Cubo-Futurist painters and Filonov by fragmenting and reconstituting word images of reality into fresh combinations, odd juxtapositions, and neologisms. But the reality that the word images now had to reflect was a Stalinist one that to free artists was increasingly absurd, which their work expressed with lighthearted irony. The *oberiut* aesthetic thus produced a rebellious, absurdist poetry and theater that was the closest Russians ever came to dada and French surrealism; needless to say, they found inspiration in the West. Kharms's poems and stories, with titles like *Blue Notebook No. 10*, *What They Sell in the Stores*

---

*His real surname was Yuvachev and Kharms was only the most common of over 10 pseudonyms. Kharms was a combination of the English "charm" and "harm."

Nowadays, *An Optical Illusion*, and *Sleep Teases a Man*, were wondrous, absurd, and had a childlike freshness:

> *On Tuesdays up above the streets*
> *A gas balloon did empty fly.*
> *It soared in silence through the air;*
> *And in it someone smoked a pipe.*
> *He gazed at squares and yards below,*
> *He gazed in peace 'til Wednesday came,*
> *On Wednesday he would douse the lamp,*
> *And say, ah well, the town's alive.*[50]

A native of Petersburg, Kharms loved the city and lamented its fate under the Communists. Among his dramatic works was his *Comedy of the City of Petersburg (Part II)* (1927), essentially a dialogue between Peter I and Nicholas II, in which Nicholas, flustered and seeing his own world and old Petersburg falling apart, asks, "O Peter, where is your Russia? Where is your city, where is pale Petersburg?"[51] Of a similar vein was another courageous and remarkable work, *Goat Song*, a roman à clef by Georgi Vaginov, a former Acmeist and alumnus of Gumilev's Poet's Guild, now an *oberiut*. The novel paints a phantasmagoric portrait of Leningrad reduced to a cultural necropolis, where former intellectuals (recognizable real life literati of the city) have been turned into faceless Sovietized philistines.

The *oberiuty* were not doctrinaire and became a beacon that united the remaining Leningrad avant-garde to defend and propagate their aesthetic. They collaborated with other avant-garde artists in what proved to be the last great modernist theater-opera production and the culminating statement of the *oberiuty*, Kharms's dadaist/surrealist opera-play of the absurd, *Elizaveta Bam*, staged in 1928 at the House of the Press on the Fontanka. The score was by Pavel Vulfius, and Filonov painted not only the stage sets but also the walls of the theater and its lobby. Drawing on Blok's *Balaganchik* as well as *Victory over the Sun*, the play, partly a parody of Glinka's *Life for the Tsar*, switches between rhythmic recitative and song, in Kharms's absurdist language. The same House of the Press then held performances of a modernist adaptation of Gogol's *Government Inspector*, staged by the avant-garde poet and director Igor Terentyev. (In the topsy-turvy world of Stalinist Leningrad, the city's artists found in Gogol's works a way to portray the absurdity of Soviet life in the city under the cover of classics that had done much the same with Tsarism a century before.) Such creations could be explained to the censors as parodies of life under the Tsars, while perceptive audiences understood that the targets were the Soviets. Terentyev's production took great liberties with Gogol's plot, was set to music, and introduced erotic themes. The toilet figured prominently in the production as a metaphor for the state of the country; at one point the hero proceeds solemnly to the toilet to the accompaniment of Beethoven's Moonlight Sonata. The effect was enhanced by sets and costumes by Filonov and his students, who utilized his Analytical method to turn the characters into "speaking costumes." Thus, to the policeman's uniform were added the paraphernalia of the prison: leg irons, chains, locks and keys; the tavern waiter had a wine bottle and hams on his head and a large sausage dangling from his groin; the postmaster was dressed as an envelope complete with wax and seal and prominent postal cancellations.[52]

The *oberiuty* wrote other librettos, and among the composers with whom they were working was Shostakovich. In 1930 appeared Shostakovich's own absurdist opera, *The Nose*, an adaptation of Gogol's story, his most "Petersburgian" work at a time when the Soviets were trying to obliterate the old city's mythos. On its surface the work was politically correct—a satire of Nicholaevan Russia—but it was probably the most experimental and surreal work ever to appear in mainstream Russian opera. The complex polyphonic though at times vaudevillian music featured subcanonical instruments like the balalaika and was punctuated by all manner of loud, novel (for an opera) sounds—drunken hiccups, the scrape of the barber's razor blade, and the beat of horses' hooves. But it was the dominant libretto, partly written by Zamyatin, that the audience and critics found most bizarre. Drawing on Mussorgsky as well as the *oberiuty*, its language was absurdist, often not synchronized with the music, declaimed as much as sung, and (to suggest that the Nose's absurdity extends to us all) was delivered by the performers in a nasal twang with their hands over their noses. The artist Vladimir Dmitriev, whose circle had inspired Balanchine's Young Ballet, produced colorful phantasmagorical sets. The Leningrad of the 1920s had indeed become carnivalesque, but not in the manner that the Communists had hoped. The work was the *Yellow Submarine* of the times.

Needless to say, Communist critics were not pleased, and their reviews were scathing. To them the opera had no redeeming proletarian or socialist themes and certainly would not attract the progressive worker. After only 16 performances, the opera was taken off the stage and would not reappear for 40 years. By then Shostakovich was already working on another opera, *The Carp*, based on the unpublished but popular absurdist poem of that name by the *oberiut* poet Nikolai Oleinikov. Through the tragic fate of a lovesick carp swimming in the Neva who ends up in a frying pan, the poem laments the tragic disappearance of the old city and its ethos and the unhappy fate of its people, but under the mask of lighthearted parody. Oleinikov himself was to write the libretto. But the project was never realized because the *oberiuty* were broken up.

Leningrad had remained a bastion for non-Soviet modernism longer than any other Russian city, but the *oberiuty* knew that they were probably doomed. But like Gumilev they were prepared to go down in flames. And they did, more than they even imagined. The *Oberiu* was disbanded by the Communists in 1930, its members branded class enemies. Eventually they were so thoroughly liquidated that the group was forgotten and rediscovered only in the 1960s, and their works were published in the West only in the 1970s and 1980s. Kharms was arrested and imprisoned in 1931, then exiled briefly in 1932 before returning to Leningrad, where he was relegated to writing children's stories. But he was arrested again in 1941, declared insane and committed to a psychological ward; he died in prison the next year either from starvation or his "treatment." Vvedensky fled the city in 1936 to Kharkov, but was arrested in 1941 and also died in confinement, as did Oleinikov. Zabolotsky was arrested in 1938 as a "terrorist," but managed to survive prison, the camps, and exile in Kazakhstan. He was released in 1946 but his health was ruined; he was eventually rehabilitated and died in 1963.

In 1932 Stalin dissolved all independent literary and artistic associations, publishing houses and journals, even sympathetic organizations like LEF and the Russian Association of Proletarian Writers, replacing them with Party-run writers and artist unions, publishers, and periodicals. (In an irony of history, the initiative was called *perestroika*, the term that Mikhail Gorbachev would later adopt for a policy which proved to be the undoing of Communism.) In 1934, Stalin's henchman for culture, Andrei Zhdanov, soon to be Party Chief in Leningrad, presented to the First All-Union Congress of Soviet Writers the doctrine of Socialist Realism as the official Soviet aesthetic, which the Union endorsed. From now on, art was to be understandable to all, heroic, and directed toward inspiring and portraying the ideal socialist world that the Party and the people were supposed to be building. But the new aesthetic's definition was left deliberately vague to give the authorities maximum scope for interpretation. It was easier to say what it was not. Any art not having clear proletarian socialist content was deemed "formalist," and its practitioners and proponents class enemies. What the Party considered "formalist" was far more encompassing than the meaning of Shklovsky's original Formalism, and here too the Party kept the definition vague. As for music, Prokofiev once quipped, "Formalism is the name given to music not understood on first hearing."[53]

Indeed, it was a work of music that Stalin did not understand at first hearing which set off the campaign against formalism in 1936. It was Shostakovich's opera, *Lady MacBeth of the Mtsensk District*, conceived as the first in a grand tetralogy that would constitute Russia's *Ring of the Nibelung*. Adapted from a 19th-century novel by Nikolai Leskov, artistically it was inspired by Alban Berg's *Wozzek* and Mussorgsky's realism and focus on the spoken word. The story is of Ekaterina Izmailova, a victim of an unhappy marriage and the decadent social and psychological environment of the prior century who, aided by her lover, strangles her husband. Both are convicted for the murder; when on their way to Siberia her lover deserts her for another convict, she kills her rival and herself. From such beginnings, the tetralogy was intended to trace the evolution and triumph of the "new Soviet woman." Its start was auspicious. The opera premiered in 1934 in Leningrad to wide acclaim and enjoyed a phenomenal run in packed houses for over two years both in the Soviet Union and abroad. Then, in January 1936 in Moscow, Stalin attended a performance, unfortunately seated in a box above the percussion section. Offended by the music's dissonance and the opera's eroticism, Stalin walked out in mid-performance, sealing its fate. Two days later, an anonymous article entitled "Muddle Instead of

Music" appeared in *Pravda* condemning the opera on all counts. It was probably written or approved personally by either Stalin or Zhdanov. *Pravda* characterized the opera as "leftist distortion" and the music as a "dissonant and muddled avalanche of sounds. Snatches of melody, embryos of musical phrases drown, escape and vanish once more in clangs, creaks and squeals. . . . The music quacks, grunts, pants, and gasps, the more naturally to depict the love scenes."[54] The initial editorial was followed by other articles condemning formalism in all fields of art—architecture, literature, ballet, and painting, thus launching the grand campaign against formalism. In one of them, only a week after the initial *Pravda* editorial, the press launched an equally vitriolic attack on Shostakovich's new ballet, *The Limpid Stream*. Shostakovich would never write another opera. But he vowed that "even if they chop my hands off, I will still continue to compose music, albeit I have to hold the pen in my teeth."[55] But after that his music was cautious and lacked its original youthful, modern vigor. Modernism in Soviet music was dead.

So too by then were modernist theater and art. In fact, the initial *Pravda* editorial condemning *Lady MacBeth* accused Shostakovich of, among the other sins, "Meyerholdism." In 1928, Meyerhold and Mayakovsky, at last disillusioned with the Soviets, staged the *Bedbug: A Fantastic Comedy in Nine Pictures* (1928–29), with sets by Alexander Rodchenko and music by Shostakovich. It parodied the vulgar trivialities of Soviet culture and life, as did their even more biting sequel, *The Bathhouse* (1930). Soon after the latter work was condemned by the Soviet cultural establishment, Mayakovsky decided that he had seen enough and shot himself; Meyerhold left with his troupe on a tour of Europe and became the bête noire of Socialist Realism. Avant-garde paintings also were banned and could not be exhibited. An order went out to the Russian Museum to take down and destroy all such paintings in its collection, which included masterpieces by Filonov and Malevich. As the priceless paintings lay in piles as garbage in the halls, fortunately one curator, at great risk to himself, hid them in the Museum's basement vaults, from which they reappeared only decades later. As for the artists themselves, Meyerhold's and Filonov's days were numbered, because the full force of the Terror was about to strike.

THE TERROR IN LENINGRAD

Stalin needed an excuse to eradicate his real or perceived opponents, beginning in the political sphere with the Party apparatus, first and foremost in Leningrad. His trusted lieutenant Kirov had built up his own following in the city, was immensely popular there among the Party and the people, and recently had dared differ with his mentor Stalin on matters of policy. At the Party Congress in 1934, Kirov received more votes than Stalin in the elections to the Central Committee. Stalin now saw him as a threat and Leningrad as a rival base of power that had to be eliminated, but Kirov's popularity, Stalin decided, precluded an immediate political solution. Yet Stalin could not wait. Apparently impressed by Hitler's purge in June 1934, he decided to have Kirov murdered.[56] On December 1, 1934, a recruited young gunman, Leonid Nikolayev, shot and killed Kirov in a corridor outside his office at Smolny. On December 16, 1934, Stalin appointed in Kirov's place Andrei Zhdanov, from Nizhny Novgorod, who served in Leningrad through World War II and over time also became Stalin's de facto commissar of culture.

Posing as Kirov's friend and mentor, Stalin seized on Kirov's murder as evidence of a broad conspiracy involving much of the city, which he used as an excuse to purge real and imagined opponents in the Party and anyone acquainted with or related to them. For this purpose he gave the NKVD unprecedented powers under which it could sentence and execute anyone by administrative process. Soon he expanded the Party purge into a broader campaign of terror over the rest of society to eliminate or reeducate "class enemies" and impose Soviet uniformity in every sphere of life. Stalin wreaked particular vengeance on Leningrad, which to him still smelled of Tsarism on the one hand and of Western cosmopolitanism, independence, and reformism on the other.[57] Whenever he launched campaigns against groups or undesirable paradigms, individuals in Leningrad were the first to be singled out as examples and targets.[58] In Leningrad the Terror was directed by the local NKVD chief who had conspired in Kirov's murder, Nikolai Yezhov, and that era in Leningrad became known as the *yezhovshchina*. The window to the West was nearly closed. Travel abroad was virtually stopped. Foreign languages were taught only to specialists with a demonstrated need for them. The circulation of foreign books and periodicals was reduced almost to nil. Western literature went largely untranslated. Those caught reading it could be arrested, as could people who received letters from the West, met with foreigners, attended social functions where diplomats or other Westerners were present, or worse yet danced with them. Even veterinarians who treated diplomats' dogs were arrested. Books were removed from libraries and destroyed, art exhibits shut down.

The arrests, interrogations, torture, show trials, executions, and deportations of exiles began promptly after Kirov's murder with the arrest and deportation of some 30,000 Leningraders to exile or the Gulag. In 1935, nearly all of the former nobility in Leningrad (which had the country's greatest concentration of them) were arrested. The Terror continued in several other "waves" through 1938, and they were curtailed only in 1939 when their damage to the economy was apparent and war appeared imminent. The statistics are staggering. Within the Party, 55 of the 71 Central Committee members and 60 of 68 of its alternates in office in 1934 had disappeared by 1939.[59] While in most locations the attrition rate of Party officials was 80 to 90 percent, the rate in Leningrad was nearly 100 percent.[60] The former Leningrad Party Chief Zinoviev was among the more prominent victims; after falsely confessing to complicity in the plot to murder Kirov, he was subjected to a show trial in 1936 and then executed. The armed forces were also decimated. Over

36,000 army officers and over 3,000 navy officers were purged right down to the company and battalion level, including 3 of 5 Marshals, 13 of 15 Army Commanders, 8 of 9 Fleet Admirals and Admirals Grade I (including the commander of the Baltic Fleet), 50 of 57 Corps Commanders, and 154 of 186 Divisional Commanders.[61] Most of them were shot. Most heads of Leningrad's industrial organizations were shot. At the Kirov (former Red Putilov) Works, hundreds of key employees were fired and then arrested, and then when production and quality inevitably suffered as a result hundreds more were arrested as "saboteurs." In the nation as a whole, just in 1937–38 about 7 million people were arrested, 1 million were executed, and 2 million died in Gulag labor camps, which then held about 8 million people; another 1 million were in prisons.[62] The executed were so numerous that they were surreptitiously carried off in the night to mass graves outside the cities. One mass grave outside Leningrad was found to contain 46,000 corpses;[63] another recently discovered in Toksovo about 20 miles northwest of St. Petersburg may contain another 30,000.[64] Leningrad's four main prisons teemed with prisoners in overcrowded conditions by which the hardships of Tsarist prisons paled. The Shpalerny and Nizhnegorodsky prisons each had a few hundred cells and were reserved for the more important prisoners, some of whom even had solitary confinement. The largest number of prisoners, about 30,000 of them, were confined in the Kresty prison in horrible conditions. Up to 16 prisoners were crammed into cells that held single prisoners in Tsarist times. A separate transfer prison held those destined for the camps.[65]

In Leningrad, as elsewhere, people tried to carry on with life as if it were normal, and the authorities hastened to preserve the appearance of normalcy while at the same time striking fear into everyone's hearts. Many prisoners were ferried around in "bread trucks" rather than the infamous Black Marias, and arrests were made at night. Except for the show trials, the authorities conducted their operations in a hushed atmosphere. The city's people, their minimum needs being met, scarcely protested, each family hoping only that they would squeak through it all by not attracting attention, that they would not be the next to hear the dreaded "knock at the door." Lyubov Yakovleva-Shaporina recalled laying out all necessities each night before going to bed in case she was arrested. She also remembered seeing the masses of exiles leaving the city by train:

> My heart froze as I approached the train station. It was terrible. What I saw there one cannot relate or describe. On the platform was a vast throng. In the air was some kind of darkness, perhaps it was smoke. It was as if the city were burning, its houses enveloped in flames, and that the fire had driven thousands of destitute people into the streets. They were attempting to save whatever they could of their belongings, to carry from the fire what their strength would let them. . . . And the tears, the tears. . . . Those leaving were crying, and those remaining were crying—but will we remain for long? No one knew what tomorrow would bring. The train cars were overflowing.[66]

Hardly a family emerged from the ordeal unaffected, but the city's artists, writers, and intellectuals were among the hardest hit. Shostakovich made it through alive, but had to endure the public ridicule of the *Lady MacBeth* affair and, worse, was forced to conform his style closer to Party norms. In that period artists accused of formalism were expected to recant before their peers in a socialist confessional public exercise called "self-evaluation" in which one identifies one's mistakes and repents. Shostakovich thus subtitled his Fifth Symphony (1937) "A Soviet artist's answer to justified criticism." Indeed, it was, on the one hand, only mildly dissonant and with little that could be criticized on formal grounds. But the music had a somber, emotional lining that made the work ambivalent. It was this aspect which impressed the Leningrad audience at its première on November 21, 1937, in Leningrad under the baton of the young Evgeny Mravinsky, who would become a city institution as conductor of the Leningrad Philharmonic. The symphony depicted realisim and heroicism, but it was the composer's own, as an artist and intellectual suffering under the pressures, demands, and horrors of the times. To Leningraders the music likewise expressed their own pain, fears, and hopes, and they interpreted the work as about life during the Terror, about the conflict between the individual and the state—a musical *Bronze Horseman*. As the music ended and Mravinsky lowered his baton, many were weeping. Then they stood up and broke into tumultuous cheering and applause as Mravinsky waved the score over his head in triumph. The ovation lasted for half an hour, the audience remaining in the hall to applaud long after the orchestra had left the stage.[67] Then they returned home to grim reality.

But many local artists suffered fates worse than Shostakovich; the liquidation of the *oberiuty* had been only a start. In 1934 the already ill Mandelstam was arrested for having written an epigram critical of Stalin in the tradition of Pushkin, was imprisoned and eventually exiled to Voronezh until 1937, when he returned to a village outside Moscow. But he was arrested again in the wave of 1938 and sent to the Gulag, where he died later that year from starvation. Nikolai Klyuev, arrested in 1933 and again in 1935, disappeared in Siberia. Boris Pilnyak was arrested in 1937 for "counter-revolutionary writing" and shot the next year. Bernard Livshits and Boris Kornilov also were shot in 1938. Gorky died under mysterious circumstances in 1936, though he was given a state funeral. The jazz musician Leopold Teplitsky was imprisoned because jazz was suspect. Meyerhold, after stating in reply to a critical 1937 *Pravda* editorial that Socialist Realism had "nothing to do with art," saw his theater closed in 1938. Then he was arrested in Leningrad and severely tortured; his interrogator broke his arm and urinated in his mouth. Then he was shot in 1940. His wife Zinaida was found dead in their flat after his arrest, with 17 knife wounds and both of her eyes gouged out—a general threat to wives. Filonov survived the Terror but would die of starvation in the first months of the Blockade, in December 1941. Malevich was only figuratively slain, but literally buried. After having been reduced to painting realist portraits, he died in 1935. He was allowed to be buried in a Suprematist coffin (but minus his trademark Suprematist cross that he wanted for it), and the public lined the former Nevsky Prospect for the funeral procession, lamenting the passage of an era; his funeral symbolically marked the death of the revolutionary avant-garde.

Even the seemingly innocuous keepers of the old art were not safe. The staff of the Hermitage was purged, a story which illustrates both the depth and absurdity to which the Terror descended as well as why Leningrad was a particular target. The Hermitage management and staff were especially suspect because many were from noble families and because they cooperated with foreign scholars and museums. Thus, a scholar in the Oriental Department who had worked in Japan was arrested and shot as a Japanese spy and terrorist. Another in the Coins and Antiquities Department, which collaborated with German scholars, was arrested as a German spy. Two specialists who had arranged an exhibition of antique weapons in Kharkov, Ukraine, were arrested for supplying arms to Ukrainian nationalists and sentenced to 10 years in the camps; one of them was then retried and shot. The Egyptologist Vera Nikolayeva was arrested and shot merely because she had the same surname as Kirov's assassin even though they were completely unrelated. In all, over 50 of the Museum's curators were arrested and imprisoned or sent to labor camps, while a dozen more were shot as spies.[68] One of them was the brilliant geographer and historian, Lev Gumilev, the son of Akhmatova and Nikolai Gumilev, who worked in the Museum's library.

Akhmatova, now living with the Silver Age critic Nikolai Punin, was losing her broad audience as a younger generation appeared, but she maintained her circle of dear and loyal friends. Mercifully, she was only watched rather than arrested, while the Soviet press normally ignored her in an attempt to isolate her; on occasion Soviet critics cited her as an anachronism whose work smelled of "bourgeois decadance." There was little new to criticize anyway since she was barely published, was careful to whom she showed her poems, and wrote less and less. In 1935 she wrote nothing at all and feared that she had lost her voice. When she was not writing poetry, she performed scholarly work on Pushkin and in fact made valuable contributions to the body of Pushkin studies. What poetry she did write reflected the times and their effect on her beloved city. In one poem she likened the city's artists to Dante, who had been exiled from his beloved Florence, which to him, like Akhmatova's Petersburg, represented an entire way of life and thought. When invited back, Dante had refused to return rather than undergo a humiliating repentance, the contemporary equivalent of "self-evaluation." In another poem written just before the war, she likened the city to the legendary invisible city of Kitezh which had drowned. But whereas Kitezh had disappeared below the waves in response to the people's prayers that it be saved from the Tatars, Petersburg was not saved from their 20th-century equivalent.[69]

Akhmatova was never arrested, but in a stratagem that was more devious and painful to her, the Communists arrested her son Lev, first in 1933, again in 1935 together with Punin, and a third time in 1938. His 1933 confinement lasted only nine days, and in 1935 Akhmatova was able to have friends intervene to secure Lev's and Punin's release. But in 1938 such tactics were no longer availing. The charge, eventually, was terrorism; in reality, Gumilev was arrested only because of his parentage. He was incarcerated and tortured for eight months but confessed to nothing. After terms in Shpalernaya and Kresty prisons totaling 18 months, he was sent to hard labor on the White Sea Canal but then brought back and condemned to be shot. Fortunately, just then Yezhov himself was purged, and Lev's sentence was commuted to five years in Siberia.

During her son's imprisonment, Akhmatova spent hundreds of hours standing in lines outside prisons with packages for him. There she saw and shared the grief of other wives and mothers whose loved ones were locked inside. They waited in silence, talking only in whispers. One frigid day a woman standing behind her, lips blue with cold, heard Akhmatova's name and recognized her. Thus roused from her stupor, she drew closer and whispered into Akhmatova's ear: "Can you describe this?" Akhmatova answered, "Yes, I can." Then, Akhmatova recalled, "something that looked like a smile passed over what had once been her face."[70]

Akhmatova set to work and in the following months composed the cycle of poems entitled *Requiem*. Its verses were so dangerous that Akhmatova was afraid to write them down. Rather, when she was ready with a set of lines, she would invite her friend Lydia Chukovskaya, the daughter of the Silver Age critic and writer Kornei Chukovsky, to her apartment. Assuming that her apartment was bugged, they made banal conversation as Akhmatova scribbled her verses on paper for Chukovskaya to commit to memory, and then burned them in an ashtray. The result was what has become recognized as the definitive poetic depiction of the Terror, set against the old Petersburg landscapes whose beauty had inspired her earlier poems. As if heeding directly the request to "describe this," the poem's dedication went:

> We rose as if for an early service,
> Trudged through the savaged capital,
> And met there, more lifeless than the dead.
> The sun is lower and Neva mistier,
> But hope keeps singing from afar.
> The verdict . . . and her tears gush forth,
> Already she is cut off from the rest,
> As if they painfully wrenched life from her heart
> As if they brutally knocked her flat,
> But she goes on . . . Staggering . . . Alone . . .[71]

The series reaches its climax in the pair of poems entitled "Crucifixion," portraying the death of the condemned:

> *A choir of angels sang the praises of that momentous hour,*
> *And the heavens dissolved in fire.*
> *To his Father He said: "Why hast Thou forsaken me!"*
> *And to his Mother: "Oh, do not weep for Me . . ."*
>
> *Mary Magdelene beat her breast and sobbed,*
> *The beloved disciple turned to stone,*
> *But where the silent Mother stood, there*
> *No one glanced and no one would have dared.*[72]

The Terror can likewise be seen as the crucifixion of the city, of which Akhmatova wrote in another poem from that time:

> *Through the crucified capital*
> *I go home.*

THE REVENGE OF MUSCOVY

Under Stalin, the city had become, through force, "the opposite of itself." From the start Petersburg culture had been modern, tolerant, experimental, skeptical, intellectual, pluralistic, and cosmopolitan, all of which encouraged spontaneous creativity in culture and the formation of society from within. But under Stalin the ideas and ways of life of old Muscovy that Petersburg had been created to destroy returned under the guise of Communism, beginning with Stalin himself. His hero and model was Ivan the Terrible, and he had no worldly perspective. Rather, he was a Georgian provincial with little education who did not write Russian until his late twenties, barely traveled abroad, and from his days as a divinity student was imbued with a crudely intolerant, fanatically religious mentality. But such qualities suited him to lead a Russian Communist crusade which drew on the main elements of Muscovite civilization (or Nicholas I's updated version, Official Nationality). Communism revived the idea that Russia is a special, chosen nation with a unique people and a great mission and destiny to teach the world. Like Muscovite ideology, Communism was an all-embracing, integrated faith that went beyond matters of government to purport to resolve all questions of social justice and personal life, and therefore encompassed private life. Both embraced collectivism and the belief in an organic society in which the state and the people were united; thus, there should and could be no dissent. Each bred fanaticism, intolerance, and an insularity from the outside world, from which, it was thought, Russia had nothing to learn and which could only contaminate Russians' minds. In their agrarian policy the Communists reverted to the traditions of state or communal ownership of land, which had originated in Muscovy's lack of Roman conceptions of property.[73]

Even the trappings and ceremonies of Muscovite and Communist culture were similar.[74] Both featured compulsive Byzantine ritualism. At Lenin's funeral Stalin essentially turned him into a saint, and his mausoleum on Red Square turned the Kremlin into a national shrine, like St. Peter's rock—symbolized by fulfilling the Slavophiles' dream of returning the capital from St. Petersburg to Moscow. Icons were replaced by portraits of Lenin, Stalin, and other Communist leaders; Communist ideology served as a liturgy; the equivalent of prayers was heard in rallies and on the ubiquitous public loudspeakers, and believers cried hallelujah in response to the revealed word; and the role of priests was filled by Soviet propagandists and agitators. The national leader in the Kremlin, thought of as a father-deliverer (batyushka), in fact was dictator. The role of the oprichnina was filled by the NKVD and the Gulag system.

By the late 1930s, the city had fallen into an abyss from which even under the best of conditions it would take time to recover and regain its culture. But matters would get worse. The city was a casualty of the war between Stalin and Hitler, where the normal ravages of war were worsened by being caught between the fanatical ideologies of the two dictators and by a nearly 900-day siege of the city.

CHAPTER 14

Hero City

Show your colors, City of Peter
And stand steadfast like Russia.

Pushkin

Leningrad—to be or not to be?

Leningrad newspaper
headline of September 17, 1941

Except for a few years of respite during NEP, the nearly three decades from World War I until June 1941 had been one continuous nightmare for the city—war, revolutions, civil war, famine, the Terror. But the worst was yet to come in World War II, much of it the result not of the Nazi attack but of the Soviet government's and military's own policies and mistakes. The city was caught between two fanatical warring ideologies and systems. The blockade's real heroes, the city's people, would face unimaginable horrors, but by facing the ordeal stoically and resourcefully they and the city passed their most severe test. Given the mobile and air warfare of the 20th century, the thought that any city could be subjected to siege, at least for any length of time, would have seemed preposterous to anyone before the war. But not only did it happen in Leningrad, it became the largest siege of the largest city in world history, with some three million people trapped inside. It was also unique in its length (29 months), the prominent role that ordinary citizens played in the city's defense, and in the hardships and losses that they suffered.

THE PRELUDE

The city had been founded by Peter in a war zone, but then, as in 1812 and World War I, the country's army, navy, great land mass, and harsh climate had kept it protected. But now, in the age of motorized armies, air warfare, and swift navies, it was vulnerable. Worse, in 1918 Lenin had given up much of Poland, the Baltics, and

Finland. The Finnish border now lay only about 20 miles northwest of the city; the Estonian border was less than 100 miles away. On August 23, 1939, Hitler's Germany and Stalin's Soviet Union signed a nonaggression pact, which contained a secret protocol dividing Europe into respective spheres of influence. It accorded Stalin most of the territories lost in 1918. Once it was signed, both sides moved quickly. Within a week, on September 1, Hitler invaded western Poland; on September 17 Stalin occupied eastern Poland. Stalin then began negotiations with Finland to push the Soviet border back from Leningrad. When the Finns refused, Stalin utilized a real or imagined border incident to organize a People's Government of Finland, with which Stalin signed a treaty under which Finland ceded the territory nearest Leningrad and leased the naval base of Hangö in exchange for other territories in Karelia. When Stalin then proceeded to occupy the territory, the legitimate government of Finland fought back.

The Finnish War gave Leningraders a taste of what was to come, both from the enemy and their own government. The Red Army had not recovered from Stalin's purge of its officers. Soldiers were sent to the front ill equipped for winter warfare and fought poorly, while able skiers, including students from the city's institutes, were drafted into service even though they were not trained soldiers, a recipe for disaster.[1] The Soviets had also underestimated the Finns, who fought valiantly and efficiently on their skis in the winter forests. After a month, the Russians had barely progressed and from early January to early February 1940 halted to regroup. The casualty rates were high, and wounded students and soldiers poured into the city. The government, which had not told the truth about the disaster, isolated the wounded returnees and ordered hospital personnel not to speak with them. When the hospitalized injured were let into the fenced park for fresh air and friends and relatives tried to speak with them through the fence, the authorities drove them away.[2] Thus did Leningraders learn about the state of the army and how their authorities would operate and treat citizen-soldiers in wartime.

The Red Army finally pushed beyond Vyborg and a treaty was signed on March 12, establishing a new border. In July 1940, Stalin occupied Estonia, Latvia, and Lithuania. With this cushion, he believed, northwest Russia was safe.

But Hitler had designs on the Soviet Union, a fact which Stalin steadfastly refused to admit against mounting evidence that Germany was preparing for an invasion. Mass German troop movements toward the Soviet border began in late May 1941; an army of some three million would attack on June 22. Stalin's attachés in Berlin as well as Winston Churchill warned Stalin repeatedly of troop buildups, but to no avail. Harrison Salisbury concluded that "Stalin could not have had more specific, more detailed, more comprehensive information. Probably no nation ever had been so well informed of an impending enemy attack."[3] But the country was more than ever an autocracy. While Stalin acknowledged that war might come eventually, he did not believe an attack was imminent. The declared policy was "No War," and no military movements that might be interpreted as a provocation or other war preparations were allowed.* The country's propaganda machine, headed by Leningrad Party boss Zhdanov, toed this line,[4] and consequently the people too did not expect an attack. Leningrad was captive of this policy and not in a position to prepare for the assault. Before the war started, not a single military unit was deployed to south of Leningrad between it and the Baltic states,[5] no measures had been taken to stock food or other supplies or to convert to wartime production, and civil defense training and firefighting capabilities against mass fires were minimal.

In Leningrad there were already telltale signs of war in the spring of 1941. German engineers had been working in Leningrad repairing ships of the Baltic Fleet, but beginning in April parts and supplies for the repairs, which previously were shipped punctually, failed to arrive. Then the engineers themselves began leaving, finding one excuse or another to return home. By the end of May only 20 remained in Leningrad, and by June 15 all were gone. German ships started leaving Soviet waters in the Baltic, and by June 16 not one remained. Then German reconnaissance planes were seen over Soviet installations on the Baltic, and on June 20 a Soviet freighter was detained in the German port of Danzig. All of this was reported to Moscow, but no instructions came other than to keep watch. Zhdanov had left for vacation in Sochi, but the local military saw what was coming. So did the director of the Hermitage, Joseph Orbeli, who flouted the ban on wartime preparations and stockpiled packing materials needed in case of an evacuation. On June 21 the Baltic Fleet was placed on alert, while that evening local army leaders gathered in Rossi's General Staff Building, ready for what might come.

Leningraders had looked forward to the weekend of June 21–22 as the highlight of the summer. That night would be the shortest of the city's White Nights, when the tradition in the city was to stroll until the early morning hours when the sun was again rising in the sky. Champagne bottles popped at midnight with the sun still not set. The weather was sunny both days, and people flocked to the parks in the city and in Pushkin and Pavlovsk, to the islands, and to the suburbs. Students had just finished their exams and were celebrating. Shostakovich had been giving exams to his composition students at the Conservatory, but he had football tickets for the 22nd. The Hermitage was full of visitors. Nevsky—no one called it by its official name, October 25th Street—was flocked with shoppers and strollers. Girls sold ice cream cones and eskimo pies on the street.

The streets, squares, and parks also were lined with loudspeakers. At noon on the 22nd, the loudspeakers crackled, and Leningraders heard the voice of Viacheslav Molotov, Commissar for Foreign Affairs, and stopped to listen with rapt attention:

Men and women, citizens of the Soviet Union! The Soviet Government, and its head, Comrade Stalin, have instructed me to make the following announcement: At 4:00 A.M.,

---

*Only on June 6, two weeks before the attack, did Stalin authorize preparations for conversion to war production *by the end of 1942.* Salisbury, *900 Days,* p. 69.

without declaration of war and without any claims being made on the Soviet Union, German troops have attacked our country. . . . The Government calls upon you, men and women citizens of the Soviet Union, to rally even more closely around the glorious Bolshevik Party, around the Soviet Government and our great leader, Comrade Stalin. Our cause is just. The enemy will be crushed. Victory will be ours.

As people recovered from the initial shock, some wondered why Stalin himself had not delivered the message. They had no way of knowing that, upon hearing of the attack, Stalin had a nervous breakdown and locked himself in a room, from which he would emerge only in early July, when Hitler's army was halfway to Leningrad.

The country was leaderless, but Leningraders had been through many wars and revolutions and knew the drill. "I am thirty-four years old. This is the fourth war of my life," the chemist Elena Kochina confided to her diary on June 22.[6] Each period of strife had been one of shortage and hunger. Within minutes after Molotov's announcement, women were in the food stores buying up sausage, canned and other preserved goods (even caviar), sugar, butter, flour, cereals, lard, and anything else on the shelves that would last. They also converged on the banks (open that Sunday) to withdraw their money. Then they spent the paper money at commission shops to buy articles of gold, silver, diamonds. And then more food, and vodka. Orbeli, fearing air raids, closed down the Hermitage early on Sunday afternoon and immediately took down the 40 most valuable paintings to the steel-clad vaults on the ground floor where the Scythian gold was kept. Knowing that the Hermitage collection would have to be evacuated as in World War I, he organized the packing, which began in earnest the next day. What people feared most was large-scale bombing of the city, as had occurred in London. But until early September the Luftwaffe dropped only propaganda leaflets on the city. They also feared that the Fascists would use gas. Leningraders prepared for gassing, but this was one of the few horrors they were spared.

Having just been through the Terror, which had reached its macabre worst in Leningrad, many Leningraders wondered whether they might be better off under the Germans. Hitler was not an attractive alternative to begin with, but in early July he announced that the Luftwaffe would raze Leningrad, and stories of Nazi mistreatment of soldiers and civilians and atrocities flowed into the city with the wounded and refugees. Had the Nazis behaved differently, believe many Leningraders from that time, they might have won Russians over and the campaign would have ended differently.[7] Except for a small few, Nazi behavior, native Russian patriotism and love for their city turned Leningraders' minds. The Leningrad poet Olga Berggolts, a victim of the Terror who had served time in prison and in the Gulag in 1937–39, expressed these feelings in a poem addressed to her Motherland:

> I did not this day forget
> The bitter years of oppression and evil.
> But in a blinding flash I understood:
> It was not I but you who suffered and waited.

No, I have forgotten nothing,
But even the dead and the victims
Will rise from the grave at your call . . . .
My Motherland with the wreath of thorns
And the dark rainbow over your head . . . .
I love you—I cannot do otherwise—
And you and I are one again, as before.[8]

But the peoples of the Baltics held no such feelings and saw the Germans as liberators. Hitler's armies waltzed through the Baltics almost without resistance.* The Soviet armies were overpowered. They were mostly infantry against Nazi artillery and armor, supplies of munitions were short, and they had no air cover. Riga fell on July 1. On July 5 the Fascists took Ostrov and on July 9 Pskov, only about 160 miles from Leningrad. The Finns joined the Fascists in order to recover their recently lost lands. They struck first on the north shore of Lake Ladoga and, with the Germans still far away, cautiously inched down the far (northeast) shore of Lake Ladoga, to take Salmi on July 21, where, much to Hitler's displeasure, they halted. On July 31 they opened a new offensive down the Karelian Ithsmus, took back Vyborg and by early September stood on the pre-1939 border. Having achieved their goal, they hesitated to move further, against Leningrad. They did not covet the city and realized that in the event of victory it would be the prize of the Nazis.

Because of the autocratic and hierarchical nature of Soviet rule, the city government operated at half-throttle until Zhdanov returned from Sochi on June 27. At first the city leadership had not been alarmed by the attack, but the rapid Nazi advance quickly woke them up. With Zhdanov's arrival, a sense of urgency set in and the bureaucratic machinery shifted to high gear. Some factories were designated for evacuation into the interior, while others were mobilized into wartime production. By early July they were turning out mortars, tanks, armored cars, mines, and flamethrowers. The distilleries produced a new invention (by the Finns in the 1939 war), the Molotov cocktail, one million of them by August. But most military production had to be exported south for use around Moscow or in the Ukraine.

Few Red Army troops were stationed in the region or would be sent from Moscow. Zhdanov realized that saving Leningrad could depend on mobilizing citizen defenders.† On Stalin's order, the call went out on June 30, mobilization points were set up, and by July 7, 160,000 People's Volunteers aged 18 to 50 were enrolled,

---

*Tallin held out as a pocket of resistance and like Leningrad was surrounded and cut off. As it fell on August 28, the defenders were evacuated by the Baltic Fleet in Dunkirk-like chaos. The Fleet suffered heavily in the retreat to Leningrad.

†In Russian *narodnoe opolchenie* or simply *opolchenie*, for which there is no satisfactory English translation but which is typically translated in Soviet Russian-English dictionaries as "emergency volunteer corps." Salisbury uses the term "People's Volunteers" which, though euphemistic and misleading given the pressures to enlist, is retained here.

including some 20,000 women and 2,500 Leningrad University students. Shostakovich signed up but was rejected as unfit; instead, he was given air raid duty and served in the fire brigade at the Conservatory. The Soviet propaganda machine soon produced a photo of him in his fireman's uniform and helmet and holding a fire hose; in America it made the cover of *Time* under the headline "Fireman Shostakovich." In reality, there were quotas to fulfill and service was hardly voluntary. As one Volunteer, the 30-year-old factory engineer Boris Sokolov recalled, "I went to war, one might say, voluntarily, that is neither resisting nor refusing, as many did, though clearly knowing better. In this [decision] my law-abiding character influenced me, as did my lack of knowledge of life outside my comfortable circle and, quite simply, my propensity not to think."[9] Most Volunteers were issued rifles or pistols (often without ammunition) but little else, and uniforms were out of the question. Virtually none of their officers had military experience. With as little as a few days' training, units were sent to the front, often without provisions. It was like World War I all over again. In addition, the NKVD also brought prisoners from the Gulag to serve as defenders and build fortifications.

From the outset Leningrad's leadership saw that all hope of keeping the Fascists away from the city's gates lay in building and defending lines of fortifications south of the city. They began with the 150-mile-long Luga Line running along the Luga River 60 to nearly 100 miles south of Leningrad, westward through the town of Luga and then to Lake Ilmen near Novgorod (see map on p. xiii). Work on the Luga Line began even before Zhdanov arrived and became the city's fixation. All possible efforts were thrown into fortifying it. Zhdanov halted all civilian construction in the city and sent the crews and their equipment, including those at work on the new Metro, to the fortification lines. Some 60,000 Leningrad civilians, mainly women, were mobilized for the Luga line to dig trenches, dugouts, gun emplacements and tank traps, build tank barriers, and help sappers lay mines. Behind the Luga Line, three rings of inner fortifications were constructed to within a few miles of the city, the innermost (if it held) putting the city outside the range of all but long-range German artillery. To build the fortifications in the city suburbs, the city's entire population was mobilized round the clock, some full time and others when they were not at their usual jobs. Even the packers at the Hermitage were not exempted and had to do double duty. No one was without a job; the concept of a "working day" had vanished. At the height of the effort, at least half a million Leningraders were at work fortifying the approaches to their city.* Almost daily, low flying German planes appeared to harass, dive upon, bomb, and strafe the workers, sending them fleeing into their ditches and killing some. One of the citizen diggers, Elena Kochina, recalled that "suddenly the wings of an airplane,

---

*Estimates of the total number of Leningraders who were involved in building the fortifications outside the city vary from 500,000 to 1,000,000. Salisbury, *900 Days*, p. 196; Werth, *op cit.*, p. 302 ("nearly a million" at the end of July and beginning of August).

gleaming, blotted out the sky. A machine gun fired and bullets plunged into the grass not far from me, rustling like small metallic lizards."[10] She ran and spent the next hour crouched in water under a bridge.

Especially at the Luga Line, the scene was chaotic, the work was done in haste and not well planned or executed (some trenches faced the wrong way[11]), and there were not enough supplies of mines, other explosives, concrete, and barbed wire to do the job. When Leningrad's military asked for more, they received a telegram stating, "To cover your needs from the Center is impossible. There are more important fronts than yours. Use your local resources."[12] They did. Even the now-antique guns from the *Aurora* were placed on Pulkovo Heights. All in all, the workers, housewives, children, students, artists, writers, and scientists of Leningrad, using mostly picks and shovels, outside the city dug 340 miles of antitank trenches, 15,875 miles of open trenches, erected 400 miles of barbed wire barriers, 190 miles of forest obstacles (felled trees, etc.), and built 5,000 wooden or concrete firing points.[13] Despite the many defects and problems, the effort ultimately worked. While Hitler's armies reached the Luga Line in less than three weeks, it took them over six more to reach the edge of the city, a delay which saved it.

Inside the city, civil defense was organized, strict police controls were imposed, and security was tightened. Within 24 hours after the onset of the war some 14,000 people were assigned to air raid duty and a round-the-clock watch was established on the rooftops. Air raid balloons hovered over the city day and night. Attics were cleaned of flammable materials. Thousands of firefighting brigades were organized at factories, offices, institutions, and apartment buildings, 500 new water hydrants were installed, and numerous water basins and firefighting platforms were built. Picture taking was prohibited and private cameras were confiscated. Both citizens and the authorities feared German spies in their midst. "Spy mania, like an infectious disease, has struck everyone without exception," observed Kochina.[14] Indeed there were spies, but anyone looking Western, speaking with an accent, or asking directions within the city was viewed with suspicion and checked and often arrested. Checkpoints were set up to control entry and exit. Forty-two processing centers were set up to process the tens of thousands of refugees pouring in from the Baltic region. On August 24 a curfew was imposed forbidding all movement in the city between 10:00 P.M. and 5:00 A.M.

The question of evacuations became a challenge of judgment and logistics. Every able-bodied individual was needed to build fortifications, so in the hope that as many of these as possible could get out later, priority was given to evacuating children, essential factories with their workers and families, and the homeless refugees who were clogging the city and becoming a burden. This was a challenge because German planes continually bombed the trains, train stations, and tracks, killing many and creating delays and backups. The railroads were overwhelmed and could not handle the volume.[15] By the beginning of the blockade nearly 100 key machine plants and other large factories representing nearly half of the city's productive capacity were completely or partially evacuated together with 164,320 of their workers; 2,000 freight cars of equipment stood trapped in the city's railroad yards when the ring closed.[16] The first order for the evacuation of children, 392,000 of them, came at the end of June, followed by another order on August 10 to evacuate 400,000 more women with their children and an order a week later to raise that number to 700,000 at a rate of 30,000 per day.[17] Initially the children were sent to whatever summer camps, children's rest homes, or similar facilities with which they were affiliated and where they could be cared for yet not far from their parents. But many of these facilities were to the south, right in the path of the attacking Germans, and soon the children had to be brought back, reprocessed, and sent to the interior. Many who were not returned were killed in the fighting.[18] In the end only 216,691 children made it out before the ring closed. Among the other evacuees were the artists of the city's major artistic ensembles, including the Philharmonic and Pushkin Drama Theater (to Novosibirsk), the Mariinsky Opera and Ballet (to Perm), the Maly Opera (to Orenburg), and the Capella. The total number of people evacuated from the city by the beginning of the blockade, including 147,500 refugees, was 636,203.[19] About three million people were trapped inside the ring when the siege began.

The number of evacuees could have been much higher. Zhdanov, under pressure to defend the city at all costs, wanted to utilize all manpower on the one hand, while on the other he like most others underestimated the threat until it was too late.[20] But another reason was that many Leningraders did not want to leave.[21] Most people did not want to become like the refugees they saw pouring in from the Baltics or to break up the family, and the route out was dangerous.[22] Thus, despite the risks of staying, most clung to their familiar apartments, friends, and the city that they loved, ready to share its fate.[23] They included prominent artists, composers and writers like Shostakovich, Akhmatova, Zoshchenko, and the dramatist and writer Yevgeny Schvarts and his wife. Some like Shostakovich and Akhmatova eventually left, but only when the Party so ordered. Others who were outside the city on June 22 decided to come and assist. The pianist Maria Yudina, who had been expelled from the Leningrad Conservatory for espousing religion, now returned from Moscow in order to play her piano for Leningraders. The poet and writer Vera Inber and her husband, a physician, arrived from Moscow, he to work at a hospital, she at the radio station.

Great effort also went into preserving the city's landmarks and cultural treasures. Initially, thought was given to submerging the Bronze Horseman into the Neva, but then it was decided to sandbag and board it up. Other statues, including Klodt's horses on the Anichkov Bridge, were buried in the Summer Garden. Many of the statues in Pavlovsk, Pushkin and Peterhof were likewise buried in their parks. Out of pride, the statues of Kutuzov and Barclay de Tolly, the heroes of 1812, remained standing in front of Kazan Cathedral but were protected by sandbags and survived the blockade intact. The statue of another war hero, Suvorov, on the Field of Mars was to be placed in the basement of a nearby building, but to accommodate the statue the basement windows had to be widened, and once the siege began moving it was beyond the strength of the weakened citizens. As it turned out, during the siege an artillery shell whistled past Suvorov's eyes and exploded in that basement, while he stood throughout the siege unscathed.[24] The Sphinxes in front of the Academy also had to meet their fate unprotected. The Hermitage, the General Staff Building, the Peter and Paul Cathedral were covered with camouflage netting like that over Smolny. The camouflage netting placed on the Hermitage complex was painted by artists to look like ruined buildings in the hope that it would not be targeted.[25] The Alexander Column on Palace Square was protected by scaffolding. The dome of St. Isaac's was painted a dirty gray. The tall spires of the Peter and Paul Cathedral and the Admiralty posed special challenges. At the Cathedral a workman had to climb the 300 feet to the top of the steeple to attach a camouflage rigging, while at the Admiralty balloonists tried and failed for two weeks to drop a similar rigging; finally, volunteer alpinists scaled the spire and splashed dirty gray paint on it.

The art, archival, and book collections of the city's palaces, museums, and libraries were boxed and either evacuated or stored in safe places. The Academy of Sciences' collection and Lenfilm Studios were evacuated. So too were 52 crates of treasures from the Catherine and Alexander Palaces in Pushkin. Other treasures from the suburban palaces were packed and brought into the cellars of St. Isaac's Cathedral and other safe places in the city, but many treasures in those palaces had to be left behind and were seized by the Nazis.[26] The Russian Museum collection, though not all of it, was sent to Gorky. The Public Library shipped out 360,000 of its most valuable items, including Voltaire's library, a Gutenburg Bible, Pushkin's archives, 7,000 incunabula, and the city's historical archives. Items that did not make it out were sent to the dungeons of the Fortress and catacombs of the Alexander Nevsky Monastery.[27] Astronomers from the Pulkovo Observatory sneaked into it one October night well after the siege had begun to rescue its telescopic lenses, valuable scientific equipment, charts and catalogues of the stars, and its library and archives, including many incunabula.[28]

But the biggest challenge was the treasures at the Hermitage. Beginning June 23, the Hermitage staff together with recruited art specialists, including Academy of Fine Arts staff and students, led by Orbeli dressed in his blue overalls, worked round the clock for six days packing the most important paintings and other treasures for evacuation, catching only brief naps when exhaustion drove them to it. Down came Rembrandt's *Prodigal Son*, *Holy Family*, and *Descent from the Cross*, together with the Raphaels, da Vincis, van Dycks, Titians, Giorgiones, Tintorettos, Rubenses, El Grecos . . . . All but the few most delicate and valuable paintings were taken off their frames and stretchers and rolled up despite the risk of damage; their empty frames were left on the walls. Crated too were Alexander Nevsky's sarcophagus, the wax figure of Peter the Great with his original clothes, the Scythian gold, and, the last item out in the first shipment, Houdon's seated Voltaire. In the semidusk on June 30, a convoy of trucks took the cargo of some half million items down

Nevsky Prospect to the train station, and at dawn on July 1 the most valuable train in human history pulled out of the station for the Urals, without blowing its whistle. One car with the most valuable items was armored, two others had antiaircraft guns, and the train was under heavy guard. As it left the station, Orbeli stood by the lamppost at the end of the platform, his hat across his heart and tears in his eyes. But then it was back to work to pack the second shipment, again toiling around the clock. Museum staff returning from duty on the suburban fortifications joined in without a rest. The second train containing a million items left on July 20. Because the Museum had run out of packing materials and substitute materials had to be found, the packing of the third and last train was delayed and the shipment never made it out. The order to halt came on August 30 after the rail line was cut off, and the 351 crates already packed spent the siege in the columned Rastrelli Gallery on the ground floor protected by sandbags.

THE BATTLE OF LENINGRAD

As the Nazis approached the Luga Line, it was far from complete. Hitler's Group North, led by Field Marshal Wilhelm von Leeb, had 20 to 23 divisions of 340,000 crack troops, 326 tanks, and 6,000 guns supported by 1,000 aircraft. This gave them a superiority of 2.4 to 1 in manpower, 4 to 1 in artillery, 5.8 to 1 in mortars, 1.2 to 1 in tanks, and nearly 10 to 1 in aircraft.[29] Half of Leningrad's 150,000 defenders facing Hitler's Panzers were People's Volunteers, which meant that the city's fate depended significantly on them.[30] The defenders were concentrated in the center near Luga and deployed more sparsely to the East and West, resulting in undefended gaps of up to 15 miles. When attacks began, sometimes the Germans would reach the Line before its defenders.[31] The scene on the Russian front lines, with inexperienced commanders, a curious mix of Red Army soldiers and ordinary citizens, and shortage of weapons, supplies, and food, was chaotic. The experience of the Volunteer Boris Sokolov was typical.

Sokolov commanded a platoon responsible for a battery of two small (three-inch), mobile (horse-drawn) artillery pieces manufactured in 1902, and (initially) with only 8 shells for each. He also had a pistol, but no bullets for it. His 30-man platoon consisted mainly of untrained students who feared mayhem from their horses as much as from the Germans. Sokolov was given the command because years earlier he had taken courses on artillery theory, where he had been instructed to locate the enemy using binoculars, make trigonometric calculations and phone in the enemy coordinates to the gunners. But now he had no binoculars or means of communication, and had no way of confirming whether Germans or Russians were in the target area. When they were not fighting, they combed the countryside for vegetables and abandoned livestock in order to feed themselves.[32] Eventually, Sokolov was taken prisoner.

When the Germans attacked the Line on July 10, the center near Luga held, but flanking attacks broke through in the east and west. In the west, the Line was permanently broken and the 60-mile road to the Winter Palace lay undefended.[33] Fortunately, the Germans had to halt because in the east, near Lake Ilmen, a Russian counterattack in mid-July drove the Germans back, forcing them to regroup and let their supply trains catch up. As a result, the Germans were held up on the Luga Line for about a month.[34] This delay not only kept open the city's connections with the interior but tripped up Hitler's schedule and probably saved the city. Hitler had already issued city guides to his officers, and, according to some accounts, he had also issued invitations to a victory celebration at the Hotel Astoria on July 21.[35] Instead, on that day he could only order that Leningrad be "finished off speedily."[36]

The German assault recommenced on the night of August 7–8. They now had 29 divisions at 80–90 percent strength against 15 considerably weakened Red Army divisions.[37] Although the regular army was soon reinforced by People's Volunteers, who suffered horrible casualties, they could not hope to hold the lines. By August 20, in the west the Germans had advanced to Krasnogvardeisk; in the east Novgorod fell on August 13 and by the 21st the Nazis were in Chudovo. Only the center near the town of Luga held, forming a precarious, exposed salient. For fear of being entrapped, the center had to pull back, chaotically, on August 21.

The Germans' main drive toward the city came from the southwest. They broke through to the Finnish Gulf near Peterhof, thus isolating Russia's 8th Army to the west in a pocket until the end of the blockade in January 1944. But the 8th Army's presence prevented an onslaught on Kronstadt and from there into the undefended mouth of the Neva. Hitler's 4th Panzers then wheeled northeast toward the city. In the east, Russia's battered 48th Army shifted eastward, partly in retreat and partly to avoid being outflanked to the east. This helped prevent the Germans from achieving their goal of linking up with the Finns on the east side of Lake Ladoga, which importantly would have closed off the Lake and prevented any supplies to the city except by air. But thus was opened a hole through which the Germans marched to sever the last rail link to the city. They cut the railroad line near the town of Mga on the 28th, occupied the town itself without a battle on the 30th, and reached the Neva on the same day. Schlüsselburg was taken on September 7th, cutting off the last land route between Leningrad and the interior. Fortunately an undefended railroad bridge across the Neva at Ostrovki was blown up on the 30th just before the Germans arrived. Lacking pontoons, they could not cross the Neva to link up with the Finns on the southeast shore of Ladoga. Blowing that bridge probably saved Leningrad. But the blockade of the city had begun.*

---

*There is no universally accepted period for the siege. Virtually all accept as the end January 27, 1944, when the siege was officially declared over, even though the counteroffensive which freed the city had commenced on January 14th. If the January 27th date is accepted, the siege lasted 882 days from when the rail line was cut (August 28, 1941), 880 days from when Mga was taken (August 30), and 872 days from the fall of Shlüsselburg (September 7). August 30 is used by Salisbury and is adopted here. See Salisbury, *900 Days*, p. 567.

Leningraders did not know of the chaos on the front lines and could not understand why the Red Army was retreating through the defenses that they had built. Zhdanov called special meetings on August 16 and 20 for frank talk about the desperate situation. Then he made a blunt appeal to the people of the city warning of the imminent danger: "Comrade Leningraders! Dear friends! Our dearly beloved city is in imminent danger of attack by the German fascist troops." Posters went up all over the city proclaiming, "The enemy is at the gates!" Zhdanov instructed citizens to prepare for mass air attacks and artillery bombardment and to create and improve air raid defenses and shelters, firefighting capabilities, and first aid facilities. He also warned that they may become involved in the fighting. "We have to teach people in the shortest possible time the main and most important methods of combat: shooting, throwing grenades, street fighting, digging trenches, crawling."[38]

Moscow grew alarmed too. Stalin sent a high-level commission including Molotov and Malenkov to Leningrad to investigate and report on the situation and weigh options, which included abandoning the city. No sooner had they arrived when they learned (on the 28th) that the last rail link to the city had just been closed off. Only on August 27, from the commission's investigation, did the scope of the food, fuel, and other shortages in the city become clear.[39] They were also displeased that so little of the population had been evacuated, and saw firsthand the chaos of the military effort. On September 1 Stalin formally reprimanded Zhdanov, as well as Marshal Voroshilov, the Leningrad Commander. But it was decided not to abandon the city. This is consistent with Stalin's policy in every other city in the Soviet Union to not yield an inch and fight to the last.[40] Stalin also knew that if Leningrad were taken or surrendered, the Germans would be free to turn on Moscow, and he needed to buy time.[41]

Hitler's plan was, in fact, to focus on Leningrad first because of its vast defense industry and also for ideological and romantic reasons. Once Leningrad was encircled he would release some units for Moscow and have others link up with the Finns east of Lake Ladoga to seal the city off completely; eventually Leningrad would capitulate from bombing, shelling, and hunger. Hitler learned about the street fighting in Minsk and Smolensk. It was slow, and the cost in men and materiel was high. While Hitler had made no final decision, taking by storm a city of three million outraged inhabitants street by street, building by building was hard even for him to contemplate.[42]

But this is exactly what Leningrad was preparing for. From the outset of the war civil defense preparations had been under way. The army raised antiaircraft balloons, installed a network of antiaircraft batteries, which proved rather effective, and pointed artillery to the south. Baltic Fleet ships also were moored on the Gulf, along the Neva within the city, and upriver toward Schlüsselburg to provide artillery cover, while guns from other ships were removed and taken into the city to be installed in permanent batteries or on converted tram or rail cars. Special defenses were set up on the Field of Mars and other open areas where enemy paratroopers might attempt to land. Citizens painted out street signs and building numbers so that entering enemy soldiers could not find their way. Windows were either boarded up or taped to withstand the shock of exploding shells and bombs. The Mariinsky Theater artists built hundreds of paper-mâché decoy tanks and guns. Thousands of citizens manned air raid watchposts on the city's rooftops. An order prohibited all whistles, chimes, and bells so they would not be confused with air raid sirens. Smolny, now also the city's military headquarters, from the first days of the war had been draped in a complex array of camouflage netting, much of it sewn by the city's theaters, the color of which changed with the seasons. Antiaircraft guns were mounted on surrounding buildings, false towers were erected nearby, and the building itself was defended by tanks, machine-gun nests, and a maze of trenches; a navy gunboat was anchored in the Neva nearby. Visitors to Smolny remarked that it was unrecognizable, and not once was it hit by an artillery shell or bomb.

As the Germans closed their ring on the city and the outer fortifications became a military theater in late August, Leningraders now focused on fortifying and defending the city itself, an effort which beginning August 29 was directed by the NKVD. On September 3, the city's population began building barricades, machine-gun nests, pillboxes, embrasures in buildings, and, eventually, booby traps. In the southern regions of the city, nearly every building was turned into a fortress, sandbagged and reinforced with steel, concrete, bricks, and wood in case the upper stories came crashing down. In order to block tanks, the perimeter was sown with concrete pyramids called "dragon's teeth" and crisscrossed with jungles of railroad iron. Factories fabricated steel-framed pillboxes nicknamed "Voroshilov hotels." In total, Leningraders built 16 to 19 miles of barricades and antitank ditches, over 4,000 pillboxes, and 17,000 other firing positions in buildings.[43] About 150 Workers' Battalions of 600 citizens each were armed with rifles, shotguns, revolvers, machine guns, knives, grenades, and Molotov cocktails and assigned to defend specific objects or sectors. Many were to defend their own factories.

The stage was now set for the final assault on the city, which came mainly from the southwest and was aimed at the new workers' region of Avtovo and the Kirov Works. The defenders not only had to keep the Nazis out of the city, but had to keep them far enough away so they could not pummel the city with short and medium-range artillery. To achieve this, on September 10th Stalin replaced Voroshilov with the legendary, fanatical Marshal Zhukov, who flew to Leningrad immediately and held a war council at Smolny. Zhukov's strategy could be summarized in one phrase: "Attack! Not one step backwards!" Against all odds. At all costs. For almost two weeks he cajoled, berated, and threatened his officers into launching counterattack after counterattack with their pathetically weakened forces. Anyone caught retreating would be shot;[44] he positioned loyal troops in the rear with machine guns to shoot anyone retreating.[45] On August 16, Stalin had issued an order calling even for the families of anyone surrendering to the Germans or deserters to be arrested, but Zhukov reinterpreted it and issued his own coded order calling for such families to be shot.[46] The casualties resulting from Zhukov's strategy were enormous.

The Baltic Fleet also played a decisive role in the city's defense at this stage. The main line of the German advance lay well within range of the artillery on Kronstadt and gunships stationed in the Gulf. The navy's guns pounded the Nazis mercilessly, slowing them down and also preventing German amphibious landings from the Gulf. Navy marines themselves staged surprise landings, disrupting the advance of the Nazis, who called the marines "Black Death" as they were dressed in black. The Luftwaffe harassed the navy's ships, damaged and sunk some, and bombed Kronstadt, but ultimately to little effect.

The German advance had slowed to a crawl but could not be stopped. Leningrad had to make plans for the worst, and did not consider surrender an option. Neither did Hitler. In early September, the Führer had instructed von Leeb not to accept the surrender of the city. Anyone trying to escape would be shot; the city's population would die from bombardment or starvation.[47]

Stalin decided to use the city itself as a weapon. Many ordinary buildings, mainly in the southeast of the city, were mined so that they could be detonated and bury advancing tanks and soldiers. But there was also a doomsday scenario. On September 13th orders approved by Stalin went out to mine all bridges, factories, ships, supply dumps, artillery pieces, institutions, all port, naval, and railroad installations, and any other objects of military value, principally in the southwest regions of the city. The full extent of the planned destruction, and what Stalin would do next, may never be known,[48] but some specialists believe that Stalin was prepared to blow up the city and march out to do final battle with the Nazis in a Russian Götterdämmerung.[49] Word of the demolition plans leaked out to the citizenry. Many felt betrayed and wondered what were the limits to what one's government could expect of its citizens as combatants. Why destroy what they had been trying to save? With their places of work and homes destroyed, how could the people live once the dust settled?[50] What they did not know was that Hitler's plans for them were even crueler.

But it never came to doomsday. Hitler waited impatiently each day for news. By now he had decided to avoid a time-consuming and costly occupation of the city. Rather, he would encircle it as closely as possible so that it could be gradually shelled into oblivion, at the first opportunity dispatching his Panzers toward Moscow. He issued the encirclement order on September 12, much to the dismay of his commanders who wanted to storm the city and claim their prize. But even to achieve his more limited goal, Hitler had to keep his armor on the Leningrad front for a few more precious days to tighten the ring. Leningraders did not fully realize it, but saving the city would be a matter of timing over just a few crucial days, of keeping the city out of range of most German artillery until the Panzers left for Moscow. The Germans pressed on slowly against Zhukov's frantic counterattacks and the Baltic Fleet's bombardment, but on the 17th Hitler could wait no longer. Convincing himself that the close encirclement would be achieved, he wheeled his armor toward Moscow. Leningrad was saved from invasion, but no one knew it just yet. The tempo and intensity of the German advance quickly slowed; in some places they pulled units back. Then they began digging in for the winter. The Russians started to notice. By the 23rd they had seen enough to realize that Zhukov and 3 million Leningraders had won the military battle for the city. Zhukov's tactics were of debatable effectiveness and had resulted in horrible sacrifices, but they worked: The German ring had been kept far enough away to save many times more lives and preserve the city from destruction.[51] Leningraders, including its leadership, expected the siege to be broken in a matter of weeks, but the German line around the city as it stood on September 21 would remain unaltered until January 1943.

On September 22 Hitler issued an order entitled "The Future of the City of Petersburg," which laid out his plans for destroying it and starving its people:

> The Führer has decided to raze the city of Petersburg from the face of the earth. After the defeat of Soviet Russia there will not be the slightest reason for the future existence of this large city. . . . It is proposed to blockade the city closely and by means of artillery fire of all caliber and ceaseless bombardment from the air to raze it to the ground. If this creates a situation in the city which produces calls for surrender, they will be refused. . . . In this war . . . we are not interested in preserving even a part of the population of this large city.[52]

The staff memo on which the order was based looked forward to the following spring: "When terror and hunger have done their work in the city, we can open a *single gate* and permit unarmed people to exit."[53]

LIFE UNDER SIEGE

Hitler had begun to implement his plan on September 4, when he first shelled the city. The first Luftwaffe bombings began two days later on the 6th. The first large-scale raids were on the 8th and 9th, the most intense on the 19th (six raids involving 264 aircraft) and the 27th (197 planes).[54] The barrage was intense throughout the autumn,* though the bombing never approached the intensity of that of London. During the winter the bombing virtually stopped due to harsh weather and a shortage of aircraft arising from the demands on other fronts. By December, the Luftwaffe could spare for Leningrad only 150 bombers and 100 fighters against 185 Soviet planes, and many of them were inoperable.[55] The artillery shelling

---

*Through November there were only 2 days without shelling. In September the city was hit with 5,364 artillery shells, 801 explosive bombs, and 31,398 incendiary bombs; in October, 7,590 shells, 991 explosive bombs, and 59,926 incendiaries; in November, 11,230 shells, 1,244 explosive bombs, and 6,544 incendiaries; in December, 5,950 shells, 259 explosive bombs, and 1,849 incendiaries. Salisbury, *900 Days*, p. 372.

continued, but also at a milder level. With too few aircraft and the use of only long-range artillery, the Germans had no hope of fulfilling Hitler's grandiloquent plan of razing the city, and the siege became a standoff. As time went on and munitions ran short, the shelling became sporadic and was carried out mainly for its psychological effect. For this purpose, holidays such as New Year's, May Day, and the anniversary of the October Revolution were slated for heavier shelling and bombing. But the casualties were still considerable. By the end of 1941, 4,481 people had been killed and 15,529 injured by the shelling and bombing; the figures for the whole siege were 16,747 civilians killed and over 33,000 wounded.[56] Others died from Luftwaffe gunfire. Many city landmarks also took hits. The Hermitage was deliberately targeted and in the course of the siege was struck by 32 shells and two bombs; another one-ton bomb exploded in Palace Square, blowing out 750 square meters of glass.[57] Engineers Castle, Gostiny Dvor, the Russian Museum, the Tauride Palace, the Mariinsky Theater, and the Church on the Spilled Blood also were hit. St. Isaac's was not hit but the scars from flying shrapnel can still be seen on its columns; a similar scar on Anichkov Bridge has been preserved for posterity. A major disruption was the many delayed-action bombs which would explode days after being dropped, designed to render useless factories and other zones in the city. Bomb disposal squads, which included many young women from the Komsomol, learned how to disarm them.

Incendiary bombs of napalm and phosphorous and the resulting fires wreaked the most havoc and panic. One of the worst incendiary attacks came early, on September 8th when the main target was the Badayev food warehouses near Vitebsk Station and the Obvodny Canal, which contained large supplies of flour, meat, sugar, oils, and other food. The flames spread over four acres and blazed all night. Many people were convinced that the city's main stocks had been destroyed and the attack had a severe impact on public morale. "Badayev has burned," the babushkas cried. "It's the end—famine."[58] In reality, the loss amounted only to about one-and-one-half days' supply at then-current rations, and some of that loss was converted into other products. But the city no longer made the mistake of concentrating many stores in one place.

The next day, September 9, a determined Dmitri Pavlov, the 36-year-old Commissar of Trade for the Russian Republic and the country's leading specialist in food distribution, arrived in the city to manage its food situation, both for civilians and the military. His appointment was another result of the Molotov commission's finding in late August that the city had only about a month's supply of most staples and only 17 days' supply of flour. Food rationing had been in place nationwide since July 1 and ration card systems since July 18, but until the beginning of the blockade Leningrad was on the same rations as other cities and the local authorities had never thought of changing them. That bread ration, 800 grams a day, was close to normal consumption. Some items such as tea, eggs, and matches were not rationed, while the sale of all foods in some kinds of outlets such as restaurants was entirely outside the rationing system. Large emergency shipments were ordered on August 29, but by then the city was blockaded. On September 2 the bread ration was cut to 600 grams for workers, 400 grams for office workers, and 300 for dependents and children under 12.

Pavlov quickly tallied the number of mouths to feed, inventoried all food supplies, compared them and did the calculation. The result was horrifying. Inside the ring were nearly 2.9 million civilians plus about 500,000 military. Even though he identified more civilian and military food inventories than had the Molotov commission, there was still just over a month's supply of flour, cereals, pasta, and meat products. But the worst part was that there was no means of shipping any additional significant quantities of food to the city. The sea, river, and rail links were all closed. The only open route lay by boat across Lake Ladoga, but there were few boats, no dock or warehouse facilities, and no road or rail links to either shore. Building this infrastructure would take time. The city would have to make do with the supplies on hand, and no one knew for how long. Even before Pavlov finished his calculations, on September 12 he reduced the bread ration again, this time to 500 grams for workers, 300 for office employees, 300 for children under 12, and only 250 for dependents.

Then Pavlov gathered what harvest he could and closed the loopholes in the system. Thousands of citizens went into the fields and orchards lying between the city and the German lines, mainly at night, to gather potatoes, cabbage, apples, and other vegetables and fruits before the snows arrived. They harvested the crop lying prone or on their hands and knees to avoid detection and resulting German shelling. But often they did work under fire. Others traveled to the city's outskirts to bargain with peasants for produce as during the Civil War. Pavlov then halted all sale and distribution of food without ration coupons. He scoured for additional caches of food in factories, rail cars, breweries, warehouses, and food plants. He closed the restaurants, stopped production of nonessential items like beer, pastries, and ice cream, and transferred the supplies to centrally managed warehouses, and eliminated ration cards held by people already receiving their food through other sources like hospitals and children's homes. He centralized storage, sale, and distribution of food, which before had been spread among several organizations, and generally banned special rations.[59] Since before the war, high military and Party officials had always enjoyed special access to better food and delicacies at special stores; these caches were soon exhausted but they were able to secure food packages from friends and relatives by air from Moscow.[60] Such special access was morally abhorrent under the circumstances, but it had no real impact on the overall situation.

Naturally speculation and a black market sprung up, and extra food could always be bought somewhere at exorbitant prices. Most Leningraders resorted to the black market at some point. Since it could never be rooted out and was insignificant enough in volume to "grease" rather than threaten the official system, the authorities kept it in check but did not attempt to eliminate it.[61] Inevitably, some police charged with fighting it were paid off. The more serious criminal racket was ration card forgery, which if not stopped in its tracks would undermine the distribution system, deplete food stores, and lead to more deaths and ultimately chaos. The authorities also feared that the Germans would drop forged cards on the city. Card forgery was made a capital offense. New ration cards were issued on October 1 and at the beginning of each month thereafter to combat fraud. Many people began claiming that their card was lost in bombardments, often simply to obtain a second card and secretly receive double rations; fraud was almost impossible to prove. The system became clogged with applications for replacement cards. Pavlov had to institute replacement policies so strict that it was nearly impossible to replace a lost or stolen card; losing one's card often meant death. Then the main problem changed to card theft.

Meanwhile Pavlov organized what supply lines he could. Meaningful quantities could be shipped only by surface transport. In the early weeks of the siege modest shipments were made by barge across Lake Ladoga, for which makeshift port facilities were hastily constructed at Osinovets on the shore nearest the city and Kobona on the opposite side. But the Germans bombed the vessels from the air and most were sunk.[62] The supply was not enough and by October 1 the city's flour supply had dropped to 15–20 days.[63] For the winter, preparations were made to ship supplies over the Ladoga ice by truck, but in the interim while the ice was forming there would be no supplies except a few by air. An airlift was organized, but only meager quantities could be brought by plane.[64]

While the soldiers fought desperately to break the siege, citizens tightened their belts and, to the background of daily bombardments, settled into a blockade routine of long shifts in factories, air raid duty, hours in air raid shelters, fire brigade work, caring for the wounded. People tried to live as normally as possible and keep their sense of humor. September was abnormally warm and sunny, and in those first weeks some theaters and cinemas still functioned, concerts were given, and even the university, depleted of many students and staff, functioned on a reduced program. Scholars, scientists, and engineers performed research and experiments that might prove useful to the survival effort or have military value. They invented substitute foods, medicines, and sources of vitamins, studied the formation of ice on Lake Ladoga, and developed substitute materials and fuels for the city's industry.

Hours in air raid shelters and cellars became a normal part of life. One university student said she suffered the worst lecture of her student life while trapped for five hours in a bomb shelter with her professor who would not shut up.[65] When Akhmatova descended to a cellar during a raid and ran into her old friend, the Pushkin scholar Boris Tomashevsky, he greeted her, smiling, "You know, Anna Andreyevna, you've come to the Stray Dog!" "It's always like this with me," she replied.[66] But not everyone retreated underground all the time. On the evening of September 27 Shostakovich was performing the incomplete piano score for his Seventh Symphony at his fifth-floor apartment for friends when the air raid sirens sounded, but he continued to play, engrossed in the music and seemingly oblivious to the outside world. When he finished the first movement, he sent his wife and children to the bomb shelter but proposed to continue and his friends assented. He played the remainder of the score to the percussion of antiaircraft guns. When his guests emerged onto the street after the all-clear had sounded, they saw that Gostiny Dvor had suffered a large hit. Ninety-eight killed, 148 wounded.

As public events became less frequent and progressively weaker Leningraders stayed more at home, Leningrad's radio became the people's link to the world and even the source of their hopes. They listened at home and in the city streets, where it was broadcast on loudspeakers. Every evening people looked forward to the last Radio News Chronicle at 11:00 P.M., hoping for encouraging news. The poet Olga Berggolts spoke on the radio daily and became the "voice" of besieged Leningrad. The authorities arranged for celebrities to address the people on the radio to give encouragement. Shostakovich spoke in September, updating people on the progress of his Seventh Symphony to show that life could go on normally. (He was, in fact, making great progress, and that September was one of the most productive months of composing in his life.) Akhmatova spent much of that September by the iron gates of the Fountain House with a gas mask over her shoulder doing air raid duty. She also aided children and sewed bags for sand which were used to protect the trenches in the garden where she later wrote *Poem without a Hero*.[67] Shortly before being evacuated she also spoke over the radio, to the women of the city:

> The city of Peter, the city of Lenin, the city of Pushkin, Dostoevsky, and Blok, this great city of culture and labor, is threatened by the enemy with shame and death. My heart, like those of all the women of Leningrad, sinks at the mere thought that our city, my city, could be destroyed. My whole life has been connected with Leningrad; in Leningrad I became a poet and Leningrad inspired and colored my poetry. I, like all of you at the moment, live only in the unshakable belief that Leningrad will never fall to the fascists.[68]

But the radio did not have a full day's program. When there was nothing else to broadcast, the sound of a metronome was heard, slowly counting away the time until the city would either perish or be freed. For survivors of the siege, the ever-present tick of the metronome, at home and from the loudspeakers in the streets, became one of its most haunting memories.

But like a metronome, inevitably the city began to wind down, and winter came early. The first snowflakes fell on October 14. As fate would have it, that winter was also the coldest in modern times, with an average temperature of only 9 degrees above Fahrenheit in December and 4 degrees below zero in January.[69] And fuel was as short as everything else. Before the war the city received 120 trainloads of fuel a day; now it received none and people gathered three to four trainloads worth of firewood at best.[70] Kerosene had been rationed in September, but by October there was none to give out. By December there was no central heating. Those who could either bought or built from barrels, brick, or scrap metal primitive wood stoves called *burzhuiki** whose stovepipes passed through the apartment windows; from January 1 to March 10, 1942, they caused 1,578 fires. And the stoves needed firewood, which was also in short supply. The authorities sent brigades to the city outskirts to chop down trees; wooden buildings and fences within the city were demolished for firewood as during the Civil War. But the temperatures inside buildings were usually below freezing and people wore their coats, hats, scarves, and gloves indoors. When there was no firewood to provide heat in apartments, residents often moved into the hallways of their buildings, which were less exposed to the cold and bombardment. Most factory workshops were unheated, as were hospitals, many of which were makeshift facilities, including in the Europe Hotel. Frost lined their walls and ice formed in the water pitchers by patients' beds. Doctors operating on patients saw blood and pus freeze on their surgical instruments and hands.

When Tikhvin was about to be taken by the Germans in early November, the Volkhov hydroelectric plant had to be dismantled and evacuated, leaving the city with only fossil fuels to generate power. The supplies of these dwindled, electricity became scarce, and the city became darker. Many factories, lacking power, fuel, and materials, and their employees either emaciated, diseased, or dead, worked on short shifts or closed entirely. By mid-December most industry had ground to a halt, and at night the city was shrouded in impenetrable blackness punctuated only by fires and explosions from bombardment. Fuel ran out for a few days at the city's main power plant with the temperature at 30 below zero, rendering the main water station unable to pump water, and the city's water system froze. So did the sewers and plumbing, meaning no baths or showers, no laundries, no barbershops. Now human waste was thrown into empty bathtubs, courtyards, or the streets. At the Hotel Europe "hospital," "all the baths and bedpans were filled with excrement and refuse, all of which froze on the spot. The medical staff could barely stand on their feet through hunger, cold and hard work beyond the limits of their strength."[71] Water was obtained by melting snow or from the river or the canals, and often could not be boiled for lack of fuel. With no fuel or water and few people having the strength to fight the fires from bombardment and the *burzhuiki*, firefighting became almost impossible and many fires burned freely. On December 9, the last of the street trams stopped running, and from then on the city lived in an eerie silence broken only by the radio and the tick, tick, tick of the metronome. All movement within the city, except for a few official vehicles, was by foot, a tremendous hardship for a citizenry already weakened by famine. Snow was not cleared except in a few major streets. The ubiquitous street symbol of the siege be-

---

*The name derives from *bourgeois*, since the stoves resembled the fat bellies of bourgeois capitalists in Soviet propaganda cartoons. There were approximately 135,000 throughout the city.

came the small children's sled, on which residents hauled food, firewood and, before long, corpses.

By November starvation and related diseases were taking a heavy toll. By November 9 the city had only seven days' supply of flour left, eight days of cereals, and no more meat. Longer-term hopes also dimmed when on November 8 the Germans captured the railroad junction of Tikhvin, which cut off transport of supplies to Lake Ladoga until a makeshift road could be built to Kobona. To prevent food supplies in the city from running out entirely, on November 13 Pavlov cut the citizens* ration to 300 grams of bread for factory workers and 150 grams for everyone else. A week later, on November 20, he had to cut it again, to 250 grams for factory workers and 125 grams (two slices) for everyone else. The city's entire population was living on only 510 tons of flour (about 30 carloads) a day. This was below the subsistence level and the new rations doomed thousands, but there was no choice. Worse, in order to stretch out supplies, by that point in time the "bread" had been adulterated over 50 percent with other ingredients like cellulose, tree bark, sawdust, and scraps of leather having scant nutritional value.[72] Pavlov's scientists invented new concoctions from ingredients never thought to be edible. One was cottonseed oil cake, formerly intended as fuel in ships and thought to be poisonous. But it was reprocessed into edible form. Perfume factories refined industrial oils for consumption. Meathouses reprocessed grease and made sausages from horse meat, peas, and soya flour. Bones were ground into soup. Vitamins were extracted from pine needles and mixed into an infusion which citizens drank daily to combat rampant scurvy.

People grew desperate as the hunger pangs gnawed inside. The city's animal population—horses, cats, dogs, crows, pigeons, rats—virtually disappeared, both from being eaten and from their own starvation. Starving rats attacked people asleep in their beds. Cats and dogs brought high prices (an average month's wage) on the black market;[73] butchers took a share as payment for cutting them up. Eventually even the police only had five dogs left in the whole city. People sold their books, nonessential clothing, gold, jewels, other valuables, even pianos for a few slices of bread. People ate wallpaper paste (partly made from flour, as people discovered) and then the wallpaper itself, likewise with bookbindings. People boiled leather, gobbled down peat, ate medicines and petroleum jelly as food, dug up flower bulbs from the Botanical Garden, and gnawed on wood. People hid dead family members in their apartments until the end of the month in order to utilize their unexpired ration cards.[74]

In the filthy conditions illnesses began to take their toll on people weakened by famine. The least infection of flu could be deadly. At one point typhus broke out

---

*Soldiers fighting the Germans received rations equal to or higher than workers. People understood and generally accepted this discrimination. Physical weakness from malnutrition was a major cause of the ineffectiveness of the troops in their attempts to break the blockade.

despite the frigid conditions, but the areas were quarantined and fortunately it did not become an epidemic. The most ubiquitous disease was that brought on by malnutrition, called dystrophy, which in its final stage was terminal.

Despite all efforts, by November people began dropping like flies. The city's death rates were without parallel in modern history. According to incomplete Soviet statistics, 11,085 people died of hunger and related diseases in November, 52,881 in December, and a total of 199,187 in January–February. But these official figures are certainly low and some estimates put the death rate at about 10,000 a day during the worst part of the winter.[75] Men and teenage boys weakened and died first because they were engaged in more physically demanding tasks without receiving a larger ration, then came those on the smallest rations.[76] But by February and March the majority of dystrophy cases were women.

Those who remained alive lost their strength. When walking on the street people would have to stop every few seconds to rest; the walk to work and climbing stairs became exhausting. As one resident wrote of the experience:

> I walked and walked and suddenly sat down in a snowdrift . . . I sit and don't understand why I have sat down. And suddenly I understood . . . it was so horrible and—above all—disgusting to die, but from what? Not from a shell fragment, not from a bomb, but from hunger . . . ! This idea made me so sick, so miserable that I jumped up—I don't know where I got the strength—and even ran a few steps.[77]

But not everyone could get up. Pedestrians staggering and collapsing to their death on the street became part of daily life.

The city's only hope lay in bringing supplies over the ice of Lake Ladoga, on what became known as the "Road of Life." In the autumn Zhdanov had ordered scientists to calculate the rate of ice formation at various temperatures and how much ice was needed to support various kinds of loads. Zhdanov and Pavlov waited desperately for the ice to form, but then they received horrible news. On November 8, just days before the ice would be ready, Tikhvin was captured by the Germans, who were attempting to link up with the Finns on the east side of the lake and seal the city off completely. This meant that supplies could not be brought near the lake by train. Unless this problem was solved, the ice road would be useless and Leningrad would perish. An army of peasants and soldiers was quickly mobilized and ordered to construct a makeshift dirt road 220 miles long through the swampy wilderness from Kobona to the closest rail depots, at Podborove and Zabore.

Fortunately, the abnormally cold weather meant that Ladoga's ice formed earlier than usual. At about 9:00 A.M. on November 17, in bitter cold a reconnaissance party ventured onto the four-inch thick ice by foot, dressed in white camouflage, roped together like alpinists and carrying ice axes. They set up flags every hundred yards or so to mark out the future ice road. Engineers advised that the road would be ready for regular transport in a few more days. But by then there were only about two days' supplies in the city at the November 13th ration, and on the 20th

Pavlov had to lower the rations again to stretch them further. Zhdanov saw that he could wait no longer and ordered the road opened. The first supply train set off on the 20th, consisting of a few hundred horses pulling sledges with light (200 to 250 pound) loads. The weight of the loads increased each day as the ice thickened, but for several days most shipments were by horse; the first trucks began running on November 22, but many fell through the ice (40 in the first 7 days). It took time to build up a meaningful daily volume. By the end of November, less than a two-day supply of starvation rations of flour had been delivered over the route. Leningrad was losing ground, and at that rate would soon run out. As the stores of supplies at Kobona were transferred, the bottleneck became the primitive road from Zabore to Kobona, which opened only on December 6 and soon was teeming with thousands of trucks. But it took a week for a truck to cover the distance to the lake, and the Germans bombed the route. Many trucks slid off the shoulder and got stuck or were wrecked; others simply broke down in the harsh conditions. Within days, of the 3,500 trucks operating on the road, 1,300 of them were out of service, awaiting repair. Ultimately over 1,000 trucks were lost.[78]

If feeding Leningrad had depended on that road, the city would have perished. But Tikhvin was recaptured on December 9. Within a few days the rail connection to Novaya Ladoga was restored, and by the end of the month to Voibokalo. Now supplies could be brought by rail near the lake. New and better trucks also were brought into service on the ice road. German bombs were ineffective as they fell through the ice and exploded underwater. Shipment volumes now increased. The number of roadways across the lake eventually multiplied to nearly 60. Zhdanov was also able to begin further evacuations of the city using trucks returning over the ice road. He set a quota of 5,000 per day, but the numbers of evacuees fell below this (only 105,000 by January 22, about two-thirds of them Baltic refugees).[79] But in January–April over half a million people were evacuated.

When Zhdanov and Pavlov met on December 23, the city was down to two days' supply of flour and people were perishing rapidly, but the outlook for sufficient supplies in the near future was promising. The pressure to increase the ration was tremendous. Zhdanov asked him, "Can you guarantee that the supplies will come in without interruption?"[80] It was hard for Pavlov to answer anything but yes, and on December 25 the ration for workers was increased by 100 grams, 75 grams for everyone else. Leningraders rejoiced, but this was a terrible gamble which at the time seemed justified by more than just the growing volume of supplies. There were fewer mouths to feed because of the many deaths and the ongoing evacuations. To Zhdanov it also appeared that the recapture of Tikhvin soon would be followed by the recovery of Mga as well, thus opening the rail line from the interior into the city and rendering the ice road a secondary route. But Mga was not retaken, and the increase in shipments coming in over the ice and of evacuees going out was painfully slow. In early January, the city still had only two days' supply of food. Never had the city been closer to perishing. If just one truck arrived late or not at all, thousands of Leningraders would not get their ration that day and scores would die. One driver who returned to his barracks from work after delivering his load late found the following note on the bulletin board: "Driver Sapozhnikov: Yesterday, thanks to you, 5,000 Leningrad women and children got no bread ration."[81] Just after New Year's, Zhdanov warned that the city's fate "hangs on a thread."[82]

But Leningraders somehow found a way to celebrate the New Year. The city authorities allowed an hour or two of extra electric light on New Year's Eve. Hungry as they were, many people had managed to save something special for the occasion—the last bottle of wine or champagne, candy, nuts, or some horse meat sausage. Families enjoyed such delicacies gathered around wick lamps or candles, and maybe a decorated evergreen branch. On the radio they heard the Spasky Chimes in Moscow playing the "Internationale," and Vera Inber read her new war poem, later entitled *Pulkovo Meridian*. The Nazis, of course, shelled the city that night, and the Baltic Fleet's guns answered back with their own New Year's greeting.

But then it was back to the grim task of survival. By then the worst days of the siege were upon the city, before the supplies from the Road of Life had increased enough to make a difference. People now lacked the strength to do the simplest chores. Those on worker's rations forced themselves to go to work just to preserve the higher ration for themselves and their families, but there was little to do other than maintain the machinery that they hoped would again be called into service. And all knew that if they did nothing they would not last long; and having nothing to do was worse than a bombing raid, many admitted. Those who gulped down their bread ration when they got it in the morning and returned home to crawl under a blanket were the first to go. "Today it is so simple to die," wrote one resident in her diary. "You just begin to lose interest, then you lie on the bed and you never again get up."[83] So people busied themselves. Ordinary citizens wrote diaries; writers planned and wrote novels and plays based on the experience. Scientists and scholars, including the Hermitage staff, continued their research work and wrote out their findings and theories, fearing that their knowledge and contributions would be lost should they die.[84] Almost as a challenge to the enemy, the Hermitage went through with its planned celebrations in honor of the birth of the Uzbek poet Alisher Navoi; it did not matter that no one there was Uzbek. Lectures were read and Navoi's poetry was recited; some participants died over the next few days, possibly from the exertions.[85] The denizens of the cellar of St. Isaac's looking after the treasures of the suburban palaces similarly held "basement evenings" of art lectures.[86] Reading in general became more than ever a pastime, especially *War and Peace*. The Public Library lost 138 members of its staff in the siege, but it never closed and was a popular venue for artists and scholars to gather. When it was too dark or people were too weak even to read, they listened to the radio. But in many people hunger brought on psychoses or a delirium that confined them to their beds. At the Hermitage the staff got through the ordeal together; about 2,000 lived in its cellars waiting for deliverance, but several died each day. Orbeli's unused packing materials were used to make coffins. The cellar in the Small Hermitage was turned into a mortuary.[87]

Meanwhile corpses piled up on the streets once most people lacked the strength to take them by sled to the cemeteries. As one siege veteran described it:

> People walked and fell, stood and toppled. The streets were littered with corpses. In pharmacies, doorways, entries, landings, and thresholds there were bodies. They lay there because people threw them there, like foundlings. The janitors swept them out in the morning like rubbish. Funerals, graves and coffins had been forgotten long ago. It was a flood of death no one could handle. The hospitals were crammed with mountains of thousands of corpses, blue, emaciated, horrible. People pulled bodies silently down the street on sleds. They sewed them up in rags or simply covered them.[88]

People without the strength to carry corpses pushed them out of windows onto the street, where they were covered by snow and pedestrians unknowingly walked over them until spring. Entrepreneurial grave diggers advertised on walls to remove and bury corpses for bread. Whole families vanished, the most famous instance being that of 11-year-old Tanya Savicheva, who recorded the deaths of all of her family members and the neighbors on seven sheets of paper that have come down to posterity: "Zhenya died 28 Dec. 1941 at 12:00 A.M. Grandma died Jan. 25 at 3 P.M. 1942. Lyoka died 17 March at 5 A.M. 1942. Uncle Vasya died Apr. 13 at 2 A.M. 1942. Uncle Lyosha May 10 at 4 P.M. 1942. Mama May 13 at 7:30 A.M. 1942. The Savichev's have died. All have died. Only Tanya remains." Tanya herself died of malnutrition in 1943.

Most people maintained order, helped at least their families and friends, and no riots broke out. Komsomols were organized to go house to house to check on families, and they saved thousands. But in these worst days of the ordeal civilization had begun to unravel. Most enterprises had closed. There were no public services, and the canal water which people now used stank of death. The city was dark with virtually no electricity, only 3,000 kilowatts from a single turbine. Fires burned freely. The Haymarket had become a den of crime and riffraff that recalled the worst of Dostoevsky's visions. Food crime rose. Evidence of cannibalism came to light, and rumors flew about cannibalist fraternities. Indeed, pedestrians did notice parts missing from corpses, and human heads were seen lying in snowbanks. One young man buying black market boots for his girlfriend on the Haymarket was invited to the seller's apartment to close the deal. As his well-fed host opened the door, he told those inside that he was bringing a "live one." The young man noticed meat hanging from hooks inside and fled.[89] No one asked what went on inside people's apartments; the streets grew more dangerous. Parents kept their children close at home, but many no longer had parents. Newly orphaned children roamed the streets or died alone in apartments. The police and fire brigades were no longer functional; governmental authority deteriorated. The streets were ruled by military patrols or criminals, reminiscent of *The Twelve*. Since empty apartments were often now looted while people were in bomb shelters and people lacked the strength to move, many now waited out the shelling at home. Life retreated inside. A journalist wrote in his diary late January: "The city is dead. . . . The city is dying as it has lived for the last half-year, clenching its teeth."[90]

RESURRECTION AND LIBERATION

But spring did come, and the city came back to life. The Road of Life was working better by late January, increasing food supplies in the city and permitting more evacuations across the ice. The Road also delivered military supplies and fuel, so the city became warmer and lighter. Rations were raised on January 24 and again on February 11, to 500 grams for workers, 400 for other employees, and 300 for dependents and children. The Road operated until April 24, and when the ice cleared shipments by boat began. Using boats also allowed larger evacuations of people (528,000 by the end of the navigation season) and of factories, while 250,000 more troops were brought in to defend the city.[91] Food lines decreased as the population was evacuated. By July only 1,100,000 million civilians remained,[92] and by the end of 1942 the city had only 637,000 people, one-fourth of its 1941 population.[93] The city now seemed deserted, like in the Civil War. Pipe was located in the abandoned Izhorsk Factory and a fuel pipeline was quickly laid under the Lake, which went into operation on June 19. The city laid in large food reserves for the next winter.

City authorities prepared for the warm weather, which posed a threat to public health potentially greater than what the city had been through. Despite the filthy conditions, disease had been kept in check so far by the cold. But if the city were not cleaned up before the warm weather came, major epidemics would wipe out much of the weakened population and the city's fabric and infrastructure would collapse. The task was like cleaning the Augean Stables or, as Vera Inber put it, "like trying to clean up the North Pole if it were covered with refuse."[94] Beginning March 8 (International Women's Day) when the snow was still on the streets and continuing into mid-April, the city authorities called all able-bodied people into the streets for official cleanup days. The first big cleanup was on March 15, when 100,000 turned out, and the numbers grew thereafter until they reached 318,000 on April 4. The enfeebled, tottering citizens, some barely able to hold a shovel, worked slowly but steadily and with determination. As one participant, an old dock worker, later recounted to a journalist:

> No one believed that it could ever be tidied up. But as soon as the sun began to have a bit of warmth in it everybody turned out, just like a single person. . . . There were housewives, schoolchildren and educated folk—professors, doctors, musicians, old

men and old women. One turned out with a crowbar, another with a shovel, another with a pick-ax; someone had a broom, somebody else had a wheelbarrow, some other person came with a child's sledge. Some of them hardly had the strength to drag their legs. Five people would harness themselves to the child's sledge and pull and pull until they had no strength left.[95]

By mid-April they had cleaned up over a million tons of debris and filth. Meanwhile city workers raced to repair the city's water and sewage systems. Corpses were buried in mass graves blasted from the earth. Damaged buildings were boarded up or given false wooden fronts, often painted to reproduce faithfully the building's (or former building's) façade. In mid-April the first trams began running again. Politeness and civility returned. Children began to play again.

Everyone knew that people would eat whatever sprouted from the ground that spring, so scientists studied what could be eaten and how, and the information was posted on bulletin boards and walls all over the city. When the first grass and weeds shot up, they were quickly eaten. Soups and other recipes appeared featuring nettles, dandelion, burdocks, plantain, chervil, sorrel, and daisies. Once the ground had thawed, people planted vegetable gardens all over the city where once there had been lawns or parks. St. Isaac's Square, the Field of Mars, the Summer Garden, and even the Hanging Gardens at the Hermitage soon boasted rows of cabbage, potatoes, and other vegetables. Those who planted and tended their individual plots proudly displayed name signs identifying their work.

In late March the city also heard the first performance of Shostakovich's Seventh Symphony, a radio broadcast of a concert in Moscow conducted by the composer himself. On the score's title page, Shostakovich had written, "dedicated to Leningrad." All of Leningrad gathered around their radios to listen to music that spoke of their burdens and emotions. Olga Berggolts, who had been ferried to Moscow to be at the concert, watched Shostakovich as he rose to the ovation. "I looked at him," she said, "small, frail, with big glasses and thought, 'This man is stronger than Hitler.'"[96] The score was sent to Leningrad in June, and rehearsals were held for six weeks before it was performed at the Philharmonic Hall on August 9. "All Leningrad" turned out for the event, for the first time in perhaps a year wearing their best suits and dresses; the motley musicians wore only sweaters, vests, jackets, even collarless shirts. The crystal chandeliers and velvet curtains still hung in the hall, though some windows had been broken and were boarded up. The audience listened to the orchestra play with inspiration and agitation against the sound of artillery fire outside. "When they played the finale, everyone in the audience stood up," wrote one witness. "It was impossible to listen to it sitting down. Impossible."[97] The troops on the front line listened by radio.

On the military front, the army made several attempts during the warm months to break the blockade, but they were never strong enough to dislodge the entrenched Germans. Eventually, a plan, called Operation Iskra ("Spark") was conceived to accumulate enough troops and munitions (which the city's remaining factories were again producing) to break through in the early winter over the Neva ice and frozen swamps near Schlüsselburg and in a pincers move join up with other units attacking from Volkhov. The Russians attacked on January 12, 1943, with over 4,500 guns and multibarreled Katyusha rockets. They broke through on January 18, at which point technically the land siege of the city was broken because the rail route from the interior to the city could be restored. Leningraders rejoiced. Olga Berggolts announced on Radio Leningrad: "The blockade is broken. . . . We shall triumph! . . . We know we have much to live through and much to bear. But we'll endure everything. Now we have already felt our strength."[98] Vera Inber added in her broadcast: "This snow-strewn moon-lit night of January 18–19 will never vanish from the memory of those who experienced it."[99] The question in many people's minds was now not if the full blockade would be lifted, but when.

Since Mga remained in German hands, the rail route into town now ran over a newly built railroad bridge at Schlüssselburg, then well north of the Neva and into the Finland Station. The first train from the interior with food, other supplies, and a delegation from Moscow arrived on February 7, pulling into a Finland Station decorated with red bunting and to the music of a band and cheers of the crowd. But the route was dangerous and might be closed down any moment. The German artillery, at one point as close as 500 yards away, shelled the tracks and trains, which usually ran at night without lights. The rail gauntlet between Volkhov and Schlüsselburg became known to some as the "road of victory," to others as the "corridor of death."[100] Over the next year, some 100,000 freight cars brought in food, fuel, and military supplies, including even some American food aid. The food ration had been increased almost to normal consumption on February 22.

Other than around the corridor of death, the German and Finnish lines remained as before, and the military siege and shelling continued. In fact, the most concentrated German shelling of the city of the entire siege was from late July to early September 1943. But otherwise life kept improving. Cinemas and theaters reopened; soccer matches resumed.

In order to break the blockade once and for all, over that summer and autumn the Red Army employed on a larger scale the same strategy of building up superior forces and attacking in the early winter that had worked in Operation Iskra. Inside the ring and near Volkhov to the east, they built up massive firepower: 21,600 guns (against Group North's 10,070), 1,475 tanks (against 385), 1,500 Katyusha rockets, together with mountains of munitions (over 1,000 freight cars of imported shells, in addition to those produced in Leningrad). The shells produced in Leningrad could be distinguished by the special inscriptions painted on them by Leningraders: "For our murdered friends," "[As payment] for the blood of Leningrad's workers," and "For our children's anguish."[101] Soviet officers and troops eventually outnumbered Germans almost 2 to 1 (1,241,000 to 741,000). This was probably the largest concentration of firepower along a short front ever assembled, more than at Stalin-grad.[102] The plan called for a three-pronged offensive from Oranienbaum, Pulkovo Heights, and the Volkhov front toward Novgorod, all under the command of General Leonid Govorov. Saving the city from massive retaliatory artillery bombardment depended on striking hard and pushing the enemy lines back rapidly so the Nazis could not regroup and fire upon the city.[103]

On the morning of January 15, 1944, the young writer Pavel Luknitsky, living at the Writers House at 9 Griboyedov Canal, got up before dawn and began reading a French novel by the light of his kerosene lamp. Suddenly the sounds of massive artillery erupted and shook the entire building. He rushed to the window, fearing another bombardment. But despite the noise there were no explosions, no air raid sirens. Suddenly someone exclaimed, "This isn't a bombardment! Those are our guns!" "It's begun!" Luknitsky said.[104] As they listened to the roar of the artillery, the whole city knew that the moment they had awaited for 29 months had finally come.

Indeed, the liberation of Leningrad had begun. On the 14th Soviet forces had attacked on the Volkhov and Oranienbaum fronts, pounding the German lines with over 100,000 rounds and moving them back about two miles. On the 15th the center joined in, firing half a million shells plus Katyusha rockets into the German lines and advancing six miles. The partisan forces behind German lines carried out coordinated attacks. Within a few days the Soviets had taken back Pushkin, Pavlovsk, Peterhof, Ropsha, Gatchina, Novgorod, and Mga. On January 22 the Germans were retreating in disorder and it was hard to keep up with them. At 8:00 P.M. on January 27, Zhdanov announced to the people of Leningrad that the longest siege ever endured by a modern city was officially over.* Then 324 guns fired 24 salvos, and golden rockets streamed across the sky in tribute to the defenders of the city and its liberation. The city celebrated that evening for the first time in years, with fireworks and joy mixed with tears. That evening Vera Inber, the poet who had spoken so often to Leningraders during the siege, tried to express her feelings in her diary. "The greatest event in the life of Leningrad: full liberation from blockade. And I, a professional writer, have no words for it. I simply say: Leningrad is free. And that is all."[105]

On the eve of the first anniversary of the city's liberation, the Presidium of the Supreme Soviet of the USSR awarded the city of Leningrad the Order of Lenin, and 470,000 of its citizens received medals "For the Defense of Leningrad," including Akhmatova for her poem *Courage*. Many more who had earned such honors had perished. More people died in the siege of Leningrad than had ever died

---

*The counteroffensive against the Finns on the Karelian peninsula was not commenced until June 10, 1944, Vyborg was taken on June 20, and the Soviets then drove the Finns across the Vuoksi River to the northeast. Then the Soviets attacked on the northeast shore of Lake Ladoga and completed the operation on August 9.

in any modern city from anything. The original Soviet figure was 632,253 civilian deaths from hunger and 16,747 from bombardments, but these figures are incomplete and cover only the city proper rather than the other areas inside the blockade. More recent estimates put the total of about 1 million civilian deaths for the area inside the blockade, and from 1.3 to 1.5 million if military deaths are included.[106] About 600,000 of the victims are buried in mass graves of about 20,000 each at Piskarevskoe Cemetery, which since December 1941 had been the official burial place of the siege. In 1960 a memorial with an eternal flame and a large statue of Mother Russia was placed there, bearing the lines of Olga Berggolts:

> *Here lie Leningraders,*
> *The men, women, and children of the city,*
> *Along with the fighting men of the Red Army.*
> *All gave their lives*
> *In defending you, O Leningrad,*
> *Cradle of the revolution.*
> *We cannot list the names*
> *Of the noble ones who lie beneath this eternal granite.*
> *But of those honored by this stone*
> *Let no one forget, let nothing be forgotten.*

On May 1, 1945, the Presidium of the USSR Supreme Soviet bestowed on Leningrad the title of "Hero City."

CHAPTER 15

Rocking the Cradle

Tell us something of St. Petersburg,
For as yet we have not seen it.
Long ago we implored the producers
Please, do not bring us all those miscellaneous films
About lovely, deserted ladies,
But bring us St. Isaac's in a movie
The Bronze Horseman, the old fortress
And all about the vast St. Petersburg.

YOUNG POET E. KUCHINSKY,
in the journal *Youth*, 1960[1]

If it's not subversive, it's not rock.

BORIS GREBENSHIKOV, local rock artist

No modern city has undergone such excruciating upheavals, violence, losses of its people, and suffering as Petersburg/Petrograd/Leningrad experienced in the first half of the 20th century. Just to take the wild population swings as an example, from 2.3 million people in 1917, the city's population fell to just 720,000 people in 1920, then rose again to over 3.1 million in 1939, yet stood at only 560,000 when the blockade ended.[2] Now the city would have to be repopulated and rebuilt, and the task was enormous. Leningrad had lost about one-third of its housing, 840 factories had been destroyed, three-fourths of its industrial equipment had been lost to bombardment or evacuation, and over 500 schools had been destroyed or damaged.[3] Miles of water mains, sewage lines, streets, and tram tracks lay in ruins, over 70 bridges were destroyed or damaged, and the port lay damaged and in disrepair. When Akhmatova returned in June 1944, she called it a "terrifying specter pretending to be my city."[4]

As Leningraders prepared to rebuild, they took a moment to reflect on the ordeal they had just survived. In December 1943, once it appeared that the city would soon be liberated, Zhdanov had ordered that an exhibition about the siege be organized, and the city's artists and craftsmen set to work gathering siege artifacts and

527

constructing panoramas and other exhibits. Held on the historical site of an 18th-century salt warehouse known as *Soleny gorodok* ("Salt Town") which shortly before the 1917 revolutions had been rebuilt as exhibit space, the exhibition opened on April 30, 1944. Outside stood rows of captured German siege guns that had bombarded the city, tanks, and other weapons. Inside were some 60,000 exhibits in 14 rooms covering some 24,000 square feet of floor space. An orchestra played in the central hall.

The city thronged to the exhibition to relive their experiences. Leningraders wandered through in reverent silence to the strains of the music, whispering only occasionally. As visitors left the exhibition, they felt secure in thinking that the memory of the siege would be preserved. But it was also now behind glass, and it was time to move on with life.

The city's defenders had pursued Hitler's armies back to Berlin, vanquished his regime, and paraded through the Brandenburg Gate much as Alexander I's army had paraded under the Arc de Triomphe in 1814. Leningrad's soldiers returned and, on July 8, 1945, held a victory parade on Palace Square. Like the veterans returning from Paris after the war with Napoleon, they had seen Europe and looked forward to a new and better life. In 1825, such visions had led to the Decembrist uprising, a point surely not lost on Stalin. He was not about to let rising expectations threaten Soviet power or his personal rule.

THE FINAL INSULT

After the war, Leningrad's leaders made grand plans for a renaissance of the city and a restoration of much of its historical vanguard role. In October 1943 the City Council commissioned an ambitious plan to transform the city into a monument of modern technology, design, and comfort.[5] Chief Architect Nikolai Baranov and his team studied other cities, including Paris and Washington, incorporating what they thought were the best features of each, and produced an elegant quarto volume of plans and sketches even before the end of the blockade.[6] After the siege was lifted, on April 11, 1944, Zhdanov gave a speech at the first postwar plenary session of the Leningrad City and Regional Party in which he outlined his grand vision for a renaissance of the city. Leningrad was not merely to be reconstructed, he said, but to be made grander and more comfortable than ever. The historical buildings and sites would be restored, a grand square would be built in front of Smolny to mark the city's governmental and administrative center, the Finland Station area would become a monument to Lenin featuring his image atop the armored car from which he once spoke, and the seacoast to the south would be developed, reviving Peter the Great's vision of a city oriented toward the sea. Zhdanov called for massive housing programs, as well as expansion of light industry to produce more consumer goods. The plan contemplated a population of 3.5 million.

But the city would be more than just buildings and factories; it was to reassume most of its former vanguard role. This was openly advocated by the Leningrad writer Vsevolod Vishnevsky in a rousing radio address: "The city cannot . . . weaken its historical push, its drive, its will. It is used to being in the front ranks— always, unfailingly. . . . We can do it!"[7] Again the city would be the Window to Europe and to trade with the West. Some prominent citizens like Ilya Ehrenburg even argued that since the Soviet Union was the victor in the war, "*We* have become the heart of Europe, the bearers of her tradition, the continuators of her boldness, her builders and her poets."[8] The city, as the bearer of the new communist vision of a just social order, would have an ecumenical role like that envisioned by Zinoviev following the October Revolution. Some leaders even spoke rashly of the city once again becoming the capital.[9]

There was some reason to believe that this ambitious vision would come to fruition. As a result of the war, the city's Party elite were in positions of national prominence from which they might be able to secure the necessary support and resources for the task.[10] And because of the siege the city had also attained unmatched moral authority. Leningrad had acquired the mythos of a martyr city, its valiant struggle symbolizing the strength, soul, and mission of the nation. It seemed to deserve special consideration. Indeed, Zhdanov's plan presupposed that the city would receive a disproportionate amount of the country's reconstruction budget, which would be needed for the plan to be fully realized. But for it to work, Stalin had to be convinced, and moral authority did not count for anything with him. He had always hated the city and had other plans for it, and the fact that the city's Party leaders were gathering strength simply meant that the time was ripe for another Leningrad purge.

After the sacrifices during the first two Five-Year Plans and the privations of the war, Russians throughout the country looked forward to a better material life with more consumer goods. But Stalin wanted to hold onto Eastern Europe, saw the Cold War looming, and wanted to provide for military needs, so he again gave priority to heavy industry, leaving few resources for consumer goods or grandiose urban plans. Zhdanov's vision for the city conflicted with Stalin's priorities, and he fell into line. The grand architectural plan vanished, and the idea of a renaissance and an ecumenical Leningrad faded. Except for industry, Stalin allocated only meager funds to the restoration of Leningrad, only about the same as the peacetime 1940 budget, and most of this was for housing.[11] A scaled-down city plan had to be prepared and approved in Moscow. Now, rather than receive a disproportionate share of the national restoration budget, Leningrad suffered discrimination, and it was the last of the country's great cities to be restored after the war, far behind Moscow, Kiev, Odessa, Minsk, and Stalingrad.[12]

Having denied the city money, Stalin then turned his wrath on the city's intelligentsia. In this Zhdanov, who had moved to Moscow in April 1944 to resume his career in the Kremlin, regained his prewar role as Stalin's factotum for ideology and culture. At the end of the siege, the city's intelligentsia hoped for a cultural renaissance that would parallel the restoration of the city. Akhmatova returned to the city and quickly became the grande dame of the city's postwar intelligentsia. Her poems were again published and were as popular as ever, she read her verses at official gatherings in Leningrad and Moscow, and her pictures appeared in the newspapers. She also received numerous visitors in her modest apartment in the former Sheremetev Palace (known as Fountain House), many of whom, like Berggolts, had experienced the whole siege and related it to her.

Another of her visitors was a young Oxford professor, Isaiah Berlin, then serving as provisional First Secretary at the British Embassy in Moscow. Born in Riga in 1909, Berlin was no stranger to the city, and wanted to see it following its liberation and to meet with members of its intelligentsia. When he arrived in late 1945, naturally one of his stops was the Writers' Bookshop on Nevsky Prospect, where as a foreign guest he was admitted to the back room not accessible to the general public. There he fell into conversation about the city and its writers with the literary scholar Vladimir Orlov, who knew Akhmatova and agreed to arrange a meeting with her. She invited Berlin over that afternoon to her flat at Fountain House. Berlin found her to be "immensely dignified, with unhurried gestures, a noble head, beautiful, somewhat severe features, and an expression of immense sadness. I bowed—it seemed appropriate for she looked and moved like a tragic queen."[13] They immediately hit it off and were soon engrossed in conversation. But suddenly they heard someone shouting Berlin's name in English from outside. It was none other than Winston Churchill's son, Randolph, who had come to Russia as a journalist and wanted Berlin to interpret for him. Realizing the danger to Akhmatova of being seen with a Westerner, Berlin rushed out and left with Churchill, but when he later called Akhmatova to apologize, she said it was all right and invited him back that evening to finish the conversation. Berlin recalled that Akhmatova spoke "without the slightest trace of self-pity, like a princess in exile, proud, unhappy, unapproachable, in a calm, even voice, at times in words of moving eloquence,"[14] and their meeting lasted until well into the next morning.* They spoke of their favorite (and not-so-favorite) writers, about the city and Akhmatova's life in it, and of Berlin's life abroad. Akhmatova read some of her poems, including *Requiem* and *Poem without a Hero*. Berlin offered to copy them down, but Akhmatova said that was not necessary because they were about to be published. Berlin visited Akhmatova again on his next trip to the city in January 1946. The visits left indelible impressions on them both. Berlin left a memoir of their conversations, while Akhmatova wrote a cycle of poems, *Cinque*, about the meetings and included Berlin as a character (the Guest from the Future) in the final version of *Poem without a Hero*.

---

*At around 3:00 A.M. her son Lev arrived. He had served in the army and participated in the capture of Berlin, was reinstated in the history faculty at the university.

The meetings also left an indelible impression on Stalin, who immediately learned about them.* "This means our nun† is now receiving visits from foreign spies,"[15] he reportedly remarked. Stalin now had his excuse to launch the campaign in Leningrad that he had been planning for some time. He wanted to show that the looser censorship and relative freedom during the war to interact with Westerners was over, and Leningrad was again made the example.

On August 14, 1946, the Central Committee of the Communist Party passed a resolution condemning the literary journals *Leningrad* and *Zvezda* for publishing the works of Akhmatova and Zoshchenko. *Leningrad* was closed and the editorial board of *Zvezda* shaken up. Stalin then dispatched Zhdanov to Leningrad to take more concrete action. Zhdanov summoned a meeting of the Leningrad branch of the Union of Writers on September 4, 1946, at which he gave a long speech denouncing Akhmatova and Zoshchenko and announcing a regulation expelling them and other local literati (including Olga Berggolts) from the Union. Extolling Socialist Realism, he claimed that Akhmatova's work "can do nothing but harm" to the morals of the young and cause them "to leave the wide paths of public life and activity for the narrow little world of personal experience."[16] "The gloomy tone of hopelessness before death, mystical experiences intermingled with eroticism—this is the spiritual world of Akhmatova, one of the leftovers from the sunken, irretrievable world of the old aristocratic culture" who is "half nun, half harlot, or rather a harlot-nun whose sin is mixed with prayer."[17] As for the city, Zhdanov continued, the denounced writers "do not hold Soviet Leningrad as the path. They want to see it as the personification of another sociopolitical order and of another ideology. Old Petersburg, the Bronze Horseman, as an image of that old Petersburg—that looms before their eyes. But we love Soviet Leningrad, Leningrad as the progressive center of Soviet culture."[18] At Zhdanov's instigation, Soviet critics also reached into Petersburg's past to condemn Dostoevsky as among the "enemies of the Soviet people and the working class" and linked his ideas to those of the "ideological lackeys of Wall Street."[19]

But that evening the victims were not present to defend themselves. Akhmatova learned that something was amiss only the next day when she went out to buy some fish and ran into a frantic Zoshchenko on the street. "Anna Andreyevna, what can we do?" he cried in despair. Not knowing what he was talking about, she tried to

---

*Akhmatova was being watched, and an NKVD agent was stationed outside her apartment. Churchill's son was certainly being watched, and probably Berlin as well.

†For some time already Akhmatova had been characterized as "half nun, half harlot" or in similar terms. The appellation derives from a 1923 lecture by the critic Boris Eikhenbaum, who used similar terms in a different, and positive, context to describe Akhmatova's mingling of erotic and religious motifs in her poems. The characterization was soon cast in negative terms in the article about her in the *Soviet Literary Encyclopedia*, and the phrase found its way into Zhdanov's and Stalin's vocabulary. See Berlin, *Akhmatova*, pp. 54–55.

reassure him and then went home. Only when she unwrapped the fish from the newspaper did she see the article about their expulsion. Life changed overnight. Her works were again banned, her ration card was canceled, and she again lived in hunger; even the shopkeepers at the food market at first refused to sell to her. People avoided her, often crossing the street when they saw her coming. But she maintained a group of loyal friends who helped her bear up. She and the other condemned writers lived like shadows in the city. She later wryly remarked to a friend, "I was famous, then I was very infamous, and I am convinced that essentially it's one and the same thing."[20]

Zhdanov's campaign was broadened into a reign of general cultural terror which became known as the *Zhdanovshchina*. Soon it swept up other poets and writers like Pasternak, as well as composers. Any music that did not contain a melody that could be hummed, said Zhdanov, was to be condemned, and so Shostakovich, Prokofiev, and Aram Khachaturian were all rebuked as formalists and silenced.[21] Part two of Eisenstein's epic film *Ivan the Terrible* was not released because it portrayed Ivan, on whom Stalin modeled himself, as "weak and indecisive, somewhat like Hamlet" and the *oprichnina* as a "degenerate band, rather like the Ku Klux Klan."[22]

Zhdanov died suddenly in August 1948 under suspicious circumstances, possibly the result of Kremlin intrigue or even Stalin's wishes. Whatever the truth, as in the case of Kirov's murder, having Leningrad's chieftain dead provided Stalin with the opportunity to launch in 1948–49 another purge of the Leningrad Party hierarchy. The Soviets called it the "Leningrad Affair," a designation which highlighted the city's ancient tensions with Moscow.[23] The charges? An alleged wartime plot to deliver the city to the Germans or, alternatively, to blow up the city and the Baltic Fleet (though Stalin himself had ordered this); and after the war, an alleged coup plot to set up a regime in league with foreign powers and to transfer the capital to Leningrad.[24] Thus Stalin completed the tragedy of the siege by arresting and executing the people who had led the struggle for the city's survival. The victims included Alexei Kuznetsov, who had led the defense of the city and was Zhdanov's successor as Leningrad Party chief; Peter Popkov, Mayor of Leningrad during the siege and now Regional Party Chief; and P.A. Tyurkin, who had managed the Road of Life.[25] Once the more influential city leaders were gone, the Leningrad Party ranks, already decimated by the war, had no influence in Moscow and it was easy to complete the purge. Eventually about 2,000 Leningrad Party members were removed, many of them arrested and shot. Thus were removed from the national leadership those Leningrad Party members who could have spoken on behalf of the city and advanced its interests. From then at least until the rise of Grigory Romanov as Leningrad Party Chief in the 1970s, the city suffered discrimination in relation to Moscow and other cities and was the target of a deliberate policy to provincialize the city and keep it down.

As in the original Terror of the 1930s, the new terror spread generally into Leningrad society and, more than before, the city itself was a victim. Though

Berggolts had proclaimed, "Let no one forget, let nothing be forgotten," erasing the memory of the siege was precisely what Stalin now tried to achieve. He began the cover-up in order to degrade the image of the city, hide the many costly mistakes of his regime during the blockade, and leave only a positive legacy of the ordeal. He began systematically to put the historical record of the siege down an Orwellian memory hole. The documents of the siege were secured, put in storage, and would not be available to historians for a quarter century, and Zhdanov's role in the siege was nearly erased. The Museum of the Defense of Leningrad was closed in 1949, and its director was arrested and sent to a concentration camp in Siberia. The Museum's exhibits disappeared; its guidebooks were confiscated. Along the sunny side of Nevsky Prospect the blue and white signs painted on buildings warning "Citizens! During bombardment this side of the street is the more dangerous!" had been retained in memory of the siege, but now Stalin had them painted out. Those writers who had lived through the blockade and planned to publish meaningful novels and plays about the experience saw their hopes dashed. Either they were not published or the "negative" and "demoralizing" elements were edited out by censors.[26] Plans for a memorial to the victims of the siege were halted. The memorial at Piskarevskoe Cemetery was dedicated only in 1960, during Khrushchev's Thaw.

At the same time, Stalin also launched a new wave of repressions against the city's intelligentsia and culture, called the purge of the "homeless cosmopolitans." Lev Gumilev was again arrested in 1949 and sent to the Gulag. So was Punin, who died in the camps in 1953. The Director of the Hermitage, Orbeli, lost his job for refusing to toe Stalin's line in a *Pravda* article condemning Orbeli's long deceased mentor at the Museum, Nikolai Marr.[27] Many leading scientists and scholars, including the Pushkin scholar Boris Tomashevsky, were denounced for "bourgeois cosmopolitanism" and "kowtowing to the West," demoted or fired, and barred from publishing. The Dean of Leningrad University, the literary critic Boris Eikhenbaum, also was fired. Lenfilm, to which Stalin had awarded the Order of Lenin in 1935, was practically shut down. The writings of Dostoevsky and the art and literature of the Silver Age were suppressed. Contacts with the West again dried up in a xenophobic campaign that brought down the Iron Curtain. The Window had closed yet again. Stalin treated Leningrad much as his hero Ivan the Terrible had treated Novgorod. Indeed, more than any leader since Ivan, Stalin had split the nation into ordinary citizens and *oprichnina*.

The city's intelligentsia were in despair. The pianist Vladimir Sofronitsky, while playing at home one day, could not go on and slammed down the lid of his piano, exclaiming, "I can't play! I keep thinking that a policeman will come and say, 'You're not playing the right way!'"[28] These were perhaps the gloomiest and most desperate days of the city's peacetime history. Many like Berggolts took to the bottle. Even Akhmatova wavered, dashing off a Socialist-Realist cycle of verses called *In Praise of Peace* in the hope that it would secure Lev's release. They appeared in *Ogonek*, but had no effect on Lev's fate. She poured her real effort into finishing *Poem without a*

Hero, which embodied the true enormity of Petersburg's 20th-century fate. While they waited for a respite from repression, Leningraders worked to restore the city and its historical treasures.

RESTORING THE CITY'S ARTISTIC HERITAGE

The Nazis had done their best to deprive the city of its cultural heritage. This was deliberate policy. Hitler considered the Slavs, like the Jews, an inferior people. He could not exterminate or enslave the entire Russian nation, but he did set upon a Final Solution to obliterate its historical and "subhuman" artistic heritage.[29] Yet he did not mind if his more cultured officers wanted to collect Russian art. The result was a random combination of looting and destruction.[30]

In the city, the Nazis could only shell or bomb historical sites, and fortunately the damage was minimal. But the story was worse at the suburban palace ensembles and parks of Peterhof, Pushkin, Pavlovsk, Strelna, and Gatchina, which the Germans had occupied. In a massive confiscation operation headed by Alfred Rosenberg, from the first hours of occupation the Germans arrived with trucks and train cars in which to cart away treasure. They loaded up paintings, tapestries, mirrors, porcelain, and other valuables, while individual soldiers looted randomly for their personal gain. The Samson fountain, bronze statues, and iron railings at Peterhof were taken away to be melted down, and even the Amber Room from the Catherine Palace at Pushkin, which the Russians considered too delicate to detach, was taken away and disappeared from history. What was not looted was destroyed. For the time being the structures of the buildings were preserved, though their interiors were defaced; parquet floors and precious furniture were used for firewood, and elegant rooms were used as garages for cars and motorcycles. German officers lived in the palaces; the top floor at Gatchina became an officers' brothel.[31] When the Nazis retreated, they took special vengeance.[32] They planted explosives in the palaces and other buildings and then set fire to them, leaving them as blackened shells.* They blew up the fountain system at Peterhof. They laid land mines in the parks as well as in the buildings, which were rigged with trip wires. Innocent objects like dolls or shoes were fastened to wires which would set off a bomb if picked up. What remained of the Catherine Palace exploded into the air when trip wires extending into the Great Pond were triggered.[33] In the Cameron Gallery, the Nazis placed 11 delayed-action bombs, but fortunately they were disarmed.[34] The Russians came upon the palaces as they were still burning. For his crimes against civilization and humanity, Rosenberg was convicted at Nuremberg and hanged in October 1946.

---

*They also planned to blow up Alexander Pushkin's grave at his family estate, but were thwarted by the speed of the Russian advance. Massie, *Pavlovsk*, p. 220.

After the German retreat, Leningraders had to decide what could be restored, how, where to find the money to do it, and when. The task would demand enormous resources at a time when priority was being given to industrial development and housing. Emotional debates arose over whether to restore suburban palaces at all. Some believed that the palaces were so badly damaged that it was not possible to restore them and urged that they be leveled, while others argued that at least some should be retained as a monument to Nazi barbarism. Their curators, of course, wanted to restore them fully, and their love and commitment won the day. Some decisions went all the way to Stalin himself. Pavlovsk and the other palaces got modest budgets first to preserve and inventory what remained and then, over many years, painstakingly restore the sites. The city's people joined in the work. Thousands of Leningraders volunteered to work on weekends to clean up the mess, remove stumps, and replant thousands of trees and bushes. Brigades of young girls like those who had defused bombs during the siege came to locate and disarm the thousands of land mines; some died or became amputees. Before the cleanup was over, every organization, establishment, school, and college in the city had participated in the work.[35] Then the city's artists, architects, and craftsmen began the slow task of lovingly restoring each element. Since free artistic expression was denied to them, the city's artists took solace in the politically safe work of restoring the monuments of art and preserving Petersburg's cultural heritage. Gradually, the palaces and their grounds were reopened as museums, at first only a few rooms while work continued on the remainder. The palace at Pavlovsk opened in 1957, Pushkin's in 1959, Peterhof's in 1964, and Gatchina's in 1985.* Restoration work continues.

By comparison, the Hermitage was restored at lightning speed. Orbeli was given tons of building materials and supplies needed to repair the building itself, and brigades of workers and artists set to work. The building was put back into order well enough so that an exhibition of works that had not been evacuated was opened on November 8, 1944. Meanwhile, the Hermitage collections that had spent the war in the Urals were quickly packed up and returned in two trains on October 10, 1945. Fortunately, very little was lost. Less than a month later, on November 4, 1945, the first 68 (out of 354) rooms of the permanent exhibit were reopened, featuring the returned treasures.

That exhibit did not feature art that had returned in the first of several trains arriving from Berlin only six days after those from the Urals. As early as 1943, the Soviet art establishment had proposed removing from conquered German territories art as compensation for the art that the Germans had destroyed, and the plan was approved by the Central Committee and Stalin. This policy found wide support

---

*Strelna was not restored following the war, but in 2000 it was chosen as the Presidential palace and full-scale renovations began. (See chapter 16, p. 582.) Oranienbaum had remained in Russian hands during the siege but was nevertheless in disrepair, and restoration, at least of some buildings, continues today.

amongst Leningraders. The British correspondent Werth reported that many Leningraders had voiced opinions like the following:

> People who deliberately destroy works of art have no right to own any. They cannot have any real love of art. . . . The least thing we can expect is that as compensation our people receive the contents of some of the German art galleries. We shall rebuild the walls of our palaces. Perhaps it is the most we can do. But at least we shall have something valuable to put into them.[36]

The allies determined not to require any formal war reparations but agreed that each could take material compensation from the territories that they occupied. In the Soviet Union's case, the Allies agreed to a $10 billion compensation scheme. Most of it was in the form of production lines and other industrial equipment, building materials, and consumer goods, but part of it was artwork.[37] The Hermitage became the recipient of new masterpieces by the Impressionists and Post-Impressionists, Raphael, Van Dyck, Botticelli and Dürer, the frieze of the altar of Zeus at Pergamum, Trojan gold discovered by Schliemann, ancient Egyptian art and artifacts, and Greek and Roman statues. Some works were briefly exhibited after the war, but then they were hidden away, to be appreciated only by specialists and those who could wrangle their way into the secret rooms. Most of these works were returned to the occupied Eastern Bloc in the 1950s as a fraternal gesture to the friendly regimes, after being put on show in two large exhibitions at the Hermitage in 1958.[38] The remainder, most of which art historians either never knew existed or thought had been lost, continued to be stored secretly until the early 1990s, when in the liberalized conditions their existence was disclosed. Some of the art has been exhibited, most notably in the 1995 *Hidden Treasures* exhibition of 74 paintings by Impressionist and Post-Impressionist masters—Degas, Gauguin, van Gogh, Manet, Monet, Renoir, Cézanne, Matisse, Pissaro, Derain, Vuillard, and others—formerly in the private collections of Otto Krebs and Otto Gerstenberg.[39] The exhibition created a world art sensation and renewed the public debate over what to do with the "treasure art." Most Russians still feel that what was once just, legally sanctioned compensation for their losses remains just compensation, while Germans consider that two wrongs do not make a right, that the world has changed and the Russians have had the art long enough. As of this writing, the fate of the art is in the hands of an intergovernmental commission and will be decided at the political level.

REBUILDING THE CITY

For the city to revive, it had to be repopulated. The population grew to 725,000 in July 1944, 920,000 by September, and 1,240,000 a year later.[40] By 1959 the figure had crossed three million, still less than the prewar number, but it took another

20 years for the four million threshold to be reached.[41] Not all evacuees returned; it was the new industrialization drive which caused the city's postwar growth. As in the 19th and early 20th centuries and in the first Five-Year Plans, peasants from the countryside flocked to the factories, and the city again became one of migrants, of peasants in workers' clothing. Because of the wartime losses of men, a historically disproportionate number of Leningraders were women. In 1945, over three-fourths of workers in industries traditionally staffed by males were female,[42] and a normal balance was achieved only after many years.

But the workplace of the mid-to-late 20th century was more sophisticated and demanded higher skills, so the city's migrant population had to be educated and trained, especially in technical fields. The city set up mass vocational training programs, as a result of which the city became the site of the Academy of Sciences' Institute of General Adult Education and the All-Union Scientific Research Institute of Professional-Technical Education.[43] The city also modernized ordinary primary and secondary education.[44] The city's school and vocational reforms became models for the rest of the country.[45]

Because so much of the city's housing stock was lost in the siege, the influx from the provinces led to a painful housing shortage, which for years perpetuated the use of communal apartments. Constructing new housing was made a priority; even prisoners from the Gulag were thrown into the effort. But significant improvements came only in the mid-1950s when the construction of large, hi-rise apartment complexes at the edge of town made of prefabricated concrete components began. Drawing on the concepts of the International Prospect project of the 1930s, these complexes were built as self-contained communities called *mikroraioni* (micro-regions) on frontage streets off the main thoroughfares, complete with schools, stores, and recreational facilities.[46] But they were aesthetically faceless and shoddily constructed, often drafty, springing leaks and needing repair before the first families moved in. These communities caused urban sprawl. Whereas the city occupied only 105 square kilometers in 1917, it had swelled to 540 by 1957 and 1,359 by 1980,[47] an increase of 13 times even though the population had less than doubled since 1917. Between 1959 and the early 1970s the population in the historical center declined by one-third,[48] and by the 1980s only 25 percent of Leningraders lived in the historical center.[49]

Since few Leningraders owned cars, they had to rely on inexpensive public transit, and huge investments were required to build the immense network. The city had begun constructing its metro in 1940, but work stopped during the siege. The first line, about 10 kilometers long with eight stations running from the center (Uprising Square on Nevsky) to the industrial regions of the Kirov Works and Avtovo, opened on November 7, 1955, the 38th anniversary of the October Revolution. As in Moscow, the metro stations were elaborate "People's Palaces" featuring heroic statues, murals and frescos, chandeliers, marble floors, columns, some made from semiprecious minerals. They were designed to glorify and make people proud of their Communist mission, though in fact they only provided a brief respite from the drabness of everyday Soviet life. The trains came every minute during rush hour, were clean, and at five kopecks (whatever the distance) were affordable to nearly all. By 2000, the metro had grown to 56 stations on over 100 kilometers of track and moved over 2.5 million passengers per day.

The city's future role in the USSR depended heavily on what direction its economy would take. With many of its factories and skilled workers permanently evacuated to the East, never to return,[50] the city's economy had suffered a severe blow, but this also provided an opportunity to develop in new directions. Indeed, Zhdanov's grand postwar plan called for more balanced development, but Stalin's plans for the city called for an even narrower focus on its traditional strengths, with light industry even decreasing.[51] The city's share of national investment eroded over time, falling from 4.6 percent before the war to 1.9 percent in the Sixth Five-Year Plan (1956–60) and only 1 percent in the Ninth and Tenth (1971–80).[52] This and the city's specialization compared to the more balanced development in Moscow meant that the city could not regain the economic importance it had before the October Revolution.[53] But within its assigned parameters, the city developed well. After having lost 75 percent of its industrial capacity during the siege, it regained its prewar level of production by 1950, and it maintained its national leadership in its traditional strengths: machinery, electronics, shipbuilding, military goods, and optical and precision instruments. In order to support its industries, the city also became a center for science, which made it the country's leader in industrial innovation.[54] The number of students in higher technical educational institutions doubled from 31,000 in 1940 to 62,000 by 1955, and by the 1970s one-fifth of its workforce was employed in scientific research at the city's many research establishments and institutions of higher learning.[55] Naturally, collaboration between these institutions and local industries and among related spheres of local industry intensified, leading in the 1960s and 1970s to the formation of numerous conglomerates called Industrial Production Associations (PPOs) and Scientific-Production Associations (NPOs). Leningrad's partnership of science and industry served and became a model for the rest of the country, though at the expense of local needs. By the mid-1970s the city's scientific establishment had performed so well, and Leningrad's Party Chief Grigory Romanov had gained such influence, that the Academy of Sciences agreed to unite all Academy scientific functions in the northwestern Russian Republic by establishing the Leningrad Scientific Center.[56]

Such rapid growth in the city's population, industry, housing, and transportation systems had to be managed pursuant to a general city plan. The 1930s International Prospect project was abandoned in favor of retaining the old historical center, though some of its individual elements like Victory Park were completed. A new plan was developed by the city's Chief Architect, Nikolai Baranov, and was adopted in 1947. It revived Peter the Great's vision of a maritime city by calling for new housing projects facing the sea, and is responsible for many of the famous landmarks seen in the city today. These include the new Finland Station (1960), the river port on the Neva, and the Victory Park on Krestovsky Island. Postwar reconstruction was symbolically brought to an end when Kirov Stadium was dedicated in July 1950 as the premier sports facility in the Soviet Union. But in the 1950s the elements in Baranov's plan dealing with housing, transportation, parks and the like, including the "movement toward the sea," were overwhelmed by the rapid pace of events and were either not realized or modified. By the early 1960s, a new plan was needed, which was adopted in 1966. Developed in the conditions of Thaw, the new plan was less utilitarian and reflected architectural, aesthetic, and environmental concerns. It called for parks and greenbelts, satellite cities and integrated planning with Leningrad Region. Such integrated social, economic, environmental, and architectural planning became a model for the rest of the country.[57] Under that plan were built many of the city's tourist hotels such as the Moskva, Leningrad, and Pribaltiskaya, and Pulkovskaya, the passenger seaport on Vasilievsky Island (1977–82), sports complexes, and the Oktyabrsky Concert Hall, some in connection with the 1980 Olympic Games, which held some competitions in Leningrad. Also erected were many of the city's war monuments, including the Monument to the Heroic Defenders of Leningrad in the mid-1970s on Moscow Prospect near Pulkovo Airport. But it proved impossible to limit population growth as planned, and the only way to meet demand was through more (and taller) large-scale prefab housing projects, which looked the same from city to city. Judging from their neighborhoods, residents might never know that they lived in the Venice of the North, which became the butt of much humor, as in the 1976 film *The Irony of Fate*, in which a Leningrader wakes up in an identical Moscow apartment building located on a street having the same name and thinks he is still at home. The 1966 plan had to be revised in the early 1980s and became known as the 1986 plan for the period 1986–2005, but it too has been overtaken by events.

Another concern became the city's ecology, which was increasingly taxed by the rapid expansion. The industrialization drive had been conceived with little attention to environmental concerns and controls. But in the early 1960s, more capital became available for urban improvements,[58] and the conditions of the Thaw permitted more open discussion about environmental and social issues. Indeed, rapid growth had created many. Despite being on the sea, the city's air was often polluted, reflected in discolored melting snow. The Baltic became overfished. To the Neva's original biological contaminants were now added toxic chemicals. Various antipollution measures and programs were ineffective. The most controversial environmental issue became the construction of the dam across the Finnish Gulf between Lisii Nos ("Fox's Nose") and Kronstadt and then from Kronstadt to Bronka, near Oranienbaum. Over 25 kilometers long and eight meters high, the dam was to contain several gates to allow the passage of ships and flow of water, and which could be closed when a flood threatens. The project bore the hallmarks of other mammoth Soviet projects of Brezhnev's time and was pushed through by Leningrad's Party Chief, Grigory Romanov, partly for political reasons: He wanted to become General Secretary following the ailing Brezhnev, and needed the glory of a successful banner project. Construction began in 1979, and from the start environmental experts raised concerns about the adverse effects it might have on the ecology of the Neva delta. Indeed, the gulf began silting up behind the dam, and it became clear that the barrier was inhibiting the outflow of wastes from the city, even after modifications were made in the mid-1980s to try and correct the problem. Once Gorbachev initiated *glasnost*, the dam became a matter of open public debate, and later was an election issue during the first democratic elections in 1989. One candidate opposed to the project declared, "Peter I Romanov opened a window to Europe, but Grigory Romanov closed it up with a dam."[59] Work was largely suspended, and as of this writing the project is not even close to completion and its status is unclear.

CITY LIFE DURING THE THAW

Life in postwar Leningrad, as in the USSR generally, was boring and lacked vitality. According to Communist propaganda, the country was already transitioning from socialism to Communism, but every day people saw that this was a lie. The promised "radiant future" kept receding like a distant horizon. Although people's basic needs were now taken care of, consumer goods were in short supply and Western luxuries were totally lacking except for the Party elite. More importantly, the freedom to speak and act, to obtain information at home and from abroad, to read what one wanted, and to listen to the music one wanted, was constrained. Instead, sports were promoted, and people were fed deadening radio and television programming, and safe or propagandistic films and music. Komsomol and Party life became bureaucratized, and these organizations became vehicles to a comfortable, privileged life and career rather than engines of progress toward Communism. Revolutionary idealism disappeared forever.

Even within the Party, hard questions were raised following Stalin's death and Beria's arrest and execution in 1953. It was now Stalin's turn to be denounced, in a famous speech of Khrushchev to the 20th Party Congress in 1956, where he laid out in detail Stalin's crimes and mistakes and accused him of creating a "cult of personality." Implicitly, Stalin personally rather than the Soviet system was at fault. To prove the point, Khrushchev quickly moved to create a kinder, gentler Communism with greater freedoms, inaugurating a period from 1956 to 1962 known as the Thaw, a term coined in the title of a novella by Ilya Ehrenburg published in *Novyi mir* in 1954. In 1956, Khrushchev also issued an amnesty under which many political prisoners were freed, including Lev Gumilev.

The Thaw did not benefit Leningraders and their city materially, but it enabled Leningraders to revive many city traditions and stimulated its cultural life. For the first time in nearly a decade, the full extent and horror of the wartime siege was acknowledged and could be discussed. A new museum of the siege was opened in 1957, and in the same year the blue and white bombardment signs reappeared on Nevsky. In 1958 Dmitry Pavlov, who had managed the city's food supplies in the crucial early months of the siege, published his groundbreaking account of the blockade.[60] Work on the Piskarevskoe memorial was begun, and it was dedicated in 1960. Akhmatova too was now in somewhat better graces. The State Literary Fund gave her a dacha in Komarovo near Finland where she would spend her last days. A small volume of her poems was published in 1957, minus, of course, *Requiem*, *Poem without a Hero*, and her other tragic works. "The path and the tragedy remained beyond the covers of the book, but the voice to which it had been given to heal souls rang out,"[61] remarked her friend, Lidia Chukovskaya. But Akhmatova still had to be careful. When Isaiah Berlin returned to the city in 1956 and tried to look Akhmatova up, she apologetically declined to see him, fearing more reprisals.

Some of Petersburg's old culture was revived. The famous statute of Pushkin on Arts Square was dedicated in 1957. Some members of *Mir iskusstva* became officially acceptable. Fokine's memoirs appeared in 1962, postcard reproductions of Benois's watercolors were printed and sold out instantly, and some books illustrated by Dobuzhinsky were also republished.[62] But the regime was not yet ready for Silver Age or *Oberiut* poetry, which remained under wraps except to those who could wrangle passes into the special sections of libraries.[63]

In music, the finale of Reingold Glier's 1949 ballet *The Bronze Horseman* was worked into the "Hymn to the Great City," the city's unofficial anthem. Beginning in the mid-1950s, at Moskovsky Train Station it began to be played when the main train to Moscow, the Red Arrow, departed and arrived. A slice of the city's history, the 1905 Revolution, was recreated in Shostakovich's 11th Symphony, entitled *1905*, premiered in November 1957 at the Leningrad Philharmonic under the baton of Evgeny Mravinsky. The greatest Russian conductor of the 20th century, Mravinsky lorded over the Philharmonic for 50 years until his death in 1988, molding it into the Soviet Union's only world-class orchestra.[64] Religious and anti-Soviet, Mravinsky had dared, in 1948 at the climax of the *Zhdanovshchina* when Shostakovich's music was being condemned, to reprise the performance of the composer's Fifth Symphony. Both he and the audience relived the famous 1937 premiere, Mravinsky again holding the score overhead and the audience standing together in an act of defiance. Now, in 1957, he got another chance with the 11th. The music was partly derived from familiar folk, revolutionary, and prison songs speaking of tyranny. One of them from the finale went:

> *Rage, you tyrants—*
> *Mock at us,*
> *Threaten us with prison and chains.*
> *We are strong in spirit, if weak in body!*
> *Shame, shame on you tyrants.*[65]

While the Symphony was ostensibly a Socialist Realist celebration of the Revolution, it was composed during the aftermath of the Soviets' repression of the 1956 Hungarian uprising and had an Aesopean subtext that was understandable to all. As one of Shostakovich's friends, Lev Lebedinsky, described it:

> What we heard in this music was not the police firing on the crowed in front of the Winter Palace in 1905, but the Soviet tanks roaring in the streets of Budapest. This was so clear to those "who had ears to listen," that his son, with whom he wasn't in the habit of sharing his deepest thoughts, whispered to Dmitri Dmitriyevich during the dress rehearsal, "Papa, what if they hang you for this?"[66]

Akhmatova, a regular at Shostakovich premieres, also understood. While Communists in the audience cheered the work's orthodoxy and anticommunists worried that he had sold out, she remarked to her friend, Lydia Chukovskaya, "In it the songs fly like angels, like birds, like white clouds against a terrible black sky."[67]

The Thaw also celebrated the return visits, in 1962, of two of the city's artistic giants who had fled for artistic freedom abroad, Igor Stravinsky and George Balanchine, who came with the New York Ballet. Until then Stravinsky's music was banned, but his visit was a triumph and reestablished at least his "Russian" works—*Firebird*, *Petrushka*, and *Rite of Spring*—in the Russian repertoire. While older balletomanes chafed at Balanchine's style, the dancing, scenery, and music laced with jazz rhythms impressed the younger artists, who thought they now saw the future of Russian ballet. The climax of the visit was Balanchine's ballet set to Stravinsky's *Agnon* performed at the Kirov. The two legends, like Diaghilev before them, represented the best of Petersburg culture, which they had taken abroad to help create a "world of art." For the city's artists who had little access to information from abroad, the ongoing vitality of the Petersburg mythos in the West was an eye-opener that gave hope and inspired them toward new experiments and greater creativity.[68]

Literary life also revived. Dostoevsky was again published and the city's literati restored his popularity, using the occasion of the 75th anniversary of his death in 1956 to publish the first Soviet edition of his complete works. The first two volumes appeared in 1956, in nearly unheard-of print runs of 300,000 copies. The Dostoevsky revival also spread to the theater. At the time the Bolshoi Dramatic Theater (then called the Gorky Dramatic Theater but always known to locals simply as "BDT") was under the direction of Georgi Tovstonogov, who had turned it into the best drama theater in the country and a showcase for the incomparable group of actors whom he had recruited and trained: Sergei Yursky, Zinaida Sharko, Tatyana Doronina, Efim Kopelyan, Yevgeny Lebedev, Kirill Lavrov, Alexander Strzhelchik and, later, Alisa Freindlich. Tovstonogov's method was to exploit each actor's unique talents to bring out his creative ideas and build the rest of the production around them. When the Thaw came and interest in Dostoevsky revived, he had the idea of staging Dostoevsky's *Idiot*, a difficult psychological work which through many failed attempts over the years has proved nearly impossible to translate to the stage, the ballet, or the silver screen. But Tovstonogov found the Prince Myshkin he needed in the relatively unknown actor Innokenty Smoktunovsky, who rehearsed tirelessly for months to perfect the role. The difficulty lay not just in getting Dostoevsky right—a nearly insurmountable challenge in itself—but in conveying latent political messages that Tovstonogov incorporated into the production without being overt or confrontational. The novel begins with Prince Myshkin returning to Petersburg after a long absence for medical treatment, and most of society treats him as a pariah because his Christian goodness sets him apart from the ambition, greed, and corruption around him. But in the play, Tovstonogov hinted, Myshkin is like Stalin's victims returning from the Gulag, and the society to which he is counterpoised is Soviet. Smoktunovsky pulled off the role spectacularly, bewitching audiences with his meekness, authenticity, and saintliness. That 1957 production is still recognized as the classic staging of the work. Tovstonogov followed *The Idiot* with productions of two plays by Alexander Volodin, *Five Evenings* (1959) and *The Older Sister* (1961), whose themes strayed far from Socialist Realism. Like *The Idiot*, the plays were not overtly political, but they brought out the banality of Soviet life by depicting scenes from the lives of ordinary Leningraders, expressing their hopes and search for happiness. Tovstonogov reigned over BDT until his death in 1989.

The city's Comedy Theater, in the former Eliseev Building on Nevsky and with Nikolai Akimov back at the helm after a seven-year absence (after being dismissed for "formalism and kowtowing before the West"),[69] also enjoyed a renaissance and wide popularity. It staged Evgeny Schvarts's 1934 play, *The Naked King*, in 1960 and subsequent revivals of two of his other plays, *The Shadow* (1940) and *The Dragon* (1943–44). The two latter plays had been performed briefly under Stalin (*The Dragon* in the guise of "antifascist" satire) but were quickly pulled once the censors saw how audiences reacted. Shvarts, known as a writer of children's stories, based the plays on the tales of Hans Christan Andersen and Charles Perrault's legend of Sir Lancelot and the Dragon, but the satire of Soviet reality was plain. In *The Dragon*, an evil dragon who can take on human shape and had the mannerisms of Stalin rules over a magical city. A knight kills the dragon, but in a city where the burghers behave like good Soviet citizens and the dragon's aide, the Mayor (now seen as Khrushchev), is ready to seize power, the tyranny continues albeit "with a human face."

It was at the end of the Thaw, in 1962, that Akhmatova completed work* on what she considered her life's masterpiece, *Poem without a Hero*. While critics differ on its literary merit compared to *Requiem* and many of her early works, the poem

---

*She wrote the first draft in 1940–42, but over the years she kept returning to it to make changes and additions, eventually doubling its length. Some specialists consider the poem unfinished.

is incomparable as the definitive poetic testament to St. Petersburg's fate in the 20th century. Akhmatova herself claims its epic quality up front by subtitling Part One "A Petersburg Tale," the subtitle Pushkin had used for *The Bronze Horseman*. The plot is structured around something of a reversal of the Pierrot-Columbine-Harlequin love triangle in Blok's *Balaganchik*, this time with Blok as Harlequin, Olga Glebova-Sudeikina as Columbine, and the poet Vsevolod Knyazev, who in real life committed suicide over his unrequited love for Sudeikina, as Pierrot. At Akhmatova's personal level, the poem is about expatiating the sins of her and her generation's bohemian past, while in parallel the city itself, a Sodom victimized (punished) by the 20th-century totalitarian state, atones for its own sins, thus bringing to a moral close (for the city) the questions that *The Bronze Horseman* had opened. A poetic record of the 20th-century city, the poem brings forth a rich and complex kaleidoscope of characters, events, and allusions tracing key events in the city from the prewar Silver Age, the Revolution and Civil War, the Terror, the siege and its aftermath up to her own meeting with Isaiah Berlin. Here the reader experiences evenings at the Stray Dog, Chaliapin singing, Anna Pavlova dancing *The Dying Swan*, Meyerhold's 1910 production of Molière's *Don Juan*, Stravinsky's and Diaghilev's *Petrushka* and the Petersburg carnival, her son Lev's imprisonment and other images of the Terror, and the city under bombardment and siege. Literary scholars and Petersburg enthusiasts are still unraveling the poem's references and subtexts, some of which will never be deciphered. And by also reaching back into the city's imperial history, tapping Pushkin, Lermontov and Dostoevsky among others, the poem for her brought to culmination the city's mythos as it had evolved since 1703, distilling its elements into an indivisible whole.[70] Akhmatova, the city's queen and moral compass, would die soon, and it was time to pass her scepter to others who would carry on and define the city's future. The poem was never published during her lifetime, but she read it often to her trusted friends, who now included a circle of young poets for whom she had become an Oracle—Dmitry Bobyshev, Anatoly Nayman, Evgeny Rein, and the future Nobel Laureate Joseph Brodsky. She dubbed them her "magic choir." Others called them "Akhmatova's orphans."

Brodsky was born in Leningrad in 1940. His father was a naval officer fighting in the war, and he barely knew him in the first eight years of his life. He and his mother survived the first horrible winter of the siege before they were evacuated, and they returned after the war. Whether by coincidence or fate, Brodsky grew up in the Dom Muruzi on Liteiny Prospect in the same apartment No. 28 in which the Merezhkovskys had lived and held their famous salons, only now it was communal and the Brodskys had only one and one-half rooms.[71] He grew up as an independent and precocious child, using the family shortwave radio as his window to the West, tuning in to the BBC and Voice of America to listen to jazz and foreign accounts and interpretations of the events in his country. When Stalin died, he could not understand what all the weeping was about. Alienated and finding no stimulation at school, at 15 he dropped out and went to work in the milling machine shop at the Arsenal, living in the worker's dormitory. This was the first of over a dozen jobs he would hold by 1962 and which took him throughout the country. One of them was dissecting corpses at a morgue in Leningrad, from which he fled when the aggrieved father of two dead Gypsy girls chased him around the premises with a knife. He thus matured in the school of hard knocks, much as Gorky had, living among illiterate and drunken characters straight from Dostoevsky and working in the hectic chaos of Soviet production. When he was ready to become a poet he had rich impressions and experiences on which to draw and something to say. He educated himself, taught himself English and Polish, and began doing translations to earn extra money.

He began reading poetry when he picked up a volume of Russian Romantic verse while working in Irkutsk on a geographical expedition, and for him it was an epiphany. He was also impressed by Dostoevsky's *Notes from Underground*. He realized his calling and soon was writing poems. Most of all he wanted to tell the unvarnished truth, to speak of his own and other people's deep alienation and sense of hopelessness. He was inspired most of all by the introspective themes and writing style of the Acmeists, though his own poems tend to be longer and more wordy and expressed a fierce emotion and temperament. Also like the Acmeists, and the *miriskusniki*, he considered himself a participant in European and world culture and touched on universal themes. Though his poems were not political and often not even particular to the Soviet Union, they were antithetical to Socialist Realism. He began reading his verses in 1958 in student halls and they struck a chord. Audiences loved his style of reading as much as the poems themselves, and his local reputation grew. Some of his poems were about the city, which he called "Piter" rather than Leningrad. *A Halt in the Wilderness* (1970) is a meditation on the destruction of a Greek church in Leningrad, contrasting the contributions that cultures make to civilization with the sacrifices that they demand. In *Stanzas to a City* (1962) he returns to the theme of the lonely, imperfect individual in the midst of the city's natural and man-made vastness, and in *From the Outskirts to the Center* (1962) he focused on the industrial landscape of the city's outskirts, evoking feelings of dislocation and loneliness. In such works he followed Gogol and Dostoevsky in portraying the isolation, alienation, and tragic fate of the individual in a large city and corrupt world.

In late 1962 Khruschev, joined now by neo-Stalinists in the Party, launched his campaigns against modern art and music. He reasserted the Bolshevik notion that all art is inherently ideological, and claimed that the West was using sympathizers in the USSR to wage an ideological battle through the arts and mass culture. As before, the Party struck first in Leningrad against a leading member of its intelligentsia. Although Brodsky was apolitical, he was chosen as the example because, like Nikolai Gumilev, he radiated independence, individualism, even arrogance; and because of his biography, he seemed to present an easy target who would not attract sympathy. The campaign began with a defamatory article about him in

Vechernii Leningrad in November 1963 which portrayed him as an uneducated vagrant, criticized poems he had not written, identified as his friends people he did not know, and charged that he was plotting to smuggle illegal manuscripts out of the country and steal a plane and defect. He was arrested on the street on February 14, 1964, on the criminal charge of "malicious parasitism" under Article 209 of the Criminal Code (i.e., willingly not taking a job and living off society). While awaiting trial, he was put in Kresty prison, where Lev Gumilev had served time and which was made famous in *Requiem*, which Akhmatova had once read to him.

Brodsky's friends, including the sympathetic journalist Frida Vigdorova, rallied to his side and tried to help. The Thaw had caused them to lose enough fear of the consequences of opposition. In the worst case they might lose their jobs or serve a few years time rather than being tortured and executed as under Stalin, and they genuinely believed that taking a stand against the state machine, at least on artistic questions, could work. The risk, they felt, was a small price to pay for the truth and a clear conscience. But there was not much time. The trial was set for February 18, only five days after his arrest. They located a skilled defense lawyer and three witnesses to speak on his behalf.

On the day of the trial, a large crowd of young supporters was gathered outside the Dzerzhinsky District Courthouse on Vosstaniya Street, while others lined the corridors inside and filled the courtroom on the second floor. They were there to show moral support, but, realizing that any incidents would only hurt Brodsky's chances, they maintained decorum and there were no demonstrations or outbursts. Judge Saveleva arrived, a conformist who would never stray from the Party line and was vulgar and ignorant about art and literature. Brodsky sat calmly and fearlessly. Though resigned to a predetermined decision, he had the inner strength of Akhmatova, and nothing the authorities could throw at him would shake his soul. He was bewildered only by how in the country of Pushkin his accusers could not comprehend the life and work of a poet.

His lawyer, Zinaida Toropova, was able to disprove the false allegations in the *Vechernii Leningrad* article, show that Brodsky worked officially and earned significant money as a translator, that this income covered his modest expenses, and that he did not live off others or the state, which in normal circumstances should have been more than enough to acquit him under the criteria of Article 209. The more interesting parts of the trial were the exchanges revealing the clash of cultures and chasm of incomprehension between the mind-set of Leningrad's intelligentsia and the Soviet regime. In a now-famous colloquy, Saveleva asked Brodsky what he did for a living. Brodsky answered that he was a poet. Correcting him, she said she meant "regular" work. Brodsky replied, "I thought that was regular work," and went on to describe how he worked with publishers. She then asked who had recognized him as a poet and "listed" him as such. "No one," he replied. "Who listed me as a member of the human race?" She then probed his qualifications, asking where he had studied to be a poet. "I don't think that comes from education," he replied. "From where?" she then asked. Bewildered, Brodsky answered "I think that it's . . . from God."[72]

Clearly there was no hope for mutual comprehension. Saveleva ordered that Brodsky be sent to a psychiatric clinic to determine his sanity, since only the sane were considered fit to be exiled. While there, he was tortured with sulfur injections. He was deemed sane, and the final phase of the proceedings began on March 13. By then his supporters had mounted a large campaign in which prominent figures, including Akhmatova, Shostakovich, and the Moscow poets Yevtushenko and Voznesensky, wrote letters, signed petitions, made phone calls, and spoke out on his behalf, but to no avail. While people who actually knew Brodsky testified on his behalf, workers and pensioners who had never met him or read his poetry were brought in to testify about his harmful influence on society. When the judge asked Brodsky how his work will help build communism, he replied, "Building communism is not just standing at a lathe or behind a plough. It is also the work of the intelligentsia."[73] The trial lasted late into the evening, and the preordained verdict was read out at 1:00 A.M. Brodsky was sentenced to five years of exile near Archangelsk. But soon after he arrived there the political climate changed. Khrushchev was removed in October 1964, and the Brodsky affair had escalated into an international incident. The foreign press, foreign governments, and intellectuals, including the existentialist philosopher Jean-Paul Sartre, a leftist generally sympathetic to the Soviet system, pressed for Brodsky's release. The case had become an embarrassment that was damaging the Soviet Union's reputation. In September 1965, the Supreme Court reviewed the case, and although the verdict was not reversed, in November, after 18 months in exile, Brodsky was freed and he returned to Leningrad.

But the damage had been done and was irreversible. Brodsky's trial was a seminal event in the city's and the country's history because it finally blew apart the assumption underlying and hopes arising from Khruschev's 1956 speech to the 20th Party Congress: that past Soviet repression was the result of Stalin's particular policies and his "cult of personality" and not an evil endemic in the system. Now people realized that nothing of essence, but only the degree of cruelty, had changed after Stalin, and that the Soviet system could not be reformed. Something now changed in people's souls, and many more were prepared to live their own lives apart from the system. From that point until Gorbachev's policy of *glasnost*, the city's intelligentsia, artists, and other nonconformists and their culture went underground, and many of the city's youth and intelligentsia lived in a counterculture of stoic dissent.

NOTES FROM UNDERGROUND

After Khrushchev's ouster, the Soviet Union was ruled by a succession of conservatives—Leonid Brezhnev until his death in 1982, then Yuri Andropov (1982–84), then Konstantin Chernenko (1984–85)—who seemed to have given up on ever achieving the ideals of communism and whose goals were limited to pre-serving the Soviet system as it was, Party power and their own privileges and ca-reers. And its center was Moscow. Leningrad was further provincialized, put under the thumb of conservative local Party Chiefs such as Vasily Tolstikov who toed the Kremlin's line. Later, when Gorbachev was in power, those years became known as the "time of stagnation." In retrospect, it is clear that the Soviet system had entered a long death spiral, though at the time it seemed that nuclear missiles and the KGB would prop it up indefinitely. Any form of dissent and nonconformity was attacked and snuffed out, and only those dissidents who attracted international attention had some means of protection. At the same time, corruption and cynicism within the system grew, and the people sensed it. People at large became alienated from the system, artists even more so, and most of all in Leningrad.

After the Thaw the artistic atmosphere in Leningrad was stifling. Anyone at-tempting to exercise artistic freedom was persecuted. Even the head of the edito-rial board who had published Dostoevsky's collected works was arrested in 1967, on the absurd charge of plotting terrorism.[74] In Brodsky's case, after his release the authorities tried the carrot-and-stick approach—to get him to confine his poems within acceptable bounds in the promise that they might be published—but he would never cooperate. He continued to write as he wanted and circulated his po-ems in the underground. In cases such as Brodsky's, where another trial would be an embarrassment, the authorities needed and adopted a new approach: deporta-tion. This would rid the country of undesirables, prevent major international em-barrassments, and hopefully the troublemakers would fade from the public eye in the West. Thus, just as Brodsky had been the first of many writers and poets to be arrested and tried under Khrushchev, under Brezhnev he was among the first in a long line of prominent writers and dissidents to be deported, in 1972. Brodsky re-gretted having to leave and made a plea to stay in a letter to Brezhnev. "I belong to Russian culture, I recognize myself as part of it and do not want to leave," he wrote. "The measure of a writer's patriotism is how he writes in the language of the peo-ple among whom he lives and not the oaths from a podium. I am bitter to have to leave Russia. I was born here, grew up here, lived here and everything I have in my soul I owe to it."[75] The plea did not work, but neither did his deportation. Brod-sky's fame only grew in the West, he continued to write great poetry, remained a thorn in the USSR's side, and went on to win the Nobel Prize for Literature in 1987. Had hard-liners still been in power then, the Prize would have been a major embarrassment, but in those changing times to most people it was already cause for pride, especially for Leningraders.

The problem was different for performing artists seeking artistic freedom. They had little choice but to defect because their art was as part of a group performance controlled by theater directors, and was in public. The Kirov's dancers had been in-spired by the artistic ideas revealed during Balanchine's visit to the city, by news of developments abroad that seeped in, and by their experiences while on foreign tours, which the USSR now promoted to earn hard currency. The best dancers could have brilliant careers abroad. The precedent had been set shortly before Balanchine's visit by Rudolf Nureyev, the Kirov's independent-minded bad boy, who was the star student of Agrippina Vaganova's male counterpart, Alexander I. Pushkin, and who graduated in 1958. Though he became the Kirov's star, he had constant run-ins with the theater's management and could not breathe artistically. In 1961 he broke loose from his KGB escorts at a Paris airport and escaped to freedom and a brilliant career in the West.[76] After Nureyev's defection, the Kirov's chief choreographer, Konstantin Sergeev, turned the theater into a mini-police state in which the repertoire was narrowed to either classics or socialist flag-wavers such as *The Distant Planet* celebrating Yuri Gagarin's space flight, while the KGB watched the dancers vigilantly for signs of insubordination or hints that they might defect.[77] One of the Kirov's star ballerinas, Natalya Makarova, endured the system for years until 1970, when she too defected in London and went on to a career in the West.[78] By then a new male star, Mikhail Baryshnikov, had made his mark. Originally considered too short and not muscular enough for the major male roles, he worked tirelessly with Pushkin to overcome his handicaps. With his musicality, grace, fine balance, and hard-earned muscular strength, he created a sensation at his graduation performance in 1967 and quickly became the Kirov's star. When the New York Ballet made a second tour of Leningrad in 1972, Baryshnikov was inspired and dreamed of working with Balanchine, remarking, "I would love to be an instrument in his wonderful hands."[79] He defected in 1974 while the Kirov was on tour in Canada. The defections of such artists made an important difference in how defectors and the Soviet system were perceived in the West. Previously, the response of the Western liberal intelligentsia and media to defectors was lukewarm because the issues were too political; embracing the defectors seemed to play into the hands of Cold Warriors, but once the issue became artistic freedom there could be no debate.[80] This in turn enabled intellectual leaders like Brodsky to step in and frame the political issues for the West more concisely. Back in Leningrad, one bright spot was the new modern dance troupe of Boris Eifman, who was classically trained and worked initially at the Kirov, choreographing *Firebird*. In 1977 he founded his own modern dance troupe, performing innovatively choreographed original short ballets which barely stayed within permissible artistic boundaries and stunned audiences. The troupe was not given state funding and had to survive on its own through gate receipts, but it survived because of the dedication of its dancers and its immense popularity.

The city's intelligentsia was forced underground, living in a surreal atmosphere of fear and depression. Many intellectuals turned to alcohol or drugs; a few committed suicide. But a spirit of rebellion remained, and a post-Thaw counterculture of bohemian artists and writers living at the margin of society arose, forming a new Dostoevskian underbelly in the city. They combined elements of the Silver Age and the Petersburg carnival with 20th-century existentialism and the beat counterculture of the West, forming a new generation of "superfluous men" similar to that which had existed under Nicholas I over a century before. Their favorite hangout was a café on the corner of Nevsky and Vladimirsky Prospects, informally known as the Saigon as it was thought of as a hot spot on the planet where things happen. It became the contemporary equivalent of the Stray Dog, a gathering place for the rebellious "stray dogs" of the city—underground artists and poets (including Brodsky), musicians and their groupies, gays, dropouts, and black marketeers. The Saigon even had its Mayakovsky in the poet Konstantin Kuzminsky, who loudly declaimed his futurist verses dressed in yellow leather pants. But mainly they stood at the round tables, drank cheap coffee and vodka, smoked, and discussed music, art, and the latest news from the BBC and Voice of America.

A symbolic low point—as well as one of transition—was the death of Akhmatova on March 5, 1966, from complications from a heart attack. As she wished, her funeral was held in Chevakinsky's Nikolsky Cathedral, and it was a seminal event in the city's history. Some 1,500 friends and supporters attended, together with press. Her four "orphans"—Brodsky, Nayman, Rein, and Bobyshev—also reunited for the occasion. Akhmatova lay in her trademark black dress, serene and noble as in life. Appropriately, a Requiem was performed. (In a separate memorial service at the House of Writers, her *Requiem* was set to music on piano, even though the poem had not yet been published.) One by one friends, admirers, students, old ladies, and the intelligentsia filed by to pay their last respects and kiss her forehead. Even the beggars outside on the church steps remembered her fondly as a kind, pious woman who gave them alms. Many civil memorial services and meetings were also held in Leningrad and Moscow in her honor. At one of them, Efim Etkind, a poet and scholar from the city's Herzen Pedagogical Institute, spoke some prophetic words: "In an article on Pushkin, Akhmatova wrote that Nicholas I and Benckendorf were now known only as the persecutors of Pushkin, as his insignificant contemporaries. . . . We live in the epoch of Akhmatova. And our descendants will refer to the persecutors of Akhmatova as we today refer to the persecutors of Pushkin."[81] Akhmatova now rests near her dacha in Komarovo, her gateway to the city.

After Akhmatova's death the city's writers regrouped. Remembering *Mir iskusstva*, they longed for world culture and fought against the growing provincialism of Soviet-sponsored poetry and literature. They tried to create a distinctly Petersburgian prose for the new times, and in doing so they studied and drew on the city's past. To them, Soviet life was so barren that nothing other than culture was worthwhile. "It started as an ordinary accumulation of knowledge but soon it became our most important occupation, to which everything could be sacrificed,"[82] Brodsky recalled. While they took menial jobs to make ends meet and avoid being condemned as parasites, their whole being revolved around literature, especially novels. Brodsky remembered:

In its ethics, this generation was among the most bookish in the history of Russia. . . . Books became the first and only reality, whereas reality itself was regarded as either nonsense or nuisance. . . . Nobody knew literature and history better than these people, nobody could write in Russian better than they, nobody despised our times more profoundly. For these characters civilization meant more than daily bread and a nightly hug. This wasn't, as it might seem, another lost generation. This was the only generation that had found itself, for whom Giotto and Mandelstam were more imperative than their own personal destinies.[83]

Most of what they wrote was unacceptable to the censors and so was copied out and circulated in *samizdat** form. Following Brodsky, some writers used the travelogue genre in the tradition of Radishchev as a vehicle to level criticism against the system. The poet Oleg Grigoriev rediscovered the *oberiuti* and wrote popular absurdist and irreverent poetry. But the culminating prose work of the period, the "requiem for the Petersburg intelligentsia,"[84] was Andrei Bitov's experimental novel, *Pushkin House* (1970). It is the closest prose equivalent to *Poem without a Hero*. The title was taken from the Pushkin House, the nickname for the Academy of Sciences' Institute for Russian Literature located on the *strekla* of Vasilievsky Island and the pinnacle of Russian literary studies. The novel's hero, Lev Odoevtsev, is a young contemporary philologist of aristocratic ancestry who works at Pushkin House and thus lives with the ghosts of Pushkin, Lermontov, Dostoevsky, and the city's 20th-century writers and poets. By lacing the plot with stories about, quotes from, and allusions to the city's writers and its history, Bitov portrays the inner world, hopes, and frustrations of the city's contemporary intelligentsia. But the novel did not make it past the censors, and for years it circulated in *samizdat* form except for some adulterated published excerpts. Although it was published abroad in 1978, in the USSR it was not published in full until the era of Gorbachev's *glasnost*.

The city's artists led similar underground lives. Some of the new generation, like Vladimir Sterligov and his wife Tatyana Glebova, were former students or colleagues of Malevich and Filonov and kept their memories and techniques alive. One young artist who was impressed by Filonov's work when he first saw it in the late 1950s was Mikhail Chemiakin, who became one of the city's leading artists of the period. Born in Moscow in 1943, he grew up mainly in East Germany and moved to Leningrad in 1957 to study at the Academy of Arts. But he was expelled in 1959 for failing to conform to Socialist Realism and made a living from odd jobs, including as a maintenance worker at the Hermitage. He was also fascinated by the history and traditions of St. Petersburg, especially its carnival. Most of his paintings at the time were contemporary renditions of Petersburg scenes or carnival

---

*Literally "self-publication." The manuscripts were typed in people's homes, preferably using carbon paper pilfered from the workplace. Often recipients of samizdat copies agreed to make one or more copies of the underground poems, stories and novels for further distribution, thus creating a chain.

characters much in the tradition of *Mir iskusstva*. Thus, when in the mid-1960s he formed his own circle of artists, he called it Sankt-Peterburg. His paintings were first exhibited in 1964 at the Hermitage, together with those of other young artists working there as maintenance workers, in a screened-off section of the Rastrelli Gallery not open to the general public. But the artists issued their own invitations, word spread, and the unofficial exhibition became a major event. When the authorities learned of the show, the KGB closed it on the second day on the ground that the art was "abstractionist," and removed the paintings. The artists, guests, and museum staff were interrogated on the spot. The artists were not arrested, but the Director of the Hermitage, Mikhail Artamonov, was fired. Despite this incident, Chemiakin's growing reputation as an artist led his liberal musical friends at the Conservatory to exhibit his work there in 1966. As with Brodsky's poems, Chemiakin's paintings were not political, but they were nonconformist and for the authorities that was enough. The Conservatory exhibit was closed a week after it had opened and Chemiakin became persona non grata. At one point he was put into a mental institution, by then a standard method of dealing with dissidents. In 1971, he was deported from the USSR and initially resided in Paris. In the West, he has become in the sphere of painting the city's leading émigré exponent of St. Petersburg culture, following in the footsteps of Diaghilev, Stravinsky, Balanchine, and Nabokov. His paintings, pastels, prints, and sculptures circulate widely, and two of his sculptures stand before the Doge's Palace in Venice (Casanova) and a public square in Paris (Petersburg Carnival). Back in Leningrad, other artists struggled on in the underground.

The leading group of artists to emerge following Chemiakin's deportation was a neorealist circle, including Richard Vasmi, Sholom Schwarz, Vladimir Shagin, and Vladimir Gromov, and led by Alexander Arefev, a veteran of the Gulag who dressed in a striped sailor's shirt (*telnyashka*) to exhibit mock patriotism, which became the favored dress of the city's bohemian counterculture. Their main subject was Dostoevskian scenes of everyday life and the city painted in the tradition of Dobuzhinsky—dirty courtyards, arrests, seedy factory neighborhoods, bathhouses. They were tailed by the KGB and detained on occasion. At the time, some modernist paintings of some artists could be legally sold on commission at the Artist's Shop on Nevsky, but most public sales were spontaneous and unofficial, often in front of the St. Catherine Church on Nevsky or on Ostrovsky Square. Most paintings were exhibited privately inside apartment-studios, or occasionally more publicly in the "red corners" at the administrative offices of apartment complexes where announcements were posted. The artists' main breakthrough of the 1970s came when the culture club at the Kirov Works held an exhibition of unofficial art in 1974. The authorities permitted the show in order to deflect international criticism of Soviet policies toward artistic freedom (Baryshnikov had just defected) and in the hope that the art would fall flat. But the strategy backfired. Although the exhibition was not advertised, word of mouth alone was enough to attract throngs to the exhibition, who formed long lines at dawn. Though the event lasted only four days, it was important because it was the first time since Chemiakin's Conservatory exhibition that the city's underground artists rose into view of the general public, and they attracted much interest in sympathy.[85]

Arefev's circle was followed in the early 1980s by several new groups, including the more traditional Hermitage Group formed around Grigory Duglach, the radical and absurdist "necro-realist" circle led by Evgeny Yufit, and the New Artists group formed around Boris Koshelokhov and which included Sergei Bugaev-Africa and Vladislav Gutsevich. Another group, calling themselves the "Mitki" after its charismatic founder, Dmitry Shagin, and which also included Vladimir Shinkarev, Victor Tikhomirov, and Alexander and Olga Florensky. They painted naïve paintings, produced films, recorded "Mitki" songs, revived the Petersburg carnival tradition with their own improvisational commedia dell'arte, and organized art exhibitions (at least one of which was broken up by the militia) and other cultural events. The group was as famous for its ritualized bohemian lifestyle as for its art, and in the early days of *glasnost* they became a favorite topic of exaggerated stories in the press. They dressed not only in the now-typical striped sailor shirts, but added old quilted jackets, felt worker's boots, and mangy fur hats with earflaps, called each other brother *(bratushka)* and sister *(sestryonka)* and kissed each other in the Orthodox manner, drank only the cheapest, rankest vodka, liked to watch old black-and-white films, and spoke in quotations from popular television serials like *One Can't Change the Meeting Place* and *17 Moments in Spring*.

Although Leningrad's youth as a whole was alienated and seethed with discontent, underground art, poetry, and literature lacked the mass appeal to serve as an outlet. But rock-and-roll music did. The arrival of rock had been preceded by a revival of American jazz during the Thaw. The first postwar club of jazz aficionados in the USSR was founded in Leningrad, followed by a second at Leningrad State University. Benny Goodman and his band, including Phil Woods and Zoot Sims, visited Leningrad in 1962, playing several concerts. But perhaps more notable was the band's late-night jam session with the enthusiastic Russian musicians beginning at the Astoria Hotel and moving on to the University, followed by a White Nights boat cruise on the Neva. Goodman's tour made a tremendous impression, but no sooner had jazz revived when it fell into official disfavor. "When I hear Jazz, it's as if I had gas on the stomach," declared Khrushchev in December 1963.[86] But it was just then when rock entered the scene and took its place in the heart of Leningrad's rebellious youth.

American rock and roll of the 50s and early 60s was little known and provoked only modest interest, but the British Invasion hit the Soviet Union the same time it hit America, and as the 60s evolved, the rock-influenced counterculture of America and Europe captivated Russia's youth, too. The rock wave began with the Beatles, whose songs were played on foreign shortwave radio broadcasts and whose records reached listeners through tourists and sailors, commanding high prices on the black market. "I went into a state of shock, total hysteria," recalled one Leningrad fan. "They put everything into focus."[87] Another remembered that, upon hearing the Beatles, "all the depression and fear ingrained over the years disappeared. I understood that everything other than the Beatles had been oppression."[88] (Eventually a Beatles museum—unofficial—was established by Nikolai Vasin at 10 Pushkin Street, a longtime bohemian hangout and colony for artists.) Soon The Dave Clark Five, The Hollies, The Rolling Stones, Jimi Hendrix, The Kinks, Led Zeppelin, Cream, and The Who also gained followings. It was impossible for the authorities to control the phenomenon, in part because of homemade tape recordings, *magnitizdat*, that circulated like *samizdat*, only faster and to a wider audience.

Before long homegrown rock bands emerged. At first they could not buy rock guitars, so they fashioned them out of planks or headboards, sometimes resorting to telephone microphones as pick-ups. Eventually they obtained proper instruments from East Germany, Poland, other East Bloc countries, and Finland. Since at first there was no original Russian rock music, they played Western songs and sang in English. During the first attempts to sing them in Russian or to perform original Russian material, audiences recoiled, preferring the more exotic English language songs. At first the bands rehearsed and performed in the "underground"— cafés, dormitories, courtyards, and empty buildings—attracting large crowds of crazed fans, often in the middle of the night. But soon most every organization in the city having a cadre of youth—schools, institutes, factories, the university—had at least one rock band.

The first prominent local group was Avant Garde-66 led by Alexander Petrenko, whose background was in jazz. The group first appeared at the fashionable Evrika Café on Prospect Energetikov, and they were quickly followed by the Forest Brothers, The Argonauts, and Flamingo. Homegrown Russian rock with original Russian lyrics began with The Nomads in the 60s, but came into its own only in the early 1970s, in Leningrad led by the pioneer band named Sankt-Peterburg, headed by Vladimir Rekshan. The authorities took offense at the band's name, accusing it of monarchism. The rockers were hardly monarchists, but soon they were singing songs of unprecedented defiance and rebellion against the communist system. As the city's most famous rocker, Boris Grebenshikov, later was fond of saying, "Rock is subversive by definition. If it's not subversive, it's not rock."[89] At first the authorities could only rail against the new music, but they soon saw that they could not stem the tide. Instead, usually through the Komsomol, they tried to co-opt rock by creating official bands and disco clubs with ideologically trained DJs who played approved songs in the hope they would attract a following.[90] After a 1969 New Year's concert of Flamingo at the Polytechnical Institute in which the audience stormed the stage, the Leningrad Party Committee asserted control over all vocal-guitar bands in the city. Thus was born the distinction between "authorized" groups, who earned state salaries, enjoyed free mass exposure, and were given large bookings, and "unauthorized" groups who played underground, were harassed by the authorities, and had to hold other jobs to avoid being arrested as parasites. The Leningrad Artistic Council was put under Party control, and no group could perform in public without passing censorship at the House of Public Creativity.[91] Until Gorbachev's *glasnost* dawned, when the distinction between official and unofficial groups was abandoned, the unofficial bands produced self-made recordings which circulated underground *(magnitizdat)*. The underground recording studio of Andrei Tropillo, a recording engineer at the state recording studio Melodiya, became a haven for bands seeking to spread their music and helped account for Aquarium's rise to stardom. A leading authorized band was the Singing Guitars led by Anatoly Vasiliev, a saxophonist and graduate of the Conservatory. Inspired by *Jesus Christ Superstar*, which had been unofficially staged in Leningrad, in 1975 the group collaborated with the composer Alexander Zhurbin to produce the country's first rock opera, *Orpheus and Eurydice*.

Eventually, Aquarium, founded in 1972, became the city's leading band. It was led by its guitarist and lead vocalist, Boris Grebenshikov, a cultured musician and poet not prone to immature or tasteless extremes whose anti-Soviet lyrics were inspired by the Acmeist poets. In fact, when Party propagandists condemned his songs, they accused him of Symbolism and "Akhmatovism."[92] Indeed, one lyric went:

> It seems that I recognize myself
> In the little boy reading verses.
> He grabs the hands of the clock
> So that the night won't end.
> And the blood flows from his hand.

For a while the group was banned from playing, which of course only increased its appeal. As Grebenshikov once remarked, "The best way to hear rock'n roll for the first time is when it's illegal."[93] Because of his folk-rock style, sophisticated musical scores, and philosophical lyrics, Aquarium became a local cult and Grebenshikov the local equivalent of John Lennon or Bob Dylan, having thousands of fans whose lives revolved around the band and its music. "Aquarium is not a band," Grebenshikov would say, "it's a way of life." Aquarium's authentic Russianness and moving lyrics derived from real life spoke to people's souls and accounted for the group's longevity. But other talented groups also had followings—Alisa, Kino, DDT, and later the jazz-rock group Popular Mechanics and the New Wave band Televizor. One of Alisa's lyrics mocked Marxist dialectics:

> Experimenter of upward-downward movement,
> He sees space where I see a wall.
> He knows the answer, he is sure of his idea.
> In every process he reaches the bottom.[94]

An early attempt of Nikolai Vasin to found a rock club in 1971 was short-lived, but in 1981 the city's first lasting club was established, on Rubinstein Street just off Nevsky, with Aquarium as its anchor band. Before long it had some 60 affiliated rock groups and about 500 club members.[95] It was not a nightclub but rather an auditorium where concerts were held about once a month. It also held an annual rock contest, which allowed new groups to gain recognition.

Western rock groups, which needed official sponsorship to perform in the USSR, were slow in coming. The groundbreaker in Leningrad was Cliff Richard in 1976, followed by Elton John in 1979, then B.B. King, the Nitty Gritty Dirt Band, and others. But in 1984 Chernenko became General Secretary and introduced a conservative cultural policy. The Ministry of Culture now banned the playing of certain foreign groups, including Black Sabbath, Alice Cooper, Pink Floyd, the Talking Heads, the Sex Pistols, AC/DC, Elvis Costello, and Van Halen. The Ministry also banned several Soviet groups, including Leningrad's Aquarium and Kino.[96]

The emergence of rock-and-roll culture was a definitive phase in the city's history. Leningrad, because of its port which served as a funnel for Western albums, magazines, news, and musical instruments, and because of its proximity to Finland, whose citizens made weekend trips on cruise ships from Helsinki and sold albums and blue jeans on the black market, became the country's Window to Rock, and rock culture's effects were felt more immediately and deeply there than elsewhere. In Leningrad, rock was a grassroots phenomenon emerging from the city's underground art community and the legions of students at the city's institutes and university, whereas in Moscow at least in the early years it was more of a fashionable hobby of the privileged children of the Party elite. Virtually an entire generation of Leningraders, including its future post-Soviet leaders, grew up under rock's influence, with more contact with the West than elsewhere in the USSR, and away from Moscow's Party apparatus. Though largely apolitical, rock culture stimulated independence of mind and creativity in other fields such as painting, poetry, and literature, whose artists often collaborated with rock musicians or portrayed them. A mind-set of discontent and rebellion formed which would explode the moment the system blinked and controls were eased. One is reminded of Blok's words from before the Revolution: "We still don't know exactly what events to expect, *but in our hearts the needle of the seismograph has already been deflected.*"[97]

CHAPTER 16

The Revenge of St. Petersburg

And Petropolis surfaced like Triton,
Submerged in water to his waist.

PUSHKIN, *The Bronze Horseman*,
describing the city emerging
from the receding flood

Just as the future ripens in the past,
So the past smolders in the future.

ANNA AKHMATOVA,
Poem without a Hero

Being a Petersburger is like a religion.

ALEXANDER POZDNYAKOV, Petersburg journalist

PETERSBURG AND GORBACHEV

B y the mid-1980s, Leningraders had endured nearly two decades of what became known as the *zastoinoe vremya* ("time of stagnation"). The Soviet state
had ossified into the opposite of what Petersburg had stood for, and it was
not working. Like Muscovy on the eve of Peter the Great's reign, the Soviet state
was inward looking rather than cosmopolitan, still clinging to the notion of the nation's special mission and superior beliefs. But few believed it anymore and the system was decrepit. The communist utopia was nowhere in sight, and the modern-
day boyars, the Communist Party, had become a conservative force serving only to
preserve its power. Like old Muscovy, the country was rapidly falling behind the
West technologically, economically, and militarily, and trade with the West was mi-
nuscule. The Party fought vainly to keep foreign ideas out of the country and from
corrupting the people, and travel abroad was restricted. Foreigners stationed
in Moscow had to live in special apartment blocs rented out by the KGB—the
modern-day equivalent of the German Quarter. Official culture was sterile and
lacked vitality, while genuine creativity in the arts was suppressed. But even as the

557

system crumbled, political debate about how to save or transform it was stifled because this would entail admissions of failure and deviations from ideological orthodoxy. Then, in 1985, Mikhail Gorbachev became General Secretary, a modern-day Nikon whose reforms exposed the system's bankruptcy and brought it crashing down in a 20th-century *raskol*.

Gorbachev sought to reform the system from within through his twin policies of *perestroika* ("restructuring") and *glasnost* ("openness"), announced in April 1985. When Gorbachev took his new policies to the people the next month, he began with a visit to Leningrad, the city that symbolizes transformation. His selection of Leningrad was not accidental. Leningrad was the city most likely to receive the new, progressive policies warmly, and it was crucial to get the policies off on the right track. The visit marked the beginning of the resurrection of the city and of old Petersburg values. Gorbachev visited the city's major factories, met with faculty at the Polytechnic Institute, dropped by the Intensification-90 economic exhibition, and ended with a political meeting at Smolny. This was also the first time that he plunged into crowds on the streets to talk with ordinary citizens. People were both shocked and delighted to see their General Secretary emerge from his limousine to parlay with the pedestrians on Nevsky Prospect. "The people in Leningrad were not simply courteous and hospitable," Gorbachev later recalled, "but listened closely to my explanations, asked questions, gave advice and encouragement. When someone yelled 'Keep it up!', this was indeed heartening."[1]

Ultimately, *perestroika* was aimed at breaking the Communist Party's monopoly of power and eventually led to the repeal of Article 6 of the Soviet Constitution, which had memorialized the Party's guiding role in the Soviet state. State power would be separated from the Party; at last, all power would really be in the soviets.[2] The USSR would become a state ruled by law, with everyone enjoying equal rights. The stranglehold of state planning over the economy would be broken. Enterprises would operate in market-like conditions and were expected to be self-sufficient. In 1986 private enterprise was first allowed in the form of cooperatives, whose number by 1991 reached 135,000 and accounted for over 18 percent of all services.[3] In order to overcome the technological and economic gap with the West, in 1987 foreign direct investment was first allowed in the form of joint ventures, and within a few years thousands of such enterprises were functioning and thousands of foreign businessmen were living in Moscow, Leningrad, and other major cities. *Glasnost* complimented *perestroika* by calling for open and free discussion of problems and issues. This meant that information, including from the West, had to be freely available and that most censorship had to be abandoned. Taken together, *perestroika* and *glasnost* implied a pluralistic decision-making process and pluralism in government. Elections would be democratic, with multiple candidates debating real issues. And since a government that exercised real power had to have strong executive, legislative, and judicial branches, a restructuring of the government would be needed. A breakthrough came at the 19th Party Conference in June 1988, at which Gorbachev got approval for a sweeping reorganization of the Soviet government, including a new, largely elected national assembly called the Congress of People's Deputies that would elect the country's standing legislature, the Supreme Soviet.[4]

Under Gorbachev the old Petersburg culture rose up in an explosion of pent-up feelings and pride to overcome the discredited Brezhnevite culture. The city's history and culture could now be researched and discussed openly, and a wealth of new publications about the city began to come out. *Mir iskusstva* and the entire Silver Age enjoyed a revival. The works of the Symbolists, Acmeists, and Futurists were again published, as were those of Zoshchenko and the Serapion Brothers, and of Kharms and the *oberiuty*. Silver Age and avant-garde paintings were brought up from the cellars of the Russian Museum and displayed, with Filonov in particular proving a revelation. Akhmatova again became an idol, and in 1989 a museum dedicated to her opened in her old apartment at Fontanka House. *Requiem* was published, as was *Poem without a Hero*. Films of the Lenfilm director Alexei German, *Checkpoint on the Road* and *My Friend Ivan Lapshin*, which had not passed the censors and had been shelved for years, were now shown and received warmly. The eminent scholar and writer Dmitry Likhachev, who had lived through the 1917 revolutions and the blockade and was a fountain of knowledge about the city, became the city's elder statesman and unofficial ambassador.

The art and writings of Petersburgers who had flourished in emigration also now appeared in the city. Nabokov was published. Balanchine's ballets appeared in the Kirov's repertoire in 1989, and Makarova and Nureyev returned to dance on the Kirov's stage. Stravinsky's music enjoyed a revival. But the greatest watershed and source of city pride was Brodsky's receipt of the Nobel Prize for Literature in 1987. It vindicated the city's many writers and intelligentsia who had not been allowed to work or publish in the postwar era, confirming to the world that their art was worthy of international recognition. Their literary works were published, with Bitov's *Pushkin House* appearing in *Novyi Mir* in 1987. By the early 1990s even Ayn Rand's works were appearing in translation.

To the extent possible, many past wrongs were also rectified. The repressions of victims of the 1930s and during the Leningrad Affair were investigated. The truth about Osip Mandelstam, Lev Gumilev, Zoshchenko, and the mythical "Leningrad opposition" of Zinoviev and Kirov became known. Most of the truth about the blockade came out. The 1946 Central Committee condemnation of Akhmatova and Zoshchenko was officially rescinded in 1988. The *Zhdanovshchina* was repudiated as a mistake, and, in a movement of de-Zhdanovization, the former Party leader's name was eliminated from that of the university and other city landmarks. Nikolai Gumilev was officially rehabilitated, his verses were again published, and the truth about his murder was made public in 1990. The 100th birthdays of Akhmatova in 1989 and Mandelstam in 1991 were celebrated. This healing process was later capped by the dedication of Chemiakin's two Sphinxes to the Victims of Political Repression (1995), strategically placed on the Neva embankment near the

KGB "Big House" where its sewage (and "the blood of its victims," as Chemiakin put it)[5] drains into the river across from Kresty prison.

The city's television station, Channel 5, became the freest and most progressive in the country, launching groundbreaking news programs of investigative journalism and public affairs that were broadcast nationally. In the ten-minute daily newscast *600 Seconds*, Alexander Nevzorov read the news at breakneck speed as the seconds ticked down in the corner of the screen. Nevzorov was TV's first muckraking journalist, and with good connections to KGB sources he was able to uncover much dirt. The show pioneered spontaneous investigation of stories, depicting the gritty details of crimes and disasters. Another show, *Fifth Wheel*, was hosted by Bella Kurkova, who was always programmed for confrontation. The program was novel in being broadcast live, introduced on-the-street interviews, and also pioneered television bridges. Kurkova helped bring many truths to light, such as the details of Gumilev's murder. The station also aired a steady diet of programming devoted to the city's history and culture, re-forming its image in the public mind.

Except for a few pensioners and Party loyalists, Leningraders reveled in the new freedoms and reforms. They gobbled up magazines, books, music, and information from the West, which was now more readily available. (Voice of America and the BBC were no longer jammed.) Since the distinction between official and unofficial rock groups was abandoned and no music was banned, the city's youth listened and danced to whatever they pleased. Quality food and good service could now be found in cooperative restaurants like Polesie and Tête à Tête. People could now say and write what they wanted, and did not hesitate to exercise their freedom of speech. Soon they were also exercising freedom of assembly and political rights.

Political groupings dedicated to various causes began to form in the city. One called Memorial was dedicated to investigating and rehabilitating the victims of Stalin's repressions, a club called Perestroika, founded in 1987 by the young economist Anatoly Chubais, sought to foster democracy and ensure that Gorbachev's reforms would not stall, and the Voter's Association likewise was dedicated to building and understanding of democracy. Prior to establishing Perestroika, since 1984 Chubais had led Leningrad's Informal Group of Young Economists, dedicated to discussing and promoting progressive economic reform. As the April 1989 elections to the Congress of People's Deputies approached, the various democratic groupings united into the Leningrad People's Front to support progressive candidates. As the Soviet Union's second city, Leningrad could send a delegation of deputies to the Congress that could help change the national life. The various hopefuls in each district began gathering supporters and planning campaigns. A free election was new to them, and they learned as they went. Never before had Soviet citizens organized and waged campaigns for the people's support or debated real issues, nor had voters been asked to decide between opposing candidates and points of view.

One of the hopefuls from the Vasilievsky Island region was a middle-aged law professor at Leningrad State University, Anatoly Sobchak. He was born in 1937 in the Siberian town of Chita, where many Decembrists had been exiled. He studied law at Leningrad State University, briefly practiced law, in 1973 joined the faculty at the University, and in the 1980s became director of its Institute of Economic Law. Both he and his wife Lyudmila Narusova had serious intellectual interests (she taught history at the Institute of Culture and was a specialist on the Decembrists), but until Gorbachev's reforms Sobchak showed no inclination toward politics or public life. He became a candidate member of the Communist Party only in 1987 and a full member in 1988. But as the April 1989 elections neared, colleagues suggested that Anatoly throw his hat into the ring. By speaking eloquently and from the heart about the need for a law-governed state, economic reform, common human values and human rights, he received enough votes at the university caucus to advance to the district level, where he faced 11 opponents, mostly workers and traditional Communists, four of whom would make it onto the ballot in the popular election. At the district caucus, held at the Baltisky Shipbuilding Plant's house of culture, Sobchak listened to his opponents give lackluster speeches, while he, speaking toward the end before a tired audience, decided to abandon his prepared text and instead improvised a short but rousing address modeled on Martin Luther King's "I Have a Dream" speech. It was enough to earn him second place in the voting and a place on the electoral ballot.[6]

Then the campaign kicked off in earnest. He was not well financed, but some 50 enthusiastic students, friends, and complete strangers rallied around him to provide the necessary support. Every day he went out to Vasilievsky Island Metro Station with a bullhorn to address the crowds of commuters. The station became a veritable Speakers Corner, with the crowds eagerly engaging the candidates on the issues. Since Sobchak had already been hosting the "Law and Economic Life" program on Channel 5, he convinced its president to hold televised debates between the candidates, the first in the country. When the voting was over, he had garnered 76 percent of the vote and went to Moscow as part of Leningrad's delegation to the Congress, which also included the 80-year-old Dmitry Likhachev and the Metropolitan of Leningrad and Novgorod, Alexei, the future Patriarch of Moscow and All Russia.

Sobchak and the Leningrad delegation quickly distinguished themselves on the national stage. Unlike in 1905 when Nicholas II had greeted Duma deputies with hostility, Gorbachev welcomed the Deputies warmly and encouraged them to speak openly. Sobchak proved an able parliamentarian who dominated the debates on law and legislative procedure, while also speaking out eloquently for human rights, governmental and economic reform, and the rights of the Union Republics. He became one of the country's most well-known, respected, and popular figures. He and other democrats, who had formed the Interregional Group of Deputies, used the Congress and Supreme Soviet as platforms to criticize past and present Soviet abuses and raise fundamental questions about the Soviet system. Meanwhile, the economy was in turmoil, and many visualized the regime disintegrating as had happened in Eastern Europe. Frightened, Communist hard-liners and nationalists claimed that the democrats were leading the country into disaster and tried to turn the clock back. One of them adopted the mantra "State, Motherland, Communism," reminiscent of Nicholas I's Official Nationality. Emotions ran high, both in the Congress and in the nation. When Article 6 of the Constitution was being repealed at the Third Congress in March 1990, in order to break the Party's monopoly it was essential to create a Presidency (a non-Party office) with real power as a substitute for Party rule, with Gorbachev serving initially as President in order to provide continuity in that time of crisis. Gorbachev's opponents on both the right and left clamored for direct elections in the hope that he would be unseated (a real possibility), while others favored indirect election by the Supreme Soviet. It was Dmitry Likhachev's short address that carried the day:

> Dear comrades, I am not a lawyer, but it seems to me that I am the oldest deputy in this hall. I have a perfect memory of the February Revolution, so I know what popular emotions mean, and I must tell you that at present our country is in the grip of emotions. In these conditions direct presidential elections will actually lead to a civil war. Believe me and trust my experience. That is why I am against a direct election. The election should be made here and now. It must not be postponed.[7]

In Sobchak's view, it was to Likhachev that Gorbachev owed his presidency.[8]

Democracy came to Leningrad too with some difficulty. It was there in the autumn of 1989 that the Communist apparat made its first counterrevolutionary power grab in a mini-putsch attempt that was a precursor to the better-known national putsch of August 1991. Elections were scheduled for the spring of 1990 for the Russian Congress of People's Deputies as well as for the Leningrad City Council (Lensoviet), and the entrenched Communist apparat, led by Leningrad Regional and City Party Chief Boris Gidaspov,[9] feared defeat. On each anniversary of the October Revolution (November 7), military and civil parades of soldiers and groups of citizens were held on Palace Square (similar to those on Red Square in Moscow), and for 1989 the Party planned on business as usual. But this year People's Deputies led the civil parade, and among the columns behind them was that of the Leningrad People's Front, which boasted some 30,000 marchers carrying democratic banners and placards. The local authorities cut the People's Front column off so that it could not enter the square, took away many of their banners and placards, and directed them toward Nevsky. A few days later, on November 10, the authorities arranged for the infamous local Stalinist reactionary Nina Andreeva to be interviewed on Channel 5, where she launched into a tirade against Gorbachev's reforms, claiming that they benefited only "shadow economy businessmen." The same day, the newspaper *Vechernyi Leningrad* reported that the Vasilievsky Island Party Committee had demanded an emergency Leningrad Party Congress, and on the 13th the Vasilievsky Island Committee held an outdoor party rally as a dry run for the city-wide Congress. Speaking from the balcony of the Kirov Palace of Culture in pouring rain, Party loyalists accused the democrats of bringing the country to ruin. On the 15th, Gidaspov authored an article in *Leningradskaya Pravda* proposing the introduction of martial law and the right of local party organizations to recall any People's Deputies who were registered with them. Since about 80 percent of the Deputies, including Sobchak, were Party members, this would have given the local Party control over the Leningrad delegation. This was actually a prescription for undoing *perestroika* and reasserting Party control over government, effectively a coup d'etat. At the joint plenary session of the Leningrad Regional and City Party Committees on November 21, Gidaspov read a report entitled *To Safeguard the Socialist Ideals of Perestroika*, in which he accused the Popular Front of betrayal, and barred liberal-minded members from speaking. The next day a city-wide public Communist Party rally was held. There Gidaspov and his supporters became the first Communists in the nation to launch an open campaign against Gorbachev's policies. The meeting, which was televised, threw the city into a state of fear; many thought that the times of repressions were returning. Sobchak was in Moscow that day, but on the 23rd he returned to Leningrad and appeared on Kurkova's *Fifth Wheel*. There Sobchak attacked Gidaspov's policies and tactics for 90 minutes. "I said that if he believed he could run the city like a munitions factory, he was grossly mistaken," Sobchak later recalled. "Because, no matter what things had been done to Leningrad over the past seventy years, the city still remained a center of world culture and science. And, perhaps, the country's spiritual center. His proposed manner of governing was, for us, quite simply impossible. Decisions on our city's affairs had to be referred to its citizens."[10] The city's democrats took heart from Sobchak's stand, and on December 6 the People's Front staged a mass anti-Gidaspov rally at the Sports and Concert Complex, which was televised. Speaker after speaker denounced the plot while the crowd chanted for Gidaspov's resignation. Gidaspov's scheme had flopped. He continued his Party career, but from that moment the Communist Party was marginalized in the city, well before the Party lost its following elsewhere. When Gidaspov finally saw that the Party had no future, he switched careers and became a banker.

And so the city elections in June 1990 went ahead. The first democratically elected Lensoviet took power. Sobchak was elected as one of the deputies and became Chairman of Lensoviet, which made him effectively Mayor. The next year the elective office of Mayor was created, to which Sobchak was elected in June 1991. But the major issue in the June 1991 elections was the proposal to restore the city's original name of St. Petersburg.

As the city regained its heritage, image, and pride, its press became almost wholly pro-democratic, and the Communist Party and Leninism became marginalized, the question of restoring the city's name arose naturally and forcefully. Even while the city was named Leningrad, many residents still fondly called it "Piter." Most deputies in Lensoviet favored the name change, but by law only the Supreme Soviet could make the decision. Therefore, Lensoviet put the question up for a referendum in the elections so that the Supreme Soviet could make its decision based on the results. The debate, waged publicly in the press, on TV, at meetings and rallies, and on the street, was heated and emotional. People knew that at the heart of the debate, as when Peter the Great founded the city, lay the deeper question over what direction the national life should take, and as such it took on national significance. Symbolically, restoring the name of Petersburg meant enlightenment, true culture, openness, freedom, cosmopolitanism, and democracy, while retaining Leningrad meant a retreat into an ideological straightjacket, isolation from the world, and authoritarian rule. Opponents of the proposal formed a Committee for the Defense of Leningrad, claiming that the city earned the name through the Bolshevik Revolution and enduring the blockade. But Brodsky, living in New York, was delighted by the proposal, commenting that it is better for the city's residents "to live in a city that bears the name of a saint than that of a devil."[11] The Orthodox Church came out in favor of St. Petersburg; Alexander Solzhenitsyn proposed essentially translating "St. Petersburg" into Russian: "Svyato-Petrograd." Sobchak was for St. Petersburg, Gorbachev for Leningrad. But ultimately the choice was in the hands of the city's people, who in the end voted in favor of St. Petersburg by a solid majority.* With so many staunch Communists in the Supreme Soviet, however, most people thought that the matter would go no further for some time.

But the Russians had also elected Boris Yeltsin as President of the Russian Republic, and he championed the sovereign rights of Russia and the other republics. The way was now open for finalizing and signing the proposed Union Treaty between the USSR and the Union Republics, which would formalize the sovereign rights of the republics and allow their laws to prevail over USSR laws in some spheres. Kremlin hard-iners saw that their power and careers would be washed up should the Treaty be signed, which was already scheduled for August 20, 1991. This impending development, together with Gorbachev's recent alliance with Boris Yeltsin at the expense of the Party's loyal old guard and the deteriorating economic situation, led the old guard to strike back. Eight of them, led by Gorbachev's own Vice President Gennady Yanaev, formed the State Committee for the State of Emergency (GKChP) with the aim of ousting Gorbachev and seizing power. In the early morning hours of August 19, they put Gorbachev and his wife under house arrest in their vacation home at Foros in the Crimea, seized the central television and radio stations, ordered armored units into Moscow and other cities, and issued a set of decrees and resolutions which were broadcast hourly on TV and radio. They also issued orders for the arrest of 69 people, mainly public figures, among them Yeltsin and Sobchak; in advance they had ordered 250,000 sets of handcuffs and 300,000 new arrest forms.[12] Yanaev purported to assume the responsibilities of

---

*The results showed that 55% of voters participating in the election voted in favor of restoring the original name while 27% voted against; the remainder of voters simply did not vote on the question. Thus, of those voicing an opinion on the question, about two-thirds were in favor.

the President pursuant to Article 127(7) of the Constitution on the false ground that Gorbachev was unable to do so "for health reasons." The health excuse was belied by the GKChP's Appeal to the Soviet People, which claimed that a "mortal danger looms over our great Motherland" and justified the State of Emergency on the grounds that Gorbachev's reforms had led to a dead end, that government was collapsing, that the economy was deteriorating, and that the people were in despair. In fact, under the Law on the State of Emergency, which Sobchak had helped draft, only the Supreme Soviet had the right to declare a state of emergency, and it could do so only on specified grounds ("natural and man-made disasters, epidemics, and large-scale public disorders"), none of which existed. Thus, the move was easily exposed as an illegal coup d'etat by conservatives seeking to turn the clock back and preserve Party rule in a unitary Soviet state.

The plotters expected the typical Soviet scenario, in which a few people seized power at the top and the rest of the country fell into line, but times had changed and they miscalculated. The GKChP had counted on Gorbachev acquiescing, but he did not, which threw the plotters off balance. By 9:00 A.M. Yeltsin had issued his "Appeal to the Citizens of Russia" declaring the GKChP's actions and decrees illegal, and the struggle for power was on. The GKChP had appointed its own local representatives in the major cities, including Leningrad, but without informing them in advance; many of them turned out to oppose the coup. The military was ambivalent, as was the KGB. In Leningrad, the GKChP ordered political leaders and heads of enterprises to meet with local GKChP representatives at Smolny on the 19th, but no one showed up. In the end the fate of the coup depended on the country's citizens and how their actions played on the minds of the military and the GKChP, none of whom turned out to be willing to be responsible for shedding the blood of unarmed citizens. Nationally, the result was largely determined in Moscow, and the story of how the coup unraveled in front of the White House is well-known. But Leningrad also played an important role, and there were many heroes there too. More importantly for the city, those three days in August were an awakening for the city's people, a psychological turning point that marked the way forward and vindicated their vote in favor of St. Petersburg. It was the moment when the city, even many old Soviet loyalists, finally threw off the shackles of Communism. Petersburgers who actively participated in resisting the coup fondly remember those three days as the best of their lives.

LENINGRAD DURING THE COUP

As August 19 dawned in Leningrad, some residents were awoken early by phone calls from friends and acquaintances telling them about the coup. Others learned through radio broadcasts at home, in taxis, or shops. Those who turned on the TV saw on all channels a rendition of *Swan Lake*, an ominous sign which Soviet citizens knew signaled either a change in power or a death in the Kremlin. But the ballet was periodically interrupted by replays of the GKChP's announcement of the State of Emergency. As Leningraders learned what had happened, many were devastated and saw their hopes for a better life evaporate in a flash. But each faced a personal choice: to go along with the GKChP or to resist. Fortunately, five years of freedoms, against the background of the city's tradition of independence, meant that a critical mass of citizens were prepared to resist. Their decision was made easier as they went into the streets that morning, where they were surprised to see no troops or tanks, not even unusual numbers of police, except in the very center of town. For a putsch, something was not quite right.

Those who were ready to play a role in events knew that the center of action would be the Mariinsky Palace, where both Lensoviet and Sobchak's office were located. Lensoviet Chairman Alexander Belyaev had already summoned the deputies for an extraordinary session that afternoon, and concerned citizens converged on the Palace spontaneously. Many quickly made banners and placards with slogans such as "Down with the Junta" and "No to Red Fascism." By mid-morning about a hundred protesters with banners, placards, and Russian tricolor flags had assembled in front of the Palace. But not all onlookers sided with them. One demonstrator remembered how an elderly man wearing his old war medals on his worn jacket—a common sight dating from Soviet times—wagged his finger and scolded the democrats for ruining his beloved country.[13]

The demonstrators were surrounded by a ring of unarmed police (their guns were in nearby police cars), who took no action since they had no orders to make arrests. When bystanders asked their captain "What's up?" he pondered for a moment and dryly replied, "I don't know." When he was asked whether one could cross the police line and join the demonstrators, his answer was the same. The previously marginalized local Communist Party officials were also confused, and remained silent as mice through the entire coup. Other than to send a few KGB agents to control Channel 5 and censor the local newspapers, no concrete action in the city had been taken to effect the coup. No public official in the city had voiced support for the GKChP. The sole public supporter was the Leningrad Military District Commander, General Viktor Samsonov, who announced the State of Emergency on local radio and TV and purported to take local power into his own hands, replacing Sobchak who he thought was being arrested. Later that day, highway police reported that a column of some 150 tanks, APCs, and other military vehicles with troops were moving along the highway from Pskov toward the city, jogging memories of the approach of Nazi tanks 50 years before. In fact, special KGB units had already infiltrated the city in unmarked vehicles and were stationed in the gymnasiums of the city's military academies. When the young soldiers ventured out on the streets for a smoke, passers-by asked them whether they would shoot Leningraders. They replied that they would do nothing and not to worry. But during the whole coup a constant worry was that plainclothes KGB agents would infiltrate the Mariinsky Palace and the crowd on St. Isaac's Square.

Sobchak[14] was in Moscow that morning and was awakened early by a telephone call from a friend in Kazakhstan, who due to the three-hour time difference learned of the coup while Moscow was still sleeping. Seeing that his building was not surrounded, Sobchak rushed to Yeltsin's dacha outside of town, where members of the Russian Republic government were already gathering. On the way he passed tanks and troops moving into town, but his car was not stopped. At the dacha, it was agreed to call an emergency session of Parliament and issue Yeltsin's Appeal to the Citizens of Russia. Sobchak then asked whether he could return to Leningrad, and Yeltsin assented. Fearing that GKChP special agents were on their way to arrest them, they left quickly in cars, Yeltsin for the White House, Sobchak for Sheremetevo Airport and the next flight to Leningrad. The GKChP agents arrived at the abandoned dacha only 10 minutes later.

Once at Sheremetevo, Sobchak, who had learned of plans to arrest him upon his arrival in Leningrad, telephoned his friend and fellow democrat Arkady Kramarev, the Leningrad commander of the Ministry of Interior special elite units (OMON), who arranged for Sobchak's protection at Pulkovo Airport. Kramarev's loyalty and the support of OMON proved invaluable as events in the city unfolded. Since Sobchak's first priority was to keep armed units out of the city and avoid bloodshed, when he arrived in Leningrad he made straight for General Samsonov's office at the General Staff Headquarters on Palace Square. When he burst into Samsonov's office, he saw that the local KGB head, other military officers, Gidaspov, and Kramarev were gathered there too. All except Kramarev were shocked to see him, and before they regained their composure Sobchak launched a furious verbal assault against the GKChP and Samsonov's actions. He attacked the State of Emergency and the GKChP itself as illegal and illegitimate, argued that it would not last, and predicted that those who supported it would be tried as criminals. Then he appealed to Samsonov not to allow troops into the city. "General, think back to Tbilisi:* you were the only one there who acted like a human being, refused to carry out a criminal order, stayed in the shadows. What are you doing getting mixed up with this bunch—this illegitimate gang?"[15] When Sobchak demanded to see the GKChP's orders, Samsonov refused, claiming they were secret. Sobchak reminded him of how the commander in Tbilisi had overstepped his own orders, and warned him against doing the same. Then Sobchak asked for Samsonov's commitment not to allow troops to enter the city. Finally, Samsonov said he would not allow it.[16] In reality, he was probably playing a waiting game, doing nothing within the city and

---

*Sobchak was referring to the infamous massacre of unarmed demonstrators in Tbilisi, Georgia, by Soviet troops in April 1989. Sobchak later chaired a commission of People's Deputies that investigated the affair.

seeing how events would unfold while the armored column made its way toward the city; he would make his final decision as the troops reached the city's gates. He was under tremendous pressure from Moscow all day, with the hysterical putschists screaming at him over the phone, accusing him of selling out to the democrats. Yet no order was forthcoming from the putschists to storm the Mariinsky Palace, just as there was none to storm the White House in Moscow. Leningrad's military would be willing to move the tanks into the city, if at all, only after the storming began in Moscow.

After the meeting with Samsonov, Sobchak went to the Mariinsky Palace to meet with Alexander Belyaev and other deputies and lay plans. Lensoviet's session began late in the afternoon. Sobchak addressed the deputies, which was broadcast on the PA to the crowd outside on St. Isaac's Square. Lensoviet passed decrees denouncing the GKChP, issued an appeal to the Leningrad garrison, KGB, and police not to support the coup, and appointed individuals to specific responsibilities in defending the palace. Leningrad's Vice Mayor, Viacheslav Shcherbakov, also arrived. As a former naval officer, he had been appointed one of the local representatives of the GKChP without his knowledge, but he wholly supported Sobchak. Sobchak also got support from the Chairman of the Leningrad Region Soviet, Yuri Yarov, who also was formally a GKChP representative in the Region but who opposed the coup and in fact co-signed with Belyaev, on behalf of the Regional Soviet, some of the proclamations denouncing the GKChP.

Sobchak had also arranged with the president of Channel 5, Boris Petrov, to make a live television appearance that evening. It was his main chance to get his message to the people; GKChP censors controlled the newspapers, the Metro had denied him access to its PA system, and the civil defense authorities likewise denied him the use of the loudspeakers on the city's streets. He arrived at Channel 5 with Shcherbakov and Yarov, whose status as GKChP representatives got them past the KGB guards and onto the air. Petrov had ensured that satellite connections were secured so that the broadcast would be heard throughout the country. This was crucial because the Moscow stations were under the control of the GKChP, making Channel 5 the only nationwide voice of resistance. Sobchak, with Shcherbakov and Yarov, denounced the coup as illegal, called upon citizens and their representatives not to recognize the GKChP and to resist, and announced a public rally on Palace Square for 10:00 A.M. the following morning. As the program progressed, excited citizens telephoned each other throughout the nation, "Turn on to Leningrad TV!" The nation's phone lines were jammed with calls. That broadcast was one of the seminal events of the coup because it was the first time Soviet citizens learned that there was organized, "legitimate" resistance to the coup. "It was as if a match had been lit under us," recalled one viewer.[17] Many fence sitters now came out against the GKChP, and the resistance was energized. Channel 5 then delivered the coup de grace to the Sobchak broadcast by airing immediately thereafter *The Defector*, an Orwellian film about a failed putsch in the USSR, which hit home. Production of the film at Lenfilm had been funded by a local bank, Vostok, and post-production had been completed only about a week before the coup. It was supposed to run at movie theaters, but on the morning of the putsch Lenfilm and the bank decided to act as citizen-patriots and gave it to Channel 5 to be broadcast that day, sacrificing their box office take.

Back on St. Isaac's Square, Leningraders had been gathering all day, and by afternoon at least 2,000 stood before the Mariinsky Palace. Belyaev spoke to the crowd from the Palace balcony, denouncing the GKChP and calling upon Leningraders to oppose it. Inside, deputies communicated with Yeltsin's team in Moscow and made copies of their and Lensoviet's decisions for distribution. But they had only two photocopy machines in the palace, both in bad condition, and little toner. They phoned a private firm (a cooperative), which quickly delivered more photocopy machines together with supplies. Cooperatives also donated fax machines, televisions, computers, and other needed equipment and supplies. Another businessman came simply to offer money. One of the new businessmen offered encouragement, "Hang in there boys. We'll bring you everything you need. After all, we understand that if you keel over, we will too."[18] A "chain" network of fax machines was set up across town to distribute Lensoviet decrees and other communications. Other copies were pasted on walls and bulletin boards on the streets. Lensoviet dispatched volunteers to fan all over town to report back on the state of affairs in each region. But by evening dozens of the city's taxi drivers—the same types who would not budge except for a pack of Marlboros or large denomination bills—had on their own initiative set up a network using their car radios to report to Lensoviet on the situation around the city.[19]

Other ordinary citizens began arriving at the Mariinsky Palace to offer Lensoviet their help. A group of doctors arrived with bandages and medical supplies to treat the wounded. Another man came and offered defenders guns. "Who are you?" he was asked. "I'm from the mafia!" he replied.[20] Soon after it dawned upon the defenders that troops could use gas on them, a truck from a private firm arrived with gas masks. No one had eaten anything all day, but at dinnertime as if by magic ordinary citizens, even elderly ladies, appeared from the street to contribute whatever food they could—bread, sausage, jam, tea, even boxes of candy. Well-off businessmen brought delicacies. By the 20th, other volunteers had set up makeshift cafés on St. Isaac's Square which provided free food to the crowd. "It was one of the most touching moments of the coup," recalled one of the defenders, "because I could see that people were beginning to lose their fear."[21]

As reports filtered in of tanks approaching the city, measures were taken to defend the Mariinsky Palace in case it was stormed. Lensoviet deputies with military backgrounds like Alexander Shchelkanov organized the defense. Shchelkanov went out to the crowd and instructed them on what to do if the troops arrived. "I told them to stay calm and to put up barricades in the streets around City Hall, . . . that they should form human chains if tanks appear, but under no circumstances should they lie down in front of them," he later recalled.[22] Barricades were erected on the approaches to the Palace. Some were fairly solid, others were flimsy, but none was a match for tanks. People siphoned gas from automobiles and obtained bottles from nearby shops to make Molotov cocktails. To the defenders' delight they received help from unexpected places. Early in the evening a convoy of water trucks arrived and blocked the approaches to the square. As they walked off, the drivers said in farewell, "Well, folks, we're going and tomorrow's a work day, but let the trucks spend the night here.* We parked them in such a way that a tank would burst before it moves them."[23] Former military men, some of them dressed in their old uniforms, came to offer their assistance. Some were veterans of the Afghanistan war dressed in their camouflage; even some Cossacks arrived in their uniforms. Kramarev's OMON troops also arrived to protect the palace, a key development since it meant that a storm of the palace would pitch one state armed force against another. The regular police, having received no orders, withdrew and officially maintained neutrality. But most police were on the side of the citizenry and some of them remained as defenders. The traffic police on the highway into Leningrad also were loyal to Lensoviet and constantly reported on the status of the armored column heading toward the city. In the south of the city, citizens erected barricades on the streets into town—Moskovsky Prospect, Prospect Stachek, and near the Kirov Works—in order to block the armored columns at the city gates. None of this was centrally directed; it came at the people's own initiative. As the barricades went up, Shcherbakov shuttled between Mariinsky and the Military District headquarters in an effort to stop the tanks. Samsonov anxiously awaited for orders from the Kremlin, but none came. Something was clearly awry in Moscow. After the tanks had passed Gatchina, Samsonov spoke with Sobchak and gave him his "officer's word" that he would not let armored vehicles into the city. In the early morning hours he diverted the main column to the military airport near Siverskaya, where they waited for further orders.

As darkness descended, the crowd on St. Isaac's Square began a night vigil. A few campfires burned. Some people strummed on guitars and sang songs, others caught some sleep. Hardly anyone drank alcohol, as was the case throughout those three days. At midnight Sobchak gave a press conference inside the palace, at which he reported that Samsonov had given his "officer's word" that no tanks would enter town. Now that it appeared that no storm would occur that night, the defenders in the palace settled down to sleep in shifts. At 2:00 A.M. Shcherbakov signed a decree authorizing a makeshift radio station, "Open City," which began broadcasting from Mariinsky shortly after 5:00 A.M. In the early morning hours Sobchak left for

---

*The drivers returned in the morning of the 20th to take the trucks back to work, but other trucks brought concrete barriers to replace the trucks as barricades.

the Kirov Works, where on the previous evening its workers' union had sent telegrams to the GKChP denouncing its actions and to Yeltsin, Sobchak, and Belyaev expressing solidarity. Sobchak appeared at an early rally of its workers, addressing them through a car's loudspeaker at the factory gate. Then they were off to Palace Square.

That morning seemingly the entire city streamed toward Palace Square for the mass rally called by Sobchak for 10:00 A.M. Even the immense Square was not enough to hold everyone standing shoulder to shoulder; many columns of citizens were turned away and stood in adjacent streets and Admiralty Park. Estimates of the crowd range from 130,000 to 300,000, about twice the estimates for the largest rally in Moscow.[24] Leningraders came with banners and placards with slogans, "Down with Fascism!," "No to the military coup!" and "Better death than slavery!" Some carried caricatures of GKChP members. As the crowd gathered and waited for the rally to begin, the windows opened in the Guards Headquarters building at the east end of the square, and soldiers could be seen milling inside. "What are they preparing to do?" some wondered nervously. But then the soldiers unfurled hand-painted bedsheets which proclaimed, "WE ARE WITH YOU!" The crowd roared with joy. "It was a fatal moment that brought tears to my eyes," one participant later said. "I knew then that we would win."[25]

Then the rally began. Sobchak said nothing extreme, but spoke emphatically and from the heart against the "usurpers," and he called the city "St. Petersburg." Belyaev, Shcherbakov, and Dmitry Likhachev also spoke, as did Father Pavel Krasnotsvetov, who appeared not on behalf of the Church (which the GKChP had silenced) but as a citizen of the city. The feeling on the square was one of pure happiness, unity, and freedom. That morning anything seemed possible. "It was the greatest day of my life," many Petersbugers still say.

That morning the first post-coup newspapers came out. In protest, they published the official versions leaving white spaces where GKChP censors had removed articles. Unofficial, uncensored short versions of *Nevskoe Vremya* ("The Nevsky Times") and *Smena* ("Change" [of generations]) were produced and photocopied on A4 sheets and distributed for free all over town. No one was thinking of money then.

The afternoon of August 20 was a waiting game. If troops stormed the White House in Moscow, the defenders of the Mariinsky Palace should be prepared for the same. But by now the change in the people's mood was palpable. Whereas people on the 19th were tentative, now they were exhilarated and determined. More of the veterans on St. Isaac's Square were now wearing their old uniforms and medals. "I saw people change before my eyes," recalled one of the defenders. "I could see it in their faces. Their fear of Soviet authority evaporated and they realized, 'We are free people!' For the first time we realized that we could go out onto the streets, make demands on our leaders, and make a difference. For the first time, we became 'citizens.' We became human beings."[26] The mind-set of an open, civil society had emerged.

As evening approached it became clear that the GKChP was preparing to order a storm of the White House in Moscow that night. Sobchak had Yeltsin appoint Shcherbakov as Military Commander of the City of Leningrad and Leningrad Region, after which many local officers began going over to his side and offering help. But the officers directly commanding the tanks were outside of town, and their loyalties were unknown. If the Mariinsky Palace was to be stormed, it would be that night. The next day it would be too late. Belyaev hastily issued a handwritten appeal to all Leningraders, which he repeated on Open Radio:

> *Fellow Citizens! The self-appointed committee is trying to liquidate the democratically elected Soviets. Society is in danger! All able-bodied men who can stand up in the defense of Lensoviet, come to St. Isaac's Square!*

The city responded, and soon St. Isaac's Square was filled all the way back to the Astoria Hotel. When a commander of the Baltic Fleet arrived and went into the palace, a cheer went up; clearly he was not with the GKChP and the Fleet would at least remain neutral. Sobchak and Belyaev spoke to the crowd from the palace balcony. Everyone knew that the barricades, the OMON and police, and the unarmed citizens would be no match for tanks. If the tanks opened fire, the affair would be over in a few minutes, just like the Decembrist rebellion that had taken place only a stone's throw away. But people remembered what had happened in Tiananmen Square in Beijing two years before. All were ready to have the matter decided by the troops' willingness to fire on citizens. Leningraders ringed the palace in a human chain, and waited. No one, inside or out, slept.

But the hours went by and no tanks came. At about 3:00 A.M. Sobchak received information that the KGB special forces that had been stationed on Kalyaev Street had been sent toward the Mayor's Office. Realizing that the defenders, even with the OMON, were no match for such special forces, Sobchak and Shcherbakov agreed to split up. Sobchak again went to the Kirov Works. On the other hand, word also came that the Baltic Fleet had stood down and refused to obey GKChP orders.[27] Soon after that news came that in Moscow the Alpha Group had refused to storm the White House and that the armor was withdrawing from it. The smell of victory was in the air. A new dawn was coming. Then, from the PA in Mariinsky Palace, the strains of Glier's "Hymn to the Great City" filled the square.

On the 21st a drizzle was falling, but it did not dampen spirits. As the day went on and nothing more was heard from the GKChP, tensions eased and the crowd started to celebrate. Even the elderly veteran with his war medals who had scolded the demonstrators on the morning of the 19th reappeared, this time with his young grandson in hand and a smile on his face. Even he, an old Communist, had seen enough of the GKChP and thanked the defenders for their courage.[28] The news that the GKChP had been arrested and of Gorbachev's return was almost anticlimactic.

In the days after the coup the mood was euphoric. The street scenes were reminiscent of 1861 when the serfs were freed. Strangers congratulated one another, people shook hands with the police, and soldiers and clapped them on the back. People knew that something great had happened, though they were not yet sure what it was or what it all meant. But they were proud of their city and what they had accomplished together, and more than ever they wanted their city to be Petersburg again. A local radio began introducing its programs with *"govorit Peterburg"* ("Petersburg speaking"), and the newspaper *Vechernii Leningrad* began adding "St. Petersburg" in parentheses at the end of its title. The city soon got its wish. On September 6, the *Russian* Supreme Soviet accepted the results of the June referendum and officially changed the city's name back to St. Petersburg. Within a short time, most of the city streets and squares bearing Communist-associated names were given back their prerevolutionary names. The Mayor's Office moved into Smolny, where the headquarters of the local Communist Party had been since 1917. The statue of Lenin inside Moscow Train Station was replaced with a bust of Peter the Great.

In the months following the coup, the Soviet Union rapidly disintegrated. On September 5, 1991, the Congress of People's Deputies dissolved itself. On October 18, Russia and eight other republics signed a treaty of economic community. On November 6, Yeltsin banned (temporarily, as it turned out) the Communist Party in Russia. On December 1, Ukraine voted for independence by a majority of 90 percent. A week later, Russia, Ukraine, and Belarus declared the USSR dissolved and founded the Confederation (or Commonwealth) of Independent States (CIS), and on December 21 eight other union republics joined the CIS. On December 25, Gorbachev resigned the presidency, two days later Yeltsin moved into Gorbachev's Kremlin office, and on December 31 the Soviet Union ceased to exist. A new Russia had appeared, and St. Petersburg had to find its place.

WHAT IS TO BE DONE?

The year or so after the coup was a heady time for the city. People rightly sensed that the country could never return to the Soviet system. In the post-coup euphoria, many thought that perhaps within a year everything would already be different. Russians would enjoy Western freedoms, the economy would be transformed, and life would be prosperous and easier. Both Sobchak and the city had made a name for themselves, within the country and abroad, epitomized by a cover story about the city in the November 4, 1991, international edition of *Newsweek*.[29] Sobchak, as politician and idealist, tried to seize the moment and realize the dream. Knowing that St. Petersburg was the country's center of progressive thinking and the most receptive location for market reforms, he visualized transformations taking hold in his city first and then spreading to the rest of the country, making Russia prosperous and allowing it to take its place in the world and foster world peace. It was the classic St. Petersburg idea.

There was some reason to believe that Sobchak and the city could pull it off, for he enjoyed Yeltsin's support and had gathered around him the most progressive team of advisors in the country, which originally included Anatoly Chubais, Alexei Kudrin, Sergei Belyaev, Mikhail Maneivich, and Ilya Yuzhanov, later joined by Alfred Koch, German Gref, and Dmitry Kozak. All eventually became leading figures in Russia's national government, except for Maneivich, who declined an invitation to Moscow and later was assassinated by mobsters. In Lensoviet, the deputies included Chubais's fellow young economists Sergei Vasiliev, who became the body's chief economic advisor, and Dmitry Vasiliev, who was appointed Deputy Head of the St. Petersburg Property Fund, which played a key role in privatization.

Also on Sobchak's team was a mild-mannered former KGB agent, Vladimir Putin. Born in Leningrad in 1952, he had a somewhat wayward childhood (he has described himself as a "hooligan"), but at age 10 or 11 he took up sport, where he learned discipline from his judo instructor; in 1976 he became the city's judo champion.[30] A year earlier, he graduated from the law faculty at Leningrad State University, where Sobchak was one of his instructors. As a child, he had always been inspired by the romantic side of spy novels and popular movies like *The Sword and the Shield*,[31] and dreamed of such an exciting life, so upon graduation he joined the KGB and worked in the Leningrad division. The work was not nearly as romantic as he had imagined and, as a lawyer, he was disappointed by the illegal methods employed by his superiors,[32] but he applied himself and performed well enough to be invited for training at the KGB's Red Banner School in Moscow and a chance to work abroad after graduation. Since he spoke German, from 1985 he was stationed in Dresden in East Germany, where until the fall of the Berlin Wall he recruited sources of information, gathered and analyzed information, and sent it to Moscow. He earned promotions but never rose to the top as he was never an insider with good connections. After the fall of the Berlin Wall, which he saw as inevitable,[33] he realized that the Soviet system had no future, ceased active service in the KGB (though he did not formally resign immediately) and began working on his dissertation in international private law at Leningrad State University. Sobchak, who had recently become Chairman of Lensoviet, needed good advisors. Mutual acquaintances at the law faculty recommended Putin, and Sobchak hired him. When Sobchak became Mayor in June 1991, he created the Committee for Foreign Relations at the Mayor's office. Putin, as one of the few in the Mayor's office who had foreign experience and knew a foreign language, became the Committee's Chairman, where he was responsible for dealings with foreign governments, handling delegations, and relations with foreign investors in the city. Shortly after Putin took this office, he and Sobchak faced the August coup. Putin stood loyal to

Sobchak and helped him through it, apparently interfacing with the KGB[34] and accompanying Sobchak to the Kirov Works.[35] People acquainted with Putin during his days at the Mayor's office remember him as a hardworking, intelligent, careful, and politically astute administrator who picked his battles carefully, played his cards close to his vest, and avoided offending Yeltsin's team. His position naturally involved protocol, but he shunned the limelight and often worked late in his office instead of going to dinners and receptions. He was thought of as a good "second man," but no one saw in him the qualities (which he turned out to have) of a political leader who could command a popular following. Few people could say they really knew him or were aware of what he really thought. But some noticed that, when following the coup the many office portraits of Lenin and Kirov were relegated to the dustbins and most Mayor's office officials replaced them with portraits of Yeltsin, Putin hung in his office a portrait of Peter the Great. For insight into Putin's mind on matters of state, one would not go far wrong by considering what Peter would think and do.

Sobchak was a visionary leader. A highly educated and cultured academic turned politician, he was at his best when his thoughts were in the clouds and when speaking of his dreams and grand plans for the city. He became an international celebrity, adapted quickly to the limelight and came to enjoy it—too much in the eyes of his critics and, eventually, the electorate. He worked energetically to bring investment and culture into Petersburg and promote the city, but this often took him to Moscow and abroad, and soon citizens noticed that he was not at the helm. In fact, Sobchak was bored by the day-to-day details of running and maintaining a city, and he was not an effective organizer or manager, and therefore did not make the best use of his talented and progressive team to achieve concrete results. Moreover, one by one, Sobchak's best and brightest helpers were plucked off by Yeltsin to serve in the Russian Government; Petersburg's government suffered a brain drain. Sobchak also had fierce and public clashes with the city council (now called Petrosoviet) about spheres of authority, the annual budget, and the city charter. Ultimately these battles did not undermine the city's development, but they cost Sobchak political capital which he could have used in the next election.

Following the coup, the outlook for the city looked rosy and everyone had high hopes. The progressive but impractical and ineffective Gavriil Popov was still Moscow's mayor, and many Russians looked to Sobchak and Petersburg as beacons to the future. Sobchak wanted to turn the city into the country's banking and financial center, as it had been before the Russian Revolution. The initial signs were hopeful, as Credit Lyonnais and BNP/Dresdner established subsidiary banks there rather than in Moscow; Deutsche Bank and ABN-AMRO opened offices. New foreign consulates—Denmark, South Africa, Norway, Greece—were opened, while others expanded, the United Kingdom's to a prestigious building on the corner of the Smolny compound. Since the country had lost its other northern ports in the Baltic states and Kaliningrad was isolated, there were high hopes for modernizing and expanding the city's port and enhancing the city's role as a center for international trade. A plan was approved to build a high-speed train between St. Petersburg and Moscow. And with the city's natural beauty, palaces, and museums, the potential for tourism was enormous. Newly completed renovations of the Hotel Astoria and Grand Hotel Europe seemed to point the way.

But in 1991 Russia's laws were confused and could not be used as a basis for realizing Sobchak's hopes. Impatient for progress and fearing that reforms at the national level may take years to realize, Sobchak decided to turn Petersburg into a free economic zone, a concept which Chubais and his economists had been developing since before the 1991 election. While still a professor of economic law, Sobchak had traveled to China to study the free economic zones there, and he became a proponent of them. In most places around the world, free (or special) economic zones consist of little more than a factory located on a few acres of territory for processing or assembling finished goods for re-export, the zone enjoying special customs privileges so that imported components and materials are not subject to customs duties and similar fees and taxes. But Sobchak's vision was much grander, and at bottom it was an assertion of limited sovereignty by the city. In addition to a special customs regime, all of Petersburg would become an island of capitalism in what was still a Russian socialist sea, with preferential rules governing foreign investment, taxation, real estate, currency regulation, and banking. This entailed working out the interface with national legislation and revenue collection and negotiating with Yeltsin's government a complex series of corresponding regulations. While the process got bogged down in the inherent complexities, Russia as a whole was liberalizing rapidly and becoming a market economy. Within a couple years, there was no longer any point to Sobchak's large zone concept and it died on the vine. Efforts continued to establish small zones and industrial parks with special legal regimes and as of this writing five exist in the city, but since the scope for special investment incentives was limited by national legislation at the insistence of domestic business interests and the International Monetary Fund, the zones function more like other zones around the world.

Meanwhile, Petersburg did enjoy some successes. Following the Russian privatization law of July 1991, the city was quick to implement a privatization program, and it privatized its small and medium-sized businesses well ahead of the rest of the country. The city also led the country in land reform, allowing the private sale of land ahead of Moscow and other regions, even though national legislation did not clearly allow it. In 1993 the university established the School of Management in cooperation with the University of California at Berkeley Haas School of Business. For a while Duke University ran local executive courses for the neophyte local businessmen. Sobchak negotiated with Ted Turner to hold the Goodwill Games in the city in 1994, hoping that this would pave the way to hosting the Olympics in 2004. The city submitted its Olympic bid, and a private "2004 Club" was formed to promote it. In 1992 the Washington-based Center for Strategic and International

Studies established an international commission cochaired by Sobchak and Henry Kissinger to develop initiatives that would make Petersburg more attractive to foreign investors. Indeed, the city scored some notable (though insufficient) successes in attracting foreign investments—Coke, Gillette, Otis Elevator, Wrigley, RJR. So did the surrounding Leningrad Region (Ford, Kraft-Jacobs, Cadbury-Schweppes, Caterpillar, and Tetra Laval later bought out by International Paper).

Ultimately the city's economy fell prey to structural limitations and to developments in Moscow. Stalin's rejection of Zhdanov's plan to diversify the local economy in favor of a hierarchically managed military-industrial complex now weighed heavily on the city.[36] When military orders dried up, the city's many large defense-related enterprises had to undergo a painful conversion and were among the last to be privatized; some enterprises never recovered. The Kirov Works became a shadow of its former self and took to leasing its now-idle space to other companies. Because of its traditional strengths in military production, heavy industry, and related technology, the city still did well in research and development work, but it was not as well placed as Moscow to develop light industry and serve the developing consumer economy. The port became mired in internal differences, difficulties with the labor union, and with infighting federal authorities in Moscow, and thus it was slow to expand and modernize. Its fees were uncompetitively high, yet ships often stood for days or even weeks waiting to be unloaded. In response, many local importers began using the ports in Riga or Helsinki instead and trucking cargoes into the city. Several joint venture projects at the main port either never got off the ground or did not work; only the operations of a Finnish investor, Containerships, flourished and helped improve the situation, although as of this writing a new refrigerator terminal was under construction. Partly as alternatives, new schemes arose to build additional ports outside of town. Some went nowhere but in 2001 an oil terminal was opened in Primorsk and a coal terminal in Ust-Luga, and a port was scheduled to open in Visotsk in 2003. The once mighty Baltic Shipping Company drifted toward bankruptcy, selling its assets or seeing them impounded around the world, and it was finally declared bankrupt in 1999.

Meanwhile, in Moscow a closely knit power elite of Russian government officials and local businessmen and bankers (many of them former Communist Party *nomenklatura*) grew up in an incestuous culture of corruption which was the antithesis of the rule of law that Sobchak had fought for. *Nomenclatura* privatization allowed insiders to snap up state assets at a pittance and build large empires.[37] Banks and so-called Financial-Industrial Groups reaped large profits first from speculation and arbitrage, then from Russian government bonds issued at high interest, to the point where they were propping up the Russian government and had its ear. They were able to lobby to prevent meaningful banking reform and enforcement of the law. (In the wake of the 1998 financial crisis it was discovered that even the Russian Central Bank had illegally stashed federal monies abroad.) As in old Muscovy and the Soviet Union, the line between state power and property and the rest of the economy and its actors was blurred. Rather than establishing a meaningful separation of powers and working within a rule-based framework, the power structure was still monolithic and unofficial, and patron–client relationships dominated—what one prominent commentator calls the "Russian system."[38] Yeltsin's regime had not overcome history. Radishchev's dream was not yet realized.

This state of affairs already favored Moscow developing as a city at Petersburg's expense. This tendency was magnified by Moscow's new Mayor, Yuri Luzhkov, who, though not known as a liberal, proved to be an effective, iron-fisted administrator and promoter of the city who got things done. Moscow businesses prospered, its real estate market skyrocketed, roads and other infrastructure were modernized; the city became a forest of construction cranes. Most money, investment, and power now flowed to Moscow. In response, many foreign companies that had originally established the center of their Russian operations in Petersburg, including Credit Lyonnais, Honeywell, Maersk, and ED&F Man Sugar, began moving their Russian headquarters to Moscow.

Resentment built up against well-off businessmen in both cities. In the popular mind, most businessmen were thought of as bandits, and indeed it was often hard to tell on what side of the law an entrepreneur stood. (In fact, it was often hard to tell where the law stood.) For years the tax burden was confiscatory, which when added to the expenses of security (whether legitimate or mafia protection payments) and bribes made it impossible to make a profit without cutting corners. One businessman said that he kept three sets of books: one which he showed the tax authorities, a second that he kept on a computer for private use, and a third (the real one) that he kept in his head. Many businessmen did no favors to their image, like NEPmen flaunting their wealth and molls ostentatiously at restaurants and nightclubs and speeding around town in S-series Mercedes, flouting traffic and parking regulations and paying off the traffic cops.

As in other Russian cities, organized crime flourished, and the authorities struggled to stop it. Their activities were the usual: car theft, smuggling, casinos, trade in alcohol, drugs, prostitution, and protection rackets against restaurants and nightclubs, retail and distribution outlets, and factories. Seemingly every business had its own *krysha* ("roof") of protection. The local and even foreign media were flush with stories of gangland wars and contract killings in Petersburg, and the city became known as "Chicago on the Neva." In fact, the situation was no worse than in Moscow, but that was still bad. Many heads of enterprises who did not yield to demands were indeed murdered. Judges and witnesses were bribed and threatened. In the famous prosecution of Alexander Malyshev, the alleged head of the notorious Tambov gang, all 63 witnesses suddenly recanted their testimony to the police and the prosecutor could not obtain a conviction. But soon afterwards one of the gang's alleged kingpins, Vladislav "The Brick" Kirpichev, was shot to death by a rival gang as he was quaffing his favorite wine in the Joy nightclub on the Griboyedov Canal. In another incident, two assassins with machine guns concealed under trenchcoats walked through the front door of the Nevsky Palace hotel on Nevsky Prospect and into its ground floor café, where they opened fire on their victim, killing also an innocent Scottish lawyer, and then strolled calmly out the back door of the building. Government officials were also not immune to threats and assassination. In August 1997, Mikhail Manevich, Chairman of the city's Committee on Management of City Property, was assassinated by a sniper while in his car on Nevsky Prospect, and in November 1998 Galina Starovoitova, the feminist psychologist and a liberal deputy to the Russian Duma, was gunned down in the stairwell of her apartment building. For a period, major hotels, restaurants, and nightclubs installed metal detectors at their entrances, and customers could check in their guns like in the Old West.

In time, however, the problem subsided. The militia and licensed private firms provided legitimate private security services that competed with the gangsters and eventually largely drove them out of the protection business. Gangland wars and contract killings became rare as underground business became rationalized. When Putin became President of Russia, he began a cleanup of crime and corruption, targeting St. Petersburg first. Federal authorities cracked down on tax evasion and prosecuted offenders, beefed up the special forces to fight crime, instituted a witness protection program, and launched criminal investigations and prosecutions against local governmental officials (though in some cases there was insufficient evidence for a conviction). Most gangsters went into legitimate businesses, began paying their taxes and contributed to charity; some like Malyshev emigrated. As of this writing, organized crime still exists but is closer to the level of major cities in the West.

Much of the above transpired over the heads of average Petersburgers, but everyone felt the nationwide shocks of Russia's transition toward a market economy, democracy, and an open society. The ruble was unstable, as were people's jobs. Many educated, highly qualified people were dislocated and could be found driving cabs. As in other cities, the safety and welfare net for pensioners, orphans, invalids, and the other disadvantaged crumbled with inflation, and many of them could be seen selling their belongings or begging on the street in despair. Shortages and long lines for even the most basic food and shoddy consumer goods had been a daily feature of Soviet life, yet in the winter of 1991–92 economic dislocations had reduced the country to needing humanitarian food and other aid from abroad, and Petersburg was one of the main recipients. But from then on the situation improved, and soon most any kind of food, clothing, or consumer goods, many of them imports, was available though for a price. Goods were expensive, but over time they became more affordable, and by the mid-1990s most people lived at a higher standard (though still under more uncertainty) than under Soviet rule.

But Petersburgers did not feel their lives had improved enough for Sobchak to retain his job in the 1996 Mayoral election. Because of his national and international reputation, his heroism during the coup, and his undeniable contributions to

Russia and the city, he went into the elections overconfident and with an inade-
quately organized and financed campaign. But he was vulnerable on several fronts.
He never had bonded with the common people and was perceived as aloof, aristocratic, living a high life, and as favoring foreigners. He was absent from the city
(often abroad) too often, attended too many balls and conferences, and in the popular perception his wife was too visible, which caused a backlash not unlike that
generated by Raisa Gorbachev. His critics raised allegations that he misappropriated
municipal apartments for favored recipients. The city's streets, apartment buildings,
and other infrastructure seemed to be deteriorating, and many Petersburgers felt
that Sobchak was ignoring the city's basic needs and that under his administration
there would never be order *(poryadok)*. There had also been some public embar-
rassments. Some venues for the Goodwill Games were not properly readied; there
was an embarrassing flap over melting ice at the ice rink. Partly as a result, the city
lost its bid for the 2004 Olympics. The city's population had noticeably declined,
to 4.8 million by 1996, hardly a sign of prosperity. In the broad scheme of things
and compared to Moscow, the city was in a funk. Still, with only a week to go before election day, many of these issues were only latent, were not part of the electoral debate, and no attractive rival had distinguished himself. Sobchak looked like
a shoe-in for lack of a clear alternative.

But Vladimir Yakovlev, Sobchak's Deputy Mayor and Chairman of the Committee on the City Economy and now Sobchak's main electoral opponent, had quietly built up support among the discontented and attracted financing from local
businesses. He also found support in Moscow, among Yeltsin's camp because
Sobchak had apparently suggested that Yeltsin would not be long in office, as well
as from Moscow bankers. A week before the election, Yakovlev attacked by surprise
with a well planned and financed media and advertising campaign that threw
Sobchak off balance and from which he never recovered. Yakovlev convinced voters that they were no better off than before Sobchak, and argued that as Deputy
Mayor he had wanted to do more to improve city infrastructure but that Sobchak
would not let him. Yakovlev struck a responsive chord, and the pent-up resentment
against Sobchak materialized in votes for Yakovlev.

Yakovlev won and installed his own team. Those who remained of Sobchak's
best and brightest went into the Russian Government, private business, or academe.
Yakovlev proved to be an astute politician, appealing to the common people and
focusing on their concerns. He indeed devoted more attention to the city's basic
needs, including reconstruction of buildings and infrastructure, and paving the
streets. And in contrast to Sobchak's focus on attracting foreign investors, Yakovlev
emphasized fostering local businesses.

But life took another turn for the worse when Russia suffered its financial crisis
in August 1998, which was ultimately caused by the symbiotic relationship between
Yeltsin's government and Moscow's power elite which had stifled banking and fi-

nancial reform, indebted the government to Moscow banks, and created an untenable budget deficit. Wages dropped, many people lost their jobs in layoffs, real estate prices and rents plummeted, and most imported goods vanished from the shelves or became unaffordable as the ruble's exchange rate deteriorated. The project for the high-speed train between Petersburg and Moscow, already under construction, fell apart that year. Many foreigners left town.

The stagnant period from August 1998 until the millennium, when Russia began to recover from the crisis, was a time for reflection and regeneration. While some businesses failed in the slowdown, in Petersburg as elsewhere the impractibility of importing goods served to protect local producers and businesses and allow them to develop and be more competitive with imports once they began to reappear. More generally, Petersburgers began to reflect on the city's future. Should Petersburg really aspire to be the country's business center, or the capital? Having seen the city of excess that Moscow had become over the past decade—overrich, overbuilt, oversatiated, corrupt, over trafficked—many Petersburgers feared that becoming the nation's capital or business center could overwhelm the city, its architecture, and traditions. In the new age of satellite telecommunications, computerization, the Internet, with Moscow only an hour's flight away, and with the abandonment of top-down political rule and economic management, there was no need for this. Better simply to influence events in Moscow.

The financial crisis had brought home the fact that too many Russians either still did not understand what an open, civil society means or were unwilling to live by it. For Russia to complete its transformation and take its place among modern democratic nations, a revolution in mentality *(myshlenie)* was still needed, which might be generational. St. Petersburg's ultimate power had always been as an idea and way of being, in the transformations that it worked in the minds of Russians and in the national life. Petersburg's resurrection should be measured not simply by the city's share of GDP, but also by how it is measuring up against Peter the Great's original vision: helping to integrate Russia with the rest of the world and changing the national life.

PETERSBURG AND WORLD CULTURE

The recovery of Petersburg culture that began in the Gorbachev years continued in the post-Soviet era. For Petersburgers, their city is a cult. Perhaps no other city in the world has its bookshops so lined with books about the city and its history— whether scholarly histories, reprints of prerevolutionary books, or albums of photos and art—and this is because there is a market for them. Dmitry Likhachev, until his death at 92 in 1999, served as the city's elder statesman and ambassador, popularizing the city's heritage. Various clubs and preservation societies emerged dedicated to conserving the city's architectural and historical treasures.

The question of preservation had come to the fore in the period of *glasnost*. In 1986–87 the city's architectural establishment openly debated at meetings and in the journal *Leningradskaya Panorama* the past mistakes of Sovietized urban development and architecture, which led to a new policy of deemphasizing utilitarian design and preserving the city's classical appearance and historical treasures.[39] Naturally, as these debates continued and the sense of the city's identity revived, disputes arose between preservationists and the proponents of new projects, and the controversies spilled into the streets. The most famous dispute, over the renovation of the Hotel Angleterre (part of the new Astoria Hotel complex), erupted suddenly in March 1987, when city residents were surprised to see Finnish-led construction crews with equipment and materials appear in front of the hotel and begin work. Preservationists feared that the Angleterre would be destroyed as a historic landmark, street demonstrations were held, and a debate in the press continued for weeks. In fact, the historic façade was preserved while only the interior (which was not particularly historic) was rebuilt—a common worldwide practice—and the furor eventually died out. This and similar incidents arose involving Dostoevsky Metro Station construction that threatened Delvig's former home and the construction of a new building on Pestel Street near the Cathedral of Transfiguration of the Savior raised the awareness of the city's leadership and the public to preservation issues at an early stage. Since then the authorities have been strict in preserving the character of the historical center. One change that they have made is to convert Malaya Konyushnaya and Malaya Sadovaya Streets into pedestrian malls. On the other hand, various proposals have been approved to restore some sites to their original appearance, such as restoring the moats around Mikhailovsky Castle. And in the suburbs, the palace at Strelna is being renovated as a presidential residence, with thousands working intensely on the project as under LeBlond.

St. Petersburg classical music, opera, and ballet have recovered well from the Soviet doldrums. The Mariinsky (also called Kirov) Orchestra and the Leningrad Philharmonic stand as Russia's two finest orchestras and are among the best in the world. In January 1988, Mravinsky died of a heart attack at age 84 after heading the Leningrad Philharmonic for 50 years. His replacement was Yuri Temirkanov, who came over from the Kirov to become Chief Conductor and Artistic Director. At that time the Philharmonic faced decreasing state funding and a difficult adjustment to operating in commercial conditions at home and independently organizing foreign tours, but it weathered the transition. And unlike in Soviet times under Mravinsky, the Philharmonic began making regular recordings, including on foreign labels, and touring abroad several times a year. Temirkanov is often a guest conductor of foreign orchestras (in 2000 becoming Chief Conductor and Music Director of the Baltimore Symphony), thus bringing St. Petersburg classical music to the world.

When Temirkanov left the Kirov, the young conductor Valery Gergiev was elected Artistic Director of the Opera and principal conductor of the orchestra. In

1996 he became Artistic and General Director of the entire Theater, which in 1992 regained its original name, the Mariinsky. Gergiev quickly reinvigorated the opera by widening the repertoire (beginning with the Russian classics), having foreign works sung in their original languages rather than Russian, improving the staging, and attracting new talent. He staged festivals devoted solely to the works of Mussorgsky, Prokofiev, and Rimsky-Korsakov. In 1993 he inaugurated the annual *Stars of the White Nights* festival at which the premières of the new season are staged, which has become an international attraction. Whereas in prior decades the Opera rarely performed overseas, under Gergiev it was soon touring abroad to rave reviews. The Mariinsky Orchestra also became a star in its own right thanks to Gergiev's talents as a conductor. Soon the Orchestra and Opera were turning out recordings and videos for foreign labels that were sold worldwide. Indeed, in 1997 Gergiev became Principal Guest Conductor at New York's Metropolitan Opera. As with the Philharmonic, St. Petersburg's best could now be appreciated throughout the world.

Revitalization at the Mariinsky ballet came more slowly. The Soviet-era Ballet Master Oleg Vinogradov had retained his position, but by the late 1980s had stopped producing new works and was touring so frequently (for commercial reasons) that the troupe's dancing and repertoire grew stale and quality suffered. The opportunity for change came when Vinogradov and the Mariinsky's administrative director, Anatoly Malkov, were arrested in 1995, accused of taking bribes from foreign impresarios. It was in the wake of this scandal that Makhabek Vaziev became Director of the ballet and Gergiev became General Director of the Theater. They began reviving the ballet with new productions, including of *Sleeping Beauty* (1999) and *The Nutcracker* (2001) featuring sets and costume designs by Chemiakin, and *La Bayadère* (2002) restoring Minkus's full score. In 2002, the troupe performed in Paris for the *Saisons Russes*, where they reprised some of the Diaghilev–Fokine classics.

The other story in Petersburg ballet was the full flowering of the Boris Eifman Ballet into Russia's leading modern ballet and one of the world's finest modern dance troupes. Since the company had been forced to operate on a self-sufficient basis even in Soviet times, it was able to weather the transition to the post-Soviet environment with aplomb and soon gained the resources to stage full-length ballets. Eifman is famous for staging original and difficult psychological works, some based on Dostoevsky, whose meaning is difficult to capture in dance, including *The Idiot, The Karamazovs, Russian Hamlet* (about Paul I), and *Red Giselle*. Prohibited from touring abroad until the late 1980s, the company did so as soon as it was allowed and began expanding its reputation abroad, as well as within Russia through television documentaries. Its quality, stature, and reputation grew so high that it debuted at the Mariinsky in 1998 and now occasionally performs there, and also has performed at the Bolshoi in Moscow. In 1998, it made a triumphant tour in New York, and thereafter began touring in the USA annually.

The Hermitage also went international. Its first attempt was through a joint venture signed in 1989 with an inexperienced American firm created solely for the project with the Hermitage, which was intended mainly to exploit international opportunities using foreign expertise.[40] It failed to produce the desired results, the partnership degenerated into legal proceedings and the venture was liquidated. Meanwhile, its longtime Director, Boris Piotrovsky, died in 1990 and his deputy, Vitaly Suslov, the new Director, picked Piotrovsky's son Mikhail as his deputy. Piotrovsky soon succeeded Suslov as Director, and under him the museum modernized. He attracted more government funding from Moscow (increasing it from $3 to $13 million in his first 3 years), persuaded Yeltsin to declare the museum a particularly valuable national treasure in 1991 and in 1996 to place the museum under the direct patronage of the presidency, giving it its own line item in the national budget (rather than being part of the Ministry of Culture budget and receiving money through the Ministry).[41] Piotrovsky also attracted a multinational group of sponsors, including international organizations, foreign governments, foreign and Russian companies, and individual patrons, including networks of "Friends" in various countries. With these funds the Hermitage has been able to retain a large and well-paid staff for its work, modernize its infrastructure, and expand, promising to become the world's largest museum complex. It has greatly expanded its temporary exhibitions and also sends its treasures to several foreign exhibitions each year. It has built a state-of-the art website in cooperation with IBM which provides visitors with virtual tours of its galleries, allowing foreigners to appreciate its treasures in the comfort of their own homes.

Petersburg drama theater, art, poetry, and literature also revived in the post-Soviet environment, but as of this writing it is premature to say who will emerge as groundbreaking historical figures in their genres. More clear is that, in the political and economic spheres, Petersburgers have helped bring about radical historical changes in the national life, as Peter the Great intended.

PETERSBURG AND THE NEW NATIONAL LIFE

Although St. Petersburg had resurrected its glorious history and traditions, it did not rest on this. Its original mission was to transform the national life. In the "time of stagnation," a feeling of resignation and powerlessness had set in, reflected in a popular Leningrad joke that the city should escape the Soviet regime by declaring war on Finland and immediately surrendering to it. Later, this separatism took a more positive direction during Sobchak's effort to make the city a free economic zone, as a model for the rest of the country. But when the Soviet Union dissolved and Yeltsin began democratic and economic reforms, new opportunities opened up. Whereas Leningraders from Zinoviev through Grigory Romanov were kept out of power in the Kremlin, now, as demonstrated by Sobchak, the city's best had more opportunities and could play a greater national role. Petersburg's leading citizens were impatient to change the national life in the direction that they visualized. Petersburg formed the most progressive large bloc of Russia's electorate and was impatient for reform. In national elections, the liberal Yabloko ("Apple") Party regularly received the largest bloc of Petersburg's votes, while the showing of the Communist Party was the weakest of any major city in the country.

As Sobchak withdrew from a national political role, members of his team began making their mark in Moscow. Yeltsin's government recognized that Sobchak had gathered some of the most progressive and talented people in the nation, and began inviting them to Moscow to assume major posts and implement Russia's reforms. The process began when in 1991 Anatoly Chubais, Sobchak's former deputy in charge of economic reform, became Chairman of the State Property Committee (GKI) and as such the architect of Russia's most fundamental reform of the early 1990s, privatization.

This story had begun several years before in Leningrad, where since 1984 Chubais had gathered his Informal Group of Young Economists, including Grigory Glazkov, Yuri Yarmagaev, Sergei Vasiliev, and eventually Dmitry Vasiliev. Influenced by the Austrian economist Friedrich von Hayek and the Hungarian economist János Kornai who had published *The Economics of Shortage*, a pathbreaking study on reforming a socialist economy, the group soon realized that the Soviet economy was doomed and discussed and held private seminars on how to transform it. Prior to *glasnost* they feared the KGB and met secretly "underground," but as controls were lifted and open discussion of reform became permissible, they learned that a group of economists in Moscow led by Yegor Gaidar were thinking along the same lines. In 1986 and again in 1987 Gaidar and members of his group, including Mikhail Dmitriev and Vitaly Naishul, attended two key seminars outside Leningrad, at which the thinking of the Leningrad and Moscow groups meshed. They concluded that market-oriented reforms, including privatization of enterprises, were necessary and inevitable. Meanwhile, Chubais became chief economic advisor to Sobchak, and together with his other young economists began making the city a model of reform. When Yeltsin appointed Gaidar as his chief economic advisor, he also tapped Chubais and his team. In November Chubais was appointed head of GKI and put in charge of privatizing the country's economy. He immediately called Dmitry Vasiliev and asked him to write a short memorandum outlining a privatization program and to join him as one of his deputies at GKI.[42] In Russia's legislature, the Supreme Soviet, the Petersburger Peter Fillipov headed the Subcommittee on Privatization and guided the necessary legislation. The triumvirate of Chubais, Vasiliev, and Fillipov led Russia's privatization effort in the early years.[43] Meanwhile, Sergei Vasiliev became an economic advisor to the Yeltsin Government, and in Petersburg he became head of a local economic think tank, the Leontief Center.

The task as Chubais and his team envisioned it was not simply economic. By introducing private property and free markets, he intended to accomplish nothing less than to smash the entire Soviet system as it had developed from Lenin to the present, so deeply that it would never return.[44] An important assumption was that he did not regard Russia as a special case exempt from well-established rules of economics or human behavior.[45] Thus, he meant to destroy the mind-set of collectivism, passivity, paternalism, authoritarianism, and statism that had flourished under Soviet rule[46] but had its roots in old Muscovy. Chubais and Gaidar realized that achieving this goal required quick, sweeping action, and not only because the economy was falling apart. If the reformers delayed for perhaps years while they created a legal structure, institutions, a welfare net, and built a political base, this would only allow Communists and other entrenched interests to sabotage the process, water down reforms, and prevent a political constituency for the hard reforms from ever developing. Under such an approach, the Soviet system might return or the country could be stuck halfway between two economic systems. Chubais and Gaidar were also encouraged by public opinion, which indicated that most people, including the workers at enterprises to be privatized, feared that delaying privatization would only enable the old corrupt elite to seize the assets.[47] Accordingly, the reformers placed their confidence in classical economic theory, believing that even if much private property ended up in the hands of *nomenklatura* and robber barons, as in the West in due course the economy would become legitimate and the necessary laws and institutions would develop, recognizing that the process might be generational.[48] Thus, with Yeltsin's blessing, they moved fast and took hard, sweeping decisions, much in the tradition of Peter the Great. Just as the legendary Giant had to create St. Petersburg all at once rather than allowing individual houses swallowed by the swamp, the reformers moved at once. On December 29, 1991—just six weeks after Vasiliev had written his memo to Chubais on how to privatize Russia—Yeltsin issued his "Basic Provisions" setting for the elements of the privatization process.

The task was daunting, the path littered with influential and bitter opponents and political land mines. Gaidar, Chubais, and their teams knew their quest would make them unpopular and they jokingly viewed themselves as kamikaze pilots.[49] "I could not have imagined in my sweetest dreams that we would achieve the results we have today," Chubais wrote afterwards. "It's not that we didn't believe we could succeed, but we didn't think that success would come . . . in our time."[50] Gaidar indeed became unpopular and his career in government was short-lived, ending in December 1992, but the more practical Chubais proved a better manager and lobbyist, and his role in reforming the economy lasted until the dismissal of the Chernomyrdin government in March 1998, shortly before the financial crisis. But the task was essentially accomplished within a few years. This was done by privatizing enterprises first and letting the market dictate their restructuring later, giving away most shares to workers, management, and (through privatization vouchers) the public, and demanding competitive procedures for the sale of the remaining shares, thus minimizing the role of *nomenklatura*, wealthy "New Russians," the mafia, and foreigners in the process.[51] Along the way Chubais was compelled to make compromises and there were some notable scandals in high profile deals, but on the whole Russia's privatization was an outstanding achievement, called by Anders Åslund "the most successful aspect of the Russian transformation."[52] It is hard to imagine that the process would have been fairer or more effective under anyone else.[53] Shortly after Chubais was promoted to First Deputy Prime Minister for Economic and Financial Policy in November 1994, a succession of other Petersburgers, Chubais's protégés, served as heads of GKI to complete the process.* In 1994 Dmitry Vasiliev left his position as Deputy Chairman of GKI to become Deputy Chairman of the Federal Commission for the Securities Market and served as its Chairman from March 1996 to October 1999, where he began the process of establishing a modern legal structure for Russia's capital markets.

Another wave of Petersburgers assumed posts in Moscow in the wake of Sobchak's electoral defeat and Yeltsin's victory in June 1996. This was facilitated by Chubais's appointment as Head of Yeltsin's Presidential Administration in June 1996, giving him influence over government appointments. Yuri Yarov, who had loyally stood by Sobchak during the coup, became Chubais's Deputy Head of Administration in July, and in August the Petersburger Alexei Bolshakov became First Deputy Prime Minister. Also in August Alexei Kudrin, who had headed Petersburg's Committee on Economy and Finance, was appointed Yeltsin's Deputy Chief of Staff and head of the Main Control Directorate, responsible for monitoring state finances, and in 1997 he became Deputy Minister of Finance. In May 1997, Sergei Vasiliev became First Deputy Chief of Staff, responsible for coordinating financial and economic policy. In May 1997, Ilya Yuzhanov, Chairman of Petersburg's Land Committee, was appointed Chairman of Russia's Land Committee and put in charge of Russia's land reforms.

Putin was also invited to Moscow following Sobchak's defeat through the influence of his Petersburg colleagues in Yeltsin's administration. Alexei Bolshakov recommended him to Yeltsin's Chief of Staff, Pavel Borodin, and was also assisted by Kudrin.[54] In August 1996 Putin began as one of Borodin's deputies and then rose rapidly. In 1997 he replaced Kudrin as head of the Main Control Directorate when Kudrin left for the Ministry of Finance. In 1998, Putin's KGB background reaped dividends when he was appointed to head the KGB's successor, the Federal Security Service, replacing the Petersburger Sergei Stepashin, who later became Prime Minister. In August 1999 Putin became acting Prime Minister upon Stepashin's dismissal from that post. When Yeltsin resigned the Presidency on New Year's Eve

---

*Sergei Belyaev, who had Chaired Petersburg's Committee for Management of City Property (KUGI) and had been on Chubais's team at GKI since 1993, took his place in February 1995. When Belyaev was elected a Duma deputy and left GKI in early 1996 to run the Our Home is Russia political party, the Muscovite Alexander Kazakov served as Chairman for a few months but was then succeeded by the former KUGI Chairman (after Belyaev) Alfred Kokh, who had served as a deputy of GKI since 1993. In 1998, German Gref, also former Chairman of KUGI, became First Deputy Minister of GKI's successor, the Ministry of Privatization.

1999, he apologized to the nation for his failures and appointed Putin acting President pending new elections. Putin then posted on the Internet his vision for Russia, "Russia at the Turn of the Millennium."[55]

The spectacular rise of this Petersburg upstart shocked the Moscow establishment. Why did the repentant Yeltsin choose him? To begin with, Putin had served loyally and had demonstrated his abilities as an effective manager who could work with others. He also had a clean record, was untouched by scandal, and could not be compromised. His KGB background and connections were an asset that would help bring law and order to the country; as Prime Minister, he had shown such abilities in handling Chechnya. More fundamentally, in the wake of the many financial scandals and financial crisis, the Moscow establishment which lived according to the "Russian system" had been discredited, which created an opportunity. While Chubais had succeeded in destroying the Soviet system, it remained to carry out the rebuilding phase of consolidating state power, creating new institutions, controlling corruption, organized crime and the new oligarchs, and realizing the rule of law. Such new reforms were crucial if Russia was to emerge from its crisis and take its rightful place in the world community. Yeltsin and his team had played an important historical role, just as Gorbachev had, but he and much of his team had a limited understanding of civil society, were creatures of the "Russian system," and operated according to its rules. Now it was important that Russia be in the hands of a fresh face from the outside who could devise and carry out the next stage of reforms with his own team. These themes indeed prevailed during the election campaign and struck a chord with the Russian people. On March 26, 2000, Putin was elected President. The challenge of finally ridding the nation of the "Russian system" and realizing Radishchev's dream fell to him. Hopefully, Chubais and Putin would prove to be an effective one-two punch.

In the months after the election, when Putin was still an unknown, speculation about his beliefs and intentions was rife. Much was made of his KGB background, his tough line with Chechnya, his restrictions on the press, and the meaning of his declared policy of establishing a "dictatorship of the law." But in the course of his key policy speeches, meetings with foreign leaders, and his actions at home and in foreign policy, it became clear that, as suggested by the portrait of Peter the Great over his desk, he falls within St. Petersburg's liberal, progressive, cosmopolitan traditions. Like Peter, Putin values a strong state, but one functioning strictly according to enlightened laws. Just as Catherine the Great maintained in her Instruction, he unambiguously regards Russia as a European nation. "Of course, Russia is a diverse country, but we are part of Western European culture. No matter where our people live, in the Far East or in the South, we are Europeans."[56] While he acknowledges that laws and policies must take account of local characteristics, he rejects the more fundamental Slavophile (and Communist) notion of Russia's special mission or path. Just as Chubais had postulated, Russia is no exception to universal rules of economics, the evolution of a democratic and civil society, and human behavior. Russia must not be strong in isolation, but rather integrate with the democratic and industrialized world. As a lawyer and former student of Sobchak, like Sobchak he stands for the rule of law and equality of citizens before the law. His ideas, like those of Radishchev and Belinsky, ultimately derive from morality, by which he means universal human values. Finally, much as Peter the Great had assembled his team of "new men," Putin assembled a team of key lieutenants from outside the Moscow power elite (in particular from St. Petersburg) in order to break its hold over the country.

Thus, Putin appointed German Gref, formerly Chairman of Petersburg's KUGI, as Minister of Economic Development and Trade and put him in charge of Russia's economic reforms. He appointed Alexei Kudrin Minister of Finance. Dmitry Kozak, formerly Chairman of the Legal Committee of the Mayor's Office under Sobchak, was appointed Deputy Head of Putin's Administration to coordinate Putin's judicial reforms. The Petersburger Nikolai Patrushev serves as head of the Federal Security Service (successor to the KGB). In March 2002, Sergei Ignatiev, a Petersburger from the faculty of the city's Institute of Economics and Finance, was appointed Chairman of Russia's Central Bank and put in charge of Russia's long-awaited banking reforms. As of this writing, other Petersburgers prominent in Putin's government include Sergei Ivanov, Minister of Defense; Boris Gryzlov, Minister of Internal Affairs; Ilya Klebanov, Minister of Industry, Science and Technology; Ilya Yuzhanov, Minister of Antimonopoly Policy and Support of Entrepreneurship; Leonid Reiman, Minister of Communications and Information Technologies; Yuri Shevchenko, Minister of Health; and Sergei Stepashin, former Prime Minister and now Chairman of the Russian Audit Chamber. Putin has placed or retained Petersburgers in charge of certain key Government-dominated companies such as Anatoly Chubais at Unified Energy Systems and Alexei Miller at Gazprom. In addition, Petersburgers are the Chairmen (Speakers) of both houses of Parliament: Sergei Mironov in the Federation Council (Russia's upper house of Parliament) and Gennady Seleznev in the Duma. Outside the government, in the wake of the financial crisis, Dmitry Vasiliev left his position as head of the Federal Commission for the Securities Market to found the Institute of Corporate Law and Corporate Governance and the Investor Protection Association, and became the country's leading crusader against corruption and for corporate reform and investor protection. For those of Putin's team who had worked together under Sobchak, this was something of a reunion. Humor arose about how Petersburgers were taking over the country. In one joke, a Muscovite answers the phone. "I'm calling from Petersburg," says the voice at the other end. "Don't begin by threatening me!" replies the Muscovite. In another, everyone arriving in Moscow on a train from Petersburg is offered a government job. In a third, an applicant for a government position is being interviewed. "Where were you born?" "Moscow," he replies. "Not good. Where did you study?" "Moscow State University." "Hmmm . . . Where do you live?" "Leningradsky Prospect." "Well, at least that's something."

With this team and the cooperation of Parliament, Putin worked deliberately, methodically, and without fanfare to begin enacting the remaining necessary legislative, judicial, economic, and financial reforms, bring about law and order, tame the oligarchs, and make the rule of law a reality, in other words to achieve the landmark transition from the "Russian system" in favor of a society in line with what Petersburg's progressives have been advocating for centuries—from Peter the Great through Catherine II, Radishchev, the Decembrists, Peter Struve, and Sobchak. Internationally, Putin's government has worked to accelerate Russia's integration into the world economy and political system, particularly through membership in the World Trade Organization, and into the group of leading industrial states, with Russia becoming a member of the Group of Eight. If the remainder of the program can be completed and the essential transition from the "Russian system" can be realized, Putin's successors will be well placed to see Russia prosper and achieve the greatness of which Peter the Great had dreamed. As the 300th anniversary of Peter's city approached, Russians and the world could see that the Petersburg idea is working after all. There is indeed something great to celebrate.

Source Notes

PREFACE

1. A. Kelly, "The Chaotic City," in A. Kelly, *Toward Another Shore: Russian Thinkers between Necessity and Chance* (1998, New Haven), pp. 206, 217.

PROLOGUE

1. N. Berdyaev, *The Russian Idea* (Hudson, New York, 1992), p. 21.
2. R. Pipes, *Russia under the Old Regime*, 2nd ed. (London, 1992), p. 83 (hereinafter cited as *Old Regime*).
3. A. Predtechenskii, ed., *Peterburg petrovskogo vremeni* (Leningrad, Academy of Sciences, 1948), p. 43 (hereinafter cited as *PPV*).
4. A. Radishchev, *A Journey from Petersburg to Moscow*, trans. L. Wiener, ed. R. Thaler (Cambridge, Massachusetts, 1958), p. 83.
5. J. Billington, *The Icon and the Axe: An Interpretive History of Russian Culture* (New York, 1966), p. 265 & n. 138 (hereinafter cited as *Icon*).
6. A. Gertsen, *Sobranie sochinenii*, 30 vols. (Moscow, 1954–65), vol. 2, pp. 43–48 (hereinafter cited as *Sobranie sochinenii*).
7. E.g., Iakov Knyazhnin's play *Vadim of Novgorod*, discussed in chapter 6, p. 206.
8. V. Kliuchevskii, *A Course in Russian History* (Armonk, New York, 1994), pp. 311–12.
9. Billington, *Icon*, p. 35.
10. Pipes, *Old Regime*, pp. 70–71.
11. V. Zenkovsky, *A History of Russian Philosophy*, 2 vols. (New York, 1953), vol. 1, p. 37.
12. Billington, *Icon*, p. 58.
13. M. Malia, *Russia under Foreign Eyes: From the Bronze Horseman to the Lenin Mausoleum* (Cambridge, Massachusetts, 1999), p. 19.
14. Billington, *Icon*, p. 59.
15. Carolyn Pouncy, ed. and trans., *The Domostroi* (Ithaca, New York, 1994).
16. Billington, *Icon*, pp. 143–44; see Revelation 13:18.
17. M. Raeff, *Understanding Imperial Russia* (New York, 1984), p. 17 (hereinafter cited as *Understanding Imperial Russia*).

CHAPTER ONE

1. Quoted in B. Sumner, *Peter the Great and the Emergence of Russia* (New York, 1962), p. 181; also M. Curtiss, *A Forgotten Empress: Anna Ivanovna and Her Era, 1730–1740* (New York, 1974), p. 222.

2. N. Riasanovsky, *The Image of Peter the Great in Russian History and Thought* (New York, 1985), p. 144 (hereinafter cited as *Image of Peter the Great*).

3. Quoted in A. Cross, *Peter the Great through British Eyes: Perceptions and Representations of the Tsar since 1698* (Cambridge, United Kingdom, 2000), pp. 3–4.

4. E. Anisimov, *The Reforms of Peter the Great: Progress through Coercion* (Armonk, New York, 1993), p. 16.

5. Quoted in R. Massie, *Peter the Great: His Life and World* (New York, 1981), p. 368 (hereinafter cited as *Peter the Great*).

6. Quoted in L. Hughes, *Russia in the Age of Peter the Great* (New Haven, 1998), p. 364; see also V. Avseenko, *Istoria goroda S.-Peterburga v litsakh i kartinkakh* (1903; reprint, St. Petersburg, 1995), p. 46.

7. B. Novikov, ed., *Masonstvo i Russkaia kultura* (Moscow, 1998), p. 22.; C. Melnikova and N. Sidorova, eds., *Masonstvo*, 2 vols. (1914; reprint, Moscow, 1991), vol. 2, p. 126; N. Mazurenko, *Muzika i Masoni* (St. Petersburg, 1994), p. 10.

8. Melnikova and Sidorova, *op cit.*, p. 126; Mazurenko, *op cit.*, p. 10.

9. See S. Soloviev, *Publichnie chtenia o Petre Velikom* (1872), reprinted in C. Dmitriev, ed., *Chtenia i raskazi po istorii Rossii* (Moscow, 1989), pp. 495–96 (hereinafter cited as *Publichnie chtenia*).

10. J.-G. Korb, *Diary of an Austrian Secretary of Legation at the Court of Czar Peter the Great*, 2 vols. (1863; reprint, London, 1968), vol. 1, p. 257.

11. K. Valishevskii, *Petr Velikii* (1912; reprint, Moscow, 1989), p. 321.

12. M. Pogodin, "Petr Velikii," in *Istorichesko-kriticheskie otryvki* (Moscow, 1846), vol. 1, 341–42. I have utilized Professor Riasanovsky's translation with minor changes. See N. Riasanovsky, *A History of Russia*, 3rd ed. (New York, 1977), pp. 266–67 (hereinafter cited as *History*).

13. Pipes, *Old Regime*, p. 67.

14. Raeff, *Understanding Imperial Russia*, pp. 25–28.

15. Anisimov, *op cit.*, p. 34.

16. Hughes, *op cit.*, p. 363.

17. Raeff, *Understanding Imperial Russia*, p. 49; Hughes, *op cit.*, p. 95; Anisimov, *op cit.*, pp. 31–32.

18. Hughes, *op cit.*, p. 135.

19. J. Staehlin von Storcksburg, *Original Anecdotes of Peter the Great* (1788; reprint, New York, 1970), p. 240.

20. Hughes, *op cit.*, p. 136.

21. J. Cracraft, *The Church Reform of Peter the Great* (Stanford, 1971), p. 306 (hereinafter cited as *Church Reform*). See also Hughes, *op cit.*, pp. 332–56.

22. Quoted in Cracraft, *Church Reform*, p. 22.

23. Quoted in Hughes, *op cit.*, p. 332.

24. Quoted in Cracraft, *Church Reform*, p. 24.

25. *Ibid.*, pp. 21–23.

26. T. Consett, *The Present State and Regulations of the Church of Russia* (London, 1729), p. xv, reprinted in J. Cracraft, ed., *For God and Peter the Great: The Works of Thomas Consett, 1723–1729* (New York, 1982).

27. Quoted in Massie, *Peter the Great*, p. 391.

28. Storcksburg, *op cit.*, p. 173.

29. Cracraft, *Church Reform*, p. 54.

30. *Ibid.*, p. 252.

31. For example, see N. Karamzin, *Memoir on Ancient and Modern Russia*, ed. R. Pipes (New York, 1966).

32. Riasanovsky, *Image of Peter the Great*, p. 158.

33. See also N. Berdyaev, *Russian Idea*, pp. 19–50; Raeff, *Understanding Imperial Russia*, pp. 223–24.

34. See Soloviev, *Publichnie chtenia*, pp. 469, 491–94.

35. Sumner, *op cit.*, p. 144.

36. See, for example, Storcksburg, *op cit.*, pp. 71, 73–75.

37. See Anisimov, *op cit.*, pp. 5, 30, 36, 238–43, 295ff.

38. E.g., *ibid.*

CHAPTER TWO

1. As translated in Avrahm Yarmolinsky, ed., *The Poems, Prose and Plays of Alexander Pushkin* (New York, 1936), pp. 95–96.

2. E.g., Massie, *Peter the Great*, p. 356; M. Pyliaev, *Staryi Peterburg* (1889; reprint, Leningrad, 1990), p. 1, fn. 1.

3. M. Viatkin, ed., *Ocherki Istorii Leningrada*, 6 vols. (Academy of Sciences, Leningrad, 1955), vol. 1, p. 13 (hereinafter cited as *OIL*; all cites are to volume 1 unless otherwise noted); V. Mavrodin, *Osnovanie Peterburga* (Leningrad, 1978), p. 66.

4. See P. Stolpianskii, *Peterburg: Kak voznik, osnovalsia i ros Sankt-Peterburg* (1918; reprint, St. Petersburg, 1991), p. 14.

5. Stolpianskii, *op cit.*, p. 15; *OIL*, p. 13, fn. 1; K. Gorbachevich and E. Khablo, *Pochemu tak Nazvani?* (St. Petersburg, 1996), p. 315.

6. Gorbachevich and Khablo, *op cit.*, p. 315.

7. *OIL*, p. 13; S. Zavarikhin, *Iavlenia Sankt-Piter-Burkha* (St. Petersburg, 1996), p. 11; Stolpianskii, *op cit.*, p. 14; Gorbacheich and Khablo, *op cit.*, p. 315.

8. *OIL*, p. 13; V. Mavrodin, *Osnovanie Peterburga* (Leningrad, 1978), p. 66.

9. Stolpianskii, *op cit.*, pp. 14–15.

10. *OIL*, p. 13.

11. Mavrodin, *op cit.*, p. 66.

12. Zavarikhin, *op cit.*, p. 12.

13. *OIL*, p. 14.

14. *Ibid.*

15. Mavrodin, *op cit.*, p. 66; *OIL*, p. 15.

16. S. Kniazkov, ed., *Ocherki iz istorii Petra Velikogo i ego vremeni* (1914; reprint, Pushkino, 1990), p. 580.

17. Stolpianskii, *op cit.*, p. 20.

18. Riasanovsky, *History*, p. 88.

19. The battle is described in detail in M. Khitrova, *Svyatii blagovernii velikii kniaz Aleksandr Iaroslavovich Nevskii* (1893; reprint, St. Petersburg, 1992), pp. 79–89.

20. L. Ermolaeva and I. Lebedeva, *Po beregam Medvezhei rechki* (St. Petersburg, 1996), p. 13; P. Semenova, ed., *Sankt-Peterburg* (1881; reprint, St. Petersburg, 1994), p. 10 (hereinafter cited as *St. Petersburg*). Some accounts place the landing at the site of the future Alexander Nevsky Monastery (e.g., Pyliaev, *op cit.*, p. 1), but the site at the mouth of the Okhta makes more sense in light of its more strategic military and commercial location and in light of the subsequent construction of a fortress on that site.

21. Pyliaev, *op cit.*, p. 1.

22. *OIL*, p. 17.

23. *Ibid.*

24. *Ibid.*, p. 16; Mavrodin, *op cit.*, p. 66.

25. Mavrodin, *op cit.*, p. 66.

26. *Ibid.*, p. 64; *PPV*, p. 12.

27. *PPV*, p. 13. According to another account, by 1500 on the territory later occupied by St. Petersburg stood 21 major settlements, as well as 37 minor ones of a few dwellings each. Kniazkov, *op cit.*, p. 581. At that time, the most populous settlement was that on Fomin Island (now Petrograd Island), which had at least 37 residences. *OIL*, p. 16; Mavrodin, *op cit.*, p. 66 (giving 38 residences).

28. Zavarikhin, *op cit.*, p. 15; Kniazkov, *op cit.*, p. 58; *PPV*, p. 14.

29. *OIL*, p. 19.

30. Kniazkov, *op cit.*, p. 581. Marsden likewise states that as many as 100 ships per year called at Nien. C. Marsden, *Palmyra of the North: The First Days of St. Petersburg.* (London, 1942), p. 46.

31. Iu. Egorov, *The Architectural Planning of St. Petersburg* (Athens, Ohio, 1969), p. xvii.

32. *Ibid.*; Zavarikhin, *op cit.*, p. 18.

33. *OIL*, p. 19.

34. Zavarikhin, *op cit.*, p. 27.

35. *OIL*, p. 19.

36. Stolpianskii, *op cit.*, pp. 20–21.

37. *PPV*, p. 15.

38. Zavarikhin, *op cit.*, p. 20.

39. M. Kagan, *Grad Petrov v istorii Russkoi kultury* (St. Petersburg, 1996), p. 27.

40. *PPV*, p. 25.

41. L. Ermolaeva and I. Lebedeva, *Zdes budet gorod* (St. Petersburg, 1996), pp. 8–9 (hereinafter cited as *Zdes budet gorod*).

42. *PPV*, p. 42. According to another account, the eagle did not appear until Peter had begun marking the spot. One account also states that the eagle's nest was found near the spot on the following day, another good omen. D. Spivak, *Severnaia stolitsa* (St. Petersburg, 1998), pp. 211–12.

43. Spivak, *op cit.*, p. 211.

44. See prologue, p. xxvi.

45. Hughes, *op cit.*, p. 210.

46. Pyliaev, *op cit.*, p. 10; Iu. Bespiatikh, ed., *Peterburg Petra I v inostrannikh opisaniakh* (St. Petersburg, 1991), pp. 258–59 (hereinafter cited as *Peterburg Petra I*). For similar accounts, see Marsden, *op cit.*, pp. 46–47; S. Volkov, *St. Petersburg: A Cultural History* (New York, 1995), 6–7.

47. Hughes, *op cit.*, p. 210. See also prologue p. xxvi.

48. Mavrodin, *op cit.*, pp. 70–71; Volkov, *op cit.*, p. 7.

49. Zavarikhin, *op cit.*, p. 20.

50. *PPV*, pp. 18–20.

51. Mavrodin, *op cit.*, p. 71.

52. *Ibid.*, p. 71.

53. I. Grey, *Peter the Great* (Philadelphia, 1960), p. 227.

54. Marsden, *op cit.*, p. 47; Ermolaeva and Lebedeva, *Zdes budet gorod*, p. 8.

55. *PPV*, p. 24.

56. F. Weber, *The Present State of Russia*, 2 vols. (1723; reprint, New York, 1968), vol. 1, p. 300.

57. Marsden, *op cit.*, p. 50.

58. These campaigns are detailed in Mavrodin, *op cit.*, pp. 77–79, and *PPV*, pp. 26–38.

59. Mavrodin, *op cit.*, p. 75; Weber, *op cit.*, p. 347.

60. S. Luppov, *Istoria stroitelstva Peterburga v pervoi chetverti XVIII veka* (Moscow-Leningrad, 1957), p. 20.

61. *PPV*, p. 36.

62. O. Ageeva, *Grad sviatogo Petra* (St. Petersburg, 1999), p. 79. Such conscripted summer labor was also used, for example, in Vorohezh, Belgorod, Azov, Taganrog, and for Novodvinsskaia fortress. *Ibid.*

63. Mavrodin, *op cit.*, p. 92; *see also* J. Cracraft, *The Petrine Revolution in Russian Architecture* (Chicago, 1988), p. 177 (hereinafter cited as *Petrine Revolution*).

64. Mavrodin, *op cit.*, p. 92; *PPV*, p. 128; Cracraft, *Petrine Revolution*, pp. 176–77.

65. *PPV*, p. 132.

66. *Ibid.*, pp. 130–31.

67. Semenova, *St. Petersburg*, p. 79.

68. F. Algarotti, *Letters from Count Algarotti to Lord Harvey and the Marquis Scipio Maffei Containing the State of the Trade, Marine, Revenues and Forces of the Russian Empire* (London, 1769), p. 120.

69. Luppov, *op cit.*, p. 94; Cracraft, *Petrine Revolution*, p. 178.

70. Ageeva, *op cit.*, pp. 79–81.

71. Luppov, *op cit.*, pp. 94–96.

72. Ageeva, *op cit.*, p. 79.

73. Zavorokhin, *op cit.*, p. 102.

74. J. Cracraft, *Petrine Revolution*, p. 175.

75. *Ibid.*, p. 126.

76. Quoted in Massie, *Peter the Great*, pp. 362–63.

77. Egorov, *op cit.*, p. xxiii.

78. Cracraft, *Petrine Revolution*, p. 179; see also L. Semenova, *Byt i naselenie Sankt-Peterburga (XVIII vek)* (St. Petersburg, 1998), p. 6 (hereinafter cited as *Byt i naselenie*); Luppov, *op cit.*, pp. 23, 28–30, 45.

79. According to Weber, official counts based on the number of houses in the city showed a population of 34,550 in 1714, over 50,000 in 1716, and approximately 60,000 by 1720. Weber, *op cit.*, pp. 9, 177, 302. But these figures are high in relation to those of historians.

80. *Ibid.*, pp. 4–5.

81. Egorov, *op cit.*, p. xx.

82. *Ibid.*

83. Hughes, *op cit.*, p. 216–17. See designs depicted in Cracraft, *Petrine Revolution*, p. 157.

84. Quoted in Mavrodin, *op cit.*, p. 129.

85. Quoted in Egorov, *op cit.*, p. 11.

86. *Ibid.*, pp. 15–16, fn. 14.

87. Marsden, *op cit.*, p. 63.

88. *OIL*, p. 159.

89. State Museum of the History of St. Petersburg, *Imperial St. Petersburg* (St. Petersburg, 1996), p. 18. With this current and a depth of 8–11 meters, the Neva has one of the largest volumes of water flow in Europe. *Ibid.*

90. Avseenko, *op cit.*, p. 41.

91. Raeff, *Understanding Imperial Russia*, p. 24ff; Malia, *op cit.*, pp. 27–29.

92. Quoted in Hughes, *op cit.*, p. 430.

93. *OIL*, p. 163.

94. *Ibid.*, p. 167.

95. Semenova, *Byt i naselenie,* p. 46.

96. Marsden, *op cit.*, p. 52.

97. Weber, *op cit.*, p. 318.

98. Semenova, *Byt i naselenia*, p. 13; Bespiatikh, *Peterburg Petra I*, pp. 51, 82.

99. Mavrodin, *op cit.*, p. 127.

100. Massie, *Peter the Great*, p. 364.

101. Described in chapter 3, p. 86.

102. Zavarikhin, *op cit.*, p. 155.

103. *PPV*, p. 56.

104. *Ibid.*

105. The history of the cathedral is detailed in G. Putnikov, *Isaakievskii sobor* (St. Petersburg, 1993).

106. Weber, *op cit.*, p. 310.

107. Pyliaev, *op cit.*, p. 68.

108. Storcksburg, *op cit.*, p. 312.

109. Marsden, *op cit.*, p. 63.

110. The history of the Summer Garden is well described in G. Bolotova, *Letnyi sad* (Leningrad, 1988).

111. See chapter 3, p. 84.

112. Semenova, *Byt i naselenie*, p. 147.

113. *Ibid.*

114. Quoted in Iu. Alianskii, *Uveselitelye zavedenia starogo Peterburga* (St. Petersburg, 1996), p. 113.

115. Billington, *Icon*, p. 185.

116. Quoted in Cracraft, *Petrine Revolution*, p. 211.

117. V. Vitiazeva, *Kamenny ostrov* (St. Petersburg, 1991), pp. 12–13.

118. Weber, *op cit.*, p. 42.

119. The history and architecture of this much-neglected palace is described in V. Gerasimov, *Bolshoi dvorets v Strelne – bez chetverti tri stoletia* (St. Petersburg, 1997).

120. Storcksburg, *op cit.*, p. 208.

CHAPTER THREE

1. Algarotti, *op cit.*, p. 70.

2. A. Pushkin, "O nichtozhestve literatury Russkoi," in *Sobranie sochinenii v odnom tome*, A. Saakiants, comp. (Moscow, 1984), p. 538 (hereinafter cited as *Sobranie sochinenii*).

3. While the details of major events in early Petersburg were recorded, little is known about the daily life of ordinary residents of the city in Peter's time. *PPV*, p. 131. Semenova, *Byt i naselenie*, contains the most comprehensive information on the subject.

4. Kagan, *op cit.*, 41–43 (quoting sources).

5. *Ibid.*, pp. 68–69.

6. *Ibid.*, pp. 52, 65–66.

7. N. Antsiferov, *Byl i mif Peterburga* (1924; reprint, St. Petersburg, n.d.), pp. 17–18 (hereinafter cited as *Byl i mif*); Billington, *Icon*, p. 184.

8. Massie, *Pavlosk*, p. 236.

9. See generally Kagan, *op cit.*, pp. 42–81.

10. *Ibid.*, p. 36.

11. Quoted in *ibid.*, p. 43.

12. *Ibid.*, pp. 43, 54, 56.

13. *Ibid.*, pp. 38–39.

14. *PPV*, p. 134.

15. *Ibid.*, p. 80.

16. *Ibid.*, p. 86, 88.

17. *Ibid.*, p. 86.

18. Semenova, *Byt i naselenie*, p. 103.

19. *PPV*, p. 85.

20. *Ibid.*, p. 88.

21. *Ibid.*, p. 90.

22. Kagan, *op cit.*, p. 56.

23. Billington, *Icon*, p. 182.

24. J. Cracraft, *Petrine Revolution*, pp. 3, 168–69.

25. *PPV,* p. 116.

26. Storcksburg, *op cit.,* p. 94.

27. J. Dressen, *Tsar Petr i ego gollandskie druzia* (St. Petersburg, 1996), p. 66.

28. Massie, *op cit.,* pp. 814–15; Mavrodin, *op cit.,* p. 197.

29. Hughes, *op cit.,* p. 325.

30. *Ibid.*

31. A. Reiber, "Politics and Technology in Eighteenth-Century Russia," *Science in Context* 8 (1995), p. 351.

32. S. Tompkins, *The Russian Mind from Peter the Great through the Enlightenment* (Norman, Oklahoma, 1953), p. 44.

33. Kagan, *op cit.,* p. 66.

34. Tompkins, *op cit.,* p. 45.

35. Quoted in Mavrodin, *op cit.,* p. 197.

36. S. Luppov, *Kniga v Rossii v pervoi chetverti XVIII v.* (Leningrad, 1973), p. 55.

37. Hughes, *op cit.,* p. 317.

38. *Ibid.*

39. Gertsen, "Moskva i Peterburg," *Sobranie sochinenii,* vol. 2, p. 37.

40. Cracraft, *Petrine Revolution,* p. 150.

41. Weber, *op cit.,* pp. 189–90.

42. See generally V. Terras, A *History of Russian Literature* (New Haven, 1991), pp. 115–30.

43. Kagan, *op cit.,* p. 74.

44. *PPV,* pp. 108, 144; see also Billington, *Icon,* p. 187.

45. Massie, *Peter the Great,* p. 619.

46. Weber, *op cit.,* pp. 31–32.

47. Volkov, *op cit.,* p. 14.

48. Weber, *op cit.,* p. 328.

49. See detailed description in Avseenko, *op cit.,* pp. 41–44; *PPV,* pp. 149–50; Hughes, *op cit.,* pp. 254–55.

50. Quoted in Stolpianskii, *op cit.,* p. 82–83.

51. *Ibid.,* p. 79.

52. Curtiss, *op cit.,* p. 32.

53. Hughes, *op cit.,* pp. 260–61.

54. Quoted in Massie, *Peter the Great,* p. 570.

55. Hughes, *op cit.,* p. 261.

56. Author's translation from Russian version quoted in A. Brikner, *Istoria Petra Velikogo* (Moscow, 1996), vol. 2, pp. 243–44. Another English translation, from Weber's German, is in Weber, *op cit.,* pp. 15–16.

57. Weber, *op cit.,* p. 16.

58. Kniazkov, *op cit.,* p. 646.

CHAPTER FOUR

1. In M. Boitsova, comp. and ed., *Dvortsovie perevoroti v Rossii 1725–1825* (St. Petersburg, 1991), pp. 69–70.

2. P. von Haven, "Travels to Russia," in Y. Bespiatikh, ed., *Peterburg Anny Ioannovny v inostrannikh opisaniakh* (St. Petersburg, 1997), p. 360 (hereinafter cited as *Peterburg Anny Ioannovny*). Peder von Haven was a Dane retained to serve in the Azov fleet in the Russo–Turkish war of 1735–39. He spent several months in Petersburg in 1736 before leaving for his duties, and completed his account of his stay there in 1743.

3. Quoted in Hughes, *op cit.*, p. 403.

4. Quoted in *ibid.*, p. 409.

5. Pyliaev, *op cit.*, pp. 110–12.

6. *Ibid.*, p. 110.

7. Volkov, *op cit.*, p. 14.

8. Pyliaev, *op cit.*, pp. 111–12.

9. These and other details of Peter's lying in state and the funeral, including pictorials, are contained in V. Gendrikov and S. Senko, *Petropavlovskii sobor: usipalnitsa imperatorskogo doma Romanovikh* (St. Petersburg, 1998), pp. 92–95; see also Hughes, *op cit.*, p. 263.

10. The eulogy is translated and reproduced in L. Weiner, ed., *Anthology of Russian Literature* (New York, 1978), pp. 214–18.

11. See contemporary (1720) description of this sentiment in Weber, *op cit.*, pp. 47–48.

12. This famous episode is described in detail in Soloviev, *History*, vol. 9, pp. 557–59, from which the quotes are taken. Author's translation.

13. Marsden, *op cit.*, p. 85.

14. *Peterburg Anny Ioannovny*, p. 262 & fn. 102.

15. Story and quote from C.H. von Manstein, *Contemporary Memoirs of Russia from the Year 1727 to 1744* (New York, 1968), pp. 11–12.

16. Quoted in Massie, *op cit.*, p. 851.

17. Quoted in W. Bruce Lincoln, *The Romanovs: Autocrats of All the Russias* (New York, 1981), p. 176 (hereinafter cited as *Romanovs*).

18. Avseenko, *op cit.*, p. 66.

19. Semenova, *Byt i naselenie*, p. 40.

20. Mrs. William Vigor, *Letters from a Lady Who Resided Some Years in Russia* (1777; reprint, New York, 1970), pp. 3–7.

21. Avseenko, *op cit.*, p. 62.

22. Marsden, *op cit.*, p. 85.

23. Curtis, *op cit.*, p. 29.

24. This famous and interesting episode is recounted in more detail than is appropriate here in Soloviev, *History*, vol. 10, pp. 218–20; M. Florinsky, *Russia: A History and an Interpretation*, 2 vols. (New York, 1953), vol. 1, pp. 440–45; Lincoln, *Romanovs*, pp. 177–83; Curtiss, *op cit.*, pp. 63–65.

25. Avseenko, *op cit.*, p. 68.

26. Quoted in Lincoln, *Romanovs*, p. 186.

27. Manstein, *op cit.*, p. 45.

28. *Ibid.*

29. T. Rice, *Elizabeth, Empress of Russia* (London, 1970), p. 31.

30. Avseenko, *op cit.*, p. 70.

31. Vigor, *op cit.,* p. 4.

32. Quoted in Curtiss, *op cit.*, p. 124.

33. Vigor, *op cit.*, pp. 93–95.

34. K. Berk, in Bespiatikh, *Peterburg Anny Ioannovny*, p. 142.

35. *Ibid.*

36. Stolpianskii, *op cit.*, pp. 212–13.

37. A. Cross, *By the Banks of the Neva: Chapters from the Lives and Careers of the British in Eighteenth–Century Russia* (Cambridge, United Kingdom, 1997), pp. 28–29 (hereinafter cited as *Banks of Neva*).

38. P. von Haven, *op cit.*, p. 315.

39. Pyliaev, *op cit.*, p. 90.

40. P. von Haven, *op cit.*, p. 316.

41. Quoted in Curtiss, *op cit.*, p. 239.

42. E.g., Volkov, *op cit.*, p. 15.

43. Curtiss, *op cit.*, p. 240.

44. The history of the design of this section of the city is well summarized in S. Sementsov, "Gradostroitelnaia istoria formirovania planirovki raiona Bolshoi i Maloi Morskikh Ulits v XVIII-nachale XIX v.," in T. Slavina et al., eds., *Peterburgskie Chtenia '96* (St. Petersburg, 1996), pp. 79–84.

45. Egorov, *op cit.*, p. 31 fn. 7.

46. Gorbachevich and Khablo, *op cit.*, p. 64.

47. *Ibid.*, pp. 50, 93.

48. Stolpianskii, *op cit.*, pp. 231–32.

49. *Ibid.*

50. *Ibid.*, pp. 291–92.

51. Semenova, *Byt i naselenie*, p. 6.

52. Quoted in Curtiss, *op cit.*, pp. 185–86.

53. Algarotti, *op cit.*, p. 80.

54. V. Cowles, *The Romanovs* (New York, 1971), p. 65.

55. *Ibid.*

56. Marsden, *op cit.*, p. 88.

57. Manstein, *op cit.*, pp. 254–55.

58. Vigor, *op cit.*, pp. 82–83.

59. *Ibid.*, pp. 83–84.

60. *Ibid.*, pp. 145–46.

61. Quoted in Marsden, *op cit.*, p. 96.

62. Quoted in Curtiss, *op cit.*, p. 261.

63. D. Sherikh, *Byli i nebylitsy Nevskogo prospekta* (St. Petersburg, 1996), p. 69.

64. Pyliaev, *op cit.*, p. 65.

65. *Ibid.*, p. 66.

66. Sherikh, *op cit.*, p. 62.

67. Quotes from Curtiss, *op cit.*, p. 223.

68. A. Lipski, "Some Aspects of Russia's Westernization during the Reign of Anna Ioannovna, 1730–1740," *American Slavic and East European Review* 18 (1959), pp. 5–6.

69. Billington, *Icon*, p. 187; Raeff, *Understanding Imperial Russia*, p. 51. Regarding the Learned Guard, see chapter 3, p. 83.

70. Lipski, *op cit.*, p. 3.

71. Berk, in *Peterburg Anny Ioannovny*, p. 144.

72. *Ibid.*

73. C. Beaumont, *A History of Ballet in Russia, 1613–1881* (London, 1930), p. 13.

74. Curtiss, *op cit.*, pp. 215–16.

75. Lipski, *op cit.*, p. 8.

76. Billington, *Icon*, p. 188.

77. Lipski, *op cit.*, p. 9.

78. *Ibid.*, p. 10.

79. Curtiss, *op cit.*, p. 276.

80. J. Addison, *The Works of the Right Honourable Joseph Addison*, 6 vols. (London, 1890), vol. 1, p. 209.

CHAPTER FIVE

1. N. Suvorova, ed., *Trekhsotletie doma Romanovikh 1613–1913: Istoricheskie ocherki* (1913, reprint, Moscow, 1992), p. 202.

2. Soloviev, *History*, vol. 12, p. 638.

3. Curtiss, *op cit.*, p. 195.

4. Manstein, *op cit.*, p. 275.

5. *Ibid.*

6. *Ibid.*, p. 276.

7. *Ibid.*, p. 317.

8. Rice, *op cit.*, p. 7.

9. Quoted in *ibid.*, p. 54.

10. Quoted in Lincoln, *Romanovs*, p. 197.

11. Marsden, *op cit.*, p. 117.

12. Vigor, *op cit.*, pp. 73, 106.

13. Rice, *op cit.*, p. 133.

14. Vigor, *op cit.*, p. 106.

15. Soloviev, *History*, vol. 12, p. 639; V. Naumov, "Elizabeth I," in D. Raleigh, ed., *The Emperors and Empresses of Russia* (New York, 1996), pp. 78–79.

16. Quoted in Naumov, *op cit.*, p. 74.

17. Manstein, *op cit.*, p. 318.

18. This account is a composite of varying and undoubtedly embellished accounts of this famous event. Compare K. Valishevskii, *Tsarstvo zhenshchin* (Moscow, 1989), p. 431; Rice, *op cit.*, p. 57; Lincoln, *Romanovs*, p. 193.

19. Catherine II, *Memoirs of Catherine the Great* (New York, 1927), pp. 125–26 (hereinafter cited as *Memoirs*).

20. Quoted in Rice, *op cit.*, p. 61.

21. Soloviev, *History*, vol. 12, p. 638.

22. Quoted in Lincoln, *Romanovs*, p. 252.

23. Cracraft, *Petrine Revolution*, p. 228.

24. Avseenko, *op cit.*, p. 82; J. Bater, *St. Petersburg: Industrialization and Change* (Montreal, 1976), p. 67.

25. Algarotti, *op cit.*, pp. 76–77.

26. Cracraft, *Petrine Revolution*, p. 232.

27. Stolpianskii, *op cit.*, p. 177 (author's translation).

28. Pyliaev, *op cit.*, pp. 155–56; Naumov, *op cit.*, p. 90.

29. Naumov, *op cit.*, p. 90.

30. J. Hanway, *An Historical Account of the British Trades over the Caspian Sea*, 2 vols. (London, 1753), vol. 2, pp. 135–36.

31. I. Grabar, *Peterburgskaia arkhitektura v XVIII i XIX vekakh* (St. Petersburg, 1994), p. 123.

32. Stolpianskii, *op cit.*, p. 173.

33. *Ibid.*, p. 174.

34. Egorov, *op cit.*, pp. 132–33.

35. Avseenko, *op cit.*, p. 86.

36. *Ibid.*, pp. 86–87.

37. B. Matveev and A. Krasko, *Fontannyi dom* (St. Petersburg, 1996), pp. 27–29; Marsden, *op cit.*, pp. 198–99.

38. Grabar, *op cit.*, p. 134.

39. Catherine II, *Memoirs*, p. 125.

40. R. Bain, *The Daughter of Peter the Great* (London, 1899), p. 138.

41. Rice, *op cit.*, pp. 135–36.

42. Catherine II, *Memoirs*, p. 97; Rice, *op cit.*, p. 104.

43. Catherine II, *Memoirs*, p. 97.

44. Quoted in G. Kates, *Monsieur d'Eon Is a Woman* (New York, 1995), pp. 75–76.

45. Catherine II, *Memoirs*, p. 56.

46. The life and career of this brilliant and fascinating individual is recounted in many books and essays, most recently in G. Kates, *op cit.*

47. Quoted in *ibid.*, p. 76.

48. Rice, *op cit.*, p. 104.

49. Catherine II, *Memoirs*, p. 205.

50. Quoted in *ibid.*, p. 69, editor's fn. 146.

51. Catherine II, *op cit.*, p. 69.

52. *Ibid.*, p. 70.

53. *OIL*, p. 240.

54. *OIL*, pp. 239–41; Rice, *op cit.*, pp. 162–63; Marsden, *op cit.*, pp. 166–68.

55. Rice, *op cit.*, p. 161.

56. Marsden, *op cit.*, p. 168.

57. *Ibid.*, p. 170.

58. *Ibid.*, p. 166.

59. Beaumont, *op cit.*, p. 22; Rice, *op cit.*, pp. 160–61.

60. Quoted in Marsden, *op cit.*, p. 179.

61. Semenova, *Byt i naselenie*, pp. 66–67.

62. Rice, *op cit.*, p. 99; Bain, *op cit.*, p. 149.

63. Rice, *op cit.*, p. 153.

64. Semenova, *Byt i naselenie*, pp. 40–41.

CHAPTER SIX

1. Billington, *Icon*, p. 217.

2. Quoted in J. Alexander, *Catherine the Great: Life and Legend* (New York, 1989), pp. 59–60 (hereinafter cited as *Catherine*).

3. C. Montesquieu, *The Spirit of the Laws* (Cambridge, 1989), p. 126.

4. The ceremony is described in chapter 5, p. 147.

5. R. Bain, *Peter III Emperor of Russia: The Story of a Crisis and a Crime* (New York, 1902), p. 30 (hereinafter cited as *Peter III*).

6. Alexander, *Catherine*, p. 55.

7. Bain, *Peter III*, p. 32.

8. Quoted in Bain, *Peter III*, p. 40.

9. E. Dashkova, *The Memoirs of Princess Dashkova* (Durham, 1995), p. 51.

10. *Ibid.*, p. 55.

11. *Ibid.*, p. 54.

12. Catherine II, *Memoirs*, p. 284.

13. Alexander, *Catherine*, p. 49.

14. Catherine II, *Memoirs*, p. 284.

15. M. Raeff, "The Domestic Policies of Peter III and His Overthrow," *American Historical Review* 75 (1970), pp. 1291, 1297–1302 (hereinafter cited as *Peter III*).

16. Bain, *Peter III*, p. 100.

17. Alexander, *Catherine*, p. 46.

18. Quoted in Bain, *Peter III*, p. 49.

19. Described in *ibid.*, pp. 73–75.

20. *Ibid.*, p. 107.

21. *Ibid.*, p. 68.

22. *Ibid.*, p. 106.

23. *Ibid.*

24. Raeff, *Peter III,* p. 1304.

25. *Ibid.,* pp. 1293–94.

26. *Ibid.,* p. 1302.

27. Bain, *Peter III,* p. 98–99.

28. A. Kamenskii, "Catherine the Great," in Raleigh, *op cit.,* p. 146.

29. Raeff, *Peter III,* pp. 1308–10.

30. Dashkova, *op cit.,* pp. 71–72.

31. *Ibid.,* p. 68.

32. Bain, *Peter III,* p. 110.

33. *Ibid.,* p. 154.

34. Catherine II, *Memoirs,* p. 25.

35. *Ibid.,* p. 124.

36. Quoted in *ibid.,* p. 162, fn. 31.

37. *Ibid.,* p. 124.

38. *Ibid.,* p. 125.

39. Alexander, *Catherine,* p. 46.

40. Quoted in Kamenskii, *op cit.,* p. 158.

41. V. Bilbasov, "The Intellectual Formation of Catherine II," in M. Raeff, ed., *Catherine the Great: A Profile* (New York, 1972), p. 34 (hereinafter cited as *Catherine*).

42. Quoted in G. Norman, *The Hermitage: The Biography of a Great Museum* (New York, 1997), p. 26.

43. Malia, *op cit.,* p. 73.

44. Lincoln, *Romanovs,* p. 293.

45. Billington, *Icon,* p. 224.

46. Quoted in Norman, *op cit.,* p. 27.

47. Quoted in *ibid.,* p. 28.

48. Letter of September 25, 1762, quoted in A. Walicki, *A History of Russian Thought from the Enlightenment to Marxism* (Stanford, 1979), p. 3 (hereinafter cited as *Russian Thought*); also I. Luppol, "The Empress and the Philosophe," in Raeff, *Catherine,* p. 48.

49. Quoted in H. Troyat, *Catherine the Great* (New York, 1980), p. 196 (hereinafter cited as *Catherine*).

50. R. McGrew, *Paul I of Russia, 1754–1801* (Oxford, 1992), p. 76 (hereinafter cited as *Paul*).

51. Quoted in P. Furbank, *Diderot: A Critical Biography* (New York, 1992), p. 379.

52. Quoted in *ibid.,* pp. 387–88.

53. Quoted in W. Durant and A. Durant, *The Story of Civilization: Rousseau and Revolution* (New York, 1967), p. 449.

54. Kamenskii, *op cit.,* p. 157.

55. Raeff, *Understanding Imperial Russia,* pp. 80, 89.

56. Quoted in Billington, *Icon,* p. 222.

57. Letter from Catherine to Madame Geoffrin of March 28, 1765, quoted in Kamenskii, *op cit.,* p. 157.

58. C. Beccaria, *An Essay on Crimes and Punishments* (Boston, 1983).

59. Reprinted in W. Reddaway, ed., *Documents of Catherine the Great* (Cambridge, United Kingdom, 1931), pp. 215–309.

60. Montesquieu, *op cit.,* pp. 126, 279–80, 283–84; see Billington, *Icon,* p. 223.

61. Billington, *Icon,* pp. 218–20.

62. M. Raeff, *Origins of the Russian Intelligentsia: The Eighteenth Century Nobility* (New York, 1966), p. 159 (hereinafter cited as *Intelligentsia*).

63. Alexander, *Catherine*, p. 100.

64. Billington, *Icon*, p. 221; Riasanovsky, *History*, pp. 285–86.

65. Walicki, *Russian Thought*, p. 4.

66. Quoted in Alexander, *Catherine*, p. 101.

67. In Reddaway, *op cit.*, pp. 17–18.

68. Quoted in Alexander, *Catherine*, p. 109.

69. Raeff, *Understanding Imperial Russia*, p. 93.

70. Walicki, *Russian Thought*, p. 7; Alexander, *Catherine*, pp. 188–89.

71. Raeff, *Intelligentsia*, pp. 154–55.

72. Alexander, *Catherine*, pp. 79, 189, 191.

73. Catherine II, *Memoirs*, p. 196.

74. Quoted in Alexander, *Catherine*, p. 45.

75. Quoted in *ibid.*, p. 44.

76. Quoted in *ibid.*, p. 45.

77. Quoted in *ibid.*, p. 158.

78. Quoted in *ibid.*, p. 116.

79. Letter to Voltaire of October 6/17, 1771, in Reddaway, *op cit.*, p. 135.

80. Reprinted in J. Alexander, "Petersburg and Moscow in Early Urban Policy," *Journal of Urban History* 8 (1982), pp. 163–64 (hereinafter cited as *Petersburg and Moscow*) and in Catherine II, *The Memoirs of Catherine the Great*, D. Maroger, ed. (London, 1955), pp. 364–65 (hereinafter cited as Maroger).

81. Platunov, *op cit.*, pp. 67–68.

82. Catherine II, autobiographical fragment reprinted in Maroger, *op cit.*, p. 373.

83. Billington, *Icon*, p. 227.

84. *OIL*, p. 365.

85. *Ibid.*, pp. 369–80.

86. G. Casanova, *History of My Life*, 12 vols. (New York, 1966–1971), vol. 10, pp. 125–26.

87. Egorov, *op cit.*, p. 42.

88. *Ibid.*, pp. 43–45.

89. Platunov, *op cit.*, p. 65.

90. Egorov, *op cit.*, p. 50.

91. Grabar, *op cit.*, pp. 175–76.

92. Bolotova, *op cit.*, p. 32.

93. Egorov, *op cit.*, pp. 77–78.

94. Quoted in A. Kaganovich, *Mednyi vsadnik: istoria sozdania monumenta* (Leningrad, 1975), p. 42.

95. Quoted in W. Bruce Lincoln, *Sunlight at Midnight: St. Petersburg and the Rise of Modern Russia* (New York, 2000), p. 94 (hereinafter cited as *Sunlight*).

96. Volkov, *op cit.*, p. 19.

97. Hamilton, *op cit.*, p. 354.

98. Quoted in Furbank, *op cit.*, p. 377.

99. Kaganovich, *op cit.*, p. 90.

100. *Ibid.*, p. 160.

101. Kaganovich, *op cit.*, p. 164.

102. *Ibid.*

103. *Ibid.*

104. Egorov, *op cit.*, pp. 65–67.

105. Cross, *Banks of Neva*, p. 16; *OIL*, p. 294.

106. *OIL*, p. 296.

107. *Ibid.*, p. 295.

108. Cross, *Banks of Neva*, p. 16. The figures, from Heinrich Storch and far from precise, were: 17,660 Germans, 3,700 Finns, 2,290 French, 1,860 Swedish, 930 British, and only 50 Dutch. *Ibid.*

109. *OIL*, p. 312.

110. In the Guards, not only the officers but also most of the soldiers came from the nobility.

111. *OIL*, p. 308.

112. *Ibid.*, p. 316.

113. *Ibid.*, p. 318. The Rogovikov galloon factory on Gagarin Street, for example, changed from using 71% serf labor and 29% free labor in 1764 to only 41% serf and 59% free in 1775. *Ibid.*, p. 271.

114. *Ibid.*, p. 318.

115. I. de Madariaga, *Catherine the Great: A Short History* (New Haven, 1990), pp. 184–85 (hereinafter cited as *Catherine*).

116. *OIL*, p. 288–89.

117. *Ibid.*, p. 288.

118. *Ibid.*, p. 289.

119. *Ibid.*, p. 290.

120. *Ibid.*, p. 266.

121. I. de Madariaga, *Russia in the Age of Catherine the Great* (New Haven, 1981), p. 327 (hereinafter cited as *Russia in the Age of Catherine*).

122. Norman, *op cit.*, p. 22.

123. *Ibid.*, p. 23.

124. Quoted in *ibid.*, p. 6.

125. Quoted in Beaumont, *op cit.*, p. 30.

126. Billington, *Icon*, p. 234.

127. *Ibid.*, pp. 237–38.

128. *Ibid.*, p. 235.

129. Karlinsky, *op cit.*, p. 81.

130. As translated in E. Bristol, *A History of Russian Poetry* (New York, 1991), p. 77.

131. *OIL*, p. 411.

132. *Ibid.*

133. *Ibid.*, pp. 416–17.

134. *Ibid.*, p. 418.

135. Dashkova, *op cit.*, p. 200.

136. Madariaga, *Catherine*, p. 93; see also Madariaga, *Russia in the Age of Catherine*, pp. 332–35.

137. Walicki, *Russian Thought*, pp. 16–17.

138. N. Novikov, *Izbrannie sochinenia* (Moscow-Leningrad, 1951), p. 85.

139. *Ibid.*, pp. 391–92.

140. *Ibid.*, p. 391.

141. Raeff, *Intelligentsia*, p. 162.

142. Tompkins, *op cit.*, p. 65.

143. Billington, *Icon*, p. 245.

144. Raeff, *Intelligentsia*, p. 164.

145. *Ibid.*, p. 161.

146. Quoted in *ibid.*, pp. 247–48.

147. Quoted in *ibid.*, pp. 246–47.

148. W. Trowbridge, *Cagliostro: Maligned Freemason and Rosicrucian* (1910; reprint, Montana, n.d.), p. 144.

149. *Ibid.*, p. 145.

150. See generally Billington, *Icon*, pp. 242–59.

151. *Ibid.*, p. 244.

152. Quoted in *ibid.*, p. 250.

153. *Ibid.*, pp. 250–51.

154. *Ibid.*, p. 256.

155. *Ibid.*, p. 248.

156. Count L.P. de Ségur, *Memoirs and Recollections of Count Ségur*, 3 vols. (London, 1827), vol. 3, p. 307.

157. *Ibid.*, p. 335.

158. Alexander, *Catherine*, p. 270.

159. Quoted in *ibid.*, p. 271.

160. McGrew, *Paul*, pp. 168–69.

161. Ségur, *op cit.*, pp. 312–13.

162. *Ibid.*, p. 226.

163. *Ibid.*, p. 420.

164. Madariaga, *Catherine*, p. 190.

165. *Ibid.*

166. Lincoln, *Romanovs*, p. 305.

167. Madariaga, *op cit.*, p. 199.

168. Ségur, *op cit.*, p. 440.

169. Alexander, *Catherine*, p. 296.

170. Troyat, *Catherine*, p. 372.

171. *Ibid.*, pp. 305–06.

172. Billington, *Icon*, p. 259.

173. Alexander, *Catherine*, p. 312.

174. L.-E. Vigée-Lebrun, *Memoirs of Madame Vigée-Lebrun* (New York, 1989), p. 84.

175. *Ibid.*, p. 126–27.

176. Quoted in Lincoln, *Romanovs*, p. 306.

177. As translated in Terras, *op cit.*, p. 143.

178. Dashkova, *op cit.*, pp. 237–40.

179. Madariaga, *Catherine*, p, 199.

180. Walicki, *Russian Thought*, p. 26.

181. Quoted in D. Lang, *The First Russian Radical: Alexander Radishchev, 1749–1802* (London, 1959), p. 77.

182. A. Radishchev, *A Journey from St. Petersburg to Moscow* (Cambridge, Massachusetts, 1958). This edition includes Catherine's own notes from reading the book.

183. *Ibid.*, p. 40.

184. Berdayev, *Russian Idea*, p. 45.

185. Radishchev, *op cit.*, pp. 102, 120.

186. In *ibid.*, p. 241.

187. A. Pushkin, "Aleksandr Radishchev," *Sobranie sochinenii*, p. 564.

188. *Ibid.*

189. Walicki, *Russian Thought*, pp. 38–39.

190. Alexander, *Catherine*, p. 78.

191. This was a popular image at the time, also expressed by Derzhavin and Ivan Betskoi. Riasanovsky, *Image of Peter the Great*, pp. 37–39.

CHAPTER SEVEN

1. V. Golovine, *Memoirs of Countess Golovine* (London, 1910), p. 133.

2. McGrew, *Paul*, p. 34.

3. *Ibid.*, pp. 57–58.

4. Quoted in *ibid.*, p. 98.

5. K. Valishevskii, *Syn Velikoi Ekaterinoi: Imperator Pavel I* (Moscow; reprint, 1990), p. 71.

6. Golovine, *op cit.*, p. 126.

7. Quoted in McGrew, *Paul*, p. 194.

8. Dashkova, *op cit.*, p. 250.

9. McGrew, *Paul*, p. 206.

10. Quoted in *ibid.*, p. 208.

11. Quoted in Sorokin, *op cit.*, p. 198.

12. *Ibid.*, p. 211.

13. McGrew, *Paul*, p. 201.

14. Golovine, *op cit.*, p. 132.

15. Quoted in J. Kenney, "The Politics of Assassination," in H. Ragsdale, ed., *Paul I: A Reassessment of His Life and Reign* (Pittsburgh, 1979), p. 126 (hereinafter cited as *Reassessment*).

16. Quoted in Sorokin, *op cit.*, p. 198.

17. McGrew, *Paul*, pp. 209–10.

18. Kenny, *op cit.*, p, 132.

19. H. Ragsdale, *Tsar Paul and the Question of Madness* (Connecticut, 1988), pp. 90–93 (hereinafter cited as *Madness*). It is still debated whether such proposals as appeared in the European press originated from Paul. Ragsdale concludes that it probably did come from him, or from his aides with Paul's knowledge, but that it was probably a joke not to be taken seriously.

20. Quoted in *ibid.*, p. 136.

21. Quoted in McGrew, *Paul*, p. 329.

22. *Ibid.*, p. 207.

23. Vigeé-Lebrun, *op cit.*, p. 125.

24. Quoted in H. Troyat, *Alexander of Russia: Napoleon's Conqueror* (New York, 1980), pp. 40–41 (hereinafter cited as *Alexander*).

25. The following account is based largely on A. Andreev, V. Zakharov, and I. Nastenko, *Istoria Maltiiskogo ordena* (Moscow, 1999), pp. 136–54, and R. McGrew, "Paul I and the Knights of Malta," in H. Ragsdale, *Reassessment*, pp. 44–75 (hereinafter cited as *Knights of Malta*).

26. Andreev et al., *op cit.*, pp. 150–51.

27. Quoted in McGrew, *Knights of Malta*, pp. 62–63.

28. Golovine, *op cit.*, p. 182.

29. Massie, *Pavlovsk*, p. 22.

30. Quoted in V. Cowles, *The Romanovs* (New York, 1971), p. 121.

31. Karamzin, *op cit.*, p. 135.

32. N. Sindalovskii, *Legendy i mify Sankt-Peterburga* (St. Petersburg, 1994), pp. 36–37 (hereinafter cited as *Legendy i mify*).

33. McGrew, *Paul*, p. 138.

34. L. Engelhardt, *Zapiski* (Moscow, 1997), p. 161 note.

35. Golovine, *op cit.*, p. 239.

36. See generally, Ragsdale, *Madness*; also McGrew, *Paul*, pp. 336–37.

37. Quoted in McGrew, *Paul*, p. 326.

38. *Ibid.*, p. 340.

39. Kenny, *op cit.*, pp. 138–39.

40. McGrew, *Paul*, p. 351.

41. Kenny, *op cit.*, p. 127.

42. McGrew, *Paul*, pp. 324–25; Sorokin, *op cit.*, p. 210.

43. McGrew, *Paul*, p. 348; see also Sorokin, *op cit.*, p. 211.

44. McGrew, *Paul*, p. 347; Golovine, *op cit.*, p. 227.

45. Golovine, *op cit.*, pp. 239–40.

46. McGrew, *Paul*, p. 356.

47. *Ibid.*, pp. 356–57; H. Ragsdale, "Conclusion," in Ragsdale, *Reassessment*, p. 177.

CHAPTER EIGHT

1. Letter to Joseph Priestly, November 29, 1802, in P. Ford, ed., *The Writings of Thomas Jefferson* (New York, 1897), vol. 8, p. 179.

2. N. Turgenev, "Ideas on the Organization of a Society," reprinted in M. Raeff, ed., *The Decembrist Movement* (Englewood Cliffs, New Jersey, 1966), p. 5 (hereinafter cited as *Decembrists*).

3. Quoted in Troyat, *Alexander*, p. 59.

4. A. McConnell, *Tsar Alexander I: Paternalistic Reformer* (Arlington Heights, Illinois, 1970), p. 4.

5. Quoted in Lincoln, *Romanovs*, p. 383.

6. Quoted in *ibid.*, p. 386.

7. McConnell, *op cit.*, p. 5.

8. Quoted in *ibid.*, p. 8.

9. *Ibid.*

10. Quoted in Troyat, *Alexander*, pp. 41–42.

11. *Ibid.*, p. 23.

12. M. Raeff, *Michael Speransky: Statesman of Imperial Russia, 1772–1839* (The Hague, 1957), p. 33 (hereinafter cited as *Speransky*).

13. Troyat, *Alexander*, p. 40.

14. Quoted in McConnell, *op cit.*, p. 22.

15. Quoted in Lincoln, *Romanovs*, p. 387.

16. *Ibid.*, p. 35.

17. M. Raeff, *Plans for Political Reform in Russia, 1730–1905* (Englewood Cliffs, New Jersey, 1966), p. 70 (hereinafter cited as *Plans for Reform*).

18. *Ibid.*, pp. 71–74.

19. Reprinted in *ibid.*, pp. 76–84.

20. Raeff, *Speransky*, p. 36.

21. T. Anderson, *Russian Political Thought: An Introduction* (Ithaca, New York, 1967), p. 150.

22. Reprinted in Raeff, *Plans for Reform*, pp. 89–91.

23. Raeff, *Speransky*, p. 46.

24. McConnell, *op cit.*, p. 35.

25. Raeff, *Speransky*, p. 55.

26. H. Troyat, *Pushkin* (New York, 1970), p. 33 (hereinafter cited as *Pushkin*).

27. Quoted in Anderson, *op cit.*, p. 153.

28. M. Jenkins, *Arakcheev: Grand Vizier of the Russian Empire* (London, 1969), p. 131.

29. E.g., Karamzin, *op cit.*, p. 184.

30. Raeff, *Speransky*, pp. 170–71.

31. *Ibid.*, p. 172.

32. *Ibid.*, p. 178.

33. *Ibid.*, p. 183.

34. Quoted in Lincoln, *Romanovs*, p. 393.

35. Quoted in I. Grey, *The Romanovs* (New York, 1970), p. 365.

36. J.Q. Adams, *John Quincy Adams in Russia*, C. Adams, ed. (New York, 1970), pp. 352–53 (diary entry of March 19th).

37. Quoted in A. Brett-James, ed., *1812: Eyewitness Accounts of Napoleon's Defeat in Russia* (London, 1966), p. 6.

38. Quoted in Lincoln, *Romanovs*, p. 391.

39. Quoted in Brett-James, *op cit.*, p. 147.

40. Quoted in *ibid.*, p. 6.

41. Quoted in E. Tarle, *Napoleon's Invasion of Russia, 1812* (New York, 1942), p. 132.

42. *Ibid.*, p. 45.

43. Quoted in Lincoln, *Romanovs*, p. 394.

44. Jenkins, *op cit.*, p. 151.

45. C. von Clausewitz, *The Campaign of 1812 in Russia* (New York, 1995), xiii–xiv, 192.

46. Quoted in Lincoln, *Romanovs*, pp. 394–95.

47. J. de Maistre, *Peterburgskie pisma* (St. Petersburg, 1995), p. 222 (letter of September 10/22, 1812).

48. Quoted in Brett-James, *op cit.*, p. 201 (letter of October 13, 1812).

49. J. de Maistre, *op cit.*, p. 220 (letter of September 2/14–3/15, 1812).

50. Jenkins, *op cit.*, p. 160.

51. Quoted in Brett-James, *op cit.*, p. 72.

52. *Ibid.*

53. Adams, *op cit.*, p. 398 (entry of September 15, 1812).

54. *Ibid.*, p. 423.

55. Brett-James, *op cit.*, pp. 70, 236–37.

56. Quoted in V. Fedorov, "Alexander I," in Raleigh, *op cit.*, p. 239.

57. Jenkins, *op cit.*, p. 157.

58. Quoted in Cowles, *op cit.*, p. 134.

59. Quoted in Jenkins, *op cit.*, p. 153.

60. Quoted in Tarle, *op cit.*, p. 315.

61. Quoted in J. Bergamini, *The Tragic Dynasty: A History of the Romanovs* (New York, 1969), p. 296.

62. Quoted in Lincoln, *Romanovs*, p. 404.

63. Quoted in Billington, *Icon*, p. 274.

64. Quoted in Grey, *op cit.*, p. 252.

65. Quoted in Troyat, *Alexander*, p. 243.

66. *Ibid.;* Billington, *Icon*, p. 286.

67. Troyat, *Alexander*, p. 243.

68. Lincoln, *Romanovs*, p. 404.

69. Grey, *op cit.*, p. 257.

70. Quoted in Lincoln, *Romanovs*, p. 407.

71. Quoted in Troyat, *Pushkin*, p. 120.

72. Quoted in *ibid.*, p. 119.

73. Quoted in *ibid.*

74. Quoted in *ibid.*

75. Constitutional Charter for the Russian Empire, Arts. 11–12, reprinted in Raeff, *Plans for Reform*, p. 111.

76. Billington, *Icon*, p. 284.

77. *Ibid.*, p. 291.

78. Quoted in *ibid.*, p. 293.

79. *Ibid.*, pp. 292–93.

80. Quoted in M. Nechkina, *Dekabristy* (Moscow, 1982), p. 18.

81. In Raeff, *Decembrists*, p. 51.

82. *Ibid.*, pp. 45 (Trubetskoi), 46 (Ryleev), 50–51 (A. Muraviev), 51 (Yakushkin), 57 (M. Muraviev-Apostol).

83. Quoted in Nechkina, *op cit.*, p. 18.

84. Quoted in A. Mazour, *The First Russian Revolution, 1825* (1937; reprint, Stanford, 1967), p. 55.

85. Raeff, *Decembrists*, pp. 19–20.

86. Quoted in Mazour, *op cit.*, p. 55.

87. Quoted in Volkov, *op cit.*, p. 26.

88. *Ibid.*, p. 56.

89. Quoted in Nechkina, *op cit.*, p. 22.

90. In Raeff, *Decembrists*, pp. 67–68.

91. *Ibid.*, pp. 22–23.

92. *Ibid.*, pp. 10, 59–60.

93. Quoted in Mazour, *op cit.*, p. 67.

94. Billington, *Icon*, p. 267.

95. Nechkina, *op cit.*, p. 33.

96. Mazour, *op cit.*, pp. 48–52.

97. Quoted in E. Feinstein, *Pushkin: A Biography* (New Jersey, 1998), p. 38.

98. Quoted in *ibid.*, p. 44.

99. F. Glinka, "Memoirs," in V. Vatsuro, ed., *Pisateli Dekabristy*, 2 vols. (Moscow, 1980), vol. 1, pp. 323–24 (hereinafter cited as *Pisateli Dekabristy*).

100. Quoted in Troyat, *Pushkin*, p. 134.

101. M. Slonim, *The Epic of Russian Literature: From Its Origins through Tolstoy* (New York, 1964), p. 78.

102. The story is reprinted in Raeff, *Decembrists*, pp. 60–66.

103. Mazour, *op cit.*, p. 75.

104. Nechkina, *op cit.*, p. 33.

105. Reproduced in Raeff, *Decembrists*, pp. 124–56.

106. Mazour, *op cit.*, p. 127.

107. As translated in *ibid.*, p. 127.

108. Quoted in *ibid.*, p. 163.

109. Quoted in Lincoln, *Romanovs*, p. 409.

110. M. Bestuzhev, "Moi tyurmi," in *Pisateli Dekabristy*, pp. 60–61.

111. Quoted in Mazour, *op cit.*, p. 164.

112. Reprinted in Raeff, *Decembrists*, pp. 101–03, and in Mazour, *op cit.*, pp. 283–84.

113. Nechkina, *op cit.*, p. 107–08.

114. *Ibid.*, p. 108.

115. Quoted in Nechkina, *op cit.*, p. 108.

116. *Ibid.*

117. Quoted in W. Bruce Lincoln, *Nicholas I: Emperor and Autocrat of All the Russias* (DeKalb, Illinois, 1989), p. 40 (hereinafter cited as *Nicholas*).

118. N. Bestuzhev, "Vospominania o Ryleeve," in *Pisateli Dekabristy*, p. 86.

119. *Ibid.*, p. 87.

120. M. Bestuzhev, *op cit.*, p. 65.

121. Quoted in Nechkina, *op cit.*, pp. 112–13. The figure of 150,000 is surely exaggerated.

122. Lincoln, *Nicholas*, p. 43.

123. Quoted in Mazour, *op cit.*, p. 178.

124. Lincoln, *Romanovs*, p. 410.

125. Mazour, *op cit.*, p. 178.

126. Nechkina, *op cit.*, p. 117.

127. The report is reproduced in substantial part in Raeff, *Decembrists*, pp. 32–43.

128. Raeff, *Decembrists*, p. 26.

129. Mazour, *op cit.*, p. 220.

CHAPTER NINE

1. As translated in Yarmolinsky, *op cit.*, p. 96.

2. Reproduced in V. Veresaev, ed., *Pushkin v zhizhi*, 4 vols. (Moscow, 1990), vol. 2, p. 275.

3. Reproduced in *ibid.*, p. 276.

4. Quoted in T. Kapustina, "Nicholas I," in Raleigh, *op cit.*, p. 258.

5. Quoted in *ibid.*

6. Quoted in *ibid.*, p. 262.

7. Quoted in *ibid.*, p. 263.

8. Marquis de Custine, *Empire of the Czar: A Journey through Eternal Russia* (New York, 1989), pp. 136–37.

9. Quoted in Lincoln, *Nicholas*, p. 60.

10. Quoted in L. Chereiskii, *Sovremenniki Pushkina* (Leningrad, 1981), p. 48.

11. Nikitenko, *op cit.*, vol. 1, p. 48.

12. *Ibid.*, p. 91.

13. *Ibid.*

14. *Ibid.*, pp. 91–92.

15. W. Bruce Lincoln, *In the Vanguard of Reform: Russia's Enlightened Bureaucrats, 1825–61* (DeKalb, Illinois, 1982), pp. 12–13.

16. Lincoln, *Nicholas*, p. 176.

17. *Ibid.*, p. 167.

18. *Ibid.*

19. Custine, *op cit.*, pp. 101–02.

20. Quoted in Lincoln, *Sunlight*, p. 116.

21. *Ibid.*, pp. 507–10.

22. *Ibid.*, p. 509.

23. M. Taranovskaia, *Karl Rossi* (Leningrad, 1978), pp. 193–94.

24. A. Rotach and O. Chekanova, *Monferran* (Leningrad, 1979), pp. 170–72.

25. Quoted in W. Mosse, *Alexander II and the Modernization of Russia* (New York, 1962), p. 11.

26. Pyliaev, *op cit.*, p. 104.

27. A. Nikitenko, *op cit.*, vol. 1, p. 107.

28. *Ibid.*

29. Lincoln, *Nicholas*, p. 273.

30. V. Belinskii, "Peterburg i Moskva," in *Fisiologia Peterburga* (Moscow, 1991), p. 32 (hereinafter cited as *Petersburg and Moscow*).

31. *Ibid.*, p. 353.

32. A. Gordin and M. Gordin, *Pushkinskii vek* (St. Petersburg, 1995), p. 363.

33. Quoted in *ibid.*, p. 365.

34. Quoted in *ibid.*, pp. 365–66.

35. *Ibid.*, p. 241.

36. A. Pushkin, *Eugene Onegin,* trans. J. Falen (Oxford, 1990), p. 15.

37. Nikitenko, *op cit.*, vol. 1, p. 198.

38. Chereiskii, *op cit.*, p. 56.

39. S. Abramovich, *Pushkin v 1833 godu* (Moscow, 1994), pp. 274–76.

40. As translated in Yarmolinsky, *op cit.*, pp. 107–08.

41. A. Amosov, in V. Brigorenko et al., eds., *A.S. Pushkin v vospominaniakh sovremennikov*, 2 vols. (Moscow, 1974), vol. 2, p. 330.

42. As translated by Avril Pyman in S. Narovchatov, ed., *Mikhail Lermontov: Selected Works* (Moscow, 1976), p. 30.

43. The details of this episode are related in P. Shchegolev, ed., *Lermontov: Vospominania, Pisma, Dnevniki* (Moscow, 1999), pp. 240–43, 258–63; V. Afanasev, *Lermontov* (Moscow, 1991), pp. 360, 368–69.

44. Quoted in W. Bruce Lincoln, *Between Heaven and Hell: The Story of a Thousand Years of Artistic Life in Russia* (New York, 1998), p. 140 (hereinafter cited as *Heaven and Hell*).

45. Letter to P. Pletnev, March 16, 1837, reprinted in V. Kunina, ed., *Poslednii god zhizni Pushkina* (Moscow, 1990), p. 597.

46. V. Erlich, *Gogol* (New Haven, 1969), p. 79.

47. Quoted in Volkov, *op cit.*, p. 31.

48. Erlich, *op cit.*, p. 79.

49. Quoted in D. Magarshack, *Gogol: A Life* (London, 1957), p. 125.

50. *Ibid.*, p. 144.

51. Quoted in Lincoln, *Heaven and Hell*, p. 142.

52. N. Gogol, *Pisma*, 4 vols. (St. Petersburg, n.d.), vol. 2, p. 508.

53. In N. Ansiferov, *Dusha Peterburga*, in *"Nepostizhimyi gorod. . ."* (Leningrad, 1991), p. 111.

54. Volkov, *op cit.*, pp. 34–35.

55. N. Gogol, "Petersburgskie zapiski 1836 goda," in *Sobranie sochinenii*, 6 vols. (Moscow, 1959), vol. 6, pp. 113–14 (hereinafter cited as *Petersburg Notes*).

56. Volkov, *op cit.*, p. 71.

57. Gogol, *Petersburg Notes*, p. 119.

58. Gordin and Gordin, *op cit.*, p. 282.

59. Quoted in Billington, *Icon*, p. 330.

60. Quoted in Lincoln, *Heaven and Hell*, p. 122.

61. Quoted in Volkov, *op cit.*, p. 68.

62. Quoted in *ibid.*

63. N. Gogol, "Poslednii den Pompeii," in *Sobranie sochinenii*, vol. 6, p. 77.

64. Gertsen, "Moskva i Peterburg," in *Sobranie sochinenii*, vol. 2, p. 40.

65. Quoted in Billington, *Icon*, p. 341.

66. Republished as *Panorama of Nevsky Prospect* (Leningrad, 1974).

67. Gordin and Gordin, *op cit.*, p. 293; Volkov, *op cit.*, pp. 60–61.

68. *Ibid.*, p. 297.

69. Norman, *op cit.*, p. 67.

70. Gertsen, "Russkie Nemtsy i Nemetskie Russkie," *Sobranie sochinenii*, vol. 14, p. 157.

71. A. Herzen, *My Past and Thoughts* (Berkeley, 1973), pp. 292–93 (hereinafter cited as *Past and Thoughts*).

72. A. Chaadaev, *Philosophical Letters & Apology of a Madman* (Knoxville, 1969), p. 41.

73. *Ibid.*, p. 42.

74. *Ibid.*, p. 43.

75. *Ibid.*, pp. 36–37.

76. *Ibid.*, p. 37.

77. *Ibid.*, pp. 165–67; see Riasanovsky, *Image of Peter the Great*, pp. 101–06.

78. Walicki, *Russian Thought*, pp. 75–76.

79. Chaadaev, *op cit.*, p. 168.

80. Gertsen, *Sobrannie sochinenia*, vol. 2, p. 38.

81. Quoted in I. Berlin, *Russian Thinkers* (New York, 1978), p. 163 (hereinafter cited as *Russian Thinkers*).

82. *Ibid.*

83. Herzen, *Past and Thoughts*, p. 238.

84. Gertsen, *Sobrannie sochinenii*, vol. 2, p. 39.

85. Belinskii, *Petersburg and Moscow*, p. 37.

86. Quoted in Berlin, *Russian Thinkers*, p. 165.

87. Quoted in *ibid.*, p. 161.

88. In R. Matlaw, ed., *Belinsky, Chernyshevsky, and Dobroliubov: Selected Criticism* (New York, 1962), p. 84.

89. *Ibid.*, p. 86.

90. *Ibid.*

91. Belinskii, *Petersburg and Moscow*, p. 36.

92. Quoted in Lincoln, *Nicholas*, p. 307.

93. Quoted in J. Seddon, *The Petrashevtsy: A Study of the Russian Revolutionaries of 1848* (Manchester, 1985), p. 42.

94. *Ibid.*, 18.

95. Walicki, *Russian Thought*, p. 153.

96. Nikitenko, *op cit.*, vol. 1, p. 298.

97. Seddon, *op cit.*, p. 44.

98. Walicki, *Russian Thought*, pp. 155–56.

99. Quoted in Seddon, *op cit.*, p. 198.

100. Lincoln, *Nicholas*, p. 281 (noting that the legend is probably apocryphal).

101. Nikitenko, *op cit.*, vol. 1, p. 320.

102. Quoted in Lincoln, *Nicholas*, p. 282.

103. Quoted in Seddon, *op cit.*, p. 224.

104. Nikitenko, *op cit.*, vol. 2, p. 67.

105. Quoted in Lincoln, *Romanovs*, p. 426.

106. Nikitenko, *op cit.*, vol. 3, p. 262.

CHAPTER TEN

1. Belinskii, *Petersburg and Moscow*, p. 34.

2. Quoted in N. Antsiferov, *Peterburg Dostoevskogo*, in *op cit.*, p. 187.

3. F. Dostoevskii, *Winter Notes on Summer Impressions*, D. Patterson, trans. (Evanston, 1988), p. 37 (hereinafter cited as *Winter Notes*).

4. Quoted in A. Yarmolinsky, *Dostoevsky: Works and Days* (New York, 1971), p. 424.

5. F. Dostoevsky, *Notes from Underground*, in F. Dostoevsky, *The Best Short Stories of Dostoevsky*, trans. D. Magarshack (New York, 1992), p. 119.

6. P. Kropotkin, *Memoirs of a Revolutionist* (Boston, 1930), p. 131.

7. *Ibid.*, p. 133.

8. Nikitenko, *op cit.*, vol. 2, pp. 179–80.

9. *Ibid.*

10. Quoted in Mosse, *op cit.*, p. 65.

11. Kropotkin, *op cit.*, p. 134.

12. Bater, *op cit.*, pp. 91–93.

13. R. Zelnik, *Labor and Society in Tsarist Russia: The Factory Workers of St. Petersburg 1855–1870* (Stanford, 1971), pp. 60–61; OIL, pp. 462–63.

14. J. McKay, *Pioneers for Profit: Foreign Entrepreneurship and Russian Industrialization, 1885–1914* (Chicago, 1970), pp. 41–42.

15. H. Schliemann, *Memoirs of Heinrich Schliemann*, L. Deuel, ed. (New York, 1977), pp. 54–56. See Generally I. Bogdanov, *Dolgaia doroga v Troiu: Genrikh Shliman v Peterburge* (St. Petersburg, 1995).

16. McKay, *op cit.*, p. 26.

17. *Ibid.*, pp. 117–18.

18. Lincoln, *Sunlight*, p. 158.

19. Bater, *op cit.*, pp. 4, 160–63, 310.

20. *Ibid.*, p. 146; Zelnik, *op cit.*, pp. 270–71.

21. Lincoln, *Sunlight*, pp. 153–54.

22. Bater, *op cit.*, pp. 55, 91–92; H. Salisbury, *Black Night, White Snow: Russia's Revolutions 1905–1917* (New York, 1978), p. 44 (hereinafter cited as *Black Night*).

23. Bater, *op cit.*, pp. 168–72.

24. Quoted in W. Brumfield, *The Origins of Modernism in Russian Architecture* (Berkeley, 1991), p. 4.

25. Stolpianskii, *op cit.*, pp. 289–90.

26. J.G. Kohl, *Russia, St. Petersburg, Moscow, Kharkoff, Riga, Odessa, the German Provinces on the Baltic, the Steppes, the Crimea, and the Interior of the Empire* (London, 1844), p. 59.

27. *Handbook for Northern Europe; including Denmark, Norway, Sweden, Finland, and Russia* (London, 1849), Part II, pp. 374–75, quoted in Bater, *op cit.*, p. 152.

28. Zelnik, *op cit.*, p. 52.

29. Lincoln, *Sunlight*, p. 154.

30. Zelnik, *op cit.*, p. 242.

31. Bater, *op cit.*, p. 177.

32. Lincoln, *Sunlight*, p. 154.

33. Bater, *op cit.*, p. 342.

34. G. Dobson, *St. Petersburg* (London, 1910), pp. 110–11.

35. Bater, *op cit.*, 353.

36. Zelnik, *op cit.*, p. 243.

37. *Ibid.*, p. 241; Lincoln, *Romanovs*, p. 479.

38. Bater, *op cit.*, p. 190.

39. *Ibid.*, pp. 251–52.

40. *Ibid.*, p. 203.

41. Lincoln, *Romanovs*, p. 479.

42. Lincoln, *Sunlight*, p. 154.

43. Zelnik, *op cit.*, p. 250.

44. *Ibid.*, p. 247.

45. *Ibid.*, p. 249.

46. *Ibid.*, p. 251.

47. *Ibid.*

48. Bater, *op cit.*, p. 201.

49. *Ibid.*, p. 206.

50. *Ibid.*, p. 208.

51. *Ibid.*, pp. 157–58.

52. Avseenko, *op cit.*, pp. 192–93.

53. *Ibid.*, pp. 209–10, 222.

54. Lincoln, *Sunlight*, p. 164.

55. Raeff, *Understanding Imperial Russia*, p. 188.

56. *Ibid.*, pp. 173–225.

57. Billington, *Icon*, pp. 392–93.

58. Berlin, *op cit.*, p. 213; Billington, *Icon*, p. 392; F. Venturi, *Roots of Revolution: A History of the Populist and Socialist Movements in 19th Century Russia* (London, 1972), p. 148.

59. Billington, *Icon*, p. 388.

60. *Ibid.*, p. 391.

61. Berlin, *op cit.*, p. 215.

62. *Ibid.*, p. 217.

63. Venturi, *op cit.*, p. 227.

64. *Ibid.*, p. 228.

65. *Ibid.*, p. 229.

66. A. Ulam, *In the Name of the People* (New York, 1977), pp. 135–36; J. Frank, "N. Chernyshevsky: A Russian Utopia," *Southern Review* 3 (1967): 68.

67. *Ibid.*, pp. 144–45.

68. *Ibid.*, p. 152.

69. Billington, *Icon*, pp. 395–97.

70. Raeff, *Understanding Imperial Russia*, pp. 185–87.

71. Billington, *Icon*, pp. 397–98.

72. Venturi, *op cit.*, p. 469–70.

73. *Ibid.*, p. 473; Billington, *Icon*, p. 394.

74. Venturi, *op cit.*, p. 503.

75. *Ibid.*, pp. 505–06.

76. Quoted in Volkov, *op cit.*, p. 93.

77. Quoted in Venturi, *op cit.*, p. 718.

78. Sindalovskii, *Legendy i mify*, p. 80.

79. N. Chernyshevsky, "The Aesthetic Relationship of Art to Reality," in N. Chernyshevsky, *Selected Philosophical Essays* (Moscow, 1953), pp. 380–81.

80. Quoted in Volkov, *op cit.*, p. 83.

81. Quoted in Lincoln, *Heaven and Hell*, p. 194.

82. Bowlt, *op cit.*, p. 32.

83. Quoted in *ibid.*, p. 187.

84. *Ibid.*, p. 196.

85. F. Dostoevskii, *The Diary of a Writer*, 2 vols. (New York, 1949), vol. 1, p. 81.

86. Volkov, *op cit.*, p. 83.

87. Norman, *op cit.*, p. 91.

88. *Ibid.*, p. 94.

89. F. Dostoevskii, "Peterburgskaia letopis," *Polnoe sobranie sochinenii*, 30 vols. (Leningrad, 1973), vol. 18, p. 26 (hereinafter cited as *Petersburg Chronicle*).

90. *Ibid.*, p. 30.

91. *Ibid.*, pp. 15–16.

92. *Ibid.*, p. 33.

93. *Ibid.*

94. Dostoevskii, *Winter Notes*, p. 19.

95. F. Dostoevskii, "Peterburgskie snovidenia v stikhakh i proze," *Polnoe sobranie sochinenii*, vol. 19, pp. 69–70.

96. Volkov, *op cit.*, pp. 73–74.

97. Quoted in H. Schonberg, *The Lives of the Great Composers* (New York, 1970), p. 338.

98. Quoted in *ibid.*, p. 343.

99. Quoted in *ibid.*, p. 348.

100. Quoted in R. Leonard, *A History of Russian Music* (New York, 1957), pp. 126–27.

101. N. Rimsky-Korsakov, *My Musical Life* (London, 1989), p. 58.

102. *Ibid.*, p. 117.

103. Volkov, *op cit.*, pp. 100, 111.

104. Quoted in Schonberg, *op cit.*, p. 340.

105. *Ibid.*, p. 358.

106. Quoted in Volkov, *op cit.*, p. 111.

107. Schonberg, *op cit.*, p. 362.

108. I. Glebov, *Chaikovskii* (Petersburg, 1923), p. 34.

109. A. Benois, *Moi vospominania*, 2 vols. (Moscow, 1980), vol. 1, p. 653 (hereinafter cited as *Memoirs*).

110. A. Poznansky, *Tchaikovsky: The Quest for the Inner Man* (New York, 1991), pp. 604–08.

111. Dostoevskii, *Petersburg Chronicle*, pp. 13–14.

112. Billington, *Icon*, p. 424.

CHAPTER ELEVEN

1. A. Bely, "Vospominania ob Aleksandre Alexandroviche Bloke," in V. Vatsuro et al., eds., *Alexander Blok v vospominaniakh sovremennikov*, 2 vols. (Moscow, 1980), vol. 1, p. 207.

2. A. Akhmatova, *My Half-Century* (Evanston, 1992), p. 91 (hereinafter cited as *My Half-Century*).

3. M. Kschessinska, *Dancing in Petersburg: The Memoirs of Kschessinska* (New York, 1961), p. 28.

4. *Ibid.*, p. 29.

5. *Ibid.*, p. 51.

6. Quoted in R. Pipes, *The Russian Revolution* (New York, 1990), p. 60 (hereinafter cited as *Russian Revolution*).

7. A.M. Romanov, *Vospominania* (Moscow, 1999), p. 164.

8. Quoted in Lincoln, *Romanovs*, p. 617.

9. McKay, *op cit.*, p. 4.

10. H. Salisbury, *Black Night*, p. 43.

11. McKay, *op cit.*, p. 26. The figures include holdings of both common stock and bonds of Russian companies.

12. Quoted in Brumfeld, *op cit.*, p. 59.

13. H. Bainbridge, *Peter Carl Fabergé* (London, 1949), p. 4.

14. V. Zlobin, *A Difficult Soul: Zinaida Gippius* (Berkeley, 1980), pp. 40–41.

15. Quoted in O. Maitch, *Paradox in the Religious Poetry of Zinaida Gippius* (Munich, 1972), p. 72.

16. Quoted in *ibid.*, p. 49.

17. See generally B. Rosenthal, ed., *Nietzsche in Russia* (Princeton, 1986).

18. Berdayev, *Russian Idea*, p. 244.

19. Billington, *Icon*, pp. 478–79.

20. N. Berdyaev, *Dream and Reality: An Essay in Autobiography* (New York, 1962), p. 142 (hereinafter cited as *Dream and Reality*).

21. Berdyaev, *Russian Idea*, p. 234.

22. Leonard, *op cit.*, p. 217.

23. Quoted in J. Kennedy, *The "Mir iskusstva" Group and Russian Art 1898–1912* (New York, 1977), p. 105.

24. Berdyaev, *Russian Idea*, p. 236.

25. *Ibid.*, p. 241.

26. Volkov, *op cit.*, p. 151.

27. The history of the building is related in A. Kobak and L. Lure, *Dom Muruzi* (St. Petersburg, 1996).

28. Berdyaev, *Dream and Reality*, p. 146.

29. Quoted in K. Mochulsky, *Aleksandr Blok* (Detroit, 1983), p. 174.

30. K. Chukovskii, "Aleksandr Blok," in Vatsuro et al., *op cit.*, vol. 2, p. 221.

31. Quoted in N. Berberova, *Alexander Blok: A Life* (New York, 1996), p. 18.

32. Mochulsky, *op cit.*, p. 98.

33. *Ibid.*, p. 99.

34. Letter of January 19, 1904, *Sobranie Sochinenii*, vol. 8, p. 88.

35. Quoted in Berberova, *op cit.*, p. 48.

36. Letter of December 30, 1905, *Sobranie sochinenii*, vol. 8, p. 144.

37. Quoted in J. Bowlt, *The Silver Age: Russian Art of the Early Twentieth Century and the "World of Art" Group* (Newtonville, Massachusetts, 1982), p. 60.

38. Kennedy, *op cit.*, p. 32.

39. A. Benois, "O Diaghileve," in *Sergei Diaghilev i russkoe iskusstvo*, 2 vols. (Moscow, 1982), vol. 2, pp. 228–29.

40. Benois, *Memoirs*, vol. 1, pp. 640–41.

41. *Ibid.*, p. 644.

42. Quoted in A. Haskell and W. Nouvel, *Diaghileff: His Artistic and Private Life* (New York, 1935), p. 60.

43. Quoted in Bowlt, *op cit.*, p. 54.

44. *Ibid.*, p. 74.

45. *Ibid.*

46. Quoted in Kennedy, *op cit.*, p. 46.

47. Quoted in *ibid.*, p. 62.

48. Quoted in Bowlt, *op cit.*, p. 56.

49. Quoted in Kennedy, *op cit.*, p. 24.

50. Quoted in Bowlt, *op cit.*, p. 61.

51. Benois, *Memoirs*, vol. 2, p. 376; Bowlt, *op cit.*, p. 62. In his memoirs Dobuzhinsky, who met Diaghilev only in 1902, gives a figure of only 5,000 rubles, but 10,000 is the generally accepted figure. See M. Dobuzhinskii, *Vospominania* (Moscow, 1987), p. 221.

52. Rimsky-Korsakov, *op cit.*, p. 286.

53. Quoted in M. Brown, *Prokofiev: A Biography* (New York, 1987), pp. 57–58.

54. Letter to Robert Godet, 1916, quoted in Schonberg, *op cit.*, p. 471.

55. R. Buckle, *Diaghilev* (New York, 1979), p. 85.

56. Dobuzhinskii, *op cit.*, p. 226.

57. Speech reprinted in *Sergei Diaghilev i russkoe iskusstvo*, 2 vols. (Moscow, 1982), vol. 1, pp. 193–94.

58. R. Pipes, *The Russian Revolution* (New York, 1990), pp. 4–9 (hereinafter cited as *Russian Revolution*).

59. Quoted in Salisbury, *Black Night*, p. 87.

60. *Ibid.*

61. Pipes, *Russian Revolution*, p. 9.

62. Bater, *op cit.*, p. 309.

63. Salisbury, *Black Night*, p. 44.

64. Bater, *op cit.*, p. 146.

65. Pipes, *Russian Revolution*, pp. 295–96.

66. K. Chukovskii, "Nat Pinkerton," in *Sobranie sochinenii*, 6 vols. (Moscow, 1969), vol. 6, pp. 122, 124. This was in a 1908 article about film and the phenomenon of the new movie theaters, which as discussed below were frequented by the lower classes.

67. Lincoln, *Romanovs*, p. 645.

68. Pipes, *Russian Revolution*, p. 22.

69. Anderson, *op cit.*, p. 284.

70. *Ibid.*

71. *Ibid.*, p. 281.

72. S. Witte, *Vospominania*, 3 vols. (Tallin, 1994), vol. 2, p. 277.

73. Quoted in Salisbury, *Black Night*, p. 91.

74. *Ibid.*, p. 92.

75. Pipes, *Russian Revolution*, pp. 22–23.

76. *Ibid.*, p. 24. Salisbury's sources put the figure at 140,000 to 150,000. Salisbury, *Black Night*, p. 117.

77. Salisbury, *Black Night*, p. 119.

78. Quoted in Lincoln, *Romanovs*, p. 43.

79. W. Sablinsky, *The Road to Bloody Sunday: Father Gapon and the St. Petersburg Massacre of 1905* (Princeton, 1976), p. 222.

80. Quoted in Salisbury, *Black Night*, p. 121.

81. Sablinsky, *op cit.*, p. 243.

82. *Ibid.*, p. 125.

83. Sablinsky, *op cit.*, p. 251; O. Figes, *A People's Tragedy: The Russian Revolution 1891–1924* (New York, 1996), pp. 177–78.

84. Salisbury, *Black Night*, p. 127.

85. Figes, *op cit.*, p. 178.

86. A. Bely, *Nachalo veka* (Moscow, 1990), p. 458.

87. Figes, *op cit.*, p. 178.

88. Z. Gippius, *Zhivie litsa: vospominania*, 2 vols. (Tbilisi, 1991), vol. 2, p. 243 (hereinafter cited as *Zhivie litsa*).

89. *Ibid.*

90. I. Duncan, *My Life* (New York, 1955), pp. 161–62.

91. Figes, *op cit.*, p. 178; Salisbury, *Black Night*, pp. 125–26.

92. Pipes, *Russian Revolution*, p. 27.

93. *Ibid.*, p. 29.

94. Z. Gippius, *Dmitry Merezhkovskii*, in *Zhivie litsa, op cit.*, vol. 2, p. 248.

95. *OIL*, vol. 3, p. 838.

96. Quoted in Pipes, *Russian Revolution*, pp. 162–63.

97. *Ibid.*, p. 163.

98. *Ibid.*

99. Figes, *op cit.*, p. 216.

100. Pipes, *Russian Revolution*, p. 179.

101. M. Buchanan, *The Dissolution of an Empire* (London, 1932), pp. 35–36.

102. E. Radzinsky, *The Rasputin File* (New York, 2000), pp. 56–58.

103. M. Paléologue, *An Ambassador's Memoirs*, F. Holt, trans., 3 vols. (New York, n.d.), vol. 1, pp. 50–51. Paléologue was the last French ambassador to the Russian court.

104. Quoted in Figes, *op cit.*, p. 251.

105. Quoted in *ibid.*, pp. 251–52.

106. Quoted in Mochulsky, *op cit.*, p. 356.

107. Quoted in Volkov, *op cit.*, p. 195.

108. Salisbury, *Black Night*, p. 261.

109. Quoted in Bowlt, *op cit.*, pp. 111–12.

110. Volkov, *op cit.*, p. 263.

111. Kschessinska, *op cit.*, pp. 72–73.

112. F. Chaliapin, *Stranitsi iz moei zhizni* (Moscow, 1990), p. 434 (quoting reminiscences of Toti dal Monte).

113. V. Teliakovskii, *Vospominania* (Leningrad and Moscow, 1965), pp. 358–59.

114. A. Benois, "The Origins of the Ballets Russes," in B. Kochno, *Diaghilev and the Ballets Russes* (New York, 1970), p. 10.

115. T. Karsavina, *Theatre Street* (New York, 1931), p. 233.

116. Mochulsky, *op cit.*, p. 267.

117. Reeder, *op cit.*, p. 34.

118. Quoted in Reeder, *op cit.*, p. 29.

119. Reeder, *op cit.*, p. 44, citing S. Gorodetskii, "Nekotorie techenia v sovremennoi russkoi poezii," *Apollon* 1 (1913), pp. 46–50.

120. Volkov, *op cit.*, p. 179.

121. In M. Kralin and I. Slobozhan, eds., *Ob Anne Akhmatove* (Leningrad, 1990), p. 90.

122. Quoted in Volkov, *op cit.*, p. 177.

123. From the unfinished play *Enuma Elish*, in A. Akhmatova, *Sochinenia v dvukh tomakh*, 2 vols. (Moscow, 1990), vol. 2, p. 284. Akhmatova wrote the play-poem, but the words in question were those of the Gumiliev character speaking to the Akhmatova character.

124. Antsiferov, *Dusha Peterburga*, in *op cit.*, p. 163.

125. N. Punin, "Iz 'vospominanii,'" in R. Timenchik and V. Morderer, comps. and eds., *Poema bez geroia* (Moscow, 1989), p. 337 (hereinafter cited as *Poema bez geroia*).

126. Quoted in Reeder, *op cit.*, p. 45.

127. K. Chukovskii, "Aleksandr Blok," in V. Vatsuro et al., vol. 2, p. 223.

128. Quoted in Volkov, *op cit.*, p. 159.

129. *Ibid.*, p. 270.

130. K. Clark, *Petersburg: Crucible of Cultural Revolution* (Cambridge, 1995), p. 32.

131. Quoted in Reeder, *op cit.*, p. 56.

132. Regarding the Crooked Mirror, see H. Segal, *Turn-of-the-Century Cabaret: Paris, Barcelona, Berlin, Munich, Vienna, Cracow, Moscow, St. Petersburg, Zurich* (New York, 1987), pp. 279–303.

133. A. Blok, *Sobranie sochinenii*, vol. 7, p. 231.

134. Volkov, *op cit.*, p. 276.

135. Quoted in Volkov, *op cit.*, p. 275.

136. Clark, *op cit.*, pp. 39, 41.

137. Quoted in *ibid.*, p. 41.

138. K. Malevich, "Suprematism," reprinted in R. Herbert, ed., *Modern Artists on Art* (Englewood Cliffs, New Jersey, 1964), pp. 93–102.

139. Quoted in Clark, *op cit.*, pp. 46–47.

140. B. Livshits, *Polutoroglazyi strelets* (Petrograd, 1923), pp. 177–78.

141. Karsavina, *op cit.*, p. 314; see Reeder, *op cit.*, p. 63.

142. A. Levinson, "*Iz ocherki 'Tri podvala,'*" in Timenchik, *Poema bez geroia*, p. 136.

143. Quoted in Reeder, *op cit.*, p. 65.

144. Livshits, *op cit.*, p. 261.

145. Reeder, *op cit.*, p. 64 (translation by Reeder).

146. Volkov, *op cit.*, pp. 188–91; Reeder, pp. 67–68.

147. E. Necheporuk and V. Kreid, comps., *Osip Mandelstam i ego vremeni* (Moscow, 1995), p. 22.

148. Salisbury, *Black Night*, p. 196.

149. A. Blok, "On Romanticism," *Sobranie sochinenii*, vol. 6, pp. 365, 368.

150. *Ibid.*, vol. 5, p. 323.

151. *Ibid.*, p. 328.
152. *Ibid.*, p. 322.
153. *Ibid.*, p. 359.

CHAPTER TWELVE

1. Quoted in Radzinsky, *op cit.*, p. 423.
2. Quoted in Lincoln, *Romanovs*, p. 703.
3. A. Blok, *Zapisnye knizhki, 1901–1920* (Moscow, 1965), p. 295.
4. Radzinsky, *op cit.*, p. 423.
5. Quoted in Salisbury, *Black Night*, p. 320.
6. *Ibid.*, p. 321.
7. *Ibid.*, p. 320.
8. Paléologue, *op cit.*, vol. 3, p. 213.
9. *Ibid.*, pp. 279–80.
10. *Ibid.*
11. Figes, *op cit.*, p. 310.
12. *Ibid.*, p. 311; Lincoln, *Romanovs*, p. 718; Salisbury, *Black Night*, pp. 343–44.
13. V. Shklovsky, *A Sentimental Journey: Memoirs 1917–1922* (Ithaca, New York, 1970), p. 9.
14. Pipes, *Russian Revolution*, p. 279.
15. Z. Gippius, *Siniaia kniga*, in *Zhivye litsa, op cit.*, p. 284 (hereinafter cited as *Siniaia Kniga*).
16. Reeder, *op cit.*, p. 107.
17. K. Rudnitsky, *Meyerhold the Director*, trans. G. Petrov (Ann Arbor, 1981), p. 235.
18. Quoted in Volkov, *op cit.*, p. 202.
19. Quoted in Lincoln, *Romanovs*, p. 719.
20. Paléologue, *op cit.*, vol. 3, p. 216.
21. Gippius, *Siniaia kniga*, p. 285.
22. Paléologue, *op cit.*, p. 217.
23. *Ibid.*, p. 221.
24. Figes, *op cit.*, pp. 313–14.
25. Paléologue, *op cit.*, vol. 3, p. 232.
26. Karsavina, *op cit.*, p. 322.
27. Figes, *op cit.*, p. 318.
28. *Ibid.*
29. *Ibid.*
30. Shklovsky, *op cit.*, p. 16.
31. Kschessinska, *op cit.*, pp. 163–64.
32. Figes, *op cit.*, p. 328.
33. Gippius, *Siniaia kniga*, p. 283.
34. *Ibid.*, pp. 324–25; Pipes, *Russian Revolution*, p. 291.
35. Figes, *op cit.*, p. 325.
36. *Ibid.*, pp. 292–93.
37. Salisbury, *Black Night*, pp. 373–74.
38. *Ibid.*, p. 321.
39. Figes, *op cit.*, p. 352.
40. Gippius, *Siniaia kniga*, p. 308.
41. Salisbury, *Black Night*, pp. 398–401.

42. Quoted in *ibid.*, p. 412.

43. *Ibid.*, p. 414; Pipes, *Russian Revolution*, pp. 392–93.

44. Salisbury, *op cit.*, p. 415.

45. *Ibid.*, pp. 448–49.

46. Quoted in *ibid.*, p. 456.

47. Gippius, *Siniaia Kniga*, p. 359.

48. *Ibid.*, p. 372.

49. *Ibid.*, p. 380.

50. V. Lenin, *Polnoe sobranie sochinenii*, 55 vols. (Moscow, 1958–65), vol. 36, pp. 15–16 (hereinafter cited as *PSS*).

51. L. Chukovskaia, *Zapiski ob Anne Akhmatovoi*, 3 vols. (Moscow, 1997), vol. 2, p. 264.

52. Karsavina, *op cit.*, p. 326.

53. Gippius, *Siniaia Kniga*, p. 383.

54. Billington, *Icon*, p. 534.

55. Letter of July 31, 1919, *PSS*, vol. 51, pp. 25–26.

56. *Ibid.*, p. 24.

57. Lincoln, *Sunlight*, p. 241.

58. De Robien, *The Diary of a Diplomat in Russia, 1917–1918* (London, 1969), pp. 165–66.

59. R.H. Bruce Lockhart, *British Agent* (New York, 1933), p. 239.

60. Norman, *op cit.*, pp. 141–42.

61. *Ibid.*, pp. 136–37.

62. *Ibid.*, pp. 138–39.

63. V. Luknitskaia, *Nikolai Gumilev: Zhizn poeta po materialam domashnego arkhiva semi Luknitskikh* (Leningrad, 1990), p. 220.

64. Figes, *op cit.*, p. 604.

65. Quoted in *ibid.*, pp. 603, 605.

66. *Ibid.*, p. 605.

67. Lincoln, *Sunlight*, p. 252.

68. Figes, *op cit.*, p. 605.

69. *Ibid.*, p. 611.

70. *Ibid.*, p. 605.

71. *Ibid.*, p. 682.

72. B. Ruble, *Leningrad: Shaping of a Soviet City* (Berkeley, 1990), p. 27 (hereinafter cited as *Leningrad*).

73. Figes, *op cit.*, p. 610.

74. M. McAuley, *Bread and Justice: State and Society in Petrograd, 1917–1922* (Oxford, 1991), p. 89.

75. Quoted in Reeder, *op cit.*, p. 135.

76. E. Goldman, *My Disillusionment in Russia* (Garden City, New York, 1923), p. 12.

77. Akhmatova, *My Half-Century*, p. 91.

78. Karsavina, *op cit.*, pp. 330–31.

79. V. Khodasevich, *Literaturnie stati i vospominia* (New York, 1954), pp. 399–400.

80. Lukhnitskaia, *op cit.*, p. 220.

81. P. Arvich, *Kronstadt 1921* (Princeton, 1970), p. 43.

82. Figes, *op cit.*, p. 762.

83. Avrich, *op cit.*, pp. 72–74.

84. R. Pipes, *Russia under the Bolshevik Regime* (New York, 1994), pp. 383–84 (hereinafter cited as *Bolshevik Regime*).

85. E. Goldman, *Living My Life*, 2 vols. (New York, 1931), vol. 2, p. 884.

86. *Ibid.*

87. M. Gorky, "To the Democracy," in *Untimely Thoughts: Essays on Revolution, Culture and the Bolsheviks 1917–18* (New Haven, 1968), p. 85.

88. The three Houses and World Literature are described in more detail in Barry Scherr, "Notes on Literary Life in Petrograd, 1918–1922: A Tale of Three Houses," *Slavic Review* 36 (June 1977), pp. 256–67.

89. A. Blok, *Sobranie sochinenii*, vol. 7, p. 297 (diary entry of August 5, 1917).

90. *Ibid*., (diary entry of August 7, 1917).

91. V. Orlov, *Gamaiun: zhizn Aleksandra Bloka* (Leningrad, 1978), p. 594.

92. Reeder, *op cit.*, p. 111.

93. In A. Akhmatova, *Requiem*, ed. and comp. R. Timenchik and K. Polivanov (Moscow, 1989), p. 31 (hereinafter cited as *Requiem*).

94. Quoted in Volkov, *op cit.*, p. 228.

95. Quoted in Reeder, *op cit.*, p. 118.

96. Quoted in Volkov, *op cit.*, p. 228.

97. V. Khodasevich, *Nekropol* (Moscow, 2000), p. 78.

98. In B. Kreid, ed. and comp., *Nikolai Gumilev v vospominaniakh sovremennikov* (Moscow, 1989), p. 244.

99. Quoted in Volkov, *op cit.*, p. 234.

100. Blok, *Sobranie sochinenii*, vol. 7, p. 365 (diary entry of June 11, 1919).

101. Orlov, *op cit.*, p. 686.

102. Iu. Annenkov, *Dnevnik moikh vstrech: Tsikl tragedii* (New York, 1966), p. 74.

103. Blok, *Sobranie sochinenii*, vol. 7, pp. 415–16 (diary entry of April 18, 1921).

104. In A. Akhmatova, *Desiatye gody*, ed. and comp. R. Timenchik and K. Polivanov (Moscow, 1989), p. 253.

105. Berberova, *op cit.*, p. 145.

106. Dobuzhinskii, *op cit.*, p. 23.

CHAPTER THIRTEEN

1. M. Fonvizn, "O Kommunizme i Sotsializme," in A. Volodin, ed., *Utopskii sotsializm v Rossii* (Moscow, 1985), pp. 221–22.

2. Billington, *Icon*, p. 534. I am indebted to Billington for the title to this chapter, who adopted the expression for a section of his book covering the same period.

3. Quoted in R. Conquest, *The Great Terror: A Reassessment* (New York, 1990), p. 3 (hereinafter cited as *Terror*).

4. Pipes, *Bolshevik Regime*, p. 394.

5. Ruble, *Leningrad*, p. 27.

6. Quoted in Reeder, *op cit.*, p. 133.

7. Volkov, *op cit.*, p. 307.

8. Quoted in Reeder, *op cit.*, p. 133.

9. Clark, *op cit.*, pp. 164, 196.

10. *Ibid.*, p. 197.

11. S. Frederick Starr, *Red and Hot: The Fate of Jazz in the Soviet Union, 1917–1980* (New York, 1983), p. 68.

12. Volkov, *op cit.*, 304.

13. A. Lourie, "Nash Marsh," in *Poema bez geroia*, p. 352.

14. Norman, *op cit.*, pp. 162–63.

15. V. Shishkin, ed., *Petrograd na perelome epokh: gorod i ego zhiteli v godi revoliutsii i grazhdanskoi voiny* (St. Petersburg, 2000), p. 329.

16. Volkov, *op cit.*, p. 283.

17. Clark, *op cit.*, pp. 125–26, 134–39.

18. N. Berdyaev, *The Origin of Russian Communism* (Ann Arbor, 1960), p. 144 (hereinafter cited as *Origin of Russian Communism*).

19. Quoted in Pipes, *Bolshevik Regime*, pp. 290–91.

20. Quoted in Conquest, *Terror*, p. 3.

21. V. Lenin, "Zadachi soiuzi molodezhi," *PSS*, vol. 41, pp. 304–05.

22. Clark, *op cit.*, p. 147, 151–52.

23. In Mochulsky, *op cit.*, p. 427.

24. Pipes, *Bolshevik Regime*, p. 289.

25. Clark, *op cit.*, p. 153.

26. *Ibid.*, pp. 157–58.

27. Volkov, *op cit.*, pp. 294, 402–03.

28. Norman, *op cit.*, p. 150.

29. *Ibid.*, pp. 183–85.

30. Clark, *op cit.*, pp. 149–50, 152, 154.

31. Terras, *op cit.*, p. 510; Clark, *op cit.*, p. 52.

32. Reprinted in G. Kern and C. Collins, eds., *The Serapion Brothers: A Critical Anthology* (Ann Arbor, 1975), pp. 133–35.

33. Volkov, *op cit.*, p. 308.

34. Clark, *op cit.*, p. 180.

35. Volkov, *op cit.*, p. 370.

36. B. Taper, *Balanchine* (New York, 1963), p. 65.

37. Berdyaev, *Origin of Russian Communism*, p. 145.

38. L. Shaumian, ed., *Leningrad entsiklopedicheskii spravochnik* (Moscow, 1957), p. 148 (hereinafter cited as *LES*).

39. Lincoln, *Sunlight*, p. 261.

40. Ruble, *Leningrad*, p. 27.

41. *LES,* p. 162.

42. Clark, *ibid.*, p. 185.

43. *Ibid.*, pp. 188, 203–06.

44. *Ibid.*, pp. 222, 238.

45. *Ibid.*, p. 266.

46. Volkov, *op cit.*, p. 404.

47. Clark, *op cit.*, p. 223.

48. Volkov, *op cit.*, pp. 401–02.

49. The Manifesto is reprinted in English in D. Kharms and A. Vvedensky, *The Man with the Black Coat: Russia's Literature of the Absurd*, trans. and ed. G. Gibian (Evanston, 1987), pp. 245–54. See also R.R. Milner–Gulland, "Left Art in Leningrad: the OBERIU Declaration," *Oxford Slavonic Papers*, vol. 3 (1970), pp. 65–75.

50. As translated in Bristol, *op cit.*, p. 261.

51. D. Kharms, "Komedia goroda Peterburg (chast II)," *Polnoe sobranie sochinenii*, 2 vols. (St. Petersburg, 1997), p. 194.

52. Volkov, *op cit.*, p. 398.

53. Quoted in Schonberg, *op cit.*, p. 516.

54. Quoted in Volkov, *op cit.*, p. 410.

55. E. Wilson, *Shostakovich: A Life Remembered* (Princeton, 1994), p. 111.

56. Conquest, *Terror*, p. 38. Stalin's role in Kirov's murder had been suspected from the start but evidence of his complicity accumulated only over time. The most complete treatments in English are R. Conquest, *Stalin and the Kirov Murder* (New York, 1989) and A. Knight, *Who Killed Kirov?* (New York, 1999). See also Conquest, *Terror*, pp. 37–52.

57. Billington, *Icon*, p. 534; Conquest, *Terror*, pp. 214–15.

58. Clark, *op cit.*, p. 300.

59. Billington, *Icon*, p. 541.

60. Conquest, *Terror*, p. 215.

61. *Ibid.*, p. 450.

62. *Ibid.*, p. 485.

63. *Ibid.*, p. 288.

64. I. Titova, "Group Discovers Terror Victims," *St. Petersburg Times*, September 20, 2002, p. 1.

65. Conquest, *Terror*, p. 269.

66. In *Requiem*, pp. 110–11.

67. Volkov, *op cit.*, p. 423.

68. Norman, *op cit.*, pp. 228, 230, 234–36.

69. Leiter, *op cit.*, pp. 99–100.

70. This episode is recounted by Akhmatova in "Instead of a Preface" at the beginning of the poem *Requiem*.

71. As translated in J. Hemschemeyer, trans., and R. Reeder, ed., *The Complete Poems of Anna Akhmatova* (Boston, 1992), p. 385 (hereinafter cited as *Complete Poems*).

72. *Ibid.*, pp. 391–92.

73. See prologue, p. xxxi.

74. Billington, *Icon*, pp. 538–39.

CHAPTER FOURTEEN

1. R. Neratova, *V dni voini: semeinaia khronika* (St. Petersburg, 1996), p. 32.

2. *Ibid.*, p. 33.

3. H. Salisbury, *The 900 Days: The Siege of Leningrad* (New York, 1969), p. 66 (hereinafter cited as *900 Days*). For a more detailed account of the country's unpreparedness on the eve of the war, see D. Glantz, *Stumbling Colossus: The Red Army on the Eve of World War* (Lawrence, Kansas, 1998).

4. *Ibid.*, pp. 73, 138.

5. *Ibid.*, p. 117.

6. E. Kochina, *Blockade Diary* (Ann Arbor, 1990), p. 31.

7. D. Konstantinov, *Cherez tunnel XX-ogo stoletia*, in *Materialy k istorii Russkoi politicheskoi emigratsii, vypusk III* (Moscow, 1997), pp. 184–85.

8. As translated in Salisbury, *900 Days*, pp. 121–22.

9. B.N. Sokolov, *V plenu* (St. Petersburg, 2000), p. 9 (hereinafter cited as *V plenu*).

10. Kochina, *op cit.*, p. 34.

11. Neratova, *op cit.*, p. 28.

12. Salisbury, *900 Days*, p. 147.

13. A. Werth, *Russia at War 1941–1945* (New York, 1964), p. 303.

14. Kochina, *op cit.*, p. 33.

15. Salisbury, *900 Days*, p. 206.

16. L. Gouré, *The Siege of Leningrad* (Stanford, 1964), pp. 51–52; Salisbury, *900 Days*, p. 207.

17. Gouré, *op cit.*, p. 53.

18. Salisbury, *900 Days*, p. 143.

19. Gouré, *op cit.*, p. 53.

20. Salisbury, *900 Days*, p. 263.

21. *Ibid.*, p. 206.

22. Gouré, *op cit.*, p. 55.

23. *Ibid.*

24. G. Goppe, *Tvoe otkritie Peterburga: zametki na poliakh istorii velikogo goroda* (St. Petersburg, 1995), pp. 86–87.

25. A. Punin, "My pomnim bomby Leningradskogo blokady," in B. Kirikov, et al., eds., *Kraevedcheskie zapiski: issledovania i materiali* (St. Petersburg, 2000), p. 281.

26. Massie, *Pavlovsk*, p. 218.

27. Salisbury, *900 Days*, p. 258.

28. *Ibid.*, p. 374.

29. *Ibid.*, pp. 182–83.

30. *Ibid.*, p. 183.

31. *Ibid.*, pp. 182–83.

32. Sokolov, *V plenu*, pp. 10–15.

33. Salisbury, *900 Days*, p. 185.

34. *Ibid.*, pp. 188–90.

35. *Ibid.*, p. 179.

36. *Ibid.*, p. 188.

37. *Ibid.*, p. 194.

38. *Ibid.*, p. 209.

39. *Ibid.*, pp. 292–93.

40. Gouré, *op cit.*, p. 94.

41. V. Krasnov, *Neizvestnyi Zhukov* (Moscow, 2000), p. 223.

42. Gouré, *op cit.*, pp. 83–84.

43. *Ibid.*, p. 97.

44. Salisbury, *900 Days*, pp. 343, 346.

45. B.V. Sokolov, *Tainy vtoroi mirovoi* (Moscow, 2001), p. 432 (hereinafter cited as *Tainy*). B.V. Sokolov should not be confused with B.N. Sokolov, author of *V plenu*.

46. *Ibid.*, pp. 429–30. Stalin's original order (No. 270), which was co-signed by Zhukov and others, is reprinted in Kraenov, *op cit.*, pp. 225–28.

47. Salisbury, *900 Days*, p. 331.

48. Gouré, *op cit.*, p. 99.

49. Salisbury, *900 Days*, p. 337.

50. See Gouré, *op cit.*, pp. 98–99.

51. Krasnov, *op cit.*, p. 230.

52. Quoted in Salisbury, *900 Days*, p. 351; Gouré, *op cit.*, p. 142.

53. Salisbury, *900 Days*, p. 350 (author's emphasis).

54. Gouré, *op cit.*, p. 100.

55. *Ibid.*, p. 143.

56. *Ibid.*, p. 102.

57. Norman, *op cit.*, pp. 251, 259.

58. Salisbury, *900 Days*, p. 292.

59. *Ibid.*, p. 369.

60. Gouré, *op cit.*, p. 193.

61. *Ibid.*, p. 159.

62. Salisbury, *900 Days*, p. 382.

63. *Ibid.*, p. 370.

SOURCE NOTES 625

64. Gouré, *op cit.*, p. 153.
65. Salisbury, *900 Days*, p. 283.
66. Reeder, *op cit.*, p. 258.
67. Salisbury, *900 Days*, p. 285.
68. Reeder, *op cit.*, p. 257.
69. Salisbury, *900 Days*, p. 437.
70. *Ibid.*, p. 456.
71. A. Fadeyev, *Leningrad in the Days of the Blockade* (Westport, Connecticut, 1971), pp. 97–98.
72. Gouré, *op cit.*, p. 155.
73. *Ibid.*, p. 156.
74. *Ibid.*, p. 158.
75. Salisbury, *900 Days*, pp. 436, 491; Gouré, *op cit.*, p. 161.
76. Salisbury, *900 Days*, p. 377.
77. Quoted in Gouré, *op cit.*, p. 161.
78. Salisbury, *900 Days*, p. 413.
79. *Ibid.*, p. 494.
80. Quoted in *ibid.*, p. 415.
81. Quoted in *ibid.*, p. 420.
82. *Ibid.*, p. 422.
83. Quoted in *ibid.*, p. 377.
84. Norman, *op cit.*, p. 253.
85. *Ibid.*, p. 252.
86. Massie, *Pavlovsk*, pp. 253–54.
87. Norman, *op cit.*, p. 254.
88. Quoted in Volkov, *op cit.*, p. 437.
89. Salisbury, *900 Days*, p. 480.
90. *Ibid.*, p. 446.
91. *Ibid.*, pp. 526–27.
92. Gouré, *op cit.*, p. 286.
93. Salisbury, *900 Days*, p. 546.
94. Quoted in Gouré, *op cit.*, p. 267.
95. Fadeyev, *op cit.*, p. 9.
96. Quoted in Salisbury, *900 Days*, p. 522.
97. Quoted in Volknov, *op cit.*, p. 441.
98. O. Berggolts, *Izbrannie proizvedenia v dvukh tomakh*, 2 vols. (Leningrad, 1967), pp. 194–95.
99. V. Inber, *Stranitsi dnei perebiraia* (Moscow, 1967), p. 161.
100. Salisbury, *op cit.*, pp. 550–51.
101. Lincoln, *Sunlight*, pp. 296–97.
102. Salisbury, *900 Days*, pp. 561–62.
103. *Ibid.*, p. 562.
104. P. Luknitskii, *Skvoz vsiu blokadu* (Moscow, 1975), pp. 361–62.
105. Quoted in Salisbury, *900 Days*, p. 568.
106. Salisbury, *900 Days*, p. 516.

CHAPTER FIFTEEN

1. As translated in Billington, *Icon*, p. 588.
2. Ruble, *Leningrad*, p. 27; Salisbury, *900 Days*, p. 575.

3. Salisbury, *900 Days*, pp. 573–74.

4. Akhmatova, *My Half-Century*, p. 28.

5. Salisbury, *900 Days*, p. 556.

6. *Ibid.*, p. 573.

7. V. Vishnevskii, "Leningradu," in *Sobranie sochinenii*, 6 vols. (Moscow, 1961), p. 164.

8. Salisbury, *900 Days*, p. 574.

9. Volkov, *op cit.*, p. 448; Salisbury, *900 Days*, p. 575.

10. B. Ruble, "The Leningrad Affair and the Provincialization of Leningrad," *Russian Review* 42 (1983), p. 302 (hereinafter cited as *Leningrad Affair*).

11. Salisbury, *900 Days*, p. 575.

12. *Ibid.*, p. 582.

13. I. Berlin, "Anna Akhmatova: A Memoir," in *Complete Poems*, p. 36.

14. *Ibid.*, p. 45.

15. Reeder, *op cit.*, p. 288.

16. A. Zhdanov, *Doklad o zhurnalakh "Zvezda" i "Leningrad"* (Gospolitizdat, 1952), p. 12.

17. *Ibid.*, pp. 9–10.

18. *Ibid.*, p. 25.

19. V. Seduro, *Dostoyevski in Russian Literary Criticism, 1846–1956* (New York, 1957), pp. 280, 283.

20. Quoted in Reeder, *op cit.*, p. 324.

21. Lincoln, *Heaven and Hell*, p. 413.

22. D. Bordwell, *The Cinema of Eisenstein* (Cambridge, Massachusetts, 1993), p. 252.

23. Billington, *Icon*, p. 551.

24. Salisbury, *900 Days*, p. 582.

25. R. Medvedev, *Let History Judge* (New York, 1989), p. 783.

26. Salisbury, *900 Days*, pp. 578–79.

27. Norman, *op cit.*, p. 289.

28. Quoted in Volkov, *op cit.*, p. 365.

29. Massie, *Pavlovsk*, pp. 204–09.

30. *Ibid.*, pp. 209–13.

31. A. Werth, *Leningrad* (New York, 1944), p. 187 (hereinafter cited as *Leningrad*).

32. See the eyewitness description only hours after the German retreat in *ibid.*, pp. 186–88.

33. Massie, *Pavlovsk*, p. 281.

34. *Ibid.*, p. 215.

35. *Ibid.*, p. 289.

36. Werth, *Leningrad*, p. 188.

37. Norman, *op cit.*, pp. 265–66.

38. *Ibid.*, pp. 273–74.

39. See the published exhibition catalogue, J. Leggio, ed., *Hidden Treasures Revealed* (New York, 1995).

40. Salisbury, *900 Days*, p. 575.

41. Ruble, *Leningrad*, p. 27.

42. Ruble, *Leningrad Affair*, p. 306.

43. Ruble, *Leningrad*, p. 148.

44. *Ibid.*, pp. 152–54.

45. *Ibid.*, p. 153.

46. Denis Shaw, "Planning Leningrad," *The Geographical Review* 68, no. 2 (April 1978), pp. 189–91.

47. Ruble, *Leningrad*, p. 66.

48. Shaw, *op cit.*, p. 191.

49. Ruble, *Leningrad*, p. 70.

50. Ruble, *Leningrad Affair*, p. 305.

51. Ruble, *Leningrad*, p. 62.

52. *Ibid.*, p. 142.

53. *Ibid.*, p. 57.

54. *Ibid.*, pp. 58–59.

55. *Ibid.*, p. 62.

56. *Ibid.*, p. 129.

57. *Ibid.*, pp. 97, 101–02.

58. Shaw, *op cit.*, p. 187.

59. Ruble, *Leningrad*, p. 87.

60. Published in English as D. Pavlov, *Leningrad 1941: The Blockade* (Chicago, 1965).

61. Chukovskaia, *op cit.*, vol. 2, p. 289.

62. Volkov, *op cit.*, p. 489.

63. *Ibid.*

64. Volkov, *op cit.*, pp. 482–83.

65. Quoted in Wilson, *op cit.*, p. 317.

66. Quoted in *ibid.*

67. Chukovskaya, *op cit.*, vol. 2, p. 273.

68. Volkov, *op cit.*, pp. 505–06.

69. *Ibid.*, p. 500.

70. *Ibid.*, p. 476.

71. See J. Brodsky, "In a Room and a Half," in J. Brodsky, *Less than One: Selected Essays* (New York, 1986), p. 452.

72. See also descriptions in Volkov, *op cit.*, pp. 476–77; Reeder, *op cit.*, pp. 441–42.

73. Quoted in Reeder, *op cit.*, p. 442.

74. V. Seduro, *Dostoevski's Image in Russia Today* (Belmont, Massachusetts, 1975), p. 165.

75. Quoted in Reeder, *op cit.*, p. 445.

76. See the account of events in L. Maybarduk, *The Dancer Who Flew* (Toronto, 1999), pp. 68–71.

77. See N. Makarova, *A Dance Autobiography* (New York, 1979), pp. 52–54; J. Ardoin, *Valery Gergiev and the Kirov: A Story of Survival* (Portland, Oregon, 2001), p. 195.

78. See account in Makarova, *op cit.*, pp. 84–93.

79. Quoted in G. Smakov, *Baryshnikov: From Russia to the West* (New York, 1981), p. 179.

80. Volkov, *op cit.*, pp. 507–08.

81. Quoted in Reeder, *op cit.*, p. 504.

82. J. Brodsky, "Less than One," in *op cit.*, p. 28.

83. *Ibid.*, pp. 28–29.

84. Volkov, *op cit.*, p. 524.

85. *Ibid.*, pp. 529–30.

86. Starr, *op cit.*, p. 270.

87. Quoted in S. Ramet, S. Zamascikov, and R. Bird, "The Soviet Rock Scene," in S. Ramet, ed., *Rocking the State: Rock Music and Politics in Eastern Europe and Russia* (Boulder, 1994), p. 182.

88. *Ibid.*

89. Quoted in Volkov, *op cit.*, p. 535.

90. Ramet et al., *op cit.*, p. 183.

91. Starr, *op cit.*, p. 300.

92. Volkov, *op cit.*, p. 533.

93. Ramet et al, *op cit.*, p. 209.

94. As quoted and translated in *ibid.*, p. 194.

95. *Ibid.*, p. 191.

96. *Ibid.*

97. See chapter 11, p. 429.

CHAPTER SIXTEEN

1. M. Gorbachev, *Memoirs* (New York, 1995), p. 175.

2. *Ibid.*, p. 258.

3. T. Gustafson, *Capitalism Russian-Style* (Cambridge, United Kingdom, 1999), pp. 116–17.

4. See Gorbachev, *op cit.*, pp. 255–59.

5. Norman, *op cit.*, p. 299.

6. A. Sobchak, *For a New Russia: The Mayor of St. Petersburg's Own Story of the Struggle for Justice and Democracy* (New York, 1992), pp. 8–10.

7. Quoted in *ibid.*, p. 120.

8. *Ibid.*, pp. 120–21.

9. Until November 21, 1989, he was only Regional Chief, but on that date he also became City Party Chief.

10. *Ibid.*, pp. 98–99.

11. Quoted in Volkov, *op cit.*, p. 544.

12. V. Bonnell, A. Cooper, and G. Freidin, eds., *Russia at the Barricades: Eyewitness Accounts of the August 1991 Coup* (Armonk, New York, 1994), p. 17 (hereinafter cited as *Russia at the Barricades*).

13. Valery Zavorotnyi in conversation with the author, September 2, 2002 (hereinafter cited as "Zavorotnyi Interview"). At the time of the coup Mr. Zavorotnyi, a writer, was one of the citizen "commandant" defenders inside the Mariinsky Palace.

14. Sobchak's version of events on the 19th, on which the following is largely based, is set forth in his interview with *Moscow News* published on August 26, 1991, and reprinted in English in *Russia at the Barricades*, pp. 218–25, and in Sobchak, *op cit.*, pp. 173–83.

15. Sobchak, *op cit.*, pp. 178–79.

16. Here Sobchak's own accounts differ. In the *Moscow News* interview, he says that Samsonov replied, "All right, I'll do it" (i.e., prevent troops from entering the city), but in his memoirs, Sobchak, *op cit.*, p. 179, he quotes Samsonov as saying, "I'll do what I can."

17. Zavorotnyi Interview.

18. Letter of Valery Zavorotnyi to Donald J. Raleigh, September 20, 1991, p. 14 (copy in author's possession) (hereinafter cited as "Zavorotnyi Letter"). This letter is reprinted in part and with omissions in *Russia at the Barricades*, pp. 147–57. The quote here is on page 154 of that book but with the second sentence omitted and translated differently.

19. Zavorotnyi Letter, p. 13 (in *Russia at the Barricades*, p. 153).

20. Zavorotnyi Interview.

21. *Ibid.*

22. Quoted in Vladimir Kovalev, "1991: The End of Leningrad," *The St. Petersburg Times*, August 17, 2001, p. 4.

23. Zavorotnyi Letter, p. 15 (in *Russia at the Barricades*, p. 155).

24. *Russia at the Barricades*, pp. 347–48.

25. Alexander Pozdnyakov in conversation with the author, August 30, 2002. Mr. Pozdnyakov is a well-known local television journalist and personality and specialist on Russian cinema, particularly Lenfilm.

26. Zavorotnyi Interview.

27. I. Ivanova et al., "Kak vystoial Peterburg [How Petersburg Stood Up]," *Vechernii Leningrad (Sankt-Peterburg)*, September 2, 1991, p. 2, col. 8.

28. Zavorotnyi Interview.

29. Fred Coleman, "St. Petersburg: Rebirth of a Great Russian City," *Newsweek* (International Edition), November 4, 1991, p. 18.

30. V. Putin, *First Person: An Astonishingly Frank Portrait by Russia's President* (New York, 2000), pp. 8–21, 32.

31. *Ibid.*, p. 22.

32. *Ibid.*, pp. 47–48.

33. *Ibid.*, p. 80.

34. V. Kovalev, "Did Putin Help Prevent Military Confrontation?" *St. Petersburg Times*, August 17, 2002, p. 4.

35. Putin, *op cit.*, p. 93.

36. Blair Ruble, "The Two Worlds of Vladimir Putin: II. Leningrad," *Wilson Quarterly*, Spring 2000, p. 37.

37. See generally Gustafson, *op cit.*, pp. 13–14; A. Åslund, *How Russia Became a Market Economy* (Washington, D.C., 1995), pp. 226–31.

38. L. Shevtsova, "Between Stabilization and a Breakthrough: Interim Results of Vladimir Putin's Presidency," Moscow Carnegie Center Briefing, January 2002, available at http://pubs.carnegie.ru/english/briefings/2002/issue02-01.asp. See also L. Shevtsova, *Yeltsin's Russia: Myths and Reality* (Washington, D.C., 1999), pp. 269–92.

39. Ruble, *op cit.*, pp. 87–89.

40. See account in Norman, *op cit.*, pp. 318–20.

41. *Ibid.*, pp. 325–26.

42. D. Hoffman, *The Oligarchs: Wealth and Power in the New Russia* (New York, 2002), pp. 87–99.

43. Åslund, *op cit.*, p. 233.

44. Hoffman, *op cit.*, p. 179.

45. *Ibid.*, p. 182.

46. *Ibid.*, pp. 182–83.

47. Åslund, *op cit.*, pp. 229–30, 241.

48. Hoffman, *op cit.*, pp. 179–80.

49. *Ibid.*, p. 182.

50. Quoted in Gustafson, *op cit.*, p. 41.

51. *Ibid.*, pp. 40–41.

52. Åslund, *op cit.*, p. 223.

53. See *ibid.*, pp. 296–97.

54. Putin, *op cit.*, pp. 125–27.

55. Available at www.publicaffairsbooks.com/books/fir-exc.html.

56. Putin, *op cit.*, p. 169.

Suggestions for Further Reading in English

The only other general history of St. Petersburg in English is W. Bruce Lincoln's *Sunlight at Midnight: St. Petersburg and the Rise of Modern Russia* (New York, 2000), which does not cover the post–Soviet period. Christopher Marsden's *Palmyra of the North: The First Days of St. Petersburg* (London, 1942), is interesting reading but goes only through Elizabeth's reign and is not always reliable. An excellent scholarly treatment of the 18th century from the perspective of the city's English community is Anthony Cross's *By the Banks of the Neva: Chapters from the Lives and Careers of the British in Eighteenth-Century Russia* (Cambridge, 1997). An excellent scholarly treatment of late 19th-century Petersburg is James Bater's *St. Petersburg: Industrialization and Change* (Montreal, 1976), while Blair Ruble's *Leningrad: Shaping a Soviet City* (Berkeley, 1990) is a valuable resource on the 20th-century period from an urbanist perspective. A valuable autobiographical account of the late 1980s and early 1990s is the late Mayor Anatoly Sobchak's *For a New Russia* (New York, 1992).

In the area of St. Petersburg culture, Solomon Volkov's *St. Petersburg: A Cultural History* (New York, 1995), the only general cultural history of the city, is enjoyable, and is strongest in music and in the 20th century. Three general cultural histories of Russia, however, contain much useful material on St. Petersburg. James Billington's *The Icon and the Axe: An Interpretive History of Russian Culture* (New York, 1966) remains the timeless classic. Also good is W. Bruce Lincoln's *Between Heaven and Hell: The Story of a Thousand Years of Artistic Life in Russia* (New York, 1998). Orlando Figes's *Natasha's Dance: A Cultural History of Russia* (New York, 2002), too recent to be used for this book, is both well written and relevant in that much of it focuses on aspects of the interaction between Muscovite and Western European culture introduced in St. Petersburg. An excellent scholarly treatment of the 20th-century avant-garde in St. Petersburg is Katrina Clark's *Petersburg: Crucible of Cultural Revolution* (Cambridge, Massachusetts, 1995).

For St. Petersburg urban planning, architecture, and art, the best general treatment of the city's urban planning in the imperial period is Iurii Egorov, *The Architectural Planning of St. Petersburg* (Athens, Ohio, 1969); for the 20th century see Blair Ruble's *Leningrad,* above. An excellent analysis of the new architecture of the Petrine period is James Cracraft's *The Petrine Revolution in Russian Architecture* (Chicago, 1988). A general Russian art history with significant attention to Petersburg is George Hamilton, *The Art and Architecture of Russia* (Frome, United Kingdom, 1983). Regarding the palaces of St. Petersburg, see Audrey Kennett, *The Palaces of Leningrad* (New York, 1973). Suzanne Massie's *Pavlovsk: The History of a Russian Palace* (Boston, 1990) is a comprehensive history of Pavlovsk through two centuries with attention to general St. Petersburg history. Regarding more modern architecture, see William Brumfeld, *The Origins of Modernism in Russian Architecture* (Berkeley, 1991). An excellent history of the Hermitage is Geraldine Norman's *The Hermitage: The Biography of a Great Museum* (New York, 1997).

On the Muscovite background, Richard Pipes's *Russia under the Old Regime* (2nd ed., London, 1995) and Nikolai Berdyaev's *The Russian Idea* (Hudson, New York, 1992), as well as Billington's *Icon,* are all brilliant must reads. On Peter the Great and his system, see Marc Raeff's *Understanding Imperial Russia* (New York, 1984), James Cracraft's *The Church Reform of Peter the*

631

Great (Stanford, 1971), Lindsey Hughes's *Russia in the Age of Peter the Great* (New Haven, 1998) and her new short biography of Peter, *Peter the Great: A Biography* (New Haven, 2002).

For accounts of Petersburg's Emperors and Empresses who impacted the city, useful surveys are W. Bruce Lincoln, *The Romanovs: Autocrats of All the Russias* (New York, 1981) and Donald Raleigh, ed., *The Emperors and Empresses of Russia* (Armonk, New York, 1996). For individual rulers after Peter the Great, see Mina Curtiss, *A Forgotten Empress: Anna Ivanovna and Her Era* (New York, 1974); Tamara Talbot Rice, *Elizabeth, Empress of Russia* (London, 1970); R. Nisbet Bain, *Peter III, Emperor of Russia* (New York, 1902); Isabel de Madariaga, *Russia in the Age of Catherine the Great* (New Haven, 1981) and *Catherine the Great: A Short History* (New Haven, 1990); John Alexander, *Catherine the Great: Life and Legend* (New York, 1989); Roderick McGrew, *Paul I of Russia, 1754–1801* (Oxford, 1992); Allen McConnell, *Tsar Alexander: Paternalistic Reformer* (Arlington Heights, Illinois, 1970); Henri Troyat, *Alexander I of Russia: Napoleon's Conqueror* (New York, 1980); and W. Bruce Lincoln, *Nicholas I: Emperor and Autocrat of All the Russias* (DeKalb, Illinois, 1989).

Regarding revolutionary history, the leading work on the Decembrist rebellion is Anatole Mazour, *The First Russian Revolution, 1825* (Reprint, Stanford, 1967). Regarding the Petrashevtsy, see J.H. Seddon, *The Petrashevtsy: A Study of the Russian Revolutionaries of 1848* (Manchester, 1985). The leading work on the 19th-century revolutionary movement and populism is Franco Venturi's *The Roots of Revolution: A History of the Populist and Socialist Movements in 19th-Century Russia* (Rev. ed., London, 1972). For accounts of the early 20th-century revolutions and Civil War, see R. Pipes's *The Russian Revolution* (New York, 1990) and *Russia under the Bolshevik Regime* (New York, 1994), Orlando Figes's *A People's Tragedy: The Russian Revolution, 1891–1924* (New York, 1996), and Harrison Salisbury's *Black Night, White Snow: Russia's Revolutions, 1905–1917* (New York, 1978). A brilliant exposition of the Muscovite background to Russian revolutionary thinking is Nikolai Berdyaev's *The Origin of Russian Communism* (Ann Arbor, 1960).

Regarding the Silver Age, the leading scholarly works are J. Kennedy, *The "Mir Iskusstva" Group and Russian Art 1898–1912* (New York, 1977) and John Bowlt, *The Silver Age: Russian Art of the Early Twentieth Century and the "World of Art" Group* (Newtonville, Massachusetts, 1982). Art books in English portraying the artists' works are readily available in the United States and Russia, most notably the State Russian Museum's *The Age of Diaghilev* (St. Petersburg, 2001).

Regarding the siege of Leningrad, the classic work is Harrison Salisbury's *The 900 Days: The Siege of Leningrad* (New York, 1969). Also good are Leon Gouré, *The Siege of Leningrad* (Stanford, 1964), and David Glantz, *The Siege of Leningrad 1941–44: 900 Days of Terror* (Osceola, Wisconsin, 2001).

For accounts of Petersburg's leading poets and writers and their work, regarding Pushkin see Robin Edmonds, *Pushkin: The Man and His Age* (New York, 1994) and Henri Troyat, *Pushkin* (New York, 1970). For Gogol, see David Magarshack, *Gogol: A Life* (London, 1957). The most useful treatment of Dostoevsky in the context of St. Petersburg is Donald Fanger, *Dostoevsky and Romantic Realism* (Evanston, 1965). Regarding Anna Akhmatova, see Amanda Haight, *Anna Akhmatova: A Poetic Pilgrimage* (New York, 1976) and Roberta Reeder, *Anna Akhmatova: Poet and Prophet* (New York, 1990). For Blok, see Konstantin Molchusky, *Aleksandr Blok* (Detroit, 1983).

The principal poems and fictional prose works about the city are discussed in the text and need not be listed here. They are available in various editions and collections. The major sources used for this book are cited in the endnotes.

Index

BNP/Dresdner, 575
Bobyshev, Dmitry, 544
Bogdanov, Alexander, 471, 473
Bogdanovich, Hippolyte, 146
Bogdanovich, Ippolit, 190
Boguslavskaya, Zhana, 424
Boheme, Jacob, 199, 253, 376
Bolotov, Andrei, 157
Bolshakov, Alexei, 587
Bolshaya Morskaya Street, 57, 148, 187, 188, 249
Bolshaya Nemetskaya Street, 59, 60
Bolshaya Neva, 29
Bolshaya Nevka, 48, 67
Bolshaya Zagorodnaya Street, 103
Bolshevik Revolution, 469
Bolsheviks: all-Bolshevik Provisional Government in Petrograd, 442–48; changes in the plastic arts by, 471–73; organic Russian state and, 22; setting up "former people," 451
Bolshoi Dom, 483
Bolshoi Dramatic Theater, 469, 542
Bolshoi Lug, 60, 63
Bolshoi Prospect, 42, 52
Bolshoi Stone Theater, 188
Bolshoi Theater, 246–47, 294, 297, 298, 314
Bolshoi Theater (Moscow), 247, 583
Bonaparte, Napoleon, 164, 220, 236, 240–45
Boris, Grand Duke, 438
Boris Eifman Ballet, 583
Boris Godunov (Pushkin), 299, 300
Boris Godunov (Rimsky-Korsakov), 363, 413
Borodin, Alexander, 361, 364
Borodin, Pavel, 587
Borodino, 244, 261
Borovikovsky, Vladimir, 201
Bourgeois Club, 187
Brandt, Karsten, 4
Braunstein, J. F., 41
Brenna, Vincenzo, 213, 222, 249
Brezhnev, Leonid, 114, 539–40, 547
The Brigadier (Fonvizin), 188

Briullov, Alexander, 315
Briullov, Karl, 315–16
Briusov, Valery, 379, 415, 416
Brodsky, Isaac, 484
Brodsky, Joseph, 544–47, 548, 549, 550–51, 559
Bronze Age, 475–79
Bronze Horseman, 179–80, 242, 248, 504
Bronze Horseman (Pushkin), 180, 302–3, 311–12, 388, 474, 479–80, 544
The Brothers Karamazov (Dostoevsky), 368
Bruce, James, 4, 8, 50, 63–64, 75, 76, 92
Bruhl, Heinrich von, 185
Bruillov, Karl, 352
Brunswick, Prince Lewis of, 125
Brunswick-Wolfenbüttel, Duke of, 122
Buchanan, Meriel, 407
Buddhist Temple, 482–83
Bugaev-Africa, Sergei, 553
Bühren, Ernst Johann, 101
Bulatov, Colonel, 272, 273
Burenin, Nikolai, 393
The Busy Bee, 153
Butashevich-Petrashevsky, Mikhail, 322
Butkov, Yakov, 312
Butter Week, 143, 414
Buturlin, Peter Ivanovich, 50, 84, 125, 187
Buzheninova, Anna, 113
Byron, Lord, 254

Cadet Corps, 192, 193
Cagliostro, Count, 198–99
Calf, Cornelius, 71
Callot, Marie-Anne, 177, 178
cameralism, 13
Cameron, Charles, 174, 182, 213, 222
Cameron Gallery, 182, 204
Campana, Giampetro, 354
Cannon Foundry, 63–64
Canziani, Joseph, 187
Capella, 504
Caravannaya Street, 115
Caravan-Sarai, 115
Caravaque, Louis, 79, 104, 125, 150
Cardel, Elisabeth, 162

OTHER TITLES OF INTEREST

BEAR HUNTING WITH THE POLITBURO
American Adventures in Russian Capitalism
Updated Edition
A. Craig Copetas
311 pp.
1-56833-238-6
$17.95
Madison Books

CLAUSEWITZ
Roger Parkinson
354 pp., 44 b/w illustrations,
    14 maps
0-8154-1233-9
$17.95
Cooper Square Press

IMPERIAL SUNSET
The Fall of Napoleon, 1813–14
R. F. Delderfield
320 pp., 12 b/w photos
0-8154-1119-7
$18.95
Cooper Square Press

IVAN THE TERRIBLE
Robert Payne and Nikita Romanoff
512 pp., 51 b/w photos
0-8154-1229-0
$18.95
Cooper Square Press

MARSHAL ZHUKOV'S GREATEST BATTLES
Georgi K. Zhukov
Edited by Harrison E. Salisbury
New introduction by David M. Glantz
328 pp., 1 b/w photo; 5 maps
0-8154-1098-0
$18.95
Cooper Square Press

NAPOLEON'S MARSHALS
R. F. Delderfield
264 pp., 26 b/w photos
0-8154-1213-4
$18.95
Cooper Square Press

A SHORT COURSE IN THE SECRET WAR
Fourth Edition
Christopher Felix
304 pp.
1-56833-179-7
$17.95
Madison Books

STALIN'S WAR
Tragedy and Triumph, 1941–1945
Edwin P. Hoyt
320 pp., 32 b/w photos and maps
0-8154-1032-8
$27.95 hc.
Cooper Square Press

TCHAIKOVSKY
Letters to His Family
Piotr Ilyich Tchaikovsky
Translated by Galina von Meck
610 pp.
0-8154-1087-5
$22.95
Cooper Square Press

**THREE WHO MADE A
REVOLUTION**
A Biographical History of Lenin,
Trotsky, and Stalin
Bertram D. Wolfe
680 pp., 54 b/w photographs and
illustrations
0-8154-1177-4
$23.95
Cooper Square Press

TOLSTOY
Tales of Courage and Conflict
Edited by Charles Neider
576 pp.
0-8154-1010-7
$19.95
Cooper Square Press

**WITH THE ARMIES OF
THE TSAR**
**A Nurse at the Russian Front,
1914–1918**
Florence Farmborough
352 pp., 48 b/w photos, 4 maps
0-8157-1090-5
$19.95
Cooper Square Press

Available at bookstores; or call 1-800-462-6420

TAYLOR TRADE PUBLISHING
200 Park Avenue South
Suite 1109
New York, NY 10003

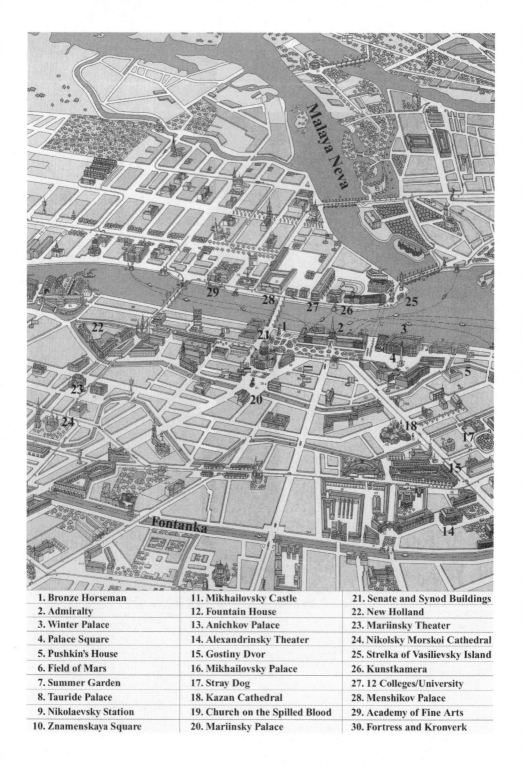

Malaya Neva

Fontanka

1. Bronze Horseman	11. Mikhailovsky Castle	21. Senate and Synod Buildings
2. Admiralty	12. Fountain House	22. New Holland
3. Winter Palace	13. Anichkov Palace	23. Mariinsky Theater
4. Palace Square	14. Alexandrinsky Theater	24. Nikolsky Morskoi Cathedral
5. Pushkin's House	15. Gostiny Dvor	25. Strelka of Vasilievsky Island
6. Field of Mars	16. Mikhailovsky Palace	26. Kunstkamera
7. Summer Garden	17. Stray Dog	27. 12 Colleges/University
8. Tauride Palace	18. Kazan Cathedral	28. Menshikov Palace
9. Nikolaevsky Station	19. Church on the Spilled Blood	29. Academy of Fine Arts
10. Znamenskaya Square	20. Mariinsky Palace	30. Fortress and Kronverk